Reel Women

An International Directory of
Contemporary Feature Films about Women

Jane Sloan

THE SCARECROW PRESS, INC.
LANHAM, MARYLAND • TORONTO • PLYMOUTH, UK
2007

SCARECROW PRESS, INC.

Published in the United States of America
by Scarecrow Press, Inc.
A wholly owned subsidary of
The Rowman & Littlefield Publishing Group, Inc.
4501 Forbes Boulevard, Suite 200, Lanham, Maryland 20706
www.scarecrowpress.com

Estover Road
Plymouth PL6 7PY
United Kingdom

British Library Cataloguing in Publication Information Available

Library of Congress Cataloging-in-Publication Data

Sloan, Jane, 1946–
  Reel women : an international directory of contemporary feature films about women / Jane Sloan.
      p. cm.
  Includes indexes.
  Filmography: p.
  ISBN-13: 978-0-8108-5738-4 (hardcover : alk. paper)
  ISBN-10: 0-8108-5738-3 (hardcover : alk. paper)
  ISBN-13: 978-0-8108-5894-7 (pbk. : alk. paper)
  ISBN-10: 0-8108-5894-0 (pbk. : alk. paper)
  1. Women in motion pictures. 2. Women in motion pictures—Catalogs. I. Title.

PN1995.9.W6S63 2007
791.43'652042—dc22   2006028794

♾ ™ The paper used in this publication meets the minimum requirements of American National Standard for Information Sciences—Permanence of Paper for Printed Library Materials, ANSI/NISO Z39.48-1992. Manufactured in the United States of America.

For my nieces,
Mary, Catherine, Elizabeth, Lily,
Janet, Linda, Allison, Jane,
Anastasia, Linda, and Nancy

CONTENTS

Preface   vii

Acknowledgments   ix

Criteria for Inclusion   xi

Organization and Codes Used in Entries   xiii

Sources for Entry Synopses   xv

A Critical Survey of Women in Leading Roles in International Cinema:
    1960 to the Present   xix

Filmography: Feature Films on the Subject of Women since 1960   1

Index of Films with Best Actress Awards and Nominations   283

Index of Actresses and Actors   291

Index of Directors, Screenwriters, Cinematographers, and Producers   321

Index of Subjects   375

Index of Titles   397

About the Author   435

PREFACE

PURPOSE

The purpose of this reference book is to list feature-length films with an adult female protagonist (or group of females) around whom the story evolves or from whose point of view the story is told. It is well known that a vast majority of central characters in fictional film narratives are men, and this list is first intended to provide some means for identifying and grouping those films centered on women. Secondarily, it is intended to fill the gap created by the two most common approaches to compiling a list of cinema about women, one relegating the topic to narrow subject matter such as domestic roles or "romance," and the other taking the subject to be coincident with the work of women filmmakers. Both imply an ideological underpinning at the same time that they limit the number of films considered.

My original goal was to list all such films produced after 1960, but comprehensiveness has proved elusive, partly because the dominance or core importance of a woman character in a film can sometimes be determined only by seeing it. Also, I discovered that synopses frequently had a different frame of reference than I, sometimes underrepresenting a character that I found important to the film. Although there are inevitably titles missing—and titles included that, had I seen the films, might not have been included—nonetheless, this list presents a larger number of films about women than one will find listed in any other source. The list is also characterized by the presence of a significant number of important films that remain inexplicably obscure—not seen, not distributed, and virtually unknown outside their niche area studies or genre markets, where they are highly valued.

The filmography both updates and expands the feature-film coverage in Kaye Sullivan's two-volume *Films For, By, and About Women* (Scarecrow, 1980, 1985). It is complementary to existing reference works that provide access to names, such as *The Women's Companion to International Films* (Virago, 1990), edited by Annette Kuhn and Susannah Radstone; *Women Film Directors: An International Bio-Critical Dictionary* (Greenwood, 1991), by Gwendolyn Foster; and *The St. James Women Filmmakers Encyclopedia* (Visible Ink, 1999), edited by Amy Unterberger. Effort was made to include all films that have gained reputation through awards, exposure in international film festivals, revival in repertory theaters, positive reviews, educational use, and wide commercial release. Special care has also been taken to include films by well-known directors that fill the subject criteria. The initial compilation was derived from the previously listed works as well as other filmographies, dictionaries, and encyclopedias.

ACKNOWLEDGMENTS

I want to extend very special thanks to Ronald Gottesman and, especially, Sumiko Higashi, who validated this project ten years ago by providing guidance in its crucial initial phase. Thanks also to John Belton, Sandy Flitterman-Lewis, and especially Maggie Humm for providing comments on its content and organization over the last three years. Catherine Geddis and Ferris Olin acted as indexing consultants, challenging and improving what I consider to be one of the most important parts of the filmography, the Index to Fictional Subjects. Jan Reinhart provided translating support in several languages. Stephen Ryan, editor at Scarecrow Press, provided detailed and very helpful feedback on the filmography. Special thanks are due to Robert Litz, Jan Schmidt, and Janet Martin for commenting on related background work, as well as to Marilyn Campbell and Richard Porton for commenting on the introductory survey. Very special thanks to Siân Murray, who watched and discussed many of these films with me while opening up her home to my frequent visits. To Chantal Lyant, Regine Boulet, Julie Marshall, and Elle-Kari Höjeberg, many thanks for the friendship and talk in what became homes away from home. Finally, this work is dedicated with love to Dosier Hammond for his sharp insights, easy laughter, and persistent encouragement.

All compilation errors are mine. Credits and other information were culled during visits to the University of Southern California Libraries, the British Film Institute National Library (London), the New York Public Library for the Performing Arts, the Rutgers University Libraries, the Princeton University Library, the Bibliothèque du film (Paris), and the Swedish Film Institute Library (Stockholm). I viewed tapes and films at these places and also attended the London Film Festival, the New York Film Festival, the Festival international de films de femmes, and FESPACO in Burkina Faso. I am grateful to the Rutgers University Faculty Council for a research grant to travel to Africa, to the Rutgers University Libraries for two annual and several short-term leaves in support of this project, and to my many colleagues in New Brunswick who facilitated my work over the last ten years, especially the staff of the Media Center and Jeris Cassel. Many other people at Rutgers provided inspiration during this period, especially the numerous women connected to the Women's and Gender Studies Department and the Institute for Women's Leadership, who model diversity in every possible mode and who have guided me over the last ten years in more ways than they know.

CRITERIA FOR INCLUSION

The following are the criteria for inclusion of entries:

- The main protagonist is a woman, either an adult or a girl taking on the responsibilities of adult relationships such as partners, children, and employment. Films about children have not been included.
- Fictional content, including non-narrative, avant-garde, or experimental types.
- Feature-length films intended for theatrical release. Made-for-television films have not been researched and are not included, though no attempt has been made to weed them out when their status was not clear. Feature-length films of anthologized short pieces are included.
- Release date is after 1960.

More than 90 percent of the films listed are dramas. All types of poetic styles, whether called non-narrative, avant-garde, or experimental, are included. Comedies, romances, and other popular commercial genres, such as martial arts, horror, exploitation, and fantasy, are included more selectively than the former categories. In these areas, selection was based on critical recognition or value as a representative example. Similarly, the list is limited to representative examples of the many international films released during the 1960s and later that focused on women by exploiting increasingly liberal standards in the depiction of sexuality. Romances where the viewpoint and emphasis is shared between a man and a woman have been excluded. The list is intended to facilitate the user in investigating the diversity of national cinemas, which by definition are opposed to hegemonic Hollywood cinema yet frequently utilize Hollywood's well-known cinematic codes to describe a culturally different visual space.

ORGANIZATION AND CODES USED IN ENTRIES

The filmography is arranged by country, and within that, chronologically. Entries are composed of the original title, an English title, and the date of release. If any of the film's production personnel are female, I have indicated this after the year of release, using the following codes:

D = director
S = screenwriter or story source
C = cinematographer
P = producer

Production personnel are then cited (using the same codes), followed by primary cast (A = actresses/actors), a synopsis, and selected awards. The films I have not seen cite the source where the synopsis information was found. Abbreviations for these sources are listed in the Sources for Entry Synopses.

All other information was culled from a variety of sources: One entry may in fact entail details from several sources in addition to the one cited for the synopsis. In the case of multinational productions, the country and language that the film was produced in is preferred. More than ninety countries and even more languages are represented in this filmography. Because the names and titles were culled from a diverse and extensive number of sources, not all in English, using transliterated words and foreign characters consistently was a challenge. French sources, for instance, present different transliterations for non-Roman names than do English sources. When the capitalization style of a non-English language has a clear standard, for example, the German capitalization of nouns, I followed that standard. When consistent guidelines were not available, I followed two generic styles: English, where most words are capitalized, or European languages, where only the first word after the article is capitalized. Transliterations are handled in the latter manner. The indexes, however, will sometimes indicate other types of styles, especially when the variation results in a wide alphabetical separation between the style used and the variant.

Two name indexes provide access to directors, screenwriters, producers, cinematographers, and selected leading actresses and actors. When I was able to determine an individual's sex, (f) and (m) follow the name in these indexes.

The Index of Titles lists the original titles and an English version. Sometimes titles in other languages have been included, particularly when title variations have made information about the film difficult to find, but effort was not made to be comprehensive in listing variant titles.

The index to fictional subjects is comprehensive within the restrictions of the synopses, allowing access to the geographic setting and time period of the film as well as events, actions, and individual characteristics portrayed.

SOURCES FOR ENTRY SYNOPSES

24 Images: La revue québécoise du cinéma (Montreal: 24 Images).

ABS-CBN film productions (www.abs-cbn.com/star-cinema).

AFI American Film Institute Catalog, 1961–1970 (Berkeley: University of California Press, 1974).

African Cinema: Politics and Culture. Manthia Diawara (Bloomington: Indiana University Press, 1992).

African Diaspora Film Festival [annual, 1993–] (www.nyadff.org).

African Media Project, University of KwaZulu-Natal, South Africa. (www.und.ac.za/und/ccms/amp/reviews/princess.htm).

Alwan past releases. Alwan Communications (www.alwanfilms.com).

AMG. All Movie Guide [accessed throughout]. All Media Guide (www.allmovie.com).

Asian Film Connections. Asian Film Foundation (www.asianfilms.org).

Atlanta Journal-Constitution (Atlanta: Cox Enterprises).

L'Attente des femmes (www.attentedes-femmes.com).

BAM [monthly film program] (New York: Brooklyn Academy of Music).

Bayami Magazine (www.bayami.com).

Belgian Cinema (Brussels: Cinématheque Royale de Belgique, 1999).

Biennale des cinémas arabes à Paris. Institut du Monde Arabe, Paris (www.imarabe.org).

BiFi fiches du cinéma [accessed throughout]. Bibliothèque du Film, Paris (www.bifi.fr).

Black African Cinema. Nwachukwu Frank Ukadike (Berkeley: University of California Press, 1994).

Bollycat: The Chronicles of Plagiarism in India's Bollywood Movies (www.bollycat.com).

Boston Turkish festival [program]. Turkish American Cultural Society of New England (http://tacsne.org/BTF-Program-2002.htm).

Bright Lights Film Journal [quarterly] (www.brightlightsfilm.com).

British Film Catalogue, vol. I: Fiction Film, 1895–1994. Denis Gifford (London: Fitzroy Dearborn, 2001).

Bullfrog [catalog]. Bullfrog Films (www.bullfrogfilms.com).

Cesko-Slovenská Filmová Databáze (http://csfd.cz/film.php).

Chaosmag: Multiperspectives on Meaningful Cinema (www.chaosmag.net).

Chicago Reader [weekly] (http://onfilm.chicagoreader.com/movies/capsules).

Chicago Sun-Times (Chicago: Chicago Sun-Times).

The *Chinese Filmography: The 2444 Feature Films Produced by Studios in the People's Republic of China from 1949 through 1995.* Donald J. Marion (Jefferson, N.C.: McFarland, 1997).

Chinese-Language Film. Sheldon H. Lu and Emilie Yueh-Yu Yeh, eds. (Honolulu: University of Hawaii, 2005).

Cine espanol [annual] (Madrid: Uniespana, 1960–).

Cineaste. America's Leading Magazine on the Art and Politics of the Cinema (New York: Cineaste).

Cinema (Bucharest: Comitetul de Stat pentru Cultura si Arta).

Le Cinéma bresilien. Antonio Paulo Paranagua (Paris: Centre Georges Pompidou, 1987).

Le Cinéma coréen. Adriano Apra, ed. (Paris: Centre Georges Pompidou, 1993).

Le Cinéma de l'Inde. Yves Thoraval (Paris: L'Harmattan, 1998).

Cinema dei paesi Arabo-Mediterranei: Arab-Mediterranean Film Festival, European Commission. Euromed Audiovisuel (Napoli: Magma, 2001).

Le Cinéma grec. Michel Demopoulos (Paris: Centre Georges Pompidou, 1995).

Cinéma hongrois, 1963–1988. Jean-Pierre Jeancolas (Paris: Editions du Centre de la Recherche Scientifique, 1989).

Cinema in Turkey: Young New Wave (Republic of Turkey: Ministry of Foreign Affairs) (www.mfa.gov.tr/grupc/cj/cja/cinema5.htm).

Le Cinéma japonais, vol. 2: 1945–. Tadao Sato (Paris: Centre Georges Pompidou, 1997).

Cinéma Méditerranéen Montpellier Festival, 27th (www.cinemed.tm.fr).

Cinema of Flames: Balkan Film, Culture, and Media. Dina Lordanova (London: BFI, 2001).

The Cinema of Ousmane Sembène. Francoise Pfaff (Westport, Conn.: Greenwood Press, 1984).

Le Cinéma polonais. Boleslaw Michalek (Paris: Centre Georges Pompidou, 1992).

Cinéma Québec: Masters in Their Own House. Janis L. Pallister (Teaneck, N.J.: Fairleigh Dickinson, 1995).

Le Cinéma turc. Mehmet Basutcu, ed. (Paris: Centre Georges Pompidou, 1996).

Les **Cinémas d'Afrique** dictionnaire. L'Association de Trois Mondes & FESPACO. (Paris: Karthala, 2000).

Les **Cinémas du** moyen-*orient: Iran, Egypte, Turquie (1896–2000).* Yves Thoraval (Paris: Séguier, 2000).

Cinemagia (www.cinemagia.ro/movie.php).

Cinematic Imagination: Indian Popular Films as Social History. Jyotika Virdi (New Brunswick, N.J.: Rutgers University, 2003).

Cinemaya, the Asian film magazine (New Delhi: A. Vasudev, 1988–).

Cinemythology: Greek Myths in World Cinema. Thessalonika International Film Festival, 2005 (www.filmfestival.gr).

Companion Encyclopedia of Middle Eastern and North African Film. Oliver Leamamn, ed. (New York: Routledge, 2001).

Contemporary Japanese Cinema. Mark Schilling (New York: Weatherhill, 1999).

Contemporary Spanish Cinema. Barry Jordan and Rikki Morgan-Tanosumas (Manchester: Manchester University, 1998).

Le Corps, l'histoire, le territoire; les rapports de genre dans le cinema algerienne. Ratiba Hadj-Moussa (Paris: Publisud, 1994).

The Cuban Filmography: 1897 through 2001. Alfonso J. García Osuna (Jefferson, N.C.: McFarland, 2003).

Danish Directors. Met Hjort and Ib Bondebjerg (Bristol, U.K.: Intellect, 2001).

Database of Philippine Movies. U. P. Film Center (www.geocities.com/philmovies/fildatafilm.html).

DEFA, East German Cinema: 1946–1992. Sean Allan (New York: Berghahn, 1997).

DEFA Film Library [catalog]. University of Massachusetts (www.umass.edu/defa).

Directory of Contemporary Dutch Films and Filmmakers. Matthew Stevens (London: Flicks, 1990).

Dizionario del cinema italiano, vol. 3: 1960–1969; vol. 4: 1970–1979; vol. 5: 1980–1989; vol. 6: 1990–1999. Roberto Chiti and Roberto Poppi (Rome: Gremese, 1991–).

Dutch Treats: New Films from Holland. Red Diaper Productions (www.reddiaper.com/Dutch2002/dutch2002.htm).

Enclitic (Los Angeles: Enclitic).

Encyclopaedia of Hindi Cinema. Govind Nihalani Gulzar and Saibal Chatterjee, eds. (New Delhi: Encyclopaedia Britannica India/Popular Prakashan, 2003).

Encyclopaedia of Indian Cinema. Ashish Rajadhyaksha and Paul Willemen (New Delhi: Oxford University Press, 1999).

Encyclopedia of Chinese Film. Zhang Yingjin (New York: Routledge, 1998).

Encyclopedia of European Cinema. Ginette Vincendeau (London: BFI, 1995).

Faber Companion to Foreign Films. Ronald Bergan and Robyn Karney, eds. (Boston: Faber and Faber, 1992).

Fassbinder:The Life and Work of a Provocative Genius. Christian Braad Thomsen (New York: Faber and Faber, 1991).

Festival de films de femmes [catalog]. Créteil, France: Festival de films de femmes, 1982–2004.

Festival des 3 Continents database. Centre de Documentation Cinématographique, Festival des 3 Continents, Paris [accessed throughout] (www.3continents.com).

Festival Internazionale Cinema Delle Donne. Turin, June 1996 (http://festivalcinemadelledonne.com).

FII Film Index International [accessed throughout]. Chadwyck-Healey.

Filipino American Films. San Francisco International Asian American Film Festival, 1991 (www.naatanet.org).

Film Criticism (Edinboro, Pa.: Film Criticism).

Film Library Quarterly (Greenwich, Conn.: Film Library Information Council).

Film Society of Lincoln Center at the Walter Reade [calendar] (New York: Film Society of Lincoln Center).

Film w Stopklatka (www.stopklatka.pl).

Films and Feminism: Essays in Indian Cinema. Jasbir Jain and Sudha Rai, eds. (New Delhi: Rawat, 2002).

Films and Filming (London: Hansom Books).

Finnish Film Forum (www.ses.fi/en).

Foundation for Hellenic Culture [calendar] (www.foundationforhellenicculture.com/cinemacalendar.htm).

Francophone Women Film Directors: A Guide. Janis L. Pallister and Ruth A. Hottell (Madison, N.J.: Fairleigh Dickinson, 2005).

Freedom Film Festival [annual]. American Cinema Foundation (www.cinemafoundation.com/fffmain.html).

French-Speaking *Women Film Directors: A Guide.* Janis L. Pallister (Madison, N.J.: Fairleigh Dickinson, 1997).

German Cinema *Book.* Tim Bergfelder and Erica Carter, eds. (London: British Film Institute, 2002).

German National *Cinema.* Sabine Hake (London: Routledge, 2002).

Greek Film Centre (www.gfc.gr).

The **Greek Filmography**: *1914 through 1996.* Dimitris Koliodimos (Jefferson, N.C.: McFarland, 1999).

Guide to Latin *American, Caribbean, and U.S. Latino Made Film and Video.* Karen Ranucci and Julie Feldman, eds. (Lanham, Md.: Scarecrow, 1998).

Histoire du cinéma *francais, vol. 2: 1961–1965; vol. 3: 1966–1970.* Maurice Bessy (Paris: Pygmalion, 1986).

Hollywood Beyond *the Wall: Cinema of East Germany.* Daniela Berghahn (Manchester: Manchester University, 2005).

Hong Kong *Filmography, 1977–1997: A Complete Reference to 1,100 Films Produced by British Hong Kong Studios.* John Charles, ed. (Jefferson, N.C.: McFarland, 2000).

Hungarian Cinema. John Cunninghman (London: Wallflower, 2004).

Hungarofilm Bulletin (Budapest: Interpress).

IMDb [Accessed throughout]. Internet Movie Database (www.imdb.com).

Indonesian Cinema. Karl G. Heider (Honolulu: University of Hawaii, 1991).

Indonesian Cinema 2. Krishna Sen (London: Zed, 1994).

The **Irish Filmography**: *Fiction Films, 1896–1996.* Kevin Rockett, ed. (Dublin: Red Mountain Media, 1996).

Japanese Cinema: *Essential Handbook.* Thomas Weisser and Yuko Mihara Weisser (Miami: Vital, 1998).

Japanese Film *Directors.* Audie Bock (Tokyo: Kodansha, 1978).

Jewish Film Archive (www.jewishfilm.com).

Journal of Modern *Greek Studies* (Baltimore, Md.: Johns Hopkins University Press).

Kinoglasnost. Anna Lawton (Cambridge: Cambridge University, 1992).

Kinoizkustvo [*Cinema Art* magazine] (Sofia: Union of Bulgarian Film Makers).

KOFIC Korean Film/Korean Cinema [annual print and electronic]. Korean Film Council, Seoul (www.koreanfilm.or.kr).

Korean Film. Eungjun Min and Jinsook Joo (Stamford, Conn.: Praeger, 2003).

Kvinnor i nordisk *film Filmfestival* [catalog, 1983]. Sweden.

lez films. Lesbian-centered European films. lez films, Europe (www.sappho.net/euro-sappho/film.html).

London Film *Festival* [catalog] (London: London Film Festival).

Los Angeles *Times* (Los Angeles: Los Angeles Times).

Post-Colonial Images: *A Study in North African Cinema.* Roy Armes (Bloomington: Indiana University Press, 2005).

The **Mexican Filmography**: *1916 through 2001.* David E. Wilt (Jefferson, N.C.: McFarland, 2004).

MFB. *Monthly Film Bulletin* (London: British Film Institute).

MOMA Film and Media Exhibitions [calendar] (New York: Museum of Modern Art).

Monash University Arts. Monash Asia Institute (www.art.monash.edu/au/mai/films).

Multiple Modernities. Jenny Kwok Wah Lau (Philadelphia: Temple, 2003).

The Nation (New York: The Nation).

National Pastime: *Contemporary Philippine Cinema.* Joel David (Manila: Anvil Publishing, 1990).

New Directors, New Films [annual program]. MOMA and Film Society of Lincoln Center, New York.

New York *Film Festival* [catalog] (New York: Film Society of Lincoln Center).

New Zealand *Films: 1912–1996.* Helen Martin and Sam Edwards (New York: Oxford, 1997).

NFDC films, detailed descriptions. Indian National Film Development Corporation (www.geocities.com/curlybraces/movies/hindimovies/htm).

Nicaragua: Retrospectiva de cine y video, 2004. Fundación Luciémaga, Managua (www.cinenica.net).

Le **Nouvel Observateur** (Paris: Nouvel Observateur).

Nouvelles du nord, *l'année Scandinave* [annual] (Nantes: L'Elan, 1997–).

NYT *New York Times* (New York: New York Times).

O Cais do olhar *cinema português de longa metragem e a ficção muda.* José de Matos-Cruz (Lisbon: Cinemateca Portuguesa, Museu do Cinema, 1999).

Once upon a Time *in China: A Guide to Hong Kong, Taiwanese, and Mainland Chinese Cinema.* Jeff Yang (New York: Atria, 2003).

PFA film notes. Pacific Film Archive, University of California, Berkeley (www.bampfa.berkeley.edu/resources/film_notes).

Pioneer Theater [calendar] (www.twoboots.com/pioneer).

Polish Feature Films: Reference Guide, 1945–1985. Oskar Sobanski (West Cornwall, Conn.: Locust Hill, 1987).

Polish National Cinema. Marek Haltof (New York: Berghahn, 2002).

Polish Women Directors. Polish Cultural Institute (www.polishculture.org.uk/events_film_women.html).

PopcornQ movies. Planetout Inc. (www.planetout.com/pno/popcornq).

À la **Recherche du cinéma** Irakien, 1945–1985. Shakir Nouri (Paris: L'Harmattan, 1986).

Reviews and Criticism of Vietnam War Theatrical and Television Dramas. Compiled by John K. McAskill. Accessed 2005, June 10 (www.lasalle.edu/library/vietnam/FilmIndex/home.htm).

Revue belge du cinéma (Brussels, Belgium: APEC).

Russian Book and Video (www.russianbookvideo.com/index.html).

Screen [incorporating Screen Education] (London: Society for Education in Film and Television).

Screen Memories: The Hungarian Cinema of Márta Mészáros. Catherine Portuges (Bloomington: Indiana University Press, 1993).

Screenonline (London: British Film Institute) (www.screenonline.org.uk).

Sight & Sound. The International Film Magazine (London: British Film Institute).

Skrien (Amsterdam: Skrien Filmscrift).

SoHo Weekly News (New York: SoHo Weekly News).

South American Cinema: A Critical Filmography, 1915–1994. Timothy Barnard and Peter Rist, eds. (Austin: University of Texas, 1996).

Soviet Film, Family Screen (www.domekan.ru/films).

The **St. James** Women Filmmakers Encyclopedia: Women on the Other Side of the Camera. Amy L. Unterburger, ed. (Farmington Hills, Mich.: Visible Ink, 1999).

The **Time Out** Film Guide. Tom Milne, ed. (London: Penguin, 1993).

Tomson Films (http://ray.com.hk/tomson/company.html).

Tribeca Film Festival Guide (New York: Tribeca Film Festival, 2003).

Twin Peeks: Australian and New Zealand Feature Films. Deb Verhoeven, ed. (Melbourne: Damned Press, 1999).

UW Film Society [calendar] (Waterloo, U.K.: University of Waterloo, 1997) (www.arts.uwaterloo.ca/~dobradov/fine%arts/pictures/juhde/fsprog7.htm).

Variety [daily] (Los Angeles: Variety).

Village Voice (New York: Village Voice).

West German Cinema Since 1945. Richard C. Helt and Marie Helt (Metuchen N.J.: Scarecrow, 1987).

West German Cinema, 1985–1990. Richard C. Helt and Marie Helt (Metuchen N.J.: Scarecrow, 1992).

Women through the Lens: Gender and Nation in a Century of Chinese Cinema. Shuquin Cui (Honolulu: University of Hawaii, 2003).

The **Women's Companion** to International Film. Annette Kuhn and Susannah Radstone, eds. (Berkeley: University of California, 1994).

Working Stiffs, Union Maids, Reds, and Riffraff: An Organized Guide to Films about Labor. Tom Zaniello (Ithaca: Cornell University Press, 1996).

World Cinema: Hungary. Byron Burns (Trowbridge, U.K.: Flicks Books, 1996).

Yale Council on Southeast Asian Studies. Southeast Asia Film Series (www.yale.edu/seas/SEAS-FilmSeries.htm).

A CRITICAL SURVEY OF WOMEN IN LEADING ROLES IN INTERNATIONAL CINEMA: 1960 TO THE PRESENT

Intelligence does not have sex . . . you do not have brains in vain. . . . Keep your eyes and ears open and don't forget me.—Sor Juana Inez de la Cruz in *I, the Worst of All* (Argentina, 1991)

FILM STUDIES CONTEXT

The history of women's representation in feature films is a story of actors working in collaboration with other individual film artists. This collective aspect of filmmaking has not always been appreciated by film critics and audiences; indeed, the auteur theory deemphasized filmmaking's group process in order to argue that the best cinema had strong individual authorship, usually in the person of the director. For women actors and their roles, however, this collective aspect of filmmaking has frequently meant some amount of independence from the typically male creative trades—directors, screenwriters, cinematographers, and so forth—involved in making a film.

In contrast to the auteur theory, a parallel critical effort of the 1970s involved deconstructing the concept of the "author" (deemed to be an instance of patriarchal control) and therefore validated the potential for shared authoring presented by the collective approach to filmmaking. When combined with feminist ideas that challenged both social hierarchies and binary oppositions, this approach allowed feminist film critics to focus on the intersection of gender and performance. Even so, little scholarly attention has been given to the work that actors do in negotiating with other production personnel; in working with a specific camera angle or framing; in illuminating the character's relationship to other objects and spaces on the screen, and in applying their craft to transcend what are frequently generic environments, characters, dialogue, and story lines. Merely identifying appropriate subject matter for such study has remained difficult, and

it is the purpose of this filmography to facilitate this effort.

Beyond these specific production contexts and theoretical questions about authorship, the representation of women also has been affected by ideas about commercial audience expectations, the contemporary social position of women, and other broad sociopolitical conditions. Progressivism, for instance, sometimes provokes the use of women characters as models of reform, while militarism and nationalism take advantage of women characters to represent the anxieties of instability. Similarly, in a culture of free speech that values liberating sexuality, the exploitation of sexual content in stories of prostitutes exposes a contradictory impulse to degrade women.

These various approaches to the representation of women overlap at any particular time with the established canon of film studies. Cerise Howard regularly polls a large number of film professionals, critics, and academics for the online journal *Senses of Cinema*, and in 2002 she posted a special "Top Five Lists of Films by Women Directors" (www.sensesofcinema.com/contents/top_tens/womens.html). Concerning the results, she asks why "the very same directors to have polled the strongest here . . . [are] all poorly represented in our ongoing, all filmmaker 'Top Tens' poll?" One reason may be that, with the exception of titles such as *Beau Travail*, a film about men made by the extraordinary woman filmmaker Claire Denis, the two hundred films by women directors that were nominated overlap almost entirely with the subject of women. The other all-filmmaker polls to which she refers are not only weak on women directors but also weak on films focused on a female protagonist. To put this in another perspective, the 2000 edition of the *International Dictionary of Films and Filmmakers* lists approximately 110 films "about women" (whether directed by women or men) out of more than 680 chosen to represent world cinema. The reason is perhaps as simple as Simone de

Beauvoir's opening line of the *Second Sex*: "For a long time I have hesitated to write a book on women. The subject is irritating, especially to women; and it is not new."

In *A Woman's View: How Hollywood Spoke to Women*, 1930–1960 (Knopf, 1993), Jeanine Basinger defines a "woman's genre" as that which "places at the center of its universe a female who is trying to deal with the emotional, social, and psychological problems that are specifically connected to the fact that she is a woman." Since most of Hollywood's better-known films were men's films, as they are to this day, her survey is based on lesser-known films of the four decades prior to 1960 that fit her main criterion of having a female protagonist. In support of this genre definition, Basinger focuses on films with white actors and describes class issues in much the same way that she describes issues of gender—as a naturalized matter of conformity and convention. Race issues are marginalized to the point of not being addressed at all, even in a lengthy discussion of both film versions of *Imitation of Life*. She concludes with the paradox that the problems of women "are represented in the story as a form of choice the woman must make between options that are mutually exclusive. The presentation of the woman's world allows for both an overt indication that women should lead conventional lives and a covert form of liberation in which they are shown doing something else or expressing anger about this need for conformity" (p. 506).

Feminist movements that entered academic discourse at the time Basinger's survey ends questioned the unproblematized "fact of woman" and the assumption of "mutually exclusive options" that Basinger presents as givens. Nonetheless, her working definition provides a useful starting point for looking at the more diverse list of films included in the present filmography, which begins where her survey left off—in 1960. One big difference in the films listed here is that they are not all generic Hollywood products. In addition, the problems these women protagonists face are broader than those "specifically connected to the fact that she is a woman" and are frequently made much more explicit and complex by placement in a larger political-historical context.

It is the implied assertion of this survey (and the filmography it introduces) that the intelligent, even brilliant, performances of female actors in the fiction films described here are as critical to enlightening content as the group of "women-authored" films generally referred to as "feminist." Classical narratives, especially dramas, constructed around a central female character illustrate the depth of women's lives through the performed expression of strength, weakness, will, and intelligence in the characters portrayed, making acting itself a kind of authorship.

The decade of the 1960s produced global sea changes that impacted film culture at the time and are still influential today: the feature-length "art" film; technical advances that allowed widespread filming outdoors; and, in popular culture, an infusion of existential philosophy, minority rights, and pacifist politics. This filmography presents an array of lesser-known films—similar in commercial standing to the set that Basinger worked with—from many different national cinemas and independent production contexts. It also includes a share of blockbusters such as *Alien* and *Erin Brockovich*, as well as popular films such as *G.I. Jane* and *Wing Chun*. *Thelma and Louise* and *The Piano* continue to define for Western audiences the modern, serious "women's film," even as they remain isolated in their successful combination of highly cinematic scenarios—of female agency struggling against worldly circumscription—and sexually commanding performances. Both continue to have great impact and appeal, provoking general audience discussion as well as classroom use and academic study. Some films about women, such as *The Comeback* (Turkey, 1973) and *Tjoet Nya Dien* (Indonesia, 1988), are described as among the best and most popular films of their national film cultures.

SOCIAL AND POLITICAL CHANGE: FILMS OF THE 1960S

All history is based on some people deciding the fate of others . . . The only way to change this is by bitter upheaval. What for? you ask. What for? conveys nothing of the fullness of life.—*Rosa Luxemburg*

By the early 1960s, there was a stream of commercial efforts, usually scripted and directed by men and following in the narrative tradition of melodrama, that described the restricted options available to women. In these narratives, the path of dependency and need was the most wide and clear, and variations from that path frequently resulted in death. The theme of single women and the power they might or might not have over their lives, alongside the responsibility they might or might not take, was acutely explored in prominent films from countries with substantial film production, most notably France. Working-class and lower-middle-class economic constraints provided the tension and excuse for exploring inequities, and frank sexuality provided commercial allure.

Upper-middle-class lives, like those of the filmmakers themselves, were more rarely depicted.

In *Butterfield 8* (United States, 1960), taken from the novel by best-selling chronicler of postwar materialism, John O'Hara, Elizabeth Taylor plays a beautiful daughter desperate to hide her true source of income as a prostitute from her single mother, who is equally desperate to hang onto their middle-class propriety. Their characters are counterweighted by a wealthy mother and daughter—her lover's in-laws—with nothing but propriety to concern them and the skills to manipulate other people that go with upper-class education and training. Taylor's role is a continuation of her efforts to bring the serious side of sexuality to Hollywood cinema, and her work is in direct contrast to the more typical female characters of the 1950s whose sexuality was expressed in comic energy called "spunk" and whose triumph was confirmed by the compliment of "You're cute when you're angry."

In *Adua and Company* (Italy, 1960), Simone Signoret reveals her own personal social awareness via the role of a prostitute, who leads a quartet of prostitutes to open a restaurant when their trade becomes illegal. Although their success is an only-in-the-movies saga, the angry resistance of the leader to a landlord who insists they resume their former trade is less so, and she is resoundingly punished for it. The Hollywood ending of *Butterfield 8* (Taylor's character dies in an accident just when her lover decides to stay with her) is profoundly countered by the one in *Adua and Company*, where the long since defeated Adua is taunted by her fellow prostitutes and refused by a john when he catches sight of her aged face. Simone Signoret was pilloried for her refusal to cover up her middle-aged appearance and remains one of the few great actresses to insist on letting audiences know what a naturally aging woman looks like. The same year, Anouk Aimée played *Lola* (France, 1960) and Stéphane Audran and Bernadette Lafont starred in *The Girls* (France, 1960), both stories of working-class women waiting for spouses to appear. In the first, the isolation and boredom of a dance-hall hostess devoted to her young son is countered by her relentless good cheer as she waits for her husband to return in his Cadillac. In the second, a group of retail-store clerks come alive at night, where they experience the continuum of teasing, seduction, and violence. In *Two Women* (Italy, 1961), Sophia Loren plays a capable shop owner who takes her daughter out of the danger of wartime Rome but discovers she cannot protect her from marauding rapists, racistly portrayed not as Italians but as turbaned Moroccans. The political rationale

for branding women witches is clearly laid out in *Trial of Joan of Arc* (France, 1962), in which Joan is a confident agent of her own fate, proud of confounding the English. As in all "witch" scenarios, it is her refusal to embrace "normal" female activity, along with her active public threat to the powers that be, that leads to her being punished.

In *The Big City* (India, 1963), an apartment-dwelling wife, played by Anil Chatterjee, gets no recognition from her family in her attempt to support them by selling vacuums door to door in the suburbs, and she eventually gives up as the job becomes just another oppression. In *Contempt* (France, 1963), Brigitte Bardot plays a wife who is deeply offended by her husband's offering of her presence to flatter his boss; so great is her need to look up to her husband that she decides she cannot live with him otherwise. In *My Life to Live* (France, 1962), a prostitute played by Anna Karina states that she begins her day with the notion that "I am responsible." This assertion affords an unusual display of confidence for a prostitute, and it leads inevitably to her resistance and gangland death. In *Mamma Roma* (Italy, 1962), Anna Magnani plays a single mother with a similar determination to improve her condition by abandoning her work as a prostitute, which, in this case, leads to the death of her son. Most of these characters have a scripted foolish (feminine) side—coy, pouting, or otherwise childish behavior, which is effectively integrated and then dismissed by the extraordinary women playing the roles. They turn such behavior into a passing whim, an inconsequential act required of them by others, making it merely a part of an otherwise fully rounded character with more important things on her mind. True to the times, the roles are given depth by the odd leftist line, such as that of the dulled wife in *The Red Desert* (Italy, 1964), played by Monica Vitti, one of the few actors able to make boredom intelligible. Referring to her mental illness, psychotherapy, and seduction by a family friend who takes advantage of her condition, she says, "Apparently, I'm cured enough to become an unfaithful wife."

During this period, lesbian sexuality is gingerly handled via a version of Lillian Hellman's *The Children's Hour* (United States, 1962), in which characters bravely played by Audrey Hepburn and Shirley MacLaine face a new understanding of their close friendship. The Hepburn character's offense at her male lover's suspicion creates the blank slate that she needs to understand her friend's suicide and walk away by herself in the end. In a considerably less mundane mode, Chinese leftist propaganda combines with a long history of theatrical cross-dressing to create the extraordinary spectacle of *The Love Eterne* (China, 1963) where a young woman, played by Betty Loh Ti, attends university dressed as a man, and a young man played by a woman, Ivy Ling Po, argue the rights of women in song. The art of these two women in acting out a heterosexual love story with a pronounced lesbian subtext in mostly song and dance results in a breathtaking collaboration.

All these films were products of either big commercial studios or well-known directors of the burgeoning international "art cinema," and all have male directors and scriptwriters. *Gertrud* (Denmark, 1964) is an appropriate cap to this first half of the 1960s. In it, Nina Pens Røde plays a former opera singer now married to a lawyer, whom she plans to leave for a callow young musician. Her first lover, a lauded national poet, along with a psychologist, who platonically stays with her to the end of her life, meet the other two men one night at a banquet. With the four men in attendance, Gertrud expounds on her theory of life as love, a performance that effectively quells the male vanity around her. To them, whether she is an unattainable ideal and the frustration of their desire, or a foolish woman easily tricked, hardly matters—they remain enthralled. Gertrud also has an odd relationship to patriotism, as evidenced by this banquet, where the poet is met with pageantry and speeches for writing of "love without bounds" despite all those "conventional people who know nothing of it." Grounded completely in her erotic life, Gertrud has nothing at all to do with motherhood or anything else of a practical nature. She is at once liberated from men and a whole product of their imagination.

In the years from 1960 to 1965, women filmmakers became more visible in international art cinema and were initially recognized by approaching women's characters in tightly focused ways. Agnès Varda investigated a two-hour period in the life of a woman waiting for the results of a cancer test in *Cleo from 5 to 7* (France, 1961). Věra Chytilová worked within an aesthetic of experimental formalism to tell stories of contrasting women—a homemaker and a gymnast—in *Something Different* (Czechoslovakia, 1963), while Monika Treut began her investigation into gender politics and sexuality with the story of a dominatrix in *Seduction: The Cruel Woman* (West Germany, 1963).

The first film of the period to make broad statements about the general condition of heterosexual white women was Mai Zetterling's *Loving Couples* (Sweden, 1964). In this film set in the nineteenth century, which combines the class themes of melodrama with themes of sexual difference, an upperclass woman, orphaned and raised by a servant,

shares the central role with an artist's model, very much at ease with her sexuality, and another servant who fell from middle-class status as a teenager when her father was killed. In each case, the formative years of preadolescence and the girls' ability to fend off sexual humiliation or victimization are emphasized. The one most in pursuit of pleasure, who gleefully marries a gay man to help out her married lover, is the most well adjusted and happy.

Following these efforts from the first half of the 1960s into the latter half of the decade, there develops a more expansive focus on female protagonists in art cinema from around the world, much of it scripted by women. Colonial entitlement and the soul destructiveness of racism are cataloged in *Black Girl* (Senegal, 1966). This film remains potent in its depiction of a middle-class couple who go to Senegal to import a girl, played by Thérèse Diop Mbissine, then install her in a tiny room in their small apartment in Marseille and refuse her freedom of movement. The husband can see that it is not right, but he is completely passive in the domestic environment and defers to his wife, who asserts abusive authority over the girl until she despairs and drowns herself in the bathtub.

The sexual liberation of a teacher (Joanne Woodward) from a restricted life caring for her lonely mother in *Rachel, Rachel* (United States, 1968) is marked by an extensive look at the tender friendship between her and another teacher, played by Estelle Parsons. The friendship is sustained by sharp intellectual exchanges, as Rachel is pragmatically agnostic, while her friend has taken to attending a faith-healing group. A declaration of love by the friend is at first met with rejection, but later, when Rachel is both desirous and fearful of a pregnancy, she attempts to reconnect. Taking strength from her friend when she leaves town, Rachel laments when they part, "Sometimes I wish I could have been different for you."

By the end of the decade, a vast range of imaginative possibilities for women characters have been opened, including the positive choice of remaining unmarried in *The Butcher* (France, 1969). "It's normal," insists the confident teacher played by Stéphane Audran, who bravely befriends and then tries to protect the village butcher from his war-induced insanity. In *A Gentle Woman* (France, 1969), a cold marriage with a very routine sense of command and control leads a young girl to suicide. As played by Dominique Sanda, the character is both mysterious and political, after "something wider than marriage" and resentful that her husband believes he can dominate her with money. In *Mama Got Married* (USSR, 1969), a muscular construction worker, played by Lyusyena Ovchinnikova, who lives in a single room with her teenage son, insists on her right to bring a new man into the household, despite the son's upset. *The Prime of Miss Jean Brodie* (United Kingdom, 1969) expands the important theme of women's commitment to the status quo in its portrait of a teacher, played by Maggie Smith, who has romanticized her unmarried status at the expense of manipulating and seducing everyone around her, including, most reliably, "the Brodie girls." Building directly from a leftist political agenda, *Lucía* (Cuba, 1969) tells stories of women from three different revolutionary time periods, each named Lucia. Focus is on the childlike naïveté of the women—each one becomes involved with a man who is not right for her, but each one grows during the process. Their emotive thrashing, mirror vanity, and relationship to the materialism and decadence of Cuban society in general is emphasized through the first two episodes, while the third has much to say about the persistence of gendered relationships through even the most extensive legal reforms intended to liberate women from male expectations.

During this period, women filmmakers increasingly found the space to look in detail at women in their specific sociopolitical environments. Larisa Shepitko shows the common instance of a competent woman turned autocrat in the story of a military pilot consigned after the war to the "more suitable" environment of a grade school in *Wings* (USSR, 1966). This film begins in a tailor shop's triple mirror, with the protagonist, played by Maya Bulgakova, surveying her head-to-toe form in her new pinstripe suit and reveling in her executive status. Back at the school, she remains insensitive and overly stern to her charges. She has a strong friendship with a museum curator and problems with her grown daughter that interest her even less than her job; all she dreams of is flying again. In *Brief Encounters* (USSR, 1968), Kira Muratova poetically mines female ambivalence via the frustrations of a city bureaucrat in love with a musician. Muratova herself plays the water utilities administrator who has worked her way into a high-level position that leaves her vulnerable to being pulled into making propaganda speeches. In the opening scene, she broods at her kitchen table, taps her pencil in time, begins to write her objections to her "comrades," then frets some more: "Leave or do the dishes . . . to do or not to do." She approaches the big stack in the sink, then instead grabs the telephone and objects to her boss that she does not want to do the conference on agriculture because her specialty is municipal economy, water supply in particular. Her lover proudly taunts her by telling her if he had a boss like hers, he would quit. Both

these Soviet characters reveal the poignant coping of educated women denied appropriate opportunity, the first by disdaining her job and lording it over children, the second by taking her job more seriously than her superiors, and in the process limiting the satisfaction of her personal life.

On this international stage of developing awareness of women's lives, Mai Zetterling laid out the continuum of class and gender in *The Girls* (Sweden, 1968), a story of a theater troupe touring Sweden with *Lysistrata*, the play by Aristophanes about Greek women who deny their men sex in order to stop war. The main actors, played by Bibi Andersson, Harriet Andersson, and Gunnel Lindblom, struggle with missing their children; competition among themselves; and derision from their partners, their colleagues, and their media entourage. The film is a catalog of women's relation to men in both the public and the domestic sphere, and its open-ended version of feminism, both cryptic and radical, has the accompanying commercial disadvantage of allowing the transgressive women to live. The search for, or lack of, community that characterizes women who are trained to be most comfortable in the home while restrained and polite in public, where they are valued first for their appearance, is related to the isolation within the frame they experience in this film; each is repeatedly left as a small figure in a large snowy landscape.

In stark contrast to these "modernist" narratives, Věra Chytilová moved confidently into a non-narrative form closely entwined with set decorating in *Daisies* (Czechoslovakia, 1966), which qualifies as postmodern in its delight with time-passing nonsense. A comment on the repressiveness of Western civilization more than the condition of women, this film focuses on the fun of childish behavior such as food fights, food orgies, and food violence, involving scissors, knives, ripping, tearing, and of course, teasing. The two friends have some of the charm and action orientation of picaresque heroes, but minimal engagement with others leaves them without much political context.

While the underlying loneliness and isolation of the two women in *Daisies* is covered up by their anarchic behavior, they relate nonetheless to many of the characters in these stories, who remain trapped and uncomfortable in both their homes and the outside world, at the extreme, compromising themselves and taunting others. Zetterling's *Night Games* (Sweden, 1966) is one of the most stark in depicting such a mother (Ingrid Thulin), spoiled by wealth and beauty, unable to take responsibility for herself or others, and abusive to her child. The main theme of the film is the destructiveness of teasing. Here the grown child, now a compulsive abuser of women, confronts his boyhood home and the memories of his selfish mother, who laughed while throwing him "doggy bones" and suggestively kissing him but getting angry when he became aroused. The film begins with a stillbirth and ends with the destruction of the family home—and the symbolic release of him from his mother.

During this period from 1960 to 1969, cinematic aesthetic norms changed markedly. However, the narrative arc of life and death, beginning and ending, which hangs over all stories, remained constant. For women, the fictional journey from cautionary to liberating tales most always begins with death. While death in battle as a hero may be romantic, when it comes to women, it's more likely senseless and stupid, a gendered relationship that *The Prime of Miss Jean Brodie* puts at its center. While Miss Brodie insists that the student she sent off to Spain died the death of a "heroine," the reality is she died seeking her brother on the wrong side of the fight, completely misled by her mentor into heading for fascist territory. Of the twenty-six films already mentioned, six end in death, suicide, or murder, and those six are the most critically acclaimed. Were we to survey the mass of films produced since the 1960s, beginning with the influential *Psycho*, the percentage of stories ending in death would be much higher, leading to mortal retribution for almost all women characters who attempt to do things differently.

By the beginning of the modern (Western, "second wave") women's movement around 1970, the themes that allowed the condition of women to be described in ways both alternative to and coincident with classical Hollywood narrative were already set in cinematic terms. These themes changed in emphasis and tone, but not in substance. They are isolation, autonomy, conservatism, appearances, race and class, abuse, punishment, family and work, friendship and love, sexuality, courage and creativity, genre fictions, and philosophical film.

FILMIC EXPLORATION OF WOMEN'S ISSUES: 1970–2004

Isolation

> I wanted to win. Though I never expected to play with God . . . I would have expected him to play fair.—*Household Saints* (United States, 1993)

Since the public sphere is male-dominated to this day, the dispersal and isolation of women is persistent. This isolation springs from the ste-

reotypical expectations of a destined future for women as a wife and mother. Any kind of passion that confounds these expectations leaves a woman character vulnerable to depression or persecution. In fictions, artists are the first to be stunned by this reality. In *Lady Sings the Blues* (United States, 1972), Diana Ross's imitations of Billie Holiday's singing run a parallel path to the ceaseless sexist and racist victimization of Holiday's life. Her mother, a live-in maid in a white suburb, is forced to board her as a child with "friends" who run brothels. Holiday runs away from the first one because she is raped. At the second one, she starts turning tricks herself, parlaying the money into freedom and a singing career. Gaining a tour with a white band, she's left out of the "whites only" relaxation and exhausts herself sufficiently to accept a "pickup" from a drug pusher. Drugs keep her career on track, but she's personally barred from venues where the band is allowed to play, and a felony drug charge, added to her too-visible talent, leaves her vulnerable to local authorities who deny her a license. The film provides grand presence in Diana Ross's singing and her onscreen romance with matinee idol Billy Dee Williams, but these elements exist entirely separate from the facts of Holiday's life, so that even within the film itself, she and her story are isolated from her public persona as a recording artist.

Self-destructive addictions, suicide, and mental illness are the inevitable by-products of isolation. In *Opening Night* (United States, 1977), Gena Rowlands plays a leading stage actress similarly isolated by her talent, which has left her surrounded by sycophants. The film suggests that she has witlessly found herself in a childless state at middle age and is so unable to cope with the death of an unknown teenage fan that she sabotages an opening night with alcohol. There is no explanation for her instability other than her vanity, and no sincere relationship to bolster her, yet the actress pulls off a drunken improvised version of her part to great applause. Years later, the same theme of aging is explored by a character played by Annette Bening in *Being Julia* (Canada, 2004), but this character is gifted with several real relationships, and her wit is persistently established throughout the film. Though she devises a scheme similar to the actress in *Opening Night*, she does not have to get drunk and execute it on her own. While *Opening Night* revels in the isolation of a lead character with no past other than that gossiped about by the people she now knows, *Being Julia* presents an actress of similar stature with a life outside her work and a past from which she has learned.

Maria Luisa Bemberg's *Camila* (Argentina, 1984) opposes the stark injunction to women that it is best to accept and await external forces with the positive quotient of irresistible sexual desire. In front of Bemberg's typically detailed and associative background of politics and history, a wealthy young woman, played by Susu Pecoraro, falls in love with a Jesuit priest who is her confessor, insisting that their passion gives them no choice but to take whatever time they have together, despite the severity of laws against it. Their flight ends with them both in front of a firing squad.

When great passion, fame, or talent are not an issue, self-destructive acting out typically follows a loss or the shocking realization of a native disinclination to fulfill expectations. In *Looking for Mr. Goodbar* (United States, 1977), from the popular book by Judith Rossner, the main character, played by Diane Keaton, is an insecure Catholic girl who becomes an accomplished and confident seducer. Humiliated by a genetic disability, she refuses to consider having children and becomes at once tougher and more reckless in pursuit of joy. Her murder is lurid, ironic, unexpected, and tragic, not only for her but for the gay man, recently bashed in the street, who murders her because she has unwittingly teased him. Her destruction is bitterly tied not to her actions, which are normal—she's a caring teacher of the deaf—but to the society around her, which has denied the gay attacker his own sexual identity. From a similar New York City Catholic upbringing, the mother and daughter (Tracey Ullman and Lili Taylor) of *Household Saints* (United States, 1993) have both internalized the hypocritical values of their family, which has left them enthralled to a husband and father familiar with the art of cheating. The mother knowingly volunteered to joust with her husband in exchange for "liberation" from singlehood, but the daughter did not. She copes with the contradiction by seeking purity in religious righteousness, which only makes her less savvy and more isolated. Instead of death, mental illness consumes her as she dreams of a God who duly informs her, "Of all My great miracles, My favorite one is tipping the scales and cheating at pinochle."

The conventional dramatic end—death—to the perils of not "settling down" is increasingly opened up and scrutinized by more individualized scenarios, many by women filmmakers. In these stories, characters who do not marry and have children assume caregiving roles. Sometimes they are sisters or aunts who fill a void, or sometimes caring for others simply becomes an addictive need. In Margarethe Von Trotta's *Sisters or the Balance of Happiness* (West Germany, 1979), a working-class woman, played by Jutta Lampe, insists on sacrificing to send her younger sister to university. When the younger one realizes that she is in love with her sister, she commits suicide, and the survivor asks another young girl from her office to move in with her. But the new girl quickly resents the strings attached to the support, and she angrily leaves her uncomprehending benefactor alone. This film is a primary example of the strong sense of specificity and depth that characterizes Von Trotta's cinema. The sisters' mother, their birth home in the country, their neighborhood bar (with folk singers), the office and its politics, and the university library all have a part to play in the story.

In Maggie Greenwald's *The Ballad of Little Jo* (United States, 1993), a teenager, played by Suzy Amis, is banished from her family after a seduction by a photographer and a pregnancy outside marriage. She is literally and tragically isolated, then attacked on the road, but finds strength enough to survive and figure out how to pass as a man, providing a convenient end to expectations and an end to social life. She is gifted with the appearance of a hired farmworker, a quiet Asian man who understands her and can keep hold of her need for privacy.

In Moufida Tlatli's *The Silences of the Palace* (Tunisia, 1994), traditional expectations are coincident with slavery and hark back to the story of *Lady Sings the Blues*. The Hollywood gloss of that film, which created a bifurcated narrative, is countered here with a flat, shallow, integrated series of confined spaces. The garden of the palace is a space of freedom only until the photographer arrives, at which point the servant child is clearly excluded from the family picture. This young woman, played by Ghalia Lacroix, is a lute player and singer who has escaped the palace, where she grew up in the servants' quarters. The escape was abetted years ago by her now-dead mother, who saw that her daughter was being invited "upstairs" to consort with the men. Unable to reveal her own privileged concubinal arrangement with the master, the mother could only telegraph the secrets of the past. Now that the daughter has been given a chance to grieve, she wants to have a child, but her lover insists she abort her pregnancy, for children have no place in their marginal existence; freedom for her has resulted in a different kind of loss.

Safi Faye's *Mossane* (Senegal, 1996) is another tale of a young girl, played by Magou Seck, caught in the grinders of relative economic status and the expectation that she will contribute her future to maintaining the family's standard of living. She is in love with a village boy, but her parents, of high status in the community, have been accepting money from her betrothed in Paris for many years. Her friend, who enjoys an active sex life with her boyfriend, nonetheless urges Mossane to remain a virgin. Mossane, who is dutiful around the house and cares for her sick brother, demands her freedom, but the village chief sides with her parents, who cannot imagine going back on their debt. The rituals by the baobab tree, fires on the beach, and animal sacrifice compete for Mossane's attention with the European gossip magazines, typifying her confused fantasies of freedom and inability to accept that it is restricted.

In Dorota Kedzierzawska's *Nothing* (Poland, 1998), isolation comes from an irrational absorption in the romantic expectations of the marital relationship. The wife in this story, played by Anita Kuskowska-Borkowska, is first seen snuggled to her husband, curled like a child in a womb aglow with photographic gold light. It develops that her husband is abusive and unkind to her without fail; that her three young children are left to their own devices, guided only by an occasional screech of "No!"; and that a fourth pregnancy has overwhelmed her. She seeks an abortion in visits to a social worker and a priest, but her sullen depressiveness inspires no help, and a neighbor has the nerve to tell her she has a bad husband. She tells her husband the lump in her belly will go away, and he nods. On its birth night, she murders the child, buries it, and throws herself at an elderly neighbor who, unable to comfort such stupidity, advises her to run away. The quality of the light shed on this woman's miserable existence is elegiac and powerful. It's an operatic treatment of the most mundane of subjects, not a vengeful, directed Medea but an ordinary woman, her ignorance reified by the advertised world of happy wedded bliss. The film is a direct aesthetic representation of her childlike dependency on her husband, where all events are concrete yet bathed in vagueness and affording no insight. It is not until she leaves her apartment that the world acquires new definition, as she takes a train and finds parentlike figures who take her in when her ticket runs out. . . . But by then the police have found her.

Autonomy

> Human loving has a long way to go.—*Women from the Lake of Scented Souls* (China, 1993)

Throughout the nineteenth century, Scandinavian authors were prominent in themes of independence for women and sexual liberation. Henrik Ibsen's *The Doll's House* has a particularly distinguished trail of influence: Before 1960 it inspired (among others) Kenji Mizoguchi in *The Love of Sumako, the Actress* (Japan, 1947), the story

of a theater troupe staging a version of the play. In this filmography, there are four versions of it. *Nora Helmer* (West Germany, 1973), two in 1973 from the United Kingdom using the original title, and *Sara* (Iran, 1993). The story, of a wife who bravely consorts with a moneylender to save her husband's life, then secretly works to pay back his debt, retains its perverse relevance. The ungrateful boorish husband, caught up in his own vanity and oblivious to the gift of love, can only think to punish her action, at which point she walks out on him and her children. The Iranian version is flushed with fear and tension, as the woman becomes exhausted from staying up all night and sewing some of the most beautiful embroidered gowns imaginable, then furtively running with them to the market to keep up with the debt. Rainer Werner Fassbinder's version is said to disdain the idealism of the end and insist on the wife's preference for maintaining her economic advantage by not leaving. Certainly economic considerations are the most common reasons for women to stay in an unfulfilling marriage, and staying with the marriage is a much more likely conclusion to such a story. Through the 1970s, this economic reality would be fantastically ignored by commercial feature films, just as it was by Ibsen, in favor of having women just walk out the door. The prime Hollywood example is *An Unmarried Woman* (United States, 1977), where Jill Clayburgh plays a happy woman married to a man who sobs pitifully when he tells her he is leaving her for a younger woman. She, on the other hand, views him with patient disgust until they part, whereupon she pauses to vomit in the gutter, then never looks back.

Ay! Carmela (Spain, 1990) brings the central conceit of *The Doll's House*—an effective role-reversal fantasy where women have integrity and men do not—to the foreground. In this film, Carmen Maura plays an actress who conflicts with her husband over how to handle the politics they face while entertaining troops at the front during the Spanish Civil War. She is offended at the ease with which he accommodates the fascists and accepts the slaughter they bring, though she understands that it allows their troupe to continue on with their business. She is willing to compromise, to be groped by a soldier to create a diversion, or dress up as a dying Republican flag, but her empathy for some captured Poles—"poor boys dying in a country whose name they can't pronounce!"—trumps her self-interest and gets her shot.

I, the Worst of All (Argentina, 1991) is the most full explication of this theme of autonomy. It is a biography of the seventeenth-century Mexican poet, scientist, and artist Sor Juana Inez de la Cruz

(Assumpta Serna), who renounced all female role expectations at a very early age, when she made up her mind to attend university. As a nine-year-old, she appears in boys' clothes and winks at the film spectator, saying that she became a nun because she could not wear "men's habit." She refuses a suitor after he informs her a woman without children is incomplete. Her university exam is a triumph of a twelve-year-old engaging with a dozen clerics around a table; they cannot stump her, and she gets her way. Like Carmela, she is too trusting, and early on she refuses to become the head of the convent, preferring her work to political power and insisting that "knowledge is always power." So while she wills herself into independence, she finds the patriarchal world is vengeful. The Archbishop pronounces her play worthy of a brothel, and, like Adua the prostitute, she is branded by the association and targeted for destruction. Though intellectuals come from Spain to debate and learn from her, one of them traps her into publishing heresy. So deprived of her comfortable existence, she falls during an attack of the plague and confesses her vanity in blood: "I, the worst of all."

In *The Story of Qiu Ju* (China, 1992), Gong Li eschews her glamorous image to portray a pregnant peasant woman furious with her village chief for punching her husband in the groin and damaging her chances for another child. When he refuses to apologize, she pursues her grievance through the elaborate court system, making several trips to the city. Everyone, especially her husband, wants her to stop, and after exhausting every possible forum, she does work out a compromise with the stubborn man. Her admirable and invigorating pursuit of justice is jarringly sullied when "justice" from on high, more harsh than she ever imagined, is suddenly meted out to the chief. The system has made a fool of her, and, more sadly, the cruel punishment of the village chief has visited shame on her, effectively proclaiming "death" to her efforts.

A unique version of the theme of personal agency is *I Don't Want to Talk about It* (Argentina, 1994), where a dwarfed girl is raised by a mother who insists she is a normal-sized child, refusing to acknowledge any limitations in her daughter and protecting her from anything that hints otherwise. This sheltering gives the woman, played by Alejandra Podesta, a strong center, and she marries a handsome older man who is charmed by her horse riding. But eventually she realizes that the self so carefully constructed by her mother is not really herself, and when the circus arrives in town one day, she is inexorably drawn to it. Nature and horses intercede to allow her to escape into a community where she actually is "normal."

Skirt Power (Mali, 1997) is a mythologized version of *The Doll's House* role reversal. In this African culture, such imaginative turns (such as reversing sex roles) are typically integrated into the spiritual fabric. Here a young village woman, played by Fanta Bereta, is disgusted at her husband's plan to acquire a second wife "so soon" and acts out a tribal story of women receiving the power to reverse the order of things. The theatrically artificial appearance of the world outside the village—where the woman scuffles with a huge demon and steals the mask of power—brilliantly sets off the insider/outsider result of the accident of birth. The village, by contrast, is normal, shot in a naturalistic style, and the dictum to the men to take on the tasks of the women, and vice versa, has its normal variations in how seriously it is taken by the individuals involved. As in *The Story of Qiu Ju*, the full meaning of the theme here is that all actions in pursuit of justice have an individual arc leading to very specific consequences, regardless of the legitimate grievances from which they have evolved. In the middle of the film a bloodied stranger appears in the village, and she is nursed secretly back to health by a child. It develops that she was attacked in the night and her valuable mask stolen; out of respect, it must be returned. As the offending woman, who has used the stolen mask to improve the condition of women in her village, is shamed into returning it, a profoundly conservative statement evolves: Change brought about by intimidation and force only serves to reinforce the acceptance of the "natural" order. The film also brings up important questions about where change leads and who it serves in the end.

Vera Drake (United Kingdom, 2004) is the most recent example of a female protagonist attempting to salve the wounds of injustice by working autonomously and in secret. Like Carmela, Vera, played by Imelda Staunton, has a strong sense of duty toward her fellow humans, and, like Carmela, she trusts that cooperating with her friends will not compromise her one true course. When it develops that she has no perspective on her work as an abortionist, either medical or social, but works only out of a blind empathy for strangers, her plight becomes a peculiarly female one. Blind to the sexist and classist world that surrounds her, she cannot effectively influence it or save herself.

Ten (Iran, 2003) is a particularly nervy twist on this self-actualizing theme. Mania Akbari plays a woman who drives a cab for a living, sharing it with the camera, which is variously placed on the dashboard or passenger seat for the duration of the film. Her riders are a typical variety of humans, but the central struggle is with her ten-year-old son, whom she ferries several times during the day and who is very angry at her for divorcing his father and marrying someone else. He treats her, as we assume he has seen his elders treat her, with intense and unwavering verbal aggression, yelling, pontificating, and hand-raising (threatening) expressions of exasperation at how she could possibly be so obtuse. Her patience, rationality, and respect for him are equally unwavering, even as she argues points with him. Of course there is a crucial difference—her opponent is a child over whom she has authority and who is not yet bigger than she is.

Conservatism

> Why don't you act like a woman?—*Ermo* (China, 1994)

> I'm so tired of wearing the pants!—*Overseas* (France, 1991)

There is another side to autonomy: the determined upholding of the sexist status quo and all that is right and good within it. In film drama, this approach rarely goes any more smoothly than striking out on one's own, and it has the added stress, where children are involved, of requiring the woman to rationalize her actions to them as well as to others. Dependent relationships resulting from a strong sense of responsibility generate harm for others in Xie Fei's *Women from the Lake of Scented Souls* (China, 1993). This fully rounded estate owner, played by Siqin Gaowa, runs a large business in high-quality sesame oil, which gets her courted by big city distributors. She detests her husband, who drinks and abuses her—abuse she is bound to passively accept—and has a long-term affair with a traveling salesman. Her developmentally disabled son begins attacking local girls and demanding a "wife." The turning point comes when she bribes the lover of a local woman to leave town so the woman can marry her son. When her son proves brutally abusive, she must face the woman with the contradictions of her own behavior. She has pursued all the traditional goals of marriage—children, and children for her children—in perverse denial of the grief those same expectations have brought to her in her own life.

This philosophy of commitment to tradition begins in the "fear" of singlehood, which is directly related to earning a living and to sexual expression. In *Sofie* (Denmark, 1982), Liv Ullmann directs Karen-Lise Mynster in the story of an only child approaching thirty, who lives with a loving Jewish family of modest middle-class means: parents, three aunts, and grandparents. She has a brief affair with

an artist, but she runs from his sexual overture and accepts an arranged marriage with a man of notably less intelligence than herself. One aunt wonders aloud about consulting Sofie regarding the proposal, but the aunts, being unmarried, are all powerless in the discussion. The grandmother determines that in the absence of anything else, the marriage must go forward. Much of Sofie's accepting view comes from the religious environment, and it is not until she is old and understands that her son will not follow in the same respectful path that she realizes the opportunities denied her by her loving family. The sexist distinction is clear: Sofie's son was raised—by a conservative woman—to trust his own judgment, while she herself was raised to be trusting, primarily of others, and not at all of herself. She learns the hard way, after an affair with her brother-in-law and her husband's mental illness, to trust her own judgment, but she blames her mother for the bad marriage, never realizing that it was her father's mother who had the most at stake and who made the decision.

In *Sh'hur* (Israel, 1994), written and acted by Hana Azoulay-Hasfari, a conservative religious family dynamic among Jewish Moroccan immigrants who live outside Jerusalem creates brutish behavior and bitter relations. The protagonist, a television producer who "succeeded" for them all, returns for her father's funeral, with her institutionalized older sister and her own young disturbed child in tow. The blind father, an expert on the Old Testament, long ago ceded his authority to an immature older brother, who abuses and dictates to his sisters, while the mother has retreated into ritual white magic. Though the producer has a responsible professional life, she is unable to cope with the reality of her family or her daughter and inevitably reverts to their aggressive abusive level. Conservatism here has produced some amount of economic progress but also a woman who knows only competition, submission, and domination as a way of life.

Competition is also the driving force of *Ermo* (China, 1994), directed by Zhou Xiaowen. It is the story of a village noodle maker, played by Alia, who supports her disabled husband and son and resents her son's spending all his time at the neighbor's watching television. Determined to keep her child at home, she decides not only to purchase a television but also to best the neighbor with the largest one she can find. To do this, she must rely on her neighbor's husband to take her into the city to sell her noodles, and he gets her an even better job making the noodles at a restaurant. When the two begin an affair, and she discovers that he is subsidizing her wage through the restaurateur, she becomes infuriated at the insult and dumps him: He was too intrusive and extravagant anyway. Meanwhile, she is comfortable selling her blood in order to gain more cash and lies to the authorities about her too frequent giving. In this culture, making a living and independence from others are points of pride. The gentility of wifely dependency is long gone, and women are expected agents of their own fate, fully invested in the status quo to the extent that rebellion is never an issue. Ermo does not want change in her life—the affair with her neighbor was passionless from her side—she only wants to make the most of what she has and believes strongly that the television will do that. In the end, she has a big screen full of snow and is exhausted from a struggle that has done nothing to enlighten her.

In *Indochine* (France, 1991), a wealthy colonial landlord, played by Catherine Deneuve, has a similar struggle that leaves her unchanged and isolated. Comfortable with her competence and "her coolies," like Ermo, she fulfills all expectations regarding her role at an ambitious level. Also, like Ermo, she is so busy she cannot love, or rather fears the dependency of it, and so finds herself isolated by racism and the wealth it has given her. Finally, there is the enigmatic story of a young woman suddenly widowed by a suicide in *Maborosi* (Japan, 1996). We first see the family blissful with their young child, then suddenly the father is dead. The woman, played by Makiko Esumi, presents a silent, competent front. She finds herself an arranged marriage in a house near the sea, where the setting is idyllic and her life appears somber but idyllic as well. The point of acceptance is unclear, but it is deep and cinematically related to the woman's "youthful beauty." A perfectly behaved, perfectly appearing, very photogenic mother with her child, this woman character is a dramatic throwback to the stillness most desired of women and mostly lacking in the liberated women in other films discussed here.

Further developing this aesthetic norm of beauty in stillness and the need for quiet in women, Marleen Gorris put Vanessa Redgrave on the screen in Virginia Woolf's *Mrs. Dalloway.* (United Kingdom, 1997). Few more perfectly caring conservative woman exist in fiction. The update in *The Hours* (United States, 2002), where a lesbian character, played by Meryl Streep, worries about being compared to Mrs. Dalloway as she goes through her own flower-buying, party-giving day, is a joking comparison based on the class privilege and comfort she shares with Woolf's character, though in fact, the comparison ends there. As a youth, Mrs. Dalloway was the epitome of the young woman

with all before her who internalizes the wisdom of her elders; chooses stability over passion; and follows through with a generous, gracious, impeccable life. Standing tall and straight, she appears to have no regrets. On the day of her party, the day of both these film stories, the arrival of her first lover brings forward a loss still unexpressed, but very much on her mind. Streep's character, on the other hand, is faced with a party fallen apart and a requirement to be gracious and hospitable to a woman who chose "rebellion and upheaval" by abandoning her husband and child, now the grown man who, the day of his modern-day party, jumps out a window because of his terminal illness.

Conservative women, comfortable with their focus on doing what's expected, go a long way toward supporting others, though they are often not granted as respectful a place as the father. In *Sugar Cane Alley* (France, 1983), Euzhan Palcy depicts the boyhood of the writer, Josef Zobel, and his rearing by his grandmother. Played by Darling Légitimus, she works hard in the cane fields of Martinique with one goal—to propel her grandson out of a similar life of grinding physical labor. She earns the money for his white schooling and is smart, stern and disciplined with him, but it is one of the village men who is granted the privilege and the time to tutor him in the reality of their racist society. In *I Love to Work* (Italy, 2004) a single mother, played by Nicoletta Braschi, works in a large office and spends all her spare time with her preadolescent daughter. When the business is sold to a large corporation restricted in its ability to lay off workers, she is targeted for removal. One day a stranger takes over her workstation, and each trip to the new boss gets her a more frivolous assignment, from spying on her fellow workers to working late, all of which lead to her becoming an unreliable mother. Having no political awareness to fall back on—she has ignored union meetings—she becomes paranoid and depressed. When her daughter seeks solace with an African family next door, she slowly begins to realize that her trust in her employers is misplaced.

Finally, autonomy reaches its apotheosis in *The Night Porter* (Italy, 1974), in which Charlotte Rampling plays a concentration camp victim who survived imprisonment because of her sadistic relationship with a Secret Service officer. She meets him years later in Rome, after she has acquired a comfortable bourgeois marriage, and he is hiding in a job as a night porter. Unable to remain living with the conditions of her survival, she seduces him again and leaves her family. He believes in their love and allows himself to be exposed by the relationship, whereupon they are executed together.

With the exception of Sofie and the woman in *The Night Porter*, these conservative characters are not thinkers or analytically inclined. They have been content with what comes at them, the modern characters having the advantage of living in a time that offers them more options. Earning a living has been accepted as hard work or the acquiring of a husband, or wealth has made it a nonissue. They are as unconcerned with thinking as they are unconcerned with their physical appearance. Several of them are beautiful enough to attract attention, but that is an aspect of the filmmaker's use of them, rather than a concern of their character.

Appearances

> I just wish I could be faceless and bodiless and be left alone.—*Klute* (United States, 1971)

The societal need to equate a woman's perceived beauty with her own desire and happiness—such beauty makes her both a desirable object and an enviable target of jealousy—is persistently expressed in films, particularly stories of prostitutes. Most of these are fantasy romances along the lines of *Pretty Woman* (United States, 1993) and are not included in this filmography because the female character is not the sole protagonist. Nonetheless, *Pretty Woman* deserves comment here because of its box office standing, its fantasy equation of the man's business with the woman's prostitution, and its placing of Julia Roberts at the highest level of stardom. She is the only actor to power a dramatic female lead part—in *Erin Brockovich* (United States, 1999)—into a blockbuster hit within the top 200 films of all time. All other titles in this rarified group with major roles for women are romantic comedies, such as *My Big Fat Greek Wedding* (United States, 2002), or thrillers, such as *Fatal Attraction* (United States, 1987).

As long as the condition of remaining single or marrying is not a "choice" made by women, but rather an event outside their control, their attractiveness remains the main tender. Earning a living outside marriage, however, is entirely up to them, and women trained to be wives have a difficult time thinking in terms other than trading on their sex appeal or becoming domestic substitutes such as nannies and governesses. Depending on economic status, prostitution is the most direct line to profit, and romanticizing prostitution has been a persistent mission of commercial cinema; it has the added advantage of not placing women in direct competition for men's jobs. Singlehood is the choice, not always conscious, of prostitutes who have had the good luck to control their busi-

ness, usually through some combination of intelligence and physical beauty. Prostitute characters in films such as *Klute* and *McCabe and Mrs. Miller* (both United States, 1971) are precursors to *Pretty Woman* because of their star performances by Jane Fonda and Julie Christie and general empowering tone, though they lack the ironic awareness of the latter's "Hey! It's only Hollywood" ending.

Another way to prostitute or take advantage of one's attractiveness for the purposes of financial gain is revealed through narratives of the restrictive nineteenth-century upper class. In stories from Henry James, such as *The Wings of the Dove* (United Kingdom, 1997) and *The Golden Bowl* (United States, 2001), penniless women played by Helena Bonham Carter and Uma Thurman see no other way to have their lovers near them than to manufacture marital relationships with wealthy acquaintances. This typical relationship of prostitution to marriage, amusingly described in *Ten* (Iran, 2003) by a prostitute—"We're the wholesalers, you're the retailers!"—is contrasted in another James story, *Washington Square* (United States, 1997). Here the tables are turned, though the "beauty" of the woman continues to play a significant part in the story of a plain young heiress, played by Jennifer Jason Leigh. Known for her awkwardness, and dominated by a father who thinks little of her because her birth led to the death of her mother, she plans to defy him by running off with her suitor and her minimal annual income. When the suitor balks—really, he wanted her and the money—she becomes strengthened in her resolve to stand up to both him and her father. Her more conventionally beautiful but less alert counterpart in *The Portrait of a Lady* (United Kingdom, 1996), played by Nicole Kidman, does not have the luck to avoid marriage to a cad. I mention these films because they do a good job of bringing out James's intricate understanding of the insidious impact wealth has on marriage; on the training that women receive, under the guise of enhancing their appearance, in manipulating marriage prospects; and on how discretion (all those things one cannot talk about) leaves women working in the dark.

These fictional stories present the quandary of upper-class women having to find an income through marriage as cautionary tales. Dramatically, the quandary can also be seen more straightforwardly as a story of prostitution, and exploited for sexual content, or it can be turned into a comedy. An expanded moral viewpoint is sometimes seen in films where women, and not male pimps, control the business. *Marketplace* (India, 1983), in which Shabana Azmi plays an autocratic madam of a luxurious bordello, is a comic rendition where prostitution is normalized as a usual business, integrated into the community and practiced by women of talent, who seek careers as performers. Likewise, though not so lighthearted, Lizzie Borden's *Working Girls* (United States, 1986) presents a hospital-like Manhattan apartment where women with other lives—one is educated and has a lesbian partner and a child—get through a boring, but lucrative and flexible, workday. Finally, the reality of prostitution as socially organized slavery is presented in *The Last Harem* (Turkey, 1997). In this film, Lucia Bosé narrates the story, from a historical perspective, of an emperor's multistory harem, which concludes with the collapse of the Ottoman Empire. In the years before the collapse, the most beautiful and favored concubine cleverly becomes partners with a savvy eunuch, who provides her with sexual gratification and information that allows her to gain early freedom. Her superior understanding of the world makes her a valuable guide to the women when they are suddenly released into an outside they have never seen. *Flowers of Shanghai* (Taiwan, 1998) is a similar peek into the nineteenth-century organized world of courtesans, who are constantly negotiating with men for money or other security and even dare to dream of buying their freedom. Here the environment is designed for groups of men to network for themselves, and the women hover in the background or wait alone in their rooms for a few minutes of intimacy and influence. As in *Adua and Company*, aging and the loss of "beauty" is a critical theme.

Race and Class

> I realized I went too far when I asked him about love.—*A Passage to India* (United Kingdom, 1984)

> 'I was a good soldier,' says the white woman jailed for antiapartheid violence. 'But you haven't been a good friend for a long time,' replies her black friend.—*Friends* (South Africa, 1993)

> Long ago, she would have been the subject of a genre painting, a water girl or a lacemaker.—*The Lacemaker* (France, 1977)

Race and class issues pervade all the thematic areas discussed in this overview: They are an integral part of women's issues. The films discussed here elaborate how racism knots the straitjacket of class around women. In post-1970 film history, it is the racism of nineteenth- and twentieth-century colonialism that first provides the perspective to explore this issue. In *A Passage to India* (United

Kingdom, 1984), based on a story by E. M. Forster, a young woman and her liberal aunt chafe at being confined in the enclaves of white colonial society. Proudly insistent on crossing racial barriers, the young woman, played by Judy Davis, goes off one day to tour a cave with an Indian doctor. When he offers his hand to help her up a rock, she is panicked by the desire that she feels and accuses the doctor of attempting to rape her. Opening the trial that ensues is the prosecutor's "universal truth" assumption that "the darker races are attracted to the lighter, but not vice versa." More confused than ever by this articulation of her fear that she is truly different, she nonetheless belatedly—after crowds of protesters have formed—frees the man with her testimony.

In *Sarraounia* (Burkina Faso, 1986), the invading French army, aided by commandeered black warriors, threatens all local kingdoms, including one led by a queen. She is known and feared as a witch because of her agnostic beliefs, her training in the manly arts of war, and her distant and imperious demeanor—not very different from the tribal kings. She is the only tribal leader to plan to fight the French invaders, but the others resent her lack of religion and refuse to allow her to organize a united front. Too late, they find the invaders' plundering ways need to be opposed with more strategy than they have developed. In the end, though the French are bumbling and do not play fair, a fierce battle takes place in the walled retreat of the queen, and her tribe is overpowered.

Sankofa (Ghana, 1994) is one of the definitive fictional depictions of the power struggles inherent in slave conditions. In it, a glamorous model is thrust back a century onto a plantation in the United States, where she feels "lucky" and superior for having been born into the main house. She endures crudely dispatched rapes from the master—guessing they are a result of the frustrations he has with the "troublemakers" in the fields—in the belief that violent objection is morally wrong. Her consciousness is raised by a man who attempts to escape and a woman who has a plan to poison the overseer. This proud woman finds despicable her grown son and other men who have been intimidated into doing the master's dirty work, for she herself would rather die. The film focuses on the intimate power struggles among the slaves, as the white characters briefly and violently stride in and out, relying on their black representatives to keep control. At one point, the model/narrator relates the fear she senses in the main house, just as the overseer groans at the stares of hatred that face him. The power of resentful observation—silent eyes—and their merging with the sea, sky, plant row, and marsh is a main theme. When the main character receives her sankofa bird and finds joy in rebellious activity in the fields, the priest—he and his lavish church are major players—laments her transformation into a witch.

Overseas (France, 1991) portrays the other world of fear in the white people's house. It presents colonial Algeria in Rashomon fashion, revealing the same incidents from the three viewpoints of three very different sisters. Promiscuity functions as the releaser of tension for the oldest one, who has unquestioningly accepted her class privileges and is so incapable of imagining what might be wrong that she becomes unstable. The Arab population emerges from hiding with the story of the middle sister, who becomes increasingly closer to the management of her farm's workers until the farm is burned up by a young worker she has trusted. Finally, there is the romantic crossover, the youngest sister who has dared to have a love affair with a rebel and who sees him shot one day outside their compound.

Almost all the films discussed in this survey depict specific class conditions. More than half depict middle- and lower-middle-class women who work outside the home. In most of them, drama comes out of the triangle of the character's work, her desire to love and be loved, and her role as a mother or similar caring figure. In the few cases where the third attribute is ignored—or the status of mother is of no interest to the character—a focus on individual spiritual destiny is sharpened in the manner of the traditional hero, bringing female figures into the mainstream of humanities narratives, as heroes, or picaresque heroes, or modern-day antiheroes.

Heroic status for women is usually an aspect of stories of the upper class—or a "classless" fantasy fiction—just as it is with male characters. In the 1960s, *Gertrud* (Denmark, 1964) set a near unreachable standard for the female antihero, refusing all respect for "honor, fame, or money"—and any man who would deign to put such considerations above her—as only an upper-class woman can. She ends up a happy hermit who has spent her life attending lectures on philosophy. Telling of her subordinate status, her life was set in this direction by a note she found one day while cleaning her lover's office: "A woman's love and a man's work are in conflict from the beginning." The amount of affront she is able to take at this inherently sexist observation recalls Basinger's "mutually exclusive options." Along with the at-once inane and obscure "heroines" of *Daisies*, this character suggests why antiheroes and picaresque heroes have since been of so little interest to those interested in telling specific, politically revealing stories about women.

Riddance (Hungary, 1973) and *The Lacemaker* (France, 1977) present similar circumstances of young working-class girls who become involved with university students. Both are beautiful women who easily catch the boys' eyes. Both are sullen and wary, and even though the relationships are sincere, they lack the interest or confidence to reassure the men and boost their egos—that crucial staple of middle-class feminine manners. In Márta Mészáros' version, the factory worker, played by Erzébet Kútvölgyi, pushes at her boyfriend to tell his parents the truth about her lack of education, and when he does not, she revels in fanciful lies to them and his friends about her background. Isabelle Huppert, in one of her first roles, plays a more timid and uncomprehending character, unable to appreciate her boyfriend's pleas to educate herself for something other than hairdressing. While both are simply too young for marriage, the first is strengthened by her experience, while the second falls into mental illness. *The Blue-Veiled* (Iran, 1995) shows a mature farmworker, played by Fatemeh Motamed-Aria, who attracts the widowed owner because of her spirited and caring nature. She insists they marry, and they run into objections from his family—a group of grown daughters who fear a "village girl" who does not know how to pour tea. Always prepared to return to her other life—she has a young son and a mother to care for—she graciously and proudly insists on doing so, leaving him to the care of his daughters when his health falters from the pressure.

Rosenstrasse (Germany, 2003) presents an interesting commentary on the impact of class on the "racial" divide of Nazi Germany. The drama, which begins with a modern-day conflict between a mother and a daughter about her marriage to a non-Jew, brings out a contrast between two families of mixed parentage. In the first, the Gentile father is threatened with the loss of his job if he does not divorce his Jewish wife, and so he leaves her to her fate of eventual imprisonment. In the same jail is a wealthy woman's husband—he has refused her father's bribe to divorce—and she has the resources (and backing of her family) to demonstrate outside the prison until he is released along with all the other Jewish men. The comparison illustrates how women, especially those without the necessary resources, are more easily abandoned and more likely to lack advocates, since they are the ones who typically provide such advocacy.

In fictions that illuminate class differences, the moment women decide to use their beauty for gain, the compromise inhibits the complete use of their mental faculties; at the same time it frequently assures them a safe and secure route through life by improving their class status. Such is the case in *The Lady and the Duke* (France, 2001), in which Lucy Russell plays an eighteenth-century countess who has amassed an independent fortune with her royal liaisons and is fully committed to royal traditions. One of her first lovers and still a dear friend is more reasonable in recognizing the abuses that have led to the French Revolution and does his bit to make peace, becoming a target of the Terror in the process. Meanwhile the Lady cleverly thwarts the revolutionaries and succeeds in saving the life of an aristocrat for whom she does not much care, just because she can and he is one of her class. Since the money women such as this character have always comes out of deference to the sexist status quo, it leaves them dependent, either literally or in their minds, and doing things they don't quite understand.

Abuse

> It's not humiliating, it's a tradition—actresses get hit!—*Opening Night* (United States, 1977)

> Your husband came to see us and he seems a peaceful man.—*The Power of Men Is the Patience of Women* (West Germany, 1978)

The abuse of women is a constant in all fictional modes—a piece of the continuum from overbearing gesture through overt intimidation to physical violence is rarely absent from any dramatic narrative. It is another theme difficult to separate from prostitution, and like prostitution, it is most common in its generic manifestation in action, thriller, and exploitation films.

Films where women play the aggressor as well as the victim or exact revenge have always been produced, but their expression within an aesthetic of graphic physical violence is part of post-1960s film culture. *Ai Nü: Intimate Confessions of a Chinese Courtesan* (Hong Kong, 1972) is in some ways a typical martial arts film, exploiting the violent abuse of women, but its two leads, Lily Ho and Betty Ting Pei, have a special formal dynamic. When Ai Nü gets dumped out of her prison box along with a group of other kidnap victims, she comes out kicking. The man and woman who run the brothel are both entranced by her stereotypical "fire," but it is the madam, proud of her own sex appeal, who sticks with the troublemaker and teaches her how to fight. The centerpiece of the film is Ai Nü's elaborate entrapment, in turn, of the three wealthy men who originally purchased and raped her. Each encounter is the sweetest of just deserts, but it is the final and powerfully

lengthy battle between the two women—leading to a climactic dismemberment—where the women get to show off their fighting, flying, ability-to-connect-with-the-camera prowess. Ai Nü's long seduction of the madam attains equal status to the madam's incredulity at her betrayal until Ai Nü's final words conclude the story: "I used love to take my revenge. I never imagined the damage love can do." Similar conditions, but of the present century, are detailed in *Lilya 4-Ever* (Sweden, 2002), the story of an abandoned Russian girl, played by Oksana Akinshina, who is kidnapped into servitude in a Swedish brothel, where she is the only, very lonely, provider. This story, however, is told in the manner of realism, so that while the basic abuse is very similar, the pitiful lead character never has a chance, and the exploitative aspects take on a more offensive quality.

Thelma and Louise (United States, 1991) develops in a less generic fashion the story of two women who take bloody revenge for attempted rape. Its connection with audiences must be attributed to the performances of Susan Sarandon and Geena Davis, their relative maturity, and general air of being justified. However, their death in the end leaves a punitive tone, despite the appearing of their being in charge of it.

The issue of endings is extremely important for any filmmaker addressing the subject of women, since Hollywood has co-opted both extremes in handling female transgression—punishment by death and wish-fulfilling triumph. Both approaches to concluding the story of a woman who has failed to meet expectations vie to this day, providing much of the interest and tension in all these stories, even though both ends are oddly unsatisfying. Either way, they respond to a damning question—will she get away with this? Or, phrased differently, will she lie down and take this?

Joan of Arc remains the primary model of heroic female role reversal, and she does not die in battle but is martyred as a witch. Women protagonists who die proudly on their feet (as Joan did) instead of their knees are still a rare instance. *Set It Off* (United States, 1996) is one of the few genre films that insists on a respectful, detailed end for each of the hunted women, allowing one (Queen Latifah) to die so that the others can live and one (Jada Pinkett) to walk defiantly away from the detective attempting to apologize and arrest her without harming her, while the last one (Vivica A. Fox) watches her friend shot to death as she sits undetected on the bus in which she escapes.

Films of abused wives struggling to get away from their unsafe homes have become an enduring genre, beginning with *Petulia* (United Kingdom, 1968), in which Julie Christie plays a San Franciscan "kook" of the times who has married into wealth—the "most beautiful man" she ever saw—and now experiments with eccentric spending and provocation. A beating from her husband lands her in the hospital, but her father-in-law commands her back, and she, bred well enough, returns home to become pregnant and "happy." By the time of *Alice Doesn't Live Here Anymore* (United States, 1974), the Zeitgeist had moved considerably, and Ellen Burstyn, no matter how meek her character in the beginning, always showed the wheels turning in Alice's head. After her husband suddenly drops dead and leaves her penniless, the film and the character integrate abuse awareness into the story, as she matures from wifely submissive childlike behavior—she is capable of escalating a Coke-spitting contest with her son—to recognizing that the men with whom she ends up do not have the right to physically abuse her or her child. While the process is not quite complete by the end of the film, there's been progress and a certain amount of articulation: "I was always trying to please him because I thought he was taking care of me, but he wasn't! It's my life, not some man's life I'm helping him out with!"

Around this time, Jean-Luc Godard and Anne-Marie Miéville put their own special didactic stamp on violence and domestic relations in *Numéro deux* (France, 1975): "Given the difficulty of conjugal life as a mode of existence, and the even greater difficulty of celibacy, women must learn to view happiness as a victory. The greatest service she can provide for the community is to be happy. . . . By refusing all help—except when absolutely needed, [women] are totally absorbed by their work, and acquire a calm and surprising sincerity." This film, which was made the same year as *Jeanne Dielman, 23 Quai du Commerce, 1080 Bruxelles* (Belgium, 1975) lays down similar political territory to Chantal Akerman's film, with a focus on the domestic day to day: cleaning, cooking, and caring for children, with the crucial difference that there is a father character in *Numéro deux*. Dramatic violence is visited on the wife, who becomes distrusted by her factory worker husband, as opposed to the violence visited on the client in *Jeanne Dielman*. Unlike the personal nature of the violence perpetrated on the woman in *Numéro deux*—her husband believes she has cheated on him—Akerman sets up a rationale of impersonal tedium and frustration for the violent murder of the john, who just happens to be the one there. This plot rationale is echoed by the murder in *A Question of Silence*, a film discussed near the end of this survey.

Through the 1980s, dramatic efforts such as Tina Turner's (as played by Angela Bassett) brave exposure of her own abuse in *What's Love Got to Do with It?* (United States, 1993) continued to be made, and the description of domestic violence as a major societal problem came frequently from action films, such as *Bandit Queen* (India, 1994), which was also biographical in inspiration. Controversial for a variety of reasons, this film nonetheless makes compelling viewing in telling the story of a child bride, played by Seema Biswas, who is raped by her husband after conflicting with his mother. She becomes a gang leader and takes to the Indian countryside with a cry, "Anyone who marries a young girl, I will kill!" Among many extremely violent episodes—the woman never stops fighting back, and she eventually becomes a politician despite her fame as a gangster—the film is also notable for a lengthy gang-rape scene that is implied through a formal focus on a creaking door.

The Battle of the Sacred Tree (Kenya, 1994) also addresses domestic violence in the story of a Nairobi middle-class woman who is regularly beaten by her suited husband. The film begins with her fleeing her home to return to her father's village, where he is a medicine man. Her father accepts her, but the villagers, particularly the Christian women, exclude her because of her shocking transgression in leaving her husband and working in a tavern. In *Dolores Claiborne* (United States, 1995) Jennifer Jason Leigh and Kathy Bates play a daughter and mother caught up with an abusive father and a violent act in the mother's past. Here, the mother has a difficult time convincing the daughter of her righteousness, the opposite circumstance of *Bastard Out of Carolina* (United States, 1996), in which Leigh now plays the mother, blinded by her own needs and disbelieving of the true cause of her daughter's physical abuse. One of the richest of these uniformly disturbing narratives is *Starry Sky* (Brazil, 1996). Directed by Tata Amaral, this thriller begins in a small São Paulo apartment where a woman, played by Alleyona Cavalli, packs her bags for Miami. Within minutes a man has forced his way inside, refusing to let her out the door. From their talk, it is clear she has known him well and for a long time. For the length of the claustrophobic film—the camera remains firmly inside with her—she never wavers from her decision to leave him, yet she persists in trying to handle him. Even the intrusion of her mother, who despises the man and whom he murders, does not change her understanding and calm in dealing with him, until finally they await the police together. The bonding of these two—victim and victimizer—recalls *The Night Porter* in its disturbing depiction of the relationship of strength and independence to collusion and survival.

Eve's Bayou (United States, 1997) is a look at domestic violence of the verbal and emotional kind, in which a mother refuses to acknowledge her husband's philandering and blames her daughter for being suspicious. The focus here is on sexual repression and a corrosive family dynamic, leading to the teenage daughter's doubting of herself and the family's overpowering romanticization of the distant mother: "What would Daddy want with Mrs. Moreau? Mama is the most beautiful woman in the whole world!" *Boys Don't Cry* (United States, 1999) goes to the heart of the relationship of violence to masculinity. Abuse and murder here is completely justified in the minds of the perpetrators by the affront of a woman who passes as a man, who only appears to have what they "really" have; the beating punishes her for attempting to fool them. It's a form of "evil spirits," the presence of which justifies physical abuse in many cultures.

In *Germany Pale Mother* (West Germany, 1979) Helma Sanders-Brahms wrote and directed a portrait of abuse as it springs from the larger political conditions of Nazi Germany, which integrated violence into the daily life of the populace as a whole. As teenagers, the main protagonist, played by Eva Mattes, and her friend have a discussion about how to respond to their Jewish friend who is crying out in the street below as she is being taken away. The main character, a survivor, is unhesitating in her response—go to sleep. By the end of the film, her kind husband has returned hardened and autocratic from the war, and she herself has been toughened by rape and homelessness. They have a young child who has been locked out of her mother's life because of neediness the mother ignores. But the child has herself learned how to taunt her mother with insistent offerings of care that annoy the older woman. By the end, there is a new political regime, but the pervasive abuse that has entered every area of life is entrenched and unreachable by political change.

Punishment

> We must tread warily in life, especially we women.—*Effi Briest* (West Germany, 1974)

> A history of brutality to women: oh spinning wheel, oh spinning wheel.—*The Wheel* (South Korea, 1983)

Aside from abuse that is illegal and hidden, there is the violence that is justified by society in dealing with the transgression of social rules such as preserving one's virginity for marriage or remaining faithful in a marriage.

The Engagement of Anna (Greece, 1972) is a tragic study in betrayal via class expectations of "proper" sexual behavior. Anna Vagena plays a young live-in servant who is thought highly of by her employers, who seek to find her a husband. The Sunday afternoon date they have arranged with a shy young man leads to disaster when she arrives home much later than expected. Met first by the lady of the house, who sniffs her body and then asks questions such as "Where did he touch you?" she recoils and her relationship with them is ruined, leading to her freedom being taken away. *Effi Briest* (West Germany, 1974) is another story of a young woman punished for unwittingly failing to meet expectations of good behavior. Though her mother is concerned about her "wildness," Effi, played by Hanna Schygulla, at seventeen readily agrees to marry a much older wealthy man when told, "You will attain what most women have at forty. You will overtake your mother." She takes a lover out of boredom and learns too late that she is not to be forgiven. Smarter than both her husband and her lover, she finds them "cold careerists: He does things over one's head and then you have to act as he wants." When she is banished from her home and child, she falters physically and dies, whereupon her mother wonders if she "wasn't too young, after all?"

Beyond informal social strictures, there is in some cultures a formal system to keep women in line, commanded by custom or religion and sometimes legally sanctioned. In the *Sealed Soil* (Iran, 1977) a young girl, played by Flora Shabaviz, deliberately refuses to engage in the search for a marriage partner and is shunned and left increasingly in silence. Alone and disbelieving, she begins to seek spiritual support, ripping off her heavy veil and vestments and raising her hands to the blessed rain. This scene remains unusual in Iranian cinema in addressing clothing as an oppression. Her actions are determined evil and an exorcist is called, assuring her further mental deterioration.

In *Moolaadé* (Senegal, 2004) a courageous wife, played by Fatoumata Coulibaly, of a liberal village man has spent her life in opposition to female genital mutilation, a procedure that left her scarred and in pain. In the past she has refused the ritual for her teenage daughter, and as the film opens she is beset by a trio of youths who have run into her compound seeking refuge (*moolaadé*) from the fate. This film is notable for the strong line it draws through the tolerance of abuse and the importance of peer pressure in adjusting that line. In this culture, the woman must repeatedly articulate her firm resolve to protect the children: first, to the other wives in her camp, where the rope has been placed to keep others away; then to her husband, who has been shamed by her actions; and finally to various and vying groups in the community. Although her refusal to give up the girls does eventually lead to a severe public beating, this comes only after simmering resentments, including the suicides of two other girls, lead to complete upheaval. In the end, the most extreme violence—a murder—is not visited upon her but upon a liberal, itinerant peddler who tries to protect her. In these less individually pathological abuser–victim scenarios, swerving from normal expectations becomes legitimate cause for physical abuse via a complex social process.

Similarly, in *To Take a Wife* (Israel, 2004), Ronit Elkabetz and her brother wrote, directed, and acted a story of a marriage that begins with a mother demanding a divorce. In response, her orthodox husband calls on his male relatives for help, and they scream and pontificate into the early hours of the morning while he sits in silence on the couch, hiding the domineering character he normally displays in his home, until she relents and agrees to stay. This kind of abuse, related to a normalized type of control, shows it deserves the name in the pretense of hurt and anguish displayed by the abuser. Viewpoint is all here; the brothers act firmly from a perception of their own generosity in "helping." Sure of their own role in their brother's marriage, they are incapable of seeing any needs that fall outside his expectations of them.

Family and Work

> Don't worry, I can manage.—*Stage Door* (Hong Kong, 1996)

Mothers appear as characters almost as frequently as there are films, and some are even simply women with caring "motherly" feelings, such as the chef, played by Stéphane Audran, in *Babette's Feast* (Denmark, 1987) from a story by Isak Dinesen, who spends her savings on a fabulous meal in honor of the two sisters who have given her a home.

Isabelle Huppert in *Story of Women* (France, 1988) plays an impoverished mother who dreams of becoming a singer but instead finds a lucrative business as an abortionist. Losing her soul mate—a Jew who is evacuated—and not understanding why, she takes up with a prostitute who sends her clients and takes over the children's room for her business. Proceeding through the days in an increasingly selfish manner, she takes a lover and finds a maid to service her husband. He does not take kindly to this and reports her to the Gestapo,

who sentence her to death. She has a venal edge that Vera Drake does not, but both are treated unfairly by their governments as "examples" of moral decrepitude. While these two characters are stark contrasts, both exist in a fog of working-class ignorance—the French woman knows nothing of Jewish persecution, and the British Vera is shocked to find her "friend" takes money for the abortions she provides at no charge. Their views of money and taking advantage of others reveal the same myopic naïveté, two sides of the simplistic coin of secretive female behavior. Both are straightforward and businesslike, and they bravely fill the void for their fellow women in need of abortion, yet the official world around them (World War II Britain and France) treats them as dangerous criminals.

Mothers with things other than children on their minds are often sympathetically portrayed by women writers and directors. In Gillian Armstrong's *High Tide* (Australia, 1987), Judy Davis plays a woman who fails to find fame as a pop singer but instead miraculously becomes good friends with a teenager who turns out to be the daughter she abandoned years ago. In *The Long Farewell* (USSR, 1971), Kira Muratova directs the portrait of a sweet but lonely single mother, played by Zinaida Sharko, by turns childish and flirtatious, who becomes obsessed with losing her teenage son after he has visited the father who ignored him for most of his life and who lives in Siberia. The cinematic portrait of her passionate love for her son and her energetic feminine presence is told in their visits to public places; at home, in their one room, they barely speak over the dresser that separates their beds. The film begins with a lengthy scene in a plant nursery, where she fusses over the choice of plant to take to a friend in the country, and he patiently waits for her to tire of the diversion. At the outdoor dinner, he flirts with the daughter of the house, while his mother throws her high heel for a dog to fetch, exclaiming, "Dogs love me!" When she suddenly loses her graciousness and yells at her son about his refusal to reveal his plans, the group falls silent, and the mother–son interpersonal dynamic becomes clear. At work, she is a very competent translator with lots of ideas, and regardless of her heavy use of "feminine wiles"—she manipulates several situations to the goal of keeping her son with her—one thing is clear: She has taught him well how to enjoy life and invest in it. At the grand finale musical event, where her frayed nerves get her into a fight over a seat, he gently moves her away and says, "Mama, I'm not going to leave. I love you."

This tragedy of the loss that is an integral part of mothering is movingly depicted in *Silent Waters*

(Pakistan, 2003), in which Kiron Kher plays a Sikh mother who was saved during the partition from a purge by a Muslim man and has been passing as Muslim ever since. As a widow, her passionate relationship with her teenage son deteriorates when he becomes insecure at his girlfriend's independent attitude and desire to educate herself, qualities his mother exhibits. When fundamentalist recruiters arrive in town, he at first makes fun of them, but he finds they boost his ego in ways his girlfriend has failed to do. Quickly, he is manipulated into active involvement in *jihad*; when a Sikh convention arrives in town and his mother's secret is revealed, her ostracization from the community only makes his radicalism more fervid. The partial roots of political radicalism in the liberalization of gender roles and the subsequent challenge to male youths to find their own way to adulthood are carefully detailed within this complex tale of religion, statehood, and gender.

The mothers of *Daughters of the Dust* (United States, 1992) are from four generations and engage at the level of broad cultural concerns more than intimate relations, though the great grandmother and her lesbian daughter work through a few minutes together in a mostly silent scene that is gravely expressive. Cora Lee Day plays the mother, dressed in significantly less finery than her progeny, who leans off her chair toward a daughter (Barbara O Jones) she has not seen in many years, a daughter elegant in dress and demeanor, who crouches and extends her back in kind toward her mother. As the old woman flicks her fingers at a lacy jabot, first to investigate, then to dismiss, the equally unbending daughter averts her eyes from the judgment. In a film where public life, family history, and communal activity are valorized over intimacy, this scene, which ends with their two heads bowed together, wordlessly communicates much empathy and understanding of a woman's need to find her own way.

In *Nargess* (Iran, 1991), a professional thief has mothered and "married" a young man she found on the streets as a child. When he falls in love and seeks "respectability," she facilitates his marriage and makes friends with the poor young girl. When the girl discovers that her new husband has no idea how to make an honest living, she patiently proceeds to look for a job for him, while his mentor offers him the opportunity of one last heist, believing she can keep him as a partner in crime. But the new wife prevails, and the booty and "old" wife are left alone on the highway. Such sadness around mothering and letting go is not a common theme, but a greatly reverberating one. In *Will It Snow for Christmas?* (France, 1996), a farm woman

(Dominique Reymond) with seven children by a married man who uses them as cheap labor is forced to recognize her weakness in maintaining her relationship with him. The theme of defeat in this documentary-like rendition of her bleak daily life contrasts with a film from India, *Genesis* (1986), set in a similarly barren countryside. Here Shabana Azmi plays a woman who has fled a flood and comes across two men who have taken over some ruins after fleeing a tyrant. She shows them how to improve their living conditions, but when she gets pregnant and they begin to argue over who is the father, she tells them the child is hers and leaves. Carmen Maura in *Between Heaven and Earth* (France, 1993) also plays out an allegory of pregnancy and women's ownership of the future. In this story, a journalist becomes pregnant but discovers that her baby does not want to be born. She consults with experts and finds other women with "talking" fetuses, who reflect on the environmental degradation of the earth.

Domineering mothers are a staple of comedic and horror cinema, and Shirley MacLaine has made them one of her specialties. In *Postcards from the Edge* (United States, 1990), she accomplishes a subtle variation in this role by leaving behind the "armor" of her makeup in a scene with her daughter, played by Meryl Streep, whom she has persistently placed in her shadow. Stuck in the hospital after a drunken fall, the mother communes with her daughter about facing the public while the daughter skillfully applies her mother's makeup, creating a scene of tenderness, intimacy, forgiveness, and understanding. It is a scene impossible to imagine with her makeup on, a scene that hints at a loving relationship less evident in the rest of the film.

In *Faat-Kine* (Senegal, 2001), Venus Seye plays a mother of two children on their way to college. As a manager of a gas station, she has garnered a middle-class life in Dakar, which is viewed covetously by the fathers of her children, who failed to take seriously their responsibilities when she was poor. In fact, her own father abused and abandoned her because of the births of her children, and it is clear that her special spirit—and that of her mother who defended her—is the reason for her present success. Rosie Perez in *The 24-Hour Woman* (United States, 1998) and Julia Roberts in *Erin Brockovich* (United States, 1999) lay out the difficulties of doing demanding work outside the home while raising children. Though they both have partners at home to help, the strains on their relationships often amount to an additional burden. Josephine Siao in *Stage Door* (Hong Kong, 1996) gives up her son at birth to a friend in order to pursue her career as an opera star. This film offers a multiplicity of views on mothering through Siao's performance as an energetic character with such strong and sincere feelings for everyone around her, including the grown son who comes to visit, that her considerable entourage is ready to be deployed in her or her family's aid at any time. Accused by her husband of treating his daughter as a friend instead of a daughter, she understands that she has never wished to command the authoritative relationship to another that mothering demands. Really, it is a social network that she commands, and they all contribute to "mothering" the many young people she has had in her life. Certainly, the combination of work and family that she has chosen requires all her concentration; at the end of the day, she replenishes with mindless time spent collecting coupons.

This notion of groups of mothers, instead of a single authority, presents an interesting alternative view of mothering as expressed in some films. As Nancy Savoca, who directed *The 24-Hour Woman*, suggests by her title, it is impossible in fact to do both, especially when children are young. Extended families have always offered intergenerational support and are buoyantly portrayed in films such as *Let's Hope It's a Girl* (Italy, 1985) and *Antonia's Line* (Netherlands, 1996), both of which focus on the responsibility of women for all the young, not just their own. Both these films are also marked by the absence of men.

Sister pairings appear to be uniformly problematic or comical. Most typically, rivalry is established or hinted at, then ignored, while the plot moves on to other matters. Films that focus on it for the duration of the narrative, such as *Georgia* (United States, 1995) or *Dancing at Lughnasa* (Ireland, 1998), take on a darkness that is emotionally wrenching. Both these character studies, one written by a woman, the other by a man, reveal the responsibility and pain of relationships not chosen. It is as though, when a writer looks hard at siblings, there is no such thing as a fictionally interesting supportive sibling relationship. Margarethe Von Trotta is one of the few writers to take persistent interest in sister relationships, and in *Sisters or the Balance of Happiness* the adoration of the younger for the older leads only to tragedy, just as it does in *Georgia* and *Dancing at Lughnasa*. However, in *Marianne and Julianne* (West Germany, 1981) Von Trotta tells the story of a pair of politically active sisters (one is a member of the Baader-Meinhof Group), whose well-known public lives allow for a plot more balanced between them. Each sister demonstrates dominance as both have clear rationales for their contrasting political philosophies of socialist activism and radical violence. The terrorist treats her sister with the same autocratic surety that she treats everyone else, while respect, even devotion, is granted her by her more moderate sister. It is on the basis of their shared goal of improving conditions for the German people and absolute lack of mothering instincts that their belief in one another sustains through every possible conflict. Each is completely her own person. And it is in the scenes of their childhood, when they found joy in shocking the community by dancing without a partner, that one sees the nascence of their strength and their ability to care for each other.

Friendship and Love

> I'm a very drunk, very pregnant lady, and I need a friend.—*Rachel, Rachel* (United States, 1968)

Friendship is a considerably more open theme than is sisterhood, and it is a rare film listed here that does not detail a friendship or offer a friend as a secondary character. The sincerity and objectivity of these movie relationships is a fine-tuned, scripted tradition. Friends can be relied on to tell the truth, so moving ahead the drama, and while they may suffer for it, it is generally not for long. The isolation of women is effectively countered by a trusted friend, capable of providing constructive advice and fresh insight. In *Two of Them* (Hungary, 1977), Marina Vlady plays an older married woman who is separated from her husband by her work residency in a youth hostel. One of her charges (Lili Monori) is a young mother with an alcoholic, but sweet, husband. Their friendship becomes admiring and close, benefiting both of them, as the older woman's marriage is as cold as the young woman's is passionate. *House Built on Sand* (Russia, 1991) presents a similarly complex relationship between old college friends who meet later in life. The film begins with the essential contrast of their feet: Ada in elegant socks and thick high heels, who efficiently taps the dirt off on the stairs to the house, and her friend Sonya in flats and thick rumpled stockings, who keeps on walking. But the latter, a museum worker, is much more clever than she appears and also more loyal. As they go through the 1930s Stalinist purges, the director, Niyole Admomenaite, paints a many-layered picture of Ada's oppression by her sexist father and faithless husband and the emotional outlet she finds in teasing her friend. By the time of the siege of Leningrad, it is Sonya who remains to nurse the dying Ada, who pleads forgiveness before they both die.

Friends (South Africa, 1993), directed by Elaine Proctor, reveals a similar aesthetic grip on its story, revealing the fissure through a group of three students (Kerry Fox, Michele Burgers, Dombisa Kente) in the very first scene. Graduation-day pictures catch the second two, an Africaaner woman set to marry an older man, who looks meekly down, and a black woman, going on to teaching, who smiles directly into the camera. The third, a British woman, looks distractedly away at a noisy political demonstration. It develops that she has associated herself with a terrorist antiapartheid cell and already is moving away from her friends, unaware that she is letting go of her true life support. It is not until she accidentally murders two people in an airport bombing and lands on the curb waiting for absolution from her black friend that she realizes how unstable she has become. Disturbingly, the film associates her revolutionary activity with her insecurity, anger, and childhood identification with a maid/nanny. *Flame* (Zimbabwe, 1995) is another story of revolutionary Africa, made by a white woman, Ingrid Sinclair. Like *Friends*, it foregrounds the daily aesthetic, especially the lightness, of African cultures, where contentious meetings are concluded with spontaneous dance and song, and the geometric arrangement of people is a norm. Here the story is of two village women, renamed in revolutionary fashion Flame and Liberty (Marian Kunonga and Ulla Mahaka). They are trained as soldiers and fight alongside the men, where Flame's courage in winning battles extends to enduring and forgiving rape. After Zimbabwe is established, Liberty, the writer, is ambitious for city life, while Flame returns to her village with her family. Though flawed as commercial productions—it's impossible to say how these films could be otherwise given the filming conditions—both films are important looks at female relations in explosive environments. They include a great deal of angry argument among the women, in itself a liberating activity. Liberty is enamored of her friend's vitality but also afraid of it: "You're a slave to anyone who smiles at you!" She knows slavery is always around the corner—in Harare her boss already treats her so, and as women, they no longer are invited to the great military gatherings that celebrate their country's victory. These are powerful films about appearances, disillusionment, and the survival of female friendship through conflict.

Adoption (Hungary, 1975) is a look at an older woman and a young girl who first approaches her in order to obtain a private place for her to make love with a boyfriend. The woodworker, played by Kati Berek, is at first reluctant but then becomes enthusiastic about helping the girl, who advises her to "drop" her longtime married lover when he refuses to father a child but also insists she should not adopt, as "adopted children are always damaged." It is as if the young girl has entered her life as a challenge to the older woman's predictable ways. In thanks, the older woman barters a marriage agreement with the young couple's respective parents—the boy's parents must agree to house the girl even in the case of divorce—and oversees a wedding. Right there, the "nice" young couple have their first tussle, but the older woman is already set to pick up her new baby. Having learned much about the bureaucracy by arranging an adult life for her teenage friend, she has garnered herself a new more permanent responsibility. Typical of Márta Mészáros's films, the actor, at first appearing dour, attains a magnetic quality that builds through scenes of great tenderness. One is in a glassed restaurant, where the two women drink wine and smoke, bowing their heads together, after both have pleasantly ignored the male attention that has come to their table.

A Woman's Tale (Australia, 1991) is a striking story of love between an old woman (Sheila Florence) and a nurse (Gosia Dobrowolska) who cares for her and who also uses her apartment to meet with her married lover. "The best men are always married," the salty old woman sympathizes, by way of showing her insistence on staying young and definite, despite her cancer. Another day, she insists her son "married the wrong woman. Most men do." Through holiday meals and helping neighbors, then conflicting with all those who want her to go to a nursing home, she remains tenaciously alive, until one day the nurse prepares a needle for her. In the end, she is desperate, "I can't face it . . . you do love me, don't you?" They hug in a very sensual way as she dies. *Granny* (Russia, 2002), directed by Lidiya Bobrova, is also an affecting tale of an old woman, played by Nina Shubina, who lives for a time with her aged sister, played by Anna Ovsyannikova, until the sister's death ends the daily life of this engagingly sturdy movie couple. Granny has adult children and grandchildren in the far north, but in the much colder environment of the "new" Russia, younger generations are preoccupied with business other than caring for their elders. The men especially find it a strange notion. A niece, who is a professional woman in Moscow, drives her aunt around to every relative she can find, then discovers a long-lost cousin just returned from Chechnya with a damaged young daughter, at which point a poetic fantasy of care is offered, very different from the frosty automobile the woman has been sitting in for a very long time.

Take Care of My Cat (South Korea, 2001) tells the story of several close friends now out of school and seeking adult lives. One has found corporate work in Seoul and left the others behind, though they all stay in touch by cell phone and with visits to the city; the film reflects their ongoing jubilance in one another by typing out their text messages in split parts of the screen. The artist, played by Ok Ji-young, who is extremely poor and lives in a shack with her grandparents, is most affected by being out of school, especially when a fire leaves her without family or shelter. Bae Doo-na plays a middle-class friend whose parents expect her to stay and work in their business but who finds inspiration in transcribing the words of a poet who cannot write for himself. The film is absolutely focused on the class divide as it impacts the girls' friendship—men barely figure in their days—but their relations are supportive enough to encourage changes that are actually more bold and decisive (and independent) than they thought possible.

Waiting for the Moon (United States, 1986) is a love story of two comfortable, engaging women, writer Gertrude Stein (Linda Bassett) and her partner, Alice B. Toklas (Linda Hunt), told in the elliptical, episodic, and relaxed manner of Stein's writings. While Stein makes herself ever smiling and indulgent of the occasional complaint that comes from Toklas, the film pays great respect, in terms of focus and time, to the quarrels between the two. Though Toklas says "criticisms are always petty," these discussions, which frequently result in angry leave-takings, go to the heart of a couple's need to challenge the moral fiber of each other when occasioned by a lack of faith or inequity. The two actors are astoundingly unified in drawing this portrait of individuals in an apparently unromantic, yet deeply romantic and happy, union that displays argument as a primary expression of love.

Sexuality

> Look at me. Am I beautiful? No, but I have loved.—*Gertrud* (Denmark, 1964)

> Give us a lick, not a prick!—*Scrubbers* (United Kingdom, 1982)

Sexual desire is a common topic among women filmmakers, more so than their male counterparts, for whom it remains an issue of appearances and seductive behavior. Eric Rohmer is a persistent exception to this, focusing on desire as it interconnects with strategies around social status. *A Good Marriage* (France, 1981) is one of his early sly stories of a young woman of both whim and precision, played by Béatrice Romand, who suddenly decides that she'll "no longer give her body away" but hold back until the marriage, so that "he will idolize"

her. *Up to a Certain Point* (Cuba, 1983) provides an equally amusing counterpart to this old-fashioned but venerable strategy in the story of a leftist married man making a film on machismo who meets a woman dockworker—the prototype for his fictional model worker and sexually liberated woman—and falls in love with her. He lies to both her and his wife, and the worker is savvy enough to tell him to go away until he makes up his mind. Finally, though, she is disappointed and saddened to have to tell him to just go away.

For most of the post-1960 period, the unexploitative depiction of sexual activity tends to be confined to relations between white heterosexual people, though there are exceptions. For instance, *Friends* (South Africa, 1993), a story of two whites and a black woman, limits its scenes of sexual relations to the white women's stories, though this is possibly more a comment on the affairs as neurotic entanglements. *Bad Timing* (United Kingdom, 1985) is on the edge of exploitation but is deepened by a dominating physical performance from Theresa Russell as a seductive woman who provokes a psychiatrist into using her however he can—to the point of his raping her when he believes she is dead. Her survival is critical to the message of sexual expression as change agent. *Y tu mama también* (Mexico, 2001) is likewise deepened by a character, played by Maribel Verdú, who is frankly articulate on sexual matters. Such openness is in contrast with *The Mother* (United Kingdom, 2004), in which sexual desire is gradually revealed to exist in a woman past the age of fifty, a woman who appears to everyone, including the spectator, to be sexually neutral. The performance here by Anne Reid as a newly widowed grandmother who propositions her daughter's lover is stunningly unusual. The useful aids to her seduction are sketches, and when the children discover them, the young man is frustrated and surprised to find himself out of a job. In *The Bitter Tears of Petra von Kant* (West Germany, 1972), Rainer Werner Fassbinder characteristically looks at a lesbian triangle as exploitative, insensitive, and perverse. Not too differently from his heterosexual male colleagues, he presents sexuality as all surface, but the presence of Hanna Schygulla, as the wily vagrant, and Irm Hermann, as the stiff, silent servant whose anger permeates the room, brings the film into a more meditative realm.

Women filmmakers have typically had less schematic views of sexuality. In *Je tu il elle* (Belgium, 1974), Chantal Akerman acts in her first film as a lesbian woman at sea in her life, bored, depressed, and finally seeking out a former lover for a sexual encounter. This final scene in a trio of set pieces is filmed to incorporate both women at all times and appears to be minimally edited, a sincere exposure of plain sex in a plain (undecorated) atmosphere. In *Scrubbers* (United Kingdom, 1982), Mai Zetterling picks up a genre prison girls story and puts a sweet lesbian at the center. Eva, played by Amanda York, shows from the opening scene determination, sensitivity, and patience, along with a big dose of overall shortsightedness. After waiting for a truck driver to be diverted into lovemaking with her friend, she breaks away, steals the truck she barely knows how to drive, and steers it into a fence so she can join her lover in prison. Unfortunately her friend (Chrissie Cotterill)—a vicious, tearful woman whose idea of motherhood is limited to being called "mummy"—is not so happy to be returned to prison, and her enmity puts in motion a series of vengeful violent acts. Eva, however, is immediately taken under the protective wing of the most powerful swaggering inmate. The soulfulness of these characters and the lesbian culture they all find comfortable and fun—regardless of their sexual orientation—is expressed in regular and frequent scenes of performance, puppet shows, bands with pots and pans as instruments, limerick singing, dancing, and most plaintively, cries out their windows at night along the lines of "I love you, Eva, I fuckin' love you."

Desert Hearts (United States, 1985), a 1940s story of a professor who goes to Reno for a divorce and finds a lesbian lover, and *Fire* (India, 1996), with Shabana Azmi as an older sister who falls in love with her faithless brother's new wife as they are left keeping house together, are prominent in the serious dramatic treatment of lesbian relationships in major feature films. *French Twist* (France, 1995) presents a more lighthearted and knowing version of a mature lesbian relationship between a married woman with a faithless husband and a local handywoman, while *Boys Don't Cry* (United States, 1999) digs into the horrors of closeted sexuality and a society that does not allow any honest expression of sexuality.

Miss Mary (Argentina, 1986) is a turn on the hypocrisy of the double standard for sexual activity. Mary, played by Julie Christie, is a governess who is approached by the young man of the house as he returns from the final event of his birthday celebration, a trip to a brothel. Naturally, he prefers her, and while she is banished for her indiscretion, she fares better than his sister, who goes mad after refusing to marry a man with whom she had a brief affair.

Nobody's Wife (Argentina, 1982) and *Danzón* (Mexico, 1991) are films that develop a gay or lesbian environment for the purpose of making a comfortable space for the heterosexual lead actor's discovery of her sexual self. In *Nobody's Wife*, one of the first films by Maria Luisa Bemberg, she describes a middle-class housewife who walks out on her husband and children the moment she discovers his infidelity, then takes an apartment with a gay man who introduces her to independence by way of nightlife and parties. In *Danzón*, a middle-aged mother, played by Maria Rojo, leaves her daughter and city job for Vera Cruz in search of her dancing partner. The trip itself, the discovery of a group of transvestites and prostitutes who help her, and the calming scene of a wharf of eroticized boats are sufficient to inspire her away from the strictures of her orderly life. *On the Way* (Hungary, 1980) is a similar story of a scientist who leaves her husband and family to attend a far-away family event and finds a much more relaxed and fun-loving culture near a lake. Here, Delphine Seyrig plays the uptight woman who looks askance at a joking flirtatious acquaintance but ultimately cannot resist him. Having been taken in, her story shows the cost of "opening up" and the devastation of her having hoped, for a long year, that their relationship might actually have substance beyond friendship. The final long scene of this film, in which she breaks down and cries in her car, recalls the final scene of *The Butcher* and the sadness of having reached out and failed to grasp.

In *Rambling Rose* (United States, 1991), Martha Coolidge directs an unusual story of a young woman, played by Laura Dern, who is taken in by a wealthy educated family as a "helper." From the first scene, this family is special in that it treats her with respect as a person and not at all like the servant she is. This quickly becomes quite challenging for all of them when she turns out to be promiscuous yet confused enough by her impulses to feel guilty. The men of the family are amused and fascinated, but the mother is protective and caring. When a doctor recommends a hysterectomy to curb her sexual appetite, the mother vociferously objects to the two men's need to "take away the girl's womanhood," suggesting they are just trying to soothe their own guilt over being attracted to her and, in the doctor's case, taking advantage of her. In adapting the Nobel Prize–winning novel by Sigrid Undset, Liv Ullman brings out her special focus on the theme of female will in *Kristen Lavransdatter* (Norway, 1996). During the middle ages, when households are compounds spread around in clearings, a spirited girl (Elizabeth Matheson) with many suitors and a talent for fending them off is forced to accept a marriage arranged by her father. When her father sends her away to keep her in line, she falls in love with an errant and much older knight and becomes proud of her "sinful body that wraps around her soul with iron bonds," expecting the loss of her virginity to get her out of the impending marriage. This first sexual encounter, which takes place outdoors, is remarkable for the teenager's decisive grasp of her man and her future. The knight has a mistress and children, but Kristen remains insistent and, after much maneuvering, succeeds in convincing her father and riding off on a horse with her knight. Her stolid demand to have the man she wants inspires her mother to confess to her husband that he may not be the father of their first child. Both old, they sit inert through the exchange, the last in the film, and swear their devotion to one another. The importance of the connection through passion, sexuality, and love, whether within the same relationship or not, is clearly expressed.

Sexuality is isolated as its own universe in *Romance* (France, 1999), directed by Catherine Breillat with a focus on spare scenes as if the woman, played by Caroline Ducey, blanked out between encounters in stairwells and apartments very specifically set up for sexual activity. Like the teacher of children in *Looking for Mr. Goodbar*, she one day finds herself in trouble in the classroom for having too much fun the night before. Unlike the latter character, who is aghast at letting down her children, this woman not only does not appear to have fun during sex but also has no connection to her work, suggesting some kind of negative relation to the world in general. Minimally, this film offers an unusual role-reversed version of sexual imagery, where orgasm is continuously sought but its pleasure so brief as not to make an appearance. *Romance* may be the title, but the film itself is a dream without the allure of romance, which makes its female authorship evident and the film more thought provoking than it seems at first.

Creativity and Courage

> It's my job to know what is and to keep my children away from it. I'd rather they had peace in heaven than hell here on earth.—*Beloved* (United States, 1998)

Since all 2,418 titles in this filmography have placed a woman in a central role, they demand a character capable of engaging an audience and capable of change. While the actions of a character within a story may be heroic, especially in the modern era, they may also go against the heroic tradition. In either case, central characters always need some amount of creativity or courage in order to push forward the narrative, be it for the good of all or errantly self-indulgent. While genre fictions are

intended to satisfy audiences by presenting clearcut characters—fantastical as they sometimes are—in this regard, the best dramatic stories of courage and creativity in women have little generic about them. On the contrary, they are characterized by in-depth depictions of a specific time and place that often as not originate in a biographical or "true" story.

In *Sambizanga* (Angola, 1972), Sarah Maldoror films a primarily political tract describing the nascent Angolan liberation movement through the story of a modest and traditional wife, played by Elisa Andrade. The first scenes are focused on her activist husband in the quarry where he works and distributes revolutionary information; suddenly he is taken away in an early-morning roundup of their small village. The women of the village advise her to take her baby with her to find her husband and use the crying child to boost her case; it is her first sense of what will be necessary to help her husband, whom she believes to be innocent of any political activity. Her trek to Luanda is slow and long, but she is helped along the way by other activists who have heard the news, and she manages to deal assertively with the officials she faces, though she never really understands why her husband has been arrested. Her courage in facing up to the government comes not from ideological ground but from her sense of responsibility for her family. It is also shaped by the network of people she finds to advise and console her, beginning with those savvy neighbors who tell her to strap her baby on her back.

This source of courage—the community—is in contrast to the source of the courage displayed in *Silkwood* (United States, 1983), where Meryl Streep plays Karen Silkwood, a real-life working-class hero who died under mysterious circumstances after actively protesting environmental conditions in a nuclear factory where she worked. In this film, her courage to speak out comes from her observation of unsafe working conditions and fear of being harmed by them. She is advised to lighten her criticism, even by the union and other workers, who are afraid for their jobs, but has a history of defiant independence that propels her forward. The film effectively folds in her unconventional personal life—children left behind with their father, as well as a lesbian best friend—to illustrate her strength of character over all. In *Rosa Luxemburg* (West Germany, 1986), Barbara Sukowa takes Rosa through scene after scene of conflict. First she argues with her lover, who tries to tell her where to work, then her family, who insists on bailing her out of jail, even though she prefers to stay as a matter of principle. Finally, she argues with friends, who expect her to lobby more for women's issues, which in her thinking take second place to pacifism and, in the Germany of the 1920s, antimilitarism. Aware of her stern persona, she swears one day to become "patience and gentleness personified," one of the many moving revelations that come from the film's extensive use of voice-over from Luxemburg's own writing. Another story of personal courage despite the opposition of others is *Black Rain* (Japan, 1989), in which Etsuko Ichihara plays a young woman who walks through Hiroshima the day of the bombing and then realizes over the next several years that she has been made sick by it. Her elders are committed to asserting her good health so she can marry, but she is ostracized anyway. Finally, she expresses her desire to live honestly and marries another victim, who has become deranged.

Olenka Cepeda plays the charismatic socialist activist Maria Elena Moyano in *Courage* (Peru, 1998). Founder of the Women's Federation of Villa El Salvador, she was assassinated at the age of thirty-three in 1993 by the Shining Path because she refused to allow them to take over her operations. Aside from her considerable charm—she easily relaxes into a night out drinking and dancing with her friends and is very close to her children and husband—the film details her negotiating skills and positive ways of interacting with bureaucrats, the media, and influential officials, creating a portrait of an exceptionally politically sophisticated woman. *Rachida* (Algeria, 2002) is also a story of political determination. Ibtissem Djouadi plays a young teacher accosted one morning on her way to school and commanded to take a bomb with her into the building; when she refuses, she is shot in the stomach. The rest of the film is her long recovery in a village outside the city, where she and her mother stay with family and where terrorists occasionally ride through wreaking havoc, forcing the villagers to be wary. After months of adjusting to the fact that her country is a war zone, and with the day-to-day support of her mother and the other women in the village, Rachida is ready to enter a demolished classroom and call the frightened children back to school.

Beloved (United States, 1998), based on the novel by Toni Morrison, intertwines themes of courage and creativity with spirituality. Sethe, played by Oprah Winfrey, is an ex-slave during the Civil War who has escaped and is tracked down by her owner. Seeing him, she takes immediate steps to murder her infant and two sons rather than have them returned to "sweet home." The film's concrete laying out of life's most extreme emotions and their relationship to injustice and the eternal is firmly grounded in every scene. The Christian

women who judge, ostracize, and pity the "murderer" arrive at the end to sing an exorcism that gets rid of the "ghost" of her dead child. This is an example of the persistent bringing in of the "outside"—in the sense of fresh air or difference—that is a powerful aspect of this film and that is directly related to its focus on women. The sensitivity and openness that Sethe emanates, without having the slightest bit of ingratiating manner, allow all kind of people to appear at her door. In fact, the image of the stream of people going down the road at the bottom of her walk suggests everyone is welcome at any time. Sethe is in constant engagement with what her preacher grandmother extolled her and everyone else who came to the gatherings in the woods to do: "Love your flesh!"

An Angel at My Table (New Zealand, 1990) is from the autobiographical writings of the New Zealand novelist Janet Frame. Like many of the films described here, it takes a strong personality who is assumed to be weak and grants her the triumph of her true self. As a little girl behind a school desk, she demands each word of her poem remain hers. It is a core of surety—in fictional ability—that does not stand her in good stead. When she gets a job as a school teacher and one day cannot speak, she goes passively to a mental institution and finds it offers her a place of nonresponsibility where she feels safe. When her novels become well known, the professionals and her family begin to look at her differently, and she herself, having written about insanity, finds that she is able to be sane and travel about as an author. We are assured of her strength when she has her first sexual encounter and the adult good sense to reject the shallow man rather than indulge his ego, no matter how painful the act is to her. There is no process here of "finding" herself, she knew herself all along, but the people around her were forced to change and recognize her.

Nonetheless, such recognition remains a matter of luck. *I, the Worst of All* (Argentina, 1991) is the story of Sor Juana Ines de la Cruz, one of the greatest Spanish-language poets. Played by Assumta Serna, she thrived all her life on doing only what she wanted to do, but then clashed one time too many with an authority she disdained. When she exclaims, "It's because I'm a woman!" to the confessor who agrees to her imprisonment for heresy, the statement has acquired a double edge. Yes, sexist men throughout her life have been jealous of her intellect, her library, her cultured life, and her freedom to defy convention. But the film also shows how she repeatedly refused to address her political environment or take responsibility for it; always, she trusted others to take care of her. In this, her story is much different and considerably more tragic than that of Janet Frame, as Sor Juana was forced by a particularly nasty political environment, the Catholic Church of the Inquisition, to abandon her writing. This event has another turn in that she is forced to swear herself "the worst" to confirm she has been too prideful of her intellect and neglected her religiosity. The film, however, puts forward a clear thesis that she did not use her intellect enough, or, rather, made choices that sustained her pure (theoretical) intellect over her independent being in the world. That she retains a saintly, pure, completely innocent aspect makes this work as important a tragic fiction as there is.

In *The Official Story* (Argentina, 1985), Norma Aleandro plays a high school teacher committed to bureaucratic rules and disciplined fairness, with a happy marriage and a much loved adopted child. Her "normality" is established early, both in her domestic relationship with her husband and at her workplace, and makes this one of the few films considered here to address the theme of a woman actually grappling with the "normal" dishonesty of her most intimate and heretofore trusted partner. When she is visited by a close friend she has not seen in years, and the woman tells her that she was tortured for her political associations, her husband's indication that the friend got what she deserved is the first clue. Immediately she suspects that her own adored daughter might be the child of one of the "disappeared" and that she herself is one who "asked no questions." Her investigation is persistent, and not once does she falter in questioning her husband, who finally and inevitably responds with violence to her demands for the truth. This is another powerful meditation on courage, life's compromises, and the creative dynamic that connects them.

GENRE FICTIONS

It's my life, not some man's life I'm helping him out with!—*Alice Doesn't Live Here Anymore* (United States, 1974)

I used love to take my revenge. I never imagined the damage love can do.—*Intimate Confessions of a Chinese Courtesan* (Hong Kong, 1972)

Genre pictures are heavily impacted by the charm and interest of the lead actors and a script that puts a different "spin" on the generic material. Many comedy-dramas have taken serious concerns about women in the workplace and commented on

them. In *9 to 5* (United States, 1980), the stellar cast of Jane Fonda, Dolly Parton, and Lily Tomlin manage to make enduring the 1970s fantasy of flexible time, day care, and salary equity, partly because in watching the film today we must be struck by what a fantasy it still is. Race relations take on a lighter but extremely effective tone in *Mama, There's a Man in Your Bed* (France, 1989), a fantasy of interracial romance that puts at its center a stout office cleaning woman, played by Firmine Richard, who has many children by different fathers, all capable of having a good time together on a holiday. She is smart and spirited enough to catch on to a scheme to embezzle from the company—out of papers she happens to see in the wastebasket—and then discreetly informs the president of the trouble facing him. Recognizing a good partner, he asks her to help him find the culprit, and their teamwork leads to love. While the true problems of class and race never surface in this happy film, its energetic lead performance is not strictly comic and provides real insight into a different kind of mother whose unglamorous presence is as "normal" as her Hollywood destiny is not. It would be interesting to compare with the similar *Claudine* (United States, 1974), played by the definitely glamorous crossover star Diahann Carroll. *The Spouse* (Iran, 1994) presents Fatemeh Motamed-Aria as a middle-class woman who works, in head scarf and long coat, beside her husband, in suit and tie, in the same soulless corporate office. The forced resignation of one of the company officers leads to extortion, which she uncovers with some elaborate intrigue at the warehouse. While incorporating comic bits of physicality to avoid detection, she saves the day and is named director over her husband, who takes to his bed at all the attention she's getting, refusing to go out of the house, while she moves ahead with her work. *Broadcast News* (United States, 1987), also almost entirely played out in the workplace, allows Holly Hunter to be the conscience and soul of a newsroom trio, a woman who starts her day every morning with a good cry. Her decision to turn her back on a suitor who fakes a tear during a report on date rape provides a major model of the independent-thinking woman. Directly related to this supremely intelligent decision is her grave insecurity regarding her attractiveness: "I have passed some line, some place. I am beginning to repel people I'm trying to seduce."

Marriage, motherhood, and the desire for both are also related to personal growth in comedies. *On a Clear Day You Can See Forever* (United States, 1970) places Barbra Streisand in two opposing roles, a clumsy Brooklyn girl with past lives and paranormal skills and a Regency-era diva with persuasive sexual confidence. "What is this ex-trasensory torture?" she screams after a final set piece of hypnotizing communication, demanding the return of her true self from people on the street, on television, and even from a dog. *La Dile-ttante* (France, 1999) presents Catherine Frot as the opposite type, completely charming and seduc-tive in the here and now to all ages, races, and gen-ders; sympathy from her is neither simply genuine or out of a bottle, but something she can always reliably produce for her own purposes.

In *The Flower of My Secret* (Spain, 1995), Marisa Paredes plays a writer in the throes of crisis because she is known for her "ladies romance" literature and not the more serious writing in which she takes pride. Her maturing away from the husband who does not love her and toward a more mundane man who appreciates her writing is the comic journey she takes. In *Heartburn* (United States, 1986), Meryl Streep effectively competes with Jack Nicholson, who is not strictly coded as male—he reads books to his child at break-fast—yet betrays her with mutual friends every chance he gets. In the end, reading to a child is not as important as being faithful, and when she leaves him for good, her reflection that she was deluded, "living a dream" of marriage, is a description that might be applied to most movie marriages.

In *Life . . . My Passion* (Egypt, 1995), three shop workers feign excuses in order to leave work early and meet for a fun night out. Living in a tene-ment, they are each attached to less competent men who get jailed, demand they wear veils, and otherwise oppress them. These women cut a large swath through Cairo, lighting up their workplaces, the streets, their apartment buildings crowded with old people and children, and even the dingy rooms they inhabit. At one point, one of the many men in their midst is dismissed: "Life has made us into men, and we don't need you anymore!" *Peking Opera Blues* (Hong Kong, 1986) is the final example of a comedy about women, and it veers into action territory. Set in the early part of the twentieth century, its trio includes a general's daughter who dresses as a man to protect herself, an actress with martial arts training, and an accidental thief; they all get involved with a guerrilla band to which the general's daughter is already committed. They must steal an important document from the general, who is loved by his daughter, but not more than she hates his politics.

Three of the more serious and interesting action films in this filmography all involve consid-eration of modern intertwined factions locked in deadly terrorist warfare. Diane Keaton gives a strong central performance in *The Little Drummer Girl* (United States, 1984), which reflects the confu-sion of the political circumstances of the Middle East, in the confusion of the film itself and in the character's own condition. As a leftist woman used to speaking out, her involvement with the more sinister elements of Israeli strategy, subsequent brainwashing, and finally, hysterical witness to a bloodbath is a "sentimental education" as only a modern liberated woman might get. Truly, she is a woman who "never knew what hit her." Likewise, *The Terrorist* (India, 1998)—which lacks a specific geographic context and therefore fails to offer the diversion of a debatable version of political "real-ity"—illustrates how little this context matters. The central character, played by Ayesha Dharkar, a girl who has lost her family during a rebellion and volunteers for a suicide mission, is similarly, and the film suggests inevitably, confused. Her training in the procedures for accomplishing her mission is so laborious—involving enigmatic mes-sages, long hikes, and mysterious tutors—that she never knows who is guiding her and finally loses interest. The men around these two lead charac-ters spend all their time playing elaborate games, while the women, focused on the caring and loss of actual people, only wonder why. In *Guardian of the Frontier* (Slovenia, 2002), Maja Weiss comments on this modern Kafkaesque condition by having three young friends take a canoe trip down the river border between Croatia and Slovenia. The three characters create a neat dominant, mild, and middle (the one with an adoring boyfriend), which lends a sense of vulnerability to the group as a whole, even though the situations they meet only provoke them to provoke each other. Again, the environment appears as "anywhere, world," with generous Bohemian artists and right-wing village demagogues holding equal sway, while the point is made that the girls do not appreciate the importance of any political philosophy. It suggests they too are confused, diverted from reality, in this instance because they are absorbed solely in con-templating their own sexual and intimate relations of the present.

PHILOSOPHICAL FILM

Why is the prospect of catastrophe so readily dissolved by poetry?—*Kristina Talking Pictures* (United States, 1976)

These common conditions and questions for women—isolation, autonomy, conservatism, ap-pearances, race and class, abuse, punishment, family and work, friendship and love, sexuality, creativity and courage—make a special appearance in films by directors who create characters specifically engaged in thinking about the condition of women. While most of the films already discussed consciously attempt to counter filmic codes that objectify women, the films in this section have a special mission to do so, whether the codes are seen as strictly a function of the cinematic apparatus (camera, editing) or as arising more broadly from scripting, acting, and the many other production elements of a film.

At the extreme opposite of action films are essay-type efforts of filmmakers such as Yvonne Rainer, who often describes her films as antinarratives. Rainer was originally a dancer of the New York avant-garde, where filmmaking was part of an integrated arts movement. Her films, especially when shot by cinematographer Babette Mangolte, present an intriguing and comprehensive mix of 1970s feminist ideas—comprising in essence what has come to be known as the feminist "label"—insofar as they combined anger over sexist injustice with a deliberate disdain for commercial "polish." In *Film about a Woman Who . . .* (United States, 1974), the line is drawn: "Compromise—life would be easier [with it]—it's always been all or nothing to me." And so, Rainer has never wavered from her own special mix of images, sound, acted set pieces, and personal voice-over distinctly intended to reflect her own sense of confessional honesty. A section titled "An emotional accretion in 48 steps" moves toward a couple's crucial moment when she invokes a "Hold me," at the moment when she actually wanted "to kick his ass." In her later films, such as *Privilege* (United States, 1990), where Rainer films a black woman interviewing other women going through menopause, she integrates observations on class and race with quotations from mostly contemporary political writings. The quotes are always apt, in this case ending with Rainer appearing as Helen Caldicott: "Utopia, the more impossible it seems, the more necessary it becomes."

Valie Export comes out of photography—and continues to be a photographer—with a different graphic sensibility from Rainer but a similar set of political concerns and avant-garde aesthetic. Both these women, along with Chantal Akerman and Marguerite Duras, show an interest in the most minute inspection of interpersonal relationships, usually through dialogue and usually in an incremental, nonlinear fashion. But there is a monologue quality to these films as well, which Export elaborates in her own deadpan way: "All my images are a mon - o - logue." In *Invisible Adversaries* (Austria, 1977), Export consistently surprises with long

shots or close-ups that are not at first decipherable, then acquire increasing interest as they reveal the movement and sound within them. An ongoing discussion of bureaucracy and personal responsibility takes place among the main character, played by Export, her male lover, and a friend who models for her. Around this is her own aggressive taboo-breaking draping of herself around public walkways. This particular project, which is also exhibited as a set of still photographs, provokes a meditation on the power of the female artist: "These images trouble me. Are they a defense mechanism against fear or do they produce fear? I don't want to protect my self against fear with means connected with fear." But the force of Export's work remains in its cinematic structural strength, such as the lengthy beginning and closing shots (night and day), which involve a very smooth pan and zoom from deep inside her bedroom out the window and over the city.

Chantal Akerman, whose career briefly paralleled Export's and Rainer's in the 1970s, quickly established herself as independent of the avant-garde, increasingly relying solely on structural images and sound and persistently using the classical narrative form of the art film. Quotations and argument, for instance, have never been part of her arsenal. Films such as *Rendez-vous d'Anna* (Belgium, 1978), *All Night Long* (Belgium, 1982), and *Night and Day* (France, 1991) establish her increasingly pared-down enigmatic style that effectively severs the work from any possible "label" yet solidifies and deepens the relevance of her poetic thinking to feminists. The end of *Night and Day*, where the lead character walks off into street traffic, never again to relate to the men with whom she has spent the time of the film, is echoed by Claire Denis in *Friday Night* (France, 2003) and adds to the sense of that ending, effectively replacing "walking into the sunset" with the citified "disappearing into traffic." In these two films, ordinary women are allowed a fictional stance that is not nice, loyal, kind, or, at the other extreme, mean and duplicitous but that simply valorizes their sexual learning experiences and right to move on from them without guilt.

Akerman bridges the space between the antinarrative and the longer line of conventional narrative films focused on broad concerns regarding women, expressed in 1968 in the previously mentioned *The Girls*, by Mai Zetterling. Similarly ambitious statements continued through the 1970s from other European filmmakers. *The All-Round Reduced Personality—Outtakes* (West Germany, 1977) is more lighthearted in style yet just as serious as Zetterling's film; Helke Sander not only wrote and directed but plays the main character as well.

The film's formal elegance and appreciation for Berlin are bound in fine tracking shots through the streets of the city. As an unmarried mother mulling over the political conditions of the time, and working on a photographic project of the city, she spends much time networking and debating politics in an attempt to fit in and earn a living, while her young daughter and the need to relax also vie for her time. Really, she just wants to be a good citizen.

A Question of Silence (Netherlands, 1982) is a flat photographic treatment of conventional events and characters: Three matter-of-fact women spontaneously murder a shopkeeper, then tell the court-appointed psychiatrist (the main character) that they have no idea why they did it. She eventually decides to pose to the court an ideological explanation—they did it because he was a man—an idea that comes after much thinking on her part and resistance from the "system," including her husband, which prefers she certify the women are insane. This film is justifiably well known and will always provoke important questions about violence and its origins. *Born in Flames* (United States, 1983), directed by a white woman, Lizzie Borden, is the only film in this group that addresses issues of race. In fact, it picks up the white bourgeois context of the previous three films in the person of a group of women intellectuals who argue the next steps in a ten-year-old revolution that has merely put more of their (mostly male) colleagues in power. The extraordinary charm and creativity of activist groups is evident everywhere, in a mixed-race "women's army" that patrols the streets and in a group of cultural radicals, led by an actor named Honey, who turn out for "not just the liberation of women, but the liberation of all to the freedom of life, which is found in music."

The May Lady (Iran, 1998) is one of the few recent additions to this set of films that combine the day-to-day lives of women actively thinking about women's issues, with excerpts of their philosophies. In it a divorced documentary filmmaker, played by Minu Farshchi, must deal with her teenage son, who is jealous of a new man with whom she has fallen in love; the son has been spoiled and believes she exists only for him. Throughout the film she writes in her journal, leaves messages for her lover, and interviews mothers in search of an "exemplary mother," an assignment she has been given by an Iranian film "council." At every free moment in her busy life, she ruminates about why a mother cannot love and also work and is depressed by the subject of her film, which puts her in touch with women much different from her and challenges her notions of mothering. Midway

through the film, she is in crisis, unable to imagine how to complete her own film, as she stands and frets over the raw interviews. One old woman tells her, "I can play the role of mother. I don't have children, but I have feelings." Another, a lawyer, asks why she is looking for an exemplary mother at all and accuses her of working out of prevailing narrow notions of gender and class. At the "council," they berate her for stalling: "No one can believe that your sharp eye failed to find a qualified mother in a patriarchal community!" Finally, an interviewee she finds in a noisy weaving factory yells at her, "My life is not good for a film! Go after your own life!" This encounter, combined with an official who tells her she has spoiled her son when she has to bail him out of jail for going to a party, breaks her creative block.

The pinnacle of philosophical film about women is the prodigious three-part, six-hour diary trilogy by Márta Mészáros, *Diary for My Children* (Hungary, 1982), *Diary for My Loves* (1987), and *Diary for My Father and Mother* (1990). This series, which chronicles a young woman's adult education—from film school in Moscow, to a search for the truth about the disappearance of her communist intellectual parents during the Stalinist era, and finally to the recognition of the repressive reality of state power during the cataclysmic uprising of 1956—is unparalleled in its depth of focus on a lone women's journey through political activism. Begun when Mészáros was already a mature, experienced filmmaker with a spare, direct black-and-white style, the series reveals most when viewed in its entirety. Mészáros takes her strong graphic style and adds to it the immediate filmed history of the period, newsreels and other found footage of demonstrations and events. These films revolve around a performance by Zsuzsa Czinkóczi that brooks not a moment of gratuitous charm. She is, from the first shot, a woman, orphaned and angry, with her own suspicions of why this has happened to her and where responsibility for her situation lies. She defines "uncompromising" in several ways. First, she refuses to look askance at the relationship between her aunt's position in the communist bureaucracy—her aunt does not use the power she has to fight for a more humane system—and the fate that befell her parents. She insists there is a relationship between individual engagement and the political hierarchy. Second, she not only testily yells through the gates of the Hungarian Embassy demanding to leave Moscow at the time of the uprising, she also "rattles the cage" of cinematic identification by maintaining her right at all times to be "unpleasant." It is not until the final segment, when the forces of history take increasing time away from the characters' daily lives, that we fully recognize the courage and intelligence—and love—behind her stance. She has insisted on seeing the sources of violence in "us," or more specifically, the aunt who owes her position to keeping quiet. As police violence sweeps over the surprised bourgeoisie, her prescience and insight is in retrospect thrilling. In the end, her character is given time to chronicle and appreciate the minor variations in people's political stances, granting them room for shopping idylls and parties where conviviality reigns, no matter how hard a line has been drawn. She is left wondering about her strong sense of righteousness as the opportunities for change in the future narrow, and forgiveness and understanding suddenly seem as important as analysis.

FILM REFERENCES AND ENTRY NUMBERS IN FILMOGRAPHY

The 24-Hour Woman United States, 1998 [2229]
9 to 5 United States, 1980 [1999]
Adoption Hungary, 1975 [934]
Adua and Company Italy, 1960 [1142]
Ai Nü: Intimate Confessions of a Chinese Courtesan Hong Kong, 1972 [900]
Alice Doesn't Live Here Anymore United States, 1974 [1946]
All Night Long Belgium, 1982 [118]
The All-Round Reduced Personality—Outtakes West Germany, 1977 [767]
An Angel at My Table New Zealand, 1990 [1392]
Antonia's Line Netherlands, 1996 [1377]
Ay! Carmela Spain, 1990 [1574]
Babette's Feast Denmark, 1987 [362]
Bad Timing United Kingdom, 1985 [1793]
The Ballad of Little Jo United States, 1993 [2150]
Bandit Queen India, 1994 [1031]
Bastard Out of Carolina United States, 1996 [2195]
The Battle of the Sacred Tree Kenya, 1994 [1284]
Being Julia Canada, 2004 [221]
Beloved United States, 1998 [2230]
Between Heaven and Earth France, 1993 [566]
The Big City India, 1963 [968]
The Bitter Tears of Petra von Kant West Germany, 1972 [751]
Black Girl Senegal, 1966 [1521]
Black Rain Japan, 1989 [1258]
The Blue-Veiled Iran, 1995 [1082]
Born in Flames United States, 1983 [2021]
Boys Don't Cry United States, 1999 [2238]
Brief Encounters USSR, 1968 [2361]
Broadcast News United States, 1987 [2069]
The Butcher France, 1969 [449]
Butterfield 8 United States, 1960 [1888]

Camila Argentina, 1984 [28]
The Children's Hour United States, 1962 [1892]
Claudine United States, 1974 [1948]
Cleo from 5 to 7 France, 1961 [425]
Contempt France, 1963 [437]
Courage Peru, 1998 [1421]
Daisies Czechoslovakia, 1966 [350]
Dancing at Lughnasa Ireland, 1998 [1119]
Danzón Mexico, 1991 [1335]
Daughters of the Dust United States, 1992 [2122]
Desert Hearts United States, 1985 [2044]
Diary for My Children Hungary, 1982 [944]
Diary for My Father and Mother Hungary, 1990 [950]
Diary for My Loves Hungary, 1987 [948]
La Dilettante France, 1999 [606]
A Doll's House United Kingdom, 1973 [1771]
Dolores Claiborne United States, 1995 [2174]
Effi Briest West Germany, 1974 [758]
The Engagement of Anna Greece, 1972 [868]
Erin Brockovich United States, 1999 [2242]
Ermo China, 1994 [301]
Eve's Bayou United States, 1997 [2223]
Faat-Kine Senegal, 2001 [1532]
Fatal Attraction United States, 1987 [2071]
Film about a Woman Who . . . United States, 1974 [1950]
Fire India, 1996 [1037]
Flame Zimbabwe, 1995 [2417]
The Flower of My Secret Spain, 1995 [1587]
Flowers of Shanghai Taiwan, 1998 [1686]
French Twist France, 1995 [579]
Friday Night France, 2003 [665]
Friends South Africa, 1993 [1543]
Genesis India, 1986 [1016]
A Gentle Woman France, 1969 [450]
Georgia United States, 1995 [2176]
Germany Pale Mother West Germany, 1979 [779]
Gertrud Denmark, 1964 [354]
The Girls France, 1960 [421]
The Girls Sweden, 1968 [1643]
The Golden Bowl United States, 2001 [2278]
A Good Marriage France, 1981 [502]
Granny Russia, 2002 [1518]
Guardian of the Frontier Slovenia, 2002 [1536]
Heartburn United States, 1986 [2056]
High Tide Australia, 1987 [57]
The Hours United States, 2002 [2300]
House Built on Sand Russia, 1991 [1514]
Household Saints United States, 1993 [2152]
I Don't Want to Talk about It Argentina, 1994 [34]
I Love to Work Italy, 2004 [1208]
I, the Worst of All Argentina, 1991 [32]
Indochine France, 1991 [550]
Intimate Confessions of a Chinese Courtesan Hong Kong, 1972 [900]

Invisible Adversaries Austria, 1977 [87]

Je tu il elle Belgium, 1974 [112]

Jeanne Dielman, 23 Quai du Commerce, 1080 Brux-elles Belgium, 1975 [113]

Klute United States, 1971 [1924]

Kristin Lavransdatter Norway, 1996 [1413]

Kristina Talking Pictures United States, 1976 [1971]

The Lacemaker France, 1977 [481]

The Lady and the Duke France, 2001 [629]

Lady Sings the Blues United States, 1972 [1932]

The Last Harem Turkey, 1997 [1737]

Let's Hope It's a Girl Italy, 1985 [1180]

Life … My Passion Egypt, 1995 [400]

Lilya 4-Ever Sweden, 2002 [1662]

The Little Drummer Girl United States, 1984 [2035]

Lola France, 1960 [422]

The Long Farewell USSR, 1971 [2365]

Looking for Mr. Goodbar United States, 1977 [1982]

The Love Eterne China, 1963 [232]

Loving Couples Sweden, 1964 [1639]

Lucía, Cuba, 1969 [329]

Maborosi Japan, 1996 [1263]

Mama Got Married USSR, 1969 [2363]

Mama, There's a Man in Your Bed France, 1989 [540]

Mamma Roma Italy, 1962 [1146]

Marianne and Julianne West Germany, 1981 [789]

Marketplace India, 1983 [1006]

The May Lady Iran, 1998 [1085]

McCabe and Mrs. Miller United States, 1971 [1925]

Miss Mary Argentina, 1986 [30]

Moolaadé Senegal, 2004 [1534]

Mossane Senegal, 1996 [1531]

The Mother United Kingdom, 2004 [1884]

Mrs. Dalloway United Kingdom, 1997 [1843]

My Big Fat Greek Wedding United States, 2002 [2308]

My Life to Live France, 1962 [434]

Nargess Iran, 1991 [1076]

Night and Day France, 1991 [553]

Night Games Sweden, 1966 [1640]

The Night Porter Italy, 1974 [1161]

Nobody's Wife Argentina, 1982 [27]

Nora Helmer West Germany, 1973 [757]

Nothing Poland, 1998 [1483]

Numéro deux France, 1975 [472]

The Official Story Argentina, 1985 [29]

On a Clear Day You Can See Forever United States, 1970 [1919]

On the Way Hungary, 1980 [1462]

Opening Night United States, 1977 [1984]

Overseas France, 1991 [555]

A Passage to India United Kingdom, 1984 [1789]

Peking Opera Blues Hong Kong, 1986 [905]

Petulia United Kingdom, 1968 [1762]

The Portrait of a Lady United Kingdom, 1996 [1836]

Postcards from the Edge United States, 1990 [2114]

The Power of Men Is the Patience of Women West Germany, 1978 [777]

The Prime of Miss Jean Brodie United Kingdom, 1969 [1764]

Privilege United States, 1990 [2115]

A Question of Silence Netherlands, 1982 [1361]

Rachel, Rachel United States, 1968 [1908]

Rachida Algeria, 2002 [21]

Rambling Rose United States, 1991 [2135]

The Red Desert Italy, 1964 [1147]

Rendez-vous d'Anna Belgium, 1978 [115]

Riddance Hungary, 1973 [931]

Romance France, 1999 [615]

Rosa Luxemburg West Germany, 1986 [828]

Rosenstrasse Germany, 2003 [717]

Sambizanga Angola, 1972 [22]

Sankofa Ghana, 1994 [847]

Sara Iran, 1993 [1078]

Sarraounia Burkina Faso, 1986 [165]

Scrubbers United Kingdom, 1982 [1784]

The Sealed Soil Iran, 1977 [1073]

Seduction: The Cruel Woman West Germany, 1963 [742]

Set It Off United States, 1996 [2216]

Sh'hur Israel, 1994 [1131]

The Silences of the Palace Tunisia, 1994 [1698]

Silent Waters Pakistan, 2003 [1416]

Silkwood United States, 1983 [2028]

Sisters or the Balance of Happiness West Germany, 1979 [782]

Skirt Power Mali, 1997 [1323]

Sofie Denmark, 1982 [360]

Something Different Czechoslovakia, 1963 [349]

The Spouse Iran, 1994 [1079]

Stage Door Hong Kong, 1996 [919]

Starry Sky Brazil, 1996 [150]

The Story of Qiu Ju China, 1992 [291]

Story of Women France, 1988 [527]

Sugar Cane Alley France, 1983 [512]

Take Care of My Cat South Korea, 2001 [1307]

Ten Iran, 2003 [1102]

The Terrorist India, 1998 [1044]

Thelma and Louise United States, 1991 [2137]

To Take a Wife Israel, 2004 [1141]

Trial of Joan of Arc France, 1962 [431]

Two of Them Hungary, 1977 [937]

Two Women Italy, 1961 [1144]

An Unmarried Woman United States, 1977 [1988]

Up to a Certain Point Cuba, 1983 [336]

Vera Drake United Kingdom, 2004 [1886]

Waiting for the Moon United States, 1986 [2064]

Washington Square United States, 1997 [2228]

What's Love Got to Do with It? United States, 1993 [2155]

The Wheel South Korea, 1983 [1293]

Will It Snow for Christmas? France, 1996 [590]

Wings USSR, 1966 [2355]

The Wings of the Dove United Kingdom, 1997 [1848]

A Woman's Tale Australia, 1991 [66]

Women from the Lake of Scented Souls China, 1993 [296]

Working Girls United States, 1986 [2065]

Y tu mama también Mexico, 2001 [1346]

FILMOGRAPHY: FEATURE FILMS ON THE SUBJECT OF WOMEN SINCE 1960

AFGHANISTAN

1. *Rabeia e Balkhi / Rabia of Balkh*   1974
D: Toryalai Shafaq
S: Abdulah Shadan
C: Sedik Aminz
A: Sima Shadan
A princess of the kingdom of Balkh, which has been at war for decades, conflicts with her father and brother. When a slave becomes the commander and wins the war, she falls in love with him, but her brother kills their father and her. *Festival des 3.*

2. *Osama*   2003 P
D: Siddiq Marmak
S: Siddiq Marmak
C: Ebrahim Ghafori
P: Julia Fraser, Julie LeBrocquy
A: Marina Golbahari, Zubaida Sahar
Kabul. With no men left in the house, a young girl is disguised as a man and sent out by her mother to work for their food in the Taliban-ruled city, which allows no women on the streets without male accompaniment. *NYT: E28. 2004, Feb. 6.*
Awards: Cannes Film Festival, AFCAE Award, 2003; London Film Festival, Sutherland Trophy, 2003; Golden Globes, Best Foreign Language Film, 2004

ALBANIA

3. *Dimeri i fundit / The Last Winter*   1976
D: Kristaq Mitro, Ibrahim Mucaj
S: Nexhati Tafa
A: Rajmonda Bullku, Dhimitra Plasari
"Group of women put up resistance to foreign occupation during World War II." *Encyclopedia of European.*

ALGERIA

4. *Elise, ou la vraie vie / Elise or Real Life* 1969 S
D: Michel Drach

S: Michel Drach, Claire Etcherelli, Claude Lanzmann
C: Claude Zidi
A: Marie-José Nat, Mohamed Chouikh, Bernadette Lafont
1950s. Woman from Bordeaux goes to Paris to stay with her radicalized brother, who gets her a job in the factory where he works. She becomes aware of the pervasive racism there and falls in love with an Algerian fellow worker. *BiFi.*
Awards: Cannes Film Festival, nomination for Golden Palm, 1970

5. *Noubat al Nissa Djebel Chenoua / The Nouba Women of Mount Chenou*   1970 DS
D: Assia Djebar
S: Assia Djebar
A: Sawan Noweir, Mohamed Haimour
Blend of fiction and documentary about a woman at a crisis in her marriage who looks back at her childhood during the Algerian War; includes abstract images of the condition of women; reenactments of a nineteenth-century native revolt; and a special focus on sound, including the music of Bela Bartók and the *nouba*, an "Andalusian urban dance form." *Post-Colonial Images: 114–122.*
Other titles: La Nouba des femmes du Mont Chenoua

6. *Remparts d'Argile / Ramparts of Clay*   1970
D: Jean-Louis Bertuccelli
S: Jean Duvignaud
C: Andreas Winding
A: Leila Schenna
Tunisia. When village men strike over their exploitative wages as rock-salt cutters, the village women transcend their subservient role within the village by joining them.
Awards: Berlin International Film Festival, Interfilm Award, 1971; Prix Jean Vigo, 1971

7. *El Fahham / The Coalburner*   1972
D: Mohamed Bouamari
S: Mohamed Bouamari

C: Daha Boukerche
A: Fattouma Ouslilha, Mohamed Debbah
Algeria, 1970s. During the agrarian revolution, a miner is commanded to become a peasant. His wife protests the layoff and, against his will, finds work in a new factory, but he angrily hopes the local council will "unveil" her for the transgression of working outside the home. *Corps, l'histoire:* 97.
Other titles: Le charbonnier

8. **Ryah El Janoub / The South Wind**   1975
D: Mohamed Slim Riad
S: Mohamed Slim Riad; based on the novel by Abdel Hamid Benhadouga
C: Daha Boukerche
A: Kelltoum, Nawal Zaatar
Algiers. A student flees her family's home when her father arranges her marriage as a payoff for security during the upheavals of the agrarian revolution. Her mother and aunt will not help, but she finds a haven in the mountains with a Berber family and becomes radicalized. *Corps, l'histoire:* 173.
Other titles: Le Vent du sud

9. **Leila wa alchwatouha / Leila and Others** 1978
D: Sid Ali Mazif
S: Sid Ali Mazif, Hamid Ait-Amara
C: Rachid Merabtine
A: Nadia Samir, Aïcha
Stories of two friends: a student who has refused an arranged marriage so she can continue her education, and her neighbor, who works in a television factory and participates in a strike for equal treatment of women, which divides the workers. *Corps, l'histoire:* 121.
Other titles: Leila et les autres

10. **Nahla**   1979
D: Farouk Beloufa
C: Allel Yahiaoui
A: Yasmine Khlat
Lebanon. During the civil war, a singer loses her voice and makes friends with a divorcée who works on a militant pro-Palestinian newspaper. *AMG.*
Awards: Moscow International Film Festival, Best Actress, 1979

11. **Imraa la ibni / A Wife for My Son**   1982
D: Ali Ghalem
S: Ali Ghalem
C: Mahmoud Lakhal
A: Isma, Rahim Lalloui

Details the arranged (forced) marriage of an eighteen-year-old, who has experienced only happiness and freedom, to an illiterate thirty-five-year-old who lives in France. *Festival de films, 10th:* 82. 1988.
Other titles: Une Femme pour mon fils

12. **Vent de sable / Sand Storm**   1982 S
D: Mohamed Lakhdar-Hamina
S: Mohamed Lakhdar-Hamina, Yamina Bachir-Chouikh
C: Youcef Sahraout
A: Leila Shenna, Albert Minska, Nadia Talbi
A desert village. A mother agitates discontent out of disappointment with her sons' children; one has a paralytic son, and the other has eight girls. Her meddling results in one daughter-in-law being felled by a vengeance killing for imagined infidelity and the other daughter-in-law being sent back to her own tribe. *Corps, l'histoire:* 199.
Awards: Cannes Film Festival, nomination for Golden Palm, 1982

13. **La Zerda ou les chants de l'oublie / Songs of Forgetting**   1982 DS
D: Assia Djebar
S: Malek Alloula, Assia Djebar
Veiled woman is a photographer; incorporates archival footage. *French-Speaking:* 16.
Awards: Berlin International Film Festival, OCIC Award, 1983

14. **El Kalaa / The Citadel**   1988
D: Mohamed Chouikh
C: Allel Yahiaoui
A: Fatima Belhadj
Life in a polygamous mountain village, where a rich, brutish man has three hard-working wives, while his son, in love with another's wife, is forced to marry a mannequin. *Festival de films, 17th:* 95. 1995.

15. **Touchia / Song of Algerian Women** 1992 DS
D: Rachid Benhadj
S: Rachid Benhadj
C: Zine Bessa
A: Nabila Nabli
A forty-year-old woman crosses Algeria to give a televised interview, but her fears rise as she encounters an increasing number of fundamentalist demonstrations. Bitter thoughts of the colonial war and its aftermath begin to focus her judgment on the male members of her own family. *Festival de films, 17th:* 94. 1994.

16. *Démon au féminin / Woman as the Devil* 1994 DS

D: Hafsa Zinai Koudil
S: Hafsa Zinai Koudil
C: A. Messaad
A: Doudja Achaichi, Djamila Haddad, Fatiha Berber, Ahmed Benaissa

1980s. An architect and his teacher wife are happy with their middle-class modern life, though one of their sons, who spends all his time at a mosque, worries them. One day the father is weakened and allows his son to convince him his wife is possessed by a demon: "It happens in couples where the woman works outside," his son assures him. Professional exorcists come to the house and the woman is locked up and submitted to a violent exorcism, which leaves her unconscious and confined to a wheelchair. *Variety: 97. 1994, Nov. 28.*

17. *La Montagne de Baya / Baya's Mountain* 1997

D: Azzedine Meddour
S: Azzedine Meddour
C: Bachir Selami
A: Djamila Amzal

Kabil, 1900s. The Berber resistance flees the French invasion. A woman is offered a huge sum for the murder of her husband, but she refuses the bribe and suffers the resentment of the villagers, who want her to accept so she can help them buy back their land. *Biennale des cinémas, 5th. Accessed 2005, June 10.*

18. *Sous les pieds des femmes / Where Women Tread* 1997 DSP

D: Rachida Krim
S: Rachida Krim, Catherine Labruyère-Colas
C: Bernard Cavalié
P: Brigitte Azoulay
A: Claudia Cardinale, Fejria Deliba, Mohommed Bakri

An Algerian woman looks back on her life as she waits the return of an old lover, whom she met in Algeria in 1958 when she and her husband hid in his house. He recruited her to raise money for the revolutionary struggle against the French. She escaped a roundup that caught her husband, but the man had her transported to Marseille, and she continued to work to free Algeria, though she was eventually arrested herself. *BiFi.*

Awards: Namur International Festival of French-Speaking Film, CICAE Award, 1997; Avignon Film Festival, Prix SACD, 1998

19. *L'Attente des femmes / Women's Expectations* 2000

D: Naguel Belouad
C: Bachir Salami
P: Naguel Belouad
A: Sonia Mekkiou

Algeria, l'Aurès region, 1920s. The twenty-year-old third wife of a respected elder becomes pregnant by a man who works for her husband. *Attente des femmes. Accessed 2005, June 11.*

20. *L'Autre monde / The Other World* 2001

D: Merzak Allouache
S: Merzak Allouache
A: Marie Brahimi

A French-Algerian woman visits Algiers to look for her fiancé and encounters a history of violence. *African Diaspora, 11th. 2003, Dec. Accessed 2004, Aug. 15.*

21. *Rachida* 2002 DSP

D: Yamina Bachir-Chouikh
S: Yamina Bachir-Chouikh
C: Mustafa Ben Mihoub
P: Margarita Seguy
A: Ibtissem Djouadi, Bahira Rachedi

1980s. A schoolteacher is shot for saying no to terrorists' demands that she plant a bomb at the school where she works. Seriously injured, she is taken away by her mother to hide in an isolated village and nursed back to health. The village seems far away from the troubles of the city, but marauders invade it too. Undeterred, she eventually and bravely is determined to teach the village children, whose classroom has been demolished.

Awards: Amiens International Film Festival, Best Film, 2002; London Film Festival, Satyajit Ray Award, 2002

ANGOLA

22. *Sambizanga* 1972 DS

D: Sarah Maldoror
S: Sarah Maldoror, Maurice Pons, Mario De Andrade; based on a story by Luandino Vieva
C: Claude Agostini
A: Elisa Andrade, Domingo De Olivera

A stone laborer is seized by police from a village hut for organizing activities. His wife then treks on foot, then bus, to Luanda (a very long way) in search of him. In the city, she displays great persistence and calm in dealing with the authorities, strongly asserting herself in requesting help from strangers as well as friends. Eventually she discovers he has died after being tortured. Based on a true story.

Awards: Berlin International Film Festival, Interfilm Award, OCIC Award, 1973

23. *O Recado das ilhas / The Message from the Islands* 1989
D: Ruy Duarte de Carvalho
S: Ruy Duarte de Carvalho
C: Joao Aboim
A: Edmea Brigham

Cape Verde. An exploration of the leading character's creation of herself through identification with characters from novels: "The beautiful Creole woman from Gonçalves' novel, which is set in the eighteenth century, becomes the Ariel of Aimé Césaire's adaptation of Shakespeare's *The Tempest.*" This sends her to the top of a volcano with a prisoner from colonial days who is now an airplane pilot. *Festival des 3.*

ARGENTINA

24. *Tres veces Ana / Three Times Ana* 1961
D: David Kohon
S: David Kohon
C: Ricardo Aronovich
P: Marcelo Simonetti
A: María Vaner

Portraits of three women, all played by the same actress: A shop clerk lives with her mother in the suburbs of Buenos Aires and has an affair with a man who persuades her to have an abortion; a carefree woman goes to a loud beachhouse party and meets an upper-class student; a man becomes obsessed with a vision of a woman, dreams of her, then discovers she is a mannequin. *South American Cinema: 37.*

Awards: Argentinean Film Critics Association, Best Screenplay, 1962

25. *La Raulito / Little Raoul* 1975 S
D: Lautaro Murúa
S: Juan Carlos Gené, Martha Mercader, José Paolantonio
C: Miguel Rodríguez
A: María Vaner, Marilina Ross

Buenos Aires, 1950s–1960s. The life of Maria Esther Duffau, a forty-year-old woman who dressed as a man, adopted a man's name, and moved in high society at the same time she lived in the rail yards and sometimes was jailed. When she felt pity coming her way, she fled; "a true rebel, who never compromises when her freedom or

pride is at stake." *Variety.* 1975, Sep. 3. Also *South American Cinema: 57.*

Other titles: Tomboy Paula

26. *Momentos* 1981 DSP
D: Maria Luisa Bemberg
S: Maria Luisa Bemberg, Marcelo Pichon Riviere
C: Miguel Rodríguez
P: Lita Stantic
A: Graciela Dufau

A landscaper, who has lost a beloved husband and married an older man, is drawn into an affair with a younger man she meets in a client's home. She expends much effort in trying to care for him and goes off with him on a vacation, but she leaves him suddenly when he becomes violent and she realizes the relationship will not be more supportive or fulfilling than the one she has.

27. *Señora de nadie / Nobody's Wife* 1982 DSP
D: Maria Luisa Bemberg
S: Maria Luisa Bemberg
C: Miguel Rodríguez
P: Lita Stantic
A: Luisina Brando

Buenos Aires. After discovering her husband's betrayal, a wife unhesitatingly leaves him and her children to make a new life for herself. She gradually returns to her children while living apart, getting a job in real estate, and trying to enjoy city life. She finds a sympathetic friend in a gay man she meets at group therapy and ends up living with him.

28. *Camila* 1984 DSP
D: Maria Luisa Bemberg
S: Maria Luisa Bemberg, Beda Docampo Feijóo, Juan Bautista Stagnaro
C: Fernando Arribas
P: Lita Stantic
A: Susu Pecoraro, Imanol Arias

1847, during the Argentine dictatorship of De Rosas. An upper-middle-class Catholic woman falls in love with a Jesuit priest; she confesses her desire to the priest, whose reticence (even illness at one point) makes him more vulnerable. Their love consummated with no turning back, she persuades him to run away with her, and they are found and executed. Political, religious, and social upheaval underlie the union and bring out the intelligence that propels the woman forward.

Awards: Havana Film Festival, Best Actress, 1984; Academy Awards, nomination for Best Foreign Film, 1985

29. *La Historia oficial / The Official Story* 1985 S
D: Luis Puenzo
S: Luis Puenzo, Aída Bortnik
C: Felix Monti
A: Norma Aleandro, Hector Alterio
A middle-class high school history teacher with a penchant for discipline and approved documentation is shocked to find that a dear school friend was "disappeared" and tortured. Hearing that pregnant women in the prison had their babies taken and sold to "people who asked no questions," she is shocked into investigating the adoption of her own child five years earlier. Her brave forays uncover the protesting grandmother of her child and the complicity of her husband in the repressive regime.
Awards: Academy Awards, Best Foreign Film, 1985; Cannes Film Festival, Best Actress, 1985; Golden Globes, Best Foreign Language Film, 1985; Toronto Film Festival, Best Picture, 1985

30. *Miss Mary* 1986 DSP
D: Maria Luisa Bemberg
S: Maria Luisa Bemberg, Jorge Goldenberg
C: Miguel Rodríguez
P: Lita Stantic
A: Julie Christie
Argentina, 1930s–1945. A British woman is a governess for a wealthy family who lives on a massive English-style estate. Conservative as they are, she does all she can to keep the girls "pure," providing lots of religion because "religion keeps women out of trouble." Hypocrisy about sexism and fascism is in the open, however, and one of the girls goes mad after a forbidden sexual experimentation. Frustrated herself, the governess allows the oldest son to enter her bedroom one night, and she is banished from the household.
Awards: Havana Film Festival, Best Actress, 1986

31. *Peros de la noche / Dogs of the Night* 1986
D: Teo Kofman
S: Pedro Espinosa
C: Julio Lencina
A: Gabriela Flores, Emilio Bardi
A brother and sister from the slums depend on one another; sent to jail, he discovers he can make a living by becoming her pimp. Eventually, she gets out from under him. *Variety. 1986, Oct. 22.*

32. *Yo, la peor de todas / I, the Worst of All*
1991 DSP
D: Maria Luisa Bemberg
S: Maria Luisa Bemberg, Antonio Larreta; based on "The Traps of Faith" by Octavio Paz

C: Felix Monti
P: Lita Stantic
A: Assumpta Serna, Dominique Sanda
Biography of the seventeenth-century Mexican poet, scientist, artist, and nun Sor Juana Inez de la Cruz. Working from the adage that "knowledge is always power," she led an independent life from childhood, insisting on going to university. Living in a convent where she is a star, she is lavishly provided with books, music, and scientific instruments and is visited by the literati of Spain. She refuses an opportunity to become the head of the convent, and the new leadership finds her spoiled, allowing the political tide of the Inquisition to engulf her. A countess briefly protects her—there is the suggestion of more than a friendship, a kiss, gifts, and dedications—but the plague takes its toll on the weakened Sor Juana, forcing her to recant. But there remains one last lecture to a group of little girls: "Intelligence does not have sex . . . you do not have brains in vain. . . . Keep your eyes and ears open and don't forget me."
Awards: Venice Film Festival, OCIC Award, 1990

33. *Un Muro de silencio / A Wall of Silence*
1993 DSP
D: Lita Stantic
S: Lita Stantic, Gabriela Massuh, Graciela Maglie
C: Felix Monti
P: Lita Stantic
A: Vanessa Redgrave, Ofelia Medina
A woman whose husband was "disappeared" and tortured is raising her child with a new man and looking forward to the future. But an old friend has written a film script based on her tragic story, and she is forced to face the tragedy again. Includes the making of the film. *Festival de films, 16th: 18. 1994.*

34. *De eso no se habla / I Don't Want to Talk about It* 1994 DS
D: Maria Luisa Bemberg
S: Maria Luisa Bemberg, Jorge Goldenberg
C: Felix Monti
P: Oscar Kramer
A: Alejandra Podesta, Luisina Brando, Marcello Mastroianni
A dwarf girl, protected by her wealthy mother, grows up strong and confident, without regard for her difference. She marries an attractive older man who is charmed by her horse riding, but one day she leaves him to join the circus.
Awards: Havana Film Festival, Special Jury Prize, 1993

35. *Sol de otoño / Autumn Sun*   1996 P
D: Eduardo Mignona
S: Eduardo Mignona
C: Marcelo Camorino
P: Lita Stantic, Eduardo Mignona
A: Norma Aleandro
A Jewish woman must quickly find a mate for her brother's visit, so she ends up tutoring a Gentile in how to be a suitor. *Film Society. 2003, Sep.*
Awards: San Sebastián International Film Festival, Best Actress, OCIC Award, 1996; Argentinean Film Critics Association, Best Film, Best Actress, 1997

36. *Cenizas del paraiso / Ashes from Paradise*
                                                  1997 S
D: Marcelo Piñeyro
S: Marcelo Piñeyro, Aída Bortnik
C: Alfredo Mayo
P: Marcelo Pavan
A: Cecilia Roth
A judge unravels a double murder case involving a prominent judge and his three sons. *IMDb.*

37. *Río Escondido / Hidden River*   1999 DSP
D: Mercedes Garcia Guevara
S: Mercedes Garcia Guevara
C: Esteban Sapir
P: Mercedes Garcia Guevara
A: Paola Krun, Inés Baum
A middle-class wife leaves Buenos Aires for Rio Escondido near the Andes mountains to ferret out a family secret; once there, she falls in love with her husband's brother, a convicted murderer. *Village Voice: 136. 2001, May 1.*
Awards: Havana Film Festival, FIPRESCI, OCIC Award, 1999; Ourense Independent Film Festival, Grand Prize, 2000

38. *Silvia Prieto*   1999 CP
D: Martin Rejtman
S: Martin Rejtman
C: Paula Grandio
P: Monica Bolan, Sandra Flomenbaum
A: Rosario Bléfari
Buenos Aires. A single woman wanders the city, passing the time by tracking down her namesakes in the phone directory; she then gets a job in a coffee bar and gives away things—her things and other people's things. Fantasy.

39. *Antigua vida mia / Antigua, My Life*   2001
D: Hector Olivera
S: Angeles Gonzalez-Sinde, Alberto Macias; based on the novel by Marcela Serrano
C: Alfredo Mayo
P: Enrique Cerezo, Luis Scalella

A: Cecilia Roth, Ana Belén
Buenos Aires. A story of two old friends, one a successful singer-songwriter who ignores her children, and the other, devoted to her husband, who goes to Guatemala to search for the remains of her grandmother, who died in the jungle with her soldier lover. *Cine espanol. 2001.*

40. *La Ciénaga / The Swamp*   2001 DSP
D: Lucretia Martel
S: Lucretia Martel
C: Hugo Colace
P: Lita Stantic
A: Mercedes Morán, Graciela Borges
Salta. The entwined life of two cousins and their families, including one who has a grown daughter who has become attached to a native servant who is departing. *Village Voice: 129. 2001, Mar. 6.*
Awards: Berlin International Film Festival, Alfred Bauer Award, 2001; Havana Film Festival, Best Film, Best Actress (Borges), 2001; Argentinean Film Critics Association, Best Film, Best Actress (Borges), 2002

41. *Ana y los otros / Ana and the Others*
                                                  2002 DSP
D: Celina Murga
S: Celina Murga
P: Carolina Konstantinovsky, Celina Murga
A: Camila Torker
Struggling economically in Buenos Aires, a young woman returns to her native city of Paraná, where she sees old friends and rethinks her life. *AMG.*
Awards: Thessaloniki Film Festival, Best Director, 2003; Venice Film Festival, Cult Network Italia Prize, 2003

42. *Un Día de suerte / A Lucky Day*   2002 DSP
D: Sandra Gugliotta
S: Sandra Gugliotta, Marcelo Schapces
C: José Guerra
P: Sandra Gugliotta
A: Valentina Bassi, Lola Berthet
A woman without prospects in Buenos Aires desires to emigrate to Italy for opportunity, just as her grandfather had emigrated to Argentina. She goes there looking for a man she knows. *Film Society. 2003, Sep.*
Awards: Berlin International Film Festival, Caligari Film Award, 2002

43. *Tan de repente / Suddenly*   2002 SP
D: Diego Lerman
S: Maria Meira, Diego Lerman
C: Luciano Zito
P: Lita Stantic

A: Carla Crespo, Véronica Hassan, Tatiana Saphir, Beatriz Thibaudin

Young lesbians kidnap a salesgirl and take her to the beach town of Rosario, where they stay at a lodge with an older woman and two young men. Action. *NYT: E3. 2003, Aug. 27.*

Awards: Havana Film Festival, Best Actress (ensemble), 2002; Viennale, FIPRESCI, 2002; Argentinean Film Critics Association, Best Supporting Actress (Thibaudin), 2004

44. *Cama adentro / Live-In Maid*   2004

D: Jorge Gaggero
S: Jorge Gaggero
A: Norma Aleandro, Norma Argentina

A "spoiled socialite" has failed in her marriage and business and is unable to pay the wage of the maid she has employed for thirty years; naturally, the maid wants to leave. *New Directors. 2005.*

Awards: Sundance Film Festival, Special Jury Prize, 2005

45. *Famila rodante / Rolling Family*   2004

D: Pablo Trapero
S: Pablo Trapero
C: Guillermo Nieto
P: Pablo Trapero
A: Graciana Chironi, Liliana Capuro, Ruth Dobel

A grandmother is determined to take her family cross-country to her birth home near the ocean, where her niece is getting married. Her two daughters, sons-in-law, and teenage grandchildren, including a new great grandchild, crowd into a small camp trailer. Breakdowns and romantic diversions force her to stay in charge and keep the focus on getting there.

Awards: Gijón International Film Festival, Best Director, Best Actress (Chironi), 2004

46. *Los Rubios / The Blonds*   2004 DSCP

D: Albertina Carri
S: Albertina Carri, Alan Pauls
C: Catalina Fernández
P: Marcelo Cespedes
A: Analia Couceyro

Fictionalized documentary view of the 1970s political wars in Argentina, during which the director's parents were imprisoned and "disappeared." *NYT: E2. 2004, Apr. 7.*

AUSTRALIA

47. *A City's Child*   1971

D: Brian Kavanaugh
S: Brian Kavanaugh, Don Battye

C: Bruce McNaughton
P: Brian Kavanaugh
A: Monica Maughan

A suburban woman with a sick mother who harangues her seeks relief in fantasy after the mother dies. Fantasy. *MFB, no. 518: 40. 1977, Mar.*

48. *Journey among Women*   1977 S

D: Tom Cowan
S: Tom Cowan, Dorothy Hewett, John Weiley; based on the novel by Diana Fuller
C: Tom Cowan
P: John Weiley
A: June Pritchard, Nell Campbell, Lillian Crombie

Eighteenth-century women's penal colony. A judge's daughter is taken as a hostage when a group of prisoners escape by killing a guard. All the women, including the hostage who comes to identify with their oppression, bond during the experience of hiding in the bush, and their solidarity leads to an organized slaughter of the soldiers who have been sent after them. *Variety: 30. 1977, July 27.*

49. *My Brilliant Career*   1979 DSP

D: Gillian Armstrong
S: Eleanor Witcombe
C: Donald McAlpine
P: Margaret Fink
A: Judy Davis, Sam Neill

Nineteenth century. A young woman insists on refusing a marriage proposal and pursuing her dream of becoming a writer.

Awards: Australian Film Institute, Best Film, Best Director, Best Screenplay, 1979; BAFTA Awards, Best Actress, 1981; London Critics' Circle Film Awards, Special Achievement, 1981

50. *Starstruck*   1982 D

D: Gillian Armstrong
S: Stephen MacLean
C: Russell Boyd
P: Richard Brennan
A: Jo Kennedy

A punk singer devises a high-wire act to succeed, and finally does, just in time to save the family business.

51. *Heatwave*   1983

D: Philip Noyce
S: Philip Noyce, Marc Rosenberg, Mark Stiles
C: Vincent Monton
P: Hilary Linstead
A: Judy Davis

"Conflict between real-estate developers and residents whose houses are to be knocked down. The battle is basically waged between the architect of the development and a female activist supporting the residents." *FII.*

Awards: Mystfest, Special Mention, 1983

52. *On Guard* 1983 DS
D: Susan Lambert
S: Susan Lambert, Sarah Gibson
C: Laurie McInnes
P: Digby Duncan
A: Liddy Clark, Jan Cornall, Kerry Dwyer

Four women who are being used as surrogate mothers discover sinister motives for the research and decide to sabotage a reproductive engineering plant. *FII.*

53. *Annie's Coming Out* 1984 S
D: Gil Brealey
S: Chris Borthwick, John Patterson; based on the novel by Rosemary Crossley and Anne McDonald
C: Mick von Bornemann
P: Don Murray
A: Angela Punch McGregor

A young victim of cerebral palsy has a teacher who goes to court to have her released from an institution. *Twin Peeks.*

Awards: Australian Film Institute, Best Film, Best Screenplay, Best Actress, 1984; Montréal World Film Festival, Special Prize, 1984

54. *My First Wife* 1984 P
D: Paul Cox
S: Paul Cox
C: Yuri Sokol
P: Jane Ballantyne, Paul Cox
A: Wendy Hughes, John Hargreaves

A wife breaks up her ten-year marriage by having an affair with a friend of her husband's. *FII.*

55. *Fran* 1985 DS
D: Glenda Hambly
S: Glenda Hambly
C: Jan Kenny
P: David Rapsey
A: Noni Hazelhurst

A mother on welfare finds that her need for a man conflicts with her responsibility to her children. *Twin Peeks.*

Awards: Australian Film Institute, Best Screenplay, Best Actress, 1985

56. *Cactus* 1986
D: Paul Cox
S: Paul Cox, Bob Ellis
C: Yuri Sokol
P: Jane Ballantyne

A: Isabelle Huppert

A French woman visiting Australia begins to go blind after a car accident, but she becomes involved with a blind doctor who helps her adjust. *AMG.*

57. *High Tide* 1987 DSP
D: Gillian Armstrong
S: Laura Jones
C: Russell Boyd
P: Sandra Levy
A: Judy Davis, Jan Adele, Claudia Karran

A pop singer is fired from her band while on the road and ends up living in a trailer park, where she becomes friends with a young woman whom she finally realizes is the daughter she abandoned years earlier.

Awards: Australian Film Institute, Best Actress (Davis), Best Supporting Actress (Adele), 1987; National Society of Film Critics Awards, Best Actress (Davis), 1989

58. *Shame* 1987 S
D: Steve Jodrell
S: Beverley Blankenship, Michael Brindley
C: Joseph Pickering
P: Paul D. Barron
A: Deborra-Lee Furness

A vacationing lawyer has her motorbike break down in a small town where she stays with the father of a teenager who has been raped. He does not know what to do with the townspeople's attitude that his daughter brought it on herself. The lawyer stays to encourage the father and the women in town to confront the authorities that ignore violence to women. *Variety: 107. 1988, Mar. 16.*

Awards: Film Critics Circle of Australia Awards, Best Screenplay, Best Actress, 1988

59. *Against the Innocent* 1988 SP
D: Daryl Dellora
S: Daryl Dellora, Jenny Hocking
C: Vladimir Kromas
P: Daryl Dellora, Jenny Hocking
A: Margaret Cameron

An academic expert on counterterrorism is hounded by the media and government security forces. *Twin Peeks.*

60. *Cry in the Dark* 1988 P
D: Fred Schepsi
S: Robert Caswell, Fred Schepsi; based on the novel by John Bryson
C: Ian Baker
P: Verity Lambert

A: Meryl Streep

When an infant is dragged off and killed by a dingo, his mother is not portrayed sympathetically by a disbelieving press. She is tried and convicted for murder, then exonerated only after serving time in prison.

Awards: New York Film Critics Association, Best Actress, 1988; Australian Film Institute, Best Film, Best Actress, 1989; Cannes Film Festival, Best Actress, 1989

61. *Sweetie*　　1989 DSC

D: Jane Campion
S: Jane Campion, Gerard Lee
C: Sally Bongers
P: John Maynard
A: Geneviève Lemon

A meek sister must contend with her boisterous sister's intrusive manic behavior, which has always been indulged by the family.

Awards: Australian Film Institute, Best Screenplay, 1989; Independent Spirit Awards, Best Foreign Film, 1991

62. *Aya*　　1990 DSP

D: Solrun Hooas
S: Solrun Hooas
C: Geoff Burton
P: Solrun Hooas
A: Eri Ishida

1950s. A Japanese war bride has a husband who insists she become "Australian," but an accident that leaves him incapacitated allows her more freedom. *Twin Peaks.*

Awards: Australian Film Awards, nomination for Best Actress, 1991

63. *Daydream Believer*　　1991 DS

D: Kathy Mueller
S: Saturday Rosenberg
C: Andrew Lesnie
P: Ben Gannon
A: Miranda Otto

A girl who was abused as a child becomes an adult with a close relationship to horses. Comedy. *AMG.*

Other titles: The Girl Who Came Late

64. *Isabelle Eberhardt*　　1991

D: Ian Pringle
S: Stephen Sewell
C: Manuel Teran
P: Jean Petit
A: Mathilda May

1900s. Based on a true story of a Russian-Swiss journalist who reported on the colonization of Algeria by the French and sided with the Arabs.

A "feminist radical who scorned authority figures." *Variety: 50. 1991, July 8.*

65. *The Last Days of Chez Nous*　　1991 DS

D: Gillian Armstrong
S: Helen Garner
C: Geoffrey Simpson
P: Jan Chapman
A: Lisa Harrow, Kerry Fox, Bruno Ganz

A successful writer, with her own distinct and commanding approach to life, travels to another town to take care of her father, leaving behind her French husband; while she is away, her sister has an affair with him.

Awards: Australian Film Institute, Best Actress (Harrow), 1992

66. *A Woman's Tale*　　1991

D: Paul Cox
S: Paul Cox, Barry Dickins
C: Nino Gaetano Martinetti
P: Paul Cox
A: Sheila Florence, Gosia Dobrowolska

An old woman with cancer resists moving and is helped by a visiting nurse in her struggle with her son and neighbors, who want her to vacate her apartment, then proceed to lock her out while she is in the hospital. Sweet and salty, she takes care of an addled neighbor, tries to help radio talk show callers, and generally lets everyone know what she thinks of them.

Awards: Flanders International Film Festival, Golden Spur, 1992

67. *Dallas Doll*　　1992 DS

D: Ann Turner
S: Ann Turner
C: Paul Murphy
P: Ross Matthews
A: Sandra Bernhard

A golf pro visits an Australian family and seduces them all. Comedy. *AMG.*

68. *Resistance*　　1992 CP

D: Paul Elliot, Hugh Keays-Byrne
S: Macau Collective
C: Sally Bongers
P: Christina Ferguson, Pauline Rosenberg, Jenny Day
A: Lorna Lesley, Helen Jones, Maya Sheridan

Migrant farmworkers are caught in a military takeover of the country. Mostly women, including a labor leader, mothers with children, and aborigines, they resist the uniformed fascists. A detailed and broad portrait of a large-scale effort to control people who are already alienated and prepared to fight. Action.

69. *Turtle Beach*   1992 S
D: Stephen Wallace
S: Blanche D'Alpuget, Ann Turner
C: Russell Boyd
P: Matt Carroll
A: Joan Chen, Greta Scacchi
An Australian journalist and a Vietnamese refugee,
   who is searching for her children, team up to
   help Vietnamese boat people in Malaysia and
   expose government atrocities. *Variety: 78. 1992,
   Mar. 30.*

70. *beDevil*   1993 DS
D: Tracy Moffatt
S: Tracy Moffatt
P: Carol Hughes
A: Diana Davidson, Tracy Moffatt
A collage exploration of the life of Australian
   aborigines in three parts: an American GI who
   disappears; a family shamed by their foreignness;
   and a man who tries to banish squatters from
   his property. *Festival de films, 21st: 80. 1999.*

71. *The Piano*   1993 DS
D: Jane Campion
S: Jane Campion
C: Stuart Dryburgh
P: Jan Chapman
A: Holly Hunter, Harvey Keitel, Anna Paquin
Nineteenth century. A mute woman is sent from
   Scotland to New Zealand to be a wife, but
   she conflicts with her straitlaced husband and
   becomes engaged via her piano playing with an
   alluring neighbor.
Awards: Cannes Film Festival, Golden Palm, Best
   Actress (Hunter), 1993; Academy Awards, Best
   Screenplay, Best Actress (Hunter), Best Support-
   ing Actress (Paquin), 1994

72. *Talk*   1993 DSP
D: Susan Lambert
S: Jan Cornall
C: Ron Hagen
P: Megan McMurchy
A: Victoria Longley, Angie Milliken
Two friends who work in a publishing house share
   their secrets and desires about sex, marriage,
   and children. *Festival de films, 17th: 15. 1995.*
Awards: Australian Film Institute, nomination for
   Best Actress (Longley), 1994

73. *Hotel Sorrento*   1995 S
D: Richard Franklin
S: Richard Franklin, Peter Fitzpatrick; based on the
   play by Hannie Rayson
C: Geoff Burton

P: Richard Franklin
A: Caroline Goodall, Caroline Gillmer, Tara
   Morice
Three sisters descend into family dysfunction when
   one of them writes a successful novel based on
   the family. *Los Angeles. 1995, July 14.*
Other titles: Sorrento Beach
Awards: Australian Film Institute, Best Screenplay,
   nominations for Best Actress (Goodall, Gillmer),
   1995

74. *Muriel's Wedding*   1995 P
D: P. J. Hogan
S: P. J. Hogan
C: Martin McGrath
P: Lynda House, Jocelyn Moorhouse
A: Toni Collette, Rachel Griffiths
An "ugly duckling" with an abusive father dreams
   of marriage though she has no boyfriend. She
   takes a vacation with a newfound friend and
   ends up marrying a man who needs citizenship.
   Comedy. *Chicago Sun-Times. 1995, Mar. 17.*
Awards: Australian Film Institute, Best Film, Best
   Actress (Colette), Best Supporting Actress
   (Griffiths), 1994

75. *Vacant Possession*   1995 DS
D: Margot Nash
S: Margot Nash
C: Dion Beebe
P: John Winter
A: Pamela Rabe
Sydney. When her mother dies, a daughter returns
   to the home from which she fled sixteen years
   earlier because her father attacked an aborigine
   neighbor with whom she was in love and who
   fathered her child. She finds her room the
   same as the day she left, with her possessions
   enshrined, and she collides with her sister who
   stayed behind. *Festival de films, 21st: 77. 1999.
   Also AMG.*

76. *Fistful of Flies*   1996 DSCP
D: Monica Pellizzari
S: Monica Pellizzari
C: Jane Castle
P: Julia Overton
A: Tasma Walton, Dina Panozzo
A sixteen-year-old and her mother battle over the
   teenager's sex life in a conservative Catholic
   Italian home.

77. *Fu sheng / Floating Life*   1996 DSP
D: Clara Law
S: Clara Law, Eddie Fong
C: Dion Beebe

P: Bridgit Ikin
A: Annette Shun Wah, Annie Yip, Cecilia Fong Sing Lee, Anthony Wong

Hong Kong. Two sisters and their young brother and parents disperse before the impending reunification with China. One, who is already established in Australia, has developed grave mental problems in her isolated suburban setting, where her nonplussed parents join her. The younger daughter moves with her husband and child to Germany but is too far away to be happy. The free-living son remains in Hong Kong with his girlfriend, who breezily engages in an abortion that suddenly leaves them both weary. Across all these borders, they try to maintain their close family ties.

Awards: Locarno International Film Festival, Silver Leopard, 1996; Créteil International Women's Film Festival, Grand Prix, 1997; Gijón International Film Festival, Best Director, 1996

78. *The Well*   1997 DSP
D: Samantha Lang
S: Laura Jones; based on the novel by Elizabeth Jolley
C: Mandy Walker
P: Sandra Levy
A: Pamela Rabe, Miranda Otto

A woman who lives on a farm with her ailing father hires a vivacious young woman to help her; their relationship becomes close until the father's death and an auto accident precipitate a crisis. Mystery. *Festival de films, 20th: 43. 1998.*

Awards: Australian Film Institute, Best Screenplay, Best Actress (Rabe), 1997; Stockholm Film Festival, Best Actress (Rabe), 1997

79. *Dance Me to My Song*   1998 S
D: Rolf De Heer
S: Rolf De Heer, Heather Rose, Frederick Stahl
C: Tony Clark
P: Rolf De Heer
A: Heather Rose

A woman with cerebral palsy is confined to a wheelchair, communicates through her computer, and has a full-time caretaker; she is left alone one day and engages with a man, inspiring jealousy in the caretaker. *AMG.*

Awards: Ft. Lauderdale International Film Festival, Humanitarian Award, 1998; Valladolid International Film Festival, Special Jury Prize, 1998

80. *Radiance*   1998 D
D: Rachel Perkins
S: Louis Nowra
C: Warwick Thornton

P: Ned Lander
A: Rachel Maza, Deborah Mailman, Trisha Morton-Thomas

North Queensland. Three Australian aborigine sisters return to their home after the death of their mother and many years of not seeing one another. The oldest is an opera singer, not inclined to look back; the second is disabled, and the youngest thinks only in terms of diversion. *Festival de films, 21st: 19. 1999.*

Awards: Australian Film Institute, Best Performance (Mailman), 1998; Melbourne International Film Festival, Most Popular Film, 1998

81. *Holy Smoke!*   1999 DS
D: Jane Campion
S: Jane Campion, Anna Campion
C: Dion Beebe
P: Jan Chapman
A: Kate Winslet, Harvey Keitel

An Australian woman traveling in India becomes devoted to a Hindu cult guru; her mother arrives in New Delhi and hires an American to "deprogram" her, but he finds that she is quite capable of programming her own life. *NYT: E15. 1999, Oct. 8.*

Awards: Venice Film Festival, Elvira Notari Prize, 1999

82. *Soft Fruit*   1999 DSP
D: Christina Andreef
S: Christina Andreef
C: Laszlo Baranyi
P: Helen Bowden, Jane Campion
A: Meany Drynan, Linal Haft, Russell Dykstra, Geneviève Lemon, Sacha Horler

After fifteen years apart, a Bulgarian immigrant family is reunited; three sisters and their ex-convict brother arrive home to care for their sick mother. The father refuses to have the son in the house, and the daughters struggle in attending to their mother, who wants only peace and quiet. *Festival de films, 22nd: 22. 2000.*

Awards: Australian Film Institute, Best Actress (Horler), 1999; San Sebastián International Film Festival, FIPRESCI, 1999

83. *Me Myself I*   2000
D: Pip Karmel
S: Pip Karmel
C: Graham Lind
P: Fabien Liron
A: Rachel Griffiths

A single woman nearing forty falls into a fantasy life, including marriage and children, with a "Mr. Right" she rejected years ago. *The Nation: 35. 2000, May 15.*

84. **The Monkey's Mask**   2000 DS
D: Samantha Lang
S: Anne Kennedy, Dorothy Porter
C: Garry Phillips
P: Robert Connolly
A: Susie Porter, Abbie Cornish, Kelly McGillis
A former cop and lesbian is hired to privately in-
  vestigate a young poet who goes missing after a
  reading; the literary world is an eye-opener for
  the detective. Thriller. *FII*.
Other titles: La Maschera di scimmia
Awards: Film Critics Circle of Australia Awards,
  nominations for Best Screenplay and Best Ac-
  tress, 2002

85. **Strange Fits of Passion**   2001 DSP
D: Elise McCredie
S: Elise McCredie
C: Jaems Grant
P: Lucy McLaren
A: Michela Noonan
A shy young woman, fond of Romantic poetry,
  seeks sexual fulfillment. *Variety: 74. May 24.*

86. **Japanese Story**   2003 DSP
D: Sue Brooks
S: Alison Tilson
C: Ian Baker
P: Sue Maslin
A: Toni Collette, Gotaro Tsunashima
Pilbara desert. A geologist takes an outback trip
  with a Japanese business client, whom she dis-
  likes from the start; he finds her rude as well.
  Action. *Festival de films, 26th: 8. 2004.*
Awards: Australian Film Institute, Best Film, Best
  Direction, Best Actress, 2003

AUSTRIA

87. **Unsichtbare Gegner / Invisible Adversaries**
                                             1977 DSP
D: Valie Export
S: Valie Export, Peter Weibel
C: Wolfgang Simon
P: Valie Export
A: Valie Export, Susanne Widl
A photographer begins a day of ruminations on the
  politics of power, the camera connecting her
  waking up in bed to the rooftops of the city outside. She develops pictures of her vagina, argues
  with her leftist lover about whether or not to
  talk back to the traffic police, and seeks help only
  to discover that everyone out there is arguing.
  Incorporated for comment are photographs she
  has taken of herself draped around the architecture and walkways of the city, images that trouble her. She makes a mustache for herself out of
  her pubic hair, confronts her psychiatrist with
  her photographic version of him as a double, and
  ends her day the same way it began.

88. **Menschen Frauen / Human Woman**
                                             1980 DSP
D: Valie Export
S: Valie Export, Peter Weibel
C: Wolfgang Dickman
P: Valie Export
A: Renée Felden, Maria Martina, Klaus Wildbolz
The story of a male journalist and his relations
  with four women: his wife, his nurse, a professor,
  and a waitress. He tells each the same stories
  and has the same expectations of being understood, but they learn his game. "An encyclopedia
  of feminine sensibility." *Festival de films, 6th: 29.
  1984.*

89. **Marianne eidn Recht für alle / Marianne
One Law for All**   1983 DS
D: Käthe Kratz
S: Käthe Kratz
C: Toni Peschke
A: Linde Prelog, Alfred Pfeifer
1918. An impoverished mother, with a husband
  in the war, lives in an abandoned train car on
  the outskirts of the city, where she works in a
  metal foundry and earns just enough to feed her
  child; she has lost a pregnancy to malnutrition.
  The soldiers—half dead from starvation—return and demand their factory jobs back from
  the women, but she leads the women to resist
  displacement and conflicts with her husband
  during the ensuing struggle. *Festival de films, 6th:
  6. 1984.*
Other titles: Marianne un droit pour tous
Awards: Erich Neuberg Award, 1985

90. **Marlene: der Amerikanishe Traum / Marlene, the American Dream**   1987 DS
D: Käthe Kratz
S: Käthe Kratz
C: Walter Kindler
A: Huberta Haubmann, Eva Linder
1955. A mother and her daughter barely survive
  in a shack, though the girl is getting a good
  education; the mother frequents the company
  of U.S. soldiers in hopes of somehow getting to
  America, and one day the men leave her a red
  motorbike. *Festival de films, 10th: 22. 1988.*

91. **Seven Women Seven Sins**   1987 DSCP
D: Chantal Akerman, Maxi Cohen, Valie Export,

Laurence Gavron, Bette Gordon, Ulrike Ottinger, Helke Sander
S: Chantal Akerman, Maxi Cohen, Valie Export, Laurence Gavron, Bette Gordon, Ulrike Ottinger, Helke Sander
C: Ulrike Ottinger
P: Maya Faber-Jansen
A: Evelyn Didi, Gabriela Nerz, Delphine Seyrig, Kate Valk, Irm Hermann
Seven women filmmakers interpret the seven "deadly sins" in contemporary life: greed (Gordon), anger (Cohen), gluttony (Sander), pride (Ottinger), sloth (Akerman), lust (Gavron), and envy (Export). *Variety: 39. 1987, Sep. 23.*

92. *Die Skorpionfrau / Scorpian Woman*
1989 DS

D: Susanne Zanke
S: Susanne Zanke
C: Tamas Ujlaki
P: Michael Von Wolkenstein
A: Angelica Domröse
After presiding over the trial of a woman who seduced and maimed a fifteen-year-old boy, a judge, who has a long-term lover, has an affair with a man the age of her son. *IMDb.*

93. *Rote Ohren fetzen durch Asche / Flaming Ears*
1991 DSCP

D: Angela Hans Schierl, Dietmar Schipek, Ursula Pürrer
S: Dietmar Schipek, Ursula Pürrer
C: Margarete Neumann, Manfred Neuwirth
P: Ursula Pürrer
A: Ursula Pürrer, Angela Hans Schierl
2700. Futuristic world populated by all lesbians. "A fragmented and bizarre drama of lust, jealousy, and revenge" develops between the film's three protagonists: a brooding cartoonist, a ruthless antagonist, and a necrophiliac nun in a red plastic outfit. *PopcornQ. Accessed 2005, Jan. 20.*

94. *Nordrand / Northern Skirts*
1999 DS

D: Barbara Albert
S: Barbara Albert
C: Christine Maier
P: Erich Lackner
A: Nina Proll, Edita Malovcic
Vienna. A group of young people, friends from childhood in Yugoslavia, try to find lives after growing up in the midst of war, but they have little knowledge of mature adult life to guide them. Two are women who meet again in an abortion clinic, where their experience only becomes more bitter. *Festival de films, 22nd: 23. 2000.*

Awards: Stockholm Film Festival, Best Debut, 1999; Venice Film Festival, Marcello Mastroiani Award (Proll), 1999; Viennale, FIPRESCI, 1999; Max Ophüls Festival, Feminina Film Awards, 2000

95. *La Pianiste / The Piano Teacher*
2001 S

D: Michael Haneke
S: Michael Haneke; based on the novel by Elfriede Jelinek
C: Christian Berger
P: Veit Heiduschka
A: Isabelle Huppert, Annie Girardot
Vienna. A conservatory piano teacher, who lives with her mother, is brought closer to her sexual obsessions by a young student. She finds gratification in both spurning and stalking him, and her sadistic and masochistic behavior is described by scenes of her public consumption of pornography and her habit of cutting herself.
Awards: Cannes Film Festival, Best Actress (Huppert), Grand Jury Prize, 2001; European Film Awards, Best Actress (Huppert), 2001; San Francisco Film Critics Circle, Best Actress (Huppert), 2002

96. *Vollgas / Step on It*
2002 DS

D: Sabine Derflinger
S: Sabine Derflinger, Maria Scheibelhofer
C: Gerald Helf
P: Michael Seeber
A: Henriette Heinze, Philomena Wolfingsede
In a ski village, a single mother struggles as a waitress. *BAM. 2003, Dec.*
Awards: Max Ophüls Festival, Promotional Award, 2002

97. *Böse Zellen / Free Radicals*
2003 DS

D: Barbara Albert
S: Barbara Albert
C: Martin Gschlacht
P: Martin Gschlacht
A: Kathrin Resetarits, Ursula Strauss
A young woman is the only survivor of a plane crash in the Gulf of Mexico; years later she is a cashier in a supermarket in a small Austrian town, surrounded by family and friends but still troubled. *New York. 2003.*

98. *Struggle*
2003 DSP

D: Ruth Mader
S: Ruth Mader, Barbara Albert
C: Bernhard Keller
P: Ruth Mader
A: Aleksandra Justa
Vienna. To improve her standard of living, a Polish woman and her child go to Austria, where she

does farm and factory work and cleaning. *Festival de films, 26th: 75. 2004.*

Awards: Max Ophüls Festival, Screenplay Award, 2003; Molodist International Film Festival, FIPRESCI, 2003

99. *Auswege* / *Sign of Escape*   2004 DSP
D: Nina Kusturica
S: Barbara Albert
C: Tim Tom
P: Nina Kusturica, Stefan Pfundner
A: Liese Lyon, Manfred Stella, Mira Milijkovic, Dagmar Schwarz
"Portrays three women, of different ages and from different social backgrounds, who are all victims of domestic violence. Gradually they realize that immediate escape from the vicious cycle that they have put up with for so long is the only solution." *FII.*

100. *Hotel*   2004 DSP
D: Jessica Hausner
S: Jessica Hausner
C: Martin Gschlacht
P: Susanne Marian
A: Franziska Weisz, Birgit Minichmayr
Austrian Alps. A new receptionist in a deserted hotel discovers that her predecessor disappeared and the police are still investigating; her own queries are met with indifference. Mystery, horror. *London Film: 42. 2004.*

**101. *Le Temps du loup* / *The Time of the Wolf*
                                          2004 P**
D: Michael Haneke
S: Michael Haneke
C: Jürgen Jürges
P: Margaret Ménégoz
A: Isabelle Huppert
A wife and mother of two is cast into the environs of her country home during a catastrophe. *Village Voice: 68. 2004, Mar. 10.*
Awards: Catalonian International Film Festival, Best Screenplay, 2003

AZERBAIJAN

102. *Yarasa* / *The Bat*   1995
D: Ajas Salajev
S: Ajas Salajev
C: Bagir Rafiyev, Saday Akhmedov
A: Mariya Lipkina
An actress and filmmaker balances life with her older husband and a younger lover. *Variety. 1995, Feb. 20.*

Awards: Angers European First Film Festival, European Jury Award, 1996

BELGIUM

103. *Monsieur Hawarden*   1968
D: Harry Kümel
S: Jan Blokker
C: Eddy Van der Enden
A: Ellen Vogel, Hilde Uytterlinden
Malmédy, 1870. A noblewoman from Paris flees after a crime of passion. Disguised as a man, she lives in a remote village with her maid. *Belgian Cinema.*

104. *Impasse de la vignette* / *One Summer after Another*   1969 DS
D: Anne-Marie Etienne
S: Anne-Marie Etienne
C: Jean-Claude Neckelbrouck
P: Alain Keytsman
A: Annie Cordy
1930s–1970s. A matriarch dominates her fifth husband and working-class family. *Belgian Cinema.*

105. *Il pleut dans ma maison* / *It's Raining in My House*   1969
D: Pierre Laroche
S: Paul Willems
C: Frederic Geilfus
P: Pierre Levie
A: Marcella Saint-Armant
A businesswoman inherits an estate from a woman whose lover committed suicide and is now a ghost in the house. *Belgian Cinema.*

106. *Plus jamais seul* / *Never Again Alone* 1969
D: Jean Delire
S: Jean Delire, Alain Quercy
C: André Goeffers
P: Liliane Weinstadt
A: Danielle Denie, Guy Heyron
A pregnant theater actress considers how to arrange the future with her egocentric husband. *Belgian Cinema.*

107. *Claudia*   1970
D: Armand Wauters
S: Armand Wauters
C: Armand Wauters
P: Armand Wauters
A: Hélène Serpieter
An old woman lives alone, wanders through Brussels remembering her past, and decides to

organize activities for senior citizens. *Belgian Cinema.*

108. *Les Lèvres rouges / Red Lips* 1971
D: Harry Kümel
S: Harry Kümel, Pierre Drouot, Jean Ferry
C: Eddy Van der Enden
P: Paul Collet
A: Delphine Seyrig, Danielle Oulmet
Ostend. In an old hotel, a descendent of the seventeenth-century Hungarian vampire countess Elizabeth Bathory toys with an American couple on their honeymoon. Horror. *Belgian Cinema.*

109. *Mira de Teleurgang van de waterhoek / Mira* 1971 S
D: Fons Rademakers
S: Hugo Claus, Magda Reypens
C: Eddy Van der Enden
P: Gérard Vercruysse
A: Willeke Von Ammelrooy
A girl has an affair with an older man, her uncle, then moves in with an engineer when the uncle is imprisoned. Throughout she insists on controlling her own sexuality and avoiding marriage. *Cinema of the Low: 91.*
Awards: Cannes Film Festival, nomination for Golden Palm, 1971

110. *Féminin-Féminin / Feminine Feminine* 1972
D: Henri Calef
S: João Correa
P: Paul Vandendries
A: Marie-France Pisier
A wealthy wife is seduced by an "emancipated" friend who then abandons her for another woman. Exploitation. *Belgian Cinema.*

111. *Miss O'Gynie et les hommes fleurs / Miss O'Gynie and the Flower Men* 1973 S
D: Samy Pavel
S: Arania Mireille, Samy Pavel; based on the play by Arania Mireille
C: Jean-Claude Neckelbrouck
P: Jacques Arnould
A: Martine Kelly, Richard Leduc, Niels Arustrup
A male gay couple's happy life is interrupted by a persistent former female lover. *Belgian Cinema.*

112. *Je tu il elle* 1974 DSP
D: Chantal Akerman
S: Chantal Akerman, Claire Wauthion
C: Bénédicte Delesalle, Renelde Dupont
P: Chantal Akerman
A: Chantal Akerman

A woman lives sparsely and passes time by eating sugar directly from a bag; she also writes letters, goes out to talk with a truck driver, and visits an old lover, who takes her in for an extended sexual encounter.

113. *Jeanne Dielman, 23 Quai du Commerce, 1080 Bruxelles* 1975 DSCP
D: Chantal Akerman
S: Chantal Akerman
C: Babette Mangolte
P: Evelyn Paul, Alain Dehan, Corinne Jénart
A: Delphine Seyrig
Three days in the life of a widow who prostitutes herself out of her apartment. Between clients she keeps house and takes care of her teenage son; the last day she murders one of the men. Includes documentary-like explications of her cooking and cleaning. Experimental.

114. *Rue Haute* 1976
D: André Ernotte
S: André Ernotte
C: Walther Van den Ende
P: Alain Guilleaume
A: Annie Cordy
An unstable woman who lost her husband during the German occupation is protected by an American painter in their working-class neighborhood. *Belgian Cinema.*

115. *Rendez-vous d'Anna* 1978 DS
D: Chantal Akerman
S: Chantal Akerman
C: Jean Penzer
P: Alain Dahan
A: Aurore Clément
A filmmaker travels persistently for her work; she meets a journalist and visits her mother and ex-lover. She is always very calm and undemonstrative. Many locations, mostly outdoors, mostly involving a form of transience, whether of actual coming and going or of temporary relations.

116. *21:12 Piano bar* 1981 DSP
D: Mary Jiminez
S: Mary Jiminez
C: Michel Houssiau
P: Carole Courtoy
A: Lucinda Childs, Anne Guerrin, Carole Courtoy
A jazz pianist becomes fascinated by "the fantasies of a suicide victim, who had sought pleasure through pain." The pianist interviews the woman's relatives after her death. *Belgian Cinema.*

117. *Le Lit / The Bed*   1982 DSP
D: Marion Hänsel
S: Marion Hänsel; based on the novel by Domi-
nique Rollin
C: Walther Van den Ende
P: Marion Hänsel
A: Natasha Perry, Francine Blistin, Heinz Bennent
A woman awaits the death of her husband. During
a twenty-four-hour period, she cares for him
and revisits memories of his illness and their
happiness, love, and life together. *Festival de films,
5th: 25. 1983.*

118. *Toute une nuit / All Night Long* 1982 DSCP
D: Chantal Akerman
S: Chantal Akerman
C: Caroline Champetier
P: Marilyn Watelet
Series of finely observed abstracted relationships,
leave-takings, and welcomes in doorways and
similar meeting spaces, involving dancing, drink-
ing, telephoning, eating, and sleeping.

119. *Benvenuta*   1983 S
D: André Delvaux
S: André Delvaux; based on the novel by Suzanne
Lilar
C: Charles Van Damme
P: Jean-Claude Batz
A: Fanny Ardant, Françoise Fabian, Vittorio
Gassman, Mathieu Carrière
A male screenwriter, wishing to adapt a novel,
interviews the novelist about the story behind
her book. It concerns the romance of a Belgian
pianist with a much older married Italian judge,
an ill-advised romance that left her emotionally
devastated. *BiFi.*

120. *Sarah dit . . . Leila dit / Never Again*
                                           1983 D
D: Frans Buyens, Lydia Chagoll
S: Frans Buyens
C: Alain Derobe
A: Myriam Boyer, Michèle Simonnet
Two women meet to converse about their experi-
ence as teenagers in concentration camps in
Auschwitz and Indonesia. *Belgian Cinema.*

121. *Dust / In the Heart of the Country*
                                           1984 DSP
D: Marion Hänsel
S: Marion Hänsel, J. M. Coetzee; based on the novel
by J. M. Coetzee
C: Walther Van den Ende
P: Marion Hänsel
A: Jane Birkin, Trevor Howard

A daughter murders her father after he seduces
the wife of their farm's black foreman, an event
that caused the woman to fall into mental illness. *MFB: 269. 1986, Sep.*
Other titles: Heart of the Country

122. *Madame P*   1984 DS
D: Eve Bonfanti
S: Eve Bonfanti
C: Patrice Payen
P: Danny Degraeve
A: Hélène Van Herck
Brussels. Follows the days of an aging lavatory
attendant in the basement of a café. *Belgian
Cinema.*

123. *Golden Eighties*   1986 DS
D: Chantal Akerman
S: Chantal Akerman, Pascal Bonitzer
C: Gilberto Azevedo
A: Myriam Boyer, Delphine Seyrig
A musical in a glittering modern shopping center,
where the shop activity bleeds out into the mall
aisles, people are always stopping by, and love is
just around the brightly lit corner.

124. *Menuet / Minuet*   1986 D
D: Lili Rademakers
S: Hugo Claus
C: Paul Van Den Bos
A: Carla Hardy, Edgar Burcksen
The wife of a beer maker who spends his free time
with his hobbies has an affair with her brother-
in-law; a young girl spies on them and manipu-
lates the husband to her own interests. *Festival
de films, 6th: 28. 1984.*

125. *Les Noces barbares / The Cruel Embrace*
                                           1987 DSP
D: Marion Hänsel
S: Marion Hänsel; based on the novel by Yann
Queffélec
C: Walther Van den Ende
P: Marion Hänsel
A: Thierry Frémont, Marianne Basler
A woman is incapable of loving her son, who was
born of rape by American soldiers; she refuses
all his appeals. *Belgian Cinema.*

126. *Eline Vere*   1991
D: Harry Kümel
S: Jan Blokker; based on the novel by Louis
Couperus
C: Eddy Van der Enden
P: Paul Breuls
A: Marianne Basler

The Hague, 1890s. A young woman is trapped in the narrow-mindedness of her bourgeois city. *Belgian Cinema.*
Awards: Joseph Plateau Awards, Best Belgian Film, 1992

127. *Rosetta* 1999
D: Jean-Pierre Dardenne, Luc Dardenne
S: Jean-Pierre Dardenne, Luc Dardenne
C: Alain Marcoen
P: Jean-Pierre Dardenne, Luc Dardenne
A: Emilie Dequenne, Anne Yernaux
A young girl travels every day from her trailer park home and alcoholic mother into town looking for work. In hopes of getting away, she impulsively steals a job from a friend, then commits suicide out of remorse and despair.
Awards: Cannes Film Festival, Golden Palm, Ecumenical Jury Prize, Best Actress (Dequenne), 1999

128. *Rosie* 1999 DS
D: Patrice Toye
S: Patrice Toye, Lieve Hellinckx
C: Richard Van Oosterhout
P: Antonio Lombardo
A: Aranka Coppens, Sara De Roo
Antwerp. A thirteen-year-old lives in a high-rise project apartment with her mother, who pretends to be her sister; the daughter lands in juvenile prison. *NYT: E22. 1999, July 23.*
Awards: Flanders International Film Festival, Silver Spur, 1998; Angers European First Film Festival, Best Actress (Coppens), 1999; Sochi International Film Festival, Grand Prix, 1999

129. *Pauline en Paulette / Pauline and Paulette* 2000
D: Lieven Debrauwer
S: Jaak Boon, Lieven Debrauwer
C: Michel Van Laer
P: Dominique Janne
A: Dora Van de Groen, Ann Petersen, Rosemarie Bergmans, Julienne De Bruyn
An older woman begins to care for her mentally ill sister when the sister she had lived with dies; a fourth sister arrives to help. *Village Voice: 122. 2002, Mar. 19.*
Awards: Cairo International Film Festival, Golden Pyramid, 2001; Cannes Film Festival, Ecumenical Jury Prize, 2001; Joseph Plateau Award, Best Actress (Van der Groen), Best Belgian Film, 2001

130. *Nuages, lettres à mon fils / Clouds: Letters to My Son* 2001 DSP
D: Marion Hänsel
S: Marion Hänsel

C: Didier Frateur
P: Marion Hänsel
A: Catherine Deneuve, Charlotte Rampling, Barbara Auer, Antje De Boeck, Carmen Maura
Letters to the filmmaker's son are read over cloudscapes. *Festival de films, 25th: 23. 2003.*

131. *Meisje* 2002 DS
D: Dorothée Van den Berghe
S: Dorothée Van den Berghe, Peter Van Kraaij
C: Jan Vancaillie
P: Jan Declercq
A: Charlotte Van den Eynde, Els Dottermans, Frieda Pittoors
A young woman moves to Brussels in hopes of working in a museum; she rooms with a single mother and sometimes takes care of her children, but she is not quite responsible enough and is finally tracked down by her own mother.

BOLIVIA

132. *Yawar Mallku / Blood of the Condor* 1969
D: Jorge Sanjines
S: Jorge Sanjines
C: Antonio Eguino
P: Ricardo Rada
A: Marcelino Yanahuaya, Benedicta Mendoza
1968. Based on actual events, the story of a Peace Corps medical clinic that sterilized native women without their consent.

BRAZIL

133. *Dona Flor e seus dois maridos / Dona Flor and Her Two Husbands* 1976
D: Bruno Barreto
S: Bruno Barreto, Jorge Amado
C: Murilo Salles
P: Newton Rique
A: Sonia Braga
At her husband's funeral, a woman reminisces over her happy life with him, even though he was a womanizer; when she becomes bored with her second husband, the first is resurrected to keep her satisfied via a mystical ceremony. *South American Cinema: 175.*

134. *Xica da Silva* 1976
D: Carlos Diegues
S: Carlos Diegues, Antonio Callado
C: José Medeiros
P: Jarbas Barbosa

A: Zezé Motta

Minas Gerais. Based on the life of an eighteenth-century black slave, who seduces her master, operator of a diamond mine, and creates controversy with her extravagance to the extent that he is banished to Portugal. *South American Cinema: 178.*

Awards: Brazilia Festival of Brazilian Cinema, Best Film, Best Director, Best Actress, 1976

135. *A Lira do delirio / The Lyre of Delight* 1978
D: Walter Lima
S: Walter Lima
C: Dib Lufti
P: Walter Lima
A: Anecy Rocha

A nightclub dancer in Rio de Janeiro has a jealous boyfriend who kidnaps her baby; she seeks help from a detective to find them. *South American Cinema: 185.*

Awards: Brazilia Festival of Brazilian Cinema, Best Director, Best Actress, 1978

136. *Mar de rosas / Sea of Roses*   1978 DS
D: Ana Carolina
S: Ana Carolina
C: Lauro Escorel
A: Norma Bengell, Christine Pereira

A woman has an altercation with her husband and runs away with their adolescent daughter; soon they are being pursued by a man the father has hired. *South American Cinema: 183.*

Other titles: A Bowl of Cherries

Awards: São Paulo Association of Art Critics Awards, Best Film, Best Director, Best Actress (Bengell), 1979

137. *Gaijin, caminhos de liberdade / Gaijin*
                                              1979 DS
D: Tizuka Yamasaki
S: Tizuka Yamasaki, Jorge Durán
C: Edgar Moura
P: Carlos Alberto Diniz
A: Kyoko Tsukamoto

1908. A Japanese woman emigrates to work in a coffee plantation in São Paulo; she learns from other migrant workers, Brazilians and Italians, to protest the near-slave conditions and eventually becomes involved with a labor leader. *South American Cinema: 192.*

Awards: Gramado Film Festival, Best Film, 1980; Havana Film Festival, Best Film, 1980

138. *Iracema*   1979
D: Jorge Bodansky, Orlando Senna
S: Jorge Bodansky

C: Jorge Bodansky
P: Orlando Senna
A: Edna De Cássia, Conceição Senna

A native girl grows up on an Amazon riverboat, then goes off with a truck driver and eventually becomes a prostitute in Bélem along the Trans-Amazon highway, where the landscape is being pillaged by industrial development. *South American Cinema: 171.*

Awards: Brazilia Festival of Brazilian Cinema, Best Film, Best Actress (Cássia), Best Supporting Actress (Senna), 1980

139. *Eles não usam black-tie / They Don't Wear Black Tie*   1981
D: Leon Hirszman
S: Leon Hirszman; based on the play by Gianfrancesco Guarnieri
C: Lauro Escorel
P: Leon Hirszman
A: Fernanda Montenegro, Gianfrancesco Guarnieri

A working-class mother and wife conflicts with the stances of her longtime leftist husband and increasingly radicalized son in the unrest of the 1970s. *Film Society. 1999, Sep.*

Awards: Havana Film Festival, First Prize, 1981; Venice Film Festival, FIPRESCI, 1981

140. *Parahyba, mulher macho / Parahyba, a Macho Woman*   1983 D
D: Tizuka Yamasaki
A: Tanya Alves

1930s. The story of Anayde Beiriz, the poet and journalist who was also a revolutionary involved in the murder of a leader of the Republican Party, an event that altered the course of Brazilian political history. *FII.*

Awards: Havana Film Festival, Best Actress, 1983

141. *A Hora da estrela / Hour of the Star*
                                              1985 DS
D: Suzana Amaral
S: Suzana Amaral; based on the novel by Clarice Lispector
A: Marcélia Cartaxo

São Paulo. A stunted country girl works as a typist and dreams of romantic fulfillment. Oblivious to those around her, she inspires bemusement and hostility but is mostly ignored. Faithful adaptation of a celebrated magic realist novel.

Awards: Brazilia Festival of Brazilian Cinema, Best Film, Best Director, Best Actress, 1985; Havana Film Festival, Best Film, Best Script, Glauber Rocha Prize, 1986

142. **Patriamada** 1986 DS
D: Tizuka Yamasaki
S: Tizuka Yamasaki, Alcione Araujo
C: Edgar Moura
P: Carlos Alberto Diniz
A: Deborah Bloch
1984. A pregnant journalist keeps her two lovers, one a leftist filmmaker and the other a liberal industrialist. *Cinéma bresilien: 216*.
Awards: Gramado Film Festival, nomination for Best Film, 1985

143. **Sonho de valsa / Dream of a Waltz**
1986 DS
D: Ana Carolina
S: Ana Carolina
C: Rodolfo Sanchez
A: Xuxa Lopes
Surreal quest for liberation from the protagonist's father, brother, ex-husband, and other men. *FII*.

144. **Eternamente Pagu** 1987 DS
D: Norma Bengell
S: Norma Bengell, Geraldo Carneiro
C: Antonio Luiz Mendes
A: Carla Camurati, Antônio Fagundes
1920s. Life of Patricia Galvão, a political activist, writer, and muse of surrealists who presented a "resistant and oppositional posture in all realms of life." *St. James: 86*.
Awards: Gramado Film Festival, Best Actress, 1988

145. **Vera** 1987 S
D: Serge Toledo
S: Serge Toledo, Sandra Mara Herzer
C: Rodolfo Sanchez
A: Ana Beatriz Nogueira
"Vera is an orphan, a juvenile delinquent, and desperately unhappy with her female body, as her desire is to be a man." *FII*.
Awards: Berlin International Film Festival, Best Actress, 1987

146. **Romance da Empregada / Story of Fausta**
1988 P
D: Bruno Barreto
S: Naum Alves de Souza
C: José Medeiros
P: Lucy Barreto
A: Betty Faria
A married woman who works as a maid for a wealthy family suffers under the abuse of her husband and plots escape. *Guide to Latin: 60*.
Awards: Havana Film Festival, Best Actress, 1988

147. **Carolota Joaquina, Princesa do Brazil**
1995 DS
D: Carla Camurati
S: Carla Camurati, Melanie Dimantas
C: Breno Silveira
A: Marieta Severo
Eighteenth century. The legend of a Spanish princess, forced into marriage with a lazy royal who became the king of Brazil; after the Portuguese conquest, she is allowed to fulfill her sexual and despotic nature, even sometimes murdering her lovers. *Festival de films, 18th: 20. 1996*.

148. **Através da janela / The Window Across**
1996 DS
D: Tata Amaral
S: Tata Amaral, Fernando Bonassi
C: Hugo Kovensky
A: Laura Cardoso, Fransergio Araujo
A retired cleaning woman is completely devoted to her grown son, who lives with her and is not interested in finding work; indeed, she herself reads the want ads in search of a job for him. During the six days of the film story, his seductive manipulation of her is replaced by fear as she suspects something is wrong. Thriller. *Festival de films, 22nd: 24. 2000*.
Awards: Miami Brazilian Film Festival, Best Director, Best Actress, 2000; São Paulo Association of Art Critics, Best Actress, 2001

149. **Tieta do Agreste / Tieta of Agreste** 1996
D: Carlos Diegues
S: João Ubaldo Ribeiro, Antonio Calmon, Carlos Diegues; based on the novel by Jorge Amado
C: Edgar Moura
P: Bruno Stroppiano
A: Sonia Braga, Marilia Pera
A wealthy São Paulo widow returns to the Brazilian village from which her father exiled her for losing her virginity; still, she must cope with her jealous older sister. *Variety. 1996, Sep. 30*.
Awards: Havana Film Festival, Best Supporting Actress (Pera), 1996

150. **Um Céu de estrelas / Starry Sky** 1996 DP
D: Tata Amaral
S: Jean-Claude Bernardet, Marcio Ferrari
C: Hugo Kovensky
P: Tata Amaral
A: Alleyona Cavalli, Paulo Garcia
São Paulo. In a small apartment where she lives with her mother, a young woman packs her bags for Miami. Suddenly, her boyfriend appears, and there follows a terror-ridden day

during which he turns increasingly violent as she tries to handle him, yet she stands her ground, insisting she will leave. They make love at one point, then he murders her mother and the police descend. A treatise on the dangers of appeasement. Thriller.
Awards: Havana Film Festival, FIPRESCI, 1997

151. *Doces poderes* / *Sweet Power*   1997 DS
D: Lúcia Murat
S: Lúcia Murat
C: Antonio Luiz Mendes
A: Marisa Orth
Brazilia. A veteran broadcaster becomes the director of a major television network. Many of her colleagues, including her predecessor, have moved to employment as media advisors in the current election. She works hard to remain objective. *Variety: 68. 1997, Feb. 16.*

152. *Central do Brasil* / *Central Station* 1998 P
D: Walter Salles
S: João Emanuel Carneiro, Marcos Bernstein
C: Walter Carvalho
P: Martine De Clermont-Tonnerre
A: Fernanda Montenegro
A jaded commercial scribe is forced to take in a young boy. She then travels into the countryside with him in search of his father.
Awards: Berlin International Film Festival, Golden Bear, 1998; Havana Film Festival, Best Film, Best Actress, 1998; BAFTA Awards, Best Film, 1999; Golden Globes, Best Foreign Language Film, 1999

153. *Eu tu eles* / *Me You Them*   2000 DSP
D: Andrucha Waddington
S: Elena Soarez
C: Breno Silveira
P: Andrucha Waddington
A: Regina Casé
A woman farmhand in northeast Brazil supports her husband and children, but she dances the night away and has lovers and children outside her marriage. *Village Voice: 140. 2001, Mar. 6.*

154. *Amélia*   2001 DS
D: Ana Carolina
S: Ana Carolina, José Pinheiro
C: Rodolfo Sanchez
P: Jaime Schwartz
A: Miriam Muniz, Camila Amado, Beatrice Agenin, Alice Borges, Betty Goffman
Fictional account of Sarah Bernhardt's visit to Brazil in 1905, where she breaks her leg and must recuperate with the help of her maid's uncultured sisters. *Variety. 2001, July 6.*

155. *O Outro lado da rua* / *The Other Side of the Street*   2003 S
D: Marcos Bernstein
S: Marcos Bernstein, Melanie Dimantas
C: Toca Seabra
P: Marcos Bernstein
A: Fernanda Montenegro
A sixty-five-year-old woman volunteers as an informant for the police; she spies a man injecting his wife and begins to investigate the case herself. *Tribeca Film. 2003.*
Awards: Berlin International Film Festival, CICAE Award, 2004; Recife Cine PE Audiovisual Festival, Best Film, Best Actress, 2004

156. *Filhas do Vento* / *Daughters of the Wind*   2004
D: Joel Zito Araújo
S: Joel Zito Araújo
C: Jacob Solitrenick
P: Marcio Curi
A: Ruth De Souza, Léa Garcia, Maria Ceiça, Elisa Lucinda
Stories of two generations: two sisters who grew up in the 1950s—one is an actress in Rio de Janeiro, the other has remained in their small town—and their two grown daughters in the present day. *NYT: E8. 2004, June 23.*

BULGARIA

157. *Poslednata Duma* / *The Last Word* 1973 DS
D: Binka Zhelyazkova
S: Binka Zhelyazkova
C: Boris Yanakiev
P: Nikola Velev
A: Iana Guirova, Tzvetana Maneva, Emilia Radeva, Leda Taseva, Dorotea Toncheva
Fascist guards play games with six women resisters who share a prison cell while they await execution. But the women manage to find space to assert humor and respect for one another. "Inventive and poetic." *Variety: 26. 1974, May 22.*
Awards: Cannes Film Festival, nomination for Golden Palm, 1973

158. *Vinata* / *Guilt*   1976 D
D: Vesselina Gerinska
S: Lyuben Stanev
C: Plamen Vagenshtain
A: Tzvetana Maneva
A rape trial. *Kinoizkustvo, vol. 31, no. 9: 59–62. 1976, Sep.*

159. *Matriarhat* / *Matriarchy*   1977 D
D: Lyudmil Kirkov

S: Georgi Mishev
C: Georgi Rusinov
A: Katia Paskaleva, Nevena Kokanova

Most men have abandoned the village to work in factories in the city, leaving the women to tend the collective farm and their own family plots. The lives of six of these women are detailed, including one with a husband who has him arrested, one who is abused at a farm prison, and one who dies. *Variety: 23. 1978, May 31.*

160. ***Bodi blagoslovena! / Be Blessed***　1978
D: Alexandre Obreshkov
S: Kiril Topalov
C: Krum Krumov
A: Mariana Dimitrova, Dorotea Toncheva

Unwed mothers in a state institution. *Kinoizkustvo, vol. 13, no. 1: 26–29. 1978, Jan.*

161. ***Zhena na trideset i tri / A Woman at 33***　1982
D: Kristo Kristov
S: Boyan Papasov
C: Atanas Tasev
A: Liliana Kovacheva

A divorced mother and secretary is harassed by her ex-husband, her coworkers, and her boss's wife, who is jealous; she "must violate even her own principles in order to survive." *IMDb.*

Other titles: Edna Zhena na trideset i tri

162. ***Hotel Tsentral / Hotel Central***　1983
D: Veselin Branev
S: Veselin Branev
C: Yatsek Todorov
A: Irène Krivoshieva

During a 1934 coup, a hotel chambermaid is put into prostitution by corrupt town officials. *FII.*

163. ***Sezonat na kanarchetat / Canary Season***　1994
D: Eugeny Mihaylov
S: Nikolai Valchinov
C: Eli Yonova
A: Paraskeva Djukelova, Plamena Getova, Mikhael Dontchev

A woman reveals the injustices of her life as a single mother to her grown son. *Film Society. 1995, Jun.*

164. ***Mila ot Mars / Mila from Mars***　2004 DSP
D: Sophia Zornitsa
S: Sophia Zornitsa
C: Alexander Krumov
P: Sophia Zornitsa
A: Vesela Kazakova

A pregnant woman flees an abusive relationship and ends up in a small town, where she is met with kindness. She remains distrustful but soon "has a new life and love." *New Directors. 2005.*

Awards: Mannheim-Heidelberg International Film Festival, Ecumenical Jury Prize, 2004; Sarajevo Film Festival, Best Film, 2004

BURKINA FASO

165. ***Sarraounia***　1986
D: Med Hondo
S: Med Hondo, Abdoulaye Mamani
C: François Catonné
P: Med Hondo
A: Aï Keïta

Nineteenth century. Queen of the Asnas of Lugu, a princess of great wealth and a complete education, is feared as a witch by neighboring lords because of her talents. She leads her people in battle with the French invaders. In the latter half, the film turns toward the bumbling of the French leaders.

Awards: Ouagadougou Panafrican Film and Television Festival, Grand Prize, 1987

166. ***Histoire d'Orokia***　1987
D: Jacob Sou, Jacques Oppenheim
S: Jacob Sou, Jacques Oppenheim, Ky Moustapha
C: Issaka Thiombiano
A: Marguerite Sou

A young girl in love and pregnant is purchased for marriage by a wealthy man, who forces her to have an abortion. After trying to poison him, she is sent to prison. Upon release, her lover is still waiting and they are married, but nonetheless he suspects her of infidelity. *BiFi.*

167. ***Yaaba***　1989
D: Idressa Ouedraogo
S: Idressa Ouedraogo
C: Matthias Kälin
P: Michael David
A: Fatimata Sanga

An old woman, thought to be a witch, is befriended by a young boy and helps him save another young boy by obtaining medicine.

Awards: Cannes Film Festival, FIPRESCI, 1989; Tokyo Film Festival, Gold Award, 1989

168. ***Sia, le rêve du python / Sia, the Dream of the Python***　2001 P
D: Dani Kouyaté
S: Moussa Diagana
C: Robert Millié
P: Elizabeth Lopez, Sylvie Maigne, Claude Gilaizeau

A: Fatoumata Diawara

A woman flees her village when the priest announces she will be sacrificed; her lover and uncle, both at the "front" fighting, help her by having the sacrifice delayed until their arrival. While her life is saved, she loses her lover in the process. *Village Voice: 110. 2001, Nov. 27.*

Awards: FESPACO, Special Jury Prize, OCIC Award, 2001; Acteurs á l'Écran, nomination for Best Actress, 2002

BURMA

169. **Main-ma le thein kywe / A Smart Lady**
                                              1994
D: Khin Maung U
C: Ko Ko Htay
A: Moe Moe Myint Aung, Waing, Moss, Nay San
In a remote village, a young woman lives with her aunt and sells fish for a living. Her business success attracts several men. Includes "traditional music and celebrations such as the Water Festival." *Yale Council. Accessed 2005, July 15.*

CAMEROON

170. **Le Prix de la liberté / The Price of Freedom**
                                              1978
D: Jean-Pierre Dikongue-Pipa
S: Jean-Pierre Dikongue-Pipa
C: Bernard Zitzermann
A: Marie-Thérèse Badje
An eighteen-year-old, oppressed by her family, runs away from her village. *FII.*

171. **Notre fille / Our Daughter**   1980
D: Daniel Kamwa
S: Daniel Kamwa
C: Hans Czap
A: Nicole Okala, Elise Atangana
An aging village Papa has seven wives, thirty children, and a new very young wife. One of his older daughters has been educated in France in order to help support the family. She has learned new ways and does not intend to follow tradition, as she has also secretly married. Her father arrives in the capital to remind her of her duties. *BiFi.*

172. **Fanta**   2000 D
D: Joséphine Bertrand Tchakoua Pouma
Paris. "Fanta lives with her husband. They quarrel over money and she wants to stop her acting lessons because they are too expensive." *Francophone Women: 23.*

CANADA

173. **Isabel**   1968
D: Paul Almond
S: Paul Almond
C: Georges Dufaux
P: Paul Almond
A: Geneviève Bujold
A young woman returns to her parents' home on the Canadian coast but becomes haunted by a family history of violence and mental illness. Mystery. *Film Society. 2000, May.*

174. **Madeleine Is . . .**   1969 DS
D: Sylvia Spring
S: Sylvia Spring, Kenneth Specht
C: Doug McKay
P: Kenneth Specht
A: Nicola Lipman, John Juliani
A young woman, trying to find her way, has several love affairs. *FII.*

175. **Les Stances à Sophie**   1971 S
D: Moshé Mizrahi
S: Moshé Mizrahi; based on the novel by Christiane Rochefort
C: Jean-Marc Ripert
A: Bernadette Lafont, Bulle Ogier
A contrast of "serious pretentious males with light hearted women in need of freedom." The first woman has many lovers but is still trapped by a comfortable bourgeois marriage; when her friend, also in a submissive marriage, is killed in an accident, the event allows her to decide to leave her possessive husband. *Festival de films, 14th: 64. 1992.*

176. **La Vraie nature de Bernadette / The True Nature of Bernadette**
                                              1971
D: Gilles Carle
S: Gilles Carle
C: René Verzier
P: Gilles Carle
A: Micheline Lanctôt
A wife leaves her wealthy Montréal lawyer husband and takes her son to live in the country, where she hopes he "will learn to become a child of nature." *FII.*
Awards: Canadian Film Awards, Best Actress, 1972

177. **La Vie rêvée / Dream Life**   1972 DS
D: Mireille Dansereau
S: Mireille Dansereau, Patrick Auzépy
C: François Gill
A: Liliane Lemaitre-Auger, Véronique Le Flaguais
Two working girls, one from a wealthy constrained

background, the other middle class, seek "the perfect man" along with "freedom, maturity and happiness." They eventually liberate themselves from the "dream life" of the socially constructed woman. *FII. Also French-Speaking: 115.*

178. *August and July* 1973 S
D: Murray Markowitz
S: Francesca Kruschen
C: James Lewis, Murray Markowitz
A: Sharon Smith, Alexa Dewiel
A lesbian couple spends the summer in a rented farmhouse; they talk about love in relation to their past, and they make love. *AMG.*

179. *Kamouraska* 1973 S
D: Claude Jutra
S: Anne Hébert, Claude Jutra
C: Michel Brault
P: Mag Bodard
A: Geneviève Bujold
Quebec, nineteenth century. A woman looks back over her life: her first husband, whom she colluded with a lover to murder; the lover who then left her; and her second husband. *AMG.*
Awards: Canadian Film Awards, Best Actress, 1973

180. *Le Temps de l'avant / Before the Time Comes* 1975 DSP
D: Anne Claire Poirier
S: Louise Carré, Marthe Blackburn
C: Michel Brault
P: Anne Claire Poirier
A: Luce Guilbeault, Paule Baillargeon, Pierre Gobeil
A happily married woman with three children agonizes over her decision to have another. *FII.*

181. *L'Autre rive / Far Shore* 1978 DSP
D: Joyce Wieland
S: Joyce Wieland, Bryan Barney
C: Richard Leiterman
P: Joyce Wieland, Judy Steel
A: Céline Lomez, Frank Moore
1919. A woman married to a mining businessman has an affair with an environmentalist. *Chicago Reader. Accessed 2005, Jan. 20.*

182. *L'Arrache-coeur / Heartbreak* 1979 DS
D: Mireille Dansereau
S: Mireille Dansereau
C: François Protat
P: Robert Ménard
A: Louise Marleau, Françoise Faucher, Michel Mondie
The painful love between a domineering mother and her daughter, a hold that is not broken until

the daughter has a child of her own. *Festival de films, 15th: 100. 1993.*

183. *Mourir à tue-tête / A Scream from Silence* 1979 DSP
D: Anne Claire Poirier
S: Anne Claire Poirier, Marthe Blackburn
C: Michel Brault
P: Jacques Gagnier, Anne Claire Poirier
A: Julie Vincent, Germain Houde, Micheline Lanctôt
A woman never recovers from a violent rape and commits suicide. A filmmaker and editor discuss their fictional footage of the rape as well as the sociological and judicial aftermath that sometimes adds to the victim's troubles. Extensive rape scene shows only the man, who talks and drinks throughout. *BiFi. Also French-Speaking: 129.*
Other titles: Primal Fear

184. *Le Sexe des étoiles / The Sex of the Stars* 1979 DS
D: Paule Baillargeon
S: Monique Prouix
C: Eric Cayla
A: Marianne Mercier, Denis Mercier
A young girl lives with her mother and spends the nights with her telescope, but she dreams only of her father; one day he appears at their door, now transformed into a woman. *Festival de films, 16th: 20. 1994.*

185. *By Design* 1981 P
D: Claude Jutra
S: Joe Weisenfeld, Claude Jutra
C: Jean Boffety
P: Beryl Fox, Werner Aellen
A: Patty Duke, Sara Botsford
Fashion designers form a lesbian couple and want to have a child, but they are rejected by adoption agencies; they ask a friend, a photographer, to be the father. *FII.*
Awards: Genie Awards, nominations for Best Actress (Botsford) and Best Foreign Actress (Duke), 1983

186. *Heartaches* 1981
D: Donald Shebib
S: Terence Heffernan
C: Vic Sarin
P: David Patterson
A: Margot Kidder, Annie Potts
Two women, one who's left a husband because she's pregnant by another man, and one who is streetwise, become friends. Comedy. *AMG.*
Other titles: Coeurs à l'envers

187. Love 1982 DSP
D: Nancy Dowd, Mai Zetterling, Annette Cohen, Liv Ullmann
S: Nancy Dowd, Joni Mitchell, Gael Greene, Edna O'Brien, Mai Zetterling, Penelope Gilliat, Liv Ullmann
C: Norman Leigh, Reginald Morris
P: Renée Perlmutter
A: pt. 1: Toni Kalem, Nicolas Campbell; pt. 2: Joni Mitchell; pt. 3: Marilyn Lightstone; pt. 4: Janet-Laine Greene; pt. 5: Candace O'Connor, Robin Ward; pt. 6: Maureen Fitzgerald, Gordon Thomson; pt. 7: Rita Tuckett, Charles Jolliffe
Seven stories. Pt. 1: "Por vida / For Life" (Dowd). A simple girl helps a wounded veteran. Pt. 2: "The Black Cat in the Black Mouse Socks" (Zetterling, Mitchell). A fairy spectacle intended to seduce. Pt. 3: "Love on Your Birthday" (Cohen, Greene). Detour from love to sex as performance and style. Pt. 4: "Julia" (Zetterling, O'Brien). Woman too often betrayed meets an ex-lover. Pt. 5: "Cliff Dwellers" (Cohen, Gilliat). Sixty years of marriage and still a young love. Pt. 6: "Love from the Marketplace" (Zetterling). Obsessive love between a mother and son, expressed over a meal. Pt. 7: "Parting" (Ullmann). An old man and his sick wife are still in love. *Festival de films, 8th: 51. 1986.*

188. Maria Chapdelaine 1983
D: Gilles Carle
S: Gilles Carle
C: Pierre Mignot
A: Carole Laure
Quebec, nineteenth century. On an isolated farm, a loving daughter attracts three men and struggles to decide. She waits for her true love but he dies, so she decides to stay near her family and marry a man she respects but does not love.
Awards: Genie Awards, nomination for Best Actress, 1984

189. La Femme de l'hotel / A Woman in Transit 1984 DSP
D: Lea Pool
S: Lea Pool, Michel Langlois
C: Georges Dufaux
P: Bernadette Payeur
A: Louise Marleau, Paule Baillargeon
A filmmaker goes to Montréal to make a film about a singer, who mysteriously crosses paths with the actress who will play her in the film. *BiFi.*

190. Anne Trister 1986 DS
D: Lea Pool
S: Lea Pool, Markel Beaulieu
C: Pierre Mignot
P: Roger Frappier
A: Albane Guilhe, Louise Marleau
A twenty-five-year-old painter lives in Israel, then moves to Canada to stay with a psychologist friend and falls in love with her. *Festival de films, 8th: 16. 1986.*

191. Diario inconcluso / Unfinished Diary 1986 DS
D: Marilu Mallet
S: Marilu Mallet
A: Marilu Mallet
"Docudrama about a Chilean woman film director who lives and works in French-speaking Canada." Her work is poorly understood, even by her Australian husband. *St. James: 359.*

192. Loyalties 1986 DS
D: Anne Wheeler
S: Anne Wheeler, Sharon Riis
C: Vic Sarin
P: William Johnston
A: Susan Wooldridge, Tantoo Cardinal
Alberta. After escaping scandal in Britain, an upper-class family moves to Canada, where the wife hires a Native American woman, who is little used to whites, as a servant; they become friends. *Festival de films, 9th: 10. 1987.*

193. Eva Guerillera 1987 DS
D: Jacqueline Levitin
S: Jacqueline Levitin
C: Jean Charles Tremblay
A: Carmen Ferland, Angela Roa
El Salvador, 1970s. A journalist goes into the jungle and interviews a female guerrilla fighter in the rebel army about her life in hiding and difficulties as a woman soldier. *Festival de films, 10th: 24. 1988.*

194. Les Fils de Marie / Marie's Sons 1987 DS
D: Carole Laure
S: Carole Laure, Pascal Arnold
C: Pascal Arnold
A: Carole Laure
A mother is completely devoted to her son, whom she loses one day in an accident, along with her husband. She places an ad in the paper: "Mother who has lost a child, seeks a child who has lost a mother." Having no other demands, she falls in love with four of the applicants, who project on her their maternal fantasies, but also their wounds. *Festival de films, 25th: 21. 2003.*
Awards: Paris Film Festival, nomination for Grand Prix, 2003

195. *I've Heard the Mermaids Singing* 1987 DSP

D: Patricia Rozema
S: Patricia Rozema
C: Douglas Koch
P: Patricia Rozema, Alexandra Raffe
A: Sheila McCarthy, Paule Baillargeon, Ann-Marie MacDonald

A daydreaming photographer has a strong but misplaced admiration for the lesbian owner of the gallery where she works, but the woman only uses her. When she is not flying through the air or walking on water, she is shocked by the cynical goings-on around her.

Awards: Cannes Film Festival, Youth Award, 1987; Genie Awards, Best Actress (McCarthy), Best Supporting Actress (Baillargeon), 1988

196. *Le Sourd dans la ville / Deaf to the City*
1987 DS

D: Mireille Dansereau
S: Mireille Dansereau, J.-J. Tremblay; based on the novel by Marie-Claire Blais
C: M. Caron
A: Béatrice Picard

An elegant noblewoman is left by her husband and installs herself in a hotel to die. *Festival de films, 15th: 100. 1993.*

197. *A Winter Tan* 1987 DS

D: Jackie Burroughs, Louise Clark, John Frizzell, John Walker, Aerlyn Weissman
S: Jackie Burroughs, John Frizzell; based on *Give Sorrow Words* by Mary Holder
C: John Walker
A: Jackie Burroughs, Diane D'Aquila

A Canadian teacher of some fifty years takes off for Mexico in search of total regeneration through sex with young men; while there are consequences to her shamelessness, her desire is not questioned. *Festival de films, 10th: 23. 1988.*

Awards: Genie Awards, Best Actress (Burroughs), 1989

198. *Bye Bye Blues* 1989 DSP

D: Anne Wheeler
S: Anne Wheeler
C: Vic Sarin
P: Anne Wheeler
A: Rebecca Jenkins

World War II. A mother leaves her military doctor husband in India and returns to Canada, then does not hear from him for several years. She gets a job in a dance band and resists having an affair, until finally her husband returns. *Variety: 29, 42. 1989, Sep. 6.*

Other titles: For the Moment

199. *The Company of Strangers* 1990 DS

D: Cynthia Scott
S: Sally Bochner, Gloria Demers
C: David De Volpi
P: David Wilson
A: Alice Diabo, Constance Garneau, Winifred Holden, Cissy Meddings, Catherine Roche, Michelle Sweeney, Beth Weber

A group of elderly women take a bus trip and become stranded in northern Quebec. *MOMA Film. 2000, Jul–Aug.*

200. *La Demoiselle sauvage / Savage Woman*
1991 DSP

D: Lea Pool
S: Laurent Gagliardi, Lea Pool
C: Georges Dufaux
P: Denise Robert
A: Patricia Tulasne

A woman murders her abusive lover, then flees; she attempts suicide but lives to become attached to an engineer, who hides her. *24 Images, no. 58: 64–65. 1991, Nov.*

201. *Deux actrices / Two Actresses* 1993 DS

D: Micheline Lanctôt
S: Micheline Lanctôt
C: André Gagnon
A: Pascale Bussières, Pascale Paroissien

A "profoundly tormented and destructive" woman reenters the life of her happily married sister and husband. *Festival de films, 16th: 19. 1994.*

202. *Double Happiness* 1994 DS

D: Mina Shum
S: Mina Shum
C: Peter Wunstorf
P: Stephen Hegyes
A: Sandra Oh

A Chinese Canadian moves out of her family home and has an affair with a white man.

Other titles: Small Happiness

Awards: Genie Awards, Best Actress, 1994; Toronto International Film Festival, Best Canadian Film, 1994

203. *Mouvements du désir / Desire in Motion*
1994 DS

D: Lea Pool
S: Lea Pool; based on the novel by Roland Barthes
C: Pierre Mignot
A: Valérie Kaprisky

A woman and her daughter take a train trip across the country; both are involved in many strange events, and a mysterious male lover appears, then goes, along with other people.

204. *Chinese Chocolate* 1995 DS
D: Yan Cui, Qi Chang
S: Yan Cui, Qi Chang
C: Michael Spicer
A: Diana Peng, Shirley Cui
Toronto. An ambitious doctor and a naïve dancer meet on a plane when they leave China to emigrate to Canada; although their desires are similar, their fortunes vary. *Festival de films, 18th: 21. 1996.*

205. *When Night Is Falling* 1995 DS
D: Patricia Rozema
S: Patricia Rozema
C: Douglas Koch
A: Pascale Bussières, Rachael Crawford
A college professor is unhappy with her relationship with a theology student who must wait to marry; one day she meets a circus artist and becomes infatuated with her. *Festival de films, 18th: 102. 1996.*

206. *Kissed* 1996 DSP
D: Lynne Stopkewich
S: Barbara Gowdy, Angus Fraser, Lynne Stopkewich
C: Gregory Middleton
P: Lynne Stopkewich
A: Molly Parker, Peter Outerbridge
Always fascinated by death, a woman with a necrophiliac side becomes a mortician. She then meets a man who wishes to make her "normal." *AMG.*

207. *War between Us* 1996 DSP
D: Anne Wheeler
S: Sharon Gibbon
C: Rene Ohashi
P: Valerie Gray, Gary Harvey
A: Shannon Lawson, Mieko Ouchi
British Columbia, 1941. A Japanese woman is interned in a small town and develops a relationship with a white woman neighbor when she becomes her housekeeper. *FII.*

208. *The Healer* 1997 DS
D: Agnieszka Holland
S: Agnieszka Holland, Arlene Sarner, Roman Gren
C: Jacek Petrycki
P: Paul Stephens
A: Miranda Otto
Despite being fiercely agnostic, a mother grabs the opportunity to take her dying child to a famous healer in Poland. The healer is seized with desire for her and makes her child a priority. After the child is healed, they have an affair.

209. *2 secondes* 1998 DS
D: Manon Briand
S: Manon Briand
C: James Gray
P: Roger Frappier
A: Charlotte Laurier
Montreal. A professional bike racer hesitates at the start of a race and is pushed into retirement. Back home, she gets a job as a bicycle messenger and becomes attached to an old Italian former racer who owns a bicycle shop. *Festival de films, 21st: 19. 1999.*
Awards: Montréal World Film Festival, Best Director, 1998

210. *C't'a ton tour Laura Cadieux / It's Your Turn, Laura* 1998 DSP
D: Denise Filiatrault
S: Denise Filiatrault
C: Daniel Jobin
P: Francine Lebrun
A: Ginette Reno, Pierrette Robitaille, Sonia Vachon
Women become friends in the waiting room of a weight-loss clinic. Also sequel *Laura Cadieux . . . La suite* (1999). *Francophone Women: 52.*
Awards: Genie Awards, nominations for Best Actress (Reno, Robitaille), 1999; Jutra Awards, nominations for Best Actress (Reno) and Best Supporting Actress (Vachon), 1999

211. *Better Than Chocolate* 1999 DSP
D: Anne Wheeler
S: Peggy Thompson
C: Gregory Middleton
P: Sharon McGowan
A: Karyn Dwyer, Christina Cox, Wendy Crewson
A mother moves in with her lesbian daughter in Vancouver. *Village Voice: 68. 1999, Aug. 17.*

212. *Felicia's Journey* 1999
D: Atom Egoyan
S: Atom Egoyan; based on the novel by William Trevor
C: Paul Sarossy
P: Bruce Davey
A: Elaine Cassidy, Bob Hoskins
A pregnant teenager looking for a boyfriend who has abandoned her accepts help from a man who turns out to be a serial killer. Thriller. *NYT: E14. 1999, Nov. 12.*
Awards: Golden Satellite Awards, nomination for Best Actress, 2000

213. *Ladies Room* 1999 DS
D: Gabriella Cristiani, Penelope Buitenhuis, Nadine Schwartz

S: Andrée Pelletier, Geneviève Lefèbvre, Leila Basen, Natalina Di Leandro, Amanda Roberts, Tony Roman
C: Pierre Mignot
P: René Malo, Claude Léger
A: Greta Scacchi, Lorraine Bracco, John Malkovich, Veronica Ferres
Two stories set in women's restrooms. First, three actresses are unexpectedly forced to share a bathroom, which leads to argument. Second, at a restroom at the opera, a woman who believes her lover is divorced meets his pregnant wife by chance. *FII.*

214. *Les Fantômes des trois Madeleine / The Three Madeleines*   2000 DSC
D: Guylaine Dionne
S: Guylaine Dionne
C: Nathalie Moliavko-Visotsky
A: Sylvie Drapeau, France Arbour, Isadora Galwey
"Surrealist road movie" about a grandmother, mother, and daughter who leave Montréal for the Gaspé region, where they seek to understand their past and find their dreams. *Francophone Women: 51.*

215. *Maelström*   2000
D: Denis Villeneuve
S: Denis Villeneuve
C: André Turpin
P: Roger Frappier
A: Marie-Josée Croze
Montreal. A wealthy woman must cope with setbacks—an abortion, a business loss, and a fall with her car into a river. *Village Voice: 104. 2002, Jan. 29.*
Awards: Berlin International Film Festival, FIPRESCI, 2001; Genie Awards, Best Actress, 2001; Jutra Awards, Best Actress, 2001

216. *Mariages / Marriages*   2001 DSP
D: Catherine Martin
S: Catherine Martin
C: Jean-Claude Labrecque
P: Lorraine Dufour
A: Marie-Eve Bertrand, Markita Boies
"Recreation of the suffocating atmosphere of matriarchs at the end of the 19th century [and] some reflection of mother-daughter relations." *Francophone Women: 61.*

217. *Suddenly Naked*   2001 DS
D: Anne Wheeler
S: Elyse Friedman
C: David Frazee
A: Wendy Crewson

An aging blockbuster novelist falls in love with a twenty-year-old man. Comedy. *IMDb.*
Awards: Leo Awards, Best Drama, 2002

218. *L'Odyssée d'Alice Tremblay / Alice's Odyssey*   2002 DSP
D: Denise Filiatrault
S: Sylvie Lussier, Pierre Poirier
C: Pierre Gill
P: Denise Robert
A: Sophie Lorain
"Subversion" of the fairy tale "Snow White and the Seven Dwarfs." Fantasy. *Francophone Women: 52.*

219. *Marion Bridge*   2003 DP
D: Wiebke von Carolsfeld
S: Daniel MacIvor
C: Stefan Ivanov
P: Bill Neven, Julia Sereny
A: Molly Parker, Stacy Smith, Rebecca Jenkins, Marguerite McNeil, Ellen Page
Youngest of three sisters returns to Cape Breton to help care for their sick mother. *NYT: E14. 2003, Apr. 18.*
Awards: Toronto International Film Festival, Best Canadian Film, 2002

220. *My Life without Me*   2003 DSP
D: Isabel Coixet
S: Isabel Coixet
C: Jean-Claude Larrieu
P: Esther Garcia, Gordon McLennan
A: Sarah Polley, Amanda Plummer, Leonor Watling
A bored wife and mother finds she has cancer and is determined to set everything straight in her family before she dies. *NYT: E15. 2003, Sep. 26.*
Awards: Berlin International Film Festival, German Art House Cinemas Prize, 2003; Sant Jordi Awards, Best Film, 2004; Vancouver Film Critics Circle, Best Actress (Polley), 2004

221. *Being Julia*   2004
D: István Szabó
S: Ronald Harwood; based on the novel by W. Somerset Maugham
C: Lajos Koltai
P: Robert Lantos
A: Annette Bening
London, 1930s. A pampered theater star has a midlife crisis and pursues a young man, who then betrays her with the same young rival with whom her liberated husband has also taken up. Undaunted, she carries out on the stage and in life a complex plot that reveals the girl's limitations and her own strength of character.

Awards: Bangkok International Film Festival, Best Actress, 2005; Golden Globes, Best Actress, 2005

CHILE

222. *La Colonia penal / The Penal Colony*
1971

D: Raoul Ruiz
S: Raoul Ruiz; based on a story by Franz Kafka
A: Mónica Echeverría

In the near future, a reporter visits an island off the coast of Peru, where all the inhabitants are men; she dutifully reports on the many bizarre events, including torture and murder. *South American Cinema: 224.*

223. *Que hacer? / What Is to Be Done?* 1973 D
D: Nina Serrano, Saul Landau, Raoul Ruiz
S: Christian Sanchez
P: James Becket
A: Sandra Archer

Chile, 1970. An American Peace Corps volunteer becomes part of a leftist group and is then used as a spy by a U.S. undercover agent. *Guide to Latin: 76.*

224. *Mi boda contigo / Our Marriage* 1984 DS
D: Valeria Sarmiento
S: Valeria Sarmiento; based on the novel by Corin Telladao
C: Acacio De Almeida
A: Nadège Clair

A young girl is adopted by childless neighbors who pay the medical bills for a lifesaving operation. Twenty years later after her adoptive mother dies, she is a seductive young woman who then marries her father, while insisting their relationship remain platonic. *Variety: 237. 1985, Mar. 6.*

Other titles: Notre mariage

225. *Amelia Lopes O'Neill*
1991 DS
D: Valeria Sarmiento
S: Valeria Sarmiento, Raoul Ruiz
C: Jean Penzer
P: Patrick Sandrin
A: Laura Del Sol, Laura Benson

Valparaiso. After the death of their father, two sisters, one who has saved herself for the perfect man, fall in love with the same man. *Variety. 1992, Feb. 25.*

Awards: Berlin International Film Festival, nominated for Best Direction, 1991

226. *Elle*
1995 DS
D: Valeria Sarmiento
S: Raoul Ruiz, Evelyne Pieiller; based on the novel by Mercedes Pinto

C: Stefan Ivanov
P: Patrick Sandrin
A: Marine Delterme

Left alone in her mansion, a woman tells the story of her marriage to an art professor who thought her beauty equal to a piece of art and who became insanely jealous; she, equally insanely, went along with his demands for attention. Luis Buñuel used the same source material for his 1952 *El. Variety: 65. 1995, Oct. 9.*

CHINA

227. *Ye meigui zhi lian / The Wild Wild Rose*
1960
D: Wang Tian-lin
S: Qin Yifu
A: Ge Lan

A seducer with a "big heart" attempts to turn away a music professor who is already engaged to someone else. *Festival des 3.*

Other titles: Sauvage, sauvage est la rose

228. *Hong se niang zijun / Red Detachment of Women* 1961
D: Xie Jin
S: Liang Xin
A: Zhu Xijuan

Hainan Island, 1940s. A woman whose father has been murdered by a cruel landowner leads a communist guerrilla group formed entirely of women to avenge him. "Not to be confused with the 1971 dance drama or the 1972 opera with the same name and story." *Festival des 3.*

229. *Huai shi zhuang / Locust Tree Village*
1962 D
D: Ping Wang
S: Hu Ke
A: Hu Peng

Reform under "tante Guo," a revolutionary mother figure who effects social change. *Women through the Lens: 253.*

Other titles: Le Village de l'Acacia

230. *Kunlun shan shang yike cao / Grass Grows on the Kunlun Mountains* 1962 D
D: Dong Kena
A: Yanjing Liu, Zhelan Wang

A woman manages a rooming house for travelers high in the mountains and befriends a young newcomer who is a geologist. *Chinese Filmography.*

Other titles: A Blade of Grass in Kunlun Mountain

231. *Li Shuang-shuang* 1962
D: Lu Ren
S: Li Zhun
A: Zhang Ruifang
The story of a model peasant woman, both "a mouthpiece for party policy and a submissive wife." *Women through the Lens: 253.*

232. *Liang Shan-bo yu Zhu Ying-tai* / *The Love Eterne* 1963
D: Li Han-hsiang
A: Betty Loh Ti, Ivy Ling Po
Fourth century. Because education is denied to women, a girl pretends to be a male doctor and advises her parents that the only way to keep her healthy is to send her off to university dressed as a man. On the way, she meets another student, a man, played in the film by a woman, and they become close friends. S/he is charmed to be enlightened by the new friend's views on women's rights, and they have persistent discussions on the subject, including an argument over whether the many dynasties "ruined by women" were not in fact led by "bad kings who ruined themselves." Most of the dialogue is sung, and it focuses on the gender confusion.

233. *Wu tai jie mei* / *Two Stage Sisters* 1964
D: Xie Jin
S: Xie Jin, Wang Lingu
C: Zhou Damin
A: Xie Fang, Cao Yindi
1930s. Two women belong to a traveling opera troupe and become close friends when they settle in Shanghai and become well known. One is seduced by materialism through gangster connections, while the other commits herself to revolution. By 1950, they have resolved their differences and vow to "remold" and always perform revolutionary operas. One of the first People's Republic films to be shown outside China in the early 1980s. *Variety. 1981, Apr. 22.*

234. *Nü feisingyuan* / *Women Pilots* 1966 D
D: Dong Kena, Cheng Yin
C: Yan Junsheng
A: Ketchun Lu
"Focuses on three women from the first squad of trainee women pilots in 'New China'." *FII.*

235. *Hong se niang zijun* / *Red Detachment of Women* 1970
D: Pan Wenzhan, Fu Jie
S: Hsin Liang; based on the 1961 film directed by Xie Jin
A: Ching Ching-hua, Lo Sing-siang

1927–1937. Ballet performed by the China Ballet Troupe, describing the birth, growth, and maturing of a women's company of soldiers and its actions in battle during the Second Revolutionary Civil War. *FII.*

236. *Hai xia* / *Island Militia Women* 1975 D
D: Qian Jiang, Chen Huan Kai, Wang Haowei
S: Xie Tieli; based on *Island Militia Women* by Li Ruquin
C: Qian Jiang
A: Wu Haiyan
A woman, abandoned as a child and saved by a fisherman, organizes the island women into a militia to fight anticommunists. *Encyclopedia of Chinese.*

237. *Qinq guo qing cheng* / *The Empress Dowager* 1975
D: Li Han-hsiang
A: Lisa Lu, Ivy Ling Po
1890s. Court intrigue around the empress "progenitor" who named her son emperor when he was a child but prefers to keep him infantilized while she reigns from behind the scenes. She indulges his attempt to root out corruption, but not when it affects her circle, and ignores the many expressions of concern about the end of the dynasty, as she refuses to wage war to protect it.

238. *Hai shang ming zhu* / *Bright Ocean Pearl* 1976 D
D: Wang Haowei
S: Shang Xiangin
C: Wang Zhaoling
A: Wang Suya
A newly wed woman conflicts with her father-in-law over corruption in her new village. She becomes director of the local fishing commission and exposes the corruption, finally educating even him. *Chinese Filmography.*

239. *A, yao lan* / *The Cradle* 1979
D: Xie Jin
S: Xu Qingding
C: Chen Zhengxiang
A: Zhe Xijuan
Chinese Civil War, 1947. "A political instructor in a front line unit is assigned to escort a group of kindergarten children to a safe area." *Chinese Filmography.*

240. *Tian yun shan chan qi* / *Legend of Tianyun Mountain* 1980
D: Xie Jin
A: Fuli Wang

A woman oversees a rehabilitation center, where she comes across the case of her former lover, who had married one of her friends, and their impoverished life; she is determined to rehabilitate them. *FII.*
Awards: Golden Rooster Awards, Best Film, 1981

241. *A Li Ma / Alima* 1981
D: Ge Gengtana, Zhang Lun
S: Yun Zhaogung
C: Zhang Lun
A: Sharen Gaowa
Mongolia, 1940s. During the Chinese Civil War, a girl is orphaned when her communist father is executed; later she becomes increasingly active in the revolution and avenges him. *Chinese Filmography.*

242. *Sha Ou / Drive to Win* 1981 DS
D: Zhang Nuanxing
S: Zhang Nuanxing
C: Pao Xiaoran
A: Chang Shanshan
An injured volleyball player watches her team lose, then moves on to help her husband with his mountain-climbing team, who are all killed in an avalanche. Finally, she coaches a successful team. *Chinese Filmography. Also Encyclopedia of Chinese.*
Awards: Golden Rooster Awards, Best Film, Best Director, 1982

243. *Jin lu er* 1982 D
D: Dong Kena
A: Leng Mei
A retail clothing store selects a woman as the "best" salesperson; others complain that she only likes to appear good, but is not sincere. *Chinese Filmography.*

244. *Tante Tao quan shui ding dong / Bubbling Spring* 1982 D
D: Shi Xiaohua
S: Wu Jianxin
C: Yu Shishan
A: Zhang Ruifang, Zhang Xiangfei
A teacher intends to take her niece to a resort but instead opens a kindergarten because the children in the neighborhood have nowhere to go. This interferes with the niece's plans to compose music, but she eventually sees the good her aunt has done. *Chinese Filmography.*

245. *Qiu Jin / Qiu Jin: A Revolutionary China* 1983
D: Xie Jin
S: Huang Zongying, Xie Jin

C: Qi Xu
A: Li Xiuming
1901. Famed revolutionary leader Qiu Jin abandons her family for exile in Japan, then returns to China to participate in an insurrection and is executed. *Chinese Filmography.*

246. *Bei gua hong dou / North China Red Beans* 1984 D
D: Wang Haowei
S: Qiao Xuezhu
C: Li Chengsheng
A: Liu Xiaoqing
A forest worker refuses to marry the man her brother-in-law has chosen for her, then becomes disenchanted with her true love when he showers the brother with gifts. *Once upon a time.*

247. *Liang jia fu nü / Woman of Good Family* 1985
D: Huang Jianzhong
A: Cong Shan
1948. An eighteen-year-old is married off to a six-year-old, then falls in love with someone her own age; she is torn because she loves both her husband and his mother. *Festival des 3.*
Other titles: Girl from Heaven

248. *Nü ren de li liang / Woman's Power* 1985
D: Jiang Shensheng, Zhao Shi
S: Xwe Ke
C: Zhang Songping
A: Li Kechun
A city chemical plant engineer is promoted at a time of crisis and experiences resistance because of her age and gender. *Chinese Filmography.*

249. *Qing shun ji / Sacrificed Youth* 1985 DS
D: Zhang Nuanxing
S: Zhang Manling, Zhang Nuanxing
C: Mu Deyuan
A: Li Fengxu
A young teacher is sent to the south to live with the peasant minority DAI during the Cultural Revolution. She discovers another way of life, including different relations between men and women, that opens a new door for her regarding love and sexuality. *Festival de films, 15th: 91. 1993.*

250. *Xiang si nü zhi ke dian / Xiangsi Woman's Hotel* 1985 D
D: Dong Kena
S: Ye Dan
A: Xiaolei Zhang

A woman put in charge of a remote hotel tries to improve it, but she is defeated by resentful former staff. *Chinese Filmography.*

251. ***Fu rong zhen / Hibiscus Town*** 1986
D: Xie Jin
S: Xie Jin, A. Cheng
C: Lu Junfu
A: Liu Xiaoqing, Xu Songzi, Wen Jiang
1960s. The owner of a successful bean curd stall is accused of graft by the communist party at the beginning of the Cultural Revolution. She loses her house and husband and must start anew, "sweeping streets." *Variety. 1988, Aug. 24.*
Awards: Golden Rooster Awards, Best Film, Best Actress (Liu), Best Supporting Actress (Xu), 1987; Karlovy Vary International Film Festival, Grand Prix, 1988

252. ***Lian ai li jie / Season of Love*** 1986 D
D: Wuer Shana
S: Wen Xiaoyu
1960s. A young professor sent to Mongolia during the Cultural Revolution falls in love over the objections of her friends. *Festival de films, 13th: 74. 1991.*
Other titles: La Saison des amours

253. ***Nü bing yuan wu qu / Woman Soldier's Song*** 1986 D
D: Dong Kena
S: Jiang Sheng
C: Zhang Wenmin
A: Wang Liyun, Fu Yiwei, Wu Lijie
Two soldiers meet on a train and reminisce about their early army days. They remember two other friends, one who died in battle. *Chinese Filmography.*

254. ***Nü er jing / A Bible for Daughters*** 1986
D: Bao Qicheng
A: Yan Xiaopin, Zhang Min, Zhang Xiaolin, Zhen Shuzhi
"A mother worries about her three daughters' prospects for marriage." *IMDb.*

255. ***Nü er lou / Army Nurse*** 1986 D
D: Hu Mei, Li Xiaojun
S: Kang Liwen, Ding Xiaoqi
C: He Qin
A: Xu Ye
1960s, Cultural Revolution. A woman rises to a high position as a nurse because of her imposed military service, but she never marries. *Encyclopedia of Chinese.*

256. ***Nü huo fuo / Woman Living Buddha*** 1986
D: Li Wei
S: Qin Wenju
C: Yan Junsheng
Tibet, 1958–1959. Living Buddha is talked into going to India with the independence movement but decides against joining and returns to China. *Chinese Filmography.*

257. ***Nü qiu da dui / Women's Group*** 1986 D
D: Wuer Shana
The story of a female warden and the charges in her all-female wing. *IMDb.*

258. ***Nü ren de gu shi / Story of Women*** 1986 DS
D: Peng Xiaolian
S: Mao Xiao
C: Liu Lihua
P: He Yijie
A: Zhang Wenrong, Zhang Min, Song Rahui
Three peasant women go to the city to sell yarn they have made and discover not just a commercial outlet but a whole different way of life. *Women through the Lens: 257.*
Other titles: San ge nü: ren / Women's Story

259. ***Hong gao liang / Red Sorghum*** 1987
D: Zhang Yimou
S: Chen Jianyu, Zhu Wei, Mo Yan
C: Gu Changwei
A: Gong Li, Wen Jiang
Sold by her parents to a leper to be his wife, a woman, along with her secret lover, takes over the man's winery after his death.
Awards: Berlin International Film Festival, Golden Bear, 1988; Golden Rooster Awards, Best Film, 1988

260. ***Huang yuan / Snowy Wilderness*** 1987 D
D: Bao Zhifang
S: Xu Yali
C: Lou Chen Sheng
A: Xu Shon Zi, Lu Xiao He
Manchuria. A fisherwoman lives alone with her child and sells her catch at the market. Periodically, a man on a horse stops by, but she greets him in stony silence. One day she makes a surprising decision about the future of her village. *Festival de films, 11th: 20. 1989.*
Other titles: Desert Blanc

261. ***Ren, gui, qing / Woman, Demon, Human*** 1987 DS
D: Huang Shuqing
S: Huang Shuqing, Li Ziyu
C: Zia Lixing

A: Pei Yan Lin, Xu Shouli

Biography of Qui Yun, a Hebei Banzi opera star. After her mother abandoned the family, she grew up with her father in a traveling theater troupe, and he introduced her to the important role of the legendary demon slayer, Zhong Kui. Normally reserved for male actors, the role made her famous. *Festival de films, 11th: 21. 1989.*

Other titles: L'Actrice et son fantôme

Awards: Golden Rooster Awards, Best Screenplay, 1988; Rio de Janeiro International Film Festival, Best Picture, 1988

262. Shan lin zhong tou yi ge nü ren / First Woman in the Forests   1987 D

D: Wang Junzheng

S: Qiao Xuezhu

C: Zhang Zhong Ping

A: Jiali Ding

A drama student researches the life of an old man she meets in the forest: In the 1940s he came to the isolated woods and fell in love with a prostitute who is now very ill, and of whom the student reminds him. *Festival de films, 13th: 16. 1991.*

Other titles: La Premiere femme de la forêt

263. Shei shi di san zhe / Who Is the Third Party?   1987 D

D: Dong Kena

S: Yao Yun

A: Li Kechun, Zhang Jie, Li Rong

An extramarital affair between a student and her professor; the film focuses on the professor's wife. *Women through the Lens.*

264. Wu ye liang dian / Two A.M.   1987 D

D: Bao Zhifang

S: Hu Huiying

C: Zhou Zhiqianq

A: Yau Xiaoping, Zhung Min

A lawyer investigates a divorce petition and finds a haunted house with a mother (who filed for divorce) and a daughter who have strange relations to two husbands/fathers. *Chinese Filmography.*

265. Xiang nü xiao xiao / Girl from Hunan   1987 D

D: Xie Fei, Wu Lan

C: Fu Jing Sheng

A: Na Renhua

At the turn of the century, a twelve-year-old village girl is married off to a toddler, then falls in love with someone her own age and becomes pregnant. *FII.*

Other titles: Married to a Child

266. Chun tao / A Woman for Two   1988

D: Ling Zifeng

S: Han Lanfang

C: Liang Ziyong

A: Liu Xiaoqing, Wen Jiang

A couple is attacked by bandits and separated. The woman goes on, supporting herself as a garbage collector and living with another man, but takes in the husband when he reappears as a legless beggar. *FII.*

Awards: 100 Flowers Awards, Best Picture, Best Actress, 1989

267. Huang tu po de po yi / The Women of Yellow Earth   1988 D

D: Dong Kena

S: Ma Feng, Sun Qian

C: Yan Junsheng

A: Ketchun Lu

In a village where men have left to get jobs elsewhere, one woman organizes the other women to till land and harvest grain. *Chinese Filmography.*

268. Jia zhuang mei gan jue / Shanghai Women   1988 DS

D: Peng Xiaolian

S: Peng Xiaolian

C: Lin Jong

P: Zhu Yongde

A: Lu Liping, Zheng Zhenyao

Shanghai. A teacher and her daughter move in with her mother when she discovers her husband is unfaithful. *FII.*

269. Nü da xue shena su she / Girl Student Dormitory   1988

D: Shi Shujin

S: Yu Shan

C: Zhao Junhong

A: Li Xia, Jiang Yiping, Luo Yan, Xu Ya, Chong Honginei

Five university students from different backgrounds share a dormitory and conflict at first, but then cooperate to help one with financial difficulties. *Chinese Filmography.*

270. Shui shi disanzhe / Who Is the Third Party?   1988 D

D: Dong Kena

A loveless marriage, providing the grounds for a study of the "threat an extramarital affair poses to society in general." *Encyclopedia of Chinese: 231.*

271. *Tai yang yu / Sun and Rain* 1988
D: Zhang Zeming
S: Liu Xihong, Zhang Zeming
C: Zheng Kangzhen
A: Yan Xiaopin, Sun Chun
A troubled young woman searches for models and encounters several women: a mother devoted to her son; a woman who goes from lover to lover, then marries a rich patron; a student energetically seeking to satisfy her desires; and a taxi driver resigned to never finding happiness. *Festival de films, 15th: 91. 1993.*
Other titles: *Sunshine and Showers*

272. *An Li Xiao / Miss An Li* 1989
D: Qin Zhiyu
S: Qin Zhiyu, Zhang Xian
C: Yuan Wenyao
A: Zhang Yanli
The manager of a large business is accused of profiteering; she fights back against the investigator (a former lover), as well as her boss, and exonerates herself. *Chinese Filmography.*

273. *Feng kang de dai jia / Obsession* 1989 DS
D: Zhou Xiaowen
S: Zhou Xiaowen, Lu Wei
C: Wang Xinsheng
A: Wu Yujuan, Li Jing
Two sisters are abandoned by their parents, and the younger girl is raped. The older one tracks the criminal and seeks revenge with the help of a retired policeman. The focus is on the guilt of the older sister, who deep down believes she is the one who should have been raped, and the strictures both girls experience in their female bodies. *Festival de films, 15th: 89, 91. 1993.*
Other titles: *Le Prix de la folie*

274. *Jin se de zhi / Golden Fingernails* 1989 D
D: Bao Zhifang
S: Zhang Chang Guang
C: Shan Liangio
P: Shen Ru-mei
A: Fu Yiwei, Wan Hui, Zhang Min, Wu Jing, Guo Yuan
Five women search for domestic happiness in a big city: Two are in love with married men; one believes she is not beautiful enough to be loved; one discovers her husband is having an affair. *Festival de films, 13th: 74. 1991.*

275. *Nü shen tan bao gaiding / Woman Detective* 1989
D: Xu Qingdong
S: Fu Xuwen
C: Zhou Jixun

A: Gong Youchun, Shen Junyi
A new detective sees less of her policeman boyfriend. She finds out why when her first murder victim turns out to be his sister, whom he had killed for consorting with mobsters. Mystery. *Chinese Filmography.*

276. *Nü zi bie dong dui / Woman Commando* 1989
D: Jin Zuoxin
S: Si Huang, Guang Yu
C: Wang Lianpin
A: He Qing, Zhy Yaying, Zhang Yukai
1940s. Eight young military recruits are tricked into a suicide mission to assassinate Japanese officers during the occupation. Two survive and defect to join the communist forces in the north. *Chinese Filmography.*

277. *Zui hou de gui zu / The Last Aristocrats* 1989
D: Xie Jin
S: Yong Bai Xin
A: Hong Pan, Lisa Lu, Linda Wang
1948. Wealthy young girls from Shanghai go to college in postwar United States. When one of them hears her parents have suddenly died, she disappears, worrying her friends. She returns severely depressed, and they help her. *FII.*

278. *Chu jia nü / The Girls to Be Married* 1990
D: Wang Jin
S: He Mengtan, Ye Weilin
C: Zhao Xiaoshi
A: Shen Rong, Tao Huiming, Ju Xue
In a remote mountain village, five girls frequent a "visiting garden," where they dream of escape from their hard lives and arranged marriages. Hearing there is a "visiting garden" in heaven for girls who remain virgins, they commit suicide together. *Once upon a time.*
Awards: Moscow International Film Festival, Special Prize, 1990

279. *Gui ge qing yuan / A Woman Pianist's Story* 1990 D
D: Zhang Huanqin
C: J. C. Calie
A: Qin Yi
A pianist is forced to marry instead of studying music in Paris as she desires. She remains resentful even though the marriage is a success. *Chinese Filmography.*

280. *Ju Dou* 1990
D: Zhang Yimou

S: Liu Heng
C: Lun Yang
P: Hu Jian
A: Gong Li, Li Baotian
A Chinese village, 1920s. An abused wife has an affair with her husband's nephew, then has a child, which belongs to her husband.
Awards: Valladolid International Film Festival, Golden Spike, 1990; Academy Awards, nomination for Best Foreign Language Film, 1991

281. *Mama*   1990 S
D: Zhang Yuan
S: Qin Yan
C: Zhang Jian
A: Qin Yan
A young mother raises alone her epileptic and mentally disabled son. Torn between hope of a cure and ending his suffering, she is shocked by the lack of understanding from her friends and family. Includes documentary-like encounters with psychiatric institutions and other mothers of disabled children. *Festival de films, 15th: 91. 1993.*

282. *Shi qu de meng / The Lost Dream* 1990 D
D: Dong Kena
A: Li Kechun
A peasant woman leaves her husband and goes to the city so that her son can have a good education; one day she accidentally kills the boy in anger. *Chinese Filmography.*

283. *O! Xi ang xue / Sweet Snow*   1990 D
D: Wang Haowei
S: Tie Ning
C: Li Chengsheng
A: Xue Bai
A young woman and her friends, excited to have the railroad arrive in their village, plan to go to Beijing; they are particularly interested in obtaining some special plastic pens. *Festival de films, 13th: 74. 1991.*

284. *Da hong deng long gao gao gua / Raise the Red Lantern*   1991
D: Zhang Yimou
S: Ni Zhen; based on the novel by Su Tong
C: Fey Zhao
P: Chiu Fu-sheng
A: Gong Li
1920s. A young woman, forced to marry a lord, finds herself in competition with the established wives over whom he will spend the night with; jealousy and treachery characterize the women's relations.

Awards: David di Donatello Awards, Best Foreign Film, 1992; BAFTA Awards, Best Film not in English, 1993

285. *Du shen nü ren / A Single Woman*   1991
D: Qin Zhiyu
S: Zhang Xian, Qin Zhiyu
C: Ru Shuiren
A: Pan Hong
The divorced head of a fashion company struggles with her workers, her young son, and her lovers. *Chinese Filmography.*

286. *Nü ren, taxi, nü ren / Woman, Taxi, Woman*
                                                         1991 D
D: Wang Junzheng
S: Qiao Xuezhu
A: Jiali Ding, Pan Hong
A taxi driver regularly chauffeurs a professor and observes her very different life, "then offers friendship and encouragement." *Women through the Lens.*

287. *Nü xing shi jie / Women's World*   1991 D
D: Dong Kena
A: Hun Bai, Yi Ding, Ting Wu
The lives of three middle-aged women, friends from school days: a reporter with *Consumer Times*, a women's rights bureaucrat, and a violinist in an orchestra. The reporter and her husband are too busy to have a relationship, and the activist demands a lot from her husband, who is secretly still in love with their old friend, the violinist. *UW Film. Accessed 2005, June 10.*

288. *Fu chu de nü ren / Women Avengers* 1992
D: Wang Wei
S: Xiao Jian
C: Zhen Kang-zhen
A: Yuan Xingzhe, Mao Haitong
1945. Japanese officers murder some local men. The widows of the murdered men organize a militia, along with other women who are rape victims, and eventually win a battle against the troops and kill the officers. *Chinese Filmography.*

289. *Hua hun / The Soul of a Painter*
                                                         1992 DS
D: Huang Shuqing
S: Huang Shuqing, Liu Meng, Min Anqi
P: Lu Le
A: Gong Li
The story of painter Pan Yuliang, who won fame painting nudes and an academic post teaching art. She conflicted with authorities over her

subject matter and past as a prostitute and was eventually exiled to Paris, where she died in 1977. *Encyclopedia of Chinese.*

Other titles: The Painter

290. *Nü huang ling xia de feng liu niang men*
                                                              1992 D
D: Dong Kena
A: Li Lan, Lu Xiaohe, Xia Yonghua

When a man takes three mistresses as a sign of financial success, his wife leaves him and becomes successful on her own. "Masterpiece of gender equality." *IMDb.*

291. *Qiu Ju da guansi / Story of Qiu Ju*   1992
D: Zhang Yimou
S: Chen Yuan Bin, Liu Heng
C: Chi Xiaoning
P: Feng Yiting
A: Gong Li

A pregnant peasant woman demands an apology for her husband's injury at the hands of the local chief. She pursues her grievance relentlessly through the courts, requiring several arduous trips to the city, but the people of the village are insistent that her passion for the truth is out of place.

Awards: Venice Film Festival, Golden Lion, Best Actress, 1992; Golden Rooster Awards, Best Film, Best Actress, 1993

292. *Shen jing qi tou / The Miraculous Policemen and the Magical Thief*   1992 D
D: Shi Xiaohua
S: Lu Shoujun
C: Lu Junfu

A successful big-city thief turns out to be a woman; she turns herself in when her daughter finds out. *Chinese Filmography.*

293. *Sun on the Roof of the World*   1992 D
D: Wang Ping, Xie Fei
S: Huang Shiying
C: Lui Baogui
A: Liang Guoqing

Beijing. A woman tells her mate that she must live in the United States, but he declines to leave. On a trip to Tibet where he is working, she becomes pregnant and leaves for America, then makes plans for him to join her. *FII.*

294. *Xuese qing chen / Bloody Morning*
                                                              1992 DS
D: Li Shaohong
S: Li Shaohong, Mao Xiao
C: Zeng Nianping

A: Kong Lin

Brothers kill a teacher for having an affair with their sister, who was discovered not to be a virgin on her wedding night. An investigation reveals that everyone knew of the plan to murder the teacher except the victim. *FII.*

Awards: Nantes Three Continents Festival, Golden Montgolfiere, 1992

295. *Di yi you huo / First Attraction*   1993 D
D: Bao Zhifang
S: Wang Tianyun
C: Ying Fukang
A: Xi Meijuan

A woman is left to raise her son alone after divorcing, and the law adds to her burden. *Chinese Filmography.*

296. *Hsiang hun nü / Women from the Lake of Scented Souls*   1993 DS
D: Xie Fei
S: Xie Fei
C: Pao Xiaoran
A: Siqin Gaowa

A matriarch creates a thriving business in sesame oil while her husband drinks and abuses her. She has had a long-term love affair and wonders why she has so indulged the men in her life, including arranging a marriage for her deranged and violent son by bribing the chosen girl's lover to leave town.

Other titles: Woman Sesame Oil Maker

Awards: Berlin International Film Festival, Golden Bear, 1992

297. *Huan nü / Illusive Girl*   1993
D: Shao Qi
S: Zhao Heqi
C: Zhao Yimin
A: Lan Lau, Ling Zonqying

"Middle aged researcher comes to China to work" and comes under the protection of a young girl, who believes the woman is her mother. Fantasy. *Chinese Filmography.*

298. *Mung sing si fan / Mary from Beijing*
                                                              1993 DS
D: Sylvia Chang
S: Sylvia Chang
C: Christopher Doyle
A: Gong Li, Wilson Lam

A Chinese woman lives in Hong Kong with a wealthy jeweler but lacks a Hong Kong identity card herself; she then gets involved with another man. *Variety: 35. 1993, Nov. 22.*

Other titles: Awakening

299. *Ao fei si xiao* / *Office Girls*   1994 D
D: Bao Zhifang
S: Yang Xinji, Shen Ningyue
C: Zhao Junhong
A: Ning Jing, Zhou Xiaoli, Li Hong
Three young Shanghai businesswomen struggle with careers and men. *Chinese Filmography*.

300. *Du shi sha ke si feng* / *Metropolitan Saxophone*   1994 D
D: Shi Xiaohua, Bao Qicheng
S: He Guopu
C: Liu Lihua
A: Xia Lixin, Tong Fan
The director of a Japanese clothing company expands into China and hires a Chinese design assistant, making her Japanese assistant unhappy. *Chinese Filmography*.

301. *Ermo*   1994 D
D: Zhou Xiaowen
S: Lang Yun
C: Lu Gengxin
P: Chen Kunming
A: Alia
A woman supports her son and husband by making and selling noodles on the street. Vexed by her son's desire to watch the neighbor's television, she is determined to purchase one herself. The neighbor's husband drives her to the city and then sets her up in a restaurant, subsidizing her wages so he can pursue his passion for her. When she finds out about the arrangement, she angrily rejects him and manages to purchase the television on her own.
Awards: Locarno International Film Festival, Ecumenical Jury Prize, 1994

302. *Hong fen* / *Blush*   1994 DS
D: Li Shaohong
S: Li Shaohong, Ni Zhen; based on the novel by Su Tong
C: Zeng Nianping
A: Wang Ji, He Saifei
Suzho, 1950s. Two friends, raised as prostitutes, must adjust to the new communist ruling that makes their trade illegal, as both are sent to be workers. One escapes to seek haven with a rich boyfriend, but his mother casts her out and she becomes a Buddhist nun, only to be cast out again because of her pregnancy. Meanwhile, her fully adjusted friend takes away her lover.

303. *Nü ren hua* / *Women Flowers*   1994
D: Wang Jin

S: Wang Jin; based on *Story of Adopted Sisters* by Su Fanggui
A: Pu Chaoying, Xie Ling, Liu Wei, Li Tuan
Pearl River delta, early twentieth century. A group of women remain unmarried and adopt young girls for the purpose of selling them to wealthy men as concubines. This leads to insanity and suicides, but one girl finds freedom. *Chinese Filmography*.
Awards: Karlovy Vary International Film Festival, nomination for Crystal Globe, 1994

304. *Yong Chun* / *Wing Chun*   1994 S
D: Yuen Woo-ping
S: Elsa Tang
C: Lee Pin Bing
A: Michelle Yeoh
Wing Chun, a local superwoman, deglamorizes herself and remains unrecognized by her childhood boyfriend, who thinks her current mask as "Soy Queen" is really just an old friend; soon they band together to vanquish the bad guys with their martial arts skills. Action.

305. *Monkey Kid*   1995 DS
D: Wang Xiaoyan
S: Wang Xiaoyan
C: Li Xiong
P: Wang Wei-wei
A: Fang Shu, Di Fu
1960s Cultural Revolution. A nine-year-old heads up her family under the long-distance direction of her doctor mother who works in the countryside; the mother returns home just often enough to keep her daughter in line.
Other titles: Le Môme Singe
Awards: Ft. Lauderdale International Film Festival, President Award, 1995; Aubervilliers International Children's Film Festival, Grand Prize, 1996

306. *Nü er gu* / *Women's Valley*   1995
D: Xie Jin
S: Zhou Jianping
C: Shen Miaorong
A: Li Cuiyan, Ma Lingyan
The warden in a women's prison tries to help several prisoners who want to reform and gain normal lives on the outside, including a sex offender, a woman who confessed to her husband's crimes, and a woman who stole medicine for her ill husband. *Chinese Filmography*.

307. *Nü er hong* / *Maiden Rose*   1995
D: Xie Yang
A: Josephine Koo, Qui Ah-lu

Follows a woman from birth in 1920s Shaoxing in Huadiao, through the birth of her daughter and the loss of her lover in the Civil War. Years later, she is politically castigated for receiving a letter from the lover, now in Taiwan, but by the 1990s, she and her daughter are able to live more freely. *Variety: 37. 1995, July 31.*
Awards: Karlovy Vary International Film Festival, Best Actress (Qui), 1995

308. *Yang Kaihui* 1995
D: Qin Zhiyu
S: Zhang Xuan
A: Yuan Chang
The story of the first wife of Mao Zedong, who refused to denounce Mao and was executed in 1930. *Chinese Filmography.*

309. *Tai yang you er / The Sun Has Ears* 1996 P
D: Yim Ho
S: Yi Ling
C: Zhao Fei
P: Zhang Yu
A: Zhang Yu
1920s. Impoverished peasants forage for food, and one of the women draws the attention of a warlord when she collapses from hunger; her husband sees an opportunity and "loans" her to the warlord, but the ploy backfires as she prefers the man to her husband. *Variety: 47. 1996, Mar. 11.*
Awards: Berlin International Film Festival, Best Director, FIPRESCI, 1996

310. *Xi xia lu tiao tiao / The Journey to the Western Zia Empire* 1997
D: Lu Wei
S: Lu Wei
C: Chang Yuhong
P: Liu Jinxi
A: Badema
China, eleventh century. The empire routinely kidnaps boys for the army, but a stubborn peasant woman pursues the kidnappers to get back her newborn. *Village Voice: 122. 2003, Mar. 5.*

311. *Hong niang / The Matchmaker* 1998
D: Huang Jianzhong
S: based on the play *Romance of the Western Chamber* by Wang Shifu
A: Liu Xin, Su Youpeng
Tang Dynasty, 619–907. A servant woman uses all her power to get the man whom her shy mistress desires. *Asian Film. Accessed: 2005 Feb. 8.*

312. *Nan fu nü zhu ren / Male Director in the Women's Department* 1998
D: Zhang Hui
A woman refuses to take responsibility for the women's department of her village and sends her husband instead to attend the Northeast gathering for women's issues; he brags of their progress. Comedy. *Chinese Filmography.*

313. *Yao wang Chalila / Longing for Chalila* 1998
D: Wang Xiaolie
P: Li Kangsheng
A: Li Lin
After a ten-year separation from her husband, a woman returns to Tibet to get a divorce, but she becomes friends with a PLA soldier on the way and decides to reunite with her husband. *Asian Film. Accessed 2005, July 15.*

314. *Guo nian hui jia / Seventeen Years* 1999
D: Zhang Yuan
S: Nig Dai, Yu Hua
C: Zhang Xigui
P: Marco Muller
A: Lin Liu
A woman leaves prison after serving seventeen years for murdering her stepsister, then tries to reunite with her parents. *NYT: 36. 1999, Dec. 26.*
Awards: Gijón International Film Festival, Best Director, 1999; Singapore International Film Festival, Best Asian Actress, 2000; Fajr Film Festival, Best Screenplay, 2001

315. *Tian yu / Xiu Xiu: The Sent Down Girl* 1999 DSP
D: Joan Chen
S: Joan Chen
C: Lu Yue
P: Alice Chan, Joan Chen
A: Lu Lu, Lopsang
1960s Cultural Revolution. A teenager is taken from her home in Chengdu to an isolated plains near Tibet to learn horse herding from a kind impotent man. Intent on getting out, she makes her body available to functionaries passing by in hopes one of them will help get her sent back home.
Awards: Golden Horse Film Festival, Best Picture, Best Actress, 1998; Paris Film Festival, Best Actress, Special Jury Prize, 1999

316. *Jin nian xia tian / Fish and Elephant* 2001
D: Li Yu
C: Fei Xiaoping
P: Cheng Yong

A: Pan Yi, Shi Tou

A zoo worker and store owner live together, though one is being pressured by her mother to marry. An ex-girlfriend appears, provoking soul searching that reveals one of the women is a child-abuse victim. *Film Criticism, vol. 28, no. 3: 21–36. 2004, Spr.*

Awards: Venice Film Festival, Elvira Notari Prize, 2001; Berlin International Film Festival, Netpac Award, 2002

317. *Ku qi de nü ren / Crying Women*　　2002
D: Liu Bingjian
S: Liu Bingjian, Deng Je
C: Xu Wei
A: Qin Liao

"Small town woman is forced to adopt an abandoned girl and to earn her living as a professional mourner." *Festival des 3.*

318. *This Side of Heaven*　　2002 DS
D: Jie Chen
S: Yan Geling, Jie Chen
C: Chi Xiaoning
P: Tan Xiangiang
A: Wu Jiaojiao

On her way to get a factory job in the city, a young girl is kidnapped, raped, and sold to an old man and his disabled son to work on their farm. She tries to flee but is caught. Pregnant, she tries to abort, but the authorities will not allow it. *Festival de films, 25th: 29. 2003.*

319. *Ho yuk / Let's Love Hong Kong*　　2003 DS
D: Yau Ching
S: Yau Ching
C: Chen Hung-yu
A: Wong Chung-ching, Erica Lam

"Three women chase, seduce, resist and fantasize about each other. A Hong Kong that is as fake as real provides the perfect setting for their games, secrets, screams and tears." *Festival de films, 27th: 71. 2005.*

320. *Xi shi yan / Eyes of Beauty*　　2003
D: Guan Hu
S: Guan Hu, Guangron Zhou
C: Wu Di
P: Jin Zhonqiang, Zhang Zhenhua
A: Ma Yili, Huang Yiqing, Yang Qianqian

Zhuji. Stories of three women. A forty-year-old opera star is famous for singing the role of Xi Shi, a legendary beauty who helped her lover defeat an enemy king; she has sacrificed her marriage to her profession but is overshadowed by a younger rival. In the mountains, a daughter serves her family, hoping that her boyfriend will take her to the city. A thirty-year-old teacher refuses marriage to a party functionary and instead takes up with a student. *Variety: 42. 2003, Jan. 13.*

Awards: Hawaii International Film Festival, Netpac Award, 2002

321. *Jingzhe / The Story of Ermei*　　2004
D: Wang Quan'an
S: Wang Quan'an
C: Lutz Reitemeier
P: Wang Quan'an, Yan Yijun
A: Yu Nan

A young woman refuses a marriage, which will bring money to her family, and moves to another town to live with a girlfriend. She becomes frustrated by a lover who refuses to commit to her, then gives up and returns to the arranged marriage. *FII.*

Awards: Paris Film Festival, Best Actress, 2004

322. *Wu die / Butterfly*　　2004 DS
D: Yan Yan Mak
S: Yan Yan Mak, Chen Xue
C: Charlie Lam
A: Josie Ho, Tian Yuan

A thirty-year-old high school teacher leads a conventional married life until one day she meets a young woman to whom she is attracted and decides to live her life according to her desires. *Festival de films, 27th: 23. 2005.*

Awards: Hong Kong Film Awards, Best New Artist (Tian), 2005

COLOMBIA

323. *María Cano*　　1990 DS
D: Camila Loboguerrero
S: Felipe Aljure, Luis Gonzalez, Camila Loboguerrero
C: Carlos Sanchez
P: Roy Marin
A: María Eugenia Dávila

Biography of María Cano, who was a poet in the first half of the century and who toured Colombia as a socialist organizer along with her union-leader lover. *South American Cinema: 263.*

Awards: San Antonio Film Festival, Best Film, 1991

CROATIA

324. *Vrijeme za ... / The Time For ...*　　1993 DS
D: Oja Kodar
S: Oja Kodar

C: Gary Graver
P: Zdravko Mihalic
A: Andrea Bakovic

A woman and her teenage son escape a Serb attack that decimates their village, and leave for the city as refugees. Though she puts him on a train to Germany so he will be safe, he jumps off and goes to join the Croat army. Eventually forced to bury him, she drags his body back the many miles to their village for burial.

Other titles: Le Temps pour . . .

325. *Prepoznavanje / Recognition* 1996 DSP
D: Snjezane Tribuson
S: Maja Gluscevic
C: Goran Mecava
P: Ankica Juric-Tilic
A: Natasa Dorcic

Zagreb. One day in a cafeteria, a woman accidentally meets the man who tortured and raped her during the war; he recognizes her and awaits orders to assassinate her. When she complains to the police, they believe she is merely experiencing psychological trauma. Thriller. *Festival de films, 19th: 20. 1997.*

326. *Tri muskarca Melite Zganger / The Three Men of Melita Zganjer* 1996 DS
D: Snjezane Tribuson
S: Snjezane Tribuson
C: Goran Mecava
P: Sanja Vejnovic, Irina Damic
A: Mirjana Rogina

A café owner seeks the ideal love she observes on her "favorite Brazilian telenovela." *Variety. 2000, Mar. 13.*

327. *Blagajnica hoce ici na more / The Cashier Wants to Go to the Seaside* 2000 P
D: Dalibor Matanic
S: Dalibor Matanic
C: Branko Linta
P: Ankica Juric-Tilic
A: Dora Polic

Comic tale of a clerk in a small-town store who desires to take her sick daughter to the sea, even though her boss objects. *NYT: E18. 2001, Mar. 23.*

CUBA

328. *Manuela* 1966
D: Humberto Solás
S: Humberto Solás
C: Jorge Herrera

P: Miguel Mendoza
A: Adela Legrá

"The daily life of Cuban partisans including a young girl who dies on maneuvers." *FII.*

329. *Lucía* 1969
D: Humberto Solás
S: Julio García Espinosa, Nelson Rodríguez, Humberto Solás
C: Jorge Herrera
A: Adela Legrá, Eslinda Núñez, Raquel Revuelta

Three stories of women named Lucía. A nineteenth-century upper-class woman with a brother fighting against the colonial government is fooled by a would-be lover into revealing where the rebels are hiding. In the 1930s, a middle-class woman, embarrassed by her chattering mother, falls in love with a socialist activist and becomes part of a cell of revolutionaries. She supports him by working in a factory, but when the government falls and the rebels assume the posture of the powerful, her husband is killed as a counterrevolutionary. In the 1960s, a young woman marries a backward man who resists the counsel of the socialist regime and insists on locking his wife in the house. A literacy teacher is attached to their home and teaches her she should not be treated like a "slave."

Awards: Moscow International Film Festival, Golden Prize, 1969

330. *Los Días del agua / Days of Water* 1971
D: Manuel Octavio Gómez
A: Idalia Anreus

A village woman with special powers becomes too powerful and is made a scapegoat. *Film Society. 1999, Feb.*

331. *De cierta manera / One Way or Another* 1974 DS
D: Sara Gómez Yera
S: Sara Gómez Yera, Tomas Gutiérrez Alea, Julio García Espinosa
C: Luis Garcia
A: Yolanda Cuellar, Mario Balsameda

Havana. A teacher in a slum confronts traditionally dominant machismo, while everyone adjusts to the new Castro order; includes documentary footage of existing conditions and real people. *Films de femmes, 12th: 79. 1990.*

332. *Aquella larga noche / That Long Night* 1979
D: Enrique Pineda Barnet
S: Antonio Benitez Rojo, Constante Diego, Tomas Gutiérrez Alea

A: Raquel Revuelta, María Eugenia Garcia
Cuban revolution. Based on a true incident about two women from Castro's guerrilla army who were captured and tortured by a commander from Batista's army. *Cuban Filmography.*

333. *Retrato de Teresa / Portrait of Teresa* 1979
D: Pastor Vega
S: Ambrosio Fornet, Pastor Vega
C: Livio Delgado
P: Evelio Delgado
A: Daisy Granados
A textile worker and mother works as a cultural secretary in the evenings; in the process of finding herself, she alienates her traditional husband, who has a wandering eye. *Guide to Latin: 129.*
Awards: Moscow International Film Festival, Best Actress, 1979

334. *Cecilia* 1982
D: Humberto Solás
S: Nelson Rodríguez, Humberto Solás; based on the novel by Cirilo Villaverde
C: Livio Delgado
P: Humberto Hernández
A: Daisy Granados
Cuba, 1800s. Slavery still exists on the plantations, and news of the Haitian revolt spreads fear among white people. A woman uses Santería to seduce the son of a rich colonialist family. *Variety. 1982, June 2.*
Awards: Cannes Film Festival, nomination for Golden Palm, 1982

335. *Amada* 1983
D: Humberto Solás, Nelson Rodríguez
S: Humberto Solás, Nelson Rodríguez
C: Livio Delgado
A: Eslinda Núñez
During World War I, an aristocratic woman, whose family has been dependent on the fading slave economy, marries a tyrant who is after her money, then falls in love with an anarchist who challenges her traditional values. *Guide to Latin: 96.*

336. *Hasta cierto punto / Up to a Certain Point* 1983
D: Tomas Gutiérrez Alea
S: Tomas Gutiérrez Alea, Sarafin Qiñones
C: Mario Garcia Joya
P: Humberto Hernández
A: Mirta Ibarra, Óscar Álvarez
A leftist married man, making a film on machismo, meets a woman dockworker who is a single mother—the prototype for his fictional model worker and liberated woman—and falls in love with her. He lies to both her and his wife, and the worker is savvy enough to tell him first to go away until he makes up his mind, and then, finally, to just go away.

337. *Se permuta / House for Swap* 1984
D: Juan Carlos Tabío
S: Juan Carlos Tabío
C: Julio Valdes
A: Rosita Fornés
A mother wheels and deals apartments during a housing shortage in order to increase her daughter's chances of marrying well. *Guide to Latin: 130.*
Awards: Havana Film Festival, Grand Coral, 1984

338. *Lejania / Parting of the Ways* 1985
D: Jesús Diaz
S: Jesús Diaz
C: Mario Garcia Joya
P: Humberto Hernández
A: Monica Guffanti, Rogelio Blain
After ten years of exile in the United States, a mother returns to Cuba with presents for her son and a materialist American outlook. *Film Society. 1999, Feb.*

339. *Demasiado miedo a la vida o Plaff / Plaff! Or Too Afraid of Life* 1988
D: Juan Carlos Tabío
C: Julio Valdes
A: Daisy Granados
A fearful widow is saved by Santería from having eggs thrown at her; the filmmakers' problems are intertwined with the narrative. Comedy. *Guide to Latin: 126.*

340. *Papeles secundarios / Supporting Roles* 1988
D: Orlando Rojas
A: Rosita Fornés, Maria Isabel, Louisa Pérez Nieto
Havana. A theater troupe, directed by an older actress, stages a classic play under contemporary socialist conditions. *Guide to Latin: 125.*
Awards: Istanbul International Film Festival, Special Jury Prize, 1991 (Nieto)

341. *La Bella del Alhambra / The Beauty of the Alhambra* 1989
D: Enrique Pineda Barnet
S: Enrique Pineda Barnet, Miguel Barnet
A: Verónica Lynn
Havana. 1920s–1930s. A young woman becomes a star in a famous men's club. *Guide to Latin: 98.*

342. *Vals de la Habana Vieja* / *Old Havana Waltz* 1989
D: Luis Felipe Bernaza
S: Luis Felipe Bernaza
C: Jorge Haydu
A: Ana Viña
A mother attempts to celebrate her daughter's fifteenth birthday with a large party, over the objections of her husband. *Guide to Latin: 130.*

343. *Alicia en el pueblo de Maravillas* / *Alice in Wondertown* 1990
D: Daniel Díaz Torres
C: Raúl Perez Ureta
P: Humberto Hernández
A: Thaïs Valdes
A young woman is trapped in a small town. *Film Society. 1999, Feb.*

344. *Mujer transparente* / *Transparent Woman* 1990 D
D: Hector Veitia, Mario Crespo, Ana Rodriguez, Mayra Segura, Mayra Vilasis
C: Julio Valdes
A: Isabel Moreno, Verónica Lynn, Leonor Arocha, Mirtha Núñez, Ibarra Rolando
Five vignettes of women: a wife and mother of two teenagers; an older woman struggling with desire; a wife having an affair; an art student; and a divorcée with two failed marriages and a friend who has fled Cuba. *Guide to Latin: 121.*

345. *Nada mas* / *Nothing* 2001 P
D: Juan Carlos Cremata Malberti
S: Juan Carlos Cremata Malberti
C: Raul Rodriguez
P: Sarah Halioua, Theirry Forte
A: Thaïs Valdes, Paula Ali
A postal worker secretly writes letters on behalf of others. *MOMA Film. 2003, Nov.*
Awards: Cartagena Film Festival, Best Supporting Actress (Ali), 2003; Havana Film Festival, Best First Work, 2003

CZECH REPUBLIC

346. *Modré z neba* / *Blue Heaven* 1997 DS
D: Eva Borusovicová
S: Jana Skorepová
C: Dodo Simonic
P: Rudolf Biermann
A: Slávká Halcáková, Emilia Kabátová, Zita Kabátová
A mother, daughter, and grandmother live in a large old house in the countryside, where the mother

makes pottery and the others enjoy erotic attachments to visitors.

347. *Pasti, pasti, pastiky* / *Traps* 1998 DS
D: Věra Chytilová
S: Věra Chytilová, Eva Kacíková
C: Stepan Kucera
A: Zusana Stivínová, Miroslav Donutil
A woman in need of gas for her car is raped by two men from whom she accepts a ride; she maneuvers them back to her home and castrates them. The two men must now hide the shame of their condition, and they also seek revenge. *Festival de films, 21st: 9. 1999.*
Awards: Venice Film Festival, Elvira Notari Prize, 1998

348. *Výlet* 2002 DS
D: Alice Nellis
S: Alice Nellis
C: Ramunas Greicius
A: Iva Janzurova, Theodora Remundova
A grandmother commands her family to help her return to their village in Slovakia to distribute her husband's ashes. The time for reflection allows them all to grow. *Festival de films, 25th: 30. 2003.*
Awards: Czech Critics Awards, Best Film, 2003; Paris Film Festival, Grand Prix, 2003

CZECHOSLOVAKIA

349. *O něčem jiném* / *Something Different* 1963 DS
D: Věra Chytilová
S: Věra Chytilová
C: Jan Èuøik
A: Eva Bosáková, Věra Uzelacová
Abstracted, alternating stories of two women, one a successful gymnast, and the other a housewife with a husband and son, both vaguely dissatisfied but also working hard in search of "something different."

350. *Sedmikrásky* / *Daisies* 1966 DSP
D: Věra Chytilová
S: Věra Chytilová, Ester Krumbachová
C: Jaroslav Kuvera
P: Věra Chytilová
A: Jitka Cerhová, Ivana Karbanová
Two insolent girls have fun wreaking havoc and displaying their bodies in an op-art animated bedroom, between frolics with old men in elegant dining rooms. Trains and complicated train-track layouts are a prominent theme, alongside dumb-

waiters, industrial sites, and drowning pools. But their main activity is food fights, food orgies, and food violence, involving scissors, knives, ripping, and tearing.

351. *Konec srpna v Hotelu Ozon* / *The End of August at the Hotel Ozone*   1967
D: Jan Schmidt
S: Pavel Jurácek
C: Jirí Macák
P: Jan Klusák
A: Beta Ponicanová, Jitka Horejsi, Vanda Kalinová, Alena Lippertová
After a nuclear devastation, eight women search for men in hopes of building the world anew; they find only an old man who holds on to "a TV set, a gramophone, and the last fragment of a newspaper that came out the day before 'it' happened." *MOMA Film. 2004, Mar.–Apr.*

352. *Hra o jablko* / *The Apple Game*   1976 DS
D: Věra Chytilová
S: Věra Chytilová, Kristina Vlachová
C: Frantisek Vlail
A: Dagmar Bláhová, Jiri Menzel
A midwife in a maternity clinic becomes pregnant by one of the doctors, who is a philanderer; a bitter commentary on masculine power, with a "gay confidence in feminine force." *Festival de films, 9th: 55. 1987.*

353. *Tichá radost* / *Quiet Joy*   1985
D: Dusan Hanák
S: Ondrej Julaj
C: Victor Svoboda
A: Magda Vásáryová
Struggles of a woman in a loveless marriage. *Cesko-Slovenská Filmová. Accessed 2005, July 15.*

DENMARK

354. *Gertrud*   1964
D: Carl Dreyer
S: Carl Dreyer; based on the play by Hjalmar Söderberg
C: Henning Bendtsen
P: Jürgen Nielsen
A: Nina Pens Røde
A former opera singer prepares to leave her husband, a prominent minister, admitting she is in love with someone else. Her musician lover meets her in the park, where her philosophy becomes clear: "I am the sky, a cloud, a mouth looking for a mouth." Her first lover, a "national poet of love," taught her about the erotic

ecstasy of which "conventional people" know nothing, as it is opposed to "honor, fame and money."

355. *Kaere Irene* / *Dear Irene*   1971 S
D: Christian Braad Thomsen
S: Christian Braad Thomsen, Mette Knudsen
C: Dirk Bruel
P: Christian Braad Thomsen
A: Mette Knudsen
A woman trapped into marriage by pregnancy has a long-term affair with a man who is more of a pushover than her husband. *FII.*

356. *Ta' det som en mand, frue!* / *Take It Like a Man, Ma'am*   1975 DSCP
D: Elisabeth Rygård, Mette Knudsen, Li Vilstrup
S: Elisabeth Rygård, Mette Knudsen, Li Vilstrup
C: Katia Petersen
P: Annelise Hovmand, Trine Hedmann
A: Tove Maës
A middle-aged middle-class housewife dreams of a society of complete gender reversal. Fantasy. *FII.*
Awards: Berlin International Film Festival, Interfilm Award, 1975

357. *Veronicas svededug* / *Veronica's Veil*   1977 DSCP
D: Jytte Rex
S: Jytte Rex
C: Jytte Rex
P: Nina Crone
A: Helle Ryslinge
"Symbolically charged cinematic language explaining women's lives and dreams." *Danish Directors: 89.*

358. *Øbjeblikket* / *The Moment*   1980 DS
D: Astrid Henning-Jensen
S: Astrid Henning-Jensen
C: Lasse Björne
P: Just Betzer
A: Ann-Marie Max-Hansen
A rocky marriage is realigned by the strength of the wife's state of mind during her illness with cancer; after her death, she is "reincarnated as a flower." *FII.*
Awards: Lübeck Nordic Film Days, Audience Prize, 1981

359. *Belladonna*   1981 DS
D: Jytte Rex
S: Jytte Rex
C: Alexander Gruszynski
A: Ilse Rande
Interior monologue of a thirty-year-old mother and her relations with men and women; a com-

bination of dreams and "small bursts of rough reality." *Variety. 1981, Nov. 4.*

360. Sofie 1982 DS
D: Liv Ullmann
S: Henri Nathansen, Peter Poulsen, Liv Ullmann
C: Jörgen Persson
P: Lars Kolvig
A: Karen-Lise Mynster, Ghita Nørby

Copenhagen, nineteenth century. After an affair with an artist, a Jewish woman settles for a loveless marriage dictated by her adored family. She tries to make the marriage work, though she has an affair with her brother-in-law, her husband goes mad, and her son disappoints her by refusing to remain religious.

Awards: Montréal World Film Festival, Ecumenical Jury Prize, Grand Jury Prize, Most Popular Film, 1992; Robert Festival, Best Supporting Actress (Nørby), 1993

361. Koks i kulissen / Ladies on the Rocks
1984 S
D: Christian Braad Thomsen
S: Helle Ryslinge, Anne Marie Helgar
C: Dirk Bruel, Jørgen Hinsch
A: Helle Ryslinge, Anne Marie Helgar

Two friends form a cabaret act. The story is inspired by the original cabaret act of the actresses/writers. *Danish Directors: 128.*

362. Babettes gaestebud / Babette's Feast
1987 S
D: Gabriel Axel
S: Gabriel Axel; based on the novel by Isak Dinesen
C: Henning Kristiansen
P: Just Betzer
A: Stéphane Audran

1871. A French chef, who has fled the conflict in Paris, makes dinner for the inhabitants of a Danish village, where she has attached herself as housekeeper to two sisters.

Awards: Academy Awards, Best Foreign Film, 1988; Golden Globes, Best Foreign Language Film, 1988; Robert Festival, Best Actress, 1988; BAFTA Awards, Best Film not in English, 1989; London Critics' Circle Film Awards, Actor of the Year (Audran), 1989

363. Flamberede hjerter / Flaming Hearts
1987 DS
D: Helle Ryslinge
S: Helle Ryslinge
C: Søren Berthelin
P: Per Holst
A: Kristen Lehfeld, Peter Hesse Overgaard

Satire of a nurse who lives a life of "humor, energy, and sincerity." After the love of her life disappears, she has an affair with a surgeon, who betrays her. *Nouvel Observateur. 1990, June 16.*
Other titles: Coeurs flambés
Awards: Bodil Awards, Best Film, Best Actress, 1987; Robert Festival, Best Film, Best Actress, 1987

364. Medea 1988
D: Lars Von Trier
S: Carl Dreyer, Preben Thomsen; based on the play by Euripides
C: Sejr Brockmann
A: Kirsten Olesen

Modern version: To exact revenge on her husband, Medea murders their sons. *NYT: E14. 2003, Apr. 18.*

365. Isolde 1989 DS
D: Jytte Rex
S: Jytte Rex, Christian Braad Thomsen
C: Manuel Sellner
A: Pia Vieth, Kim Jansson

"Myths and symbolic dream images mixed in a labyrinth manner." *Danish Directors: 89.*

366. Freud flyttar hemifrån / Freud Leaves Home 1991 DS
D: Susanne Bier
S: Marianne Goldman
C: Erik Zappon
A: Gunilla Röor

Stockholm. A twenty-five-year-old Jewish woman still lives with her family; during a birthday celebration, she seizes the day and goes off to the country with a man she barely knows. *Festival de films, 15th: 105. 1993.*
Other titles: Freud quitte la maison

367. Breaking the Waves 1996
D: Lars Von Trier
S: Lars Von Trier, Peter Asmussen
C: Robby Müller
P: Peter Jensen
A: Emily Watson, Katrin Cartlidge, Stellan Skarsgård

A young woman, encouraged in her simplicity by her conservative, isolated, community, leaps out to gain a husband who works on an oil rig and who makes her extremely happy. When he becomes disabled in a sea accident after she has prayed for his permanent return, she falls into self-destructive sexual activity.

Awards: Cannes Film Festival, Grand Prize, 1996; European Film Awards, Best Film, Best Actress (Watson), 1996; New York Film Critics Association, Best Film, Best Actress, 1996; Bodil Awards,

Best Film, Best Actress (Watson), Best Supporting Actress (Cartlidge), 1997

368. *Barbara*   1997
D: Nils Malmros
S: Jürgen-Frantz Jacobsen
C: Jan Weincke
P: Per Holst
A: Anneke Von der Lippe
Faroe Islands, eighteenth century. A woman marries, and is widowed by, two successive vicars; a third new vicar falls in love with her despite her reputation.
Awards: Robert Festival, Best Film, 1998

369. *Let's Get Lost*   1997
D: Jonas Elmer
S: Jonas Elmer
C: Bo Tengberg
P: Mogens Dester
A: Sidse Babett Knudsen
A woman who has just been jilted by her boyfriend flirts with other men and plots revenge. *Film Society. 1999, Sep.*
Awards: Bodil Awards, Best Film, Best Actress, 1998; Robert Festival, Best Film, Best Actress, 1998

370. *Sekten / Credo*   1997 DS
D: Susanne Bier
S: Susanne Bier
C: Göran Nilsson
P: Peter Jensen
A: Sofie Gråbøl, Ellen Hillinsø
Two women fight against a "powerful sect." Fantasy. *Danish Directors: 247.*
Awards: Robert Festival, Best Supporting Actress (Hillinsø), 1998; Fantasporto, Best Actress (Gråbøl), 1999

371. *Fruen på Hamre / The Lady of Hamre*
                                                   2000 DS
D: Katrine Wiedemann
S: Vinca Wiedemann; based on the novel by Morten Korch
C: Morten Søborg
P: Ib Tardini
A: Bodil Jørgensen
Nineteenth century. Two sisters live on their rural family farm. The older one promises her father on his deathbed that she will marry his choice, a man who will bring money into the farm, but afterward she struggles with the reality of marrying a man she does not love. *Festival de films, 25th: 67. 2003.*
Awards: Festróia–Tróia International Film Festival, Best Actress, 2000

372. *Dancer in the Dark*   2001 P
D: Lars Von Trier
S: Lars Von Trier
C: Robby Müller
P: Vibeke Windeløv
A: Björk, Catherine Deneuve
Washington State, United States. A Scandinavian immigrant works at a metal factory in a small town and volunteers for the local musical play because she loves to sing. She is going blind and fears that her son will, too; betrayed by a neighbor, she accidentally murders him and is sentenced to death.
Awards: Cannes Film Festival, Best Actress (Björk), 2000; Bodil Awards, Best Actress (Björk), 2001

373. *En Kaerligheds historie / Kira's Reason: A Love Story*   2001
D: Ole Christian Madsen
S: Ole Christian Madsen, Mogens Rukov
C: Jürgen Johansson
P: Bo Ehrhardt
A: Stine Stengade
A mentally disturbed mother returns home to her husband and children after a hospital stay. Her husband breaks off his affair with her sister, but his attraction for and enabling of his wife's wild side inhibits his helping her.
Awards: Bodil Awards, Best Film, Best Actress, 2002; Robert Festival, Best Film, Best Actress, 2002

374. *Elsker dig for evigt / Open Hearts*   2002 DSP
D: Susanne Bier
S: Susanne Bier, Anders Thomas Jensen
C: Morten Søborg
P: Vibeke Windeløv
A: Sonia Richter, Paprika Steen
A woman's fiancé is paralyzed from the neck down just before their wedding; as she waits for his recovery, she begins an affair with his doctor. Dogme. *Village Voice: 103. 2003, Feb. 18.*
Awards: Toronto International Film Festival, FIPRESCI, 2002; Bodil Awards, Best Film, Best Supporting Actress (Steen), 2003; Robert Festival, Best Film, 2003

375. *Dogville*   2003 P
D: Lars Von Trier
S: Lars Von Trier
C: Anthony Dod Mantle
P: Vibeke Windeløv
A: Nicole Kidman
A fugitive hides in a small town (a two-dimensional representation of 1930s United States). *Village Voice: 58. 2004, Mar. 24.*

Awards: European Film Awards, Best Direction, 2003; Bodil Awards, Best Film, 2004

376. *Forbrydelser / In Your Hands* 2004 DS
D: Annette K. Olesen
S: Annette K. Olesen, Kim Fupz Aakeson
C: Boje Lomholdt
P: Ib Tardini
A: Ana Eleonora Jorgensen, Trine Dyrholm, Sarah Boberg
The chaplain in a women's prison becomes attracted to a prisoner who killed her child through neglect. The inmate is also known to have spiritual powers, and she predicts the chaplain's long-hoped-for pregnancy. Tragedy follows when a sonogram shows that the fetus may be defective, and the chaplain chooses to abort.

EGYPT

377. *El Haram / The Sin* 1964
D: Henry Barakat
S: Saad Eldin Wahba, Yusef Idris
C: Dia el-Deen El-Mahdi
A: Faten Hamama
An impoverished farmworker is unable to feed her family because her husband is gravely ill. One day she is raped by the landowner's guard; after giving birth in a field, she murders the baby. Pursued by the authorities, she commits suicide. *Cinémas du moyen: 282.*
Other titles: Le Péché

378. *El Kahira thalatin / Carra 30* 1966
D: Salah Abu Seif
S: Salah Abu Seif, Ali El-Zurhani, W. Kahiry, Nagib Mahfuz; based on the novel by Nagib Mahfuz
C: Wahid Farid
A: Suad Husni
1930s. A student is forced to prostitute herself to survive. *Cinémas du moyen: 296.*

379. *Zawgati, mudir am / My Wife Is Director-General* 1966
D: Fatin Abdel Wahab
S: Abdel Hamid, Gouda Sahar
C: Mahmoud Fahmy
A: Chadia
A comedy of manners results when a wife is made the chief executive of the company where her husband works, but the real difficulties fall on the second wife, who remains in charge of their family life. *Festival de films, 10th: 84. 1988.*
Other titles: Karamat zawgati / Ma femme est PDG

380. *Al Zawga el tania / The Second Wife* 1967
D: Salah Abu Seif
S: Mostafa Sami, Saad Eldin Wahba
C: Abdou Nasr
A: Suad Husni
An eighty-year-old mayor of the town decides he must have a second wife because his first wife is rich but sterile. He forces a peasant to repudiate his wife and mother of their three children in order to obtain her for himself, but she revolts. *Festival de films, 10th: 84. 1988.*
Other titles: La Seconde épouse

381. *Za'ir al-Fajr / Visitor at Dawn* 1973
D: Mamduh Shukri
A: Magda Al-Khatib
An activist journalist is murdered, but the investigation of her death is stopped. *Companion Encyclopedia: 86.*

382. *Uridu hallan / I Want a Solution* 1975
D: Said Marzuq
S: Saad Eldin Wahba
C: Said El Cheikh
A: Faten Hamama
A woman demands a divorce after twenty years of marriage but meets only legislative and administrative roadblocks. This film provoked modifications in the Muslim legal system. *Festival de films, 10th: 85. 1988.*
Other titles: Ouridou hallan /Je demande une solution

383. *Ualla azae lel sayedat / No Cordiality for the Woman* 1981
D: Henry Barakat
A: Faten Hamama
A middle-class divorced woman with a daughter finds a new life and job working at a newspaper; when her husband decides he wants to return, she refuses him. *AMG.*

384. *Laylat el-kaped alla Fatma / The Night They Arrested Fatma* 1984
D: Henry Barakat
S: Sekiena Fouad
A: Faten Hamama
A story told in flashback: A young woman refuses to leave with her lover so that she can remain home and take care of her brothers; "years later the lover returns to marry her but her brother has him sent to prison and tries to get [his sister] sent to a mental institution." *FII.*

385. *Al Kanour ayuha al-qanun / Sorry, It's the Law* 1985 D
D: Inas Al-Dighidi

A woman lawyer defends a wife on a charge of murdering her abusive husband, citing the "double standard" whereby a man convicted for the same crime would not be punished as severely. *Cinémas du moyen: 171. Also Companion Encyclopedia.*
Other titles: Afwan ayuha al-qanun /Désolé, c'est la loi

386. *Al Nissa / The Women*   1985 DS
D: Nadia Hamza
S: Nadia Gade, Nadia Hamza
C: Ghoneim Bahnassi
A: Passy, Leila Olwi, Magda Zaki
Stories of three women: an ambitious lawyer, a passive housewife, and a teacher eager to emigrate. *Festival de films, 10th: 83. 1988.*
Other titles: Les Femmes

387. *Al-Youm as-Sadiss / The Sixth Day*   1986
D: Youssef Chahine
S: Youssef Chahine
C: Mohsen Nasr
A: Dalida
Cairo, 1947. A forty-year-old laundry woman cares especially for one of her clients, a favorite actress who plays in "Sacrifice of a Mother." She also cares for her paralytic husband and son, who brings home a monkey trainer one day to live with them in their basement apartment. There is a cholera epidemic; the son contracts it and they wait out the six-day life of the disease, but he dies. *Cinémas du moyen: 285.*
Other titles: Le Sixième jour

388. *Ahlam Hind wa Kamilya / Dreams of Hind and Camelia*   1988
D: Mohamed Khan
S: Mohamed Khan, Mustapha Jouma
A: Nagla Fathy, Aida Ryad, Ahmet Zaki
Cairo. Two friends live in a slum and work as house servants. One cannot have children, and the other is a widow with a lover in prison. Without men, they suffer low standing in Muslim culture, but they live together to help with expenses and dream of finding happiness together, especially when they find they are awaiting a child. *Cinémas du moyen: 283–84.*

389. *Al Tahaddi / The Challenge*   1988 D
D: Inas Al-Dighidi
The struggle of a divorced woman to counter the Muslim law that gives her husband the right to raise their son after he reaches the age of seven. *Cinémas du moyen: 171.*
Other titles: Le Défi

390. *Yawm murr yawm hulu / Good Day, Bad Day*   1988
D: Khairy Beshara
S: Fayez Ghali, Ounsi Abu Seif
C: Tarek El Telmessani
A: Faten Hamama
Cairo, Shubra quarter. A widow with five children struggles to pay off her husband's debts and marry off her four daughters. *Cinema dei.*
Other titles: Bitter Day, Sweet Day

391. *Zawjat rajul muhim / Wife of an Important Man*   1988
D: Mohamed Khan
S: Raoul Tewfik
C: Mohsen Ahmed
A: Mervet Amin, Zizi Moustafa, Ahmet Zaki
The wife of an ambitious secret service officer suffers a mental breakdown when he develops into a fascist. *Cinémas du moyen: 279.*
Awards: Moscow International Film Festival, nomination for Golden Prize, 1987

392. *Emraa waheda la takri / One Woman Is Not Enough*   1989 D
D: Inas Al-Dighidi
C: Mohsen Nasr
A: Yousra, Fifi Aida
A man has relations with three women, each unaware of the others, until one day the truth comes out. "An attack on polygamy." *Festival des 3. Also Cinémas du moyen: 171.*
Other titles: Une Seule femme ne suffit pas / Imra'ah wahidah la takfi

393. *Sayyidati anisati / Dear Ladies!*   1990
D: Ra'fat Al-Mihi
A: Maali Zayed, Abla Kamel, Mahmoad Abdel
Existential, absurd treatment of the problem of dominant and repressive gender norms. *Cinémas du moyen: 167.*
Other titles: Mesdames et mesdemoiselles

394. *Emraa ayla lel sekout / Fall of a Woman*   1992
D: Medhat El-Sebai
C: Tarek El-Telmessani
A: Yousra
A cabaret performer testifies against a gang member in a murder trial; he takes revenge by planting the incriminating weapon in her wardrobe. *Festival des 3.*
Other titles: La Chute d'une femme

395. *Al Qatilla / The Murderess*   1992 D
D: Inas Al-Dighidi
A: Farouk Al-Fichawa, Fifi Abdou, Sarah, Imane

The tale of a woman who murders. *Companion Encyclopedia: 37.*

396. *Marcides* 1993
D: Yousry Nasrallah
S: Yousry Nasrallah
C: Ramses Marzouk
A: Yousra
Cairo. A bourgeois daughter has an affair with a black African diplomat; her pregnancy forces her to marry an aged Egyptian, but she is defiant and insists on naming the blond child "Noubi." The child grows up to have a difficult emotional life. *Festival des 3.*
Awards: Locarno International Film Festival, nomination for Golden Leopard, 1993

397. *Laham rakhis / Cheap Flesh* 1994 D
D: Inas Al-Dighidi
The real condition of young girls sent to Saudi Arabia to couple with aging men for the purpose of providing them with a son; once accomplished, the women are abandoned. *Cinémas du moyen: 171.*
Other titles: Chair á bon marché

398. *Atabit al-sittat / Ladies' Threshold* 1995
D: Ali Abd El-Khalek
"Childless woman seeks the help of a supposed magician, but when she gets pregnant her husband repudiates her in the belief she has committed adultery." *Companion Encyclopedia: 57.*

399. *Al Jaraj / The Garage* 1995
D: Ala Karim
An impoverished woman, who works in a garage, loses her husband and must give up her children because she has not participated in family planning. *Companion Encyclopedia: 57.*

400. *Ya donya ya gharami / Life . . . My Passion* 1995
D: Magdi Ahmed Ali
S: Mohaned Hilmi Hilal
C: Mohsen Nasr
A: Layla Alaqui, Alham Chahine, Hala Sidki
Cairo, Darassa quarter. Three women, attached to traditional men, work in sweatshops and retail stores; adopting a philosophical view, they find enjoyment and support with each other and refuse to wear veils. Still, one must contend with passing a "wedding test" by getting her vagina sewn up, and another must object to her fiancé's suggestion that she wear a veil.

401. *Istakusa / Lobster* 1996 D
D: Inas Al-Dighidi

S: based on the play *The Taming of the Shrew* by William Shakespeare
A free adaptation of *The Taming of the Shrew.* An unusual picture of intimate life in a traditional "oriental" marriage. *Cinémas du moyen: 171–72.*
Other titles: Langouste / Stakoza

402. *El Akhar / The Other* 1999
D: Youssef Chahine
S: Youssef Chahine, Khaled Youssef
C: Mohsen Nasr
A: Nabila Ebeid, Hanan Tork, Mahmoud Hemida
A prince, the son of Egypt's wealthiest man and a politically ambitious American woman, meets and marries a journalist of modest background, great independence, and unhesitating integrity. She makes an enemy of her new mother-in-law by writing about his family's corrupt business practice, and she pushes her husband to do the right thing.
Other titles: L'Autre
Awards: Cannes Film Festival, Francois Chalais Award, 1999

403. *Al Bahethat an al horeya / Women in Search of Freedom* 2004 DP
D: Inas Al-Dighidi
S: Rafiq El-Sabban
C: Mohsen Ahmed
P: Inas Al-Dighidi
A: Nicole Bardawil, Dalila El-Beheiry, Sanaa Mozian
Paris. Three homesick Arab women struggle to make a life: a journalist who fled the war in Beirut; a painter who left her controlling husband and children to pursue a career; and a working-class Moroccan who has become a slave to a shopkeeper. *Variety: 50. 2005, Jan. 10.*

404. *Hob el banat / Women's Love* 2004
D: Khaled El Hagar
A: Laila Eloui, Ashraf Abdel Baki, Hana Shiha, Hanan Tork
Cairo suburbs. Three half sisters have grown up separately, one in London, one in Alexandria, and one in Cairo with their wealthy father. After his death, they must live together for a year in order to receive their inheritance. *London Film: 64. 2004.*
Awards: Cairo International Film Festival, Special Mention, 2003

ECUADOR

405. *La Tigra / The Tigress* 1990 P
D: Camilo Luzuriaga
S: Camilo Luzuriaga; based on the novel by José de la Cuadra

C: Diego Falconi
P: Lilia Lemos
A: Lissette Cabrera, Verónica Garcia, Rossana Iturralde
Amazon region. Three sisters own the general store; the eldest believes a witch doctor's prediction that the youngest must remain a virgin in order for the three to hold on to their property. Conflict ensues. *Guide to Latin: 141.*

ESTONIA

406. **Varastatud kohtumine / Stolen Meeting**
                                    1989 DSP
D: Leida Laïus, Piret Tibbo
S: Marina Zveryeva
C: Jüri Sillart
P: Piret Tibbo
A: Maria Klenskaja
Released from prison, a woman seeks to retrieve her relationship with the boy child she was forced to abandon. The child is a ward of the state, but she insists on her maternal right, attempting to remove him from what seems to be a happy home. *Festival de films, 12th: 30. 1990.*
Other titles: *Une Recontre volée / Ukradennoye svidaniye*
Awards: Kalinin Film Festival, Best Actress, 1989

ETHIOPIA

407. **Mogzitwa / The Nanny**   2003
D: Nikodimos Fikru
A: Nafkote Fikru
A woman tries to find success in the United States. *African Diaspora, 11th. 2003, Dec. Accessed 2004, Aug. 15.*

FINLAND

408. **Att älska / To Love**   1964
D: Jörn Donner
S: Jörn Donner
C: Sven Nykvist
P: Rune Waldekranz
A: Harriet Andersson, Zbigniew Cybulski
"A recently widowed young woman is taught the true values of love by a foreigner." *FII.*
Awards: Venice Film Festival, Best Actress, 1964

409. **Anna**   1970 S
D: Jörn Donner
S: Eija-Elina Bergholm, Jörn Donner

A: Harriet Andersson, Maarit Hyttinen, Marja Packalén
A thirty-eight-year-old woman takes a holiday trip with her daughter and teenage maid. *Faber Companion.*

410. **Marja Pieni**   1972 DS
D: Eija-Elina Bergholm
S: Eija-Elina Bergholm
C: Pirjo Honkasalo
P: Jörn Donner
A: Liisamaija Laaksonen
"An office girl, unmarried and free, gets involved in various affairs with different men. She finally has a major affair with one man, and the film studies how this changes her." *FII.*

411. **Maa on syntinen laulu / Earth Is a Sinful Song**   1973
D: Rauni Mollberg
S: Rauni Mollberg, Pirjo Honkasalo
C: Hannu Peltomaa
P: Rauni Mollberg
A: Maritta Mäkelä
Lapland, 1950s. Erotic tale of a Finnish girl's affair with a reindeer herdsman. Though she has a child, her father refuses to acknowledge the cross-cultural marriage and accidentally kills the man. *FII.*
Awards: Berlin International Film Festival, nomination for Golden Bear, 1974

412. **Aika hyva ihmiseksi / Pretty Good for a Human Being**   1977
D: Rauni Mollberg
S: Rauni Mollberg, Veikko Korkala
A: Irma Seikkula, Raili Veivo
1920s. In a small town dominated by a black market and smuggling, a woman takes care of the small son of a widower who has lost interest in life. *Variety: 20. 1978, Aug. 9.*
Awards: Jussi Awards, Best Direction, Best Actress (Seikkula, Veivo), 1978

413. **Landet som icke är / Land That Does Not Exist**   1977 DS
D: Tuija-Maija Niskanen
S: Eija-Elina Bergholm; based on the poems and diaries of Edith Södergran
1892–1923. The story of Russian-born poet Edith Södergran, who wrote in the Swedish language and brought Swedish-language poetry into the modern era. *Women's Companion: 296.*
Other titles: *Maa jota ei ole*

414. **Avskedet / The Farewell**   1982 DS
D: Tuija-Maija Niskanen

S: Eija-Elina Bergholm, Vivica Bandler
C: Esa Vuorinen
A: Stina Ekblad, Gunnar Björnstrand
A woman defies her tyrannical father to have an affair with a German woman. *Women's Companion: 296.*

415. *Angelan sota / Angela's War* 1984 DS
D: Eija-Elina Bergholm
S: Eija-Elina Bergholm, Jörn Donner
C: Kari Sohlberg
P: Jörn Donner
A: Ida-Lotta Backman, Mathieu Carrière
World War II. A wealthy woman has an affair with a hospitalized German army captain after her Finnish lover dies in combat. Her family and friends are not pleased at this further assault on Finnish integrity. *Variety: 16. 1984, Aug. 29.*

416. *Palava enkeli / Burning Angel* 1984 S
D: Lauri Törhönen
S: Lauri Törhönen, Hannelore Torronen
C: Esa Vuorinen
P: Kaj Holmberg
A: Riita Viiperi, Eva Eloranta
A newly graduated nurse works in a psychiatric hospital but cannot forget her father's suicide or her "domineering mother." When a female patient she has been close to incinerates herself, the nurse falls into an affair with a shallow doctor and then becomes mentally ill herself. *Variety: 19. 1984, May 23.*
Awards: Jussi Awards, Best Actress (Eloranta), 1984

417. *Tulitikkutehtaan tyttö / The Match Factory Girl* 1990 P
D: Aki Kaurismäki
S: Aki Kaurismäki
C: Timo Salminen
P: Katinka Faragó
A: Kati Outinen, Elina Salo
A passive factory worker seeks adventure one night and becomes pregnant by a man who thinks making payments is the solution to his "problem"; she seeks revenge.
Awards: Berlin International Film Festival, Interfilm Award, 1990; Jussi Awards, Best Director, Best Actress (Outinen), Best Supporting Actress (Salo), 1991

418. *Pelon maantiede / The Geography of Fear* 2000 DS
D: Auli Mantila
S: Auli Mantila
C: Heikki Färm
P: Tero Kaukomaa

A: Tanjalotta Räikkä, Leena Klemola, Anna-Elina Lyytikainen
"A band of bad girls strikes out at male pigs." A dentist and her sister are part of the "mysteriously close group." *AMG.*
Awards: Sochi International Film Festival, FIPRESCI, 2000; Jussi Awards, Best Script, 2001

419. *Eila* 2003 S
D: Jarmo Lampela
S: Tove Idström
C: Harri Räty
A: Sari Mällinen
A cleaner's place of employment is being privatized. Some workers strike and are replaced by younger workers. She continues to work until one day she revolts as well. *Nouvelles du nord, no. 16: 87. 2003.*
Awards: Jussi Awards, Best Director, Best Actress, 2004

420. *Jumalan morsian / A Bride of the Seventh Heaven* 2003 DS
D: Markku Lehmuskallio, Anastasia Lapsui
S: Anastasia Lapsui
C: Johannes Lehmuskallio
P: Kristina Pervilä
A: Angelina Saraleta, Viktoria Hudi
"An old woman, betrothed for life to a god, meaning she can take no earthly husband, recounts the story of her lonely life to a blind girl: Where the river Seregg ngyne begins, that is where she who has seven braids started singing ... The trimming of her bonnet is whiter than the first snow of winter." *Finnish Film. Accessed 2005, Feb. 14.*

FRANCE

421. *Les Bonnes femmes / The Girls* 1960
D: Claude Chabrol
S: Claude Chabrol, Paul Gégauff
C: Henri Decaë
P: Robert Hakim
A: Bernadette Lafont, Stéphane Audran, Clotilde Joano, Lucile Saint-Simon
Paris. Four girls who work in an appliance shop endure their humdrum workday in anticipation of the excitement of the nights. One has a night job as a singer and keeps it a secret. Another has a boyfriend who preps her in class distinctions by insisting she impress his parents by dropping certain names. Another forms an attachment to a stalker.

422. *Lola* 1960
D: Jacques Demy

S: Jacques Demy
C: Raoul Coutard
P: Carlo Ponti
A: Anouk Aimée

Nantes. A cabaret dancer and single mother is courted by a variety of men but insists on waiting for the return of the father of her child. She refuses the offer of marriage from a childhood friend, hurt to find he wanted something other than friendship. Eventually, her man returns in a fancy white suit and Cadillac to match.

423. *La Proie pour l'ombre / Shadow of Adultery*   1960 S
D: Alexandre Astruc
S: Alexandre Astruc; based on the novel by Françoise Sagan
C: Marcel Grignon
P: Leopold Schlosberg
A: Annie Girardot

A dissatisfied bourgeois woman runs an art gallery and takes an artist lover whom she finds more exciting than her executive husband, a man completely understanding and generous toward her. When she realizes her husband's good qualities and tries to get him back, it is too late. *BiFi.*

424. *La Vérité / Truth*   1960 S
D: Henri-Georges Clouzot
S: Henri-Georges Clouzot, Véra Clouzot, Jérôme Géronimi, Michèle Perrein
C: Armand Thirard
P: Raoul Lévy
A: Brigitte Bardot

Justice in France; a provincial woman goes on trial in Paris for murdering her lover. *Variety. 1960, Nov. 23.*
Awards: Golden Globes, Best Foreign Language Film, 1961

425. *Cléo de 5 à 7 / Cleo from 5 to 7*   1961 DS
D: Agnès Varda
S: Agnès Varda
C: Jean Rabier
P: Carlo Ponti
A: Corinne Marchand

Two hours in the life of a singer who has a significant entourage and is waiting for the results of a test for cancer. She tries to go outside herself in speaking with a friend, and then with a stranger on his way to the war in Algeria, and succeeds.
Awards: French Syndicate of Cinema Critics, Best Film, 1963

426. *Une Femme est une femme / A Woman Is a Woman*   1961
D: Jean-Luc Godard
S: Jean-Luc Godard
C: Raoul Coutard
P: Carlo Ponti
A: Anna Karina, Jean-Claude Brialy

A woman wants to have a child but her lover is not ready; he responds by inviting a friend of theirs over when she threatens to have the child with someone else. Since both are readers, their arguments take on an arch literary tone. *Film Criticism, vol. 25, no. 1: 36. 2000, Fall.*
Awards: Berlin International Film Festival, Best Actress, Special Prize, 1961; Cannes Film Festival, Best Actress, 1961

427. *La Fille aux yeux d'or / The Girl with the Golden Eyes*   1961
D: Jean-Gabriel Albicocco
S: Jean-Gabriel Albicocco, Pierre Pélégri; based on the novel by Honoré de Balzac
C: Quinto Albicocco
P: Gilbert de Goldschmidt
A: Marie Laforet, Françoise Prévost, Paul Guers, Françoise Dorléac

A superficial fashion photographer pursues a young girl who turns out to be a lesbian, as well as the partner of his business associate, who is not happy with his interest in her lover. *AMG.*

428. *Le Quatrième sexe / The Fourth Sex* 1961
D: Michel Wichard
S: Jean Mitry, Alphonso Gimeno
C: Marcel Combes
P: Jose Benazeraf
A: Brigitte Juslin, Richard Winckler, Nicole Arnaud

Paris. An American woman dresses as a man and lives as a lesbian. However, when a man implies she is a lesbian, she decides to get back by "corrupting his sister." Exploitation. *FII.*

429. *Vie privée / A Very Private Affair*   1961 P
D: Louis Malle
S: Louis Malle
C: Henri Decaë
P: Christine Gouze-Rénal
A: Brigitte Bardot

"Melodrama of a film star who is suddenly famous and then comes to a tragic end." *FII.*

430. *Baie des anges / Bay of Angels*   1962
D: Jacques Demy
S: Jacques Demy
C: Jean Ravier
P: Paul-Edmond Decharme

A: Jeanne Moreau

A compulsive gambler goes on an extended spree at the Riviera, corrupting a banker in the process. *Histoire du cinéma.*

431. *Procès de Jeanne d'Arc / Trial of Joan of Arc* 1962 P

D: Robert Bresson

S: Robert Bresson; based on transcripts of the trial

C: Leonce-Henri Burel

P: Agnès Delahaie

A: Florence Carrez

Set in the courtroom, where the interrogation is hostile, and the jail, where she is spied on and threatened. The film portrays a grounded and intelligent Joan of Arc, resistant to sentimentality, though her fate to be burned as a witch is set.

Awards: Cannes Film Festival, Jury Prize, OCIC Award, 1962

432. *La Prostitution* 1962

D: Maurice Boutel

S: Maurice Boutel, Marcel Sicot

C: Quinto Albicocco

P: Maurice Boutel

A: Etchika Choureau, Evelyne Dassas

An immigrant tells the story of her arrival in Paris and immediate encounter with a pimp, who has one of his girls (who has been blinded by him) train her to be a prostitute. She eventually flees to Hong Kong and turns him in to Interpol. *Histoire du cinéma.*

433. *Thérèse Desqueroux* 1962

D: Georges Franju

S: Georges Franju; based on the novel by François Mauriac

C: Christian Matras

P: Eugene Lepicier

A: Emmanuelle Riva

A woman marries because she is in love with the man's sister. Stifled, she attempts to poison her husband, is imprisoned, and is then released to his home and the confines of her room. Finally, he allows her to move to Paris, but she considers going back to him.

Awards: Venice Film Festival, Best Actress, 1962

434. *Vivre sa vie / My Life to Live* 1962

D: Jean-Luc Godard

S: Jean-Luc Godard

C: Raoul Coutard

P: Pierre Braunberger

A: Anna Karina, Monique Messine

A salesgirl in a record store cannot pay her rent and falls into prostitution. She goes from glistening eyes and a sense that "I am responsible" to a hard-edged silence over her plight. Refusing a client because "sometimes it's degrading," she is punished and shot.

Awards: Venice Film Festival, Special Jury Prize, 1962

435. *L'Autre femme / The Other Woman* 1963 S

D: Francois Villiers

S: Francois Villiers, Jacques Sigurd; based on the novel by Maria-Luisa Linarès

C: Cecilio Paniagua

P: Roger Cauvin

A: Annie Girardot, Alida Valli

A decorator finds refuge on a Spanish island and becomes obsessed with an English writer, whom she eventually discovers is married. *Histoire du cinéma.*

436. *La Derive* 1963 DS

D: Paule Delsol

S: Paule Delsol

C: Jean Malige

P: Sacha Kamenka

A: Paulette Dubost, Jacquelline Vandal, Anne-Marie Coffinet

A shiftless woman, without a job, moves from lover to lover and visits her mother in between. *BiFi.*

437. *Le Mépris / Contempt* 1963

D: Jean-Luc Godard

S: Jean-Luc Godard; based on the novel by Alberto Moravia

C: Raoul Coutard

P: Carlo Ponti

A: Brigitte Bardot, Michel Piccoli

Rome. A typist comes to resent her screenwriter husband's relationship with a manipulative producer because she realizes her husband is using her to manipulate the producer in turn. Her anger is clear, but her husband is evasive and believes he is doing it for her benefit. During a shoot on Capri, they suffer complete alienation.

438. *Muriel, ou le temps d'un retour / Muriel* 1963

D: Alain Resnais

S: Jean Cayrol

C: Sacha Vierny

P: Philippe Dusart

A: Delphine Seyrig

A widowed art dealer lives with her grown son, who cannot forget an atrocity he witnessed in

Algeria. An old lover and his "niece" come to stay with her.

Awards: Venice Film Festival, Best Actress, 1963

439. *Une Femme mariée / A Married Woman*
                                                      1964
D: Jean-Luc Godard
S: Jean-Luc Godard
C: Raoul Coutard
P: Phillipe Dusart
A: Macha Méril

Paris. A young wife, a writer for women's magazines, becomes pregnant but does not know if the child is her husband's or her lover's. *Histoire du cinéma.*

440. *Les Parapluies de Cherbourg / The Umbrellas of Cherbourg*   1964
D: Jacques Demy
S: Jacques Demy
C: Jean Rabier
P: Mag Bodard
A: Catherine Deneuve

A girl's mother dislikes her lover because he is a mechanic. The girl sees him off to the war in Algeria, then finds herself pregnant and marries another. Musical.

Awards: Prix Louis Delluc, 1963; Cannes Film Festival, Golden Palm, 1964

441. *Le Bonheur / Happiness*   1965 DS
D: Agnès Varda
S: Agnès Varda
C: Claude Beausoleil
P: Mag Bodard
A: Marie-France Boyer, Claire Drouot, Jean-Claude Drouot

A carpenter wants his wife and the mother of his children to accept his mistress; instead she drowns herself, and he lives happily ever after.

Awards: Prix Louis Delluc, 1964; Berlin International Film Festival, Silver Bear (Varda), 1965

442. *Le Journal d'une femme en blanc / Diary of a Woman in White*   1965
D: Claude Autant-Lara
S: Jean Aurenche, René Sheeler; based on the novel by André Saubiran
C: Michel Kelber
A: Marie-José Nat

A gynecologist in a hospital is concerned about the necessary abortions and takes care of a young woman, who dies during a miscarriage. Pregnant herself, she allows the father to leave the country without knowing that she is pregnant because she wants to devote herself to medicine. But she also

hopes to keep the child. There is a sequel, *Le Nouveau journal d'une femme en blanc* (1966), in which she continues her career as a single mother. *BiFi.*

443. *Viva Maria!*   1965
D: Louis Malle
S: Louis Malle
C: Henri Decaë
P: Óscar Dancigers
A: Jeanne Moreau, Brigitte Bardot

South America, 1910. Comic tale of the daughter of an IRA terrorist, trained in explosives, who is being hunted by the authorities. She hides out with a dancer from a traveling circus, and together they "invent" the striptease, take up a revolutionary cause, and outwit the military, then the church.

444. *Deux ou trois choses que je sais d'elle / Two or Three Things I Know about Her* 1966
D: Jean-Luc Godard
S: Jean-Luc Godard
C: Raoul Coutard
P: Raoul Lévy
A: Marina Vlady

Paris. A housewife works the stairwells of an apartment in the banlieue as a prostitute; the filmmaker engages with her and the world around her.

445. *La Religieuse / The Nun*   1966
D: Jacques Rivette
S: Jacques Rivette, Jean Gruault; based on a story by Denis Diderot
C: Alain Levant
P: Georges de Beauregard
A: Anna Karina

Eighteenth century. A young woman, forced by her parents to enter a convent, is offered a chance to escape by a priest, who demands she become his lover in return.

Awards: Cannes Film Festival, nomination for Golden Palm, 1966

446. *Belle de jour*   1967
D: Luis Buñuel
S: Luis Buñuel, Jean-Claude Carrière
C: Sacha Vierny
P: Henri Baum
A: Catherine Deneuve

Paris. A young bourgeois woman who prefers to express her sexuality outside her marriage becomes a prostitute.

447. *Les Biches / Bad Girls*   1968
D: Claude Chabrol
S: Paul Gégauff, Claude Chabrol
C: Jean Rabier

P: André Génovès
A: Stéphane Audran, Jacqueline Sassard, Jean-Louis Trintignant
A young woman is courted by a stylish wealthy woman who takes her to St. Tropez. She falls in love with a man, who is then seduced by her benefactor. *BiFi.*
Awards: Berlin International Film Festival, Silver Bear (Audran), 1968

448. *La Femme infidèle / The Unfaithful Wife* 1968

D: Claude Chabrol
S: Claude Chabrol
C: Jean Rabier
P: André Génovès
A: Stéphane Audran, Michel Bouquet
A wealthy woman lives a perfect life with her husband and child in a Paris suburb; not realizing her boredom, she falls into a passionate affair. Her husband becomes suspicious and accidentally murders the man, and they conspire to cover up the crime.

449. *Le Boucher / The Butcher* 1969

D: Claude Chabrol
C: Jean Rabier
P: André Génovès
A: Stéphane Audran, Jean Yanne
Southern France. After a failed love affair, a village teacher is confidently determined to live her life as a single woman. She struggles with her habitual openness and kindness when it conflicts with clues that her friend, a local butcher obsessed with his war experiences, may be a violent psychopath. Mystery.

450. *Une Femme douce / A Gentle Woman* 1969

D: Robert Bresson
S: Robert Bresson; based on a story by Fyodor Dostoevsky
C: Ghislain Cloquet
P: Mag Bodard
A: Dominique Sanda
A young, poor woman marries a pawnbroker but resents his attempts to control her. The routine of their shop, which she sees as taking advantage of needy people, also offends her. She commits suicide after considering murdering him, and he recalls their life together while pacing around her dead body.

451. *La Fiancée du pirate / A Very Curious Girl* 1969 DS

D: Nelly Kaplan

S: Nelly Kaplan, Claude Makovski
C: Jean Badal
P: Jean Cotet
A: Bernadette Lafont
After her mother's funeral, a woman decides she wants to stay and be the town's prostitute; she ends up conflicting with the townspeople and avenging their snobbery. Comedy. *BiFi.*
Other titles: *Dirty Mary*

452. *Lions Love* 1969 DSP

D: Agnès Varda
S: Agnès Varda
C: Stevan Larner
P: Agnès Varda
A: Viva, Jerome Ragni, James Rado, Shirley Clarke
Characters mimic their real lives as an avant-garde filmmaker attempts to finance her project through a major Hollywood studio. The experience pushes her to the "brink of suicide." *AMG.*

453. *Mon nuit chez Maud / My Night with Maud* 1969

D: Eric Rohmer
S: Eric Rohmer
C: Nestor Almendros
P: Barbet Schroeder
A: Françoise Fabian, Jean-Louis Trintignant
A conservative man is challenged by an evening of discussion of ethical issues with a worldly intellectual woman.
Awards: French Syndicate of Cinema Critics, Best Film, 1970; New York Film Critics Circle Awards, Best Screenplay, 1970

454. *Pean d'ane / Donkey's Skin* 1970

D: Jacques Demy
S: Jacques Demy
C: Ghislain Cloquet
A: Delphine Seyrig, Catherine Deneuve
Fairy tale of a princess "so beautiful" that her widowed father wants to marry her. The desperate princess confides in the lily fairy, who gets around by helicopter from her oyster shell in the forest, and has an egotistical and even infuriating human character. She advises the princess to place impossible conditions on the marriage. Fantasy. *Festival de films, 11th: 73. 1989.*

455. *La Rupture* 1970 S

D: Claude Chabrol
S: Claude Chabrol; based on a novel by Charlotte Armstrong
C: Jean Rabier
A: Stéphane Audran, Jean Pierre Cassel
A drug-crazed father throws his child across a

room while the mother manages to pick up a frying pan and subdue him. He returns to his wealthy family, and she stays in a boardinghouse near the hospital while the child recuperates, but her husband's family schemes against her. Mystery.

456. *Mourir d'aimer / To Die of Love*   1971
D: André Cayatte
S: André Cayatte, Pierre Dumayet
C: Maurice Fellous
P: Henri Jaquillard
A: Annie Girardot
1960s. A teacher who is prosecuted for an affair with a student commits suicide; based on a true story. *BiFi.*

457. *Papa, les petits bateaux / Papa, the Little Boats*   1971 DS
D: Nelly Kaplan
S: Nelly Kaplan, Jean Laborder
C: Ricardo Aronovich
A: Sheila White
An eccentric heiress is imprisoned as a public nuisance by her arms merchant father in an attempt to teach her a lesson. She escapes, disguised as a police officer, but is then kidnapped by gangsters, with whom she proceeds to collaborate to get ransom money from her father, which, in the end, all comes to her. *BiFi.*

458. *Paulina 1880*   1971 S
D: Jean-Louis Bertuccelli
S: Albina De Boisrouvray
C: Andreas Winding
A: Olga Karlatos, Eliana De Santis, Maximilian Schell
1860–1880. A young, wealthy Italian has an affair with a count; when her beloved father dies, she believes it is payment for her sin, and she refuses marriage in favor of refuge in a convent. *BiFi.*

459. *César et Rosalie*   1972 P
D: Claude Sautet, Claude Néron
S: Jean-Loup Dabadie
C: Jean Boffety
P: Michelle De Broca
A: Romy Schneider, Yves Montand, Sami Frey
Caught between two men, her ex-husband and a former lover, a woman tires of the exclusive games the men play and rejects both. A turn on George Bernard Shaw's *Candida. West German Cinema.*

460. *Coup pour coup / Blow for Blow*   1972
D: Marin Karmitz
A: Simone Aubin, Anne-Marie Bacquié

Rouen. A fictional reconstruction of the successful occupation by women of a French textile factory. *MFB, no. 481: 25. 1974, Feb.*

461. *Nathalie Granger*   1972 DS
D: Marguerite Duras
S: Marguerite Duras
C: Ghislain Cloquet
A: Jeanne Moreau, Lucia Bosé
Two women live in a house in the country: The housekeeper takes great care with the house and the garden and gives piano lessons to children, while the Madame worries about the future of her daughter. A salesman's talk of his failure convinces her to leave her daughter alone. *BiFi.*

462. *Vivre ensemble / Living Together*   1972 DSP
D: Anna Karina
S: Anna Karina
P: Anna Karina
A: Anna Karina
A serious married man leaves his wife and teaching position to live with a carefree woman who has many friends and access to drugs. They enjoy Paris and then New York until she has a child and becomes more serious, even getting a job, while he becomes increasingly lost. *BiFi.*

463. *La Femme du Gange / Woman of the Ganges*   1973 DS
D: Marguerite Duras
S: Marguerite Duras
C: Bruno Nuytten
A: Catherine Sellers, Nicole Hiss, Gérard Depardieu
Two female voices ("a sort of multiplicity one carries in oneself") describe the sea while the camera pictures the sea, the sand, people pacing in the sand, a casino, and a "crazy person." Experimental. *Enclitic, vol. 7, no. 2: 55–62. 1983, Fall.*

464. *Aloïse*   1974 DS
D: Liliane De Kermadec
S: Liliane De Kermadec, André Téchiné
C: Jean Penzer
P: Alain Dahan
A: Delphine Seyrig, Isabelle Huppert
Life of Aloise Corbaz, the Swiss primitive painter (1886–1964), who suffered through World War I in Germany. She never recovered from the shock and was incarcerated in a mental institution in Switzerland for the remainder of her life.

465. *Céline et Julie vont en bateau / Celine and Julie Go Boating*   1974 S
D: Jacques Rivette

S: Jacques Rivette, Juliet Berto, Eduardo De Gregorio, Dominique Labourier, Bulle Ogier, Marie-France Pisier
C: Jacques Renard
P: Barbet Schroeder
A: Bulle Ogier, Juliet Berto, Dominique Labourier
Paris. A magician inspires a librarian to enter into a fantasy game that takes them all over the city and into the countryside.
Awards: Locarno International Film Festival, Special Jury Prize, 1974

466. *Femmes femmes* / *Women Women*   1974
D: Paul Vecchiali
S: Paul Vecchiali, Noël Simsolo
C: Georges Strouvé
P: Paul Vecchiali
A: Helen Surgere, Sonia Saviange
Two middle-aged actresses, neither successful, engage in songs, fantasy, and alcohol in and around their shared apartment; finally, one commits suicide. *BiFi.*

467. *India Song*   1974 DS
D: Marguerite Duras
S: Marguerite Duras
C: Bruno Nuytten
P: Stéphane Tchalgadjieff
A: Delphine Seyrig
Calcutta. The bored wife of the French consul bitterly reminisces, particularly about her resentment of people who "get used to India." All sound consists of voice-over; images are sets of a colonial embassy and a hotel lounge.
Awards: César Awards, nomination for Best Actress, 1976

468. *La Veuve Couderc* / *The Widow Couderc*   1974
D: Pierre Granier-Deferre
S: Pierre Granier-Deferre; based on the novel by Georges Simenon
C: Walter Wottitz
P: Raymond Danon
A: Simone Signoret, Alain Delon
1940s. A widow is emotionally isolated at her farm, surrounded by her late husband's family, who wait only for their property to be returned. She takes in a fugitive, fifteen years her junior, and has an affair with him, leading to tragedy. *BiFi.*

469. *Docteur Françoise Gailland*   1975 S
D: Jean-Louis Bertuccelli
S: Jean-Louis Bertuccelli, André Brunelin, Noëlle Loriot; based on the novel by Noëlle Loriot
C: Claude Renoir
P: Lise Fayolle
A: Isabelle Huppert, Annie Girardot, Jean-Pierre Cassel
A doctor who discovers she has cancer is determined to make things better with her husband and children, whom she has neglected because of her professional dedication. *BiFi.*

470. *Folle à tuer* / *Mad Enough to Kill*   1975
D: Yves Boisset
S: Yves Boisset
C: Jean Boffety
P: Jean Bolvary
A: Marlène Jobert
A former mental patient becomes a guardian for a wealthy young boy, and they are kidnapped; she manages their escape. Thriller. *BiFi.*

471. *L'Histoire d'Adèle H* / *The Story of Adele H*   1975 S
D: Francois Truffaut
S: Jean Gruault, Suzanne Schiffman, Francois Truffaut; based on the diaries of Adèle Hugo
C: Nestor Almendros
P: Marcel Berbert
A: Isabelle Adjani
Nineteenth century. The daughter of a famous author has an obsessive love for a soldier and follows him to the island where he is stationed, refusing to accept his lack of interest.
Awards: National Society of Film Critics Awards, Best Actress, 1975; New York Film Critics Circle Awards, Best Actress, 1975; Cartagena Film Festival, Best Actress, 1976

472. *Numéro deux*   1975 DS
D: Anne-Marie Miéville, Jean-Luc Godard
S: Anne-Marie Miéville, Jean-Luc Godard
C: William Lubtchansky
A: Sandrine Battistella
Split screens tell the story of a working-class family of two young children, their grandparents, and their sexual lives. Woman's work—washing, ironing, mopping, listening to children—is central to the Marxist analysis of social and environmental ills.

473. *Duelle*   1976 SP
D: Jacques Rivette
S: Jacques Rivette, Eduardo De Gregorio, Marilu Parolini
C: William Lubtchansky
P: Stéphane Tchalgadjieff
A: Bulle Ogier, Juliet Berto
A sun goddess and a moon goddess arrive in Paris and duel over a precious stone that will allow one of them to remain on earth. *BiFi.*

474. *Lumière* 1976 DSP
D: Jeanne Moreau
S: Jeanne Moreau
C: Ricardo Aronovich
P: Claire Duval
A: Jeanne Moreau, Lucia Bosé, Caroline Cartier, Marie Henriau, Francine Racette
An actress vacations with three friends and reflects (in flashback) on her many involvements of the past, her busy life as a film star, and the suicide of an adored elderly friend with whom she had assumed a platonic relationship.
Awards: César Awards, nomination for Best Supporting Actress (Racette), 1977

475. *Maitresse* 1976
D: Barbet Schroeder
S: Barbet Schroeder, Paul Voufargol
C: Nestor Almendros
A: Bulle Ogier, Gérard Depardieu
A dominatrix begins an affair with a thief she finds burgling her apartment; includes details of her work and clients in a "ritual rather than sensational treatment." *Variety: 21. 1976, Feb. 11.*

476. *Mon coeur est rouge / Paint My Heart Red* 1976 DSP
D: Michèle Rosier
S: Michèle Rosier
C: Bruno Nuytten
P: Michèle Rosier
A: Françoise Lebrun
A blond woman engages in feminist activities, including a feminist fete with slides and a party with women, including Mai Zetterling and Anne Wizemsky, dressed as famous male writers.

477. *Néa / A Young Emmanuelle* 1976 DS
D: Nelly Kaplan
S: Nelly Kaplan, Jean Chapot
C: Andreas Winding
P: Yvon Guézel
A: Ann Zacharias, Sami Frey
A sixteen-year-old writer reads mostly erotic literature and convinces a publisher to accept a manuscript, but it lacks the reality that practical experience would give it, so she has the publisher show her. The book is a triumph, but the publisher ignores her, so she seeks revenge by accusing him of rape. *BiFi.*

478. *L'Une chante, l'autre pas / One Sings, the Other Doesn't* 1976 DS
D: Agnès Varda
S: Agnès Varda
C: Charles Van Damme

A: Valérie Mairesse, Thérèse Liotard
The story of two friends through the 1960s and 1970s; one is a popular singer, the other runs a family-planning clinic.

479. *L'Amour violé / Rape of Love* 1977 DSP
D: Yannick Bellon
S: Yannick Bellon
C: Georges Barsky
P: Jacqueline Doye
A: Nathalie Nell
Grenoble. A nurse who has been gang-raped searches for meaning and resolution of the crime. *AMG.*

480. *Le Camion* 1977 DS
D: Marguerite Duras
S: Marguerite Duras
C: Bruno Nuytten
P: François Barat
A: Marguerite Duras, Gérard Depardieu
Actors read a script about a truck driver who picks up a middle-aged woman. *BiFi.*

481. *La Dentellière / The Lacemaker* 1977
D: Claude Goretta
S: Claude Goretta, Pascal Lainé
C: Jean Boffety
P: Daniel Toscan du Plantier
A: Isabelle Huppert
Normandy. A young hairdresser has her first affair with a university student. The couple lives together, but their different lives—he persists in encouraging her to "improve herself" by studying some other trade—his disapproving mother, and his own insecurity end their relationship. She does not have the resources to cope and is institutionalized.
Awards: Cannes Film Festival, Ecumenical Jury Prize, 1977; BAFTA Awards, Best Newcomer (Huppert), 1978

482. *Le Dernier baiser / The Last Kiss* 1977 DS
D: Dolores Grasian
S: Dolores Grasian, Jean Curtelin, Jean Reznikow
C: Alain Derobe
P: Pierre Druout
A: Annie Girardot
A taxi driver, who has her own problems with men, bonds with a passenger she picks up who is searching for her philandering husband; they track him down as he's picking up another woman. Comedy.

483. *Une Femme, un jour / A Woman, One Day* 1977 S
D: Léonard Keigel

S: Simone Bach
C: Ricardo Aronovich
P: Léonard Keigel
A: Mélanie Brévan, Caroline Céllier
A lesbian relationship between an unconventional woman and a middle-class mother is ended by the latter's need for "respectability." *FII.*

484. *Les Indiens sont encore loin / The Indians Are Still Far Away* 1977 DSP
D: Patricia Moraz
S: Patricia Moraz
C: Renato Berta
P: Agnès Chaulier
A: Isabelle Huppert, Christine Pascal
An introverted girl has many friends, all with their own problems. Some she has helped at various times, but one day when all of them have forgotten her, she is unable to cope and commits suicide. *BiFi.*
Awards: Locarno International Film Festival, Ecumenical Jury Prize, 1977

485. *Jambon d'Ardenne / Ham and Chips* 1977
D: Benoît Lamy
S: Benoît Lamy, Rudolph Pauli
C: Michel Baudour
P: Pierre Druout
A: Annie Girardot
A hotel owner dominates the staff, the tourists in the neighborhood, and her family. *Belgian Cinema.*

486. *La Vie devant soi / Madame Rosa* 1977
D: Moshé Mizrahi
S: Moshé Mizrahi
C: Nestor Almendros
P: Jean Bolvary
A: Michal Bat-Adam, Simone Signoret
An old woman, formerly a prostitute, cares for children of prostitutes and is particularly close to an unruly Arab boy. *BiFi.*

487. *Violette Nozière* 1977 S
D: Claude Chabrol
S: Odile Barski, Hervé Bromberger
C: Jean Rabier
P: Roger Morand
A: Isabelle Huppert, Stéphane Audran
True crime: A daughter kills her father and tries to kill her mother. Tried and convicted, then released from prison ten years later, she becomes a cause for women's groups. *Variety: 36. 1978, May 24.*
Awards: Cannes Film Festival, Best Actress (Huppert), 1978; César Awards, Best Supporting Actress (Audran), 1979

488. *Une Histoire simple / A Simple Story* 1978
D: Claude Sautet
S: Claude Sautet, Jean-Loup Dabadie
C: Jean Boffety
A: Romy Schneider
A divorced fashion designer with a fifteen-year-old son has an abortion when a relationship fails but decides to get pregnant again and remain single. *BiFi.*
Other titles: Eine einfache Geschichte
Awards: César Awards, Best Actress, 1979; Academy Awards, nomination for Best Foreign Language Film, 1980

489. *Judith Therpauve* 1978
D: Patrice Chéreau
S: Patrice Chéreau, Georges Conchon
C: Pierre Lhomme
P: Daniel Toscan du Plantier
A: Simone Signoret
A widow, who was heavily involved in the resistance, comes out of retirement to take over a failing liberal paper, but the forces against her are too great. *BiFi.*

490. *Félicité* 1979 DS
D: Christine Pascal
S: Christine Pascal
C: Yves Lafaye
A: Christine Pascal, Monique Chaumette
A woman leaves her brother at a hotel and goes to the cinema with her lover, who meets an old friend there. Becoming jealous, she leaves them and goes to her room to think, then harasses him when he returns early the next morning. *Festival de films, 23rd: 93. 2001.*

491. *La Femme flic / The Woman Cop* 1979
D: Yves Boisset
S: Yves Boisset, Claude Veillot
C: Jacques Loiseleux
P: Alain Sarde
A: Miou-Miou
A small-town police inspector uncovers a child-prostitution ring involving the local elite. *BiFi.*

492. *Regaeim / Moments* 1979 DS
D: Michal Bat-Adam
S: Michal Bat-Adam
C: Yves Lafaye
P: Moshé Mizrahi
A: Michal Bat-Adam, Brigitte Catillon
Two women, an Israeli novelist and a French photographer, become close friends when they meet on a train to Jerusalem. *FII.*
Other titles: Each Other

493. *Les Soeurs Brontë / The Brontë Sisters*
1979

D: André Téchiné
S: Pascal Bonitzer, André Téchiné
C: Bruno Nuytten
P: Yves Gasser
A: Isabelle Adjani, Isabelle Huppert, Marie-France Pisier

The story of the famous trio of female writers and their relationship with their self-destructive brother. *BiFi.*

Awards: Cannes Film Festival, nomination for Golden Palm, 1979

494. *Tapage nocturne / Nocturnal Uproar* 1979 DS

D: Catherine Breillat
S: Catherine Breillat
C: Jacques Boumendil
A: Dominique Laffin

A film director, married with a child, pursues sexual excitement with an actor and then with another filmmaker, who manages to turn the seduction on her and make her submissive to him. *Festival de films, 23rd: 93. 2001.*

495. *Les Ailes de la colombe / The Wings of the Dove* 1980 S

D: Benoît Jacquot
S: Florence Delay; based on the novel by Henry James
C: Ennio Guarnieri
A: Dominique Sanda, Isabelle Huppert

Venice. A woman who prostitutes herself to support her luxurious lifestyle meets an heiress with a deadly malady and persuades her own lover to seduce and marry the girl to obtain her fortune. *Festival de films, 10th: 95. 1988.*

496. *La Banquiere / The Banker* 1980

D: Francis Girod
S: Francis Girod
C: Bernard Zitzermann
P: Ariel Zeitoun
A: Romy Schneider, Marie-France Pisier

Paris, 1920s. The rise and fall of a self-made bank president; based on the life of Marthe Hanau. *BiFi.*

Other titles: The Woman Banker

497. *Cocktail Molotov* 1980 DS

D: Diane Kurys
S: Diane Kurys, Alain Le Henry, Philippe Adrieu
C: Philippe Rousselot
P: Alexandre Arcady
A: Elise Carron, Philippe Le Bas

May, 1968. A woman flees her mother's house to join a kibbutz with her boyfriend, but he backs out and she goes on her own. Finding herself pregnant, she decides not to keep the child.

498. *Je vous aime / I Love You All* 1980

D: Claude Berri
S: Claude Berri
C: Etienne Becker
A: Catherine Deneuve

A woman, content to be alone, breaks up with her current lover and indulges in happy memories of a Christmas eve when she was reunited with the three men she has loved. *Festival de films, 16th: 71. 1994.*

499. *Loulou* 1980

D: Maurice Pialat
S: Maurice Pialat
A: Isabelle Huppert, Gérard Depardieu

After three years of marriage to a successful advertising executive, a woman becomes obsessed with a lout who scorns her, and she leaves her husband for him. *Film Society. 2004, Apr.*

500. *Agatha et les lectures illimitées / Agatha* 1981 DSC

D: Marguerite Duras
S: Marguerite Duras
C: Dominique Le Rigoleur, Jean-Paul Meruisse
A: Bulle Ogier, Yann Andréa

A woman inhabits a large, lonely beach house with her brother, who is also her lover. *BiFi.*

501. *L'Amour nu* 1981 DS

D: Yannick Bellon
S: Yannick Bellon, Françoise Prévost
A: Marlène Jobert

A translator in her forties meets an oceanographer and potential lover, but she develops breast cancer and flees into hiding. *AMG.*

502. *Le Beau mariage / A Good Marriage* 1981 P

D: Eric Rohmer
S: Eric Rohmer
C: Bernard Lutic
P: Margaret Ménégoz
A: Béatrice Romand

A proud woman gets fed up with her married lover and decides to marry someone else. She tells her friends and family she is going to marry a man she has just met. The new man suspects a plot to trap him and refuses to see her, but one day she confronts him, he admits he is attracted to her, and she creates a scene of indignant affront at his suggestion that she is chasing him.

503. **Le Pont du Nord**   1981 SC
D: Jacques Rivette
S: Jacques Rivette, Suzanne Schiffman
C: Caroline Champetier, William Lubtchansky
P: Barbet Schroeder
A: Bulle Ogier, Pascale Ogier
Paris. A former terrorist just out of prison finds an old friend who is not pleased to see her. When he disappears, she searches for him with the help of a mysterious woman who has been following her, but they find that no one is pleased to see either of them. Mystery. *BiFi.*

504. **La Posesión / Possession**   1981
D: Andrzej Zulawski
S: Andrzej Zulawski
C: Bruno Nuytten
P: Daniel Toscan du Plantier
A: Isabelle Adjani
A woman abandons her husband, child, and lover to indulge in encounters with a strange creature; in the process, she creates bloody havoc. Thriller. *Film Society. 2002, Oct.*
Awards: Cannes Film Festival, Best Actress, 1981; César Awards, Best Actress, 1982; Fantasporto, Best Actress, Audience Award, 1983

505. **Balles perdues / Stray Bullets**   1982
D: Jean-Louis Comolli
S: Jean-Louis Comolli, Serge Valleti, Clarence Woff
C: William Lubtchansky
A: Maria Schneider, Andréa Ferréol
A wealthy diamond merchant is murdered and robbed; his assistant discovers the body but hesitates to call the police because she knows too much. She takes the body to a busy detective, and she and he pursue separate investigations. Thriller. *Festival de films, 23rd: 71. 2001.*

506. **Le Grain de sable / Grain of Sand**   1982
D: Pomme Meffre
S: Pomme Meffre
C: Jean-Noël Ferragut
A: Delphine Seyrig
A theater cashier with a normal life finds herself unemployed; she enjoys exploring the city, but anxiety and boredom interfere, and she seeks companionship with a businessman, who turns up dead. Mystery. *Festival de films, 11th: 77. 1989.*

507. **Jument vapeur / Dirty Dishes**   1982 D
D: Joyce Buñuel
A: Carole Laure
Comic rendering of an angry woman with two sons, an "average housewife: after 10 years of cooking, cleaning, and mending, she can't get excited about anything." *French-Speaking: 56.*

508. **La Truite / The Trout**   1982 S
D: Joseph Losey
S: Joseph Losey, Monique Lange
C: Henri Alekan
P: Yves Rousset-Rouard
A: Isabelle Huppert, Jeanne Moreau
Paris. A country girl raised on a trout farm, who vowed as a teenager to never grant a man any of her true self, lives with a gay friend. A businessman tries to seduce her and brings her into the corporate world. *BiFi.*

509. **Coup de foudre / At First Sight**   1983 DS
D: Diane Kurys
S: Diane Kurys, Alain Le Henry
C: Bernard Lutic
P: Ariel Zeitoun
A: Miou-Miou, Isabelle Huppert
1950s. A Jewish refugee and a woman who both have children and unsatisfying marriages become close friends and set up a dress shop together. They become very involved with each other and their work, leaving their husbands, and sometimes their children, behind.
Other titles: Entre nous
Awards: San Sebastián International Film Festival, FIPRESCI, 1983; Academy Awards, nomination for Best Foreign Language Film, 1984

510. **L'Été meurtrier / One Deadly Summer**
                                             1983
D: Jean Becker
S: Jean Becker, Sébastien Japrisot
C: Etienne Becker
P: Christine Beyout
A: Isabelle Adjani, Suzanne Flon
A young woman becomes deranged in an attempt to avenge the rape of her mother that resulted in her birth. *BiFi.*
Awards: César Awards, Best Actress (Adjani), Best Supporting Actress (Flon), 1984

511. **Les Mots pour le dire / The Words to Say It**   1983 SP
D: José Pinheiro
S: Suso Cecchi D'Amico, Marie-Francois Leclère; based on the novel by Marie Cardinal
C: Gerry Fisher
P: Vera Belmont
A: Marie-Christine Barrault, Nicole Garcia, Daniel Mesguich
The psychoanalysis of a woman endangered by inexplicable uterine bleeding in her adulthood.

Born in Algeria, she was frozen out by her French mother, who was embittered by the changes forced by the end of French control there. *BiFi.*

Awards: César Awards, nomination for Best Actress (Garcia), 1984

512. *Rue Cases Nègres* / *Sugar Cane Alley*
                                              1983 DS
D: Euzhan Palcy
S: Euzhan Palcy, Josef Zobel
C: Dominique Chapuis
A: Darling Légitimus, Garry Cadenat
Martinique. A grandmother works in the sugar-cane fields while she raises her young grandson in a strict but loving and energetic manner. She sacrifices her life for his education.
Other titles: Black Shack Alley
Awards: Venice Film Festival, Silver Lion, Best Actress, 1983; César Awards, Best First Work, 1984

513. *Bérénice* 1984
D: Raoul Ruiz
S: based on the play by Jean Racine
A: Anne Alvaro
"Queen from the East, the daughter of Herod, is loved by the Roman emperor, but refused acceptance by the Roman court because she was not pure Latin." Filmed as a shadow play with one character. *Variety. 1984, Mar. 7.*

514. *Les Nuits de la pleine lune* / *Full Moon in Paris* 1984
D: Eric Rohmer
S: Eric Rohmer
C: Renato Berta
A: Pascale Ogier
Paris. A young woman conflicts with the man she loves over how they spend their free time; she likes to stay out late, and he gets up early. To indulge more in nightlife, she acquires an apartment of her own in the city, but eventually he finds someone else. *BiFi.*
Awards: Venice Film Festival, Best Actress, 1984

515. *La Pirate* 1984
D: Jacques Doillon
S: Jacques Doillon
C: Bruno Nuytten
P: Olivier Lorsac
A: Jane Birkin, Maruschka Detmers
A woman renews her relationship with a former lover even though her husband objects. The woman has reappeared suddenly with her teenage daughter in tow, who becomes upset by the intrigue and interferes tragically. *BiFi.*

Awards: Cannes Film Festival, nomination for Golden Palm, 1984

516. *San toit ni loi* / *Vagabond* 1985 DS
D: Agnès Varda
S: Agnès Varda
C: Patrick Blossier
P: Oury Milshtein
A: Sandrine Bonnaire
A homeless and sullen young woman wanders the south of France and attaches herself to a series of strangers. Some even try to help her, but she eventually self-destructs in the cold.
Awards: Venice Film Festival, FIPRESCI, 1985; César Awards, Best Actress, 1986; Los Angeles Film Critics Association, Best Actress, Best Foreign Film, 1986

517. *Voyage à Paimpol* 1985 SP
D: John Berry
S: John Berry, Josiane Lévêque; based on the novel by Dorothée Letessier
C: Bernard Zitzermann
P: Myriam Boyer
A: Myriam Boyer, Michel Boujenah, Dora Doll
A factory worker has married for the sake of her child and now feels more trapped than ever; she takes a day trip to Paimpol to meet a journalist whom she met during a strike and who encouraged her to write about her life in the factory. *Bifi (Ital.).*

518. *4 Aventures de Reinette et Mirabelle* / *4 Adventures of Reinette and Mirabelle*
                                              1986 SC
D: Eric Rohmer
S: Eric Rohmer, Joëlle Miguel
C: Sophie Maintigneux
A: Joëlle Miguel, Jessica Forde
A Paris girl and a country girl meet on vacation, then decide to room together at university, where their different personalities conflict. *AMG.*

519. *L'Amant magnifique* 1986 DSC
D: Aline Isserman
S: Aline Isserman, Michel Dufresne
C: Dominique Le Rigoleur
A: Isabel Otero
A woman is married to a man who breeds horses. She has an affair with a groom and decides to leave her husband, but the groom also chooses his horse over her. *Bifi.*

520. *Cours privé* / *Private Class* 1986
D: Pierre Granier-Deferre
S: Pierre Granier-Deferre, Christopher Frank

C: Robert Fraisse
P: Alain Sarde
A: Elizabeth Bourgine

A high school teacher seduces colleagues and students but is exposed with a letter-writing campaign that spreads through the whole school. *BiFi.*

521. *Le Rayon vert / The Green Ray* 1986 SCP

D: Eric Rohmer
S: Marie Rivière, Eric Rohmer
C: Sophie Maintigneux
P: Margaret Ménégoz
A: Marie Rivière

A young secretary has trouble spending her summer vacation time; her first is canceled and she decides to try out Normandy, then the mountains, and finally Biarritz, where a friend lends her apartment. *BiFi.*

522. *Signé Charlotte* 1986 DS

D: Caroline Huppert
S: Caroline Huppert
A: Isabelle Huppert

"Rock singer is blamed for her boyfriend's murder . . . so [she] escapes with her former lover." Mystery. *French-Speaking: 79.*

523. *Thérèse* 1986 S

D: Alain Cavalier
S: Camille De Casabianca, Alain Cavalier
C: Philippe Rousselot
A: Catherine Mouchet

The life of St. Therese of Lisieux (1873–1897), the Little Flower of Jesus. Young Therese goes off to join her older sisters in a convent; there she maintains a special devotion to Christ, despite the variable lifestyles of the other nuns. Her mysticism is finely and humorously described, but it "remains utterly rational." *NYT: C28. 1986, Dec. 17.*
Awards: Cannes Film Festival, Jury Prize, 1986; César Awards, Best Film, Best Director, 1987

524. *Jupon rouge / The Red Skirt* 1987 DSP

D: Geneviève Lefèbvre
S: Nicole Berckmans, Geneviève Lefèbvre
C: Ramon Suárez
P: Geneviève Lefèbvre
A: Marie-Christine Barrault, Alida Valli

A concentration camp survivor, who devotes herself to political work with Amnesty International, has a fashion-designer lover who falls in love with a younger woman. The fashion designer tries to keep both relationships, but the older woman becomes mentally unstable. *Variety. 1987, Sep. 23.*
Other titles: Manuela's Loves

525. *Le Petit amour / Kung Fu Master* 1987 DS

D: Agnès Varda
S: Agnès Varda, Jane Birkin
C: Pierre-Laurent Chénieux
A: Jane Birkin, Mathieu Demy

A forty-year-old mother has a long-term affair with her teenage daughter's fifteen-year-old friend; he strains under the social disgrace, but she remains blinded by her passion for him.
Awards: Berlin International Film Festival, nomination for Golden Bear, 1988

526. *La Vieille quimboiseuse et le majordome* 1987

D: Julius-Amédée Laou
S: Julius-Amédée Laou
C: Jean-Paul Miotto
A: Jenny Alpha

Paris, 1921. A chambermaid and a valet form a married couple and move with their masters to Paris from the Antilles. Within a year, the wife is dancing with the "Revue nègre." Soon she is an usher, then a concierge, and she eventually acquires the status of a quimboiseuse, or healer. *Festival de films, 25th: 24. 2003.*

527. *Une Affaire de femmes / Story of Women* 1988 S

D: Claude Chabrol
S: Colo Tavernier, Claude Chabrol
C: Jean Rabier
P: Marin Karmitz
A: Isabelle Huppert

Based on a true story of an impoverished village woman who falls into the lucrative abortion business during the Vichy era. By the time her husband returns from the front, she is attached to her affluent lifestyle, dreams of becoming a singer, and coldly ignores him. He turns her in, and she becomes an example of loose morality, the last woman to suffer the death penalty in France.
Other titles: Secrets of Women
Awards: Venice Film Festival, Best Actress, 1988; Bogota Film Festival, Best Actress, 1989; New York Film Critics Circle Awards, Best Foreign Film, 1989

528. *La Bande des quatre / The Gang of Four* 1988 SCP

D: Jacques Rivette
S: Pascal Bonitzer, Christine Laurent, Jacques Rivette
C: Caroline Champetier
P: Martine Marignac
A: Bulle Ogier, Laurence Côte, Fejria Deliba, Natalie Richard

A drama teacher and her all-woman troupe, who room together, become immersed in a Pierre Marivaux play. *AMG.*

Awards: Acteurs à l'Écran, Best Actress (Richard), 1989; Berlin International Film Festival, FIPRESCI, 1989

529. *Camille Claudel* 1988 SP

D: Bruno Nuytten
S: Bruno Nuytten, Marilyn Goldin
C: Pierre Lhomme
P: Isabelle Adjani
A: Isabelle Adjani, Gérard Depardieu

The story of Auguste Rodin's student lover, whose skill and ideas influenced him but who fell into unbalanced behavior; the film spends equal time charting both. Detailed scenes of her lugging stone, consulting with her male model, and advising Rodin on composition end abruptly when her family's, especially her mother's, refusal to support her make her vulnerable and dependent on Rodin.

Awards: Berlin International Film Festival, Best Actress, 1989; César Awards, Best Actress, Best Film, 1989

530. *Chocolat* 1988 DS

D: Claire Denis
S: Claire Denis, Jean-Pol Fargeau
C: Robert Alazraki
P: Alain Belmondo
A: Mireille Perrier, Isaach De Bankolé

A woman returns to Cameroon, where she grew up with an absent father, the colonial director of the territory, and a beautiful mother, who was attracted to their black manservant. The humiliating position of the manservant is related to his interactions with the young girl.

531. *La Lectrice / The Reader* 1988 SCP

D: Michel Deville
S: Michel Deville, Rosalinde Deville, Raymond Jean
C: Dominique Le Rigoleur
P: Rosalinde Deville
A: Miou-Miou

A woman reads a novel aloud at night to her lover. It's about a "professional reader," telling of the varied sensual reactions that her reading has on her clients and of her abandonment of the trade when she is faced with a professor who brings in a crowd of friends to hear her read the Marquis de Sade's *120 Days of Sodom.* Undaunted by its cautions, the "reader" decides to try the profession herself. Includes recitations from the works of Marguerite Duras, Guy de Maupassant, Émile Zola, and others.

Awards: Montréal World Film Festival, Grand Prix, 1988; Prix Louis Delluc, 1988

532. *La Maison de Jeanne / Jeanne's House* 1988 DS

D: Magali Clément
S: Magali Clément
C: Pierre Novion
A: Christine Boisson

Clermont-Ferrand. Jeanne runs an inn where her husband is the chef, and her sisters work as well. One day the proprietor upsets their daily life when he reveals a secret love. *Festival de films, 14th: 92. 1988.*

533. *Mon cher sujet / My Favorite Story* 1988 DS

D: Anne-Marie Miéville
S: Anne-Marie Miéville
C: Jean-Paul Rosa da Costa
A: Gaël Le Roi, Hélène Roussel, Anny Romand

A daughter, mother, and grandmother are reunited by the death of the grandfather and the birth of a child. They reveal to one another the difficulties of their relationships with men. *Festival de films, 11th: 141. 1989.*

Awards: Cannes Film Festival, Award of Youth, 1988

534. *La Passion Béatrice / Passion of Beatrice* 1988 S

D: Bertrand Tavernier
S: Colo Tavernier
C: Bruno De Keyzer
P: Pierre Saint-Blancat
A: Julie Delpy, Bernard-Pierre Donnadieu

Fourteenth century. A nobleman with a violent past is released from prison with a ransom raised by his daughter, then returns home only to conflict with her, eventually provoking her to murder him. *BiFi.*

535. *Prisonnières* 1988 DS

D: Charlotte Silvera
S: Charlotte Silvera
C: Bernard Lutic
A: Marie-Christine Barrault, Fanny Bastien, Annie Girardot

A woman who has murdered her child is jailed; she is soon deprived of privileges and rejected by both the guards and the other prisoners. *Festival de films, 11th: 140. 1989.*

536. *Chimère* 1989 DS

D: Claire Devers
S: Arlette Langmann, Claire Devers
C: Renato Berta

A: Béatrice Belle, Wadeck Stanczak

After living with her lover for a year, a woman desires a child and becomes pregnant; when she tells her partner, he reproaches her for not consulting him about the decision, and their relationship falls apart. *Festival de films, 12th: 131. 1990.*

Awards: Cannes Film Festival, nomination for Golden Palm, 1989

537. *Et la lumière fut / And Then There Was Light*   1989 S

D: Otar Ioseliani

S: Otar Ioseliani, Mina Kindl

C: Robert Alazraki

P: Alain Quefféléan

A: Saly Badji

"Life in an African village with a matriarchal society is virtually destroyed by the invasion of civilization." *West German Cinema, 1985.*

Awards: Venice Film Festival, Grand Special Jury Prize, 1989

538. *Le Moine et la sorcière / The Sorceress*   1989 DSP

D: Suzanne Schiffman

S: Suzanne Schiffman, Pamela Berger; based on the writings of Etienne de Bourbon

C: Patrick Blossier

P: Pamela Berger

A: Christine Boisson

France, thirteenth century. Monks conflict with a forest woman over church attitudes toward unmarried women healers, finally accusing her of heresy. Taken from the writings of a Dominican friar who pursued heretics. *Variety: 28. 1987, Sep 23.*

539. *Pentimento*   1989 DS

D: Tonie Marshall

S: Tonie Marshall

C: Pascal Lebègue

A: Patricia Dinev

An alcoholic mother and her young daughter are very close. One day over a death notice, the mother tells her daughter of her father, whom she has never met, and the daughter runs off to find her other family. *Festival de films, 14th: 93. 1992.*

540. *Romuald & Juliette / Mama, There's a Man in Your Bed*   1989 DS

D: Coline Serreau

S: Coline Serreau

C: Jean-Noël Ferragut

P: Philippe Carcassonne

A: Firmine Richard, Daniel Auteuil

Lyon. An African immigrant night office cleaner raises a lively group of children, each with a different father. She saves the head of the yogurt company from corporate sabotage by sharing information she has found in the wastebaskets and advising him how to pursue the matter. She and the executive become friends. Comedy.

Awards: BAFTA Awards, nomination for Best Film not in English, 1991

541. *Aventure de Catherine C.*   1990 S

D: Pierre Beuchot

S: Pierre Beuchot, Catherine Breillat

C: Willy Kurant

A: Fanny Ardant, Hanna Schygulla

Five years after the end of an affair, an actress remains despondent because of the rejection of a lover; while making a film in Vienna, she is invited to stay in the home of a baroness with a violent past, and their friendship turns violent as well when she discovers the baroness is involved with her ex-lover. *BiFi.*

542. *La Captive du désert / Captive of the Desert*   1990 P

D: Raymond Depardon

S: Raymond Depardon

C: Raymond Depardon

P: Pascale Dauman

A: Sandrine Bonnaire

A researcher is held captive and made to join in the monotonous life of a tribe of rebel nomads in the Sahara, then inexplicably let go. *BiFi.*

543. *Le Jour des rois / Epiphany Sunday*   1990 DS

D: Marie-Claude Treilhou

S: Marie-Claude Treilhou

C: Jean-Bernard Menoud

A: Danielle Darrieux, Paulette Dubost, Micheline Presle

Three aged sisters get together every Sunday. Two live with husbands, the third is in a retirement home. They still see things very differently, compete, and quarrel, but they also support one another. *Festival de films, 23rd: 103. 2001.*

544. *La Femme Nikita / Nikita*   1990

D: Luc Besson

S: Luc Besson

C: Thierry Arbogast

P: Patrice LeDoux

A: Anne Parillaud

"A violent and inarticulate girl is convicted of a police-killing" and jailed. She is saved from execution by government intelligence, who then tutor her in social graces and political assassination. Action. Remakes: *Hei Mao / Black Cat* (Hong Kong, 1991) and *Point of No Return* (United States, 1992). *FII.*

Awards: César Awards, Best Actress, 1991; David di Donatello Awards, Best Foreign Actress, 1991

545. *Un Weekend sur deux / Every Other Weekend* 1990 DS
D: Nicole Garcia
S: Nicole Garcia, Anne-Marie Etienne
C: William Lubtchansky
P: Alain Sarde
A: Nathalie Baye
A divorced actress takes her two children, who live with their father, away for the weekend in hopes of patching up their relationship, but she takes them too far, provoking the older boy to contact his father and demand he come get them. *BiFi.*

546. *Blanche et Marie* 1991 S
D: Jacques Renard
S: Jacques Renard, Sophie Goupil
C: Gérard de Battista
P: Yannick Bernard
A: Emmanuelle Béart, Miou-Miou, Maria Casarès
1941. A woman is drawn into working with the resistance to the Germans, after realizing that her mother is already active. They and a young girl become increasingly involved. The mother is arrested and tortured but never informs. When France is liberated, she is released. *BiFi.*

547. *Border Line* 1991 DS
D: Danièle Dubroux
S: Danièle Dubroux
C: Fabio Conversi
A: Danièle Dubroux
A woman visits a lover she has not seen in twenty years; finding that he has died, she moves to become the lover of his son, though her relationship with him is more maternal. *Festival de films, 14th: 101. 1992.*

548. *Boulevard des Hirondelles* 1991 DS
D: Josée Yanne
S: Josée Yanne; based on *Ils partiront dans l'ivresses* by Lucie Aubrac
C: Carlo Vanni
A: Elizabeth Bourgine, Pierre-Loup Rajot
Lyon, 1943. The true story of Lucie Aubrac, who, with her husband, organized a resistance group based in the Boulevard des Hirondelles and managed to free him from the Gestapo. *Festival de films, 23rd: 76. 2001.*

549. *Un Homme et deux femmes / A Man and Two Women* 1991 DS
D: Valerie Stroh
S: Valerie Stroh; based on stories by Doris Lessing
C: Peter Suschitzky
P: René Féret
A: Valerie Stroh, Diane Pierens, Lambert Wilson, Olivia Bruneaux
1950s. A writer, worried that her lover is moving to Paris, writes three stories: "A Man and Two Women," where a new mother offers her husband to her friend on the grounds she has time only for her baby, but the friend refuses; "The One, the Other," where a married woman begins a long-unfulfilled romantic relationship with her brother; and "Our Friend, Judith," where two friends wonder about a single friend, who does not care about how she looks but goes to Italy and has an affair with the local barber. *BiFi.*

550. *Indochine* 1991 S
D: Régis Wargnier
S: Erik Orsenna, Louis Gardel, Catherine Cohen
C: François Catonné
P: Jean Labadie
A: Catherine Deneuve, Vincent Perez
Vietnam, 1950s and 1960s. A rubber plantation owner is proud of her commanding and attentive relations with the Asian population, "my coolies," and adopts a local girl. The story follows their relationship for twenty-five years, including the strain of her daughter running away with a former lover with whom she had experienced her only real passion.

551. *Madame Bovary* 1991
D: Claude Chabrol
S: Claude Chabrol; based on the novel by Gustave Flaubert
C: Jean Rabier
P: Marin Karmitz
A: Isabelle Huppert
Nineteenth century. A bored young housewife prostrates herself in the name of romantic attachments to men other than her husband.

Awards: Moscow International Film Festival, Best Actress, 1991

552. *Milena* 1991 DS
D: Vera Belmont
S: Vera Belmont, Jana Cerna
C: Dietrich Lohmann
P: Vera Belmont
A: Valérie Kaprisky
Czechoslovakia, 1920s. Instead of following her father's wish that she become a doctor like

him, a young woman marries a music critic and pursues a free life as a leftist journalist and translator of Kafka, eventually ending up in a concentration camp. *IMDb*.

553. *Nuit et jour / Night and Day* 1991 DSP
D: Chantal Akerman
S: Chantal Akerman, Pascal Bonitzer
C: Jean-Claude Neckelbrouck
P: Martine Marignac
A: Guilaine Londez
Paris. A shiftless young woman inhabits a very spare apartment with her lover, who drives a taxi at night. One day she meets a man who drives a taxi during the day, and she makes alternating sleeping arrangements with him.

554. *Olivier, Olivier* 1991 DS
D: Agnieszka Holland
S: Agnieszka Holland, Yves Lapointe, Régis Debray
C: Bernard Zitzermann
P: Marie-Laure Reyre
A: Brigitte Roüan, Grégoire Colin
A woman falls into alcoholism while waiting for the return of her missing favorite young son, who suddenly reappears years later. The teenager, found on the streets of Paris, is accepted by the family, and only the jealous older sister wonders if this boy is really her brother. An experienced con artist, the boy suspects a neighbor of being predatory, and soon the real son's body is found in a nearby basement. *BiFi*.
Awards: Valladolid International Film Festival, Best Actress, 1992

555. *Outremer / Overseas* 1991 DS
D: Brigitte Roüan
S: Brigitte Roüan, Cedric Kahn
C: Dominique Chapuis
P: Serge Cohen Solal
A: Brigitte Roüan, Nicole Garcia, Marianne Basler
Algeria, 1950s. Three sisters from a wealthy family move into their adult lives under the specter of colonial relations. Their stories are told in individual segments, repeating scenes from their different viewpoints. The first is married to a navy man who abuses her, but she is inconsolable when he goes missing. The second runs a large farm and faces the resentment of the Arab workers, but she is unable to convince her husband to take action. The third resists marriage and has a secret affair with a rebel, who is killed.

556. *Au pays des Juliets / In the Country of Juliets* 1992 S
D: Mahdi Charef

S: Christine Brière, Mahdi Charef
C: Gérard De Battista
A: Maria Schneider, Laure Duthilleul, Claire Nebout
Three prisoners have been granted a free day and wait at the train station, where a strike interferes with their plans. They take off in a stolen auto for the city, where one plans to see a lover, the second does not know what she will do, and the third hopes to see her son. They confess their crimes to one another (all abuse related) and bond, in the end wondering if they will return to prison or not. Mystery. *Festival de films, 23rd: 71. 2001.*
Awards: Cannes Film Festival, Ecumenical Jury Prize, 1992

557. *Céline* 1992
D: Jean-Claude Brisseau
S: Jean-Claude Brisseau
C: Romain Winding
A: Lisa Hérédia, Isabelle Pasco
A desperate young woman is found crying on the street by a nurse, who takes her to live in the country. *Film Society. 2004, Feb.*

558. *Les Histoires d'amour finissent mal ... en général / Love Affairs Usually End Badly* 1992 DS
D: Anne Fontaine
S: Anne Fontaine, Claude Arnaud
C: Christophe Pollack
A: Marie Boudet
Paris. A worker in a theater lives with a taxi driver she plans to marry within the month; but then she meets another man. *Festival de films, 15th, 108. 1993.*
Awards: Prix Jean Vigo, 1993

559. *Après l'amour / After Love* 1993 DS
D: Diane Kurys
S: Diane Kurys, Antoine Lacomblez
C: Fabio Conversi
P: Jean-Bernard Fetoux
A: Isabelle Huppert
A novelist meanders through a life crowded with intimates: her lover, her husband, and his lovers and their children. Without any desire to have children of her own, she eventually becomes pregnant.

560. *L'Evanouie* 1993 DS
D: Jacqueline Veuve
S: Jacqueline Veuve, Jacques Nollo
C: Bruno De Keyzer
A: Stéphane Audran, Daniel Gélin

A woman goes to a hospital for tests, but she decides to evade the tests and her son and goes off to live in a hotel. There she meets an old man who helps her. *Francophone Women: 217.*

561. Jeanne la pucelle / Joan the Maid 1993 S
D: Jacques Rivette
S: Jacques Rivette, Pascal Bonitzer, Christine Laurent
C: William Lubtchansky
P: Peter Wallon
A: Sandrine Bonnaire
Primarily focused on the political intrigue that surrounded the phenomenon of this charismatic figure. Part I: The battles. Joan pleads with the French to believe in her divine mission to save them from the English and crown the Dauphine. Part II: Prison. Challenged in battles, Joan is captured, imprisoned, placed on trial, and burned at the stake. *Variety: 46. 1994, Feb. 21.*

562. Loin des barbares / Far from the Barbarians 1993 DS
D: Liria Bégéja
S: Liria Bégéja
C: Patrick Blossier
A: Dominique Blanc, Timo Floko
A young Albanian woman is ready to move to the United States with her husband when she gets a telephone call from a mysterious man who says that her father, who died in Albania under mysterious conditions twenty-five years earlier, may still be alive and living in France. She goes to help the man search for her father. *Festival de films, 26th: 60. 2004.*
Awards: Angers European First Film Festival, Best Film, 2000

563. Lou n'a pas dit non / Lou Didn't Say No 1993 DS
D: Anne-Marie Miéville
S: Anne-Marie Miéville
C: Edwin Horak
P: Serge Houppin
A: Marie Bunel, Caroline Micla, Manuel Blanc
A film director has a jealous lover. *Village Voice: 108. 2003, May 7.*
Awards: Entrevues Film Festival, Grand Prix, 1994

564. Ma saison preferée / My Favorite Season 1993
D: André Téchiné
S: André Téchiné, Pascal Bonitzer
C: Thierry Arbogast
P: Alain Sarde
A: Catherine Deneuve, Daniel Auteuil

A middle-aged daughter cares for her mother and conflicts with her brother.
Awards: César Awards, nomination for Best Actress, 1994; Boston Society of Film Critics Awards, Best Foreign Film, 1996

565. Une Nouvelle vie / A New Life 1993
D: Oliver Assayas
S: Oliver Assayas
C: Denis Lenoir
P: Bruno Pésary
A: Judith Godrèche, Sophie Aubrey
After the death of her mother, a woman changes. She begins a search for her father and finds a half sister. *MOMA Film. 2003, Sep.*

566. Sur la terre comme au ciel / Between Heaven and Earth 1993 DSP
D: Marion Hänsel
S: Jaco van Dormael, Marion Hänsel; based on a story by Laurette Vankeerberghen
C: Josep Civit
P: Marion Hänsel
A: Carmen Maura, André Delvaux
Paris. A television journalist gets pregnant, then questions her condition as her child wonders aloud from the womb about the world into which she will be born. Her colleagues have difficulty appreciating this, especially when she discovers the phenomenon has spread and there are other cases of fetuses refusing to be born. A young neighbor boy helps her through the crisis.
Other titles: Entre el cielo y la tierra / In Heaven as on Earth
Awards: Karlovy Vary International Film Festival, nomination for Crystal Globe, 1992

567. Trois couleurs: Bleu / Blue 1993 S
D: Krysztof Kieslowski
S: Agnieszka Holland, Slawomir Idziak
C: Slawomir Idziak
P: Marin Karmitz
A: Juliette Binoche
A music composer copes with the accidental death of her child and husband by attempting suicide and then going into hiding; resurfacing, she faces betrayal over her collaborative relationship with her husband and his infidelity.
Awards: Venice Film Festival, Golden Lion, Best Actress, 1993; César Awards, Best Actress, 1994; Goya Awards, Best European Film, 1994

568. L'Ange noir / The Black Angel 1994
D: Jean-Claude Brisseau
S: Jean-Claude Brisseau

C: Romain Winding
P: Alain Sarde
A: Sylvie Vartan

A respectable woman has a gangland past; she murders a mobster she claims tried to rape her, then manipulates her lawyer. *Film Society. 2004, Feb.*

569. *Une Femme francaise / A French Woman* 1994

D: Régis Wargnier
S: Régis Wargnier, Alain Le Henry
C: François Catonné
P: Yves Marmion
A: Emmanuelle Béart, Daniel Auteuil

A military officer's wife loves him but has affairs during his absences; one is a serious one with a German who follows her from post to post, knowing she will not leave her husband. *BiFi.*

570. *Personne ne m'aime / Nobody Loves Me* 1994 DS

D: Marion Vernoux
S: Marion Vernoux
C: Eric Gautier
A: Bernadette Lafont, Bulle Ogier

A mother thrown out of her home and first lives with her grown daughter, then moves on to her sister, who takes her to a resort to spy on the sister's philandering husband. Comedy. *BiFi.*

Awards: Locarno International Film Festival, Special Prize, 1994

571. *La Piste du télégraphe / The Telegraph Route* 1994 DS

D: Liliane De Kermadec
S: Liliane de Kermadec
C: Aurique Delannoy
A: Elena Safonova

New York, 1927. A woman in search of her roots and identity sets out on foot across North America for the Siberian land where she was born. *Festival de films, 17th: 100. 1995.*

572. *La Reine Margot / Queen Margot* 1994 S

D: Patrice Chéreau
S: Danièle Thompson; based on the novel by Alexandre Dumas
C: Philippe Rousselot
P: Claude Berri
A: Isabelle Adjani, Daniel Auteuil, Virna Lisi, Vincent Perez

Sixteenth century. The Catholic daughter of Catherine de Medici is forced into marriage with a Huguenot Protestant to facilitate peace, but she attempts to keep her independence and lovers.

Awards: Cannes Film Festival, Best Actress (Lisi), Jury Prize, 1994; César Awards, Best Actress (Adjani), Best Supporting Actress (Lisi), 1995

573. *Rosine* 1994 DS

D: Christine Carrière
S: Christine Carrière, Jean Aurel
C: Christophe Pollack
P: Alain Sarde
A: Eloïse Charretier, Mathilde Seigner

A factory worker is loved beyond deserving by her fourteen-year-old daughter, who behaves more maturely than she. One day the girl discovers her mother with a man, who turns out to be her father; at first, he is loving, then violent, and finally he rapes the child. *Festival de films, 19th: 95. 1997. Also Variety. 1994, Aug. 22.*

Awards: Locarno International Film Festival, Bronze Leopard, 1994; Acteurs à l'Écran, Best Actress (Seigner), 1995

574. *Trois couleurs: Rouge / Red* 1994

D: Krysztof Kieslowski
S: Krysztof Kieslowski
C: Piotr Sobocinski
P: Marin Karmitz
A: Irène Jacob, Jean-Louis Trintignant

A young fashion model is passive and curious at the same time; she makes friends with an aging judge when she runs over his dog, and he turns out to have qualities similar to her.

575. *La Cérémonie / The Ceremony* 1995 S

D: Claude Chabrol
S: Caroline Eliacheff, Claude Chabrol; based on the novel by Ruth Rendell
C: Bernard Zitzermann
P: Marin Karmitz
A: Isabelle Huppert, Sandrine Bonnaire, Jacqueline Bisset

Brittany. A young woman is hired to work as a maid in a mansion; she is terrified that her illiteracy will be uncovered. She becomes friends with the local postmaster, a wild woman the same age who schemes to get back at the world and uses her connection to the maid to execute a violent rampage.

Other titles: *Judgment in Stone*
Awards: César Awards, Best Actress (Huppert), 1996; Los Angeles Film Critics Association, Best Foreign Film, 1996

576. *Circuit carole* 1995 DS

D: Emmanuelle Cuau
S: Emmanuelle Cuau, Arlette Langmann
C: Benoit Delhomme

P: Philippe Martin
A: Bulle Ogier, Laurence Côte

A working-class mother has grave emotional difficulties with her daughter's rebellion into the world of motorcycle racing. *Festival de films, 10th: 103. 1995.*

577. *En Avoir (ou pas) / To Have (or Not)*
1995 DSC

D: Laëtitia Masson
S: Laëtitia Masson
C: Caroline Champetier
P: Georges Benayoun
A: Sandrine Kiberlain

Suddenly one day, a young worker in a fish factory leaves town and her eager-to-marry boyfriend; she finds life in a small city somewhat more interesting and eventually takes up with another man.

Awards: Berlin International Film Festival, CICAE Award, 1996; Brussels International Film Festival, Best Actress, 1996

578. *Fugueuses*
1995 DSP

D: Nadine Trintignant
S: Gilles Perrault, Nadine Trintignant
C: Acacio De Almeida
P: Anne François
A: Irène Jacob, Marie Trintignant, Nicole Garcia

Lisbon. Two Parisian women meet on a train to Lisbon and become close friends; one, who has accidentally killed a friend during a brawl, takes the other's identity when she drowns. *BiFi.*

579. *Gazon maudit / French Twist*
1995 DS

D: Josiane Balasko
S: Josiane Balasko, Patrick Aubrée
C: Gérard De Battista
P: Pierre Grunstein
A: Victoria Abril, Josiane Balasko

A handywoman's car breaks down in front of a Spanish immigrant's suburban home, and she falls in love with the wife and mother of the house, whose husband has affairs himself. Comedy.

Awards: César Awards, Best Writing, 1996

580. *Mina Tannenbaum*
1995 DS

D: Martine Dugowson
S: Martine Dugowson
C: Dominique Chapuis
P: Georges Benayoun
A: Romaine Bohringer, Elsa Zylberstein

A bright, talented, but troubled artist and her more prosaic and conventional friend remain close throughout their lives. They have many differences, and even experience betrayal, but they

hold on to an almost religious faith and respect for one another.

Awards: Sochi International Film Festival, Grand Prix, 1994; Boston Society of Film Critics Awards, Best Foreign Film, 1995

581. *Souviens-toi de moi*
1995 DSC

D: Zaïda Ghorab-Volta
S: Zaïda Ghorab-Volta
C: Hélène Louvart
P: Danièle Incalcaterra
A: Zaïda Ghorab-Volta

Paris. A young woman in her twenties must remain with her traditional Algerian immigrant parents in the banlieu, denying herself freedom and a better job in deference to them, yet observant of the repression and violence her mother accepts. *BiFi.*

Other titles: Elyes, baccar

582. *L'École de la chair / The School of Flesh*
1996 CP

D: Benoît Jacquot
S: Jacques Fieschi; based on the novel by Yukio Mishima
C: Caroline Champetier
P: Fabienne Vonier
A: Isabelle Huppert, Vincent Martinez

A middle-aged fashion designer picks up a young working-class bisexual boxer, who is sometimes abusive. Still, she pays his debts and keeps him, even taking him on a vacation to Morocco. *Village Voice: 139. 1996, Mar. 2.*

Awards: César Awards, nomination for Best Actress, 1999

583. *La Fille seule / Single Girl*
1996 C

D: Benoît Jacquot
S: Benoît Jacquot, Jerome Beaujour
C: Caroline Champetier
A: Virginie Ledoyen

A girl discovers she is pregnant, then spends the next hour of the film beginning her new job as a hotel waitress. *BiFi.*

584. *Marius et Jeanette / Marius and Jeanette*
1996

D: Robert Guédiguian
S: Robert Guédiguian
C: Bernard Cavalié
P: Robert Guédiguian
A: Ariane Ascaride, Gerard Meylan

Marseille. A working-class woman with two children lives in an apartment in an intimate neighborhood. She has a temper and suddenly quits her job as a grocery checkout clerk, then meets a nice man.

585. *Mécaniques célestes / Celestial Clockwork*
1996 DSP
D: Fina Torres
S: Yves Belaubre, Telsche Boorman, Chantal Pelletier
C: Ricardo Aronovich
P: Fina Torres
A: Ariadna Gil
An aspiring opera diva abandons her wedding ceremony in Caracas and moves to Paris to join other young immigrants.

586. *Nénette and Boni*   1996 DSC
D: Claire Denis
S: Claire Denis, Jean-Pol Fargeau
C: Agnès Godard
P: Georges Benayoun
A: Alice Houri, Grégoire Colin
A fifteen-year-old pregnant girl, alone in the world, clings to her eighteen-year-old brother for support.
Awards: Locarno International Film Festival, Golden Leopard, 1996

587. *La Petite Lola / Clubbed to Death* 1996 DS
D: Yolande Zauberman
S: Yolande Zauberman, Noëmie Lvovsky
C: Denis Lenoir
A: Elodie Bouchez, Béatrice Dalle, Julie Bataille
A young woman is drugged and raped at a rave, but she remains attracted to the multicultural environment, the hypnotic music, and an older man, who is one of the locals. She returns to the warehouse district and contends with his current lover, a woman his own age.
Other titles: Dançar Até Morrer
Awards: Valladolid International Film Festival, nomination for Golden Spike, 1997

588. *Post-coitum, animal triste / After Sex*
1996 DS
D: Brigitte Roüan
S: Brigitte Roüan, Santiago Amigorena, Guy Zilberstein
C: Pierre Dupouey
P: Humbert Balsan
A: Brigitte Roüan, Boris Terral, Patrick Chesnais, Françoise Arnoul
A married woman with two children risks her career and home by having a painful love affair with a man twenty years her junior. In a parallel story, her lawyer husband defends a woman accused of murdering her philandering husband. *Variety. 1997, June 1.*

589. *Temps de chien / Heavy Weather*   1996
D: Jean Marboeuf

S: Jean Marboeuf, Eric-Emmanuel Schmitt
C: Dominique Bouilleret
A: Julie Marboeuf, Catherine Arditi, Françoise Arnoul, Evelyn Bouix
Personal and work problems of an all-female workforce in a multinational insurance company; one rises to an executive position, then fails. *Variety: 88. 1997, Apr. 6.*
Awards: Namur International Festival of French-Speaking Film, Best Screenplay, 1996

590. *Y aura-t-il de la neige à Noël? / Will It Snow for Christmas?*   1996 DSC
D: Sandrine Veysset
S: Sandrine Veysset, Antoinette De Robien
C: Hélène Louvart
P: Humbert Balsan
A: Dominique Reymond
The South. A mother and her seven children live in a cold farm building down the road from the warm house where the father and his "legitimate" family live. The father picks up the children every day to work on his farm. Isolated by her status, the woman is kind and loving to the fault of accepting this man's abusive terms, but she begins to wake up when she sees him flirting with their daughter.
Awards: Paris Film Festival, Best Actress, 1996; Prix Louis Delluc, 1996; Viennale, FIPRESCI, 1996

591. *Anna Karenina*   1997
D: Bernard Rose
S: Bernard Rose; based on the novel by Leo Tolstoy
A: Sophie Marceau
A woman gives up her child and position for a romance with a younger man but commits suicide when the romance ends.

592. *Artemisia*   1997 DS
D: Agnès Merlet
S: Agnès Merlet, Patrick Amos
C: Benoit Delhomme
P: Patrice Haddad
A: Valentina Cervi
Seventeenth century. The true story of Artemisia Gentileschi, a famous painter and the talented daughter of a well-known artist who encouraged her interest in drawing, after she persisted in secret. He then arranged training from one of his peers, and a scandal and rape trial ensued. The film, controversially in regard to the historical record, describes their sexual relationship as consensual and the rape accusation as a cover.
Awards: Avignon/New York Film Festival, Best Film, 1998

593. *Lucie Aubrac* 1997 S
D: Claude Berri
S: Claude Berri; based on an autobiography by Lucie Aubrac
C: Vincenzo Marano
P: Pierre Grunstein
A: Carole Bouquet, Daniel Auteuil
A woman of the French resistance successfully maneuvers to free her husband from a series of Gestapo prisons.
Awards: Berlin International Film Festival, nomination for Golden Bear, 1997

594. *Marquise* 1997 DSP
D: Vera Belmont
S: Jean-Francois Josselin, Vera Belmont
C: Jean-Marie Dreujou
P: Vera Belmont
A: Sophie Marceau
Eighteenth century. A young woman born into poverty uses her beauty to earn a living by seducing men. When Molière and his theater troupe arrive in her village, the leading actor asks to marry her, and she agrees if she is allowed to become an actress and join the troupe. *Cine espanol. 1997.*
Awards: AFI Fest, nomination for Grand Jury Prize, 1997

595. *Nous sommes tous encore ici / We're All Still Here* 1997 DS
D: Anne-Marie Miéville
S: Anne-Marie Miéville
C: Christophe Beaucarne
A: Bernadette Lafont, Aurore Clément, Jean-Luc Godard
A triptych: the philosophy of a suburban woman, spoken in dialogue from Plato and Socrates, while she irons and sews; Jean-Luc Godard reads from Hannah Arendt's *On Totalitarianism*; and a couple comment on their romance and on being artists. *Variety. 1997, Apr. 21.*

596. *On connait la chanson / Same Old Song* 1997 SP
D: Alain Resnais
S: Agnès Jaoui, Jean-Pierre Bacri
C: Renato Berta
P: Catherine Chouridis
A: Sabine Azéma, Agnès Jaoui, André Dussollier
Paris. Two sisters, one who gives tours of the city while finishing her thesis, the other a married executive, have four men in their lives. Their banter and activity is organized around famous popular song fragments that are lip-synched to the original versions. *Variety. 1977, Nov. 17.*

Awards: Prix Louis Delluc, 1997; César Awards, Best Film, Best Supporting Actress (Jaoui), 1998; French Syndicate of Cinema Critics, Best Film, 1998

597. *Les Palmes de M. Shutz* 1997
D: Claude Pinoteau
S: Claude Pinoteau, Richard Dembo
C: Pierre Lhomme
P: Pierre Sayag
A: Isabelle Huppert, Charles Berling, Philippe Noiret
The story of Madame Curie, a Polish woman who arrived at the Paris School of Physics and Chemistry and was put to work with two top researchers, Pierre Curie and Gustave Belmont, in hopes of gaining a prestigious prize (palmes). At first reluctant to collaborate with her, Curie ended up marrying her, and the trio discovered radioactivity and won the Nobel Prize in 1903. *BiFi.*

598. *Romaine* 1997 DS
D: Agnès Obadia
S: Agnès Obadia
C: Luc Pagés
A: Agnès Obadia, Eva Ionesco
A woman loses her lover to a transvestite friend, then vacations and finds a couple of other women friends. They go to a chateau where they find "an ex-assassin who is taciturn but also a poet." *Francophone Women: 176.*

599. *Sinon, oui / A Foreign Body* 1997 DSP
D: Claire Simon
S: Claire Simon
C: Richard Copans
P: Catherine Jacques
A: Cathérine Mendez
A woman who claims she is pregnant finds it difficult to hold on to the secret that she is not, but her family relationships depend on it. *FII.*
Awards: Avignon Film Festival, Prix SACD, 1997

600. *Á vendre / For Sale* 1998 DS
D: Laëtitia Masson
S: Laëtitia Masson
C: Antoine Héberlé
P: Nicolas Daguet
A: Sandrine Kiberlain
A young woman, who is soon to be wed to an older man, her employer, disappears; he hires a detective, who traces her pattern of moving on, first from the countryside where she was raised, and then to the city, where she supported herself in many ways, including prostitution. *Variety: 39. 1998, June 1.*

601. *Conte d'automne / Autumn's Tale* 1998 C
D: Eric Rohmer
S: Eric Rohmer
C: Diane Baratier
P: Françoise Etchegaray
A: Béatrice Romand, Marie Rivière
A middle-aged widow with two children is a hard-working vintner and extremely proud of her wine. Though she enjoys life with her friends and family and is resigned to not find love, she is surprised to meet a man one day at a social event.
Other titles: A Tale of Autumn

602. *Laisse un peu d'amour* 1998 DSC
D: Zaïda Ghorab-Volta
S: Zaïda Ghorab-Volta
C: Hélène Louvart
A: Andrée Damant, Aurelia Petit, Lise Payen
An immigrant single mother is forced into early retirement from her job and spends her days going from office to office. Her two daughters, one a graduate from drama school, the other just out of the hospital after a suicide attempt, live with her. *Festival de films, 22nd: 82. 2000.*

603. *Un Pont entre deux rives / The Bridge* 1998
D: Gérard Depardieu, Frédéric Aubertin
S: François Dupeyron
A: Carole Bouquet, Gérard Depardieu
After fifteen years of marriage, a mother meets an engineer, falls in love, and considers leaving her family. *BiFi.*

604. *Serial Lover* 1998
D: James Huth
S: James Huth, Romain Berthomieu
C: Jean-Claude Thibaut
P: Philippe Rousselot
A: Michèle Laroque
A woman decides to marry and invites three potential husbands to her house for her birthday, but things go awry when she accidentally kills one of them. Comedy. *AMG.*
Awards: Chicago International Film Festival, FIPRESCI, 1998; Paris Film Festival, Special Jury Prize, 1998

605. *Vie rêvée des anges / The Dreamlife of Angels* 1998 C
D: Erick Zonca
S: Erick Zonca
C: Agnès Godard
P: Michel Saint-Jean
A: Elodie Bouchez, Natacha Régnier

Lille. A young drifter moves in with another young woman; the lodging is temporary, as is much of their lives.

606. *La Dilettante* 1999
D: Pascal Thomas
S: Jacques Lourcelles, Pascal Thomas
C: Christophe Beaucarne
P: Pascal Thomas
A: Catherine Frot
Bored with her life in Switzerland, a woman returns to Paris, where she leans on two children she has not seen in many years, teaches school in a tough district, sells antiques, and becomes a criminal defendant and a model prisoner, all with a panache that only her children cannot appreciate.
Awards: Moscow International Film Festival, Best Actress, 1999

607. *Les Enfants du siècle / Children of the Century* 1999 DSP
D: Diane Kurys
S: Diane Kurys, Murray Head
C: Vilko Filac
P: Diane Kurys
A: Juliette Binoche, Benoît Magimel
Paris, 1830s. Early life of novelist George Sand, chronicling her beginnings as an author of feminist manifestos that attracted the poet Alfred de Musset; a trip to Venice leads to their breakup when both are unfaithful. *Francophone Women: 153.*

608. *Haut les coeurs! / Chin Up!* 1999 DSCP
D: Sólveig Anspach
S: Sólveig Anspach, Pierre-Erwan Guillaume
C: Mathilde Jaffre
P: Diana Elbaum
A: Karin Viard
A pregnant woman undergoes treatment for cancer. *London Film. 1999.*
Awards: César Awards, Best Actress, 2000; Flanders International Film Festival, Silver Spur, 1999; Lumiere Awards, Best Actress, 2000

609. *Une Liaison pornographique / An Affair of Love* 1999 C
D: Frédéric Fonteyne
S: Philippe Blasband
C: Virginie Saint-Martin
A: Nathalie Baye, Serge Lopez
A single woman places an ad for a "pornographic" relationship, nothing personal. They meet weekly in the same café and go to the same hotel; then, one day, she asks that they make love "normally." *Festival de films, 24th: 30. 2002.*
Awards: Venice Film Festival, Best Actress, 1999

610. Love Me 1999 DS
D: Laëtitia Masson
S: Laëtitia Masson
C: Antoine Héberlé
P: Alain Sarde
A: Sandrine Kiberlain, Johnny Hallyday
An amnesiac happens to be in an airport without a name or papers, somewhere in the United States. She asks a rock star, whom she idolizes, to help her, but he disappears. She thinks only of connecting with him, though mostly she daydreams. *Festival de films, 22nd: 103. 2000.*
Awards: Berlin International Film Festival, nomination for Golden Bear, 2000

611. The Messenger: The Story of Joan of Arc
1999
D: Luc Besson
S: Luc Besson, Andrew Birkin
C: Thierry Arbogast
P: Patrice Ledoux
A: Milla Jovovich
Fifteenth century. The life of Joan of Arc as an action film.
Awards: Lumiere Awards, Best Film, 2000

612. Nadia et les hippopotames / Nadia and the Hippos 1999 DSC
D: Dominique Cabrera
S: Dominique Cabrera
C: Hélène Louvart
A: Ariane Ascaride
During a transportation strike, a mother with an infant believes she sees the father, with whom she is not in contact, on the television news among a group of protestors. She decides to go and find him. *Festival de films, 22nd: 101. 2000.*

613. La Nouvelle Eve / The New Eve 1999 DSC
D: Catherine Corsini
S: Catherine Corsini, Marc Syrigas
C: Agnès Godard
P: Paulo Branco
A: Karin Viard
A thirty-year-old single woman, uninterested in marriage, accidentally meets and fixates on a happily married man. *BiFi.*
Other titles: A Nova Eva

614. Portraits chinois 1999 DS
D: Martine Dugowson
S: Martine Dugowson
C: Vincenzo Marano
P: Georges Benayoun
A: Romaine Bohringer, Helena Bonham Carter
A group of young friends, who work in fashion and filmmaking, struggle with jealousy and success. *Village Voice: 140. 1999, Nov. 16.*
Awards: Karlovy Vary International Film Festival, Best Director, 1997

615. Romance 1999 DS
D: Catherine Breillat
S: Catherine Breillat
C: Yorgos Arvanitis
P: Jean-François Lepetit
A: Caroline Ducey
A school teacher, unhappy with her lover's lack of interest in sex, picks up a stud—a real-life porn star—in a bar and then pursues an older man with a taste for bondage.
Awards: British Independent Film Awards, nomination for Best Foreign Film, 1999

616. Vénus Beauté Institut / Venus Beauty Institute 1999 DS
D: Tonie Marshall
S: Tonie Marshall
C: Gérard De Battista
P: Gilles Sandoz
A: Nathalie Baye, Bulle Ogier, Mathilde Seigner
A beauty parlor manager suffers the crisis of her fortieth year while living alone. She plays around with her ex-husband, who has left her physically scarred, and also with a stranger who becomes taken with her. The lives of some of the other hairdressers are also revealed, particularly a young one with a regular client, an older, kindly man.
Other titles: Venus Beauty Salon
Awards: César Awards, Best Film, Best Director, 2000; Seattle International Film Festival, Best Actress (Baye), 2000

617. Voyages 1999
D: Emmanuel Finkiel
S: Emmanuel Finkiel
P: Yael Fogiel
A: Shulamit Adar, Liliane Rovère, Regine Gorintin
Three stories of women "attempting to reclaim their lost Eastern European Jewish heritage" One is left behind at a cemetery stop of a bus tour of Jewish cultural sites; one "receives a call from a man claiming to be the father she believed died in a concentration camp"; and one "traverses Tel Aviv on a hot day in search of her cousin." *Film Society. 2001, Feb.*
Awards: Cannes Film Festival, Youth Award, 1999; Viennale, FIPRESCI, 1999

618. Baise-moi / Rape Me 2000 DS
D: Virginie Despentes, Coralie Trinh
S: Virginie Despentes, Coralie Trinh

C: Benoît Chamaillard
P: Dominique Chiron
A: Raffaela Anderson, Karen Lancoume
Two (real-life) porn stars take violent assaults in stride; after meeting on a train platform, they bond and proceed to indiscriminately rob and kill both men and women for revenge. Horror. *Village Voice: 113. 2001, July 10.*

619. *Les Blessures assassinés / Murderous Maids* 2000 SP
D: Jean-Pierre Denis
S: Jean-Pierre Denis, Michèle Pétin; based on the novel by Paulette Houdyer
C: Jean-Marc Fabre
P: Michèle Pétin
A: Julie-Marie Parmentier, Sylvie Testud, Isabelle Renauld
The story of the infamous Pepin sisters, domestic workers who murder their employer; this version includes childhood scenes with their mother. *Village Voice: 133. 2002, Apr. 23.*

620. *La Bûche* 2000 DS
D: Danièle Thompson
S: Danièle Thompson, Christopher Thompson
C: Robert Fraisse
P: Alain Sarde
A: Emmanuelle Béart, Sabine Azéma, Charlotte Gainsbourg
Three sisters return at Christmas to their stepfather's funeral and long-divorced Russian Jewish and Catholic parents; each has a relationship marred by "cheating"—the parents had dueling affairs throughout their marriage—and then they discover an attractive half brother of whom they were unaware.

621. *Le Conte du ventre plein / A Belly Full* 2000
D: Melvin Van Peebles
S: Melvin Van Peebles
C: Philippe Pavans de Ceccatty
P: Jean-Pierre Saire
A: Andréa Ferréol, Jacques Boudet, Meiji U Tum'si
France, 1960s. A white restaurant couple go to an orphanage and find a young black girl to replace their daughter and main waitress; trouble develops as they badmouth the girl and then ask her to pretend she is pregnant. Satire. *FII.*
Awards: Acapulco Black Film Festival, Best International Film, 2000

622. *Une Femme d'exterieur / An Outgoing Woman* 2000 SP
D: Christophe Blanc

S: Christophe Blanc, Eve Deboise
C: Pascal Poucet
P: Nathalie Mesuret, Bertrand Gore
A: Agnès Jaoui
Lyon. A nurse finds her husband cheating, then kicks him out and begins a slide away from her children and into mental breakdown. *AMG.*

623. *Merci pour le chocolat / Nightcap* 2000 S
D: Claude Chabrol
S: Claude Chabrol, Caroline Eliacheff; based on the novel by Charlotte Armstrong
C: Renato Berta
P: Marin Karmitz
A: Isabelle Huppert
A wealthy heiress places a sleeping potion in hot chocolate then sends her victims to their cars; in the end she blithely admits her inability to resist these perverse actions intended to get her way.

624. *Place Vendôme* 2000 DS
D: Nicole Garcia
S: Nicole Garcia, Jacques Fieschi
C: Laurent Dailland
P: Alain Sarde
A: Catherine Deneuve
The alcoholic wife of a wealthy gem dealer gets a grip on her life and his business after he commits suicide. She becomes involved again with an ex-lover, who betrayed her when she was first a gem dealer herself.
Awards: Venice Film Festival, Best Actress, 1998

625. *Saint-Cyr* 2000 DS
D: Patricia Mazuy
S: Patricia Mazuy, Yves Dangerfield
C: Thomas Mauch
P: Denis Freyd
A: Isabelle Huppert
The story of the wife of Louis XIV, the Madame de Maintenon, who founded a boarding school for impoverished young girls. *Film Society. 2001, Mar.*
Awards: Cannes Film Festival, Award of Youth, 2000; Prix Jean Vigo, 2000

626. *Samia* 2000 S
D: Philippe Faucon
S: Philippe Faucon, Soraya Nini; based on *Je suis une beurette* by Soraya Nini
C: Jacques Loiseleux
P: Humbert Balsan
A: Lynda Benahouda
Marseille. The daughter of an Algerian immigrant family struggles for independence and clashes

with her older brother over Islamic moral values. *Film Society. 2001, Mar.*

Awards: Amiens International Film Festival, Prize of the City, 2000

627. *La Veuve de Saint-Pierre / The Widow of St. Pierre*   2000
D: Patrice Leconte
S: Patrice Leconte
C: Eduardo Serra
P: Gilles Legrand
A: Juliette Binoche, Daniel Auteuil
Nineteenth century. A military fort in an isolated Canadian seaport suddenly must incarcerate a condemned murderer while they await the arrival of a guillotine, the only legal mode of execution; the commander's wife insists on caring for him.
Awards: Moscow International Film Festival, FIPRESCI, 2000; César Awards, nomination for Best Actress, 2001

628. *Amélie*   2001
D: Jean-Pierre Jeunet
S: Jean-Pierre Jeunet, Guillaume Laurant
C: Bruno Delbonnel
P: Jean-Marc Deschamps
A: Audrey Tatou
A young waitress in Paris fancifully spends her time improving others' lives.
Other titles: Le Fabuleux destin d'Amélie Poulain

629. *L'Anglaise et le duc / The Lady and the Duke*   2001 SCP
D: Eric Rohmer
S: Eric Rohmer; based on *Journal of My Life During the French Revolution* by Grace Elliot
C: Diane Baratier
P: Françoise Etchegaray
A: Lucy Russell, Jean-Claude Dreyfus
Paris, eighteenth century. A Scottish noblewoman endowed with great social cunning survives the Terror despite her passionate royalist attachments. She risks her life to save aristocratic friends she does not like and argues politics with her dear friend, a Duke who supports the revolutionaries and is executed while trying to influence the course of events.

630. *Avec tout mon amour / With All My Love*   2001 DSC
D: Amalia Escriva
S: Amalia Escriva
C: Jeanne Lapoirie
A: Jeanne Balibar, Bruno Todeschini, Dominique Blanc

Algeria, 1903. Seven Europeans have been killed during a revolt in a small town. The wife of the lawyer for the accused, the daughter of a Spanish colonial family, commits suicide; the trial brings out more secrets and lies. *Festival de films, 24th: 103. 2002.*

Awards: Angers European First Film Festival, Best Film, 2000

631. *Betty Fisher et autres histoires / Alias Betty*   2001 S
D: Claude Miller
S: Claude Miller; based on *The Tree of Hands* by Ruth Rendell
C: Christophe Pollack
P: Yves Marmion
A: Sandrine Kiberlain, Nicole Garcia, Mathilde Seigner
A novelist and single parent loses her young son in an accident; her mother then kidnaps the child of a neglectful waitress to give to her in hopes it will assuage her grief. *Village Voice: 108. 2002, Sep. 11.*
Other titles: Betty Fisher and Other Stories
Awards: Chicago International Film Festival, Best Actress (Garcia, Kiberlain), 2001; Montréal World Film Festival, Best Actress (Garcia, Kiberlain, Seigneur), 2001

632. *La Captive*   2001 DSC
D: Chantal Akerman
S: Chantal Akerman, Eric De Kuyper; based on *La Prisonniere* by Marcel Proust
C: Sabine Lancelin
P: Paulo Branco
A: Sylvie Testud
A wealthy writer brings a lesbian into his home, hoping to some day change her sexual orientation. *Film Society. 2001, Mar.*
Awards: European Film Awards, nomination for Best Actress, 2000

633. *Cet amour-là*   2001 DSC
D: Josée Dayan
S: Josée Dayan
C: Caroline Champetier
P: Alain Sarde
A: Jeanne Moreau, Aymeric Demarigny
Fictionalization of a relationship between an elderly Marguerite Duras and a young male devotee. *NYT: E5. 2003, Apr. 2.*

634. *Chaos*   2001 DS
D: Coline Serreau
S: Coline Serreau
C: Jean-François Robin

P: Alain Sarde
A: Rachida Brakni, Catherine Frot, Vincent Lindon
A middle-class couple watch from their car while a prostitute who has asked for their help is beaten up in the street; the wife returns the next day to help the woman escape her enslavement.
Awards: César Awards, Most Promising Actress (Brakni), 2002; Norwegian International Film Festival, Film Critics Award, 2002

635. *The Girl*   2001 DSP
D: Sande Zeig
S: Sande Zeig; based on a story by Monique Wittig
C: Georges Lechaptois
P: Dolly Hall
A: Claire Keim, Agathe De La Boulaye
Paris. A singer and an artist have an affair, though each has other attachments. *AMG.*

636. *Une Hirondelle a fait le printemps / Girl from Paris*   2001
D: Christian Carion
S: Christian Carion, Eric Assous
C: Antoine Héberlé
P: Christophe Rossignon
A: Mathilde Seigner, Michel Serrault
A Parisian decides to become a farmer by purchasing land from an old farmer who remains there with her until his new home is ready. *FII.*
Awards: Cabourg Romantic Film Festival, Best Actress, 2002

637. *Inch'Allah dimanche / Inch'Allah Sunday*   2001 DS
D: Yamina Benguigui
S: Yamina Benguigui
C: Antoine Roch
P: Philippe Dupuis-Mendel
A: Fejria Deliba
A wife, along with her three children and mother-in-law, leaves Algeria for a small town in France where her husband has worked for ten years. It is an isolating existence, and she conflicts with her family over her desire for free movement outside the house; one day she hears of another Algerian family nearby and decides to find them, whatever the cost. *Festival de films, 24th: 101. 2002.*
Awards: Arcachon Film Festival, Best Film, Best Actress, 2001; Marrakech Film Festival, Grand Prix, 2001; Toronto International Film Festival, International Critics Prize, 2001

638. *Jeunesse dorée / Golden Youth*   2001 DS
D: Zaïda Ghorab-Volta

S: Zaïda Ghorab-Volta
C: Pierre Milon
P: Nicolas Blanc
A: Alexandra Jeudon, Alexandra Laflandre
With a summer grant from a local club, two teenagers take to the road, where they document families and homes with their cameras.

639. *Martha ... Martha*   2001 DSC
D: Sandrine Veysset
S: Sandrine Veysset, Sebastien Regnier
C: Hélène Louvart
P: Humbert Balsan
A: Valérie Donzelli, Yann Goven
An impoverished, irresponsible woman lets her husband take care of their young girl, whom she herself abuses. *Film Society. 2002, Feb.*

640. *La Répétition*   2001 DSC
D: Catherine Corsini
S: Catherine Corsini, Pascale Breton
C: Agnès Godard
P: Philippe Martin
A: Emmanuelle Béart, Pascale Bussières
Two childhood friends, both interested in the theater, separate traumatically. Years later, they meet when one attends a performance by the other. Overwhelmed by passion, the married woman leaves her husband to pursue the actress. Thriller. *Variety: 23. 2001, May 21.*
Awards: Cannes Film Festival, nomination for Golden Palm, 2001

641. *Sa mère, la pute*   2001 DS
D: Brigitte Roüan
S: Brigitte Roüan, Marc Villard
C: Jimmy Glasberg
A: Brigitte Roüan
Police determine that a teenager has died from a drug overdose, but her mother believes bruises on the body indicate murder. Knowing there is much to discover, she persists in investigating herself, posing as a drug user and a prostitute. *Francophone Women: 187.*

642. *Le Secret*   2001 DS
D: Virginie B. Wagon
S: Virginie B. Wagon, Erick Zonca
A: Anne Coesens
Wishing to "vary her existence," a married mother takes an African American dancer as a lover. They do not love each other, but only use one another. *Francophone Women: 211.*
Awards: Avignon Film Festival, Prix Tournage, 2000; Deauville Film Festival, Best French Script, 2000

643. **Sous la sable / Under the Sun** 2001 SC
D: François Ozon
S: Emanuèle Bernheim, François Ozon, Marina De Van, Marcia Romano
C: Jeanne Lapoirie
P: Olivier Delbosc
A: Charlotte Rampling
A Parisian English teacher is widowed on a vacation trip; over the next year, she remains in denial, speaking of her husband as if he were alive and sometimes seeing him in their home, even as she attempts to lead a normal life and engages in a new sexual relationship. Her mother-in-law blames his suicide on the couple's inability to have children.
Awards: César Awards, nomination for Best Actress, 2002

644. **Le Stade de Wimbledon / Wimbledon Stadium** 2001
D: Mathieu Amalric
S: Mathieu Amalric
C: Christophe Beaucarne
P: Paulo Branco
A: Jeanne Balibar
A woman goes to Trieste to research an influential intellectual who stopped writing. *FII.*

645. **Zaïde, un petit air de vengeance / Zaide** 2001 DS
D: Josée Dayan
S: Odile Barski
P: Jean-Pierre Guérin
A: Jeanne Moreau
A sixty-year-old woman murders several men in revenge. *IMDb.*

646. **8 femmes / 8 Women** 2002 SC
D: François Ozon
S: Marina De Van, François Ozon, Robert Thomas
C: Jeanne Lapoirie
P: Olivier Delbosc
A: Catherine Deneuve, Isabelle Huppert, Fanny Ardant, Emmanuelle Béart, Virginie Ledoyen, Danielle Darrieux, Firmine Richard, Ludivine Sagnier
Relatives and friends, all women, gather in a country mansion where the man of the house has been murdered. Mystery, comedy.
Awards: Berlin International Film Festival, Silver Bear (all actresses), 2002; European Film Awards (all actresses), 2002; Lumiere Awards, Best Director, 2003

647. **À la folie, pas du tout / He Loves Me, He Loves Me Not** 2002 DS
D: Laetitia Colombani
S: Laetitia Colombani, Caroline Thivel
C: Pierre Aim
P: Charles Gassor
A: Audrey Tatou, Isabelle Carré, Sophie Guillemin
Bordeaux. A painter tells her side of an affair with a married cardiologist, then he tells his side, revealing how little he knows of her stalking behavior. *Village Voice: 132. 2003, July 12.*

648. **Choses secretes / Secret Things** 2002
D: Jean-Claude Brisseau
S: Jean-Claude Brisseau
C: Wilfrid Sempé
P: Jean-Claude Brisseau
A: Sabrina Seyvecou, Coralie Revel
Workers in a strip joint quit in a huff, then scheme to take over a bank by seducing male employees. *NYT: E13. 2004, Feb. 20.*

649. **Deux / Two** 2002
D: Werner Schroeter
S: Werner Schroeter
A: Bulle Ogier, Isabelle Huppert
Twin girls (played by the same actress) grow up separately and unaware of each other; both "seek human connection through impersonal sex." *Film Society. 2005, Feb.*

650. **Fleurs de sang / Blood Flowers** 2002 DS
D: Myriam Mézières, Alain Tanner
S: Myriam Mézières
A: Myriam Mézières, Tess Barthes
"14 year old has just killed her first lover, a man much older." Flashbacks tell the story of her childhood taking care of her mother, a cabaret performer. *Francophone Women: 172.*

651. **Bord de mer / Seaside** 2003 DS
D: Julie Lopes-Curval
S: Julie Lopes-Curval, François Favrat
C: Stephan Massis
P: Alain Benguigui
A: Hélène Fillières, Bulle Ogier, Ludmila Mikaël, Liliane Rovère
A factory worker in a seaside town becomes involved with a local married patron, then leaves town with him. Her boyfriend's mother is an aging gambler who wonders what happened to the pair.
Awards: Cannes Film Festival, Golden Camera, 2002

652. **Cette femme-là / Hanging Offense** 2003
D: Guillaume Nicloux
S: Guillaume Nicloux
C: Pierre-William Glenn

P: Frédéric Bourboulon
A: Josiane Balasko
Fontainebleau. A police captain finds an unsolved murder taking over her life—and perhaps her mind. *Film Society. 2004, April.*
Awards: César Awards, nomination for Best Actress, 2004

653. *Dans ma peau / In My Skin*   2003 DS
D: Marina De Van
S: Marina De Van
C: Pierre Barougier
P: Laurence Farenc
A: Marina De Van
An executive with a new job and a loving boyfriend accidentally gashes her leg and uncovers an obsession with cutting herself.

654. *Demain on démènage / Tomorrow We Move*   2003 DSC
D: Chantal Akerman
S: Chantal Akerman, Eric De Kuyper
C: Sabine Lancelin
P: Paulo Branco
A: Sylvie Testud, Aurore Clément
Comic look at a woman who invites her widowed mother to live with her but resents it when the apartment gets crowded; she decides to move, but the apartment buyers annoy her as well. *Film Society. 2005, Jan.*

655. *Demonlover*   2003
D: Oliver Assayas
S: Oliver Assayas
C: Denis Lenoir
P: Xavier Giannoli
A: Connie Nielsen, Chloë Sevigny, Gina Gershon
Dot-com executive women spy, abduct, maneuver, and wreak havoc within a "videogame aesthetic." *NYT: E15. 2003, Sep. 19.*

656. *Les Égarés / Strayed*   2003 C
D: André Téchiné
S: Gilles Taurand, André Téchiné
C: Agnès Godard
P: Jean-Pierre Ramsay-Levi
A: Emmanuelle Béart
France, June 1940. At the beginning of the occupation, a woman leaves Paris with her two children; after a bomb targeting the crowd of refugees is dropped on the road, they follow an illiterate young man into the wilderness. *Film Society. 2004, Feb.*

657. *Elle est des nôtres / She's One of Us*   2003 DSP
D: Siegrid Alnoy

S: Siegrid Alnoy, Jerome Beaujour, François Favrat
C: Christophe Pollack
P: Beatrice Caufman
A: Sasha Andres, Catherine Mouchet
An office worker is "efficient but alienated" from her environment; one day she accidentally murders a woman with whom she's been trying to make friends. Thriller. *NYT: E13. 2003, Mar. 12.*
Awards: Stockholm Film Festival, FIPRESCI, 2003; Thessaloniki Film Festival, Special Mention, 2003

658. *Nathalie*   2003 DS
D: Anne Fontaine
S: Anne Fontaine, Jacques Fieschi
C: Jean-Marc Fabre
P: Alain Sarde
A: Emmanuelle Béart, Fanny Ardant
A happily married woman hires a young prostitute to seduce her husband, whom she suspects of having an affair; she then becomes irrationally involved with the prostitute. Mystery. *NYT: E13. 2004, Mar. 12.*
Awards: European Film Awards, nominations for Best Actress (Béart, Ardant), 2004

659. *Une Part du ciel / A Piece of the Sky*   2003 CP
D: Bénédicte Liénard
S: Bénédicte Liénard
C: Hélène Louvart
P: Jacques Bidou, Marianne Dumoulin
A: Séverine Caneele, Sofia Lebotte
The story of two women: One works in a bakery; the other is in prison, where she resists her confinement. *Village Voice: 68. 2003, Sep. 24.*
Awards: Buenos Aires International Festival of Independent Cinema, Best Actress (Caneele), 2003

660. *La Petite prairie aux bouleaux / Birch Tree Meadow*   2003 DS
D: Marceline Loridan-Ivens
S: Marceline Loridan-Ivens, Jeanne Moreau
C: Emmanuel Machuel
P: Alain Sarde
A: Anouk Aimée
An Auschwitz-Birkenau survivor returns to the camp with a group of other survivors. *Film Society. 2004, Jan.*

661. *Qui a tué Bambi? / Who Killed Bambi?*   2003 P
D: Gilles Marchand
S: Gilles Marchand
C: Pierre Milon
P: Carole Scotta, Caroline Benjo

A: Sophie Quinton
A student nurse faints and is cared for by a doctor, whom she suspects of murder. Mystery. *NYT: E13. 2004, Mar. 12.*

662. Raja   2003 CP
D: Jacques Doillon
S: Jacques Doillon
C: Hélène Louvart
P: Souad Lamriki, Margaret Ménégoz
A: Najat Benssellem, Pascal Gregory
A young Moroccan woman employed in a wealthy Frenchman's garden becomes an object of desire for him. *Village Voice: 58. 2004, Mar. 24.*
Awards: Marrakech International Film Festival, Best Actress, 2003; Cannes Film Festival, France Culture Award, 2004

663. Stupeur et tremblements / Fear and Trembling   2003 S
D: Alain Corneau
S: Amélie Nothomb, Alain Corneau
C: Yves Angelo
P: Alain Sarde
A: Sylvie Testud, Kaori Tsuji
Tokyo. A French woman, born in Japan, works as a translator in a large multinational firm. Trying to be helpful, she violates the rigorous hierarchical arrangements that govern the workforce and gets caught in dangerous games with her female boss. *NYT: E13. 2004, Nov. 19.*
Awards: César Awards, Best Actress (Testud), 2004; Karlovy Vary International Film Festival, Best Actress (Testud), 2004

664. Swimming Pool   2003
D: François Ozon
S: Emanuèle Bernheim, François Ozon
C: Yorick Saux
P: Olivier Delbosc
A: Charlotte Rampling, Ludivine Sagnier
A British mystery novelist retreats to her editor's country house in France, then conflicts with his young daughter, who appears unexpectedly and has a provocative manner. Mystery.
Awards: European Film Awards, Best Actress (Rampling), 2003

665. Vendredi soir / Friday Night   2003 DSC
D: Claire Denis
S: Emanuèle Bernheim, Claire Denis
C: Agnès Godard
P: Bruno Pésary
A: Valérie Lemercier, Vincent Lindon
Paris. A woman packs up her apartment in anticipation of moving in with her fiancé, then finds herself in a traffic jam and a one-night stand with a stranger.

666. La Vie promise / The Promised Life 2003 S
D: Olivier Dahan
S: Agnès Fustier-Dahan, Olivier Dahan
C: Alex Lamarque
P: Éric Névé
A: Isabelle Huppert
A prostitute flees Nice with her fourteen-year-old daughter.
Awards: San Sebastián International Film Festival, nomination for Golden Seashell, 2002

667. À tout de suite / Right Now   2004 SC
D: Benoît Jacquot
S: Benoît Jacquot, Elisabeth Fanger
C: Caroline Champetier
P: Raoul Saada
A: Isild Le Besco, Ouassini Embarek
1970s. A young art student falls in love with a Moroccan, who depends on her when he is sought by the police for robbery. She runs away with him to Madrid, Tangiers, and finally Greece, where everything unravels and she is left on her own. *London Film: 36. 2004.*

668. Anatomie de l'enfer / Anatomy of Hell
                                                   2004 D
D: Catherine Breillat
S: Catherine Breillat; based on her novel *Pornocratie*
C: Yorgos Arvanitis
P: Jean-François Lepetit
A: Amira Casar
A straight woman teams with a gay man for sexual experimentation. *Village Voice: 64. 2004, Feb. 11.*
Awards: Philadelphia Film Festival, Best Feature, 2004

669. La Blessure / The Wound   2004 SCP
D: Nicolas Klotz
S: Elisabeth Perceval
C: Hélène Louvart
P: Elisabeth Perceval
A: Noëlla Mobassa, Adama Doumbia
Paris. An African arrives at the airport, expecting to be united with her husband as an asylum-seeker. Instead, she is jailed, and her husband is left searching for her. A sympathetic employee connects her with her husband, but the impoverished communal squat where he takes her sends her into a mental tailspin. *London Film: 36. 2004.*

670. Brodeuses / Sequins   2004 DS
D: Éléonore Faucher

S: Éléonore Faucher, Gaëlle Macé
C: Pierre Cottereau
P: Alain Benguigui
A: Lola Naymark, Ariane Ascaride

A supermarket clerk in a small town is distant from her boyfriend, as well as her nearby family, and absorbs herself in embroidery design. When she finds herself pregnant, she leaves her job in order to hide better. She finds work with a woman who has connections to Parisian haute couture and who is grieving the loss of her son. They bond over their shared passion of large-scale intricate beading and embroidery, a process the film documents.

Other titles: A Common Thread
Awards: Cannes Film Festival, Grand Prize, 2004

671. *Comme une image / Look at Me* 2004 DS
D: Agnès Jaoui
S: Jean-Pierre Bacri, Agnès Jaoui
C: Stéphane Fontaine
P: Christian Bérard
A: Marilou Berry, Agnès Jaoui

A voice teacher has a struggling novelist husband; when she discovers that a famous author's daughter is in her class, she devotes extra time to her. The husband is suddenly successful, hobnobbing with the famous author, but as the teacher gets closer to the girl, she finds the courage to object to both men's selfishness, just as the overweight daughter finds the courage to accept herself.

672. *Pourquoi (pas) le Brésil / Why (Not) Brazil?* 2004 DS
D: Laëtitia Masson
S: Laëtitia Masson
C: Crystel Fournier
P: Jean-Michel Rey
A: Elsa Zylberstein, Laëtitia Masson

A filmmaker runs into problems getting her own projects funded; reluctantly she agrees to adapt a difficult novel—*Pourquoi le Brésil* by Christine Angot—knowing that, from her point of view, the project is impossible. Combines documentary and fictional narrative. "An engaging and frequently self-deprecating study of the creative process." *London Film: 35. 2004.*

673. *Since Otar Left* 2004 DS
D: Julie Bertuccelli
S: Julie Bertuccelli, Bernard Renucci
C: Christophe Pollack
P: Yael Fogiel
A: Esther Gorintin, Nino Khomassouridze, Dinara Droukarova

Tbilisi, Georgia. Three generations of women live together in a small apartment. When an adored son dies after emigrating to France, the daughter and granddaughter fabricate letters from him to protect the older woman. Then one day the mother surprises them with tickets to Paris to see him.
Awards: Cannes Film Festival, Critics Grand Prize, 2003; Viennale, FIPRESCI, 2003; Warsaw International Film Festival, Special Mention, 2003

GABON

674. *Ayouma* 1978 S
D: Pierre-Marie Dong, Charles Mensah
S: Joséphine Kana Bongo
A: Fidèle Gomez, Charlotte Ndong

A modern African takes his fiancée away from her village; this action puts them into conflict with the tradition that sees her as a negotiable commodity. *Revue belge, no. 11: 37. 1978, Oct/Nov.*

GEORGIA

675. *Walsi Petschorase / Waltzing on the River Pecora* 1992 DS
D: Lana Gogoberidze
S: Zaira Arsenishvili, Lana Gogoberidze
C: Georgi Beridze
P: Alexander Sharashidze
A: Irina Kupchenko

Tbilisi, 1937. Two stories. A woman is declared an enemy of the state and deported to a camp in the north, but the camp is full, so those not able to engage in forced labor are set out to roam in the glacial winter. Next, a thirteen-year-old girl escapes from a state orphanage, then makes friends with a KGB officer who has taken over her arrested parents' apartment. *Festival de films, 15th: 21. 1993.*
Other titles: Une Valse au bord de la Petchora
Awards: Berlin International Film Festival, Ecumenical Jury Prize, 1993

GERMANY

676. *Eine Frau namens Harry / Harry and Harriette* 1990
D: Cyril Frankel
S: Frank Lenart, Vivian Naefe
C: Heinz Hölscher
P: Karl Spiehs
A: Petra Wagner, Barbara Von Baur, Fiona Fullerton, Thomas Gottschalk

A woman "makes a pact with the devil to change her gender and see what it is like to have the professional and financial advantages of men." Fantasy. *West German Cinema, 1985.*

677. Die Rückkehr / The Woman from Africa
1990 DS

D: Margarethe Von Trotta
S: Margarethe Von Trotta
C: Tonino Delli Colli
P: Augusto Caminito
A: Barbara Sukowa, Stefania Sandrelli

Paris. A doctor, bitter at her lover's marriage to her best friend, returns home from Africa when the friend becomes ill. *FII.*
Other titles: L'Africana

678. Das serbische Mädchen / The Serbian Girl
1990

D: Peter Sehr
S: Peter Sehr
C: Dietrich Lohmann
P: Dirk Düwel
A: Mirjana Jokovic

An eighteen-year-old Serbian from Yugoslavia goes to Hamburg to search for a man with whom she had a holiday romance. *MOMA Film. 2003, Dec.*
Awards: German Film Awards, nomination for Outstanding Feature Film, 1991

679. Im Kreise der Lieben / The Trio
1991 DS

D: Hermine Huntgeburth
S: Hermine Huntgeburth
C: Bernd Meiners
A: Barbara Auer, Karin Baal, Ruth Hellberg

Hamburg. A grandmother of eighty years, her fifty-year-old daughter, and her thirty-year-old granddaughter live together in an old apartment. Their emotional dependence on each other is complete: The youngest engages in matrimonial swindles, her mother is in constant search of a man's love, and the grandmother is always in charge. *Festival de films, 14th: 21. 1992.*
Other titles: Le Trio terrible
Awards: German Film Awards, Outstanding Feature Film by a New Director, 1992

680. My Father Is Coming
1991 DSCP

D: Monika Treut
S: Monika Treut, Bruce Benderson
C: Elfi Mikesch
P: Monika Treut
A: Shelley Kästner, Annie Sprinkle

New York City. A German lesbian actress must scramble to find a substitute husband when her father, who believes she is married, arrives for a visit. A gay friend takes on the role, but her father is not fooled and not worried; he finds a porn-star lover of his own and even gets a role in a film. Comedy. *Festival de films, 14th: 22. 1992.*

681. Salmonberries
1991 P

D: Percy Adlon
S: Percy Adlon
C: Newton Thomas Sigel
P: Eleonore Adlon
A: k.d. lang, Rosel Zech

A German librarian goes to Alaska, where an Eskimo mine worker who passes as a boy falls in love with her; they travel to Berlin together. *NYT. 1994, Sep. 2.*
Awards: Montréal World Film Festival, Grand Prix, 1991; Bavarian Film Awards, Best Film, Best Actress (Zech), 1992

682. Das alte Lied
1992 DSP

D: Ula Stöckl
S: Ula Stöckl
C: Rali Raltschev
P: Clara Burchner

A reading from the novel *Hyperion* by Hölderlin that reflects the "profound malaise of the sad and torn German heart" introduces the story of an old woman who returns to Dresden to celebrate Christmas with her family after the fall of the Berlin Wall. *Festival de films, 14th: 20. 1992.*
Other titles: L'Eternel retour

683. Antigone
1992 DSP

D: Danièle Huillet, Jean-Marie Straub
S: Danièle Huillet, Jean-Marie Straub; based on the play by Sophocles
C: William Lubtchansky
P: Regina Ziegler
A: Astrid Ofner

A daughter defies the burial customs decreed by the king for her brother's funeral and is executed, though the gods recognize her righteousness. *Cinemythology. Accessed 2005, July 13.*

684. Der Brocken / The Broken Mountain
1993 S

D: Vidim Glowna
S: Knut Boeser, Christine Roesch
C: Franz Ritschel
P: Harald Reichebner
A: Elsa Grube-Deister

An old woman defends her "idyllic life on the island of Rügen." *German National: 189.*
Awards: Berlin International Film Festival, nomination for Golden Bear, 1992

685. *Zeit des zorns / The Long Silence*
1993 DSP

D: Margarethe Von Trotta
S: Felice Laudadio
C: Marco Sperduti
P: Felice Laudadio
A: Carla Gravina

Rome. When a judge investigating mob ties to influential politicians is murdered, his widow resolves to continue the investigation herself. She provides the press with information and produces a television documentary showing other widows speaking out. Thriller. *Variety: 33/34. 1993, Sep. 1.*

Other titles: Il Lungo silenzio

Awards: Montréal World Film Festival, Best Actress, Ecumenical Jury Prize, 1993

686. *Mutters Courage / My Mother's Courage*
1995

D: Michal Verhoeven
S: Michal Verhoeven
C: Theo Bierkens
P: Veit Heiduschka
A: Pauline Collins

Budapest. A son narrates the story of his mother's escape from deportation when 4,000 Jews were rounded up on a summer day in 1944. She is naïve—"apart from the yellow star on her dress," everything seems normal to her—and the escape is an accidental impulse. *Variety: 94. 1995, Sep. 25.*

Awards: Bavarian Film Awards, Best Production, 1996; German Film Awards, Silver Award, 1996

687. *Das Versprechen / The Promise*   1995 DS
D: Margarethe Von Trotta
S: Margarethe Von Trotta, Peter Schneider
C: Franz Rath
P: Eberhard Junkersdorf
A: Corinna Hartouch, Meret Becker

1961. An East German is separated from her boyfriend when he decides at the last minute not to flee with her to the west. They meet later but again he hangs back, while she is arrested, and, unknown to him, pregnant. They meet again when the wall falls in 1989, and their child is grown, but both have married others.

Awards: Bavarian Film Awards, Best Direction, Best Actress (Becker), 1995

688. *Engelchen / Little Angel*   1996 DS
D: Helke Misselwitz
S: Helke Misselwitz
C: Thomas Plenert
P: Thomas Wilkening

A: Susanne Lothar

East Berlin. A woman lives alone and works in a factory. One day, she meets a Polish black marketeer at the train station. He sets up house with her, but when she becomes pregnant, he tells her he already has a family in Poland and says goodbye.

Awards: Max Ophüls Festival, Interfilm Award, 1997; San Sebastián International Film Festival, Special Prize, 1997; Seattle International Film Festival, Showcase Award, 1997

689. *Jenseits der Stille / Beyond Silence* 1996 DS
D: Caroline Link
S: Caroline Link, Beth Serlin
C: Gernot Roll
P: Jakob Claussen
A: Sylvie Testud, Tatjana Trieb

A girl grows up ministering to her deaf-mute parents; when she begins to play the clarinet and desire a musical career, there is conflict with the demands of her caretaking. *Village Voice: 148. 1998, June 9.*

690. *Keiner liebt mich / Nobody Loves Me*
1996 DSP

D: Doris Dörrie
S: Doris Dörrie
C: Helge Weindler
P: Renate Seefeldt, Gerd Huber
A: Maria Schrader

A woman in her twenties, with a job at airport security, lives alone and fearful in a high-rise, where she makes friends with a young, gay African eccentric.

Awards: Bavarian Film Awards, Best Actress, 1995; German Film Awards, Outstanding Actress, 1995

691. *Alles wird gut / All Ends Well*   1997 DSCP
D: Angelina Maccarone
S: Angelina Maccarone, Fatina El-Tayeb
C: Judith Kaufmann
P: Claudia Schröder
A: Kati Stüdemann, Chantal De Freitas

An African lesbian is left bereft by her punk-rock lover and takes a job as a housekeeper in the building where the ex-lover lives in order to be near her; she then falls for the advertising executive who employs her. *Variety. 1998, July 28.*

Awards: L.A. Outfest, Audience Award, 1998; Toronto Inside Out Lesbian and Gay Film and Video Festival, Best Feature, 1998

692. *Bandits*   1997 DS
D: Katja Von Garnier

S: Katja Von Garnier, Uwe Wilhelm
C: Torsten Breuer
P: Harald Kügler
A: Katja Riemann, Jasmin Tabatabai, Nicolette Kre-
bitz, Jutta Hoffmann
Four convicts form a rock band, then escape when
they play outside the walls; they head for South
America. *AMG.*

693. *Frost* 1997
D: Fred Kelemen
S: Fred Kelemen
C: Fred Kelemen
A: Anna Schmidt
An impoverished woman and her young son flee
her abusive husband and make their way on foot
through a barren winter countryside toward
her hometown. *Village Voice: 108. 2003, Jan. 8.*
Awards: Rotterdam International Film Festival,
FIPRESCI, 1998

694. *Gesches / Gift* 1997 DS
D: Walburg Von Waldenfels
S: Walburg Von Waldenfels
C: Christel Orthmann
A: Geno Lechner
1900s. A reputedly devoted wife and mother turns
out to be a serial poisoner of many of her family
and friends, including three husbands and three
children; she admits guilt but has no explanation.
Thriller. *Festival de films, 20th: 42. 1998.*

695. *Mein Herz—Niemandem! / My Heart Is Mine Alone* 1997 DSP
D: Helma Sanders-Brahms
S: Helma Sanders-Brahms
C: Roland Dressel
P: Helma Sanders-Brahms
A: Lena Stolze, Cornelius Obonya
1930s. The story of Jewish Else Lasker-Schüller and
Protestant Gottfried Benn, poets of the Nazi
era who were lovers. He supported Nazism, and
she was forced to flee the country. *FII.*

696. *Plätze in Städten / Places in the City* 1998 DS
D: Angela Schanelec
S: Angela Schanelec
C: Reinhold Vorschneider
P: Florian Koerner von Gustorf
A: Sophie Aigner
Berlin. A young woman is dissatisfied, does not
get along with her family or boyfriend, and gets
pregnant on a trip to Paris. *FII.*
Awards: Max Ophüls Festival, nomination for Max
Ophüls Award, 1999

697. *Aimée & Jaguar* 1999 S
D: Max Färberböck
S: Erica Fischer, Max Färberböck; based on the
biography of Aimée Färberböck Kohler
C: Tony Imi
P: Hanno Huth
A: Maria Schrader, Juliana Köhler
Berlin, 1943. A Jewish woman works at a Nazi
paper and creates false identification papers
for the German resistance; at the same time,
she has an affair with an SS wife and mother
of three children. *Festival de films, 23rd: 96.
2001.*
Awards: Bavarian Film Awards, Best Actress
(Schrader, Köhler), Best Director, 1999; Berlin In-
ternational Film Festival, Best Actress (Schrader,
Köhler), 1999; German Film Awards, Outstanding Actress (Schrader, Köhler), 1999

698. *Lola rennt / Run Lola Run* 1999
D: Tom Twyker
S: Tom Twyker
C: Frank Griebe
P: Stefan Arndt
A: Franka Potente
A woman has only twenty minutes to raise money
to save her petty-thief boyfriend. Her predica-
ment is played out in three different scenarios.
Action. *NYT: E15. 1999, Mar. 26.*

699. *Nicht nichts ohne Dich / Ain't Nothing without You* 1999 DSP
D: Pia Frankenberg
S: Pia Frankenberg
C: Thomas Mauch
P: Pia Frankenberg
"Ambitious director of B movies tries living with
foreigners." *West German Cinema, 1985.*
Awards: Max Ophüls Festival, Max Ophüls Award,
1986

700. *Yara* 1999
D: Yilmaz Arslan
S: Yilmaz Arslan
C: Jürgen Jürges
P: Yilmaz Arslan
A: Yelda Reynaud
A German Turkish woman is sent suddenly back
to Turkey by her conservative father; thought
strange and offensive by her Islamic family be-
cause she yearns to be German, she runs away
and ends up in a mental institution.
Awards: Antalya Golden Orange Film Festival,
Best Film, Best Actress, 1998; Istanbul In-
ternational Film Festival, Special Jury Prize,
1999

701. *Fernweh* / *The Opposite of Homesick*

2000 DS

D: Liza Johnson
S: Liza Johnson
C: Ulrich Malik
A: Veronika Nowag-Jones

A worker in a film archives is uncertain about her future in the united Germany. She begins to engage with a gay couple, a cynical American and his lover who romanticizes the United States, and a power struggle ensues. *Cineaste, vol. 25, no. 4: 52. 2000.*

702. *Marlene*

2000 P

D: Joseph Vilsmaier
S: Don Bohlinger, Christian Pfannenschmidt
C: Joseph Vilsmaier
P: Katherina Trebitsch
A: Katja Flint

The life of Marlene Dietrich, focusing on her rise to stardom and her relationship with Josef von Sternberg in the 1930s. *MOMA Film. 2000, Nov.*

Awards: Guild of German Art House Cinemas, Silver Award, 2000

703. *Die Polizisten* / *The Policewoman* 2000 S

D: Andreas Dresen
S: Laila Stieler
C: Michael Hammon
P: Christian Granderath
A: Gabriela Maria Schmeide

Rostock. A police academy graduate is assigned to a new city and becomes attached to a young shoplifter. *MOMA Film. 2000, Nov.*

Awards: Adolf Grimme Awards, Gold Award, Best Script, Best Actress, 2001

704. *Die Stille nach dem Schuß* / *The Legend of Rita*

2000

D: Volker Schlöndorff
S: Volker Schlöndorff, Wolfgang Kohlhaase
C: Andreas Höfer
P: Arthur Hofer
A: Bibiana Beglau, Nadja Uhl

A radical terrorist lives through her revolutionary period in the West to become an ordinary worker in East Germany, but she must remain undercover. *Village Voice: 117. 2001, Jan. 30.*

Awards: Berlin International Film Festival, Best Actress (Beglau, Uhl), 2000

705. *Die Unberührbare* / *No Place to Go*

2000 P

D: Oskar Roehler
S: Oskar Roehler; based on the life of Gisela Elsner

C: Hagen Bogdanski
P: Ulrich Caspar, Käte Ehrmann
A: Hannelore Elsner

Fictionalized life of writer Gisela Elsner (the director's mother), who wrote novels of life in East German socialist society and was rejected after reunification. *AMG.*

Awards: Chicago International Film Festival, Best Actress, 2000; German Film Awards, Outstanding Feature Film, Outstanding Actress, 2000; Bavarian Film Awards, Best Actress, 2001

706. *Anna Wunder*

2001 DSC

D: Ulla Wagner
S: Ulla Wagner
C: Jolanta Dylewska
P: Christoph Friedel
A: Renée Soutendijk, Alice Deekeling

1960s. A waitress and part-time prostitute with two children turns to drink after her husband abandons her; the young daughter, disguised as a boy, sets out on her own to find her father, now living in the French countryside. *Variety: 41. 2001, Dec. 17.*

707. *Drei Sterne* / *Mostly Martha*

2001 DS

D: Sandra Nettelbeck
S: Sandra Nettelbeck
C: Michael Bertl
P: Karl Baumgartner
A: Martina Gedeck

Hamburg. A chef at a French restaurant is hardnosed and obsessed with her work, but she must care for her young niece when her sister dies.

Other titles: Bella Martha

708. *Heidi M.*

2001 SCP

D: Michael Klier
S: Karin Aström
C: Sophie Maintigneux
P: Manuela Stehr
A: Katrin Sass

A Berlin store owner and single mother resists romance in favor of her responsibilities. *MOMA Film. 2001, Nov.*

Awards: German Film Awards, Outstanding Actress, 2001; German Film Critics Association, Best Actress, 2002

709. *Nirgendwo in Afrika* / *Nowhere in Africa*

2001 DS

D: Caroline Link
S: Caroline Link; based on an autobiographical novel by Stefanie Zweig
C: Gernot Roll

P: Bernd Eichinger
A: Juliana Köhler, Lea Kurka, Karoline Echertz
Kenya, World War II. A German Jewish family flee to an isolated shack in the countryside, where the wife refuses to unpack. She eventually learns to relax and be happy, even succeeding as a farmer. *NYT: E18. 2003, Mar. 7.*
Awards: German Film Awards, Outstanding Feature Film, 2002; Academy Awards, Best Foreign Film, 2003

710. *Annas sommer / Anna's Summer* 2002 DSP
D: Jeanine Meerapfel
S: Jeanine Meerapfel
C: Andreas Sinambs
P: Dagmar Jacobsen, Jeanine Meerapfel
A: Angela Molina
A Jewish widow, the daughter of a Spanish mother and a Greek father, returns to Greece to sell the family property; memories and new relationships affect her, and she decides to stay. *Variety. 2001, Sept. 17.*
Other titles: *El varano de Anna*

711. *Der Felsen / A Map of the Heart*   2002
D: Dominik Graf
S: Dominik Graf
C: Benedict Neuenfels
P: Christine Berg
A: Karoline Eichhorn
Abandoned by her lover while on vacation in Corsica, a woman takes up with a teenage boy. *MOMA Film. 2002, Aug.*

712. *Goodbye Lenin*   2002
D: Wolfgang Becker
S: Wolfgang Becker
C: Martin Kukula
P: Stefan Arndt
A: Katrin Sass
A passionately socialist woman misses the fall of the Berlin Wall because she is in a coma; afterward, her dissident son attempts to hide from her the political changes outside. *NYT: E1. 2002, Apr. 2.*
Awards: Berlin International Film Festival, Blue Angel, 2003; Bavarian Film Awards, Audience Award, 2004

713. *In den Tag hinein / The Days Between*
**   2002 DS**
D: Maria Speth
S: Maria Speth
C: Reinhold Vorschneider
P: Holger Lochar
A: Sabine Timoteo

Berlin. A young woman has two lovers—one Japanese—and a vague future as she lives with her brother's family. *Festival de films, 23rd: 22. 2001.*
Awards: Baden-Baden Days, MFG Star, 2001; Créteil International Women's Film Festival, Grand Jury Prize, 2001

714. *Mein letzter / My Last Film*   2002 P
D: Oliver Hirschbiegel
S: Bodo Kirchhoff
C: Rainer Klausmann
P: Claudia Schröder
A: Hannelore Elsner
An actress, "betrayed by her husband yet again," decides to leave their apartment and asks a cameraman to record her packing and reminiscing. *MOMA Film. 2003, Nov.*
Awards: German Film Awards, Outstanding Actress, 2003

715. *Ahnungslosen / Valley of the Innocent*
**   2003 DS**
D: Branwen Okpako
S: Branwen Okpako
C: Andreas Höfer
P: Jon Handschin
A: Nisma Cherrat
Dresden. A police officer visits the orphanage where she was raised and discovers her father was a black Kenyan; at the same time she must investigate the murder of her mother's husband. Thriller. *Film Society. 2004, Apr.*

716. *Die Farbe der Seele / The Color of the*
Soul*   2003 DSP
D: Helma Sanders-Brahms
S: Helma Sanders-Brahms
C: Raimund Von Scheibner
P: Helma Sanders-Brahms
A: Eva Mattes, Gilbert Diop
Berlin. A singer from Senegal loses his voice while on tour and finds that he must have an operation. A German nurse takes him into her home in order to help him through. *Festival de films, 26th: 22. 2004.*
Other titles: *La Couleur de l'ame*

717. *Rosenstrasse*   2003 DS
D: Margarethe Von Trotta
S: Pamela Katz, Margarethe Von Trotta
C: Franz Rath
P: Henrik Meyer, Markus Zimmer
A: Maria Schrader, Katja Riemann
New York. A Jewish woman investigates her mother's family when her liberal father dies and her mother bans the daughter's Gentile fiancé from

the house. She interviews a Gentile woman who protected her mother during the Holocaust. It's a tangled story of the mother's abandonment, first by her Gentile father (who was advised to divorce) and then by her adoptive mother, the interviewee, when an aunt requested she be sent to New York. The interviewee found the mother as a child outside a Gestapo prison on Rosenstrasse, where Jews, including the mother and the interviewee's husband, were interred and where a Gentile crowd demonstrated for weeks in 1943 against their imprisonment.

Awards: Venice Film Festival, UNICEF Award, Best Actress (Riemann), 2003; David di Donatello Awards, Best Film, 2004

718. *Die Andere Frau / The Other Woman*
2004 DS

D: Margarethe Von Trotta
S: Pamela Katz
C: Martin Langer
A: Barbara Sukowa, Barbara Auer

1990s. A woman "who worked for the West German government and who was seduced into giving state secrets to an East German agent masquerading as an international peace worker is now a prisoner. She writes an insinuating letter to another woman, a stranger in a contented marriage." *MOMA Film. 2004, Dec.*

EAST GERMANY

719. *Minna von Barnhelm oder das Soldatenglück / Minna von Barnhelm* 1962

D: Martin Hellberg
S: Martin Hellberg; based on the play by Gotthold Ephraim Lessing
A: Johanna Matz

Nineteenth century. A wealthy woman is engaged to a soldier, who refuses her love because he is penniless, insisting that equality is too important. "Minna has to resort to female cunning to make him face the deeper meaning of his words." *DEFA Film. Accessed 2005, Jan. 18.*

720. *Der geteilte Himmel / Divided Heaven* 1964

D: Konrad Wolf
S: Konrad Wolf; based on the novel by Christa Wolf
A: Renate Krössner

1961. A small-town teacher follows a scientist, who is unable to adapt to the new "collective-oriented culture" in the city of Halle. However, she struggles to reconcile with the new order,

and when he goes to West Berlin, she refuses to go with him. *Hollywood Beyond: 190–91.*

721. *Karla / Carla* 1965

D: Herrmann Zschoche
S: Herrmann Zschoche, Ulrich Plenzdorf
C: Gü Ost
P: Gert Golde
A: Jutta Hoffmann

A teacher works against the system and tries to teach her students to be open and truthful. *DEFA Film. Accessed 2005, Jan. 18. Also DEFA, East.*

Awards: Berlin International Film Festival, FIPRESCI, 1990

722. *Das siebente Jahr / The Seventh Year* 1969

D: Frank Vogel
S: Frank Vogel
C: Roland Graf
P: Erich Kühne
A: Jessy Rameik

"Episodes from the domestic life of a female doctor on the eve of the seventh anniversary of her marriage to an actor." *FII.*

723. *Der Dritte / The Third* 1972

D: Egon Gunther
S: Günther Rücker
C: Erich Gusko
A: Jutta Hoffmann

A never-married mother with two children looks for a husband and has a feminist struggle between her yearning for directness and the need to use her "feminine" wiles. *FII.*

724. *Die Legende von Paul und Paula / The Legend of Paul and Paula* 1973

D: Heiner Carow
S: Heiner Carow, Ulrich Plenzdorf
C: Jürgen Brauer
A: Angelica Domröse

A single mother with two small children has a boring job in a supermarket and dreams only of a better life. She has an affair with a government official trapped in a bourgeois marriage. *Hollywood Beyond: 197.*

725. *Bis daß der Tod Euch scheidet, Leben mit Uwe / Living with Uwe* 1974

D: Lothar Warneke
A: Katrin Sass

A woman resents that her career suffers because she must care for her child, while her husband is able to devote himself to furthering his own science career. *Hollywood Beyond: 204.*

726. *Hostess* / *Bird-Walking Weather*   1976
D: Rolf Römer
S: Rolf Römer
C: Siegfried Mogel
P: Siegfried Kabitzke
A: Angela Brunner
A woman questions the meaning of her live-in lover's proposal of marriage. *DEFA Film. Accessed 2005, Jan. 18.*

727. *Alle meine Mädchen* / *All My Girls*
                                              1979 DS
D: Iris Gusner
S: Iris Gusner, Gabriele Kotte
A: Lissy Tempelhof, Monica Bielenstein, Ella Lierck, Susi Barbara Schnitzler, Anita Viola Schweizer
Stories of a group of women who work in a light-bulb factory. *Hollywood Beyond: 195.*

728. *Die Beunruhigung* / *Apprehension* 1980 S
D: Lothar Warneke
S: Helga Schubert
C: Thomas Plenert
A: Christine Schorn
A divorced psychologist learns she may have cancer and questions her former priorities. *DEFA Film. Accessed 2005, Jan. 18.*

729. *Solo Sunny*   1980
D: Konrad Wolf, Wolfgang Kohlhaase
S: Wolfgang Kolhlhaase
C: Eberhard Geick
A: Renate Krössner
A former factory worker sings in a pop band but chafes under the restrictions of her band mates, as well as her relationships with men in general. *AMG.*
Awards: Berlin International Film Festival, Best Actress, FIPRESCI, 1980

730. *Die Verlobte* / *The Fiancée*   1980 S
D: Günther Rücker
S: Günther Rücker; based on the novel by Eva Lippold
C: Jürgen Brauer
P: Hans-Erich Busch
A: Jutta Wachowiak
A communist spends ten years in prison for anti-fascist activities. She is always tended by her lover, who is arrested and condemned to death just when she is released. Focus is on the loneliness and isolation of prison life. *Variety: 20. 1980, July 23.*
Awards: Karlovy Vary International Film Festival, Crystal Globe, 1980

731. *Bürgschaft für ein Jahr* / *On Probation*
                                                1981 S
D: Herrmann Zschoche
S: Gabriele Kotte, Tine Schulze-Gerlach, Tamara Trampe
C: Günter Jaeuthe
A: Katrin Sass, Monika Lennartz
The state determines that a single mother is unfit and she loses her children; two professionals attempt to help her become more competent, but the woman gives up. *DEFA Film. Accessed 2005, Jan. 18.*

732. *Unser kurzes Leben* / *Our Short Life*
                                                1981 S
D: Lothar Warneke
S: Brigitte Reimann, Regine Kühn
C: Claus Neumann
P: Horst Hartwig
A: Simone Frost
A young architect on her first assignment confronts the problems of designing public housing. *German National.*
Awards: Moscow International Film Festival, nomination for Golden Prize, 1981

733. *Das Fahrrad* / *The Bicycle*   1982 D
D: Evelyn Schmidt
S: Ernst Wenig
C: Roland Dressel
A: Heidemarie Schneider
A single mother and factory worker with a history of bad judgment commits fraud to get some money for her sick child, but she loses her lover, who is an engineer, when she tells him the truth. *DEFA Film. Accessed 2005, Jan. 18.*

734. *Kaskade rückwärts* / *Leap Backward*
                                               1984 DS
D: Iris Gusner
S: Iris Gusner, Roland Kästner
A: Gertraud Kreissig, Johanna Schall
"Middle aged woman changes jobs and moves to the city to find love." *German National: 140.*

735. *Der Traum vom Elch* / *The Dream of the Elk*   1986 S
D: Siegfried Kühn
S: Christa Müller, Siegfried Kühn
C: Peter Brand
A: Katrin Sass, Marie Gruber
A woman who rarely sees her lover has an affair with a man her friend is in love with; when her friend commits suicide, the woman must reconsider her behavior. *FII.*

736. Einer trage des anderen Last / Bear Ye Another's Burdens 1988
D: Lothar Warneke
S: Wolfgang Held
C: Peter Ziesche
A: Karin Gregorek, Susanne Lüning
The story of a friendship between two women in a sanatorium, one a Christian, the other a Marxist. *German National: 141.*
Awards: Berlin International Film Festival, Interfilm Award, 1988

737. Die Schauspielerin / The Actress 1988 S
D: Siegfried Kühn
S: Regine Kühn, Siegfried Kühn, Hedda Zimmer
C: Peter Ziesche
P: Volkmar Leweck
A: Corinna Harfouch
1930s. A theater actress takes on a Jewish identity in order to be with her lover. *German National: 143.*

WEST GERMANY

738. Eine Frau fürs ganze Leben / A Woman for Life 1960
D: Wolfgang Liebeneiner
A: Ruth Leuwerik
"Anecdotes about women through three phases of German history between 1902 and 1946." *West German Cinema.*

739. Die Rote / The Redhead 1962
D: Helmut Käutner
S: Alfred Andersch
A: Ruth Leuwerik, Rossano Brazzi
A woman leaves her "disappointing" husband and lover to go to Venice, where she hopes to find a new job and a new life, but she learns she cannot run away from herself. *AMG.*
Awards: Berlin International Film Festival, nomination for Golden Bear, 1962

740. Der Besuch / The Visit 1963
D: Bernhard Wicki
S: Ben Barzman; based on the play by Friedrich Dürrenmatt
C: Armando Nannuzi
P: Anthony Quinn
A: Ingrid Bergman, Anthony Quinn
A wealthy woman returns to her hometown to seek revenge on the man who abandoned her when she was pregnant as a youth. She proposes paying the locals to murder him, then demands they reprieve him so he will have to live with his betrayal. *FII.*

741. Venusberg / Mount Venus 1963
D: Rolf Thiele
S: Rolf Thiele
C: Wolf Wirth
P: Rolf Wilhelm
A: Marisa Mell, Nicole Badal, Jane Axell
Seven women "meet at the vacation resort of a gynecologist, where they attempt to find themselves." *West German Cinema.*

742. Verführung: Die grausame Frau / Seduction: The Cruel Woman 1963 DSCP
D: Monika Treut, Elfi Mikesch
S: Monika Treut, Elfi Mikesch
C: Monika Treut, Elfi Mikesch
P: Monika Treut, Elfi Mikesch
A: Mechtild Grossmann, Sheila McLaughlin, Udo Kier
"A gallery owner specializes in S/M art. Being a dominatrix isn't easy for her as she insists all is performance, but her clients want a 'real' relationship." *lez films. Accessed 2005, June 10.*

743. Abschied von gestern / Yesterday Girl 1966
D: Alexander Kluge
S: Alexander Kluge
C: Edgar Reitz
P: Alexander Kluge
A: Aleksondra Kluge
An impoverished East German with a knack for petty crime flees to West Germany, where attempts to rehabilitate her do not succeed. *Time Out.*
Awards: Venice Film Festival, Special Jury Prize, 1966; German Film Awards, Outstanding Feature Film, Outstanding Actress, 1967

744. Die Artisten in der Zirkuskuppel: ratlos / Artists at the Top of the Big Top: Disoriented 1968
D: Alexander Kluge
S: Alexander Kluge
C: Guenter Hoermann
A: Hannelore Hoger
A circus director, the daughter of a performer who has died, seeks perfection and funding for the circus but meets obstacles. *Faber Companion.*
Awards: German Film Awards, Outstanding Feature Film, 1969; Venice Film Festival, Golden Camera, 1969

745. Chronik de Anna Magdalena Bach / Chronicles of Anna Magdalena Bach 1968 DS
D: Danièle Huillet, Jean-Marie Straub
S: Danièle Huillet, Jean-Marie Straub

C: Ugo Piccone
P: Gian Vittorio Baldi
A: Christiane Lang, Gustav Leonhardt
The career and family life of Johannes Sebastian Bach, as seen through the imagined diaries of his wife; the emphasis is on the music and the economic stresses of raising children and maintaining Bach's financial advantage with his church employers and benefactors.
Awards: Berlin International Film Festival, nomination for Golden Bear, 1968

746. Gib mir Liebe / All for Love   1968
D: Günter Schlesinger
S: Rubin Sharon
A: Monica Teuber, Evelyn Künneke
A woman's marriage comes to an end because she is childless. After numerous affairs, including a brief lesbian relationship, she finds herself pregnant. *FII.*

747. Neun Leben hat die Katze / The Cat Has Nine Lives   1968 DS
D: Ula Stöckl
S: Ula Stöckl
C: Dietrich Lohmann
A: Heidi Stroh
A non-narrative portrayal of a woman who rejects conventional relationships. "First German film to address female identity." *German National.*

748. 1 + 1 = 3   1970 DSP
D: Heidi Genée
S: Heidi Genée
C: Gernot Roll
P: Heidi Genée
A: Adelheid Arndt
An unmarried actress decides to keep her child, but having observed the tensions in her sister's marriage, she decides to avoid marriage. *MFB: 137. 1981, July.*

749. Der Fall Lena Christ / The Case of Lena Christ   1970
D: Hans W. Geissendörfer
S: Hans W. Geissendörfer
C: Robby Müller
A: Heidi Stroh, Edith Volkmann
The life of Lena Christ, the turn-of-the-twentieth-century German author who committed suicide at thirty-nine. *West German Cinema.*

750. Der Tod der Maria Malibran / Death of Maria Malibran   1971
D: Werner Schroeter
S: Werner Schroeter

A: Magdalena Montezuma
"Inspired by the character of Maria Malibran, the nineteenth-century prima donna who died during a performance, when she was only 28." *FII.*

751. Die bitteren Tränen der Petra von Kant / The Bitter Tears of Petra von Kant   1972
D: Rainer Werner Fassbinder
S: Rainer Werner Fassbinder
C: Michael Ballhaus
A: Margit Carstensen, Hanna Schygulla, Irm Hermann
A neurotic, wealthy fashion designer takes in a charming loafer, falls in love, and is finally painfully rejected. In the background is her silent, abused servant.

752. Der scharlachrote Buchstabe / The Scarlet Letter   1972 S
D: Wim Wenders
S: Tankred Dorst, Ursula Ehler; based on the novel by Nathaniel Hawthorne
C: Robby Müller
P: Peter Genée
A: Senta Berger
Seventeenth century, Massachusetts. A woman is marked because of her child and single status; her secret affair with the local minister is threatened with exposure when her husband resurfaces.

753. Angst essen Seele auf / Ali, Fear Eats the Soul   1973
D: Rainer Werner Fassbinder
S: Rainer Werner Fassbinder
C: Jürgen Jürges
P: Rainer Werner Fassbinder
A: Brigitte Mira, El Hedi Ban Salem
A widow, who works as a cleaning woman, marries a much younger Moroccan mechanic. She conflicts with her grown children over her decision, baring her own deep prejudices in the process.
Awards: Cannes Film Festival, FIPRESCI, 1974; German Film Awards, Outstanding Actress, 1974

754. Gelegenheitsarbelt einer Sklavin / Occasional Work of a Female Slave   1973
D: Alexander Kluge
S: Alexander Kluge, Hans Drawe
C: Thomas Mauch
A: Aleksondra Kluge
A poor woman performs illegal abortions and has her consciousness raised when her practice is shut down by the police. In response, she becomes a socialist activist. *Variety: 16. 1974, May 29.*

Other titles: Part Time Work of a Domestic Slave

755. *Martha* 1973
D: Rainer Werner Fassbinder
S: Rainer Werner Fassbinder
C: Michael Ballhaus
P: Peter Märthesheimer
A: Margit Carstensen
A selfish wealthy woman marries into a sadomasochistic relationship, which she resists until she is paralyzed by an accident. *FII.*

756. *Mutter Küsters Fahrt zum Himmel / Mother Kuster Goes to Heaven* 1973
D: Rainer Werner Fassbinder
S: Rainer Werner Fassbinder, Kurt Raab
C: Michael Ballhaus
A: Brigitte Mira
A woman, whose husband kills his boss and commits suicide over layoffs at his factory, is politicized and joins a leftist group. *Faber Companion.*

757. *Nora Helmer* 1973
D: Rainer Werner Fassbinder
S: Berhnard Schulze; based on *A Doll's House* by Henrik Ibsen
C: Günter Steinke
P: Karlhans Reuss
A: Margit Carstensen
A modern, pared-down version, where Nora is not "a capricious being . . . but a society lady hungry for money and power." Ibsen's world of "idealism, where things can be upended" and suddenly changed is challenged with a new ending. *Fassbinder: 174–178.*

758. *Effi Briest* 1974
D: Rainer Werner Fassbinder
S: Rainer Werner Fassbinder; based on the novel by Theodor Fontane
P: Rainer Werner Fassbinder
A: Hanna Schygulla
Berlin countryside, nineteenth century. A seventeen-year-old agrees to a marriage with an aristocrat twice her age. Though her mother is concerned, the girl cannot resist when told of the wealth she will attain. She has a brief affair, which is discovered many years later, at which point her husband kills the man in a duel and banishes his wife from her home and her child.
Awards: Berlin International Film Festival, Interfilm Award, 1974

759. *Die Praxis der Liebe / Practice of Love* 1974 DS
D: Valie Export
S: Valie Export
C: Jörg Schmidt-Reitwein
A: Adelheid Arndt
Hamburg. A journalist, assigned to peep shows, gets involved with an old friend, a smuggler, who investigates his friend's murder. A mix of her dreams and fantasies accompanies a thriller-type story. *Variety: 8. 1985, Mar. 13.*
Awards: Berlin International Film Festival, nomination for Golden Bear, 1985

760. *Strohfeuer / A Free Woman* 1974 S
D: Volker Schlöndorff
S: Volker Schlöndorff, Margarethe Von Trotta
C: Sven Nykvist
A: Margarethe Von Trotta
A divorced woman feels liberated, tries tap dancing and working as a typist, but jousts with her husband over custody of their son. Having trouble supporting herself, they both decide it is best to marry again.
Other titles: Summer Lightning
Awards: German Film Critics Association, Best Actress, 1974

761. *Die verlorene Ehre der Katharina Blum / The Lost Honor of Katharina Blum* 1975 DS
D: Volker Schlöndorff, Margarethe Von Trotta
S: Volker Schlöndorff, Margarethe Von Trotta; based on a story by Heinrich Böll.
C: Jost Vacano
A: Angela Winkler
A woman unwittingly spends the night with a terrorist being followed by the police, then becomes the object of a journalist's intrusive investigation.
Awards: San Sebastián International Film Festival, OCIC Award, 1975; German Film Awards, Outstanding Actress, 1976

762. *Chinesisches Roulette / Chinese Roulette* 1976
D: Rainer Werner Fassbinder
S: Rainer Werner Fassbinder
C: Michael Ballhaus
A: Margit Carstensen, Anna Karina, Alexander Allerson
A woman arranges for her parents, who have always cheated on one another, a surprise meeting in the country with their past and present lovers. *West German Cinema.*

763. *Der Fangschuss / Coup de grâce* 1976 S
D: Volker Schlöndorff
S: Jutta Brückner, Margarethe Von Trotta, Geneviève Dormann; based on the novel by Marguerite Yourcenar

C: Igor Luther
P: Anatole Dauman
A: Margarethe Von Trotta, Matthais Habich
1919. In wartime, a bright, wealthy woman, the center of a large country house that is a refuge for government soldiers, falls for a German commander who is more attracted to her brother. His rejection and general cold demeanor bolster her sympathy for the Bolsheviks, and she becomes an active participant in the war.
Awards: German Film Awards, Outstanding Direction, 1977

764. *Grete Minde*   1976 DS
D: Heidi Genée
S: Heidi Genée; based on the novel by Theodor Fontane
A: Katarina Jacob, Hannelore Elsner
Sweden, seventeenth century. A Catholic daughter is protected by her father from the rest of his Protestant family, but they deny her all status when he dies. In revenge, she takes her stepbrother's child and her own child into a church and starts a fire. *Variety: 26. 1977, May 25.*
Awards: Berlin International Film Festival, nomination for Golden Bear, 1977; German Film Awards, Outstanding Feature Film, 1977

765. *Die Marquise von O / The Marquise of O*
1976
D: Eric Rohmer
S: Eric Rohmer; based on the novel by Henrich von Kleist
C: Nestor Almendros
P: Barbet Schroeder
A: Edith Clever, Bruno Ganz
Eighteenth century. A widow with two children "is drugged and raped by an officer from the invading Russian army, a count. Discovering she is pregnant, she confronts her rapist and demands that he marry her; the Count agrees." *Film Society. 2004, July*
Awards: Cannes Film Festival, Jury Prize, 1976; German Film Awards, Outstanding Actress, 1976

766. *Shirins Hochzeit / Shirin's Wedding*
1976 DS
D: Helma Sanders-Brahms
S: Helma Sanders-Brahms
C: Thomas Mauch
A: Ayten Erten
A young Turkish woman flees from an arranged marriage into Germany, where she loses her job and her only friend and is raped and murdered. *FII.*
Awards: Baden-Baden Days of Teleplay, Teleplay Award, 1976

767. *Die Allseitig reduzierte Persönlichkeit— Redupers / The All-Round Reduced Personality: Outtakes*   1977 DSCP
D: Helke Sander
S: Helke Sander
C: Katia Forbet, Hille Sagel
P: Maya Faber-Jansen
A: Helke Sander, Eva Gagel
Berlin. A photographer and single mother confronts her complex world. Devotion to her eight-year-old does not prevent impatience when the girl desperately grabs her shirt to keep her from going to work. In the process of becoming politicized, she attempts to engage in a city-funded project, only to find the officials expect her photographs to be about women's issues rather than the urban landscapes that interest her. She concedes points in a variety of social and professional encounters and takes up fads, such as tae kwon do, in search of balance and well-being.
Other titles: Redupers—Die Allseitig reduzierte Persönlichkeit

768. *Ein ganz und gar verwahrlostes Mädchen / A Thoroughly Neglected Girl*   1977 DSP
D: Jutta Brückner
S: Jutta Brückner
C: Edward Windhäger
P: Jutta Brückner
A: Rita Rischak, Brigitte Türk
Documentary and fictional story of an actress's life—her past, her future plans, and her son. *West German Cinema.*
Other titles: A Completely Neglected Girl

769. *Die linkshändige Frau / The Left-Handed Woman*   1977 P
D: Peter Handke
S: Peter Handke
C: Robby Müller
P: Renée Gundelach
A: Edith Clever
A suburban wife is bored with her husband, son, and friends and decides to leave them.

770. *Madame X—Eine absolute Herrscherin / Madame X: An Absolute Ruler*   1977 DSC
D: Ulrike Ottinger, Tabea Blumenschein
S: Ulrike Ottinger
C: Ulrike Ottinger
A: Tabea Blumenschein, Yvonne Rainer, Monica Von Cube
Madame X, a pirate of the China Sea, lures a crew to her ship with a telegram—"All women of the world - stop - full of gold love adventure - stop."

The fabulously costumed women are transformed, via a carnival, into even more fantastic versions of themselves. Not at all ordinary, they are true cinematic spectacles. *Screen Fantasy, vol. 28, no. 4: 82–83. 1987, Aug.*

771. *Das zweite Erwachen der Christa Klages / The Second Awakening of Christa Klages*
1977 DS
D: Margarethe Von Trotta
S: Margarethe Von Trotta, Luisa Francia
C: Franz Rath
P: Gunther Witte
A: Tina Engle, Sylvia Reize
A teacher in a progressive nursery robs a bank to save the school from bankruptcy, then flees and seeks out old friends for help. *FII.*
Awards: Berlin International Film Festival, Interfilm Award, 1978; German Film Awards, Outstanding Feature Film, Outstanding Actress (Engle), 1978

772. *Die Ehr der Maria Braun / The Marriage of Maria Braun*
1978
D: Rainer Werner Fassbinder
S: Peter Märthesheimer, Pea Frölich, Rainer Werner Fassbinder
C: Michael Ballhaus
P: Michael Fengler
A: Hanna Schygulla, Gisela Uhlen
Germany, World War II. An ambitious and confident woman is married to a German soldier, but she makes friends in high places, and so loses him.
Awards: Berlin International Film Festival, Silver Bear (Schygulla), 1979; David di Donatello Awards, Special David (Schygulla), 1980; German Film Awards, Outstanding Direction, Outstanding Actress (Schygulla, Uhlen), 1980

773. *Erikas Leidenschaften / Erika's Passions*
1978 DS
D: Ula Stöckl
S: Ula Stöckl
C: Nicole Gasquet
P: Christoph Holch
A: Vera Tschechowa, Karin Baal
A woman returns to her lover's apartment four years after the breakup of their romance. They spend time confronting the emotional realities of their disappointing relationship, not entirely without humor, as they manage to get locked in the bathroom at one point. *Variety: 18. 1978, Nov. 8.*

774. *Eine Frau mit Verantwortung / A Woman with Responsibility*
1978 DS
D: Ula Stöckl

S: Jutta Brückner
C: Mario Masini
A: Christina Scholz, Niklaus Dutsch
"Young woman cannot cope with the role of housewife since she has never learned to stand up for herself." *West German Cinema.*
Awards: Baden-Baden Days of Teleplay, Teleplay Award, 1979

775. *Geschichten aus dem Wienerwald / Stories of the Vienna Woods*
1978
D: Maximilian Schell
S: Maximilian Schell, Christopher Hampton
C: Klaus König
A: Birgit Doll
Vienna, 1930. A young woman "tries, but fails to escape her social milieu." *West German Cinema.*
Awards: German Film Awards, Outstanding Feature Film, 1980

776. *Gina Wildkatze / Gina Wildcat*
1978 DSP
D: Gina Arnold
S: Gina Arnold
C: Peter Baudendistel
P: Gina Arnold
A: Gina Von Freiburg
The story of a Freiburg bar owner and her difficulties. *West German Cinema.*

777. *Die Macht der Männer ist die Geduld der Frauen / The Power of Men Is the Patience of Women*
1978 DS
D: Christine Perincioli
S: Christine Perincioli
Berlin. Real women from a shelter for battered women perform in a story about a woman who lives with a violent husband in a cycle of abuse that is accepted by their friends. Worsened by an attempt to live on her own that is thwarted by having no address, no day care, and no job, she finally enters "Frauenhaus," where they help her to divorce and begin again. *Variety: 1980, Sep. 17. Also SoHo: 40. 1982, Mar. 2.*

778. *Bildinis einer Trinkerin / Ticket of No Return*
1979 DSCP
D: Ulrike Ottinger
S: Ulrike Ottinger
C: Ulrike Ottinger
P: Renée Gundelach
A: Tabea Blumenschein, Magdalena Montezuma
Berlin. An "ideal woman" leaves the countryside and heads for the city to drink herself to death; there she becomes involved with another alcoholic, and they tour the seedy side of the city. *St. James: 319.*

Other titles: Portrait of a Female Alcoholic

779. Deutschland bleiche Mutter / Germany
Pale Mother   1979 DSP
D: Helma Sanders-Brahms
S: Helma Sanders-Brahms
C: Jürgen Jürges
P: Helma Sanders-Brahms
A: Eva Mattes, Elizabeth Stepanek
Berlin, 1930s–1940s. An apolitical woman marries
   a man who is not a Nazi, but he is drafted into
   the army and separated for many years from his
   already tormented wife and daughter. Their life
   is bleak, especially toward the end of the war
   when her house is demolished. She wanders
   through the country, where she is raped by
   American soldiers, to a shelter where she finds
   her best friend. Deprivation envelops them further when the father returns with a petty focus
   on his own career in the postwar bureaucracy.
   Depicts the full cycle of abuse and its relationship with control, involving everyone, including
   the daughter.
Awards: Berlin International Film Festival, nomination for Golden Bear, 1980; Créteil International
   Women's Film Festival, Grand Prix, 1980

780. Etwas tut weh / Something Hurts 1979 DSP
D: Recha Jungmann
S: Recha Jungmann
C: Rüdiger Laske
P: Recha Jungmann
A: Simone Maul
Rhone river village. A filmmaker traces her past.
   West German Cinema.

781. Hungerjahre—in einem reichen Land /
Hunger Years   1979 DSP
D: Jutta Brückner
S: Jutta Brückner
C: Jörg Jeshel
P: Jutta Brückner
A: Britta Pohland, Sylvia Ulrich, Helga Lehner
1950s. During a period defined by an "upsurge of
   material prosperity, the increasing grip of cold
   war politics and the rehabilitation of numerous
   Nazis," a young girl grows up with a controlling
   mother, who is anxious to deny both of them
   their sexuality. The daughter attempts to cope
   through overeating, self-mutilation, and a suicide
   attempt. *St. James: 58.*
Other titles: Years of Hunger

782. Schwestern oder die Balance des Glücks /
Sisters or the Balance of Happiness 1979 DS
D: Margarethe Von Trotta

S: Luisa Francia, Martje Grohmann, Jutta Lampe,
   Margarethe Von Trotta
C: Franz Rath
A: Jutta Lampe, Gudrun Gabriel
Two sisters are very close; the older one, an executive secretary, supports the younger, who is a
   student with a critical outlook on the workaday
   world. When she realizes she is in love with her
   sister, she commits suicide, and the older one
   attempts to replace her by asking a girl from the
   office to move in. The new roommate finds the
   dead girl's diaries one day and is angered by the
   strings being tightened around her.
Awards: German Film Awards, Outstanding Actress
   (Lampe), 1980; Créteil International Women's
   Film Festival, Grand Prix, 1981

783. Die Jager / Deadly Game   1980
D: Károly Makk
S: Károly Makk
C: Lothar Stickelbrucks
P: Dieter Geisslen
A: Barbara Sukowa, Helmut Berger
"Diplomat's wife, who has committed a murder,
   returns to the scene of the crime." *West Ger-*
   man Cinema.

784. Laufen lernen / Learning to Run 1980 DS
D: Jutta Brückner
S: Uta Geiger-Berlet
C: Hille Sagel
A: Sylvia Ulrich
A middle-aged mother of two children tries to
   change her life. *FII.*
Other titles: The First Steps

785. Lili Marleen   1980
D: Rainer Werner Fassbinder
S: Rainer Werner Fassbinder, Manfred Purzer
C: Michael Ballhaus
P: Luggi Waldleitner
A: Hanna Schygulla
1940s. Story of the singer who made the titular
   song famous in Germany and her relationship
   with a Jew.

786. Malou   1980 DSP
D: Jeanine Meerapfel
S: Jeanine Meerapfel
C: Michael Ballhaus
P: Regina Ziegler
A: Ingrid Caven, Grischa Huber
A young married woman confronts the memory
   of her Catholic mother, who died an alcoholic
   in Argentina, where she fled with her husband,
   a German Jew, who subsequently abandoned

her. The daughter visits Strasbourg, where her mother was born and buried, to confront her mother's dependency on men.

787. *Die Reise nach Lyon / Blind Spot* 1980 DS
D: Claudia Von Alemann
S: Claudia Von Alemann
C: Hille Sagel
A: Rebecca Pauly
A historian takes a train to Lyon to research nineteenth-century socialist feminist Flora Tristan. *Variety: 21. 1981, Feb. 25.*

788. *Die Berührte / No Mercy, No Future*
1981 DS
D: Helma Sanders-Brahms
S: Helma Sanders-Brahms
C: Thomas Mauch
A: Elizabeth Stepanek
Chronicle of the mental illness of a middle-class girl who acts out in sexual liaisons between suicide attempts. *AMG.*

789. *Die bleirne Zeit / Marianne and Juliane*
1981 DS
D: Margarethe Von Trotta
S: Margarethe Von Trotta
C: Franz Rath
A: Barbara Sukowa, Jutta Lampe
1970s. Two sisters have grown up in the postwar denial of Germany's recent past. One is a terrorist member of the Baader-Meinhof Group, intent on waking Germans out of their complacency, and the other is a journalist who writes as a militant feminist and who supports her sister when she is arrested and condemned to life in prison.
Other titles:The German Sisters / Leaden Times
Awards: Venice Film Festival, Golden Lion, 1981

790. *Celeste* 1981 S
D: Percy Adlon
S: Percy Adlon; based on a book by Celeste Albaret
C: Jürgen Martin
A: Eva Mattes, Jürgen Arndt
Memoirs of Celeste Albaret, who was the housekeeper and nurse for Marcel Proust at the end of his life. *West German Cinema.*

791. *Dabbel Trabbel / Double Trouble* 1981 DS
D: Dorothea Neukirchen
S: Dorothea Neukirchen
C: Jacques Steyn
A: Gudrun Landgrebe, Jochen Schroeder
A professional couple have a crisis because she wants to have a child and he does not. *FII.*

792. *Deutschland kann manchmal sehr schön sein / Germany Can Sometimes Be Very Nice* 1981 DSP
D: Solveig Hoogesteijn
S: Solveig Hoogesteijn
P: Jörg Schmidt, Solveig Hoogesteijn
A: Julia Siemers, Hanns Zischler
A young woman in rebellion rejects language as a means of communication and is lured by a musician to an interest in life. *West German Cinema.*

793. *Freak Orlando* 1981 DSCP
D: Ulrike Ottinger
S: Ulrike Ottinger
C: Ulrike Ottinger
P: Renée Gundelach
A: Magdalena Montezuma, Delphine Seyrig
A fantastical reworking of the androgynous person who exists through the centuries, originally created by Virginia Woolf in her novel *Orlando*. *MOMA Film. 2003, Dec.*

794. *Der subjektive Faktor / The Subjective Factor* 1981 DS
D: Helke Sander
S: Helke Sander
C: Martin Schäfer
A: Angelika Rommel
Berlin, 1967–1970. A woman and her young son live in a commune with students active in alternative politics; there she learns to demand more from her relationships with men. *Festival de films, 4th: 32. 1982.*

795. *Der Tag der Idioten / Day of the Idiots*
1981
D: Werner Schroeter
S: Werner Schroeter
C: Ivan Slapeta
A: Carole Bouquet
A woman mysteriously finds herself in a mental institution; a female doctor tries to help her, but she remains out of reach and eventually becomes the victim of an accident. *Festival de films, 19th: 62. 1997.*

796. *Die weiße Rose / The White Rose* 1981
D: Michal Verhoeven
S: Michal Verhoeven, Mario Krebs
C: Axel de Roche
A: Lena Stolze, Wulf Kessler
Munich, 1930s. The history of a resistance group named the White Rose, which was led by two students during the Nazi regime; both were executed in 1943. *West German Cinema.*
Awards: German Film Awards, Outstanding Actress, 1983

797. *Catherine Chérie*   1982
D: Hubert Frank
C: Franz Lederle
A: Berta Cabre, Micha Kapteijn
"Rising pop singer is backed by an author of por-
   nography and becomes involved in his drug deal-
   ings." Exploitation. *West German Cinema.*

798. *Fünf letzte Tage / The Last Five Days*
                                                    1982
D: Percy Adlon
S: Percy Adlon
C: Horst Lermer
A: Lena Stolze
"Final days of resistance fighter Sophie Scholl,
   who was executed by the Nazis." *West German
   Cinema.*
Awards: Bavarian Film Awards, Best Director, 1983;
   German Film Awards, Outstanding Actress,
   1983

799. *Grenzenlos*   1982 P
D: Josef Rödl
S: Josef Rödl
C: Frank Brühne
P: Gudrun Ruzicková-Steiner
A: Therese Affolter
"Village woman, an outsider, flees to the city, but
   returns determined to stand up for herself."
   West German Cinema.

800. *Heller Wahn / Sheer Madness*   1982 DS
D: Margarethe Von Trotta
S: Margarethe Von Trotta
C: Michael Ballhaus
P: Eberhard Junkersdorf
A: Hanna Schygulla, Angela Winkler
A married woman is afraid of people and spends
   her time in museums copying paintings. When
   she attempts suicide one day, she is saved by
   the intervention of a writer, an associate of
   her husband's. The two women become close
   friends, and while the husband encourages the
   friendship in hopes of curing his wife's depression, he also becomes jealous, provoking
   another suicide attempt. *Festival de films, 5th:
   42. 1983.*
Other titles: L'Amie
Awards: Berlin International Film Festival, OCIC
   Award, 1983

801. *Rote Liebe / Red Love*   1982 SP
D: Rosa Von Präunheim
S: Alexandra Kollantai
C: Rosa Von Präunheim, Mike Kuchar
P: Renée Gundelach

A: Olga Demetriscu, Eddie Constantine, Sascha
   Hammer
Two women decide to liberate themselves from
   marriage: In 1919 revolutionary Russia, a woman
   leaves her philandering husband; and in 1980s
   Vienna, a mother of seven has left her marriage
   to join a commune. *AMG.*

**802. *Die Sehnsucht der Veronika Voss / Veron-
   ika Voss***   1982
D: Rainer Werner Fassbinder
S: Rainer Werner Fassbinder
C: Xaver Schwarzenberger
P: Thomas Schühly
A: Rosel Zech, Annemarie Düringer, Hilmar
   Thate
Munich, 1955. A wealthy, aged film actress is con-
   trolled by a female doctor, who supplies her
   with drugs in order to get her money. *FII.*
Awards: Berlin International Film Festival, Golden
   Bear, 1982; Toronto International Film Festival,
   FIPRESCI, 1982

**803. *Weggehen um Anzukommen / Leaving in
   Order to Arrive***   1982 DSP
D: Alexandra Von Grote
S: Alexandra Von Grote
C: Hille Sagel
P: Alexandra Von Grote
A: Gabriele Osberg, Ute Cremer
Berlin. Two women live together for a year, but
   their conception of the relationship has always
   been opposed; a trial separation forces the end
   as one falls in love with another woman. The
   other takes a trip alone to the south of France,
   wondering why she was so hurt, but gains
   strength in a new conception of love. *Festival de
   films, 4th: 33. 1982.*
Other titles: Nouveau départ

804. *Zuckerhut / Sugar Hat*   1982 DS
D: Vivian Naefe
S: Vivian Naefe, Ulrich Limmer
C: Klaus Eichhammer
A: Despina Papanou, Gundi Ellert, Dominique
   Raacker
Three "impulsive women are disappointed in rela-
   tionships." *West German Cinema.*

805. *Canale Grande*   1983 DSCP
D: Friederika Pezold
S: Friederika Pezold
C: Elfi Mikesch
P: Friederika Pezold
A: Friederika Pezold
"Turned off by normal television channels, a young

woman tries to establish her own program."
West German Cinema.

806. *Cherie, mir ist schlecht / Cherie, I'm Not Well* 1983 DSP
D: Marian Kiss
S: Marian Kiss, Ed Canter
C: Gusztav Hamos
P: Marian Kiss
A: Marie Canter, Lotti Huber
Threatened with murder, "a model finds refuge with a woman who collects television commercials." Thriller. *West German Cinema.*

807. *Dorian Gray im Spiegel der boulevard Presse / The Image of Dorian Gray in the Yellow Press* 1983 DSCP
D: Ulrike Ottinger
S: Ulrike Ottinger
C: Ulrike Ottinger
P: Renée Gundelach
A: Delphine Seyrig, Irm Hermann, Tabea Blumenschein
A media news conglomerate creates a new human being. Science fiction. *Festival de films, 6th:* 15. 1984.
Other titles: The Mirror Image of Dorian Gray

808. *Die flambierte Frau / A Woman in Flames* 1983 S
D: Robert Von Ackeren
S: Robert Von Ackeren, Catharina Zwerenz
C: Jürgen Jürges
P: Robert Von Ackeren
A: Gudrun Landgrebe
A bored housewife finds freedom in prostitution and falls in love with a male prostitute.

809. *Grat Wanderung / Dangerous Climb* 1983 DS
D: Barbara Kappen
S: Barbara Kappen
C: Claus Deubel
A: Irina Hoppe, Petra Seeger
"Two women from Berlin vacation in the mountains of Norway and are disturbed by a male climber." *West German Cinema.*

810. *Eine Liebe in Deutschland / A Love in Germany* 1983 S
D: Andrzej Wajda
S: Agnieszka Holland
C: Igor Luther
A: Hanna Schygulla
1941. While her husband is at the eastern front, a woman falls in love with a Polish worker. She writes a letter to him, and it is intercepted by the Gestapo, who murder him.

Other titles: Un Amor en Allemagne

811. *Mitten ins Herz / Right in the Heart* 1983 DS
D: Doris Dörrie
S: Doris Dörrie
C: Michael Gobel
A: Beate Hensen
A woman moves in with a passive man and lies to him that she is pregnant; she then steals a baby to keep up the facade that is making him happy. *Variety: 24. 1983, July 14.*
Other titles: Straight to the Heart

812. *Der Beginn Aller Schrecken ist Liebe / The Trouble with Love* 1984 DS
D: Helke Sander
S: Helke Sander, Dörte Haak
C: Martin Schäfer
P: Jürgen Mohrbutter
A: Rebecca Pauly, Helke Sander, Lou Castel
Two old friends vie over a longtime boyfriend of one of the women. *PFA. Accessed 2004, July 10.*
Other titles: Love Is the Beginning of All Terror

813. *Der Biß / The Bite* 1984 DSP
D: Marianne Enzenberger
S: Marianne Enzenberger
C: Jeff Preiss
P: Marianne Enzenberger
A: Marianne Enzenberger, Marianne Rosenberg
"Vampire tries to liberate her bourgeois friends from their career obsessions." Horror, fantasy. *West German Cinema.*

814. *Christines Schwester / Christine's Sister* 1984 DS
D: Silke Lähndorf
S: Silke Lähndorf
C: Jürgen Jürges
A: Angela Stresemann, Maria Hartmann
"Sensitive young woman confronts the emotional superficiality of life in the big city." *West German Cinema.*

815. *Ediths Tagebuch / Edith's Diary* 1984 S
D: Hans W. Geissendörfer
S: Hans W. Geissendörfer; based on the novel by Patricia Highsmith
C: Michael Ballhaus
P: Hans W. Geissendörfer
A: Angela Winkler
"Disappointed by life, a woman escapes into her diary," and unreality in general. *West German Cinema.*

816. *Flugel und Fesseln / The Future of Emily*
1984 DSP
D: Helma Sanders-Brahms
S: Helma Sanders-Brahms
C: Sacha Vierny
P: Helma Sanders-Brahms
A: Brigitte Fossey, Hildegarde Knef, Camille Raymond
Normandy. A film star returns from Berlin to her family home to pick up her young daughter. The weekend is characterized by argument and struggle with her mother, who criticizes her daughter's scandal-ridden life, believing bourgeois strictures to be better for her grandchild. *Festival de films, 7th: 8. 1985.*
Other titles: L'Avenir d'Émilie

817. *Novembermond / November Moon*
1984 DS
D: Alexandra Van Grote
S: Alexandra Van Grote
C: Bernard Zitzermann
A: Gabriele Osberg, Christiane Millet
1930s. A German girl leaves for Paris, survives the occupation, and has an affair with a French woman, who hides her. *West German Cinema, 1985.*

818. *Der Schlaf der Vernunft / Sleep of Reason*
1984 DSP
D: Ula Stöckl
S: Ula Stöckl
C: Axel Block
P: Renée Gundelach
A: Ida Di Benedetto
A gynecologist organizes opposition to a pharmaceutical company that produces the Pill, causing conflict with her husband, who is an executive there; eventually she discovers he has betrayed her, and she leaves him. *Festival de films, 6th: 17. 1984.*
Other titles: Reason Asleep
Awards: German Film Awards, Silver Award, 1985

819. *Bolero*
1985 SP
D: Rüdiger Nüchtern
S: Rüdiger Nüchtern, Monika Nüchtern
C: Jacques Steyn
P: Monika Nüchtern
A: Katja Rupé, Michael König
"Gallery owner sacrifices her career for the sake of her marriage and family." *West German Cinema.*

820. *German Dreams*
1985
D: Lienhard Wawrzyn

S: Lienhard Wawrzyn
C: Claus Deubel
A: Angela Lieberg
After being imprisoned for trying to escape, a woman and her teenage daughter gain visas from the East but are confounded in their expectation of economic prosperity in the West. *West German Cinema, 1985.*

821. *Die Kümmeltürkin geht / The Turkish Spice Lady Is Leaving*
1985 DS
D: Jeanine Meerapfel
S: Jeanine Meerapfel
C: Johann Feindt
A: Melek Tez
"Turkish woman returns to Turkey after living in Berlin for 18 years." *West German Cinema, 1985.*
Other titles: Melek Leaves
Awards: Berlin International Film Festival, Interfilm Award, 1985

822. *Männer / Men*
1985 DS
D: Doris Dörrie
S: Doris Dörrie
C: Helge Weindler
P: Helmut Rasp
A: Ulrike Kriende, Heiner Lauterbach
A wife having an affair is left by her husband, who moves in with her lover. Comedy.
Awards: German Film Awards, Outstanding Screenplay, 1986

823. *Die Wolfsbraut / The Wolf's Bride*
1985 DSP
D: Dagmar Beiersdorf
S: Dagmar Beiersdorf
C: Christoph Gies
P: Dagmar Beiersdorf
A: Imke Barnstedt, Martine Felton
A filmmaker has a "creative crisis" and begins an affair with "a mulatto woman she encounters cleaning a cinema." *FII.*

824. *Yerma*
1985
D: Barna Kabay, Imre Gyöngyössy
S: Imre Gyöngyössy, Katalin Petanyi; based on the play by Federico Garcia Lorca
C: Gabor Szabó
A: Gudrun Landgrebe
An Andalusian village. "Young woman caught in a traditional marriage." *West German Cinema.*

825. *Zuckerbaby / Sugarbaby*
1985 CP
D: Percy Adlon
S: Percy Adlon

C: Johanna Heer
P: Eleonore Adlon
A: Marianne Sägebrecht
A bored, overweight woman who works in a funeral parlor seduces a subway train driver. *West German Cinema*.
Awards: Valladolid International Film Festival, Silver Spike, 1985

826. *Auf immer und ewig / Now or Never*
1986 DSP
D: Christel Buschmann
S: Christel Buschmann
C: Frank Brühne
P: Christel Buschmann
A: Eva Mattes
A young mother learns she has a terminal disease and finds hope in reestablishing contact with the father of her child. *West German Cinema*.
Other titles: For Ever and Ever

827. *Francesca*
1986 DSP
D: Verena Rudolph
S: Verena Rudolph
C: Eberhard Gieck
P: Heide Breitel, Verena Rudolph
A: Eva Lissa
The story of a woman raised in a Bavarian convent who became a star of the Italian cinema in the 1950s. *West German Cinema*.

828. *Rosa Luxemburg*
1986 DSP
D: Margarethe Von Trotta
S: Margarethe Von Trotta
C: Franz Rath
P: Regina Ziegler
A: Barbara Sukowa
The adult life of the revolutionary thinker begins in a prison cell, with her torture and mock execution. It then flashes back through her romance with a revolutionary Pole, who refuses her desire for motherhood, and to her antiwar work in Germany. A dedicated, powerful pacifist and internationalist, Luxemburg firmly stood her ground in both her professional and personal life.
Awards: Cannes Film Festival, Best Actress, 1986; German Film Awards, Outstanding Feature Film, Outstanding Actress, 1986

829. *Anita: Tänze des Lasters / Anita: Dances of Vice*
1987 SCP
D: Rosa Von Präunheim
S: Rosa Von Präunheim, Marianne Enzenberger, Lotti Huber
C: Elfi Mikesch

P: Hannelore Limpach
A: Lotti Huber, Ina Blum
The life of Anita Berber, a famous dancer of 1920s Germany, as expressed by an aging modern-day mental patient who thinks she is Berber. *Time Out*.

830. *Bagdad Cafe*
1987 SP
D: Percy Adlon
S: Percy Adlon, Eleonore Adlon
C: Bernd Heinl
P: Eleonore Adlon, Percy Adlon
A: Marianne Sägebrecht, CCH Pounder
California. While on the road, a German woman fights with her husband and flees to an old motel, which she helps the owner make commercially viable. *FII*.
Other titles: Out of Rosenheim
Awards: Seattle International Film Festival, Best Film, 1988; César Awards, Best Foreign Film, 1989; German Film Awards, Outstanding Actress (Sägebrecht), 1989; Independent Spirit Awards, Best Foreign Film, 1989

831. *Ein Blick—und die Liebe bricht aus / One Look and Love Breaks Out*
1987 DS
D: Jutta Brückner
S: Jutta Brückner
C: Marcello Carmorino
P: P. Von Vietinhoff
An experimental film of feminist issues, exploitation, sexism, relationships: "compulsive and stylized reenactment of women's enslavement to romantic love." *German Cinema: 194. Also West German Cinema, 1985*.

832. *Die Geirwally*
1987 S
D: Walter Bockmayer
S: Walter Bockmayer; based on the novel by Wilhelmine von Hillern
C: Wolfgang Simon
A: Samy Orfgen
"Daughter is forced by her father to marry someone other than the man she loves." *West German Cinema, 1985*.

833. *Komplizinnen / Serving Time*
1987 DSP
D: Margit Czenki
S: Margit Czenki
C: Hille Sagel
P: Renée Gundelach
A: Pola Kinski, Therese Affolter
A woman is sentenced to prison for robbing a bank, then works with other inmates to accomplish prison reforms. *West German Cinema, 1985*.
Other titles: Accomplices

834. *Rage to Kill* 1987
D: Ernst Ritter von Theumer
S: James Dallessandro, Louis La Russo
C: Mario DiLeo
A: Maud Adams
"Daughter of a murdered Nazi-hunter continues her mother's work and uncovers a concentration camp doctor in the jungles of Paraguay." *West German Cinema, 1985.*
Other titles: Hell Hunters

835. *Die Verliebten / Days to Remember*
1987 DS
D: Jeanine Meerapfel
S: Jeanine Meerapfel
C: Predrag Popovic
P: Udo Heiland
A: Barbara Sukowa
Montenegro. A German television journalist visits her Yugoslav family and has an affair with a young German man. *FII.*
Awards: Berlin International Film Festival, nomination for Golden Bear, 1987

836. *La Amiga / The Girlfriend* 1988 DSP
D: Jeanine Meerapfel
S: Jeanine Meerapfel, Osvaldo Bayer, Alcides Chiesa, Agnieszka Holland
C: Axel Block
P: Renée Gundelach
A: Liv Ullmann, Cipe Lincovsky
1980s. A woman with a son "disappeared" in Argentina campaigns to find him, and she finds support from an old friend in similar circumstances. *Variety. 1988, Oct. 5.*
Awards: Berlin International Film Festival, Peace Award, 1990; San Sebastián International Film Festival, Best Actress (Ullmann, Lincovsky), 1990

837. *Bittere ernte / Bitter Harvest* 1988 DS
D: Agnieszka Holland
S: Agnieszka Holland, Paul Hengge
C: Joseph Ort-Snep
A: Armin Müller-Stahl, Elisabeth Trissenaar
World War II. An educated Jew jumps from the train that is taking her husband and family to the death camps. After wandering the countryside, she is taken in by an illiterate peasant, who hides her in his basement during the day and brings her into his home at night to pursue a sexual relationship. *Festival de films, 11th: 142. 1989.*
Other titles: Angry Harvest

838. *Herbstmilch / Autumn Milk* 1988 S
D: Joseph Vilsmaier

S: Peter Steinbach; based on an autobiography by Anna Winschneider
C: Joseph Vilsmaier
P: Joseph Vilsmaier
A: Dana Vávrová
Bavaria, World War II. A woman "cares for her family and farm, then her husband's family when he is drafted." *West German Cinema, 1985.*
Awards: German Film Awards, Outstanding Actress, 1989; Valladolid International Film Festival, Best Actress, 1989

839. *Johanna d'Arc de Mongolia / Joan of Arc of Mongolia* 1988 DSCP
D: Ulrike Ottinger
S: Ulrike Ottinger
C: Ulrike Ottinger
P: Renée Gundelach
A: Delphine Seyrig, Irm Hermann, Xu Re Huar
An affluent older woman, an anthropologist, an American actress, and other Westerners ride the Trans-Siberian railway in "Oriental" splendor; there is an occasional peek into the crowded third-class coach as well. Somewhere in the terrain of mountainous desert and plains, they are kidnapped by female Mongolian warriors; the captives remain, for the most part, calm, accepting, and civilized. Fantasy.
Other titles: Johanna d'Arc of Mongolia

840. *Die Jung Frauenmaschine / The Virgin Machine* 1988 DSC
D: Monika Treut
S: Monika Treut
C: Elfi Mikesch
A: Ina Blum, Suzie Sexpert
A German journalist flees her relationship for California and finds the San Francisco lesbian scene as she researches romance as a disease. Marked by an enthusiasm for sex toys (detailed by Suzie Sexpert) and expressionistic imagery of female genitalia.

841. *Martha Jellneck* 1988 S
D: Kai Wessel
S: Beate Langmaack
C: Achim Poulheim
A: Heidemarie Hatheyer
A woman, who is "confined to her apartment, discovers that her brother's murderer, an ex-Nazi, is passing himself off as her brother. She plans revenge." *West German Cinema, 1985.*
Awards: German Film Awards, Outstanding Actress, 1989

842. *Die Gottesanbeterin / Georgette Meunier* 1989 DSP
D: Tania Stöcklin, Cyrille Rey-Coquais

S: Tania Stöcklin, Cyrille Rey-Coquais
C: Ciro Cappellari
P: Anka Schmid
A: Tiziana Jelmini
A deranged woman, in love with her brother, goes on a killing spree of all the men in her village. *West German Cinema, 1985.*

843. Ich bin dir Verfallen / I'm Your Slave 1989
D: Jean-Pierre Thorn
S: Jean-Pierre Thorn, Orette Cordie, Dominique Lancelot
C: Denis Gheerbrant
A: Solveig Dommartin
Follows the persistent disillusionment of a woman "who has been a nun, a worker, a priest's lover, and a trade union-functionary." *West German Cinema, 1985.*

844. Martha und ich / Martha and Me 1989
D: Jiri Weiss
S: Jiri Weiss
C: Viktor Ruzicka
A: Marianne Sägebrecht, Michel Piccoli
Prague, 1938. "Wife of a Jewish doctor refuses to divorce and save herself" from the fate she knows awaits him. *West German Cinema, 1985.*
Awards: Vancouver International Film Festival, Most Popular Film, 1991; Seattle International Film Festival, Best Actress, 1992

845. Tiger, Löwe, Panther / Tiger, Lion, Panther 1989 S
D: Dominik Graf
S: Sherry Hormann
C: Klaus Eichhammer
P: Michael Hild
A: Natja Bruckhorst, Martina Gedeck, Sabine Kaack
The story of three women, their men, and their relationships with one another. *MOMA Film. 2004, Jan.*
Awards: Baden-Baden Days of Teleplay, Teleplay Award, 1989

GHANA

846. Love Brewed in the African Pot 1981
D: Kwaw Painstil Ansah
S: Kwaw Painstil Ansah
C: Chris Tsui Tesse
A: Jumoke Debayo
1951. An educated dressmaker, whose father wants her to marry a lawyer, falls in love with a semiliterate automobile mechanic. The father

relents, but she finds only disappointment in the relationship she has romanticized. *Black African: 132–34.*

847. Sankofa 1994
D: Haile Gerima
S: Haile Gerima
C: Augustin Cubano
P: Haile Gerima
A: Olufunnike Ogunlano, Mutabaruka, Alexandra Duah
An African American model does a photo shoot in a tourist slave fort, where she is sent back to the time of slavery in the United States and reborn. The focus is on the routine rapes and beatings of daily life on the plantation and the intimate power struggles among the slaves: the division between those born on the plantation and those who knew free life, between the "privilege" of the house slaves and the banished field "niggers," and between those who stay and those who try to escape. The church is represented by a manipulative priest, while escaped slaves in the hills hold on to African beliefs and train for war.
Awards: Berlin International Film Festival, nomination for Golden Bear, 1993

GREECE

848. To Agrimi / The Wildcat 1960
D: Kostos Karayiannis
S: Kostos Karayiannis
A: Christina Sylva
A young working woman clashes with employers who try to dictate to her; she also refuses the attention of a rich man, preferring more sincere relationships. *Greek Filmography.*

849. Antigoni / Antigone 1960
D: Yorgas Tzavellas
S: Yorgas Tzavellas; based on the play by Sophocles
C: Dinos Katsouridis
P: James Paris
A: Irene Papas, Manos Katrakis
A daughter defies the command of the king and pursues a proper burial for her brother, despite his rebellion against the throne; she is executed by the king, her father. *Cinéma grec.*
Awards: Berlin International Film Festival, nomination for Golden Bear, 1960

850. Electra 1961
D: Michael Cacoyannis

S: Michael Cacoyannis; based on the play by Euripides
C: Walter Lassally
P: Michael Cacoyannis
A: Irene Papas, Aleka Catselli, Yannis Fertis

After witnessing the murder of her father by her mother's lover, Electra waits for the help of her brother, then avenges the murder by murdering the perpetrator, as well as her mother. *Festival de films, 22nd: 67. 2000.*

Awards: Academy Awards, nomination for Best Foreign Film, 1963

851. *Phaedra* 1961
D: Jules Dassin
S: Jules Dassin; based on a play by Euripides
C: Jacques Natteau
P: Jules Dassin
A: Melina Mercouri

Athens, Paris, London. A modern update of *Hippolytus* by Euripides. The second wife of a powerful ship owner seduces his son, who prefers to marry a ship magnate's daughter. Rejected, she confesses her love to her husband anyway, and he banishes his son. *Cinemythology. Accessed 2005, July 13.*

852. *Dhio manes sto stavro tou ponou / Two Mothers on the Cross* 1962
D: Orestis Laskos
S: Nestoras Matsas, Kostas Assimakopoulos
C: Yiannis Athanassiadis
A: Antigoni Mylonas, Miranda Myrat

A poor woman gives away her son for adoption, then a year later tries to get him back from his loving adoptive mother. *Greek Filmography.*

853. *Ta Kokkina fanaria / The Red Lanterns* 1963
D: Vassilas Georgiades
S: Alekos Galanos
C: Nikos Gardelis
P: Victor Michaelides
A: Jenny Karezi, Katarina Helmi, Alexandra Ladikou

Piraeus, Traumba district. Six stories of people struggling to escape a marginal existence in a house of prostitution. *Greek Filmography.*

Awards: Academy Awards, nomination for Best Foreign Film, 1964

854. *Adhikimeni / She Was Wronged* 1964
D: Yiorgas Papakostas
S: Yiorgas Papakostas
A: Marianna Koirakou

A woman lives alone with her alcoholic father; she gets a job in a nightclub and is encouraged to become a singer. *Greek Filmography.*

855. *Despoinis dieuthyntes / Miss Director* 1964
D: Dinos Dimopoulos
S: Asimakis Gialamas, Costas Pretederis
C: Nikos Kavoukidis
A: Jenny Karezi

A civil engineer "replaces the director of a construction company and falls in love with one of the employees" but has difficulties making him see her as a woman. *Journal of Modern, vol. 18, no. 1: 109. May 2000.*

856. *Dhiogmos / Persecution* 1964
D: Grigoris Grigoriou
S: Panos Kontelis
C: Grigoris Danalis
A: Voula Zoumboulak

An island woman cares for a wounded leader of the resistance, then returns with him to the mainland to search for her son, who was lost when they were exiled in 1922. *Greek Filmography.*

Awards: Thessaloniki Film Festival, Best Director, Best Screenplay, Grand Prize, 1964

857. *Moderna stahtopouta / Modern Cinderella* 1964
D: Alekos Sakellarios
S: Alekos Sakellarios
C: Nikos Gardelis
A: Aliki Vouyouklaki, Dimitris Papamichael

A woman is the secretary for the "General Director of a shipping company. She falls in love with him, is successful in her job but has a hard time making him fall in love with her. Eventually, she also succeeds in that." *Journal of Modern, vol. 18, no. 1: 109. 2000, May.*

858. *O Nikitis / The Winner* 1965 DS
D: Maria Plyta
S: Maria Plyta
C: Syrokos Danalis
A: Miranda Kounelaki, Dimitris Papamichael

Against her family's wishes, a wealthy younger sister waits for an opportunity to marry the chauffeur's son, her true love. *Greek Filmography.*

859. *I Dhaskalitsa me tin kali kardhia / The Teachers with the Golden Heart* 1966
D: Giancarlo Zagni
S: Fausto Tozzi
C: Aldo Scavarda
P: Apostolos Tegopoulos

A: Gigliola Ginguetti

Tuscany, 1861. A teacher is appointed to create a school in a village where there has never been one. Her effort is resented by both the parents and the landowners. *Greek Filmography.*

860. *Stefania* 1966

D: Yannis Dalianidis

S: Yannis Dalianidis

C: Mimis Plessas

A: Zoe Laskari

To escape the advances of her stepfather, a girl leaves her family but falls into a child prostitution ring; she is arrested and put into a house, where she is abused by the guards and falls in love with a doctor, but she cannot seem to get away from unwanted advances. Exploitation. *Cinéma grec: 237.*

861. *Ap' ta Ierossolima me agapi / From Jerusalem with Love* 1967

D: Yiorgas Papakostas

S: Yiorgas Papakostas

C: Nikos Milas

P: Apostolos Tegopoulos

A: Gelly Mavropoulou

A mother takes her disabled child to Jerusalem for curing, causing conflict with her selfish husband. *Greek Filmography.*

862. *Konserto yia polivola / A Case of High Treason* 1967

D: Dinos Dimopoulos

S: Nikos Fossis

C: Nikos Kavoukidis

A: Jenny Karezi

1930s, the eve of World War II. A civil servant delivers military documents to an Italian spy, who is blackmailing her with death threats against her brother. Caught, she becomes a double agent. *Greek Filmography.*

863. *Mia gynaika stin antistassi / A Woman in the Resistance* 1970

D: Dinos Dimopoulos

S: Dinos Dimopoulos, Lazeros Montanais

C: Carl Heinz

A: Jenny Kerezi

World War II. A woman whose father, brother, and lover have gone to war becomes a nurse, then befriends a German commander to extract secrets for the resistance. *Greek Filmography.*

864. *Mando mavroyenous* 1971

D: Kostos Karayiannis

S: Kostos Karayiannis, Nikos Kambauis

C: Vassilis Vassiliadis

A: Jenny Karezi

Vienna, 1820. A wealthy socialite works to convince European governments to support Greece's freedom. She avoids marriage and returns to her home to participate in the Filiki Eteria, a secret revolutionary group. *Greek Filmography.*

865. *Aliko Dohiktator, I / Aliki Dictator* 1972

D: Takis Vouyouklakis

S: Lakis Mihailidis

C: Yorgos Arvanitis

A: Aliki Vouyouklaki

A traveling performer, famous for her impersonation of Charlie Chaplin, continues on alone after the death of her father and finally finds a friend in a blind student. *Greek Filmography.*

866. *Erotiki symfonia / Erotic Symphony*
1972 SP

D: Kostas Kazakos

S: Jenny Karezi

C: Vassilis Vassiliadis

P: Jenny Karezi, Kostas Kazakos

A: Jenny Karezi

A famous pianist, who secretly loves her twin sister's husband, returns to her home island, where her sister still lives. On a sailing trip the sister dies, and the pianist has the opportunity to substitute herself, but she shrinks from the effort required to make it happen. *Greek Filmography.*

867. *Lyssistrati / Lysistrata* 1972

D: Yiorgas Zervoulakos

S: Yiznnis Negrepontis; based on the play by Aristophanes

C: Nikos Milas

A: Jenny Karezi, Anna Fonsou

A censored version of the play about an Athenian woman who leads all Greek women, including the Spartans, in a campaign to deny their men sex in order to stop the war between Athens and Sparta. *Greek Filmography.*

868. *To Proxenio tis Anna / The Engagement of Anna* 1972

D: Pantelis Voulgaris

S: Pantelis Voulgaris, Menis Koumantareas

C: Nikos Kavoukidis

P: Dinos Katsouridis

A: Anna Vagena

Athens. A shy servant has protective employers who think highly of her and wish to see her married; she appears to be one of the family. When she has a date with someone they have chosen for her, it takes her all day to get used to him, and their joy at finally connecting with one another at an amusement park makes them forget the time. The frantic return home is for nothing; the family accuses her of immoral behavior and has only scorn for him. There will be no more outings.

Awards: Berlin International Film Festival, FIPRESCI, OCIC Award, 1974

869. *I Fonissa / The Murderess*   1974
D: Kostas Ferris
S: Kostas Ferris, Dimos Theos; based on the novel by Alexandros Papadiamantis
C: Stavros Hassapis
A: Maria Alkeou

An old woman reminisces over her hard life while caring for two grandchildren; she murders them, believing she is saving them from a similar cruel life, then flees from the police and drowns herself in the sea. *Greek Filmography.*

870. *I Dhemonisement / Possessed Woman*
                                              1975
D: Dimis Dadiras
S: Melpo Zarokosta
C: Kostas Papayiannakis
A: Katia Dandoulaki, Amalia Giza

A psychiatrist treats a schizophrenic girl whose parents are allowing an exorcist to treat her. The situation leaves the doctor herself vulnerable. *Greek Filmography.*

871. *Kravyi yinekon / A Dream of Passion* 1978
D: Jules Dassin
S: Jules Dassin
C: Yorgos Arvanitis
P: Yorgos Arvanitis
A: Melina Mercouri, Ellen Burstyn

A famous actress returns to Greece after the military junta and befriends an American woman imprisoned for killing her three children; the film culminates in a performance of *Medea.* *AMG.*

Awards: Cannes Film Festival, nomination for Golden Palm, 1978

872. *I Dhromi tis agapis ine nihterini / Love Wanders in the Night*   1981 DS
D: Frieda Liappa
S: Frieda Liappa
C: Nikos Smaragadis
A: Maria Skountzou, Mirka Papakonstantinou

Athens. Two isolated sisters have abandoned their village and share an apartment; when their sole relative, an artist cousin with whom they are both in love, arrives from Paris, the older sister

commits suicide, and the younger leaves the country with the cousin. *Cinéma grec.*

873. *Kataskopos Nelly / Nelly, the Spy*   1981
D: Takis Vouyouklakis
S: Nikos Foskolos
C: Aris Stavro
A: Aliki Vouyouklaki

Berlin, 1930s. A Greek student drops out of university and becomes a successful singer, loved by the SS. When war starts, she returns to Greece and joins the resistance, but she becomes suspect because of her past association. *Greek Filmography.*

874. *Rembetiko*   1983 S
D: Kostas Ferris
S: Kostas Ferris, Sotira Leonardou
C: Takis Zervoulakos
A: Sotira Leonardou

Athens. The true story of rembetico singer Marika Ninou, who lived over the first half of the twentieth century; the film chronicles her personal life, as well as the history of the cultural, social, and political times. *AMG.*

Awards: Thessaloniki Film Festival, Best Actress, 1983; Berlin International Film Festival, Silver Bear (Ferris), 1984

875. *Adhexios erastis / Clumsy Lover*   1984 DS
D: Maria Skourti
S: Maria Skourti
A: Anna Paspati

A woman moves to her husband's house upon marriage; he ignores her as she raises their children, and when she discovers he is having an affair, she kicks him out. *Greek Filmography.*

876. *I Timi tis agapis / The Price of Love* 1984 DS
D: Tonia Marketaki
S: Tonia Marketaki; based on the novel by Konstantinos Theotokis
C: Stavros Hassapis
A: Toula Stathopoulou, Anny Loulou

Corfu, 1900. A factory worker and her daughter tangle with a man whose family demands a large dowry after he has seduced the daughter. The daughter decides to raise the child on her own. *Cinéma grec: 246.*

877. *To Aroma tis violettas / The Scent of Violets*   1985 D
D: Maria Gavala
A: Yota Festa, Martina Passari

A girl and her cousin steal from their grandmother, then clash over their action and its consequences. *Greek Filmography.*

878. Manía 1985
D: Yiogas Panoussopoulos
S: Yiogas Panoussopoulos
C: Yiogas Panoussopoulos
P: Yiogas Panoussopoulos
A: Alesandra Vanzi
A computer analyst, on her way to the United States for training, is possessed by a strange desire while at the National Garden in Athens. She provokes the zoo animals, creating a panic that leads to her being hunted by the police. *Variety: 16. 1985, Oct. 23.*

879. Mia tosso makrini apoussia / A Very Long Absence 1985
D: Stavros Tsiolis
S: Stavros Tsiolis
C: Yorgos Arvanitis
A: Pemy Zouni, Dimitra Hatoupi
A young woman is determined to keep her mentally ill sister with her, against the wishes of others who advise her to place her in an institution. The inevitable conflicts drive the woman, like her sister, into isolation and silence. *Cinéma grec: 247.*
Other titles: Une Aussi longue absence

880. Petrina chronia / Stone Years 1985
D: Pantelis Voulgaris
S: Pantelis Voulgaris
C: Yorgos Arvanitis
P: Nikos Doukas
A: Themis Bazaka
1954–1974. A communist is jailed while his lover escapes; years later he is released, but after a brief idyll, she is jailed. Pregnant, she raises the child in prison, where he joins her a few years later until they are released when the dictatorship falls in 1974. *Variety: 20. 1985, Sep. 11.*
Awards: Venice Film Festival, Best Actress, OCIC Award, 1985

881. Itan enas isichos thanatos / A Quiet Death 1986 D
D: Frieda Tiappa
A: Eleanora Stathopoulou, Pemy Zouni
A writer decides to give up her career and flees her husband and psychiatrist. As she wanders the city, the night becomes stormy, reflecting her inner turmoil. *AMG.*
Awards: San Sebastián International Film Festival, Best New Director, 1986

882. Apoussies / Absences 1987
D: Yiorgas Katakouzinos
S: Yiorgas Katakouzinos

A: Themis Bazaka, Pemy Zouni, Maria Konstandarou, Katarina Sarri
1920s. Three grown daughters, abandoned by their mother, struggle to live on their own after their father dies. *Greek Filmography.*

883. Ta Chronia tis megalis zestis / The Years of the Big Heat 1991 DS
D: Frieda Liappa
S: Frieda Liappa, Martina Passari
C: Nikos Smaragadis
A: Electra Alexandropoulou, Periklis Moustakis
A heat wave affects visitors at a beach house that is owned by a woman who knows nothing of her past. She and a man whose memory has also been destroyed act out "festive rites of community, ceremonies of the past, and secret murder." *Greek Filmography.*

884. Kristallines nichtes / Crystal Nights 1991 DS
D: Tonia Marketaki
S: Tonia Marketaki
C: Stavros Hassapis
A: Michele Valley, Tania Tripi
1930s. During the German occupation, a German member of a satanic organization acquires the qualities of a modern "witch," such as telepathic power. She falls in love with a young Jewish boy, but he leaves her because of her age. She commits suicide, then is born again as a young girl who attempts to seduce him. *Variety: 120. 1992, May 11.*

885. Agria triandafylla / Wild Roses 1993
D: Angelos Provelangios
S: Angelos Provelangios
P: Angelos Provelangios
A: Loukia Papadaki, Maria Degleri
Two women become sexually involved and connected to political murders; a detective is pulled into their intrigue. Exploitation. *Greek Filmography.*

886. I Ariadhni meni sti Lero / Ariadne Lives in Leros 1993
D: Thanassis Rakintzis
A: Eleftheria Rigou
A woman who witnesses the murder of her mother by her father gains employment at the mental institution where he is incarcerated and plots revenge. *Greek Filmography.*

887. Dhromi ke portokalia / Roads and Oranges 1994 DS
D: Aliki Danezi-Knutsen
S: Aliki Danezi-Knutsen

C: Cornelius Schultze-Kraft
A: Vana Tabota, Stella Frogeui
Cyprus, 1970s. Two sisters search in the hostile territory of southern Turkey for their father, who went missing in action during the 1974 Turkish invasion of Cyprus. *Greek Filmography.*

888. Tράito / Transit　　1995 DS
D: Isavella Mavraki
S: Anna Andianou
A: Anna Andianou
A confident, well-organized journalist falls in love with a mysterious man who is passing through Greece; she is attracted to his lack of roots. *Festival Internazionale. Accessed 2005, July 13.*
Other titles: Tranzito

889. Tris epoches / Three Seasons　1996 DS
D: Maria Ilioú
S: Maria Ilioú
C: Stamatis Yannoulis
A: Yiota Tetsa, Yioland Kaperda, Dioni Kortaki
Three sisters—one a chemist in a dye factory, one a fabric dyer, and one a journalist—uncover an ecological scandal regarding the chemicals used to make the dyes; their activism causes problems in their lives. *Festival de films, 19th: 73. 1997.*
Other titles: Trois saisons
Awards: Würzburg International Filmweekend, Audience Award, 1997

890. Maria Electra　　1997 DS
D: Stella Belessi
S: Stella Belessi
C: Vangelis Katritzidatis
A: Alexandra Batsalia
Thessalonica. A mathematics student takes the train most days into the countryside, where she sells books and her body, which she prostitutes under the name Electra. One day she meets an accomplished acrobat, and her life is changed. *Festival de films, 22nd: 84. 2000.*

891. Alexandria　　2001 DSP
D: Maria Ilioú
S: Maria Ilioú, Stephen Cleary
C: Yannis Drakoularakos
P: Sylvain Bursztejn, Maria Ilioú
A: Camille Panonacle, Michele Valley, Irene Inglessi, Silvia De Santis
A woman travels with her daughter to Alexandria and shares with her the story of her youth there. *Foundation for Hellenic. Accessed: 2004 July 22.*

892. Bar　　2001 DS
D: Aliki Danezi-Knutsen
S: Aliki Danezi-Knutsen
C: Cornelius Schultze-Kraft
P: Anna Tsiarta
A: Stela Fyrogeni
Two women, played by the same actress, cross paths in a tavern: a Cyprus cab driver and a Uruguayan stowaway. Fantasy. *Variety: 56. 2002, Jan. 4.*
Awards: Thessaloniki Film Festival, nomination for Golden Alexander, 2001

893. O Evdemos ilios tou erota / The 7th Sun of Love　　2001
D: Vangelis Serdaris
A: Elena Maria Kavoukidou, Katerina Papadaki
1920s. "A young maidservant becomes an object of desire, pursued by a major in the Greek army, his ineffectual groom, and his wife ... as Greece's Asia Minor disaster draws near." *Foundation for Hellenic. Accessed 2004, Jan. 18.*
Awards: Thessaloniki Film Festival, Greek Union of Film and Television Technicians Award, 2001

894. Kato apo t'astra / Under the Stars　2001
D: Christos Georgiou
S: Christos Georgiou
C: Roman Osin
P: Sam Taylor
A: Mirto Alikaki, Akis Sakellariou
Cyprus. A Turkish woman who smuggles goods over the Greek–Turkish border agrees to take money to help a battle-scarred man visit his village on the Turkish side. Once there, they find "the spirits of their lost relatives." *Greek Film. Accessed 2005, Feb. 14.*

GUINEA

895. Naitou　　1982
D: Moussa Kemoko Diakite
S: Moussa Kemoko Diakite
A: African Ballet of Guinea
Two wives in a polygamous house have young daughters coming of age; one is jealous and poisons the other wife, but she is also jealous of her own daughter, who is a stepchild. Musical. *Variety: 21. 1984, July 25.*

GUINEA-BISSAU

896. Mortu Nega　　1987 D
D: Flora Gomes
C: Dominique Gentil

A: Flora Gomes
1973–77. A woman searches for her husband, who is a guerilla, and experiences the realities of war; after liberation from Portugal, she must learn how to live in peace. Includes re-creations of historic events. *FII.*

897. *Udju azul di Yonta* / *Blue Eyes of Yonta*
1992 DS
D: Flora Gomes
S: Flora Gomes
C: Dominique Gentil
A: Maysa Marta
A young woman receives anonymous love letters and imagines they are from a local hero, who is very busy otherwise trying to establish his future.
Awards: Würzburg International Filmweekend, Audience Award, 1994

HAITI

898. *Corps plongés* / *Falling Bodies*   1999
D: Raoul Peck
S: Raoul Peck
C: Pascal Marti
P: Jacques Bidou
A: Geno Lechner
A Manhattan pathologist becomes uncomfortable when she is asked to "soften" testimony; she also has a relationship with a married judge. An old classmate arrives in town, a Haitian diplomat whose wife has been assassinated, and he helps her gain perspective on her life. *Variety: 60. 1998, Sep. 28.*
Awards: Montréal World Film Festival, nomination for Grand Prix, 1998

HONG KONG

899. *Dong fu ren* / *The Arch*   1968
D: Tang Shu Shuen
S: Tang Shu Shuen
A: Lisa Lu
A kind widow is so adored by villagers that they plea for an arch of "chastity" in her name. This status leads to the loss of a potential lover, who instead leaves with her daughter. *Chinese Filmography.*

900. *Ai Nü: Intimate Confessions of a Chinese Courtesan*   1972
D: Chor Yuen
S: Chiu Kang Chien

P: Shaw Run Me
A: Lily Ho, Betty Ting Pei
A woman, kidnapped for deployment in a brothel, resists and kicks back at every opportunity, attracting brutal treatment and unlikely romantic attachments at the same time. After being sold to the three highest bidders, she becomes passive and accepts tutelage in the martial arts, as well as the love of the madam. Surpassing her mentor's skill, she sets about trapping and murdering the three men who first bought and raped her. Action.

901. *Chang bei* / *My Young Aunt*   1981 P
D: Lau Kar-leung
S: Lau Kar-leung, Li Tai-hung
C: Peter Ngor
P: Mona Fong
A: Kara Hui, Lau Kar-leung
A widow and martial artist carries a will to her family in Canton, then teams up with a young cousin to recoup stolen deeds. Action. *Hong Kong.*
Awards: Hong Kong Film Awards, Best Actress, 1982

902. *Qing cheng zhi lian* / *Love in a Fallen City*   1984 DS
D: Ann Hui
S: Eileen Chang
C: Tony Hope
A: Cora Miao, Chow Yun- Fat
Hong Kong, 1940s. A divorced woman, looking for a comfortable marriage, is courted by a rich playboy during the Japanese occupation. *Variety: 23. 1984, Aug. 29.*

903. *Si shui liu nian* / *Homecoming*   1984
D: Yim Ho
S: Kong Liang
C: Poon Hang-sang
P: Xia Meng
A: Josephine Koo, Siqin Gaowa
A Hong Kong woman returns to her childhood village in Guongdong-Fujian and reconnects with an old friend, exposing the disparity in living standards between their provincial existence and mainland China. *Hong Kong.*
Awards: Hong Kong Film Awards, Best Film, Best Actress (Siqin), 1985

904. *Tong chiu ho fong nü i* / *An Amorous Woman of the Tang Dynasty*   1984
D: Eddie Fong
S: Eddie Fong
A: Patricia Xia
A bright, talented high-born woman attempts to toe the Taoist path but instead has an affair with

a wanderer. When he moves on, she begins a relationship with her female maid, which gets them both banished. *Variety. 1984, Sep. 5.*

905. *Dao ma dan / Peking Opera Blues*   1986
D: Tsui Hark
S: Raymond To
C: Poon Hang-sang
P: Tsui Hark
A: Cherie Chung, Sally Yeh, Brigitte Lin
China, 1913. During the rise of Sun Yat-sen's re-publican movement, three women—a general's daughter who dresses as a man to protect herself, an actress with martial-arts training, and an accidental thief—get involved with a guerrilla band to which the general's daughter is already committed. They must steal an important document from the general, who is loved by his daughter, but not more than she hates his politics. Comedy, action.
Other titles: Knife Horse Dawn

906. *Passion*   1986 DS
D: Sylvia Chang
S: Sylvia Chang
C: Ma Chor-shing
A: Sylvia Chang, Cora Miao
Two women have been friends for thirty years; now they are widows, each with a child. In the afternoons while the children play, they talk, and tension mounts when the facts of the love affair of one with the other's husband are revealed. *Festival de films, 13th: 77. 1991.*

907. *Yan kou / Rouge*   1987 S
D: Stanley Kwan
S: Yau Tai, Lillian Lee
C: Bill Wong
P: Jackie Chan
A: Anita Mui
Hong Kong, 1930s. "Courtesan, a victim of an un-successful suicide pact, returns to earth 50 years later to find her lover." *Hong Kong.*
Other titles: Yin ji kau
Awards: Golden Horse Film Festival, Best Actress, 1988; Asia-Pacific Film Festival, Best Actress, 1989; Hong Kong Film Festival, Best Film, Best Actress, 1989

908. *Ai zai Beiang de jijie / Farewell China*
                                                   1990 DS
D: Clara Law
S: Clara Law
C: Ma Jingle
P: Teddy Robin Kwan
A: Maggie Cheung, Tony Leung

A woman, desperate to go to America, becomes pregnant to obtain a visa. She leaves her husband behind, though he eventually arrives in the United States to search for her. *Hong Kong.*
Awards: Hong Kong Film Awards, nominations for Best Film and Best Actress, 1991

909. *Miao jie huang hou / Queen of Temple Street*   1990
D: Lawrence Ah Mon
S: Chan Man-keung
C: Chan Ying
P: William Tam
A: Sylvia Chang, Ha Ping, Josephine Koo, Rain Lau, Carol Cheng
The story of a madam and her rebellious teenage daughter in a documentary-like depiction of a Hong Kong brothel. *Hong Kong.*
Awards: Hong Kong Film Awards, Best Screenplay, Best New Performer (Lau), Best Supporting Actress (Cheng), 1991

910. *Ren zai niu yue / Full Moon in New York*
                                                   1990
D: Stanley Kwan
S: Tau Tai
C: Bill Wong
A: Sylvia Chang, Maggie Cheung, Siqin Gaowa, Jo-sephine Koo
Three Chinese friends live in New York City: an actress, a housewife, and a businesswoman. *Hong Kong.*
Awards: Golden Horse Film Festival, Best Actress (Cheung), 1989

911. *The Twin Bracelets*   1990 DS
D: Huang Yu Shan
S: Huang Yu Shan
C: Bob Thompson
A: Chen Te Jung, Liu Hsiao Hui
Two village girls have sworn to be faithful to each other by the exchange of bracelets. Though they marry, village custom allows only a few days a year with their husbands; to complicate things, one marries happily and the other mar-ries a man she detests. There is trouble when the happy one receives authorization to leave town with her husband. *Festival de films, 13th: 77. 1991.*

912. *Sha sha jia jia zhan qi lai / Sisters of the World Unite*   1991 DSP
D: Sylvia Chang, Maisy Tsue
S: Eveline Au, Sylvia Chang
C: Jingle Ma

P: Sylvia Chang
A: Sylvia Chang, Sally Yeh
Two sisters seek diversion from the frustrations of their relationships with men. Comedy. *Hong Kong.*

913. *Yuen ling-juk / Actress* 1991
D: Stanley Kwan
S: Yautai On-ping
C: Poon Hang-sang
P: Leonard Ho
A: Maggie Cheung
1930s. Biography of a silent-film actress, Ruan Ling Yu, who rose from poverty and committed suicide during a scandal over an affair with a married man; includes documentary footage of her films. *FII.*
Other titles: Ruan Ling Yu / Center Stage
Awards: Berlin International Film Festival, Silver Bear (Cheung), 1992; Hong Kong Film Festival, Best Actress, 1992

914. *Xiao ao jiang hu zhi dong fang bu bai /*
   Swordman II 1992
D: Ching Siu-tung, Tsui Hark
S: Hanson Chan
A: Brigitte Lin, Jet Li
A villain, "neither male nor female, with an ability to do needlework and love excessively," overpowers with her martial arts skills but fails to obtain the object of her lust. Action. *Multiple Modernities: 212.*
Awards: Hong Kong Film Awards, nomination for Best Actress, 1993

915. *Qing she / Green Snake* 1993 S
D: Tsui Hark
S: Tsui Hark, Lillian Lee
C: Ko Chiu-lam
P: Tsui Hark
A: Maggie Cheung, Joey Wang
A story based on a folktale of two snake sisters who, with training, pass as humans. *Hong Kong.*

916. *Nü ren si shi / Summer Snow* 1994 DP
D: Ann Hui
S: Chan Man-keung
C: Mark Li
P: Ann Hui, Raymond Chow
A: Josephine Siao
Hong Kong. A woman with a teenager and husband deals with her father-in-law's Alzheimer's disease after he is brought to live in their house. *Hong Kong.*
Awards: Berlin International Film Festival, Best Actress, 1995; Créteil International Women's Film Festival, Grand Prix, 1996

917. *Xian dai bao xia zhuan / The Execution-*
   ers 1995 S
D: Johnny To, Ching Siu-tung
S: Susanne Chan, Sandy Shaw
C: Hang-sang Poon
P: Ching Siu-tung
A: Maggie Cheung, Michelle Yeoh, Anita Mui
The sequel to *The Heroic Trio* (1993), where three women warriors bonded and then dispersed to become a mercenary, a political resister, and a mother who has sworn off being a superhero. Here, they reunite to stave off the apocalypse that has already sent the mother to jail. Action. *Multiple Modernities: 214.*
Other titles: The Heroic Trio

918. *Ah kam / The Stuntwoman* 1996 DP
D: Ann Hui
S: Kin Chung Chan
C: Ardy Lam
P: Raymond Chow, Catherine Hun
A: Michelle Yeoh
The life and gangster entanglements of a woman who becomes a successful stuntwoman after substituting on a set one day for a friend. Action. *Variety, March 3, 1977.*

919. *Hu du men / Stage Door* 1996
D: Shu Kei
S: Raymond To
C: Bill Wong
A: Josephine Siao
A charismatic Cantonese opera star, who plays male parts on the stage and has a fervid lesbian audience, struggles with leaving her troupe and retiring to Australia. She spiritedly copes with her feelings for a grown son, whom she left with a friend when he was a baby; a stepdaughter whose lesbian relationship has upset her father; and a new young singer who suffers parental beatings.
Awards: Golden Horse Film Festival, Best Actress, 1996

920. *Si mian xia wa / Four Faces of Eve* 1996
D: Kam Kwok-leung, Jan Lamb
S: Kam Kwok-leung, Jan Lamb
C: Chris Doyle
A: Sandra Ng
The stories of five women played by the same actress: a prostitute in love with her therapist; a mute immigrant abused wife; twin sisters with opposing personalities; and a housewife who makes it on a television game show. *Variety. 1998. Mar. 16.*

921. *Song jia huang chao / Soong Sisters* 1996 D
D: Mabel Cheung

S: Alex Law
C: Arthur Wong
P: Raymond Chow
A: Maggie Cheung, Michelle Yeoh, Vivian Wu
Three sisters, daughters of the wealthy financier Charlie Soong, become powerful: Ching-ling marries Sun Yat-sen, May-ling marries Chiang Kai-shek, and Ai-ling marries wealthy industrialist H. H. Kung. *Variety. 1997, Mar. 16.*
Other titles: The Sung Sisters / Chant d'exile
Awards: Hong Kong Film Awards, Best Actress (Cheung), 1998

922. *Ban sheng yuan / Eighteen Springs* 1997 DS
D: Ann Hui
S: John Chan; based on the novel by Eileen Chang
C: Mark Lee
A: Wu Chien-lien, Leon Li, Anita Mui
Shanghai, 1930s. An older sister becomes a courtesan in order to support her orphaned siblings. The younger sister is in love with a man of good family, but he disdains her compromised background, so she decides to remain with her family, knowing she is still needed there. *Festival de films, 20th: 45. 1998.*
Awards: Hong Kong Film Awards, Best Actress (Mui), 1998; Hong Kong Film Critics Association, Best Actress (Wu), 1998

923. *Gu huo zai qing yi pian zhi hong xing shi san mei / Portland Street Blues*   1998
D: Raymond Yip
S: Manfred Wong
C: Yiu-fai Lai
P: Raymond Chow
A: Sandra Ng, Shu Qi
When a lesbian gang is challenged, their leader reflects on her rise to power. Action. *FII.*
Awards: Hong Kong Film Awards, Best Actress (Ng), Best Supporting Actress (Qi), 1999; Hong Kong Film Critics Society Awards, Best Actress (Ng), 1999

924. *Maisat sam lam / The Mistress*   1999 DS
D: Crystal Kwok
S: Crystal Kwok
C: Gigo Lee
A: Ray Lui, Jacqueline Peng, Vicky Chen
Hong Kong. A young, educated woman is hired to tutor a wealthy man's mistress. She ends up becoming the man's mistress herself but finds that he continues to be unfaithful. *FII.*

925. *You yuan jing meng / Peony Pavilion*
2001 SP
D: Yonfan

S: Yonfan, Rie Miyazawa
C: Henry Chung
P: Ann Hui
A: Joey Wong, Rie Miyazawa
Suzhou, 1930s. A singer and courtesan is married to an opium-addicted aristocrat; her cousin is a teacher with modern values. They bond together through their difficulties. *FII.*
Awards: Moscow International Film Festival, Best Actress, FIPRESCI, 2001

926. *Lian zhi feng jing / The Floating Landscape*   2003 DS
D: Carol Lai Miu-suet
S: Carol Lai Miu-suet
C: Arthur Wong
A: Karena Lam
A young woman has lost her lover to illness; just before his death he became obsessed with memories of his childhood in China. She goes to the rural Qingdao area in the middle of winter and finds a China much different from the one she knows. *Festival de films, 26th: 24. 2004.*
Awards: Goya Awards, Best Film, Best Director, 2004

HUNGARY

927. *Eltávozott nap / The Girl*   1968 DS
D: Márta Mészáros
S: Márta Mészáros
C: Tamás Somló
A: Kati Kovács
When she becomes an adult, an orphan searches for her mother and discovers a hard woman married to a peasant who constantly watches television. The woman is ashamed and introduces the daughter as her niece. *Cinéma hongrois: 124.*

928. *Holdudvar / Binding Sentiments*   1969 DS
D: Márta Mészáros
S: Márta Mészáros
C: János Kende
A: Mari Töröcsik
The "widow of a famous economist" is unable to let go of her grief, even under pressure from her son and his wife to live normally. *Screen Memories: 36.*

929. *Sziget a szárazföldön / Lady from Constantinople*   1969 D
D: Judit Elek
S: Iván Mándy
C: Elemér Ragályi

A: Marian Kiss

Budapest. An old woman isolates herself by living in the past, then suddenly discovers an invalid in her building and takes care of him until he dies. The other tenants, who have come to know her through her charity, then ask her to move so they can take advantage of her larger apartment; finally, she does, settling on a place in the country. *Variety: 32. 1969, Feb. 26.*

Other titles: Island on the Continent

Awards: Hungarian Film Week, Best Actress, 1970

930. *Szép lányok, ne sirjatok / Don't Cry, Pretty Girls* 1970 DS

D: Márta Mészáros

S: Yvette Biró, Peter Zimre

C: János Kende

A: Jaroslava Schallerova

A young woman leaves the provinces to work in a Budapest factory and live in a hostel with other young people, who are sustained by a youth culture of rock music and dance. *Screen Memories: 39.*

931. *Szabad lélegzet / Riddance* 1973 DS

D: Márta Mészáros

S: Márta Mészáros

C: Lajos Koltai

A: Erzsébet Kútvölgyi, Gábor Nagy

A young weaver in a factory, who has been abandoned by her mother and then abused by her boyfriend, goes to a dance and passes as a student. She attracts a young man, who loves her even after he discovers the truth. He tries to integrate her into his family but is hesitant to tell them the truth, so she vents her frustration by lying to them even more.

932. *Szerelmem, Electra / Electra* 1974 S

D: Miklós Jancsó

S: László Gyurkó, Gyula Hernádi; based on the play by Sophocles

C: János Kende

P: József Bajusz

A: Mari Töröcsik, György Cserhalmi

The modern Hungarian plains. Electra avenges the murder of her father. *Hungarian Cinema.*

Other titles: Elektra

Awards: Cannes Film Festival, nomination for Golden Palm, 1975

933. *Ha megjön József / When Joseph Returns* 1975

D: Zsolt Kézdi Kovács

S: Zsolt Kézdi Kovács

C: János Kende

A: Lili Monori, Eva Ruttkai

The new bride of a seaman is left home with a philandering mother-in-law. *Variety: 24. 1976, July 28.*

934. *Örökbefogadás / Adoption* 1975 DS

D: Márta Mészáros

S: Márta Mészáros, Gyula Hernádi, Ferenc Grunwalsky

C: Lajos Koltai

A: Kati Berek, Gyöngyver Vigh

A middle-aged woman, who works in a woodworking factory, wants to have a child with a married man, who refuses. At the same time, she befriends a teenager from the local "institute" and helps her marry. The woman adopts an infant child right after the wedding. Includes scenes of work in the factory; the routine of her home; and encounters with a series of bureaucrats, social workers, and doctors, who advise her on how to help the girl and herself.

Awards: Berlin International Film Festival, Golden Bear, OCIC Award, 1975; Chicago Film Festival, Gold Plaque, 1975

935. *Déryné, hol Van? / Madame Dery* 1976 DS

D: Gyula Maar

S: Gyula Maar, János Pilinszky; based on the book by Rosa Dery

C: Lajos Koltai

A: Mari Töröcsik

Based on a memoir of a nineteenth-century actress who struggles with her career as she ages. *Variety: 20. 1976, May 26.*

Other titles: Where Are You, Mrs. Dery / In the Wings

Awards: Cannes Film Festival, nomination for Golden Palm, 1976

936. *Kilenc hónap / Nine Months* 1976 DS

D: Márta Mészáros

S: Gyula Hernádi, Márta Mészáros, Ildikó Kórodi

C: János Kende

A: Lili Monori, Jan Nowicki

A pregnant single mother and worker in an iron factory has an affair with the foreman, but he becomes jealous when he discovers that her child's father is a married professor and that she wants to go to university herself. She stands up to his domination and bears his child, her second, on her own. The film ends with a live birth by the pregnant actress.

Awards: Tehran International Film Festival, Best Actress, 1976; Berlin International Film Festival, OCIC Award, 1977; Cannes Film Festival, FIPRESCI, 1977

937. **Ök Ketten / Two of Them**   1977 DS
D: Márta Mészáros
S: Ildikó Kórodi, Josef Balázs, Géza Bereményi
C: János Kende
A: Marina Vlady, Lili Monori
Separated from her family because she lives in the women's work hostel that she manages, a woman befriends a younger woman who is married to an alcoholic.

938. **Angi Vera**   1978
D: Pál Gábor
S: Endre Vészi, Pál Gábor
C: Lajos Koltai
A: Veronika Papp, Éva Szabó
An eighteen-year-old factory worker is sent to be "trained" after complaining about management; eventually she becomes a Stalinist hack, even though she is befriended by a more moderate party operative.
Awards: Cannes Film Festival, FIPRESCI, 1979; Sao Paulo International Film Festival, Best Feature Film, 1979; David di Donatello Awards, Best Film, 1981; London Critics' Circle Film Awards, Best Foreign Language Film, 1981

939. **Örökség / The Heiresses**   1980 DS
D: Márta Mészáros
S: Ildikó Kórodi, Márta Mészáros
C: Elemér Ragályi
A: Isabelle Huppert, Lili Monori
1930s–1940s. A wealthy infertile woman supports another woman to have a child by her husband so she can inherit her father's money. But her husband and the woman fall in love, and, as the other woman is Jewish, the wife reports them to the fascist Arrow Cross. *Screen Memories: 64.*
Other titles: Les Heritieres / The Inheritance
Awards: Cannes Film Festival, nomination for Golden Palm, 1980

940. **Anna / Mother and Daughter**   1981 DS
D: Márta Mészáros
S: Márta Mészáros, Gyula Hernádi
C: Tamás Andor
A: Marie-José Nat
A successful Hungarian clothes designer believes a young woman she sees while visiting Paris is her daughter, who was lost during the 1956 uprising. *Screen Memories: 79–81.*

941. **Adj király katonát! / The Princess**   1982
D: Pal Erdöss
S: István Kardos
C: Lajos Koltai
A: Erika Ozsada, Andrea Szendrei

Budapest. Two country girls work in a cotton mill; both become pregnant, one from a rape. *World Cinema: 192.*
Awards: Cannes Film Festival, Golden Camera, 1983; Locarno International Film Festival, Golden Leopard, 1983

942. **Egymásra nézve / Another Way**   1982 S
D: Károly Makk
S: Károly Makk; based on an autobiographical novel by Ersébet Galgócsi
C: Tamás Andor
A: Jadwiga Jankowska-Cieúlak, Grazyna Szapolowska
Hungary, 1956. Journalists who focus on the repressiveness of the communist regime in their work form a lesbian couple; when the husband of one finds out, he murders his wife. *Variety: 15. 1982, June 2.*
Awards: Cannes Film Festival, Best Actress (Jankowska-Cieúlak), FIPRESCI, 1982; São Paulo International Film Festival, Audience Award, 1983

943. **Guernica**   1982
D: Ferenc Kósa
S: Ferenc Kósa
C: Lajos Koltai
A: Ottila Kovács
"Young woman's life takes on meaning when she learns of a sculptor working on a monument against war." *West German Cinema.*

944. **Napló gyermekeimnek / Diary for My Children**   1982 DS
D: Márta Mészáros
S: Márta Mészáros
C: Nyika Jancsó
A: Zsuzsa Czinkóczi, Anna Polony
Part I of the diary trilogy. Budapest, 1947. A young girl returns from Moscow to her aunt's home in Hungary. Her artist parents were exiled as communists before World War II and then subjected to Stalinist purges, while her aunt, also formerly of the communist underground, has gained relative wealth and high uniformed status in the new government. The aunt clashes with her niece, who refuses to be co-opted. The disparity of their political viewpoints reaches a crisis when the aunt becomes the new prison warden. The film incorporates documentary footage and fictional film of the period. The severe thoughtfulness of the lead performance gains impact through parts II and III of the trilogy: *Diary for My Loves* (948) and *Diary for My Father and Mother* (950).

Awards: Budapest Film Festival, Grand Prix, Acting Award (Czinkóczi), 1984; Chicago International Film Festival, Bronze Hugo, 1984; Munich Film Festival, Interfilm Award, 1984; Hungarian Film Critics Prize, Best Direction, 1985

945. *Névtelen vär / The Nameless Castle*
1983 DS
D: Éva Zsures
S: Éva Zsures
C: Lóránt Lukács
A: Vera Pap, Teri Tordai, Gábor Koncz
Eighteenth century. A Bourbon princess hides under a veil in a chateau and remains a "nameless" mystery to the community. A baroness buys the estate and falls in love with the count who cares for the princess, but the baroness does not find out why the princess is hiding until Napoleon's army is defeated. *Hungarofilm Bulletin, no. 12: 14–15. 1983.*

946. *Maria nap / Maria's Day*
1984 DP
D: Judit Elek
S: Luca Karall, Gyorgy Petho
C: Emil Novak
P: Judit Ordody
A: Edit Handel, Eva Igo
1866. At an aristocratic family reunion marked by conflict and the political pressures of the time, the oldest daughter is encouraged to leave her husband by her family, who dislikes him, while the younger one, unhappily married and celebrating her birthday, dies. *Variety: 216. Mar. 7.*

947. *Öszi almanach / Autumn Almanac*
1985
D: Béla Tarr
S: Béla Tarr
C: Sandor Kardos
A: Hédi Temessy
An older woman and her nurse, her son, the nurse's lover, and a lodger "quarrel, maneuver, and betray in a crumbling apartment" owned by the old woman. *MOMA Film. 2001, Oct.*
Awards: Locarno International Film Festival, Ernest Artaria Award, 1984

948. *Napló szerelmeinmnek / Diary for My Loves*
1987 DS
D: Márta Mészáros
S: Márta Mészáros, Eva Pataki
C: Nyika Jancsó
A: Zsuzsa Czinkóczi, Anna Polony, Jan Nowicki
Part II of the diary trilogy. A student refuses the care of her functionary aunt, whom she considers compromised, and eventually goes to study economics in Moscow. Once there, she fights to go to film school instead. She also searches for her father, a sculptor, and eventually makes a film in the Hungarian countryside. See also *Diary for My Children* (944) and *Diary for My Father and Mother* (950).
Awards: Berlin International Film Festival, OCIC Award, 1987

949. *Az én XX szazadom / My 20th Century*
1989 DS
D: Ildikó Enyedi
S: Ildikó Enyedi
C: Tibor Máthé
A: Dorota Segda
A surreal collage of the lives of twin sisters who are raised in different families; one lives an irresponsible life, the other is a radical activist. The film includes lectures and demonstrations of light and electric inventions. Fantasy.
Awards: Cannes Film Festival, Golden Camera, 1989

950. *Napló apámnak anyámnak / Diary for My Father and Mother*
1990 DS
D: Márta Mészáros
S: Márta Mészáros, Eva Pataki
C: Nyika Jancsó
A: Zsuzsa Czinkóczi, Anna Polony
Part III of the diary trilogy. A filmmaker documents events of the 1956 uprising in Budapest, particularly from the viewpoint of her friends and family. This is the culminating episode of a complex autobiographical portrait—incorporating details of Hungarian history and culture as they relate to the psychology of personal relationships. See also *Diary for My Children* (944) and *Diary for My Loves* (948).

951. *Anna filmje / Anna's Film*
1992
D: György Molnár
S: György Molnár
A: Anna Ráczlevei
A comfortable middle-class woman with three children is pregnant with a fourth she does not want; fantasy prevails in her life. *Variety: 68. 1993, Feb. 22.*

952. *A Csalás gyönyöre / Rapture of Deceit*
1992 D
D: Livia Gyarmathy
S: Géza Böszörményi
C: Gábor Balog
A: Rita Tushingham, Anikô Für
Late 1980s. An engineer loses her position during the changeover to capitalism, then finds her husband having an affair with the boss's daughter.

She moves in with an older widow, then gets a job as a waitress, but she becomes involved with gangsters who threaten the restaurant. *Variety: 73. 1992, Dec. 7.*
Other titles: *Le Plaisir de tromper*

953. Fényérzékeny történet / A Light Sensitive Story   1994
D: Pal Erdöss
S: Pal Erdöss, István Kardos
A: Erika Ozsada
A photographer and single mother allows her in-laws to take her child to Germany for a visit to his father, but they return without him. *AMG.*

954. A Magzat / Foetus   1994 DS
D: Márta Mészáros
S: Márta Mészáros, Eva Pataki
C: Nyika Jancsó
A: Adel Kovats, Aliona Antonova
A young mother of two children finds she is pregnant. She agrees, for a large payment, to go into seclusion and sign over her child at birth to her boss at the store where she works. *Variety. 1994, Feb. 21.*
Awards: Berlin International Film Festival, nomination for Golden Bear, 1994

955. Csókkal es körömmel / Kisses and Scratches   1995
D: György Szomjas
S: György Szomjas
C: Ferenc Grunwalsky
A: Beáta Papp, Ildikó Bakos, Bea Kálmán
Budapest. A social worker in a working-class district also babysits for a single mother. They pursue their relationship within the local lesbian subculture, and another friend takes the mother's affection away from the social worker. *FII.*

956. Siódmy pokój / The Seventh Chamber   1995 DS
D: Márta Mészáros
S: Márta Mészáros, Eva Pataki, Roberta Mazzoni
C: Piotr Sobocinski
P: Francesco Pamphili
A: Maia Morgenstern, Jan Nowicki, Adriana Asti, Fanny Ardant
Breslau, Germany, 1891–1942. The life of philosopher Edith Stein, a German Jew who became a philosopher and Catholic Carmelite nun at the start of the war, only to be removed by the Nazis and taken to Auschwitz, where she died. *Variety. 1995, Sep. 25.*
Other titles: *La Settima stanza*

Awards: Venice Film Festival, OCIC Award, 1995

957. Csajok / Bitches   1996 DS
D: Ildiko Szabó
S: Ildiko Szabó
C: Péter Jankura
P: István Kardos
A: Dorotya Udvaros, Eniko Eszenyi, Mariann Szalay
The story of three "disappointed wives," their husbands, and their families. *AMG.*

958. A Szerencse lányai / Daughter of Luck   1999 D
D: Márta Mészáros
S: Zoltan Jancsó
C: Piotr Wojtowicz
P: Filip Bajon
A: Olga Drozdova, Masha Petraniuk, Ewa Telega
A Russian woman on vacation is forced into prostitution in Warsaw after her friend is murdered and she is left alone and destitute. *AMG.*
Other titles: Cory scescie
Awards: Polish Film Festival, Best Supporting Actress (Telega), 1999

959. Kisvilma: az utolsó napló / Little Vilma: The Last Diary   2000 DS
D: Márta Mészáros
S: Márta Mészáros, Eva Pataki
C: Nyika Jancsó
P: Csaba Bereczki, Károly Makk
A: Lili Monori
Kirgizstan. A woman searches for details of her father's disappearance during the Stalinist purges of the 1930s. As a child, she and her revolutionary communist family were exiled there from fascist Hungary. See also *Napló gyermekeimnek / Diary for My Children*, *Napló szerelmeinmnek / Diary for My Loves*, and *Napló apámnak anyámnak / Diary for My Father and Mother. Variety. 2000, Feb. 28.*

ICELAND

960. A Hjara veraldar / Rainbow's End 1983 DS
D: Kristín Johannesdóttir
S: Kristín Johannesdóttir
A: Tóra Friðriksdóttir
In a "lyrical and personal" account, a mother gives up a music career for her two children. *Encyclopedia of European.*

961. Ungfrúin góða og húsið / Honor of the House   1999 DS
D: Guðný Halldórsdóttir

S: Guðný Halldórsdóttir
C: Per Källberg
P: Snorri Þórisson
A: Ragnhildur Gisladóttir, Tinna Gunnlaugsdóttir
1900. A mother is disturbed by the jealousy that develops between her two daughters when the younger one is sent to Copenhagen to develop her talent in embroidery. The girl becomes pregnant there, and when her sister finds out, she takes charge of the family's honor by arranging a fake marriage and giving the baby away to an orphanage. *Festival de films, 23rd: 24. 2001.*
Awards: Edda Awards, Best Film, Best Actress, 1999; Sochi International Film Festival, Best Actress, 2000

962. *Mávahlátur / Seagull's Laughter* 2001 S
D: Ágúst Guðmundsson
S: Ágúst Guðmundsson, Kristin Marja Baldursdóttir
C: Peter Krause
P: Kristín Atladóttir
A: Margrét Vijhálmsdóttir, Ugala Egilsdóttir
1950s. A woman returns to a small fishing village in Iceland where she grew up. Her glamour and ideas about liberation are viewed suspiciously by the community. *Village Voice: 64. 2004, Feb. 11.*
Awards: Edda Awards, Best Film, Best Director, Best Actress (Vijhálmsdóttir), 2001; Karlovy Vary International Film Festival, Best Actress (Egilsdóttir), 2002

INDIA

963. *Devi / The Goddess* 1960
D: Satyajit Ray
S: Satyajit Ray, Prabhat Mukherjee
C: Subrata Mitra
P: Satyajit Ray
A: Sharmila Tagore
A father dreams that his daughter-in-law is the goddess Kali reincarnated. Frightened, she sends for her husband, who arrives to find a trail of people awaiting the attention of the goddess. The couple decide to run away, but she becomes guilty about running from her responsibility, and they return. When she fails to cure her nephew, her goddess status, which has already left her depressed and isolated, now leaves her vulnerable to "the demons."

964. *Meghe dhaka tara / Hidden Star* 1960
D: Ritwik Ghatak
S: Ritwik Ghatak
C: Dinen Gupta

A: Supriya Choudhury, Geeta Ghatak, Geeta Dey
Calcutta, 1950s. An East Bengali refugee family struggles to survive in a shantytown on the city's outskirts. When their father is injured, they become entirely dependent on the eldest daughter, who ends her education to help them. When the eldest daughter's lover falls in love with her selfish sister and an accident to her brother increases her burden, she begins to deteriorate with tuberculosis. *Sight & Sound, vol. 7, no. 9: 39. 1997, Sep.*
Other titles: The Cloud Capped Star

965. *Sahib bibi aur ghulam / The Lord, His Wife and Slave* 1962
D: Abrar Alvi
S: Abrar Alvi; based on the novel by Bimal Mitra
A: Meena Kumari
An upper-class wife attempts to seduce her husband, who relies on courtesans for his sexual needs. As she adopts the ways of a courtesan, she becomes an alcoholic. *Cinematic Imagination: 134.*
Awards: Filmfare Awards, Best Film, Best Director, Best Actress, 1963

966. *Bandini* 1963
D: Bimal Roy
S: Nabendu Ghosh
C: Kamal Bose
P: Bimal Roy
A: Nutan, Ashok Kumar
After a village affair with a freedom fighter, a woman moves to the city and accidentally murders his wife. In prison, she is pursued by the prison doctor, but upon release, she finds her former lover is ill and needs her. *FII.*
Awards: Filmfare Awards, Best Film, Best Actress, 1964

967. *Gumrah / Deception* 1963
D: B. R. Chopra
S: Akhtar-Ul-Iman
P: B. R. Chopra
A: Mala Sinha, Sunil Dutt, Shashikala
A woman who has married her brother-in-law in order to raise her sister's children engages in a secret relationship with a former lover. *Cinematic Imagination: 127.*
Awards: Filmfare Awards, Best Supporting Actress (Shashikala), 1964

968. *Mahanagar / The Big City* 1963
D: Satyajit Ray
S: Satyajit Ray, Narendranath Mitra
C: Subrata Mitra

P: R. D. Bansal
A: Anil Chatterjee
New Delhi, 1950s. The wife of an unemployed
   bank clerk gets a job selling vacuum cleaners, then clashes over her decision with her
   children, husband, and his father, who live with
   her in a cramped city apartment. Soon enough,
   the job—going from door to door in a suburb
   of single-family homes—becomes another oppression, as she clashes with her boss and the
   customers and then finally resigns over unfair
   treatment.

969. *Charulata / The Lonely Wife*   1964
D: Satyajit Ray
S: Satyajit Ray, Rabindranath Tagore
C: Subrata Mitra
A: Madhabi Mukherjee
Calcutta, nineteenth century. A bored housewife of
   a political writer falls in love with a young poet,
   whom she imagines will be more sympathetic to
   her writing than her husband. *Faber Companion.*
Awards: Berlin International Film Festival, Silver
   Bear (Ray), OCIC Award, 1965

970. *The Guide*   1965 S
D: Vijay Anand
S: Vijay Anand
P: Tad Danielewski
A: Waheeda Rehman, Dev Anand
A railway guide encourages a woman to leave her
   husband and pursue her passion for dance. She
   becomes a star and separates from the guide.
   There is a dubbed English version written by
   Pearl S. Buck. *Encyclopaedia of Hindi.*
Awards: Filmfare Awards, Best Film, Best Actress,
   1967

971. *Mamta*   1966
D: Asit Sen
P: Charu Chitra
A: Suchitra Sen
The same actress plays the twin roles of a cour-
   tesan mother and her lawyer daughter. *Encyclo-
   paedia of Hindi.*
Awards: Moscow International Film Festival, Best
   Actress, 1966

972. *Bombay Talkie*   1970 S
D: James Ivory
S: James Ivory, Ruth Prawer Jhabvala
C: Subrata Mitra
P: Ismail Merchant
A: Jennifer Kendal
A middle-aged British writer has her novel made
   into a film in Bombay and ends up flirting with

the screenwriter as well as the leading man.
   AMG.

973. *Khilona*   1970
D: Chander Vohra
P: L. V. Prasad
A: Mumtaz, Sanjeer Kumar
A mentally ill poet is nursed back to health by a
   poor woman. *Encyclopaedia of Hindi.*
Awards: Filmfare Awards, Best Film, Best Actress, 1971

974. *Amar prem / Immortal Love*   1971
D: Shakti Samanta
S: Arvind Mukherjee
A: Sharmila Tagore
A woman is tricked into becoming a prostitute af-
   ter being forced out of her home because she is
   unable to have children. Musical. *Festival des 3.*
Awards: Filmfare Awards, Best Screenplay, 1973

975. *Oru penninte katha / Story of a Woman*
                                               1971
D: K. S. Sethumadhavan
A: Sheela
Returning to her native village, a woman takes
   revenge against a former lover and his wife.
   Encyclopedia of Indian: 410.

976. *Pakeezah / Pure Heart*   1971
D: Kamal Amrohi
S: Kamal Amrohi
C: Josef Wirschling
P: Kamal Amrohi
A: Meena Kumari, Ashok Kumar
Lucknow, 1900. A Muslim courtesan suffers the
   rejection of her husband's family and dies giving
   birth to her daughter; the daughter becomes a
   courtesan, but she is saved by marriage to her
   father's nephew. *Encyclopedia of Indian: 410.*

977. *Anta mana manchike / All for the Best*
                                               1972 D
D: Bhanumathi Ramakrishna
C: Lakshman Gorey
A: Bhanumathi Ramakrishna
A widow raises her sister, who gets involved with
   a pimp. *Encyclopedia of Indian: 410.*

978. *Maya darpan / Mirror of Illusion*   1972
D: Kumar Shahani
S: Kumar Shahani
C: K. K. Mahajan
A: Aditi
The unmarried daughter of a wealthy Rajasthani
   has a sexual relationship with an engineer. *Ency-
   clopedia of Indian: 413.*

979. *Ankur / The Seedling* 1973
D: Shyam Benegal
S: Shyam Benegal
C: Govind Nihalani
P: Lalit Bijlani
A: Shabana Azmi
A servant, married off to a deaf-mute, has an affair with the son of the owner of the country estate where she works. *New York. 2002.*

980. *Avalum penn thaane / She Too Is a Woman* 1974
D: Durai
A: Sumithra
A prostitute tries to find better employment. *Encyclopedia of Indian: 420.*

981. *Rajanigandha / Tube Rose* 1974 DS
D: Basu Chatterjee
S: Basu Chatterjee
C: K. K. Mahajan
P: Suresh Jindal
A: Vidya Sinha
A woman has two suitors, one she is engaged to, and the other she meets when applying for a job. *Encyclopedia of Indian: 420.*
Awards: Filmfare Awards, Best Film, 1975

982. *Stir patra / Letter from the Wife* 1974
D: Purnendu Pattrea
S: Purnendu Pattrea
C: Shakti Banerjee
A: Madhabi Mukherjee
A daughter-in-law writes poetry and conflicts in general with the traditional expectations of her husband's wealthy family. *FII.*

983. *Aandhi / The Storm* 1975
D: Gulzar
S: Bhushan Banmali, Gulzar
C: K. Vaikunth
P: J. Om Prakash
A: Suchitra Sen
During her election campaign, a Hindu woman is smeared because of continuing ties to her estranged husband. *Encyclopedia of Indian: 422.*

984. *Jai Santoshi maa / In Praise of Mother Santoshi* 1975
D: Vijay Sharma
A: Anita Guha, Kanan Kaushal
A mother goddess is vaulted into the pantheon by an earthly disciple. *Encyclopedia of Indian: 424.*

985. *Julie* 1975
D: K. S. Sethumadhavan

S: Inder Raj Anand, Chakrapani
P: Chakrapani
A: Laxmi Narayan, Nadira
A pregnant young woman tries to save herself by sending her child far away. *Encyclopedia of Indian: 424.*
Awards: Filmfare Awards, Best Actress (Narayan, Nadira), 1976

986. *Mausam* 1975
D: Gulzar
S: Gulzar
C: K. Vaikunth
A: Sharmila Tagore
A young woman in a brothel is suddenly offered a new life by a man she does not realize is the doctor who abandoned her mother when she was born. He hesitates to tell her that he is the father she despises. Musical. *Festival des 3.*
Awards: National Film Awards, Best Actress, 1976; Filmfare Awards, Best Film, Best Director, 1977

987. *Tapasya* 1975
D: Anil Ganguly
P: Tarachand Barjatya
A: Raakhee Gulzar
An older sister sacrifices her own future happiness to raise her siblings. *Encyclopaedia of Hindi.*
Awards: Filmfare Awards, Best Actress, 1977

988. *Bhadrakali* 1976
D: A. C. Trilogchander
A: Rani Chandra
A woman's marriage ends when she is raped by a "chandalan" Kandeepan. Her ex-husband then marries another woman sought after by the Kandeepan, but the first woman finds and kills the criminal before the second wife is harmed. *Encyclopedia of Indian: 427.*

989. *Chuvanna vithukal / Red Seedling* 1976
D: P. A. Backer
A: Shantakumari
A prostitute tries to help her younger sister improve her lot but is arrested; eventually released, she finds that her sister, who has been abandoned by her lover and has a child, is more dependent than ever. *Encyclopedia of Indian: 427.*

990. *Avargal / Characters* 1977
D: K. Balachander
A: Sujatha, Leelavathi
A woman, abandoned and shunted from man to man, forges a bond with her mother-in-law. *Encyclopedia of Indian: 431.*

991. *Bhumika* / *The Role*   1977
D: Shyam Benegal
S: Shyam Benegal, Satyadev Dubey
C: Govind Nihalani
P: Lalit Bijlani
A: Smita Patil
1930s. A woman from the Maharashtra becomes a music and film star in Bombay. Based on the life of Hansa Wadkar. *Encyclopaedia of Hindi.*
Awards: Filmfare Awards, Best Film, 1978; National Film Awards, Best Actress, 1978

992. *Chilakamma c heppindi*   1977
D: Eranki Sharma
A: Sripriya, Sangeetha
A girl sets out for the city to find a job, then is seduced and abandoned when she becomes pregnant. Helped for a time by the man's sister, she finally returns to the countryside and marries. *Encyclopedia of Indian: 431.*

993. *Ghattashraddha* / *The Ritual*   1977
D: Girish Kasaravalli
A: Meena Kuttappa
A child widow lives with her father, who runs a Brahmin school, and becomes pregnant by a teacher; she enlists the help of a young male student in an attempt to abort the fetus, and then commits suicide. *Encyclopedia of Indian: 431.*

994. *Kulavadhu*   1977
D: Krishnakant
P: Babubhai Desai
A: Asha Parekh
A rich woman's sexual past, involving a murder and jail sentence, is revealed when she marries. *Encyclopedia of Indian: 432.*

995. *Ek din prati din* / *And Quiet Rolls the Dawn*   1979
D: Mrinal Sen
S: Mrinal Sen
C: K. K. Mahajan
P: Mrinal Sen
A: Gita Sen, Mamata Shankar
A lower-middle-class family waits for news of their daughter, the sole support of the family, who has failed to return on time from her office job; it is forbidden for her to spend the night away from home. *Films and Feminism: 145.*

996. *Meera*   1980
D: Gulzar
S: Gulzar, Bhushan Banmali
C: K. Vaikunth

P: Premji
A: Hema-Malini
The musical story of Meera Bai, a medieval poet, here given supernatural qualities, who refused to marry on the grounds she was destined to be the bride of Krishna. *AMG.*

997. *36 Chowringhee Lane*   1981 DS
D: Aparna Sen
S: Aparna Sen
C: Ashok Mehta
P: Shashi Kapoor
A: Jennifer Kendal, Debashree Roy
Late 1970s. A student visits her former Shakespeare teacher, a British woman who has remained in Calcutta, and persuades her to let her and her boyfriend use her flat; after they marry, the couple abandons her. *Cinéma de l'Inde: 317.*

998. *Chakra* / *Vicious Circle*   1981
D: Rabindra Dharmaraj
S: Jaywant Dalvi, Rabindra Dharmaraj
C: Barun Mukherjee
P: Manmohan Shetty
A: Smita Patil, Naseeruddin Shah
When a man kills another for attempting to rape his wife, he is forced to flee with his family; in the city he is murdered, and his wife and children become completely impoverished. *FII.*
Awards: Locarno International Film Festival, Golden Leopard, 1981; Filmfare Awards, Best Actress, 1982

999. *Umbartha* / *The Threshold*   1981 S
D: Jabbar Patel
S: Vijay Tendulkar, Shanta Nisal
C: Rajan Kinagi
P: Sujata Chitra
A: Smita Patil
The wife of a progressive lawyer decides to manage a safe house for female abuse victims, but she loses her husband and is forced to resign the job. *Encyclopedia of Indian: 452.*
Other titles: Dawn / Subah

1000. *Umrao jaan*   1981 S
D: Muzaffar Ali
S: Muzaffar Ali, Shama Zaidi
P: Muzaffar Ali
A: Rekha, Javed Siddiqui
A nineteenth-century courtesan (tawaif) from Lucknow is trained in music and dance and becomes much sought after; she lives with a series of men. *Encyclopedia of Indian: 453.*
Awards: National Film Awards, Best Actress 1982

1001. *Namkeen* 1982
D: Gulzar
A: Shabana Azmi
A "no nonsense" mother and her daughters take in boarders and sell spices for a living. The middle daughter does not speak because she was kidnapped and held captive for a time as a child. *Encyclopaedia of Hindi: 182.*

1002. *Phaniyamma* 1982 DSP
D: Prema Karanth
S: Prema Karanth; based on the novel by M. K. Indira
C: Madhu Ambat
P: Prema Karanth
A: Dasharathi Dixit
An upper-caste Hindu girl, married at nine and visited with the purification of widowhood at fifteen, grows up to be a wise, progressive, and caring member of her village, even though she believes that "traditions are meaningless." Based on a true story of a woman who lived from 1870 to 1952. *Films and Feminism: 180.*

1003. *Adaminte variyellu / Adam's Rib* 1983
D: K. G. George
S: K. G. George
C: Ramachandra Babu
A: Suhasini, Sreevidya, Soorya
Follows three women: one becomes mentally ill under the weight of family responsibility, one attempts divorce, and one is a housemaid who finds salvation in a home for women. *Encyclopedia of Indian: 457.*

1004. *Ardh satya / Half Truths* 1983
D: Govind Nihalani
S: Vasant Dev, S. D. Panwalker
C: Govind Nihalani
P: Pradeep Kapoor
A: Smita Patil, Om Puri
A teacher becomes involved with an idealistic police officer and helps him fight the corruption of the justice system. *Variety. 1984, Aug. 29.*

1005. *Arth / The Meaning* 1983
D: Mahesh Bhatt
S: Mahesh Bhatt, Sujit Sen
C: Pravin Bhatt
P: Kuljit Pal
A: Shabana Azmi, Smita Patil, Rohini Hattangadi
A filmmaker struggles to become independent after her husband leaves her; at the same time she becomes intrigued by the plight of her cleaning woman, who murders her husband after he abandons her. Even more boldly, the servant adopts a child while she is imprisoned and insists on remaining a single mother. *Films and Feminism: 166.*
Awards: National Film Awards, Best Actress (Azmi), 1983; Filmfare Awards, Best Film, Best Actress (Azmi), Best Supporting Actress (Hattangadi), 1984

1006. *Mandi / Marketplace* 1983 S
D: Shyam Benegal
S: Shama Zaidi
C: Ashok Mehta
P: Lalit Bijlani
A: Shabana Azmi, Smita Patil
Comic portrayal of the magnetic, autocratic madam of a luxurious bordello, who has a favorite among the girls whom she protects and would like to see become a singer. She is also forced to move the bordello outside of town to make way for progress, an elaborate political and construction process that leaves the women thriving.

1007. *Masoom / Innocent* 1983
D: Shekhar Kapur
S: Gulzar
C: Pravin Bhatt
A: Shabana Azmi, Naseeruddin Shah
The death of a mistress brings a heretofore unknown boy child into a happy family. The wife must love and accept him. *Encyclopedia of Indian.*
Awards: Filmfare Awards, Best Film, 1983

1008. *Ponirah* 1983
D: Slamet Rahardjo
S: Slamet Rahardjo
C: Tantra Suryadi
A: Nani Vidya, Christine Hakim
A woman, persecuted by her father for the death in childbirth of her mother, is finally sent away in the care of an impoverished nurse. The nurse must turn to prostitution to survive and takes the child to live in a brothel, where she learns to hate men. *Variety: 21. 1984, Nov. 28.*

1009. *Smriti chitre / Memory Episodes* 1983 D
D: Vijaya Mehta
S: Mangesh Kulkarni; based on an autobiography by Laxmibai Tilak
C: R. C. Mapashi
A: Vijaya Mehta, Suhas Joshi, Pallavi Patil, Rarindra Mankani
1868–1936. The story of Laxmibai Tilak, the author of a "major social reform text," who was also the wife of a philosopher famous for converting from Hinduism to Christianity. *Encyclopedia of Indian.*

1010. *Khandar / The Ruins*   1984
D: Mrinal Sen
S: Premendra Mitra, Mrinal Sen
C: K. K. Mahajan
P: Jagdish Chowhani
A: Shabana Azmi, Gita Sen
A woman lives with her sick mother near some famous ruins; one day she is visited by a man who pretends to be her former fiancé, who had married someone else years earlier. *Film Society. 2002, Sep.*
Awards: Chicago International Film Festival, Best Film, 1984; Montréal World Film Festival, Special Jury Prize, 1985; National Film Awards, Best Actress, 1984

1011. *Tarang / Wave*   1984
D: Kumar Shahani
S: Kumar Shahani
C: K. K. Mahajan
A: Smita Patil
A woman's husband is killed in a factory accident, and she goes to work as a servant in the factory owner's home. *FII.*
Other titles: Vibrations

1012. *Utsav / The Festival*   1984
D: Girish Karnad
S: Girish Karnad, Krishna Basrur, Bhasa
C: Ashok Mehta
P: Shashi Kapoor
A: Rekha
Fourth century. The poetic love story between a beautiful courtesan of Ujjain and a Brahmin. *Encyclopedia of Indian: 469.*

1013. *Aakhir kyon*   1985
D: J. Om Prakash
P: J. Om Prakash
A: Smita Patil
A pregnant woman discovers that her sister and husband began an affair while she was in the hospital; her husband intends to continue the relationship. The wife then turns to writing and becomes a famous author. *Encyclopaedia of Hindi: 389. Also IMDb.*

1014. *Kamla*   1985
D: Jag Mundhra
S: Vasant Dev, Vijay Tendulkar
C: Pravin Bhatt
P: Jag Mundhra
A: Shabana Azmi, Deepti Naval
A woman wonders about her own exploitation when her journalist husband purchases a slave girl to expose trafficking, then exploits her himself in their own home. *New York. 2002.*

1015. *Anjuman / Congregation*   1986
D: Muzaffar Ali
S: Muzaffar Ali
C: Ishan Arya
P: Muzaffar Ali
A: Shabana Azmi
A poor woman lives with her mother and siblings, does embroidery for a living, and ends up organizing an embroiderers' union. Includes musical sequences. *Village Voice: 114. 2002, Sep. 25.*

1016. *Genesis*   1986
D: Mrinal Sen
S: Mohit Chattopadhya, Mrinal Sen
C: Carlo Varini
A: Shabana Azmi
Two men who have fled a possessive royal master commandeer some ruins in the desert to begin a new life. A woman, who has fled a flood on the other side of the country, joins them and stays to help organize. She clues them in to a trader who is taking advantage of them and generally improves their living conditions. When she becomes pregnant, they fight over which is the father.

1017. *Mirch marsala / Spices*   1986
D: Ketan Mehta
S: Ketan Mehta, Shafi Hakim
A: Smita Patil
Gujarat, 1940s. The village men agree to send a desirable woman to the tax collector in exchange, but she takes refuge in a spice factory; violence ensues, and she and other women band together to fight back. *Variety: 21. 1987, Aug. 5.*
Other titles: Hot Spices; A Touch of Spice; Chili Bouquet
Awards: Hawaii International Film Festival, Best Feature Film, 1987

1018. *Paroma*   1986 DS
D: Aparna Sen
S: Aparna Sen
C: Ashok Mehta
P: Nirmal Kumar
A: Raakhee Gulzar
A wealthy Bengali wife has an affair with a younger man, then is exposed and must recover from the condemnation of her family. *Cinéma de l'Inde: 318.*

1019. *Rao Saheb / The Barrister*   1986 DS
D: Vijaya Mehta
S: Vijaya Mehta; based on the novel by Jaywant Dalvi
C: Adeep Tamdon

P: Vinay Willing
A: Anupam Kher (m), Tanvi (f)
Rao Saheb is devoted to Western progressivism and tries to reform India's treatment of women by treating the wife of one of his retainers as an equal. This puts both in the midst of a scandal. *FII.*

1020. *Antarjali yatra / Voyage Beyond* 1987
D: Goutam Ghose
S: Goutam Ghose, Kamal Majumdar
C: Ravi Malik
A: Shampa Ghose
1830s. A father encourages his daughter to marry an older man for his wealth; when the dying husband attempts to take his young wife with him in a suttee ritual, an untouchable counsels her to rebel. *Variety. 1988, Nov. 30.*
Awards: Tashkent Film Festival, Grand Prix, 1988

1021. *Ek Pal / A Moment* 1987 DSP
D: Kalpana Lazmi
S: Kalpana Lazmi, Gulzar
C: K. K. Mahajan
P: Bhupen Hazarika
P: Kalpana Lazmi
A: Shabana Azmi
A woman settles for marriage with a workaholic, then eventually seeks out a former lover. *FII.*

1022. *Khoon bhari maang* 1988
D: Rakesh Roshan
S: Ravi Kapoor, Mohan Kaul
P: Rakesh Roshan
A: Rekha, Sonu Walia
A "Casanova husband" attempts to murder his wife, but she survives and returns after plastic surgery as a "glamorous wife" to seek revenge. *Encyclopaedia of Hindi.*
Awards: Filmfare Awards, Best Actress (Rekha), Best Supporting Actress (Walia), 1989

1023. *Main zinda noon / I Am Living* 1988
D: Sudhir Mishra
S: Sudhir Mishra
C: Rajesh Joshi
A: Deepti Naval
Bombay. An orphan girl moves to the city with her husband, who deserts her. She becomes the main economic support of his family, and they resent it when she meets another man. When her husband returns, she loses all sympathy and support and becomes mentally unbalanced. *Chaosmag. Accessed 2005, June 10.*

1024. *Rihatee / Liberation* 1988 DSP
D: Patil Arunaraje
S: Patil Arunaraje
C: S. R. K. Murthy
P: Patil Arunaraje
A: Hema Malini
In a village near Bombay where the men work in the city for long periods and frequent prostitutes, the women are sometimes seduced by other opportunities. Three become pregnant: one aborts, one commits suicide, and one decides to keep the child even though her husband is not the father. The village council determines that she must be expelled, but women object to the double standard. Musical. *Festival de films, 12th: 25. 1990.*
Other titles: Rihaee

1025. *Main azaad hoon* 1989
D: Tinnu Anand
S: Javed Akhtar
A: Shabana Azmi
A reporter writes letters against city corruption from an imaginary poor man. The stories prove so powerful that she must find an ordinary man to pose as the fighter; then one day she prints a letter that he is going to end his life fighting. Version of *Meet John Doe* (United States). *Bollycat. Accessed 2005, June 10.*

1026. *Sati* 1989 D
D: Aparna Sen
S: Arun Bannerjii, Kamal Majumdar
C: Ashok Mehta
A: Shabana Azmi
1828. A young woman is married to a tree to avoid premature widowhood and the capital punishment that goes with it (suttee). *Cinéma de l'Inde: 318.*
Awards: Montréal World Film Festival, Jury Distinction, 1989

1027. *Kasba* 1990
D: Kumar Shahani
S: Kumar Shahani
C: K. K. Mahajan
P: Ravi Malik
A: Mita Vashisht
A lower-caste adopted daughter is used by her crime-syndicate father to run his business. When a son is arrested and the father flees, she moves quickly take over the business. *Variety: 62. 1991, Nov. 4.*

1028. *Mahaprithivi / World Within, World Without* 1991
D: Mrinal Sen
S: Mrinal Sen, Anjan Dutt

C: Shashi Anand
P: Goutam Goswami
A: Gita Sen, Soumitra Chatterjee, Aparna Sen
Calcutta, 1980s. "Four days before German unification a mother of a middle-class family is found hanging dead in a locked up room. A story constructed from her diary runs alongside the story of the unification in Germany." *AMG.*

1029. *Miss Beatty's Children*   1992 DS
D: Pamela Rooks
S: James Killough, Pamela Rooks
C: Venu
A: Jenny Seagrove
An idealistic British missionary who works in the Indian countryside has appeared for years in native garb, which has made her an outcast. When she is accused of kidnapping, she is let go from her work with an organization that buys (and saves) young girls from families who otherwise would sell them into temple prisons. She proceeds to adopt and raise children on her own.

1030. *Shwet paatharer thaalaa*   1992
D: Shankar Gope
A: Aparna Sen
A wife and mother is shattered when her husband is killed in a car accident and she is shunned by his family, and even her son, because of her status. *NFDC. Accessed 2005, July 13.*

1031. *Bandit Queen*   1994 S
D: Shekhar Kapur
S: Ranjit Kapoor, Mala Sen; based on biographies of Phoolan Devi
C: Ashok Mehta
P: Bobby Bedi
A: Seema Biswas, Sunita Bhatt
The true story of Phoolan Devi, who was sold at the age of eleven by her impoverished family to an older man. After fleeing a marital rape, she became an easy target as a woman who has left her husband, as well as a threat because of her resistance to the local rulers. Unwelcome at home, she joins a gang and is tutored in guns, thievery, and leadership. Eventually she rules her own gang and becomes famous, then jailed. After her release, she was elected to a seat in the Indian parliament representing Uttar Pradesh. Action.

1032. *Mammo*   1994
D: Shyam Benegal
S: Khalid Mohamed
C: Prasann Jain
P: Raj Pius
A: Farida Jalal

A woman moves to Lahore with her husband and becomes a Pakistani citizen; after his death, she is rejected by his relatives but is also barred from returning to her own family in India. *FII.*
Awards: Filmfare Awards, Best Actress, 1995

1033. *Mohra*   1994
D: Rajiv Rai
S: Rajiv Rai, Shabbir Boxwala
C: Damodar Naidu
P: Gulshan Rai
A: Raveena Tandon
A warden's daughter is a journalist who visits the jail to write a story. Some prisoners try to rape her, but she is saved by an inmate who was imprisoned for murdering his wife's rapists. Intrigue develops when she attempts to get him freed. Action. *IMDb.*

1034. *Unishe April / April the Nineteenth* 1995
D: Rituparno Ghosh
S: Rituparno Ghosh
C: Sunirmal Majumdar
A: Debashree Roy, Aparna Sen
Conflict grows and leads to accusations of selfishness between a mother, who is a celebrity dancer, and her doctor daughter. *FII.*
Awards: National Film Awards, Best Film, Best Actress (Roy), 1995

1035. *Yugant / What the Sea Said*   1995 DS
D: Aparna Sen
S: Aparna Sen
C: A. Shashikant
A: Roopa Ganguly
Orrisa. A couple, separated for seventeen years, "because neither of them is willing to compromise on an intellectual or professional level," attempt to renew their relationship at a holiday by the beach. *FII.*

1036. *Doghi / Two Women*   1996 D
D: Sumitra Bhave, Sunil Sukhatankar
A: Uttara Baokar, Sonali Kulkarni, Renuka Daftardar
Maharashtra. Two sisters live in a farming community; one suffers the accidental loss of her betrothed and is sent to a brothel to make up the payment to his family; this money supports her other sister. *Variety: 84. 1996, Feb. 12.*

1037. *Fire*   1996 DS
D: Deepa Mehta
S: Deepa Mehta
C: Giles Nuttgens
P: Bobby Bedi

A: Shabana Azmi, Nandita Das

A new bride enters her husband's household, but he is often away visiting his true love; eventually she falls into an affair with her sister-in-law, who has also been made lonely by a husband who has retreated into religion in response to their lack of children.

1038. *Maachis* 1996

D: Gulzar

S: Gulzar

P: R.V. Pandit

A: Tabu, Chandrachur Singh

"An ordinary girl is driven to become a terrorist" after her brother is beaten by the police. *Encyclopaedia of Hindi: 634.*

Awards: National Film Awards, Best Actress, 1996

1039. *Sardari Begum* 1996

D: Shyam Benegal

S: Khalid Mohamed

C: Sanjay Dharankar

P: Amit Khanna

A: Smiriti Mishra, Kiron Kher, Rajeshwari Sachdev

New Delhi. A famous singer, now faded, is killed in a riot; a woman reporter investigates her death and uncovers the details of her life struggle, beginning with being disowned by her family, and ending with her fame as a recording star.

Awards: Moscow International Film Festival, nomination for Golden St. George, 1997

1040. *Bandh jharokhe* 1997 DS

D: Prema Karanth

S: Prema Karanth; based on *The Dark Holds No Terrors* by Deshpande Shashi

A Brahmin pediatrician leaves her home in Mumbai because she is unhappily married to a man who rapes her. After her mother dies and she patches relations with her father, her marital problems are revealed in flashback, along with the harsh treatment she received from her mother, who blamed her for her brother's death. *Films and Feminism: 184.*

1041. *Hazaar chaurasi ki maa* / *Mother of 1084* 1997

D: Govind Nihalani

S: Govind Nihalani, Tripurari Sharma

C: Govind Nihalani

P: Govind Nihalani

A: Jaya Bachchan, Nandita Das, Seema Biswas

Calcutta, 1970s. A wealthy woman loses her politically involved son to an assassin's bullet, then investigates his life and finds he was a militant leftist. She then begins to "question her own

submissive role as a traditional wife within a complacent bourgeois society." *FII.*

1042. *Mrityudand* / *Death Sentence* 1997

D: Prakash Jha

S: Prakash Jha, Rajan Kothari; based on the novel by Sahiwal

C: Rajan Kothari

P: Prakash Jha

A: Shabana Azmi, Madhuri Dixit

Bihar. A woman marries into an upper-class family and becomes friends with her sister-in-law; both have weak husbands but accept abuse from them. Their story is countered by one of a "servant who turns to prostitution to pay off a debt." One day their troubles become too much, and they all fight back. *New York. 2002.*

Awards: Bangkok Film Festival, Best Film, 1998

1043. *Janmadinam* / *Day of Birth* 1998 DS

D: Suma Josson

S: Suma Josson

C: Hari Nair

A: Nandita Das, Surekha Sikri

A pregnant woman and her mother spend a night in a hospital waiting for the birth; during the night, "time and space lose their meaning." *AMG.*

1044. *The Terrorist* 1998

D: Sanatosh Sivan

S: Sanatosh Sivan

C: Sanatosh Sivan

P: Shree Prasad

A: Ayesha Dharkar

A woman who has lost her family during a rebellion volunteers for a suicide assassination of a politician. Her training in the procedures for accomplishing this is laborious, involving enigmatic messages, long hikes, and mysterious tutors, and she never knows exactly who is guiding her.

Awards: Sarajevo Film Festival, Special Jury Prize, 2000

1045. *Godmother* 1999

D: Vinay Shukla

S: Vinay Shukla

C: Rajan Kothari

A: Shabana Azmi

When a woman's politically active husband is murdered, she takes up the cause of their oppressed community and becomes a brutal leader in the cause of justice. Musical. *FII.*

Awards: National Film Awards, Best Actress, 1999; Filmfare Awards, Best Story, 2000

1046. *Paromitar ek din / House of Memories*
1999 DS
D: Aparna Sen
S: Aparna Sen
C: Abhik Mukherjee
P: Rejesh Agarwal
A: Aparna Sen, Soumitra Chatterjee
A woman continues to be close to her mother-in-law even after the end of her marriage, and she goes to nurse her when she becomes ill. *FII.*
Awards: Bombay International Film Festival, FIPRESCI, 2000; Karlovy Vary International Film Festival, Ecumenical Jury Prize, 2000

1047. *Hari bhari / Fertility*
2000 S
D: Shyam Benegal
S: Shama Zaidi, Priya Chandrasekhar
C: Rajan Kothari
A: Shabana Azmi, Nandita Das, Surekha Sikri, Rajeshwari, Alka Trivedi
The lives of five Muslim women in a market town: a grandmother, two daughters-in-law, and a grand-daughter. *FII.*

1048. *Bavandar / The Sandstorm*
2001 S
D: Jag Mundhra
S: Ashok Mishra, Sudha Arora
C: Ashok Kumar
P: Jag Mundhra
A: Nandita Das, Laila Rouass
Rajasthan. A lower-caste woman works for the "women's development program" and speaks against child marriage and other sexist customs; the establishment takes revenge on her, but she persists in demanding justice. *FII.*
Awards: Bermuda International Film Festival, Audience Award, 2001

1049. *Chandni Bar*
2001
D: Madhur Bhandarkar
S: Mohan Azad, Masood Mirza
C: Rajeev Ravi
P: R. Mohan
A: Tabu
Bombay, 1985. A woman has left her native Sitapur because of riots there; she finds work as a dancer at the Chandni Bar, where she is tutored in the art by another dancer; eventually she attracts the attention of a gangster. *FII.*
Awards: International Indian Film Academy Awards, Most Popular Actress, 2002; National Film Awards, Best Actress, 2002

1050. *Daman*
2001 DS
D: Kalpana Lazmi
S: Kalpana Lazmi
C: Sudeep Chatterjee
A: Raveena Tandon, Sayaji Shinde, Raima Dev Sen
Assam. An illiterate girl is forced to marry a wealthy tea estate owner, who rapes and beats her. The man's brother is sympathetic to her plight, however, and intervenes in his brother's plan to marry off their young daughter, allowing her and the mother to escape. *FII.*
Awards: National Film Awards, Best Actress (Tandon), 2001

1051. *Daughters of This Century*
2001
D: Tapan Sinha
S: Tapan Sinha
C: Soumendu Roy
P: S. N. Bannerfee
A: Shabana Azmi, Jaya Bachchan, Nandita Das, Deepa Sahi, Sulbha Deshpandey
"Five short stories about female oppression by renowned Indian writers, the film was intended as a millennial tribute to Indian women." *FII.*
Awards: Cairo International Film Festival, nomination for Golden Pyramid, 2001

1052. *Lajja*
2001
D: Rajkumar Santoshi
S: Rajkumar Santoshi
P: Rajkumar Santoshi
A: Minisha Koirala, Jackei Shroff, Madhuri Dixit, Rekha
Kanpur, Uttar Pradesh. A woman leaves her philandering husband and is then beaten and raped in reprisal. She eventually finds other women in similar circumstances. *FII.*
Awards: Zee Cine Awards, Best Supporting Actress (Dixit), 2002

1053. *Filhaal*
2002 DS
D: Meghna Gulzar
S: Meghna Gulzar
C: Manmohan Singh
P: Jhamu Sughand
A: Tabu, Sushmita Sen
Two friends are very close, though one has married. The married woman is unable to bear children, and her friend volunteers to be a surrogate mother. Complications arise when she thinks of keeping the child herself. *IMDb.*

1054. *Manda meyer upakhyan / Tale of a Naughty Girl*
2002
D: Buddhadev Dasgupta
S: Buddhadev Dasgupta
C: Venu
P: Arya Bhattacharya
A: Samata Das

1969. A village prostitute sells her daughter into servitude. *BAM. 2003, Dec.*

Awards: Bangkok International Film Festival, Best Asian Film, 2003; National Film Awards, Best Film, 2003

1055. *Mr. and Mrs. Iyer* 2002 DS
D: Aparna Sen
S: Aparna Sen, Dulal Dey
C: Goutam Ghose
P: N. Venkatesan
A: Konkona Sensharma

During a bus journey, a Hindu woman provides a Muslim man with cover from a Hindu mob that attacks the bus looking for Muslims on whom to take revenge; she then falls in love with him. *NYT: E17. 2003, Apr. 25.*

Awards: Locarno International Film Festival, Netpac Award, 2002; Cinemanila International Film Festival, Best Screenplay, 2003; National Film Awards, Best Direction, Best Actress, 2003

1056. *Swaraaj / The Little Republic* 2002
D: Anwar Jamal
S: Sehjo Singh
C: S. Chokalingham
P: George Mathew
A: Alka Amin, Tanishita Chatterjee

"Drama about a group of women workers in a small village who band together to dig a vital water well when their men folk are unable to do it themselves." *FII.*

Awards: Munich Film Festival, Future Award, 2003

1057. *Kandukondain, kandukondain / I Have Found It* 2004
D: Rajiv Menon
S: Rajiv Menon; based on *Sense and Sensibility* by Jane Austen
C: Rajiv Chandran
P: A. M. Rathnam
A: Aishwarya Rai, Tabu

Set in contemporary India, an otherwise faithful version of the novel about sisters who lose their inheritance to a brother, along with some of their marriageability quotient. *Village Voice: 66. 2004, Apr. 14.*

INDONESIA

1058. *Apa yang kau cari Palupi / What Are You Searching for, Palupi?* 1970
D: Asrul Sani

An actress leaves her husband in search of an unidentified "something, which she sees as happiness, and the film sees as greed, immorality, and rejection of men." *Indonesian Cinema 2.*

Other titles: What Do You Search for, Palupi?

1059. *Suci sang primadona / Suci the Divine Primadonna* 1977
D: Arifin C. Nur
A: Joice Erna

A singer and prostitute balances three benefactors and a new young lover. *Indonesian Cinema 2.*

Awards: Festival Film Indonesia, Best Actress, 1977

1060. *Guruku contik sekali / My Teacher Is Very Pretty* 1980 D
D: Ida Farida

A teacher takes schoolgirls to a nature camp and carefully keeps them away from the nearby boys. *Indonesian Cinema 2.*

1061. *Para perintis kemerdekaan / Pioneers of Freedom* 1980
D: Asrul Sani
A: Mutiara Sani

West Sumatra, 1920s. Oppressed by her husband, a wife seeks help from an Islamic reformer, then serves a prison sentence for being a member of a religious sect that preaches against the Dutch; freed, she finds other activists and eventually joins the women's movement. *FII.*

1062. *Bukan isteri pilihannya / Not the Wife of His Choice* 1981
D: Edward Pesta Sirait
A: Ita Mustafa, Adi Kudir

A woman finds work and supports herself and her mother-in-law after being abandoned by her husband. *Indonesian Cinema 2: 134.*

1063. *Kadarwati, wanita dengan lima nama / Five Faces of Kadarwati* 1983
D: Sophan Sophiaan
S: Satmowi Atmowiloto
C: Adrian Susanto
A: Joice Erna, Frans Tumbuan

World War II. A Japanese woman is offered a medical education by the Japanese during the occupation but instead is sent to Malaysia as a "comfort woman." After the war, she takes revenge. *Monash University. Accessed 2005, June 1.*

1064. *Roro Mendut* 1983
D: Ami Priyono
C: Adrian Susanto
P: Bambang Widitomo
A: Meriam Bellina

1910s. A woman, given to a general as booty, refuses to surrender and uses her sex appeal to acquire money and the freedom to resist him. *Indonesian Cinema 2: 51.*

1065. Titan serambut dibelah tujuh / Narrow Bridge   1983
D: Chaerul Uman
S: Asrul Sani
C: Soleh Ruslani
A: Marlia Hardi
A progressive teacher in a small town is accused of rape, while a woman is accused of being immoral for refusing the advances of an important villager. *Variety: 22. 1986, Jan. 15.*

1066. Doea tanda mata / Mementos   1984
D: Teguh Karya
A: Jenny Rachman
1950s. A singer and a teacher resist the Dutch colonial government, one in planning an assassination, the other in instructing youth. *Indonesian Cinema 2: 150.*

1067. 7 wanita dalam tugas rahasia / Seven Women on a Secret Mission   1985
Women escape a renegade nationalist camp in the forest and journey into the wilderness. Action. *Indonesian Cinema.*

1068. Ibunda / Mother   1986
D: Teguh Karya
S: Teguh Karya
C: George Kamarullah
A: Tuti Indra Malaon
Jakarta. A widow conflicts with her grown, but still immature, children when she becomes involved with an Irian Javan, whom they view with racial prejudice. *Monash University. Accessed 2005, Feb. 13.*

1069. Ayu dan Ayu   1988
A woman with two daughters suffers through her husband's affair with a dancer, who conveniently dies and contributes the desired son to the family. *Indonesian Cinema.*

1070. Tjoet Nya Dien   1988
D: Eros Djarot
S: Eros Djarot
C: George Kanarullah Penata
P: Alwin Arifen
A: Christine Hakim
1887–1910. Based on the true story of Tjoet Nya Dien, a woman who, after her husband was killed in an ambush, led a battalion during the colonial wars against the Dutch. A well-

known and "inspiring saga." *Variety: 33. 1989, May 17.*

1071. Lady Dragon   1992
D: David Worth
S: Clifford Mohr
C: David Worth
A: Cynthia Rothrock
A former CIA agent learns the martial arts of the Lady Dragon and goes after the drug dealer who murdered her husband. Action. *IMDb.*

1072. Pasir berbisik / Whispering Sands
                                                        2003 DS
D: Nan Trevini Achinas
S: Nan Trevini Achinas
C: Yadi Sugandhi
A: Christine Hakim, Slamet Djarot, Dian Sastrowardoyo
A woman and her daughter live on the Java coast, where the mother grows and sells medicinal herbs and secretly provides abortions; the father has been gone a long time. They are forced to flee farther inland because of marauding bands of men, and in the next village, the daughter finds a friend. *Festival de films, 27th: 71. 2005.*
Awards: Seattle International Film Festival, Special Jury Prize, 2002; Singapore International Film Festival, Best Actress (Sastrowardoyo), 2002

IRAN

1073. Khak-e mohr shode / The Sealed Soil
                                                       1977 DSP
D: Marva Nabili
S: Marva Nabili
C: Barbod Teheri
P: Marva Nabili
A: Flora Shabaviz
A woman in prerevolutionary Iran is ostracized for daring to turn down marriage proposals, and she eventually has a nervous breakdown. Increasingly mute and motionless inside the walls of the barren courtyard of her home, her only positive gesture is an appreciation of the rain. She is seen to be evil, and a cleric is called in to exorcise her.

1074. Bon bast / Dead End   1977
D: Parviz Sayyad
S: Parviz Sayyad
C: Houshang Baharlou
P: Parviz Sayyad
A: Mary Apik

Life under the Shah: "Young woman is pursued by a man she thinks is a suitor but who turns out to be a security agent tailing her brother." *Companion Encyclopedia: 158.*

Awards: Moscow International Film Festival, Best Actress, 1977

1075. *Jahizieh bara-ye Robab / Dowry for Robaab* 1986

D: Syamak Shayeghi
S: Asghar Abdollahi
C: Hassan Gholizadeh
A: Parvaneh Massoomi

The daughter of a poor fishing family is forced to marry her cousin but must wait until the dowry is sufficient, a difficulty that falls on her little brother to solve. *Festival des 3.*

Other titles: Une Dot pour Robab

1076. *Nargess* 1991 DSP

D: Rakhshan Bani-Etemad
S: Rakhshan Bani-Etemad, Fereydun Jeyrani
C: Hossein Djafarian
P: Rakhshan Bani-Etemad
A: Atefah Razavi, Farimah Farjani

An older woman, a professional thief, is "married" to a young accomplice she found on the streets as a child. When he falls in love and seeks "respectability," she facilitates his marriage to a poor, honest, young girl. The women become friends, but the girl is adamant about his earning a living, even though he does not know how. He engages in one last heist, then abandons his mentor along with the stash.

1077. *Mosaferan* 1992

D: Bahram Bayzai
S: Bahram Bayzai
C: Mehrdad Fakhimi
P: Bahram Bayzai
A: Homa Rusta, Majid Mozaffari

Tehran. A woman's sister and her family are killed in a car crash on the way to her wedding; their grandmother insists that life must continue, that the wedding must proceed even in the midst of a funeral. *Cinémas du moyen: 274.*

Other titles: Les Voyageurs

1078. *Sara* 1993

D: Dariush Mehrjui
S: Dariush Mehrjui
C: Mahmoud Kalari
P: Dariush Mehrjui
A: Niki Karimi

A wife incurs a debt to save her husband's life, then spends her nights secretly embroidering lavish gowns and furtively selling them at the open market to pay it off. When her husband finds out, he punishes her, and she is forced to conclude that her submissiveness has limits. A modern version of *A Doll's House.*

Awards: Nantes Three Continents Festival, Audience Award, 1993; San Sebastián International Film Festival, Golden Seashell, Best Actress, 1993

1079. *Hamsar / The Spouse* 1994

D: Mehdi Fakhimzadeh
S: Mehdi Fakhimzadeh
A: Fatemeh Motamed-Aria, Mehdi Hashemi

Tehran. A married couple work at the same soulless corporate office; he wears Western suits, she goes about in a scarf and long coat. The wife uncovers an extortion plot by creating a trap at the warehouse, where her husband has been locked up. He tries to take credit for revealing the scheme, but nonetheless she is made the new director over him. He takes to bed at home, but she stands her ground with the help of friends and family. Comedy.

1080. *Zinat* 1994

D: Ebrahim Moktari
S: Ebrahim Moktari
C: Homayun Pievar
P: Farhang-Sara Bahman
A: Atefah Razavi

A young doctor is pressured by her husband and his family to give up her job in a rural health clinic, even though this would be a tremendous loss to the clinic; as a result she becomes frustrated in her marital relationship. *FII.*

Awards: Cinéma du Réel, Special Mention, 2000

1081. *Pari* 1995

D: Dariush Mehrjui
S: Dariush Mehrjui
C: Ali Reza Zarin Dast
A: Niki Karimi

The story of a crisis in the life of a twenty-year-old university-educated woman, who has been raised in a wealthy intellectual family and is habitually fully veiled. She quarrels with a professor about sterile thinking, finding no "heart" in her culture, only received ideas. She and her brother travel to their family home, which is in a state of disrepair, and where all the men argue as she continues to fall into depression.

1082. *Rousari-abi / The Blue-Veiled* 1995 DS

D: Rakhshan Bani-Etemad
S: Rakhshan Bani-Etemad

C: Azia Sa'ati
P: Majid Modaresi
A: Fatemeh Motamed-Aria, Ezatolla Entezami

An assertive farmworker supports her mother, siblings, and a young son. Capable of demanding fair treatment in the lines for food and for work, her character gets noticed by the widowed, lonely owner. They have a long-term affair; she demands marriage, but his daughters object to the alliance with "a village girl."

Awards: Locarno International Film Festival, Bronze Leopard, 1995; Thessaloniki Film Festival, FIPRESCI, 1995

1083. *Gabbeh* 1996
D: Mohsen Makhmalbaf
S: Mohsen Makhmalbaf
C: Mahmoud Kalari
P: Khalil Daroudchi
A: Shaghayegh Djodat

An impressionistic narrative of an aging couple and their nomadic tribal existence. The story takes off from the motif of their gabbeh (carpet), which depicts the wife's youthful desire for a horseman and her father's refusal to allow the marriage.

Awards: Catalonian International Film Festival, Best Direction, 1996; Tokyo International Film Festival, Best Artistic Contribution, 1996

1084. *Leila* 1997
D: Dariush Mehrjui
S: Dariush Mehrjui, Mahnaz Ansarian
C: Mahmoud Kalari
P: Dariush Mehrjui
A: Leila Hatami

A husband accepts that his much-loved young wife cannot have children. Pushed relentlessly by her mother-in-law, the wife insists that her husband take a second wife. The couple's shock and resentment build as they realize what this does to their relationship, but it is the wife who suffers the most extreme mental anguish.

1085. *Banoo-ye ordibehesht / The May Lady* 1998 DS
D: Rakhshan Bani-Etemad
S: Rakhshan Bani-Etemad
C: Hossein Jafarian
P: Jahangir Kosari
A: Minu Farshchi

A divorced documentary filmmaker must deal with her teenage son, who is jealous of a new man with whom she has fallen in love. Throughout the film she writes in her journal, calls her lover, and interviews mothers for a film she is making

on the "exemplary mother." In free moments, she ruminates about why a mother cannot also have love and work, and she is depressed by the subject of her film, which challenges the conventional view that has guided her own mothering.

Awards: Fajr Film Festival, Special Jury Award, 1998

1086. *Banoo / The Lady* 1999
D: Dariush Mehrjui
C: Naser Mansuri
A: Bita Farehi

A pious woman responds to her husband's betrayal and abandonment by taking into her house those in need. *Film Society. 2000, Jun.*

Other titles: Banu

Awards: Berlin International Film Festival, Don Quixote Award, 1999

1087. *Do Zan / Two Women* 1999 DS
D: Tahmineh Milani
S: Tahmineh Milani
C: Hossein Djafarian
A: Niki Karimi, Marila Zare'i

1980s. Two architecture students at Tehran University are friends. One, from the country, has problems with her father, her husband, and a stalker; the other, from the city, becomes a successful career woman. *New Directors. 2000.*

Other titles: Deux femmes

1088. *Ghermez / Red* 1999
D: Fereydun Jeyrani
S: Fereydun Jeyrani
C: Mahmoud Kalari
A: Hedyeh Tehrani

A hospital worker with a child marries a younger man, but he proves to be suspicious and violently repressive toward her, so she leaves him. Though the courts support her with an alimony judgment, she returns to him for another cycle of abuse. *Festival des 3.*

1089. *Arous-e atash / Bride of Fire* 2000
D: Khosro Sinai

A medical student is in love with her professor but engaged to an illiterate trader in southern Iran; not allowed to break the engagement, she douses her wedding bed with gasoline and sets it on fire, as one of her aunts stabs the bridegroom. *Variety: 31. 2000, May 29.*

Other titles: Arus atash

1090. *Baran / Rain* 2000
D: Majid Majidi
S: Majid Majidi
C: Mohammad Davudi

P: Majid Majidi
A: Zahra Bahrami, Hossein Abedini
An Afghan girl disguises herself as her dead father in order to keep his job as a construction worker across the Iran border.
Awards: Fajr Film Festival, Best Film, 2001; Gijon International Film Festival, Best Director, Best Screenplay; Montréal World Film Festival, Grand Prix, 2001

1091. *Dayereh / The Circle* 2000
D: Jafar Panahi
S: Kambuzia Partovi
C: Bahram Badakshani
P: Jafar Panahi
A: Nargess Mamizadeh, Maryiam Parvin Almani, Fereshteh Sadr-Orafai, Elham Saboktakin
Several women let out of prison one morning go through their first day of freedom in different ways; all under siege, they seek refuge and engage with other women on the margins of society. *The Nation: 34–36. 2001, Apr. 30.*
Other titles: Il Cerchio

1092. *Dokhtaran khorshid / Daughters of the Sun* 2000 DS
D: Maryam Shahriar
S: Maryam Shahriar
C: Homayun Payvar
P: Jahangir Kosari
A: Altinay Ghelich Taghani, Soghra Karimi
A young woman, the oldest of six children, is banished by her father to a servitude that requires her passing as a man so that she can send back money to the family. She lives at the isolated carpet-making factory, and one of the other working girls there falls in love with her. *Festival de films, 23rd: 24. 2001.*

1093. *Roozi khe zan shodam / The Day I Became a Woman* 2000 DS
D: Marziyeh Meshkini
S: Marziyeh Meshkini, Mohsen Makhmalbaf
C: Nohamad Ahmadi
P: Mohsen Makhmalbaf
A: Fatemeh Cherag Akhar, Shahr Banou Sisizadeh, Ameneh Passand
Three stories of women at different stages of life: A nine-year-old girl tries to free herself of the veil; a married woman seeks freedom in bicycle racing, but the men in her family oppose it; and an old woman takes the risk of seeking her dream by purchasing everything she ever wanted and sending it to a beach. *Festival des 3.*
Awards: Chicago International Film Festival, Silver Hugo, 2000; Thessaloniki Film Festival, Best

Director, 2000; Venice Film Festival, Best First Film, 2000

1094. *Sagkoshi / Killing Mad Dogs* 2000
D: Bahram Bayzai
S: Bahram Bayzai
C: Asghar Rafiyie Jam
P: Bahram Bayzai
A: Mozhde Shamsai
Tehran. A middle-class woman returns to the city after the revolution, but she is harassed by her husband's business enemies. *Village Voice: 120. 2001, Feb. 27.*
Other titles: Killing Rabids
Awards: Fajr Film Festival, Best Actress, 2001

1095. *Zir-e poost-e shahr / Under the City's Skin* 2000 DS
D: Rakhshan Bani-Etemad
S: Rakhshan Bani-Etemad, Farid Mostafavi
C: Hossein Jafarian
P: Jahangir Kosari
A: Golab Adineh, Homeira Riazi, Baran Kowsari
Tehran. A mother and textile-factory worker balances the demands of her children around the abuse to which women, particularly her grown daughters, are routinely subjected. *The Nation: 37. 2003, Mar. 24.*
Other titles: Under the Skin of the City
Awards: Karlovy Vary International Film Festival, Netpac Award, 2001; Moscow International Film Festival, Special Jury Prize, 2001

1096. *Nimeh-ye penhan / The Hidden Half* 2001 DSP
D: Tahmineh Milani
S: Tahmineh Milani
C: Mahmoud Kalari
P: Tahmineh Milani
A: Niki Karimi
The wife of a judge, who has been sent to the countryside to hear the appeal of a woman sentenced to death, gives him her diary of her past life of activism in hopes of giving him empathy for the accused; the judge knew nothing of his wife's past. *Variety: 43. 2001, Feb. 19.*
Awards: Cairo International Film Festival, Best Actress, 2001

1097. *Safar e ghandehar / Kandahar* 2001
D: Mohsen Makhmalbaf
S: Mohsen Makhmalbaf
C: Ebrahim Ghafori
P: Mohsen Makhmalbaf
A: Nelofer Pazira
A Canadian immigrant barters her way back into

Afghanistan to find her sister, who has threat-ened to commit suicide. *The Nation: 37. 2001, Dec. 10.*

Awards: Cannes Film Festival, Ecumenical Jury Prize, 2001; Thessaloniki Film Festival, FIPRESCI, 2001

1098. *Bemani / Stay Alive* 2002 P
D: Dariush Mehrjui
S: Dariush Mehrjui, Vahidéa Mohammadi
C: Bahram Badakshani
P: Dariush Mehrjui, Tahmineh Milani
A: Neda Aghaei
A young woman fights the dullness of her imposed marriage to an older man. *MOMA Film. 2003, May.*

1099. *Emtehan / Exam* 2002
D: Nasser Refaie
S: Nasser Refaie
C: Farzad Judat
P: Davoud Rashidi
A: Raya Nasiri
Tehran. Women arrive at a school to take the university entrance exam; there are many con-flicts because very few of the women will be accepted into university. *FII.*

Awards: Mannheim-Heidelberg International Film Festival, Special Jury Prize, 2002

1100. *Zendan-e zanan / Women's Prison* 2002 DSP
D: Manijeh Hekmat
S: Manijeh Hekmat, Farid Mostafavi
C: Dariush Ayyari
P: Manijeh Hekmat
A: Roya Teymourian, Roya Nonahali, Pegah Ahan-garani
A woman is "in jail for killing her abusive stepfa-ther." The film follows two decades of her mal-treatment by an oppressive female warden. *FII.*

Awards: Fribourg International Film Festival, Ecu-menical Jury Prize, 2003; Rotterdam Inter-national Film Festival, Amnesty International Award, 2003

1101. *Panj é asr / At Five in the Afternoon* 2003 DSC
D: Samira Makhmalbaf
S: Samira Makhmalbaf, Mohsen Makhmalbaf
C: Samira Makhmalbaf
P: Mohsen Makhmalbaf
A: Agheleh Rezaie
Kabul, Afghanistan. A young woman is desperate for an education and attends a Muslim school until she must flee into the desert, taking her infant nephew and father with her. *Film Society. 2005, Feb.*

Awards: Cannes Film Festival, Jury Prize, 2003

1102. *Ten* 2003
D: Abbas Kiarostami
S: Abbas Kiarostami
C: Abbas Kiarostami
P: Marin Karmitz
A: Mania Akbari
Tehran. While working in her cab, a taxi driver contends with several passengers: her sister; a friend who has been abandoned by her husband; an acquaintance who does not want to marry; an elderly conservative woman; a prostitute ("We're the wholesalers, you're the retailers"); and most persistently, her preteen son, who hates his new stepfather and lets her know at every opportunity.
Other titles: 10

IRAQ

1103. *Gazala* 1967
D: Mohamed Ali Safa
C: Androws Isa
A: Salim Siwis, Abdl Hamed
A poor family wishes to marry off its oldest daughter to a wealthy old man in expectation of gaining his estate quickly; she commits suicide. *Recherche du Cinéma: 177.*

1104. *Al Zawraq / The Boat* 1977
D: Groupe de jeunes cinéastes
S: Qa'id Al Nomani, Ahmed Al Iman
C: Adrian Al Iman
A: Sami Oaftan
A pregnant woman is saved from suicide by a fish-erman, who marries her after hearing her sad story, but the village gossips torment her until she flees. *Recherche du Cinéma: 181.*
Other titles: La Barque

1105. *Al Tejruba / The Experiment* 1980
D: Fuad Al Tohami
A: Alima Khudhair
1960s, before the revolution. Two stories: one of peasant resistance, the other of a pregnant girl who demands that she and her baby live. *FII.*

IRELAND

1106. *I Can't . . . I Can't* 1969
D: Piers Haggard
S: Piers Haggard, Lee Dunne, Robert I. Holt
C: Ray Sturgess

P: Philip Krasne
A: Tessy Wyatt, Dennis Waterman
Dublin. At a wedding, the bride's mother dies because of a miscarriage with her seventh child. Subsequently, the woman so fears pregnancy and the church's prohibition against contraception that she is unable to consummate her marriage, frustrating her husband and leading her to attempt suicide. *Irish Filmography: 24.*
Other titles: *Wedding Night*

1107. *Images* 1972 S
D: Robert Altman
S: Susannah York, Robert Altman
C: Vilmos Zsigmond
P: Tommy Thompson
A: Susannah York, Rene Auberjonois
A woman is immersed in the chaotic imagery of a woman writer, who is in turn plagued by visions of former lovers and painful events from her past. She wreaks havoc on herself and her husband. Horror.
Awards: Cannes Film Festival, Best Actress, 1972

1108. *Maeve* 1981 DSP
D: Pat Murphy, John Davies
S: Pat Murphy
C: Robert Smith
P: Pat Murphy
A: Mary Jackson, Brid Brennan, John Keegan
Belfast. A woman returns from London to the Republican enclave where her family lives; the apartment is street level, and the entire neighborhood is surrounded by checkpoints. She takes offense at her lover's view of women's rights as a danger to the Republican cause.

1109. *Ascendancy* 1982 P
D: Edward Bennett
S: Edward Bennett, Nigel Gearing
C: Clive Tickner
P: Penny Clark
A: Julie Covington
Belfast, 1920s. A sheltered woman from a wealthy Protestant Unionist family grows to ally herself with Irish independence after her brother is killed in World War I. *Time Out.*
Awards: Berlin International Film Festival, Golden Bear, 1983

1110. *Attracta* 1983
D: Kieran Hickey
S: William Trevor
C: Sean Corcoran
P: Douglas Kennedy
A: Wendy Hiller, Kate Thompson
County Cork, 1950s. An elderly woman breaks down at the grave of a friend; with the help of a doctor, she looks back on her years as a Protestant schoolteacher during the middle of the century and the political violence that surrounded her. *Irish Filmography.*

1111. *Anne Devlin* 1984 DSP
D: Pat Murphy
S: Pat Murphy
C: Thaddeus O'Sullivan
P: Pat Murphy
A: Brid Brennan
Ireland, 1798. The true story of an activist member of the Republicans, who poses as a housekeeper and provides cover for rebels while they execute an uprising, then are quickly caught. She is jailed and tortured, but she remains righteous and proud and never informs on the men, many of whom do inform.

1112. *Cal* 1984
D: Pat O'Connor
S: Bernard MacLaverty
C: Jerzy Zielinski
P: David Putnam
A: Helen Mirren, John Lynch
A woman, whose constable husband has been murdered by the Irish Republican Army, has an affair with a teenager involved in the IRA mission that killed him.
Awards: Cannes Film Festival, Best Actress, 1984; Evening Standard British Film Awards, Best Actress, 1985

1113. *Fragments of Isabella* 1989 S
D: Ronan O'Leary
S: Ronan O'Leary; based on the novel by Isabella Leitner
C: Walter Lassally
A: Gabrielle Reidy
A monologue from a Hungarian Jew recalling her life at Auschwitz—and her escape. *FII.*

1114. *Undercurrents* 1990
D: Stephen Rooke
A: Mary McGuckian, Sighle Tóibín
Dublin. A musician becomes jealous and abandons a roommate from school when a man falls in love with her and they marry. Their closeness returns when the friend and her daughter attend a concert of the musician, who confides in her friend the abuse she experienced as a child from her father. *Irish Filmography: 49.*

1115. *Circle of Friends* 1995 S
D: Pat O'Connor
S: Andrew Davies; based on the novel by Maeve Binchy
C: Kenneth MacMillan
P: Frank Price
A: Minnie Driver, Geraldin O'Rawe, Saffron Burrows
High school seniors split up during summer, then reunite at Trinity College in Dublin.

1116. *Words upon the Window Pane* 1995 DSP
D: Mary McGuckian
S: Mary McGuckian; based on the play by W. B. Yeats
C: William Diver
P: Anna Devlin
A: Geraldine Chaplin, Geraldine James
Dublin, 1920s. An American from England is invited to a séance, where the ghost of Jonathan Swift is avenged by the ghost of his unacknowledged lover. *FII.*

1117. *Snakes and Ladders* 1996 DSP
D: Trish McAdam
S: Trish McAdam
C: Dietrich Lohmann
P: Lilyan Sievernich
A: Pam Boyd, Gina Moxley, Sean Hughes
Dublin. Young roommates find a modest living and enjoyment being street performers. When a boyfriend proposes, they turn away from their free life toward the wedding and pregnancy, which wreaks havoc on both relationships.

1118. *Some Mother's Son* 1996
D: Terry George
S: Terry George, Jim Sheridan
C: Geoffrey Simpson
P: Edward Burke
A: Helen Mirren, Fionnula Flanagan
1981. Two mothers, one apolitical, the other an IRA supporter, both have sons in prison for IRA activity; they alternately clash and join forces in dealing with their sons' participation in the hunger strike of 1981.
Awards: San Sebastián International Film Festival, Audience Award, 1996

1119. *Dancing at Lughnasa* 1998
D: Pat O'Connor
S: Brian Friel, Frank McGuinness
C: Kenneth MacMillan
P: Noel Pearson
A: Meryl Streep, Catherine McCormack, Kathy Burke, Brid Brennan

Donegal, 1930s. Five unmarried sisters, one with a young son, struggle economically. The oldest performs a matriarchal role, supporting them with her position as a teacher and using two of them as servants. When she loses her job because of her strict manner, their close ties are loosened forever.
Awards: IFTA Awards, Best Actress (Brennan), 1999

1120. *Nora* 2000 DS
D: Pat Murphy
S: Pat Murphy; based on a biography by Brenda Maddox
C: Jean-François Robin
P: Bradley Adams
A: Susan Lynch, Ewan McGregor
Nora Barnacle, a hotel maid, meets and seduces James Joyce; despite his higher education, they remain lovers throughout life, move to Venice, and have children.
Other titles: James Joyce's Nora
Awards: Cherbourg-Octeville Festival of Irish & British Film, Best Actress, 2000; IFTA Awards, Best Actress, 2000

1121. *When the Sky Falls* 2000
D: John MacKenzie
S: Michael Sheridan, Ronan Gallagher
C: Seamus Deasy
P: Michael Wearing
A: Joan Allen, Patrick Bergin
Based on the case of Dublin newspaper reporter Veronica Guerin, who was assassinated for investigating the drug trade. *FII.*

1122. *Silent Grace* 2002 DSP
D: Maeve Murphy
S: Maeve Murphy
C: David Katznelson
P: Maeve Murphy
A: Orla Brady, Cathleen Bradley, Cara Seymour
"Drama set in Armagh women's prison during the 1981 hunger strikes." *FII.*

1123. *Magdalene Sisters* 2003 P
D: Peter Mullan
S: Peter Mullan
C: Nigel Willoughby
P: Frances Higson
A: Anne-Marie Duff, Geraldine McEwan, Nora-Jane Noone, Dorothy Duffy
1960s. Young, single women who are pregnant, aggressive, or otherwise shunned are sent off by their families to a commercial laundry run by nuns, who treat them as slaves.

ISRAEL

1124. *Matzor / Siege* 1969 S
D: Gilberto Tofano
S: Gilberto Tofano, Dahn Ben Amotz, Gila Almagor
C: David Gurfinkel
P: Ya'ackov Agmon
A: Gila Almagor
A woman is widowed in the Six Day War; even though she has a young child, she despairs. *Companion Encyclopedia: 292.*

1125. *Ani ohev otach Rosa / I Love You Rosa* 1972
D: Moshé Mizrahi
S: Moshé Mizrahi
C: Adam Greenberg
P: Menahem Golan
A: Michal Bat-Adam, Zivi Avramson, Naomi Bachar
A Sephardic Jew is widowed, then promised to her husband's eleven-year-old brother. *Companion Encyclopedia: 242.*

1126. *Michael sheli / My Michael* 1975 S
D: Dan Wolman
S: Esther Mor, Dan Wolman
C: Adam Greenberg
A: Efrat Lavi, Oded Kotler
Jerusalem, 1950s. An Israeli teacher goes mad and withdraws into her fantasies of play with Palestinian childhood friends. *Companion Encyclopedia: 294.*

1127. *Ma'agalim shel shishabat / Weekend Circles* 1980 DS
D: Idit Shechori
S: Idit Shechori
C: Nurit Aviv
P: Yehezkel Alani
A: Rahel Shein, Hava Ortman, Noa Cohen-Raz, Galit Gil
Four women spend a weekend together drinking, playing, and discussing sex. *Companion Encyclopedia: 288.*

1128. *Atalia* 1984
D: Akiva Tevet, Tzvika Kretzner
S: Tzvika Kretzner
C: Nurit Aviv
P: Omri Maron
A: Michal Bat-Adam
A widow who lives on a kibbutz takes a younger lover, but pressures from the community drive them into the city. *Companion Encyclopedia: 243.*

1129. *Ahavata ha'ahronah shel Laura Adler / Laura Adler's Last Love Affair* 1990
D: Avraham Heffner
S: Avraham Heffner
C: David Gurfinkel
P: Marek Rozenbaum
A: Rita Zohar
A stage actress gets a job in Hollywood but then discovers she has cancer. *Companion Encyclopedia: 238.*

1130. *Autobiographia dimionit / Imagined Autobiography* 1994 DS
D: Michal Bat-Adam
S: Michal Bat-Adam
C: Yoav Kosh
P: Marek Rozenbaum
A: Michal Bat-Adam
A filmmaker takes care of her children and father while she makes a film about her childhood and mentally ill mother. *Companion Encyclopedia: 245.*

1131. *Sh'hur* 1994 S
D: Shmuel Hasfari
S: Hana Azoulay-Hasfari
C: David Gurfinkel
A: Hana Azoulay-Hasfari, Gila Almagor, Ronit Elkabetz
A television journalist returns for her father's funeral to the small town near Jerusalem where her Moroccan immigrant family lives. Picking up her institutionalized sister and her own young silent daughter on the way, she recalls the rape her sister endured because their brother took advantage of a neighbor girl. At home, other childhood memories flood her mind: her mother's penchant for white magic, her older sister's bitter arranged marriage, and her father's repressiveness.
Awards: Israeli Film Academy, Best Film, Best Director, Best Screenplay, Best Supporting Actress (Elkabetz), 1994; Berlin International Film Festival, Special Mention, 1995

1132. *Ahava mimabat sheni / Love at Second Sight* 1998 D
D: Michal Bat-Adam
S: Michal Bat-Adam
A: Michal Zoharetz
A newspaper photographer shares her home with an elderly man, cares for her grandfather, and covers the story of a threatened suicide.

1133. *Chronika shel ahava / Chronicle of Love* 1999 DS
D: Tzipi Trope

S: Tzipi Trope
A: Sharon Alexander, Tanya Sobolev, Nitzan Bartana
A social worker visits battered women during the day, lives with her architect husband, and hides the secret of her own victimization. *Jewish Film. Accessed 2005, Jan. 9.*

1134. *Ahot zara / Foreign Sister*   2000
D: Dan Wolman
S: Dan Wolman
C: Itamar Hadar
P: Dan Wolman
A: Tamar Yerushalmi, Askala Marcus
A happy housewife and mother hires an Ethiopian Christian woman as a maid and becomes aware of the problems of illegal migrant workers. *African Diaspora. 2001. Accessed 2004, Aug. 15.*

1135. *Chaverim shel Yana, ha / Yana's Friends*
                                                      2000
D: Arik Kaplun
S: Arik Kaplun, Semyon Vinokur
C: Valentin Belonogov
P: Anet Bikel
A: Evlyn Kaplun
A pregnant woman from Moscow is abandoned in Tel Aviv by her husband, so she makes friends with a photographer and the landlady. *Companion Encyclopedia: 269.*

1136. *Kadosh*   2000 S
D: Amos Gitai
S: Amos Gitai, Eliette Abecassis
C: Renato Berta
P: Amos Gitai
A: Meital Barda, Yaël Abecassis
Jerusalem, Mea Shearim quarter. Two sisters struggle with the pressures of their ultra-Orthodox Jewish culture; the childless elder sister sees her husband encouraged to find another woman, and the younger must give up her true love. *Companion Encyclopedia: 280.*

1137. *Mars Turkey / Clean Sweep*   2000 S
D: Oded Davidoff
S: Limor Nachmias, Gal Zaid
C: Gideon Porath
A: Yael Hadar, Dalit Kahan
An undercover police detective investigates a drug dealer but is betrayed by a superior officer, also her lover. Thriller. *Variety: 28. 2003, June 30.*
Awards: Israeli Film Academy, Best Supporting Actress (Kahan), 2001

1138. *Avanim / Stones*   2003
D: Raphaël Nadjari

S: Raphaël Nadjari
C: Laurent Brunet
P: Geoffroy Grison
A: Asi Levi
A married woman with a small child has an affair, while she also struggles with "her father's financially questionable affiliation with orthodox religious institutions." *MOMA Film. 2004, Nov.*
Awards: Geneva Cinéma Tout Ecran, Grand Prix, 2004

1139. *Knafayim shvurot / Broken Wings*   2004
D: Nir Bergman
S: Nir Bergman
C: Valentin Belonogov
P: Assaf Amir
A: Orli Zilberschatz-Banai, Maya Maron
Haifa. A recently widowed mother of four copes with her job and conflicts with her children, particularly the oldest, a seventeen-year-old daughter. *Village Voice: 63. 2004, Mar. 10.*
Awards: Israeli Film Academy, Best Film, Best Director, Best Actress (Zilberschatz-Banai), Best Supporting Actress (Maron), 2002; Tokyo International Film Festival, Grand Prix, 2002; Berlin International Film Festival, Jury Prize, 2003

1140. *Or (mon trésor) / Or (My Treasure)*
                                                      2004 DS
D: Karen Yedaya
S: Karen Yedaya, Sari Ezouz
C: Laurent Brunet
P: Emmanuel Agneray
A: Dana Ivgi, Ronit Elkabetz
An unstable mother, who sometimes works as a prostitute, depends on her teenage daughter, who works in a restaurant and has her own problems with her boyfriend. *London Film: 59. 2004.*
Awards: Bratislava International Film Festival, Grand Prix, 2004; Cannes Film Festival, Golden Camera, 2004

1141. *Ve'lakhta lehe isha / To Take a Wife*
                                                      2004 DS
D: Ronit Elkabetz, Shlomi Elkabetz
S: Ronit Elkabetz, Shlomi Elkabetz
C: Yaron Scharf
P: Eric Cohen
A: Ronit Elkabetz, Simon Abkarian
Haifa, 1970s. A woman demands a divorce and gets in response a nightlong caucus with her husband's male relatives, who scream and pontificate until she relents. Daily life is painful; her husband participates only in religious activities, while she works as a beautician, fends off

his demands, and deals with their four young children. A brief afternoon with a former lover gives a respite.

Awards: Bratislava International Film Festival, Grand Prix, 2004; Cannes Film Festival, Golden Camera, 2004

ITALY

1142. *Adua e le compagne / Adua and Company* 1960
D: Antonio Pietrangelo
S: Antonio Pietrangelo, Ruggero Maccari, Ettora Scola
C: Armando Nannuzi
P: Moris Ergas
A: Simone Signoret, Gina Rovere, Sandra Milo, Emmanuelle Riva

Rome, 1958. Four friends are put out of business when a new law closes brothels. The oldest succeeds in setting them up in a restaurant in the country, but a man buys out their lease and insists they use the business as a cover for prostitution. Having seen a chance for a different kind of life, they refuse.

Other titles: Hungry for Love

1143. *L'Avventura* 1960
D: Michelangelo Antonioni
S: Michelangelo Antonioni, Elio Bartolini, Tonino Guerra
C: Aldo Scavarda
A: Monica Vitti, Lea Massari, Gabriel Ferzetti

A woman disappears while touring a deserted island with friends; her fiancé and a woman friend search for her but give up over time as they grow to form a couple themselves.

1144. *La Ciociara / Two Women* 1961
D: Vittorio De Sica
S: Cesare Zavattini; based on the novel by Alberto Moravia
C: Gabor Pogany
P: Carlo Ponti
A: Sophia Loren, Eleanora Brown, Jean-Paul Belmondo

1943. A mother and teenage daughter leave Rome after an air raid; bombings infest the countryside as well, but they find brief refuge with relatives in their hometown; Germans threaten them there, and the mother decides to return to Rome. On the way back, the pair are gang-raped by marauding "Moroccans." The stunned girl seeks to clean herself in a creek but remains speechless; finding out that a dear friend has been killed by the Germans, both finally are able to grieve.

Awards: Academy Awards, Best Actress (Loren), 1962

1145. *La Ragazza con la valiglia / The Girl with the Suitcase* 1961
D: Valerio Zurlini
S: Valerio Zurlini, Leo Benvenuti
C: Tino Santoni
P: Maurizo Lodi
A: Claudia Cardinale

A nightclub singer leaves her job for a rich man, who abandons her. She follows him to his country home and becomes involved with his sixteen-year-old brother. *Dizionario del cinema, vol. 2.*

Awards: Cannes Film Festival, nomination for Golden Palm, 1961

1146. *Mamma Roma* 1962
D: Pier Paolo Pasolini
S: Pier Paolo Pasolini, Sergio Citti
C: Tonino Delli Colli
P: Alfred Bini
A: Anna Magnani, Franco Citti

Rome. A middle-aged ex-prostitute with an ambitious and extroverted character—she crashes her old lover's wedding with a pig as her date—tries to lift herself and her beloved young son above their social station. But the projects outside the city where she tries to establish a new life are not far enough away.

1147. *Deserto rosso / The Red Desert* 1964
D: Michelangelo Antonioni
S: Michelangelo Antonioni, Tonino Guerra
C: Carlo Di Palma
P: Angelo Rizzoli
A: Monica Vitti

Ravenna. The wife of an engineer suffers with depression and is directly affected by the environmentally devastated landscape around the factory where the film is set, finding no pleasure even in her child. A man tries to "help" by seducing her, but her detached view remains unchanged: "Apparently, I'm cured enough to become an unfaithful wife."

1148. *La Fuga / The Escape* 1964
D: Paolo Spinola
S: Paolo Spinola, Piero Bellanova, Sergio Amidei
C: Marcello Gatti
P: Alberto Casati
A: Giovanna Ralli, Anouk Aimée

"A young married woman who is desperately unhappy" finds happiness in a lesbian relationship with an interior decorator, but nevertheless commits suicide. *FII. Also lez films. Accessed 2005, June 10.*

Awards: Italian National Syndicate of Film Journalists, Best Actress (Ralli), 1966

1149. *Goodbye in the Mirror* 1964 D
D: Storm De Hirsch
A: Charlotte Bradley
Rome. The story of "the relationships an American girl living in Rome has with her flat mates and her lover." The only feature film of an experimental filmmaker well known for her shorts. *FII.*

1150. *Giulietta degli spiriti* / *Juliet of the Spirits* 1965
D: Federico Fellini
S: Federico Fellini, Tullio Pinelli
C: Gianni Di Venanzo
P: Angelo Rizzoli
A: Giulietta Masina
A film director's wife, a middle-aged bourgeois woman, dreams of leaving her unfaithful husband; fantasies regarding her past, her friends, and her family invade the equally fantastical present.
Awards: New York Film Critics Circle Awards, Best Foreign Language Film, 1965; Golden Globes, Best Foreign Language Film, 1966

1151. *Madamigella di Maupin* / *Mademoiselle de Maupin* 1965
D: Mauro Bolognini
S: Théophile Gautier, Luigi Magni
C: Roberto Gerardi
A: Catherine Spaak
Disguised as a man, a woman joins the army to find out more about men. Comedy. *FII.*
Awards: San Sebastián International Film Festival, Best Director, 1966

1152. *Le Soldatesse* / *The Camp Followers* 1965
D: Valerio Zurlini
S: P. De Bernadi
C: Tonino Delli Colli
P: Moris Ergas
A: Anna Karina, Lea Massari, Valeria Moriconi, Tomas Milian
Fifteen Athens prostitutes are escorted by an infantry truck to work among the Italian soldiers; empathy and love develop among them. *Film Society. 2000, Sep.*
Awards: Moscow International Film Festival, nomination for Grand Prix, 1965

1153. *Vaghe stelle dell'Orsa* / *Sandra* 1965 S
D: Luchino Visconti
S: Suso Cecchi D'Amico, Enrico Medioli
A: Claudia Cardinale
Volterra. A woman returns "for the commemoration of a public park in honor of her Jewish father, who died in Auschwitz." Her brother, with whom she has an incestuous relationship, tells her that it was their mother who surrendered their father. *MOMA Film. 2004, Nov. Also Festival de films, 22nd: 73. 2000.*
Awards: Venice Film Festival, Golden Lion, 1965

1154. *Diario di una schizofrenica* / *Diary of a Schizophrenic Girl* 1968 S
D: Nelo Risi
S: Nelo Risi, Fabio Carpi; based on *Journal d'une schizofrène* by Margeurite Ardrée Sechehaye
P: Gian Vittorio
A: Ghislaine D'Orsay, Margarita Lozano
A young woman is treated in a clinic by a woman psychiatrist. *Dizionario del cinema, vol. 2.*

1155. *I Cannibali* / *The Cannibals* 1969 DS
D: Liliana Cavani
S: Liliana Cavani, Italo Moscati; based on *Antigone* by Sophocles
C: Guilio Albonico
P: Enzo Doria
A: Britt Eklund
A loose reworking in contemporary fascist Italy of the story of Antigone, her father, and her brother, who, in this version, wants to become an animal. *AMG.*
Other titles: Antigone

1156. *Medea* 1970 P
D: Pier Paolo Pasolini
S: Pier Paolo Pasolini; based on the play by Euripides
C: Ennio Guarnieri
P: Marina Cicogna
A: Maria Callas
Medea, thought to be a witch, falls in love with Jason, for whom she kills her brother. Then Jason decides he must leave her to marry a king's daughter. To exact revenge on him, Medea murders the woman, him, and then Jason's sons. "Febrile version." *Variety: 26. 1970, Mar. 11. Also Cinemythology. Accessed 2005, July 13.*

1157. *L'Ospite* / *The Guest* 1972 DS
D: Liliana Cavani
S: Liliana Cavani
C: Guilio Albonico
A: Lucia Bosé

A seventy-year-old writer is released after many years in a mental hospital. She tries to live with her brother but eventually returns to the security of confinement. *Dizionario del cinema, vol. 3.*

1158. *Pianeta Venere / Planet Venus* 1972 DS
D: Elda Tattoli
S: Elda Tattoli
C: Dario DiPalma
P: Turi Vasile
A: Marina Berti, Lilla Brignone, Bedi Moratti
1940s–1970s. An ambitious politician dominates a young girl, forcing her to have an abortion and accepting the donation of her eye (he had lost his in the war). Finally she is able to leave him, and she then becomes involved in the women's movement. *AMG. Also Dizionario del cinema, vol. 3.*

1159. *Una Breve vacanza / A Brief Vacation*
1973 P
D: Vittorio De Sica
S: Cesare Zavattini
C: Ennio Guarnieri
P: Marina Cicogna
A: Florinda Bolkan
A factory worker contracts tuberculosis and leaves her macho husband and children for a sanitarium in the Alps, where she finds she can enjoy life. *FII.*

1160. *Cari genitori / Dear Parents* 1973 S
D: Enrico Maria Salerno
S: Enrico Maria Salerno, Lina Wertmüller
C: Dario Di Palma
A: Maria Schneider, Florinda Bolkan, Catherine Spaak
London. A bourgeois Italian goes to England to find her eighteen-year-old daughter, whom she has not seen in many years, and finds her living in a hippie commune, creating avant-garde theater that promotes abortion rights for women. Their meeting becomes further strained when the daughter announces she has a lesbian lover. *Festival de films, 23rd: 70. 2001.*
Awards: David di Donatello Awards, Best Actress (Bolkan, Schneider), 1973

1161. *Il Portiere di notte / The Night Porter*
1974 DSP
D: Liliana Cavani
S: Barbara Albert, Liliana Cavani
C: Alfio Contini
P: Esa De Simone
A: Charlotte Rampling, Dirk Bogarde
A concentration camp survivor freely walks away

from a comfortable life, her family, and children and resumes her former sadistic relationship with her Nazi torturer, now a night porter in a hotel. He has been carefully hiding his past and current ties to other former Nazis, who all fear exposure, but succumbs to her insistence that they resume their relationship. They become trapped as he imagines they have a love.

1162. *Travolti da un insolito destino nell'azzurro mare d'Agosto / Swept Away . . . By an Unusual Destiny in the Blue Sea of August*
1975 DS
D: Lina Wertmüller
S: Lina Wertmüller
C: Giulio Battiferri
P: Mano Cardarelli
A: Mariangela Melato, Giancarlo Giannini
"Upper class Milanese factory owner is stranded with a yacht hand on a tiny island where they fall in love. After being rescued, he goes back to wife and family, and she returns to her usual life." *FII.*

1163. *L'Erdità Ferramonti / The Inheritance*
1976
D: Mauro Bolognini
S: Ugo Pirro, Sergio Bazzini
C: Ennio Guarnieri
P: Gianni Lucari
A: Fabio Testi, Dominique Sanda, Adriani Asti
"Period drama. A woman of petit bourgeois origins sets about making a fortune by marrying into the rich Ferramonti family." *FII.*
Awards: Cannes Film Festival, Best Actress (Sanda), 1976; Italian National Syndicate of Film Journalists, Best Supporting Actress (Asti), 1977

1164. *Io sono mia / I Belong to Me* 1977 DS
D: Sofia Scandurra
S: Lu Leone, Sofia Scandurra; based on the novel by Dacia Maraini
C: Nurit Aviv
P: Lu Leone
A: Maria Schneider, Stefania Sandrelli
A rich, disabled young woman befriends a housewife and raises her "feminist consciousness." *FII.*

1165. *Mogliamante / Wifemistress* 1977
D: Marco Vicario
S: Rodolfo Somego
C: Ennio Guarnieri
P: Franco Cristaldi
A: Laura Antonelli
A wife takes over her husband's wine business while he hides from the police. *FII.*

1166. *Un Fatto di sangue fra due uomini per cause di una vedova—si sospettano moventi politici / Blood Feud*   1978 DS
D: Lina Wertmüller
S: Lina Wertmüller
C: Tonino Delli Colli
P: Arrigo Colombo
A: Sophia Loren, Marcello Mastroianni, Giancarlo Giannini
Sicily. A woman is widowed by a mafia murder, then falls in love with two men. One is an organizer of the resistance against Mussolini, and the other is a gangster. *Variety: 20. 1979, Feb. 7.*

1167. *La Fine del mondo nel nostro solito letto in una notte piena di pioggia / Night Full of Rain*   1978 DS
D: Lina Wertmüller
S: Lina Wertmüller
C: Guiseppe Rotunno
P: Gil Shiva
A: Candice Bergen, Giancarlo Giannini
An American photographer marries an Italian journalist, an "old line communist." She's liberated, but he is not. *AMG.*
Other titles: The End of the World (In Our Usual Bed in a Night Full of Rain)

1168. *Immacolata e concetta / Two Women in Love*   1979 S
D: Salvatore Piscicelli
S: Salvatore Piscicelli, Carla Apuzzo
C: Emilio Bestetti
A: Ida Di Benedetto, Marcella Michelangeli
Naples. Two women meet in prison and fall in love. One is in prison for murdering her lover's husband, the other for facilitating prostitution. *FII.*
Awards: Locarno International Film Festival, Silver Leopard, 1979; Italian National Syndicate of Film Journalists, Best Actress (Di Benedetto), 1980

1169. *La Luna*   1979 S
D: Bernardo Bertolucci
S: Bernardo Bertolucci, Franco Arcalli, Clare Peploe
C: Vittorio Storaro
P: Giovanni Bertolucci
A: Jill Clayburgh
A preoccupied opera singer tries to focus more on her teenage son when she learns he is addicted to drugs.
Awards: Golden Globes, nomination for Best Actress, 1980

1170. *Salto nel vuoto / Leap into the Void* 1980
D: Marco Bellocchio
S: Vincenzo Cerami, Marco Bellocchio

C: Giuseppe Lanci
A: Anouk Aimée, Michel Piccoli
"A forty-year-old woman discovers that she has thrown her youth away in order to take care of her brother." *FII.*
Other titles: Le Saut dans le vide
Awards: Cannes Film Festival, Best Actress, Best Actor, 1980; David di Donatello Awards, Best Director, 1980

1171. *Oltre la porta / Beyond the Door* 1982 DS
D: Liliana Cavani
S: Liliana Cavani, Enrico Medioli
C: Luciano Tovoli
P: Francesco Giorgi
A: Eleanora Giorgi, Marcello Mastroianni
A daughter who believes her father caused her mother's death withholds information that could free him from prison. *FII.*

1172. *Il Processo di Caterina Ross / The Trial of Caterina Ross*   1982 DS
D: Gabriella Rosaleva
S: Gabriella Rosaleva
C: Renato Tafori
A: Daniela Moretti
Switzerland, seventeenth century. A young girl, the progeny of witches, is put on trial in a small Italian-speaking village. The film setting is a modern warehouse near a railway station; long takes are focused on the accused, with the prosecutor offscreen. *Variety: 25. 1982, Aug. 25.*

1173. *Storia di Piera / Piera's Story*   1983 S
D: Marco Ferreri
S: Piera Degli Esposti, Marco Ferreri
C: Ennio Guarnieri
P: Achille Manzotti
A: Isabelle Huppert, Hanna Schygulla, Marcello Mastroianni
The story of an actress and her relationship with her mother, an unfaithful wife who eventually went into a psychiatric hospital. *FII.*
Awards: Cannes Film Festival, Best Actress (Schygulla), 1983; Sant Jordi Awards, Best Foreign Actress (Schygulla), Best Foreign Actor, 1985

1174. *Pianoforte*   1984 DS
D: Francesca Comencini
S: Francesca Comencini
C: Armando Nunnuzzi
A: Giulia Boschi, Marie-Christine Barrault, François Siener
Two heroin addicts try to become normal by living apart, but when reunited, they fall into bad

habits again; finally, he commits suicide and she lives on. *AMG.*

Awards: Italian National Syndicate of Film Journalists, Best New Actress (Boschi), 1985

1175. *Sotto, sotto . . . strapazzato da anomala passione / A Jealous Man* 1984 DS
D: Lina Wertmüller
S: Lina Wertmüller, Enrico Oldoini
A: Veronica Lario, Luisa De Santis, Enrico Montesano

Rome. Two friends enjoy walking in the park and discover an attraction for one another; the carpenter husband of one becomes very jealous.
Other titles: Softly, softly

1176. *Un Complicato intrigo di donne, vicoli e delitte / The Naples Connection* 1985 DS
D: Lina Wertmüller
S: Lina Wertmüller, Elvio Porta
C: Giuseppe Lanci
P: Menahem Golan, Yoram Globus
A: Angela Molina, Harvey Keitel, Isa Danieli

Naples. A former child prostitute runs a boarding house while her young son sells drugs; around them gangsters are being murdered by a group of mothers whose children have been murdered. *FII.*
Other titles: Camorra: The Naples Connection
Awards: Berlin International Film Festival, Interfilm Award, 1986; David di Donatello Awards, Best Actress (Molina), 1986

1177. *Fuori dal mondo / Not of This World*
1985 S
D: Giuseppe Piccioni
S: Giuseppe Piccioni, Gualtiero Rosella, Lucia Maria Zei
C: Luca Bigazzi
P: Lionella Cerri
A: Margherita Buy

A nun is handed a lost baby in a park, and after taking it to the hospital, makes an effort to find the parents. Her search leads to a dry-cleaning shop and an unhappy man, whose employee may be the baby's mother. The episode makes the nun question her vocation. *IMDb.*
Awards: AFI Fest, Best Film, Grand Jury Prize, 1999; David di Donatello Awards, Best Film, Best Screenplay, Best Actress, 1999

1178. *Il Futuro è donna / The Future Is Woman* 1985 S
D: Marco Ferreri
S: Marco Ferreri, Dacia Maraini, Piera Degli Esposti, Christine Lembach

C: Tonino Delli Colli
P: Achille Manzotti
A: Ornella Muti, Hanna Schygulla

A childless middle-class couple develop a relationship with a single pregnant woman who moves in with them. *West German Cinema.*
Other titles: Die Zukunft

1179. *Interno Berlinese / The Berlin Affair*
1985 DS
D: Liliana Cavani
S: Liliana Cavani, Roberta Mazzoni; based on the novel by Junichiro Tanizaki
C: Dante Spinotti
P: Fulvio Luciano
A: Gudrun Landgrebe, Mio Takaki, Kevin McNally

Berlin, 1930s. A Japanese woman of the elite international community is a powerful seducer who engages a husband and wife in a suicide pact. *Variety: 28. 1985, Nov. 6.*

1180. *Speriamo che sia femmina / Let's Hope It's a Girl* 1985 S
D: Mario Monicelli
S: Mario Monicelli, Suso Cecchi D'Amico
C: Camillo Bazzoni
P: Giovanni Di Clemente
A: Liv Ullmann, Catherine Deneuve, Stefania Sandrelli, Athina Cenci

Sisters, one the matriarch of the family farm, the other a famous actress in Rome, take care of business while the men in their lives are either gone, abusive, or dreaming. The funeral of an ex-husband attracts his mistress to the farm, who adds to the easygoing camaraderie. One of the younger generation awaits a newborn, and the women acknowledge that they get along best with one another and "hope it's a girl."
Awards: David di Donatello Awards, Best Director, Best Supporting Actress (Cenci), 1986; Italian National Syndicate of Film Journalists, Best Director, Best Screenplay, 1986

1181. *La Ballata di Eva / The Ballad of Eve*
1986
D: Francesco Longo
S: Francesco Longo
C: Claudio Meloni
P: Francesco Longo
A: Ida Di Benedetto

Naples. A fifteen-year-old has been left with her grandmother while her mother works in a factory in Turin. When she disappears, the mother must fight the pimps who've befriended her daughter. *Variety. 1986, June 11.*

1182. **Cronaca di u na morte annunciata /
Chronicle of a Death Foretold**   1986
D: Francesco Rosi
S: Tonino Guerra; based on the novel by Gabriel
   García Márquez
C: Pasqualino De Santis
A: Irene Papas, Ornella Muti
Sicily. After her marriage, a daughter is returned
   to her parents when the son-in-law discovers
   she is not a virgin. To avenge the family's honor,
   her brothers murder the culprit. *Festival de films,
   22nd: 66. 2000.*
Other titles: Chronique d'une mort annoncée

1183. **Didone non è morta**   1987 DS
D: Lina Mangiacapre
S: Lina Mangiacapre, Adèla Cambria, Lucia Brundi
C: Antonio Modica
A: Daniela Silverio, Mauro Cruciano
Naples. In the champs Phlégréens, Didone, the queen
   of Carthage, returns to meet one more time her
   great love; "she will lose him and also her dream of
   a great civilization." *Festival de films, 25th: 21. 2003.*

1184. **La Maschera / The Mask**   1987 DS
D: Fiorella Infascelli
S: Adriano Apra, Fiorella Infascelli
C: Acacio De Almeida
A: Helena Bonham Carter, Michael Maloney
Eighteenth century. A nobleman attempts to
   seduce an actress in a traveling troupe who
   is eager to know more about life than just
   the stage. She refuses him and he follows the
   troupe, taking on various masks, in order to
   continue his pursuit of her; soon, she has seduced him. *Festival de films, 11th: 141. 1989.*

1185. **Gentili Signore**   1988 DS
D: Adriana Monti
S: Adriana Monti, Angelo Cordini
C: Angelo Cordini
A: Anna Bonaiuto, Marina Confalone
Three workers outside Milan form a cooperative
   union. *Dizionario del cinema, vol. 5.*

1186. **Il Demino clandestino / To Save Nine**
                                    1989 DS
D: Lina Wertmüller
S: Lina Wertmüller
P: Carlo Vanzina
A: Piera Degli Esposti, Dominique Sanda, Hartmut
   Becker
A widowed mother with nine children leaves her
   impoverished life on a farm and goes to Bolo-
   gna, where she tells the landlord that she lives
   alone. *AMG.*

1187. **Paura e amore / Three Sisters**   1990 DS
D: Margarethe Von Trotta
S: Dacia Maraini, Margarethe Von Trotta
C: Giuseppe Lanci
P: Eberhard Junkersdorf
A: Greta Scacchi, Fanny Ardant, Valeria Golino,
   Agnes Sorel
A portrait of three sisters born into an educated
   family: The oldest is a literature professor, the
   middle one is bored with her husband, and the
   youngest studies medicine and has lost her boy-
   friend in an accident. Loosely based on the play
   by Anton Chekhov. *Le Monde, July 17, 1988.*
Other titles: Love and Fear / Fürchten und Lieben
Awards: Cannes Film Festival, nomination for
   Golden Palm, 1988

1188. **Sabato, Domenica, Lunedi / Saturday,
Sunday, Monday**   1990 DS
D: Lina Wertmüller
S: Lina Wertmüller, Eduardo De Filippo
C: Carlo Tafani
A: Sophia Loren, Luca De Filippo
"Comedy about a marital crisis." *FII.*

1189. **Scandalo segreto / Secret Scandal**   1990
DS
D: Monica Vitti
S: Monica Vitti
C: Luigi Kuveiller
A: Monica Vitti
A happy woman married for two decades to an
   artist receives a camera as a gift and discovers
   that it fills her idle time to the point of obses-
   sion. *Festival de films, 14th: 96. 1992.*

1190. **Ambrogio**   1992 D
D: Wilma Labate
S: Sandro Petraglia
C: Guiseppe Maccari
P: Giuseppe Giovannini
A: Francesca Antonelli, Anita Ekberg
A woman wants to go to the Italian Naval Academy,
   but she is not encouraged by her family and
   friends or by the institution. *Variety. 1992, Oct 19.*

1191. **Con gli occhi chiusi / With Closed Eyes**
                                    1994 DS
D: Francesca Archibugi
S: Francesca Archibugi, Federigo Tozzi
C: Giuseppe Lanci
P: Guido De Laurentiis
A: Stefania Sandrelli, Deborah Caprioglio
Sienna, early twentieth century. A farmworker's
   daughter is in love with the master's son. *MOMA
   Film. 2003, Nov.*

1192. ***Stealing Beauty*** 1996 S
D: Bernardo Bertolucci
S: Susan Minot, Bernardo Bertolucci
C: Darius Khondji
P: Jeremy Thomas
A: Liv Tyler, Sinead Cusack, Jeremy Irons
Tuscany. A nineteen-year-old whose mother has just committed suicide goes to live in a compound for intellectuals and artists, where she plays out a search for her birth father and begins her adult life and, more cautiously, her sexual life.
Awards: Cannes Film Festival, nomination for Golden Palm, 1996

1193. ***Va' dove ti porta il cuare / Go Where the Heart Leads You*** 1996 DS
D: Christina Comencini
S: Christina Comencini, Roberta Mazzoni; based on the novel by Susanna Tamaro
C: Roberto Forza
P: Sandro Parenzo
A: Virna Lisi, Margherita Buy, Valentina Chico
Trieste. A woman returns home from the United States when her grandmother dies, and she reads her grandmother's diary. The film uses flashback to relate the grandmother's loveless marriage and affair, as well as her view of her daughter and granddaughter. *Festival de films, 19th: 103. 1997.*
Other titles: Follow Your Heart / Geh wohin dein herz dich Trägt
Awards: Italian National Syndicate of Film Journalists, Best Actress (Lisi), 1997

1194. ***Domenica*** 2000 DS
D: Wilma Labate
S: Wilma Labate
C: Allessandro Pesci
P: Maurizio Tini
A: Domenica Guiliano
A twelve-year-old street kid, a determined survivor of an orphanage and rape, runs money schemes and spars with a detective, who wants her to identify a corpse as her rapist. *Film Society. 2001, Jun.*

1195. ***Guarda il cielo / Watch the Sky*** 2000
D: Piergiorgio Gay
S: Piergiorgio Gay, Elena Calogero
C: Fabio Olmi
A: Sandra Ceccarelli
Three stories of women struggling with conflict. 1940s: A farm woman wants to purchase more land, but her husband would rather have more children to work than more land to work.

Early 1970s: A woman wants to go to Rome to study, but her boyfriend insists that his wife be a housewife. Late 1990s: A woman and her husband are on opposite sides of a labor union dispute at their factory. *Film Society. 2001, Jun.*

1196. ***Pane e tulipani / Bread and Tulips*** 2000 S
D: Silvio Soldini
S: Silvio Soldini, Doriana Leondeff
C: Luca Bigazzi
P: Daniele Maggioni
A: Licia Maglietta, Bruno Ganz
When a wife and mother, who is tired of her routine, is left behind by her tour bus, she heads for Venice and gets a job. *FII.*
Awards: David di Donatello Awards, Best Film, Best Actress, 2000; Italian National Syndicate of Film Journalists, Best Actress, Best Screenplay, 2000

1197. ***Sud side stori / South Side Story*** 2000 DSP
D: Roberta Torre
S: Roberta Torre
C: Daniele Cipri
P: Elizabetta Riga
A: Forstine Ehobor
Palermo. A Nigerian prostitute falls in love with a street singer. *FII.*
Awards: Istanbul International Film Festival, nomination for Golden Tulip, 2001

1198. ***Le Fate ignoranti / Blind Fairies*** 2001
D: Ferzan Ozpetek
S: Ferzan Ozpetek
C: Pascal Marti
P: Tilde Corsi
A: Margherita Buy
A doctor discovers at the death of her husband that he had a long-term love affair with a man; she seeks the man out. *Village Voice: 150. 2001, June 5.*
Awards: Italian National Syndicate of Film Journalists, Best Actress, 2001; New York Lesbian and Gay Film Festival, Best Feature, 2002

1199. ***Tre moglie / Three Wives*** 2001 S
D: Marco Risi
S: Marco Risi, Silvia Napolitano
C: Italo Petriccione
P: Marco Guidone, Marco Risi
A: Francesca D'Aloja, Iaia Forte, Silke
Three wives travel to Buenos Aires to search for their bank-robber husbands, who have abandoned them. Comedy. *Variety. 2001, Nov. 21.*

1200. ***Vipera / Mother Viper*** 2001 P
D: Sergio Citti

S: Vincenzo Cerami, Sergio Citti
C: Blasco Giurato
P: Elide Melli
A: Elide Melli, Harvey Keitel, Giancarlo Giannini, Annalisa Schettino
1940s. Abandoned by her mother, a child is raped and made pregnant, making her motherly relationship to her father more complete; he dies and the child is taken from her. As an adult, she searches for her son and finds her mother, who has a son the same age. *FII.*

1201. **Angela**   2002 DSP
D: Roberta Torre
S: Massimo D'Anolfi, Roberta Torre
C: Daniele Cipri
P: Rita Cecchi Gori, Lierka Rusic
A: Donatella Finocchiaro
Palermo, 1980s. A woman, who manages her criminal husband's shoe store business front, has an affair with one of his young lieutenants. *NYT: E12. 2003, April 4.*
Awards: Tokyo International Film Festival, Best Actress, 2002

1202. **Callas Forever**   2002
D: Franco Zeffirelli
S: Martin Sherman, Franco Zeffirelli
C: Ennio Guarnieri
A: Fanny Ardant
A tour organizer tries to convince the aging, unsocial Maria Callas to lip-synch her most memorable old performances for video. Finally, she agrees. The first one, *Carmen*, is received well, but then she changes her mind about the next one. *Cine espanol. 2002.*

1203. **Il più bel giorno della mia vita / The Best Day of My Life**   2002 DS
D: Christina Comencini
S: Christina Comencini, Giulia Calenda
C: Fabio Cianchetti
A: Virna Lisi, Margherita Buy
A family reunites for a communion, but the mother only worries about her children: a daughter who has affairs, a son who goes out with men, and another daughter who is raising her children alone. *Festival de films, 25th: 30. 2003.*
Awards: Montréal World Film Festival, Grand Prix, 2002; Créteil International Women's Film Festival, Grand Prix, 2003

1204. **Scarlet Diva**   2002 DS
D: Asia Argento
S: Asia Argento
C: Frederic Fasano

P: Claudio Argento
A: Asia Argento
A contemporary movie star fights her way to the top of the film industry, experiencing rape and beatings as well as revealing the "lonesome passion and unspigoted woe" of the actual director and star. *Village Voice: 140. 2002, Aug. 13.*
Awards: Williamsburg Brooklyn Film Festival, Best New Director, 2001

1205. **Vecchie / Old Women**   2002
D: Daniele Segre
S: Daniele Segre
C: Paolo Ferrari
P: Daniele Segre
A: Maria Grazia Grassini, Barbara Valmorin
"In the living room of a seaside holiday home, two old women in their nightdresses use any excuse to avoid leaving the apartment." *FII.*

1206. **Benzina / Gasoline**   2003 DS
D: Monica Stambrini
S: Monica Stambrini, Anne Ciccone; based on the novel by Elena Stancanelli
C: Fabio Cianchetti
P: Galliano Juson
A: Regina Orioli, Maya Sansa
Two gas station workers accidentally kill one of their mothers, then head for the road. Action. *Village Voice: 104. 2004, July 2.*

1207. **Respiro**   2003
D: Emanuele Crialese
S: Emanuele Crialese
C: Fabio Zamarion
P: Domenico Procacci
A: Valeria Golino
A high-spirited mother of two boys is manic-depressive. A warm relationship with her fisherman husband does not stave off the relatives who think she would be better off in a mental institution, so she flees to live in a cave, where her oldest son cares for her while the island population believes she is dead.
Awards: Cannes Film Festival, Grand Prize, 2002; Italian National Syndicate of Film Journalists, Best Actress, 2002

1208. **Mi piace lavorare (mobbing) / I Love to Work**   2004 DS
D: Francesca Comencini
S: Francesca Comencini
C: Luca Bigazzi
P: Donatella Botti
A: Nicoletta Braschi

A divorced single mother is targeted by new management and moved to job after job. Apolitical and trusting, she attempts to take on isolating assignments, such as timing factory workers and asking coworkers the reasons for the copies they are making. The pressures of all this break down her confidence and reliability, pushing her daughter into the home of an African neighbor. Forced to resign, she belatedly engages the help of the union. Based on a court case that documented a corporate phenomenon called "mobbing," where older workers are set against one another to force them to quit.

Awards: Berlin International Film Festival, Ecumenical Jury Prize, 2004; Mar del Plata Film Festival, Best Actress, 2004

IVORY COAST

1209. *La Femme au couteau / The Woman with a Knife* 1969
D: Bassori Timite
S: Bassori Timite
A: Bassori Timite, Mary Vieyra

A woman helps a man who has just returned from studying in Europe and finds himself sexually inhibited, terrorized by the image of a woman wielding a knife at him. Doctors and medicine men are of no help, but the woman makes him understand the trauma of his childhood with a repressive mother. *Cinémas d'Afrique: 457.*

1210. *L'Herbe sauvage / Wild Grass* 1977
D: Henri DuParc
S: Henri DuParc
C: Christian Lacoste
A: Clémentine Tikado, Donaldo Fofana

Abidjan. A bureaucrat and his doctor wife have trouble balancing their professional lives and their relationship. He takes a mistress, who traditionally would have an acceptable place supporting the wife with domestic chores. But instead the wife declares her independence and begins a new life of her own. Includes a critique of genital mutilation. *Cinémas d'Afrique: 182.*

1211. *Djeli / The Griot* 1981
D: Fadika Kramo-Lanciné
S: Fadika Kramo-Lanciné
C: N-Gouan Kacou
A: Fatou Ouatara

A young woman, close to her traditional father, commits suicide at his disapproval of her marriage to one of the griot caste; the film includes many scenes of female griots performing.

Other titles: Djeli, conte d'aujourd'hui

1212. *Visages de femmes / Faces of Women* 1985
D: Désiré Ecaré
S: Désiré Ecaré
C: François Migeat
P: Désiré Ecaré
A: Sijiri Bakaba, Eugenie Cisse-Roland, Carmen Levry

An essay on feminism and economics in Africa, telling a story of three women who "try to break out of their traditional roles and enter the male-dominated business world." *FII.*

Awards: Cannes Film Festival, FIPRESCI, 1985

1213. *Bal poussière / Dancing in the Dust* 1989
D: Henri DuParc
C: Bernard Déchet
A: Therese Taba, Tchelly Hanny

The richest man in town takes a sixth wife, a young woman who causes revolt among his other wives by encouraging them to demand more sexual relations with him. *African cinema: 144.*

1214. *Rue Princesse* 1994 P
D: Henri DuParc
S: Henri DuParc
C: Bernard Déchet
P: Henriette DuParc
A: Félicité Wouassi

A house of prostitution on rue Princesse (Princess Street). One of the women meets a musician, the kind son of a rich man who frequents the street, but the man advises his son to work elsewhere. The film includes scenes of the women organizing to protect themselves against AIDS. *African Media.* Accessed 2005, July 15; cached 2004, Nov. 22.

JAPAN

1215. *Akibiyori / Late Autumn* 1960
D: Yasujiro Ozu
S: Yasujiro Ozu, Kogo Noda; based on the novel by Ton Satomi
C: Yuhara Atsuta
A: Setsuko Hara, Chishu Rya

A widowed mother looks for a suitor for her daughter.

1216. *Oginsama / Love under the Crucifix* 1960 D
D: Kinuyo Tanaka
S: Masashige Narusawa; based on the novel by Toko Kon

C: Yoshio Miyajima
P: Sennosuke Tsukimori
A: Ineko Arima, Ganjiro Nakamura, Mieko Takamine

A young woman is in love with a married Christian convert but marries someone else. Their affair continues into a time when Christians are forced into hiding, and she commits suicide. *AMG*.

Other titles: *Lady Ogin*

1217. *Onna ga kaidan o agaru toki / When a Woman Ascends the Stairs*   1960
D: Mikio Naruse
S: Ryuzo Kikushima
C: Masao Tamai
A: Hideko Takamine

Tokyo, Ginza district. A widow who runs a bar to support her family must consider marriage as a more respectable alternative. Nonetheless, she pushes away a suitor. *Japanese Film*.

1218. *Taiyo no hakaba / The Sun's Burial* 1960
D: Nagisa Oshima
S: Toshirô Ishido
C: Ko Kawamata
A: Kayoko Hanoo

"Slum girl lives by selling black market blood by day and prostituting herself by night." *Japanese Film*.

Awards: Blue Ribbon Awards, Best New Director, 1961

1219. *Eien no hito / Immortal Love*   1961
D: Keisuke Kinoshita
S: Keisuke Kinoshita
C: Hiroshi Kusada
A: Hideko Takamine

A rural woman loses her lover to war and is forced to marry a man who rapes her. She carries resentment and helps her children flee the house. *Japanese Film*.

Other titles: *The Bitter Spirit*

Awards: Mainichi Film Concours, Best Actress, 1961; Academy Awards, nomination for Best Foreign Film, 1962

1220. *Tsuma toshite onna toshite / As a Wife, as a Woman*   1961
D: Mikio Naruse
S: Toshiro Ide, Zenzo Matsuyama
C: Jun Yasumoto
A: Hideko Takamine

The mistress of a wealthy professor has two children by him. He takes them away from her and into his own childless home after setting her up as a bar madam. *Japanese Film*.

1221. *Tsuma wa kokuhaku sura / A Wife's Confession*   1961
D: Yasuzo Masumura
S: Masato Ide
C: Setsuo Kobayashi
A: Ayako Wakao

A young widow on trial for murdering her husband reveals her "manipulative ego under her submissiveness." *Cinéma japonais*.

Awards: Kinema Junpo Awards, Best Actress, 1961; Blue Ribbon Awards, Best Actress, 1962

1222. *Gan no tera / Temple of the Wild Geese*   1962
D: Yuzo Kawashima
S: Yuzo Kawashima
C: Hiroshi Murai
A: Ayako Wakao

When a famous artist dies, his mistress goes to live with a monk according to her lover's bequest. There lives there another apprentice, a peasant with whom she develops a relationship. *Festival des 3*.

Other titles: *Le Temple des oies sauvages*

1223. *Horoki / Her Lonely Lane*   1962 S
D: Mikio Naruse
S: Toshiro Ide, Sumie Tanaka; based on the novel by Fumiko Hayashi
C: Jun Yasumoto
P: Sanezumi Fujimoto
A: Hideko Takamine, Kinuyo Tanaka

An impoverished woman writes autobiographical novels and struggles to earn a living for herself and her mother when they are abandoned. As she becomes successful, she loses the love of a writer who cannot get published. *Japanese Film*.

Other titles: *Lonely Lane; A Wandering Life*

1224. *Konojo to kare / She and He*   1963
D: Susumu Hami
S: Susumu Hami, Kunio Shimizu
C: Juichi Nagano
A: Hidari Sachiko

A disaster in the neighborhood makes a middle-class woman aware of an impoverished man who used to be a student of her husband's, but she is unable to overcome the limitations of her social position to do anything about it. *AMG*.

Awards: Kinema Junpo Awards, Best Actress, 1963; Berlin International Film Festival, Best Actress, 1964

1225. *Nippon konchuki / Insect Woman*   1963
D: Shohei Imamura
S: Shohei Imamura, Keiji Hasebe

C: Shinsaku Himeda

A: Sachiko Hidari

An unmarried farm mother, herself an illegitimate daughter, tires of her impoverished life and seeks independence. She takes her daughter to the city, becomes a prostitute, then a madam, and her daughter does the same. *Japanese Film.*

Awards: Kinema Junpo Awards, Best Actress 1963; Berlin International Film Festival, Best Actress, 1964

1226. *Akai satsui / Intentions of Murder* 1964

D: Shohei Imamura

S: Shohei Imamura, Keiji Hasebe

C: Shinsaku Himeda

A: Misuni Harukawa

Sendai. Home alone, a country wife is raped by an intruder, who returns to proclaim love. Pregnant, she agrees to go to Tokyo with him, but when the train is stopped in a snowdrift, she leaves him to die. *Japanese Film.*

Other titles: Unholy Desire

1227. *Koge / The Scent of Incense* 1964

D: Keisuke Kinoshita

S: Keisuke Kinoshita

C: Hiroshi Kusada

A: Mariko Okada, Nobuko Otana

"Bitter relations between a mother and a daughter in the Geisha world," where the mother dominates. *Japanese Film.*

Other titles: Le Parfum de l'encens

1228. *Manji / All Mixed Up* 1964

D: Yasuzo Masumura

S: Kaneto Shindo, Junichiro Tanizaki

C: Setsuo Kobayashi

P: Yonejiro Saito

A: Ayako Wakao, Kyoko Kishida

A married woman has an affair with a young girl who is ashamed of her lesbianism. *Japanese Cinema.*

1229. *Onna no rekishi / A Woman's Story* 1964

D: Mikio Naruse

S: Ryozo Kashara

C: Jun Yasumoto

A: Hideko Takamine

"The life history of a woman who faced disillusion from her husband and disappointment from her son, but lives to welcome her grandson." *Japanese Film.*

1230. *Seisaku no tsuma / Seisaku's Wife* 1965

D: Yasuzo Masumura

S: Kaneto Shindo; based on the novel by Genjiro Yoshida

C: Tomohiro Akino

P: Masaichi Nagata

A: Ayako Wakao

A woman in a small village is sold to an older man by her impoverished parents, then "saved" by a communist "model youth." But their illicit love is not acceptable to the villagers. *Festival des 3.*

Awards: Blue Ribbon Awards, Best Actress, 1966; Kinema Junpo Awards, Best Actress, 1966

1231. *Utsukushisa to kanashimi to / With Beauty and Sorrow* 1965

D: Masahiro Shinoda

S: Nobuo Yamada

C: Masao Kosugi

A: Keoru Yachigusa, Mariko Kaga

A young woman seeks revenge by seducing the son of a middle-aged man who seduced her. *Japanese Film.*

Awards: Asia-Pacific Film Festival, Best Actress (Yachigusa), 1965

1232. *Akai tenshi / The Red Angel* 1966

D: Yasuzo Masumura

S: Kaneto Shindo; based on the novel by Yoriyoshi Arima

C: Setsuo Kobayashi

A: Ayako Wakao

1939, Sino-Japanese War. A nurse works closely with a surgeon in a military hospital at the front. Horrors, and even her rape, are routine, and one day, she sexually assaults the surgeon. Exploitation. *Festival des 3.*

1233. *Andesu no hanayome / Bride of the Andes* 1966

D: Susumu Hani

S: Susumu Hani

C: Juichi Nagano

A: Sachiko Hidari

A mail-order bride struggles to adapt to life in the mountains of Peru, but her husband is good, and she stays there after he is accidentally killed. *AMG.*

1234. *Hikinige / Hit and Run* 1966

D: Mikio Naruse

S: Zenzo Matsuyama

C: Rokuro Hishigaki

P: Sanezumi Fujimoto

A: Hideko Takamine, Yôko Tsukasa

A woman's son is killed in a car accident, and she discovers by accident that the true culprit—"a spoiled wife"—was provided a cover story by her wealthy husband. The woman gets a job as a servant in the rich man's house, intending to harm their son, but she decides to focus her revenge on the wife instead. Thriller. *IMDb.*

Awards: Kinema Junpo Awards, Best Actress (Tsukasa), 1967

1235. *Ai no kawaki* / *The Thirst for Love* 1967
D: Koreyoshi Kurahara
S: Koreyoshi Kurahara; based on the novel by Yukio Mishima
C: Yoshio Miyajima
P: Kazu Otsuka
A: Ruriko Asaoka
A dissatisfied bourgeois woman becomes her father-in-law's mistress after her husband's death. *Cinéma japonais: 119.*
Other titles: Soif d'amour

1236. *Hanaoka Seishu no tsuma* / *The Wife of Seishu Hanaoka* 1967
D: Yasuzo Masumura
S: Kaneto Shindo; based on the novel by Sawako Ariyoshi
C: Setsuo Kobayashi
A: Ayako Wakao, Hideko Takamine
A woman stays with her mother-in-law while her husband studies medicine in another city, but the relationship becomes ridden with jealousy. When he returns, they vie to please him by volunteering for his experiments with anesthesia. The wife loses her eyesight, and the mother dies, leaving the couple, finally, alone. *Festival des 3.*

1237. *Hibotan bakuto* / *Red Peony Gambler* 1968
D: Kasaku Yameshita
A: Junko Fuji
A woman warrior takes revenge on her father's murderers, becoming a great swordswoman and avenging angel for everyone. Yakusa series, first of eight ending in 1972. Action. *Cinéma japonais.*
Other titles: La Pivoine rouge

1238. *Shinjû ten no amijima* / *Double Suicide* 1969
D: Shinoda Masahiro
S: Taeko Tomioka, Shinoda Masahiro
C: Toichiro Narushima
A: Shima Iwashita
Early eighteenth century. The story is framed in a Burraku puppet-theater style. A merchant abandons his wife and family for a courtesan (played by the same actress as the wife), whom he can no longer afford. This is unbearable to the couple, and they commit suicide. *Japanese Film.*

1239. *Nippon sengoshi* / *History of Postwar Japan* 1970
D: Shohei Imamura
S: Shohei Imamura
C: Masao Tochizawa
A fictional "interview" with a middle-aged bar owner who has married an American half her age. *Japanese Cinema.*

1240. *Ichijo sayuri: nureta yokujo* / *Following Desire* 1972
D: Tatsumi Kumashiro
S: Tatsumi Kumashiro
C: Shinsaku Himeda
P: Akira Miura
A: Ichijo Sayuri
A real-life stripper, who believes her act is art, plays a stripper in a soft-porn drama involving her boyfriend and club manager. *AMG.*
Awards: Kinema Junpo Awards, Best Screenplay, Best Actress, 1972

1241. *Kototsu no hito* / *Twilight Years* 1973
D: Shiro Toyoda
S: Zenzo Matsuyama
A: Hideko Takamine
A daughter-in-law nurses her husband's senile father until his death. "Despite the fact that he had been a burden to her, she finds that she is overwhelmed with grief." *FII.*

1242. *Himiko* 1974
D: Masahiro Shinoda
S: Taeko Tomioka
C: Tatsuo Suzuki
A: Shima Iwashita
"Drama about a semi-legendary pre-historic shaman queen named Himiko." *Japanese Film.*
Awards: Cannes Film Festival, nomination for Golden Palm, 1974

1243. *Keiko* 1974 C
D: Claude Gagnon
C: Andrée Pelletier
A: Junko Wakashiba, Akiko Kitamura
A city working girl is dissatisfied with men and has a lesbian relationship, but her father intervenes and arranges a marriage that she consents to. *FII.*
Awards: Hochi Film Awards, Special Award, 1979

1244. *Maruhi: shikijo mesu ichiba* / *Secret Chronicle: Shebeast Market* 1974
D: Noboru Tanaka
S: Akio Ido
C: Shohei Anso
A: Meika Seri, Genshu Hanayagi

Three stories of prostitution in different eras: nineteenth-century Tokyo, an Edo temple, and modern Osaka. The film was made for the exploitation market, with a reputed subversive tone. *Contemporary Japanese.*

1245. *Sandakan hachiban shokan: bokyo / Sandakan 8*   1975 S
D: Kei Kumai
S: Kei Kumai, Ei Hirosawa
C: Mitsuji Kaneo
P: Masajuki Sato
A: Kinuyo Tanaka, Yoko Takashi, Komaki Kurihara
A Japanese woman tells her story of wartime prostitution—a somber, straightforward tale of the Karajuki-san in Borneo—to a female journalist.
Awards: Kinema Junpo Awards, Best Film, Best Director, Best Actress (Tanaka), 1974; Berlin International Film Festival, Best Actress (Tanaka), OCIC Award, 1975; Academy Awards, nomination for Best Film, 1976

1246. *Daichi no komoruta / Lullaby of the Earth*   1976
D: Yasuzo Masumura
S: Yoshio Shirasaka
C: Yoshihisa Nakagawa
P: Hiroaki Fuji
A: Mieko Harada
1930s. A sensitive girl who is left orphaned lives in a house of prostitution on an isolated island in a lake, from where she struggles to escape. *Cinéma japonais.*
Awards: Kinema Junpo Awards, Best Actress, 1976; Blue Ribbon Awards, Best Film, Best Actress, 1978

1247. *Hanare goze Orin / Banished Orin*   1977
D: Masahiro Shinoda
S: Masahiro Shinoda, Keiji Hasebe
C: Kazuo Miyagawa
A: Shima Iwashita
Early twentieth century. "A blind shanisen player is banished from her troupe for having sexual relations. She then becomes friends with an army deserter." *Japanese Film.*
Awards: Kinema Junpo Awards, Best Actress, 1977; Awards of the Japanese Academy, Best Actress, 1978

1248. *Toi ippon no michi / The Far Road*   1977 D
D: Sachiko Hidari
S: Ken Miyamoto
C: Junichi Segawa
A: Sachiko Hidari
"Working class woman cares for her children and

husband, denies him his sexual needs because of her fatigue, [does] piecework at home," and objects to the injustice of her husband's layoff in the name of "progress." *Women's Companion: 199.*
Awards: Berlin International Film Festival, nomination for Golden Bear, 1978

1249. *Oginsama / Love and Faith*   1978 S
D: Kei Kumai
S: Yoskitaka Yoda; based on the novel by Toko Kon
C: Kozo Okazaki
P: Tsuneyasu Matsumoto
A: Ryoko Nakano, Toshiro Mifune
Sixteenth century. A daughter defends her father, who chooses death over supporting the Emperor's invasion of Korea. *Cinéma japonais.*
Other titles: Mademoiselle Ogin

1250. *Ah! Nomugi toge / Nomugi Pass*   1979
D: Satsuo Yamamoto
S: Yoshi Hattori
C: Setsuo Kobayashi
P: Takero Ito
A: Shinobu Otake
Early 1900s, late Meiji period. An action film depicting the young women who cross the dangerous Nomugi Pass in order to work in silk mills near Lake Suwa. *Contemporary Japanese.*
Awards: Mainichi Film Concours, Best Film, 1979

1251. *Kazetachi no gogo / Afternoon Breezes*   1980
D: Hitoshi Yazaki
S: Shunichi Nagasaki
P: Shunichi Nagasaki
A: Setsuko Aya, Naomi Ito
A woman is in love with her roommate and tries to come between her and her boyfriend; when the other woman realizes the betrayal, she turns her roommate out. *FII.*

1252. *La Reipu / The Rape*   1982
D: Yoichi Higashi
A: Yuko Tanaka
A woman is raped in the street by someone she recognizes. She chooses to proceed with an investigation and trial; they are humiliating for her, but the man is convicted. *Variety: 18. 1982, Apr. 14.*

1253. *Narayama bushiko / The Ballad of Narayama*   1983
D: Shohei Imamura
S: Shohei Imamura
C: Masao Tochizawa
P: Goro Kusakabe
A: Sumiko Sakamote, Ken Ogata

An old woman heads to a mountaintop to die, as tradition demands of the elderly in her impoverished village. Before going, she wraps up her duties by marrying off her children and even murdering a potential wife of whom she disapproves. *Japanese Cinema.*

1254. *Sasame yuki / The Makioka Sisters* 1983
D: Kon Ichikawa
S: Kon Ichikawa, Shinya Hidaka; based on the novel by Junichiro Tanizaki
C: Kyoshi Hasegawa
P: Tomoyuki Tanaka, Kon Ichikawa
A: Keiko Kishi, Yûko Kotegawa, Yoshiko Sakuma, Sayuri Yoshinaga, Juzo Itami
Osaka, 1930s. Four sisters from a wealthy family, the older two married, are left with nothing but the family home after their father's death. The younger two both insist on living with the second-oldest sister because of the first husband's interfering. Everyone awaits the arrival of wealthy suitors, which works out in one case. *Variety: 20. 1983, Sep. 21.*
Other titles: Les Quatres soeurs

1255. *Sekando rabu / Second Love* 1983
D: Yoichi Higashi
S: Yoichi Higashi, Masako Tanaka
C: Taseshi Kurihara
A: Reiko Ohara
A woman is in a second marriage to a younger man, whose insecurity leads him to constantly suspect her of infidelity. Typical of a film director whose "heroines are strong, intelligent, and, above all, adult." *Variety. 1983, May 11.*

1256. *Eiga joyu / Actress* 1987
D: Kon Ichikawa
S: Kon Ichikawa, Shinya Hidaka
C: Yukio Isohata
P: Tomoyuki Tanaka, Kon Ichikawa
A: Sayuri Yoshinaga, Bunta Sugawara
A biography of actress Kinuyo Tanake and her conflicts with Kenji Mizoguchi, the director whose films made her famous. *Contemporary Japanese.*

1257. *Marusa no onna / A Taxing Woman* 1987
D: Juzo Itami
S: Juzo Itami
C: Yonezo Maeda
P: Yasushi Tamaoki
A: Nobuko Miyamoto
A satire of a tax agent pursuing the wealthy for tax evasion.
Awards: Kinema Junpo Awards, Best Film, Best

Actress, 1987; Awards of the Japanese Academy, Best Film, Best Actress, 1988

1258. *Kuroi ame / Black Rain* 1989
D: Shohei Imamura
S: Shohei Imamura, Masuji Ibuse
C: Takashi Kawamata
P: Hisao Iino
A: Etsuko Ichihara, Yoshiko Tanaka
Hiroshima, World War II. A young woman, along with her aunt and uncle, walks through Hiroshima in search of shelter on the day of the bombing. Several years later, her elders attempt to prove her good health so she can marry, but she is ostracized anyway. Finally, knowing she is ill, she expresses her desire to live "honestly" and asks to marry another victim, who has become deranged.
Awards: Cannes Film Festival, Ecumenical Jury Prize, Technical Grand Prize, 1989; Hochi Film Awards, Best Actress, 1989; Kinema Junpo Awards, Best Film, Best Director, Best Actress, 1989

1259. *Afureru atsui namida / Swimming with Tears* 1992
D: Hirotaka Tashiro
S: Hirotaka Tashiro
A: Ruby Moreno
A young Filipina runs away from her husband's home in the Japanese countryside and goes to Tokyo, where she searches for the Japanese father who abandoned her as a child. *Contemporary Japanese.*

1260. *Yume no onna / Yearning* 1993
D: Tamasaburo Bando
S: Myoko Sakurai
C: Mutsuo Noganumo
A: Sayuri Yoshinaga, Sumie Kotaoka
Meiji period, 1868–1912. A woman is forced to become a courtesan and board her daughter. She persists in winning her independence with the help of her servant, a friend. *Contemporary Japanese.*
Awards: Berlin International Film Festival, nomination for Golden Bear, 1993

1261. *Onna zakari / Turning Point* 1994
D: Nobuhiko Obayashi
S: Nobuhiko Obayashi
A: Sayuri Yoshinaga
A journalist is promoted to the editorial page, but her first editorial is critical of a minister's antiabortion stance and brings the pressure of religious groups down on her. *Contemporary Japanese.*

Awards: Mainichi Film Concours, Best Actress, 1994

1262. *Kaze no katami / After the Wind Has Gone* 1996 D
D: Yukiko Takayama
S: Kaori Takahishi; based on the novel *Konjaku Monogatari* by Takehiko Fukunaga
P: Meneko Okomot
A: Shima Iwashita
China, Heian Dynasty. A princess is loved by three men. The film has special focus on material culture. *Contemporary Japanese.*
Other titles: Le Veut à laisse une trace

1263. *Maborosi* 1996
D: Hirokazu Kore-eda
S: Yoshihisa Ogita
C: Masao Nakabori
P: Naoe Gozu
A: Makiko Esumi
A young husband suddenly and inexplicably commits suicide, leaving a wife and child; the quiet and disciplined widow takes her child to live in an arranged marriage in the isolated seaside.
Awards: Venice Film Festival, Best Director, 1995; Blue Ribbon Awards, Best New Actress, 1996

1264. *Yume no ginga / Labyrinth of Dreams* 1996
D: Sogo Ishii
S: Sogo Ishii; based on the novel by Kyusaku Yumeno
C: Norimichi Kasamatsu
P: Atsuyuki Shimoda
A: Rena Komine
A bus conductor in a small town suspects a new driver of murdering her friend, who was also a conductor. *Contemporary Japanese.*
Awards: Sochi International Film Festival, Special Jury Prize, 1997

1265. *Himutsu no h anazono / My Secret Garden* 1997
D: Shinobu Yaguchi
S: Shinobu Yaguchi
C: Masahiro Kishimoto
A: Naomi Nichida
A bank teller is used as a hostage, then thrown down a mountain road, where she watches the robbers get killed and the money sink into a pond near Mt. Fuji. She attends university to study geology so she can trek into the wilderness to find it. Comedy. *Contemporary Japanese.*

1266. *Ai o kou hito / Begging for Love* 1998
D: Hideyoshi Hirayama

S: Yoshinobu Tei, Chong Wui Sin
P: Kadokawa Shoten
A: Mieko Harada
A widow and bar hostess physically abuses her daughter throughout her childhood; the daughter searches for her as an adult, even while remaining unforgiving. *Contemporary Japanese.*
Awards: Kinema Junpo Awards, Best Actress, 1998; Montréal World Film Festival, FIPRESCI, 1998; Awards of the Japanese Academy, Best Film, Best Director, Best Actress, 1999

1267. *Midori* 1998 DS
D: Sachi Hamano
S: Kuninori Yamazaki; based on *Wandering in the Seventh World* by Midori Osaki
C: Joji Tanaka
A: Kayoko Shiraishi
The life of Midori Osaki, a writer who was famous in the 1920s, then rediscovered just before she died in 1971 at the age of seventy-four. The film tells the story of why her very modern "female" writing was forgotten, alongside the story of her best-known novel about a young girl who wants to write erotic poetry and finds a passionate love who helps her discover her sexuality. An "Asiatic Simone de Beauvoir." *Festival de films, 22nd: 29. 2000.*

1268. *Onna keiji riko: seibo no fukako fuchi / Riko* 1998 S
D: Satoshi Isaka
S: Rika Tanaka
A: Riko Takizawa
A single mother and detective runs into a murder case that becomes personal. *Contemporary Japanese.*

1269. *I.K.U.* 2000 DS
D: Shu Lea Cheang
S: Shu Lea Cheang
C: Tetsuya Kamoto
A: Ayumu Tokito
A "seduction machine" is programmed to accumulate all possible sexual experience. She is programmed unlike any other robot. Other robots, like the audience, lose their cyberspace bearings when faced with her. The latest in digital technology creates a "hypermedia ballet." *Festival de films, 23rd: 94. 2001.*

1270. *Love Juice* 2000 DS
D: Shindô Kaze
S: Shindô Kaze
C: Kanaya Koji

A: Okuno Mika, Fujimura Chika

Two young women who are very close live together and get the same job in a nightclub; one is heterosexual, the other is a lesbian. When the first is raped by the club owner, the other woman consoles her and declares her love, but then regrets it and separates herself. *Festival de films, 23rd: 26. 2001.*

Awards: Berlin International Film Festival, CICAE Award, 2001

1271. *Avalon* 2001
D: Mamoru Oshii
S: Kazunori Itô
C: Grzegorz Kedzierski
P: Shinji Kubo
A: Malgorzata Foremniak

A woman leads the charge to the final "level of reality" in a virtual reality game. Science fiction. *Film Society. 2004, Nov.*

1272. *Kao / Face* 2001
D: Junji Sakamoto
S: Junji Sakamoto, Isamu Uno
C: Norimichi Kasamatsu
P: Yukiko Shii
A: Naomi Fujiyama

A seamstress heads for the road after assaulting her sister. *New Directors. 2001.*

Awards: Hochi Film Awards, Best Film, Best Actress, 2000; Kinema Junpo Awards, Best Film, Best Actress, 2000; Awards of the Japanese Academy, Best Director, 2001

1273. *Kasei-no kanon / The Mars Canon* 2001 DSP
D: Shiori Kazama
S: Tomoko Ogawa, Shotaro Oikawa
C: Isao Ishii
P: Naokatsu Ito, Midori Sato
A: Makiko Kuno, Mami Nakamura

Tokyo. A thirty-year-old retail clerk has had a long affair with a married man whom she sees once a week; she meets a new friend who is more independent and helps her get out of the dead-end relationship.

Awards: Tokyo International Film Festival, Asian Film Award, 2001

1274. *Yurisai / Lily Festival* 2001 DS
D: Sachi Hamano
S: Kuninori Yamazaki
C: Houko Momotani
A: Kazuko Yoshiyuki, Mickey Curtis, Utae Shoji

Six women, aged sixty-nine to ninety-one, live together in a residence hall for the retired; one

day an attractive elderly man moves in and proceeds to set off a revolution in the sexual mores of the group when he seduces three of them in turn. Everyone joins in, inspiring as well a lesbian relationship. *Festival de films, 27th: 74. 2005.*

Awards: Philadelphia International Gay & Lesbian Film Festival, Jury Prize, 2003

1275. *Hebi ichigo / Wild Berries* 2002 DS
D: Miwa Nichikawa
S: Miwa Nichikawa
C: Hideo Yamamoto
P: Hirokazu Kore-eda
A: Miho Tsumiki

A sensible young teacher tries to reassure her boyfriend about her insecure family, but she is plagued by her manipulative brothers and an expensive funeral for her grandfather, which leads to a confrontation with gangsters. Comedy.

1276. *Umi wa miteita / The Sea Is Watching* 2002
D: Kei Kumai
S: Akira Kurosawa, Shugoro Yamamoto
C: Teizo Okuhara
P: Naoto Sarukawa
A: Misa Shimizu, Nagiko Tohno

Nineteenth century, Edo period. A young, strong, accepting woman and her older, more cynical mentor work as courtesans in a brothel near the rural Tokyo Bay. They flirt with romance on the outside but never attempt to escape. *Variety: 31. 2002, Nov. 17.*

Awards: San Sebastián International Film Festival, nomination for Golden Seashell, 2002

1277. *Kôhî jikô / Café Lumière* 2004
D: Hou Hsiao-hsien
S: Hou Hsiao-hsien, Chu Tien-wen
C: Lee Ping-ping
A: Yo Hitoto

Tokyo. A young writer becomes pregnant by a man she does not want to marry; her best friend is a man who owns a bookstore. She comes and goes for her research, visits her parents in the country, and then receives them in her tiny apartment. Primary emphasis is on the getting there, restaurants and cafés, and especially the city's elaborate rail network of public transport.

KAZAKHSTAN

1278. *Byegushaya mishen / The Running Target* 1991
D: Talgat Temenov

S: Oleg Mandzhiyev
C: Bek Bakhtybekov
A: Nonna Mordjukova

"Friendship between persecuted German woman and a hunted adolescent after 1986 demonstrations in Alma Ata." *Companion Encyclopedia: 10.*

1279. *Zhizn—zhenshchina / Life Is a Woman*
1991 DS

D: Zhanna Serikbayeva
S: Zhanna Serikbayeva, Nina Filippova
C: Saparbek Koychumanov
P: Talgat Shagiev

A woman who murdered a criminal who hurt her boyfriend is put into jail with eight other women; she informs on a drug ring and receives an improved cell, where she is seduced by another inmate. *FII.*

1280. *Azhal auzynda / A Hunter's Family*
1995 DS

D: Shapiga Musina
S: Shapiga Musina
A: Aygul Bagaeva, Meruert Utekesheva

A hunter captures and brings home a wife to his compound isolated in snowbound mountains, where they live in a single round room, elaborately furnished, with cloth dividers. The bride is left for weeks at a time with the hunter's openly hostile mother, who is disgusted with the wife's frank sexuality and lack of experience in housekeeping. One day the wife falls into a bear trap and miscarries. Delirious, she takes revenge on the mother.

1281. *Namis / The Honor* 1996 D

D: Ulzhan Koldauova
S: Isabekov Dulat
C: Sapar Koichumanov
P: Nuraly Suleimenov
A: Shynar Askarova, Bayan Alim-Akyn

1950s. A pregnant girl is raped by the servant of the family of a suitor who had been rejected by her father and is then banished from the family home; she ends up with a widow, who takes the newborn from her. *Variety: 61. 1996, July 29.*

1282. *Jylama / Don't Cry* 2003

D: Amir Karakulor

Trained and working in China, an opera singer returns to her Kazakh village to take care of her sick niece; her main struggle is to acquire the costly medicine she needs. *Film Society. 2003, May.*

Awards: Hawaii International Film Festival, nomination for Best Feature Film, 2003

KENYA

1283. *Saikati* 1992 DS

D: Anne Mungai
S: Anne Mungai
A: Lynette Mukami Kinoti

A Masaai girl is being forced to marry the chief's son, but a friend from Nairobi convinces her to go to Nairobi to work instead. It develops that the work is prostitution, so the girl decides to return to her village and marry. *St. James: 222.*

Awards: FESPACO, Plan International Award, 1999

1284. *The Battle of the Sacred Tree* 1994 DS

D: Wanjiru Kinyanjui
S: Wanjiru Kinyanjui, Barbara Kimenye
C: François Kotlarski
A: Margaret Nyacheo, Catherine Kariuki, Roslynn Kimani

After being beaten by her husband on a regular basis, a free-thinking woman takes her young daughter and leaves Nairobi to live with her medicine man father in their Kikuyu village. The village is appalled at her action, but she and her father are close, and she obtains work in the local bar. Because of her status, she is ineligible for membership in the local Christian ladies' club, and when they connive to chop down a large and very old tree because it is believed to have magical powers, she helps the town organize against the move.

1285. *Metamo* 1997

D: Albert Wandago

A woman who became pregnant as a teenager keeps her child but must leave her community. She becomes an actress, then returns to school, where she excels and becomes a judge in the High Court of Kenya. *Alwan past. Accessed 2005, June 10.*

1286. *Dangerous Affair* 2002 DSP

D: Judy Kibinge
S: Judy Kibinge, Njeri Karago
P: Njeri Karago

Nairobi. The life of a middle-class socialite "involving movies, pubs, discos, and other entertainment facilities for young adventurous adults in the age of leisure, pleasure and AIDS." *FII.*

NORTH KOREA

1287. *Our Rail Ticket Clerk* 1973

D: Goh Hak Rim
A: Chol Gwi Bok

A ticket taker on a train mobilizes the train passengers to improve the community. *Asian Film.
Accessed: 2005, Feb. 8.*

1288. *Naeui haengbok / My Happiness*   1987
D: Kim Yeong-ho
S: Oh Hye Young
C: Byung Ryul Choi
A: Kim Jeong-hwa, Kim Ok-heui, Kim Kwang-ryeol
Pyongyang. A mother tells her grown daughter of
the medals she and her friend earned as soldiers
during the Korean War. *Asian Film. Accessed 2005,
Feb. 18.*

SOUTH KOREA

**1289. *Sarang bang sonnim omoni / My Mother
and Her guest***   1961
D: Shin Sang-okk
C: Choi Su-yeong
P: Shin Sang-okk
A: Choi Eun-hie
A widow with a young daughter takes in a roomer
and falls in love with him, scandalizing her small
town. *MOMA Film. 2002, Mar./Apr.*
Other titles: The Houseguest and My Mother

**1290. *Ijo yeoinjanhoksa / Women of the Cho-
sun Dynasty***   1969
D: Shin Sang-okk
S: Ahn Dae-seong
C: Choi Seung-woo
P: Shin Sang-okk
A: Choi Eun-hie, Hwang Jeong-sun, Kim Ji-mi, Nam
Jeong-im, Yun Jeong-hie
"Four stories of women as prostitutes and moth-
ers: 1: 'Wives Should Be Submissive.' A father
tries to marry his daughter into a wealthy fam-
ily. 2: 'A Daughter-in-Law Is No Better Than a
Stranger.' A woman thinks that her daughter-in-
law has turned her son against her, so she tries
to kill the younger woman. 3: '7 Grounds for
Divorce.' A wife begins an affair with her servant
because of her husband's impotence. 4: 'Prohibit
Sex in Court.' A concubine's life is at risk when
it is revealed that her infant child is not the
king's." *MOMA Film. 2002, Mar./Apr. Also IMDb.*

1291. *She-pen / A Woman Reporter*   1977
D: Kim Soo-yang
S: Jo Moon-jin
C: Jun Jo-myung
A: Wang Chung-a
1945–1965. Twenty years in the life of Korea's
first woman reporter and the problems she

confronted as a woman in a male profession.
KOFIC. 1977.
Other titles: Yeogija 20nyeon

1292. *Angae maul / The Misty Village*   1982
D: Im Kwon-taek
S: Lee Mun-yeol, Song Kil-han
C: Jeon Il-seong
P: Park Jong-chan
A: Ahn Seong-ki
A young teacher takes a post in an isolated village,
where the population is one large inbred com-
munity. *MOMA Film. 2004, Feb.*
Other titles: Village in the Mist / Angemaeul

1293. *Moul le ya, moul le ya / The Wheel* 1983
D: Lee Doo-yong
S: Lim Chung
C: Seong-choon Lee
P: Woong-ki Jeong
A: Won Mi-kyong
Chosun Dynasty. A woman is sold to a man who
dies before the wedding. Obliged to remain with
her in-laws as a servant, she is raped one night
and they banish her. She finds a kind man who
marries her, but he is sterile and she is subjected
to a servant in order to provide him with an
heir. Literal translation of title: "A history of bru-
tality to women: oh spinning wheel, oh spinning
wheel." *Variety: 20. 1984, Dec. 5.*
Other titles: Yoinchanhoksa: moul le ya moul le ya

1294. *Ma nim / The Tree of Adultery*   1985
D: Chung Jin-woo
S: Sang-hak Jee
C: Seong-choon Lee
A: Choi Byoung-keun
In a feudal society, a wealthy woman who has not
had children—because her husband is sterile—
is made to commit suicide for failing to become
a mother. *KOFIC. 1985.*

1295. *Pong / The Mulberry Tree*   1986
D: Lee Doo-yong
S: Na Dohyang
C: Son Hyunchae
P: Lee Tae-won
A: Lee Mi-suk
Japanese-occupied Korea, 1920s. "In a small village,
a woman's husband is frequently away on busi-
ness; in order to survive she starts to sleep with
men in the village who give her rice and other
commodities." *FII.*

1296. *Ticket*   1986
D: Im Kwon-taek

S: Song Kil-han
C: Ku Jung-mo
P: Jin Seong-man
A: Kim Ji-mi

A coffeehouse at the seashore provides its servers with opportunity for prostitution; the owner is left by her husband and made to accept money (the same "ticket" all the women accept for their services) from the husband, whom she loves, as well as others, in order to survive. *Cinéma coréen: 123.*

1297. *Adada* 1987
D: Im Kwon-taek
S: Gye Yong-muk
C: Jung Il-sung
P: Park Jong-chan
A: Shin Hye-soo

A woman with a stutter has a large dowry, but she is rejected because of her imperfection by her husband's family as well as her own. *MOMA Film. 2004, Feb.*
Awards: Montréal International Film Festival, Best Actress, 1987

1298. *Sibaji / The Surrogate Woman* 1987
D: Im Kwon-taek
S: Kil-han Song
C: Ku Jung-mo
P: Jeong Do-hwan
A: Kang Soo-yeon, Yun Hyung-ja

Chosun Dynasty. A wife cannot conceive, though her husband loves her and is willing to accept her condition. But his mother insists on bringing in a surrogate to maintain the family line; the surrogate becomes attached to the man and eventually commits suicide. *Cinéma coréen: 118.*
Other titles: La Mère porteuse
Awards: Venice Film Festival, Best Actress (Kang), 1987

1299. *Aje, aje, bara aje / Come, Come, Come Upward* 1989
D: Im Kwon-taek
S: Han Sung-won
C: Ku Jung-mo
P: Lee Tae-won
A: Kang Soo-yeon

A young woman tries to become a Buddhist nun, but she is forced to leave after being sexually compromised by a traveler. She meanders through a varied life, losing several husbands and children, then eventually returns to the retreat.
Awards: South Korea Grand Bell, Best Film, 1989; Moscow International Film Festival, Best Actress, 1989

1300. *Gyae-got-un nalui ohu / The Hot Roof* 1995
D: Lee Min-yong
S: Lee Min-yong, Cho Min-ho
C: Jeong-min Seo
P: Sun-yeol Lee
A: Ha You-mi, Jeong Seon-keyong

Various women in abusive relationships sweat through the hottest day of the summer in their high-rise apartments. Suddenly a battered women runs out the front door, fleeing the blows of her husband, and a riot ensues when a group of women beat him up. When the police arrive, the women band together and flee to the roof in resistance, creating a platform for a media satire of diverse characters, including a transvestite, the leader of the building's women's club, and the frustrated cops.
Awards: Hawaii International Film Festival, Best Feature Film, 1996

1301. *San bu in koa / Push! Push!* 1997
D: Park Chul-soo
S: Byun Won Mi, Ji Sang-hak
C: Sung Kwang-jae
P: Hwang Kyung Sang
A: Hwang Sin-hye, Bang Eun-jin

The story of two nurses in a large hospital maternity ward and their many and varied patients; includes a live birth. Comedy. *AMG.*

1302. *Chunyeo dului gernyuk siksa / Girls' Night Out* 1998
D: Lim Sang Soo
A: Yeon Kang Soo, Kyung Jin Hee, Jin Kim Yeo

Three single women "talk candidly and crudely of their sex life, their pleasure, and their marginalized roles in society." *Korean Film: 169.*

1303. *Jeongsa / An Affair* 1998
D: Lee Jae-yong
S: Kim Dae-u
C: Kim Yeong-cheol
P: Oh Jeong-wan
A: Lee Mi-suk

A married woman with a son falls in love with her sister's fiancé. *Korean Film: 170.*

1304. *Paran daemun / Birdcage Inn* 1998
D: Kim Ki-duk
S: Kim Ki-duk
A: Lee Ji-eun

A prostitute from a seedy district in Seoul that is slated for urban renewal takes her trade to Pohang, where she boards with a family. When the way she makes her living becomes apparent, she conflicts with the university-educated daughter of the family. *Film Society. 2004, Nov.*

1305. *Chunhyang* 2000

D: Im Kwon-taek
S: Cho Sang-hyun, Kang Hye-yun
C: Jung Il-sung
A: Lee Hyo-jeong

The daughter of a courtesan is brutalized by a new governor while her husband is away at school. *MOMA Film. 2004, Feb.*

Awards: Hawaii International Film Festival, Best Feature Film, 2000

1306. *Ggot seom / Flower Island* 2001

D: Song Il Gon
S: Song Il Gon
C: Kim Myong-joon
P: Ahn Hun-chan
A: Seo Joo-hee, Im Yoo-jin, Kim Hye-na

Three women meet on their way to "Flower Island—where all pain and sorrow will disappear. . . . they come to realize that the journey itself is what heals their inner wounds." *FII.*

Awards: Venice Film Festival, CinemAvvenire Award, 2001; Fribourg International Film Festival, FIPRESCI, 2002

1307. *Go-yang-i-rul boo-tak-hae / Take Care of My Cat* 2001 DS

D: Jeong Jae-eun
S: Jeong Jae-eun
C: Yeong-hwan Choi
P: Ki-min Oh
A: Bae Doo-na, Lee Yo-won, Ok Ji-young, Lee Eun-shil, Lee Eun-joo

Inchon. Five young girls tied together through their cell phones seek adult life after they finish school; one moves to Seoul to work in a brokerage, disturbing the security of the others, particularly the artist, whose family is less affluent and who feels abandoned. The rebel and the twins, who are most concerned with getting their cat a good home, cope with the loss better. A fire in the shanty home of the artist brings her closer to the rebel.

Awards: Pusan International Film Festival, Netpac Award, 2001; Hong Kong International Film Festival, FIPRESCI, 2002; Rotterdam International Film Festival, KNF Award, 2002

1308. *Apeurika / A.F.R.C.A.* 2002

D: Shin Seung-soo
C: Jang Jun-yeong
A: Lee Yo-won, Kim Min-sun, Lee Young-jin, Cho Eun-ji

Two women, frustrated with college and jobs, take a trip to Gangleung; they discover guns in their borrowed car and meet two other women with revenge on their minds. Action. *KOFIC. 2002.*

Other titles: Afrika

1309. *Milae / Ardor* 2002 D

D: Byun Young-joo
C: Kim Mi-hee
A: Kim Yoon-jin

A couple is forced to move to the countryside to rebuild their relationship after the husband's affair with a student, but once there, the wife gets involved with a married doctor. *Asian Film. Accessed 2004, July 18.*

1310. *Daehan minguk / The First Amendment*
2003 S

D: Song Gyeong Shik
S: Kim Jin-su, Choi Jong-tae
C: Lee Dong-sahm
A: Ye Ji-weon

An election tie and a candidate running on a platform to abolish prostitution bring out an unexpected third candidate: a prostitute. Comedy. *FII.*

1311. *Miso / A Smile* 2003 DS

D: Kyung-hee Park
S: Kyung-hee Park
C: Jae-soo Lim
A: Sang-mi Chu

A photographer has a condition that will make her blind; the film shows her eventual acceptance of her condition, after she takes a trip to the United States and learns how to fly an airplane. *Festival de films, 26th: 23. 2004.*

LEBANON

1312. *Leila wal ziab / Leila and the Wolves*
1984 DS

D: Heiny Srour
S: Heiny Srour
C: Curtis Clark
A: Nabila Zeitouni

An exploration of "the collective memory of Arab women and their hidden role in the modern history of Palestine and Libya." A Lebanese student, unhappy with the sexism of her culture, undertakes a voyage back in time to the colonial period of the 1920s and the revolution of the 1930s, when women took up arms. *Festival de films, 7th: 14. 1985.*

Awards: Mannheim Film Festival, Grand Prix, 1984

1313. *Les Écrans de sable / Sand Screens*
                                                   1990 DS
D: Randa Chahal-Sabbag
S: Randa Chahal-Sabbag
C: Yorgou Avernatis
A: Maria Schneider
Two old friends view life very differently; the younger one grew up during the oil boom and believes that everything can be obtained with money; the other has memories of the war in Libya and the need to adapt oneself to different situations. *Festival de films, 17th: 94. 1995.*

1314. *Civilizées / Civilized People*   1998 DS
D: Randa Chahal-Sabbag
S: Randa Chahal-Sabbag
C: Ricardo Jacques Gale
A: Jalila Baccar, Tamin Chahal, Myrna Maakaron
1970s–1980s. House servants—Filipinos, Egyptians, and Sri Lankans—are abandoned in Beirut by their wealthy employers during the civil war. *Cinema dei.*
Awards: Venice Film Festival, UNESCO Award, 1999; Human Rights Watch International Film Festival, Nestor Almendros Award, 2000

1315. *Le Cerf-volant / The Kite*   2003 D
D: Randa Chahal-Sabbag
A: Flavia Bechara
A sixteen-year-old must cross the barbed-wire border between Lebanon and Israeli-annexed territory in order to connect with the fiancé on the other side that her father has arranged for her. *Film Society. 2004, Jun.*
Awards: Venice Film Festival, Special Prize, Laterna Magica Prize, 2003

MALAYSIA

1316. *Perempuan, isteri dan ...? / Woman, Wife, and Whore*   1993
D: Haji Shaari U-wei
S: Haji Shaari U-wei
P: Pansha
A: Sofia Jane
A woman flees on her wedding day with her true love but is tracked down by the bridegroom, who kills the lover, rapes the woman, and sends her to be a prostitute. Later he retrieves her and she tricks him into marrying her, but she has only revenge on her mind. *IMDb.*

1317. *Layar lara*   1997
D: Shuhaimi Baba
S: Shuhaimi Baba

C: Aida Fitri Buyung
A: Azean Irdwaty, Ida Nerina, Man Bai
An actress must learn to collaborate and adjust her notion of what it is to be the star. In the film, she plays a real estate agent working with "greedy urban developers." *St. James: 235.*

MALI

1318. *Den Muso / The Girl*   1975
D: Souleymane Cissé
S: Abdoulaye Sidibé
A: Dounamba Dany Coulibaly
Bamako. A mute rich girl is raped and made pregnant by an unemployed boy, who resents her. *Festival des 3.*
Other titles: La Fille

1319. *Moko-dakhan / Destiny*   1976
D: Sega Coulibaly
A: Fanta Berthe
A powerful man seduces young girls; one becomes pregnant. Her father blames the girl and her mother, who is responsible for her conduct, and banishes them both from the village. They move to the city without resources and become prostitutes to survive. *Festival des 3.*
Other titles: Le Destin

1320. *Finzan*   1989
D: Cheick Sissoko Oumar
S: Cheick Sissoko Oumar
A: Hélène Diarra, Diarrah Sanogo
A young widow, forced to marry an old man, refuses to submit to a tradition that states her dead husband's brother has the right to inherit her, which angers her family and the village elders. *FII.*

1321. *Waati / Time*   1995
D: Souleymane Cissé
S: Souleymane Cissé
C: Jean-Jacques Bouhon
P: Xavier Castano
A: Linéo Tsolo
A poor woman living under South African apartheid flees her country after killing the policeman who murdered her father. She travels through the Ivory Coast and Mali, eventually moving to the new South Africa with an adopted Tuareg daughter. *Variety. 1995, May 19.* Also *FII.*
Other titles: Le temps
Awards: Cannes Film Festival, nomination for Golden Palm, 1995

1322. *Faraw, une mère de sable / Faraw! Mother of the Dunes* 1997
D: Abdoulaye Ascofare
S: Abdoulaye Ascofare
C: Yorgos Arvanitis
A: Amïna Keïta
A rural woman cares for her three children and husband, who is disabled from being in jail on a false charge. Her daughter wants to help by working for foreigners, but the mother contacts one of her former suitors for support instead.
Awards: FESPACO, Best Actress, 1997

1323. *Taafe fanga / Skirt Power* 1997
D: Adama Drabo
S: Adama Drabo
C: Lionel Cousin
P: Adama Drabo
A: Fanta Bereta, Ramata Drabo, Hélène Diarra
A Dogon village wife who is informed by her husband that he will take a second wife is so angry she wrests a mask from one of the evil spirits that haunt the night. At first fearful, she confidently takes on the persona of the most powerful spirit in her village and commands the men and women to reverse their roles and work responsibilities. A wounded woman who is recuperating in the village turns out to be the original owner of the mask and demands it back. A mixture of griot-told tale, theatrical night staging, electric effects, and bright days near spectacular caves and streams.
Awards: FESPACO, Special Jury Prize, 1997; Namur International Festival of French-Speaking Film, Special Jury Prize, 1997

MEXICO

1324. *Os Cafajestes / The Beach of Desire* 1962
D: Ruy Guerra
S: Miguel Torres, Ruy Guerra
C: Tony Rabatoni
A: Norma Bengell
Two shiftless men use women whenever they can; one day they devise a scheme of stealing a woman's clothes from the beach, then speeding off in a car and photographing the nude woman as she runs after the car, "exhausted and humiliated." *Festival de films, 24th: 80. 2002.*

1325. *El Amor no es pecado / Love Is Not a Sin* 1964
D: Rafael Baledón
S: José María Fernández Unsáin

C: Raul Solares
P: Jesus Martinez
A: Marga López
A woman loses her son in an accident; distraught, she provokes her husband into leaving her, then opens a home for abandoned children. *Mexican Filmography.*

1326. *Un Ángel de la calle / Angel of the Street* 1966
D: Zacarias Gómez Urquisa
S: Julio Luzardo
C: Manuel Gómez Urquisa
P: Joaquin Bernal
A: Sofia Álvarez
A mother opposes her son's marriage to a poor woman. *Mexican Filmography.*

1327. *Doña Herlinda y su hijo / Doña Herlinda and Her Son* 1969
D: Jaime Humberto Hermosillo
S: Jaime Humberto Hermosillo
C: Miguel Ehrenberg
P: Manuel Barbachano Ponce
A: Guadalupe Del Toro
A middle-class woman and matriarch works to hide her son's homosexuality and even invites his male lover to live with them. *Guide to Latin: 167.*

1328. *Anacrusa o de como la música viene después del silencio / Anacrusa or How the Music Comes after the Silence* 1978
D: Ariel Zúñiga
A: Adriana Roel
A professor investigates her activist daughter's disappearance and becomes more politically aware when she discovers her daughter was murdered. *Mexican Filmography.*
Awards: Berlin International Film Festival, Interfilm Award, 1979

1329. *Erendira* 1982
D: Ruy Guerra
S: Gabriel García Márquez
C: Denys Clerval
P: Alain Queffélean
A: Irene Papas, Claudia Ohana
A young girl causes the destruction by fire of her imperious grandmother's mansion. To get payback for a new house, the grandmother sets the girl up as a prostitute, dragging her across the desert and creating lines of eager customers.

1330. *Frida* 1984
D: Paul Leduc
S: José Joaquín Blanco, Paul Leduc

C: Ángel Goded
P: Manuel Barbachano Ponce
A: Ofelia Medina
Abstract reflections on the painter Frida Kahlo, her life, and her relationships with Diego Rivera and Leon Trotsky. *Guide to Latin: 169.*
Awards: Havana Film Festival, Best Actress, 1985; Ariel Awards, Golden Ariel, Best Actress, 1986; Bogota Film Festival, Best Actress, 1986

1331. *Amor a la vuelta de la esquina / Love around the Corner*   1985 S
D: Alberto Cortés
S: Alberto Cortés, José Agustín; based on the novel by Albertine Sarrazin
C: Guillermo Navarro
P: Miguel Camacho
A: Gabriela Roel
A criminal escapes from prison, prostitutes herself, and steals until she is picked up by the police and sent back. *Guide to Latin: 161.*

1332. *Nocturno amor que te vas / Departed Love in the Evening*   1987 DS
D: Marcela Fernández Violante
S: Jorge Perez Grovas, Marcela Fernández Violante
C: Arturo De la Rosa
A: Patricia Reyes Spindola
A working-class woman with two children confronts the establishment over the disappearance of her companion. *Variety: 16. 1988, Jan. 6.*

1333. *El Secreto de Romelia / Romelia's Secret*   1988
D: Busi Cortés
S: based on the novel by Rosario Castellanos
C: Francisco Bojorquez
A: Diana Bracho, Dolores Beristáin, Arcelia Remirez, Lumi Cavazos
A woman returns to her hometown with her daughter and granddaughters to claim the estate of her recently deceased husband, and she confronts her past with this man she had left many years before. Mystery. *Guide to Latin: 183.*
Awards: Ariel Awards, Best First Work, Best Supporting Actress (Beristáin), 1989

1334. *Lola*   1989 DS
D: Maria Novaro
S: Maria Novaro, Beatriz Novaro
C: Rodrigo Garcia
P: Jorge Sánchez
A: Leticia Huijara
Mexico City. A mother has been abandoned by her rock musician lover. She and her young daughter

sell clothing on the street to survive and must contend with the police, who hold raids to ferret out unlicensed vendors. *Variety: 26. 1990, Jan. 17.*

1335. *Danzón*   1991 DS
D: Maria Novaro
S: Maria Novaro
C: Rodrigo Garcia
P: Jorge Sánchez
A: Maria Rojo
A woman with a teenage daughter suddenly loses her dancing partner and takes off for Vera Cruz to find him. She meets a drag queen, who helps in the search, and has an affair with a handsome sailor.

1336. *Angel de fuego / Angel of Fire*   1992 D
D: Dana Rotberg
C: Toni Kuhn
P: Leon Constantiner
A: Evangelina Sosa
A young circus artist becomes pregnant by her father and is ostracized; eventually she commits suicide by setting herself and the circus on fire. *Mexican Filmography.*
Awards: Guadalajara Mexican Film Festival, FIPRESCI, 1992; Fantasporto, Best Actress, Special Jury Award, 1993

1337. *Novia que te vea / Bride to Be* 1992 DSP
D: Guita Schyfter
S: Hugo Hiriart, Guita Schyfter; based on the novel by Rosa Nissan
C: Toni Kuhn
P: Guita Schyfter
A: Angélica Aragón, Claudette Maillé
Mexico City, 1950s. Two women from immigrant Jewish families, one Polish Ashkenazi, the other Turkish Sephardim, become friends. The more wealthy and conservative Turk, whose family owns a cloth mill, is a painter attracted to the more free life of the socialist activist Pole. The differences in orthodox and conservative Jewish upbringing are described in detail via portraits of the mothers and contrasting parental approaches to acquiring marriage partners for their daughters.
Other titles: Like a Bride
Awards: Guadalajara Mexican Film Festival, Audience Award, 1993; Ariel Awards, Best First Film, Best Supporting Actress (Aragón), 1994

1338. *Serpientes y escaleras / Snakes and Ladders*   1992 P
D: Busi Cortés

S: Busi Cortés
C: Francisco Bojorquez
P: Georgina Terán
A: Diana Bracho, Arcelia Ramírez, Lumi Cavazos, Gregorio Cisneros
Guanajuato. A politician helps one of his daughter's childhood friends find stability when her own father dies; but he ends up seducing the friend and leaving her pregnant. *FII.*

1339. *La Reina de la noche / Queen of the Night* 1994 S
D: Arturo Ripstein
S: Paz Alicia Garciadiego
C: Bruno De Keyzer
P: Jean-Michel Lacor
A: Reyes Spínolda, Blanca Guerra, Ana Ofelia Murguía
1930s. A biography of famed folk singer Lucha Reyes, who committed suicide in 1948. *FII.*
Awards: Gramado Film Festival, Special Mention, 1994; Havana Film Festival, Best Supporting Actress (Guerra), 1994; Ariel Awards, Best Actress (Spínolda), Best Supporting Actress (Murguía), 1996

1340. *Profundo carmesi / Deep Crimson* 1996 S
D: Arturo Ripstein
S: Paz Alicia Garciadiego
C: Guillermo Granillo
A: Regina Orozco, Julietta Egurrola
A nurse with two children leaves them in an orphanage to pursue a romantic attachment to a man who steals from rich women. Soon enough, her jealousy leads her to murder his victims. Comedy. *AMG.*
Awards: Venice Film Festival, Best Screenplay, 1996; Ariel Awards, Best Actress (Orozco), Best Supporting Actress (Egurrola), 1997

1341. *Un Embrujo / Under a Spell* 1998 P
D: Carlos Carrera
S: Carlos Carrera, Martín Salinas
C: Rodrigo Prieto
P: Bertha Navarro
A: Blanca Guerra
Mexico, 1920s. A teacher has an affair with a student but loves another; years later, she is branded a witch when the dead body of her lover turns up. *Film Society. 1999, Aug.*
Awards: Ariel Awards, Best Direction, Best Actress, 1999

1342. *Así es la vida / Such Is Life* 2000 SP
D: Arturo Ripstein
S: Paz Alicia Garciadiego; based on the play *Medea*

by Euripedes
C: Guillermo Granillo
P: Laura Imperiale
A: Arcelia Ramírez
Mexico City. A slum-dwelling woman is abandoned by her boxer husband, who also threatens to take away her children; she plots to murder the children for revenge. *Variety. 2000, May 29.*
Other titles: C'est la vie
Awards: Havana Film Festival, FIPRESCI, 2000; Lleida Latin-American Film Festival, Best Actress, 2001

1343. *La Perdición de los Hombres / The Ruination of Men* 2000 SP
D: Arturo Ripstein
S: Paz Alicia Garciadiego
C: Guillermo Granillo
P: Laura Imperiale
A: Patricia Reyes Spindola
"Two women argue over the corpse of a no-good husband they shared." *Village Voice. 2001, Jan. 16.*
Awards: San Sebastián Film Festival, FIPRESCI, 2000; Gramado Film Festival, Best Director, 2002

1344. *De piel de víbora* 2000 DS
D: Marcela Fernández Violante
S: Marcela Fernández Violante
C: Arturo De la Rosa
A: Ana Colchero
A divorced dentist returns from vacation to find her apartment has been vandalized. Among the objects stolen is an irreplaceable album of photos from her childhood. Insisting on her rights as a victim, she pushes the justice system relentlessly in order to gain retribution for her loss. *Festival de films, 12th: 93. 2002.*

1345. *Sin dejar huella / Without a Trace* 2000 DSP
D: Maria Novaro
S: Maria Novaro
C: Serguei Saldívar
P: Dulce Kuri
A: Aitana Sánchez-Gijón, Thiare Scanda
Ciudad Juarez. A single mother who works in an assembly plant has her maternity leave coming to an end and a boyfriend who deals drugs. One day, she is asked for a lift by a woman, a dealer in pre-Columbian art who is being chased by a gang of drug dealers; the two go off together across Mexico to Cancun, becoming friends on the way. *Cine espanol. 2000.*
Awards: Sundance Film Festival, Latin America Cinema Award, 2001

1346. *Y tu mamá también* / *And Your Mother Too* 2001
D: Alfonso Cuarón
S: Alfonso Cuarón, Carlos Cuarón
C: Emmanuel Lubezki
P: Alfonso Cuarón
A: Maribel Verdú, Diego Luna, Gael García Bernal
Two young men take up with an older woman for a trip across the country; she makes love to, teases, and dominates them by turn, creating a sexual agenda that so tantalizes them with an "anything goes" philosophy that they turn to one another for pleasure. The gay encounter leads one of them to deny the friendship.
Awards: Venice Film Festival, Best Screenplay, 2001; Chicago Film Critics Association Awards, Best Film, 2003; New York Film Critics Circle Awards, Best Foreign Film, 2003

MONGOLIA

1347. *Suuder* 1986
D: Begziin Baljinnyam
C: Begziin Baljinnyam
A: Suren Dolgor, G. Ravdan
A married woman wants to live with another man, but when her husband is called to war, she has second thoughts. *Festival des 3.*
Other titles: L'Ombre

1348. *Khuin kholboo* / *The Maternal Link* 1992
D: Jigjidiin Binder
C: J. Binder
A girl is very close to another villager, who marries someone else. Weakened, she becomes accidentally blind, then decides to have a child, which she agrees to leave with her old lover and his wife because she cannot take care of it. *Festival des 3.*
Other titles: Le Lien maternel

MOROCCO

1349. *El Chergui* / *The Violent Silence* 1975
D: Moumen Smihi
S: Moumen Smihi
C: Mohamed Sekkat
A: Leila Shenna
Tangiers, 1950. "Young married woman resorts to magic to stop her husband from taking a second wife. . . . during one last ritual, she drowns." *Festival des 3.*

1350. *Arayiss min kasab* / *The Reed Dolls* 1981 DS
D: Jilalli Ferhati

S: Farida Belyazid
C: Abdel Darkaoui
A: Chaabia Adraoui, Souad Thami, Ahmed Gerhati
1950s. A young girl is arranged in marriage to an older cousin, who dies. She refuses to marry her brother-in-law, the traditional solution to her plight, and is left alone with two children—as well as the heavy consequences of insisting on going her own way. *Festival de films, 10th: 85. 1988.*
Other titles: Poupées de roseaux

1351. *Bab al-Sama maftouh* / *A Door in Heaven* 1988 D
D: Farida Benlyazid
A: Zakia Tahiri, Chaabia Adraoui, Eva Saint-Paul
A wealthy young Moroccan woman, who lives in Paris, moves back to Fez after her father's death. She turns increasingly toward Islam and makes his home into a refuge for other women. *AMG.*

1352. *Badis* 1988
D: Mohamed Abderahman
S: Nourredine Sail
C: Federico Ribes
A: Jilalli Ferhati, Maribel Verdú
1974. A teacher transfers to a remote village to better confine his wife, whom he suspects of infidelity, but then he becomes involved with a young girl. Gossip leads the two women to try to run away together. *Festival des 3.*

1353. *Keïd ensa* / *Women's Wiles* 1999 DSP
D: Farida Benlyazid
S: Farida Benlyazid
C: Serge Palatsi
P: Hassen Daldoul, Silvia Vosser
A: Samira Akariou
Fairy tale of a merchant's educated daughter, who marries a sultan and then is imprisoned for her attempts to prove her equality to him; finally she outwits him. *AMG.*

1354. *Al Ouyoune al jaffa* / *Cry No More* 2003 DSP
D: Narjiss Nejjar
S: Narjiss Nejjar
C: Denis Gravouil
P: Narjiss Nejjar
A: Raouia, Siham Assif
Atlas Mountains. An old woman leaves prison after twenty-five years and returns to her village, where she finds her daughter has established a prostitution ring for men who pay to enter the women-only village. Daughters are harshly initiated into the way of life, and the visitor is

determined to liberate them. *Festival de films, 26th: 9. 2004.*

Other titles: Les Yeux secs

Awards: Marrakech International Film Festival, Best Screenplay, 2003; Paris Film Festival, Francophone Award, 2004

1355. **Tarfaya** 2004
D: Daoud Aoulad-Syad
S: Youssef Fadel, Daoud Aoulad-Syad
C: Thierry Lebigre
A: Touria Alaoui
A woman arrives in a northern Moroccan village intent on crossing over to Spain. She has lost most of her belongings, but she waits with the others to attempt the voyage until her former boss shows up. *Festival des 3.*

NETHERLANDS

1356. **Twee vrouen / Twice a Woman** 1979 P
D: George Sluizer
S: George Sluizer, Rood Jurriën
C: Mat Van Hensbergen
P: Anne Lorden, George Sluizer
A: Bibi Andersson, Sandra Dumas
Divorced because of infertility, a museum curator has an affair with a younger woman. *Cinema of the Low: 152.*

1357. **Een Vrouw als Eva / A Woman like Eve**
1979 DS
D: Nouchka Von Brakel
S: Nouchka Von Brakel, Judith Herzberg
C: Nurit Aviv
P: Matthijs Van Heijningen
A: Monique Van de Ven, Maria Schneider
A married Dutch woman falls in love with a French woman, and a custody battle over the former's children ensues. *Directory of Contemporary.*

1358. **Charlotte** 1981 S
D: Frans Weisz
S: Frans Weisz, Judith Herzberg
C: Jerzy Lipman
P: Ferenc Kálman
A: Birgit Doll
"Life of Charlotte Salomon, a Jew who perished at Auschwitz." *Directory of Contemporary.*

1359. **Het meisje met het rode haar / The Girl with the Red Hair** 1981
D: Ben Verbong
S: Ben Verbong, Pieter De Vos
C: Theo Van de Sande

P: Chris Brouwer
A: Renée Soutendijk
Dutch resistance worker Hanny Schaft transforms into an executioner of traitors. She is executed herself by the Germans in 1945. *Directory of Contemporary.*

Awards: Berlin International Film Festival, nomination for Golden Bear, 1982

1360. **Ademloos / Breathless** 1982 DS
D: Mady Saks
S: Mady Saks
C: Cees Samsom
P: Roeland Kerbasch
A: Monique Van de Ven, Linda Van Dijck
"Woman has a nervous breakdown after an attack of hyperventilation." *Directory of Contemporary.*

1361. **De Stilte rond Christine M. / A Question of Silence** 1982 DS
D: Marleen Gorris
S: Marleen Gorris
C: Frans Bromet
P: Matthijs Van Heijningen
A: Edda Barends, Nelly Frijda, Henriette Tol, Cox Habbema
Amsterdam. A prison psychiatrist is assigned to analyze three women who have been arrested for murdering a shop owner. When one of the women was caught shoplifting, the others spontaneously defended her, and the three beat the shop owner to death. The women, who were not acquainted before the incident, are comfortable with their action, and the psychiatrist is forced to consider factors outside her normal professional understanding, which affects her relationship with her husband.
Awards: Créteil International Women's Film Festival, Grand Prix, 1982; Nederlands Film Festival, Best Film, 1982

1362. **Ven de koele meren des doods / Hedwig, or the Cool Lakes of Death** 1982 DS
D: Nouchka Von Brakel
S: Nouchka Von Brakel; based on the novel by Frederik van Eden
C: Theo Van de Sande
P: Matthijs Van Heijningen
A: Renée Soutendijk
Around 1900, a wealthy woman becomes a drug addict. *Directory of Contemporary.*

1363. **De Stille oceaan / Silent Ocean**
1983 DSP
D: Digna Sinke
S: Annemarie Vandeputter

C: Albert Vanderwildt
P: Marion Hänsel, Hans Klap
A: Josée Ruiter, Josée De Pauw
The story of the difficulties faced by a journalist returned from assignment in Latin America, including issues about euthanasia and her marriage for the purpose of immigration. *Directory of Contemporary.*
Other titles: *The Silent Pacific*
Awards: Berlin International Film Festival, nomination for Golden Bear, 1984

1364. *Desirée*   1984
D: Felix De Rooy
S: Norman De Palm
C: Ernest Dickerson
P: Norman De Palm
A: Marianne Rolle
Brooklyn. A pregnant black woman must deal with an insecure lover, a fundamentalist priest, and a racist employer. She believes her child is the source of this evil. *African Diaspora. 2001. Accessed 2004, Aug. 15.*

1365. *Emma Zunz*   1984
D: Peter Delpeut
S: Peter Delpeut
C: Herman Boogaerdt
P: Frank Van Reemst
A: Willemien Van Dartel
"Young woman murders the director of a factory where she works to avenge her father's being wrongfully accused of embezzlement." *Directory of Contemporary.*
Awards: Nederlands Film Festival, Tuschinski Award, 1984

1366. *Gebroken spiegels / Broken Mirrors*   1984 DS
D: Marleen Gorris
S: Marleen Gorris
C: Frans Bromet
P: Matthijs Van Heijningen
A: Lineke Rijxman, Henriette Tol, Edda Barends
A woman lives with a drug addict, and her child, while she prostitutes herself; the film engages with the house where she works, the daily routine of the prostitutes and their clients. Parallel to this is the story of a wife who is suddenly removed from her home, tied to a bed, and tortured: Her assailant is not shown. *Festival de films, 7th: 12. 1985.*

1367. *Iris*   1985 DS
D: Mady Saks
S: Mady Saks, Felix Thijssen

C: Frans Bromet
P: Frans Rasker
A: Monique Van de Ven
A thirty-year-old veterinarian leaves the city and the man she lives with to settle in a country village and assert her independence. But she is persistently confronted with "jealous and lustful" men, which leaves her vulnerable to gossip. She worries about her reputation, until one night she is raped and her house ransacked, at which point she finds she must assert herself for good.

1368. *Dagboek van een oude dwaas / Diary of a Mad Old Man*   1986 DS
D: Lili Rademakers
S: Hugo Claus, Claudine Bouvier; based on the novel by Junichiro Tanizaki
C: Paul Van Den Bos
A: Ralph Michael, Beatie Edney
A rich banker is fixated on his beautiful daughter, whom he has spoiled. When his wife dies and he has a heart attack and must stay at home, his passion knows no reason, and the young woman knows the game well enough to get whatever she wants. *Festival de films, 11th: 142. 1989.*
Other titles: *Journal d'un vieux fou*

1369. *Een Maand later / A Month Later*   1987 DS
D: Nouchka Von Brakel
S: Nouchka Von Brakel, Jan Donkers
C: Peter de Bont
P: Matthijs Van Heijningen
A: Renée Soutendijk, Monique Van de Ven
A journalist answers an ad to exchange lives for a month with a housewife who manages a "perfectly run" household, with three teenagers and an understanding "master of the household" husband, who is also a psychiatrist. Comedy. *Variety. 1987, Sep. 23.*

1370. *Krokodillen in Amsterdam / Crocodiles in Amsterdam*   1989 DS
D: Annette Apon
S: Annette Apon, Yolanda Entius
C: Bernd Wouthuysen
A: Joan Nederlof, Yolanda Entius
Two friends are opposites—one extroverted, rebellious, and in charge, the other dreamy and project driven; they travel together to Amsterdam. Comedy. *Festival de films, 12th: 27. 1990.*

1371. *De onfatsoenlijke vrouw / The Indecent Woman*   1991 S
D: Ben Verbong
S: Ben Verbong, Marianne Dikker

C: Lex Wertwijn
P: Haig Balian
A: José Way, Huub Stapel
A married mother pursues her sexual fantasies with a strange man, but she objects when the man interferes in her domestic life. *AMG.*

1372. Belle   1993 DS
D: Irma Achten
S: Irma Achten
C: Nestor Sanz
P: Kees Kasander
A: Wivineke Van Groningen
A woman is determined not to be like her cold mother; early in life she has a lesbian relationship with her mother's housekeeper, then marries, has children, and founds a chain of clothing stores. Through it all, she remains attached to her first love and, therefore, unhappy with herself. *FII. Also lez films. Accessed 2005, June 10.*

1373. Belle Van Zuylen / Madame de Charrière
                                                        1993 DS
D: Digna Sinke
S: Digna Sinke
C: Goert Giltay
P: René Scholten
A: Will Van Kralingen
Eighteenth century. A biography of a Dutch noblewoman who, at twenty-three, wrote a scathing critique of her class, then married a noble Swiss and continued to publish and write music. Tiring of the oppressive society at Neuchâtel, she moved to Paris and fell in love with Benjamin Constant, twenty-seven years her junior. Their eight-year correspondence represents a historical documentation of the condition of women at the time. *Festival de films, 16th: 25. 1994.*

1374. Die tödliche Maria / Deadly Maria 1993 S
D: Tom Twyker
S: Tom Twyker, Christiane Voss
C: Frank Griebe
P: Tom Twyker
A: Nina Petri, Katia Studt
A young woman cares for her needy father and narrow-minded husband, then snaps when her husband steals the household money she has been saving; she murders them both. *FII.*
Awards: Sochi International Film Festival, Special Jury Prize, 1994; Bavarian Film Awards, Best Actress (Petri), 1995

1375. Marie-Antoinette is niet dood / Marie Antoinette Is Not Dead   1995 DS
D: Irma Achten

S: Irma Achten
C: Tinus Holthius
A: Antje De Boeck, Karlijn Silleghem
The rehabilitation of Marie Antoinette: "oppressed by her father, she grows up to be a fickle and difficult woman," the predecessor of Lady Di. Fantasy. *Festival de films, 18th: 27. 1996.*

1376. Tot ziens / Goodbye   1995 DSP
D: Heddy Honigmann
S: Heddy Honigmann, Helena Van der Meulen
C: Stef Tijdink
P: Suzanne Van Voorst
A: Johanna ter Steege
A couple find themselves in an unrealistic relationship, as he is married. *FII.*
Awards: Locarno International Film Festival, Special Prize, 1995; Nederlands Film Festival, Dutch Film Critics Award, 1995

1377. Antonia's Line   1996 DSP
D: Marleen Gorris
S: Marleen Gorris
C: Willy Stassen
P: Hans De Weers, Judy Cournihan
A: Willeke Von Ammelrooy, Els Dottermans
A dying, never-married matriarch looks back on her life and the lives of her unmarried daughters and granddaughters. They all live in a village where they have been central and active, even dominant, participants in the community.
Other titles: Antonian maailma

1378. Licht / When the Light Comes   1997 S
D: Stijn Coninx
S: Jean Van der Velde; based on the novel by Heleen van der Laan
C: Theo Bierkens
P: Paul Voorthuysen
A: Francesca Vanthielen
Arctic Circle. A young woman seeks adventure in the northern ice floes and decides to spend the winter in a hut with a loner and his dogs. *FII.*
Awards: Rouen Nordic Film Festival, Grand Jury Prize, 1999; Tromsø International Film Festival, Audience Award, 1999

1379. Hauptsache Leben / Life Is the Main Thing   1998 DS
D: Connie Walther
S: Connie Walther
C: Frank Griebe
P: Tobias Stiller
A: Renée Soutendijk
A woman with two daughters undergoes a mastectomy for breast cancer; her lover proposes

marriage, but another man has come into her life. *FII*.

1380. *Twee koffers / Left Luggage* 1998
D: Jeroen Krabbé
S: Edwin De Vries
C: Walther Van den Ende
P: Ate de Jong
A: Laura Fraser, Marianne Sägebrecht, Isabella Rossellini
Antwerp, 1970s. A woman takes a job as a nanny in a strict Hasidic household; her liberal Jewish background conflicts with their daily life. *Film Society. 1999, Jan.*
Awards: Berlin International Film Festival, Special Award (Rossellini), 1998; Enden International Film Festival, Best Picture, 1998; Nederlands Film Festival, Grolsch Film Award, 1998

1381. *Babs* 2000 DS
D: Irma Achten
S: Irma Achten
C: Reinier Van Brummelen
A: Brigitte Kaandorp
An unmarried mother lives above a café with her eight-year-old daughter. Musical comedy. *Skrien, vol. 32, no. 10: 32–33. 2000, Dec.*

1382. *Îles flottantes* 2001 DS
D: Nanouk Leopold
S: Nanouk Leopold
C: Benito Strangio
P: Jeroen Beker
A: Maria Kraakman, Manja Topper, Halina Reijn
Three thirtyish women are close friends and continue to support one another as they try to find mates. Comedy. *Dutch Treats. Accessed 2004, Aug. 15.*
Awards: Nederlands Film Festival, Prize of the City, 2001

1383. *Nynke* 2001
D: Pieter Verhoeff
S: Pieter Verhoeff; based on the life of Sjoukje Bokma de Boer, who wrote under the pseudonym Nynke Van Hichtum
C: Paul Van den Bos
P: Hans De Weers
A: Monic Hendrickx
A writer of children's books lives in the shadow of her famous sexist husband, a socialist statesman. Burdened with two children, she succumbs to a nervous breakdown but is healed through the support of "some enlightened women." *Variety: 24. 2001, Nov. 5.*
Awards: Nederlands Film Festival, Best Film, Best

Actress, 2001; Newport Beach Film Festival, Best Actress, 2002

1384. *Zus & Zo* 2001 DSP
D: Paula Van der Oest
S: Paula Van der Oest
C: Bert Pot
P: Jacqueline De Goeij
A: Monic Hendrickx, Anneke Blok, Sylvia Poorta, Jacob Derwig
Three sisters try to thwart their family seaside home being inherited by their gay brother, who plans to marry a girlfriend for the purpose of gaining the inheritance. *Variety: 41. 2001, Oct. 15.*
Awards: Academy Awards, nomination for Best Foreign Film, 2003

NEW ZEALAND

1385. *Constance* 1984
D: Bruce Morrison
S: Jonathan Hardy
C: Kevin Hayward
P: Larry Paar
A: Donogh Rees
Auckland, 1948. A teacher, who mimics the vamps of Hollywood and wanders from one job to another, is raped by a visiting Hollywood photographer. *New Zealand.*
Awards: Taorima Film Festival, Bronze Award, 1984

1386. *Iris* 1984
D: Tony Isaac
S: Keith Aberdein
C: James Bartle
P: John Barnet
A: Helen Morse
The life of writer Iris Wilkonson, pen name Robin Hyde, who was born in South Africa and moved from Australia to England to China during the 1930s and 1940s. The story is told from the viewpoint of the screenwriter and actress researching her life. *New Zealand.*
Other titles: Out of Time

1387. *Mr. Wrong* 1984 DSP
D: Gaylene Preston
S: Gaylene Preston, Geoff Murphy; based on a story by Elizabeth Jane Howard
C: Thom Burstyn
P: Robin Laing
A woman buys a Jaguar automobile that is haunted by a murdered woman and that does not unlock for men. Pursued by a series of men herself, she

eventually finds a solution to her troubles with the car. Thriller. *New Zealand.*

Awards: Créteil International Women's Film Festival, Most Popular Film, 1986; New Zealand Film and TV Awards, Best Female Performance, 1986

1388. *Other Halves* 1984 S
D: John Laing
S: Sue McCauley; based on the novel by Sue Mc-Cauley
C: Leon Narbey
P: Tom Finlayson
A: Lisa Harrow, Mark Pilisi
Auckland. A thirtyish white woman who is separated from her husband meets a Polynesian teenager in a mental hospital, and they make a life together on the outside. *New Zealand.*

1389. *Trial Run* 1984 DS
D: Melanie Read
S: Melanie Read
C: Allen Guilford
P: Don Reynolds
A: Annie Whittle
A former champion distance runner leaves her family to photograph penguins near the coast. Suspecting she is being stalked, she discovers she is being followed by her teenage son. Mystery. *New Zealand.*
Other titles: Austral

1390. *Sylvia* 1985 S
D: Michael Firth
S: Michael Firth, Michele Quill; based on books by Sylvia Ashton-Warner
P: Don Reynolds, Michael Firth
A: Eleanor David
The life of Sylvia Ashton-Warner, a rural teacher of Maori, who developed a new teaching method and became famous when her books documenting her success were published in the 1950s. She was also a novelist. See also *The Spinster* (1891), based on one of her novels. *New Zealand.*
Awards: New Zealand Film and TV Awards, Best Actress, 1986

1391. *Mauri* 1988 DSP
D: Merata Mita
S: Merata Mita
C: Graeme Cowley
P: Merata Mita
A: Eva Rickard
In a traditional "north Island settlement," the unity of "land and life force" (Mauri) is threatened. Women, in particular a grandmother, propose an open yet preservation-minded environment. An all-Maori production. *New Zealand.*

1392. *An Angel at My Table* 1990 DSP
D: Jane Campion
S: Laura Jones; based on an autobiographical novel by Janet Frame
C: Stuart Dryburgh
P: Bridgit Ikin
A: Kerry Fox, Alexia Keogh, Karen Fergusson
The story of Janet Frame, her childhood as a chubby, stubborn, and shy child lost in a loving but large working-class family and her troubled early adulthood when she repeatedly submitted herself to confinement in mental institutions. She eventually extricated herself from institutional life through the accomplishment of her novels and became strong enough to withstand abandonment by her first lover. Three red-haired actresses play the part.
Awards: Film Critics Circle of Australia Awards, Best Foreign Film, 1990; Venice Film Festival, Special Jury Prize, 1990; Berlin International Film Festival, Film Prize, 1991

1393. *Bread and Roses* 1990 DSP
D: Gaylene Preston
S: Gaylene Preston, Graeme Tetley
C: Allen Guilford
P: Robin Laing
A: Genevieve Picot, John Laing
Early 1900s. A biography of an early women's rights advocate, Australian Sonja Davies. Born of an unmarried mother and divorced by the age of seventeen, she nonetheless managed to become a "trainee nurse" during World War II. She then became a socialist activist and led the women's rights movement in Australia in the 1950s. This very popular film was made into a four-hour miniseries for Australian television. *AMG.*
Awards: New Zealand Film and TV Awards, Best Actress, 1994

1394. *Ruby and Rata* 1990 DP
D: Gaylene Preston
S: Graeme Tetley
C: Leon Narbey
P: Robin Laing, Gaylene Preston
A: Yvonne Lawley, Vanessa Rare
An Auckland suburbanite rents a room in her house to a single mother. *New Zealand.*

1395. *Crush* 1992 DSP
D: Alison MacLean
S: Alison MacLean, Anne Kennedy
C: Dion Beebe
P: Bridget Ilkin
A: Marcia Gay Harden, Donogh Rees, Caitlin Bossley

Two old school friends, one aimless, the other a literary critic, take a trip to interview a prize-winning author; a car crash leaves the critic hospitalized, while the other seduces the author and his daughter.

1396. *Heavenly Creatures* 1994
D: Peter Jackson
S: Frances Walsh, Peter Jackson
C: Alun Bollinger
P: Jim Booth
A: Kate Winslet, Melanie Lynskey
Two friends, bonded through an intense fantasy life, murder the working-class mother of one when they are threatened with separation by the leave-taking of the wealthy other mother.
Awards: New Zealand Film and TV Awards, Best Actress (Lynskey), 1994; Venice Film Festival, Silver Lion, 1994; London Critics' Circle Film Awards, Best Actress (Winslet), 1996

1397. *Once Were Warriors* 1994 S
D: Lee Tamahori
S: Riwia Brown, Alan Duff
C: Stuart Dryburgh
P: Robin Scholes
A: Rena Owen, Manaengaroa Kerr-Bell, Temerua Morrison
Auckland. A mother from a proud Maori heritage engages in a drinking, partying lifestyle with her abusive husband. The children suffer greatly: One son is jailed, another is a gang member, and the daughter commits suicide after being raped.
Awards: Montréal World Film Festival, Best Film, Best Actress (Owen), 1994; Rotterdam International Film Festival, Best Film, 1995; San Diego Film Festival, Best Actress (Owen), 1995

1398. *Broken English* 1996 S
D: Gregor Nicholas
S: Gregor Nicholas, Johanna Pigott
C: John Toon
P: Robin Scholes
A: Aleksandra Vujcic, Madeline McNamara, Elizabeth Mavric
Adult sisters and their mother suffer under an autocratic Croatian father in Auckland, where they have emigrated. The neighborhood also includes Pacific Islanders, Chinese, and Maori.
Awards: TV Guide Film and Television Awards, Best Supporting Actress (McNamara), 1996

1399. *Topless Women Talk about Their Lives*
1997
D: Harry Sinclair
S: Harry Sinclair

C: Dale McCready
P: Harry Sinclair
A: Danielle Cormack
A woman misses an abortion appointment and realizes she now must have the baby and decide how to cope with the fact that her current boyfriend is not the father. *FII.*
Awards: New Zealand Film and TV Awards, Best Director, Best Actress, 1997; Thessaloniki Film Festival, Special Mention, 1997

1400. *Perfect Strangers* 2003 DSP
D: Gaylene Preston
S: Gaylene Preston
C: Alun Bollinger
P: Gaylene Preston
A: Sam Neill, Rachael Black
A woman leaves a pub with a man and ends up kidnapped on his boat in the middle of the sea. Thriller. *Festival de films, 26th: 25. 2004.*
Awards: Fantasporto, Best Actress, 2004

NICARAGUA

1401. *Mujeres de la frontera / Frontier Women*
1986
D: Iván Arguello
Under siege by the Contras, village women take an active part in the revolution. *Nicaragua: Retrospectiva. Accessed 2005, July 15.*

NIGERIA

1402. *Emotional Crack* 2003
D: Lancelot Oduwa-Imasuen
A: Uduak Akrah, Emma Ayalogu
A woman, used to forgiving her husband for his battering, is befriended by someone who "gives her confidence to deal with him, and leads her down a path where modern values and tradition collide." *Film Society.* 2004, Apr.

NORWAY

1403. *Hustruer / Wives* 1975 DS
D: Anja Breien
S: Anja Breien
C: Halvor Naess
P: Hans Lindgren
A: Frøydis Armand, Katja Medbøe, Anne-Marie Ottersen
Three wives, one pregnant, take some days away from family responsibilities when they meet at a

school reunion after many years of separation. They have fun talking, touring around town, and flirting with men; much of the dialogue is improvised by the actresses. The film inspired two sequels. *Encyclopedia of European. Also Variety: 14. 1975, Aug. 27.*
Awards: Locarno International Film Festival, Ecumenical Jury Prize, 1975

1404. *Apenbaringen / Revelation*   1977 DS
D: Vibeke Løkkeberg
S: Vibeke Løkkeberg
A: Marie Takvam
A wife and mother nears sixty; her children gone, she tries to find employment, but ends up having a nervous breakdown. *Variety. 1979, Jan. 10.*

1405. *Forfolgelsen / Witch Hunt*   1981 DS
D: Anja Breien
S: Anja Breien
C: Erling Thurmann-Andersen
P: Gunnar Svensrud
A: Lil Terselius
Seventeenth century. A woman who lives in a remote mountain community decides to seek work in a farm village. A woman "of independent spirit and open sexuality," she is executed for being a witch. *St. James: 55.*
Awards: Venice Film Festival, Best Actress, 1981

1406. *Liten Ida / Little Ida*   1981 DS
D: Laila Mikkelsen
S: Laila Mikkelsen, Marit Paulsen
C: Hans Welin
P: Harald Ohrvik
A: Lise Fjeldstad, Sunniva Lindeklejv
A single mother has an affair with a German soldier in Nazi-occupied Norway; the older siblings disappear and the youngest, seven years old, is made to take the abuse from the community as well as from her mother. *Variety: 22. 1981, Sep. 9.*
Other titles: *Growing Up*
Awards: Guldbagge Awards, Best Actress (Fjeldstad, Lindeklejv), 1982

1407. *Papirfügien / Paper Bird*   1984 DS
D: Anja Breien
S: Anja Breien
C: Erling Thurmann-Andersen
P: Bente Erichsen
A: Elisabeth Mortensen
Oslo. A lawyer investigates the suicide death of her father, an actor. Mystery. *Festival de films, 7th: 18. 1985.*
Other titles: *Le Cerf volant*
Awards: Mystfest, nomination for Best Film, 1985

1408. *Snart Sjutton / Sweet 17*   1984 D
D: Laila Mikkelsen
S: Karin Sveen
C: Rolv Håan
A: Gerd Brotnow
An overweight woman with little confidence clashes with her friends and family and learns to rely on her inner strength. She falls in love and becomes pregnant, but she makes up her mind that she cannot keep the child and decides to have an abortion. *Kvinnor i nordisk: 63.*

1409. *Hustruer ti ar etter / Wives: Ten Years After*   1985 DS
D: Anja Breien
S: Anja Breien, Knut Faldbakken
C: Erling Thurmann-Andersen
P: Bente Erichsen
A: Frøydis Armand, Katja Medbøe, Anne-Marie Ottersen
Three old school friends spend a drunken Christmas eve on the streets of Oslo, then run away briefly to a Swedish luxury hotel. Sequel to *Hustruer / Wives* (1403). *Variety. 1985, Nov. 13.*
Awards: Amanda Awards, Best Film, Best Actress (Ottersen), 1986

1410. *Hud / Skin*   1986 DS
D: Vibeke Løkkeberg
S: Vibeke Løkkeberg
P: Terje Kristiansen
A: Vibeke Løkkeberg
Bergen, turn of the century. A woman who is controlled by her father is promised to a man against her will. *FII.*
Other titles: *Vilde, the Wild One*

1411. *Måker / Seagulls*   1991 DS
D: Vibeke Løkkeberg
S: Vibeke Løkkeberg, Kristiansen Terje
C: Paul Roestad
P: Kristiansen Terje
A: Vibeke Løkkeberg
1915. A mentally ill woman returns to her family. *Variety: 54. 1991, Feb. 25.*

1412. *Hustruer III / Wives III*   1996 DS
D: Anja Breien
S: Anja Breien
C: Halvor Naess
P: Bente Erichsen
A: Frøydis Armand, Katja Medbøe, Anne-Marie Ottersen
Oslo. Three old school friends leave their husbands for a few days to experience independence.

The sequel reprises a few scenes from the two earlier films (1403, 1409) and finds the women celebrating being fifty on a streetcar, bickering a lot, and ending up in a hot-air balloon. Improvised dialogue shows the depth and character in the actresses' relations; in one scene, they spy an old woman creaking along the street, then stop to imagine how they will feel and be acting at that age.

1413. *Kristin Lavransdatter* 1996 DS
D: Liv Ullmann
S: Liv Ullmann; based on the novel by Sigrid Undset
C: Sven Nykvist
P: Göran Lindström
A: Elizabeth Matheson
Norway, middle ages. A wealthy young woman's beauty and passion for a friend over her betrothed lead her to a convent, where she falls in love—across the walls of the convent—with a knight who is socially above her but "banned" because he is a father, and a married woman is his mistress. The knight is also in love, but it is the girl who transcends the barriers of her parents' opposition and the mistress's anger and guarantees their union. Almost all the arranged marriages in the film involve mismatches due to different ages.

1414. *Salige er de som törster / Blessed Are Those Who Thirst* 1997 S
D: Carl Jörgen Kiönig
S: Axel Hellstenius; based on the novel by Ann Holt
C: Kjell Vassdal
P: Petter Borgli
A: Kjersti Elvik
A lesbian motorcycle police detective has a live-in lover and a male partner on the force; they investigate a rape and murder. Thriller. *Variety: 56. 1998, Oct. 26.*
Awards: Amanda Awards, Best Film, Best Actress, 1998

1415. *Det Storste i verden / The Greatest Thing* 2001 S
D: Thomas Robsahm
S: Riri Senje; based on *The Fisherman's Daughter* by Bjornstjerne Bjornson
C: Gaute Gunnari
P: Truls Kontny
A: Herborg Krakevik
Nineteenth century. A young woman who is forced to leave her hometown because of marauders takes refuge with a minister and his daughter,

with whom she becomes close friends. It develops that she lied and left home because she was engaged to three men at once, and her friend is now in love with one of them. *Variety: 31. 2001, Nov. 18.*
Awards: Amanda Awards, nomination for Best Actress, 2002

PAKISTAN

1416. *Khamosh pani / Silent Waters* 2003 DS
D: Sabiha Sumar
S: Sabiha Sumar, Paromita Vohra
C: Ralph Netzer
P: Helge Albers
A: Kiron Kher
A widowed Sikh woman was forced into the Muslim faith as a teenager; her village was overrun, and she was commanded by her father to throw herself down a well, but instead she ran away and was taken in by a Muslim, who married her. She hides her true faith, teaches a liberal Muslim doctrine, and never goes near the well. Her beloved son, threatened by the ambition of his young love and insecure about not having a father, becomes an Islamic extremist in his adulthood.
Awards: Locarno International Film Festival, Best Actress, Golden Leopard, 2003; Nantes Three Continents Festival, Silver Montgolfiere, 2003

PALESTINE

1417. *Al Zakira al khasba* 1980
D: Michel Khleifi
S: Michel Khleifi
C: Yves Meeren
A: Farah Hatoum, Sahar Khalifa
The stories of two women: a widow of fifty years who struggles to regain a plot of ground seized by the Israelis in 1948, and a young novelist who fights to obtain a divorce and keep her children. *Festival de films, 10th: 86. 1988.*

1418. *Rana's Wedding* 2003 SC
D: Hany Abu-Assad
S: Liana Badr, Ihab Lamey
C: Brigit Hillenius
P: Bero Beyer
A: Clara Khoury
A wealthy young woman negotiates checkpoints on her way to Israeli-occupied territory, where her boyfriend lives. *Village Voice: 64. 2003, Aug. 13.*

PERU

1419. *Du verbe aimer / About the Verb Love*
                                              1984 DS
D: Mary Jimeniz
S: Mary Jiminez
A: Mary Jiminez
A "poetic explosion" in the first person of "unre-
quited desire for a mother." *French-Speaking: 35.*

1420. *Malabrigo*   1986
D: Alberto Durant
S: Alberto Durant
C: Mario Garcia Joya
P: Andres Malatesta
A: Charo Verástegui
Malabrigo. A woman arrives to join her accountant
husband in an economically dying fishing port,
but he has disappeared. *Guide to Latin: 197.*

1421. *Coraje / Courage*   1998 SP
D: Alberto Durant
S: Alberto Durant, Ana Caridad Sanchez
C: Mario Garcia Joya
P: Beatriz De la Gándara
A: Olenka Cepeda
Lima. The story of charismatic activist Maria Elena
Moyano, founder of the Women's Federation of
Villa El Salvador, who was assassinated in 1993
at the age of thirty-three by the Shining Path
because she refused to allow them to take over
her operations. The film details the difficulties
caused by her extraordinary commitment as
well as her many warm relationships with family,
friends, and government officials, which along
with her courage and intelligence made her so
powerful. She was supported by the press with
the nickname "Mama *Coraje*."

1422. *La Carnada*   1999 D
D: Marianne Eyde
C: Cesar Perez
A: Monica Sanchez, Gabriela Velásquez
In a small fishing village, a pregnant wife and her
husband have a spiritual relationship with nature. The woman is threatened by another local
woman, who lives a free sexual life, having many
love affairs while still living with a husband. *Festival de films, 24th: 97. 2002.*
Awards: Havana Film Festival, FIPRESCI, 1999

1423. *El Destino no tiene favoritos / Destiny
Has No Favorites*   2002
D: Alvaro Velarde
S: Alvaro Velarde
C: Micaela Cajahuaringa

P: Alvaro Velarde
A: Celine Aguirre, Tatiana Astengo
A bored housewife gets left behind in a house
where a TV soap opera is being filmed. Comedy.
Film Society. 2003, Sep.
Awards: Lima Latin American Film Festival, Best
Actress (Astengo), 2003

PHILIPPINES

1424. *Insiang*   1976
D: Lino Brocka
S: Lamberto Antonio, Mario O'Hara
C: Conrado Baltazar
A: Hilda Koronel, Mona Lisa
Manila. In a slum where they are market vendors,
a daughter is raped by her mother's hoodlum
lover; disbelieved by her mother, the girl plots
revenge and eventually provokes the mother
into murdering the offender. *Database of Philip-
pine. Accessed 2003, Aug. 13.*
Awards: FAMAS Awards, Best Supporting Actress
(Lisa), 1977; Manila Film Festival, Best Actress
(Koronel), Best Supporting Actress (Lisa), 1977;
Filipino Film Critics, Best of the 1970s

1425. *Mins'y isang gamu-gamo / Corazon de la
Cruz*   1976 DSP
D: Lupita Aquino-Kashiwahara
S: Marina Feleo Gonzalez
C: Joe Batac
P: Digna Santiago
A: Nora Aunor
A nurse who has been raised near an American
military base wants to immigrate to the United
States, but an American soldier accidentally kills
her brother, and she must reevaluate her ambi-
tion. *Database of Philippine. Accessed 2003, Aug. 13.*
Awards: FAMAS Awards, Best Picture, Best Direc-
tor, 1977

1426. *Tatlong taong walong Diyos / Three God-
less Years*   1976
D: Mario O'Hara
S: Mario O'Hara
A: Nora Aunor
"Young girl survives during the Japanese occupation."
Database of Philippine. Accessed 2003, Aug. 13.
Awards: FAMAS Awards, Best Actress, 1977; Gawad
Urian Awards, Best Actress, 1977

1427. *Ina, kapatid, anak / Mother, Sister, Daugh-
ter*   1979 P
D: Lino Brocka
S: Mel Chionglo

C: Conrado Baltazar
P: Lily Monteverde
A: Lolita Rodriguez, Charito Solis

A daughter returns to her village after working in the United States for twenty years. The house is in disarray, and her half sister who lives there with their father is an alcoholic. The two have always conflicted, and tension leads to their father's death. *Festival des 3.*

Awards: Gawad Urian Awards, Best Actress (Solis), 1980

1428. *Brutal* 1980 D
D: Marilou Díaz Abaya
S: Ricardo Lee
C: Manolo Anaya
A: Amy Austria, Gina Alajar, Chara Santos

A journalist investigates murders of a husband and two of his friends, committed by a battered woman. The perpetrator refuses to speak when the case becomes a media sensation, and the journalist must interview others, including a prostitute, to uncover the truth. *Database of Philippine. Accessed 2005, June 10.*

Awards: Manila Film Festival, Best Picture, Best Actress (Austria), 1980; FAMAS Awards, Best Actress (Austria), 1981; Gawad Urian Awards, Best Actress (Alajar), 1981

1429. *Bona* 1981 P
D: Lino Brocka
S: Cenen Ramones
C: Conrado Baltazar
P: Nora Aunor
A: Nora Aunor, Rustica Carpio

Manila. An eighteen-year-old middle-class woman is abused by her father, then her boyfriend, but eventually fights back. *MOMA Film. 2000, Dec.*

1430. *Salome* 1981 D
D: Laurice Guillen
S: Ricardo Lee
A: Gina Alajar

Camarines Norte, in the countryside. Three versions of a murder by a woman of her lover involve "legends and folk tales" and provide a "play on [the] Filipina's virtuous image." *AMG. Also Bayami Magazine. Accessed 2006, July 10.*

Awards: Gawad Urian Awards, Best Director, Best Actress, 1981

1431. *Moral* 1982 D
D: Marilou Díaz Abaya
S: Ricardo Lee
C: Manolo Abaya

A: Lorna Tolentino, Anna Martin, Gina Alajar, Sandy Andolong

The stories of four young women with "intertwining" lives: "a promiscuous drug addict in love with an activist, a singer who sleeps her way to fame, a lawyer devoted to a homosexual husband, and an expectant mother frustrated by a chauvinist husband." *Database of Philippine. Accessed 2005, June 10.*

Awards: FAMAS Awards, Best Supporting Actress (Andolong), 1982

1432. *Bulaklak ng City Jail / Flowers of the City Jail* 1984
D: Mario O'Hara
S: Lualhati Bautista
C: Johnny Araojo
A: Nora Aunor, Perla Bautista, Gina Alajar

A pregnant woman, arrested for murder, is sent to Manila City Prison, then escapes and bears the child while hiding in the city zoo. After recapture, she eventually gains legal custody of the child. Most of the film takes place in prison. *National Pastime: 100.*

Awards: Metro Manila Film Festival, Best Film, Best Actress (Aunor), 1984; FAMAS Awards, Best Actress (Aunor), Best Supporting Actress (Bautista), 1985

1433. *Karnal / Of the Flesh* 1985 D
D: Marilou Díaz Abaya
S: Ricardo Lee
C: Manolo Abaya
A: Charito Solis, Philip Salvador, Cecille Castillo, Grace Amilbangsa

The story is narrated directly to the camera by a middle-aged woman who has been stultified by family tragedy. Her father fled his abusive wealthy father but was forced to return to their charcoal plantation with his city-bred wife, who never adjusted to the patriarchal culture. Events escalated into a patricide, and then, while the husband is in jail, the aborting of his pregnant wife's "red devil."

1434. *Inay* 1992 P
D: Derek Dee, Artemio Marquez
S: Ricardo Lee
C: Humilde Roxas
P: Melanie Marquez
A: Nora Aunor

After her husband commits incest with their child, a wife takes justice into her own hands and a trial ensues. *IMDb.*

1435. *Lucia* 1992
D: Mel Chionglo

S: Ricardo Lee
A: Lolita Rodriguez, Gina Alajar
A woman takes her family away from a fishing village after an oil spill; they end up living outside Manila in a ghetto, where the law is corrupt, leaving them vulnerable to crime and poverty. *Database of Philippine. Also Bullfrog. Accessed 2005, June 10.*

1436. *Dahil mahal kita / The Dolzura Cortez Story* 1993 D
D: Laurice Guillen
S: Ricardo Lee
A: Vilma Santos
The true story of the first Filipina HIV/AIDS patient to come out to the media and raise consciousness about the disease: a film "ready to challenge the Filipino idea of what is right and wrong." *IMDb.*
Awards: FAP Awards, Best Actress, 1994; Gawad Urian Awards, Best Actress, 1994

1437. *The Fatima Buen Story* 1994
D: Mario O'Hara
S: Frank Rivera
C: Johnny Araojo
A: Kris Aquino
A story of women in prison: "Based on an actual case, film mixes tabloid sensationalism with paranormal symbolism and features [the film director's] trademark qualities: incipient violence and heroic love." Thriller. *Film Society. 1998, Aug.*
Awards: Gawad Urian Awards, Best Picture, Best Direction, 1994

1438. *Ika-11 utos: Mahalin mo asawa mo* 1994 D
D: Marilou Díaz Abaya
A: Aiko Melendez
The story of a battered wife and three friends who try to help her; they are all charged with the murder of her husband. *ABS-CBN. Accessed 2005, June 10.*

1439. *The Flor Contemplacion Story* 1995
D: Joel Lamangan
S: Bonifacio Ilagan, Ricardo Lee
C: Romeo Vitug
P: William C. Leary
A: Nora Aunor, Jacklyn Jose
Singapore. An immigrant domestic worker is hanged for the murder of another Filipina maid and the boy in her care. The case unleashed sympathy for the plight of domestics working in foreign countries, and the film argues her innocence. *FII.*

Awards: Cairo International Film Festival, Golden Pyramid, 1995; FAP Awards, Best Director, Best Actress (Aunor), Best Supporting Actress (Jose), 1996; Gawad Urian Awards, Best Director, Best Actress (Aunor), Best Supporting Actress (Jose), 1996

1440. *Ipaglaban mo / Redeem Her Honor* 1995 D
D: Marilou Díaz Abaya
S: Ricardo Lee
C: Eduardo Jacinto
P: Chard Santos-Concio
A: Sharmaine Arnaiz, Gina Alajar, Elizabeth Oropesa
The story of two legal cases: a girl abused by her uncle, whose mother prosecutes when she finds out, and a middle-class woman stalked by a man. *AMG.*

1441. *May nag mamahal sa iyo / May Motherhood Be Yours* 1996 DS
D: Marilou Díaz Abaya
S: Olivia Lamasan, Ricardo Lee
A: Lorna Tolentino
Hong Kong. A domestic servant returns to her hometown in the Philippines to find the son she gave up for adoption. *IMDb.*

1442. *Babae / Woman* 1997 D
D: Lupita Aquino-Kashiwahara
S: Ruel Bayani
A: Nora Aunor, Judy Ann Santos
A story of three generations: A woman copes with the death of her husband; her daughter considers changing her career and family life; the teenage granddaughter tries to keep the family together. *Database of Philippine. Accessed 2003, Aug. 13.*

1443. *Milagros* 1997 D
D: Marilou Díaz Abaya
S: Rolando Tinio
C: Eduardo Jacinto
A: Sharmaine Arnaiz, Raymond Bagatsing, Elizabeth Oropesa
A prostitute becomes a maid for a widower and his three sons. *Film Society. 2000, Aug.*
Awards: Gawad Urian Awards, Best Picture, Best Direction, Best Supporting Actress (Oropesa), 1998

1444. *Sidhi / The Story of Ah* 1998
D: Joel Lamangan
S: Ricardo Lee
C: Romulo Araojo

P: Vic Del Rosario
A: Vilma Santos
Before her father's death, a mute woman is married by him to a brutish bigamist. *Film Society. 2000, Jul.*

1445. *Babae sa bubungang lata / Woman on a Tin Roof* 1999
D: Mario O'Hara
S: Mario O'Hara, Agapito Joaquin
C: Rey De Leon
A: Aya Medel, Anita Linda
A woman and her husband, both prostitutes, go to live with her aunt, a "faded movie queen." *Village Voice: 112. 2000, Aug. 1.*
Awards: FAMAS Awards, Best Supporting Actress (Linda), 1999

1446. *Bata, bata . . . Paano ka ginawa / Lea's Story* 1999
D: Chito S. Roño
S: Lualhati Bautista
C: Charlie Peralta
P: Malou Santos
A: Vilma Santos, Serena Dalrymple
A woman's rights activist and mother of two children is threatened with losing them when her work takes her away from her family. *Film Society. 2000, Jul.*
Awards: Asia-Pacific Film Festival, Special Jury Award, 1999; FAP Awards, Best Actress (Santos, Dalrymple), 1999; Gawad Urian Awards, Best Picture, Best Actress, 1999

1447. *Bulaklak ng Maynila / Ada of Manila* 1999 P
D: Joel Lamangan
S: Domingo Landicho, Ricardo Lee
C: Monino Duque
P: Veronique Del Rosario-Corpus
A: Elizabeth Oropesa
Manila. A woman, her husband, and her teenage daughter live in a shanty on a garbage heap; the daughter is an object of desire for the local "vending rights" lord, and the relationship leads to trouble. *Film Society. 2000, Aug.*
Awards: FAMAS Awards, Best Actress, 2000; FAP Awards, Best Film, Best Director, Best Screenplay, Best Actress, 2000; Gawad Urian Awards, Best Actress, 2000

1448. *Pila balde / Fetch a Pail of Water* 1999
D: Jeffrey Jeturian
S: Armando Lao
C: Shayne Clemente
A: Ana Capri
An eighteen-year-old survives in a slum by selling fried bananas and helping her grandmother do laundry; she also takes care of her younger siblings and negotiates with suitors in hopes of getting out of the slum. *Film Society. 2000, Aug.*
Awards: Worldfest Houston, Gold Award, 2000

1449. *Anak* 2000
D: Rory B. Quintos
S: Raymond Lee, Ricardo Lee
C: Joe Batac
P: Trina Dayrit
A: Vilma Santos, Amy Austria
A woman returns to her children and family in Manila after many years of working in Hong Kong. *Filipino American. Accessed 2004, June 30.*
Awards: FAP Awards, Best Screenplay, Best Supporting Actress (Austria)

1450. *Taning yaman* 2000 DS
D: Laurice Guillen
S: Laurice Guillen
C: Lee Meily
A: Gloria Romero
A grandmother and matriarch holds the family together until they discover she has Alzheimer's disease. *AMG.*
Awards: FAP Awards, Best Picture, Best Actress, 2001; Gawad Urian Awards, Best Director, Best Actress, 2001

1451. *Hubog / Wretched Lives* 2001
D: Joel Lamangan
S: Roy C. Iglesias
C: Romulo Araojo
P: Roselle Monteverde-Teo
A: Assunta De Rossi, Alessandra De Rossi
An impoverished woman cares for her mentally unstable younger sister after the death of their parents; both sisters are raped. *Village Voice: 60. 2003, Nov. 12.*
Awards: Gawad Urian Awards, Best Actress (Assunta De Rossi), 2002

1452. *Santa Santita / Magdalena, the Unholy Spirit* 2004 D
D: Laurice Guillen
S: Johnny Delgado, Michiko Yamamoto
A: Angelica Panganiban
A woman supports herself as a magdadasal—a woman who prays for others in exchange for contributions. When she dies of worry over her free-living daughter, who sometimes prostitutes herself, the daughter takes over the job and finds her inner spirit transformed. *AMG.*

POLAND

1453. Matka Joanna od aniolóu / Mother Joan of the Angels 1961
D: Jerzy Kawalerowicz
S: Jerzy Kawalerowicz, Tadeusz Konwicki
C: Jerzy Wojcik
A: Lucyna Winnicka
A deranged abbess protects the nuns in her convent from a priest charged to relieve them from the devil's possession. *Film Society. 2004, Feb.*
Other titles: The Devil and the Nun
Awards: Cannes Film Festival, Special Jury Prize, 1961

1454. Jak byæ kochana / Art of Loving 1962
D: Wojciech J. Has
S: Brandys Kazimierz
C: Stefan Matyjaszkiewicz
A: Barbara Krafftówna, Zbigniew Cybulski
An actress on her way to Paris recalls a cowardly leading man who seduced her, a man she had sheltered from the Gestapo. *Variety. 1963, May 29.*
Other titles: How to Be Loved

1455. Za sciana / Behind the Wall 1971
D: Krzysztof Zanussi
S: Krzysztof Zanussi, Edward Zebrowski
C: Jan Hesse
A: Maja Komorowska
A science writer seeks solace from a more successful chemistry professor who lives nearby, but he is solely dedicated to his own advancement. *FII.*
Awards: San Remo International Film Festival, Grand Prix, 1971

1456. Bilans kwartalny / Balance Sheet 1974
D: Krzysztof Zanussi
S: Krzysztof Zanussi
C: Slawomir Idziak
A: Maja Komorowska, Peotr Franczewski
An accountant becomes more involved with her job, but remains bored with her husband, and begins an affair with a "free spirited" man. *Polish National: 129.*
Other titles: Quarterly Balance-Taking
Awards: Berlin International Film Festival, OCIC Award, 1975; Polish Film Festival, Best Actress, 1975

1457. Czlowiek z marmuru / Man of Marble 1977
D: Andrzej Wajda
S: Aleksander Scibor-Rylski
C: Edward Klosinski
A: Krystyna Janda, Jerzy Radziwittowicz
A filmmaker researches a famous labor leader, a "model worker" of the 1950s, and faces censorship in uncovering the oppression he experienced. A 1981 sequel, *Czlowiek z zelaza / Man of Iron*, follows the years of the filmmaker's marriage to the labor leader's son, who works at the shipyards in Gdansk, and her life in his shadow. Both films chronicle attempts to reform the Soviet empire and the beginnings of its demise.
Awards: Polish Film Festival, Critics Award, 1977; Cannes Film Festival, FIPRESCI, 1978

1458. To ja Pani Bavary / Madame Bovary, It's Me 1977
D: Zbigniew Kaminski
S: Zbigniew Kaminski
C: Zdzislaw Kaczmarek
A: Jadwiga Jankowska-Cieúlak, Krystyna Janda
A young married woman seems happy, but she seeks escape from her daily life. *Cinéma polonais: 107.*
Awards: Locarno International Film Festival, FIPRESCI, 1977

1459. Pasázerka / The Passenger 1978 S
D: Andrzej Munk
S: Andrzej Munk; based on the novel by Zofia Posmysz
C: Krysztof Winiewicz
A: Aleksandra Slaska, Anna Ciepielewska
A former female SS warden at Auschwitz sees a passenger on a plane many years later whom she thinks was a prisoner there and recalls their relationship. *Polish Feature.*
Awards: Cannes Film Festival, Special Mention, 1964; Venice Film Festival, Italian Film Critics Award, 1964

1460. Kobieta i kobieta / A Woman and a Woman 1979
D: Ryszard Bugajski
S: Ryszard Bugajski, Janusz Dymek
C: Janusz Kalicinski
A: Halina Labonarska, Anna Romantowska
Two friends uncover corruption in a garment factory and denounce the culprit, who is the lover of one; years later, one of them becomes a corrupt mayor herself. *AMG.*

1461. Bez mitosci / Without Love 1980 DS
D: Barbara Sass
S: Barbara Sass
C: Wieslaw Zdort
A: Dorota Stalínska

A journalist "yearns for a career at all costs," in the process losing her ability to love and her values so she can be "tougher than men." *Polish National: 151.*

Awards: Polish Film Festival, Best Debut Director, Best Actress, 1980

1462. *Útközben / On the Way* 1980 DS
D: Márta Mészáros
S: Márta Mészáros, Jan Nowicki, Marek Piwowski
C: Tamás Andor
A: Delphine Seyrig, Beata Tyszkiewicz, Jan Nowicki
A happily married scientist leaves her home to attend to the sudden death of a friend. She becomes involved with a fun-loving man, whom she keeps at arm's length during the series of family events that throw them together. His charm moves her, however, and a year later when he suddenly calls and asks her to meet him at the airport, she is not prepared for his "good" news.
Other titles: Po Drodze / On the Move

1463. *Kobieta samotna / A Woman Alone*
1981 DS
D: Agnieszka Holland
S: Agnieszka Holland, Maciej Karpinski
C: Jacek Petrycki
A: Maria Chwalibóg, Boguslaw Linda
A single mother, who lives next to the train tracks and barely gets by on her wage as a postal worker, meets a strange young man while on her beat. One day, she leaves her child and goes off with him. This film was originally banned in Poland.
Other titles: A Woman on Her Own / The Lonely Woman
Awards: Polish Film Festival, Best Actress, Special Jury Prize, 1988

1464. *Przesluchanie / The Interrogation* 1981
D: Ryszard Bugajski
S: Ryszard Bugajski
A: Krystyna Janda
1949. A singer is imprisoned and tortured for six years by Stalinist secret police but refuses to implicate others; she also must endure the separation from her daughter, who was born in prison. This film was originally banned in Poland. *Polish National: 213.*
Awards: Cannes Film Festival, Best Actress, 1990

1465. *W obronie wlasnej / In Self Defense* 1981
D: Zbigniew Kaminski
A: Beata Tyszkiewicz, Teresa Budzisz-Krzyzanowska, Krzysztof Jasinski

An emergency-room doctor is abandoned by her lover. Bereft, she seeks out her mother, brother, and sister, but they cannot help her. She runs into an old college friend, who has all the time she needs, but then admits that he is in love with her. *Film w Stopklatka. Accessed 2005, July 15.*

1466. *Epitafium la Barbary Radizwillowny / The Epitaph for Barbara Radizwill* 1982 S
D: Janusz Majewski
S: Janusz Majewski, Halina Auderska; based on the "Queen Bona" television serial
C: Zygmunt Samosiuk
A: Anna Dymna
Sixteenth century. A story told in flashback of a wealthy Italian who became involved with the Polish king. *FII.*

1467. *Krzyk / The Scream* 1983 DS
D: Barbara Sass
S: Barbara Sass
C: Wieslaw Zdort
A: Dorota Stalínska
A young ex-convict negotiates life outside by moving away from the influence of her old friends and family. *Polish National: 152.*
Awards: Polish Film Festival, Best Actress, 1984

1468. *Rok spokojnego slonca / Year of the Quiet Sun* 1984
D: Krzysztof Zanussi
S: Krzysztof Zanussi
C: Wojciech Idziak
P: Hartwig Schmidt
A: Maja Komorowska, Scott Wilson
A woman whose life was destroyed by the war has a tragic affair with an American soldier who is searching for American bodies from the Nazi camps. *Polish Feature.*
Awards: Venice Film Festival, Golden Lion, 1984

1469. *Dziewczeta z Nowolipek / Girls from No-wolipki Street* 1985 DS
D: Barbara Sass
S: Barbara Sass; based on the novel by Pola Goja-wiczyñska
C: Janusz Gauer
A: Ewa Kasprzyk, Izabela Drobotowicz-Orkisz, Maria Ciunelis, Marta Klubowicz
Warsaw, 1900. Four working-class girls finish school and attempt to find love and husbands even while they come to understand the difficulties of finding happiness. There is a sequel: *Rajska Jablòn / The Apple Tree of Paradise*, 1986. *Polish National: 171, 195.*

1470. *Kobieta w kapeluszu / The Woman with a Hat* 1985
D: Stanislaw Rozewicz
S: Stanislaw Rozewicz
C: Wojcik Jerzy
A: Hanna Mikuc
A young theater actress plays a puppet dancer on the stage, takes care of her neighbor, visits an older actress, conflicts with her mother, and searches for meaning. *Polish National: 170.*
Awards: Moscow International Film Festival, Silver Prize, 1985; Polish Film Festival, Golden Lion, 1985

1471. *Kobieta z prowincji / A Provincial Woman* 1985
D: Andrzej Baranski
S: Andrzej Baranski
C: Ryszard Lenczewski
A: Ewa Dalkowska, Katarzyna Rubacha
In a small town, a sixty-year-old woman looks back on her adult life, which began when she refused a passionate love for a more solid man, who then died after their second child. She then married a baker with a house but still sold rugs at the market to give support to her first family. Always, her efforts are focused on her children. *Cinéma polonais: 292.*
Other titles: Une Femme de la province
Awards: Gdansk Film Festival, Special Jury Award, 1985; Berlin International Film Festival, FIPRESCI, 1986

1472. *Nadzór / Custody* 1985
D: Wieslaw Saniewski
S: Wieslaw Saniewski
A: Ewa Blaszczyk
1967. A bride is arrested at her wedding for embezzlement, then sentenced to life in prison; she must fight to see her child, who is born there. *Polish National: 167.*
Awards: Gdansk Film Festival, Best Actress, Audience Award, 1985

1473. *Przez dotyk / Touching, at a Touch* 1986 DS
D: Magdalena Lazarkiewicz
S: Magdalena Lazarkiewicz, Ilona Lepkowska
C: Krzysztof Pakulski
A: Grazyna Szapolowska, Maria Ciunelis
"The story of two women who share a hospital room—one is severely mentally disturbed, the other is pregnant, happily married, and terminally ill with cancer." *FII.*
Awards: Créteil International Women's Film Festival, Grand Prix, 1986

1474. *Historia niemoralna / An Immoral Story* 1990 DS
D: Barbara Sass
S: Barbara Sass
C: Wieslaw Zdort
A: Dorota Stalínska
The filmmaker comments on the editing of a film within the film, a story of an actress who is reflecting on being an artist, faced with the same challenges of representation as the director. *Polish National: 195.*

1475. *Diably, diably / The Devils, the Devils* 1991 DS
D: Dorota Kedzierzawska
S: Dorota Kedzierzawska
C: Zdzislaw Nadja
A: Justyna Ciemny
Attracted to the singing and dancing of a band of gypsies, a young girl in a small town attaches herself to them, despite their outcast status in the community. *Festival de films, 14th: 106. 1992.*

1476. *Le Double vie de Véronique / The Double Life of Véronique* 1991
D: Krysztof Kieslowski
S: Krysztof Kieslowski
C: Slawomir Idziak
P: Leonardo De La Fuente
A: Irène Jacob
A singer dies suddenly in a concert, then turns up as an actress in another life in Paris.
Awards: Cannes Film Festival, Best Actress, FIPRESCI, 1991; National Society of Film Critics Awards, Best Foreign Language Film, 1992

1477. *Biale matzeństwo / White Marriage* 1993 DS
D: Magdalena Lazarkiewicz
S: Magdalena Lazarkiewicz, Tadeusz Rózewicz
A: Teresa Budzisz-Krzyzanowska, Jolanta Fraszynska
1930s. In a mix of "subjective and objective reality, dreams and waking," a wealthy young woman, who observes the limited lives of the other women in her family, resists the traditional role of wife, preferring instead to discover her sexuality on her own. *Polish National: 195.*

1478. *Pozegnanie z Maria / Farewell to Maria* 1993
D: Filip Zylber
S: Filip Zylber
C: Dariusz Kuc
A: Danuta Szaflarska, Katarzyna Jamróz
Two sisters escape from the Jewish ghetto; one

chooses to return to be with her friends and family, the other insists on raising awareness of the violence inside the ghetto. *Polish National: 234.*

Awards: Polish Film Festival, Best Debut Director, Best Supporting Actress (Szaflarska), 1993

1479. *Tylko strach / Only Fear* 1993 DS
D: Barbara Sass
S: Barbara Sass
C: Wieslaw Zdort
A: Anna Dymna
"Successful television journalist struggles to overcome alcoholism." *Polish National: 195.*
Awards: Polish Film Festival, Best Actress, 1993

1480. *Pestka / Pip* 1995 DS
D: Krystyna Janda
S: Krystyna Janda
A: Krystyna Janda, Daniel Olbrychski, Anna Dymna
"The story of a 40-year old radio editor who falls for an architect and family man. He has doubts about his feelings and she is distraught that she is destroying someone's happiness." *Polish Women. Accessed 2005, Mar. 8.*
Awards: Polish Film Festival, Best Debut Director, 1995

1481. *Pokuszenie / Temptation* 1995 DS
D: Barbara Sass
S: Barbara Sass
C: Wieslaw Zdort
A: Magdalena Cielecka
A young woman joins a convent after falling in love with a priest. Years later, in order to free herself from prison, she agrees to collaborate with Stalinist agents and betray him as an anticommunist.
Awards: Polish Film Festival, Best Actress, 1995; Karlovy Vary International Film Festival, International Critics Prize, 1996

1482. *Wielki tydzien / Holy Week* 1996
D: Andrzej Wajda
S: Andrzej Wajda
C: Wit Dabal
P: Lew Rywin
A: Beata Fudalej, Magdalena Warzecha, Jan Malecki
Warsaw, April 1943. During the siege of Easter week, a Jewish woman, who has escaped from the ghetto, moves in with Catholic friends to hide, but she makes no attempt to be discreet and lashes out at her hosts. *Polish National: 231.*
Other titles: Die Karwoche
Awards: Berlin International Film Festival, nomination for Golden Bear, 1996

1483. *Nic / Nothing* 1998 DS
D: Dorota Kedzierzawska
S: Dorota Kedzierzawska
A: Anita Kuskowska-Borkowska
A young wife adores her brutish husband; she has three young children, who are isolated by poverty and growing up in ignorance. She is so incapable of connecting with anyone that when the smallest child covets someone else's orange, and the stranger offers it, she can only grab the child and run. Pregnant again, she tries to abort, then hides her pregnancy, telling her husband the lump will go away, and murders the newborn.
Awards: Brussels International Film Festival, Best Actress, 1999; Denver International Film Festival, Best European Film, 1999; Polish Film Awards, Best Director, 1999; Sochi International Film Festival, FIPRESCI, 1999

1484. *Na koniec swiata / To the End of the World* 1999 DS
D: Magdalena Lazarkiewicz
S: Joanna Zolkowska; based on *Therese Raquin* by Emil Zola
C: Tomasz Dobrowolski
P: Piotr Lazarkiewicz
A: Joanna Steczkowska
"Story of a young woman's initiation into love and sensuality," though she remains a victim. *Polish Women. Accessed 2005, Mar. 8.*

1485. *Torowisko / The Junction* 1999 DS
D: Urszula Urbaniak
S: Urszula Urbaniak
C: Bartek Prokopowicz
A: Karolina Dryzner, Ewa Lorska
A modest young woman wonders if she will ever escape her isolated town, where she works alone in the railroad crossing station and deals with her mother, layabout brother, and promiscuous best friend. The vicious rape of her friend illustrates the vulnerable, cowed nature of everyone in the town and leads to the victim's decision to settle down and marry.
Awards: Montréal World Film Festival, Special Award, 1999

1486. *Wrota Europy / Gates of Europe* 1999
D: Jerzy Wojcik
S: Melchior Wankowicz, Andrzej Mularczyk
C: Witold Sobocinski
P: Dariusz Jablonski
A: Alicja Bachleda-Curus, Kinga Pries, Agnieszka Sitek
1918. Three close friends decide to become nurses at the front, where the Bolsheviks are winning. *Freedom Film. 2000. Accessed 2005, Mar. 6.*

Awards: Cairo International Film Festival, nomination for Golden Pyramid, 2000

PORTUGAL

1487. *Ana*　　　　　　　　　　　　　　1982 DS
D: Margarida Cordeiro, António Reis
S: Margarida Cordeiro, António Reis; based on a story by Rainer Maria Rilke
C: Acacio De Almeida, Elso Rogue
P: António Reis
A: Ana Maria Martins Guerra, Manuel Eanes
A girl recalls her grandmother in a "liturgical" filmic meditation on place, death, and the past. *Variety. 1985, Oct. 9.*

1488. *À Flor do mar / By the Seaside*　　　1986 P
D: João César Monteiro
S: João César Monteiro
C: Acacio De Almeida
P: Margarida Gil
A: Laura Morante
A woman takes her children to live in Rome, believing she will never return to Portugal. Nonetheless, one year later, she returns to her provincial home near the sea and meets again her remaining family. *O Cais do olhar: 226.*

1489. *Relacão fiel e verdadeira / A Faithful and True Rehabilitation*　　　　　　1986 DSP
D: Margarida Gil
S: Margarida Gil, João César Monteiro
C: Manuel Costa e Silva
P: João César Monteiro, Margarida Gil
A: Caterina Alves Costa
Seventeenth century. A young woman is married off by her mother to the jaded son of an aristocratic family in the rural north; he has a reputation for debauchery and violence. Trapped and abused, she goes with her husband through "barren lands and increasingly inhospitable homes," finding only misery. *O Cais do olhar: 230.*

1490. *Três menos eu / Three Minus Me*　　1988
D: João Canijo
S: João Canijo, Paulo Tunhas
C: José Luis Carvalhosa
A: Rita Blanco, Anne Gauthier, Isabel De Castro
An eighteen-year-old is employed in a discotheque and takes care of her young sister; her cousin visits from France, and intrigue develops around a common lover. *O Cais do olhar: 242.*

1491. *Solo de violino / Violin Solo*　　1990 DS
D: Monique Rutler

S: Monique Rutler, Gonsalves Preto
C: Manuel Costa e Silva
A: Fernanda Lapa, Victor Santos
1917. The life of Adelaide Coelho da Cunha, daughter of the founder of the Diário de notícias and a journalist and intellectual in her own right. She fell in love with a chauffeur and abandoned her social duty, whereupon her husband had her committed to a psychiatric hospital. *O Cais do olhar: 123.*

1492. *Nuvem*　　　　　　　　　　　　1991 DS
D: Ana Luìsa Guimarães
S: Ana Luìsa Guimarães
C: Manuel Costa e Silva
A: Rosa Castro André
A woman witnesses a murder and makes friends with the leader of the perpetrators, even falling in love with him; but she never tells him the truth, and he becomes suspicious of the danger she might pose. Mystery. *Festival de films, 14th: 107. 1992.*
Other titles: Nuages

1493. *Rosa negra / Black Rose*　　　1992 DSC
D: Margarida Gil
S: Margarida Gil, Maria Velho da Costa
C: Sophie Maintigneux
A: Catarina Correia, Fernando Luis, Manuela De Freitas
Two people take a train to a small industrial city: One is a teacher set to substitute for a colleague on maternity leave, and the other is a man who set fire to the local factory, returning after years of exile to find an old lover; he is not well received. *O Cais do olhar: 267.*

1494. *Chá forte com limão / Black Tea with Lemon*　　　　　　　　　　　　1993
D: António De Macedo
S: António De Macedo
C: Manuel Costa e Silva
A: Eugénia Bettencourt, Isabel De Castro, Jean-Pierre Cassel
Summer, 1870. An aging landowner lives in a mansion with her servants and rarely ventures away from the large estate. She invites an old friend who used to live with her and her daughter to stay for a couple of weeks, and their afternoon conversations take them back to the wounds of the past. *O Cais do olhar: 272.*

1495. *Vale Abraão / Abraham's Valley*　1993 S
D: Manoel De Oliveira
S: Manoel De Oliveira; based on a story by Augustina Bessa-Luís
C: Mario Barroso

P: Paulo Branco

A: Leonor Silveira, Luis Miguel Cintra

A young woman, who marries an older man she does not love, is also vain, "like Madame Bovary," and has several lovers until one day she inexplicably dies. *O Cais do olhar: 278.*

Awards: Tokyo International Film Festival, Best Film, 1993

1496. *Três irmãos / Two Brothers, My Sister*
1994 DS

D: Teresa Villaverde

S: Teresa Villaverde

C: Volker Tittel

A: Maria De Medeiros

Lisbon. A mother forces her grown daughter to cook for the family while she herself goes to school and has a job. The daughter is stifled in every way and, as her mother ignores the father's violence, is also victimized, along with her two brothers, who try to intercede. *FII.* Also *O Cais do olhar: 283.*

Other titles: Three Siblings

Awards: Venice Film Festival, Best Actress, 1994

1497. *Ossos / Bones*
1997

D: Pedro Costa

S: Pedro Costa

C: Emmanuel Machuel

P: Paulo Branco

A: Vanda Duarte, Mariya Lipkina

Lisbon, the ghetto of Estrela d'Africa. A young mother abuses her infant, even trying to gas the baby, which her husband stops, but then he tries to sell the child on the street. The mother and her close friend attempt to get the child back. *Variety: 59. 1997, Oct. 6.*

Awards: Entrevues Film Festival, Grand Prix, 1997

1498. *O Anjo da guarda*
1998 DSP

D: Margarida Gil

S: Margarida Gil, Maria Velho da Costa

C: Carlos Assis

P: Antonia Seabra

A: Isabel De Castro, Natália Luísa, Dalila Carmo

A woman returns to her village in search of a letter from her father, an anthropologist who lived in Timor. There she meets a man, a "guardian angel," who helps her. *O Cais do olhar: 112.*

Awards: Fantasporto, Best Actress (Carmo), 1999; Rome Festival, Grand Prize, 1999

1499. *Os Mutantes / The Mutants*
1998 DS

D: Teresa Villaverde

S: Teresa Villaverde

C: Acacio De Almeida

P: Jacques Bidou

A: Ana Moreira

Lisbon, 1996. A young girl who lives on the streets of the city with other children eventually has a child of her own. *O Cais do olhar: 240.*

Awards: Seattle International Film Festival, New Director Award, 2000

1500. *La Carta / The Letter*
2000 S

D: Manoel De Oliveira

S: Manoel De Oliveira; based on *La Princesse de Clèves* by Madame de la Fayette

C: Emmanuel Machuel

P: Paulo Branco

A: Chiara Mastroianni

A young girl, disappointed in love, marries an older successful man, then falls in love with a popular singer. She tells her husband, and when he dies of disappointment, she abandons the singer and goes to Africa "to help people suffering from civil war, disease, and starvation." *Cine espanol. 2000.*

Awards: Cannes Film Festival, Jury Prize, 1999

1501. *Agua e sal / Water and Salt*
2001 DS

D: Teresa Villaverde

S: Teresa Villaverde

C: Emmanuel Machuel

P: Paulo Branco

A: Galatea Ranzi

A young photographer lives with her husband and daughter in a village near the sea. When her husband goes away for a few days, she plans to finish a long-overdue project but is diverted by a couple she meets on the beach, who leave her insecure. *Festival de films, 24th: 30. 2002.*

1502. *Nha fala / My Voice*
2002 DS

D: Flora Gomes

S: Flora Gomes, Franck Moisnard

P: Serge Zeitoun, Luis Galvão Teles

A: Fatou N'Diaye, Bia Gomes, Jean-Christophe Dollé

A singer from Guinea Bissau leaves for Paris even though there is a curse on her family commanding that she not sing. Encouraged to sing professionally by a French man, she finds the curse does not carry through and returns home to stage her death and rebirth and to appease her mother. Musical. *Festival des 3.*

Awards: Amiens International Film Festival, SIGNIS Award, 2002; Venice Film Festival, Laterna Magica Prize, 2002

1503. *A Mulher que acreditava ser presidente dos EUA / The Woman Who Imagined She Was President of the United States*
2003 S

D: João Botelho

S: João Botelho, Leonor Pinhão
C: Inês Carvalho
P: Paulo Branco
A: Alexandra Lencastre
Lisbon. On Washington Street, a woman believes she is the president, outfitting herself as "a tall blond socialite with upswept hair, a red power suit, an unseen First Gentleman, and an all-female retinue." Fantasy. *Village Voice: 111. 2003, May 21.*

ROMANIA

1504. ***Nunta de piatra* / *Stone Wedding***   1973
D: Mircea Veroiu, Dan Pita
S: Dan Pita, Mircea Veroiu
A: Leopodina Balanuta
Part 1: A stone worker loses her husband and children, then buries her last daughter with money she earns from selling the horse she uses for work. Part 2: A bride leaves her wedding ceremony to go off with a musician. *Variety: 18. 1973, May 16.*

1505. ***Pe malul stîng al Dunarii albastre* / *On the Left Bank of the Blue Danube***   1984 DS
D: Malvina Ursianu
S: Malvina Ursianu
C: Vivi Dragan Vasile
A: Gina Patrichi
At end of World War II, a former cabaret dancer, now widowed, seeks an important document hidden in her house. *FII.*

1506. ***O Lumina la etajul 10* / *A Light on the 10th Floor***   1985 DS
D: Malvina Ursianu
S: Malvina Ursianu
C: Sorin Iliesiu
A: Irina Petrascu
The story of a released political prisoner. *Cinemagia. Accessed 2005, June 30.*

1507. ***Sanda***   1990 DS
D: Christiana Nicolae
S: Christiana Nicolae
C: Adrian Dragusin
A: Florentine Morcanu, Iarina Demian
The daily life of a woman obliged by law to remain pregnant. *Festival de films, 14th: 80. 1992.*

1508. ***Le Chêne* / *The Oak***   1992 P
D: Lucian Pintilie
S: Lucian Pintilie, Ion Baiesu
C: Doru Mitran
P: Sylvain Bursztejn, Eliane Stutterheim

A: Maia Morgenstern
During the violence of the Ceauşescu years, a woman goes to the countryside to teach; gang-raped at the station, she then develops a relationship with a doctor. *FII.*
Awards: European Film Awards, Best Actress, 1993

1509. ***O Primavara de neuitat* / *An Unforgettable Summer***   1994
D: Lucian Pintilie
S: Lucian Pintilie
C: Calin Ghibu
A: Kristen Scott-Thomas
Danube valley village, 1925. A Romanian officer's wife befriends Bulgarian hostages her husband is expected to kill. *Cinema of Flames: 62.*
Awards: Cannes Film Festival, nomination for Golden Palm, 1994

1510. ***Aici nu mai locuieste nimeni* / *Nobody Lives Here***   1996 D
D: Malvina Ursianu
A: Maria Rotaru
A woman tries to rebuild her life after the traumas of 1989. *Cinema, vol. 14, no. 11: 10–11. 1976, Nov.*

1511. ***Stare de fapt* / *State of Things***   1996
D: Stere Gulea
C: Vivi Dragan Vasile
A: Mara Grigore, Dan Condurache
1989. A woman seeks justice for her rape but encounters a corrupt system. *Cinema of Flames: 203.*

1512. ***Fata în fata* / *Face to Face***   1998
D: Marius Theodor Barna
S: Marius Theodor Barna
C: Alex Solomon
A: Maia Morgenstern
"Famous poet and political dissident Iona Petroni finds that her husband was an informer for the Securitate," and the media descends on her. *Freedom Film. 2000. Accessed 2005, Mar. 6.*

1513. ***Binecuvintata fii inchisoare* / *Bless You Prison***   2002 S
D: Nicolae Margineanu
S: Nicolae Margineanu; based on the novel by Nicole Valery-Grossu
C: Doru Mitran
P: Nicolae Margineanu
A: Maria Ploae, Dorina Lazar, Ecaterina Nazarie
1949. True story of a woman who was imprisoned on a false charge of espionage but who helps the other prisoners through religious faith. *Freedom Film. 2003. Accessed 2005, Mar. 6.*

Awards: Montréal World Film Festival, Ecumenical Jury Prize, 2003; Romanian Union of Filmmakers, Best Actress (Ploae), 2003

RUSSIA [SEE ALSO USSR]

1514. *Dom na peske / House Built on Sand*
1991 DS

D: Niyole Admomenaite
S: Natalya Chepik, Tatyana Tolstaya
C: Aleksandr Shumovich
A: Yelena Shiffers, Yelena Tkachyova

Leningrad, 1930s. A daughter of a Russian family of professors, which is torn apart by Stalinism and World War II, renews a friendship with a woman from school, who now works in a museum. The friend is aggressive in pointing out the foibles of the men in the family, and she makes herself the butt of jokes. In the family's emptied townhouse, the two care for each other through the German siege of the city.

Awards: Angers European First Film Festival, Procirep Award, 1993

1515. *S dnjom rozhdenya / Happy Birthday*
1998 DS

D: Larisa Sadilova
S: Larisa Sadilova
C: Alexander Kazarenskov
P: Gennadi Sidorov
A: Gulya Stolyarova, Irina Proshina

Five women are the last patients in the maternity ward of a decrepit village hospital that is set for tearing down. Documentary-like scenes complement the self-deprecating humor of the women, who are happy to relax during a time of little responsibility. *Festival de films, 21st: 27. 1999.*

Other titles: Longue vie

Awards: Créteil International Women's Film Festival, Grand Prix, 1999

1516. *Strana gluchich / The Land of the Deaf*
1998 S

D: Valery Todorovsky
S: Renata Litvinova, Yuri Korotkov
C: Yuri Shajgardanov
P: Sergei Livnev
A: Chulpan Khamatova, Dina Korzun

A woman flees Moscow just as her boyfriend is going to use her to pay off a gambling debt; there she takes up with a mute, who convinces her prostitution is the only way to freedom. *Freedom Film. 1999. Accessed 2005, Mar. 6.*

Awards: Russian Guild of Film Critics, Golden Aries, 1998; Seattle International Film Festival, New

Director's Showcase Award, 1998; Nika Awards, Best Actress (Korzun), 1999

1517. *Sobstvennaya tien / One's Own Shadow*
2000 DS

D: Olga Narutskaya
S: Olga Narutskaya
C: Dmitri Dolinin
A: Natalia Riazantseva, Marina Cheptounova

A famous writer and a doctor, very close in their youth, unexpectedly meet again after many years apart. The reality of their present—the doctor is separated from her husband and supports a child on her own—brings back their dreams and allows their attachment to once again thrive. *Festival de films, 23rd: 30. 2001.*

Other titles: Sa propre ombre

Awards: Créteil International Women's Film Festival, Special Mention, 2001

1518. *Babusya / Granny*
2002 DS

D: Lidiya Bobrova
S: Lidiya Bobrova
C: Valeri Revich
P: Andrei Zertsalov
A: Anna Ovsyannikova, Nina Shubina

In northern Russia, a grandmother, who has raised her daughter's children while the parents worked for an airline, is shunned by her son-in-law when the daughter dies. Her niece arrives from Moscow to try to find someone else in the family to take the grandmother in, but like her, they all have other obligations. Finally, she succeeds with the most humble relatives, who have survived a stay in Chechnya at the cost of a damaged daughter and who are joyful to see the kindly old woman.

Awards: Copenhagen International Film Festival, Golden Swan, Special Jury Prize (Ovsyannikova, Shubina), 2003; Cottbus Film Festival, Grand Prize, 2003; Karlovy Vary International Film Festival, Special Jury Prize, 2003

1519. *S ljubov'ju, Lilya / With Love, Lilya*
2002 DS

D: Larisa Sadilova
S: Larisa Sadilova, Gennadi Sidorov
C: Anatoly Petriga
A: Marina Zubanova, Valentina Berezutskaya

A young woman works in a poultry factory and thinks only of finding a husband, "a passionate quest with an essential emptiness" that makes it difficult for her to succeed. *Festival de films, 25th: 32. 2003.*

Awards: Brussels European Film Festival, Best Actress (Zubanova), 2003; Warsaw International Film Festival, Grand Prix, 2003

1520. *Vremya zhatvy* / *Harvest Time*
2004 DSCP
D: Marina Razbezhkina
S: Marina Razbezhkina
C: Irina Uralskaya
P: Natalia Zheltukhina
A: Ludmila Motornaya
After the end of World War II, a mother in a village has a small child and must contend with having to drive a tractor; her husband lost his legs in combat. *Festival de films, 27th: 25. 2005.*
Awards: Moscow International Film Festival, FIPRESCI, 2004; Thessaloniki Film Festival, Silver Alexander, 2004

SENEGAL

1521. *La Noire de ...* / *Black Girl* 1966
D: Ousmane Sembène
S: Ousmane Sembène
A: Anne-Marie Jelinek, Thérèse Diop Mbissine
A Senegalese girl takes a position as a maid for a French couple in Marseille; she is isolated in their cramped apartment, dominated by the wife, and excluded from any social life. The husband is sympathetic but passive throughout the events, ceding all domestic territory to his wife until the girl commits suicide.

1522. *Kodou* 1971 S
D: Ababacar Samb-Makharam
S: Annette Mbaye D'Erneville
A: Madeleine Diallo
A young girl unable to endure the pain of a lip tattoo ritual becomes insane with the ensuing rejection, as tradition dictates she must kill herself. *Cinéma Québec, vol. 1, no. 10: 28–31. 1972, Jul./Aug.*
Other titles: Codou

1523. *Emitai* / *The Thundergod* 1972
D: Ousmane Sembène
S: Ousmane Sembène
C: Michel Remaudeau
Casamance, World War II. The French military have bled a Diola village of its young men and increased the rice tax. The women of the village resist by protecting the rice despite armed opposition. *Cinema of Ousmane: 141–42.*
Other titles: Dieu de tonnerre
Awards: Moscow International Film Festival, Silver Prize, 1971; Berlin International Film Festival, OCIC Award, 1972

1524. *Xala* / *The Curse* 1974
D: Ousmane Sembène

S: Ousmane Sembène
C: Georges Caristan
A: Seune Samb, Thierno Leye, Myriam Niang
A wealthy man takes a third wife, which makes his other wives and daughter unhappy; he then suffers impotence on his wedding night.
Awards: Moscow International Film Festival, nomination for Golden Prize, 1975

1525. *Kaddu beykat* / *Peasant Letter* 1975 DS
D: Safi Faye
S: Safi Faye
C: Patrick Fabry
A: Assane Faye, Maguette Gueye
A bad peanut harvest—an unreliable monoculture imposed by the French colonizers—inhibits a young woman from marrying; her suitor returns from Dakar, where he tried but failed to find a trade, so they both lack the means to marry. *Festival de films, 20th: 96. 1998.*
Other titles: Lettre Paysanne

1526. *Ceddo* 1976
D: Ousmane Sembène
S: Ousmane Sembène
C: Georges Caristan
A: Tabata Ndiaye
An Imam, with the collusion of the king, tries to convert a tribe to Islam; the king's daughter, Princess Dior, is kidnapped by the Iman when she ascends to the throne, but she refuses conversion and returns to slay the Imam and triumph.

1527. *Fad'jal* 1979 DSP
D: Safi Faye
S: Safi Faye
C: Patrick Fabry
P: Safi Faye
A: Ibou Ndong
A village community is named after the woman who founded it; an elder tells the children the history of their oral civilization, where "the passing of an old person is like a library being burned." Industrial civilization fast approaches. *Festival de films, 11th: 111. 1989.*

1528. *Jom* / *Dignity* 1981
D: Ababacar Somb-Makharan
C: Peter Chappell
A: Makhourédia Guèye, Zator Sarr, Aminata Fall
A labor strike is on the verge of being broken because of bribes distributed by the boss, but the "men who give in" are driven out by the village women. In solidarity with the strikers, the women hold on to their "jom." *Variety: 17. 1982, May 26.*

1529. *Hyènes / Hyenas* 1992
D: Djibril Diop Mambéty
S: Djibril Diop Mambéty; based on *The Visit* by Friedrich Dürrenmatt
C: Matthias Kälin
P: Pierre-Alain Meier
A: Ami Diakhate, Mansour Diouf
A wealthy woman returns to the village where she was left pregnant and abandoned years earlier by one of the local businessmen; she tells the villagers she will give them all her money if they kill him.

1530. *Quartier Mozart* 1992
D: Jean-Pierre Bekolo
S: Jean-Pierre Bekolo
C: Regis Blondeau
P: Jean-Pierre Bekolo
A: Pauline Andela
A witch uses sorcery on a young girl that allows her to inhabit the body of a man and feel what it's like.
Awards: Locarno International Film Festival, Special Prize, 1992

1531. *Mossane* 1996 DS
D: Safi Faye
S: Safi Faye
C: Jürgen Jürges
A: Magou Seck, Isseu Niang
A teenager wonders how to respond to her much-loved boyfriend, observing the active sex life of her girlfriend. Within the village, she is isolated by the high financial position of her family, and she discovers their prosperity is funded by her fiancé, who works in Paris. She tries to refuse the marriage, but the chief dictates that she must marry the fiancé, so she drowns herself. Many rituals are detailed: fires on the beach, gifts of milk at the baobab tree, drum calls for rain, animal sacrifice, and gifts of money.
Awards: International Festival of Films for Children and Young People, Lucas Award, 1997

1532. *Faat-Kiné* 2001
D: Ousmane Sembène
S: Ousmane Sembène
C: Dominique Gentil
P: Wongue Mbengue
A: Venus Seye
Dakar. An unmarried mother of two college students manages a gas station, takes care of her mother, and generally enjoys life—she is prosperous even without a husband, and her children are becoming well educated. Her style is always open and generous, and she handles visits

to a graduation party from the children's fathers with aplomb, even though the men offend her.

1533. *Karmen Geï / Karmen* 2002
D: Joseph Gai Ramaka
S: Joseph Gai Ramaka; based on *Carmen* by Prosper Merimee
C: Bertrand Chatry
P: Richard Sadler
A: Djeïnaba Diop Gaï, Stéphanie Biddle
Karmen dances herself out of jail, then on to other challenges. *The Nation: 35–36. 2002. Apr. 29.*
Awards: San Francisco International Film Festival, SKYY Prize, 2002

1534. *Moolaadé* 2004
D: Ousmane Sembène
S: Ousmane Sembène
C: Dominique Gentil
P: Ousmane Sembène
A: Fatoumata Coulibaly, Maimouna Hélène Diarra, Salimata Traoré
Four young girls escape from their "purification" rite and find protection (moolaadé) from a village mother, who refused to allow her own daughter to be cut because she herself suffered all her life from the wound. Her husband becomes exasperated at being denounced by the other villagers for her action. The women in charge of purification brood outside the rope, and her daughter is threatened with not being able to marry because she is unclean. Positions begin to harden, leading to a public beating of the offending mother, until a royal son announces he will marry her unclean daughter. In between there is music, dance, and frank talk.
Awards: Cannes Film Festival, Ecumenical Jury Prize, 2004; Los Angeles Pan African Film Festival, Jury Award, 2005; National Society of Film Critics Awards, Best Foreign Film, 2005

SLOVENIA

1535. *Slepa pega / Blind Spot* 2002 DSC
D: Hanna A. Wojcik-Slak
S: Hanna A. Wojcik-Slak
C: Karina Kleszczewska
P: Francie Slak
A: Manca Dorrer
"A woman tries to help her drug-addict boyfriend kick his habit." *FII.*

1536. *Varuh meje / Guardian of the Frontier*
2002 DSP
D: Maja Weiss

S: Norman Brock, Zoran Hocevar, Maja Weiss
C: Boris Kastelic
P: Ida Weiss
A: Tanja Poto, Pia Zemlji, Iva Krajnc
Three friends take a canoe trip down the river Kolpa, which marks the border between Croatia and Slovenia. They encounter the "other" in an anonymous border guard, outsider artists, village fascists, sexual predators, and, most painfully, each other. Their sexuality is detailed, and it inhibits their attending to the complicated social and political events that confront them on the trip. Action.
Awards: Berlin International Film Festival, Manfred Salzgebar Award, 2002; San Francisco International Lesbian & Gay Film Festival, Best First Feature, 2002

SOUTH AFRICA

1537. *Mamza*　　　　　　　　　　　　1985
D: Johan Blignaut
S: Johan Blignaut
C: Dirk Mostert
A: Lulu Strachan
Mamza, known for her solid stature and temperament, refuses charity and earns a living for herself and her teenage daughter by running an illegal bar. But dignity is hard to come by for the second-class citizens of apartheid. *Festival des 3.*

1538. *Fiela se Kind / Fiela's Child*　　1987 DS
D: Katinka Heyns
S: Chris Barnard; based on the novel by Dalene Matthee
A: Sharleen Surtie-Richards
A black woman raises an abandoned white child. When the child is twelve, he is discovered by the white authorities and sent to live with an impoverished rural Afrikaans woman with an abusive husband. *St. James: 334.*

1539. *Quest for Truth, Quest for Love*　1988 DS
D: Helena Nogueira
S: Helena Nogueira; based on "Q.E.D." by Gertrude Stein
C: Roy McGregor
P: Shan Moodley
A: Jana Cillers, Sandra Prinsloo, Andrew Buckland
Two women, a journalist who is militantly antiapartheid and a biologist doing research in the local ecology, are attracted to one another, but the activist is involved with a boyfriend, who is killed, and then is imprisoned for her press reports on his death. *Festival de films, 10th: 20. 1988.*
Other titles: *Fire in Their Hearts*

1540. *On the Wire*　　　　　　　　　　1990 DS
D: Elaine Proctor
S: Elaine Proctor
C: Yoshi Tezuka
P: Laurie Borg
A: Aletta Bezuidenhout, Michael O'Brien
An Afrikaners couple live in a rural all-white community increasingly terrorized by revolutionary blacks. They experience tragedy when the husband, an ex-soldier unable to come to grips with his own complicity in racist crimes, has his mind unravel and slides into domestic violence. *Festival de films, 13th: 19. 1991.*

1541. *Taxo to Soweto / Taxi to Soweto*　1991 S
D: Manie Van Rensburg
S: Manie Van Rensburg, Marina Bekker
C: Nick Herholdt
A: Elize Cawood, Patrick Shair
Johannesburg. A white bourgeois South African whose car breaks down takes a taxi driven by a black man, which leads to trouble. *Cinémas d'Afrique.*
Other titles: *Taxi pour Soweto*

1542. *Die Storie van Klara Viljee / The Story of Klara Viljee*　　　　　　　　　　　1992 D
D: Katinka Heyns
A: Anna-Mart Van der Merwe
"Blend of allegory and social realism" shot in the Arniston dunes of the south Cape. An Afrikaans orphan is betrayed by a lover, who has a child with someone else. When the man dies, she becomes a hermit, living in a cottage behind a sand dune. When his death turns out to be a ruse, she unburies herself. *St. James: 337.*

1543. *Friends*　　　　　　　　　　　　1993 DSP
D: Elaine Proctor
S: Elaine Proctor
C: Dominique Chapuis
P: Judith Hunt
A: Kerry Fox, Dombisa Kente, Michele Burgers
Three friends graduate from college and try to find their way in a volatile South Africa. One is white (she joins a terrorist group); one is black, a teacher of small children; and one is Boer, and she is immediately married to an older family friend and begins a bourgeois life. Her wedding results in a racist encounter and begins the struggle between the other two over violent versus peaceful means of change. The radical activist gradually becomes unstable after she accidentally kills someone in a terrorist action at an airport.

1544. *Yesterday* 2004 P

D: Darrell Roodt
S: Darrell Roodt
C: Michael Brierley
P: Anant Singh, Helena Spring
A: Leleti Khumalo, Kenneth Khambula, Harriet Lenabe

A Zulu village. After long trips to a doctor in another village, Yesterday discovers she is HIV positive. When she confronts her husband with the news, he beats her, but he eventually returns to be cared for by her as he dies of AIDS. A teacher helps her through her ordeal and eases her grief over leaving her young child.

Awards: Venice Film Festival, EIUC Award, 2004; Academy Awards, nomination for Best Foreign Language Film, 2005

SPAIN

1545. *Cambio de sexo / Sex Change* 1976

D: Vincente Aranda
S: Vincente Aranda, Carlos Duran
C: Jose Luis Alcaine, Nestor Almendros
P: Jaime Fernández-Cid
A: Victoria Abril, Bibi Andersson

A teenage boy, always in trouble for his womanly inclinations, dreams of becoming a woman after he makes friends with a transsexual who is a stage performer.

Other titles: I Want to Be a Woman

1546. *La Peticion / The Engagement Party*
1976 DS

D: Pilar Miró
S: Pilar Miró, Leo Anchoriz; based on a story by Emile Zola
C: Hans Burman
A: Ana Belén

Nineteenth century. A wealthy young woman engages in sadistic relationships and murders the man who helps her dispose of the body of her lover. *FII.*

Other titles: The Request

1547. *Elisa vida mia / Elisa, My Life* 1977

D: Carlos Saura
S: Carlos Saura
C: Teodoro Escamilla
A: Geraldine Chaplin, Fernando Rey

A young woman leaves her husband because he has an affair with her best friend. She goes to visit her father, whom she has not seen in twenty years. *Festival de films, 13th: 56. 1991.*

1548. *Vámonos, Barbara / Let's Go Barbara*
1977 DS

D: Cecilia Bartolomé
S: Cecilia Bartolomé
C: Jose Luis Alcaine
A: Amparo Soler Leal, Julieta Serrano

A middle-aged woman leaves her loveless marriage and takes her twelve-year-old daughter on a car trip up the coast of Spain. *Cine espanol. 1977.*

1549. *Jaque la dama / Check to the Queen*
1978

D: Francisco Rodriguez
C: José María Alarcón, Heinrich Starhemberg
A: Ana Belén, Concha Velasco

"Concerned with a latent lesbian relationship between an amateur actress and a bored housewife." *FII.*

1550. *De Criada a señora / From Maid to Lady* 1979

D: Vitorio De Sisti
S: Domenico Calandruccio
C: Raúl Pérez Cubero
A: Carmen Villani

Rome. A young woman arrives in the city only to be rebuffed by her boyfriend, who had promised to marry her; she accuses him of rape, and he is jailed. She becomes a success as a boutique manager, but her old lover reappears and promises to make his rape conviction "real." *Cine espanol. 1980–1981.*

1551. *Gary Cooper que estás en los cielos / Gary Cooper Who Art in Heaven* 1980 DS

D: Pilar Miró
S: Pilar Miró, Antonio Larreta
C: Carlos Suárez
A: Carmen Maura, Mercedes Sampietro

Three days in the life of a young woman who has become a television director after a long struggle in the male-dominated media industry; she faces surgery for what could be cancer, as well as her own incompletely balanced life. *Contemporary Spanish: 121. Also Festival de films, 4th: 21. 1982.*

Awards: Fotogramas de Plata, Best Film, 1981; Moscow International Film Festival, Best Actress (Sampietro), 1981

1552. *Historias de mujeres / A Women's Story*
1980

D: Mauricio Walerstein
S: Santiago San Miguel, Mauricio Walerstein
C: Carlos Suárez
A: Charo López, Perla Vonasek, Hilda Vera

Caracas. Three daughters return to the deathbed of their father; each of them has been frustrated in life, and they look back on their lives before an event that changed everything. *Cine espanol. 1980–1981.*

1553. *Una Chica llamada Marilyne / A Girl Called Marilyne* 1981
D: Jean Luret
S: Jean Luret
C: Domingo Solano
A: Françoise Givernau, Veronica Miriel
Paris. A young woman is happy with a lover, but her mother arrives and seduces the boyfriend away. She seeks support from a friend, and they go to Spain to visit her father, where he, in turn, falls in love with her friend. On their return to Paris, the two women become closer and decide to live together. *Cine espanol. 1980–1981.*

1554. *Naftalina / Mothballs* 1981
D: Pep Callis
S: Toni Agusti, Pep Callis
C: Juan Costa
A: Pilar Dominguez, Toni Agusti
A Catalonian village. A traditional family is upset when their eldest daughter and her friend decide to start up a dance academy. The women persist, even through the mother's death, risking the family's unity with their enterprise. *Cine espanol. 1980–1981.*

1555. *Vida perra / A Dog's Life* 1981
D: Javier Aguirre
S: Javier Aguirre
C: Manuel Rojas
A: Esperanza Roy
An unmarried woman in a small town resents both her sister, who demonstrated sufficient independence to run away with a man, and her mother, whom she believes left her without the resources to succeed. *Cine espanol. 1980–1981.*

1556. *Antonieta* 1982
D: Carlos Saura
S: Jean-Claude Carrière, Carlos Saura
C: Teodoro Escamilla
P: Pablo Buelna
A: Isabelle Adjani, Hanna Schygulla, Diana Bracho
While researching famous suicides, a French journalist goes to Mexico to investigate the life of Antonieta Rivas Mercado, a wealthy participant in the art scene and the politics of revolutionary Mexico, who committed suicide in Paris in 1931. *Faber Companion.*

1557. *Coto de caza / Game Reserve* 1983
D: Jorge Grau
S: Jorge Grau, Manuel Summers
C: Antonio Cuevas Ortiz
A: Assumpta Serna
A lawyer believes that society itself is responsible for youthful violence, until the day her home is raided, her husband is murdered, and she herself is raped in front of her children. After that, she decides to take the law into her own hands, despite her former principles. Thriller. *Cine espanol. 1983.*

1558. *Entre tinieblas / Dark Habits* 1983
D: Pedro Almodóvar
S: Pedro Almodóvar
C: Angel Luis Fernández
P: Luis Calvo
A: Cristina Sanchez Pascual, Marisa Paredes, Mary Carrillo
A young singer is distraught when her boyfriend is killed by bad drugs, and she decides to hide in a convent directed by a Mother Superior "with a fascination for evil." Comedy. *FII.*

1559. *Inseminacion artificial / Artificial Insemination* 1983
D: Arturo Martinez
S: Alberto Vazquez Figueroa
C: Agustin Lara
A: Maria Jose Cantudo
A woman marries the man who has bought from her the publishing firm she inherited. Finding that he is sterile, she decides to have a child through artificial insemination, but he becomes jealous and leaves her. When he changes his mind, it is too late. *Cine espanol. 1983.*

1560. *Akelarre / Witches' Sabbath* 1984
D: Pedro Olea
S: Pedro Olea, Gonzalo Goikoetxea
C: Jose Luis Alcaine
A: Silvia Munt, Mary Carrillo
Navarra, end of the seventeenth century. In a Basque village, a young woman, whose grandmother was burned as a witch, has had two lovers: first, the son of a local lord, and second, a peasant in revolt. This history leaves her vulnerable to persecution. *Cine espanol. 1984.*

1561. *Fanny "Pelopaja" / Towhaired Fanny* 1984
D: Vincente Aranda
S: Vincente Aranda
C: Juan Amorós
A: Fanny Cottençon, Bruno Cremer
"Fanny" has survived her life only through violence.

An ex-cop thrown off the force for beating her spends his time hunting her for revenge, but she intends to find him first. Thriller. *Cine espanol. 1984.*

1562. *El Anillo de niebla* / *The Ring of Mist*
1985

D: Antonio Gomez-Olea

S: Arnoldo Garcia Del Vall

C: Augusto Balbuena

A: Beatriz Galbó, Sally Sitton, Mercedes Sampietro

A scientist travels to Madrid to investigate a strange formation of flies that inhabit the garbage dumps; her sister, an entomologist and photographer, joins her for technical assistance. Horror. *Cine espanol. 1985.*

1563. *Extramuros* / *Beyond the Walls*   1985

D: Miguel Picazo

S: Miguel Picazo

C: Teodoro Escamilla

A: Carmen Maura, Mercedes Sampietro, Aurora Bautista, Assumpta Serna

End of the sixteenth century. Colonial wars have forced many people either to emigrate, enlist in the army, or join a religious order. Lack of resources is forcing a convent to close, but two of the nuns, who form a lesbian couple, scheme to falsify stigmata to attract attention, pilgrims, and money. Despite their success, they are viewed jealously by the convent's prioress, and the Inquisition is called in. *Cine espanol. 1985.*

Awards: San Sebastián International Film Festival, Best Actress (Sampietro), 1985; Sant Jordi Awards, Best Actress (Maura), 1986

1564. *Perras callejeras* / *Street Bitches*   1985

D: José Antonio de La Loma

S: José Antonio de La Loma

C: Alejandro Ulloa

A: Teresa Giménez, Sonia Martínez, Susana Sentís

Three young criminals are hunted for robberies and knife attacks; one is a Gypsy who has been taught to steal by her father, one is an ex-convict who prostitutes but hates it, and one is kept by an old man but still needs money for her drug habit. *Cine espanol. 1985.*

1565. *Calé* / *Gypsy*   1986

D: Carlos Serrano

S: Carlos Serrano, Joaquin Oristrell

C: Federico Ribes

A: Rosario Flores, Joan Miralles

A famous actress prepares for a role as the flower seller in *Pygmalion* by spending time with a gypsy in the gypsy world. Their friendship turns into a violent passion that requires the gypsy to flee her tribe and the actress to question her otherwise free-thinking world, which she knows will not accept the relationship. *Cine espanol. 1986.*

1566. *Lola*   1986

D: Bigas Luna

S: Bigas Luna

C: Josep Civit

A: Angela Molina

A factory worker is plagued by a violent lover; she manages to separate from him and move to Barcelona, where she meets an executive and acquires a bourgeois existence for herself and her new daughter. Five years later, she runs into her old boyfriend on the street, and he proceeds to stalk her, especially after he discovers that her daughter is his child. *Cine espanol. 1986.*

Awards: Mystfest, Best Actress, 1986

1567. *Luna de Agosto* / *August Moon*   1986

D: Juan Minon

S: Juan Minon

C: Miguel Trujillo

A: Patricia Adriani

At Ramadan, a young woman takes a ship to Tangiers, where she expects to meet her boyfriend. She discovers that he went to Marrakech and left a silver pendant for her with a command to follow him there, so she does. *Cine espanol. 1986.*

1568. *La Mitad del cielo* / *Half of Heaven* 1986

D: Manuel Gutiérrez Aragon

S: Manuel Gutiérrez Aragon

C: Jose Luis Alcaine

P: Luis Megino

A: Angela Molina, Margarita Lozano

Madrid. A story of three generations of women. The mother runs a meat stand and then a restaurant. The grandmother and daughter have powers of premonition. *Cine espanol. 1986.*

Awards: San Sebastián International Film Festival, Best Actress (Molina), 1986; Fotogramas de Plata, Best Film, 1987

1569. *Tata mia* / *Nanny Dear*   1986

D: Jose Luis Borau

S: Jose Luis Borau

C: Teodoro Escamilla

A: Imperio Agenentica, Carmen Maura

The daughter of one of Franco's generals was raised by a kind nanny, then sent to a convent until being released at the age of forty. Beset by a lack of knowledge about how to act or contain her sexual urges, she finds her nanny and brings her to Madrid to help her figure out life. *Cine espanol. 1986.*

1570. **La Casa de Bernarda Alba / The House of Bernarda Alba**   1987
D: Mario Camus
S: Antonio Larreta; based on the play by Federico Garcia Lorca
C: Fernando Arribas
A: Irene Gutiérrez Caba, Ana Belén, Florinda Chico, Aurora Pastor, Enriqueta Caballeria
Andalusia, 1920s. A mother forces her daughters into the traditional mourning after their father's death. Realizing she will never marry and escape the matriarchal household, one of them commits suicide. *Variety: 18. 1987, May 20.*

1571. **Brumal**   1988 DS
D: Cristina Andreu
S: Cristina Andreu, Cristina Fernandez Cubas
C: Juan Molina
A: Paola Gonzalez Bose, Lucia Bosé
A daughter is disturbed by memories of life with her mother in Brumal, which they both left for the city when she was still a child. She returns to the town at the age of thirty-five when her mother dies, and her memories turn into an emotional crisis. *Cine espanol. 1988.*

1572. **La Diputada / The Deputy**   1988
D: Javier Aguirre
S: German Álvarez Blanco
C: Domingo Solano
A: Victoria Vera
The true story of Begoña Ansúrerz, "who went from being a businesswoman in the world of fashion to being a figure in the world of politics at the hands of a relentless team of image builders." *Cine espanol. 1988.*

1573. **Mujeres al bordo de un ataque de nervios / Women on the Verge of a Nervous Breakdown**   1988
D: Pedro Almodóvar
S: Pedro Almodóvar
C: Jose Luis Alcaine
P: Pedro Almodóvar
A: Carmen Maura, Antonio Banderas, Maria Barranco
Comic tale of a woman who pursues her ex-lover, along with his wife and child, in order to uncover the truth of their breakup and destroy her memories of him.
Awards: European Film Awards, Best Actress (Maura), 1988; Goya Awards, Best Screenplay, Best Actress (Maura), Best Supporting Actress (Barranco), 1989

1574. **Ay! Carmela**   1990
D: Carlos Saura

S: Carlos Saura, Rafael Azcona
C: Jose Luis Alcaine
P: Andres Gómez
A: Carmen Maura, Andrés Pajares
Near the end of the Spanish Civil War, a husband and wife team perform for the Republicans; they get arrested and then perform for the fascists. The wife resists her husband's deal with the fascist leader and courageously objects to the treatment of prisoners by the new regime, then suffers fatal consequences.
Awards: European Film Awards, Best Actress, 1990; Goya Awards, Best Picture, Best Actress, 1991

1575. **Boom boom**   1990 DSP
D: Rosa Verges
S: Rosa Verges, Jordi Beltrán
C: Josep Civit
P: Benoît Lamy, Rosa Romero
A: Viktor Lazlo, Sergi Mateu
Barcelona. Comic tale of an intelligent and energetic dentist who enjoys sex but has sworn off love. She crosses paths with a man, recently abandoned by his wife, who has also sworn off love, so it takes time for them to connect. *Festival de films, 15th: 106. 1993.*
Awards: Fotogramas de Plata, Best Film, 1991; Goya Awards, Best New Director, 1991

1576. **Alas de mariposa / Butterfly Wings**   1991
D: Juanma Bajo Ulloa
S: Juanma Bajo Ulloa
C: Aitor Mantxola
A: Silvia Munt
A couple has a six-year-old girl, but the wife is obsessed with giving her husband a son. When she becomes pregnant, she fears the girl's potential jealousy, and her own strong sense of guilt leads her to exclude her daughter from the event, which turns their life into a nightmare. *Cine espanol. 1991.*
Awards: Goya Awards, Best Director, Best Screenplay, Best Actress, 1992

1577. **Chatarra / Scrap Metal**   1991 P
D: Felix Rotaeta
S: Michel Gaztambide, Felix Rotaeta
C: Josep Civit
P: Victoria Borrás, Rosa Romero
A: Carmen Maura, Mario Gas
A woman and her young child are pursued by a mysterious policeman, so she leaves Bilbao and goes to another industrial city, where she works again in a nightclub. The policeman finds them and insists he is the child's father and they must all live together as a "happy family," but the

woman takes her child and flees again. Thriller. *Cine espanol. 1991.*

Awards: Venice Film Festival, nomination for Golden Lion, 1991

1578. *Cómo ser mujer y no morir en el intento / How to Be a Woman and Not Die Trying* 1991 DS

D: Ana Belén
S: Carmen Rico-Godoy
C: Juan Amorós
P: Andres Gómez
A: Carmen Maura, Antonio Resines

A forty-two-year-old mother, wife, and journalist "tries to do her job professionally, without neglecting her amorous relationship, the practical organization of the house, her friendships or the emotional needs of her children." A normal woman who "works like a man and still plays the role of a married woman." *Cine espanol. 1991.*

1579. *Tacones lejanos / High Heels* 1991

D: Pedro Almodóvar
S: Pedro Almodóvar
C: Alfredo Mayo
A: Victoria Abril, Marisa Paredes

A self-obsessed cabaret singer returns home after fifteen years to find her daughter married to one of her former lovers. Comedy. *Cine espanol. 1991.*

Awards: Spanish Actors Union, Best Actress (Paredes), 1992; César Awards, Best Foreign Film, 1993

1580. *Dime una mentira / Lie to Me* 1992 S

D: Juan Bollaín
S: Juan Bollaín, Icíar Bollaín, Marina Bollaín
C: Angel Luis Fernández
A: Icíar Bollaín, Marina Bollaín

Two look-alikes, an actress and a woman who lives with her mother, meet accidentally and trade lives in hopes their dissatisfactions will be eased. Comedy. *Cine espanol. 1992.*

1581. *Sublet (Realquiler) / Sublet* 1992 DSP

D: Chus Gutiérrez
S: Chus Gutiérrez
C: Juan Molina
P: Angélica Huete
A: Icíar Bollaín

New York City. A woman leaves Madrid in search of a new life; she finds a sublet in "Hell's Kitchen," along with all the big-city trouble that goes with life in an inner-city neighborhood. *Cine espanol. 1992.*

Awards: Cinema Writers Circle Awards, Best New Artist (Gutiérrez), 1993

1582. *Trampa para una esposa / Trap for a Wife* 1992

D: Joaquin Blanco
S: Joaquin Blanco
C: Manuel Valverde
A: Analia Ivars, Antonio Mayans, Marisa Oliver

After three years of marriage, a woman is disappointed in her husband's sexual drive; on the advice of a friend, she tries other men but finds that her real love is her girlfriend. *Cine espanol. 1992.*

1583. *El Pájaro de la felicidad / The Bird of Happiness* 1993 D

D: Pilar Miró
S: Mario Camus
C: Jose Luis Alcaine
A: Mercedes Sampietro

An art restorer is raped on the street by a gang; getting little support from her lover, she leaves him and is determined to change her life. *Contemporary Spanish.*

Awards: Ondas Awards, Best Actress, 1993

1584. *Sombras en una batalla / Shadows in a Conflict* 1993

D: Mario Camus
S: Mario Camus
C: Manuel Velasco
P: Carlos Ramon
A: Carmen Maura

Near the Portuguese border, a middle-aged mother with a young daughter begins an affair with a man who smuggles arms; she then becomes involved in his trade. *FII.*

Awards: Cinema Writers Circle Awards, Best Film, 1994

1585. *Costa Brava / Family Album* 1995 DSP

D: Marta Balletbò-Coll
S: Marta Balletbò-Coll, Ana Simon Cerezo
C: Teo López Garcia
P: Marta Balletbò-Coll
A: Desi Del Valle, Marta Balletbò-Coll, Montserrat Gausachs

Barcelona. An actress who is a tour guide during the day begins a relationship with a bisexual woman who works at the university; they then move in together. *FII.*

Awards: San Francisco International Lesbian & Gay Film Festival, Best Feature, 1995

1586. *Entre rojas* 1995 DSP

D: Azucema Rodriguez
S: Myriam de Maeztu, Mercedes de Blas
C: Javier Salmones

P: Fernando Colomo, Beatriz De la Gándara
A: Penelope Cruz, Cristina Marcos, Maria Pujalte
1970s. A story set in the "political wing of a women's prison." *Contemporary Spanish: 124.*
Awards: Bogota Film Festival, Best Film, 1996; Spanish Actors Union, Newcomer Award (Pujalte), 1996

1587. La Flor de mi secreto / The Flower of My Secret   1995 P
D: Pedro Almodóvar
S: Pedro Almodóvar
C: Affonso Beato
P: Esther Garcia
A: Marisa Paredes
A pseudonymous romance novelist with aspirations to be a serious writer spurns but eventually falls in love with an admiring editor, who is more available than her husband. Comedy.
Awards: Karlovy Vary International Film Festival, Best Actress, 1996; Sant Jordi Awards, Best Spanish Actress, 1996

1588. Hola, estàs sola? / Hi, Are You Alone?
                                               1995 DS
D: Icíar Bollaín
S: Icíar Bollaín
C: Teo Delgado
A: Silke, Candela Peña
Two twenty-year-old friends who have grown up without mothers enjoy living from day to day; they travel together and discover more about their loves and losses. *Festival de films, 24th: 89. 2002.*
Awards: Sant Jordi Awards, Best First Work, 1997

1589. Nadie hablara de nosotras cuando hayamos muerto / Nobody Will Speak of Us When We're Dead   1995
D: Agustin Diaz Yanes
S: Agustin Diaz Yanes
C: Paco Femenia
P: Edmundo Gil
A: Victoria Abril, Pilar Barden
Mexico. A prostitute witnesses a drug murder, then flees for her native Spain, followed by a hit man who has been sent to silence her. An alcoholic with a "comatose bullfighter" husband, she is supported by her mother-in-law in her efforts to extract money from the gang. *Variety. 1995, Oct. 2.*
Awards: San Sebastián Film Festival, Best Actress (Abril), Special Jury Prize, 1995; Goya Awards, Best Film, Best Actress (Abril), 1996

1590. Actrius / Actresses   1996
D: Ventura Pons

S: Ventura Pons, J. M. Benet
C: Tomàs Pladevall
P: Ventura Pons
A: Rosa María Sardá, Nuria Espert, Anna Lizaran, Mercé Pons
Three self-absorbed actresses relate different versions of an old secret to a young actress investigating the life of one of their colleagues.
Awards: Butaca Awards, Best Catalan Film, Best Catalan Actress (Sardá, Espert, Lizaran, Pons), 1997

1591. Cuerpo en el bosque / A Body in the Forest   1996
D: Joaquín Jordá
S: Joaquín Jordá
C: Carles Gusi
P: Julio Fernández
A: Rossy De Palma
A Civil Guard lieutenant investigates the murder of a woman found in the woods, then runs into intrigue among the victim's family and friends. *Cine espanol. 1996.*
Other titles: Un Cos al bosc
Awards: Montpellier Mediterranean Film Festival, Special Mention, 1997

1592. Lejos de África / Black Island   1996 DS
D: Cecilia Bartolomé
S: Cecilia Bartolomé
C: Pancho Alcaine
P: Adrian Lipp
A: Alicia Bogo, Isabel Mestres, Anelis Bonifacio, Ademelis Fernandez
1950s. A young white girl grows up in Equatorial Guinea during the last days of the colonial empire; she is very close to a black girl the same age. When they are twenty years old, a man comes between them. *Cine espanol. 1996.*

1593. Libertarias / Freedom Fighters   1996
D: Vincente Aranda
S: Antonio Rabinad
C: Jose Luis Alcaine
P: Andres Gómez
A: Victoria Abril, Ana Belén, Ariadna Gil
Spanish Civil War, 1936. A nun who is forced from her convent by revolutionary troops takes refuge in a house of prostitution. The women there have become a fighting unit, and she joins them, but they are denied full participation at the war front. *Variety: 86. 1996, May 6.*

1594. El Perro del hortelano / Dog in the Manger   1996 DS
D: Pilar Miró

S: Pilar Miró; based on the play by Felix Lope de Vega

C: Javier Aguirresarobe

P: Enrique Cerezo

A: Emma Suárez, Carmelo Gómez

Seventeenth century. A countess in love with her secretary must figure a way to justify her desire, as the relationship is beneath her status. Comedy.

Awards: Mar del Plata Film Festival, Best Film, 1996; Goya Awards, Best Director, Best Actress (Suarez), 1997

1595. *Por un hombre en tu vida* / *Put a Man in Your Life* 1996 DS

D: Eva Lesmes

S: Eva Lesmes, Joaquin Oristrell

C: Juan Amorós

P: César Benitez

A: Cristina Marcos, Toni Canto

"Football manager and feminist pop singer dive into a hotel swimming pool and crack their heads together. At first they think they have died, in fact they have swapped bodies." Comedy. *FII.*

1596. *Tu nombre en venena mis sueños* / *Your Name Poisons My Dreams* 1996 DS

D: Pilar Miró

S: Pilar Miró, Ricardo Franco

C: Javier Aguirresarobe

P: Rafael Díaz-Salgado

A: Emma Suárez

Madrid, 1950s. A woman returns after being involved in the 1942 murder investigation of three leftist militants. Mystery. *Contemporary Spanish: 124.*

Awards: Ondas Awards, Best Actress, 1996

1597. *De qué se ríen las mujeres?* / *What Are Women Laughing About?* 1997 S

D: Joaquin Oristrell

S: Joaquin Oristrell, Yolanda Garcia Serrano

C: Fernando Arribas

A: Veronica Forqué, Candela Peña, Adriana Ozores

Three sisters are a comedy team. One of their husbands dies, and the widow discovers that he has been continually unfaithful to her all their married life; she seeks revenge by picking up as many men as she can. Comedy. *Cine espanol. 1997.*

1598. *Resultado final* / *The Outcome* 1997

D: Juan Antonio Bardem

S: Juan Antonio Bardem

C: Manuel Velasco

A: Mar Flores

1996. A woman looks back on her life, particularly the excitement of her student days in the 1970s and her first lover, who was an unsatisfactory

partner; later she married a man who rose "to money and power." *Cine espanol. 1997.*

Awards: Cairo International Film Festival, nomination for Golden Pyramid, 1998

1599. *Todo está oscuro* / *Everything Is Dark* 1997 DSC

D: Ana Díez

S: Ana Díez, Angel Amigo

C: Teresa Medina

A: Silvia Munt

A stock market executive travels to Colombia to "repatriate the body of her brother, a journalist who has been murdered." Thriller. *Cine espanol. 1997.*

Awards: Bogota Film Festival, nomination for Best Film, 1997

1600. *Ave Maria* 1998 S

D: Eduardo Rossoff

S: Camille Thomasson

C: Henner Hofman

P: Andrea Kreuzhage

A: Teresa Lopez-Tarin, Ana Torrent

Seventeenth century. The daughter of a duke, born in Mexico of an American native woman, returns to Spain with him and is educated in a convent. Her high intelligence allows her to become a teacher of cartography, fine arts, and science, but she becomes an object of jealousy for an ambitious priest because she teaches men. *Cine espanol. 1999.*

Awards: Havana Film Festival, Best Director, 1999; Newport Beach Film Festival, Audience Award, 2000

1601. *Me llamo Sara* / *My Name Is Sara* 1998 DS

D: Dolores Payás

S: Dolores Payás

C: Andreu Rebes, Ricard Figueras

A: Elvira Minguez, Elena Castells

Barcelona. At forty years, a bourgeois woman is content with her job, her teenage daughter, and a longtime partner, but her comfortable certainties begin to reveal "cracks of considerable size." *Cine espanol. 1998.*

Other titles: Em dic Sara

Awards: Miami Hispanic Film Festival, Best Actress (Minguez), 1999

1602. *Cuando vuelvas a mi lado* / *Come Back to My Side* 1999 DS

D: Gracia Querejeta

S: Gracia Querejeta, Elias Querejeta, Manuel Gutiérrez Aragon

C: Alfredo Mayo

P: Elias Querejeta
A: Mercedes Sampietro, Julieta Serrano, Marta Belaustegui, Adriana Ozores, Rosa Mariscal
Three sisters leave Madrid to return home to Galicia to be with their dying mother and carry out her will. *Cine espanol. 1999.*

1603. *Ellas / Women*   1999
D: Luis Galvão Teles
S: Luis Galvão Teles
C: Alfredo Mayo
A: Carmen Maura, Guesch Patti, Miou-Miou, Marisa Berenson, Marthe Keller
A journalist interviews her friends about what women want. *NYT: E24. 1999, Oct. 29.*
Awards: Hamptons International Film Festival, Vision Award, 1999

1604. *Flores de otro mundo / Flowers from Another World*   1999 DS
D: Icíar Bollaín
S: Icíar Bollaín, Julio Lilamazares
C: Teo Delgado
A: Lissete Mejía, Marilyn Torres, Elena Irureta, Jose Sanchez
A busload of women is imported from the city to a small-town social so the local men can find wives; immigrants from the Caribbean are most attracted to the arrangement, and two attempt to make it work.
Awards: Bogota Film Festival, Silver Precolumbian Circle, 1999; Bordeaux International Festival of Women in Cinema, Best Actress (ensemble), 1999; Cannes Film Festival, Mercedes-Benz Award, 1999

1605. *Sobreviviré / I Will Survive*   1999 S
D: Alfonso Albacete, David Menkes
S: David Menkes, Lucía Etxebarría
C: Gonzalo Fernández-Berridi
P: Francisco Ramos
A: Emma Suárez, Mirta Ibarra, Juan Diego Botto
A first-person narrative of a woman, widowed by an accident, who has a young son and works at a video store. She begins a relationship with a younger gay sculptor and insists that her depressive moods signal "vitality." *Cine espanol. 1999.*
Awards: Torino International Gay & Lesbian Film Festival, Best Film, 2000

1606. *Todo sobre mi madre / All About My Mother*   1999
D: Pedro Almodóvar
S: Pedro Almodóvar
P: Affonso Beato
A: Cecilia Roth, Marisa Paredes, Penelope Cruz, Candela Péna, Rosa María Sardá

A woman who has just lost her teenage son in an accident returns to Barcelona, where she makes contact with the friends of her youth and the father of her dead son.
Awards: Cannes Film Festival, Best Film, Best Director, 1999; Academy Awards, Best Foreign Film, 2000

1607. *Yerma*   1999 DS
D: Pilar Távora
S: Chus Gutiérrez, Juan Cordoba; based on the play by Federico Garcia Lorca
C: Acacio De Almeida
A: Aitana Sánchez-Gijón, Amaya Carmona
A woman goes along with the traditions of her family and marries the man her father chooses for her. She is attracted to another man but remains faithful, believing a child will transcend her husband's unloving nature, but he becomes more and more jealous until, finally, she kills him. *Festival de films, 22nd: 79. 2000.*

1608. *Yoyes*   1999 DS
D: Helena Taberna
S: Helena Taberna, Andres Martoreli
C: Federico Rives
P: Enrique Cerezo
A: Ana Torrent
The former leader of the ETA, a Basque separatist organization, Yoyes returns to Spain from a seven-year exile in Mexico. She has a child and wants only to forget her past, but in Spain she is a news item, propaganda for the government, and an apparent betrayer to her former comrades. Yoyes was assassinated in 1986. Based on a true story. *Festival de films, 12th: 90. 2002.*
Awards: Cartagena Film Festival, Best First Work, 2001; Gramado Film Festival, Audience Award, 2001

1609. *La Comunidad / Common Wealth*   2000
D: Alex De la Iglesia
S: Alex De la Iglesia, Jorge Guerrica
C: Kiko De la Rica
P: Andres Gómez
A: Carmen Maura
A real estate agent discovers cash in an apartment, then must deal with the anger of the residents in the community. *Cine espanol. 2000.*
Awards: Cinema Writers Circle Awards, Best Actress, 2001; Fotogramas de Plata, Best Film, 2001; Goya Awards, Best Actress, 2001

1610. *El Este de la brujula / East on the Compass*   2000
D: Jordi Torrent
S: Jordi Torrent
C: Xavier Gil

A: Sarita Choudhury

Barcelona. An Indian woman and her young son arrive in Spain without knowing the language; she is looking for someone in particular and is helped by some of the people in the boarding house where they stay. *Cine espanol. 2000.*

1611. *El Harén de Madame Osmane / Harem of Madame Osmane* 2000 P
D: Nadir Moknèche
S: Nadir Moknèche
C: Xavier Gil
P: Sarah Halioua, Gerardo Herrero
A: Carmen Maura, Myriam Amarouchène

Algeria, 1993. An owner of a boardinghouse and a former fighter in the resistance is insecure and afraid of being alone since her husband abandoned her; she tries to control her daughter, along with all the boarders. *Cine espanol. 2000.*

1612. *Nosotras / Women* 2000 DS
D: Judith Colell
S: Jordi Cadena, Isabel Clara Simo
C: Josep Civit
P: Aureli De Luna
A: Mercedes Sampietro, Eva Santolaria

A collage of women in many different roles and events: on the street, in shops, in boardrooms, in brothels, and in doctor's offices. All describe the difficulties women and girls have with their appearances, their relationships, and their jobs. *Cine espanol. 2000.*

Awards: Catalonian International Film Festival, Best Actress (Sampietro), 2000; Butaca Awards, Best Catalan Film, 2001

1613. *La Reina Isabel en persona / Queen Isabella in Person* 2000
D: Rafael Gordon
S: Rafael Gordon
C: David Aranguren
A: Isabel Ordaz

Queen Isabella looks back on her fifteenth-century reign from the perspective of today: "She throws scorn on the coarse portrayals of her person and makes a lively appeal for people to look more deeply at the transition from medieval feudalism to the Modern State." She comments on her controversial expulsion of the Jews via a law on foreigners and on "the tragedies of her intimate life as a wife, daughter, mother, Christian, and queen." *Cine espanol. 2000.*

1614. *Sé quién eres / I Know Who You Are* 2000 DS
D: Patricia Ferreira

S: Daniela Fejerman, Inéz París
C: Jose Luis Alcaine
P: Pancho Casal
A: Ana Fernández, Miguel Sola

Galacia. A young psychiatrist falls in love with her first patient, an amnesiac with a terrorist past. *Film Society.* 2000, Dec.

Awards: Lleida Latin-American Film Festival, Audience Award, 2000

1615. *Sexo por compasión / Compassionate Sex* 2000 DSP
D: Laura Mañá
S: Laura Mañá
C: Henner Hofman
P: Miguel Hernandez, Fina Torrente
A: Elizabeth Margoni

After her husband leaves her because of her generosity, a fifty-year-old woman decides to brighten the lives of her fellow villagers by engaging in sex with all the men of the village. *Cine espanol. 2000.*

Awards: Guadalajara Mexican Film Festival, Best Director, 2001; Málaga Spanish Film Festival, Best Film, 2001

1616. *Solas* 2000
D: Benito Zambrano
S: Benito Zambrano
C: Tote Trenez
P: Antonio Pérez
A: María Galiana, Ana Fernández

Seville. A mother stays in her daughter's apartment while tending to her husband in the hospital; the daughter is stuck in life doing cleaning work, and the mother attempts to improve her condition.

Awards: Berlin International Film Festival, Ecumenical Jury Prize, 1999; Brussels International Film Festival, Best Actress (Fernández), FIPRESCI, 2000; Cartagena Film Festival, Critics Award, Best Supporting Actress (Galiana), 2000; Goya Awards, Best Screenplay, Best Actress (Fernández, Galiana), 2000

1617. *Time's Up!* 2000 DS
D: Cecilia Barriga
S: Cecilia Barriga
C: Edgar Gil
A: Leonor Benedetto

New York. An Argentinean psychiatrist decides to avoid renting an office space and holds her sessions in a mobile home. In dealing with tearing herself away from her patients for her annual vacation, she realizes that she herself needs some therapy. *Festival de films, 23rd: 23. 2001.*

Awards: Amiens International Film Festival, Best Actress, 2000

1618. *Viaje de Arián / Journey of Arian*   2000
D: Eduard Bosch
S: Jordi Gasull, Patxi Amezcua
C: Xavier Gil
A: Ingrid Rubio

A young woman has been active in the Basque liberation movement since her childhood. She is in love with a terrorist, who gets her more deeply involved until she becomes hunted by police and is forced into a safe house; from there, she works with a group to kidnap the daughter of an industrialist from Navarre. Thriller. *Cine espanol. 2000.*

Awards: Málaga Spanish Film Festival, Special Mention (Rubio), 2000

1619. *Juana la loca / Mad Love*   2001
D: Vincente Aranda
S: Vincente Aranda, Antonio Larreta
C: Paco Femenia
P: Enrique Cerezo
A: Pilar López de Ayala, Daniele Liotti

Spain, 1496. Queen Juana, who has developed a great passion for her husband after a state-arranged marriage, is declared insane by him so that he can depose her and become king himself. *Cine espanol. 2001.*

Other titles: *Juana the Mad*

Awards: San Sebastián International Film Festival, Best Actress, 2001; Goya Awards, Best Actress, 2002

1620. *El Juego de Luna / Luna's Game* 2001 DS
D: Mónica Laguna
S: Mónica Laguna, Jorge Guerricaechevarria
C: Teo Delgado
P: Andres Gómez
A: Ana Torrent

A professional gambler, raised by a gambler father, looks for a big win. *Film Society. 2001, Dec.*

Awards: Málaga Spanish Film Festival, Best Director, 2001

1621. *El Palo / Hold Up*   2001 D
D: Eva Lesmes
S: Luis Marias
C: Gonzalo Fernández-Berridi
A: Adriana Ozores, Malena Alterio, Maribel Verdú, Carmen Maura

Four women plan a robbery: the bank cleaner, a bourgeois who has lost her income, a pregnant hairdresser, and a "punk with no future." They comically bond over the preparation, but the robbery "is something very serious." *Cine espanol. 2001.*

1622. *Silencio roto / Broken Silence*   2001
D: Montxo Armendáriz
S: Montxo Armendáriz
C: Guillermo Novarro
P: Montxo Armendáriz
A: Lucia Jiménez, Juan Diego Botto, Mercedes Sampietro, María Botto, Asunción Balaguer

1944. A woman returns to her family village, where the *maquis* (Republican guerrillas) continue to fight Franco after his victory. She becomes involved in protecting the men, who flee periodically into the hills when government forces arrive seeking to purge them, but she realizes the futility of their isolation as she falls in love with one.

Awards: Butaca Awards, Best Catalan Actress (Sampietro), 2001

1623. *Deseo / Beyond Desire*   2002
D: Gerardo Vera
S: Angelos Caso
C: Javier Aguirresarobe
P: Andres Gómez
A: Leonor Watling, Cecilia Roth, Rosa María Sardá, Leonardo Sbaraglia

World War II. A woman's husband and father are executed by the Franco regime; she finds work as a housekeeper for an Argentinean, whom she discovers deals with the Nazis. *Film Society. 2002, Dec.*

1624. *Lisístrata / Lysistrata*   2002
D: Francesc Bellmunt
S: Ralf König; based on the play by Aristophanes
C: Julian Elizalde
A: Maribel Verdú, Juan Luis Galiardo

A modern version of the play about Greek women denying their men sex in order to stop the Peloponnesian wars; here, the military commanders follow a gay leader who commands the troops to satisfy themselves by engaging in "forced homosexuality" on the battlefield. *Cine espanol. 2002.*

1625. *Piedras / Stones*   2002
D: Ramón Salazar
S: Ramón Salazar
C: David Carretero
P: Francisco Ramos
A: Victoria Peña, Antonia San Juan, Angela Molina, Majwa Nimri, Monica Cervera

Madrid. Intertwined stories of five women who work in a brothel at the edge of the city. Humor gets them through the days. *AMG.*

Awards: Flanders International Film Festival, Audience Award, 2002; Stockholm Film Festival, Best Actress (Peña), 2002

1626. *La Soledad era esto* / *That Was Loneliness*
2002 S
D: Sergio Renan
S: Manuel Matji, Aída Bortnik
C: Antonio Saiz
P: Enrique Cerezo
A: Charo López
A divorced woman who barely speaks to her grown daughter is compelled to change her thinking when her own mother, with whom she had not gotten along, dies. Finding her mother's diaries and audiotapes, she reads and listens, finding a woman more like herself than she knew. *Cine español. 2002.*

1627. *La Hija del canibál* / *Lucía, Lucía* 2003 SP
D: Antonio Serrano
S: Marcela Fuentes-Berain, Antonio Serrano; based on the novel by Rosa Montera
C: Xavier Pérez Grobet
P: Inna Payan, Epigmenio Ibarra
A: Cecilia Roth
A woman's husband disappears at the Mexico City airport as they are heading for a vacation; she examines her life with the help of two men, one older and one younger than she. *FII.*
Other titles: *The Cannibal's Daughter*

1628. *Una Preciosa puesta de sol* / *A Beautiful Sunset*
2003 P
D: Alvaro Del Amo
S: Alvaro Del Amo
C: Carlos Suárez
P: Jacobo Echeverría-Torres, Beatriz Navarrete
A: Marisa Paredes, Ana Torrent, Marta Larralde
A grandmother, daughter, and granddaughter vacation in the mountains. *Film Society. 2003, Dec.*

1629. *Soldados de Salamina* / *Soldiers of Salamina*
2003 P
D: David Trueba
S: David Trueba; based on the novel by Javier Cercas
C: Javier Aguirresarobe
P: Christina Huete, Andres Gómez
A: Ariadna Gil
A novelist seeks a new subject and finds a story of a fascist writer who was mysteriously saved by his captor during the Civil War. *Film Society. 2003, Dec.*
Awards: Copenhagen International Film Festival, Best Screenplay, 2003

1630. *Te doy mis ojos* / *Take My Eyes* 2003 DS
D: Icíar Bollaín
S: Icíar Bollaín, Alicia Luna
C: Carles Gusi
P: Santiago García de Leániz
A: Laia Marull
A woman flees her house with her son after a beating by her husband; he follows them with contrition, pleading for their return. After living with her sister and taking a job, she feels stronger, and her husband has entered therapy, so she returns to him. *Festival de films, 26th: 23. 2004.*
Awards: Goya Awards, Best Film, Best Director, 2004

1631. *Los Nombres de Alicia* 2004 D
D: Pilar Ruiz-Gutierrez
S: Pablo Alonzo
C: Carles Gusi
A: Ana Morreira
An English woman arrives in a provincial Spanish town to learn Spanish and teach English to the children of the family with whom she stays; her highly sexual presence has an unsettling effect on the quiet household. *Festival de films, 27th: 24. 2005.*

1632. *A mi madre le gustan las mujeres* / *My Mother Likes Women*
2004 DSP
D: Inéz París, Daniela Fejerman
S: Inéz París, Daniela Fejerman
C: David Omedes
P: Beatriz De la Gándara
A: Rosa María Sardá, Eliska Sirová, Leonor Watling, Maria Pujalte, Silvia Abascal
A concert pianist introduces her Czech female lover to her three daughters and tells them she is turning over her retirement income to the woman, a piano student who is their age. *Village Voice: 62. 2004, May 19.*
Awards: Miami Hispanic Film Festival, Best Actress (Watling), Audience Award, 2002; Cartagena Film Festival, Best Actress (Watling), 2003; Dublin Gay & Lesbian Film Festival, Audience Award, 2003

1633. *Yo Puta* / *Whore* 2004 DS
D: Maria Luna Lidon
S: Adela Ibanez; based on the novel by Isabel Pisano
C: Ricardo Aronovich
P: Jose Magag
A: Daryl Hannah, Denise Richards
A pretend documentary where female and male prostitutes around the world discuss their work in interviews; includes some real interviews. *Tribeca Film. 2003.*

SRI LANKA

1634. ***Gehenu Lamai / The Girls***   1977 DS
D: Sumitra Peries
S: Sumitra Peries
C: M. S. Anandan
P: Lester Peries
A: Vasanthi Chaturani, Jenita Samaraweera
Sinhal. Two impoverished sisters have difficulties;
   one has a child while still unmarried, the other
   "submits" to an "economically suitable arranged
   marriage." *FII.*

1635. ***Yahalou yeheli / Friends***   1983 D
D: Sumitra Peries
S: Karunasena Jayalath
C: Donald Darunaratna
A: Nadika Gunasekeva, Tony Ranasinghe
A landowner, wishing to gain more property, is
   against all social reforms in his village but is
   opposed in his schemes by his sister and one
   of his daughters. *Festival de films, 10th: 113.
   1988.*
Other titles: Les Ami(e)s

1636. ***Lokuduwa / The Eldest Daughter*** 1994 D
D: Sumitra Peries
S: Tissa Abeysekera, Edward Mallawarachchi
C: Willie Blake
A: Geetha Kumarasinghe
A woman works in a clothing firm and becomes
   mistress of the owner, her father's friend. She
   then rises to the top position but eventually
   quits to regain her self-esteem. *FII.*

1637. ***Duvata Mawaka Misa / A Mother Alone***
                                              1997 D
D: Sumitra Peries
S: Tony Ranasinghe
C: K. A. Dharmasena
P: Milina Sumathipala
A: Sangeetha Weeraratne, Sriyani Amarasena
A young woman is sent off to live with various
   aunts because she is pregnant. While waiting,
   she finds they are hypocritical, having their own
   sexual liaisons, and her emboldened attitude
   toward them provokes jealousy.

SWEDEN

1638. ***Tystnaden / The Silence***   1963
D: Ingmar Bergman
C: Sven Nykvist
P: Allan Ekelund
A: Ingrid Thulin, Gunnel Lindblom

Two sisters and a young son stay in a large foreign
   hotel, where the younger sister has an affair,
   then tells the other about it.
Awards: Guldbagge Awards, Best Director, Best
   Actress (Thulin), 1964

1639. ***Älskande pär / Loving Couples*** 1964 DS
D: Mai Zetterling
S: Mai Zetterling, David Hughes; based on the
   novel by Agnes von Krusenstjerna
C: Sven Nykvist
P: Goran Lindren, Rune Waldekranz
A: Harriet Andersson, Gunnel Lindblom, Gio
   Petré
Three women rest in a maternity ward at the
   beginning of the twentieth century. A wealthy
   landowner, orphaned as a child, was cared for
   by a servant when no one else in the family
   volunteered; she grows up to love a shallow
   man with whom the servant had had a longtime
   affair. Another servant is married to a kind man,
   but she still feels the humiliation of her fall from
   bourgeois comfort after the death of her father
   and suffers greatly when she miscarries. The
   third woman is a carefree artist's model who
   has always found joy in her provocative sexuality, even when it gets her into trouble. The film
   ends with a live birth.

1640. ***Nattlek / Night Games***   1966 DS
D: Mai Zetterling
S: Mai Zetterling, David Hughes
C: Rune Ericson
P: Göran Lindgren
A: Ingrid Thulin
A man returns to his childhood home with his
   fiancé, whom he blindfolds as they enter the
   opulent round house. Flashbacks describe his
   adolescent days with his vain mother, who took
   joy in teasing him and who stayed at home only
   to entertain sycophantic friends. To entertain
   her guests, she throws him sugar as if he's a
   "Doggy," but when he masturbates after she
   arouses him with kisses, she turns into a prud-
   ish tyrant.

1641. ***Persona***   1966
D: Ingmar Bergman
S: Ingmar Bergman
C: Sven Nykvist
P: Ingmar Bergman
A: Liv Ullmann, Bibi Andersson
An actress in a mute depression recuperates with a
   nurse attendant at a remote seaside resort. The
   nurse wonders if she will be strong enough to
   deal with the actress's will and is personally be-

trayed when she finds a letter the actress wrote about the nurse's most personal revelations.

Awards: Guldbagge Awards, Best Film, Best Actress (Andersson), 1967; National Society of Film Critics Awards, Best Actress (Andersson), 1968

1642. *Yngsjömordet* / *Woman of Darkness*
1966 S
D: Arne Mattsson
S: Eva Dahlbeck; based on the novel by Yngve Lyttkens
C: Lasse Björne
P: Lorens Marmstedt
A: Gunnel Lindblom

Nineteenth century. A woman is executed for murdering her son's wife; she and her son were lovers, and she reflects on the events leading up to the violence. *FII.*

1643. *Flikorna* / *The Girls*   1968 DS
D: Mai Zetterling
S: Mai Zetterling, David Hughes
C: Rune Ericson
P: Göran Lindgren
A: Bibi Andersson, Harriet Andersson, Gunnel Lindblom, Gunnar Björnstrand, Erland Josephson

Three actresses tour the north of Sweden with Aristophanes' *Lysistrata*, about women who deny their husbands sex in order to stop war. One actress is childless and married to a broker with two mistresses, one loves her husband and children but is bored, and one is a doctor's mistress caring for his child; all are torn between their domestic circumstances and their work. One night, the lead actress is inspired by the play to make a public appeal for dialogue about the state of the world. The attempt is clumsy, and the troupe must deal with the fallout from the press and their own embarrassment at being associated with her.

Other titles: Lysistrata

1644. *Georgia Georgia*   1971 S
D: Stig Björkman
S: Maya Angelou
C: Andreas Bellis
P: Jack Jordan
A: Diana Sands

A black singer living in Stockholm has an attraction for a white man, but her assistant objects.

Awards: Berlin International Film Festival, nomination for Golden Bear, 1973

1645. *Viskningar och Rop* / *Cries and Whispers*
1972
D: Ingmar Bergman

S: Ingmar Bergman
C: Sven Nykvist
P: Lars-Owe Carlberg
A: Harriet Andersson, Ingrid Thulin, Kari Sylwan, Liv Ullmann

Two sisters move to the family mansion to tend to their third sister, who is dying of cancer.

Awards: Guldbagge Awards, Best Film, Best Actress (Andersson), 1973

1646. *Den Vita Väggen* / *The White Wall*   1974
D: Stig Björkman
S: Stig Björkman
C: Petter Davidson
P: Bengt Forslund
A: Harriet Andersson

A divorced woman with a young son looks for employment. *FII.*

Other titles: Trå Kvinnor: den Vita Väggen

1647. *Ansikte mot ansikte* / *Face to Face*   1975
D: Ingmar Bergman
S: Ingmar Bergman
C: Sven Nykvist
P: Lars-Owe Carlberg
A: Liv Ullmann

A psychiatrist has a mental breakdown while her husband and daughter are away. *Faber Companion.*

Awards: Los Angeles Film Critics Association, Best Foreign Film, Best Actress, 1976; Golden Globes, Best Foreign Language Film, 1977; New York Film Critics Circle Awards, Best Actress, 1977

1648. *Långt Borta och Nära* / *Far Away and Close*   1976 DS
D: Marianne Ahrne
S: Marianne Ahrne, Bertrand Hurault
C: Hans Welin
P: Jörn Donner
A: Lilga Kovanko

A doctor intern in a state mental hospital helps a mute young man. *Variety: 26. 1976, Dec. 29.*

Other titles: Near and Far Away
Awards: Gulbagge Awards, Best Direction, 1977

1649. *Paradistorg* / *Summer Paradise*   1976 DS
D: Gunnel Lindblom
S: Gunnel Lindblom, Ulla Isaksson
C: Tony Forsberg
P: Ingmar Bergman
A: Birgitta Valberg, Sif Ruud

Two friends, a doctor and a divorced grandmother, who is a social worker, conflict while on summer vacation; the doctor is a "creature of reason," and the social worker is "considerate of her fellow human beings." *FII.*

Awards: Guldbagge Awards, Best Actress (Valberg), 1977

1650. Höstsonaten / Autumn Sonata 1978
D: Ingmar Bergman
S: Ingmar Bergman
C: Sven Nykvist
P: Richard Brick
A: Ingrid Bergman, Liv Ullmann
A concert pianist returns to visit her grown daughter, whom she has not seen in many years; their relationship is strained and lacking respect. She is surprised to find her other daughter, whom she had institutionalized as disabled, being cared for there.
Awards: New York Film Critics Circle Awards, Best Actress (Bergman), 1978; Golden Globes, Best Actress (Bergman), 1979

1651. Gräset Sjunger / The Grass Is Singing 1981 S
D: Michael Raeburn
S: Michael Raeburn; based on the novel by Doris Lessing
C: Bille August
P: Mark Forstater
A: Karen Black
Zimbabwe. A woman who works in the city decides she must marry and so goes to live with a farmer in the bush; she becomes disturbed by the isolation, and she eventually breaks down from exhaustion and the strain of her relationship with a black servant. *Variety: 20. 1981, June 3.*
Other titles: Killing Heat

1652. Mamma 1982 DS
D: Suzanne Osten
S: Tove Ellefsen, Suzanne Osten
C: Hans Welin
P: Bert Sundberg
A: Malin Ek
The story of the director's mother, who began to make films in the 1940s but gradually lost her mind to surreal visions that the film renders with avant-garde techniques. *AMG.*
Awards: Guldbagge Awards, Best Actress, 1984

1653. Berget pa manens baksida / Hill on the Dark Side of the Moon 1983 S
D: Lennart Hjulström
S: Agneta Pleijel
C: Sten Holmberg
P: Bert Sundberg
A: Gunilla Nyroos, Bibi Andersson
The last years in the life of Sonya Kovalevsky, a Soviet mathematician and Sweden's first woman

professor, who died at forty-one after having a daughter with a man who insisted they not marry. *AMG.*
Awards: Guldbagge Awards, Best Actress (Nyroos), 1985

1654. Amorosa 1986 DS
D: Mai Zetterling
S: Mai Zetterling
C: Rune Ericson
A: Stina Ekblad, Erland Josephson
A portrait of Swedish novelist Agnes Von Krusenstjerna, a disturbed woman who persistently broke societal taboos around sexuality in her scandalous novels of the 1930s, then suffered ostracism from her aristocratic family. Both defiant and brittle, she found refuge with an older man, an editor who persisted in publishing her work and feeding her erotic fantasies through years of mental illness.
Awards: Guldbagge Awards, Best Actress, Best Actor, 1987

1655. På Liv och död / A Matter of Life and Death 1986 DS
D: Marianne Ahrne
S: Marianne Ahrne, Bertrand Hurault
C: Hans Welin
P: Stefan Hencz
A: Lena Olin
A journalist refuses assignment in Japan in order to write about a maternity hospital and remain near a doctor she loves from afar. *FII.*

1656. Änglagård / House of Angels 1992
D: Colin Nutley
S: Colin Nutley
C: Jens Fischer
P: Lars Dahlquist
A: Helena Bergström, Rikard Wolff
A cabaret singer moves from the continent to a farm she has inherited; she and her gay motorcycle friend conflict with the locals, but they make peace and stay. There is a 1994 sequel: *Änglagård—andra sommaren. AMG.*
Awards: Guldbagge Awards, Best Film, 1993; Rouen Nordic Film Festival, Press Award, Audience Award, 1993

1657. Bara du och jag / Just You and Me 1994 DS
D: Suzanne Olsten
S: Suzanne Olsten, Barbro Smeds
C: Göran Nilsson
P: Anders Birkeland
A: Francesca Quartey

Sweden's Minister of Youth, a young black woman, has an affair with a teacher twice her age who has five children; they are harassed by racists. *FII.*

1658. *Enskilda samtal* / *Private Confessions*
1996 DP
D: Liv Ullmann
S: Ingmar Bergman
C: Sven Nykvist
P: Ingrid Dahlberg
A: Pernilla August, Samuel Fröler, Max Von Sydow
In talks with her confessor, a minister's wife looks back on her affair with a young divinity student and her frustration over his withdrawal from her. After confessing to her husband, she suffers his anger as well as the loss of her lover.

1659. *Trolösa* / *Faithless*
1998 D
D: Liv Ullmann
S: Ingmar Bergman
C: Jörgen Persson
P: Kaj Larsen
A: Lena Endre, Erland Josephson
A director writing a script calls up the ghost of an actress to help him draft his tale of infidelity; he gets her to tell the story by spontaneously creating the character of an actress who has an affair with a friend of the family and ruins her marriage. *FII.*
Other titles: *L'Infidele*
Awards: Cannes Film Festival, nomination for Golden Palm, 2000; Guldbagge Awards, Best Actress, 2001

1660. *Fyra kvinnor* / *Four Women*
2002
D: Baker Karim
S: Baker Karim
C: Baker Karim
A: Nomika Miheller, Annette Johnson, Karen Helen Hargaard, Malin Bjorklund
A woman returning to her hometown for the wedding of one of her friends brings along a video camera. *Film Society. 2002, Nov.*

1661. *Hus i helvete* / *All Hell Let Loose*
2002 DSP
D: Susan Taslami
S: Susan Taslami
C: Robert Nordström
P: Anita Oxburgh
A: Melinda Kinnaman
The oldest daughter of an Iranian Muslim family returns from the United States bent on becoming a nightclub dancer; she hides her ambition from her father. Her mother also goes against his wishes as she pursues her professional ca-

reer, and the youngest daughter is about to get married, making the father even more sensitive. *Festival de films, 25th: 83. 2003.*
Awards: Montréal World Film Festival, First Film Special Award, 2002

1662. *Lilya 4-Ever*
2002
D: Lukas Moodysson
S: Lukas Moodysson
C: Ulf Brantas
P: Lars Jönsson
A: Oksana Akinshina
An Eastern European sixteen-year-old is abandoned by her mother and never recuperates from the loss; left to fend for herself, she becomes a prostitute and is lured to Sweden, where she is forced into sex slavery.
Awards: Gijon International Film Festival, Best Actress, Grand Prix, 2002; Stockholm Film Festival, FIPRESCI, 2002; Guldbagge Awards, Best Film, Best Actress, 2003

SWITZERLAND

1663. *La Salamandre* / *The Salamander* 1971
D: Alain Tanner
S: Alain Tanner, John Berger
C: Renato Berta
P: Gabriel Auer
A: Bulle Ogier
A checkout clerk at a grocery store becomes the fixation of a couple of male journalists, who are writing a story about her murdered uncle.
Awards: Berlin International Film Festival, OCIC Award, 1971

1664. *Der Ruf der blonden Göttin* / *Voodoo Passion* 1977
D: Jesus Franco
S: Erwin Dietrich
A: Nanda Van Bergen, Ada Tauler
Haiti. The wife of the British consul arrives to live again with her estranged husband; she gets involved with the lesbian housekeeper, a nymphomaniac "sister," and suffers from nightmares about voodoo ceremonies. Exploitation. *FII.*

1665. *Messidor*
1979
D: Alain Tanner
S: Alain Tanner
C: Renato Berta
P: Yves Gasser
A: Clémentine Amouroux, Catherine Rétoré
Two girls abandon their jobs and homes for life on the road; after an attempted rape, they gradually

become thieves. The plot is similar to the later *Thelma and Louise* (2136).

Awards: Berlin International Film Festival, nomination for Golden Bear, 1979

1666. La Femme de Rose Hill / Woman from Rose Hill 1989
D: Alain Tanner
S: Alain Tanner
C: Hugues Ryffel
P: Paulo Branco
A: Marie Gaydu
A woman arrives in a small Swiss town to marry her pen pal, then falls in love with a younger man. *BiFi.*

1667. Le Journal de Lady M / Diary of Lady M 1993 S
D: Alain Tanner
S: Myriam Mézières
C: Denis Jutzeler
P: Alain Tanner
A: Myriam Mézières, Juanjo Puigcorbe, Félicité Wouassi
A single nightclub singer pursues a painter to his home in Barcelona; when she discovers he is married, she invites him and his wife to live with her in Paris. *Belgian Cinema.*

1668. Die Reise nach Kafiristan / The Journey to Kafiristan 2001 S
D: Fosco Dubini, Donatello Dubini
S: Fosco Dubini, Donatello Dubini, Barbara Marx
C: Matthias Kälin
P: Fosco Dubini, Donatello Dubini
A: Nina Petri, Jeanette Hain
The story of author Anne Marie Schwarzenbach and ethnologist Ella Maillart, who traveled together in 1939 from Geneva through the Balkans to Turkey, Persia, and finally Kabul. *Film Society. 2003, Apr.*

1669. Julie's Geist / Julie's Ghost 2002 DP
D: Bettina Wilhelm
P: Gudrun Ruzicková-Steiner
A: Sylvie Testud
Two young women meet on the street; one is killed by a car and becomes a ghostly conscience for the other. Fantasy. *Film Society. 2003, Apr.*
Awards: WorldFest Houston, Grand Award, 2002

1670. Les Petites couleurs / A Little Color 2002 DS
D: Patricia Plattner
S: Patricia Plattner, Jean Bobby
C: Matthias Kälin

P: Paulo Branco
A: Anouk Grinberg, Bernadette Lafont
A young woman flees her violent husband, then meets an older widow, who initiates her into a new life as a prostitute at a truck-stop hotel. *Film Society. 2003, Apr.*
Awards: Swiss Film Prize, nomination for Best Film, 2003

TAIWAN

1671. Hai tan de yi tian / That Day on the Beach 1983
D: Edward Yang
S: Edward Yang, Nien-jen Wu
C: Christopher Doyle
A: Sylvia Chang, Hsu Ming
Two women, a concert pianist and a divorcée with a new business, discuss in flashback their childhood and choices. *AMG.*

1672. Kan hai de rizi / A Flower in the Rainy Night 1983
D: Wang Tong
S: Huang Chunming
C: Lin Hongzhong
P: Mei Changkun
A: Lu Xiaofen, Ma Rufeng, Sue Ming-ming
A woman, sold by her stepfather at the age of fourteen, continues to support her family with the money she earns as a prostitute. However, they spurn her low status, so she decides to separate from them and have a family of her own. *Asian Film. Accessed 2005, Feb. 14.*
Awards: Golden Horse Awards, Best Actress, Best Supporting Actress, 1983

1673. Kuei mei / Jade Women 1983
D: Yi Chang
S: Yi Chang, Sho Sa
C: Yang Wei-han
P: Lin Deng-fei
A: Loretta Yang
1950s–1970s. A mainland Chinese woman is forced into relocation to Taiwan and a loveless marriage to a widower. From there the couple go to Japan as domestic servants, where they learn the restaurant trade so they can open their own restaurant in Taiwan. The result is "educated successful children and middle class affluence." *Variety. 1986, Jan. 29.*

1674. You ma caizi / Rapeseed Girl 1983
D: Wan Ren
S: Hou Hsiao-hsien

C: Lin Zanting
P: Lin Rongfeng
A: Ko I-cheng, Chen Qioyan, Li Shuping
A mother dominates her family and weak husband, who struggles with financial stress; she fails to respect and support her daughter, who eventually marries against her mother's will. *Asian Film. Accessed 2005, Feb. 14.*

Other titles: Ah Fei

Awards: Golden Horse Awards, Best Supporting Actress, 1984

1675. *Sha fu / Woman of Wrath*   1984
D: Zeng Zhuangxiang
S: Wu Nien-chen
C: Chang Hui-kung
A: Hsia Wen-shi, Pai Ying
Taiwan, Japanese occupation. A woman is being starved by her butcher husband and is also routinely raped by him, which reminds her of her mother, who was raped by Japanese soldiers and then committed suicide. One day she butchers her husband as she has seen him butcher animals. *Festival des 3. Also Tomson Films. Accessed 2005, July 15.*

1676. *Wo te ai / This Love of Mine*   1986
D: Chang Yi
S: Chang Yi
C: Yang Wei-han
A: Yang Hui-shan
A woman struggles with "urban pollution," constantly cleaning her bathroom, washing and peeling fruit, and finally chopping off her hair in an attempt to "reinvent" herself and win back her husband. *Chinese-Language: 271. Also AMG.*

1677. *Huang se gu shi / Story of a Woman*
1987 D
D: Sylvia Chang
S: Choi Ming Leung, So Wai Ching
C: Cheung Wai-kung
P: Bun Hsu
A: Sylvia Chang, Maggie Cheung
"Trilogy of stories, tracing the youth, marriage and divorce of a young woman." *FII.*

1678. *Kuei-hua hsiang / Osmanthus Alley* 1987
D: Chen Kun-hou
S: Ding Yah Ming; based on the novel by Hsiao Li-hung
C: Chen Kun-hou
P: Lin Deng Fei
A: Lu Hsiao-fen
An orphaned girl with attractive bound feet and embroidery skills marries into a wealthy family after refusing a sincere but poor love. *Once upon a Time: 174.*

Other titles: Guihuaxiang

1679. *Yuan nü / Rouge of the North*   1988 S
D: Tan Han-chang
S: Tan Han-chang; based on the novel by Eileen Chang
C: Yang Wei-han
A: Hsia Wen-shi
Shanghai, 1910. A poor young woman is married to a rich, blind, and demanding man, who drives her to attempt suicide. She never recovers from the abuse and treats her son with worse callousness. *Festival des 3.*

1680. *Fan mu an kao / A Woman and Seven Husbands*   1990
D: Terry Tong
S: Tang Chi-ming
A: Lu Hsiao-fen
A widow unwittingly sells herself to seven men in a poor village. The arrangement is illegal, so she suffers from hiding it as well as from dealing with the men, but she comes to sympathize with their predicament. *IMDb.*

1681. *Ke tu chiu hen / Song of the Exile* 1990 D
D: Ann Hui
S: Wu Nien-jen
C: David Chung
P: Nai Chung-chou
A: Maggie Cheung, Lu Hsiao-fen, Shwu-fen Chang
Hong Kong. A woman returns from London for her sister's wedding and finds herself at odds with both her sister and her Japanese-born mother. Their reconciliation begins when the mother returns to Japan after a fifty-year absence. *Festival de films, 13th: 78. 1991.*

Awards: Hong Kong Film Awards, nomination for Best Picture, 1991

1682. *Hao nan hao nü / Good Men, Good Women*   1995
D: Hou Hsiao-hsien
S: Bo-chow Lan, Bi-yi Chiang
C: Huai-en Chen
P: Katsuhiro Mizuno
A: Annie Shizuka Inoh
A young actress, preparing for an important role in a film about the resistance to the Japanese occupation of China and the communist revolution, is forced to confront her sordid past because of a stolen diary.

Awards: Fribourg International Film Festival, Special Jury Award, 1996; Hawaii International Film

Festival, Best Feature Film, 1996; Singapore Film Festival, Best Film, 1996

1683. *Qunian dong tian / Heartbreak Island*
                                                    1995
D: Hsu Hsiao-ming
S: Hsu Hsiao-ming, Guo Chang
C: Yang Wei-han
P: Jessie Huang
A: Vicky Wei
A woman, released after ten years in prison for antigovernment terrorism, discovers that her former lover and mentor lives a complacent, apolitical, middle-class life. *AMG.*
Awards: Rotterdam International Film Festival, Net-pac Award, 1996

1684. *Shao nü Siao Yu / Siao Yu*   1995 DSP
D: Sylvia Chang
S: Sylvia Chang, Ang Lee
C: Joe DeSalvo
P: Dolly Hall, Ang Lee
A: Rene Liu, Daniel Travanti
Manhattan. A Chinese illegal alien working in a sweatshop marries a radical journalist to gain a green card, but her boyfriend becomes jealous. The film provides a detailed portrayal of the stresses of her workplace and life and how they relate to the politics of her husband.
Other titles: Xiao Yu
Awards: Asia-Pacific Film Festival, Best Actress, 1995

1685. *Mei-li zai chang ge / Murmur of Youth*
                                                    1997 DS
D: Lin Cheng-sheng
S: Ko Shu-ching, Lin Cheng-sheng
C: Tsai Cheng-hui
P: Chiu Shun-ching
A: Rene Liu, Tseng Jing
Two young women, one middle class, the other working class, fall in love while working in a movie theater. *AMG.*
Awards: Tokyo International Film Festival, Best Actress (Liu, Tseng), 1997

1686. *Hai shang hua / Flowers of Shanghai*
                                                    1998
D: Hou Hsiao-hsien
S: Tien-wen Chu
C: Pin Bing Lee
P: Shozo Ichiyama
A: Fang Shuan, Michiko Hada, Annie Shizuka Inoh
Shanghai, 1880s. The film documents the activities in a house of courtesans, viewed entirely from the darkened inside, detailing the financial ar-rangements and political intrigue among the generations of women as well as between the women and the men. Issues of independence, freedom, and security are always on the wom-en's minds.

1687. *San ju chi lian / The Love of Three Oranges*   1998
D: Hung Hung
S: Hung Hung
C: Chih-yuan Chang
A: Lee Jiunn-jye, Angela Ma, Chen Wei-chi
An old boyfriend stops in on a lesbian couple, and one of the women gives in to him, leaving the other sobbing but willing to wait out the infi-delity. Then she becomes a target for the man. *Festival des 3.*

1688. *Siao bai wa jin ju / Hidden Whisper*
                                                    2000 DS
D: Vivian Chang
S: Vivian Chang
C: Shen Rei-yuan
P: Chiu Shun-ching
A: Hsiao Shu-shen, Shu Qi
Three portraits: a "small girl, whose gambling, par-tially disabled father mistreats her mother;" a teenager who steals identity cards so she can escape her life; and a thirty-year-old woman and her dying mother. *FII.*
Awards: Fribourg International Film Festival, Special Mention, 2001

1689. *Zheng hun qi shi / The Personals*   2000
D: Chen Kuo-fu
S: Chen Kuo-fu
C: Ho Nan-hung
P: Hsu Li-kong
A: Rene Liu
An eye doctor posts an ad for a mate, then in-terviews responders in a tea shop. *MOMA Film. 2000, Jul./Aug.*
Awards: Golden Horse Film Festival, Best Actress, 1998; Taipei Film Festival, Best Actress, 1998; Asia-Pacific Film Festival, Best Actress, 1999

1690. *Qian xi man bo / Millennium Mambo*
                                                    2001
D: Hou Hsiao-hsien
S: Chu Tien-wen
C: Pin Bing Lee
P: Chu Tien-wen
A: Shu Qi
Taipei. A bar hostess tries to get out from under her youthful gangster lover, who stalks her ev-ery move. *Variety: 19. 2001, May 28.*

Awards: Chicago International Film Festival, Silver Hugo, 2001; Flanders International Film Festival, Silver Spur, 2001

1691. 20 : 30 : 40   2002 DS
D: Sylvia Chang, Angelica Lee, Rene Liu
S: Sylvia Chang
C: Chien Hsiang
A: Sylvia Chang, Angelica Lee, Rene Liu
Three separate stories of different women at the ages of twenty, thirty, and forty: The first wants to become a pop musician, the second is a stewardess torn between two lovers, and the third is adjusting to a recent divorce. *FII.*
Awards: Berlin International Film Festival, nomination for Golden Bear, 2004

TANZANIA

1692. *Maangamizi: The Ancient One*   2001 S
D: Martin M'Hando, Ron Mulvihill
S: Willie E. Dawkins, Martin M'Hando, Queenae Taylor Mulvihill
C: Willie E. Dawkins
P: Martin M'Hando
A: Amandina Lihamba, Barbara O Jones
Two women share terrifying memories of their youth. Now a doctor, one tries to help the other, who is in extreme psychological crisis, unable to speak. Upon seeing her friend, the mental ward patient opens up and proclaims they have been brought together by an imaginary shaman, "Maangamizi." At first skeptical, the doctor begins to appreciate this manifestation of their "psychic and spiritual bond against a hostile world." *Variety: 42–43. 2001, Oct. 1; AMG.*

THAILAND

1693. *Puen-Paeng / Puen and Paeng*   1983
D: Cherd Songsri
S: Thom Thatree
C: Cherd Songsri
A: Chanuteporn Visitsophon
1930s. A young girl is in love with a young man who is in love with her more beautiful sister. The wedding is planned, but he becomes sick. When his betrothed disappears, leaving the rejected one to nurse him, he begins to understand his mistake. *Variety: 17. 1983, July 6.*

1694. *Amdaeng Muen kab nai Rid / Muen and Rid*   1994
D: Cherd Songsri

S: Channipa, Thom Thatree
C: Anupap Buachand
A: Jintara Sukapatana
A biography of the nineteenth-century feminist Amdang Muen, who was sold by her father to a rich man as a second wife but fled; she then fought for equal rights for women in Thailand and for her freedom to love a Buddhist monk. *Monash University. Accessed 2004, Aug. 8.*

TUNISIA

1695. *Aziza*   1979
D: Abdellatif Ben Ammar
S: Abdellatif Ben Ammar, Taoufik Jebali
C: Youssef Sharaqui
A: Yasmine Khlat, Dalila Rammes
A young woman, orphaned as a child, moves with her uncle to the city of Tunis, where she gets a job in a textile factory. *Faber Companion.*
Awards: Carthage Film Festival, Best Film, 1980

1696. *Sama / The Trace*   1982 DS
D: Néjia Ben Mabrouk
S: Néjia Ben Mabrouk
C: Marc-André Batigne
A: Fatma Khemiri, Mouna Noureddine
A village woman struggles against discrimination in order to get her degree, studying by candle at night and refusing all male advances; only her mother respects her efforts. "Authentic locations in a militant tract." *Variety: 12. 1988, Aug. 24.*
Awards: Berlin International Film Festival, Caligari Film Award, 1989

1697. *H'Biba M'Sika*   1994 DS
D: Selma Baccar
S: Sayda Ben Mahmoud
C: Allel Yahiaoui
A: Souad Amidou
The life of celebrated singer Habiba M'sika, who became wealthy, was adulated by many, and had a large group of devoted friends, until one day she fell in love with a young poet. *Festival de films, 22nd: 92. 2000.*
Other titles: Habiba M'sika

1698. *Shamt al kushur / The Silences of the Palace*   1994 DS
D: Moufida Tlatli
S: Nouri Bouzid, Moufida Tlatli
C: Youssef Ben Youssef
P: Ahmed Baha
A: Amel Hedhili, Hend Sabri, Ghalia Lacroix, Sami Bouajila

A singer and lute player struggles with an unwed pregnancy that her lover of ten years insists must be aborted. The daughter of a servant and (unknown to her) the master of the house, she returns to the palace of her youth and relives the painful memories of her life there and her relationship with her mother, who was sold by her own parents at the age of ten. They lived in luxurious conditions, alongside the "legitimate" girl child of similar age. When the singer's beauty and talent attracted the attention of the men "upstairs," she fled with the man who now oversees her singing career.

Awards: Cannes Film Festival, Golden Camera, 1994; Istanbul International Film Festival, Tanit d'Or, 1994; Toronto International Film Festival, FIPRESCI, 1994

1699. *Miel et cendres / Honey and Ashes*
                                              1996 DS
D: Nadia Farès
S: Nadia Farès, Yves Kropf, Mahmoud Larnaout
C: Ismael Ramirez
P: Karin Koch
A: Nozha Khouadra, Samia Mzali, Amel Hedhili

Two women, one in love with someone other than her arranged spouse-to-be, the other battered by her professor husband, come to be helped by an older successful doctor whose life has been constricted in similar ways. *Variety. 1996, Oct. 7.*

Awards: Gijón International Film Festival, Best Screenplay, 1996; Locarno International Film Festival, Ecumenical Jury Prize, 1996

1700. *Bent familia / The Daughter of a Good Family*   1997
D: Nouri Bouzid
S: Nouri Bouzid
C: Armand Marco
A: Amel Hedhili, Nadia Kaci, Leila Nassim

Tunis. The story of three middle-class friends: One grows out of her submissiveness to a domineering husband; one is divorced with a young son; and one has fled the Muslim fundamental uprising in Algeria. *Cinema dei.*

1701. *Les Siestes grenadine / Pomegranate Siestas*   1999 S
D: Mahmoud Ben Mahmoud
S: Moncef Dhouib, Maryse Leon Garcia
C: Gilberto Azevedo
P: Hassen Daldoul
A: Yasmine Bahri

A young woman who has been raised in Paris and Dakar returns to Tunisia, where the rigid conservatism offends her. She searches out her

mother, whom she has not seen for many years, but connects mostly with outsiders—black musicians and a family servant, a woman the same age as she. *Variety: 112. 1999, Dec. 13.*

Awards: Torino International Festival of Young Cinema, Special Jury Prize, 1999

1702. *La Saison des hommes / Season of Men*   2000 DS
D: Moufida Tlatli
S: Moufida Tlatli, Nouri Bouzid
C: Youssef Ben Youssef
A: Rabiaa Ben Abdallah

Djerba. Women maintain the patriarchal system on an island where they weave carpets; the men are gone for most of the year, selling the work at markets in Tunis or France. *Francophone Women: 34.*

1703. *Arais al tein / Clay Dolls*   2002
D: Nouri Bouzid
S: Nouri Bouzid
C: Gilberto Azevedo
P: Hassen Daldoul
A: Hend Sabri, Oumeyma Ben Afsia

Two young girls have been bartered from their families and brought to the city to work as maids; one makes clay dolls to soothe herself, the other leaves her employers and discovers she is pregnant. *Variety: 38. 2003, Mar. 17.*

Other titles: Poupeés d'argile

Awards: Namur International Festival of French-Speaking Film, Best Actress (Sabri), 2002; Fribourg International Film Festival, Ecumenical Jury Prize, 2003

1704. *Bedwin Hacker*   2002 DSP
D: Nadia El Fani
S: Nadia El Fani
C: Tarek Ben Abdallah
P: Nadia El Fani
A: Sonia Hamza

In a desert town, a computer genius hacks into European television channels and sends political messages in Arabic. *African Diaspora, 11th. 2003, Dec. Accessed 2004, Aug. 15.*

1705. *Satin Rouge / Red Satin*   2002 DSCP
D: Raja Amari
S: Raja Amari
C: Diane Baratier
P: Dora Bouchoucha Fourati
A: Hiam Abbass, Hend El Fahem

Tunis. A widow, saddened by the recent death of her husband, finds joy and liberation in the world of cabaret belly dancing, where she goes looking for her teenage daughter. *NYT: AE11. 2002, Aug. 25.*

Awards: Montréal World Film Festival, Best African Film, 2002; Seattle International Film Festival, Showcase Award, 2002

1706. *Viva Laldjérie / Viva Algeria* 2003 P

D: Nadir Moknèche
S: Nadir Moknèche
C: Jean-Claude Larrieu
P: Bertrand Gore, Nathalie Mesuret
A: Lubna Azabal, Biyouna, Nadia Kaci

Algiers. A dancer mother and her grown daughter try to survive after the fundamentalist culture deprives them of pursuing their livelihood. When a historic café is proposed to be turned into a mosque, the mother becomes angry and insists on resuming performing. *Variety: 26. 2004, May 17.*

Awards: Thessaloniki Film Festival, nomination for Best Film, 2004

TURKEY

1707. *Yilanlarin öcü / Revenge of the Serpents*
1962

D: Metin Erksan
S: Metin Erksan
C: Mengü Yegin
P: Musret Ikbal
A: Hurhan Nur, Fikret Hakan

A capable mother stands in the way of a rich villager who wants to build a house for himself in front of her son's home in the center of the village; much intrigue follows, and the villagers are forced to exile her. *Cinémas du moyen: 300.*

Other titles: La Vengeance des serpents

1708. *Häremde dört kadýn / Four Women in a Harem* 1964

D: Halit Refig
S: Halit Refig, Kemal Tahir
C: Mike Rafaelyan
P: Özdemir Birsel
A: Nilüfer Aydan

Istanbul, end of the Ottoman Empire. An official chooses a fourth wife, but she loves a young doctor who is part of the liberation army intent on overthrowing the monarchy. *Cinémas du moyen: 200.*

1709. *Kuyu / The Well* 1968

D: Metin Erksan
S: Metin Erksan
C: Mengü Yegin

A: Nil Göncü, Mayati Hamzaoglu

A young village girl is raped by a man she refuses to marry, so he drags her away at the end of a rope. Though she returns home, her honor is lost. Saved once from suicide by a bandit, she tries again after he's jailed and succeeds in throwing herself down a well. *Cinémas du moyen: 296.*

Other titles: Le Puits

1710. *Bir türke gönül verdim / I Loved a Turk*
1969

D: Halit Refig
S: Halit Refig
C: Cengiz Tacer
P: Hürrem Erman
A: Eva Bender, Ahmet Mekin

A German woman is abandoned by her lover, a Turkish worker who leaves her with a five-year-old son; she immigrates to Turkey to find him but falls in love with another man, whom her former lover murders during their wedding. *IMDb.*

1711. *Asiye nasil kurtulur?* 1973

D: Nejat Saydam
S: Safa Önal, Vasif Ongören
C: Melih Sertesen
A: Türkan Soray

In response to complaints about the treatment of prostitutes, a political group gathers and organizes protests. *BiFi.*

Other titles: Comment sauver Asiye?

1712. *Dönüs / The Comeback* 1973 D

D: Türkan Soray
S: Safa Önal
A: Türkan Soray

A peasant leaves his wife to go work in Germany; the film focuses on her struggle to fend for herself. When he returns many years later, he is shocked at the contrast of the "feudal" culture of the village with what he now knows about life. *Cinéma turc: 201.*

1713. *Gelin / The Bride* 1973

D: Lüfti Ömer Akad
S: Lüfti Ömer Akad
C: Gani Turanli
A: Hülya Koçyigit, Kerem Yilmazer

Istanbul. A young couple and their child move to an impoverished quarter where the husband's family has already settled. His parents have sacrificed to open a shop and incurred much debt, and so they are not inclined to pay the expenses of a serious illness affecting the couple's small child, but the daughter-in-law confronts them. *Cinémas du moyen: 291.*

Other titles: La Bru

1714. Kizgin toprak / The Grave   1973
D: Feyzi Tuna
S: Feyzi Tuna
C: Kaya Erenrz
A: Fatma Girik

Having trouble earning a living, a wife decides to ferry people across the river in her small boat, despite the disapproval of a man with a large ferry farther upstream. One day her boat is damaged, and her husband retaliates; she is then raped in retaliation. *Cinéma turc: 260.*

Other titles: Hot Land / La Terre brullante
Awards: Tashkent Film Festival, Special Award (Girik), 1974

1715. Bedrana   1974 DP
D: Süreyya Duru
S: Vedat Türkali, Bekir Yildiz
C: Ali Ugar
P: Süreyya Duru
A: Perihan Savaç

A woman flees with her lover to another village, where he is forced to run contraband in exchange for their safety. A man attempts to rape her, leaving her significantly wounded and vulnerable to being killed for the outrage. Her lover is helpless to aid her, and she commits suicide. *Cinéma turc: 260.*

1716. Yatik Emine / Emine, the Leaning One
1974
D: Ömer Kavur
A: Türkan Soray

World War I. "Prostitute is banished to an Anatolian village, where her beauty causes so much trouble between the men and their wives that the local mayor puts her in jail." *Cinema in Turkey.* Accessed November 14, 2002.

1717. Selvi boylum al yazmalim / The Girl with the Red Scarf   1977
D: Atif Yilmaz
S: Ali Özgentürk; based on the novel by Chinguiz Aitmatov
C: Çetin Tunca
A: Türkan Soray

A young peasant woman takes her child and leaves her truck driver husband when he falls into drink after losing his job. She lives with another man who is kind to her, but her husband returns. Even though she still loves him, she tells him she must remain loyal to the other man, whom her child considers his father. *Cinémas du moyen: 195–96.*

1718. Yilani oldürseler / To Crush the Serpent
1982 DS
D: Türkan Soray
S: Arif Keskiner, Isil Özgentürk, Türkan Soray
C: Günes Karabuda
P: Abdurrahman Keskiner
A: Türkan Soray

Villagers accuse a woman of murdering her husband; even though a young man is caught and killed for the deed, the people still believe the woman is responsible for provoking it. *Festival de films, 19th: 78. 1997.*

Other titles: Tu ecraseras le serpent

1719. Derman   1983
D: Serif Gören
S: Ahmet Soner
C: Erdogan Engin
A: Hülya Koçyigit

To repay her education expenses, a woman must go from her family's village to a larger one built around cattle breeding and subject to climate extremes. Despite her fears, she decides to build her life there and have a family and children, until she and a poacher, fleeing a prison sentence, fall in love. *Cinémas du moyen: 296.*

Awards: Valencia Film Festival, Jury Award, 1983; Karlovy Vary International Film Festival, International Film Critics Award, 1984

1720. Ayna / The Mirror   1984
D: Erden Kiral
S: Erden Kiral
C: Kenan Ormanlar
P: Joachim Von Vietinghof
A: Nür Surer, Suavi Eren, Vera Deludi

A lord sexually dominates another man's wife, who lives in a shanty on the village outskirts; he trades her silence for a mirror and a piece of cloth. The terrorized wife tells her husband, and he murders the man one day, but they are forced to hide, and the wife descends into madness. *Cinémas du moyen: 295.*

Other titles: Le Miroir
Awards: Istanbul International Film Festival, Special Jury Prize, 1985

1721. Bir yudum sevgi / A Sip of Love   1984
D: Atif Yilmaz
A: Hale Soyagazi

To support her children, a peasant woman grips her own destiny and leaves her alcoholic husband to work in a factory. There she falls in love with a man, also unhappily married; despite the hostility of neighbors, she and her children begin to live with him. *Cinémas du moyen: 196.*

Other titles: Une Gouette d'amour

1722. Kasik düsmani / The Wedding Chamber
1984 DS
D: Bilgé Olgaç
S: Bilgé Olgaç
C: Umit Gulzoy
P: Mustafa Ozbey
A: Perihan Savaç, Halil Ergün
1978. Based on a news account of a village wedding; on the day, an explosion kills all the women, who were together in one house, except for one survivor who has lost her mind. "The men realize the impossibility of living without women." *FII.*
Other titles: Spoon Enemy / La Chambre de mariage
Awards: Créteil International Women's Film Festival, Grand Prix, 1985

1723. Adi Vasfiye
1985
D: Atif Yilmaz
S: Necati Cumali
C: Orhan Oguz
A: Müjde Ar, Macit Koper
A male writer, lacking inspiration, stops on the street before a poster of a singer and imagines what kind of woman she might be: modern, seeking her own life, yet available to many men. Suddenly he disappears, and many men are "giving body" to Vasfiye with their own stories, a turn on the 1001 nights of Sheherazade. *Cinémas du moyen: 197, 296.*
Other titles: Prénom Vasfiyé

1724. Gülüsan
1986 DS
D: Bilgé Olgaç
S: Bilgé Olgaç
C: Hüseyin Ozsahin
A: Yaprak Özdemiroglu, Meral Orhonsay
A man with two wives but no children (he does not acknowledge that he is the one who is sterile) decides to marry again and accidentally chooses a blind woman. She is most vulnerable to the jealous revenge of the first two wives. *Festival de films, 8th: 1986.*

1725. Aah, Belinda
1987
D: Atif Yilmaz
S: Baris Pirhasan
A: Müjde Ar
A sophisticated actress with a "swank apartment" and a rich boyfriend does a commercial for a shampoo called "Belinda." Suddenly the crew disappears, and she becomes the wife and mother in the commercial, trapped in a drab apartment and working in a bank. None of her old friends recognize her. Comedy. *Variety: 22. 1987, Mar. 4.*

1726. Afife Jale
1987 S
D: Sahin Kaygun
S: Nezihe Araz
C: Erdogan Engin
A: Müjde Ar, Tarik Tarkan
Istanbul, 1900s, near the end of the Ottoman Empire. The biographical story of Afife Jale, who was the first Muslim woman to appear on the Turkish stage. At that time, female parts were played by non-Muslims or by men. She persists over the objections of her family as well as the authorities, and she is arrested on the stage. *Cinémas du moyen: 312.*

1727. Degirmen
1987
D: Atif Yilmaz
S: Baris Pirhasan
C: Orhan Oguz
P: Cengiz Ergun
A: Serap Aksoy
Istanbul, 1914. A Bulgarian immigrant is accused of prostitution and exiled to Saripinar, a nearby village where the residents object to her presence. *Cinéma Méditerranéen. Accessed 2005, Jan. 9.*
Other titles: Le moulin

1728. On kadin / 10 Women
1987
D: Serif Gören
S: Hüseyin Kuzu
C: Erdal Kahraman
A: Türkan Soray
Ten portraits of Turkish women, all played by the same actress, including a journalist, provincial mother, bourgeois mother, feminist, wily *tzigane*, mother, and daughter. *Cinémas du moyen: 292.*
Other titles: Dix femmes

1729. Bez bebek / Cloth Doll
1988
D: Engin Ayça
C: Erdogan Engin
A: Hülya Koçyigit, Hakan Balamir
A woman and her daughter live alone while her husband is in prison; she falls in love with a stonemason, then must watch her husband murder him when he returns. *AMG.*
Other titles: The Rag Doll
Awards: Amiens International Film Festival, Best Actress, 1989

1730. Hanim / Madam
1989 S
D: Halit Refig
S: Nezihe Araz
C: Çetin Tunca

P: Cengiz Ergun
A: Pamira Bezman
A woman of noble birth acquires non-noble status as she ages and remains unmarried. *Cinémas du moyen: 200.*
Other titles: *La Dame*

1731. Berdel   1990
D: Atif Yilmaz
S: Esma Ocak
C: Erdal Kahraman
A: Türkan Soray
A woman with five daughters loves them; she tries another time to have a boy, but again has a girl. Her husband decides to get another wife but does not have a dowry, so he offers to exchange (berdel) one of his girls for a second wife. *Cinémas du moyen: 197.*
Other titles: *Troc de mariées*

1732. Soguktu ve yagmur ciseliyordu / It Was Cold and Raining   1990
D: Engin Ayça
S: Engin Ayça
C: Ertunc Senkay
A: Türkan Soray
A professional singer better understands her relationship with her accompanist through a long conversation with his sister at the time of his death. *AMG.*

1733. Iki kadýn / Two Women   1992
D: Yavuz Özkan
S: Yavuz Özkan
C: Orhan Oguz
P: Yavuz Özkan
A: Zuhal Olcay, Serap Aksoy, Haluk Bilginer
A prostitute sues a prominent politician for rape, which brings the media down on him; his wife seeks the woman out, and they become friends. *FII.*

1734. Bir sonbahar hikayesi / An Autumn Story
                                                           1994
D: Yavuz Özkan
A: Zuhal Olcay
1978–1981. During a period of great political tension, a professor marries an ambitious banker obsessed with his career, and their marriage falters. *AMG.*

1735. Dus gezginleri / Walking after Midnight
                                                           1994
D: Atif Yilmaz
S: Atif Yilmaz, Yildirim Turker
C: Metin Erabaci

A: Meral Oguz, Lale Mansur, Deniz Türkali
A doctor gives regular checkups to the local prostitutes; one of the women turns out to be a childhood friend, and the two begin a lesbian relationship. *FII.*

1736. Ask ölümden soguktur / Love Colder Than Death   1995 DSP
D: Canan Gerede
S: Canan Gerede
C: Jürgen Jürges
P: Eliane Stutterheim
A: Bennu Gerede, Kadir Inanir
Istanbul. Based on a true story of a popular singer and her jealous husband, with whom she has a sadomasochistic relationship. In a violent fit, he causes her to miscarry and then abandons her. With the help of her mother, she regains her health and an even more successful career, but her husband returns and demands that she stop performing. *Cinémas du moyen: 290.*
Other titles: *L'amour plus froid*
Awards: Angers European First Film Festival, Jean Carment Award, 1996; Sochi International Film Festival, Best Actress, 1996

1737. Harem suare / The Last Harem   1997
D: Ferzan Ozpetek
S: Ferzan Ozpetek, Gianni Romoli
C: Pasaquale Mari
P: Gianni Romoli
A: Marie Gillain, Lucia Bosé, Valeria Golino, Alex Descas
Istanbul, 1904. An aging servant tells stories to the harem, particularly of a favored concubine who gained power with her great political skill and the help of a beloved black eunuch, in fact, her lover. When the sultan flees the collapsing empire and the concubines are suddenly freed, this sophisticated woman, the sultan's favorite, helps them find their way into the new world.
Other titles: *Le Dernier harem*
Awards: AFI Fest, nomination for Grand Jury Prize, 1999

1738. Filler ve çimen / Elephants and Grass
                                                           2001
D: Dervis Zaim
S: Dervis Zaim
C: Ertunc Senkay
P: Ali Akdeniz
A: Sanem Çelik
A marathon runner hopes to get into a European race so she can use the prize money to take care of her soldier brother, who has been wounded in east Turkey. Unfortunately, she finds

that her hotel sponsor is so corrupt that she cannot avoid being involved. Thriller. *Boston Turkish, 7th. 2002. Accessed 2005, June 10.*
Other titles: *Les Eléphants et la pelouse*

1739. *Anam / My Mother* 2002 DS
D: Buket Alakus
S: Buket Alakus
C: Marcus Lambrecht
P: Stefan Schubert
A: Nursel Koese
Hamburg. A Turkish cleaning woman tries to save her grown son from drug addiction. *Village Voice: 112. 2002, Oct. 16.*

1740. *Hiçbiryerde / In Nowhereland* 2002
D: Tayfun Pirselimoglu
S: Tayfun Pirselimoglu
C: Collin Mounier
P: Zeynep Ozbatur
A: Zuhal Olcay
A woman faces the bureaucracy in searching for her son, a missing person and possible political prisoner. *Village Voice: 74. 2003, Oct. 15.*
Awards: Istanbul Film Festival, Best Actress, 2002; Montréal World Film Festival, Special Grand Prize, 2002

1741. *Bulutlari beklerken / Waiting for the Clouds* 2004 DS
D: Yesim Ustaoglu
S: Yesim Ustaoglu, Yorgos Andreadis
C: Jacek Petrycki
A: Ruchen Ciliskur
An old Greek woman lives in Turkey; when her sister, with whom she lived and was extremely close, dies, she stops speaking with the other villagers, except for a young boy. Gradually, they become friends, and she tells him of her past, her brother who disappeared, and the family's flight from Greece in 1947. *Festival de films, 27th: 26. 2005.*

UKRAINE

1742. *Tri istorii / Three Stories* 1997 DS
D: Kira Muratova
S: Renata Litvinova, Vera Storozheva
C: Genadij Karjuk
P: Igor Tolstunov
A: Renata Litvinova
Three separate films, of which the longest, "Ophelia," is about a woman who works in an orphanage, where she discovers the records room and looks up the names of mothers who have given

up babies for adoption, like her own. Finding two, she murders them.
Awards: Berlin International Film Festival, nomination for Golden Bear, 1997

1743. *Vtorostepenniye lyudi / Second Class Citizens* 2001 DSP
D: Kira Muratova
S: Kira Muratova, Sergei Chetvertkov
C: Gennadi Karyuk
P: Anna Emil
A: Natalya Buzko
"An illegal resident in a nouveau riche area becomes involved in the unintentional murder of her boyfriend. Unable to inform the police, she is forced to hide the body. Then his identical twin turns up." Satire. *FII.*

UNITED KINGDOM

1744. *And Women Shall Weep* 1960
D: John Lemont
S: John Lemont, Leigh Vance
P: Norman Williams
A: Ruth Dunning
A widow saves her teenage son from a crime by exposing his brother as a murderer. *British Film.*

1745. *The Innocents* 1961
D: Jack Clayton
S: William Archibald, Truman Capote; based on *The Turn of the Screw* by Henry James
C: Freddie Francis
P: Jack Clayton
A: Deborah Kerr
"Governess fights the ghost of a dead predecessor for the souls of her two orphaned charges." Horror. See also the 2001 remake, *The Others* (2281).

1746. *Taste of Honey* 1961 S
D: Tony Richardson
S: Shelagh Delaney, Tony Richardson
C: Walter Lassally
P: Tony Richardson
A: Rita Tushingham, Dora Bryan
"Widow's teenage daughter is seduced by a Negro sailor and looked after by a homosexual." *British Film.*
Awards: BAFTA Awards, Best Film, Best Screenplay, Best Actress (Bryan), 1962; Cannes Film Festival, Best Actress (Tushingham), 1962

1747. *I Thank a Fool* 1962 S
D: Robert Stevens

S: Karl Turnheg; based on the novel by Audrey Erskine Lindop
C: Harry Waxman
P: Anatole de Grunwald
A: Susan Hayward, Diane Cilento, Peter Finch
Ireland. A doctor performs euthanasia on her ailing lover and is prosecuted unjustly; upon her release from prison, she is destitute and is contacted by the prosecutor, who wants her to tend to his ailing wife. *AMG.*

1748. The L-Shaped Room   1962 S
D: Bryan Forbes
S: Lynne Reid Banks, Bryan Forbes
C: Douglas Slocombe
P: Richard Attenborough
A: Leslie Caron
London. A young French woman, pregnant and unmarried, takes a room in a boardinghouse to try to come to terms with her condition.
Awards: BAFTA Awards, Best Actress, 1963; Golden Globes, Best Actress, 1964

1749. Mix Me a Person   1962
D: Leslie Norman
S: Ian Dalrymple
P: Victor Seville
A: Anne Baxter
A psychiatrist "proves that a convicted teenager did not kill a policeman." *British Film.*

1750. Chalk Garden   1964 S
D: Ronald Neame
S: John Michael Hayes; based on the play by Enid Bagnold
P: Ross Hunter
A: Deborah Kerr, Hayley Mills
A governess realizes that her wealthy employer is trying to keep her teenage charge, the latter's grandchild, away from her mother. *British Film.*

1751. Girl with Green Eyes   1964 S
D: Desmond Davies
S: Edna O'Brien; based on her novel *The Lonely Girl*
P: Tony Richardson
A: Rita Tushingham, Peter Finch, Lynn Redgrave
Dublin. A shy farm girl moves to the city, where she rooms with a more sophisticated woman and ends up in an affair with an older man. *AMG.*
Awards: Golden Globes, Best English Language Foreign Film, 1965

1752. The Pumpkin Eater   1964 S
D: Jack Clayton
S: Harold Pinter; based on the novel by Penelope

Mortimer
C: Oswald Morris
P: James Woolf
A: Anne Bancroft, Peter Finch
A woman with seven children marries for the third time but breaks down under pressure from her husband and consents to an abortion, only to find he is unfaithful. *British Film.*
Awards: BAFTA Awards, Best Screenplay, Best Actress, 1964; Cannes Film Festival, Best Actress, 1964; Golden Globes, Best Actress, 1965

1753. Seance on a Wet Afternoon   1964
D: Bryan Forbes
S: Bryan Forbes
C: Gerry Turpin
P: Richard Attenborough
A: Kim Stanley
A psychic weakened by the death of her son convinces her husband to kidnap a wealthy girl in order to provide a showcase for her "powers." *AMG.*
Awards: New York Film Critics Circle Awards, Best Actress, 1964

1754. Darling   1965
D: John Schlesinger
S: Frederic Raphael
P: Joseph Janni
A: Julie Christie, Dirk Bogarde, Laurence Harvey
London, 1960s. A working-class beauty prostitutes herself to move up in fashionable society and eventually marries an Italian count. The character comments cynically on her own story.
Awards: Academy Awards, Best Actress, 1965; BAFTA Awards, Best Actress, 1965

1755. Lady L.   1965
D: Peter Ustinov
S: Peter Ustinov; based on the novel by Romain Gary
C: Henri Alekan
P: Carlo Ponti
A: Sophia Loren
"80 year old Corsican tells a biographer of her life as a laundress, a prostitute, a thief, an anarchist and wife of an English lord." *British Film.*

1756. Repulsion   1965
D: Roman Polanski
S: Roman Polanski, Gérard Brach
C: Gilbert Taylor
P: Gene Gutowski
A: Catherine Deneuve
A visibly fearful manicurist in a beauty parlor lives with her sexually active sister; when the sister goes away, she suffers violent dreams and fanta-

sies, and she murders two men who happen to appear at her apartment door.

Awards: Berlin International Film Festival, FIPRESCI, Silver Bear (Polanski), 1965

1757. *Mademoiselle* 1966 S
D: Tony Richardson
S: Marguerite Duras; based on the play by Jean Genet
C: David Watkin
P: Oscar Lewenstein
A: Jeanne Moreau
France. A village schoolteacher commits arson, then blames a local woodcutter. *FII.*
Awards: Cannes Film Festival, nomination for Golden Palm, 1966

1758. *Modesty Blaise* 1966
D: Joseph Losey
S: Evan Jones; based on the comic strip by Jim Holdaway
C: Jack Hildyard
P: Joseph Janni
A: Monica Vitti, Terence Stamp
A female agent, "whose body English transcends all language barriers," gets in the middle of a government espionage ring. "One of the nuttiest, screwiest pictures ever made." Action, comedy. *Variety.* 1966, May 11.

1759. *Far from the Madding Crowd* 1967
D: John Schlesinger
S: Frederic Raphael; based on the novel by Thomas Hardy
C: Nicolas Roeg
P: Joseph Janni
A: Julie Christie, Terence Stamp, Alan Bates, Peter Finch
Dorset, 1866. A free-spirited woman inherits a farm while involved with an adoring farmer, who comes to work for her. She then moves on to more advantageous relationships and chooses to marry a shiftless soldier.

1760. *Poor Cow* 1967 S
D: Ken Loach
S: Nell Dunn, Ken Loach
P: Joseph Janni
A: Carol White
"Thief's young wife moves in with his friend while he is in jail." *British Film.*
Awards: Golden Globes, nomination for Best English Language Foreign Film, 1969

1761. *Isadora* 1968 S
D: Karel Reisz

S: Melvyn Bragg, Clive Extan, Margaret Drabble; based on *My Life* by Isadora Duncan
P: Robert Hakim, Raymond Hakim
A: Vanessa Redgrave
The story of dancer Isadora Duncan, who brought a special interest in sexuality to formal dance and lived a life free of convention.
Other titles: Loves of Isadora
Awards: Academy Awards, nomination for Best Actress, 1969; Cannes Film Festival, Best Actress, 1969

1762. *Petulia* 1968 S
D: Richard Lester
S: Laurence Marcus, Barbara Turner
C: Nicolas Roeg
P: Richard Wagner
A: Julie Christie, George C. Scott, Shirley Knight
San Francisco. A wealthy socialite escapes from her disappointing marriage with "kooky" and provocative behavior, pursuing a man the opposite of her husband, a doctor who tries to help her. She epitomizes proud fashion beauty, but after a beating from her husband that leaves her in the hospital, she returns home to her duty and becomes pregnant. The film abstracts the characters, foregrounding the classist, racist context to which they do not relate.

1763. *Madwoman of Chaillot* 1969
D: Bryan Forbes
S: Edward Anhalt; based on the play by Jean Giraudoux
P: Ely Landau
A: Katherine Hepburn, Charles Boyer
Paris. A countess exacts justice on evil businessmen who are conspiring to drill for oil. *FII.*

1764. *The Prime of Miss Jean Brodie* 1969 S
D: Ronald Neame
S: Jay Presson Allen; based on the novel by Muriel Spark
P: Robert Fryer
A: Maggie Smith, Pamela Franklin, Celia Johnson
Edinburgh, 1932. The motto at a tony high school for girls is "Who can find a virtuous woman? For her price is far beyond rubies." Jean Brodie schools her "girls, the creme de la creme," in "truth and beauty," which she sees as thwarting the local authority (the principal who suspects her teaching methods are unorthodox), while admiring autocrats such as Mussolini, Franco, and herself. She leads the students through extracurricular games involving her lovers.
Awards: Academy Awards, Best Actress (Smith), 1969; BAFTA Awards, Best Actress (Smith), Best Supporting Actress (Johnson), 1969

1765. Women in Love   1969
D: Ken Russell
S: Larry Kramer; based on the novel by D. H. Lawrence
C: Billy Williams
P: Larry Kramer
A: Glenda Jackson, Alan Bates, Oliver Reed, Jennie Linden
England, 1920s. Two sisters, an artist and a school-teacher who debate the worth of marriage, become close to two upper-class friends. They marry and honeymoon together in Switzerland, where a gay artist easily draws one of them away from the husband she already finds too stuffy.
Awards: Academy Awards, Best Actress (Jackson), 1971; Golden Globes, Best English Language Foreign Film, 1971

1766. My Lover, My Son   1970 S
D: John Newland
S: William Marchant, Jennie Hall
C: David Muir
P: Wilbur Stark
A: Romy Schneider
"Second wife has an incestuous affair with her son." British Film.

1767. Three Sisters   1970 S
D: Laurence Olivier
S: Moura Budberg; based on the play by Anton Chekhov
C: Geoffrey Unsworth
P: John Goldstone
A: Jeanne Watts, Joan Plowright, Louise Purnett
Russia, 1900. A story of the lives and loves of three orphaned sisters who have been displaced from Moscow into the countryside. British Film.

1768. Mary, Queen of Scots   1971
D: Charles Jarrot
S: John Hale
C: Christopher Challis
P: Hal B. Wallis
A: Vanessa Redgrave, Glenda Jackson
England, sixteenth century. Queen Elizabeth is forced to defend her throne from Mary, Queen of Scots, who claims it by virtue of her birth by Henry VIII. AMG.
Awards: Academy Awards, nomination for Best Actress (Redgrave), 1971; David di Donatello Awards, Special Award (Jackson), 1972

1769. Pope Joan   1972
D: Michael Anderson
S: John Briley

C: Billy Williams
P: Kurt Unger
A: Liv Ullmann, Olivia De Havilland
Based on the legend of the "female pope" of the ninth century. A "raped German girl poses as a monk, and becomes the pope." British Film.

1770. Daddy   1973 DS
D: Niki de Saint Phalle, Peter Whitehead
S: Niki de Saint Phalle
C: Peter Whitehead
P: Tom G. Neuman
A: Niki de Saint Phalle
"After her father's death, a woman begins to realize that he made her hate all men." West German Cinema, 1985.

1771. A Doll's House   1973
D: Joseph Losey
S: Michael Meyer, David Mercer; based on the play by Henrik Ibsen
C: Gerry Fisher
P: Richard Dalton, Joseph Losey
A: Jane Fonda, Delphine Seyrig, David Warner
Oslo, nineteenth century. A woman attempts to help her husband by secretly acquiring a loan; when he discovers it and is only angered by her action, she is deeply hurt and walks out the door, leaving him and her beloved children. There is a second British version, the same year, directed by Patrick Garland and written by Christopher Hampton, with Claire Bloom, Anthony Hopkins, and Anna Massey.

1772. Hedda   1975
D: Trevor Nunn
S: Trevor Nunn; based on the play Hedda Gabler by Henrik Ibsen
C: Douglas Slocombe
A: Glenda Jackson
Hedda is a newly married, thoroughly bored bourgeois housewife who cannot resist meddling in her husband's and relatives' affairs. FII.
Awards: Academy Awards, nomination for Best Actress, 1975

1773. Riddles of the Sphinx   1977 DSC
D: Laura Mulvey, Peter Wollen
S: Laura Mulvey, Peter Wollen
C: Diane Tammes
A: Dinah Stabb
A mother and her four-year-old daughter are close; the father decides to leave. Much emphasis is placed on the daily life, cooking, cleaning, and interpersonal workings of the family. Experimental. Screenonline. Accessed 2005, Feb. 23.

1774. *Rapunzel Let Down Your Hair*

1978 DSCP

D: Susan Shapiro, Esther Ronay, Francine Winham
S: Susan Shapiro, Esther Ronay, Francine Winham
C: Diane Tammes
P: Susan Shapiro, Esther Ronay, Francine Winham
A: Margaret Ford

A mother reads the Rapunzel fairy tale to her daughter, until the mother becomes the witch and the child enters the world of witchcraft and maternal love. A detective arrives as the prince and spies on the mother/witch and daughter. Finally, the mother works in a family-planning clinic, the daughter is pregnant, and they both end up at a feminist festival. *Screenonline. Accessed 2005, Feb. 23.*

1775. *Stevie*   1978

D: Robert Enders
S: Hugh Whitmore
C: Freddie Young
P: Robert Enders
A: Glenda Jackson, Mona Washbourne

The story of modern poet Stevie Smith and her quiet life living with her aunt.

Awards: Boston Society of Film Critics Awards, Best Supporting Actress (Washbourne), 1978; Montréal World Film Festival, Best Actress (Jackson), 1978; New York Film Critics Circle Awards, Best Actress (Jackson, Washbourne), 1981

1776. *Heartland*   1979 SP

D: Richard Pearce
S: Beth Ferris, William Kittredge
C: Fred Murphy
P: Beth Ferris
A: Conchita Ferrell, Rip Torn

Wyoming, nineteenth century. A single mother answers an advertisement for a housekeeper in the U.S. frontier and eventually marries her employer. *AMG.*

Awards: Berlin International Film Festival, Golden Bear, 1980

1777. *The Song of the Shirt*   1979 DP

D: Susan Clayton, Jonathan Curling
P: Anne Cottringer
A: Martha Gibson, Geraldine Pilgrim

1840s. A fiction and documentary blend of working women in the garment industry in Britain of the 1840s. *MFB, no. 556: 95. 1980.*

1778. *Richard's Things*   1980

D: Anthony Harvey
S: Frederic Raphael
C: Freddie Young
P: Mark Shivas

A: Liv Ullmann, Amanda Redman

After her husband dies, a wife discovers he had a mistress, and the two women develop a relationship. *British Film.*

Awards: Venice Film Festival, Best Actress (Ullmann), 1980

1779. *Burning an Illusion*   1981 P

D: Menelik Shabazz
S: Menelik Shabazz
C: Ray Cornwall
P: Vivien Pottersman
A: Cassie McFarlane

After one of her friends is beaten by the police, a secretary is transformed from someone who clubs every night into a serious black militant. *MFB, no. 583: 165. 1982, Aug.*

1780. *Raggedy Man*   1981

D: Jack Fisk
S: William Wittliff
C: Ralf Bode
P: William Wittliff
A: Sissy Spacek, Eric Roberts

Texas, 1940s. A divorced woman with two children is shunned by the community because of her marital status and falls into a relationship with a violent man. *AMG.*

Awards: Golden Globes, nomination for Best Actress, 1982

1781. *Doll's Eye*   1982 SP

D: Jan Worth
S: Annie Brown Worth, Anne Cottringer, Jan Worth
C: Mike Tomlinson
P: Jill Pack
A: Sandy Ratcliffe, Bernice Stegers, Lynne Worth

Three single mothers live near one another in a London neighborhood. One is a journalist researching prostitution, one is a telephone operator, and one is a prostitute. *British Film.*

1782. *Gold Diggers*   1982 DSCP

D: Sally Potter
S: Lindsay Cooper, Rose English, Sally Potter
C: Babette Mangolte
P: Nita Amy, Donna Grey
A: Julie Christie, Colette Lafont

"Fantasy of a black French computer operator and a blond dancer." *British Film.*

Awards: Berlin International Film Festival, Reader Jury, 1984

1783. *Heat and Dust*   1982 S

D: James Ivory

S: Ruth Prawer Jhabvala; based on her novel
C: Walter Wassally
P: Ismail Merchant
A: Julie Christie, Greta Scacchi
India, 1970s. A woman investigates the life of her aunt, married in the 1920s to a British colonial officer in India. Both women have love affairs with Indians and attempt to have abortions, but the modern woman decides to keep the child.
Awards: BAFTA Awards, Best Adapted Screenplay, 1983; London Critics' Circle Film Awards, Best Screenplay, 1984

1784. *Scrubbers*   1982 DS
D: Mai Zetterling
S: Roy Minton, Jeremy Watt, Mai Zetterling
C: Ernst Vincze
P: Don Boyd, George Harrison
A: Amanda York, Chrissie Cotterill, Elizabeth Edmonds, Kathy Burke
Two teenagers escape jail, one to see her child, the other to commit another crime so she can reunite with her imprisoned lover. Their return also leads to enmity, as the lover has already found someone else, and the mother blames her friend for ratting. "Out" lesbian culture combines with performance and punk, as the girls are fond of dancing, putting on shows, and hanging out their windows at night to cry out songs, limericks, and plaintive assertions.

1785. *Educating Rita*   1983
D: Lewis Gilbert
S: Willy Russell
C: Frank Watts
P: Lewis Gilbert
A: Julie Walters, Michael Caine
A working-class wife is determined to complete her education. She meets a professor who teaches her to be strong in her ideas, and conflict develops with her husband.

1786. *Loose Connections*   1983 S
D: Richard Eyre
S: Maggie Brooks
C: Clive Tickner
P: Simon Perry
A: Lindsay Duncan, Stephen Rea
A woman posts a sign for a companion to drive to a feminist convention in Germany; she ends up with a gay man. *FII.*

1787. *The Bostonians*   1984 S
D: James Ivory
S: Ruth Prawer Jhabvala; based on the novel by Henry James

C: Walter Lassally
P: Ismail Merchant
A: Vanessa Redgrave, Jessica Tandy, Linda Hunt, Christopher Reeve
Boston, 1876. A faith healer's daughter, who is a gifted speaker, rejects marriage to follow a charismatic feminist leader, who expects that she not marry. She wavers painfully between her commitment to the older woman and her attraction to a man.

1788. *The Company of Wolves*   1984 S
D: Neil Jordan
S: Angela Carter, Neil Jordan; based on stories by Angela Carter
C: Bryan Loftus
P: Chris Brown
A: Angela Lansbury, Sarah Patterson
A grandmother tells her granddaughter horror tales of werewolves. "Granny knows a great deal, but she doesn't know everything. And if there is a beast inside every man, he meets his match in the beast inside of every woman." Horror. *Chicago Sun-Times.* 1984, Jan. 1.

1789. *A Passage to India*   1984
D: David Lean
S: David Lean, Santha Rammi Rau; based on the novel by E. M. Forster
C: Ernest Day
P: Richard Goodwin
A: Judy Davis, Peggy Ashcroft, Victor Banerjee, James Fox
Chandrapore, 1920s. An English woman and her liberal future mother-in-law cause concern in the colonial compound by insisting on relating to Indians as people. The younger woman accuses an Indian friend of attempted rape when she cannot face the fact of her attraction to him. Opening the ensuing trial is the prosecutor's "universal truth" assumption that "the darker races are attracted to the lighter, but not vice versa."
Awards: Academy Awards, nomination for Best Actress (Davis), Best Supporting Actress (Ashcroft), 1984; BAFTA Awards, Best Actress (Ashcroft), 1984

1790. *Steaming*   1984 S
D: Joseph Losey
S: Patricia Losey; based on the play by Nell Dunn
P: Paul Mills
A: Vanessa Redgrave, Sarah Miles, Diana Dors
"Set in a Turkish bath which is faced with demolition. On ladies day a group of women congregate to discuss their problems." *FII.*

1791. *Supergirl*   1984
D: Jeannot Szwark
S: David O'Dell
C: Alan Hume
P: Timothy Burrill
A: Faye Dunaway, Helen Slater
Supergirl goes to earth to save the planet from a witch who has stolen a precious "power source." Action. *AMG.*

1792. *Assam Garden*   1985 DS
D: Mary McMurray
S: Elizabeth Bond
C: Bryan Loftus
P: Nigel Stafford-Clark
A: Deborah Kerr, Madhur Jaffrey
England. The widow of a colonial officer in India cultivates an Indian-style garden and is helped by an Indian woman from a nearby housing estate. *Time Out.*

1793. *Bad Timing*   1985
D: Nicolas Roeg
S: Yale Udoff
C: Anthony Richmond
P: Jeremy Thomas
A: Theresa Russell, Art Garfunkel
Vienna. A magnetic but vulnerable woman, desperate to be seen for herself, seduces a mean-spirited American psychiatrist; a detective investigates her near death.

1794. *Dance with a Stranger*   1985 S
D: Mike Newell
S: Shelagh Delaney
C: Peter Hannan
P: Roger Randall-Cutler
A: Miranda Richardson, Rupert Everett
1950s. A single mother has an affair with a powerful politician; scandal ensues when she murders him. She is tried and executed, becoming the last woman submitted to the death penalty in Britain. *Awards:* Evening Standard British Film Awards, Best Actress, 1986

1795. *A Room with a View*   1985 S
D: James Ivory
S: Ruth Prawer Jhabvala; based on the novel by E. M. Forster
C: Tony Pierce-Roberts
P: Ismail Merchant
A: Maggie Smith, Helena Bonham Carter, Judi Dench
Florence, 1900s. A young English woman and her chaperone visit Italy, where danger lurks in the form of an unconventional suitor.

Awards: Academy Awards, Best Screenplay, 1987; BAFTA Awards, Best Film, Best Actress (Smith), Best Supporting Actress (Dench), 1987, Golden Globes, Best Actress (Smith), 1987

1796. *Ursula and Glenys*   1985 P
D: John Davies
S: John Davies
C: Robert Smith
P: Angela Topping
A: Brid Brennan, Gaylie Runciman
"Soho prostitute tells her half-sister of her incestuous affair with her stepfather." *British Film.*

1797. *Zina*   1985
D: Ken McMullen
S: Ken McMullen, Terry James
C: Bryan Loftus
A: Domiziana Giordano
Berlin, 1930. The daughter of Leon Trotsky, deluded into thinking that she is her father, is treated by a psychoanalyst in Vienna; she eventually commits suicide. *British Film.*
Awards: San Sebastián International Film Festival, Special Jury Prize, 1985; Rotterdam International Film Festival, KNF Award, 1986

1798. *Nanou*   1986 DS
D: Conny Templeman
S: Conny Templeman, Antoine Lacomblez
C: Martin Fuhrer
P: Simon Perry
A: Imogen Stubbs
An English woman on holiday has an affair with a French political extremist and finds she is pregnant. *FII.*

1799. *The Passion of Remembrance*   1986 DS
D: Maureen Blackwood, Isaac Julien
S: Maureen Blackwood, Isaac Julien
C: Stephen Bernstein
A: Anni Domingo
London. A series of set pieces about a West Indian immigrant family, documentary-like scenes of the community's history, a woman who collects videos of political struggle, and finally, an interview by a black woman of a "brother" on the question of sexual identity and the place of women in the leftist movement. *Festival de films, 9th: 11. 1987.*

1800. *Business as Usual*   1987 DSP
D: Lezli-An Barrett
S: Lezli-An Barrett
C: Ernst Vincze
P: Sara Geater

A: Glenda Jackson, Cathy Tyson, John Thaw
A store manager, fired on the excuse of indulging a harassment suit from one of the workers, struggles against the owners of her dress shop chain and organizes a successful picket line; the film includes many details of labor organizing in contemporary Liverpool, England. *Working Stiffs.*

1801. *High Season*   1987 DSP
D: Clare Peploe
S: Clare Peploe, Mark Peploe
C: Chris Menges
P: Clare Downs
A: Jacqueline Bisset, Irene Papas, James Fox
Greece. A photographer and her sculptor husband are involved in a plot to smuggle an antique vase. *British Film.*

1802. *The Lonely Passion of Judith Hearne*
                                              1987
D: Jack Clayton
S: Peter Nelson; based on the novel by Brian Moore
C: Peter Hannan
P: Peter Nelson
A: Maggie Smith, Bob Hoskins
Dublin. A woman is fooled by the attentions of a tenant in her boardinghouse, who imagines she has money.
Awards: BAFTA Awards, Best Actress, 1989

1803. *Shag*   1987 DSP
D: Zelda Barron
S: Lanier Laney, Zelda Barron, Robin Swicord
C: Peter MacDonald
P: Julia Chasman
A: Phoebe Cates, Bridget Fonda, Annabeth Gish
1960s. Four friends vacation in Myrtle Beach, South Carolina, a last fling before one gets married; "shag" is the current dance craze. *Variety: 80. 1988, Aug. 24.*

1804. *A World Apart*   1987 P
D: Chris Menges
S: Shawn Slovo
C: Peter Biziou
P: Sarah Radclyffe
A: Barbara Hershey, Jodhi May, Linda Mvusi, Jeroen Krabbé
South Africa, 1963. "A woman's stand against apartheid splits her family. Based on the true story of Ruth First, a committed journalist and ANC supporter who was assassinated in 1982." *FII.*
Awards: BAFTA Awards, Best Screenplay, 1988; Cannes Film Festival, Best Actress (Hershey, May, Mvusi), Special Jury Grand Prize, 1988

1805. *Scandal*   1988
D: Michael Caton-Jones
S: Michael Thomas
C: Mike Molloy
P: Stephen Woolley
A: Joanne Whalley, Bridget Fonda
1960s. Call girls Christine Keeler and Mandy Rice-Davies consort with the British Conservative Party elite, causing a national scandal when it is revealed that one of the women is also involved with a Russian official.
Awards: Golden Globes, nomination for Best Actress (Fonda), 1990; Political Film Society, Award, 1990

1806. *Strapless*   1988 P
D: David Hare
S: David Hare
C: Andrew Dunn
P: Rich McCullum, Patsy Pollack
A: Blair Brown, Bridget Fonda, Bruno Ganz
Two sisters vie for the same man. One sister is a doctor, the other is pregnant and unmarried. *British Film.*

1807. *Impromptu*   1989 S
D: James Lapine
S: Sarah Kernochan
C: Bruno De Keyzer
P: Stuart Oken
A: Judy Davis, Bernadette Peters, Hugh Grant
France, nineteenth century. George Sand, Frederic Chopin, and their artist friends live the bohemian life and take advantage of rich patrons, as well as one another.

1808. *Oranges Are Not the Only Fruit* 1989 DSP
D: Beeban Kidron
S: Jeanette Winterson
C: Ian Punter
P: Philippa Giles
A: Charlotte Coleman, Geraldine McEwan
A girl who has been raised in a strict evangelical family scandalizes them with her lesbian relationship. *AMG.*
Awards: San Francisco International Lesbian & Gay Film Festival, Best Feature, 1990; BAFTA Awards, Best Drama, Best Actress (McEwan), 1991; Prix Italia, Special Prix, 1991

1809. *She's Been Away*   1989
D: Peter Hall
S: Stephen Poliakoff
C: Philip Bonham-Carter
P: Kenith Trodd
A: Peggy Ashcroft, Geraldine James

At the age of sixty, a woman is released from a mental institution and discovers "that little has changed in the world, but the effects are different." *FII.*

Awards: Venice Film Festival, Best Actress (Ashcroft, James), 1989

1810. *Shirley Valentine* 1989
D: Lewis Gilbert
S: Willy Russell
C: Alan Hume
P: Lewis Gilbert
A: Pauline Collins, Tom Conti, Julia McKenzie
A Liverpool housewife goes on a trip to Greece with her friend. *AMG.*

Awards: BAFTA Awards, Best Actress (Collins), 1990

1811. *Hidden Agenda* 1990
D: Ken Loach
S: Jim Allen
C: Clive Tickner
P: Eric Fellner
A: Frances McDormand, Brian Cox, Mai Zetterling
Belfast. The husband of a human rights lawyer is assassinated by police, and the lawyer pursues the investigation along with a local inspector. When they uncover a CIA conspiracy and the inspector's job is threatened, she is left to continue the investigation on her own. *British Film.*

Awards: Cannes Film Festival, Jury Prize, 1990

1812. *Women in Tropical Places* 1990 DSCP
D: Penny Woolcock
S: Candy Guard, Penny Woolcock
C: Janet Tovey
P: Felicity Oppé
A: Alison Doody, Scarlet O'Hara, Huffy Reah
Newcastle. An Argentinean is engaged to marry a man, who sends his chauffeur to meet her at the airport; at a hotel she meets a "standup comedienne and her daughter who provide her with wild diversions while she waits for her man." Comedy. *FII.*

1813. *Antonia and Jane* 1991 DS
D: Beeban Kidron
S: Marcy Kahan
C: Rex Maidment
P: George Faber
A: Imelda Staunton, Saskia Reeves
Two friends with opposite styles actively dislike each other's quirks; one is married to a former lover of the other.

1814. *Dream On* 1991 DS
D: Ellin Hare, Lorna Powell
S: Kitty Fitzgerald
C: Peter Roberts
A: Maureen Harold, Amber Styles
North Shields. A sixty-year-old "leather mama" arrives on her motorcycle to join her son, who owns a pub. Three women friends who shoot darts at the pub look to her for support. *Festival de films, 14th: 28. 1992.*

Awards: Prix Europa, Special Award, 1997; Emden International Film Festival, Award of the German Unions, 1998

1815. *Enchanted April* 1991 SP
D: Mike Newell
S: Peter Barnes; based on the novel by Elizabeth von Arnim
C: Rex Maidment
P: Ann Scott
A: Miranda Richardson, Joan Plowright, Josie Lawrence
1920. Two married English women and two single friends vacation together in Italy.

Awards: Cleveland International Film Festival, Best Film, 1992; Golden Globes, Best Performance (Richardson, Plowright), 1993

1816. *Blue Black Permanent* 1992 DSP
D: Margaret Tait
S: Margaret Tait
C: Alex Scott
P: Barbara Grigor
A: Celia Imrie, Gerda Stevenson
Edinburgh. "Photographer tells her lover about her mother's love affair and eventual suicide." *British Film.*

1817. *Orlando* 1992 DS
D: Sally Potter
S: Sally Potter, Walter Donohue; based on the novel by Virginia Woolf
C: Alexei Rodionov
P: Christopher Sheppard
A: Tilda Swinton
Orlando traverses the centuries in the royal courts of England. He eventually becomes disgusted at the behavior of the male power structure, and he changes sex. She ends up with a baby and a book.

Awards: Venice Film Festival, OCIC Award, 1992; Seattle International Film Festival, Best Actress, 1993

1818. *Anchoress* 1993 S
D: Chris Newby

S: Judith Stanley-Smith, Christine Watkins
C: Michel Baudour
P: Paul Breuls
A: Natalie Morse
Britain, fourteenth century. A young rural girl, inspired by a pagan cult of the earth seen as witchcraft, agrees to live as a devotee of the Virgin Mary by sealing herself behind the stone wall of a church. *Variety. 1993, May 17.*
Awards: Montréal World Film Festival, First Film Special Award, 1993

1819. *Camilla*   1993 DP
D: Deepa Mehta
S: Paul Quarrington
C: Guy Dufaux
P: Christina Jennings
A: Jessica Tandy, Bridget Fonda
A singer on vacation with her husband meets an older woman who is a cellist and takes a trip with her to a concert.

1820. *The Summer House*   1993 SP
D: Waris Hussein
S: Martin Sherman; based on the novel by Alice Thomas Ellis
C: Rex Maidment
P: Norma Heyman
A: Jeanne Moreau, Julie Walters, Joan Plowright, Lena Headey
1950s. Arriving for a wedding, an older woman, a friend of the mother, tries to prevent the imminent marriage of the daughter to an older man she does not love. *FII.*
Other titles: The Clothes in the Wardrobe

1821. *Bhaji on the Beach*   1994 DSP
D: Gurinder Chadha
S: Gurinder Chadha, Meera Syaa
C: John Kenway
P: Nadine Marsh-Edwards
A: Kim Vithana, Jimmi Harkishin, Sarita Khajuria
A group of Indian women take a bus trip to Blackpool for amusement; some use the free time and camaraderie to make important life decisions.

1822. *Ladybird, Ladybird*   1994 SP
D: Ken Loach
S: Rona Munro
C: Barry Ackroyd
P: Sally Hibbin
A: Crissy Rock
Liverpool. A welfare mother has several children with a series of sometimes abusive men. After a fire breaks out when she has left the chil-

dren alone, she conflicts with Social Services, who eventually take the children away from her.

1823. *Sister My Sister*   1994 DSP
D: Nancy Meckler
S: Wendy Kesselman
C: Ashley Rowe
P: Norma Heyman
A: Jodhi May, Joely Richardson, Julie Walters
France, 1932. Based on the true story of two servants, the Pepin sisters, who have an incestuous relationship and eventually murder their domineering mistress and her daughter.

1824. *The Snapper*   1994 P
D: Stephen Frears
S: Roddy Doyle
C: Oliver Stapleton
P: Lynda Myles
A: Tina Kellegher, Colm Meany
Dublin. A twenty-year-old becomes pregnant by a neighborhood family man, but she works through the difficulties with the help of her father. *British Film.*
Awards: Goya Awards, Best European Film, 1995; Prix Italia, 1994

1825. *Thin Ice*   1994 DSCP
D: Fiona Cunningham Reid
S: Fiona Cunningham Reid, Geraldine Sherman
C: Belinda Parson
P: Fiona Cunningham Reid
A: Charlotte Avery, Sabra Williams
"Lesbian romantic comedy about an ambitious photographer and a previously straight" woman who win the gold medal in figure skating for Britain at the Gay Games in New York in 1994. *FII.*

1826. *Widow's Peak*   1994
D: John Irvin
S: Hugh Leonard
C: Ashley Rowe
P: Jo Manuel, Tracey Seaward
A: Mia Farrow, Joan Plowright, Natasha Richardson
1920s. Comic mystery and intrigue in an Irish rural town dominated by wealthy widows.
Awards: Karlovy Vary International Film Festival, Best Actress (Richardson), 1994

1827. *Butterfly Kiss*   1995 P
D: Michael Winterbottom
S: Frank Cottrell Boyce
C: Seamus McGarvey

P: Julie Baines
A: Amanda Plummer, Saskia Reeves
A woman searches the countryside for her lost lover, murdering anyone in the way, until she finds a new woman who joins up for the killing spree. Action. *AMG.*

1828. *Carrington* 1995
D: Christopher Hampton
S: Christopher Hampton
C: Denis Lenoir
P: Ronald Sheldo
A: Emma Thompson, Jonathan Pryce
1910s. The intensely close relationship between Dora Carrington, a painter, and the much more well known and gay Lytton Strachey, biographer of Bloomsbury literati.
Awards: National Board of Review, Best Actress, 1995

1829. *The Scar* 1995
D: The Amber Collective
S: The Amber Collective
A: Charlie Hardwick
A woman with two teenage children, a former leader of a miner's strike, falls in love with the new mine supervisor. *Screenonline. Accessed 2005, Feb. 23.*
Awards: Prix Europa, Special Award, 1997; Emden International Film Festival, Award of the German Unions, 1998

1830. *Sense and Sensibility* 1995 SP
D: Ang Lee
S: Emma Thompson; based on the novel by Jane Austen
C: Michael Coulter
P: Lindsay Doran
A: Emma Thompson, Harriet Walter, Kate Winslet
An estate goes to the first son, as required by law, leaving a wife and three daughters without many options.
Awards: Academy Awards, Best Screenplay, 1996; BAFTA Awards, Best Film, Best Actress (Thompson), 1996; Berlin International Film Festival, Golden Bear, 1996

1831. *Swann* 1995 DSP
D: Anna Benson Gyles
S: Carol Shields, David Young
C: Gerald Packers
P: Christina Jennings, Ann Scott
A: Miranda Richardson, Brenda Fricker
Ontario. A feminist author researches a poet's life and makes friends with the woman who takes care of the poet's "memorial room." *FII.*

1832. *Welcome to the Terrordrome* 1995 DS
D: Ngozi Onwurah
S: Ngozi Onwurah
C: Alwin Kuchler
A: Suzette Liwellyn
Beginning with a re-creation of a slave market in Africa, the film moves to the people's descendents in a "futuristic, decaying, racially segregated city." A mixed-race couple awaits a child and lives in fear of being discovered. Thriller. *Festival de films, 17th: 23. 1995.*

1833. *Edie and Pen* 1996 SCP
D: Matthew Irmas
S: Victoria Tennant
C: Alicia Weber
P: Victoria Tennant
A: Stockard Channing, Meg Tilly
Two women of very different backgrounds and ages, both in the process of divorcing husbands, meet accidentally while traveling, and they bond.

1834. *Flight* 1996
D: Alex Pillai
S: Tanika Gupta
C: Mike Spragg
P: Behroze Gandhy
A: Mina Anwar
An Indian British college-age daughter of a morally rigid, disabled father is caught making love to her boyfriend in an empty warehouse; her father punishes her so severely that her mother helps her run away to a safe house.

1835. *Moll Flanders* 1996
D: Pen Densham
S: Pen Densham; based on the novel by Daniel Defoe
C: David Tattersall
P: Pen Densham
A: Robin Wright Penn, Stockard Channing
London, eighteenth century. An orphan fights the odds to find her way as a prostitute in the city.

1836. *The Portrait of a Lady* 1996 DS
D: Jane Campion
S: Laura Jones; based on the novel by Henry James
C: Stuart Dryburgh
P: Steve Golin
A: Nicole Kidman, John Malkovich, Barbara Hershey
Nineteenth century. A young and idealistic American heiress is taken in by a suave art collector

and his mistress, who are after her money; she accidentally discovers their relationship.

Awards: Los Angeles Film Critics Association, Best Supporting Actress (Hershey), 1996; National Society of Film Critics Awards, Best Supporting Actress (Hershey), 1997

1837. *The Proprietor*   1996

D: Ismail Merchant
S: Jean-Marie Besset, George Trow
C: Larry Pizer
P: Humbert Balsan
A: Jeanne Moreau, Sean Young

Expatriated novelist Adrienne Mark, author of the 1950s memoir *Je m'appelle France*, returns to Paris to deal with her family home and childhood memories of wartime France. *Variety. 1996, Oct. 7.*

1838. *Secrets & Lies*   1996

D: Mike Leigh
S: Mike Leigh
C: Dick Pope
P: Simon Channing-Williams
A: Brenda Blethyn, Marianne Jean-Baptiste

London. An adopted black optometrist with a comfortable middle-class life seeks out her white working-class mom, a factory worker, after her adoptive parents die.

Awards: Academy Awards, nominations for Best Picture, Best Actress (Blethyn), and Best Supporting Actress (Jean-Baptiste), 1997

1839. *Y fargen / The Proposition*   1996 P

D: Strathford Hamilton
S: Paul Matthews
C: David Lewis
P: Elizabeth Matthews
A: Theresa Russell

Wales, eighteenth century. A widow saves her farm by driving a cattle herd the long route to the market; she is aided by an arrogant cowboy.

1840. *A Business Affair*   1997 DSP

D: Charlotte Brandström
S: Charlotte Brandström, William Stadiem, Lucy Flannery; based on the novel by Barbara Skelton
C: Willy Kurant
P: Clive Parsons, Diana Belling
A: Carole Bouquet, Christopher Walken

A famous writer's wife writes a successful novel, then leaves him because of his lack of moral support. She takes up with her publisher, who then acts in a fashion similar to her husband by losing interest in her second effort.

Other titles: D'une Femme a l'autre

1841. *Career Girls*   1997

D: Mike Leigh
S: Mike Leigh
C: Dick Pope
A: Katrin Cartlidge, Lynda Steadman

Two friends from college meet years later as adults and spend a weekend together in London. *IMDb.*

Awards: Evening Standard British Film Awards, Best Actress (Cartlidge), 1998

1842. *Mrs. Brown*   1997 P

D: John Madden
S: Jeremy Brock
C: Stephen Greatrex
P: Sarah Curtis
A: Judi Dench

Nineteenth century. Near the end of her reign, Queen Victoria is soothed after her husband's death by a devoted servant; their relationship is a scandal.

Awards: BAFTA Awards, Best Actress, 1998; Golden Globes, Best Actress, 1998; London Critics' Circle Film Awards, Best Actress, 1998

1843. *Mrs. Dalloway*   1997 DSCP

D: Marleen Gorris
S: Eileen Atkins; based on the novel by Virginia Woolf
C: Sue Gibson
P: Stephen Bayly, Lisa Katselas Paré
A: Vanessa Redgrave, Natascha McElrone

London, 1923. On the day of a party, an older wealthy woman looks back on her perfect life, particularly her youth when she chose stability over a more challenging relationship. She is uncomprehendingly disturbed by a shell-shocked World War I veteran she runs into by chance.

Awards: Evening Standard British Film Awards, Best Screenplay, 1999

1844. *Nil by Mouth*   1997

D: Gary Oldman
S: Gary Oldman
C: Ron Fortunato
P: Luc Besson, Gary Oldman
A: Kathy Burke, Laila Morse, Ray Winstone

A pregnant woman lives with her mother, grandmother, brother, and brutish husband in modern London. *AMG.*

Awards: Cannes Film Festival, Best Actress (Burke), 1997; BAFTA Awards, Best Film, 1998

1845. *The Tango Lesson*   1997 DS

D: Sally Potter
S: Sally Potter

C: Robby Müller
P: Christopher Sheppard
A: Sally Potter
A fictional documentary of the filmmaker's attraction to the tango, her search for teachers and journey to Buenos Aires, her affair with a master dancer, her flirtations with Hollywood, and the renovation of her apartment in London.

1846. *Under the Skin* 1997 DSP
D: Carine Adler
S: Carine Adler
C: Barry Ackroyd
P: Kate Ogborn
A: Samantha Morton, Claire Rushbrook, Rita Tushingham
A young woman watches her mother die, quarrels with her sister, and compensates with a sex spree fueled in nightclubs.
Awards: Boston Society of Film Critics Awards, Best Actress (Morton), Best New Filmmaker, 1998; Toronto International Film Festival, FIPRESCI, 1997

1847. *Wara mandel / Dance of the Wind* 1997
D: Rajan Khosa
S: Rajan Khosa, Robin Mukherjee
C: Piyush Shah
P: Nalin Pan
A: Kitu Gidwani
New Delhi. A young singer loses her voice when her mother, also her music teacher, dies; she finds her mother's teacher and guru and begins to revive. *FII.*

1848. *The Wings of the Dove* 1997
D: Iain Softley
S: Hossein Amini; based on the novel by Henry James
C: Eduardo Serra
P: Stephen Evans
A: Helena Bonham Carter, Alison Elliot, Linus Roache
London, nineteenth century. A penniless woman, bound to a controlling wealthy aunt, is separated from the love she desires and becomes attached to a dying wealthy American girl, who invites her and her lover to Venice.
Awards: Boston Society of Film Critics Awards, Best Actress (Carter), 1997; Los Angeles Film Critics Association, Best Actress (Carter), 1997

1849. *The Winter Guest* 1997 S
D: Alan Rickman
S: Alan Rickman, Sharman Macdonald
C: Seamus McGarvey

P: Ken Lipper
A: Emma Thompson, Phyllida Law
A recently widowed photographer in a small Scottish town conflicts with her mother. The actresses are a real-life mother and daughter.
Awards: Brussels International Film Festival, Audience Award, 1998; Chicago International Film Festival, Gold Hugo, 1998

1850. *Elizabeth* 1998
D: Shekhar Kapur
S: Michael Hirst
C: Remi Adefarasin
P: Tim Bevan
A: Cate Blanchett
England, sixteenth century. The rise to power of Elizabeth I; the film focuses on her extraordinary intellect. Spared by her sister from imprisonment as a youth, she is thereafter able to negotiate the pressures related to the political intrigue of the court. She has lovers, evades marriage, and crowns herself the "virgin queen."
Awards: BAFTA Awards, Best Actress, 1999; Chicago Film Critics Association Awards, Best Actress, 1999; Golden Globes, Best Performance, 1999; London Critics' Circle Film Awards, Actress of the Year, 1999

1851. *The Governess* 1998 DSP
D: Sandra Goldbacher
S: Sandra Goldbacher
C: Ashley Rowe
P: Sarah Curtis
A: Minnie Driver, Tom Wilkinson
Nineteenth century. A governess hides her Jewish heritage while contributing ideas on inventing a chemical process for photography to the father of the household where she works. Discredited by him because of her forthright sexuality, which has frightened him, she moves to London to be a photographer herself.
Awards: Karlovy Vary International Film Festival, Special Prize, 1998

1852. *Hilary and Jackie* 1998 S
D: Anand Tucker
S: Frank Cottrell Boyce; based on *A Genius in the Family* by Hilary and Piers du Pré
C: David Johnson
P: Nicolas Kent
A: Emily Watson, Rachel Griffiths
The story of Jacqueline du Pré, famed concert cellist, and her sister, Hilary, an accomplished flutist who settled sensibly for a home and family but who was overshadowed and burdened by her more talented and emotionally fragile sister.

Awards: British Independent Film Awards, Best Actress (Watson), 1999; London Critics' Circle Film Awards, Best Actress (Watson), 2000

1853. *Little Voice*   1998 P
D: Mark Herman
S: Mark Herman, Jim Cartright
C: Andy Collins
P: Elizabeth Karlsen
A: Jane Horrocks, Brenda Blethyn, Michael Caine
A shy woman who still lives with her mother becomes famous doing musical impersonations.
Awards: Screen Actors Guild Awards, nomination for Outstanding Cast, 1999

1854. *Sliding Doors*   1998 P
D: Peter Howitt
S: Peter Howitt
C: Remi Adefarasin
P: Philippa Braithwaite
A: Gwyneth Paltrow
Two versions of a woman's fate: One day she takes a train and sees her fiancé with someone else, then ditches him and finds a life of her own; another day she misses the train and marries him. Comedy. *IMDb.*
Awards: Russian Guild of Film Critics, Best Foreign Actress, 1998; Florida Film Critics Circle, Best Actress, 1999

1855. *Conceiving Ada*   1999 DSP
D: Lynn Hershman Leeson
S: Lynn Hershman Leeson, Eileen Jones
C: Bill Zarchy
P: Lynn Hershman Leeson
A: Tilda Swinton, Francesca Faridany
The story of Ada Lovelace, a Victorian-era mathematician credited with the first computer program, and her collaboration with a modern computer scientist working in artificial intelligence. Science fiction. *Village Voice. 1999, Feb. 24.*

1856. *Cotton Mary*   1999 S
D: Ismail Merchant
S: Alexandra Viets
C: Pierre Lhomme
P: Gil Donaldson
A: Greta Scacchi, Madhur Jaffrey
Just after Indian independence in the 1950s, a British woman alone in southern India seeks help from an Indian servant nurse for her premature baby. *Village Voice: 144. 2000, Mar. 21.*

1857. *Hideous Kinky*   1999 SP
D: Gillies MacKinnon
S: Billy MacKinnon; based on the novel by Esther

Freud
C: John De Borman
P: Ann Scott
A: Kate Winslet
Based on an autobiographical novel, a British woman, with her two young daughters, seeks meaning in Morocco in the 1970s. *FII.*

1858. *Stella Does Tricks*   1999 D
D: Corky Giedroyc
S: A. L. Kennedy
C: Barry Ackroyd
P: Adam Barker
A: Kelly Macdonald
A teenage prostitute, a favorite of her pimp, seeks revenge on her abusive father, who sent her into the streets, as well as the pimp; taking energy from her fantasy life, she exacts pain but does not improve her situation. *Village Voice. 2000, Jan. 26.*

1859. *The Sticky Fingers of Time*   1999 DSP
D: Hilary Brougher
S: Hilary Brougher
C: Ethan Mass
P: Isen Robbins, Susan Stover
A: Nicole Zaray, Terumi Matthews, Belinda Becker
1950s. A Brooklyn science fiction writer finds her lost lover in the future 1990s of the East Village, where she also meets another attractive woman. *NYT: E26. 1999, Mar. 26.*

1860. *Tea with Mussolini*   1999
D: Franco Zeffirelli
S: Franco Zeffirelli
C: David Watkin
P: Clive Parsons
A: Cher, Judi Dench, Joan Plowright, Maggie Smith, Lily Tomlin
Florence, 1930s. A group of apolitical British expatriates, all older women, take care of a young orphan and wait for the war to end.
Awards: BAFTA Awards, Best Supporting Actress (Smith), 2000

1861. *Wonderland*   1999 P
D: Michael Winterbottom
S: Laurence Coriat
C: Sean Bobbitt
P: Gina Carter, Michele Camarda
A: Shirley Henderson, Molly Parker, Gina McKee
South London. One weekend in the lives of three sisters, a waitress, a hair stylist with a child, and an expectant single mother, all trying to find a way out of their economically prescribed lives.
Awards: British Independent Film Awards, Best British Film, 1999

1862. *Aberdeen* 2000 S
D: Hans Petter Moland
S: Kristen Amundsen
C: Philip Ogaard
P: Petter Borgli
A: Lena Headey, Charlotte Rampling
A London lawyer is commanded by her dying mother to go to Norway and bring back to Scotland her long-lost alcoholic father. *NYT: AR10. 2001, July 29.*
Awards: Brussels Film Festival, Best Actress (Headey), 2000; Hamptons International Film Festival, Best Feature Film, 2000

1863. *Agnes Browne* 2000 DP
D: Anjelica Huston
S: John Goldsmith, Brendan O'Carroll
P: Anjelica Huston, Arthur Lappin, Jim Sheridan
A: Anjelica Huston, Marion O'Dwyer
Dublin, 1960s. The suddenly widowed mother of seven young children tries to maintain economic stability as a produce vendor. She is greatly aided by a close relationship with another woman.

1864. *Babymother* 2000 SP
D: Julian Henriques
S: Julian Henriques, Vivienne Howard
C: Peter Middleton
P: Parminder Vir
A: Anjela Lauren Smith
A young Jamaican mother brings up her two children in a London housing project and starts a reggae band, with herself as the lead singer. Musical. *AMG.*

1865. *Between Two Women* 2000
D: Steven Woodcock
S: Steven Woodcock
A: Barbara Marten, Andrina Carroll
Postwar 1940s. In a small northern town, a married mother with a talented child meets his art teacher, and their friendship turns to love. *AMG.*

1866. *Esther Kahn* 2000
D: Arnaud Desplechin
S: Arnaud Desplechin, Emmanuel Bourdieu
C: Eric Gautier
P: Chris Curling
A: Summer Phoenix, Ian Holm
London, nineteenth century. A Jewish teenager escapes her impoverished family, her mocking mother, and the ghetto by becoming a stage actress. This detailed portrait focuses on her intelligence, her training, and her devotion to the work, which goes far in explaining the success of an odd, willful girl.

Awards: Viennale, Honorable Mention, 2000

1867. *The House of Mirth* 2000 SP
D: Terence Davies
S: Terence Davies; based on the novel by Edith Wharton
C: Remi Adefarasin
P: Olivia Stewart
A: Gillian Anderson, Eric Stoltz
A young woman of modest income haunts upper-class New York society, waiting for a husband she loves who also has enough money; her one friend is a bachelor of insufficient means. Manipulated by others who are jealous of her sincerity and beauty, she is humiliated and she despairs.
Awards: British Independent Film Awards, Best Actress, 2000; Istanbul International Film Festival, People's Choice, 2001

1868. *Last Resort* 2000 P
D: Pawel Pawlikowski
S: Pawel Pawlikowski, Rowan Joffe
C: Ryszard Lenczewski
P: Ruth Caleb
A: Dina Korzun
A Russian immigrant and her son arrive in London expecting to be met by her British fiancé, but they end up in a barbed-wire "holding area." *Village Voice: 113. 2001, Feb. 27.*

1869. *Bread and Roses* 2001 P
D: Ken Loach
S: Paul Laverty
C: Barry Ackroyd
P: Rebecca O'Brien
A: Pilar Padilla, Elpidia Carrillo
Los Angeles. A newly arrived Mexican woman is helped by her already established sister to get work at a cleaning company, which is ripe for union organizing; she is a union supporter, but her sister, responsible for an ailing husband, is not. *NYT: E14. 2001, June 1.*
Awards: Santa Barbara International Film Festival, Phoenix Prize, 2001; ALMA Awards, Outstanding Supporting Actress (Carrillo), 2002; Imagen Foundation Awards, Best Theatrical Film, 2002

1870. *Charlotte Gray* 2001 DP
D: Gillian Armstrong
S: Jeremy Brock
C: Dion Beebe
P: Sarah Curtis
A: Cate Blanchett
World War II. A Scottish woman is recruited out of blitzkrieged London for British Special Op-

erations in wartime France in support of the resistance.

1871. *Iris*   2001
D: Richard Eyre
S: Richard Eyre, John Bayley
C: Roger Pratt
P: Robert Fox
A: Kate Winslet, Judi Dench, Jim Broadbent
The story of the youth and later Alzheimer's period of novelist Iris Murdoch, told from the viewpoint of her husband. *Village Voice: 124. 2002, Dec. 12.*
Awards: BAFTA Awards, Best Actress (Dench), 2002

1872. *One Life Stand*   2001 DSCP
D: May Miles Thomas
S: May Miles Thomas
C: May Miles Thomas
P: Karen Smyth
A: Maureen Carr
A working-class divorced woman deals with her son and her abusive boss at a tarot-reading telephone service. *Village Voice: 148. 2001, Apr. 17.*

1873. *Very Annie Mary*   2001 DS
D: Sara Sugarman
S: Sara Sugarman
C: Barry Ackroyd
P: Damian Jones
A: Rachel Griffiths
A young, already fading opera singer is dominated by her father and left only to dream of a life of her own. Comedy. *NYT: E29. 2002, Mar. 29.*
Awards: U.S. Comedy Arts Festival, Best Screenplay, Best Actress, 2002

1874. *Bend It like Beckham*   2002 DSP
D: Gurinder Chadha
S: Gurinder Chadha, Paul Mayeda Berges
C: Jong Lin
P: Gurinder Chadha
A: Parminder K. Nagra, Keira Knightley
A young woman is recruited for a soccer team, but her traditional Sikh family would rather see her married.
Awards: Locarno International Film Festival, Audience Award, 2002; Sydney Film Festival, Grand Prix, 2002; GLAAD Media Awards, Outstanding Film, 2004

1875. *Crush*   2002
D: Jim McKay
S: Jim McKay
C: Henry Braham

P: Lee Thomas
A: Andie MacDowell, Anna Chancellor, Imelda Staunton
Three friends in a small English town quarrel when one of them marries a younger man, one of her former students. Comedy.

1876. *Do I Love You?*   2002 DSP
D: Lisa Gornick
S: Lisa Gornick
P: Lisa Gornick
A: Lisa Gornick, Harri Alexander, Birghitta Bernhard, Darren Black, Raquel Cassidy
A thirty-year-old lesbian, "on a quest to unravel the riddles in her life," believes her lesbian friends have better careers and love lives and wonders why. *FII.*

1877. *Me without You*   2002 DSP
D: Sandra Goldbacher
S: Sandra Goldbacher, Laurence Coriat
C: Denis Crossan
P: Finola Dwyer
A: Anna Friel, Michelle Williams
The story of two friends over twenty years, one of whom betrays the other. *NYT: E11. 2002, July 5.*

1878. *Morvern Callar*   2002 DSP
D: Lynne Ramsay
S: Lynne Ramsay, Liana Dognini
C: Alwin Kuchler
P: George Faber, Robyn Slovo
A: Samantha Morton, Kathleen McDermott
A woman finds her author boyfriend dead from a suicide on Christmas Day. She takes the manuscript he has left her, puts her name on it, sends it to an editor, and takes off on a vacation to Spain with her friend. Suddenly, she receives a big check and is pursued by editors as the "next big thing."

1879. *Secret Society*   2002 DS
D: Imogen Kimmel
S: Catriona McGowan
C: Glynn Speeckaert
P: Vesna Jovanoska, David Pupkewitz
A: Charlotte Brittain
Yorkshire. A factory worker becomes a successful member of a group of women Sumo wrestlers. Comedy. *Village Voice: 154. 2002, June 11.*

1880. *Triumph of Love*   2002 DS
D: Clare Peploe
S: Clare Peploe, Marilyn Goldin, Bernardo Bertolucci; based on the play by Pierre de Marivaux
C: Fabio Cianchetti

P: Bernardo Bertolucci

A: Mira Sorvino, Fiona Shaw

France, eighteenth century. A princess disguises herself as a boy in order to win over the rightful heir. *FII.*

Awards: Venice Film Festival, nomination for Golden Lion, 2001

1881. *Calendar Girls*　　　　　2003 SP

D: Nigel Cole

S: Tim Firth, Juliette Towhidi

C: Ashley Rowe

P: Nick Barton, Suzanne Mackie

A: Helen Mirren

Middle-aged women decide to create a calendar of nudes of themselves for charity; the project and its success underscore differences in their characters. Comedy.

1882. *Dear Frankie*　　　　　2003 DSCP

D: Shona Auerbach

S: Andrea Gibb

C: Shona Auerbach

P: Caroline Wood

A: Emily Mortimer

A single mother forges letters to her son from the boy's brutal father. *Tribeca Film. 2003.*

Awards: Seattle International Film Festival, Women in Cinema Lena Sharpe Award, 2004

1883. *Sylvia*　　　　　2003 DP

D: Christine Jeffs

S: John Brownlow

C: John Toon

P: Alison Owen

A: Gwyneth Paltrow

The life of poet Sylvia Plath, who went mad while tending to her two toddlers. Rightly suspecting her husband of infidelity, she leaves him, writes the poetry that made her famous, but never fully recuperates.

1884. *The Mother*　　　　　2004

D: Roger Michell

S: Hanif Kureishi

C: Alwin Kuchler

P: Kevin Loader

A: Anne Reid, Catherine Bradshaw, Daniel Craig

A newly widowed woman in her sixties propositions her daughter's boyfriend, a carpenter working on her son's house. In this belated letting go of her bland motherliness and uncovering of her own sexuality, she shocks her children out of their complacency.

Awards: London Critics' Circle Film Awards, Best Actress (Reid), 2004

1885. *Vanity Fair*　　　　　2004 DP

D: Mira Nair

S: Matthew Faulk, Mark Skeet; based on the novel by William Thackeray

C: Declan Quinn

P: Janette Day

A: Reese Witherspoon

London, eighteenth century. An orphan, the impoverished daughter of a French mother and artist father, defies the odds and lives a life in castles and mansions; more cloying than calculating, she has a fascination for India.

1886. *Vera Drake*　　　　　2004

D: Mike Leigh

S: Mike Leigh

C: Dick Pope

P: Simon Channing-Williams

A: Imelda Staunton

London, late 1940s. A genial, energetic woman cleans homes during the day and takes care of numerous neighbors and her husband, grown son, and daughter. They are unaware of her other life as an abortionist. When one of the "girls" lands in the hospital, Vera is arrested and breaks down under the mortification. Though she was only "helping the girls out" and never accepted money, she is made an example of and given a long sentence.

Awards: BAFTA Awards, Lean Award for Direction, Best Actress, 2005

1887. *Yasmin*　　　　　2004 P

D: Kenneth Glenaan

S: Simon Beaufoy

C: Tony Slater-Ling

P: Sally Hibbin

A: Archie Panjabi

Industrial urban England. A young Muslim woman changes clothes every day for her job as a social worker—from black scarf and long dress to tight jeans and high heels. She has a white boyfriend at work, then returns home to serve the men in the family. Things change after the attacks of September 11, 2001, and the divisions between the white world and her own sharpen when her husband is arrested.

Awards: Locarno International Film Festival, Ecumenical Jury Prize, 2004

UNITED STATES

1888. *Butterfield 8*　　　　　1960

D: Daniel Mann

S: John Michael Hayes; based on the novel by John O'Hara

C: Charles Harten
P: Pandro Berman
A: Elizabeth Taylor

A high-priced prostitute lives with her sweet mother, who turns a blind eye; she falls in love with one of her clients, who is treated like a child by his wealthy wife's parents. The two mothers, one upper class and controlling, the other lower middle class and naïve, are contrasted in their dealings with their daughters.
Awards: Academy Awards, Best Actress, 1960

1889. *Sappho, Darling* 1960
D: Gunnar Steele
S: Albert Zugsmith
P: Hal Senter
A: Carol Young, Yvonne D'Angers, Alan Darnay

Sappho "discovers that all men want is sex" and so falls in love with a female friend. Exploitation. *Variety: 6. 1969, Mar. 12.*

1890. *A Raisin in the Sun* 1961 S
D: Daniel Petrie
S: Lorraine Hansberry
C: Charles Lawton Jr.
P: David Susskind
A: Claudia McNeil, Ruby Dee, Diana Sands, Sidney Poitier

A widowed matriarch attempts to balance her desire to escape the ghetto with the needs of her children, particularly her son, who supports them as a chauffeur and desires a less demeaning position. *Working Stiffs.*

1891. *The Spinster* 1961 S
D: Charles Walters
S: Sylvia Ashton-Warner, Ben Maddow; based on the novel by Sylvia Ashton-Warner
C: Joseph Ruttenberg
P: Julian Blaustein
A: Shirley MacLaine

An American goes to rural New Zealand to teach Maori children; their lifestyle shocks her, but she is determined to be as effective as she can and devises new methods to teach them. See also *Sylvia* (1390), based on the life of the novelist. *AMG.*
Other titles: Two Loves
Awards: Berlin International Film Festival, nomination for Golden Bear, 1961

1892. *The Children's Hour* 1962 S
D: William Wyler
S: John Michael Hayes; based on the play by Lillian Hellman
C: Franz Planer

P: William Wyler
A: Shirley MacLaine, Audrey Hepburn

Two friends own an exclusive girls' boarding school and become outcasts because of a rumored lesbian relationship. Their rigid society offers only one response to the thought of them loving one another "that way"—horror—and they themselves are ill-equipped to deal with the crisis.
Awards: Laurel Awards, Top Female Performance (MacLaine), 1962

1893. *The Miracle Worker* 1962
D: Arthur Penn
S: William Gibson
C: Ernest Caparros
P: Fred Coe
A: Anne Bancroft, Patty Duke

The story of the blind and deaf Helen Keller and the teacher who brings her into the world of communication.
Awards: San Sebastián International Film Festival, OCIC Award, 1962; Academy Awards, Best Actress (Bancroft), Best Supporting Actress (Duke), 1963

1894. *Love with the Proper Stranger* 1963
D: Robert Mulligan
S: Arnold Schulman
C: Milton Krasner
P: Alan J. Pakula
A: Natalie Wood, Steve McQueen

New York City. A girl from a strict Italian American family finds she is pregnant by a man with whom she has spent one night; after an attempt at an abortion, she grows up fast, and they both find they love one another.
Awards: Mar del Plata Film Festival, Best Actress, 1964; Academy Awards, nomination for Best Actress, 1964

1895. *Kisses for My President* 1964
D: Curtis Bernhardt
S: Robert G. Kane
C: Robert Surtees
P: Curtis Bernhardt
A: Polly Bergen, Fred MacMurray

Comedy about the first woman president and the troubles her husband has as first lady, which are solved when the president becomes pregnant and resigns. *AFI.*

1896. *The Naked Kiss* 1964
D: Sam Fuller
S: Sam Fuller
C: Stanley Cortez
P: Sam Fuller

A: Constance Towers

A prostitute is frightened out of her living by a local sheriff, and she turns to caring for handicapped children. Mystery.

1897. *Bad Girls Go to Hell* 1965 DS
D: Doris Wishman
S: Doris Wishman
A: Gigi Darlene

After killing a would-be rapist, a newly abandoned wife flees to New York city and lives under an assumed name, where she moves from a "drunken lout" who abuses her to a lesbian who abuses her to the home of the mother of a detective looking for her. Exploitation. *AMG.*

1898. *Inside Daisy Clover* 1965
D: Robert Mulligan
S: Gavin Lambert
C: Charles Lang
P: Alan J. Pakula
A: Natalie Wood, Ruth Gordon

A teenager becomes a star in the 1930s Hollywood studio system, losing her grounding in the process.

1899. *One Potato, Two Potato* 1965
D: Larry Pearce
S: Raphael Hayes, Orville Hampton
C: Andrew Laszlo
P: Anthony Spinelli
A: Barbara Barrie, Bernie Hamilton

A divorced white mother fights for custody of her children after marrying a black man. *AMG.*

Awards: Cannes Film Festival, Best Actress, 1964

1900. *Seven Women* 1965 S
D: John Ford
S: Janet Green, Norah Lofts
C: Joseph LaShelle
P: Bernard Smith
A: Anne Bancroft, Margaret Leighton, Sue Lyon

China, 1930s. A doctor who talks tough, drinks, and chain-smokes attempts to help a group of nurses in a missionary hospital, though their leader finds her insensitive and a bad influence. They are challenged by a cholera epidemic, a marauding group of warriors, and a hysterical older woman who is pregnant and stranded with them.

1901. *The Group* 1966 S
D: Sidney Lumet
S: Sidney Buchman; based on the novel by Mary McCarthy
C: Boris Kaufman

P: Sidney Buchman
A: Candice Bergen, Joan Hackett, Elizabeth Hartman, Shirley Knight, Joanna Pettet, Mary-Robin Redd, Jessica Walter, Kathleen Widdows

Eight women graduate from an elite college in the early 1930s and begin their separate lives.

1902. *The Trouble with Angels* 1966 DS
D: Ida Lupino
S: Jane Trahey, Blanche Hanalis
C: Lionel Lindon
P: William Frye
A: Rosalind Russell

Comedy about a Mother Superior dealing with a couple of new high school students intent on countering her authority. *AMG.*

1903. *The Plastic Dome of Norma Jean*
1967 DS
D: Juleen Compton
S: Juleen Compton
C: Roger Barlow
A: Sharon Henesy, Robert Vance

Ozark mountains. A young girl with clairvoyant powers is exploited by a circus-tent entrepreneur, which revives his business and the town; she suffers a breakdown from the pressure. *AFI.*

1904. *Wait until Dark* 1967 S
D: Terence Young
S: Frederick Knott, Jane Howard-Carrington
C: Charles Lang
P: Mel Ferrer
A: Audrey Hepburn

A blind woman fends off intruders in her home who have business with her husband. Thriller.

Awards: Academy Awards, nomination for Best Actress, 1968

1905. *For Love of Ivy* 1968
D: Daniel Mann
S: Robert Alan Aurthur, Sidney Poitier
C: Joseph F. Coffey
P: Jay Weston
A: Abbey Lincoln, Sidney Poitier

When the family maid decides she wants to seek a better life, one of the sons hires a man to woo her, but not marry her, so she will stay. Comedy. *AMG.*

Awards: Golden Globes, nomination for Best Supporting Actress, 1969

1906. *Funny Girl* 1968 S
D: William Wyler
S: Isobel Lennart
C: Harry Stradling Sr.
P: Ray Stark

A: Barbra Streisand, Omar Sharif, Kay Medford
The life of Broadway star Fanny Brice (1891–1951). Musical.
Awards: Academy Awards, Best Actress, 1969; David di Donatello Awards, Best Foreign Actress (Streisand), 1969; Golden Globes, Best Motion Picture, 1969

1907. *The Killing of Sister George*   1968
D: Robert Aldrich
S: Lukas Heller, Frank Marcus
C: Joseph Biroc
P: Robert Aldrich
A: Beryl Reid, Susannah York
London. An actress loses her role on a soap opera, and the grief puts her long-term relationship with a younger woman on the skids as well.
Awards: Golden Globes, nomination for Best Actress (Reid), 1969

1908. *Rachel, Rachel*   1968 S
D: Paul Newman
S: Stewart Stern, Margaret Laurence
C: Gayne Rescher
P: Paul Newman
A: Joanne Woodward, Estelle Parsons
A thirty-five-year-old teacher who lives with her demanding mother has alternating fantasies of disaster and seizing control. When her good friend insists she go to a Christian revival and then makes a pass at her, her vulnerability becomes raw, but she pushes on into an affair with an old school friend looking for "action." When he disappears, she again seeks help from her girlfriend to take charge of her life.
Awards: New York Film Critics Circle Awards, Best Director, Best Actress (Woodward), 1968; Golden Globes, Best Director, Best Actress (Woodward), 1969; Laurel Awards, Best Supporting Actress (Parsons), 1970

1909. *Rosemary's Baby*   1968
D: Roman Polanski
S: Ira Levin
C: William Fraker
P: William Castle
A: Mia Farrow, John Cassavetes, Ruth Gordon
An innocent wife is manipulated by those closest to her, including her husband, who joins a devil's cult. They inflict on her a devil-child. Horror.
Awards: Academy Awards, Best Supporting Actress (Gordon), 1969; French Syndicate of Cinema Critics, Best Foreign Film, 1970

1910. *Three in the Attic*   1968
D: Richard Wilson

S: Stephen Yafa
C: J. Burgi Contner
P: Richard Wilson
A: Yvette Mimeux, Judy Pace, Maggie Thrett, Christopher Jones
A comedy about three girls, white, black, and Jewish, who are offended when they discover a man who is sleeping with all of them; they lock him in an attic and "try to kill him with sex." Exploitation. *AMG.*

1911. *Up Tight!*   1968 SP
D: Jules Dassin
S: Jules Dassin, Ruby Dee, Julian Mayfield
C: Boris Kaufman
P: Jules Dassin, Ruby Dee
A: Ruby Dee, Raymond St. Jacques
Cleveland. A prostitute makes friends with a black militant snitch who has a price on his head. *Chicago Sun-Times. 1969, Feb. 19.*

1912. *The Happy Ending*   1969
D: Richard Brooks
S: Richard Brooks
C: Conrad Hall
P: Richard Brooks
A: Jean Simmons, John Forsyth
The suburban wife of a successful lawyer falls into addiction to pills and alcohol; their normal lifestyle involves sexual betrayal among their friends. After a dinner party that ends with her suicide attempt, her husband suggests she "needs a hobby." *AMG.*
Awards: Academy Awards, nomination for Best Actress, 1969

1913. *The Rain People*   1969
D: Francis Coppola
S: Francis Coppola
C: Bill Butler
P: Bart Patton
A: Shirley Knight
A woman leaves her husband to hitchhike around the country.
Awards: San Sebastián International Film Festival, Golden Seashell, 1969

1914. *That Tender Touch*   1969
D: Russel Vincent
S: Russel Vincent
C: Robert Caramico
P: Russel Vincent
A: Sue Bernard, Bee Tompkins, Rick Cooper
The story of "the relationship between a younger and an older woman" and the older woman's anxiety when her lover finds a man. Exploitation. *Variety: 26. 1969, Nov. 26.*

1915. *Beyond the Valley of the Dolls* 1970
D: Russ Meyer
S: Roger Ebert
C: Fred Koenekamp
P: Russ Meyer
A: Marcia McBroom
An all-girl rock group moves to Los Angeles to make it big. Comedy. *AFI.*

1916. *Bloody Mama* 1970
D: Roger Corman
S: Don Peters, Robert Thom
C: John Alonzo
P: Roger Corman
A: Shelley Winters
Loosely based on the true story of Ma Barker, a child abuse victim who led her four sons in a life of bank robbery and incestuous sex; the film has a large cult following. Exploitation, action.

1917. *The Dark Side of Tomorrow* 1970 D
D: Barbara Peters
S: Jack Deerson
C: Jack Deerson
P: David Novak
A: Elizabeth Plumb, Alisa Courtney
"Two lonely suburban housewives engage in a lesbian affair." Exploitation. *FII.*

1918. *Diary of a Mad Housewife* 1970 S
D: Frank Perry
S: Sue Kaufman, Eleanor Perry
C: Gerald Hirschfeld
P: Frank Perry
A: Carrie Snodgress, Richard Benjamin
New York City. The story of the frustrations faced by a graduate of the elite Smith College, who becomes a Central Park housewife. Comedy.
Awards: Golden Globes, Best Actress, 1971; Laurel Awards, Best Actress, 1971

1919. *On a Clear Day You Can See Forever*
1970
D: Vincente Minnelli
S: Alan Jay Lerner
C: Harry Stradling Sr.
P: Howard Koch
A: Barbra Streisand
A girl trying to quit smoking undergoes hypnosis, only to find that she is able to enter past lives, one in particular as a nineteenth-century heiress. Musical.

1920. *Puzzle of a Downfall Child* 1970 S
D: Jerry Schatzberg
S: Jerry Schatzberg, Carole Eastman

C: Adam Holender
P: John Foreman
A: Faye Dunaway
A former fashion model retires to a beach house to write memoirs of her rise to celebrity and her bitter experience with fame. *Film Society. 2002, Apr.*
Awards: Golden Globes, nomination for Best Actress, 1971

1921. *Student Nurses* 1970 DSP
D: Stephanie Rothman
S: Don Spencer, Stephanie Rothman
C: Stevan Larner
P: Stephanie Rothman
A: Elaine Giftos, Karen Carlson, Brioni Farrell, Barbara Leigh
A story of nurses and their romances: "One falls for a poet with a terminal illness; one takes acid and becomes pregnant; one becomes involved with Hispanic revolutionaries; another has an affair with a gynecologist." Exploitation. *IMDb.*

1922. *Wanda* 1970 DS
D: Barbara Loden
S: Barbara Loden
C: Nicholas T. Proferes
P: Harry Shuster
A: Barbara Loden
Pennsylvania. A depressed mother married to a miner does not take care of her two children. Accepting a divorce, she has no home or way of earning a living, so she follows a thief around.

1923. *Bury Me an Angel* 1971 DS
D: Barbara Peters
S: Barbara Peters
C: Sven Walnum
P: Paul Norbert
A: Dixie Peabody
A biker goes on the road with a shotgun to avenge her brother's murder. Action. *IMDb.*

1924. *Klute* 1971
D: Alan J. Pakula
S: Andy Lewis, Dave Lewis
C: Gordon Willis
P: Alan J. Pakula
A: Jane Fonda, Donald Sutherland
An upscale prostitute is approached by a small-town detective (Klute) looking for his missing friend. She resists involvement, but they develop a relationship, if uneasy, when it becomes clear that she is in danger and he does have some clues as to why. Always, she feels trapped and angry. Mystery.

Awards: New York Film Critics Circle Awards, Best Actress, 1971; Academy Awards, Best Actress, 1972; Golden Globes, Best Actress, 1972

1925. *McCabe and Mrs. Miller*   1971
D: Robert Altman
S: Edmund Naughton, Robert Altman
C: Vilmos Zsigmond
P: Mitchell Brower
A: Julie Christie, Warren Beatty
Nineteenth century. A prostitute goes into business with a local hustler.
Awards: Academy Awards, nomination for Best Actress, 1972

1926. *Such Good Friends*   1971 S
D: Otto Preminger
S: Elaine May, Joan Didion; based on the novel by Lois Gould
C: Gayne Rescher
P: Otto Preminger
A: Dyan Cannon
While her husband is in a hospital bed, a wealthy wife discovers he has been sleeping with her friends, and she seeks revenge by sleeping with his friends. However, he dies before leaving the hospital. *Films and Filming, vol. 18, no. 8: 55–56. 1972, May.*
Awards: Golden Globes, nomination for Best Actress, 1972

1927. *The Velvet Vampire*   1971 DS
D: Stephanie Rothman
S: Stephanie Rothman, Charles Swartz
C: Daniel Lacambre
P: Charles Swartz
A: Celeste Yarnall, Sherry Miles
A wealthy vampire invites a couple to her desert home; the wife is taken with the woman, but when she finds her husband dead, she attempts escape. Horror. *AMG.*

1928. *What's the Matter with Helen?*   1971
D: Curtis Harrington
S: Henry Farrell
C: Lucien Ballard
P: George Edwards
A: Debbie Reynolds, Shelley Winters, Agnes Moorehead
1920s. A voice coach and a dance instructor open an acting school for children; both have sons convicted of murder, and the mysterious man who spies on them sets them against one another. See also *Whoever Slew Auntie Roo?* (Curtis Harrington, 1971), where the Shelley Winters character invites two children from a local

orphanage into her home and terrorizes them. Horror. *AMG.*

1929. *Boxcar Bertha*   1972 S
D: Martin Scorsese
S: John William Corrington, Joyce Hooper Corrington; based on *Sisters of the Road* by Bertha Thompson
C: John M. Stephens
P: Roger Corman
A: Barbara Hershey, David Carradine
1930s. A woman becomes involved with a railroad union and its radical leader; a series of nonviolent robberies ensures a violent end at the hands of "company thugs." Action. *Working Stiffs.*

1930. *The Effect of Gamma Rays on Man-in-the-Moon Marigolds*   1972
D: Paul Newman
S: Based on the play by Paul Zindel
C: Adam Holender
P: Paul Newman
A: Joanne Woodward
A forever dreaming widow is unable to manage her life or provide direction for her two daughters.
Awards: Cannes Film Festival, Best Actress, 1973

1931. *Group Marriage*   1972 DS
D: Stephanie Rothman
S: Stephanie Rothman, Charles Swartz
C: Daniel Lacambre
A: Claudia Jennings, Aimée Eccles, Victoria Vetri
Six professionals arrange a communal marriage in order to save money. Comedy. *AMG.*

1932. *Lady Sings the Blues*   1972 S
D: Sidney J. Furie
S: Chris Clark, Suzanne De Passe
C: John Alonzo
P: Brad Dexter
A: Diana Ross
New York, 1930s. Jazz singer Billie Holiday is sent twice into brothels by a mother who worked as a live-in maid. A dreamy singing teenager, she is raped, turns to prostitution, and then transforms herself into a musician. A jazz tour through the segregated South, where she sees a lynching, gets her started on heroin.

1933. *Lives of Performers*   1972 DSC
D: Yvonne Rainer
S: Yvonne Rainer
C: Babette Mangolte
A: Valda Setterfield, John Erdman, Shirley Soffer
Subtitled a "melodrama," the film is actually a collage rendering of a dance troupe, its leader, and

the piles of her scripts and photos; the focus is on the performers and rehearsals.

1934. *Play It as It Lays*   1972 S
D: Frank Perry
S: Joan Didion, John Gregory Dunne
C: Jordan Cronenweth
P: Dominick Dunne
A: Tuesday Weld, Anthony Perkins
Los Angeles. An aspiring young actress has problems coping with the superficiality of her milieu, and she breaks down after the failure of her career, an abortion, and the suicide of one of her few genuine friends.
Awards: Golden Globes, nomination for Best Actress, 1973

1935. *Season of the Witch*   1972 P
D: George Romero
S: George Romero
C: Bill Hinzman
P: Nancy Romero
A: Jan White
An affluent, bored housewife gets into witchcraft through a local practitioner. Exploitation. *AMG.*
Other titles: Jack's Wife / Hungry Wives

1936. *Sisters*   1972 S
D: Brian De Palma
S: Brian De Palma, Louisa Rose
C: Gregory Sandor
P: Edward Pressman
A: Margot Kidder, Jennifer Salt
A horror tale of conjoined twins who become a split personality in adulthood, one a serial killer. A female reporter investigates.

1937. *Up the Sandbox*   1972 S
D: Irvin Kershner
S: Paul Zindel; based on the novel by Anne Richardson Roiphe
C: Gordon Willis
P: Irwin Winkler
A: Barbra Streisand
A neglected housewife and mother fantasizes wild adventures while she attempts to tell her husband that she is pregnant.

1938. *Autobiography of Miss Jane Pittman*
                                                              1973
D: John Korty
S: Tracy Keenan Wynn; based on the novel by Ernest J. Gaines
C: James Crabe
P: Philip Barry Jr.
A: Cicely Tyson

An ex-slave, a woman born in the 1850s, lives to work in the civil rights movement of the 1960s.

1939. *Black Girl*   1973
D: Ossie Davis
S: J. E. Franklin
C: Glenwood J. Swanson
P: Lee Savin
A: Louise Stubbs, Peggy Pettit, Leslie Uggams, Claudia McNeil, Ruth Ann Greene, Ruby Dee
Two sisters, grown but shiftless, are jealous of their adopted stepsister, who drops out of school to dance, and also of a neighbor woman, who is a favorite of their mother's because she is going to college. *Chicago Sun-Times. 1973, Feb. 6.*

1940. *Cleopatra Jones*   1973
D: Jack Starrett
S: Max Julien
C: David Walsh
P: William Tennant
A: Tamara Dobson, Shelley Winters
Los Angeles. A government agent, who is a martial artist, is assigned to cleaning up the drug trade in Turkey and must contend with a female drug lord. Blaxploitation. *AMG.*

1941. *Coffy*   1973
D: Jack Hill
S: Jack Hill
C: Paul Lohmann
P: Samuel Arkoff
A: Pam Grier
A nurse avenges her eleven-year-old sister's fatal drug overdose by luring the suspects and gunning them down. Blaxploitation. *Variety. 1973, May 16.*

1942. *Five on the Black Hand Side*   1973
D: Oscar Williams
C: Gene Polito
P: Brock Peters
A: Clarice Taylor, Leonard Jackson
Los Angeles. A middle-class family is ruled by an autocrat; the three children "make their own way in the world of new black consciousness," while the "mother finally rebels and submits a list of demands that the husband must sign or else." Comedy. *FII.*

1943. *Summer Wishes, Winter Dreams*   1973
D: Gilbert Cates
S: Stewart Stern
C: Gerald Hirschfeld
P: Jack Brodsky
A: Joanne Woodward, Martin Balsam, Sylvia Sidney

"After one of her routine days is interrupted by the death of her mother, a woman goes to Europe with her husband. The focus shifts from her woes to his as he recalls the horror of two frightened days under attack during World War II." *FII*.

Awards: Academy Awards, nomination for Best Supporting Actress (Sidney), 1974; BAFTA Awards, Best Actress (Woodward), 1974

1944. *Terminal Island*   1973 DS
D: Stephanie Rothman
S: Stephanie Rothman, Charles Swartz
C: Daniel Lacambre
P: Charles Swartz
A: Marta Kristen, Phyllis David
Four women struggle to survive on an island penal colony inhabited mostly by male convicts. Exploitation. *AMG*.

1945. *The Way We Were*   1973
D: Sydney Pollack
S: Arthur Laurents
C: Harry Stradling Jr.
P: Ray Stark
A: Barbra Streisand, Robert Redford
A politically active woman marries and divorces a good-looking writer, the man of her dreams.

Awards: David di Donatello Awards, Best Foreign Actress, 1974

1946. *Alice Doesn't Live Here Anymore* 1974 P
D: Martin Scorsese
S: Robert Getchell
C: Kent Wakeford
P: Audrey Maas, David Susskind
A: Ellen Burstyn, Diane Ladd, Lelia Goldoni, Kris Kristofferson
A widow, used to the role of submissive wife, dreams of returning to her old singing career and so heads west with her eleven-year-old son, from New Mexico to Tucson, Arizona. Her relationships with her son and two men she meets, one extremely violent, create a portrait of a thirty-five-year-old woman in the process of understanding the relationship between jokes, teasing, threats, and violence.

Awards: Academy Awards, Best Actress (Burstyn), 1975; BAFTA Awards, Best Film, Best Actress (Burstyn), Best Supporting Actress (Ladd), 1976

1947. *Caged Heat*   1974 S
D: Jonathan Demme
S: Jonathan Demme, Evelyn Purcell
C: Tak Fujimoto

P: Roger Corman
A: Juanita Brown, Erica Gavin, Barbara Steel
A girl sent to prison on a drug charge eventually organizes an escape, all in the spirit of a "quasi feminist melodrama of camaraderie and revolution." Action. *Village Voice: 58. 1975, Jan. 6.*

1948. *Claudine*   1974 SP
D: John Berry
S: Tina Pine, Lester Pine
C: Gayne Rescher
P: Hannah Weinstein
A: Diahann Carroll, James Earl Jones
Harlem. An African American welfare mother with six children by several men works clandestinely as a maid to help her children get out of the ghetto. She falls in love with a garbageman, who pridefully rejects welfare. *NYT: 34. 1974, Apr. 23.*

Awards: Academy Awards, nomination for Best Actress, 1975

1949. *Daisy Miller*   1974
D: Peter Bogdanovich
S: Frederic Raphael; based on the novel by Henry James
C: Alberto Spagnoli
P: Peter Bogdanovich
A: Cybill Shepherd, Cloris Leachman
Nineteenth century. An American girl visiting Italy causes resentment and gossip among the upper crust because of her "American" accent and forthright style; just obnoxious enough to assure them of her difference, she changes and grows, while they remain static.

1950. *Film about a Woman Who ...*   1974 DSC
D: Yvonne Rainer
S: Yvonne Rainer
C: Babette Mangolte
A: John Erdman, Shirley Soffer
A collage of the filmmaker's professional engagements and heterosexual dissatisfaction, using all types of reading, voice-over, dialogue, and silent action; from the kitchen table to the beach, from the dance studio to a subway script reading, from contretemps over hurt feelings in bed to a museum full of seduction and death, and in between "an emotional accretion in 48 steps."

1951. *Foxy Brown*   1974
D: Jack Hill
S: Jack Hill
C: Brick Marquard
P: Buzz Feitshans
A: Pam Grier

A woman takes revenge for the death of her lover and goes after the mob by posing as a prostitute. Blaxploitation. *AMG.*

1952. *Hester Street* 1974 DS
D: Joan Micklin Silver
S: Joan Micklin Silver
C: Kenneth Van Sickle
P: Raphael D. Silver
A: Carol Kane, Steven Keats
Manhattan, 1900. A Russian Jewish wife arrives to join her immigrant husband and finds that he has modern ideas about marital fidelity, much different from hers.
Awards: Academy Awards, nomination for Best Actress, 1976

1953. *Just the Two of Us* 1974 DS
D: Jack Deerson, Barbara Peters
S: Barbara Peters, David Novak
C: Jack Deerson
P: David Novak
A: Elizabeth Plumb, Alisa Courtney
"Two women whose husbands are away on business decide to rectify their problems by having an affair." Exploitation. *FII.*

1954. *Rape Squad* 1974 S
D: Bob Kelljian
S: Betty Conklin, H. R. Christian
C: Brick Marquard
P: Buzz Feitshans
A: Jo Ann Harris
A woman who has been raped by a masked man organizes other women to train in karate in order to find, punish, and reform him and other rapists. Exploitation. *Variety: 18. 1974, June 12.*
Other titles: *Act of Vengeance*

1955. *Savage Sisters* 1974
D: Eddie Romero
S: Harry Corner
C: Justo Paulino
P: Eddie Romero
A: Gloria Hendry, Cheri Caffaro, Rosanna Ortiz
A "tough cop" helps a couple of revolutionaries escape from their "banana republic" jail and thwart a corrupt general. Exploitation. *IMDb.*

1956. *Smile* 1974
D: Michael Ritchie
S: Jerry Belson
C: Conrad Hall
P: Michael Ritchie
A: Barbara Feldon, Annette O'Toole, Melanie Griffith, Bruce Dern
A satire behind the scenes at a major Southern California beauty pageant.

1957. *The Sugarland Express* 1974
D: Steven Spielberg
S: Steven Spielberg, Hal Barwood
C: Vilmos Zsigmond
P: Richard Zanuck
A: Goldie Hawn
A mother works to get her husband out of prison and her child out of foster care. Action.
Awards: Cannes Film Festival, Best Screenplay, 1974

1958. *Truck Stop Women* 1974
D: Mark Lester
S: Mark Lester
C: John Arthur Morrill
P: Mark Lester
A: Claudia Jennings, Lieux Dressler
A woman who runs a truck stop, including prostitution and hijacking rings, is helped by her daughter in a power struggle with the mob. Exploitation. *AMG.*

1959. *A Woman under the Influence* 1974
D: John Cassavetes
S: John Cassavetes
C: Mitch Breit
P: Sam Shaw
A: Gena Rowlands, Peter Falk
A mentally ill woman is committed to a home by her husband.
Awards: Golden Globes, Best Actress, 1975; San Sebastián International Film Festival, Best Actress, OCIC Award, 1975

1960. *The Working Girls* 1974 DS
D: Stephanie Rothman
S: Stephanie Rothman
C: Daniel Lacambre
P: Charles Swartz
A: Sarah Kennedy, Denise Brooks, Lynne Guthrie
Los Angeles. Three young women share an apartment, try to act like men, and "will do anything for money." Exploitation. *MFB, no. 525: 217. 1977, Oct.*

1961. *Zandy's Bride* 1974 S
D: Jan Troell
S: Marc Norman; based on the novel by Lillian Bos Ross
C: Jordan Cronenweth
P: Harvey Matofsky
A: Liv Ullmann, Gene Hackman
A rancher is surprised by the unexpectedly strong personality of his mail-order bride. *AMG.*

Other titles: For Better or for Worse
Awards: David di Donatello Awards, European Award, 1976

1962. *Crazy Mama* 1975
D: Jonathan Demme
S: Frances Doel, Robert Thom
C: Bruce Logan
P: Lamar Card
A: Cloris Leachman, Ann Southern
1950s. The story of three generations of women on a crime spree, during which they travel from California to their home in Arkansas. Action. *AMG.*

1963. *Legacy* 1975 DSP
D: Karen Arthur
S: Joan Hotchkis
C: John Bailey
P: Karen Arthur
A: Joan Hotchkis
"Insightful look at an upper class woman cracking up, founded on a tour-de-force" performance. An ironic view of insanity established in the context of the "boorish" husband and the woman's own fantasies of the "American dream." *Variety: 14. 1975, Aug. 27.*

1964. *Love among the Ruins* 1975
D: George Cukor
S: James Costigan
C: Douglas Slocombe
P: Alan Davis
A: Katherine Hepburn, Laurence Olivier
A wealthy widow is sued for breach of promise by a younger man.
Awards: Emmy Awards, Outstanding Direction, Outstanding Actress, 1975; Los Angeles Film Critics Association, Special Award, 1975

1965. *Mahogany* 1975
D: Berry Gordy
S: John Byrum
C: David Watkin
P: Jack Ballard
A: Diana Ross
A poor African American woman becomes famous as a fashion model and latches onto white men in the process; she eventually finds her happiness with a black man. *Variety: 22. 1975, Oct. 8.*

1966. *Not a Pretty Picture* 1975 DSP
D: Martha Coolidge
S: Martha Coolidge
C: Don Lenzer
P: Martha Coolidge
A: Michele Manenti, Jim Carrington

A mix of narrative and documentary filming of the making of the film; the director and the actress have both been raped in the past, and they discuss their feelings for the camera while they make the film of her rape by a schoolmate. *NYT. 1976, Apr. 1.*

1967. *Sheila Levine Is Dead and Living in New York* 1975 S
D: Sidney J. Furie
S: Gail Parent, Kenny Solms
C: Donald Morgan
P: Harry Korshak
A: Jeannie Berlin, Roy Scheider
1960s, New York City. An ordinary woman moves to the city to meet men and falls for the first one she dates; he is less enthusiastic. Comedy. *AMG.*

1968. *The Virginia Hill Story* 1975 S
D: Joel Schumacher
S: Juleen Compton, Joel Schumacher
C: Jack Woolf
P: Aaron Rosenberg
A: Dyan Cannon, Harvey Keitel
A woman involved with gangster Bugsy Siegel testifies in a congressional hearing. *AMG.*

1969. *Bush Mama* 1976
D: Haile Gerima
S: Haile Gerima
C: Charles Burnett
P: Haile Gerima
A: Barbara O Jones, Cora Lee Day
Watts, Los Angeles. A mother is left on her own in an inner-city neighborhood after her lover is jailed. She struggles with bureaucrats and violence in attempting to cope with her impoverishment. A close-up, cinema vérité–style drama.

1970. *Jackson County Jail* 1976
D: Michael Miller
S: Michael Miller
C: Willy Kurant
P: Jeff Begun
A: Yvette Mimeux, Tommy Lee Jones
A businesswoman leaves her job and unfaithful lover to drive to New York from Los Angeles. Robbed and raped along the way by a jail warden, she goes after him and murders him. Exploitation. *Variety: 19. 1976, May 5.*

1971. *Kristina Talking Pictures* 1976 DSC
D: Yvonne Rainer
S: Yvonne Rainer
C: Babette Mangolte

A: Kate Parker, Bert Barr

San Francisco. A couple sit in bed and have normal discussions and arguments. Dialogue alternates with silent film (though the couples continue to speak) and then a dinner party; the story of a dream; and a very large party, dancing, and other performance art. Experimental.

1972. *Lipstick*   1976
D: Lamont Johnson
S: David Rayfiel
C: Bill Butler
P: Freddie Fields
A: Margaux Hemingway, Mariel Hemingway, Anne Bancroft

A model is raped by her sister's music teacher and humiliated in court because he gets off on a technicality. She then seeks revenge. Exploitation. *Variety: 22. 1976, Apr. 7.*

1973. *Regrouping*   1976 DS
D: Lizzie Borden
S: Lizzie Borden

A filmmaker meets with four women who are appearing in her film, and they all agree to the final script. Conflicts arise during the shooting; the film becomes a mix of the original idea and a commentary on collaboration, group functioning, and individual thinking. Other scenes are of supermarket shoppers, a women's group shower, lesbian lovemaking, a car ride where one of the original women tells the filmmaker how they all distrusted her, and a new group of women who become studio commentators. Experimental. *Film Library, vol. 9, no. 4: 50–52. 1977.*

1974. *Sparkle*   1976
D: Sam O'Steen
S: Sam O'Steen, Joel Schumacher
C: Bruce Surtees
P: Howard Rosenman
A: Irene Cara, Lonette McKee, Philip Michael Thomas, Dwan Smith

Three sisters, daughters of a house maid, find fame as popular singers, but they respond differently to the demands of performing and flounder in "casual dope and sex." *Variety: 26. 1976, Apr. 7.*

1975. *The War Widow*   1976
D: Paul Bogart
S: Harvey Perr
A: Pamela Bellwood, Frances Lee McCain

"Story of a lesbian love affair, set during World War I." *FII.*
Awards: San Francisco International Lesbian & Gay Film Festival, Audience Award, 1988

1976. *Widow*   1976 S
D: J. Lee Thompson
S: Lynn Caine, Barbara Turner
C: Billy Goldenberg
P: John Furia
A: Michael Learned

"Vulnerable widow tries to deal with her own substantial grief, that of her children, and the prospect of raising them alone with no money." *AMG.*

1977. *Coma*   1977
D: Michael Crichton
S: Michael Crichton; based on the novel by Robin Cook
C: Victor J. Kemper
P: Martin Erlichman
A: Geneviève Bujold

A doctor investigates unexplained deaths in the hospital where she works. Thriller.

1978. *Demon Seed*   1977
D: Donald Cammell
S: Robert Jaffe
C: Bill Butler
P: Herb Jaffe
A: Julie Christie

A woman is impregnated by a computer created by her husband. Special effects by Jordan Belson.

1979. *I Never Promised You a Rose Garden*
                                                 1977 S
D: Anthony Page
S: Lewis John Carlino, Gavin Lambert; based on the novel by Joanne Greenberg
C: Bruce Logan
P: Edgar Scherick
A: Kathleen Quinlan, Bibi Andersson

A young woman in a mental hospital struggles with an overpowering fantasy life but is helped by a therapist.
Awards: Academy Awards, nomination for Best Screenplay, 1978

1980. *I Spit on Your Grave*   1977
D: Meir Zarchi
S: Meir Zarchi
C: Yuri Haviv
P: Meir Zarchi
A: Camille Keaton

A novelist rents a cabin, where she is raped (for thirty minutes of the film); subsequently, she pursues her own bloody revenge. Exploitation. *AMG.*
Other titles: Day of the Woman
Awards: Catalonian International Film Festival, Best Actress, 1978

1981. *Julia*   1977
D: Fred Zinnemann
S: Alvin Sargent; based on *Pentimento*, a memoir by
    Lillian Hellman
C: Douglas Slocombe
P: Richard Roth
A: Jane Fonda, Vanessa Redgrave
1930s. A Broadway playwright is persuaded by
    her wealthy longtime friend to carry a large
    amount of cash into Germany to the antifascist
    resistance.
Awards: Academy Awards, Best Screenplay, Best
    Supporting Actress (Redgrave), 1978; Golden
    Globes, Best Actress (Fonda, Redgrave), 1978;
    BAFTA Awards, Best Film, Best Screenplay, Best
    Actress (Fonda), 1979

1982. *Looking for Mr. Goodbar*   1977 S
D: Richard Brooks
S: Richard Brooks; based on the novel by Judith
    Rossner
C: William Fraker
P: Freddie Fields
A: Diane Keaton, Tuesday Weld
After an affair with an abusive college teacher ends,
    a woman insists on leaving her Catholic family
    home and supporting herself on her salary as
    a teacher of deaf children. Scarred by a genetic
    condition, she refuses to think of having chil-
    dren and digs into sexual gratification, becoming
    experienced enough to take money if offered.
    Independence makes her tough and aggressive,
    but one day she brings home the wrong man.
Awards: Academy Awards, nomination for Best Sup-
    porting Actress (Weld), 1978; Golden Globes,
    nomination for Best Actress (Keaton), 1978

1983. *The Mafu Cage*   1977 DP
D: Karen Arthur
S: Don Chastain
C: John Bailey
P: Diana Young
A: Lee Grant, Carol Kane
Sisters, one psychotic, live in the shadow of their
    dead father, who raised them in Africa, where he
    worked with Mafu chimpanzees. Horror. *Festival
    de films, 9th: 96. 1987.*

1984. *Opening Night*   1977
D: John Cassavetes
S: John Cassavetes
C: Al Ruban
P: Al Ruban
A: Gena Rowlands, Joan Blondell, John Cassavetes
An actress in previews with a new play loses her
    focus when a young and ardent fan is killed in

an accident. Increasingly unhappy with the script,
    which addresses the bothersome subject of ag-
    ing, and requiring sycophantic treatment from
    her "friends"—the writer, the director, and the
    male lead—she shows up for opening night too
    drunk to stand up.
Awards: Berlin International Film Festival, Best Ac-
    tress (Rowlands), Interfilm Award, 1978

1985. *Summer School Teachers*   1977 DSP
D: Barbara Peters
S: Barbara Peters
C: Eric Saarinen
P: Julie Corman
A: Candice Rialson, Pat Anderson
Southern California. Three teachers arrive from
    Idaho in hopes of stirring up the student body.
    Exploitation. *AMG.*

1986. *Three Women*   1977
D: Robert Altman
S: Robert Altman
C: Charles Rosher Jr.
P: Robert Altman
A: Shelley Duvall, Sissy Spacek, Janice Rule
Three eccentric women are isolated from them-
    selves and others; two work as aides in a spa for
    the elderly, the other is a mysterious artist.
Awards: Cannes Film Festival, Best Actress (Du-
    vall), 1977; Los Angeles Film Critics Association,
    Best Actress (Duvall), 1977; New York Film
    Critics Circle Awards, Best Supporting Actress
    (Spacek), 1977

1987. *The Turning Point*   1977
D: Herbert Ross
S: Arthur Laurents
C: Robert Surtees
P: Arthur Laurents
A: Anne Bancroft, Shirley MacLaine, Leslie Browne
Two friends reflect on their choices, one for a
    career in ballet, the other for motherhood and
    teaching in a school for ballet.
Awards: Academy Awards, nominations for Best Ac-
    tress (Bancroft, MacLaine) and Best Supporting
    Actress (Browne), 1978; Golden Globes, Best
    Motion Picture, 1978

1988. *An Unmarried Woman*   1977
D: Paul Mazursky
S: Paul Mazursky
C: Arthur Ornitz
P: Paul Mazursky
A: Jill Clayburgh, Alan Bates, Michael Murphy
New York City. A dreamer with a passion for
    ballet and regular outings with her friends is

suddenly betrayed by her husband; he sobs at having to leave her for a younger woman. She slowly begins a new life, and when he is ready to return, she is far beyond wanting back her former life.

Awards: Cannes Film Festival, Best Actress, 1978; Academy Awards, nominations for Best Film and Best Actress, 1979

1989. *The China Syndrome* 1978
D: James Bridges
S: James Bridges, T. S. Cook
C: James Crabe
P: Michael Douglas
A: Jane Fonda, Jack Lemmon
A television reporter witnesses a nearly catastrophic accident at a nuclear plant but is rebuffed when pursuing the story. Intrigue develops around an insider providing information, a murder, and plant safety weaknesses brought on by cost-cutting.
Awards: BAFTA Awards, Best Actress, 1979

1990. *Girlfriends* 1978 DSP
D: Claudia Weill
S: Vicki Polon
C: Fred Murphy
P: Claudia Weill
A: Melanie Mayron, Anita Skinner
A photographer struggles with her close friend's decision to marry.

1991. *Old Boyfriends* 1978 DP
D: Joan Tewkesbury
S: Leonard Schrader, Paul Schrader
C: William Fraker
P: Edward Pressman, Michele Rappaport
A: Talia Shire
A psychologist attempts suicide and seeks to know herself through meeting up again with old boyfriends. *AMG.*

1992. *Remember My Name* 1978
D: Alan Rudolph
S: Alan Rudolph
C: Tak Fujimoto
P: Robert Altman
A: Geraldine Chaplin, Anthony Perkins
A convict leaves prison after twelve years and seeks out her former husband, even though the marriage is long over. *Festival de films, 13th: 56. 1991.*

1993. *Woman Called Moses* 1978 S
D: Paul Wendkos
S: Marcy Heidish, Lonne Elder

C: Robert Hauser
P: Michael Jaffe
A: Cicely Tyson
Nineteenth century. The life of Harriet Tubman, the escaped slave who founded the Underground Railroad, allowing hundreds of other slaves to escape from the South. *AMG.*
Awards: Writers Guild of America, Anthology Adaptation, 1979

1994. *Alien* 1979
D: Ridley Scott
S: Dan O'Bannon, Ronald Shusett
C: Derek Vanlint
P: Walter Hill
A: Sigourney Weaver
A woman crew member survives attacks by an alien on a spaceship. The film inspired three sequels: *Aliens* (1986), *Alien³* (1992), and *Alien: Resurrection* (1997). Action.

1995. *Gal Young 'Un* 1979 S
D: Victor Nuñez
S: Victor Nuñez; based on the novel by Marjorie Kinnan Rawlings
C: Victor Nuñez
P: Victor Nuñez
A: Dana Preu, David Peck
Florida, 1930s. A widow is taken in by a bootlegger who marries her, but she fights back when he brings home a younger woman to be his mistress.

1996. *The Lady in Red* 1979
D: Lewis Teague
S: John Sayles
C: Daniel Lacambre
P: Roger Corman
A: Pamela Sue Martin
The story of a woman who was a key figure in the capture of the infamous Chicago gangster John Dillinger. Action. *AMG.*

1997. *Norma Rae* 1979 P
D: Martin Ritt
S: Irving Ravetch, Harriet Frank Jr.
C: John Alonzo
P: Tamara Asseyev, Alexandra Rose
A: Sally Field
A textile worker, tired of the company and the "company town" in which her entire family is trapped, decides to become a union organizer in the factory.
Awards: Cannes Film Festival, Best Actress, 1979; Academy Awards, Best Actress, 1980; Golden Globes, Best Actress, 1980

1998. The Rose   1979
D: Mark Rydell
S: Michael Cimino, Bo Goldman
C: Vilmos Zsigmond
P: Aaron Russo
A: Bette Midler
1960s. The rise and fall into addiction of a popular
    blues singer, based on the life of Janis Joplin.
Awards: Golden Globes, Best Actress, 1980

1999. 9 to 5   1980 S
D: Colin Higgins
S: Colin Higgins, Patricia Resnick
C: Reynaldo Villalobos
P: Bruce Gilbert
A: Jane Fonda, Lily Tomlin, Dolly Parton
Three office workers, exasperated with their "pink
    ghetto," kidnap the boss and manage the depart-
    ment without him, instituting flexible time, day
    care, and salary equity.
Other titles: Nine to Five

2000. Coal Miner's Daughter   1980 S
D: Michael Apted
S: Thomas Rickman, George Vecsey; based on an
    autobiography by Loretta Lynn
C: Ralf D. Bode
P: Bernard Schwartz
A: Sissy Spacek, Tommy Lee Jones
The life of country singer Loretta Lynn, born in
    Kentucky in 1932 and married at thirteen to a
    kind man who pushed her to reveal her talent.
Awards: Los Angeles Film Critics Association, Best
    Actress, 1980; Academy Awards, Best Actress,
    1981; Golden Globes, Best Actress, 1981

2001. Gloria   1980
D: John Cassavetes
S: John Cassavetes
C: Fred Schuler
P: Sam Shaw
A: Gena Rowlands
A neighbor picks up a boy whose parents have just
    been murdered and protects him from the mob.

2002. It's My Turn   1980 DS
D: Claudia Weill
S: Eleanor Bergstein
C: Bill Butler
P: Martin Elfand
A: Jill Clayburgh, Michael Douglas
A married professor falls in love with an athlete
    who lives in another state.

2003. Private Benjamin   1980 SP
D: Howard Zieff

S: Nancy Meyers, Charles Shyer, Harvey Miller
P: Nancy Meyers, Charles Shyer, Harvey Miller
A: Goldie Hawn, Eileen Brennan
Comedy about a spoiled Jewish woman who loses
    her husband and then impulsively enters the U.S.
    Army, expecting special treatment; she buckles
    down and becomes a good soldier.
Awards: Academy Awards, nominations for Best
    Actress (Hawn) and Best Supporting Actress
    (Brennan), 1980

2004. Resurrection   1980 P
D: Daniel Petrie
S: Lewis John Carlino
C: Mario Tosi
P: Renée Missel
A: Ellen Burstyn, Eva Le Gallienne
After her lover dies and she is injured in an acci-
    dent, a woman mysteriously becomes a miracle
    healer, but she remains modest and refuses to
    consider herself a religious leader.
Awards: Academy Awards, nominations for Best
    Actress (Burstyn) and Best Supporting Actress
    (Le Gallienne), 1981

2005. Absence of Malice   1981
D: Sydney Pollack
S: Kurt Luedtke
C: Owen Roizman
P: Sydney Pollack
A: Sally Field, Paul Newman
A journalist hounds a businessman in trouble, but she
    is humiliated to find she has been duped by being
    fed wrong information and unjustly harmed him.

2006. Broken English   1981 DS
D: Michie Gleason
S: Michie Gleason
P: Bert Schneider
A: Beverley Ross, Jacques Martial, Greta Ronnin-
    gen, Oona Chaplin
Paris. A young woman from the United States be-
    comes involved with a Namibian rebel and takes
    on his revolutionary aims. She goes with him to Tu-
    nis and Senegal, where she breaks him out of jail.

2007. The End of August   1981 SP
D: Bob Graham
S: Leon Heller, Gregory Nava, Eula Seaton; based
    on the novel by Kate Chopin
C: Robert Elswit
P: Sally Sharp
A: Sally Sharp
At the turn of the century, a woman has an affair and
    eventually leaves her home and family. AMG.
Other titles: The Awakening

2008. *The Entity* 1981
D: Sidney J. Furie
S: Frank De Felitta
C: Stephen H. Burum
P: Harold Schneider
A: Barbara Hershey
A single mother of three is repeatedly raped by a ghost; she is treated by psychologists and, finally, university experts in the supernatural. Horror. *AMG.*

2009. *The Incredible Shrinking Woman* 1981 SP
D: Joel Schumacher
S: Jane Wagner, Richard Matheson
C: Bruce Logan
P: Hank Moonjean, Jane Wagner
A: Lily Tomlin, Charles Grodin
Household chemicals make a suburban housewife shrink, increasing her abuse by and usability to others; at one point she is found sleeping in a doll's house. Comedy.

2010. *Missing* 1981
D: Costa-Gavras
S: Costa-Gavras, Thomas Hauser, Donald Stewart
C: Ricardo Aronovich
P: Edward Lewis
A: Sissy Spacek, Jack Lemmon
Chile, 1973. An American goes missing during the coup; his wife and father go there to find him, but they discover the U.S. Embassy is not interested in helping them.
Awards: Academy Awards, nomination for Best Actress, 1982; Cannes Film Festival, Golden Palm, 1982

2011. *Only When I Laugh* 1981
D: Glenn Jordan
S: Neil Simon
C: David Walsh
P: Neil Simon
A: Marsha Mason, Kristy McNichol
New York City. "Comedy about the adjustments a successful actress and her daughter have to make when the daughter begins to live with the mother after a six year separation." *FII.*
Awards: Academy Awards, nomination for Best Actress (Mason), 1981

2012. *Rich and Famous* 1981 P
D: George Cukor
S: Gerald Ayres, John Van Druten
C: Donald Peterman
P: William Allyn, Jacqueline Bisset
A: Jacqueline Bisset, Candice Bergen
College friends become writers, one of serious fiction, the other of commercially successful romance novels.

2013. *White Dog* 1981
D: Sam Fuller
S: Sam Fuller, Curtis Hanson, Romain Gary
C: Bruce Surtees
P: Jon Davison
A: Kristy McNichol, Paul Winfield
An actress takes in a dog she has hit with her car and nurses it back to health. One day it attacks and kills an intruder, and she discovers that the dog has been trained to attack black people. *AMG.*

2014. *Chained Heat* 1982
D: Paul Nicolas
S: Paul Nicdas, Vincent Mengel
C: Mac Ahlberg
P: Billy Fine
A: Linda Blair, Sybil Danning, Tamara Dobson, Stella Stevens
Violent conditions push the white and black factions in a women's prison to band together in revolt. Exploitation. *Variety: 16. 1983, June 1.*

2015. *Come Back to the 5 and Dime Jimmy Dean, Jimmy Dean* 1982
D: Robert Altman
S: Ed Graczyk, based on his play
C: Pierre Mignot
P: Scott Bushnell
A: Sandy Dennis, Cher, Karen Black, Kathy Bates
The "Disciples of James Dean" unite on the anniversary of his death and reminisce about their lives.

2016. *Frances* 1982
D: Graeme Clifford
C: László Kovács
P: Jonathan Sanger
A: Jessica Lange, Kim Stanley
1950s. The story of actress Frances Farmer, whose will, talent, and anger at the system made her vulnerable to addiction; her domineering mother had her institutionalized.
Awards: Academy Awards, nominations for Best Actress (Lange) and Best Supporting Actress (Stanley), 1983; Moscow International Film Festival, Best Actress (Lange), 1983

2017. *Lianna* 1982 P
D: John Sayles
S: John Sayles
C: Austin De Besche
P: Maggie Renzi

A: Linda Griffiths, Jane Hallaren
A married mother falls in love with another woman.

2018. ***Personal Best***   1982
D: Robert Towne
S: Robert Towne
C: Michael Chapman
P: Robert Towne
A: Mariel Hemingway, Patrice Donnelly
A young athlete forms a sexual triangle around herself, with her male coach and another female athlete.

2019. ***Smithereens***   1982 DSP
D: Susan Seidelman
S: Susan Seidelman, Peter Askin
C: Chirine El Khadem
P: Susan Seidelman
A: Susan Berman
New York City. An obnoxious self-promoter on the lower east side of Manhattan wants a music career but just gets in everyone's way, including her own.
Awards: Cannes Film Festival, nomination for Golden Palm, 1982

2020. ***Sophie's Choice***   1982
D: Alan J. Pakula
S: Alan J. Pakula; based on the novel by William Styron
C: Nestor Almendros
P: Alan J. Pakula
A: Meryl Streep, Kevin Kline
Brooklyn. A woman who lives with a scholar looks back on her life with her children in a Nazi concentration camp, where she made many painful choices in order to survive.
Awards: Academy Awards, Best Actress, 1983; Golden Globes, Best Actress, 1983; Kinema Junpo Awards, Best Foreign Film, 1983

2021. ***Born in Flames***   1983 DP
D: Lizzie Borden
S: Ed Bowes
C: Ed Bowes
P: Lizzie Borden
A: Honey, Adele Bertei, Pat Murphy, Kathryn Bigelow, Sheila McLaughlin
The near future. Ten years after a socialist victory, there is continuing revolution over still unaddressed economic discrimination. The result is radical feminism on the radio and a "women's army" in the streets. All gets dryly critiqued— the socialists, who are blind to the classist, racist status quo; the cultural radicals; and the

political radicals, as the president proposes pay for housewives. An explosive cover-up of the murder of a black lesbian leader brings this quintessential mix of New York rap, reggae, and punk expression to its ongoing topic end, a terrorist bombing.
Awards: Berlin International Film Festival, Jury Prize, 1983; Créteil International Women's Film Festival, Grand Prix, 1983

2022. ***Committed***   1983 DSP
D: Sheila McLaughlin, Lynne Littman
S: Sheila McLaughlin, Lynne Littman
C: Heinz Emigholz
P: Sheila McLaughlin, Lynne Littman
A: Sheila McLaughlin, Victoria Boothby
1950s. The life of Frances Farmer, a Hollywood actress who was committed to a mental institution. *FII.*

2023. ***Cross Creek***   1983 S
D: Martin Ritt
S: Dalene Young; based on memoirs by Marjorie Kinnan Rawlings
C: John Alonzo
P: Robert Radnitz
A: Mary Steenburgen, Alfre Woodard
Marjorie Kinnan Rawlings, author of *The Yearling*, moves to the Florida bayou for peace and quiet, where she is cared for by an African American servant.
Awards: Academy Awards, nomination for Best Supporting Actress (Woodard)

2024. ***Heart like a Wheel***   1983
D: Jonathan Kaplan
S: Ken Friedman
C: Tak Fujimoto
P: Charles Roven
A: Bonnie Bedelia
A race-car driver struggles to keep the support of the men around her and to win.
Awards: Golden Globes, nomination for Best Actress, 1984

2025. ***Love Letters***   1983 DS
D: Amy Holden Jones
S: Amy Holden Jones
C: Alex Birschfeld
P: Don Levin
A: Jamie Lee Curtis, James Keach, Amy Madigan
Los Angeles, Venice. A classical disc jockey uncovers her mother's love affair after her death and struggles with her repellent feelings for her father, whom she knows her mother married because she was pregnant. She begins an affair

with a married photographer and stalks his family, but she has a friend to help her.

2026. *El Norte* 1983 SP
D: Gregory Nava
S: Anna Thomas, Gregory Nava
C: James Glennon
P: Trevor Black, Anna Thomas, Bertha Navarro
A: Zaide Silvia Gutiérrez, David Villalpando
A sister and brother flee violence in Guatemala for a new life as illegal immigrants in Los Angeles, where she works cleaning large homes.
Awards: Montréal World Film Festival, Grand Prix, 1984

2027. *Scarred* 1983 DSP
D: Rose-Marie Turko
S: Rose-Marie Turko
C: Michael Miner
P: Rose-Marie Turko
A: Jennifer Mayo
A teenage mother is forced into prostitution in order to take care of her baby. *AMG*.

2028. *Silkwood* 1983 S
D: Mike Nichols
S: Alice Arlen, Nora Ephron
C: Miroslav Ondricek
P: Michael Hausman
A: Meryl Streep, Cher, Kurt Russell
Workers at a nuclear plant suffer contamination and blow the whistle on unsafe conditions. One, Karen Silkwood, is particularly confrontational and begins to talk to the media, gain celebrity, and gather evidence until she is suspiciously killed in an auto accident. Her unconventional domestic life—children left with their father, a current lover, and a lesbian best friend—is related to her character. Based on a true story.
Awards: Academy Awards, nominations for Best Screenplay, Best Actress (Streep), and Best Supporting Actress (Cher), 1984; Golden Globes, Best Supporting Actress (Cher), 1984

2029. *Terms of Endearment* 1983
D: James L. Brooks
S: James L. Brooks; based on the novel by Larry McMurtry
C: Andrzej Bartkowiak
P: James L. Brooks
A: Debra Winger, Shirley MacLaine, Jack Nicholson
A domineering mother and her daughter are very close until Mom disapproves of her daughter's choice of husband. Years go by, grandchildren arrive, the daughter becomes terminally ill with cancer, and Mom never lets go of her obnoxious, occasionally kindly, "mother knows best" persona.
Awards: Academy Awards, Best Picture, Best Director, Best Actress (MacLaine), 1984; David di Donatello Awards, Best Foreign Actress (MacLaine), 1984; Golden Globes, Best Screenplay, Best Actress (MacLaine), 1984

2030. *Testament* 1983 DSP
D: Lynne Littman
S: Carol Amen, John Sacret Young
C: Stephen Poster
P: Lynne Littman
A: Jane Alexander
California suburbia. A woman and her children survive a nuclear bomb attack but are left completely isolated and on their own.
Awards: Academy Awards, nomination for Best Actress, 1984

2031. *Variety* 1983 DSP
D: Bette Gordon
S: Bette Gordon, Kathy Acker
C: John Forster, Tom DiCillo
P: Renée Shatransky, Arnold Abelson
A: Sandy McLeod
A feminist sells tickets at a porno theater in Times Square to earn a living; one patron attracts her, and she follows him into an adult video store, then continues to stalk him. *Variety: 22. 1983, Sep. 21.*

2032. *Choose Me* 1984 P
D: Alan Rudolph
S: Alan Rudolph
P: David Blocker, Carolyn Pfeiffer
A: Geneviève Bujold, Lesley Ann Warren, Rae Dawn Chong, Keith Carradine
A radio psychiatrist, herself maladjusted, tries to solve problems of people who call.
Awards: Toronto International Film Festival, FIPRESCI, 1984

2033. *The Dollmaker* 1984 S
D: Donald Petrie
S: Susan Cooper, Hume Cronyn; based on the novel by Harriet Arnow
C: Paul Lohmann
P: Bill Finnegan
A: Jane Fonda
A doll maker from rural Kentucky moves to the slums of Detroit when her husband seeks work as a mechanic. *Working Stiffs.*
Awards: Emmy Awards, Outstanding Lead Actress in a Limited Series or a Special, 1984; Directors

Guild of America, Outstanding Achievement, 1985

2034. *Goodbye New York*   1984
D: Amos Kollek
S: Amos Kollek
C: Amnon Salomon, Amos Kollek
A: Julie Hagerty
An American woman leaves for Paris, where she finds her husband with someone else, then goes on to Tel Aviv, where she settles in a kibbutz. *AMG.*

2035. *The Little Drummer Girl*   1984
D: George Roy Hill
S: Loring Mandel; based on the novel by John Le Carré
C: Wolfgang Treu
P: Robert Crawford
A: Diane Keaton
An actress, outspoken in her support of the Palestinian cause, is lured by an attraction to an Israeli intelligence man into infiltrating a Palestinian family by impersonating a friend of theirs. The Palestinians then send her to be trained as a terrorist, and she becomes increasingly confused by her many close relationships and her understanding of both sides.

2036. *Mrs. Soffel*   1984 D
D: Gillian Armstrong
S: Ron Nyswaner
C: Russell Boyd
P: Scott Rudin, Edgar Sherick
A: Diane Keaton, Mel Gibson
1900s. A warden's wife leaves her family to help a prisoner, with whom she has fallen in love, escape. Based on a true story.

2037. *Not for Publication*   1984 P
D: Paul Bartel
S: Paul Bartel
C: George Tirl
P: Anne Kimmel
A: Nancy Allen
A farce about a *National Enquirer* writer who moonlights as a political aide, uncovers corruption, and regains control of her father's newspaper. *AMG.*

2038. *Places in the Heart*   1984 P
D: Robert Benton
S: Robert Benton
C: Nestor Almendros
P: Arlene Donovan
A: Sally Field
Waxahachie, Texas, 1930s. After a town sheriff is murdered by a young black boy, his wife must work their cotton farm and take care of their two children; two men help, a black field worker and a blind World War I veteran. *FII.*
Awards: Academy Awards, Best Actress, 1984

2039. *Streetwalkin'*   1984 DS
D: Joan Freeman
S: Joan Freeman, Robert Alden
C: Steven Fierberg
P: Roger Corman
A: Melissa Leo
New York City. A young runaway falls in love with a pimp, then prostitutes to support herself and her brother; when she see the pimp nearly murder another of his girls who wants to quit, she runs away. "Emphasizes the physical abuse of young women." Exploitation. *AMG.*

2040. *Swing Shift*   1984 S
D: Jonathan Demme
S: Nancy Dowd, Bo Goldman
C: Tak Fujimoto
P: Jerry Bick
A: Goldie Hawn, Christine Lahti
World War II. Two women enjoy their newfound work in an airplane factory; one must contend with a husband away at the front and has an affair with a coworker.
Awards: New York Film Critics Circle Awards, Best Supporting Actress (Lahti), 1984

2041. *Agnes of God*   1985
D: Norman Jewison
S: John Pielmeier
C: Sven Nykvist
P: Norman Jewison
A: Jane Fonda, Anne Bancroft, Meg Tilly
The abbess of a convent warily receives a court-appointed psychiatrist assigned to assess a novice who has been found with a dead infant and who believes she had a "virgin birth." The doctor inserts her personal secular values into the religious environment and conflicts with the abbess.
Awards: Golden Globes, Best Supporting Actress (Tilly), 1985

2042. *The Color Purple*   1985 S
D: Steven Spielberg
S: Menno Meyjes; based on the novel by Alice Walker
C: Allen Daviau
P: Quincy Jones
A: Whoopi Goldberg, Margaret Avery, Oprah Winfrey

Early twentieth century. Chronicles thirty years in the life of a young African American girl, who at fourteen becomes pregnant by her father and suffers many more abuses. She is forced into marriage to a man who brings his mistress into their home, and she becomes attracted to the woman, even running away with her for a brief period of time.

Awards: Golden Globes, Best Actress (Goldberg), 1986; Image Awards, Outstanding Motion Picture, Outstanding Actress (Goldberg), 1988

2043. *Compromising Positions*   1985 S
D: Frank Perry
S: Susan Isaacs
C: Barry Sonnenfeld
P: Frank Perry
A: Susan Sarandon

A former newspaperwoman and suburban matron gets involved in solving the neighborhood murder of a dentist. Comedy. *Chicago Sun-Times. 1985, Aug. 30.*

2044. *Desert Hearts*   1985 DSP
D: Donna Deitch
S: Natalie Cooper; based on the novel by Jane Rule
C: Robert Elswit
P: Donna Deitch
A: Helen Shaver, Patricia Charbonneau

Reno, Nevada, 1950s. An east coast professor, not very happy, arrives for a divorce and becomes involved with a local woman.

Awards: Locarno International Film Festival, Bronze Leopard (Shaver) 1985; Sundance Film Festival, Honorable Mention, 1986

2045. *Desperately Seeking Susan*   1985 DSP
D: Susan Seidelman
S: Leora Barish
C: Edward Lachman
P: Midge Sanford
A: Rosanna Arquette, Madonna

A story of games between an attractive, free-spirited woman and her suburban housewife admirer. Comedy.

Awards: BAFTA Awards, Best Actress (Arquette), 1986

2046. *Marie*   1985
D: Roger Donaldson
S: John Briley, Peter Maas
C: Chris Menges
P: Elliot Schick
A: Sissy Spacek

Tennessee. A mother walks out on an abusive relationship, then gets herself an education

and a good job with the government, eventually becoming the head of the parole board. There she finds that her mentor is involved in corruption, but she insists on exposing it, even at great risk to her livelihood. Based on a true story.

2047. *Mask*   1985 S
D: Peter Bogdanovich
S: Anna Hamilton Phelan
C: László Kovács
P: Martin Starger
A: Cher, Eric Stoltz

California. A biker mother of a very bright teenager disfigured with a fatal illness works hard to keep him happy and to get her own life together. They are both given solid support from other kind and caring gang members.

Awards: Cannes Film Festival, Best Actress, 1985; Writers Guild of America, nomination for Best Screenplay, 1986

2048. *Naked Vengeance*   1985
D: Cirio Santiago
S: Reilly Askew
C: Ricardo Remias
P: Anthony Maharaj
A: Deborah Tranelli

An actress seeks solace at her parents' home after her husband is murdered, but she only runs into more trouble and is forced to pursue revenge. Exploitation. *Variety: 16. 1986, June 11.*

2049. *Out of Africa*   1985 S
D: Sydney Pollack
S: Kurt Luedtke; based on an autobiography by Isak Dinesen
C: David Watkin
P: Sydney Pollack
A: Meryl Streep, Robert Redford

The story of Isak Dinesen's early, romantic life. She marries a titled gentlemen, who settles her in Kenya but takes little responsibility for the home. Strong willed, she takes care of the ranch by herself and falls in love with a local adventurer.

Awards: Los Angeles Film Critics Association, Best Actress, 1985; Academy Awards, Best Picture, 1986

2050. *Plenty*   1985
D: Fred Schepisi
S: David Hare
C: Ian Baker
P: Joseph Rapp, Edward Pressman
A: Meryl Streep

A World War II resistance fighter moves aggressively into the postwar world, determined to find a fulfilling life yet remaining dissatisfied. *AMG.*

2051. *Sweet Dreams* 1985
D: Karel Reisz
S: Robert Getchell
C: Robbie Greenberg
P: Bernard Schwartz
A: Jessica Lange, Ed Harris
1950s. The story of Patsy Cline, her rise from humble origins, and her working-class marriage, which is put under pressure by her ambition and success. Songs are dubbed with the real voice of Patsy Cline.
Awards: Academy Awards, nomination for Best Actress, 1985

2052. *Wildrose* 1985 P
D: John Hanson
S: Eugene Corr
C: Peter Stein
P: Sandra Schulberg
A: Lisa Eichhorn
A woman drives a dump truck in a Minnesota strip mine for a living and builds herself a log cabin in her spare time. *Working Stiffs.*

2053. *84 Charing Cross Road* 1986 S
D: David Jones
S: Helen Hanff; based on her book
C: Brian West
P: Geoffrey Helman
A: Anne Bancroft, Anthony Hopkins
1940s. A literary enthusiast in New York City corresponds at length with a bookseller in the United Kingdom; after many years, she travels to London and meets him.
Awards: BAFTA Awards, Best Actress, 1988; USC Scripter Award, 1989

2054. *Crimes of the Heart* 1986 S
D: Bruce Beresford
S: Beth Henley
C: Dante Spinotti
P: Freddie Fields
A: Diane Keaton, Jessica Lange, Sissy Spacek
Three sisters reunite for the oldest sister's birthday.

2055. *Extremities* 1986
D: Robert M. Young
S: William Mastrosimone
C: Curtis Clark
P: Burt Sugarman
A: Farrah Fawcett
A woman is frightened by a man who assaulted her; the police do nothing, so the next time he visits she vigorously does battle with him, locking him up in her house.
Awards: Golden Globes, nomination for Best Actress, 1987

2056. *Heartburn* 1986 S
D: Mike Nichols
S: Nora Ephron; based on her novel
C: Nestor Almendros
P: Mike Nichols
A: Meryl Streep, Jack Nicholson
Washington, D.C. A marriage between two journalists endures a house renovation, the births of two children, and a separation over the man's affair. The marriage ends when he continues to be unfaithful and the wife realizes she was deluded, "living a dream."
Awards: Valladolid International Film Festival, Best Actress, 1986

2057. *Magdalena Viraga* 1986 DSCP
D: Nina Menkes
S: Nina Menkes
C: Nina Menkes
P: Nina Menkes
A: Claire Aguilar, Tinka Menkes
An experimental narrative of a prostitute and nine clients, each encounter the same, all shot in a grainy blue-tinged light. *Festival de films, 9th: 21. 1987.*

2058. *The Morning After* 1986
D: Sidney Lumet
S: James Hicks
C: Andrzej Bartkowiak
P: Bruce Gilbert
A: Jane Fonda, Jeff Bridges
An alcoholic woman wakes up in a strange apartment next to a murdered man. Thriller.
Awards: Academy Awards, nomination for Best Actress, 1987

2059. *'Night, Mother* 1986 S
D: Tom Moore
S: Marsha Norman, based on her play
C: Stephen Katz
P: Alan Greisman
A: Sissy Spacek, Anne Bancroft
A mother deals with her epileptic middle-aged daughter's determination to commit suicide. *AMG.*
Awards: Golden Globes, nomination for Best Actress (Bancroft), 1987

2060. *Nobody's Fool*				1986 DS
D: Evelyn Purcell
S: Beth Henley
C: Mikhail Suslov
P: Jon Denny
A: Rosanna Arquette, Eric Roberts
Los Angeles. A pregnant woman gives up her baby after attacking her lover for refusing to marry her, then regrets it. He marries a wealthy woman instead, and she finds an affair with a stage technician helps her recover. *MFB, no. 641: 182–83. 1987, Jun.*

2061. *Peggy Sue Got Married*			1986 S
D: Francis Coppola
S: Jerry Leichtling, Arlene Sarner
C: Jordan Cronenweth
P: Paul Gurian
A: Kathleen Turner
At her high school reunion, a woman travels back into her teenage days and revisits her decision to marry the husband who has disappointed her. Comedy.
Awards: Academy Awards, nomination for Best Actress, 1987; National Board of Review, Best Actress, 1987

2062. *She's Gotta Have It*			1986 P
D: Spike Lee
S: Spike Lee
C: Ernest Dickerson
P: Pamm R. Jackson
A: Tracy Camilla Johns
Brooklyn. An African American woman has three lovers but refuses to commit to any one.
Awards: Independent Spirit Awards, Best First Feature, 1987

2063. *Sleepwalk*					1986 DSP
D: Sara Driver
S: Sara Driver, Lorenzo Mans
C: Jim Jarmusch
P: Kathleen Brennan
A: Ann Magnuson, Suzanne Fletcher
A typesetter is hired to translate a Chinese manuscript, and the effort provokes mysterious, even supernatural, events. She becomes involved in a murder, and her son is kidnapped. She searches for him on her own. Mystery. *Variety: 22. 1986, May 14.*

2064. *Waiting for the Moon*			1986 DP
D: Jill Godmilow
S: Mark Magill
C: André Neau
P: Sandra Schulberg
A: Linda Hunt, Linda Bassett
A portrait of the charmed life of noted lesbian couple Gertrude Stein and Alice B. Toklas, in their Paris apartment, country home, and imported automobile. The film is stripped down to readings and rewritings, neighborly generosity, the casual taking on of a baby, a rehearsal for one of Stein's plays, meetings with Hemingway and Apollonaire, and petty quarrels. The bickering is a special theme, revealing intimacy of the kind that film scripts usually omit.
Awards: Sundance Film Festival, Grand Jury Prize, 1987

2065. *Working Girls*				1986 DSCP
D: Lizzie Borden
S: Lizzie Borden, Sandra Kay
C: Judy Irola
P: Lizzie Borden
A: Louise Smith, Deborah Banks, Liz Caldwell
New York City. A documentary-like day in the life of upscale prostitutes, with an emphasis on the worklike environment, the functional architecture, the routine practicalities of pleasing clients, and the women's support of one another. The main character is a Yale-educated woman with a lesbian partner and a child.
Awards: Sundance Film Festival, Special Jury Prize, 1987; Independent Spirit Awards, nomination for Best Female Lead (Smith), 1988

2066. *Anna*					1987 DS
D: Linda Christanell
S: Agnieszka Holland, Yurek Bogayevicz
A: Sally Kirkland, Pauline Porizkova
A Czech immigrant arrives in New York City looking for her hero, an exiled Czech actress; they become friends, but the older woman becomes jealous of the younger woman's success. *Time Out.*
Awards: Golden Globes, Best Actress (Kirkland), 1988; Independent Spirit Awards, Best Female Lead (Kirkland), 1988; Los Angeles Film Critics Association, Best Actress (Kirkland), 1988

2067. *Baby Boom*					1987 SP
D: Charles Shyer
S: Charles Shyer, Nancy Myers
C: William Fraker
P: Nancy Myers, Bruce Block
A: Diane Keaton, Sam Shepard
New York City. A businesswoman suddenly inherits a newborn, whom she does her best to reject, but they bond without her realizing it. Stuck alone with the child, she leaves her job and buys a farm in Vermont, where she sets up a successful applesauce business—and finds love, too. Comedy.

2068. Black Widow   1987
D: Bob Rafelson
S: Ronald Bass
C: Conrad Hall
P: Laurence Mark
A: Debra Winger, Theresa Russell
A detective becomes intrigued by a serial killer of
   wealthy husbands and demands to be sent out
   to pursue the suspect; following the suspect to
   Hawaii, the detective makes friends with her, but
   she is discovered and becomes a target herself.

2069. Broadcast News   1987
D: James L. Brooks
S: James L. Brooks
C: Michael Ballhaus
P: James L. Brooks
A: Holly Hunter, William Hurt
An extremely bright producer becomes upset
   when her male friend is passed over for hir-
   ing as a newscaster in favor of a polished man
   who is not as bright as they are. The new man
   does offer a groundbreaking story on date rape,
   however, and wins the producer's heart—until
   she discovers that he faked his own tears dur-
   ing the show.
Awards: Berlin International Film Festival, Best
   Actress, 1988; Boston Society of Film Critics
   Awards, Best Actress, 1988

2070. Call Me   1987 DS
D: Sollace Mitchell
S: Karyn Kay, Sollace Mitchell
C: Zoltan David
P: Kenneth Martel
A: Patricia Charbonneau
A woman is intrigued by an obscene phone call and
   becomes involved in a murder. AMG.
Awards: Mystfest, Best Story, 1988

2071. Fatal Attraction   1987 P
D: Adrian Lyne
S: Nicholas Meyer
C: Howard Atherton
P: Sherry Lansing
A: Glenn Close, Michael Douglas, Anne Archer
A woman seduces a cynical married man, then
   decides to make him pay for his cheating and
   attacks him in his home. Thriller.
Awards: Academy Awards, nominations for Best
   Actress (Close) and Best Supporting Actress
   (Archer), 1988

2072. Forever, Lulu   1987 C
D: Amos Kollek
S: Amos Kollek

C: Lisa Rinzler
P: Amos Kollek
A: Hanna Schygulla, Debbie Harry
New York. "Emigrant writer has adventures that
   bring her fame and fortune." Comedy. West Ger-
   man Cinema.
Other titles: Für immer: Lulu

2073. Housekeeping   1987 S
D: Bill Forsyth
S: Bill Forsyth; based on the novel by Marilynne
   Robinson
C: Michael Coulter
P: Robert Colesberry
A: Christine Lahti
1950s. Two orphaned girls live with a liberated,
   eccentric aunt and over time develop very dif-
   ferent views of her. One needs the approval of
   the conventional world, while the other remains
   captivated by her caretaker.
Awards: Tokyo International Film Festival, Best
   Screenplay, Special Jury Prize, 1987

2074. Lady Beware   1987 DS
D: Karen Arthur
S: Susan Miller, Charles Zev Cohen
C: Tom Neuwirth
P: Tony Scotti
A: Diane Lane
Pittsburgh. A window dresser acquires fame with
   "punky avant-garde displays" and is stalked by
   a married man. She responds "not in the tradi-
   tional film manner" by turning the tables on him.
   Thriller. AMG. Also Variety. 1987, Sep. 23.

2075. Light of Day   1987
D: Paul Schrader
S: Paul Schrader
C: John Bailey
P: Keith Barish
A: Gena Rowlands, Joan Jett, Michael J. Fox
A singer fronts a punk band with her more strait-
   laced younger brother, then conflicts with him
   over their mother's sickbed.

2076. Making Mr. Right   1987 DS
D: Susan Seidelman
S: Floyd Byars, Laurie Frank
C: Edward Lachman
P: Joel Tuber
A: Ann Magnuson, John Malkovich
A woman helps a scientist give his robot human
   emotions and behavior. Comedy.

2077. Outrageous Fortune   1987 S
D: Arthur Hill

S: Leslie Dixon
C: David Walsh
P: Ted Field
A: Bette Midler, Shelley Long
Two acting classmates discover they share a lover, then find adventure in searching for him. Comedy.
Awards: Golden Globes, nomination for Best Actress (Midler), 1988

2078. *Overboard*   1987 SP
D: Garry Marshall
S: Leslie Dixon
C: John Alonzo
P: Alexandra Rose
A: Goldie Hawn, Kurt Russell
A millionaire falls out of her yacht and into an amnesiac relationship with a carpenter and his family. Comedy.

2079. *She Must Be Seeing Things*   1987 DSP
D: Sheila McLaughlin
S: Sheila McLaughlin
C: Mark Daniels
P: Sheila McLaughlin
A: Sheila Dabney, Lois Weaver
A black Brazilian civil rights lawyer and a white filmmaker are lovers. When the director is away making a film about a seventeenth-century nun, the lawyer reads her diary and becomes jealous imagining the encounters in the diary are with men; her fantasies blend with scenes from the film, allowing the film to comment on the relationship of lesbian eroticism to voyeurism. *Festival de films, 9th: 20. 1987.*

2080. *Shy People*   1987 S
D: Andrei Konchalovsky
S: Gérard Brach, Marjorie David
C: Chris Menges
P: Menahem Globus
A: Jill Clayburgh, Barbara Hershey, Martha Plimpton
Louisiana. A New York magazine writer and her daughter, who are already having trouble getting along, visit their family in the bayou and run into a strong-minded aunt and cousins, which provides the stage for a culture clash. *Variety: 28. 1987, May 20.*
Awards: Cannes Film Festival, Best Actress (Hershey), 1987

2081. *Siesta*   1987 DS
D: Mary Lambert
S: Patrice Chaplin, Patricia Louisianna Knop
C: Bryan Loftus

P: Gary Kurfirst
A: Ellen Barkin, Gabriel Byrne, Jodie Foster, Isabella Rossellini
A daredevil skydiver wakes up at the end of an airport runway in Spain. The fragmented story relates her decision five days earlier to find a man she still loves but who, like her, is married to someone else. He does not respond, but she stays around an expatriate English crowd in hopes of seducing him. *Variety: 15. 1987, Oct. 21.*

2082. *Summer Heat*   1987 DS
D: Michie Gleason
S: Michie Gleason, Louise Shivers; based on *Here to Get My Baby Out of Jail* by Louise Shivers
C: Elliot Davis
P: William Tennant
A: Lori Singer, Anthony Edwards, Kathy Bates
North Carolina, 1930s. A bored wife has an affair with a new man in town, who ingratiates himself to her husband, then boards on their farm, then plots to harm the husband. *Variety: 108. 1987, May 20.*

2083. *The Whales of August*   1987 P
D: Lindsay Anderson
S: David Berry
C: Mike Fash
P: Carolyn Pfeiffer
A: Bette Davis, Lillian Gish, Ann Sothern
One aged sister takes care of the other, who is blind. A male neighbor attempts to take advantage by suggesting they all live together, and another younger woman neighbor is an old friend.
Awards: Academy Awards, nomination for Best Supporting Actress (Sothern), 1987; National Board of Review, Best Actress (Gish), 1987

2084. *The Witches of Eastwick*   1987
D: George Miller
S: Michael Cristofer; based on the novel by John Updike
C: Vilmos Zsigmond
P: Neil Canton
A: Cher, Susan Sarandon, Michelle Pfeiffer, Jack Nicholson
Three single women conjure up a new neighbor and then grovel for "the little devil's" attention. Comedy.

2085. *The Accused*   1988 P
D: Jonathan Kaplan
S: Tom Topor
C: Ralf Bode
P: Sherry Lansing
A: Kelly McGillis, Jodie Foster

A waitress has a fight with her trailer-park boyfriend and flees to a neighborhood bar. The story of her gang rape that follows is told in flashback from the perspective of the trial that ensues and the victim's relationship with her lawyer.
Awards: Academy Awards, Best Actress (Foster), 1989; Berlin International Film Festival, Golden Bear, 1989; David di Donatello Awards, Best Actress (Foster), 1989; Golden Globes, Best Actress (Foster), 1989

2086. *Another Woman* 1988
D: Woody Allen
S: Woody Allen
C: Sven Nykvist
P: Robert Greenhut
A: Gena Rowlands, Sandy Dennis, Mia Farrow
The sessions of a male psychiatrist and female patient are overheard by a professor who has rented the apartment next door in order to write a book; hearing the patient's questioning, the professor begins to question her own relationships and life. *Time Out.*

2087. *Beaches* 1988 SP
D: Garry Marshall
S: Mary Agnes Donoghue; based on the novel by Iris Rainer Dart
C: Dante Spinotti
P: Bonnie Bruckheimer, Bette Midler
A: Bette Midler, Barbara Hershey
An entertainer and a wealthy lawyer, who met in Atlantic City in their youth, remain friends for many years.

2088. *Cannibal Women in the Avocado Jungle of Death* 1988
D: J. F. Lawton
S: J. F. Lawton
C: Robert Knouse
P: Gary Goldstein
A: Shannon Tweed, Adrienne Barbeau, Bill Maher
Comedy of a feminist professor hired to investigate an avocado shortage in a jungle ruled by the Piranha Women.

2089. *Crossing Delancey* 1988 DS
D: Joan Micklin Silver
S: Susan Sandler
C: Theo Van de Sande
P: Michael Nozik
A: Amy Irving, Peter Riegert, Reizl Bozyk
A Jewish single woman, who is happy with her life and job in a New York bookshop, resists her family's matchmaking but eventually warms to the traditional man her grandmother's match-

maker has found for her.

2090. *The Good Mother* 1988 S
D: Leonard Nimoy
S: Michael Bortman; based on the novel by Sue Miller
C: David Watkin
P: Arne Glimcher
A: Diane Keaton, Liam Neeson
A mother is determined to raise a liberated child but loses custody of her daughter to her ex-husband over a sexual incident with her lover.

2091. *Gorillas in the Mist* 1988 S
D: Michael Apted
S: Anna Hamilton Phelan, Tab Murphy
C: John Seale
P: Terence A. Clegg
A: Sigourney Weaver
A biography of scientist Dian Fossey, who studied endangered apes in Africa and fought the Ugandan government to save them from being poached.
Awards: Golden Globes, Best Actress, 1989

2092. *Heart of Midnight* 1988
D: Matthew Chapman
S: Matthew Chapman
C: Ray Rivas
P: Andrew Gaty
A: Jennifer Jason Leigh, Peter Coyote
While recovering from a nervous breakdown, a woman inherits a nightclub from her uncle. Thriller. *AMG.*
Awards: Catalonian International Film Festival, Best Film, 1989

2093. *Married to the Mob* 1988
D: Jonathan Demme
S: Barry Strugatz, Mark R. Burns
C: Tak Fujimoto
P: Kenneth Utt
A: Michelle Pfeiffer, Mercedes Ruehl, Dean Stockwell
A woman tries to escape her mob associations but can't. Comedy.
Awards: Golden Globes, nomination for Best Actress (Pfeiffer), 1989; National Society of Film Critics Awards, Best Supporting Actress (Ruehl), 1989

2094. *Mystic Pizza* 1988 S
D: Donald Petrie
S: Amy Holden Jones
C: Tim Suhrstedt
P: Mark Levinson
A: Annabeth Gish, Julia Roberts, Lili Taylor
Mystic, Connecticut. Three waitresses, just out of

high school, work in a pizza parlor and negotiate their ambitions with their working-class
backgrounds.
Awards: Independent Spirit Awards, Best First Feature, 1989

2095. *Punchline* 1988
D: David Seltzer
S: David Seltzer
C: Reynaldo Villalobos
P: Daniel Melnick
A: Sally Field, Tom Hanks
New York City. A suburban housewife pursues her
dream of being a stand-up comic, with the help
of a man who knows the ropes.

2096. *Sticky Fingers* 1988 DSP
D: Catlin Adams
S: Catlin Adams, Melanie Mayron
C: Gary Thieltges
P: Catlin Adams, Melanie Mayron
A: Helen Slater, Melanie Mayron, Eileen Brennan
Two impoverished musicians find $1 million in drug
money and cannot resist spending it, adding ten-
sion to their close relationship and getting them
chased. Comedy. *Variety: 244. 1988, May 4.*

2097. *The Wash* 1988
D: Michael Toshiyuki Uno
S: Philip Kan Gotanda
C: Walt Lloyd
P: Calvin Skaggs
A: Nobu McCarthy, Mako
A seventy-year-old Japanese American, dissatisfied
with a cold marital relationship, separates from
her husband but continues to do his wash, even
as she begins a new relationship. *Variety: 24.
1988, May 25.*
Awards: Independent Spirit Awards, nomination for
Best Female Lead, 1989

2098. *Working Girl* 1988
D: Mike Nichols
S: Kevin Wade
C: Michael Ballhaus
P: Douglas Wick
A: Melanie Griffith, Sigourney Weaver, Harrison
Ford
An assistant who has her ideas stolen by her fe-
male boss gets back by taking advantage and
posing as the boss when the boss is away.
Awards: Golden Globes, Best Film, Best Actress
(Griffith), Best Supporting Actress (Weaver), 1989

2099. *Zelly and Me* 1988 DSP
D: Tina Rathborne

S: Tina Rathborne
C: Mikael Salomon
P: Sue Jett
A: Isabella Rossellini, Alexandra Jones, Glynis Johns
Virginia. An orphaned rich girl being raised by her
wealthy, cold grandmother grows closer to her
nanny, who tries to save her. She is denied even the
expression of affection for dolls, and so she turns a
pair of socks into dolls she can confide to at night;
these fantasies of resistance lead her to identify
with Joan of Arc. *Festival de films, 11th: 23. 1989.*

2100. *Brenda Starr* 1989 S
D: Robert Ellis Miller
S: Noreen Stone, James D. Buchanan, Jenny Wol-
kind; based on the comic strip by Dale Messick
C: Freddie Francis
P: Myron Hyman
A: Brooke Shields
A reporter has problems being appreciated by her
comic-strip artist, so she disappears and goes off
to the Amazon jungle to find a scientist with a
secret formula. Comedy, action. *Atlanta Journal-
Constitution: C5. 1992, May 12.*

2101. *Long Walk Home* 1989
D: Richard Pearce
S: John Cork, Randy Meyer
C: Roger Deakins
P: Dave Bell
A: Sissy Spacek, Whoopi Goldberg
Montgomery, Alabama, 1950s. Two women, one
black, one white, become activists during the
bus boycotts of the civil rights movement.
Awards: Image Awards, nomination for Outstanding
Actress (Goldberg), 1993

2102. *Music Box* 1989
D: Costa-Gavras
S: Joe Eszterhas
C: Patrick Blossier
P: Irwin Winkler
A: Jessica Lange
A criminal attorney defends her Hungarian father,
who is threatened with deportation for war
crimes committed during World War II. *FII.*
Awards: Academy Awards, nomination for Best
Actress, 1989

2103. *Steel Magnolias* 1989
D: Herbert Ross
S: Robert Harling
C: John Alonzo
P: Ray Stark
A: Sally Field, Dolly Parton, Shirley MacLaine, Daryl
Hannah, Olympia Dukakis, Julia Roberts

A mother conflicts with her grown diabetic daughter when she insists on bearing a child even though she and her husband have been warned of the risks. After the birth leaves her debilitated, the mother offers one of her kidneys, but the daughter dies. Friends who congregate around the beauty parlor help them through the ordeal, which takes place in a spacious small town.

Awards: Golden Globes, Best Supporting Actress (Roberts), 1990

2104. *True Love*   1989 DSC
D: Nancy Savoca
S: Nancy Savoca, Richard Guay
C: Lisa Rinzler
P: Richard Guay, Shelley Houis
A: Annabella Sciorra, Ron Eldard
An Italian American couple has been engaged a long time; the film closely documents the wedding and its preparations. But the bride's suspicions that something is wrong are confirmed when her husband announces he is going to spend their wedding night drinking with his friends. *Chicago Sun-Times. 1989, Sep. 15.*

Awards: San Sebastián International Film Festival, OCIC Award, 1989; Sundance Film Festival, Grand Jury Prize, 1989

2105. *The Witches*   1989
D: Nicolas Roeg
S: Roald Dahl, Allan Scott
C: Harvey Harrison
P: Mark Shivas
A: Anjelica Huston, Mai Zetterling
A nine-year-old boy and his grandmother discover a "convention of witches" with "a plan to turn all the children of England into mice." *AMG.*

Awards: Los Angeles Film Critics Association, Best Actress (Huston), 1990; Boston Society of Film Critics Awards, Best Actress (Huston), 1991

2106. *Blue Steel*   1990 DS
D: Kathryn Bigelow
S: Kathryn Bigelow, Eric Red
C: Amir Mokri
P: Oliver Stone
A: Jamie Lee Curtis
A rookie cop with a difficult relationship with her cop father also has a perceived history of poor judgment that gets her grounded; she dates a psychopath, whom she is unaware has stolen her gun and taken to stalking her. Action.

Awards: Mystfest, Best Actress, 1990

2107. *The End of Innocence*   1990 DS
D: Dyan Cannon

S: Dyan Cannon
C: Alex Nepomniaschy
P: Vince Cannon
A: Dyan Cannon, Rebecca Schaeffer
A woman looks back on her selfish parents and her eventual breakdown and placement in a mental institution. *AMG.*

2108. *The Handmaid's Tale*   1990 S
D: Volker Schlöndorff
S: Harold Pinter; based on the novel by Margaret Atwood
C: Igor Luther
P: Daniel Wilson
A: Natasha Richardson, Faye Dunaway, Elizabeth McGovern
Reproduction in a future religious fundamentalist society is organized for the purpose of making babies for a mostly sterile upper class through surrogate slaves.

Awards: GLAAD Media Awards, Outstanding Film, 1991

2109. *Henry and June*   1990 S
D: Philip Kaufman
S: Philip Kaufman, Rose Kaufman; based on *The Diaries of Anaïs Nin*
C: Philippe Rousselot
A: Maria De Medeiros, Fred Ward, Uma Thurman
Paris, 1930s. Anaïs Nin, in a conventional marriage, meets the bohemian-living Henry and June Miller and falls in love with both. They experiment with their love lives but mostly write and talk about their writing. *Festival de films, 23rd: 82. 2001.*

2110. *Impulse*   1990 DS
D: Sondra Locke
S: John DeMarco, Leigh Chapman
C: Dean Semler
P: Albert Ruddy
A: Theresa Russell
Los Angeles. An undercover vice cop with a smart mouth and a sexist boss has trouble curbing her impulses, as she likes the power she has over the men she entraps. Action.

2111. *In the Spirit*   1990 DSP
D: Sandra Seacat
S: Jeannie Berlin, Laurie Jones
C: Richard Quinlan
P: Julian Schlossberg, Beverly Irby
A: Jeannie Berlin, Marlo Thomas, Elaine May, Olympia Dukakis
Comedy about a New Yorker who hires a "ditzy psychic" to decorate her apartment. *AMG.*

2112. The Lemon Sisters 1990 DP
D: Joyce Chopra
S: Jeremy Pikser
C: Bobby Byrne
P: Diane Keaton
A: Diane Keaton, Carol Kane, Kathryn Grody
Atlantic City, 1980s. Three friends cover songs from 1960s "girl groups" in Atlantic City. Comedy. *AMG.*

2113. Men Don't Leave 1990 S
D: Paul Brickman
S: Barbara Benedek, Paul Brickman
C: Bruce Surtees
P: Jon Avnet
A: Jessica Lange, Kathy Bates
A widow with two sons suffers a lower standard of living because of her husband's death and gets a job as a shop clerk. *AMG.*

2114. Postcards from the Edge 1990 S
D: Mike Nichols
S: Carrie Fisher
C: Michael Ballhaus
P: John Calley, Mike Nichols
A: Meryl Streep, Shirley MacLaine
An actress wakes up in a rehabilitation center after a drug overdose. Smart and swaggering, she suffers under the influence of her histrionic mother, who is a famous musical comedy star inclined to put others in the shade.
Awards: Academy Awards, nomination for Best Actress (Streep), 1991; BAFTA Awards, nomination for Best Actress (MacLaine), 1991

2115. Privilege 1990 DSP
D: Yvonne Rainer
S: Yvonne Rainer
C: Mark Daniels
P: Yvonne Rainer
A: Alice Spivak, Novella Nelson
A black filmmaker interviews women about menopause, beginning with old instruction films; moving through references and cited readings on racism, classism, and change of life; and on to more personal stories of a couple who fight and a professor who loved Emma Goldman and Margaret Mead. Experimental.

2116. She-Devil 1990 DSP
D: Susan Seidelman
S: Barry Strugatz, Mark R. Burns; based on the novel by Fay Weldon
C: Oliver Stapleton
P: Susan Seidelman
A: Roseanne Barr, Meryl Streep

A suburban wife gains revenge on her philandering husband by destroying his home life and career. Comedy. *AMG.*
Awards: Golden Globes, nomination for Best Actress (Streep), 1990

2117. The Silence of the Lambs 1990
D: Jonathan Demme
S: Ted Tally
C: Tak Fujimoto
P: Ronald Bozman
A: Jodie Foster, Anthony Hopkins
An FBI agent tangles with an evil imprisoned murderer in an attempt to get information from him about another serial killer. Horror.
Awards: Academy Awards, Best Picture, Best Actress, 1992

2118. Stella 1990 S
D: John Erman
S: Robert Getchell; based on the novel by Olive Higgins Prouty
C: Billy Williams
P: Samuel Goldwyn Jr.
A: Bette Midler
A waitress who has insisted on raising her daughter on her own gives up the child to her wealthy doctor father when she reaches marriageable age. Remake of the 1937 Barbara Stanwyck vehicle *Stella Dallas. NYT. 1990, Feb. 2.*

2119. Streets 1990 DS
D: Katt Shea Ruben
S: Katt Shea Ruben, Andy Ruben
C: Phedon Papamichael
P: Roger Corman
A: Christina Applegate
Los Angeles. A drug-addicted teenage prostitute lives on the streets, befriends a young man, and staves off a serial killer. Thriller. *AMG.*

2120. A Thousand Pieces of Gold 1990 DSP
D: Nancy Kelly
S: Ruthanne Lum McCunn, Ann Makepeace
C: Bobby Bukowski
P: Nancy Kelly
A: Rosalind Chao
Idaho, 1880s. The true story of a Chinese woman sold by her family as a wife but who ends up in slavery as a prostitute in a mining camp; she resists.
Awards: Deauville Film Festival, nomination for Critics Award, 1990

2121. Closet Land 1991 DSP
D: Radha Bharadwaj

S: Radha Bharadwaj
C: Bill Pope
P: Janet Meyers
A: Madeleine Stowe, Alan Rickman
A one-room set of Greek columns and tiled floor evolves into a futuristic setting, as a sadistic policeman interrogates and tortures a children's-book author arrested for subversive writings; she refuses to give him what he wants. *Festival de films, 14th: 13. 1992.*
Awards: San Sebastián International Film Festival, OCIC Award, 1991

2122. *Daughters of the Dust*   1991 DSP
D: Julie Dash
S: Julie Dash
C: Arthur Jafa
P: Julie Dash
A: Cora Lee Day, Alva Rogers, Barbara O Jones, Trula Hoosier
1902. A picnic day in the life of freed slaves who originally made their home on an island off the Atlantic coast. All are now leaving for the more prosperous north and expect to take along the great grandmother, who refuses to go. The Gullah community is portrayed in lush visual detail, beautiful clothing, hair fashion, and the physicality of hugging and dancing. A prosperous lesbian couple, a young daughter in love with a local Cherokee, and many other family members inhabit the primarily outdoor set pieces that revolve around the conflict between past folkways and the attraction to the "wealth of the mainland."
Awards: Sundance Film Festival, Cinematography Award, 1991

2123. *Defenseless*   1991
D: Martin Campbell
S: Jeff Burkhart
C: Phil Meheux
P: Renée Missel
A: Mary Beth Hurt, Barbara Hershey
A lawyer gets romantically involved with a client, who turns out to be married to one of her old friends. Mystery. *AMG.*

2124. *Dogfight*   1991 D
D: Nancy Savoca
S: Bob Comfort
C: Bobby Bukowski
P: Richard Guay
A: Lili Taylor, River Phoenix
1963. Four Marines have a "dogfight" (whoever finds the "ugliest" date gets the cash) before heading out to Vietnam. One of the chosen girls is a sensible and intelligent folksinger who works as a waitress in a café. She figures out the game and takes her date to task for the offense.

2125. *Fried Green Tomatoes*   1991 S
D: Jon Avnet
S: Fannie Flagg, Carol Sobieski; based on the novel by Fannie Flag
C: Geoffrey Simpson
P: Jon Avnet
A: Kathy Bates, Mary Stuart Masterson, Mary Louise Parker, Jessica Tandy, Cicely Tyson
An insecure housewife makes friends with a woman in a nursing home. The older woman tells her the story of her life in the American south of the 1920s, where she was raised by a black woman and in love with a woman married to a racist man. *Chicago Sun-Times. 1992, Jan. 10.*

2126. *Gas Food Lodging*   1991 DS
D: Allison Anders
S: Allison Anders
C: Dean Lent
P: William Ewart
A: Brooke Adams, Ione Skye, Fairuza Balk
New Mexico. A waitress works at an isolated truck stop and deals with her two teenage daughters and their coming of age.

2127. *Grand Isle*   1991 DSP
D: Mary Lambert
S: Hesper Anderson; based on *The Awakening* by Kate Chopin
C: Toyomichi Kurita
P: Carolyn Pfeiffer
A: Kelly McGillis
Louisiana, nineteenth century. A wealthy socialite falls in love with a Creole artist and moves away from her family and friends. *AMG.*
Awards: Deauville Film Festival, nomination for Critics Award, 1991

2128. *Leaving Normal*   1991 P
D: Edward Zwick
S: Ed Solomon
C: Ralf D. Bode
P: Lindsay Doran
A: Christine Lahti, Meg Tilly
A "hard-boiled" waitress meets an abused wife fleeing her husband; they take to the road together and end up in Alaska. *NYT: C14. 1992, Apr. 29.*

2129. *Little Man Tate*   1991 DP
D: Jodie Foster

S: Scott Frank
C: Mike Southon
P: Peggy Rajski
A: Jodie Foster, Dianne Wiest
A woman raises a genius and conflicts with a teacher who attempts to help him. *AMG.*

2130. *Love Crimes* 1991 DSP
D: Lizzie Borden
S: Allan Moyle, Laurie Frank
C: Jack Green
P: Lizzie Borden
A: Sean Young
A young district attorney turns detective and becomes obsessed with a criminal who preys on women who refuse to prosecute him. Thriller.

2131. *Mississippi Masala* 1991 DSP
D: Mira Nair
S: Sooni Taraporevala
C: Edward Lachman
P: Mira Nair
A: Sarita Choudhury, Denzel Washington
An exiled Indian Ugandan family settles in Mississippi; their daughter has an affair with a local African American. She is dark enough to inhibit her chances of marriage within the Indian community, and her parents forbid her to see him.
Awards: São Paulo International Film Festival, Special Award, 1991; Venice Film Festival, Golden Osella, 1991

2132. *Mortal Thoughts* 1991
D: Alan Rudolph
S: William Reilly, Claude Kerven
C: Elliot Davis
P: John Fiedler
A: Demi Moore, Glenne Headly
An abused wife, a best friend, and a murdered husband lead to an investigation. Thriller. *AMG.*

2133. *Not without My Daughter* 1991 SP
D: Brian Gilbert
S: David Rintels, Betty Mahmoody, William Hoffer
C: Peter Hannan
P: Mary Jane Ufland, Harry Ufland
A: Sally Field
An Iranian doctor takes his American wife and daughter to Iran for a visit, where they become trapped. *AMG.*

2134. *Queen of Diamonds* 1991 DSCP
D: Nina Menkes
S: Nina Menkes
C: Nina Menkes
P: Nina Menkes

A: Tinka Menkes, Claudia Cardinale
Las Vegas. The life of a young blackjack dealer, including a fourteen-minute scene of her at work. In her off time she wanders the city and cares for an old man. *AMG.*
Awards: Sundance Film Festival, nomination for Grand Jury Prize, 1991

2135. *Rambling Rose* 1991 D
D: Martha Coolidge
S: Calder Willingham
C: Johnny Jensen
P: Renny Harlin
A: Laura Dern, Robert Duvall, Diane Ladd
1930s. A young girl is taken in by a wealthy, educated family as a "helper." Abused as a child, the teenager is impulsively promiscuous but exceptionally loving and cheerful, and the family accepts her, until a doctor recommends a hysterectomy to curb her sexual appetite. The mother objects to the recommendation.
Awards: Montréal World Film Festival, Best Actress (Dern), 1991; Independent Spirit Awards, Best Film, Best Director, Best Supporting Female (Ladd), 1992

2136. *Sleeping with the Enemy* 1991 S
D: Joseph Ruben
S: Nancy Price, Ronald Bass
C: John Lindley
P: Leonard Goldberg
A: Julia Roberts
A woman creates a new identity to escape her wealthy, abusive husband, but he stalks her and eventually she is forced to fight him. Thriller.

2137. *Thelma and Louise* 1991 SP
D: Ridley Scott
S: Callie Khouri
C: Adrian Biddle
P: Ridley Scott, Mimi Polk
A: Susan Sarandon, Geena Davis
Two women leave their lovers behind and take to the road; they become the object of a manhunt when they violently thwart a rape attempt. Action.
Awards: Academy Awards, Best Screenplay, 1992; David di Donatello Awards, Best Foreign Actress (Sarandon, Davis), 1992

2138. *V. I. Warshawski* 1991 S
D: Jeff Kanew
S: Edward Taylor; based on the novel by Sara Paretsky
C: Jan Kiesser
P: Jeffrey Lurie

A: Kathleen Turner

A smart-aleck detective with martial arts skills and a lot of friends is left with a young girl when the girl's father is murdered. The two instinctively become a team, outsmarting the bad guys on the basis of the detective's maxim: "Never underestimate a man's ability to underestimate a woman."

2139. Basic Instinct   1992

D: Paul Verhoeven

S: Joe Eszterhas

C: Jan De Bont

P: Alan Marshall

A: Sharon Stone, Michael Douglas

A take-charge and very wealthy novelist becomes the prime suspect in the vicious murder of her mob boyfriend; the detective investigating cannot resist getting sexually involved with her. Exploitation, thriller.

Awards: Golden Globes, nomination for Best Actress, 1993

2140. Crazy in Love   1992 DSP

D: Martha Coolidge

S: Gerald Ayres; based on the novel by Luanne Rice

C: Johnny Jensen

P: Karen Danager-Dorr

A: Holly Hunter, Gena Rowlands, Frances McDormand, Herta Ware

A grandmother, mother, and two daughters live together on an island in Washington State. *Variety:* 59. 1992, Aug. 10.

2141. Death Becomes Her   1992

D: Robert Zemeckis

S: Martin Donovan, David Koepp

C: Dean Cundey

P: Robert Zemeckis

A: Meryl Streep, Goldie Hawn, Bruce Willis

Two women share the same plastic surgeon and eventually become immortal. Comedy.

2142. The Hand That Rocks the Cradle 1992 S

D: Curtis Hanson

S: Amanda Silver

C: Robert Elswit

P: David Madden

A: Annabella Sciorra, Rebecca De Mornay

A nanny has a history of previous loss—her husband and a child—which she blames on the mother who hires her.

Awards: Cognac Festival du Film Policier, Best Actress (De Mornay), 1992

2143. A League of Their Own   1992 D

D: Penny Marshall

S: Kim Wilson, Lowell Ganz, Babaloo Mandel

C: Miroslav Ondricek

P: Elliot Abbott

A: Geena Davis, Madonna, Lori Petty, Rosie O'Donnell

1940s. Two sisters play professional baseball in the women's league.

2144. Lorenzo's Oil   1992

D: George Miller

S: George Miller, Nick Enright

C: John Seale

P: George Miller

A: Susan Sarandon, Nick Nolte

A mother cares for a child dying of a rare disease; she lobbies with her husband to find a cure, persists beyond all sane and contrary advice, and keeps him alive for longer than anyone expected.

Awards: Academy Awards, nomination for Best Actress, 1993; Golden Globes, nomination for Best Actress, 1993

2145. Love Field   1992 P

D: Jonathan Kaplan

S: Don Roos

C: Ralf Bode

P: Sarah Pillsbury, Midge Sanford

A: Michelle Pfeiffer, Dennis Haysbert

The South, 1963. A Dallas woman, obsessed with the Kennedys, decides to leave her husband and take a bus to the president's funeral in Washington, D.C. She befriends an African American and his child, but her naïveté gets them in trouble, and they end up running from the law.

Awards: Berlin International Film Festival, Best Actress, 1993

2146. Me and Veronica   1992 SP

D: Don Scardino

S: Leslie Lyles

C: Michael Barrow

P: Leslie Urdang, Nellie Nugiel

A: Elizabeth McGovern, Patricia Wettig

A self-destructive mother on her way to prison seeks help from her sister after many years of separation.

2147. Passion Fish   1992 P

D: John Sayles

S: John Sayles

C: Roger Deakins

P: Sarah Green, Maggie Renzi

A: Mary McDonnell, Alfre Woodard

A newly disabled actress returns to her southern home to recuperate and has an imperious attitude toward her nurse.

Awards: Academy Awards, nomination for Best Actress (McDonnell), 1993; Independent Spirit Awards, Best Supporting Female (Woodward), 1993

2148. *This Is My Life*　　　　1992 DSP
D: Nora Ephron
S: Nora Ephron, Delia Ephron; based on *This Is Your Life* by Meg Wolitzer
C: Bobby Byrne
P: Lynda Obst
A: Julie Kavner
A single mother moves to Manhattan and begins a career as a comedian, but her two teenage daughters become resentful. *AMG.*

2149. *Alma's Rainbow*　　　　1993 DSP
D: Ayoka Chenzira, Ronald K. Gray
S: Ayoka Chenzira
P: Ayoka Chenzira, Charles Lane, Howard M. Brickner
A: Victoria Gabriella Platt, Kim Weston-Moran, Mizan Nunes
A beauty parlor owner and her sister, who has recently returned from Europe, attempt to help the owner's teenage daughter understand her sexual urges. *AMG.*

2150. *The Ballad of Little Jo*　　　　1993 DSP
D: Maggie Greenwald
S: Maggie Greenwald
C: Declan Quinn
P: Brenda Goodman, Fred Berner
A: Suzy Amis
United States, nineteenth century. After a seduction by a photographer and banishment from an eastern city, a girl strikes out into the west on her own. After being attacked, she trains herself to pose like a man and to use a gun, and she successfully passes as a man for the duration of her life, allowing only an Asian male servant into her home.

2151. *A Dangerous Woman*　　　　1993 SP
D: Stephen Gyllenhaal
S: Naomi Foner, Mary McGarry Morris
C: Robert Elswit
P: Naomi Foner
A: Debra Winger, Laurie Metcalf
A childlike woman lives with her aunt and is fired from her job, then taken advantage of by a neighbor. *IMDb.*
Awards: Tokyo International Film Festival, Best Actress (Winger), 1994

2152. *Household Saints*　　　　1993 DS
D: Nancy Savoca

S: Richard Guay, Nancy Savoca; based on the novel by Francine Prose
C: Bobby Bukowski
P: Richard Guay
A: Lili Taylor, Tracey Ullman
A wife survives under the thumb of Italian Catholic parents who met when the mother noticed the father cheating her on her meat purchase. After her life is lightened by her mother's death, it develops that her own daughter does not have the same resources to cope and has retreated into religious fanaticism. After several engagements with reality, including college and a boyfriend, the girl ends up institutionalized.
Awards: Independent Spirit Awards, Best Supporting Female (Taylor), 1994

2153. *Lillian*　　　　1993
D: David D. Williams
S: David D. Williams
C: Robert Griffith
P: David D. Williams
A: Lillian Folley
Virginia. A "fictional documentary-like study of a middle-aged black woman" who cares for children, some relatives and some foster children, as well as elderly boarders in her home. *Variety. 1993, Feb. 15.*

2154. *Ruby in Paradise*　　　　1993
D: Victor Nuñez
S: Victor Nuñez
C: Alex Vlacos
A: Ashley Judd
A girl leaves Tennessee for Panama City, Florida, where she finds a job and lovers.
Awards: Sundance Film Festival, Grand Jury Prize, 1993; Independent Spirit Awards, Best Female Lead, 1994

2155. *What's Love Got to Do with It?*　　　1993 S
D: Brian Gibson
S: Kate Lanier; based on an autobiography by Tina Turner
C: Jamie Anderson
P: Barry Krost
A: Angela Bassett, Laurence Fishburne
The life of Tina Turner, chronicling her path to stardom as a pop singer and her eventual separation from her abusive husband, Ike Turner, who was also her partner and band leader.
Awards: Academy Awards, nomination for Best Actress, 1994; Golden Globes, Best Actress, 1994

2156. *Angie*　　　　1994 DS
D: Martha Coolidge

S: Todd Graff; based on the novel by Avra Wing
C: Johnny Jensen
P: Larry Brezner
A: Geena Davis
A pregnant young woman frees herself from the boyfriend she does not love but keeps the child after considering motherhood and adoption.

2157. *Blue Sky* 1994 S
D: Tony Richardson
S: Rama Laurie Stagner, Jerry Leightling, Arlene Sarner
C: Steve Yaconelli
P: Robert H. Solo
A: Jessica Lange, Tommy Lee Jones
1962. A wife and mother has an exaggerated sense of self-worth based on her feminine charm that becomes dangerous when combined with her poor judgment. She jeopardizes the well-being of her family when she collaborates with the U.S. Army to suppress her husband's antinuclear ideas by having him committed to a mental institution.
Awards: Academy Awards, Best Actress, 1994; Berlin International Film Festival, Silver Bear (Lange), 1994

2158. *Boulevard* 1994 DS
D: Penelope Buitenhuis
S: Rae Dawn Chong
C: David Frazee
P: Peter Simpson
A: Rae Dawn Chong, Kari Wuhrer, Lou Diamond Phillips
Toronto. A woman leaves her abusive husband to live with a prostitute who gives her shelter; but her friend is deported, leaving her alone again, and she learns the trade at the hands of a violent pimp. Exploitation, thriller. *FII.*

2159. *The Client* 1994
D: Joel Schumacher
S: Akiva Goldsman, Robert Getchell; based on the novel by John Grisham
C: Tony Pierce-Roberts
P: Arnon Milchan
A: Susan Sarandon, Brad Renfro, Tommy Lee Jones
A recovering alcoholic lawyer takes on the case of an eleven-year-old child who has witnessed a murder, and she must contend with him as well as the district attorney. Mystery.
Awards: BAFTA Awards, Best Actress, 1995

2160. *Crooklyn* 1994 S
D: Spike Lee

S: Joie Lee, Cinqué Lee, Spike Lee
C: Arthur Jaffe
A: Alfre Woodard, Delroy Lindo, Zelda Harris
Brooklyn, 1970s. A teacher and her youngest child, a nine-year-old daughter, form the strong core of a struggling lower-middle-class family; the father is a jazz musician who wants to make it on his own in music. *IMDb.*

2161. *Fanci's Persuasion* 1994 SP
D: Charles Herman-Wurmfeld
S: Eden Wurmfeld, Caroline Libresco, Stephanie Rosenbaum
C: David Morrison
P: Eden Wurmfeld, Caroline Libresco
A: Jessica Patton, Boa
San Francisco. A young Jewish lesbian prepares for her wedding; her best friends, who are magicians, cast a spell creating "pandemonium" among her relatives. *FII.*

2162. *Fresh Kill* 1994 DSCP
D: Shu Lea Cheang
S: Jessica Hagedorn
C: Jane Castle
P: Shu Lea Cheang
A: Sarita Choudhury, Erin McMurtry
New York City. A lesbian couple, an African American and an Indian, raise a daughter and have gay friends who work in their favorite sushi bar; they uncover a scandal involving poisoned fish. *Festival de films, 16th: 22. 1994.*

2163. *Go Fish* 1994 DSCP
D: Rose Troche
S: Rose Troche, Guinevere Turner
C: Ann T. Rossetti
P: Rose Troche
A: Guinevere Turner
Chicago. Two young women begin a romance in the lesbian hangouts—bookstores and cafés—of the city and in their apartments.
Awards: Berlin International Film Festival, Best Feature Film, 1994; Deauville Film Festival, Audience Award, 1994; GLAAD Media Awards, Outstanding Film, 1995

2164. *Mi Vida Loca / My Crazy Life* 1994 DS
D: Allison Anders
S: Allison Anders
C: Rodrigo Garcia
P: Carl Colpaert
A: Angel Aviles
Los Angeles. Latinas form a strong group of friends, taking care of each other's children and even forming a gang to provide protection. They per-

sist in romantic escapades, yet they suffer the casual betrayals of the men around them and the hatred and suspicion of the law.

2165. *Mrs. Parker and the Vicious Circle* 1994 S
D: Alan Parker
S: Alan Parker, Randy Sue Coburn
C: Jan Kiesser
P: Robert Altman
A: Jennifer Jason Leigh
New York City. The adult life of writer Dorothy Parker, whose political passion and literary wit made her a famous member of an elite male crowd. In the long run, her political passion left her at odds with her intellectual and more dispassionate friends.
Awards: Chicago Film Critics Association Awards, Best Actress, 1995; National Society of Film Critics Awards, Best Actress, 1995

2166. *Risk* 1994 DS
D: Deirdre Fishel
S: Deirdre Fishel
C: Peter Pearce
P: Hank Blumenthal
A: Karen Sillas
New York. An artist gets involved with a violent man. *Village Voice. 1994, Oct. 11.*
Awards: Sundance Film Festival, nomination for Grand Jury Prize, 1994

2167. *Souvenir* 1994 DSCP
D: Lisa Cholodenko
S: Lisa Cholodenko
C: Tami Reiker
P: Lisa Shapiro, Lisa Cholodenko
A: Erin McMurtry, Britta Couris, Barbara Sinclair
"Road movie in which a quarreling lesbian couple is sexually and emotionally reconciled during an ambiguous nocturnal encounter with the eccentric manager of a run-down roadside motel." *FII.*

2168. *Two Small Bodies* 1994 DS
D: Beth B.
S: Neal Bell, Beth B.
C: Phil Parmet
P: Daniel Zuta
A: Suzy Amis, Fred Ward
A sexist detective repeatedly confronts a waitress who has lost two children by accusing her of their murders. The story is a "powerful exercise in female humiliation," though she does fight back. *Variety: 30. 1993, Sep. 20.*
Awards: Locarno International Film Festival, nomination for Golden Leopard, 1993

2169. *Art for Teachers of Children* 1995 DSCP
D: Jennifer Montgomery
S: Jennifer Montgomery
C: Jennifer Montgomery
P: Jennifer Montgomery
A: Caitlin Grace McDonnell
A woman tells the story of her boarding school seduction by a married photography teacher and dormitory leader; as an adult she finds that he is wanted for child pornography.

2170. *Bar Girls* 1995 DSP
D: Marita Giovanni
S: Laura Hoffman
C: Michael Ferris
P: Marita Giovanni
A: Nancy Allison Wolfe
Affairs of the heart in a lesbian bar.

2171. *Barb Wire* 1995 S
D: David Glenn Hogan
S: Ilene Chaiken, Chuck Pfarrer
C: Rick Bota
P: Brad Wyman
A: Pamela Anderson
United States, second civil war, 2017. The only free zone in the country, the fictional Steel Harbor, is run by club owner and bounty hunter Barb Wire. She accidentally comes by valuable property that allows her to escape government surveillance and is pushed to use her resources to defend freedom for everyone. Exploitation. *FII.*

2172. *Beyond Rangoon* 1995
D: John Boorman
S: Alex Lasker, Bill Rubenstein
C: John Seale
P: John Boorman
A: Patricia Arquette
1988. A doctor suffering from grief visits Burma and attends a political rally where Aung San Suu Kyi, leader of the Free Burma movement, speaks; drawn in, she ends up fleeing with a revolutionary leader through the countryside, which is in violent upheaval. Action.

2173. *Boys on the Side* 1995
D: Herbert Ross
S: Don Roos
C: Donald Thorin
P: Arnon Milchan
A: Drew Barrymore, Whoopi Goldberg, Mary-Louise Parker
A cross-country trip gets serious when a sadistic boyfriend is accidentally killed by three

newfound friends, including a lesbian woman and another with AIDS; they end up in Tucson, Arizona.

2174. *Dolores Claiborne*   1995
D: Taylor Hackford
S: Tony Gilroy; based on the novel by Stephen King
C: Gabriel Beristain
P: Taylor Hackford
A: Jennifer Jason Leigh, Kathy Bates
The troubled daughter of an abusive father doubts the sanity of her mother, who has been accused of murdering a woman in whose home she works as a servant.

2175. *Érotique*   1995 DS
D: Lizzie Borden, Clara Law, Monika Treut
S: Lizzie Borden, Susie Bright, Eloi Calage, Monika Treut, Ana Maria Magalhães
A: Camilla Soeberg, Priscilla Barnes, Liane Alexandra Curtis, Kamala Lopez, Hayley Man, Marianne Sägebrecht
Three stories: A Chinese actress has a day job as a phone-sex operator; two lesbians pick up a man for sex; an Australian Chinese man finds a former lover. *AMG.*

2176. *Georgia*   1995 S
D: Ula Grosbard
S: Barbara Turner
C: Jan Kiesser
P: Ula Grosbard
A: Jennifer Jason Leigh, Mare Winningham
A punk-rock singer, addicted to drugs, yearns for an appreciative audience but cannot perform consistently. She adores and depends on her older sister, married with children, who is a famous folk-rock singer. The two poles of sibling rivalry, from proud independence to smug middle-class life, are played out within the two distinct music subcultures.
Awards: Montréal World Film Festival, Best Actress (Leigh), Grand Prix, 1995; New York Film Critics Circle Awards, Best Actress (Leigh), 1995; Independent Spirit Awards, Best Supporting Actress (Winningham), 1996

2177. *How to Make an American Quilt*
                                             1995 DSP
D: Jocelyn Moorhouse
S: Jane Anderson
C: Janusz Kaminski
P: Sarah Pillsbury, Midge Sanford
A: Winona Ryder, Anne Bancroft, Ellen Burstyn, Kate Nelligan, Alfre Woodard

A graduate student on the verge of marriage spends the summer writing her thesis with her mother, her aunts, and their friends.

2178. *I Like It like That*   1995 DSP
D: Darnell Martin
S: Darnell Martin
C: Alexander Gruszynski
P: Ann Carli, Lane Janger
A: Lauren Velez, Rita Moreno, Jon Seda
Bronx. A Puerto Rican wife with young children hides in the bathroom to get away from the chaos of her apartment. Her husband's susceptibility to other women, along with his macho ways in general (he times their lovemaking), makes her angry. Eventually, she gets a job and considers her options after he steals something for her and is imprisoned.
Awards: New York Film Critics Circle Awards, Best New Director, 1994; Independent Spirit Awards, nominations for Best Female Lead and Best First Feature, 1995

2179. *Little Women*   1995 DSP
D: Gillian Armstrong
S: Robin Swicord; based on the novel by Louisa May Alcott
C: Geoffrey Simpson
P: Robin Swicord
A: Winona Ryder, Trini Alvarada, Kirsten Dunst, Claire Danes, Susan Sarandon
Massachusetts, 1860s. A mother helps her four growing daughters negotiate the move into adulthood and its relationship to marriage. All are encouraged to find happiness for themselves, and one resists marriage to take up a career as a writer.

2180. *Losing Isaiah*   1995 SP
D: Stephen Gyllenhaal
S: Naomi Foner, Seth Margolis
C: Andrzej Bartkowiak
P: Naomi Foner
A: Halle Berry, Jessica Lange
A white social worker takes in a crack baby for foster care but is forced by the court to return the child to the mother after she's been rehabilitated.
Awards: Image Awards, nomination for Outstanding Actress (Berry), 1996

2181. *Manny and Lo*   1995 DS
D: Lisa Krueger
S: Lisa Krueger
C: Tom Krueger
P: Dean Silvers

A: Mary Kay Place, Scarlett Johansson

Two orphaned sisters escape from their foster home and kidnap a woman to help them get through a pregnancy. She ends up helping them as much as they hoped. *NYT: C3. 1996, July 26.*

2182. *The Midwife's Tale*   1995 DSP
D: Megan Silver
S: Megan Silver
C: Adam Teichman
P: Megan Silver
A: Stacey Havener, Carla Milford, Gayle Cohen

A lesbian mother tells her child a fairy tale: In medieval times, a "sporty, headstrong young noblewoman" agrees to marry at her father's insistence. She fears that she will die in childbirth and so finds a midwife to abort her pregnancy, but her husband suspects and the midwife is arrested. Though imprisoned by her husband, she does figure a way of escape for herself and the midwife. *FII.*

2183. *Now and Then*   1995 DSP
D: Leslie Linka Glatter
S: Leslie Linka Glatter, I. Marlene King
C: Ueli Steiger
P: I. Marlene King, Demi Moore
A: Demi Moore, Rosie O'Donnell, Rita Wilson, Christina Ricci, Thora Birch, Melanie Griffith, Melanie Hoffman

Childhood friends—an actress, a gynecologist, a housewife, and an author—meet again and recall their years together as adolescents. *AMG.*

2184. *Picture Bride*   1995 DSP
D: Kayo Hatta
S: Kayo Hatta
C: Claudio Rocha
P: Lisa Onodera
A: Youki Kudoh

Nineteenth century. A Japanese woman travels to Hawaii to become the wife of an older man who has hidden his age from her. They work in the cane fields, and eventually she falls in love with him.
Awards: Sundance Film Festival, Audience Award, 1995

2185. *The Quick and the Dead*   1995
D: Sam Raimi
S: Simon Moore
C: Dante Spinotti
P: Joshua Donen
A: Sharon Stone, Gene Hackman

A strange gunfighter arrives in a town dominated by a corrupt mayor who stages single-draw gun-fights for fun; she ends up facing him down to exact revenge for her father's death at his hands years ago. Action.

2186. *Safe*   1995 P
D: Todd Haynes
S: Todd Haynes
C: Alex Nepomniaschy
P: Christine Vachon
A: Julianne Moore

A bored suburban housewife becomes obsessed with germs and disease, then finally moves out of her home to an antiseptic community.
Awards: Seattle International Film Festival, American Independent Award, 1995; Rotterdam International Film Festival, FIPRESCI, 1996

2187. *The Spitfire Grill*   1995
D: Lee David Zlotoff
S: Lee David Zlotoff
C: Robert Draper
P: Forrest Murray
A: Alison Elliot, Ellen Burstyn, Marcia Gay Harden

Vermont. A girl released from prison goes to live in a small town where she can begin anew; there she works as a waitress and becomes close to the owner and another waitress. *AMG.*
Awards: Sundance Film Festival, Audience Award, 1996

2188. *Tale of Love*   1995 DSC
D: Trinh T. Minh-ha, Jean-Paul Bourdier
S: Trinh T. Minh-ha
C: Kathleen Beeler
A: Juliette Chen, Mai Huynh

Poetic rendition of the story of a Vietnamese woman who emigrates to the United States and sends money back to her family. Her story alternates with a meditation on the "Tale of Kieu," a traditional poem of a woman's passion and suffering. *Variety: 47. 1995, Oct. 23.*

2189. *Tank Girl*   1995 DS
D: Rachel Talalay
S: Tedi Sarafian; based on the comic strip by Jamie Hewlett
C: Gale Tattersall
P: Pen Densham
A: Lori Petty, Naomi Watt

A story set in the future, where the world and its water are controlled by the evil Water & Power, fought off by the Rippers, who are half man and half kangaroo, and Tank Girl, a supergirl. Action.

2190. *To Die For*   1995 SP
D: Gus Van Sant

S: Buck Henry; based on the novel by Joyce May-
   nard
C: Eric Alan Edwards
P: Laura Ziskin
A: Nicole Kidman, Illeana Douglas
Darkly comic look at an irrational, willful, and dan-
   gerous woman who becomes full of herself as
   a local television star, then bonds with a group
   of teenagers and convinces one to murder her
   husband.
Awards: Golden Globes, Best Actress, 1996; London
   Critics' Circle Film Awards, Best Actress, 1996

2191. *Waiting to Exhale*   1995 SP
D: Forest Whitaker
S: Terry McMillan, Ronald Bass
C: Toyomichi Kurita
P: Deborah Schindler
A: Whitney Houston, Angela Bassett, Loretta
   Devine, Lela Rochon
Four middle-class friends meet regularly and often
   discuss their problems with men. Two of the
   women are professionals in love with married
   men; one is powerfully angry at her husband,
   who is leaving her for a white woman; and one
   is a sweet single mother with a son.

2192. *Watermelon Woman*   1995 DSC
D: Cheryl Dunye
S: Cheryl Dunye
C: Michelle Crenshaw
P: Barry Swimar
A: Cheryl Dunye, Guinevere Turner, Valerie
   Walker
An African American filmmaker who works in a
   video store has an affair with a white woman
   and discovers a black lesbian actress—"Water-
   melon Woman"—from the 1930s. She decides
   to discover more about her. *Festival de films,
   18th: 24. 1996.*

2193. *Alchemy*   1996 DSC
D: Suzanne Myers
S: Suzanne Myers
C: Tami Reiker
P: Kelly Forsythe
A: Rya Kihstedt, Marian Quinn
A young artist loses a boyfriend; visits her sister,
   who is dying of cancer, in upstate New York;
   then goes to an artists' retreat.

2194. *The Associate*   1996
D: Donald Petrie
S: Nick Thiel; based on a screenplay by Jean-
   Claude Carrière and René Gainville and the
   novel by Jenaro Prieto

C: Alex Nepomniaschy
P: Adam Leipzig
A: Whoopi Goldberg, Dianne Wiest
A finance expert starts her own business when she
   is passed over for promotion; in order to suc-
   ceed, she invents a male partner. Comedy.

2195. *Bastard Out of Carolina*   1996 DSP
D: Anjelica Huston
S: Anne Meredith; based on the novel by Dorothy
   Allison
C: Anthony Richmond
P: Amanda Di Giulio
A: Jennifer Jason Leigh, Glenne Headly, Jena
   Malone
1950s, American South. A woman, widowed with
   two young children, marries unwisely to a man
   who sexually abuses her daughter; she refuses
   to acknowledge the evidence, and eventually her
   daughter is forced to live elsewhere.
Awards: San Francisco International Film Festival,
   Certificate of Merit, 1997

2196. *Bound*   1996
D: Andy Wachowski, Larry Wachowski
S: Andy Wachowski, Larry Wachowski
C: Bill Pope
P: Andrew Lazar
A: Jennifer Tilly, Gina Gershon
Two women used to hanging around convicts and
   gangsters develop a romantic relationship and
   decide to do some thieving themselves; natu-
   rally, they are pursued. *FII.*
Awards: Stockholm Film Festival, Honorable Men-
   tion, 1996; Fantasporto, Best Film, Best Actress
   (Tilly), 1997

2197. *Citizen Ruth*   1996 P
D: Alexander Payne
S: Alexander Payne, Jim Taylor
C: James Glennon
P: Cathy Konrad
A: Laura Dern, Swoosie Kurtz
Pro-life activists take up the case of an addict who has
   been told by a judge to get an abortion because
   she has already lost custody of four children.
Awards: Montréal World Film Festival, Best Actress
   (Dern), 1996; Thessaloniki Film Festival, Best
   Screenplay, 1996

2198. *Dead Man Walking*   1996 S
D: Tim Robbins
S: Tim Robbins; based on the book by Helen
   Prejean
C: Roger Deakins
P: Tim Robbins

A: Susan Sarandon, Sean Penn

A nun counsels a murderer and rapist who is on death row, finally witnessing his capital punishment out of devotion to his soul.

Awards: Academy Awards, Best Actress, 1996; Berlin International Film Festival, Best Actress, Ecumenical Jury Prize, 1996; Screen Actors Guild, Best Actress, 1996

2199. *Everything Relative*   1996 DSP

D: Sharon Pollack
S: Sharon Pollack
C: Zak Othmer
P: Sharon Pollack
A: Monica Bell, Carol Schneider, Ellen McLaughlin, Olivia Negron, Andre Weber

Northampton, Massachusetts. Seven women college friends gather for a reunion when one has a baby. *Los Angeles. 1996, Sep. 20.*

2200. *Fargo*   1996

D: Joel Coen
S: Joel Coen
C: Roger Deakins
P: Ethan Coen
A: Frances McDormand

Minneapolis. Comic rendering of an investigation by a pregnant detective into a kidnapping-turned-murder.

Awards: Academy Awards, Best Actress, 1996; BAFTA Awards, Best Director, 1996

2201. *Female Perversions*   1996 DSCP

D: Susan Stratfeld
S: Julie Hébert, Susan Stratfeld
C: Teresa Medina
P: Mindy Affrime
A: Tilda Swinton, Amy Madigan

Los Angeles. A lawyer, who is nominated for a judgeship, tries to help her shoplifting younger sister.

2202. *The First Wives Club*   1996 S

D: Hugh Wilson
S: Olivia Goldsmith, Robert Harling
C: Donald Thorin
P: Scott Rudin
A: Diane Keaton, Bette Midler, Goldie Hawn

New York City. Three middle-aged women lose an old school friend, who commits suicide over the loss of her husband to a younger woman. Each finds she has the same problem, and they bond together, at first to take revenge and then to establish a posh counseling center for women.

Awards: Blockbuster Entertainment Awards, Favorite Actress (Hawn), 1997; National Board of Review, Best Acting Ensemble, 1997

2203. *Girl 6*   1996 S

D: Spike Lee
S: Suzan-Lori Parks
C: Malik Sayeed
P: Spike Lee
A: Theresa Randle

New York. An actress, out of luck because she is disinclined to take advantage of her body, takes a job as a phone-sex operator, where the voyeurism begins to arouse her as well as her clients. Her model is Dorothy Dandridge.

2204. *Girls Town*   1996 SP

D: Jim McKay
S: Denise Casano, Anna Grace
C: Russell Lee Fine
P: Lauren Zalaznick
A: Lili Taylor, Anna Grace, Bruklin Harris

Three teenagers, one who is raising a child, decide to avenge the suicide of a friend who had been raped.

Awards: Seattle International Film Festival, Best Actress (Taylor), 1996; Sundance Film Festival, Filmmaker Trophy, 1996

2205. *Grace of My Heart*   1996 DSP

D: Allison Anders
S: Allison Anders
C: Jean-Yves Escoffier
P: Ruth Charny
A: Illeana Douglass

1960s. Fictional biography of a songwriter, similar to Carole King. The film recounts the sea change of popular music from performed hits with anonymous songwriting to the more personal and eccentric era of the singer-songwriter.

2206. *I Shot Andy Warhol*   1996 DSCP

D: Mary Harron
S: Mary Harron, Daniel Minahan
C: Ellen Kuras
P: Christine Vachon
A: Lili Taylor

New York City. A caustic portrait of Valerie Solanas, author of the *SCUM Manifesto*, one of the earliest and most radical feminist tracts of the 1960s. Imagining the downtown scenesters who hung around Andy Warhol's factory to be her friends, she became a laughable fixture to them, then gains infamy for injuring Warhol in a shooting.

Awards: Seattle International Film Festival, Best Actress, 1996; Stockholm Film Festival, Best Actress, 1996; Sundance Film Festival, Special Recognition (Taylor), 1996

2207. *If These Walls Could Talk*   1996 DSCP
D: Nancy Savoca, Cher
S: Pamela Wallace, Earl Wallace, Nancy Savoca, Susan Nanus, I. Marlene King
C: Bobby Bukowski, Ellen Kuras, John Stanier
P: Demi Moore, Suzanne Todd
A: Demi Moore, Sissy Spacek, Shirley Knight
Three stories of the struggle that women go through in considering whether to have a child or abort: a 1950s nurse, a 1970s housewife with four children, and a modern-day student.

2208. *Inn Trouble*   1996 DSP
D: Cristina Rey
S: Cristina Rey, Stephani Shope
C: Mark Petersen
P: Cristina Rey
A: Cristina Rey, Stephani Shope, Melissa Aronson
At the funeral of their friend, a group of lesbians discover that the will leaving them her inn property is missing, and her homophobic relatives intend to take over; comedy and intrigue develop. *FII.*

2209. *Lena's Dreams*   1996 DS
D: Heather Johnston, Gordon Eriksen
S: Heather Johnston, Gordon Eriksen
C: Armando Basulto
P: Chip Garner
A: Marlene Forte, Gary Perez, Judy Reyes
New York City. A Cuban American actress suffers through her thirty-second birthday, having promised herself she would give up her acting career at thirty if she was not able to earn a living. During the week she attends several tryouts, where she is stymied by racial stereotyping.

2210. *The Long Kiss Goodnight*   1996 P
D: Renny Harlin
S: Shane Black
C: Guillermo Navarro
P: Stephanie Austin
A: Geena Davis, Samuel L. Jackson
A teacher and mother has her past as a government assassin exposed and must resurrect her defensive skills in order to protect herself and her daughter. Action.

2211. *The Mirror Has Two Faces*   1996 DP
D: Barbra Streisand
S: Richard LaGravenese; based on *Le Miroir à deux faces* (France, 1958), a film by André Cayatte
C: Dante Spinotti
P: Arnon Milchan, Barbra Streisand
A: Barbra Streisand, Jeff Bridges, Lauren Bacall
A professor marries another professor who is better looking than she is, but he is wary of women who are after him for his sex appeal and doesn't want to be bothered with sex. *Variety.* 1996. Nov. 11.

2212. *MURDER and murder*   1996 DSP
D: Yvonne Rainer
S: Yvonne Rainer
C: Stephen Kazmierski
P: Yvonne Rainer
A: Joanna Merlin, Kathleen Chalfont
New York City. Chronicle of a love affair between middle-age lesbians, one a professor, the other uneducated, along with treatises on aging and the medical and social treatment of breast cancer. Experimental.

2213. *Naked Acts*   1996 D
D: Bridgett Davis
A: Jake-Ann Jones, Patricia DeArcy, Rene Cox
An aspiring African American actress, whose mother was a blaxploitation star, is faced with pressure from her mother and the director to perform nude scenes she is uncomfortable with. *Village Voice.* 1998, Oct. 7.

2214. *Party Girl*   1996 DSP
D: Daisy Von Scherler Mayer
S: Sheila Gaffney, Harry Birckmayer
C: Michael Slovis
P: Harry Birckmayer, Stephanie Koules
A: Parker Posey
A party girl is redeemed by a job in a library. Comedy.
Awards: Sundance Film Festival, nomination for Grand Jury Prize, 1995

2215. *Rich Man's Wife*   1996 DSP
D: Amy Holden Jones
S: Amy Holden Jones
C: Haskell Wexler
P: Roger Birnbaum, Julie Bergman Sender
A: Halle Berry, Clive Owen
A wealthy mixed-race couple flounder in a bad marriage. After a flirtation, a man kills the husband "for" the wife, but it develops that the murder for hire was commanded by the wife's lover. Thriller.

2216. *Set It Off*   1996 S
D: F. Gary Gray
S: Kate Lanier, Takashi Bufford
C: Marc Reshovsky
P: Dale Pollack
A: Jada Pinkett, Queen Latifah, Vivica A. Fox, Kimberly Elise
Los Angeles. A bank teller is fired because she recognizes a robber from her neighborhood. Angry,

she teams up to rob banks with two friends who work as office night cleaners, one a lesbian, the other a single mother, and another friend who wants her brother to go to college. Action.

Awards: Acapulco Black Film Festival, Best Director, Best Actress (Latifah), 1997; Cognac Festival du Film Policier, Special Jury Prize, 1997

2217. ***Things I Never Told You***   1996 DSCP
D: Isabel Coixet
S: Isabel Coixet
C: Teresa Medina
P: Dora Medrano
A: Lili Taylor, Andrew McCarthy

A depressed young woman attempts suicide and begins a relationship with the hotline counselor. *FII.*

Awards: Thessaloniki Film Festival, Best Actress, Silver Alexander, 1996; Fotogramas de Plata, Best Film, 1997

2218. ***Unhook the Stars***   1996 S
D: Nick Cassavetes
S: Nick Cassavetes, Helen Caldwell
C: Phedon Papamichael
P: René Cleitman
A: Gena Rowlands, Marisa Tomei, Gérard Depardieu

A suburban widow with an unruly teenage daughter makes friends with and helps out a young neighbor mother who is being abused by her husband.

2219. ***Walking and Talking***   1996 DS
D: Nicole Holofcener
S: Nicole Holofcener
C: Michael Spiller
P: Ted Hope
A: Catherine Keener, Anne Heche

Manhattan. The story of two friends in their twenties; one is getting married, which makes the other nervous, but then the marriage jitters arrive. *Variety. 1996, Jan. 1.*

Awards: Sundance Film Festival, nomination for Grand Jury Prize, 1996

2220. ***Work***   1996 DSP
D: Rachel Reichman
S: Rachel Reichman
P: Susan Stover
A: Sonha Sohn, Cynthia Kaplan

A young working-class married woman looks for work that does not interest her and has an affair with the college-bound African American woman next door. *Bright Lights. 2004, May. Accessed 2005, Mar. 6.*

2221. ***Clockwatchers***   1997 DSP
D: Jill Sprecher
S: Jill Sprecher, Karen Sprecher
C: Jim Denault
P: Gina Resnick
A: Toni Collette, Parker Posey, Lisa Kudrow, Alanna Ubach

Four young women work temporary jobs at Global Credit, struggle with the realities of a nine-to-five office world, and become friends. Comedy. *AMG.*

Awards: Torino International Film Festival, Best Film, 1997; Arizona International Film Festival, Most Popular Independent Film, 1998

2222. ***Contact***   1997 S
D: Robert Zemeckis
S: Carl Sagan, Ann Druyan
C: Don Burgess
A: Jodie Foster, Jena Malone

An astronomer is convinced she has heard signals from deep space and sets up a station to continue communication with the "aliens." When they respond, much of the official science and media world becomes engaged with her and her work, not always positively.

Awards: Academy of Science Fiction, Fantasy, and Horror Films, Best Actress (Foster), 1998

2223. ***Eve's Bayou***   1997 DSC
D: Kasi Lemmons
S: Kasi Lemmons
C: Amy Vincent
P: Caldecott Chubb
A: Jurnee Smollett, Meagan Good, Lynn Whitfield, Samuel L. Jackson

Louisiana, 1960s. A small-town African American doctor dominates his daughters with his charm until his youngest daughter sees him with another woman. His wife and his sister, who is a clairvoyant, turn away from his infidelities, but the older daughter is set off by the revelation and punished by her mother.

Awards: Acapulco Black Film Festival, Black Film Award, 1998

2224. ***It's in the Water***   1997 DS
D: Kelli Herd
S: Kelli Herd
C: Michael Off
A: Keri Jo Chapman, Teresa Garrett

Texas. A local mother in a boring marriage volunteers at the new AIDS hospice, where she finds an old school friend working as a nurse. Their lesbian relationship inspires gossip and other gay relationships as well as an antigay support group. Action. *AMG.*

2225. *Jackie Brown* 1997

D: Quentin Tarantino
S: Quentin Tarantino; based on the novel *Rum Punch* by Elmore Leonard
C: Guillermo Navarro
A: Pam Grier, Samuel L. Jackson

Los Angeles. A woman collaborates with a gun dealer but gets arrested; even though he bails her out, she knows his evil game, so she gets involved with the bail bondsman and cooperates with the police. Action.

2226. *Loved* 1997 DS

D: Erin Dignam
S: Erin Dignam
C: Reynaldo Villalobos
P: Sean Penn
A: Robin Wright Penn, Amy Madigan, Joanna Cassidy

Los Angeles. A suicidal champion swimmer from a wealthy suburban family has a long-term involvement with an abusive man.

Awards: Seattle International Film Festival, Best Actress (Wright Penn), 1997

2227. *Selena* 1997

D: Gregory Nava
S: Gregory Nava
C: Edward Lachman
P: Moctesuma Esparze
A: Jennifer Lopez, Edward James Olmos

A biography of the Mexican pop singing star and the father who promoted her; she was murdered by the president of her fan club.

Awards: ALMA Awards, Outstanding Feature Film, Outstanding Actress, 1998; Imagen Foundation Awards, Best Film, Best Actress, 1998

2228. *Washington Square* 1997 DSP

D: Agnieszka Holland
S: Carol Doyle; based on the novel by Henry James
C: Jerzy Zielinski
P: Roger Birnbaum, Julie Bergman Sender
A: Jennifer Jason Leigh, Albert Finney, Maggie Smith, Judith Ivey

New York, 1950s. A shy heiress is in love with a penniless man, but her father, convinced the man is a gold digger, insists that he will disinherit her if she marries. She decides to defy him, but her lover gets cold feet. Over the years, she grows stronger by standing up to her father, and her insecurity disappears along with the desire for her lover, who attempts to return after her father dies.

2229. *The 24-Hour Woman* 1998 DSC

D: Nancy Savoca
S: Nancy Savoca, Richard Guay
C: Teresa Medina
P: Richard Guay
A: Rosie Perez, Marianne Jean-Baptiste, Patti LuPone

A high-powered TV director, a Puerto Rican Brooklynite, has an unexpected child and faces conflicts with her coworkers and husband, as well as her own sense that her life is overfull.

2230. *Beloved* 1998 SP

D: Jonathan Demme
S: Akosua Busia, Richard LaGravenese, Adam Brooks; based on the novel by Toni Morrison
C: Tak Fujimoto
P: Kate Forte, Jonathan Demme
A: Oprah Winfrey, Thandie Newton, Kimberly Elise, Danny Glover

Cincinnati, nineteenth century. A slave, who gave birth during her escape from "sweet home," ekes out a living with her daughter in a haunted home off the main road leading into town. A feral girl/ghost arrives to stay and discomfits the household with her tantrums, exacerbated by a pregnancy; an exorcism by the Christian women forces her out. The mother becomes involved with a man, who leaves her when he finds out she is shunned for murdering her children. Spirits are ever present, and the grandmother is a woodland preacher.

2231. *High Art* 1998 DSCP

D: Lisa Cholodenko
S: Lisa Cholodenko
C: Tami Reiker
P: Dolly Hall
A: Ally Sheedy, Radha Mitchell, Patricia Clarkson

A photography magazine editor is attracted to a photographer who lives in her apartment building. The photographer is a drug addict with a German live-in lover.

Awards: Deauville Film Festival, Jury Prize, 1998; GLAAD Media Awards, Outstanding Film, 1999; Independent Spirit Awards, Best Female Lead (Sheedy), 1999; National Society of Film Critics Awards, Best Actress (Sheedy), 1999

2232. *How Stella Got Her Groove Back* 1998 SP

D: Kevin Rodney Sullivan
S: Ronald Bass, Terry McMillan
C: Jeff Jur
P: Jennifer Ogden
A: Angela Bassett, Whoopi Goldberg, Taye Diggs

A newly divorced woman takes a vacation with a friend and finds love in the Caribbean. Comedy.

Awards: Acapulco Black Film Festival, Best Actress (Bassett), 1999; Image Awards, Outstanding Motion Picture, Outstanding Actress (Bassett, Goldberg), 1999

2233. *One True Thing* 1998 SP
D: Carl Franklin
S: Karen Croner; based on the novel by Anna Quindlen
C: Declan Quinn
P: Jesse Beaton
A: Meryl Streep, Renée Zellweger, William Hurt
A daughter is pushed by her father to leave her job as a journalist in New York and return home to take care of her dying mother, whom she has never respected. Revelations about her father's affairs with students leave her more angry and then more understanding. *Variety: 4. 1998, Sep. 8.*
Awards: Academy Awards, nomination for Best Actress (Streep), 1999

2234. *The Players Club* 1998 P
D: Ice Cube
S: Ice Cube
C: Malik Sayeed
P: Patricia Charbonnet
A: LisaRaye
A young African American mother working in a shoe store is lured into stripping at a local club; her cousin gets involved too, and rapes and prostitution follow, leading the woman to take revenge. *AMG.*

2235. *A Price Above Rubies* 1998
D: Boaz Yakin
S: Boaz Yakin
C: Adam Holender
P: John Penotti
A: Julianna Margulies, Renée Zellweger
Brooklyn. A Hasidic woman is forced to marry a scholar; stifled, she is led into the outside world by a predatory brother-in-law, who has her work in his jewelry business and then betrays her when she befriends another man.
Awards: Deauville Film Festival, nomination for Grand Prize, 1998

2236. *Stepmom* 1998 S
D: Chris Columbus
S: Gigi Levangie, Jessie Nelson
C: Donald McAlpine
P: Chris Columbus
A: Susan Sarandon, Julia Roberts
A divorced mother gets cancer, then tries to make friends, for her children's sake, with her ex-husband's new wife, with whom she has heretofore competed.
Awards: San Diego Film Critics Society, Best Actress (Sarandon), 1998

2237. *Anywhere but Here* 1999 S
D: Wayne Wang
S: Alvin Sargent; based on the novel by Mona Simpson
C: Roger Deakins
P: Laurence Mark
A: Susan Sarandon, Natalie Portman
A single mother and her teenage daughter move from Wisconsin to Beverly Hills, where the daughter suffers her mother's high spirits, class pretension, and romantic failures.

2238. *Boys Don't Cry* 1999 DS
D: Kimberly Pierce
S: Kimberly Pierce, Andy Bienen
C: Jim Denault
P: John Hart
A: Hilary Swank, Chloë Sevigny
Nebraska. A teenager who is tired of hiding her true passions runs away to a new town, where she passes as a boy. Her appeal in this new role attracts many new friends, male and female, and she falls in love with one of them. But her identity is eventually uncovered, and she is murdered by some of the men, who react in hysterical revenge to the betrayal. Based on the story of Brandon Teena.
Awards: Boston Society of Film Critics Awards, Best New Filmmaker, Best Actress (Swank), Best Supporting Actress (Sevigny), 1999; London Film Festival, FIPRESCI, 1999; Academy Awards, Best Actress (Swank), nomination for Best Supporting Actress (Sevigny), 2000

2239. *Brokedown Palace* 1999
D: Jonathan Kaplan
S: Adam Fields, David Arata
C: Newton Thomas Sigel
P: Adam Fields
A: Kate Beckinsale, Claire Danes
Two young women vacationing in Thailand are conned into being drug mules and thrown into prison; inside, one learns to speak Thai and saves the other at a public hearing, while sacrificing herself.

2240. *A Cooler Climate* 1999 DS
D: Susan Seidelman
S: Zena Collier, Marsha Norman
C: John Bartley
A: Judy Davis, Sally Field

A middle-class woman divorces for a younger man, who leaves her; without resources, she ends up as a maid for a wealthy woman in her summer home in Maine, where they become friends. *NYT: E24. 1999, Aug. 20.*

2241. *Double Jeopardy* 1999
D: Bruce Beresford
S: David Weisberg
C: Peter James
P: Leonard Goldberg
A: Ashley Judd, Tommy Lee Jones
Jailed for the murder of her wealthy spouse, who disappeared from a boat they were on together, a woman becomes suspicious when she is released and cannot find her child. She leads her parole officer on a chase across the country to New Orleans, where she finds her husband alive. Action.

2242. *Erin Brockovich* 1999 S
D: Steven Soderbergh
S: Susannah Grant
C: Edward Lachman
P: Danny DeVito
A: Julia Roberts, Albert Finney
California. Based on the true story of a cancer-ridden community—polluted by a plant owned by Pacific Gas & Electric—and a financially desperate single mother who demands and gets the job of investigating and prosecuting the company.
Awards: Academy Awards, Best Actress, 2001; BAFTA Awards, Best Actress, 2001; London Critics' Circle Film Awards, Actress of the Year, 2001

2243. *Freak Weather* 1999 DS
D: Mary Kuryla
S: Mary Kuryla
A: Jacqueline McKenzie
Kicked out of her abusive boyfriend's house, a woman goes on the road with her son. *Pioneer Theater. Accessed 2005, March 8.*

2244. *Girl, Interrupted* 1999 S
D: James Mangold
S: James Mangold, Lisa Loomer, Anna Hamilton Phelan; based on the book by Susana Kaysen
C: Jack Green
P: Douglas Wick
A: Winona Ryder, Angelina Jolie, Clea Duvall
A young woman who has attempted suicide is placed in a mental hospital, which is dominated by one particularly aggressive patient.
Awards: Academy Awards, Best Supporting Actress (Jolie), 2000

2245. *Guinevere* 1999 DS
D: Audrey Wells
S: Audrey Wells
C: Charles Minsky
P: Jonathan King
A: Sarah Polley
A wealthy and unhappy young woman on her way to Harvard Law School gets involved with a burnt-out photographer thirty years her senior. *Village Voice: 126. 1999, Sep. 29.*
Awards: Deauville Film Festival, Special Jury Prize, 1999; Sundance Film Festival, Waldo Salt Screenwriting Award, 1999

2246. *I Love You ... Don't Touch Me!* 1999 DSP
D: Julie Davis
S: Julie Davis
C: Mark Putnam
P: Julie Davis
A: Marla Schaffel
A young woman saves her virginity for the perfect man but wonders about the different approach taken by her friend, who experiments sexually. *Variety: 68. 1997, Feb. 10.*

2247. *Limbo* 1999 P
D: John Sayles
S: John Sayles
C: Haskell Wexler
P: Maggie Renzi
A: Mary Elizabeth Mastrantonio, David Strathairn
Alaska. A lounge singer and her teenage daughter go on a boat trip with a new man; it turns dangerous and they begin to bond, then it turns evil.
Awards: Seattle International Film Festival, Best Direction, 1999

2248. *A Map of the World* 1999 SP
D: Scott Elliott
S: Jane Hamilton, Peter Hedges, Polly Platt
C: Seamus McGarvey
P: Kathleen Kennedy, Frank Marshall
A: Sigourney Weaver, Julianne Moore, Chloë Sevigny
Wisconsin. A mother and nurse is ostracized by the community because of her responsibility for the death of a neighbor child, whose mother is her friend.

2249. *Music of the Heart* 1999 SP
D: Wes Craven
S: Pamela Gray
C: Peter Deming
P: Susan Kaplan, Marianne Magdalena
A: Meryl Streep, Angela Bassett, Cloris Leachman

A homemaker is abandoned by her husband, then finds a position teaching violin in schools. *NYT: E13. 1999, Oct. 29.*

Awards: Academy Awards, nomination for Best Actress (Streep), 2000

2250. *Passion of Mind* 1999
D: Alain Berliner
S: Ronald Bass, David Field
C: Eduardo Serra
P: Ronald Bass
A: Demi Moore

An American widow lives with her two children in Provence, France, during the day and in Manhattan at night. Fantasy. *Variety: 21. 2000, May 22.*

2251. *Sugar Town* 1999 DS
D: Allison Anders, Kurt Voss
S: Allison Anders, Kurt Voss
C: Kristian Bernier
P: Daniel Hassid
A: Jade Gordon, Ally Sheedy

Los Angeles. The pop music scene through the eyes of several participants, particularly an aspiring rock star who steals a music producer boyfriend from her boss. *AMG.*

Awards: Fantasporto, Best Screenplay, 2000

2252. *Tumbleweeds* 1999 S
D: Gavin O'Connor
S: Gavin O'Connor, Angela Shelton
C: Dan Stoloff
P: Greg O'Connor
A: Janet McTeer

A woman and her twelve-year-old daughter hit the roads of the American South in search of a man and a home; they move on without a look back whenever things get tough.

Awards: Golden Globes, Best Actress, 2000

2253. *28 Days* 2000 DSP
D: Betty Thomas
S: Susannah Grant
C: Declan Quinn
P: Celia Costas
A: Sandra Bullock

An alcoholic New Yorker is sent to a rehabilitation center by court order and becomes a convert to the mores of Alcoholics Anonymous. Comedy.

2254. *The Business of Strangers* 2000
D: Patrick Stettner
S: Patrick Stettner
C: Teodoro Maniaci
P: Robert Nathan
A: Stockard Channing, Julia Stiles

An executive away from home spends a night drinking with a younger woman who was supposed to assist her. She and a headhunter flirt, a story of rape emerges, and the game turns to revenge.

Awards: London Critics' Circle Film Awards, Actress of the Year (Channing), 2003; Paris Film Festival, Jury Prize, 2003

2255. *Chutney Popcorn* 2000 DSP
D: Nisha Ganatra
S: Nisha Ganatra, Susan Carnival
C: Erin King
P: Susan Carnival
A: Jill Hennessy, Nisha Ganatra, Madhur Jaffrey, Sakina Jaffrey

An Indian American woman has a baby for her sister, who is not able to have one, over the objections of her lesbian lover. *NYT: E14. 2000, Sep. 26.*

2256. *Claire Dolan* 2000 P
D: Lodge Kerrigan
S: Lodge Kerrigan
C: Teodoro Maniaci
P: Ann Ruark
A: Katrin Cartlidge

Manhattan. An upper east side prostitute seeks a normal life of motherhood after the death of her mother; however, she must first deal with her pimp. *Film Society. 2000, Feb.*

2257. *Committed* 2000 DSP
D: Lisa Krueger
S: Lisa Krueger
C: Tom Krueger
P: Marlen Hecht
A: Heather Graham

A woman follows her wayward husband from New York to Texas, then befriends his new girlfriend to take revenge. *Village Voice: 130. 2000, May 2.*

Awards: Sundance Film Festival, nomination for Grand Jury Prize, 2000

2258. *The Contender* 2000
D: Rod Lurie
S: Rod Lurie
C: Denis Maloney
P: Marc Frydman
A: Joan Allen, Gary Oldman

A senator nominated for vice-president is smeared by a sex scandal.

Awards: Academy Awards, nomination for Best Actress, 2001

2259. *Hanging Up* 2000 DSP
D: Diane Keaton

S: Delia Ephron, Nora Ephron
C: Howard Atherton
P: Nora Ephron
A: Meg Ryan, Diane Keaton, Lisa Kudrow
Los Angeles. Three sisters face the decline and death of their father, long divorced from their mother, who will have nothing to do with him and little to do with her daughters; the focus is on the middle sister and her in-between, must-care-for-everyone nature. Comedy.

2260. *If These Walls Could Talk 2*   2000 DSP
D: Jane Anderson, Martha Coolidge, Anne Heche
S: Jane Anderson, Anne Heche, Sylvia Sichel, Alex Sichel
P: Mary Kane
A: Chloë Sevigny, Natasha Lyonne, Vanessa Redgrave, Sharon Stone, Michelle Williams, Ellen DeGeneres
Three stories of lesbians who live in the same house at different times: in the 1960s, a woman whose partner suddenly dies; in the 1970s, a student whose lesbian politics do not coincide with campus feminists; and in the 1990s, a couple who decide to have a child by going to a sperm bank.

2261. *Isn't She Great*   2000
D: Andrew Bergman
S: Paul Rudnick
C: Karl Lindenlaub
P: Mark Lobell
A: Bette Midler, Stockard Channing, Nathan Lane
A biopic of Jacqueline Susann, author of *Valley of the Dolls* and other 1960s runaway best sellers about the sex lives of suburbanites. *The Nation: 34. 2000, Feb. 21.*

2262. *Love and Basketball*   2000 DS
D: Gina Prince-Bythewood
S: Gina Prince-Bythewood
C: Reynaldo Villalobos
P: Spike Lee
A: Sanaa Lathan, Monica Wright, Alfre Woodard
Los Angeles. An African American gets a scholarship to USC with her basketball talent and parallels the sports career of a good male friend. *Village Voice: 121. 2000, Feb. 15.*
Awards: Black Reel Awards, Best Director, Best Actress (Lathan), 2001; Image Awards, Outstanding Actress (Lathan), 2001

2263. *Luminarias*   2000 S
D: Jose Luis Valenzuela
S: Evelina Fernández
C: Alex Phillips

P: Sal Lopez
A: Evelina Fernández, Marta DuBois, Angela Moya, Dyana Ortelli
A Hispanic lawyer is left by her faithless husband. She seeks male companionship by going out with her friends, who are supportive of her and her divorce. *NYT: E20. 2000, Oct. 6.*
Awards: Toulouse Latin America Film Festival, Special Mention, 2000

2264. *Nurse Betty*   2000 P
D: Neil LaBute
S: John C. Richards
C: Jean Yves Escoffier
P: Gail Mutrux, Steve Golin
A: Renée Zellweger
After her husband is murdered, a Kansas nurse heads for Hollywood to be near her favorite soap opera doctor, whom she believes is real. Fantasy. *NYT: E1. 2000, Sep. 8.*
Awards: Golden Globes, Best Actress, 2001

2265. *Sleepy Time Gal*   2000 SP
D: Christopher Münch
S: Christopher Münch, Alice Elliott Dark
C: Marco Fargnoli
P: Ruth Charny
A: Jacqueline Bisset, Martha Plimpton
New York. A radio DJ learns she has cancer, so she seeks out the son and daughter she gave up for adoption, as well as an ex-lover. *NYT. 2002, Feb. 10.*
Awards: Sundance Film Festival, nomination for Grand Jury Prize, 2001

2266. *Things behind the Sun*   2000 DSP
D: Allison Anders
S: Allison Anders, Kurt Voss
C: Terry Stacey
P: Robin Alper
A: Kim Dickens
A young singer-songwriter is driven to alcoholism by a rape in her youth; a music journalist, tormented himself by impotence, recalls his part in the rape (as a child, he lived with his violent older brother) when she writes a song about it, and he decides to interview her.

2267. *Things You Can Tell Just By Looking at Her*   2000 P
D: Rodrigo Garcia
S: Rodrigo Garcia
C: Emmanuel Lubezki
P: Marsha Oglesby, Lisa Lindstrom
A: Glenn Close, Cameron Diaz, Calista Flockhart, Holly Hunter, Kathy Baker

Southern California. Five stories of women whose paths cross: an unmarried doctor caring for her aging mother; a tarot card reader with a lesbian lover; a pregnant bank manager having an affair with a married man; a single mother who is an author of children's books; and two sisters, a medical examiner and a police detective. *AMG.*

Awards: Cannes Film Festival, Un Certain Regard Award, 2000

2268. *The Weight of Water*   2000 DS
D: Kathryn Bigelow
S: Alice Arlen, Christopher Kyle; based on the novel by Anita Shreve
C: Adrian Biddle
P: Sigurjon Sighvatsson
A: Catherine McCormack, Sarah Polley
A modern-day writer investigates the hundred-year-old murders of the sister and sister-in-law of a nineteenth-century Norwegian immigrant. She discovers that a man was framed and condemned to death by the testimony of the woman because her incestuous relationship with her brother was suddenly uncovered.

2269. *What's Cooking?*   2000 DS
D: Gurinder Chadha
S: Gurinder Chadha
C: Lin Jong
P: Jeffrey Taylor
A: Mercedes Ruehl, Kyra Sedgwick, Julianna Margulies, Joan Chen, Alfre Woodard
Los Angeles. Thanksgiving dinner in four different households: Latino, Vietnamese, African American, and Jewish. *Village Voice: 140. 2000, Nov. 21.*

Awards: London Critics' Circle Film Awards, Best British Director, 2002

2270. *Where the Heart Is*   2000
D: Matt Williams
S: Babaloo Mandel
C: Richard Greatrex
P: David McFadean
A: Natalie Portman, Ashley Judd, Stockard Channing
A pregnant young woman is abandoned by her boyfriend on their trip from Tennessee to California; she camps out in the local Wal-Mart in Oklahoma, has the baby, and eventually finds a life there. *NYT: E11. 2002, Apr. 23.*

Awards: YoungStar Awards, Best Young Actress (Portman), 2000

2271. *Woman Wanted*   2000 S
D: Kiefer Sutherland

S: Joanna McClelland Class
C: Ric Waite
P: Damian Lee
A: Holly Hunter
A housekeeper attracts her new employer and his grown son, and she responds sexually to both. *AMG.*

Awards: Ajijic International Film Festival, Best Independent Feature, 2002

2272. *An American Rhapsody*   2001 DSP
D: Eva Gardos
S: Eva Gardos
C: Elemér Ragályi
P: Colleen Camp
A: Nastasja Kinski, Scarlett Johansson
1956. A woman, left behind at a farm in Hungary when her parents flee communism in 1950, finally rejoins them and her fully assimilated older sister in southern California. *NYT: E15. 2001, Aug. 10.*

Awards: Hollywood Film Festival, Best Feature, 2001

2273. *The Blue Diner*   2001 SCP
D: Jan Egelson
S: Natacha Estébanez, Jan Egelson
C: Teresa Medina
P: Natacha Estébanez
A: Lisa Vidal, Miriam Colón
A Boston woman suddenly loses her ability to speak Spanish under the pressure of her nagging immigrant mother's needs.

2274. *Bridget Jones's Diary*   2001 DS
D: Sharon McGuire
S: Helen Fielding, Andrew Davies, Richard Curtis; based on the book by Helen Fielding
C: Stuart Dryburgh
P: Tim Bevan
A: Renée Zellweger
A young woman diets, drinks, and seeks a mate while at the office and at family gatherings. Comedy.

Awards: Academy Awards, nomination for Best Actress, 2002

2275. *The Deep End*   2001 S
D: Scott McGhee, David Siegel
S: Scott McGhee; based on the novel by Elisabeth Sanxay Holding
C: Giles Nuttgens
P: David Siegel
A: Tilda Swinton
Lake Tahoe, Nevada. A mother attempts to cover up her teenage son's involvement in his gay lover's murder. *AMG.*

2276. *Everything Put Together*   2001 S
D: Marc Forster
S: Adam Forgash, Catherine Lloyd Burns
C: Roberto Schaefer
P: Sean Furst
A: Radha Mitchell
A young suburban mother loses her baby to sudden infant death syndrome; overwhelmed by grief, she becomes alienated from and shunned by other neighborhood mothers. *Village Voice: 133. 2001, Nov. 13.*
Awards: Sundance Film Festival, nomination for Grand Jury Prize, 2000

2277. *Ghost World*   2001
D: Terry Zwigoff
S: Terry Zwigoff; based on the comic book by Daniel Clowes
C: Affonso Beato
P: John Smith
A: Thora Birch, Scarlett Johansson, Illeana Douglas
Two girls just out of high school look for an apartment and jobs; while their different styles conflict, they find diversion with an aging hipster and his pop-culture-collector friends. Comedy.

2278. *The Golden Bowl*   2001 S
D: James Ivory
S: Ruth Prawer Jhabvala; based on the novel by Henry James
C: Tony Pierce-Roberts
P: Ismail Merchant
A: Kate Beckinsale, Anjelica Huston, Uma Thurman, Nick Nolte
A woman of the world, unfortunately lacking finances, stands by as her lover insists on marrying a wealthy American friend. She then marries the friend's father, the "world's first billionaire," so she can remain near her lover.

2279. *Lift*   2001 D
D: DeMane Davis, Khari Streeter
S: DeMane Davis
C: David Phillips
P: Mark Hankey
A: Kerry Washington, Lonette McKee
Boston. An inner-city girl has a job in a downtown department store, where she moves well in high-style culture and expertly shoplifts, but her heart is in the neighborhood. *NYT. 2001, Mar. 29.*

2280. *The New Women*   2001 C
D: Todd Hughes, P. David Ebersole
S: Todd Hughes
C: Larra Anderson

P: John Schliesser
A: Mary Woronov, Jamie Tolbert, Sandra Kinder, Cheryl Dunye
"Science-fiction thriller about a strange storm that puts the entire male population of the planet to sleep, leaving women to band together for survival." *FII.*

2281. *The Others*   2001
D: Alejandro Amenabar
S: Alejandro Amenabar; based on the film *The Innocents* (see entry 1745)
C: Javier Aguirresarobe
P: Fernando Bovaira
A: Nicole Kidman, Fionnula Flanagan
England, 1940s. A mother with two weak children, unable to withstand sunlight, is trapped in an isolated mansion struck by frightening supernatural events. Horror.
Awards: Flanders International Film Festival, FIPRESCI, 2001; London Critics' Circle Film Awards, Best Actress (Kidman), 2002

2282. *Series 7*   2001 P
D: Daniel Minahan
S: Daniel Minahan
C: Randy Drummond
P: Christine Vachon, Joana Vicente, Katie Roumel
A: Brooke Smith
A "TV reality show" drama of a pregnant woman out to win by murdering the other contestants in her old hometown. Exploitation, horror. *Village Voice: 134. 2001, Mar. 6.*
Awards: Sweden Fantastic Film Festival, Best Feature, 2002

2283. *Songcatcher*   2001 DS
D: Maggie Greenwald
S: Maggie Greenwald
C: Enrique Chediak
P: Richard Miller
A: Janet McTeer
1907. A professor visits Appalachia to record native folk songs that she believes are related to traditional folk ballads. Her educated ways lead to a clash with the locals. *AMG.*
Awards: Deauville Film Festival, Audience Award, 2000; Sundance Film Festival, Special Jury Prize, 2000

2284. *Stranger Inside*   2001 DSCP
D: Cheryl Dunye
S: Cheryl Dunye, Catherine Crouch
C: Nancy Schreiber
P: Effie Brown, Jim McKay
A: Rain Phoenix, Yolanda Ross, Davenia McFadden

Minnesota. A young woman is transferred to a high-security prison, where she is taken into a gang that is led by the mother she thought was dead. The film was shot and improvised at the Sybil Brand Institute for Women in Los Angeles. *Festival de films, 24th: 25. 2002.*

Awards: Miami Gay and Lesbian Film Festival, Special Jury Prize, 2001; Créteil International Women's Film Festival, Audience Award, 2002

2285. *What Makes a Family*   2001 DP
D: Maggie Greenwald
S: Robert Freedman
C: Rhett Morita
P: Wendy Grean
A: Brooke Shields, Anne Meara
"A lesbian, who has been artificially inseminated, dies after giving birth. Her partner is then involved in a legal fight to regain custody of the baby from the dead woman's parents." *FII.*

Awards: GLAAD Media Awards, Outstanding Television Movie, 2002

2286. *Wit*   2001 S
D: Mike Nichols
S: Emma Thompson, Margaret Edson, Mike Nichols
C: Seamus McGarvey
P: Simon Bosanquet
A: Emma Thompson
A college literature professor, in the end stage of cancer and bedridden in a hospital, is not down and out yet, insistent on devising witty monologues on her condition.

Awards: Berlin International Film Festival, Ecumenical Jury Prize, 2001; Emmy Awards, Outstanding Television Movie, 2001

2287. *30 Years to Life*   2002 DSP
D: Vanessa Middleton
S: Vanessa Middleton
C: Cliff Charles
P: Vanessa Middleton, Tim Mosley
A: Melissa De Sousa, Erika Alexander
An African American works on Wall Street and suffers through singlehood with her friends. *NYT: E12. 2002, Apr. 5.*

Awards: Black Reel, Best Independent Actress (Alexander), 2003

2288. *The Banger Sisters*   2002
D: Bob Dolman
S: Bob Dolman
C: Karl Walter Lindenlaub
P: Mark Johnson
A: Goldie Hawn, Susan Sarandon

Two old friends, rock band groupies in their younger days, meet again twenty years later; one finds that the other has become a well-to-do conservative housewife who is embarrassed by her past and her friend. Comedy.

2289. *Daydream Believer*   2002 DSCP
D: Debra Eisenstadt
S: Debra Eisenstadt
C: Debra Eisenstadt
P: Debra Eisenstadt
A: Sybil Kempson
A talented small-town Vermont girl tries her luck in Manhattan as an actress. *NYT: E5. 2002, Sep. 25.*

2290. *Discombobbled*   2002 DS
D: Xiao-yen Wang
S: Xiao-yen Wang
C: Li Xiong
A: Qu Ying
San Francisco. An artist who emigrated from China is looking forward to experiencing the modern world. She gets a job in a restaurant and learns English, but she misses her boyfriend, who has stayed behind, and has trouble assimilating because of her regrets. *Festival de films, 25th: 29. 2003.*

2291. *Divine Secrets of the Ya-Ya Sisterhood*   2002 DSP
D: Callie Khouri
S: Mark Andrus; based on the novel by Rebecca Wells
C: John Bailey
P: Bonnie Bruckheimer
A: Ellen Burstyn, Shirley Knight, Fionnula Flanagan, Maggie Smith, Sandra Bullock
A New York playwright is kidnapped by her mother's friends and taken to Louisiana so she can learn to appreciate her distant mother.

2292. *Enough*   2002
D: Michael Apted
S: Nicholas Kazan
C: Rogier Stoffers
P: Rob Cowan
A: Jennifer Lopez
A mother attempts to flee from a vengeful and violent spouse, even changing her name. Finally she does combat training in order to keep from being murdered and to save her daughter from him. Thriller.

2293. *Far from Heaven*   2002 P
D: Todd Haynes
S: Todd Haynes

C: Edward Lachman
P: Christine Vachon
A: Julianne Moore, Dennis Quaid
1950s. A happily married suburban housewife deals with her closeted husband, her children, and an attraction to the African American gardener.
Awards: Broadcast Film Critics Association, Best Actress, 2003; Chicago Film Critics Association Awards, Best Picture, Best Actress, 2003; Independent Spirit Awards, Best Director, Best Female Lead, 2003

2294. *Femme Fatale*   2002 P
D: Brian De Palma
S: Brian De Palma
C: Thierry Arbogast
P: Marina Gefter
A: Rebecca Romijn-Stamos
A thief, trained in elaborate seduction, finds refuge from her pursuers in a look-alike's apartment, then plays out her evil destiny in a reformist spirit. Thriller.

2295. *Frida*   2002 DSP
D: Julie Taymor
S: Clancy Sigal, Diane Lake, Gregory Nava, Anna Thomas
C: Rodrigo Prieto
P: Lindsay Flickinger, Salma Hayek
A: Salma Hayek, Alfred Molina
A biography of Frida Kahlo, her proud upbringing and aggressive confidence in her art, the severe and lifelong pain inflicted by a streetcar accident in her youth, her Marxist politics, and her relationships with Diego Rivera and Leon Trotsky.

2296. *The Good Girl*   2002
D: Miguel Arteta
S: Mike White
C: Enrique Chediak
P: Matthew Greenfield
A: Jennifer Aniston
"Unhappy 30 year old clerk at a Texas store is stuck in a dull, barren marriage to a housepainter" and has an affair with younger worker. *NYT: E10. 2002, Aug. 30.*

2297. *Happy Here and Now*   2002
D: Michael Almereyda
S: Michael Almereyda
C: Jonathan Herron
P: Callum Greene
A: Shalom Harlow, Liane Baliban, Ally Sheedy
A "woman investigates the disappearance of her sister" through her Internet relationships. *Film Society. 2003, Feb.*

2298. *Harrison's Flowers*   2002 S
D: Elie Chouraqui
S: Elie Chouraqui, Isabel Ellsen
C: Nicola Pecorini
P: Albert Cohen
A: Andie MacDowell
A wife travels to Vukovar, Croatia, during the civil war to search for her missing journalist husband. *Village Voice: 118. 2002, Mar. 19.*

2299. *High Crimes*   2002 P
D: Carl Franklin
S: Cary Bickley, Yuri Zeltzer; based on the book by Joseph Finder
C: Theo Van de Sande
P: Janet Yang, Jesse Beaton
A: Ashley Judd, Morgan Freeman
A pregnant lawyer's husband is suddenly arrested for war crimes when he was in the Marines in Central America. She insists on defending him herself and hires a jaded ex-alcoholic lawyer to help her with the military trial. But the witnesses have all disappeared. Thriller.

2300. *The Hours*   United States 2002
D: Stephen Daldry
S: David Hare, Michael Cunningham; based on the novel by Michael Cunningham
C: Seamus McGarvey
P: Robert Fox
A: Nicole Kidman, Meryl Streep, Julianne Moore
Three intertwining stories focusing on intimate relationships: Virginia Woolf and her husband at the end of her life, just before she committed suicide; a contemporary New York lesbian and editor of a famous poet; and the poet's mother, alienated from her 1950s suburban husband and child, who abandons her family after considering suicide.
Awards: Academy Awards, Best Actress (Kidman), 2003; BAFTA Awards, Best Actress (Kidman), 2003; Berlin International Film Festival, Best Actress (Kidman, Streep, Moore), 2003

2301. *Hysterical Blindness*   2002 DSP
D: Mira Nair
S: Laura Cahill
C: Declan Quinn
P: Janette Day
A: Uma Thurman, Gena Rowlands, Juliette Lewis
New Jersey, 1987. Two thirtyish women seek love in the local bars. One has a child she is raising on her own, one has a mother who surprises her daughter by finding love herself. *Festival de films, 26th: 8. 2004.*
Awards: Golden Globes, Best Actress (Thurman), 2003

2302. *Janice Beard* 2002 DS
D: Claire Kilner
S: Claire Kilner, Ben Hopkins
C: Richard Greatrex
P: Jonathan Olsberg
A: Eileen Walsh, Patsy Kensit
A young temporary worker bucks the office political tide, then falls into a romance with an industrial saboteur. Comedy. *NYT: E14. 2002, May 10.*
Awards: Cinequest San Jose Film Festival, Best First Feature, 2000

2303. *Kissing Jessica Stein* 2002 S
D: Charles Herman-Wurmfeld
S: Heather Juergensen, Jennifer Westfeld
C: Lawrence Sher
P: Brad Zions
A: Jennifer Westfeld, Heather Juergensen
A New York journalist responds to an ad for female companionship that's been placed by a thrill-seeking "hipster" gallery owner. *Village Voice: 122. 2002, Mar. 19.*
Awards: Louisville Jewish Film Festival, Best Film, 2002; GLAAD Media Awards, Outstanding Film, 2003; Glitter Awards, Best Lesbian Feature, 2003

2304. *Leela* 2002
D: Somanth Sen
S: Somanth Sen
C: S. Douglas Smith
P: Raj Munjal
A: Dimple Kapadia
California. A visiting professor from the University of Bombay has an affair with one of her male students. *NYT. 2002, Nov. 8.*

2305. *Lovely and Amazing* 2002 DS
D: Nicole Holofcener
S: Nicole Holofcener
C: Harlan Bosmajian
P: Ted Hope
A: Catherine Keener, Brenda Blethyn, Emily Mortimer
Two sisters—one an actress, the other a mother and artist—help their mother through liposuction surgery by taking care of their adopted African American ten-year-old sister; in between they deal with their own anger and romantic disappointments. Comedy.
Awards: Independent Spirit Awards, Best Supporting Female (Mortimer), 2002

2306. *Margarita Happy Hour* 2002 DSP
D: Ilya Chaiken
S: Ilya Chaiken

C: Gordon Chou
P: Susan Leber
A: Eleanor Hutchins
Brooklyn. An artist immersed in the loft scene cares for her two-year-old child and irresponsible boyfriend. *Village Voice: 116. 2002, Mar. 26.*

2307. *Monsoon Wedding* 2002 DSP
D: Mira Nair
S: Sabrina Dhawan
C: Declan Quinn
P: Caroline Baron, Mira Nair
A: Lillete Dubey, Naseeruddin Shah, Vasundhara Das
New Delhi. Two upper-class families come together for a large wedding; many characters participate, and the bride is not yet over her affair with someone who is not her arranged American partner.
Awards: Canberra International Film Festival, Audience Award, 2001; British Independent Film Awards, Best Foreign Film, 2002

2308. *My Big Fat Greek Wedding* 2002 SP
D: Joel Zwick
S: Nia Vardalos
C: Jeff Jur
P: Tom Hanks, Rita Wilson
A: Nia Vardalos
Chicago. The thirty-year-old daughter of a Greek restaurant family causes havoc with her marriage to a Protestant. Comedy. *Village Voice: 138. 2002, Apr. 23.*
Awards: Golden Satellite Awards, Best Motion Picture, 2003; Independent Spirit Awards, Best Debut Performance, 2003

2309. *Personal Velocity* 2002 DSCP
D: Rebecca Miller
S: Rebecca Miller
C: Ellen Kuras
P: Alexis Alexanian
A: Kyra Sedgwick, Parker Posey, Fairuza Balk, Maria Hobel
A triptych: A small-town waitress leaves her abusive husband; a Manhattan publishing house editor ignores her husband; and a third woman narrowly escapes injury from the car accident that the others hear about on the news.
Awards: Sundance Film Festival, Grand Jury Prize, 2002; Independent Spirit Awards, Best Director, 2003

2310. *Real Women Have Curves* 2002 DSP
D: Patricia Cardozo
S: Josefina Lopez
C: Jim Denault

P: Effie Brown
A: America Ferrera, Lupe Ontiveros, Ingrid Loiu
A Mexican American girl wins a scholarship to Columbia University, but she must contend with her mother's insistence that she work in her sister's sweatshop in East Los Angeles.
Awards: Humanitas Prize, 2002; Imagen Foundation Awards, Best Supporting Actress (Ontiveros), 2003

2311. *The Rising Place*   2002
D: Tom Rice
S: Tom Rice
C: Jim Dollarhide
P: Tracy Ford
A: Laurel Holloman, Elise Neal
1940s, Mississippi. Told through flashback dramatizations of old letters, a young small-town southern woman is isolated by her friendship with a black woman and her pregnancy outside marriage. *Village Voice: 118. 2002, Nov. 16.*
Awards: Heartland Film Festival, Grand Prize, 2000; Stony Brook Film Festival, Best Film, 2002

2312. *Secretary*   2002 SP
D: Steven Shainberg
S: Erin Cressida Wilson, Mary Gaitskill; based on the story by Mary Gaitskill
C: Steven Fierberg
P: Andrew Fierberg, Amy Hobby
A: Maggie Gyllenhaal, James Spader
A young woman returns to her protective mother after a stay in a mental hospital; on the job with her rigidly demanding lawyer boss, she finds that making errors gets her spankings that she enjoys. Fantasy and reality collide as the boss resists her game, and she devises ever more elaborate ploys to engage his attention. Comedy. *NYT: E12. 2002, Sep. 20.*
Awards: Boston Society of Film Critics Awards, Best Actress, 2002; Fantasporto, Best Actress, 2003; Paris Film Festival, Best Actress, 2003

2313. *Something to Talk About*   2002 SP
D: Lasse Hallström
S: Callie Khouri
C: Sven Nykvist
P: Anthea Sylbert
A: Julia Roberts, Kyra Sedgwick, Dennis Quaid, Gena Rowlands
A woman, the manager of her father's horse stable business, discovers her husband's affair and moves in with her sister, thereby beginning the process of questioning her male relationships, including the one with her father. AMG.

2314. *Unfaithful*   2002
D: Adrian Lyne
S: Claude Chabrol, Alvin Sargent
C: Peter Biziou
P: Adrian Lyne
A: Diane Lane, Richard Gere
A happily married suburban woman suddenly takes up with an attractive rake she meets in lower Manhattan. When her husband discovers the affair, he visits the man and accidentally murders him. Remake of *La Femme infidèle* (448).
Awards: National Society of Film Critics Awards, Best Actress, 2003; New York Film Critics Circle Awards, Best Actress, 2003

2315. *White Oleander*   2002 S
D: Peter Kosminsky
S: Mary Agnes Donoghue; based on the novel by Janet Fitch
C: Elliot Davis
P: Jon Wells
A: Robin Wright Penn, Michelle Pfeiffer, Allison Lohman, Renée Zellweger
A dominating mother murders a boyfriend who jilts her. Imprisoned, she continues to control her teenager as the girl passes through a series of foster homes and stepmothers.

2316. *Acts of Worship*   2003 DS
D: Rosemary Rodriguez
S: Rosemary Rodriguez
C: Luke Geissbuhler
P: Nadia Leonelli
A: Ana Reeder, Michael Hyatt
A drug addict on New York's lower east side is befriended by a successful young photographer who is a recovering addict herself. *NYT: E12. 2003, Nov. 21.*
Awards: Santa Barbara International Film Festival, Best Actress (Reeder), 2001; Magnolia Independent Film Festival, Best Feature, 2002

2317. *Casa de los Babys*   2003
D: John Sayles
S: John Sayles
C: Mauricio Rubinstein
P: Hunt Lowry
A: Marcia Gay Harden, Lili Taylor, Daryl Hannah, Mary Steenburgen, Maggie Gyllenhaal, Vanessa Martinez
A group of women from the United States wait in a Latin American town for approval to take home the babies they are in the process of adopting. *NYT: E15. 2003, Sep. 19.*

2318. *Civil Brand*   2003 DSP
D: Neema Barnette

S: Preston A. Whitmore II, Joyce Renee Lewis
C: Yuri Neyman
P: Neema Barnette
A: LisaRaye, Lark Voorhies, N'Bushe Wright
African Americans in a women's prison work with a prison guard who is a law student to object to corporate abuse of their labor. *NYT: E16. 2003, Oct. 10.*

2319. *Deliver Us from Eva* 2003
D: Gary Hardwick
S: Gary Hardwick, B. E. Brauner
C: Alexander Gruszynski
P: Paddy Cullen
A: Gabrielle Union, LL Cool J
An African American woman who raised her three sisters after their parents died cannot refrain from interfering in their lives; her in-laws pay someone to date her. Comedy. *Village Voice: 110. 2003, Feb. 5.*
Awards: Black Reel Awards, Best Screenplay, 2004

2320. *Down & Out with the Dolls* 2003
D: Kurt Voss
S: Kurt Voss
C: Tony Croll
P: Matt Hill
A: Zoë Poledouris, Kinnie Starr, Nicole Barrett, Melody Moore
The story of an all-girl punk rock band in Portland, Oregon. Lots of music. *Village Voice: 108. 2003, Mar. 19.*

2321. *Freaky Friday* 2003 S
D: Mark Waters
S: Heather Hach, Leslie Dixon
C: Oliver Wood
P: Andrew Gunn
A: Jamie Lee Curtis, Lindsay Lohan
A mother and her guitar-playing daughter switch bodies for a day after being charmed by an Asian restaurateur who noticed their bickering. Comedy.

2322. *Gaudi Afternoon* 2003 DSP
D: Susan Seidelman
S: James Myhre, Barbara Wilson
C: Josep Civit
P: Susan Seidelman
A: Judy Davis, Marcia Gay Harden, Lili Taylor, Juliette Lewis
Barcelona. A translator is hired by an American "femme fatale" to locate her husband; she runs into a kidnapping plot. *Cine espanol. 2001.*

2323. *In the Cut* 2003 DSP
D: Jane Campion
S: Jane Campion; based on the novel by Susanna Moore

C: Dion Beebe
P: Nicole Kidman, Laurie Parker
A: Meg Ryan, Jennifer Jason Leigh, Mark Ruffalo
A teacher stumbles upon a murder clue, then becomes involved with the detective investigating the crime. Thriller.

2324. *Laurel Canyon* 2003 DSP
D: Lisa Cholodenko
S: Lisa Cholodenko
C: Wally Pfister
P: Susan Stover
A: Frances McDormand, Kate Beckinsale, Natascha McElhone
Los Angeles. A hip record producer, in the midst of an affair with a rock singer with whom she is making a record, receives her conservative doctor son and his girlfriend in her home.

2325. *Legally Blonde I and II* 2003 S
D: Robert Luketic, Charles Herman-Wurmfeld
S: Amanda Brown, Karen Lutz, Kirsten Smith, Eve Ahlert
C: Anthony Richmond
P: Marc Platt
A: Reese Witherspoon, Sally Field
In *Legally Blonde* (2001), a Beverly Hills fashion student decides to follow her boyfriend to Harvard Law School. In the sequel, *Legally Blonde II*, she becomes a congressional aide and pursues a crusade against animal testing, with Sally Field as the congresswoman. Comedy.

2326. *Mango Kiss* 2003 DSP
D: Sascha Rice
S: Sascha Rice, Sarah Brown
C: John Pirozzi
P: Sascha Rice
A: Michelle Wolff, Danièle Ferraro, Sally Kirkland
"Comedy about two young lesbians who find their relationship strained by the temptations of San Francisco's gay scene." *FII.*

2327. *Marathon* 2003
D: Amir Naderi
S: Amir Naderi
C: Michael Simmonds
P: Amir Naderi
A: Sara Paul
A woman attempts to solve seventy-seven crossword puzzles while riding the New York subway for a day. *Village Voice: 43. 2004, Mar. 31.*

2328. *Mona Lisa Smile* 2003 P
D: Mike Newell
S: Lawrence Konner

C: Anastas Michlos
P: Paul Schiff, Deborah Schindler
A: Julia Roberts, Kirsten Dunst, Julia Stiles, Maggie Gyllenhaal
Wellesley, Massachusetts, 1953. A young art teacher at an elite college faces down overprivileged students who do not expect to have jobs themselves. *AMG.*

2329. *Monster*   2003 DSP
D: Patty Jenkins
S: Patty Jenkins
C: Steven Bernstein
P: Mark Damon, Charlize Theron
A: Charlize Theron, Christina Ricci
The adult life of a serial murderer and her attachment to a needy schoolgirl, who urges on her criminality and then testifies against her. Based on true story.
Awards: Academy Awards, Best Actress (Theron), 2004; Berlin International Film Festival, Best Actress (Theron), 2004; Golden Globes, Best Actress (Theron), 2004

2330. *Pieces of April*   2003 CP
D: Peter Hedges
S: Peter Hedges
C: Tami Reiker
P: Alexis Alexanian, John Lyons
A: Katie Holmes, Patricia Clarkson
Manhattan. A woman who lives in a rundown apartment attempts to offer her Pennsylvania family and dying mother a Thanksgiving meal. *Village Voice: 72. 2003, Oct. 1.*
Awards: Chicago International Film Festival, Audience Award, FIPRESCI, 2003; Vancouver Film Critics Circle, Best Supporting Actress (Clarkson), 2004

2331. *Robin's Hood*   2003 DSCP
D: Sara Millman
S: Sara Millman, Khahtee Turner
C: Sara Millman
P: Sara Millman
A: Khahtee Turner, Clody Cates
San Francisco. An African American social worker is suspended for not being hard enough on her clients. She turns to bank robbery with a French-speaking lesbian lover, and they turn their proceeds over to a community center. *Variety: 24. 2003, Aug. 4.*

2332. *The Safety of Objects*   2003 DSP
D: Rose Troche
S: Rose Troche; based on stories by Amy Michael Homes
C: Enrique Chediak

P: Dorothy Berwin, Christine Vachon
A: Glenn Close, Patricia Clarkson, Mary Kay Place, Jessica Campbell
Four families in a modern suburban development, two headed by single mothers, are challenged by a fatal car accident involving their children; it brings to the fore other pressures in their lives.
Awards: Deauville Film Festival, Best Female Performance (Clarkson), Critics Award, 2002

2333. *Teknolust*   2003 DSP
D: Lynn Hershman Leeson
S: Lynn Hershman Leeson
C: Hiro Narita
P: Lynn Hershman Leeson
A: Tilda Swinton
A genetic scientist creates RedGreenBlue color-coded clones of herself. Science fiction. *NYT: 13. 2004, Jan. 20.*

2334. *Under the Tuscan Sun*   2003 DSP
D: Audrey Wells
S: Audrey Wells; based on the book by Frances Mayes
C: Geoffrey Simpson
P: Audrey Wells
A: Diane Lane, Sandra Oh, Lindsay Duncan
Betrayed by her husband, a writer moves to Tuscany to recuperate. *Village Voice: 69. 2003, Oct. 22.*

2335. *Veronica Guerin*   2003 S
D: Joel Schumacher
S: Carol Doyle, Mary Agnes Donoghue
C: Brendan Galvin
P: Jerry Bruckheimer
A: Cate Blanchett
Based on a true story. A journalist exposes the Dublin drug trade and is executed by the mob.
Awards: San Sebastián International Film Festival, Solidarity Award, 2003; Golden Globes, nomination for Best Actress, 2004

2336. *What Alice Found*   2003
D: A. Dean Bell
S: A. Dean Bell
C: Richard Connors
P: Richard Connors
A: Judith Ivey, Emily Grace
A young woman headed for Miami from New Hampshire gets taken in by an aging truck-stop prostitute and her pimp, who initiate her into the trade in expectation of her supporting them. *Village Voice: 66. 2003, Dec. 3.*
Awards: Deauville Film Festival, Grand Special Prize, 2003; Sundance Film Festival, Special Jury Prize, 2003

2337. *Catwoman* 2004 S

D: Pitof

S: Theresa Rebeck, John Brancato, Michael Ferris; based on the comic book by Bob Kane

C: Thierry Arbogast

P: Edward McDonnell

A: Halle Berry, Sharon Stone

Catwoman emerges to fight her alter ego's employer, a corporate cosmetics company. Action. *Village Voice: 60. 2004, July 21.*

2338. *Cavedweller* 2004 DS

D: Lisa Cholodenko

S: Anne Meredith; based on the novel by Dorothy Allison

C: Xavier Pérez Grobet

P: Michael Levine

A: Kyra Sedgwick, Kevin Bacon

A singer returns to Georgia to regain custody of the two daughters she left behind with her abusive ex-husband. *Tribeca Film. 2003.*

Awards: Karlovy Vary International Film Festival, Ecumenical Jury Award, 2004; Seattle International Film Festival, New American Cinema Award, 2004

2339. *Connie and Carla* 2004 S

D: Michael Lembeck

S: Nia Vardalos

C: Richard Greatrex

P: Gary Barber

A: Nia Vardalos, Toni Collette

Two women escape the mob by passing as drag performers. Comedy. *NYT: E20. 2004, Apr. 16.*

2340. *Iron Jawed Angels* 2004 DS

D: Katja Von Garnier

S: Sally Robinson, Eugenia Bostwick-Singer, Raymond Singer, Jennifer Friedes

C: Robbie Greenberg

A: Hilary Swank, Frances O'Connor, Julia Ormond, Anjelica Huston, Molly Parker, Carrie Snodgrass

The true story of Alice Paul, who began a radical campaign to gain the vote for women in the United States through a constitutional amendment, conflicting with the more conservative approach of the National American Women's Suffrage Association and its president, Carrie Chapman Catt, which went state by state. *Variety: 84. 2004, Feb. 2.*

Awards: Golden Globes, Best Supporting Actress (Huston), 2005

2341. *Kill Bill Vols. 1 and 2* 2004 S

D: Quentin Tarantino

S: Quentin Tarantino, Uma Thurman

C: Robert Richardson

P: Lawrence Bender

A: Uma Thurman, David Carradine, Lucy Liu

The Bride, an assassin out to take revenge on those who murdered her family at her wedding, finally gives in to motherly sentiment after vanquishing her many foes. Action.

2342. *Maria Full of Grace* 2004

D: Joshua Marston

S: Joshua Marston

C: Jim Denault

P: Paul Mezey

A: Catalina Sandino Moreno

Colombia. A pregnant flower plantation worker, disgusted with the expectations of financial support from her family and the lack of ambition of her boyfriend, signs on as a drug mule and ends up in Queens, where she slowly takes charge of her life.

Awards: Berlin International Film Festival, Silver Bear (Moreno), 2004; Deauville Film Festival, Grand Prize, 2004

2343. *Million Dollar Baby* 2004

D: Clint Eastwood

S: Paul Haggis, based on short stories by F. X. Toole

C: Tom Stern

A: Hilary Swank, Clint Eastwood, Morgan Freeman

A thirty-year-old woman works out in a gym at night and waitresses during the day; she insists that a boxing trainer take her on, and he reluctantly agrees. She wins fights but one day takes a crippling beating, which leads to a request for euthanasia.

Awards: Academy Awards, Best Picture, Best Director, Best Actress, 2005; Golden Globes, Best Director, Best Actress, 2005

2344. *A Slipping-Down Life* 2004 DS

D: Toni Kalem

S: Toni Kalem; based on the novel by Anne Tyler

C: Michael Barrow

P: Richard Raddon

A: Lili Taylor, Guy Pearce

North Carolina. A woman works in an amusement park in a small town, where she falls for a local singer and carves his name in her forehead, thereby impressing him with her devotion. *NYT: E12. 2004, May 14.*

Awards: Indianapolis International Film Festival, Special Jury Prize (Taylor), 2004

2345. *The Stepford Wives* 2004

D: Frank Oz

S: Paul Rudnick
C: Rob Hahn
P: Donald DeLine
A: Nicole Kidman, Bette Midler, Glenn Close
A Connecticut suburban town grows robotic wives to fulfill husbands' needs with the proper sunshine disposition; one of the new wives resists her planned transformation. Remake of the 1972 film of same title. Comedy.

2346. *The Time We Killed*   2004 DSCP
D: Jennifer Reeves
S: Jennifer Reeves
C: Jennifer Reeves
P: Jennifer Reeves
A: Lisa Jamot
New York City. An agoraphobic poet dreams of life outside while "confined in her Brooklyn apartment." *Village Voice. 2004, Feb. 25.*
Awards: Berlin International Film Festival, FIPRESCI, 2004; L.A. Outfest, Outstanding Achievement, 2004

2347. *Twisted*   2004 SP
D: Philip Kaufman
S: Sarah Thorp
C: Peter Deming
P: Anne Kopelson, Barry Baeres
A: Ashley Judd
A new homicide inspector finds that her blackouts coincide with a string of murders. *Village Voice: 70. 2004, Mar. 10.*

2348. *Woman Thou Art Loosed*   2004
D: Michael Schultz
S: Stan Foster; based on the novel by T. D. Jakes
C: Reinhart Peschke
P: Reuben Cannon
A: Kimberly Elise, T. D. Jakes, Loretta Devine
A woman who has led a life of drugs, prostitution, and prison guns down the stepfather who raped her when she was twelve. Her attempt to return to her community in the care of a preacher leads to the shooting, which takes place at a revival meeting.
Awards: American Black Film Festival, Best Film, 2004; Black Reel Awards, Best Director, Best Actress (Elise), 2005

URUGUAY

2349. *Transatlantique / Transatlantic* 1997 DSC
D: Christine Laurent
S: Christine Laurent, André Téchiné
C: Jeanne Lapoirie

P: Paulo Branco
A: Laurence Côte
A French woman goes to Montevideo to meet her lover but ends up having to search for him. *Film Society. 1999, Sep.*
Other titles: Transatlántico
Awards: Locarno International Film Festival, nomination for Golden Leopard, 1997

2350. *En la puta vida / The Tricky Life* 2001 DS
D: Beatriz Flores Silva
S: János Kovácsi, Beatriz Flores Silva; based on the novel by Maria Urruzola
C: Francisco Gozon
A: Mariana Santángelo, Andrea Fantoni, Placido El Cara
Montevideo. A single mother with two children leaves her married lover and goes into prostitution with a friend. She dreams of opening a beauty salon but instead follows a pimp to Spain. When she witnesses a transvestite murdered by her protector, she testifies against him at his trial. *Festival de films, 12th: 97. 2002.*
Awards: Bogota Film Festival, Best Director, 2002; Miami Hispanic Film Festival, Audience Award, 2002

2351. *La Espera / The Wait*   2002 S
D: Aldo Garay
S: Sebastian Bednarik, Coral Godoy
C: Diego Varela
A: Elena Zuasti, Veronica Perrotta
"A mother, a daughter, and a neighbor harbor frustrations and reproaches in anonymous, empty spaces." They are "doomed" in their mutual dependency. *Festival des 3.*

USSR

2352. *Skaz o materi / A Mother's Epic*   1963
D: Aleksandr Karpov
S: Dj. Tachenov
A: Amina Oumourzakova
Kazakhstan. A mother pushes ahead with her life, caring for the people around her, even though her son has been killed at the front. *Festival des 3.*

2353. *Sledy ukhodiat za gorizont / Footsteps Disappear on the Horizon*   1964
D: Majit Begaline
S: A. Tarazi
C: A. Achrapov
A: F. Charipova
Kazakhstan. A young woman has reluctantly gone to live with her husband's family in the wintry, re-

mote north, where they are shepherds. One day she falls in love with someone else. *Festival des 3.*

2354. *Belye, belye ajsty* / *The White, White Storks* 1966

D: Ali Khamraev
S: Ali Khamraev, Odelsha Agishev
C: Dilshat Fatkhulin
A: Sairam Isayeva

Uzbekistan. A married woman falls in love with another man, then clashes with villagers and her father, who tries to understand but is hindered by tradition. *Companion Encyclopedia: 20.*
Other titles: Belyye, belyye aisty / The White Cranes

2355. *Krylia* / *Wings* 1966 DS
D: Larisa Shepitko
S: Natalya Ryazantseva, Valentin Yeshov
C: Igor Slabnevich
A: Maya Bulgakova

A school principal remains famous and proud of her career as a fighter pilot. She struggles with the children and bumbles through the crisis of a boy who goes missing after refusing to publicly apologize to her. She treats them all in the authoritarian manner that has alienated her from her daughter. She has a lover, other friends, and a full life, yet she mostly yearns for her former life, marked regularly by subjective views of flying through clouds.

2356. *Anna Karenina* 1967
D: Alexander Zarkhi
S: Vasili Katanyan; based on the novel by Leo Tolstoy
A: Tatiana Samoilova

A woman gives up her child and position for a romance with a younger man but commits suicide when the romance ends.

2357. *Istoriya Asi Klyachinoi kotoraya lyubila, da ni vyshla zamuzh* / *Asya's Happiness* 1967
D: Andrei Konchalovsky
S: Yuri Klepikov
C: Georgi Rerberg
A: Iya Savvina

A cook in a Russian village becomes pregnant by a local bully, who then avoids her. She has an affair with a truck driver, but she prefers to live alone with her son. *Kinoglasnost: 120.*
Awards: Berlin International Film Festival, FIPRESCI, 1988; Nika Awards, Best Director, Best Screenplay, 1989

2358. *Komissar* / *The Commissar* 1967
D: Aleksandr Askoldov
S: Aleksandr Askoldov, Vasili Grossman

C: Valeri Ginzburg
A: Nonna Mordjukova, Rolan Bykov

1919–1921. During the civil war, a female commissar becomes pregnant and spends her internment with a Jewish family, where she is touched by their caring for her. Afterward, she returns to the revolutionary struggle.
Awards: Berlin International Film Festival, FIPRESCI, Silver Bear (Askoldov), 1988; Flanders International Film Festival, Silver Spur, 1988

2359. *V ogne broda net* / *No Ford in the Fire* 1967
D: Gleb Panfilov
S: Gleb Panfilov
C: Dmitri Dolinin
A: Inna Churikova

A young peasant becomes a prolific and talented painter. *Kinoglasnost: 21.*
Awards: Locarno International Film Festival, Golden Leopard, 1969

2360. *Virineya* / *Story of a Woman* 1967 S
D: Vladimir Fetin
S: Lidiya Sejfullina, Albina Shulgina
C: Yevgeni Shapiro
A: Lyudmila Chursina

Siberia, 1918–1920. In a small village, a woman takes the lead in the partisan struggle during the civil war. *Soviet Film. Accessed 2005, July 15.*

2361. *Korotkie vstretchi* / *Brief Encounters* 1968 DS
D: Kira Muratova
S: Kira Muratova, Leonid Zhukhovitsky
C: Gennadi Karyuk
A: Kira Muratova, Nina Ruslanova

Leningrad. A city housing official is competent but frustrated by superiors demanding she make propaganda speeches, which takes her away from her specialty of municipal water. Her guitar-playing, mostly absent geologist lover wants her to leave with him, without regard for her career. She takes in and tutors a girl from the steppes who works as a maid, not realizing that the girl came to her door because she is in love with the geologist too.
Other titles: Short Encounters
Awards: Nika Awards, Best Actress (Ruslanova), 1988

2362. *Samancynyn zolu* / *The Mother's Field* 1968
D: Chinguiz Aitmatov
S: Chinguiz Aitmatov
C: V. Vilenski

A: B. Kydykeeva
Kirgizstan. A woman loses her husband, sons, and
daughter-in-law to the war but revives herself
by talking to her husband's portrait and teaching
her grandson how to farm. *Festival des 3.*

2363. *Mama vyshla zamuzh / Mama Got Married*   1969
D: Vitaly Melnikov
S: Yuri Klepikov
C: Dmitri Dolinin
A: Lyusyena Ovchinnikova
A construction worker raises her sullen teenage
son in a small apartment and also tries to deal
with a new man in her life. Insisting on her own
future, she eventually asks the man to share
their one-room apartment, and the new man
and her son begin their uneasy relationship.

2364. *Nachalo / The Beginning*   1970
D: Gleb Panfilov
S: Gleb Panfilov
C: Dmitri Dolinin
A: Inna Churikova
A factory worker who loves the theater is offered
the role of Joan of Arc and triumphs in it. *Kinoglasnost: 21.*
Other titles: The Debut

2365. *Dolgiye provody / The Long Farewell*   1971 DS
D: Kira Muratova
S: Natalya Ryazantseva
C: Gennadi Karyuk
A: Zinaida Sharko
A mother shares a one-room apartment with her
teenage son, who is embarrassed by her love for
him. He has recently vacationed in Siberia with
his father, who abandoned them years ago, and
is considering living with him. His mother spies
on him, though she herself is fully engaged with
her job as a translator.
Awards: Nika Awards, nomination for Best Film,
Best Actress, 1988

2366. *Bez strakha / Without Fear*   1972
D: Ali Khamraev
S: Andrei Konchalovsky
A: Tamara Shakirova, Khikmat Latypov
Uzbekistan, 1920s. A Red Army officer forces the
Muslim women in a village to unveil, provoking
honor killings. *Film Society. 2003, May.*

2367. *Nevestka / The Daughter-in-Law*   1972
D: Khodjakuli Narliev
C: Anatoli Ivanov

A: Maya-Gozel Aimedova
During World War II, a woman waits in a Turkoman
desert town for the return of her pilot husband.
AMG. Also FII.

2368. *Kseniya, lyubimaya zhene Fyordora / Kseniya, Beloved Wife of Feodor*   1974
D: Vitaly Melnikov
S: Vitaly Melnikov
A: Alla Meshcheryakova
A woman moves into a housing development with
her new husband. *Film Society. 2003, Dec.*

2369. *Chuzhiye pisma / Strange Letters* 1975 S
D: Ilya Averbakh
S: Natalya Ryazantseva
C: Dmitri Dolinin
A: Irina Kupchenko, Svetlana Smirnova
A teacher has a destructive relationship with a
sixteen-year-old pupil, who has been brought up
emotionally impoverished. *AMG.*

2370. *Perepolokh / Disturbance*   1976 DS
D: Lana Gogoberidze
S: Lana Gogoberidze, Zaira Arsenishvili
A: Najda Haradze, Sofiko Chiaureli
Georgia. An aging actress returns to her hometown
to enjoy the activities: dancing, a town meeting
on whether to build a museum or a restaurant,
and a cooking contest. She even manages to
reunite her daughter with her lover. Primarily
"greatly spirited performances" in dance. *Variety:
38. 1977, Jan. 19.*
Other titles: Commotion

2371. *Proshu slova / May I Have the Floor* 1976
D: Gleb Panfilov
S: Gleb Panfilov
C: Aleksandr Antipenko
A: Inna Churikova
The mayor of a village sees her son killed in a
gun accident. A successful, dedicated bureaucrat, she must reconcile her desire to build a
bridge—and the new housing that will come
with it—with the reality of resistance from the
townspeople and her own grief. *Kinoglasnost: 21.
Also Variety: 22. 1976, July 28.*
Other titles: Je demande la parole

2372. *Byeda / Disaster*   1977 D
D: Dinara Asanova
S: Izrail Metter
C: Anatoli Lapshov
A: Yelena Kuzmina, Lidiya Fedoseyeva-Shukshina
Russia. In a northern town, a woman who barely survives economically suffers a blow that leaves her

family even more vulnerable and dependent on the local social services. *Film Society. 2003, Nov.*
Other titles: Beda

2373. *Strannaya zhenshchina / A Strange Woman*
1977
D: Yuly Raizman
S: Yevgeni Gabrilovich
A: Irina Kupchenko
"A beautiful, successful and prominent career woman, married to a diplomat, and the mother of a teenage boy, suddenly decides one day to leave her husband for a lover." *FII.*

2374. *Torgovka i poet / A Market Woman and a Poet*
1978
D: Samson Samsonov
S: Ivan Shamiakin
A: Natalia Andreichenko
A woman member of the underground in Russia goes to a prisoner-of-war camp to try to ransom one of her group; there, she meets her "destiny." *Russian Book. Accessed 2005, Mar. 4.*

2375. *Moskva slezam ne verit / Moscow Does Not Believe in Tears*
1979
D: Vladimir Menshov
S: Valentin Chernykh
C: Igor Slabnevich
A: Vera Alentova, Raisa Ryazanova, Irina Murayeva
Moscow. Three young women move to the city; the film tells the story of their lives at different times, 1958 and 1978.
Awards: Academy Awards, Best Foreign Film, 1981

2376. *Neskolko interviu palichnim voprosam / Some Interviews on Personal Matters*
1979 DS
D: Lana Gogoberidze
S: Lana Gogoberidze, Erlom Akhvlediani
C: Nugzar Erkomaishvili
A: Sofiko Chiaureli
Georgia. A newspaper journalist responds to reader inquiries and gets so absorbed that her husband asks her to choose between work and family, which includes teenage children and her mother. *FII.*

2377. *Poznavaia bely svet / Getting to Know the Big Wide World*
1979 D
D: Kira Muratova
S: Grigori Baklanov
C: Youri Klimenko
A: Nina Ruslanova
A group of workers travel to a tractor factory in a new city. They live like nomads, but one

woman mason never stops in her quest for love; she builds walls with a particular flourish and attracts many men. *Festival de films, 10th: 72. 1988.*
Other titles: En decouvrant le vaste monde

2378. *Proshchanie / Farewell*
1981 S
D: Elem Klimov
S: Larisa Shepitko, Rudolf Tyurin, Valentin Rasputin
C: Vladimir Chukhnov
A: Stefaniya Stayuta, Maya Bulgakova
Developers prepare an island village community for its submersion by a dam. One old woman refuses to leave, and others stay with her. Their plight is metaphorically paralleled with a "futile attempt by demolition workers to destroy an ancient tree." "A film elegy, one of the few in world cinema," as it makes reference to the death of Shepitko during the making of the film. *Variety: 22. 1983, Aug. 3.*

2379. *Odin den i vsya zhian / One Day and a Whole Life*
1982 DS
D: Lana Gogoberidze
S: Lana Gogoberidze, Zaira Arsenishvili
C: Nugzar Erkomaishvili
A: Daredjan Kharshiladze, Tamara Skhirtladze
Georgia, 1920s. A young woman grows to resent her brutish second husband, but she later begins to appreciate him when he joins in the communist movement. *AMG.*
Awards: Cannes Film Festival, nomination for Golden Palm, 1984

2380. *Vassa*
1983
D: Gleb Panfilov
S: Gleb Panfilov; based on the play by Maxim Gorky
C: Leonid Kalashinikov
A: Inna Churikova, Valentina Telichkina
Nizhny Novogorod, 1913. A shipping empire wife tries to save her husband from criminal charges, then pushes him to suicide in order to save the reputation of their two young daughters. Hardened by this, she conflicts with her daughter-in-law, who is involved in revolutionary activities, over control of her grandson. *Variety: 22. 1983, Aug. 3.*
Awards: Moscow International Film Festival, Golden Prize, 1983

2381. *Den dlinnee notchi / Day Longer than Night*
1984 DS
D: Lana Gogoberidze
S: Lana Gogoberidze, Zaira Arsenishvili
C: Nugzar Erkomaishvili

A: Daredjan Kharshiladze, Tamara Skhirtladze

The struggles of a Georgian woman and her family, from the turn of the century to the present, and the history that surrounds her. *Kinoglasnost: 26.*

2382. *Milyi, dorogoi, lyubimyi, yedinstvennyi ... / Sweetheart, Dear, Beloved, the Only One ...*   1984 D

D: Dinara Asanova

S: Valery Priemikhov

C: Vladimir Ilyin

A: Olga Mashnaya, Valeri Priyomykhov

A young woman kidnaps an infant to get back her boyfriend, then appeals to a cab-driver stranger for help. *Kinoglasnost: 44.*

Other titles: *Dear, Dearest, Beloved, Unique ...*

2383. *Oglianis / Look Back*   1984 D

D: Aida Mansarova

S: Eduard Volodarsky

A: Anastasiya Voznesenskaya

A mother reflects on the causes of her teenage son's extreme anger. *Kinoglasnost: 42.*

2384. *Iskrenne vash ... / Sincerely Yours ...*   1985 D

D: Alla Surikova

S: Valentin Azernikov

C: Vsevolod Simakov

A: Vera Glagoleva

A woman enjoys a newfound material existence. *Kinoglasnost.*

2385. *Sestra moja Ljusia / My Sister Lucy* 1985

D: Ermek Chinarbaev

S: Anatoli Kim

C: Geuorgui Guidt

A: Olga Ostrooumova

Kazakhstan, 1940s. Following the war, a Russian widow lives with her daughter and a Kazakh woman and her son in a small village; the story is told from the viewpoint of the grown boy. *Festival des 3.*

2386. *Krugovorot / Full Circle*   1986 DS

D: Lana Gogoberidze

S: Lana Gogoberidze, Zaira Arsenishvili

C: Nugzar Erkomaishvili

A: Leila Abashidze, Lia Eliava

Tbilsi. Two aged friends who have not seen one another in a long time meet again. One is a nearly incapacitated actress who lives with her daughter and an aunt and who has lost none of her generosity; the other is a scientist who has remained single, with a married lover, and adopted a child. *Soviet Film, no. 8: 36. 1986.*

Other titles: *Oromtriali / Succession of Events*

Awards: Tokyo International Film Festival, Best Director, 1987

2387. *Odinokaya zhenshchina zhelayet pozna-komitsya / A Lonely Woman Seeks a Lifetime Companion*   1987

D: Vyacheslav Krishtofovich

S: Viktor Merezhko

C: Vasili Trushkovsky

A: Irina Kupchenko

Russia. A seamstress posts a lonely hearts ad, which results in a relationship with an abusive homeless man. *AMG.*

Awards: Montréal World Film Festival, Best Actress, 1987

2388. *Peremena uchasti / Twist of Fate*   1987 DS

D: Kira Muratova

S: Kira Muratova; based on a story by W. Somerset Maugham

C: Valeri Myulgaut

A: Natalya Leble

A woman kills her lover and presents the act as self-defense, lying about it to both her husband and her lawyer, but the investigation uncovers the truth. *Festival de films, 10th: 73. 1988.*

2389. *Malenkaya Vera / Little Vera*   1988 S

D: Vasil Pichul

S: Mariya Khmelik

C: Yefim Reznikov

A: Natalya Negoda

A rebellious young woman with punk hair and lay-about friends gets pregnant, and her boyfriend moves in with her disapproving family. Her father accidentally stabs the boy one day, and she is pressured not to tell the police. *Variety. 1988, July 20.*

Awards: Montréal World Film Festival, Special Prize, 1988; Venice Film Festival, FIPRESCI, 1988; European Film Awards, Best Screenwriting, 1989; Bogota Film Festival, Best Actress, 1990

2390. *Asteniceskij sindrom / The Aesthenic Syndrome*   1989 DS

D: Kira Muratova

S: Kira Muratova, Aleksandr Chernykh, Sergei Popov

C: Vladimir Pankov

P: Micha Lampert

A: Olga Antonova, Natalya Buzko, Galina Zachurdaewa, Aleksandra Svenskaja

Stories of the glasnost era. First, a doctor has grave difficulties living alone when her husband dies, lashing out at friends and coworkers. It develops that this story is a film within the film, but the audience has little interest in it. Outside the theater, a second story begins about a complacent teacher, comfortable with the bureaucratic stalemate in the classroom, who gets nowhere with her layabout son. Third, a narcoleptic male teacher is subject to fits of wonderment from his mother and wife and to chaos in the classroom, but he mostly just sleeps through it all.

Awards: Berlin International Film Festival, Silver Bear (Muratova), 1990; Nika Awards, Best Film, 1991

2391. *Interdevochka* / *Intergirl* 1989
D: Pyotr Todorovsky
S: Vladimir Kunin
C: Valeri Shuvalov
P: Anders Birkeland
A: Elena Yakovleva
A prostitute, who has a day job as a nurse and lives with her mother, marries a client so she can live in Sweden, but she quickly gets homesick. *Kinoglasnost: 211.*

2392. *Koma* / *Coma* 1989 D
D: Niyole Admomenaite, Boris Gorlov
A: Nataliya Nikulenko
1940s. A gulag prisoner has a child by one of the camp guards, then must betray her lover in order to keep the child. *Variety: 38. 1989, Sep. 13.*

2393. *Spasi i sokhrani* / *Save and Protect* 1989
D: Alexander Sokurov
S: Yuri Arabov; based on the novel by Gustave Flaubert
C: Sergei Yurizditsky
A: Cecile Zervoudaki
A bored housewife turns to sexual affairs. The film is a loose adaptation of Gustave Flaubert's *Madame Bovary*, which focuses on "the essence of her earthly journey toward the grave." *Kinoglasnost: 229.*

Awards: Montréal World Film Festival, FIPRESCI, 1989

2394. *Oultougan* 1990
D: Yedygué Bosylbaiev
S: Yedygué Bosylbaiev
C: Marat Douganov
Kazakhstan. A woman lives in a depressed village near the Aral Sea; its declining condition and the prevailing alcoholism of the people profoundly affect her, to the point of suicide. *Festival des 3.*

2395. *Rebro Adama* / *Adam's Rib* 1990
D: Vyacheslav Krishtofovich
S: Vyacheslav Krishtofovich, Vladimir Kunin
C: Pavel Lebeshev
A: Inna Churikova, Svetlana Ryabava, Yelena Bogdanova
Moscow. Three generations of women live together in a cramped apartment: a dying, demanding grandmother; the mother, who entertains two ex-husbands one day for a celebration; and two near-grown daughters.

Awards: Nika Awards, Best Actress (Churikova), 1992

VENEZUELA

2396. *Oriana* 1985 DSP
D: Fina Torres
S: Fina Torres, Antoine Lacomblez
C: Jean-Claude Larrieu
P: Fina Torres
A: Doris Wells
Flashbacks of three generations of women as a niece returns to inherit the hacienda where her aunt was held hostage. *Guide to Latin: 243.*

Awards: Cannes Film Festival, Golden Camera, 1985; Cartagena Film Festival, Best Film, Best Screenplay, 1985

2397. *Macu, la mujer del policia* / *Macu, the Policeman's Wife* 1987 DS
D: Solveig Hoogesteijn
S: Solveig Hoogesteijn, Milagros Rodriguez
C: Andres Agusti
P: Olegario Barrera
A: Ana Castell
Caracas. A woman, married at eleven to a much older policeman, later has an affair with someone her own age; her husband kills the lover and two of his friends. *Guide to Latin: 240.*

2398. *Disparen a matar* / *Shoot to Kill* 1991
D: Carlos Azpúrua
S: David Suárez
C: Adriano Moreno
P: Carlos Azpúrua
A: Amalia Pérez
A mother sees her son murdered by police in their slum apartment complex; she crusades to uncover the truth of the incident and is eventually helped by a journalist. *Guide to Latin: 236.*

2399. *Santera* / *Santeria* 1994 DS
D: Solveig Hoogesteijn
S: Solveig Hoogesteijn, Senal Paz

C: Andres Agusti
A: Laura Del Sol, Irma Salcedo
A doctor who works for Amnesty International investigates the Venezuelan prison system. There she meets a woman, a priest of the Santería, who has been unjustly jailed for murdering her stepfather. *Festival de films, 24th: 98. 2002.*

2400. *Golpes a mi puerta* / *Knocks at My Door*   1996
D: Alejandro Saderman
S: Alejandro Saderman, Juan Carlos Gené
C: Adriano Moreno
P: Alejandro Saderman
A: Verónica Oddo, Elba Escobar
Two nuns protect a fugitive from political persecution. *Film Society. 1995, Jun.*
Awards: Havana Film Festival, FIPRESCI, 1993; Gramado Film Festival, Best Actress (Oddo), 1994

2401. *Manuela Sáenz*   2000
D: Diego Risquez
S: Padrón Leonardo
C: Cezany Jawarski
P: Pedro Mezquita
A: Beatriz Valdèz, Mariano Alvarez
South America, nineteenth century. The story of Simon Bolívar's lover, a woman of "avant-garde feminism" who fought with him in the struggle for the union of all South America. *Le Monde, September 26, 2001.*

2402. *Woman on Top*   2000 DS
D: Fina Torres
S: Vera Blasi
C: Thierry Arbogast
P: Alain Poul
A: Penelope Cruz
A chef leaves Brazil and her husband, who objects to her need to be on top during lovemaking, and moves to San Francisco, where she becomes the star of a cooking show. Comedy. *FII.*
Awards: Bogota Film Festival, nomination for Best Film, 2000

VIETNAM

2403. *Bao gio cho toi thang muoi* / *October Won't Return*   1984
D: Nhat Minh Dang
S: Nhat Minh Dang
C: Lan Nguyen
A: Huu Muoi Nguyen

A wife returns to her in-laws' house after her husband is killed in the Vietnam War, but she is unable to tell them of the tragedy. During a Buddhist day of forgiveness, her husband's soul "tells her that he would like to see her living happy." *FII.*
Other titles: When the 10th Month Comes
Awards: Moscow International Film Festival, nomination for Golden Prize, 1985

2404. *Co gai tren song* / *Girl on the River* 1988
D: Nhat Minh Dang
S: Nhat Minh Dang
C: Viet Thanh Pham
A: Minh Chau
During the Vietnam War, a prostitute works from her *sang pan* (boat); though she has mostly nationalist clients, she helps a wounded communist fighter. *Cinemaya, no. 7: 10–13. 1990.*

2405. *Kiep phu du* / *Ephemeral Fate*   1990
D: Hai Ning
C: Tran Trung Nhan
A: Hoang Cuc
The last days of the Trinh Sam Dynasty. Two warring clan brothers are directed and manipulated by their respective mothers, courtesans insistent on gaining whatever power and status they can. *Festival des 3.*
Other titles: Destin éphémère

2406. *Dau an cua quy* / *The Devil's Mark*
                                              1992 D
D: Linh Viêt
S: Pham Thuy Nhon
C: Doan Quoc
A: Hiep Ngoc, Don Duong
A girl condemned for witchcraft is banished from society. She falls in love, but the man is arrested when he enters the village; she insists on a purge of fire to rid herself of her problems. *Festival des 3.*
Other titles: La Marque du démon

2407. *Luoi dao* / *The Knife*   1995
D: Hoang Le
S: Nguyen Ho
South Vietnam. An old woman confronts the liberation army and is killed; her granddaughter swears revenge and is given a knife by an officer to exact it. Years later, she unknowingly falls in love with the perpetrator. *Reviews and Criticism. Accessed 2005, June 10.*
Other titles: Le Couteau

2408. *Mua he chieu thang dung* / *The Vertical Ray of the Sun*   2000
D: Fran Anh Hung

S: Fran Anh Hung
C: Pin Bing Lee
P: Christophe Rossignon
A: Tran Nu Yen-khe, Le Khanh, Nguyen Nhu Quyng

Three sisters in Hanoi have recently lost their parents. The oldest, married, is having an affair, which she one night divulges to the middle sister, who is newly married to a man who travels a lot. The youngest lives with their brother and likes to pretend he and she are a couple—every morning they wake up together to American music.

Other titles: À la verticale de l'été

2409. *Nga ba Dong Loc / Ten Girls of Dong Loc* 2001
D: Tien-hanem Duy
S: Quang Vinh Nguyen
C: Huu Tuan Nguyen
P: Kim Cuong Nguyen

A group of young women, the "Assault Youth Unit," is assigned the cleanup of unexploded air bombs in Vietnam. Based on real events. *FII.*

2410. *Gai nhay / Bar Girls* 2002
D: Hoang Le
S: Nguy Ngu
A: Anh Vu, Minh Thu

A journalist investigates dancers in a nightclub but is attacked by them. The violent encounter encourages her to be more circumspect, and she discovers more about their lives. *Festival des 3.*

YUGOSLAVIA

2411. *Deveti Krug / The Ninth Circle* 1960 DS
D: France Štiglic
S: France Štiglic, Vladimir Koch
C: Ivan Marincek
A: Dusica Zegarac, Boris Dvornik

Croatia, 1940s. An upper-class Jewish girl hides among a Catholic family after her parents are deported. They kindly arrange a marriage with their son, but both young people suffer under the deception. *Variety. 1960, May 18.*

Awards: Academy Awards, nomination for Best Foreign Language Film, 1961

2412. *Na Klancu / In the Gorge* 1971
D: Vojko Duletic
S: Vojko Duletic; based on the novel by Ivan Cankar
C: Mile De Gleria
A: Stefka Drolc

1930s. A woman is seduced by a rich man, then ends up marrying an impoverished young man. *FII.*

Other titles: On the Hill of Desire

2413. *Vdovstvo Karoline Zasler / Widowhood of Karolina Zasler* 1975
D: Matjaz Klopcic
S: Matjaz Klopcic
C: Tomislav Pinter
A: Milena Zupancic

In a village near the Austrian border, a widow is dispirited by her position in the community; men lust after her, but she is blamed for the death of one of them. Made a social outcast, she longs for a family and sets her sights on a stranger. *FII.*

Awards: Berlin International Film Festival, CIDALC Award, 1977

2414. *Montenegro* 1981
D: Dusan Makavejev
S: Dusan Makavejev, Branko Vucicevic
C: Tomislav Pinter
P: George Zecevic
A: Susan Anspach

A Swedish housewife with easygoing inclinations makes friends with a community of free-wheeling Yugoslavs who live, drink, have free sex, and allow her to be herself.

Awards: São Paulo International Film Festival, Best Film, 1981

2415. *Azra* 1988 D
D: Mirza Idrizovic
C: Danijel Sukalo
A: Dara Dzovic

A woman officer who fought the Germans in World War II has difficulties returning to the traditional life of her village. *Variety. 1988, Aug. 31.*

ZIMBABWE

2416. *Neria* 1992 SP
D: Godwin Mawuru
S: Tsitsi Dangarembga, Louise Riber
C: John Riber
P: Louise Riber
A: Jesesi Mungoshi

A widow must grapple with her husband's family, whose tradition is to acquire everything left by their son. *FII.*

2417. *Flame* 1995 DS
D: Ingrid Sinclair
S: Barbara Jago, Philip Roberts, Ingrid Sinclair

C: João Costa
P: Simon Bright
A: Marian Kunonga, Ulla Mahaka

1970s. Two village girls join the revolution in Rhodesia and take on new names. Flame becomes a brave soldier, and Liberty becomes a journalist, the thoughtful narrator. Both try to pick up their lives after liberation in 1980; Flame returns to their village to have a family, and Liberty goes to a job in Harare, where many years later she is frightened by the sight of Flame. As they watch a military parade to which they've not been invited, she explains, "We're just women now."

2418. *Everyone's Child*   1996
D: Tsitsi Dangarembga
S: Tsitsi Dangarembga
C: Patrick Lindsell
P: Jonny Persey
A: Nomsa Mlambo, Killness Nyati, Thulani Sandhla, Nkululeko Phiri

When their parents suddenly die, the oldest sister becomes mother to her many siblings; her oldest brother goes to Harare. Though she is in love with someone else, the girl sleeps with a man to get money and becomes branded as a prostitute. *AMG.*

INDEX OF
FILMS WITH BEST ACTRESS AWARDS
AND NOMINATIONS

30 Years to Life (United States, 2002), 2287
84 Charing Cross Road (United States, 1986), 2053
Aberdeen (United Kingdom, 2000), 1862
The Accused (United States, 1988), 2085
Acts of Worship (United States, 2003), 2316
Adada (South Korea, 1987), 1297
Une Affaire de femmes / Story of Women (France, 1988), 527
Agnes of God (United States, 1985), 2041
Ai o kou hito / Begging for Love (Japan, 1998), 1266
Ai zai Beiang de jijie / Farewell China (Hong Kong, 1990), 908
Aika hyva ihmiseksi / Pretty Good for a Human Being (Finland, 1977), 412
Aimée & Jaguar (Germany, 1999), 697
Aje, aje, bara aje / Come, Come, Come Upward (South Korea, 1989), 1299
Alas de mariposa / Butterfly Wings (Spain, 1991), 1576
Alice Doesn't Live Here Anymore (United States, 1974), 1946
La Amiga / The Girlfriend (West Germany, 1988), 836
Amorosa (Sweden, 1986), 1654
Anak (Philippines, 2000), 1449
Angel de fuego / Angel of Fire (Mexico, 1992), 1336
Angela (Italy, 2002), 1201
Angst essen Seele auf / Ali, Fear Eats the Soul (West Germany, 1973), 753
O Anjo da guarda (Portugal, 1998), 1498
Anna (United States, 1987), 2066
Annie's Coming Out (Australia, 1984), 53
Ansikte mot ansikte / Face to Face (Sweden, 1975), 1647
Arais al tein / Clay Dolls (Tunisia, 2002), 1703
Arth / The Meaning (India, 1983), 1005
Así es la vida / Such Is Life (Mexico, 2000), 1342
Ask ölümden soghktur / Love Colder Than Death (Turkey, 1995), 1736
Através da janela / The Window Across (Brazil, 1996), 148
Att älska / To Love (Finland, 1964), 408
Ay! Carmela (Spain, 1990), 1574

Aya (Australia, 1990), 62

Babae sa bubungang lata / Woman on a Tin Roof (Philippines, 1999), 1445
Babettes gaestebud / Babette's Feast (Denmark, 1987), 362
Bagdad Cafe (West Germany, 1987), 830
Ban sheng yuan / Eighteen Springs (Hong Kong, 1997), 922
La Bande des quatre / The Gang of Four (France, 1988), 528
Bandini (India, 1963), 966
Basic Instinct (United States, 1992), 2139
Bata, bata . . . Paano ka ginawa / Lea's Story (Philippines, 1999), 1446
Being Julia (Canada, 2004), 221
Berget pa manens baksida / Hill on the Dark Side of the Moon (Sweden, 1983), 1653
Betty Fisher et les autres histoires / Alias Betty (France, 2001), 631
Bez bebek / Cloth Doll (Turkey, 1988), 1729
Bez mitosci / Without Love (Poland, 1980), 1461
Bhumika / The Role (India, 1977), 991
Les Biches / Bad Girls (France, 1968), 447
Bilans kwartalny / Balance Sheet (Poland, 1974), 1456
Binecuvintata fii inchisoare / Bless You Prison (Romania, 2002), 1513
Blue Sky (United States, 1994), 2157
Blue Steel (United States, 1990), 2106
Bon bast / Dead End (Iran, 1979), 1074
Bound (United States, 1996), 2196
Boys Don't Cry (United States, 1999), 2238
Bread and Roses (New Zealand, 1990), 1393
Bread and Roses (United Kingdom, 2001), 1869
Breaking the Waves (Denmark, 1996), 367
Broadcast News (United States, 1987), 2069
Broken English (New Zealand, 1996), 1398
Brutal (Philippines, 1980), 1428
Bulaklak ng City Jail / Flowers of the City Jail (Philippines, 1984), 1432
Bulaklak ng Maynila / Ada of Manila (Philippines, 1999), 1447

Butterfield 8 (United States, 1960), 1888
By Design (Canada, 1981), 185

Cal (Ireland, 1984), 1112
Camila (Argentina, 1984), 28
Camille Claudel (France, 1988), 529
La Captive (France, 2001), 632
Career Girls (United Kingdom, 1997), 1841
Cari genitori / Dear Parents (Italy, 1973), 1160
Carrington (United Kingdom, 1995), 1828
Central do Brasil / Central Station (Brazil, 1998), 152
La Cérémonie / The Ceremony (France, 1995), 575
Cette femme-là / Hanging Offense (France, 2003), 652
Chakra / Vicious Circle (India, 1981), 998
Chandni Bar (India, 2001), 1049
Chang bei / My Young Aunt (Hong Kong, 1981), 901
Le Chêne / The Oak (Romania, 1992), 1508
The China Syndrome (United States, 1978), 1989
Chun tao / A Woman for Two (China, 1988), 266
La Ciénaga / The Swamp (Argentina, 2001), 40
Citizen Ruth (United States, 1996), 2197
Claudine (United States, 1974), 1948
The Client (United States, 1994), 2159
Coal Miner's Daughter (United States, 1980), 2000
The Color Purple (United States, 1985), 2042
Un Complicato intrigo di donne, vicoli e delitte / The
    Naples Connection (Italy, 1985), 1176
La Comunidad / Common Wealth (Spain, 2000), 1609
Contact (United States, 1997), 2222
The Contender (United States, 2000), 2258
Cry in the Dark (Australia, 1988), 60

Dahil mahal kita / The Dolzura Cortez Story
    (Philippines, 1993), 1436
Daichi no komoruta / Lullaby of the Earth (Japan,
    1976), 1246
Daman (India, 2001), 1050
Dance with a Stranger (United Kingdom, 1985), 1794
Dancer in the Dark (Denmark, 2001), 372
Dancing at Lughnasa (Ireland, 1998), 1119
A Dangerous Woman (United States, 1993), 2151
Darling (United Kingdom, 1965), 1754
Dead Man Walking (United States, 1996), 2198
Desperately Seeking Susan (United States, 1985), 2045
El Destino no tiene favoritos / Destiny Has No
    Favorites (Peru, 2002), 1423
Det Storste i verden / The Greatest Thing (Norway,
    2001), 1415
Diary of a Mad Housewife (United States, 1970), 1918
La Dilettante (France, 1999), 606
Dolgiye provody / The Long Farewell (USSR, 1971),
    2365
Double Happiness (Canada, 1994), 202
Le Double vie de Véronique / The Double Life of
    Véronique (Poland, 1991), 1476

L'École de la chair / The School of Flesh (France,
    1996), 582
The Effect of Gamma Rays on Man-in-the-Moon
    Marigolds (United States, 1972), 1930
Egymásra nézve / Another Way (Hungary, 1982), 942
Eien no hito / Immortal Love (Japan, 1961), 1219
Eila (Finland, 2003), 419
Elizabeth (United Kingdom, 1998), 1850
Elsker dig fo evigt / Open Hearts (Denmark, 2002), 374
Un Embrujo / Under a Spell (Mexico, 1998), 1341
En Avoir (ou pas) / To Have (or Not) (France, 1995),
    577
En Kaerligheds historie / Kira's Reason: A Love Story
    (Denmark, 2001), 373
L'Erdità Ferramonti / The Inheritance (Italy, 1976), 1163
Erin Brockovich (United States, 1999), 2242
L'Été meurtrier / One Deadly Summer (France, 1983),
    510
Eternamente Pagu (Brazil, 1987), 144
Extramuros / Beyond the Walls (Spain, 1985), 1563
Extremities (United States, 1986), 2055

Famila rodante / Rolling Family (Argentina, 2004), 45
Far from Heaven (United States, 2002), 2293
Faraw, une mère de sable / Faraw! Mother of the
    Dunes (Mali, 1997), 1322
Fargo (United States, 1996), 2200
Fatal Attraction (United States, 1987), 2071
Le Fate ignoranti / Blind Fairies (Italy, 2001), 1198
Felicia's Journey (Canada, 1999), 212
Une Femme est une femme / A Woman Is a Woman
    (France, 1961), 426
The First Wives Club (United States, 1996), 2202
Flamberede hjerter / Flaming Hearts (Denmark,
    1987), 363
The Flor Contemplacion Story (Philippines, 1995),
    1439
La Flor de mi secreto / The Flower of My Secret
    (Spain, 1995), 1587
Flores de otro mundo / Flowers from Another
    World (Spain, 1999), 1604
For Love of Ivy (United States, 1968), 1905
Forfolgelsen / Witch Hunt (Norway, 1981), 1405
Fran (Australia, 1985), 55
Frances (United States, 1982), 2016
Frida (Mexico, 1984), 1330
Fruen på Hamre / The Lady of Hamre (Denmark,
    2000), 371
Fu rong zhen / Hibiscus Town (China, 1986), 251
La Fuga / The Escape (Italy, 1964), 1148
Fünf letzte Tage / The Last Five Days (West Germany,
    1982), 798
Funny Girl (United States, 1968), 1906
Fuori dal mondo / Not of This World (Italy, 1985),
    1177

Gary Cooper que estás en los cielos / Gary Cooper
　Who Art in Heaven (Spain, 1980), 1551
Georgia (United States, 1995), 2176
Girl, Interrupted (United States, 1999), 2244
Girls Town (United States, 1996), 2204
Godmother (India, 1999), 1045
Golpes a mi puerta / Knocks at My Door
　(Venezuela, 1996), 2400
Gorillas in the Mist (United States, 1988), 2091
Gu huo zai qing yi pian zhi hong xing shi san mei /
　Portland Street Blues (Hong Kong, 1998), 923
The Guide (India, 1965), 970
Gumrah / Deception India (India, 1963), 967
Guo nian hui jia / Seventeen Years (China, 1999), 314

Hanare goze Orin / Banished Orin (Japan, 1977), 1247
The Hand That Rocks the Cradle (United States,
　1992), 2142
The Happy Ending (United States, 1969), 1912
Haut les coeurs! / Chin Up! (France, 1999), 608
Heart like a Wheel (United States, 1983), 2024
Heartburn (United States, 1986), 2056
Heavenly Creatures (New Zealand, 1994), 1396
Hedda (United Kingdom, 1975), 1772
Heidi M. (Germany, 2001), 708
Herbstmilch / Autumn Milk (West Germany, 1988), 838
Hester Street (United States, 1974), 1952
Hiçbiryerde / In Nowhereland (Turkey, 2002), 1740
High Art (United States, 1998), 2231
High Tide (Australia, 1987), 57
Hikinige / Hit and Run (Japan, 1966), 1234
Hilary and Jackie (United Kingdom, 1998), 1852
Une Hirondelle a fait le printemps / Girl from Paris
　(France, 2003), 636
L'Histoire d'Adèle H / The Story of Adele H (France,
　1975), 471
Une Histoire simple / A Simple Story (France, 1978),
　488
La Historia oficial / The Official Story (Argentina,
　1985), 29
A Hora da estrela / Hour of the Star (Brazil, 1985), 141
Höstsonaten / Autumn Sonata (Sweden, 1978), 1650
Hotel Sorrento (Australia, 1995), 73
The Hours (United States, 2002), 2300
The House of Mirth (United Kingdom, 2000), 1867
How Stella Got Her Groove Back (United States,
　1998), 2232
Hu du men / Stage Door (Hong Kong, 1996), 919
Hubog / Wretched Lives (Philippines, 2001), 1451
Hustruer ti ar etter / Wives: Ten Years After
　(Norway, 1985), 1409
Hysterical Blindness (United States, 2002), 2301

I Like It like That (United States, 1995), 2178
I Shot Andy Warhol (United States, 1996), 2206

I Spit on Your Grave (United States, 1977), 1980
Ichijo sayuri: nureta yokujo / Following Desire (Japan,
　1972), 1240
Images (Ireland, 1972), 1107
Immacolata e concetta / Two Women in Love (Italy,
　1979), 1168
Ina, kapatid, anak / Mother, Sister, Daughter
　(Philippines, 1979), 1427
Inch'Allah dimanche / Inch'Allah Sunday (France,
　2001), 637
India Song (France, 1974), 467
Insiang (Philippines, 1976), 1424
Iracema (Brazil, 1979), 138
Iris (United Kingdom, 2001), 1871
Iron Jawed Angels (United States, 2004), 2340
Isadora (United Kingdom, 1968), 1761

Japanese Story (Australia, 2003), 86
Jingzhe / The Story of Ermei (China, 2004), 321
Juana la loca / Mad Love (Spain, 2001), 1619
Julia (United States, 1977), 1981
Julie (India, 1975), 985

Kamouraska (Canada, 1973), 179
Kan hai de rizi / A Flower in the Rainy Night
　(Taiwan, 1983), 1672
Kao / Face (Japan, 2001), 1272
Keiner liebt mich / Nobody Loves Me (Germany,
　1996), 690
Khamosh pani / Silent Waters (Pakistan, 2003), 1416
Khandar / The Ruins (India, 1984), 1010
Khilona (India, 1970), 973
Khoon bhari maang (India, 1988), 1022
Kilenc hónap / Nine Months (Hungary, 1976), 936
The Killing of Sister George (United States, 1968), 1907
Kizgin toprak / The Grave (Turkey, 1974), 1714
Klute (United States, 1971), 1924
Knafayim shvurot / Broken Wings (Israel, 2004), 1139
Kobieta samotna / A Woman Alone (Poland, 1981),
　1463
Konojo to kare / She and He (Japan, 1963), 1224
Korotkie vstretchi / Brief Encounters (USSR, 1968),
　2361
Krzyk / The Scream (Poland, 1983), 1467
Kuroi ame / Black Rain (Japan, 1989), 1258

Lajja (India, 2001), 1052
The Last Days of Chez Nous (Australia, 1991), 65
Let's Get Lost (Denmark, 1997), 369
Une Liaison pornographique / An Affair of Love
　(France, 1999), 609
Lilya 4-Ever (Sweden, 2002), 1662
A Lira do delirio / The Lyre of Delight (Brazil, 1978),
　135
Liten Ida / Little Ida (Norway, 1981), 1406

Lola (Spain, 1986), 1566
The Lonely Passion of Judith Hearne (United
    Kingdom, 1987), 1802
Long Walk Home (United States, 1989), 2101
Looking for Mr. Goodbar (United States, 1977), 1982
Lorenzo's Oil (United States, 1992), 2144
Losing Isaiah (United States, 1995), 2180
Love and Basketball (United States, 2000), 2262
Love Field (United States, 1992), 2145
Love with the Proper Stranger (United States, 1963),
    1894
Loved (United States, 1997), 2226
Lovely and Amazing (United States, 2002), 2305
The L-Shaped Room (United Kingdom, 1962), 1748
Lumière (France, 1976), 474
La Luna (Italy, 1979), 1169

Ma saison preferée / My Favorite Season (France,
    1993), 564
Maachis (India, 1996), 1038
Maborosi (Japan, 1996), 1263
Madame Bovary (France, 1991), 551
Maelström (Canada, 2000), 215
Malenkaya Vera / Little Vera (USSR, 1988), 2389
Mamma (Sweden, 1982), 1652
Mammo (India, 1994), 1032
Mamta (India, 1966), 971
Mar de rosas / Sea of Roses (Brazil, 1978), 136
Maria Chapdelaine (Canada, 1983), 188
Maria Full of Grace (United States, 2004), 2342
Die Marquise von O / The Marquise of O (Germany,
    1976), 679
Married to the Mob (United States, 1988), 2093
Mars Turkey / Clean Sweep (Israel, 2000), 1137
Martha und ich / Martha and Me (West Germany,
    1989), 844
Marusa no onna / A Taxing Woman (Japan, 1987), 1257
Mary, Queen of Scots (United Kingdom, 1971), 1768
Mask (United States, 1985), 2047
Mausam (India, 1975), 986
Mávahlátur / Seagull's Laughter (Iceland, 2003), 962
McCabe and Mrs. Miller (United States, 1971), 1925
Me ilamo Sara / My Name Is Sara (Spain, 1998), 1601
Mei-li zai chang ge / Murmur of Youth (Taiwan, 1997),
    1685
Mein letzter / My Last Film (Germany, 2002), 714
A mi madre le gustan las mujeres / My Mother Likes
    Women (Spain, 2004), 1632
Mi piace lavorare (mobbing) / I Love to Work (Italy,
    2004), 1208
Miao jie huang hou / Queen of Temple Street (Hong
    Kong, 1990), 909
Milagros (Philippines, 1997), 1443
Million Dollar Baby (United States, 2004), 2343
The Miracle Worker (United States, 1962), 1893

Miss Mary (Argentina, 1986), 30
Missing (United States, 1981), 2010
La Mitad del cielo / Half of Heaven (Spain, 1986), 1568
The Monkey's Mask (Australia, 2000), 84
Monster (United States, 2003), 2329
Moral (Philippines, 1982), 1431
The Morning After (United States, 1986), 2058
The Mother (United Kingdom, 2004), 1884
Les Mots pour le dire / The Words to Say It (France,
    1983), 511
Mr. and Mrs. Iyer (India, 2002), 1055
Mrs. Brown (United Kingdom, 1997), 1842
Mrs. Parker and the Vicious Circle (United States,
    1994), 2165
Mujeres al bordo de un ataque de nervios / Woman
    on the Verge of a Nervous Breakdown (Spain,
    1988), 1573
Muriel, ou le temps d'un retour / Muriel (France,
    1963), 438
Muriel's Wedding (Australia, 1995), 74
Music Box (United States, 1989), 2102
My Brilliant Career (Australia, 1979), 49
My Life without Me (Canada, 2003), 220

Nada mas / Nothing (Cuba, 2001), 345
Nadie hablara de nosotras cuando hayamos muerto
    / Nobody Will Speak of Us When We're Dead
    (Spain, 1995), 1589
Nadzór / Custody (Poland, 1985), 1472
Nahla (Algeria, 1979), 10
Nathalie (France, 2003), 658
Nics / Nothing (Poland, 1998), 1483
'Night, Mother (United States, 1986), 2059
Nikita (France, 1990), 544
Nil by Mouth (United Kingdom, 1997), 1844
Nimeh-ye penham / The Hidden Half (Iran, 2001),
    1096
Nippon konchuki / Insect Woman (Japan, 1963), 1225
Nora (Ireland, 2000), 1120
Norma Rae (United States, 1979), 1997
Nosotras / Women (Spain, 2000), 1612
Novia que te vea / Bride to Be (Mexico, 1992), 1337
Nü er hong / Maiden Rose (China, 1995), 307
Nü ren si shi / Summer Snow (Hong Kong, 1994), 916
Les Nuits de la pleine lune / Full Moon in Paris
    (France, 1984), 514
Nynke (Netherlands, 2001), 1383

Odinokaya zhenshchina zhelayet poznakomitsya /
    A Lonely Woman Seeks a Lifetime Companion
    (USSR, 1987), 2387
Olivier, Olivier (France, 1991), 554
On connait la chanson / Same Old Song (France,
    1997), 596
Once Were Warriors (New Zealand, 1995), 1397

One Potato, Two Potato (United States, 1965), 1899
One True Thing (United States, 1998), 2233
Only When I Laugh (United States, 1981), 2011
Onna zakari / Turning Point (Japan, 1994), 1261
Opening Night (United States, 1977), 1984
Oranges Are Not the Only Fruit (United Kingdom, 1989), 1808
Orlando (United Kingdom, 1992), 1817
The Others (United States, 2001), 2281
Out of Africa (United States, 1985), 2049
Outrageous Fortune (United States, 1987), 2077
O Outro lado da rua / The Other Side of the Street (Brazil, 2003), 155

El Pájaro de la felicidad / The Bird of Happiness (Spain, 1993), 1583
Palava enkeli / Burning Angel (Finland, 1984), 416
Pane e tulipani / Bread and Tulips (Italy, 2001), 1196
Papeles secundarios (Cuba, 1988), 340
Paradistorg / Summer Paradise (Sweden, 1976), 1649
Parahyba, mulher macho / Parahyba, a Macho Woman (Brazil, 1983), 140
Une Part du ciel / A Piece of the Sky (France, 2003), 659
Pasir berbisik / Whispering Sands (Indonesia, 2003), 1072
A Passage to India (United Kingdom, 1984), 1789
Passion Fish (United States, 1995), 2147
Pauline en Paulette / Pauline and Paulette (Belgium, 2000), 129
Peggy Sue Got Married (United States, 1986), 2061
Perfect Strangers (New Zealand, 2003), 1400
El Perro del hortelano / Dog in the Manger (Spain, 1996), 1594
Persona (Sweden, 1966), 1641
Petrina chronia / Stone Years (Greece, 1985), 880
La Pianiste / The Piano Teacher (Austria, 2001), 95
The Piano (Australia, 1993), 71
Pianoforte (Italy, 1984), 1174
Pieces of April (United States, 2003), 2330
Piedras / Stones (Spain, 2002), 1625
Place Vendôme (France, 2000), 624
Places in the Heart (United States, 1984), 2038
Play It as It Lays (United States, 1972), 1934
Pokuszenie / Temptation (Poland, 1995), 1481
Die Polizisten / The Policewoman (Germany, 2000), 703
La Posesión / Possession (France, 1981), 504
Postcards from the Edge (United States, 1990), 2114
Pozegnanie z Maria / Farewell to Maria (Poland, 1993), 1478
The Prime of Miss Jean Brodie (United Kingdom, 1969), 1764
Private Benjamin (United States, 1980), 2003
Przesluchanie / The Interrogation (Poland, 1981), 1464

The Pumpkin Eater (United Kingdom, 1964), 1752
Puzzle of a Downfall Child (United States, 1970), 1920

Qiu Ju da guansi / Story of Qiu Ju (China, 1992), 291

Rachel, Rachel (United States, 1968), 1908
Raggedy Man (United Kingdom, 1981), 1780
Raja (France, 2003), 662
Rambling Rose (United States, 1991), 2135
Real Women Have Curves (United States, 2002), 2310
Rebro Adama / Adam's Rib (USSR, 1993), 2395
La Reina de la noche / Queen of the Night (Mexico, 1994), 1339
La Reine Margot / Queen Margot (France, 1994), 572
Rembetiko (Greece, 1983), 874
Ren zai niu yue / Full Moon in New York (Hong Kong, 1990), 910
Respiro (Italy, 2003), 1207
Resurrection (United States, 1980), 2004
Retrato de Teresa / Portrait of Teresa (Cuba, 1979), 333
Richard's Things (United Kingdom, 1980), 1778
Romance da Empregada / Story of Fausta (Brazil, 1988), 146
A Room with a View (United Kingdom, 1985), 1795
Rosa Luxemburg (West Germany, 1986), 828
The Rose (United States, 1979), 1998
Rosemary's Baby (United States, 1968), 1909
Rosenstrasse (Germany, 2003), 717
Rosetta (Belgium, 1999), 127
Rosie (Belgium, 1999), 128
Rosine (France, 1994), 573
Ruby in Paradise (United States, 1993), 2154
Rue Cases Nègres / Sugar Cane Alley (France, 1983), 512

S ljubov'ju, Lilya / Without Love, Lilya (Russia, 2002), 1519
Sagkoshi / Killing Mad Dogs (Iran, 2000), 1094
Sahib bibi aur ghulam / The Lord, His Wife and Slave (India, 1962), 965
Salige er de som törster / Blessed Are Those Who Thirst (Norway, 1997), 1414
Salmonberries (Germany, 1991), 681
Salome (Philippines, 1981), 1430
Salto nel vuoto / Leap into the Void (Italy, 1980), 1170
San toit ni loi / Vagabond (France, 1985), 516
Sandakan hachiban shokan: bokyo / Sandakan 8 (Japan, 1975), 1245
Sara (Iran, 1993), 1078
Scandal (United Kingdom, 1988), 1805
Schwestern oder die Balance des Glücks / Sisters or the Balance of Happiness (West Germany, 1979), 778
Seance on a Wet Afternoon (United Kingdom, 1964), 1753

Secretary (United States, 2002), 2312

El Secreto de Romelia / Romelia's Secret (Mexico, 1988), 1333

Secrets & Lies (United Kingdom, 1996), 1838

Seisaku no tsuma / Seisaku's Wife (Japan, 1965), 1230

Sekten / Credo (Denmark, 1997), 370

Selena (United States, 1997), 2227

Sense and Sensibility (United Kingdom, 1995), 1830

Set It Off (United States, 1996), 2216

Sh'hur (Israel, 1994), 1131

Shame (Australia, 1987), 58

Shao nü Siao Yu / Siao Yu (Taiwan, 1995), 1684

She-Devil (United States, 1990), 2116

She's Been Away (United Kingdom, 1989), 1809

Shirley Valentine (United Kingdom, 1989), 1810

Shy People (United States, 1987), 2080

Si shui liu nian / Homecoming (Hong Kong, 1984), 903

Sia, le rêve du python / Sia, the Dream of the Python (Burkina Faso, 2001), 168

Sibaji / The Surrogate Woman (South Korea, 1987), 1298

The Silence of the Lambs (United States, 1990), 2117

Silencio roto / Broken Silence (Spain, 2001), 1622

Silkwood (United States, 1983), 2028

Sliding Doors (United Kingdom, 1998), 1854

Sofie (Denmark, 1982), 360

Soft Fruit (Australia, 1999), 82

Sol de otoño / Autumn Sun (Argentina, 1996), 35

Solas (Spain, 2000), 1616

Solo Sunny (East Germany, 1980), 729

Song jia huang chao / Soong Sisters (Hong Kong, 1996), 921

Sophie's Choice (United States, 1982), 2020

Sous la sable / Under the Sun (France, 2001), 643

Speriamo che sia femmina / Let's Hope It's a Girl (Italy, 1985), 1180

Steel Magnolias (United States, 1989), 2103

Stepmom (United States, 1998), 2236

Stevie (United Kingdom, 1978), 1775

Die Stille nach dem Schuß / The Legend of Rita (Germany, 2000), 704

Storia di Piera / Piera's Story (Italy, 1983), 1173

Strana gluchich / The Land of the Deaf (Russia, 1998), 1516

Strohfeuer / A Free Woman (West Germany, 1974), 760

Stupeur et tremblements / Fear and Trembling (France, 2003), 663

Such Good Friends (United States, 1971), 1926

Suci sang primadona / Suci the Divine Primadonna (Indonesia, 1977), 1059

Summer Wishes, Winter Dreams (United States, 1973), 1943

Sweet Dreams (United States, 1985), 2051

Swimming Pool (France, 2003), 664

Swing Shift (United States, 1984), 2040

Sylvia (New Zealand, 1985), 1390

A Szerencse lányai / Daughter of Luck (Hungary, 1999), 958

Sziget a szárazföldön / Lady from Constantinople (Hungary, 1969), 929

Tacones lejanos / High Heels (Spain, 1991), 1579

Talk (Australia, 1993), 72

Tan de repente / Suddenly (Argentina, 2003), 43

Taning yaman (Philippines, 2000), 1450

Tapasya (India, 1975), 987

Taste of Honey (United Kingdom, 1961), 1746

Tatlong taong walong Diyos / Three Godless Years (Philippines, 1976), 1426

Tea with Mussolini (United Kingdom, 1999), 1860

Terms of Endearment (United States, 1983), 2029

Testament (United States, 1983), 2030

Thelma and Louise (United States, 1991), 2137

Thérèse Desqueroux (France, 1962), 433

Things I Never Told You (United States, 1996), 2217

Three Women (United States, 1977), 1986

Tian yu / Xiu Xiu: The Sent Down Girl (China, 1999), 315

Time's Up! (Spain, 2000), 1617

To Die For (United States, 1995), 2190

Die tödliche Maria / Deadly Maria (Netherlands, 1993), 1374

Topless Women Talk about Their Lives (New Zealand, 1997), 1399

Três irmãos / Two Brothers, My Sister (Portugal, 1994), 1496

Trois couleurs: Bleu / Blue (France, 1993), 567

Trolösa / Faithless (Sweden, 1998), 1659

Tsuma wa kokuhaku sura / A Wife's Confession (Japan, 1961), 1221

Tu nombre en venena mis sueños / Your Name Poisons My Dreams (Spain, 1996), 1596

Tulitikkutehtaan tyttö / The Match Factory Girl (Finland, 1990), 417

Tumbleweeds (United States, 1999), 2252

Tylko strach / Only Fear (Poland, 1993), 1479

Tystnaden / The Silence (Sweden, 1963), 1638

Umrao jaan (India, 1981), 1000

Die Unberührbare / No Place to Go (Germany, 2000), 705

Under the Skin (United Kingdom, 1997), 1846

Unfaithful (United States, 2002), 2314

Ungfrúin góða og húsið / Honor of the House (Iceland, 1999), 961

Unishe April / April the Nineteenth (India, 1995), 1034

An Unmarried Woman (United States, 1977), 1988

Utsukushisa to kanashimi to / With Beauty and Sorrow (Japan, 1965), 1231

Va' dove ti porta il cuare / Go Where the Heart Leads You (Italy, 1996), 1193
Varastatud kohtumine / Stolen Meeting (Estonia, 1989), 406
Vénus Beauté Institut / Venus Beauty Institute (France, 1999), 616
Vera (Brazil, 1987), 145
Vera Drake (United Kingdom, 2004), 1886
Veronica Guerin (United States, 2003), 2335
Das Versprechen / The Promise (Germany, 1995), 687
Very Annie Mary (United Kingdom, 2001), 1873
La Veuve de Saint-Pierre / The Widow of St. Pierre (France, 2000), 627
Violette Nozière (France, 1977), 487
Viskningar och Rop / Cries and Whispers (Sweden, 1972), 1645
La Vraie nature de Bernadette / The True Nature of Bernadette (Canada, 1971), 176

Wait until Dark (United States, 1967), 1904
The Wash (United States, 1988), 2097
The Way We Were (United States, 1973), 1945
The Well (Australia, 1997), 78
The Whales of August (United States, 1987), 2083
What's Love Got to Do with It? (United States, 1993), 2155
Where the Heart Is (United States, 2000), 2270

Widow's Peak (United Kingdom, 1994), 1826
Wings of the Dove (United Kingdom, 1997), 1848
A Winter Tan (Canada, 1987), 197
The Witches (United States, 1989), 2105
Woman Thou Art Loosed (United States, 2004), 2348
A Woman under the Influence (United States, 1974), 1959
Women in Love (United Kingdom, 1969), 1765
Working Girl (United States, 1988), 2098
Working Girls (United States, 1986), 2065
A World Apart (United Kingdom, 1987), 1804

Xiao ao jiang hu zhi dong fang bu bai / Swordman II (Hong Kong, 1992), 914
Xica da Silva (Brazil, 1976), 134

Y aura-t-il de la neige à Noël? / Will It Snow for Christmas? (France, 1996), 590
Yan kou / Rouge (Hong Kong, 1987), 907
Yara (Germany, 1999), 700
You ma caizi / Rapeseed Girl (Taiwan, 1983), 1674
You yuan jing meng / Peony Pavilion (Hong Kong, 2001), 925
Yuen ling-juk / Actress (Hong Kong, 1991), 913

Zeit des zorns / The Long Silence (Germany, 1993), 685
Zheng hun qi shi / The Personals (Taiwan, 2000), 1689

INDEX OF
ACTRESSES AND ACTORS

Abascal, Silvia (f), 1632
Abashidze, Leila (f), 2386
Abbass, Hiam (f), 1705
Abdel Baki, Ashraf (m), 404
Abdel, Mahmoad, 393
Abdou, Fifi, 395
Abecassis, Yaël (f), 1136
Abedini, Hossein, 1090
Abkarian, Simon (m), 1141
Abril, Victoria (f), 579, 1545, 1579, 1589, 1593
Achaichi, Doudja (f), 16
Adams, Brooke (f), 2126
Adams, Maud (f), 834
Adar, Shulamit (f), 617
Adele, Jan (f), 57
Adineh, Golab (f), 1095
Aditi (f), 978
Adjani, Isabelle (f), 471, 493, 504, 510, 529, 572, 1556
Adraoui, Chaabia (f), 1350, 1351
Adriani, Patricia (f), 1567
Affolter, Therese (f), 799, 833
African Ballet of Guinea, 895
Agenentica, Imperio (f), 1569
Agenin, Beatrice (f), 154
Aghaei, Neda (f), 1098
Aguilar, Claire (f), 2057
Aguirre, Celine (f), 1423
Agusti, Toni (m), 1554
Ahangarani, Pegah (f), 1100
Ahn Seong-ki (f), 1292
Aïcha, 9
Aida, Fifi (f), 392
Aigner, Sophie (f), 696
Aimedova, Maya-Gozel (f), 2367
Aimée, Anouk (f), 422, 660, 1148, 1170
Akariou, Samira, 1353
Akbari, Mania (f), 1102
Akerman, Chantal (f), 112
Akhar, Fatemeh Cherag (f), 1093
Akinshina, Oksana (f), 1662
Akrah, Uduak (f), 1402
Aksoy, Serap (f), 1727, 1733

Al-Fichawa, Farouk, 395
Al-Khatib, Magda (f), 381
Alajar, Gina (f), 1428, 1430, 1431, 1432, 1435, 1440
Alaoui, Touria (f), 1355
Alaqui, Layla (f), 400
Aleandro, Norma (f), 29, 35, 44
Alentova, Vera (f), 2375
Alexander, Erika (f), 2287
Alexander, Harri (f), 1876
Alexander, Jane (f), 2030
Alexander, Sharon (f), 1133
Alexandropoulou, Electra (f), 883
Ali, Paula (f), 345
Alia (f), 301
Alikaki, Mirto (f), 894
Alim-Akyn, Bayan (m), 1281
Alkeou, Maria (f), 869
Allen, Joan (f), 1121, 2258
Allen, Nancy (f), 2037
Allerson, Alexander (m), 762
Almagor, Gila (f), 1124, 1131
Almani, Maryiam Parvin (f), 1091
Alpha, Jenny (f), 526
Alterio, Hector (m), 29
Alterio, Malena (f), 1621
Alvarada, Trini (f), 2179
Alvarez, Mariano (m), 2401
Álvarez, Óscar (m), 336
Álvarez, Sofia (f), 1326
Alvaro, Anne (f), 513
Alves, Tanya (f), 140
Amado, Camila (f), 154
Amarasena, Sriyani (f), 1637
Amarouchène, Myriam (f), 1611
Amidou, Souad (f), 1697
Amilbangsa, Grace (f), 1433
Amin, Alka (f), 1056
Amin, Mervet (f), 391
Amis, Suzy (f), 2150, 2168
Amouroux, Clémentine (f), 1665
Amzal, Djamila (f), 17
Anand, Dev (m), 970

Andela, Pauline (f), 1530
Anderson, Gillian (f), 1867
Anderson, Pamela (f), 2171
Anderson, Pat (f), 1985
Anderson, Raffaela (f), 618
Andersson, Bibi (f), 1356, 1545, 1641, 1643, 1653,
	1979
Andersson, Harriet (f), 408, 409, 1639, 1643, 1645,
	1646
Andianou, Anna (f), 888
Andolong, Sandy (f), 1431
Andrade, Elisa (f), 22
André, Rosa Castro, 1492
Andréa, Yann, 500
Andreichenko, Natalia (f), 2374
Andres, Sasha (f), 657
Anniston, Jennifer (f), 2296
Anreus, Idalia (f), 330
Anspach, Susan (f), 2414
Antonelli, Francesca (f), 1190
Antonelli, Laura (f), 1165
Antonova, Aliona (f), 954
Antonova, Olga (f), 2390
Anwar, Mina (f), 1834
Apik, Mary (f), 1074
Applegate, Christina (f), 2119
Aquino, Kris (f), 1437
Ar, Müjde (f), 1723, 1725, 1726
Aragón, Angélica (f), 1337
Araujo, Fransergio (m), 148
Arbour, France (f), 214
Archer, Anne (f), 2071
Archer, Sandra (f), 223
Ardant, Fanny (f), 119, 541, 646, 658, 956, 1187, 1202
Arditi, Catherine (f), 589
Argentina, Norma (f), 44
Argento, Asia (f), 1204
Arias, Imanol (m), 28
Arima, Ineko (f), 1216
Armand, Frøydis (f), 1403, 1409, 1412
Arnaiz, Sharmaine (f), 1440, 1443
Arnaud, Nicole (f), 428
Arndt, Adelheid (f), 748, 759
Arndt, Jürgen (m), 790
Arnoul, Françoise (f), 588, 589
Arocha, Leonor (f), 344
Aronson, Melissa (f), 2208
Arquette, Patricia (f), 2172
Arquette, Rosanna (f), 2045, 2060
Arustrup, Niels (m), 111
Asaoka, Ruriko (f), 1235
Ascaride, Ariane (f), 584, 612, 670
Ashcroft, Peggy (f), 1789, 1809
Askarova, Shynar (f), 1281
Assif, Siham, 1354

Astengo, Tatiana (f), 1423
Asti, Adriana (f), 956
Atangana, Elise (f), 171
Auberjonois, Rene (m), 1107
Aubin, Simone, 460
Aubrey, Sophie (f), 565
Audran, Stéphane (f), 362, 421, 447, 448, 449, 455,
	487, 560
Auer, Barbara (f), 130, 679, 718
August, Pernilla (f), 1658
Aunor, Nora (f), 1425, 1426, 1429, 1432, 1434, 1439,
	1442
Austria, Amy (f), 1428, 1449
Auteuil, Daniel (m), 540, 564, 569, 572, 593, 627
Avery, Charlotte (f), 1825
Avery, Margaret (f), 2042
Aviles, Angel (f), 2164
Avramson, Zivi (f), 1125
Axell, Jane (f), 741
Aya, Setsuko (f), 1251
Ayalogu, Emma (f), 1402
Aydan, Nilüfer (f), 1708
Azabal, Lubna (f), 1706
Azéma, Sabine (f), 596, 620
Azmi, Shabana (f), 979, 1001, 1005, 1006, 1007, 1010,
	1014, 1015, 1016, 1021, 1025, 1026, 1037, 1042,
	1045, 1047, 1051
Azoulay-Hasfari, Hana (f), 1131

Baal, Karin (f), 679, 773
Bacall, Lauren (f), 2211
Baccar, Jalila (f), 1314
Bachar, Naomi (f), 1125
Bachchan, Jaya (f), 1041, 1051
Bachleda-Curus, Alicja (f), 1486
Backman, Ida-Lotta (f), 415
Bacon, Kevin (m), 2338
Bacquié, Anne-Marie (f), 460
Badal, Nicole (f), 741
Badema, 310
Badje, Marie-Thérèse (f), 170
Badji, Saly (f), 537
Bae Doo-na (f), 1307
Bagaeva, Aygul, 1280
Bagatsing, Raymond (m), 1443
Bahrami, Zahra (f), 1090
Bahri, Yasmine (f), 1701
Bai, Man, 1317
Baillargeon, Paule (f), 180, 189, 195
Bakaba, Sijiri, 1212
Baker, Kathy (f), 2267
Bakos, Ildikó (f), 955
Bakovic, Andrea (f), 324
Bakri, Mohommed (m), 18
Balaguer, Asunción (f), 1622

Balamir, Hakan (m), 1729
Balanuta, Leopodina (f), 1504
Balasko, Josiane (f), 579, 652
Baliban, Liane (f), 2297
Balibar, Jeanne (f), 630, 644
Balk, Fairuza (f), 2309
Balletbò-Coll, Marta (f), 1585
Balsam, Martin (m), 1943
Balsameda, Mario (m), 331
Ban Salem, El Hedi (m), 753
Bancroft, Anne (f), 1752, 1893, 1900, 1972, 1987,
    2041, 2053, 2059, 2177
Banderas, Antonio (m), 1573
Banerjee, Victor (m), 1789
Bang Eun-jin (f), 1301
Banks, Deborah (f), 2065
Baokar, Uttara (f), 1036
Barbeau, Adrienne (f), 2088
Barda, Meital (f), 1136
Bardawil, Nicole (f), 403
Barden, Pilar (f), 1589
Bardi, Emilio (f), 31
Bardot, Brigitte (f), 424, 429, 437, 443
Barends, Edda (f), 1361, 1366
Barkin, Ellen (f), 2081
Barnes, Priscilla (f), 2175
Barnstedt, Imke (f), 823
Barr, Bert, 1971
Barr, Roseanne (f), 2116
Barranco, Maria (f), 1573
Barrault, Marie-Christine (f), 511, 524, 535, 1174
Barrett, Nicole (f), 2320
Barrie, Barbara (f), 1899
Barrymore, Drew (f), 2173
Bartana, Nitzan (m), 1133
Barthes, Tess (f), 650
Basler, Marianne (f), 125, 126, 555
Bassett, Angela (f), 2155, 2191, 2232, 2249
Bassett, Linda (f), 2064
Bassi, Valentina (f), 42
Bastien, Fanny (f), 535
Bat-Adam, Michal (f), 486, 492, 1125, 1128, 1130
Bataille, Julie (f), 587
Bates, Alan (m), 1759, 1765, 1988
Bates, Kathy (f), 2015, 2082, 2113, 2125, 2174
Batsalia, Alexandra (f), 890
Battistella, Sandrine (f), 472
Baum, Inés (f), 37
Bautista, Aurora (f), 1563
Bautista, Perla (f), 1432
Baxter, Anne (f), 1749
Baye, Nathalie (f), 545, 609, 616
Bazaka, Themis (f), 880, 882
Béart, Emmanuelle (f), 546, 569, 620, 640, 646, 656,
    658

Beatty, Warren (m), 1925
Bechara, Flavia (f), 1315
Becker, Belinda (f), 1859
Becker, Hartmut (m), 1186
Becker, Meret (f), 687
Beckinsale, Kate (f), 2239, 2278, 2324
Bedelia, Bonnie (f), 2024
Beglau, Bibiana (f), 704
Belaustegui, Marta (f), 1602
Belén, Ana (f), 39, 1546, 1549, 1570, 1593
Belhadj, Fatima (f), 14
Bell, Monica (f), 2199
Belle, Béatrice (f), 536
Bellina, Meriam (f), 1064
Bellwood, Pamela (f), 1975
Belmondo, Jean-Paul (m), 1144
Ben Abdallah, Rabiaa (f), 1702
Ben Afsia, Oumeyma (f), 1703
Benahouda, Lynda (f), 626
Benaissa, Ahmed (m), 16
Bender, Eva (f), 1710
Benedetto, Leonor (f), 1617
Bengell, Norma (f), 136, 1324
Benjamin, Richard (m), 1918
Bennent, Heinz (m), 117
Bening, Annette (f), 221
Benson, Laura (f), 225
Benssellem, Najat (f), 662
Berber, Fatiha (f), 16
Berek, Kati (f), 934
Berenson, Marisa (f), 1603
Bereta, Fanta (f), 1323
Berezutskaya, Valentina (f), 1519
Bergen, Candice (f), 1167, 1901, 2012
Bergen, Polly (f), 1895
Berger, Helmut (m), 783
Berger, Senta (f), 752
Bergin, Patrick (m), 1121
Bergman, Ingrid (f), 740, 1650
Bergmans, Rosemarie (f), 129
Bergström, Helena (f), 1656
Beristáin, Dolores (f), 1333
Berlin, Jeannie (f), 1967, 2111
Berling, Charles (m), 597
Berman, Susan (f), 2019
Bernard, Sue (f), 1914
Bernhard, Birghitta (f), 1876
Bernhard, Sandra (f), 67
Berry, Halle (f), 2180, 2215, 2337
Berry, Marilou (f), 671
Bertei, Adele (f), 2021
Berthe, Fanta (f), 1319
Berthet, Lola (f), 42
Berti, Marina (f), 1158
Berto, Juliet (f), 465, 473

Bertrand, Marie-Eve (f), 216
Bettencourt, Eugénia (f), 1494
Bezman, Pamira (f), 1730
Bezuidenhout, Aletta (f), 1540
Bhatt, Sunita (f), 1031
Biddle, Stéphanie (f), 1533
Bielenstein, Monica (f), 727
Bigelow, Kathryn (f), 2021
Bilginer, Haluk (m), 1733
Binoche, Juliette (f), 567, 607, 627
Birch, Thora (f), 2183, 2277
Birkin, Jane (f), 121, 515, 525
Bisset, Jacqueline (f), 575, 1801, 2012, 2265
Biswas, Seema (f), 1031, 1041
Biyouna (f), 1706
Björk (f), 372
Bjorklund, Malin, 1660
Björnstrand, Gunnar (m), 414, 1643
Black, Darren (m), 1876
Black, Karen (f), 1651, 2015
Black, Rachael (f), 1400
Bláhová, Dagmar (f), 352
Blain, Rogelio, 338
Blair, Linda (f), 2014
Blanc, Dominique (f), 562, 630
Blanc, Manuel (m), 563
Blanchett, Cate (f), 1850, 1870, 2335
Blanco, Rita (f), 1490
Blaszczyk, Ewa (f), 1472
Bléfari, Rosario (f), 38
Blethyn, Brenda (f), 1838, 1853, 2305
Blistin, Francine (f), 117
Bloch, Deborah (f), 142
Blok, Anneke (f), 1384
Blondell, Joan (f), 1984
Bloom, Claire (f), 1771
Blum, Ina (f), 829, 840
Blumenschein, Tabea (f), 770, 778, 807
Boa (f), 2161
Boberg, Sarah (f), 376
Bogarde, Dirk (m), 1161, 1754
Bogdanova, Yelena (f), 2395
Bogo, Alicia (f), 1592
Bohringer, Romaine (f), 580, 614
Boies, Markita (f), 216
Boisson, Christine (f), 532, 538
Bolkan, Florinda (f), 1159, 1160
Bollaín, Icíar (f), 1580, 1581
Bollaín, Marina (f), 1580
Bonaiuto, Anna (f), 1185
Bonham Carter, Helena (f), 614, 1184, 1795, 1848
Bonifacio, Anelis (f), 1592
Bonnaire, Sandrine (f), 516, 542, 561, 575
Boothby, Victoria (f), 2022
Borges, Alice (f), 154

Borges, Graciela (f), 40
Bosáková, Eva (f), 349
Boschi, Giulia (f), 1174
Bosé, Lucia (f), 461, 474, 1157, 1571, 1737
Bossley, Caitlin (f), 1395
Botsford, Sara (f), 185
Botto, María, 1622
Bouajila, Sami (m), 1698
Bouchez, Elodie (f), 587, 605
Boudet, Jacques (m), 621
Boudet, Marie (f), 558
Bouix, Evelyn (f), 589
Boujenah, Michel (m), 517
Bouquet, Carole (f), 593, 603, 795, 1840
Bouquet, Michel (m), 448
Bourgine, Elizabeth (f), 520, 548
Boyd, Pam (f), 1117
Boyer, Charles (m), 1763
Boyer, Marie-France (f), 441
Boyer, Myriam (f), 120, 123, 517
Bozyk, Reizl (f), 2089
Bracco, Lorraine (f), 213
Bracho, Diana (f), 1333, 1338, 1556
Bradley, Cathleen (f), 1122
Bradley, Charlotte (f), 1149
Bradshaw, Catherine (f), 1884
Brady, Orla (f), 1122
Braga, Sonia (f), 133, 149
Brahimi, Marie (f), 20
Brakni, Rachida (f), 634
Brando, Luisina (f), 27, 34
Braschi, Nicoletta (f), 1208
Brazzi, Rossano (m), 739
Brennan, Brid (f), 1108, 1111, 1119, 1796
Brennan, Eileen (f), 2003, 2096
Brévan, Mélanie (f), 483
Brialy, Jean-Claude (m), 426
Bridges, Jeff (m), 2058, 2211
Brigham, Edmea (f), 23
Brignone, Lilla (f), 1158
Brittain, Charlotte (f), 1879
Broadbent, Jim (m), 1871
Brooks, Denise (f), 1960
Brotnow, Gerd (f), 1408
Brown, Blair (f), 1806
Brown, Eleanora (f), 1144
Brown, Juanita (f), 1947
Bruckhorst, Natja (f), 845
Bruneaux, Olivia (f), 549
Brunner, Angela, 726
Bryan, Dora (f), 1746
Buckland, Andrew (m), 1539
Budzisz-Krzyzanowska, Teresa (f), 1465, 1477
Bujold, Geneviève (f), 173, 179, 1977, 2032
Bulgakova, Maya (f), 2355, 2378

Bullku, Rajmonda (f), 3
Bullock, Sandra (f), 2253, 2291
Bunel, Marie (f), 563
Burcksen, Edgar (m), 124
Burgers, Michele (f), 1543
Burke, Kathy (f), 1119, 1784, 1844
Burroughs, Jackie (f), 197
Burrows, Saffron (f), 1115
Burstyn, Ellen (f), 871, 1946, 2004, 2177, 2187, 2291
Bussières, Pascale (f), 201, 205, 640
Buy, Margherita (f), 1177, 1193, 1198, 1203
Buzko, Natalya (f), 1743, 2390
Bykov, Rolan, 2358
Byrne, Gabriel (m), 2081

Caba, Irene Gutiérrez (f), 1570
Caballeria, Enriqueta (f), 1570
Cabre, Berta (f), 797
Cabrera, Lissette (f), 405
Cadenat, Garry (m), 512
Caffaro, Cheri (f), 1955
Caine, Michael (m), 1785, 1853
Caldwell, Liz (f), 2065
Callas, Maria (f), 1156
Cameron, Margaret (f), 59
Camilla Johns, Tracy (f), 2062
Campbell, Jessica (f), 2332
Campbell, Nell (f), 48
Campbell, Nicolas (m), 187
Camurati, Carla (f), 144
Caneele, Séverine (f), 659
Cannon, Dyan (f), 1926, 1968, 2107
Canter, Marie (f), 806
Canto, Toni (m), 1595
Cantudo, Maria Jose (f), 1559
Cao Yindi (f), 233
Capri, Ana (f), 1448
Caprioglio, Deborah (f), 1191
Capuro, Liliana (f), 45
Cara, Irene (f), 1974
Cardinal, Tantoo (f), 192
Cardinale, Claudia (f), 18, 1145, 1153, 2134
Cardoso, Laura (f), 148
Carlson, Karen (f), 1921
Carmo, Dalila (f), 1498
Carmona, Amaya (f), 1607
Caron, Leslie (f), 1748
Carpio, Rustica (f), 1429
Carr, Maureen (f), 1872
Carradine, David (m), 1929, 2341
Carradine, Keith (m), 2032
Carré, Isabelle (f), 647
Carrez, Florence (f), 431
Carrière, Mathieu, 119, 415
Carrillo, Elpidia (f), 1869

Carrillo, Mary (f), 1558, 1560
Carrington, Jim (m), 1966
Carroll, Andrina (f), 1865
Carroll, Diahann (f), 1948
Carron, Elise (f), 497
Carstensen, Margit (f), 751, 755, 757, 762
Cartaxo, Marcélia (f), 141
Cartier, Caroline (f), 474
Cartlidge, Katrin (f), 367, 1841, 2256
Casar, Amira (f), 668
Casarès, Maria (f), 546
Casé, Regina (f), 153
Cassavetes, John (m), 1909, 1984
Cassel, Jean-Pierre (m), 455, 469, 1494
Cassidy, Elaine (f), 212
Cassidy, Joanna (f), 2226
Cassidy, Raquel (f), 1876
Castel, Lou (m), 812
Castell, Ana (f), 2397
Castells, Elena (f), 1601
Castillo, Cecille (f), 1433
Cates, Clody (f), 2331
Cates, Phoebe (f), 1803
Catillon, Brigitte (f), 492
Catselli, Aleka (f), 850
Cavalli, Alleyona (f), 150
Cavazos, Lumi (f), 1333, 1338
Caven, Ingrid (f), 786
Cawood, Elize (f), 1541
Ceccarelli, Sandra (f), 1195
Ceiça, Maria (f), 156
Çelik, Sanem (f), 1738
Céllier, Caroline (f), 483
Cenci, Athina (f), 1180
Cepeda, Olenka (f), 1421
Cerhová, Jitka (f), 350
Cervera, Monica (f), 1625
Cervi, Valentina (f), 592
Cever, Edith (f), 765, 769
Chadia (f), 379
Chahal, Tamin (f), 1314
Chahine, Alham (f), 400
Chalfont, Kathleen (f), 2212
Chancellor, Anna (f), 1875
Chandra, Rani (f), 988
Chang Shanshan (f), 242
Chang, Shwu-fen, 1681
Chang, Sylvia (f), 906, 909, 910, 912, 1671, 1677, 1691
Chang, Yuan (f), 308
Channing, Stockard (f), 1833, 1835, 2254, 2261, 2270
Chao, Rosalind (f), 2120
Chaplin, Geraldine (f), 1116, 1547, 1992
Chaplin, Oona (f), 2006
Chapman, Keri Jo (f), 2224
Charbonneau, Patricia (f), 2044, 2070

Charipova, F., 2353
Charretier, Eloïse (f), 573
Chatterjee, Anil (f), 968
Chatterjee, Soumitra (f), 1028, 1046
Chatterjee, Tanishita (f), 1056
Chaturani, Vasanthi (f), 1634
Chau, Minh, 2404
Chaumette, Monique (f), 490
Chen, Joan (f), 69, 2269
Chen, Juliette (f), 2188
Chen Qioyan (f), 1674
Chen Te Jung, 911
Chen, Vicky (f), 924
Chen Wei-chi, 1687
Cheng, Carol (f), 909
Cheptounova, Marina (f), 1517
Cher (f), 1860, 2015, 2028, 2047, 2084
Cherrat, Nisma (f), 715
Chesnais, Patrick (m), 588
Cheung, Maggie (f), 908, 910, 913, 915, 917, 921, 1677, 1681
Chiaureli, Sofiko (f), 2370, 2376
Chico, Florinda (f), 1570
Chico, Valentina (f), 1193
Chika, Fujimura (f), 1270
Childs, Lucinda (f), 116
Ching Ching-hua, 235
Chironi, Graciana (f), 45
Cho Eun-ji (f), 1308
Choi Byoung-keun, 1294
Choi Eun-hie (f), 1289, 1290
Chol Gwi Bok (f), 1287
Chong Honginei, 269
Chong, Rae Dawn (f), 2032, 2158
Choudhury, Sarita (f), 1610, 2131, 2162
Choudhury, Supriya (f), 964
Chouikh, Mohamed (m), 4
Choureau, Etchika (f), 432
Chow Yun-Fat (m), 902
Christie, Julie (f), 30, 1754, 1759, 1762, 1782, 1783, 1925, 1978
Chu, Sang-mi (f), 1311
Chung, Cherie (f), 905
Churikova, Inna (f), 2359, 2364, 2371, 2380, 2395
Chursina, Lyudmila (f), 2360
Chwalibóg, Maria (f), 1463
Cielecka, Magdalena (f), 1481
Ciemny, Justyna (f), 1475
Ciepielewska, Anna (f), 1459
Cilento, Diane (f), 1747
Ciliskur, Ruchen (f), 1741
Cillers, Jana (f), 1539
Cintra, Luis Miguel (m), 1495
Cisneros, Gregorio (f), 1338
Cisse-Roland, Eugenie, 1212

Citti, Franco (m), 1146
Ciunelis, Maria (f), 1469, 1473
Clair, Nadège (f), 224
Clark, Liddy (f), 52
Clarke, Shirley (f), 452
Clarkson, Patricia (f), 2231, 2330, 2332
Clayburgh, Jill (f), 1169, 1988, 2002, 2080
Clément, Aurore (f), 115, 595, 654
Close, Glenn (f), 2071, 2267, 2332, 2345
Coesens, Anne (f), 642
Coffinet, Anne-Marie (f), 436
Cohen, Gayle (f), 2182
Cohen-Raz, Noa (f), 1127
Colchero, Ana (f), 1344
Coleman, Charlotte (f), 1808
Colin, Grégoire (m), 554, 586
Collette, Toni (f), 74, 86, 2221, 2339
Collins, Pauline (f), 686, 1810
Colón, Miriam (f), 2273
Condurache, Dan, 1511
Confalone, Marina (f), 1185
Cong Shan (f), 247
Constantine, Eddie (m), 801
Conti, Tom (m), 1810
Cooper, Rick (m), 1914
Coppens, Aranka (f), 128
Cordy, Annie (f), 104, 114
Cormack, Danielle (f), 1399
Cornall, Jan (f), 52
Cornish, Abbie (f), 84
Correia, Catarina (f), 1493
Costa, Caterina Alves (f), 1489
Côte, Laurence (f), 528, 576, 2349
Cottençon, Fanny (f), 1561
Cotterill, Chrissie (f), 1784
Couceyro, Analia (f), 46
Coulibaly, Dounamba Dany, 1318
Coulibaly, Fatoumata (f), 1534
Couris, Britta (f), 2167
Courtney, Alisa (f), 1917, 1953
Courtoy, Carole (f), 116
Covington, Julie (f), 1109
Cox, Brian (m), 1811
Cox, Christina (f), 211
Cox, Rene (f), 2213
Coyote, Peter (m), 2092
Craig, Daniel (m), 1884
Crawford, Rachael (f), 205
Cremer, Bruno (m), 1561
Cremer, Ute (f), 803
Crespo, Carla (f), 43
Crewson, Wendy (f), 211, 217
Crombie, Lillian (f), 48
Croze, Marie-Josée (f), 215
Cruciano, Mauro (m), 1183

Cruz, Penelope (f), 1586, 1606, 2402
Cserhalmi, György (m), 932
Cuellar, Yolanda (f), 331
Cui, Shirley (f), 204
Curtis, Jamie Lee (f), 2025, 2106, 2321
Curtis, Liane Alexandra (f), 2175
Curtis, Mickey (m), 1274
Cusack, Sinead (f), 1192
Cybulski, Zbigniew (m), 408, 1454
Czinkóczi, Zsuzsa (f), 944, 948, 950

D'Aloja, Francesca (f), 1199
D'Angers, Yvonne (f), 1889
D'Aquila, Diane (f), 197
D'Orsay, Ghislaine (f), 1154
Dabney, Sheila (f), 2079
Daftardar, Renuka (f), 1036
Dalida (f), 387
Dalkowska, Ewa (f), 1471
Dalle, Béatrice (f), 587
Dalrymple, Serena (f), 1446
Damant, Andrée (f), 602
Dandoulaki, Katia (f), 870
Danes, Claire (f), 2179, 2239
Danieli, Isa (f), 1176
Danning, Sybil (f), 2014
Darlene, Gigi (f), 1897
Darnay, Alan (m), 1889
Darrieux, Danielle (f), 543, 646
Das, Nandita (f), 1037, 1041, 1043, 1047, 1048, 1051
Das, Samata (f), 1054
Das, Vasundhara (f), 2307
Dassas, Evelyne (f), 432
David, Eleanor (f), 1390
David, Phyllis (f), 1944
Davidson, Diana (f), 70
Dávila, María Eugenia (f), 323
Davis, Bette (f), 2083
Davis, Geena (f), 2136, 2143, 2156, 2210
Davis, Judy (f), 49, 51, 57, 1789, 1807, 2240, 2322
Day, Cora Lee (f), 1969, 2122
De Bankolé, Isaach (m), 530
De Boeck, Antje (f), 130, 1375
De Bruyn, Julienne (f), 129
De Cássia, Edna (f), 138
De Castro, Isabel (f), 1490, 1494, 1498
De Filippo, Luca (m), 1188
De Freitas, Chantal (f), 691
De Freitas, Manuela (f), 1493
De Havilland, Olivia (f), 1769
De La Boulaye, Agathe (f), 635
De Medeiros, Maria (f), 1496, 2109
De Mornay, Rebecca (f), 2142
De Olivera, Domingo (m), 22
De Palma, Rossy (f), 1591

De Pauw, Josée, 1363
De Roo, Sara (f), 128
De Rossi, Alessandra (f), 1451
De Rossi, Assunta (f), 1451
De Saint Phalle, Niki (f), 1770
De Santis, Eliana (f), 458
De Santis, Luisa (f), 1175
De Santis, Silvia (f), 891
De Sousa, Melissa (f), 2287
De Souza, Ruth (f), 156
De Van, Marina (f), 653
DeArcy, Patricia (f), 2213
Debayo, Jumoke (f), 846
Debbah, Mohamed (m), 7
Dee, Ruby (f), 1890, 1911, 1939
Deekeling, Alice (f), 706
DeGeneres, Ellen (f), 2260
Degleri, Maria (f), 885
Degli Esposti, Piera (f), 1186
Del Sol, Laura (f), 225, 2399
Del Toro, Guadalupe (f), 1327
Del Valle, Desi (f), 1585
Deliba, Fejria (f), 18, 528, 637
Delon, Alain (m), 468
Delpy, Julie (f), 534
Delterme, Marine (f), 226
Deludi, Vera (f), 1720
Delvaux, André (m), 566
Demarigny, Aymeric, 633
Demetriscu, Olga (f), 801
Demian, Iarina (f), 1507
Demy, Mathieu (m), 525
Dench, Judi (f), 1795, 1842, 1860, 1871
Deneuve, Catherine (f), 130, 372, 440, 446, 454, 498, 550, 564, 624, 646, 1180, 1756
Denie, Danielle (f), 106
Dennis, Sandy (f), 2015, 2086
Depardieu, Gérard, 463, 475, 480, 499, 529, 603, 2218
Dequenne, Emilie (f), 127
Dern, Bruce (m) 1956
Dern, Laura (f), 2135, 2197
Derwig, Jacob (m), 1384
Descas, Alex (m), 1737
Deshpandey, Sulbha, 1051
Detmers, Maruschka (f), 515
Devine, Loretta (f), 2191, 2348
Dewiel, Alexa (f), 178
Dey, Geeta (f), 964
Dharkar, Ayesha (f), 1044
Di Benedetto, Ida (f), 818, 1168, 1181
Di Fu (f), 305
Diabo, Alice (f), 199
Diakhate, Ami (f), 1529
Diallo, Madeleine (f), 1522
Diarra, Hélène (f), 1320, 1323

Diarra, Maimouna Hélène (f), 1534
Diawara, Fatoumata (f), 168
Diaz, Cameron (f), 2267
Dickens, Kim (f), 2266
Didi, Evelyn (f), 91
Diego Botto, Juan (m), 1605, 1622
Diggs, Taye, 2232
Dimitrova, Mariana (f), 160
Dinev, Patricia (f), 539
Ding, Jiali (f), 262, 286
Diop Gaï, Djeïnaba (f), 1533
Diop, Gilbert (m), 716
Diop Mbissine, Thérèse (f), 1521
Diouf, Mansour (m), 1529
Dixit, Dasharathi (f), 1002
Dixit, Madhuri (f), 1042, 1052
Djarot, Slamet (f), 1072
Djodat, Shaghayegh (f), 1083
Djouadi, Ibtissem (f), 21
Djukelova, Paraskeva (f), 163
Dobel, Ruth (f), 45
Dobrowolska, Gosia (f), 66
Dobson, Tamara (f), 1940, 2014
Dolgor, Suren, 1347
Doll, Birgit (f), 775, 1358
Doll, Dora (f), 517
Dollé, Jean-Christophe (m), 1502
Domingo, Anni (f), 1799
Dominguez, Pilar (f), 1554
Dommartin, Solveig (f), 843
Domröse, Angelica (f), 92, 724
Donnadieu, Bernard-Pierre (m), 534
Donnelly, Patrice (f), 2018
Dontchev, Mikhael (m), 163
Donutil, Miroslav (m), 347
Donzelli, Valérie (f), 639
Doody, Alison (f), 1812
Dorcic, Natasa, 325
Dorléac, Françoise (f), 427
Dorrer, Manca (f), 1535
Dors, Diana (f), 1790
Dottermans, Els (f), 131, 1377
Douglas, Michael (m), 2002, 2071, 2139
Douglas, Illeana (f), 2190, 2205, 2277
Doumbia, Adama (m), 669
Drabo, Ramata (f), 1323
Drapeau, Sylvie (f), 214
Dressler, Lieux (f), 1958
Dreyfus, Jean-Claude, 629
Driver, Minnie (f), 1115, 1851
Drobotowicz-Orkisz, Izabela (f), 1469
Drolc, Stefka (f), 2412
Droukarova, Dinara (f), 673
Drouot, Claire (f), 441
Drouot, Jean-Claude (m), 441

Drozdova, Olga (f), 958
Drynan, Meany (f), 82
Dryzner, Karolina (f), 1485
Duah, Alexandra (f), 847
Duarte, Vanda (f), 1497
Dubey, Lillete (f), 2307
DuBois, Marta (f), 2263
Dubost, Paulette (f), 436, 543
Dubroux, Danièle (f), 547
Ducy, Caroline (f), 615
Dufau, Graciela (f), 26
Duff, Anne-Marie (f), 1123
Duffy, Dorothy (f), 1123
Dukakis, Olympia (f), 2103, 2111
Duke, Patty (f), 185, 1893
Dumas, Sandra (f), 1356
Dunaway, Faye (f), 1791, 1920, 2108
Duncan, Lindsay (f), 1786, 2334
Dunning, Ruth (f), 1744
Dunst, Kirsten (f), 2179, 2328
Dunye, Cheryl (f), 2192, 2280
Duong, Don, 2406
Duras, Marguerite (f), 480
Düringer, Annemarie (f), 802
Dussollier, André (m), 596
Duthilleul, Laure (f), 556
Dutsch, Niklaus (m), 774
Dutt, Sunil (m), 967
Duval, Clea (f), 2244
Duvall, Robert (m), 2135
Duvall, Shelley (f), 1986
Dvornik, Boris (m), 2411
Dwyer, Karyn (f), 211
Dwyer, Kerry (f), 52
Dykstra, Russell (m), 82
Dymna, Anna (f), 1466, 1479, 1480
Dyrholm, Trine (f), 376
Dzovic, Dara (f), 2415

Eanes, Manuel (m), 1487
Eastwood, Clint (m), 2343
Ebeid, Nabila (f), 402
Eccles, Aimée (f), 1931
Echertz, Karoline (f), 709
Echeverría, Mónica (f), 222
Edmonds, Elizabeth (f), 1784
Edney, Beatie (f), 1368
Edwards, Anthony (m), 2082
Egilsdóttir, Ugala (f), 962
Egurrola, Julietta (f), 1340
Ehobor, Forstine (f), 1197
Eichhorn, Karoline (f), 711
Eichhorn, Lisa (f), 2052
Ek, Malin (f), 1652
Ekberg, Anita (f), 1190

Ekblad, Stina (f), 414, 1654
Eklund, Britt (f), 1155
El-Beheiry, Dalila (f), 403
El Cara, Placido (m), 2350
El Fahem, Hend (f), 1705
Eldard, Ron, 2104
Eliava, Lia (f), 2386
Elise, Kimberly (f), 2216, 2230, 2348
Elkabetz, Ronit (f), 1131, 1140, 1141
Ellert, Gundi (f), 804
Elliot, Alison (f), 1848, 2187
Eloranta, Eva (f), 416
Eloui, Laila (f), 404
Elsner, Hannelore (f), 705, 714, 764
Elvik, Kjersti (f), 1414
Embarek, Ouassini (m), 667
Endre, Lena (f), 1659
Engle, Tina (f), 771
Entezami, Ezatolla (m), 1082
Entius, Yolanda (f), 1370
Enzenberger, Marianne (f), 813
Erdman, John (m), 1933, 1950
Eren, Suavi (m), 1720
Ergün, Halil (m), 1722
Erna, Joice (f), 1059, 1063
Erten, Ayten (f), 766
Escobar, Elba (f), 2400
Espert, Nuria (f), 1590
Esumi, Makiko (f), 1263
Eszenyi, Eniko (f), 957
Everett, Rupert (m), 1794

Fabian, Françoise (f), 119, 453
Fagundes, Antônio, 144
Falk, Peter (m), 1959
Fall, Aminata, 1528
Fang Shu (f), 305
Fang Shuan (f), 1686
Fantoni, Andrea (f), 2350
Farehi, Bita (f), 1086
Faria, Betty (f), 146
Faridany, Francesca (f), 1855
Farjani, Farimah (f), 1076
Farrell, Brioni (f), 1921
Farrow, Mia (f), 1826, 1909, 2086
Farshchi, Minu (f), 1085
Fathy, Nagla (f), 388
Faucher, Françoise (f), 182
Fawcett, Farrah (f), 2055
Faye, Assane, 1525
Fedoseyeva-Shukshina, Lidiya, 2372
Felden, Renée (f), 88
Feldon, Barbara (f), 1956
Felton, Martine (f), 823
Fergusson, Karen (f), 1392

Ferhati, Jilalli (f), 1352
Ferland, Carmen (f), 193
Fernandez, Ademelis (f), 1592
Fernández, Ana (f), 1614, 1616
Fernández, Evelina (f), 2263
Ferraro, Danièle (f), 2326
Ferrell, Conchita (f), 1776
Ferréol, Andréa (f), 505, 621
Ferrera, America (f), 2310
Ferres, Veronica (f), 213
Fertis, Yannis, 850
Ferzetti, Gabriel (m), 1143
Festa, Yota, 877
Field, Sally (f), 1997, 2005, 2038, 2095, 2103, 2133,
    2240, 2325
Fikru, Nafkote (f), 407
Fillières, Hélène (f), 651
Finch, Peter (m), 1747, 1751, 1752, 1759
Finney, Albert (m), 2228, 2242
Fitzgerald, Maureen (f), 187
Fjeldstad, Lise (f), 1406
Flanagan, Fionnula (f), 1118, 2281, 2291
Fletcher, Suzanne (f), 2063
Flint, Katja (f), 702
Flockhart, Calista (f), 2267
Floko, Timo (m), 562
Flon, Suzanne (f), 510
Florence, Sheila (f), 66
Flores, Gabriela (f), 31
Flores, Mar (f), 1598
Flores, Rosario (f), 1565
Fofana, Donaldo (m), 1210
Folley, Lillian (f), 2153
Fonda, Bridget (f), 1803, 1805, 1806, 1819
Fonda, Jane (f), 1771, 1924, 1981, 1989, 1999, 2033,
    2041, 2058
Fong Sing Lee, Cecilia (f), 77
Fonsou, Anna (f), 867
Ford, Harrison (m), 2098
Ford, Margaret (f), 1774
Forde, Jessica (f), 518
Foremniak, Malgorzata, 1271
Fornés, Rosita (f), 337, 340
Forqué, Veronica (f), 1597
Forsyth, John, (m) 1912
Forte, Iaia (f), 1199
Forte, Marlene (f), 2209
Fossey, Brigitte (f), 816
Foster, Jodie (f), 2081, 2085, 2117, 2129, 2222
Fox, James (m), 1789, 1801
Fox, Kerry (f), 65, 1392, 1543
Fox, Michael J. (m), 2075
Fox, Vivica A. (f), 2216
Franczewski, Peotr (m), 1456
Franklin, Pamela (f), 1764

Fraser, Laura (f), 1380
Fraszynska, Jolanta (f), 1477
Freeman, Morgan (m), 2299, 2343
Frémont, Thierry (m), 125
Frey, Sami (m), 459, 477
Fricker, Brenda (f), 1831
Friel, Anna (f), 1877
Frijda, Nelly (f), 1361
Friðriksdóttir, Þóra (f), 960
Frogeui, Stella, 887
Fröler, Samuel, 1658
Frost, Simone (f), 732
Frot, Catherine (f), 606, 634
Fu Yiwei (f), 253, 274
Fudalej, Beata (f), 1482
Fuji, Junko, 1237
Fujiyama, Naomi (f), 1272
Fullerton, Fiona (f), 676
Für, Anikô (f), 952
Furness, Deborra-Lee (f), 58
Fyrogeni, Stela (f), 892

Gabriel, Gudrun (f), 782
Gagel, Eva (f), 767
Gainsbourg, Charlotte (f), 620
Galbó, Beatriz (f), 1562
Galiana, María (f), 1616
Galiardo, Juan Luis (m), 1624
Galwey, Isadora (f), 214
Ganatra, Nisha (f), 2255
Ganguly, Roopa (f), 1035
Ganz, Bruno (m), 65, 765, 1196, 1806
García Bernal, Gael (m), 1346
Garcia, Léa (f), 156
Garcia, María Eugenia (f), 332
Garcia, Nicole (f), 511, 555, 578, 631
Garcia, Paulo (m), 150
Garcia, Verónica (f), 405
Garfunkel, Art (m), 1793
Garneau, Constance (f), 199
Garrett, Teresa (f), 2224
Gas, Mario (m), 1577
Gassman, Vittorio (m), 119
Gausachs, Montserrat (f), 1585
Gauthier, Anne (f), 1490
Gavin, Erica (f), 1947
Gaydu, Marie (f), 1666
Ge Lan, 227
Gedeck, Martina (f), 707, 845
Gélin, Daniel (m), 560
Gere, Richard (m), 2314
Gerede, Bennu (f), 1736
Gerhati, Ahmed (m), 1350
Gershon, Gina (f), 655, 2196
Getova, Plamena (f), 163

Ghatak, Geeta (f), 964
Ghorab-Volta, Zaïda (f), 581
Ghose, Shampa (f), 1020
Giannini, Giancarlo (m), 1162, 1166, 1167, 1200
Gibson, Martha (f), 1777
Gibson, Mel (m), 2036
Gidwani, Kitu (f), 1847
Giftos, Elaine (f), 1921
Gil, Ariadna (f), 585, 1593, 1629
Gil, Galit (f), 1127
Gillain, Marie (f), 1737
Gillmer, Caroline (f), 73
Giménez, Teresa (f), 1564
Ginguetti, Gigliola (f), 859
Giordano, Domiziana (f), 1797
Giorgi, Eleanora (f), 1171
Girardot, Annie (f), 95, 423, 435, 456, 469, 482, 485, 535
Girik, Fatma (f), 1714
Gish, Annabeth (f), 1803, 2094
Gish, Lillian (f), 2083
Gisladóttir, Ragnhildur (f), 961
Givernau, Françoise (f), 1553
Giza, Amalia (f), 870
Glagoleva, Vera (f), 2384
Glover, Danny (m), 2230
Gobeil, Pierre (m), 180
Godard, Jean-Luc (m), 595
Godrèche, Judith (f), 565
Goffman, Betty (f), 154
Golbahari, Marina (f), 2
Goldberg, Whoopi (f), 2042, 2101, 2173, 2194, 2232
Goldoni, Lelia (f), 1946
Golino, Valeria (f), 1187, 1207, 1737
Gomes, Bia (f), 1502
Gomes, Flora (f), 896
Gómez, Carmelo (m), 1594
Gomez, Fidèle (m), 674
Göncü, Nil (f), 1709
Gong Li (f), 259, 280, 284, 289, 291, 298
Gong Youchun (f), 275
Gonzalez Bose, Paola (f), 1571
Good, Meagan (f), 2223
Goodall, Caroline (f), 73
Gordon, Jade (f), 2251
Gordon, Ruth (f), 1898, 1909
Gorintin, Esther (f), 673
Gorintin, Regine (f), 617
Gornick, Lisa (f), 1876
Gottschalk, Thomas (m), 676
Goven, Yann (m), 639
Gråbøl, Sofie (f), 370
Grace, Anna (f), 2204
Grace, Emily (f), 2336
Graham, Heather (f), 2257

Granados, Daisy (f), 333, 334, 339
Grant, Hugh (m), 1807
Grant, Lee (f), 1983
Gravina, Carla (f), 685
Grazia Grassini, Maria (f), 1205
Greene, Janet-Laine, 187
Greene, Ruth Ann (f), 1939
Gregorek, Karin (f), 736
Gregory, Pascal (m), 662
Grier, Pam (f), 1941, 1951, 2225
Griffith, Melanie (f), 1956, 2098, 2183
Griffiths, Linda (f), 2017
Griffiths, Rachel (f), 74, 83, 1852, 1873
Grigore, Mara (f), 1511
Grinberg, Anouk (f), 1670
Grodin, Charles (m), 2009
Grody, Kathryn (f), 2112
Grossmann, Mechtild (f), 742
Grube-Deister, Elsa (f), 684
Gruber, Marie (f), 735
Guarnieri, Gianfrancesco, 139
Guerra, Blanca (f), 1339, 1341
Guerrin, Anne (f), 116
Guers, Paul (m), 427
Gueye, Maguette, 1525
Guèye, Makhourédia, 1528
Guffanti, Monica (f), 338
Guha, Anita (f), 984
Guilbeault, Luce (f), 180
Guilhe, Albane (f), 190
Guiliano, Domenica (f), 1194
Guillemin, Sophie (f), 647
Guirova, Iana (f), 157
Gulzar, Raakhee (f), 987, 1018
Gunasekeva, Nadika (f), 1635
Gunnlaugsdóttir, Tinna (f), 961
Guo Yuan (f), 274
Guthrie, Lynne (f), 1960
Gutiérrez, Zaide Silvia (f), 2026
Gyllenhaal, Maggie (f), 2312, 2317, 2328

Ha, Pat. See Hsia Wen-shi
Ha Ping (f), 909
Ha You-mi (f), 1300
Habbema, Cox (f), 1361
Habich, Matthais (m), 763
Hackett, Joan (f), 1901
Hackman, Gene (m), 1961, 2185
Hada, Michiko (f), 1686
Hadar, Yael (f), 1137
Haddad, Djamila (f), 16
Haft, Linal (m), 82
Hagerty, Julie (f), 2034
Haimour, Mohamed, 5
Hain, Jeanette (f), 1668

Hakan, Fikret, 1707
Hakim, Christine (f), 1008, 1070, 1072
Halcáková, Slávká (f), 346
Hallaren, Jane (f), 2017
Hallyday, Johnny (m), 610
Hamama, Faten (f), 377, 382, 383, 384, 390
Hamed, Abdl, 1103
Hamilton, Bernie (m), 1899
Hammer, Sascha (f), 801
Hamza, Sonia (f), 1704
Hamzaoglu, Mayati (m), 1709
Hanayagi, Genshu (f), 1244
Handel, Edit (f), 946
Hanks, Tom (m), 2095
Hannah, Daryl (f), 1633, 2103, 2317
Hanny, Tchelly (f), 1213
Hanoo, Kayoko, 1218
Hara, Setsuko (f), 1215
Harada, Mieko (f), 1246, 1266
Haradze, Najda (f), 2370
Harden, Marcia Gay (f), 1395, 2187, 2317, 2322
Hardi, Marlia (f), 1065
Hardy, Carla (f), 124
Harfouch, Corinna (f), 737
Hargaard, Karen Helen (f), 1660
Hargreaves, John (m), 54
Harkishin, Jimmi (m), 1821
Harlow, Shalom (f), 2297
Harold, Maureen (f), 1814
Harris, Bruklin (f), 2204
Harris, Ed (m), 2051
Harris, Jo Ann (f), 1954
Harris, Zelda (f), 2160
Harrow, Lisa (f), 65, 1388
Harry, Debbie (f), 2072
Hartman, Elizabeth (f), 1901
Hartmann, Maria (f), 814
Hartouch, Corinna (f), 687
Harukawa, Misuni (f), 1226
Harvey, Laurence (m), 1754
Harwick, Charlie (f), 1829
Hashemi, Mehdi (f), 1079
Hassan, Véronica (f), 43
Hatami, Leila (f), 1084
Hatheyer, Heidemarie (f), 841
Hatoum, Farah (f), 1417
Hatoupi, Dimitra (f), 879
Hattangadi, Rohini (f), 1005
Haubmann, Huberta (f), 90
Havener, Stacey (f), 2182
Hawn, Goldie (f), 1957, 2003, 2040, 2078, 2141, 2202, 2288
Hayek, Salma (f), 2295
Haysbert, Dennis (m), 2145
Hayward, Susan (f), 1747

Hazelhurst, Noni (f), 55
He Qing, 276
He Saifei (f), 302
Headey, Lena (f), 1820, 1862
Headly, Glenne (f), 2132, 2195
Heche, Anne (f), 2219
Hedhili, Amel (f), 1698, 1699, 1700
Heinze, Henriette (f), 96
Helgar, Anne Marie (f), 361
Hellberg, Ruth (f), 679
Helmi, Katarina (f), 853
Hema-Malini (f), 996
Hemida, Mahmoud, 402
Hemingway, Margaux (f), 1972
Hemingway, Mariel (f), 1972, 2018
Henderson, Shirley (f), 1861
Hendrickx, Monic (f), 1383, 1384
Hendry, Gloria (f), 1955
Henesy, Sharon (f), 1903
Hennessy, Jill (f), 2255
Henriau, Marie (f), 474
Hensen, Beate (f), 811
Hepburn, Audrey (f), 1892, 1904
Hepburn, Katherine (f), 1763, 1964
Hérédia, Lisa (f), 557
Hermann, Irm (f), 91, 751, 807, 839
Hershey, Barbara (f), 1804, 1836, 1929, 2008, 2080,
    2087, 2123
Heyron, Guy, 106
Hidari, Sachiko (f), 1225, 1233, 1248
Hiller, Wendy (f), 1110
Hillinsø, Ellen (f), 370
Hiss, Nicole (f), 463
Ho, Josie (f), 322
Ho, Lily (f), 900
Hoang Cuc (f), 2405
Hobel, Maria (f), 2309
Hoffman, Melanie (f), 2183
Hoffmann, Jutta (f), 692, 721, 723
Hoger, Hannelore (f), 744
Holden, Winifred (f), 199
Holloman, Laurel (f), 2311
Holm, Ian (m), 1866
Holmes, Katie (f), 2330
Honey (f), 2021
Hoosier, Trula (f), 2122
Hopkins, Anthony (m), 1771, 2053, 2117
Hoppe, Irina (f), 809
Horejsi, Jitka (f), 351
Horler, Sacha (f), 82
Horrocks, Jane (f), 1853
Hoskins, Bob (m), 212, 1802
Hotchkis, Joan (f), 1963
Houde, Germain (m), 183
Houri, Alice (f), 586

Houston, Whitney (f), 2191
Howard, Trevor (m), 121
Hsia Wen-shi (f), 1675, 1679
Hsiao Shu-shen (f), 1688
Hu Peng, 229
Huang Yiqing (f), 320
Huar, Xu Re (f), 839
Huber, Grischa (f), 786
Huber, Lotti (f), 806, 829
Hudi, Viktoria (f), 420
Hughes, Sean, 1117
Hughes, Wendy (f), 54
Hui, Kara (f), 901
Huijara, Leticia (f), 1334
Hun Bai (f), 287
Hunt, Linda (f), 1787, 2064
Hunter, Holly (f), 71, 2069, 2140, 2267, 2271
Huppert, Isabelle (f), 56, 95, 101, 464, 469, 481, 484,
    487, 493, 495, 499, 508, 509, 522, 527, 551, 559,
    575, 582, 597, 623, 625, 646, 649, 666, 939, 1173
Hurt, Mary Beth (f), 2123
Hurt, William (m), 2069, 2233
Husni, Suad (f), 378, 380
Huston, Anjelica (f), 1863, 2105, 2278, 2340
Hutchins, Eleanor (f), 2306
Huynh, Mai (f), 2188
Hwang Jeong-sun (f), 1290
Hwang Sin-hye (f), 1301
Hyatt, Michael (f), 2316
Hyttinen, Maarit, 409

Ibarra, Mirta (f), 336, 1605
Ibou Ndong, 1527
Ichihara, Etsuko (f), 1258
Igo, Eva (f), 946
Im Yoo-jin (f), 1306
Imane, 395
Imrie, Celia (f), 1816
Inanir, Kadir (m), 1736
Inglessi, Irene (f), 891
Inoh, Annie Shizuka (f), 1686
Ionesco, Eva (f), 598
Irdwaty, Azean (f), 1317
Irons, Jeremy (m), 1192
Irureta, Elena (f), 1604
Irving, Amy (f), 2089
Isabel, Maria (f), 340
Isayeva, Sairam (f), 2354
Ishida, Eri (f), 62
Isma, 11
Itami, Juzo (m), 1254
Ito, Naomi (f), 1251
Iturralde, Rossana (f), 405
Ivars, Analia (f), 1582
Ivey, Judith (f), 2228, 2336

Ivgi, Dana (f), 1140
Iwashita, Shima (f), 1238, 1242, 1247, 1262

Jackson, Glenda (f), 1765, 1768, 1772, 1775, 1800
Jackson, Leonard, 1942
Jackson, Mary (f), 1108
Jackson, Samuel L. (m), 2210, 2223, 2225
Jacob, Irène (f), 574, 578, 1476
Jacob, Katarina (f), 764
Jaffrey, Madhur (f), 1792, 1856, 2255
Jaffrey, Sakina (f), 2255
Jakes, T. D., 2348
Jalal, Farida (f), 1032
James, Geraldine (f), 1116, 1809
Jamot, Lisa (f), 2346
Jamróz, Katarzyna (f), 1478
Janda, Krystyna (f), 1457, 1458, 1464, 1480
Jane, Sofia (f), 1316
Jankowska-Cieúlak, Jadwiga (f), 942, 1458
Jansson, Kim (f), 365
Janzurova, Iva (f), 348
Jaoui, Agnès (f), 596, 622, 671
Jasinski, Krzysztof (m), 1465
Jean-Baptiste, Marianne (f), 1838, 2229
Jelinek, Anne-Marie (f), 1521
Jelmini, Tiziana, 842
Jenkins, Rebecca (f), 198, 219
Jennings, Claudia (f), 1931, 1958
Jeong Seon-keyong (f), 1300
Jett, Joan (f), 2075
Jeudon, Alexandra (f), 638
Jiang Yiping, 269
Jiménez, Lucia (f), 1622
Jiminez, Mary (f), 1419
Jin Kim Yeo (f), 1302
Joano, Clotilde (f), 421
Jobert, Marlène (f), 470, 501
Johansson, Scarlett (f), 2181, 2272, 2277
Johns, Glynis (f), 2099
Johnson, Annette (f), 1660
Johnson, Celia (f), 1764
Jokovic, Mirjana (f), 678
Jolie, Angelina (f), 2244
Jolliffe, Charles (m), 187
Jones, Alexandra (f), 2099
Jones, Barbara O (f), 1692, 1969, 2122
Jones, Christopher, 1910
Jones, Helen (f), 68
Jones, Jake-Ann (f), 2213
Jones, James Earl (m), 1948
Jones, Tommy Lee (m), 1970, 2000, 2157, 2159, 2241
Jorgensen, Ana Eleonora (f), 376
Jørgensen, Bodil (f), 371
Jose, Jacklyn (f), 1439
Josephson, Erland (m), 1643, 1654, 1659

Joshi, Suhas (f), 1009
Jovovich, Milla (f), 611
Ju Xue (f), 278
Judd, Ashley (f), 2154, 2241, 2270, 2299, 2347
Juergensen, Heather (f), 2303
Juliani, John (m), 174
Juslin, Brigitte (f), 428
Justa, Aleksandra (f), 98

Kaack, Sabine (f), 845
Kaandorp, Brigitte (f), 1381
Kabátová, Emilia (f), 346
Kabátová, Zita (f), 346
Kaci, Nadia (f), 1700, 1706
Kaga, Mariko (f), 1231
Kahan, Dalit (f), 1137
Kalem, Toni (f), 187
Kalinová, Vanda (f), 351
Kálmán, Bea (f), 955
Kamel, Abla, 393
Kane, Carol (f), 1952, 1983, 2112
Kang Soo-yeon (f), 1298, 1299
Kapadia, Dimple (f), 2304
Kaperda, Yioland (f), 889
Kaplan, Cynthia (f), 2220
Kaplun, Evlyn (f), 1135
Kaprisky, Valérie (f), 203, 552
Kapteijn, Micha (m), 797
Karbanová, Ivana (f), 350
Karezi, Jenny (f), 853, 855, 862, 864, 866, 867
Karimi, Niki (f), 1078, 1081, 1087, 1096
Karimi, Soghra (f), 1092
Karina, Anna (f), 426, 434, 445, 462, 762, 1152
Kariuki, Catherine (f), 1284
Karlatos, Olga (f), 458
Karran, Claudia (f), 57
Kasprzyk, Ewa (f), 1469
Kästner, Shelley (f), 680
Katrakis, Manos (m), 849
Kaushal, Kanan (f), 984
Kavner, Julie (f), 2148
Kavoukidou, Elena Maria, 893
Kazakova, Vesela (f), 164
Keach, Stacey (m), 2025
Keaton, Camille (f), 1980
Keaton, Diane (f), 1982, 2035, 2036, 2054, 2067, 2090, 2112, 2202, 2259
Keats, Steven (m), 1952
Keegan, John (m), 1108
Keener, Catherine (f), 2219, 2305
Keim, Claire (f), 635
Keïta, Aï (f), 165
Keïta, Amïna (f), 1322
Keitel, Harvey (m), 71, 81, 1176, 1200, 1968
Kellegher, Tina (f), 1824

Keller, Marthe (f), 1603
Kelltoum, 8
Kelly, Martine (f), 111
Kempson, Sybil (f), 2289
Kendal, Jennifer (f), 972, 997
Kennedy, Jo (f), 50
Kennedy, Sarah (f), 1960
Kensit, Patsy (f), 2302
Kente, Dombisa (f), 1543
Keogh, Alexia (f), 1392
Kerezi, Jenny (f), 863
Kerr, Deborah (f), 1745, 1750, 1792
Kerr-Bell, Manaengaroa (f), 1397
Kessler, Wulf (m), 796
Khajuria, Sarita (f), 1821
Khalifa, Sahar (f), 1417
Khamatova, Chulpan (f), 1516
Khanh, Le (f), 2408
Kharshiladze, Daredjan (f), 2379, 2381
Khemiri, Fatma (f), 1696
Kher, Anupam (m), 1019
Kher, Kiron (f), 1039, 1416
Khlat, Yasmine (f), 10, 1695
Khomassouridze, Nino (f), 673
Khouadra, Nozha (f), 1699
Khoury, Clara (f), 1418
Khudhair, Alima (f), 1105
Kiberlain, Sandrine (f), 577, 600, 610, 631
Kidder, Margot (f), 186, 1936
Kidman, Nicole (f), 375, 1836, 2190, 2281, 2300, 2345
Kier, Udo (m), 742
Kihstedt, Rya (f), 2193
Kim Hye-na (f), 1306
Kim Jeong-hwa (f), 1288
Kim Ji-mi (f), 1290, 1296
Kim Kwang-ryeol (f), 1288
Kim Min-sun (f), 1308
Kim Ok-heui (f), 1288
Kim Yoon-jin (f), 1309
Kimani, Roslynn (f), 1284
Kinder, Sandra (f), 2280
Kinnaman, Melinda (f), 1661
Kinoti, Lynette Mukami (f), 1283
Kinski, Nastasja (f), 2272
Kinski, Pola (f), 833
Kirkland, Sally (f), 2066, 2326
Kishi, Keiko (f), 1254
Kishida, Kyoko (f), 1228
Kiss, Marian (f), 929
Kitamura, Akiko (f), 1243
Klemola, Leena (f), 418
Klenskaja, Maria (f), 406
Kline, Kevin (m), 2020
Klubowicz, Marta (f), 1469

Kluge, Aleksondra (f), 743, 754
Knef, Hildegarde, 816
Knight, Shirley (f), 1762, 1901, 1913, 2207, 2291
Knightley, Keira (f), 1874
Knudsen, Mette (f), 355
Knudsen, Sidse Babett (f), 369
Ko I-cheng (m), 1674
Koçyigit, Hülya (f), 1713, 1719, 1729
Koese, Nursel (f), 1739
Köhler, Juliana (f), 697, 709
Koirakou, Marianna (f), 854
Koirala, Minisha (f), 1052
Kokanova, Nevena (f), 159
Komine, Rena (f), 1264
Komorowska, Maja (f), 1455, 1456, 1468
Koncz, Gábor (m), 945
Kong Lin (f), 294
König, Michael (m), 819
Konstandarou, Maria (f), 882
Koo, Josephine (f), 307, 903, 909, 910
Koper, Macit (m), 1723
Koronel, Hilda (f), 1424
Kortaki, Dioni (f), 889
Korzun, Dina (f), 1516, 1868
Kotaoka, Sumie (f), 1260
Kotegawa, Yûko (f), 1254
Kotler, Oded (m), 1126
Kounelaki, Miranda (f), 858
Kovacheva, Liliana (f), 161
Kovács, Kati (f), 927
Kovács, Ottila (f), 943
Kovanko, Lilga (f), 1648
Kovats, Adel (f), 954
Kowsari, Baran (f), 1095
Kraakman, Maria (f), 1382
Krabbé, Jeroen (m), 1804
Krafftówna, Barbara (f), 1454
Krajnc, Iva (f), 1536
Krakevik, Herborg (f), 1415
Krebitz, Nicolette (f), 692
Kreissig, Gertraud, 734
Kriende, Ulrike (f), 822
Kristen, Marta (f), 1944
Kristofferson, Kris (m), 1946
Krivoshieva, Irène (f), 162
Krössner, Renate (f), 720, 729
Krun, Paola (f), 37
Kudir, Adi, 1062
Kudoh, Youki (f), 2184
Kudrow, Lisa (f), 2221, 2259
Kulkarni, Sonali (f), 1036
Kumar, Ashok (m), 966, 976
Kumar, Sanjeer (m), 973
Kumarasinghe, Geetha (f), 1636
Kumari, Meena (f), 965, 976

Künneke, Evelyn (f), 746
Kuno, Makiko (f), 1273
Kunonga, Marian (f), 2417
Kupchenko, Irina (f), 675, 2369, 2373, 2387
Kurihara, Komaki (f), 1245
Kurka, Lea (f), 709
Kurtz, Swoosie (f), 2197
Kuskowska-Borkowska, Anita (f), 1483
Kuttappa, Meena (f), 993
Kútvölgyi, Erzébet (f), 931
Kuzmina, Yelena, 2372
Kydykeeva, B., 2362
Kyung Jin Hee (f), 1302

Laaksonen, Liisamaija (f), 410
Labonarska, Halina (f), 1460
Labourier, Dominique (f), 465
Lacroix, Ghalia (f), 1698
Ladd, Diane (f), 1946, 2135
Ladikou, Alexandra (f), 853
Laffin, Dominique (f), 494
Laflandre, Alexandra (f), 638
Lafont, Bernadette (f), 4, 175, 421, 451, 570, 595, 1670
Lafont, Colette, 1782
Laforet, Marie (f), 427
Lahti, Christine (f), 2040, 2073, 2128
Laing, John (m), 1393
Lalloui, Rahim, 11
Lam, Erica (f), 319
Lam, Karena (f), 926
Lam, Wilson (m), 298
Lampe, Jutta (f), 782, 789
Lan Lau (f), 297
Lancoume, Karen (f), 618
Lanctôt, Micheline (f), 176, 183
Landgrebe, Gudrun (f), 791, 808, 824, 1179
Lane, Diane (f), 2074, 2314, 2334
Lane, Nathan (m), 2261
Lang, Christiane (f), 745
Lang, k.d. (f), 681
Lange, Jessica (f), 2016, 2051, 2054, 2102, 2113, 2157, 2180
Lansbury, Angela (f), 1788
Lapa, Fernanda, 1491
Lario, Veronica (f), 1175
Laroque, Michèle (f), 604
Larralde, Marta (f), 1628
Laskari, Zoe (f), 860
Lathan, Sanaa (f), 2262
Latypov, Khikmat, 2366
Lau Kar-leung (m), 901
Lau, Rain (f), 909
Laure, Carole (f), 188, 194, 507
Laurier, Charlotte (f), 209

Lauterbach, Heiner, 822
Lavi, Efrat (f), 1126
Law, Phyllida (f), 1849
Lawley, Yvonne (f), 1394
Lawrence, Josie (f), 1815
Lawson, Shannon (f), 207
Lazar, Dorina (f), 1513
Lazlo, Viktor (f), 1575
Le Bas, Philippe (m), 497
Le Besco, Isild (f), 667
Le Flaguais, Véronique (f), 177
Le Gallienne, Eva (f), 2004
Le Roi, Gaël (f), 533
Leachman, Cloris (f), 1949, 1962, 2249
Learned, Michael (f), 1976
Leble, Natalya (f), 2388
Lebotte, Sofia (f), 659
Lebrun, Françoise (f), 476
Lechner, Geno (f), 694, 898
Ledoyen, Virginie (f), 583, 646
Leduc, Richard (m), 111
Lee, Angelica (f), 1691
Lee Eun-joo (f), 1307
Lee Eun-shil (f), 1307
Lee Hyo-jeong (f), 1305
Lee Ji-eun (f), 1304
Lee Jiunn-jye, 1687
Lee Mi-suk (f), 1295, 1303
Lee Yo-won (f), 1307, 1308
Lee Young-jin (f), 1308
Leelavathi (f), 990
Légitimus, Darling (f), 512
Legrá, Adela (f), 328, 329
Lehfeld, Kristen (f), 363
Lehner, Helga (f), 781
Leigh, Barbara (f), 1921
Leigh, Jennifer Jason (f), 2092, 2165, 2174, 2176, 2195, 2228, 2323
Leighton, Margaret (f), 1900
Lemaitre-Auger, Liliane (f), 177
Lemercier, Valérie (f), 665
Lemmon, Jack (m), 1989, 2010
Lemon, Geneviève (f), 61, 82
Lencastre, Alexandra (f), 1503
Lennartz, Monika (f), 731
Leo, Melissa (f), 2039
Leonardou, Sotira (f), 874
Leonhardt, Gustav (m), 745
Lesley, Lorna (f), 68
Leung, Tony (m), 908
Leuwerik, Ruth (f), 738, 739
Levi, Asi (f), 1138
Levry, Carmen, 1212
Lewis, Juliette (f), 2301, 2322
Leye, Thierno (m), 1524

Li Baotian (m), 280
Li Cuiyan, 306
Li Fengxu (f), 249
Li Hong (f), 299
Li, Jet (m), 914
Li Jing (f), 273
Li Kechun (f), 248, 263, 282
Li Lan (f), 290
Li, Leon (m), 922
Li Lin (f), 313
Li Rong, 263
Li Shuping (f), 1674
Li Tuan, 303
Li Xia, 269
Li Xiuming, 245
Liang Guoqing (f), 293
Lieberg, Angela, 820
Lierck, Ella (f), 727
Lightstone, Marilyn (f), 187
Lihamba, Amandina (f), 1692
Lin, Brigitte (f), 905, 914
Lin Liu (f), 314
Lincoln, Abbey (f), 1905
Lincovsky, Cipe (f), 836
Linda, Anita (f), 1445
Linda, Boguslaw, 1463
Lindblom, Gunnel (f), 1638, 1639, 1642, 1643
Lindeklejv, Sunniva (f), 1406
Linden, Jennie (f), 1765
Linder, Eva (f), 90
Lindo, Delroy (m), 2160
Lindon, Vincent (m), 634, 665
Ling Zonqying (f), 297
Liotard, Thérèse (f), 478
Liotti, Daniele (m), 1619
Lipkina, Mariya (f), 102, 1497
Lipman, Nicola (f), 174
Lippertová, Alena (f), 351
Lisa, Mona (f), 1424
LisaRaye (f), 2234, 2318
Lisi, Virna (f), 572, 1193, 1203
Lissa, Eva (f), 827
Litvinova, Renata (f), 1742
Liu Hsiao Hui, 911
Liu, Lucy (f), 2341
Liu, Rene (f), 1684, 1685, 1689, 1691
Liu Wei, 303
Liu Xiaoqing (f), 246, 251, 266
Liu Xin (f), 311
Liwellyn, Suzette (f), 1832
Lizaran, Anna (f), 1590
LL Cool J (m), 2319
Lo Sing-siang, 235
Loden, Barbara (f), 1922
Lohan, Lindsay (f), 2321

Lohman, Allison (f), 2315
Loiu, Ingrid (f), 2310
Løkkeberg, Vibeke (f), 1410, 1411
Lomez, Céline (f), 181
Londez, Guilaine (f), 553
Long, Shelley (f), 2077
Longley, Victoria (f), 72
Lopes, Xuxa (f), 143
López, Charo (f), 1552, 1626
López de Ayala, Pilar (f), 1619
Lopez, Jennifer (f), 2227, 2292
Lopez, Kamala (f), 2175
López, Marga (f), 1325
Lopez, Serge (m), 609
Lopez-Tarin, Teresa (f), 1600
Lopsang (m), 315
Lorain, Sophie (f), 218
Loren, Sophia (f), 1144, 1166, 1188, 1755
Lorska, Ewa (f), 1485
Lothar, Susanne (f), 688
Loulou, Anny (f), 876
Lozano, Margarita (f), 1154, 1568
Lu Hsiao-fen (f), 1678, 1680, 1681
Lu, Ketchun (f), 234, 267
Lu Liping (f), 268
Lu, Lisa (f), 237, 277, 899
Lu Lu (f), 315
Lu Xiao He, 260
Lu Xiaofen (f), 1672
Lu Xiaohe (m), 290
Lucinda, Elisa (f), 156
Lui, Ray (m), 924
Luis, Fernando (m), 1493
Luísa, Natália (f), 1498
Luna, Diego (m), 1346
Lüning, Susanne (f), 736
Luo Yan, 269
LuPone, Patti (f), 2229
Lynch, John (m), 1112
Lynch, Susan (f), 1120
Lynn, Verónica (f), 341, 344
Lynskey, Melanie (f), 1396
Lyon, Liese (f), 99
Lyon, Sue (f), 1900
Lyonne, Natasha (f), 2260
Lyytikainen, Anna-Elina (f), 418

Ma, Angela (f), 1687
Ma Lingyan, 306
Ma Rufeng (f), 1672
Ma Yili (f), 320
Maakaron, Myrna (f), 1314
MacDonald, Ann-Marie (f), 195
Macdonald, Kelly (f), 1858
MacDowell, Andie (f), 1875, 2298

MacLaine, Shirley (f), 1891, 1892, 1987, 2029, 2103, 2114
MacMurray, Fred (m), 1895
Madigan, Amy (f), 2025, 2201, 2226
Madonna (f), 2045, 2143
Maës, Tove (f), 356
Magimel, Benoît (m), 607
Maglietta, Licia (f), 1196
Magnani, Anna (f), 1146
Magnuson, Ann (f), 2063, 2076
Mahaka, Ulla (f), 2417
Maher, Bill (m), 2088
Maillé, Claudette (f), 1337
Mailman, Deborah (f), 80
Mairesse, Valérie, 478
Mäkelä, Maritta (f), 411
Mako (m), 2097
Malaon, Tuti Indra (f), 1068
Malecki, Jan (m), 1482
Malini, Hema (f), 1024
Malkovich, John (m), 213, 1836, 2076
Mallet, Marilu (f), 191
Mällinen, Sari (f), 419
Malone, Jena (f), 2195, 2222
Maloney, Michael, 1184
Malovcic, Edita (f), 94
Mamizadeh, Nargess (f), 1091
Man, Hayley (f), 2175
Manenti, Michele (f), 1966
Maneva, Tzvetana (f), 157, 158
Mankani, Rarindra (m), 1009
Mansur, Lale (f), 1735
Mao Haitong, 288
Marbeouf, Julie (f), 589
Marceau, Sophie (f), 591, 594
Marchand, Corinne (f), 425
Marcos, Cristina (f), 1586, 1595
Marcus, Askala (f), 1134
Margoni, Elizabeth (f), 1615
Margulies, Julianna (f), 2235, 2269
Mariscal, Rosa (f), 1602
Marleau, Louise (f), 182, 189, 190
Maron, Maya (f), 1139
Marta, Maysa (f), 897
Marten, Barbara (f), 1865
Martial, Jacques (m), 2006
Martin, Anna (f), 1431
Martin, Pamela Sue (f), 1996
Martina, Maria (f), 88
Martínez, Sonia (f), 1564
Martinez, Vanessa (f), 2317
Martinez, Vincent (m), 582
Martins Guerra, Ana Maria (f), 1487
Marull, Laia (f), 1630
Mashnaya, Olga (f), 2382

Masina, Giulietta (f), 1150
Mason, Marsha (f), 2011
Massari, Lea (f), 1143, 1152
Massey, Anna (f), 1771
Masson, Laëtitia (f), 672
Massoomi, Parvaneh (f), 1075
Masterson, Mary Stuart (f), 2125
Mastrantonio, Mary Elizabeth (f), 2247
Mastroianni, Chiara (f), 1500
Mastroianni, Marcello (m), 34, 1166, 1171, 1173
Mateu, Sergi (m), 1575
Matheson, Elizabeth (f), 1413
Mattes, Eva (f), 716, 779, 790, 826
Matthews, Terumi (f), 1859
Matz, Johanna (f), 719
Maughan, Monica (f), 47
Maul, Simone, 780
Maura, Carmen (f), 130, 566, 1551, 1563, 1569, 1573, 1574, 1577, 1578, 1584, 1603, 1609, 1611, 1621
Mavric, Elizabeth (f), 1398
Mavropoulou, Gelly (f), 861
Max-Hansen, Ann-Marie (f), 358
May, Elaine (f), 2111
May, Jodhi (f), 1804, 1823
May, Mathilda (f), 64
Mayans, Antonio (m), 1582
Mayo, Jennifer (f), 2027
Mayron, Melanie (f), 1990, 2096
Maza, Rachel (f), 80
McBroom, Marcia (f), 1915
McCain, Frances Lee (f), 1975
McCarthy, Andrew (m), 2217
McCarthy, Nobu (f), 2097
McCarthy, Sheila (f), 195
McCormack, Catherine (f), 1119, 2268
McDermott, Kathleen (f), 1878
McDonnell, Caitlin Grace (f), 2169
McDonnell, Mary (f), 2147
McDormand, Frances (f), 1811, 2140, 2200, 2324
McElrone, Natascha (f), 1843, 2324
McEwan, Geraldine, 1123, 1808
McFadden, Davenia (f), 2284
McFarlane, Cassie (f), 1779
McGillis, Kelly (f), 84, 2085, 2127
McGovern, Elizabeth (f), 2108, 2146
McGregor, Angela Punch (f), 53
McGregor, Ewan (m), 1120
McGuckian, Mary (f), 1114
McKee, Gina (f), 1861
McKee, Lonette (f), 1974, 2279
McKenzie, Jacqueline (f), 2243
McKenzie, Julia (f), 1810
McLaughlin, Ellen (f), 2199
McLaughlin, Sheila (f), 742, 2021, 2022
McLeod, Sandy (f), 2031

McMurtry, Erin (f), 2162, 2167
McNally, Kevin, 1179
McNamara, Madeline (f), 1398
McNeil, Claudia (f), 1890, 1939
McNeil, Marguerite (f), 219
McNichol, Kristy (f), 2011, 2013
McQueen, Steve (m), 1894
McTeer, Janet (f), 2252, 2283
Meany, Colm (m), 1824
Meara, Anne (f), 2285
Mercouri, Melina (f), 851, 871
Medbøe, Katja (f), 1403, 1409, 1412
Meddings, Cissy (f), 199
Medel, Aya (f), 1445
Medford, Kay (f), 1906
Medina, Ofelia (f), 33, 1330
Mehta, Vijaya (f), 1009
Mei, Leng (f), 243
Mejía, Lissete (f), 1604
Mekin, Ahmet (m), 1710
Mekkiou, Sonia (f), 19
Melato, Mariangela (f), 1162
Melendez, Aiko (f), 1438
Mell, Marisa (f), 741
Melli, Elide (f), 1200
Mendez, Cathérine (f), 599
Mendoza, Benedicta (f), 132
Menkes, Tinka (f), 2057, 2134
Menzel, Jiri, 352
Mercier, Denis, 184
Mercier, Marianne (f), 184
Méril, Macha (f), 439
Merlin, Joanna (f), 2212
Mesguich, Daniel (m), 511
Meshcheryakova, Alla (f), 2368
Messine, Monique (f), 434
Mestres, Isabel (f), 1592
Metcalf, Laurie (f), 2151
Meylan, Gerard (m), 584
Mézières, Myriam (f), 650, 1667
Miao, Cora (f), 902, 906
Michael, Ralph (m), 1368
Michelangeli, Marcella (f), 1168
Micla, Caroline (f), 563
Midler, Bette (f), 1998, 2077, 2087, 2118, 2202, 2261, 2345
Mifune, Toshiro (m), 1249
Miguel, Joëlle (f), 518
Miheller, Nomika (f), 1660
Mika, Okuno (f), 1270
Mikaël, Ludmila (f), 651
Mikuc, Hanna (f), 1470
Miles, Sarah (f), 1790
Miles, Sherry (f), 1927
Milford, Carla (f), 2182

Milian, Tomas (m), 1152
Milijkovic, Mira, 99
Millet, Christiane, 817
Milliken, Angie (f), 72
Mills, Hayley (f), 1750
Milo, Sandra (f), 1142
Mimeux, Yvette (f), 1910, 1970
Ming, Hsu, 1671
Minguez, Elvira (f), 1601
Minichmayr, Birgit (f), 100
Minska, Albert (m), 12
Miou-Miou (f), 491, 509, 531, 546, 1603
Mira, Brigitte (f), 753, 756
Miralles, Joan, 1565
Miriel, Veronica (f), 1553
Mirren, Helen (f), 1112, 1118, 1881
Mishra, Smiriti (f), 1039
Mitchell, Joni (f), 187
Mitchell, Radha (f), 2231, 2276
Miyamoto, Nobuko, 1257
Miyazawa, Rie (f), 925
Mlambo, Nomsa (f), 2418
Mobassa, Noëlla (f), 669
Moe Moe Myint Aung, 169
Moffatt, Tracy (f), 70
Molina, Alfred (m), 2295
Molina, Angela (f), 710, 1176, 1566, 1568, 1625
Mondie, Michel (m), 182
Monori, Lili (f), 933, 936, 937, 939, 959
Montand, Yves (m), 459
Montenegro, Fernanda (f), 139, 152, 155
Montesano, Enrico (m), 1175
Montezuma, Magdalena (f), 750, 778, 793
Moore, Demi (f), 2132, 2183, 2207, 2250
Moore, Frank (m), 181
Moore, Julianne (f), 2186, 2248, 2293, 2300
Moore, Melody (f), 2320
Moorehead, Agnes (f), 1928
Morán, Mercedes (f), 40
Morante, Laura (f), 1488
Moratti, Bedi (f), 1158
Morcanu, Florentine (f), 1507
Mordjukova, Nonna (f), 1278, 2358
Moreau, Jeanne (f), 430, 443, 461, 474, 508, 633, 645, 1757, 1820, 1837
Moreira, Ana (f), 1499
Moreno, Isabel (f), 344
Moreno, Rita (f), 2178
Moreno, Ruby (f), 1259
Moretti, Daniela (f), 1172
Morgenstern, Maia (f), 956, 1508, 1512
Morice, Tara (f), 73
Moriconi, Valeria (f), 1152
Morreira, Ana (f), 1631
Morrison, Temerua (m), 1397

Morse, Helen (f), 1386
Morse, Laila (f), 1844
Morse, Natalie (f), 1818
Mortensen, Elisabeth (f), 1407
Mortimer, Emily (f), 1882, 2305
Morton, Samantha (f), 1846, 1878
Morton-Thomas, Trisha (f), 80
Moss, 169
Motamed-Aria, Fatemeh (f), 1079, 1082
Motornaya, Ludmila (f), 1520
Motta, Zezé (f), 134
Mouchet, Catherine (f), 523, 657
Moustafa, Zizi (f), 391
Moustakis, Periklis, 883
Moxley, Gina (f), 1117
Moya, Angela (f), 2263
Mozaffari, Majid, 1077
Mozian, Sanaa (f), 403
Mui, Anita (f), 907, 917, 922
Mukherjee, Madhabi (f), 969, 982
Müller-Stahl, Armin (m), 837
Mumtaz (f), 973
Mungoshi, Jesesi (f), 2416
Muniz, Miriam (f), 154
Munt, Silvia (f), 1560, 1576, 1599
Muratova, Kira (f), 2361
Murayeva, Irina (f), 2375
Murguía, Ana Ofelia (f), 1339
Murphy, Michael (m), 1988
Murphy, Pat (f), 2021
Mustafa, Ita (f), 1062
Mutabaruka, 847
Muti, Ornella (f), 1178, 1182
Mvusi, Linda (f), 1804
Mylonas, Antigoni (f), 852
Mynster, Karen-Lise (f), 360
Myrat, Miranda (f), 852
Mzali, Samia (f), 1699

Nabli, Nabila (f), 15
Nadira (f), 985
Nagra, Parminder K. (f), 1874
Nagy, Gábor (m), 931
Nakamura, Ganjiro (m), 1216
Nakamura, Mami (f), 1273
Nakano, Ryoko (f), 1249
Nam Jeong-im (f), 1290
Narayan, Laxmi (f), 985
Nasiri, Raya (f), 1099
Nassim, Leila (f), 1700
Nat, Marie-José (f), 4, 442, 940
Naval, Deepti (f), 1014, 1023
Nay San, 169
Naymark, Lola (f), 670
Nazarie, Ecaterina (f), 1513

N'Diaye, Fatou (f), 1502
Ndiaye, Tabata (f), 1526
Ndong, Charlotte (m), 674
Neal, Elise (f), 2311
Nebout, Claire (f), 556
Nederlof, Joan (f), 1370
Neeson, Liam (m), 2090
Negoda, Natalya (f), 2389
Negron, Olivia (f), 2199
Neill, Sam (m), 49, 1400
Nell, Nathalie (f), 479
Nelligan, Kate (f), 2177
Nelson, Novella (f), 2115
Nerina, Ida (f), 1317
Nerz, Gabriela (f), 91
Newman, Paul (m), 2005
Newton, Thandie (f), 2230
Ng, Sandra (f), 920, 923
Ngoc, Hiep, 2406
Nguyen, Huu Muoi (f), 2403
Niang, Isseu (f), 1531
Niang, Myriam (f), 1524
Nichida, Naomi (f), 1265
Nicholson, Jack (m), 2029, 2056, 2084
Nielsen, Connie (f), 655
Nieto, Louisa Pérez (f), 340
Nikulenko, Nataliya, 2392
Nimri, Majwa (f), 1625
Ning Jing (f), 299
Nogueira, Ana Beatriz (f), 145
Noiret, Philippe (m), 597
Nolte, Nick (m), 2144, 2278
Nonahali, Roya (f), 1100
Noonan, Michela (f), 85
Noone, Nora-Jane, 1123
Nørby, Ghita (f), 360
Noureddine, Mouna (f), 1696
Nowag-Jones, Veronika (f), 701
Noweir, Sawan (f), 5
Nowicki, Jan (m), 936, 948, 956, 1462
Nunes, Mizan, 2149
Núñez, Eslinda (f), 329, 335
Núñez, Mirtha (f), 344
Nur, Hurhan (f), 1707
Nutan (f), 966
Nyacheo, Margaret (f), 1284
Nyati, Killness, 2418
Nyroos, Gunilla (f), 1653

O'Brien, Michael (m), 1540
O'Connor, Candace (f), 187
O'Connor, Frances (f), 2340
O'Donnell, Rosie (f), 2143, 2183
O'Dwyer, Marion (f), 1863
O'Hara, Scarlet (f), 1812

O'Rawe, Geraldin (f), 1115
O'Toole, Annette (f), 1956
Oaftan, Sami, 1104
Obadia, Agnès (f), 598
Obonya, Cornelius (m), 695
Oddo, Verónica (f), 2400
Ofner, Astrid (f), 683
Ogata, Ken (m), 1253
Ogier, Bulle (f), 175, 465, 473, 475, 500, 503, 528, 570,
    576, 616, 649, 651, 1663
Ogier, Pascale (f), 503, 514
Ogunlano, Olufunnike (f), 847
Oguz, Meral (f), 1735
Oh, Sandra (f), 202, 2334
Ohana, Claudia (f), 1329
Ohara, Reiko (f), 1255
Ok Ji-young (f), 1307
Okada, Mariko (f), 1227
Okala, Nicole (f), 171
Olbrychski, Daniel (m), 1480
Olcay, Zuhal (f), 1733, 1734, 1740
Oldman, Gary (m), 2258
Olesen, Kirsten (f), 364
Olin, Lena (f), 1655
Oliver, Marisa (f), 1582
Olivier, Laurence (m), 1964
Olmos, Edward James (m), 2227
Olwi, Leila, 386
Ontiveros, Lupe (f), 2310
Ordaz, Isabel (f), 1613
Orfgen, Samy, 832
Orhonsay, Meral, 1724
Orioli, Regina (f), 1206
Ormond, Julia (f), 2340
Oropesa, Elizabeth (f), 1440, 1443, 1447
Orozco, Regina (f), 1340
Ortelli, Dyana (f), 2263
Orth, Marisa (f), 151
Ortiz, Rosanna (f), 1955
Ortman, Hava (f), 1127
Osberg, Gabriele (f), 803, 817
Ostrooumova, Olga (f), 2385
Otake, Shinobu (f), 1250
Otana, Nobuko, 1227
Otero, Isabel (f), 519
Ottersen, Anne-Marie (f), 1403, 1409, 1412
Otto, Miranda (f), 63, 78, 208
Ouatara, Fatou, 1211
Ouchi, Mieko (f), 207
Oulmet, Danielle (f), 108
Oumourzakova, Amina (f), 2352
Ouslilha, Fattouma (f), 7
Outerbridge, Peter, 206
Outinen, Kati (f), 417
Ovchinnikova, Lyusyena (f), 2363

Overgaard, Peter Hesse (m), 363
Ovsyannikova, Anna (f), 1518
Owen, Clive (m), 2215
Owen, Rena (f), 1397
Özdemiroglu, Yaprak, 1724
Ozores, Adriana (f), 1597, 1602, 1621
Ozsada, Erika (f), 941, 953

Pace, Judy (f), 1910
Packalén, Marja (f), 409
Padilla, Pilar (f), 1869
Page, Ellen (f), 219
Pai Ying, 1675
Pajares, Andrés, 1574
Paltrow, Gwyneth (f), 1854, 1883
Pan Hong (f), 277, 285, 286
Pan Yi (f), 316
Panganiban, Angelica (f), 1452
Panjabi, Archie (f), 1887
Panonacle, Camille (f), 891
Panozzo, Dina (f), 76
Pap, Vera (f), 945
Papadaki, Katerina, 893
Papadaki, Loukia (f), 885
Papakonstantinou, Mirka (f), 872
Papamichael, Dimitris (m), 857, 858
Papanou, Despina (f), 804
Papas, Irene (f), 849, 850, 1182, 1329, 1801
Papp, Beáta (f), 955
Papp, Veronika (f), 938
Paquin, Anna (f), 71
Paredes, Marisa (f), 1558, 1579, 1587, 1606, 1628
Parekh, Asha (f), 994
Parillaud, Anne (f), 544
Parker, Kate (f), 1971
Parker, Mary-Louise (f), 2125, 2173
Parker, Molly (f), 206, 219, 1861, 2340
Parmentier, Julie-Marie (f), 619
Paroissien, Pascale (f), 201
Parsons, Estelle (f), 1908
Parton, Dolly (f), 1999, 2103
Pascal, Christine (f), 484, 490
Pasco, Isabelle (f), 557
Paskaleva, Katia (f), 159
Paspati, Anna (f), 875
Passand, Ameneh (f), 1093
Passari, Martina (f), 877
Passy, 386
Pastor, Aurora (f), 1570
Patil, Pallavi (f), 1009
Patil, Smita (f), 991, 998, 999, 1004, 1005, 1006, 1011,
    1013, 1017
Patrichi, Gina (f), 1505
Patterson, Sarah (f), 1788
Patti, Guesch (f), 1603

Patton, Jessica (f), 2161
Paul, Sara (f), 2327
Pauly, Rebecca (f), 787, 812
Payen, Lise (f), 602
Pazira, Nelofer (f), 1097
Peabody, Dixie (f), 1923
Pearce, Guy (m), 2344
Peck, David (m), 1995
Pecoraro, Susu (f), 28
Pei, Betty Ting (f), 900
Pei Yan Lin (f), 261
Peña, Candela (f), 1588, 1597, 1606
Peña, Victoria (f), 1625
Peng, Diana (f), 204
Peng, Jacqueline (f), 924
Penn, Robin Wright (f), 1835, 2226, 2315
Penn, Sean (m), 2198
Pens Røde, Nina (f), 354
Pera, Marilia (f), 149
Pereira, Christine (f), 136
Pérez, Amalia (f), 2398
Perez, Gary (m), 2209
Perez, Rosie (f), 2229
Perez, Vincent (m), 550, 572
Perkins, Anthony (m), 1934, 1992
Perrier, Mireille (f), 530
Perrotta, Veronica (f), 2351
Perry, Natasha (f), 117
Peters, Bernadette (f), 1807
Petersen, Ann (f), 129
Petit, Aurelia (f), 602
Petraniuk, Masha (f), 958
Petrascu, Irina (f), 1506
Petré, Gio (f), 1639
Petri, Nina (f), 1374, 1668
Pettet, Joanna (f), 1901
Pettit, Peggy (f), 1939
Petty, Lori (f), 2143, 2189
Pezold, Friederika (f), 805
Pfeifer, Alfred, 89
Pfeiffer, Michelle (f), 2084, 2093, 2145, 2315
Phillips, Lou Diamond (m), 2158
Phiri, Nkululeko, 2418
Phoenix, Rain (f), 2284
Phoenix, River (m), 2124
Phoenix, Summer (f), 1866
Picard, Béatrice (f), 196
Piccoli, Michel (m), 437, 844, 1170
Picot, Genevieve (f), 1393
Pierens, Diane (f), 549
Pilgrim, Geraldine (f), 1777
Pilisi, Mark (m), 1388
Pinkett, Jada (f), 2216
Pisier, Marie-France (f), 110, 493, 496
Pittoors, Frieda (f), 131

Place, Mary Kay (f), 2181, 2332
Plasari, Dhimitra (f), 3
Platt, Victoria Gabriella (f), 2149
Plimpton, Martha (f), 2080, 2265
Ploae, Maria (f), 1513
Plowright, Joan (f), 1767, 1815, 1820, 1826, 1860
Plumb, Elizabeth (f), 1917, 1953
Plummer, Amanda (f), 220, 1827
Po, Ivy Ling (f), 232, 237
Podesta, Alejandra (f), 34
Pohland, Britta (f), 781
Poitier, Sidney (m), 1890, 1905
Poledouris, Zoë (f), 2320
Polic, Dora (f), 327
Polley, Sarah (f), 220, 2245, 2268
Polony, Anna (f), 944, 948, 950
Ponicanová, Beta (f), 351
Pons, Mercé (f), 1590
Poorta, Sylvia (f), 1384
Porizkova, Pauline (f), 2066
Porter, Susie (f), 84
Portman, Natalie (f), 2237, 2270
Posey, Parker (f), 2214, 2221, 2309
Potente, Franka (f), 698
Poto, Tanja (f), 1536
Potter, Sally (f), 1845
Potts, Annie (f), 186
Pounder, CCH (f), 830
Prelog, Linde (f), 89
Presle, Micheline (f), 543
Preu, Dana (f), 1995
Prévost, Françoise (f), 427
Pries, Kinga (f), 1486
Prinsloo, Sandra (f), 1539
Pritchard, June (f), 48
Priyomykhov, Valeri (f), 2382
Proll, Nina (f), 94
Proshina, Irina (f), 1515
Pryce, Jonathan (m), 1828
Pu Chaoying, 303
Puigcorbe, Juanjo, 1667
Pujalte, Maria (f), 1586, 1632
Puri, Om, 1004
Purnett, Louise (f), 1767
Pürrer, Ursula (f), 93

Qin Liao, 317
Qin Yan (f), 281
Qin Yi (f), 279
Qu Ying (f), 2290
Quaid, Dennis (m), 2293, 2313
Quartey, Francesca (f), 1657
Queen Latifah (f), 2216
Qui Ah-lu (f), 307
Quinlan, Kathleen (f), 1979

Quinn, Anthony (m), 740
Quinn, Marian (f), 2193
Quinton, Sophie (f), 661
Quyng, Nguyen Nhu (f), 2408

Raacker, Dominique (f), 804
Rabe, Pamela (f), 75, 78
Racette, Francine (f), 474
Rachedi, Bahira (f), 21
Rachman, Jenny (f), 1066
Ráczlevei, Anna (f), 951
Radeva, Emilia (f), 157
Rado, James (m), 452
Radziwittowicz, Jerzy (m), 1457
Ragni, Jerome (m), 452
Rai, Aishwarya (f), 1057
Räikkä, Tanjalotta (f), 418
Rainer, Yvonne (f), 770
Rajeshwari, 1047
Rajot, Pierre-Loup (m), 548
Ralli, Giovanna (f), 1148
Ramakrishna, Bhanumathi (f), 977
Rameik, Jessy (f), 722
Ramírez, Arcelia (f), 1338, 1342
Rammes, Dalila (f), 1695
Rampling, Charlotte (f), 130, 643, 664, 1161, 1862
Ranasinghe, Tony, 1635
Rande, Ilse (f), 359
Randle, Theresa (f), 2203
Ranzi, Galatea (f), 1501
Raouia, 1354
Rare, Vanessa (f), 1394
Ratcliffe, Sandy (f), 1781
Ravdan, G., 1347
Raymond, Camille (f), 816
Razavi, Atefah (f), 1076, 1080
Rea, Stephen (m), 1786
Reah, Huffy (f), 1812
Redd, Mary-Robin (f), 1901
Redford, Robert (m), 1945, 2049
Redgrave, Lynn (f), 1751
Redgrave, Vanessa (f), 33, 1761, 1768, 1787, 1790, 1843, 1981, 2260
Redman, Amanda (f), 1778
Reed, Oliver (m), 1765
Reeder, Ana (f), 2316
Rees, Donogh (f), 1385, 1395
Reeve, Christopher (m), 1787
Reeves, Saskia (f), 1813, 1827
Régnier, Natacha (f), 605
Rehman, Waheeda (f), 970
Reid, Anne (f), 1884
Reid, Beryl (f), 1907
Reidy, Gabrielle (f), 1113
Reijn, Halina (f), 1382

Reize, Sylvia (f), 771
Rekha (f), 1000, 1012, 1022, 1052
Remirez, Arcelia (f), 1333
Remundova, Theodora (f), 348
Renauld, Isabelle (f), 619
Renfro, Brad, 2159
Renhua, Na (f), 265
Reno, Ginette (f), 210
Resetarits, Kathrin (f), 97
Resines, Antonio (m), 1578
Rétoré, Catherine (f), 1665
Revel, Coralie (f), 648
Revuelta, Raquel (f), 329, 332
Rey, Cristina (f), 2208
Rey, Fernando (m), 1547
Reyes, Judy (f), 2209
Reyes Spindola, Patricia (f), 1332, 1343
Reymond, Dominique (f), 590
Reynaud, Yelda (f), 700
Reynolds, Debbie (f), 1928
Rezaie, Agheleh (f), 1101
Rialson, Candice (f), 1985
Riazantseva, Natalia (f), 1517
Riazi, Homeira (f), 1095
Ricci, Christina (f), 2183, 2329
Richard, Firmine (f), 540, 646
Richard, Natalie (f), 528
Richards, Denise (f), 1633
Richardson, Joely (f), 1823
Richardson, Miranda (f), 1794, 1815, 1831
Richardson, Natasha (f), 1826, 2108
Richter, Sonia (f), 374
Rickard, Eva, 1391
Rickman, Alan (m), 2121
Riegert, Peter (m), 2089
Riemann, Katja (f), 692, 717
Rigou, Eleftheria (f), 886
Rijxman, Lineke (f), 1366
Rischak, Rita, 768
Riva, Emmanuelle (f), 433, 1142
Rivière, Marie (f), 521, 601
Roa, Angela (f), 193
Roache, Linus (m), 1848
Roberts, Eric (m), 1780, 2060
Roberts, Julia (f), 2094, 2103, 2136, 2236, 2242, 2313, 2328
Rocha, Anecy (f), 135
Roche, Catherine (f), 199
Rochon, Lela (f), 2191
Rock, Crissy (f), 1822
Rodriguez, Lolita (f), 1427, 1435
Roel, Adriana (f), 1328
Roel, Gabriela (f), 1331
Rogers, Alva (f), 2122
Rogina, Mirjana, 326

Rojo, Maria (f), 1335
Rolando, Ibarra (f), 344
Rolle, Marianne (f), 1364
Romand, Anny (f), 533
Romand, Béatrice (f), 502, 601
Romantowska, Anna (f), 1460
Romero, Gloria (f), 1450
Romijn-Stamos, Rebecca (f), 2294
Rommel, Angelika (f), 794
Ronningen, Greta (f), 2006
Röor, Gunilla (f), 366
Rose, Heather (f), 79
Rosenberg, Marianne (f), 813
Ross, Beverley (f), 2006
Ross, Diana (f), 1932, 1965
Ross, Marilina (f), 25
Ross, Yolanda (f), 2284
Rossellini, Isabella (f), 1380, 2081, 2099
Rotaru, Maria (f), 1510
Roth, Cecilia (f), 36, 39, 1606, 1623, 1627
Rothrock, Cynthia (f), 1071
Roüan, Brigitte (f), 554, 555, 588, 641
Rouass, Laila (f), 1048
Roussel, Hélène (f), 533
Rovere, Gina (f), 1142
Rovère, Liliane (f), 617, 651
Rowlands, Gena (f), 1959, 1984, 2001, 2075, 2086,
    2140, 2218, 2301, 2313
Roy, Debashree (f), 997, 1034
Roy, Esperanza (f), 1555
Rubacha, Katarzyna (f), 1471
Rubio, Ingrid (f), 1618
Ruehl, Mercedes (f), 2093, 2269
Ruffalo, Mark (m), 2323
Ruiter, Josée (f), 1363
Rule, Janice (f), 1986
Runciman, Gaylie (f), 1796
Rupé, Katja (f), 819
Rushbrook, Claire (f), 1846
Ruslanova, Nina (f), 2361, 2377
Russell, Kurt (m), 2028, 2078
Russell, Lucy (f), 629
Russell, Rosalind (f), 1902
Russell, Teresa (f), 1793, 1839, 2068, 2110
Rusta, Homa (f), 1077
Ruttkai, Eva (f), 933
Ruud, Sif (f), 1649
Rya, Chishu (f), 1215
Ryabava, Svetlana (f), 2395
Ryad, Aida (f), 388
Ryan, Meg (f), 2259, 2323
Ryazanova, Raisa (f), 2375
Ryder, Winona (f), 2177, 2179, 2244
Ryslinge, Helle (f), 357, 361
Saboktakin, Elham (f), 1091

Sabri, Hend (f), 1698, 1703
Sachdev, Rajeshwari (f), 1039
Sachiko, Hidari (f), 1224
Sadr-Orafai, Fereshteh (f), 1091
Safonova, Elena (f), 571
Sägebrecht, Marianne (f), 825, 830, 844, 1380, 2175
Sagnier, Ludivine (f), 646, 664
Sahar, Zubaida (f), 2
Sahi, Deepa, 1051
Saint-Armant, Marcella (f), 105
Saint-Paul, Eva (f), 1351
Saint-Simon, Lucile (f), 421
Sakamote, Sumiko (f), 1253
Sakellariou, Akis (m), 894
Sakuma, Yoshiko (f), 1254
Salcedo, Irma (f), 2399
Salo, Elina (f), 417
Salvador, Philip (f), 1433
Samaraweera, Jenita (f), 1634
Samb, Seune (f), 1524
Samir, Nadia (f), 9
Samoilova, Tatiana (f), 2356
Sampietro, Mercedes (f), 1551, 1562, 1563, 1583,
    1602, 1612, 1622
San Juan, Antonia (f), 1625
Sanchez, Jose (m), 1604
Sanchez, Monica (f), 1422
Sanchez Pascual, Cristina (f), 1558
Sánchez-Gijón, Aitana (f), 1345, 1607
Sanda, Dominique (f), 32, 450, 495, 1163, 1186
Sander, Helke (f), 767, 812
Sandhla, Thulani (f), 2418
Sandino Moreno, Catalina (f), 2342
Sandrelli, Stefania (f), 677, 1164, 1180, 1191
Sands, Diana (f), 1644, 1890
Sanga, Fatimata (f), 167
Sangeetha (f), 992
Sani, Mutiara (f), 1061
Sanogo, Diarrah, 1320
Sansa, Maya (f), 1206
Santángelo, Mariana (f), 2350
Santolaria, Eva (f), 1612
Santos, Chara (f), 1428
Santos, Judy Ann (f), 1442
Santos, Victor (m), 1491
Santos, Vilma (f), 1436, 1444, 1446, 1449
Saphir, Tatiana (f), 43
Sarah, 395
Saraleta, Angelina (f), 420
Sarandon, Susan (f), 2043, 2084, 2136, 2144, 2159,
    2179, 2198, 2236, 2237, 2288
Sardá, Rosa María (f), 1590, 1606, 1623, 1632
Sarr, Zator, 1528
Sarri, Katarina (f), 882
Sass, Katrin (f), 708, 712, 725, 731, 735

Sassard, Jacqueline (f), 447
Sastrowardoyo, Dian (f), 1072
Savaç, Perihan (f), 1715, 1722
Saviange, Sonia (f), 466
Savvina, Iya (f), 2357
Sayuri, Ichijo (f), 1240
Sbaraglia, Leonardo (m), 1623
Scacchi, Greta (f), 69, 213, 1187, 1783, 1856
Scanda, Thiare (f), 1345
Schaeffer, Rebecca (f), 2107
Schaffel, Marla (f), 2246
Schall, Johanna, 734
Schallerova, Jaroslava, 930
Scheider, Roy (f), 1967
Schell, Maximilian (m), 458
Schenna, Leila (f), 6
Schettino, Annalisa (f), 1200
Schierl, Angela Hans (f), 93
Schmeide, Gabriela Maria (f), 703
Schmidt, Anna (f), 693
Schneider, Carol (f), 2199
Schneider, Heidemarie (f), 733
Schneider, Maria (f), 505, 556, 1160, 1164, 1313, 1357
Schneider, Romy (f), 459, 488, 496, 1766
Schnitzler, Susi Barbara (f), 727
Scholz, Christina (f), 774
Schorn, Christine (f), 728
Schrader, Maria (f), 690, 697, 717
Schroeder, Jochen (m), 791
Schwarz, Dagmar, 99
Schweizer, Anita Viola (f), 727
Schygulla, Hanna (f), 541, 751, 758, 772, 785, 800, 810, 1173, 1178, 1556, 2072
Sciorra, Annabella (f), 2104, 2142
Scott, George C. (m), 1762
Scott-Thomas, Kristen (f), 1509
Seagrove, Jenny (f), 1029
Seck, Magou (f), 1531
Seda, Jon (m), 2178
Sedgwick, Kyra (f), 2269, 2309, 2313, 2338
Seeger, Petra (f), 809
Segda, Dorota (f), 949
Seigner, Mathilde (f), 573, 616, 631, 636
Seikkula, Irma (f), 412
Sellers, Catherine (f), 463
Sen, Aparna (f), 1028, 1030, 1034, 1046
Sen, Gita (f), 995, 1010, 1028
Sen, Raima Dev (f), 1050
Sen, Suchitra (f), 971, 983
Sen, Sushmita (f), 1053
Senna, Conceição (f), 138
Sensharma, Konkona (f), 1055
Sentís, Susana (f), 1564
Seo Joo-hee (f), 1306
Seri, Meika (f), 1244

Serna, Assumpta (f), 32, 1557, 1563
Serpieter, Hélène (f), 107
Serrano, Julieta (f), 1548, 1602
Serrault, Michel (m), 636
Setterfield, Valda (f), 1933
Severo, Marieta (f), 147
Sevigny, Chloë (f), 655, 2238, 2248, 2260
Sexpert, Suzie (f), 840
Seye, Venus (f), 1532
Seymour, Cara (f), 1122
Seyrig, Delphine (f), 91, 108, 113, 123, 438, 454, 464, 467, 506, 793, 807, 839, 1462, 1771
Seyvecou, Sabrina (f), 648
Shabaviz, Flora (f), 1073
Shadan, Sima (f), 1
Shah, Naseeruddin (m), 998, 1007, 2307
Shair, Patrick (m), 1541
Shakirova, Tamara (f), 2366
Shamsai, Mozhde (f), 1094
Shankar, Mamata (m), 995
Shantakumari (f), 989
Sharen Gaowa (f), 241
Sharif, Omar (m), 1906
Sharko, Zinaida (f), 2365
Sharp, Sally (f), 2007
Shashikala (f), 967
Shaver, Helen (f), 2044
Shaw, Fiona (f), 1880
Sheedy, Ally (f), 2231, 2251, 2297
Sheela (f), 975
Shein, Rahel (f), 1127
Shen Junyi (m), 275
Shen Rong (f), 278
Shenna, Leila (f), 12, 1349
Shepard, Sam (m), 2067
Shepherd, Cybill (f), 1949
Sheridan, Maya (f), 68
Shi Tou (f), 316
Shields, Brooke (f), 2100, 2285
Shiffers, Yelena (f), 1514
Shiha, Hana (f), 404
Shimizu, Misa (f), 1276
Shin Hye-soo (f), 1297
Shinde, Sayaji (m), 1050
Shiraishi, Kayoko (f), 1267
Shire, Talia (f), 1991
Shizuka Inoh, Annie (f), 1682
Shoji, Utae (f), 1274
Shope, Stephani (f), 2208
Shroff, Jackei (m), 1052
Shu Qi (f), 923, 1688, 1690
Shubina, Nina (f), 1518
Shun Wah, Annette (f), 77
Siao, Josephine (f), 916, 919
Siddiqui, Javed (m), 1000

Sidki, Hala (f), 400
Sidney, Sylvia (f), 1943
Siemers, Julia (f), 792
Siener, François (m), 1174
Signoret, Simone (f), 468, 486, 489, 1142
Sikri, Surekha (f), 1043, 1047
Sillas, Karen (f), 2166
Silke (f), 1199, 1588
Silleghem, Karlijn (f), 1375
Silveira, Leonor (f), 1495
Silverio, Daniela (f), 1183
Simmons, Jean (f), 1912
Simonnet, Michèle (f), 120
Sinclair, Barbara (f), 2167
Singer, Lori (f), 2082
Singh, Chandrachur (m), 1038
Sinha, Mala (f), 967
Sinha, Vidya (f), 981
Siqin Gaowa (f), 296, 903, 910
Sirová, Eliska (f), 1632
Sisizadeh, Shahr Banou (f), 1093
Sitek, Agnieszka (f), 1486
Sitton, Sally (f), 1562
Siu Fong-Fong. *See* Siao, Josephine
Siwis, Salim, 1103
Skarsgård, Stellan (m), 367
Skhirtladze, Tamara (f), 2379, 2381
Skinner, Anita, 1990
Skountzou, Maria (f), 872
Skye, Ione (f), 2126
Slaska, Aleksandra (f), 1459
Slater, Helen (f), 1791, 2096
Smirnova, Svetlana (f), 2369
Smith, Anjela Lauren (f), 1864
Smith, Brooke (f), 2282
Smith, Dwan (f), 1974
Smith, Louise (f), 2065
Smith, Maggie (f), 1764, 1795, 1802, 1860, 2228, 2291
Smith, Sharon (f), 178
Smith, Stacy (f), 219
Smollette, Jurnee (f), 2223
Snodgrass, Carrie (f), 1918, 2340
Sobolev, Tanya (f), 1133
Soeberg, Camilla (f), 2175
Soffer, Shirley (f), 1933, 1950
Sohn, Sonha (f), 2220
Sola, Miguel (m), 1614
Soler Leal, Amparo (f), 1548
Solis, Charito (f), 1427, 1433
Song Rahui (f), 258
Soorya (f), 1003
Soray, Türkan (f), 1711, 1712, 1716, 1717, 1718, 1728, 1731, 1732
Sorel, Agnes (f), 1187
Sorvino, Mira (f), 1880

Sosa, Evangelina (f), 1336
Sou, Marguerite (f), 166
Soutendijk, Renée (f), 706, 1359, 1362, 1369, 1379
Southern, Ann (f), 1962
Soyagazi, Hale (f), 1721
Spaak, Catherine (f), 1151, 1160
Spacek, Sissy (f), 1780, 1986, 2000, 2010, 2046, 2054, 2059, 2101, 2207
Spader, James (m), 2312
Spínolda, Reyes (f), 1339
Spivak, Alice (f), 2115
Sprinkle, Annie (f), 680
Sreevidya (f), 1003
Sripriya (f), 992
St. Jacques, Raymond (m), 1911
Stabb, Dinah (f), 1773
Stalínska, Dorota (f), 1461, 1467, 1474
Stamp, Terence (f), 1758, 1759
Stanczak, Wadeck (m), 536
Stanley, Kim (f), 1753, 2016
Stapel, Huub (m), 1371
Starr, Kinnie (f), 2320
Stathopoulou, Eleanora (f), 881
Stathopoulou, Toula (f), 876
Staunton, Imelda (f), 1813, 1875, 1886
Stayuta, Stefaniya (f), 2378
Steadman, Lynda (f), 1841
Steczkowska, Joanna (f), 1484
Steege, Johanna ter (f), 1376
Steel, Barbara (f), 1947
Steen, Paprika (f), 374
Steenburgen, Mary (f), 2023, 2317
Stegers, Bernice (f), 1781
Stella, Manfred, 99
Stengade, Stine (f), 373
Stepanek, Elizabeth (f), 779, 788
Stevens, Stella (f), 2014
Stevenson, Gerda (f), 1816
Stiles, Julia (f), 2254, 2328
Stivínová, Zusana (f), 347
Stockwell, Dean (m), 2093
Stoltz, Eric (m), 1867, 2047
Stolyarova, Gulya (f), 1515
Stolze, Lena (f), 695, 796, 798
Stone, Sharon (f), 2139, 2185, 2260, 2337
Stowe, Madeleine (f), 2121
Strachan, Lulu (f), 1537
Strathairn, David, 2247
Strauss, Ursula (f), 97
Streep, Meryl (f), 60, 1119, 2020, 2028, 2049, 2050, 2056, 2114, 2116, 2141, 2233, 2249, 2300
Streisand, Barbra (f), 1906, 1919, 1937, 1945, 2211
Stresemann, Angela (f), 814
Stroh, Heidi (f), 747, 749
Stroh, Valerie (f), 549

Stubbs, Imogen (f), 1798
Stubbs, Louise (f), 1939
Stüdemann, Kati (f), 691
Studt, Katia (f), 1374
Styles, Amber (f), 1814
Su Youpeng (f), 311
Suárez, Emma (f), 1594, 1596, 1605
Sue Ming-ming (f), 1672
Sugawara, Bunta (m), 1256
Suhasini (f), 1003
Sujatha (f), 990
Sukapatana, Jintara (f), 1694
Sukowa, Barbara (f), 677, 718, 783, 789, 828, 835
Sumithra (f), 980
Sun Chun (f), 271
Surer, Nür (f), 1720
Surgere, Helen (f), 466
Surtie-Richards, Sharleen, 1538
Sutherland, Donald (m), 1924
Svenskaja, Aleksandra (f), 2390
Swank, Hilary (f), 2238, 2340, 2343
Sweeney, Michelle (f), 199
Swinton, Tilda (f), 1817, 1855, 2201, 2275, 2333
Sylva, Christina (f), 848
Sylwan, Kari (f), 1645
Szabó, Éva (f), 938
Szaflarska, Danuta (f), 1478
Szalay, Mariann (f), 957
Szapolowska, Grazyna (f), 942, 1473
Szendrei, Andrea (f), 941

Taba, Therese (f), 1213
Tabatabai, Jasmin (f), 692
Tabota, Vana (f), 887
Tabu (f), 1038, 1049, 1053, 1057
Taghani, Altinay Ghelich (f), 1092
Tagore, Sharmila (f), 963, 974, 986
Tahiri, Zakia (f), 1351
Takaki, Mio (f), 1179
Takamine, Hideko (f), 1217, 1219, 1220, 1223, 1229,
    1234, 1236, 1241
Takamine, Mieko (f), 1216
Takashi, Yoko (f), 1245
Takizawa, Riko, 1268
Takvam, Marie (f), 1404
Talbi, Nadia (f), 12
Tanaka, Kinuyo (f), 1223, 1245
Tanaka, Yoshiko (f), 1258
Tanaka, Yuko (f), 1252
Tandon, Raveena (f), 1033, 1050
Tandy, Jessica (f), 1787, 1819, 2125
Tanvi (f), 1019
Tao Huiming (f), 278
Tarkan, Tarik (m), 1726
Taseva, Leda (f), 157

Tatou, Audrey (f), 628, 647
Tauler, Ada (f), 1664
Taylor, Clarice (f), 1942
Taylor, Elizabeth (f), 1888
Taylor, Lili (f), 2094, 2124, 2152, 2204, 2206, 2217,
    2317, 2322, 2344
Tehrani, Hedyeh (f), 1088
Telega, Ewa (f), 958
Telichkina, Valentina (f), 2380
Temessy, Hédi (f), 947
Tempelhof, Lissy (f), 727
Terral, Boris (m), 588
Terselius, Lil (f), 1405
Testi, Fabio (m), 1163
Testud, Sylvie (f), 619, 632, 654, 663, 689, 1669
Tetsa, Yiota (f), 889
Teuber, Monica (f), 746
Teymourian, Roya (f), 1100
Tez, Melek, 821
Thami, Souad, 1350
Thate, Hilmar (m), 802
Thaw, John (m), 1800
Theron, Charlize (f), 2329
Thibaudin, Beatriz (f), 43
Thomas, Marlo (f), 2111
Thomas, Philip Michael (m), 1974
Thompson, Emma (f), 1828, 1830, 1849, 2286
Thompson, Kate (f), 1110
Thomson, Gordon (m), 187
Thrett, Maggie (f), 1910
Thu, Minh, 2410
Thulin, Ingrid (f), 1638, 1640, 1645
Thurman, Uma (f), 2109, 2278, 2301, 2341
Ti, Betty Loh (f), 232
Tian Yuan (f), 322
Tikado, Clémentine (f), 1210
Tilly, Jennifer (f), 2196
Tilly, Meg (f), 1833, 2041, 2128
Timite, Bassori (m), 1209
Timoteo, Sabine (f), 713
Ting Wu (f), 287
Tkachyova, Yelena (f), 1514
Todeschini, Bruno (m), 630
Tohno, Nagiko (f), 1276
Tóibín, Sighle (f), 1114
Tokito, Ayumu (f), 1269
Tol, Henriette (f), 1361, 1366
Tolbert, Jamie (f), 2280
Tolentino, Lorna (f), 1431, 1441
Tomei, Marisa (f), 2218
Tomlin, Lily (f), 1860, 1999, 2009
Tompkins, Bee (f), 1914
Toncheva, Dorotea (f), 157, 160
Tong Fan (m), 300
Topper, Manja (f), 1382

Tordai, Teri (f), 945
Tork, Hanan (f), 402, 404
Torker, Camila (f), 41
Torn, Rip (m), 1776
Töröcsik, Mari (f), 928, 932, 935
Torrent, Ana (f), 1600, 1608, 1620, 1628
Torres, Marilyn (f), 1604
Towers, Constance (f), 1896
Tranelli, Deborah (f), 2048
Traoré, Salimata (f), 1534
Travanti, Daniel (m), 1684
Trieb, Tatjana (f), 689
Trintignant, Jean-Louis (m), 447, 453, 574
Trintignant, Marie (f), 578
Tripi, Tania (f), 884
Trissenaar, Elisabeth (f), 837
Trivedi, Alka, 1047
Tschechowa, Vera (f), 773
Tseng Jing (f), 1685
Tsolo, Linéo (f), 1321
Tsuji, Kaori (f), 663
Tsukamoto, Kyoko (f), 137
Tsukasa, Yôko (f), 1234
Tsumiki, Miho (f), 1275
Tsunashima, Gotaro (m), 86
Tuckett, Rita (f), 187
Tulasne, Patricia (f), 200
Tumbuan, Frans, 1063
Türk, Brigitte, 768
Türkali, Deniz (f), 1735
Turner, Guinevere (f), 2163, 2192
Turner, Kathleen (f), 2061, 2138
Turner, Khahtee (f), 2331
Tushingham, Rita (f), 952, 1746, 1751, 1846
Tweed, Shannon (f), 2088
Tyler, Liv (f), 1192
Tyson, Cathy (f), 1800
Tyson, Cicely (f), 1938, 1993, 2125
Tyszkiewicz, Beata (f), 1462, 1465

U Tum'si, Meiji (f), 621
Ubach, Alanna (f), 2221
Udvaros, Dorotya (f), 957
Uggams, Leslie (f), 1939
Uhl, Nadja (f), 704
Uhlen, Gisela (f), 772
Ullman, Tracey (f), 2152
Ullmann, Liv (f), 836, 1180, 1641, 1645, 1647, 1650,
    1769, 1778, 1961
Ulrich, Sylvia (f), 781, 784
Union, Gabrielle (f), 2319
Utekesheva, Meruert, 1280
Uytterlinden, Hilde (f), 103
Uzelacová, Vera (f), 349
Vagena, Anna (f), 868

Valberg, Birgitta (f), 1649
Valdes, Thaïs (f), 343, 345
Valdèz, Beatriz (f), 2401
Valk, Kate (f), 91
Valley, Michele (f), 884, 891
Valli, Alida (f), 435, 524
Valmorin, Barbara (f), 1205
Van Bergen, Nanda (f), 1664
Van Dartel, Willemien (f), 1365
Van de Groen, Dora (f), 129
Van de Ven, Monique (f), 1357, 1360, 1367, 1369
Van den Eynde, Charlotte (f), 131
Van der Merwe, Anna-Mart (f), 1542
Van Dijck, Linda (f), 1360
Van Groningen, Wivineke (f), 1372
Van Herck, Hélène (f), 122
Van Kralingen, Will (f), 1373
Vance, Robert, 1903
Vandal, Jacquelline (f), 436
Vaner, María (f), 24, 25
Vanthielen, Francesca (f), 1378
Vanzi, Alesandra (f), 878
Vardalos, Nia (f), 2308, 2339
Vartan, Sylvie (f), 568
Vásáryová, Magda (f), 353
Vashisht, Mita (f), 1027
Vávrová, Dana (f), 838
Veivo, Raili (f), 412
Velasco, Concha (f), 1549
Velásquez, Gabriela (f), 1422
Velez, Lauren (f), 2178
Vera, Hilda (f), 1552
Vera, Victoria (f), 1572
Verástegui, Charo (f), 1420
Verdú, Maribel (f), 1346, 1352, 1621, 1624
Vetri, Victoria, 1931
Viard, Karin (f), 608, 613
Vidal, Lisa (f), 2273
Vidya, Nani (f), 1008
Vieth, Pia (f), 365
Vieyra, Mary (f), 1209
Vigh, Gyöngyver (f), 934
Viiperi, Riita (f), 416
Vijhálmsdóttir, Margrét (f), 962
Villalpando, David (m), 2026
Villani, Carmen, 1550
Viña, Ana, 342
Vincent, Julie (f), 183
Visitsophon, Chanuteporn (f), 1693
Vithana, Kim (f), 1821
Vitti, Monica (f), 1143, 1147, 1189, 1758
Viva (f), 452
Vlady, Marina (f), 444, 937
Vogel, Ellen (f), 103
Volkmann, Edith (f), 749

Von Ammelrooy, Willeke (f), 109, 1377
Von Baur, Barbara (f), 676
Von Cube, Monica (f), 770
Von der Lippe, Anneke (f), 368
Von Freiburg, Gina (f), 776
Von Sydow, Max (m), 1658
Von Trotta, Margarethe (f), 760, 763
Vonasek, Perla (f), 1552
Voorhies, Lark (f), 2318
Vouyouklaki, Aliki (f), 857, 865, 873
Voznesenskaya, Anastasiya (f), 2383
Vu, Anh, 2410
Vujcic, Aleksandra (f), 1398

Wachowiak, Jutta (f), 730
Wagner, Petra (f), 676
Waing, 169
Wakao, Ayako (f), 1221, 1222, 1228, 1230, 1232, 1236
Wakashiba, Junko (f), 1243
Walia, Sonu (f), 1022
Walken, Christopher (m), 1840
Walker, Valerie (f), 2192
Walsh, Eileen (f), 2302
Walter, Harriet (f), 1830
Walter, Jessica (f), 1901
Walters, Julie (f), 1785, 1820, 1823
Walton, Tasma (f), 76
Wan Hui (f), 274
Wang Chung-a (f), 1291
Wang, Fuli (f), 240
Wang Ji (f), 302
Wang, Joey (f), 915
Wang, Linda (f), 277
Wang Liyun, 253
Wang Suya (f), 238
Ward, Fred (m), 2109, 2168
Ward, Robin, 187
Ware, Herta (f), 2140
Warner, David (m), 1771
Warren, Lesley Ann (f), 2032
Warzecha, Magdalena (f), 1482
Washbourne, Mona (f), 1775
Washington, Denzel (m), 2131
Washington, Kerry (f), 2279
Waterman, Dennis (m), 1106
Watling, Leonor (f), 220, 1623, 1632
Watson, Emily (f), 367, 1852
Watt, Naomi (f), 2189
Watts, Jeanne (f), 1767
Way, José (f), 1371
Weaver, Lois (f), 2079
Weaver, Sigourney (f), 1994, 2091, 2098, 2248
Weber, Andre (f), 2199
Weber, Beth (f), 199
Weeraratne, Sangeetha (f), 1637

Wei, Vicky (f), 1683
Weisz, Franziska (f), 100
Weld, Tuesday (f), 1934, 1982
Wells, Doris (f), 2396
Wen Jiang (m), 251, 259, 266
Westfeld, Jennifer (f), 2303
Weston-Moran, Kim (f), 2149
Wettig, Patricia (f), 2146
Whalley, Joanne (f), 1805
White, Carol (f), 1760
White, Jan (f), 1935
White, Sheila (f), 457
Whitfield, Lynn (f), 2223
Whittle, Annie (f), 1389
Widdows, Kathleen (f), 1901
Widl, Susanne (f), 87
Wiest, Dianne (f), 2129, 2194
Wildbolz, Klaus (m), 88
Wilkinson, Tom (m), 1851
Williams, Michelle (f), 1877, 2260
Williams, Sabra (f), 1825
Willis, Bruce (m), 2141
Wilson, Lambert (m), 549
Wilson, Rita (f), 2183
Wilson, Scott (m), 1468
Winckler, Richard (m), 428
Winfield, Paul (m), 2013
Winfrey, Oprah (f), 2042, 2230
Winger, Debra (f), 2029, 2068, 2151
Winkler, Angela (f), 761, 800, 815
Winnicka, Lucyna (f), 1453
Winningham, Mare (f), 2176
Winslet, Kate (f), 81, 1396, 1830, 1857, 1871
Winstone, Ray (m), 1844
Winters, Shelley (f), 1916, 1928, 1940
Witherspoon, Reese (f), 1885, 2325
Wolfe, Nancy Allison (f), 2170
Wolff, Michelle (f), 2326
Wolff, Rikard (m), 1656
Wolfingsede, Philomena (f), 96
Won Mi-kyong (f), 1293
Wong, Anthony (m), 77
Wong Chung-ching (f), 319
Wong, Joey (f), 925
Wood, Natalie (f), 1894, 1898
Woodard, Alfre (f), 2023, 2147, 2160, 2177, 2262, 2269
Woodward, Joanne (f), 1908, 1930, 1943
Wooldridge, Susan (f), 192
Woronov, Mary (f), 2280
Worth, Lynne (f), 1781
Wouassi, Félicité (f), 1214, 1667
Wright, Monica (f), 2262
Wright, N'Bushe (f), 2318
Wu Chien-lien (f), 922
Wu Haiyan (f), 236

Wu Jiaojiao (f), 318
Wu Jing (f), 274
Wu Lijie, 253
Wu, Vivian (f), 921
Wu Yujuan (f), 273
Wuhrer, Kari (f), 2158
Wyatt, Tessy (f), 1106

Xi Meijuan (f), 295
Xia Lixin (f), 300
Xia, Patricia (f), 904
Xia Yonghua (f), 290
Xie Fang (f), 233
Xie Ling, 303
Xu Shon Zi, 260
Xu Shouli, 261
Xu Songzi (f), 251
Xu Ya, 269
Xu Ye (f), 255
Xue Bai (f), 283

Yachigusa, Keoru (f), 1231
Yakovleva, Elena (f), 2391
Yan Xiaopin (f), 254, 271
Yanahuaya, Marcelino (m), 132
Yang Hui-shan (f), 1676
Yang, Loretta (f), 1673
Yang Qianqian (f), 320
Yanjing Liu (f), 230
Yanne, Jean (m), 449
Yarnall, Celeste (f), 1927
Yau Xiaoping, 264
Ye Ji-weon (f), 1310
Yeh, Sally (f), 905, 912
Yen-khe, Tran Nu (f), 2408
Yeoh, Michelle (f), 304, 917, 918, 921
Yeon Kang Soo (f), 1302
Yernaux, Anne (f), 127
Yerushalmi, Tamar (f), 1134
Yi Ding (f), 287
Yilmazer, Kerem, 1713
Yip, Annie (f), 77
Yo Hitoto (f), 1277
York, Amanda (f), 1784
York, Susannah (f), 1107, 1907
Yoshinaga, Sayuri (f), 1254, 1256, 1260, 1261
Yoshiyuki, Kazuko (f), 1274
Young, Carol (f), 1889
Young, Sean (f), 1837, 2130

Yousra (f), 392, 394, 396
Yu Nan (f), 321
Yuan Xingzhe, 288
Yun Hyung-ja (f), 1298
Yun Jeong-hie (f), 1290

Zaatar, Nawal, 8
Zacharias, Ann (f), 477
Zachurdaewa, Galina (f), 2390
Zaki, Ahmet (m), 388, 391
Zaki, Magda, 386
Zaray, Nicole (f), 1859
Zare'i, Marila (f), 1087
Zayed, Maali, 393
Zech, Rosel (f), 681, 802
Zegarac, Dusica (f), 2411
Zeitouni, Nabila (f), 1312
Zellweger, Renée (f), 2233, 2235, 2264, 2274, 2315
Zemlji, Pia (f), 1536
Zervoudaki, Cecile (f), 2393
Zetterling, Mai (f), 1811, 2105
Zhang Jie, 263
Zhang Min (f), 254, 258, 274
Zhang Ruifang (f), 231, 244
Zhang Wenrong (f), 258
Zhang Xiangfei (f), 244
Zhang, Xiaolei (f), 250
Zhang Xiaolin (f), 254
Zhang Yanli (f), 272
Zhang Yu (f), 309
Zhang Yukai, 276
Zhe Xijuan (f), 239
Zhelan Wang (f), 230
Zhen Shuzhi (f), 254
Zheng Zhenyao (f), 268
Zhou Xiaoli (f), 299
Zhu Xijuan (f), 228
Zhung Min, 264
Zhy Yaying, 276
Zilberschatz-Banai, Orli (f), 1139
Zischler, Hanns (m), 792
Zohar, Rita (f), 1129
Zoharetz, Michal (f), 1132
Zoumboulak, Voula, 856
Zouni, Pemy (f), 879, 881, 882
Zuasti, Elena (f), 2351
Zubanova, Marina (f), 1519
Zupancic, Milena (f), 2413
Zylberstein, Elsa (f), 580, 672

INDEX OF
DIRECTORS, SCREENWRITERS,
CINEMATOGRAPHERS, AND PRODUCERS

Aakeson, Kim Fupz, 376
Abaya, Manolo, 1431, 1433
Abbott, Elliot, 2143
Abdel Wahab, Fatin, 379
Abderahman, Mohaned, 1352
Abdollahi, Asghar, 1075
Abecassis, Eliette (f), 1136
Abelson, Arnold, 2031
Aberdein, Keith, 1386
Abeysekera, Tissa, 1636
Aboim, Joao, 23
Abu Seif, Ounsi, 390
Abu Seif, Salah, 378, 380
Abu-Assad, Hany (m), 1418
Achinas, Nan Trevini (f), 1072
Achrapov, A, 2353
Achten, Irma (f), 1372, 1375, 1381
Acker, Kathy (f), 2031
Ackroyd, Barry, 1822, 1846, 1858, 1869, 1873
Adams, Bradley, 1120
Adams, Catlin (f), 2096
Adefarasin, Remi, 1850, 1854, 1867
Adjani, Isabelle (f), 529
Adler, Carine (f), 1846
Adlon, Eleonore (f), 681, 825, 830
Adlon, Percy (m), 681, 790, 798, 825, 830
Admomenaite, Niyole (f), 1514, 2392
Adrieu, Philippe, 497
Aellen, Werner, 185
Affrime, Mindy, 2201
Agarwal, Rejesh, 1046
Agishev, Odelsha (m), 2354
Agmon, Ya'ackov, 1124
Agneray, Emmanuel, 1140
Agostini, Claude, 22
Aguirre, Javier, 1555, 1572
Aguirresarobe, Javier, 1594, 1596, 1623, 1629, 2281
Agusti, Andres, 2397, 2399
Agusti, Toni (m), 1554
Agustín, José, 1331
Ah Mon, Lawrence (m), 909
Ahlberg, Mac, 2014

Ahlert, Eve (f), 2325
Ahmadi, Nohamad, 1093
Ahmed Ali, Magdi (m), 400
Ahmed, Mohsen, 391, 403
Ahn Dae-seong, 1290
Ahn Hun-chan, 1306
Ahrne, Marianne (f), 1648, 1655
Aim, Pierre, 647
Ait-Amara, Hamid, 9
Aitmatov, Chinguiz, 1717, 2362
Akdeniz, Ali, 1738
Akerman, Chantal (f), 91, 112, 113, 115, 118, 123, 553, 632, 654
Akhmedov, Saday, 102
Akhtar, Javed, 1025
Akhtar-Ul-Iman, 967
Akhvlediani, Erlom, 2376
Akino, Tomohiro, 1230
Al-Dighidi, Inas (f), 385, 389, 392, 395, 397, 401, 403
Al Iman, Adrian, 1104
Al Iman, Ahmed, 1104
Al-Mihi, Ra'fat (m), 393
Al Nomani, Qa'id, 1104
Al Tohami, Fuad (m), 1105
Alakus, Buket (f), 1739
Alani, Yehezkel, 1127
Alarcón, José María, 1549
Alazraki, Robert, 530, 537
Albacete, Alfonso, 1605
Albaret, Celeste (f), 790
Albers, Helge, 1416
Albert, Barbara (f), 94, 97, 98, 99, 1161
Albicocco, Jean-Gabriel, 427
Albicocco, Quinto, 427, 432
Albonico, Guilio, 1155, 1157
Alcaine, Jose Luis, 1545, 1548, 1560, 1568, 1573, 1574, 1583, 1593, 1614
Alcaine, Pancho, 1592
Alcott, Louisa May, 2179
Alden, Robert, 2039
Aldrich, Robert (m), 1907
Alekan, Henri, 508, 1755

Alexanian, Alexis (f), 2309, 2330
Ali, Muzaffar, 1000, 1015
Aljure, Felipe, 323
Allen, Jay Presson (f), 1764
Allen, Jim, 1811
Allen, Woody (m), 2086
Allison, Dorothy (f), 2195, 2338
Allouache, Merzak (m), 20
Alloula, Malek, 13
Allyn, William, 2012
Almagor, Gila (f), 1124
Almendros, Nestor, 453, 471, 475, 486, 765, 1545, 2020, 2038, 2056
Almereyda, Michael (m), 2297
Almodóvar, Pedro (m), 1558, 1573, 1579, 1587, 1606
Almond, Paul (m), 173
Alnoy, Siegrid (f), 657
Alonzo, John, 1916, 1932, 1997, 2023, 2078, 2103
Alonzo, Pablo, 1631
Alper, Robin, 2266
Altman, Robert (m), 1107, 1925, 1986, 1992, 2015, 2165
Álvarez Blanco, German, 1572
Alves de Souza, Naum, 146
Alvi, Abrar, 965
Amado, Jorge, 133, 149
Amalric, Mathieu (m), 644
Amaral, Suzana (f), 141
Amaral, Tata (f), 148, 150
Amari, Raja (f), 1705
Ambat, Madhu, 1002
The Amber Collective, 1829
Amen, Carol (f), 2030
Amenabar, Alejandro (m), 2281
Amezcua, Patxi, 1618
Amidei, Sergio, 1148
Amigo, Angel, 1599
Amigorena, Santiago, 588
Amini, Hossein, 1848
Aminz, Sedik, 1
Amir, Assaf, 1139
Amorós, Juan, 1561, 1578, 1595
Amos, Patrick, 592
Amotz, Dahn Ben, 1124
Amrohi, Kamal, 976
Amundsen, Kristen (f), 1862
Amy, Nita, 1782
Anand, Inder Raj, 985
Anand, Shashi, 1028
Anand, Tinnu (m), 1025
Anand, Vijay, 970
Anandan, M. S., 1634
Anaya, Manolo, 1428
Anchoriz, Leo, 1546
Anders, Allison (f), 2126, 2164, 2205, 2251, 2266

Andersch, Alfred, 739
Anderson, Hesper, 2127
Anderson, Jamie, 2155
Anderson, Jane (f), 2177, 2260
Anderson, Larra, 2280
Anderson, Lindsay (m), 2083
Anderson, Michael (m), 1769
Andianou, Anna (f), 888
Andor, Tamás, 940, 942, 1462
Andreadis, Yorgos, 1741
Andreef, Christina (f), 82
Andreu, Cristina (f), 1571
Andrus, Mark, 2291
Angelo, Yves, 663
Angelou, Maya, 1644
Angot, Christine (f), 672
Anhalt, Edward, 1763
Ansah, Kwaw Painstil (m), 846
Ansarian, Mahnaz, 1084
Anso, Shohei, 1244
Anspach, Sólveig (f), 608
Antipenko, Aleksandr, 2371
Antonio Bardem, Juan, 1598
Antonio de La Loma, José, 1564
Antonio, Lamberto, 1424
Antonioni, Michelangelo (m), 1143, 1147
Aoulad-Syad, Daoud, 1355
Apon, Annette (f), 1370
Apra, Adriano, 1184
Apted, Michael (m), 2000, 2091, 2292
Apuzzo, Carla (f), 1168
Aquino-Kashiwahara, Lupita (f), 1425, 1442
Arabov, Yuri, 2393
Aragon, Manuel Guiérrez (m), 1568
Aranda, Vincente (m), 1545, 1561, 1593, 1619
Aranguren, David, 1613
Araojo, Johnny, 1432, 1437
Araojo, Romulo, 1444, 1451
Arata, David, 2239
Araujo, Alcione, 142
Araújo, Joel Zito (m), 156
Araz, Nezihe (f), 1726, 1730
Arbogast, Thierry, 544, 564, 611, 2294, 2337, 2402
Arcady, Alexandre, 497
Arcalli, Franco, 1169
Archibald, William, 1745
Archibugi, Francesca (f), 1191
Argento, Asia (f), 1204
Argento, Claudio, 1204
Arguello, Iván (m), 1401
Arifen, Alwin, 1070
Arima, Yoriyoshi, 1232
Aristophanes, 867, 1624, 1643
Ariyoshi, Sawako (f), 1236
Arkoff, Samuel, 1941

Arlen, Alice (f), 2028, 2268
Armendáriz, Montxo (m), 1622
Armstrong, Charlotte (f), 455, 623
Armstrong, Gillian (f), 49, 50, 57, 65, 1870, 2036, 2179
Arnaud, Claude, 558
Arndt, Stefan, 698, 712
Arnold, Gina (f), 776
Arnold, Pascal, 194
Arnould, Jacques, 111
Aronovich, Ricardo, 24, 457, 474, 483, 585, 1633, 2010
Arora, Sudha (f), 1048
Arribas, Fernando, 28, 1570, 1597
Arsenishvili, Zaira (f), 675, 2370, 2379, 2381, 2386
Arslan, Yilmaz (m), 700
Arteta, Miguel (m), 2296
Arthur, Karen (f), 1963, 1983, 2074
Arunaraje, Patil (f), 1024
Arvanitis, Yorgos, 615, 668, 865, 871, 879, 880, 1322
Arya, Ishan, 1015
Asanova, Dinara (f), 2372, 2382
Ascofare, Abdoulaye (m), 1322
Ashton-Warner, Sylvia (f), 1390, 1891
Askew, Reilly, 2048
Askin, Peter, 2019
Askoldov, Aleksandr (m), 2358
Asmussen, Peter, 367
Assayas, Oliver (m), 565, 655
Asseyev, Tamara (f), 1997
Assimakopoulos, Kostas, 852
Assis, Carlos, 1498
Assous, Eric, 636
Aström, Karin (f), 708
Astruc, Alexandre (m), 423
Athanassiadis, Yiannis, 852
Atherton, Howard, 2071, 2259
Atkins, Eileen (f), 1843
Atladóttir, Kristín, 962
Atmowiloto, Satmowi, 1063
Atsuta, Yuhara, 1215
Attenborough, Richard, 1748, 1753
Atwood, Margaret (f), 2108
Au, Eveline (f), 912
Aubertin, Frédéric (m), 603
Aubrac, Lucie (f), 548, 593
Aubrée, Patrick, 579
Auderska, Halina (f), 1466
Auer, Gabriel, 1663
Auerbach, Shona (f), 1882
August, Bille, 1651
Aunor, Nora (f), 1429
Aurel, Jean, 573
Aurenche, Jean, 442
Aurthur, Robert Alan, 1905
Austen, Jane (f), 1057, 1830

Austin, Stephanie (f), 2210
Autant-Lara, Claude (m), 442
Auzépy, Patrick, 177
Averbakh, Ilya (m), 2369
Avernatis, Yorgou, 1313
Aviv, Nurit, 1127, 1128, 1164, 1357
Avnet, Jon (m), 2113, 2125
Axel, Gabriel (m), 362
Ayça, Engin (m), 1729, 1732
Ayres, Gerald, 2012, 2140
Ayyari, Dariush, 1100
Azad, Mohan, 1049
Azcona, Rafael, 1574
Azernikov, Valentin, 2384
Azevedo, Gilberto, 123, 1701, 1703
Azoulay, Brigitte (f), 18
Azoulay-Hasfari, Hana (f), 1131
Azpúrua, Carlos (m), 2398

B., Beth (f), 2168
Baba, Shuhaimi (f), 1317
Babu, Ramachandra, 1003
Baccar, Selma (f), 1697
Bach, Simone (f), 483
Bachir-Chouikh, Yamina (f), 12, 21
Backer, P. A. (m), 989
Bacri, Jean-Pierre, 596, 671
Badakshani, Bahram, 1091, 1098
Badal, Jean, 451
Badr, Liana (f), 1418
Baeres, Barry, 2347
Bagnold, Edid (f), 1750
Baha, Ahmed, 1698
Baharlou, Houshang, 1074
Bahman, Farhang-Sara, 1080
Bahnassi, Ghoneim, 386
Baiesu, Ion, 1508
Bailey, John, 1963, 1983, 2075, 2291
Baillargeon, Paule (f), 184
Baines, Julie (f), 1827
Bajo Ulloa, Juanma, 1576
Bajon, Filip, 958
Bajusz, József, 932
Baker, Ian, 60, 86, 2050
Bakhtybekov, Bek, 1278
Baklanov, Grigori, 2377
Balachander, K. (m), 990
Balasko, Josiane (f), 579
Balázs, Josef, 937
Balbuena, Augusto, 1562
Baldi, Gian Vittorio, 745
Baldursdóttir, Kristin Marja (f), 962
Baledón, Rafael (m), 1325
Balian, Haig, 1371
Baljinnyam, Begziin, 1347

Ballantyne, Jane (f), 54, 56
Ballard, Jack, 1965
Ballard, Lucien, 1928
Balletbò-Coll, Marta (f), 1585
Ballhaus, Michael, 751, 755, 756, 762, 772, 785, 786, 800, 815, 2069, 2098, 2114
Balog, Gábor, 952
Balsan, Humbert, 588, 590, 626, 639, 1837
Baltazar, Conrado, 1424, 1427, 1429
Balzac, Honoré de, 427
Bandler, Vivica (f), 414
Bando, Tamasaburo, 1260
Banerjee, Shakti, 982
Bani-Etemad, Rakhshan (f), 1076, 1082, 1085, 1095
Banks, Lynne Reid (f), 1748
Banmali, Bhushan, 983, 996
Bannerfee, S. N., 1051
Bannerjii, Arun, 1026
Bansal, R. D., 968
Bao Qicheng (m), 254, 300
Bao Zhifang (f), 260, 264, 274, 295, 299
Barakat, Henry, 377, 383, 384
Baranski, Andrzej (m), 1471
Baranyi, Laszlo, 82
Barat, François, 480
Baratier, Diane (f), 601, 629, 1705
Barbachano Ponce, Manuel, 1327, 1330
Barber, Gary, 2339
Barbosa, Jarbas, 134
Barish, Keith, 2075
Barish, Leora (f), 2045
Barjatya, Tarachand, 987
Barker, Adam, 1858
Barlow, Roger, 1903
Barna, Marius Theodor, 1512
Barnard, Chris, 1538
Barnes, Peter, 1815
Barnet, Enrique Pineda (m), 332, 341
Barnet, John, 1386
Barnet, Miguel, 341
Barnette, Neema (f), 2318
Barney, Bryan (m), 181
Baron, Caroline (f), 2307
Barougier, Pierre, 653
Barrera, Olegario, 2397
Barreto, Bruno (m), 133, 146
Barreto, Lucy (f), 146
Barrett, Lezli-An (f), 1800
Barriga, Cecilia (f), 1617
Barron, Paul D., 58
Barron, Zelda (f), 1803
Barroso, Mario, 1495
Barrow, Michael, 2146, 2344
Barry, Philip, Jr., 1938
Barski, Odile (f), 487, 645

Barsky, Georges, 479
Bartel, Paul (m), 2037
Barthes, Roland, 203
Bartkowiak, Andrzej, 2029, 2058, 2180
Bartle, James, 1386
Bartley, John, 2240
Bartolini, Elio, 1143
Bartolomé, Cecilia (f), 1548, 1592
Barton, Nick, 1881
Barwood, Hal, 1957
Barzman, Ben, 740
Basen, Leila (f), 213
Basrur, Krishna, 1012
Bass, Ronald, 2068, 2136, 2191, 2232, 2250
Basulto, Armando, 2209
Batac, Joe, 1425, 1449
Bat-Adam, Michal (f), 492, 1130, 1132
Batigne, Marc-André, 1696
Battiferri, Giulio, 1162
Battista, Gérard de, 546
Battye, Don, 47
Batz, Jean-Claude, 119
Baudendistel, Peter, 776
Baudour, Michel, 485, 1818
Baum, Henri, 446
Baumgartner, Karl, 707
Bautista, Lualhati, 1432, 1446
Bautista Stagnaro, Juan, 28
Bayani, Ruel (m), 1442
Bayer, Osvaldo, 836
Bayley, John, 1871
Bayly, Stephen, 1843
Bayzai, Bahram, 1077, 1094
Bazzini, Sergio, 1163
Bazzoni, Camillo, 1180
Beato, Affonso, 1587, 1606, 2277
Beaton, Jesse (f), 2233, 2299
Beaucarne, Christophe, 595, 606, 644
Beaufoy, Simon, 1887
Beaujour, Jerome, 583, 657
Beaulieu, Markel, 190
Beauregard, Georges de, 445
Beausoleil, Claude, 441
Becker, Etienne, 498, 510
Becker, Jean (m), 510
Becker, Wolfgang (m), 712
Becket, James, 223
Bedi, Bobby, 1031, 1037
Bednarik, Sebastian, 2351
Beebe, Dion, 75, 77, 81, 1395, 1870, 2323
Beeler, Kathleen, 2188
Begaline, Majit, 2353
Bégéja, Liria (f), 562
Begun, Jeff, 1970
Beiersdorf, Dagmar (f), 823

Beker, Jeroen, 1382
Bekker, Marina (f), 1541
Bekolo, Jean-Pierre (m), 1530
Belaubre, Yves, 585
Belén, Ana (f), 1578
Belessi, Stella (f), 890
Bell, A. Dean (m), 2336
Bell, Dave, 2101
Bell, Neal, 2168
Bellanova, Piero, 1148
Belling, Diana (f), 1840
Bellis, Andreas, 1644
Bellmunt, Francesc, 1624
Bellocchio, Marco, 1170
Bellon, Yannick (f), 479, 501
Belmondo, Alain, 530
Belmont, Vera (f), 511, 552, 594
Belonogov, Valentin, 1135, 1139
Belouad, Naguel (m), 19
Beloufa, Farouk (m), 10
Belson, Jerry, 1956
Belson, Jordan, 1978
Beltrán, Jordi, 1575
Belyazid, Farida (f), 1350
Bemberg, Maria Luisa (f), 26, 27, 28, 30, 32, 34
Ben Abdallah, Tarek, 1704
Ben Ammar, Abdellatif (m), 1695
Ben Mabrouk, Néjia (f), 1696
Ben Mahmoud, Mahmoud (m), 1701
Ben Mahmoud, Sayda (f), 1697
Ben Mihoub, Mustafa, 21
Ben Youssef, Youssef, 1698, 1702
Benayoun, Georges, 577, 580, 586, 614
Benazeraf, Jose, 428
Bender, Lawrence, 2341
Benderson, Bruce, 680
Bendtsen, Henning, 354
Benedek, Barbara (f), 2113
Benegal, Shyam (m), 979, 991, 1006, 1032, 1039, 1047
Benet, J. M., 1590
Bengell, Norma (f), 144
Benguigui, Alain, 651, 670
Benguigui, Yamina (f), 637
Benhadj, Rachid (f), 15
Benitez, César, 1595
Benitez Rojo, Antonio, 332
Benjo, Caroline (f), 661
Benlyazid, Farida (f), 1351, 1353
Bennett, Edward (m), 1109
Benson Gyles, Anna (f), 1831
Benton, Robert, 2038
Benvenuti, Leo, 1145
Bérard, Christian, 671
Berbert, Marcel, 471
Berckmans, Nicole (f), 524

Bereczki, Csaba, 959
Bereményi, Géza, 937
Beresford, Bruce (m), 2054, 2241
Berg, Christine, 711
Berger, Christian, 95
Berger, John (m), 1663
Berger, Pamela (f), 538
Berges, Paul Mayeda, 1874
Bergholm, Eija-Elina (f), 409, 410, 413, 414, 415
Bergman, Andrew (m), 2261
Bergman, Ingmar (m), 1638, 1641, 1645, 1647, 1649, 1650, 1658, 1659
Bergman, Nir (m), 1139
Bergren, Eric, 2016
Bergstein, Eleanor (f), 2002
Beridze, Georgi, 675
Beristain, Gabriel, 2174
Berlin, Jeannie (f), 2111
Berliner, Alain (m), 2250
Berman, Pandro, 1888
Bernal, Joaquin, 1326
Bernard, Yannick, 546
Bernardet, Jean-Claude, 150
Bernaza, Luis Felipe (m), 342
Berner, Fred, 2150
Bernhardt, Curtis (m), 1895
Bernheim, Emanuèle, 643, 664, 665
Bernier, Kristian, 2251
Bernstein, Marcos (m), 152, 155
Bernstein, Stephen, 1799
Bernstein, Steven, 2329
Berri, Claude, 498, 572, 593
Berry, David, 2083
Berry, John (m), 517, 1948
Berta, Renato, 484, 514, 536, 596, 623, 1136, 1663, 1665
Berthelin, Søren, 363
Berthomieu, Romain, 604
Bertl, Michael, 707
Berto, Juliet (f), 465
Bertolucci, Bernardo (m), 1169, 1192, 1880
Bertolucci, Giovanni, 1169
Bertrand Tchakoua Pouma, Joséphine (f), 172
Bertuccelli, Jean-Louis (m), 6, 458, 469
Bertuccelli, Julie (f), 673
Berwin, Dorothy (f), 2332
Beshara, Khairy (m), 390
Bessa, Zine, 15
Bessa-Luís, Augustina (f), 1495
Besset, Jean-Marie, 1837
Besson, Luc, 544, 611, 1844
Bestetti, Emilio, 1168
Betzer, Just, 358, 362
Beuchot, Pierre, 541
Bevan, Tim, 1850, 2274

Beyer, Bero, 1418
Beyout, Christine, 510
Bhandarkar, Madhur, 1049
Bharadwaj, Radha (f), 2121
Bhasa, 1012
Bhatt, Mahesh (m), 1005
Bhatt, Pravin, 1005, 1007, 1014
Bhattacharya, Arya, 1054
Bhave, Sumitra, 1036
Bick, Jerry, 2040
Biddle, Adrian, 2137, 2268
Bidou, Jacques, 659, 898, 1499
Bienen, Andy, 2238
Bier, Susanne (f), 366, 370, 374
Bierkens, Theo, 686, 1378
Biermann, Rudolf, 346
Bigazzi, Luca, 1177, 1196, 1208
Bigelow, Kathryn (f), 2106, 2268
Bijlani, Lalit, 979, 991, 1006
Bikel, Anet, 1135
Binchy, Maeve (f), 1115
Binder, J., 1348
Binder, Jigjidiin, 1348
Bini, Alfred, 1146
Birckmayer, Harry, 2214
Birkeland, Anders, 1657, 2391
Birkin, Andrew, 611
Birkin, Jane (f), 525
Birnbaum, Roger, 2215, 2228
Biró, Yvette (f), 930
Biroc, Joseph, 1907
Birschfeld, Alex, 2025
Birsel, Özdemir, 1708
Bisset, Jacqueline (f), 2012
Biziou, Peter, 1804, 2314
Bjornson, Bjornstjerne, 1415
Björkman, Stig (m), 1644, 1646
Björne, Lasse, 358, 1642
Black, Shane, 2210
Black, Trevor, 2026
Blackburn, Marthe (f), 180, 183
Blackwood, Maureen (f), 1799
Blais, Marie-Claire (f), 196
Blake, Willie, 1636
Blanc, Christophe (m), 622
Blanc, Nicolas, 638
Blanco, Joaquin, 1582
Blanco, José Joaquín, 1330
Blankenship, Beverley (f), 58
Blas, Mercedes de (f), 1586
Blasband, Philippe, 609
Blasi, Vera (f), 2402
Blaustein, Julian, 1891
Blignaut, Johan, 1537
Block, Axel, 818, 836

Block, Bruce, 2067
Blocker, David, 2032
Blokker, Jan, 103, 126
Blondeau, Regis, 1530
Blossier, Patrick, 516, 538, 562, 2102
Blumenschein, Tabea (f), 770
Blumenthal, Hank, 2166
Bobbitt, Sean, 1861
Bobby, Jean, 1670
Bobrova, Lidiya (f), 1518
Bochner, Sally (f), 199
Bockmayer, Walter, 832
Bodansky, Jorge, 138
Bodard, Mag, 179, 440, 441, 450
Bode, Ralf, 1780, 2085, 2145
Bode, Ralf D., 2000, 2128
Boeser, Knut, 684
Boffety, Jean, 185, 459, 470, 481, 488
Bogart, Paul, 1975
Bogayevicz, Yurek, 2066
Bogdanovich, Peter (m), 1949, 2047
Bogdanski, Hagen, 705
Bohlinger, Don, 702
Boisset, Yves (m), 470, 491
Bojorquez, Francisco, 1333, 1338
Bolan, Monica (f), 38
Bollaín, Icíar (f), 1580, 1588, 1604, 1630
Bollaín, Juan, 1580
Bollaín, Marina (f), 1580
Bollinger, Alun, 1396, 1400
Bolognini, Mauro (m), 1151, 1163
Bolvary, Jean, 470, 486
Bonassi, Fernando, 148
Bond, Elizabeth, 1792
Bonfanti, Eve (f), 122
Bongers, Sally (f), 61, 68
Bonham-Carter, Philip, 1809
Bonitzer, Pascal, 123, 493, 528, 553, 561, 564
Bont, Peter de, 1369
Boogaerdt, Herman, 1365
Boon, Jaak, 129
Boorman, John (m), 2172
Boorman, Telsche, 585
Booth, Jim, 1396
Borau, Jose Luis, 1569
Borden, Lizzie (f), 1973, 2021, 2065, 2130, 2175
Borg, Laurie, 1540
Borgli, Petter, 1414, 1862
Bornemann, Mick von, 53
Borrás, Victoria (f), 1577
Borthwick, Chris (f), 53
Bortman, Michael, 2090
Bortnik, Aída (f), 29, 36, 1626
Borusovicová, Eva (f), 346
Bosanquet, Simon, 2286

Bosch, Eduard, 1618
Bose, Kamal, 966
Bosmajian, Harlan, 2305
Bostwick-Singer, Eugenia (f), 2340
Bosylbaiev, Yedygué, 2394
Böszörményi, Géza, 952
Bota, Rick, 2171
Botelho, João (m), 1503
Botti, Donatella, 1208
Bouamari, Mohamed (m), 7
Bouchoucha Fourati, Dora (f), 1705
Bouhon, Jean-Jacques, 1321
Bouilleret, Dominique, 589
Boukerche, Daha, 7, 8
Boumendil, Jacques, 494
Bourboulon, Frédéric, 652
Bourdier, Jean-Paul, 2188
Bourdieu, Emmanuel, 1866
Boutel, Maurice, 432
Bouvier, Claudine (f), 1368
Bouzid, Nouri (m), 1698, 1700, 1702, 1703
Bovaira, Fernando, 2281
Bowden, Helen (f), 82
Bowes, Ed, 2021
Boxwala, Shabbir, 1033
Boyce, Frank Cottrell, 1827, 1852
Boyd, Don, 1784
Boyd, Russell, 50, 57, 69, 2036
Boyer, Myriam (f), 517
Bozman, Ronald, 2117
Brach, Gérard, 1756, 2080
Brand, Peter, 735
Bragg, Melvyn (m), 1761
Braham, Henry, 1875
Braithwaite, Philippa (f), 1854
Brancato, John, 2337
Branco, Paulo, 613, 632, 644, 654, 1495, 1497, 1500, 1501, 1503, 1666, 1670, 2349
Brandström, Charlotte (f), 1840
Branev, Veselin (m), 162
Brantas, Ulf, 1662
Brauer, Jürgen, 724, 730
Brault, Michel, 179, 180, 183
Braunberger, Pierre, 434
Brauner, B. E., 2319
Brealey, Gil (m), 53
Breien, Anja (f), 1403, 1405, 1407, 1409, 1412
Breillat, Catherine (f), 494, 541, 615, 668
Breit, Mitch, 1959
Breitel, Heide (f), 827
Brennan, Kathleen (f), 2063
Brennan, Richard, 50
Bresson, Robert (m), 431, 450
Breton, Pascale (f), 640
Breuer, Torsten, 692

Breuls, Paul, 126, 1818
Brezner, Larry, 2156
Briand, Manon (f), 209
Brick, Richard, 1650
Brickman, Paul (m), 2113
Brickner, Howard M., 2149
Bridges, James, 1989
Brière, Christine (f), 556
Bright, Simon, 2417
Bright, Susie (f), 2175
Briley, John, 1769, 2046
Brindley, Michael, 58
Brisseau, Jean-Claude (m), 557, 568, 648
Brock, Jeremy, 1842, 1870
Brock, Norman, 1536
Brocka, Lino (m), 1424, 1427, 1429
Brockmann, Sejr, 364
Brodsky, Jack, 1943
Bromberger, Hervé, 487
Bromet, Frans, 1361, 1366, 1367
Brooks, Adam, 2230
Brooks, James L., 2029, 2069
Brooks, Maggie (f), 1786
Brooks, Richard (m), 1912, 1982
Brooks, Sue (f), 86
Brougher, Hilary (f), 1859
Brouwer, Chris, 1359
Brower, Mitchell, 1925
Brown, Amanda (f), 2325
Brown, Chris, 1788
Brown, Effie (f), 2284, 2310
Brown, Riwia (f), 1397
Brown, Sarah (f), 2326
Brownlow, John, 1883
Bruckheimer, Bonnie, 2087, 2291
Bruckheimer, Jerry, 2335
Brückner, Jutta (f), 763, 768, 774, 781, 784, 831
Bruel, Dirk, 355, 361
Brühne, Frank, 799, 826
Brundi, Lucia (f), 1183
Brunelin, André (m), 469
Brunet, Laurent, 1138, 1140
Bryson, John, 60
Buachand, Anupap, 1694
Buchanan, James D., 2100
Buchman, Sidney (m), 1901
Buck, Pearl S. (f), 970
Budberg, Moura (f), 1767
Buelna, Pablo, 1556
Bufford, Takashi, 2216
Bugajski, Ryszard (m), 1460, 1464
Buitenhuis, Penelope (f), 213, 2158
Bukowski, Bobby, 2120, 2124, 2152, 2207
Bun Hsu, 1677
Buñuel, Joyce (f), 507

Buñuel, Luis (m), 446
Burchner, Clara (f), 682
Burel, Leonce-Henri, 431
Burgess, Don, 2222
Burke, Edward, 1118
Burkhart, Jeff, 2123
Burman, Hans, 1546
Burnett, Charles, 1969
Burns, Catherine Lloyd, 2276
Burns, Mark R., 2093, 2116
Burrill, Timothy, 1791
Burroughs, Jackie (f), 197
Burstyn, Thom, 1387
Bursztejn, Sylvain, 891, 1508
Burton, Geoff, 62, 73
Burum, Stephen H., 2008
Busch, Hans-Erich, 730
Buschmann, Christel (f), 826
Bushnell, Scott, 2015
Busia, Akosua (f), 2230
Butler, Bill, 1913, 1972, 1978, 2002
Buyens, Frans, 120
Buyung, Aida Fitri, 1317
Byars, Floyd, 2076
Byrne, Bobby, 2112, 2148
Byrum, John, 1965
Byun Won Mi, 1301
Byun Young-joo (f), 1309

Cabrera, Dominique (f), 612
Cacoyannis, Michael (m), 850
Cadena, Jordi, 1612
Cahill, Laura (f), 2301
Caine, Lynn (f), 1976
Cajahuaringa, Micaela, 1423
Calage, Eloi (f), 2175
Calandruccio, Domenico, 1550
Caldwell, Helen (f), 2218
Caleb, Ruth, 1868
Calef, Henri, 110
Calenda, Giulia (f), 1203
Calie, J. C., 279
Callado, Antonio, 134
Calley, John, 2114
Callis, Pep, 1554
Calmon, Antonio, 149
Calogero, Elena, 1195
Calvo, Luis, 1558
Camacho, Miguel, 1331
Camarda, Michele, 1861
Cambria, Adèla (f), 1183
Caminito, Augusto, 677
Cammell, Donald (m), 1978
Camorino, Marcelo, 35
Camp, Colleen (f), 2272

Campbell, Martin (m), 2123
Campion, Anna (f), 81
Campion, Jane (f), 61, 71, 81, 82, 1392, 1836, 2323
Camurati, Carla (f), 147
Camus, Mario, 1570, 1583, 1584
Canijo, João, 1490
Cankar, Ivan, 2412
Cannon, Dyan (f), 2107
Cannon, Reuben, 2348
Cannon, Vince, 2107
Canter, Ed, 806
Canton, Neil, 2084
Caparros, Ernest, 1893
Capote, Truman (m), 1745
Cappellari, Ciro, 842
Caramico, Robert, 1914
Carcassonne, Philippe, 540
Card, Lamar, 1962
Cardarelli, Mano, 1162
Cardinal, Marie (f), 511
Cardozo, Patricia (f), 2310
Caridad Sanchez, Ana (f), 1421
Carion, Christian (m), 636
Caristan, Georges, 1524, 1526
Carlberg, Lars-Owe, 1645, 1647
Carle, Gilles, 176, 188
Carli, Ann (f), 2178
Carlino, Lewis John, 1979, 2004
Carlos Gené, Juan, 2400
Carmorino, Marcello, 831
Carneiro, Geraldo, 144
Carneiro, João Emanuel, 152
Carnival, Susan (f), 2255
Carolina, Ana (f), 136, 143, 154
Carolsfeld, Wiebke von (f), 219
Caron, M., 196
Carow, Heiner (m), 724
Carpi, Fabio, 1154
Carré, Louise (f), 180
Carrera, Carlos (m), 1341
Carretero, David, 1625
Carri, Albertina (f), 46
Carrière, Christine (f), 573
Carrière, Jean-Claude, 446, 1556, 2194
Carroll, Matt, 69
Carter, Angela (f), 1788
Carter, Gina (f), 1861
Cartright, Jim, 1853
Carvalho, Inês, 1503
Carvalho, Walter, 152
Carvalhosa, José Luis, 1490
Casal, Pancho, 1614
Casano, Denise, 2204
Casati, Alberto, 1148
Caso, Angelos, 1623

Caspar, Ulrich, 705
Cassavetes, John (m), 1959, 1984, 2001
Cassavetes, Nick (m), 2218
Castano, Xavier, 1321
Castellanos, Rosario, 1333
Castle, Jane (f), 76, 2162
Castle, William, 1909
Caswell, Robert, 60
Cates, Gilbert, 1943
Caton-Jones, Michael (m), 1805
Catonné, François, 165, 550, 569
Caufman, Beatrice (f), 657
Cauvin, Roger, 435
Cavalié, Bernard, 18, 584
Cavalier, Alain, 523
Cavani, Liliana (f), 1155, 1157, 1161, 1171, 1179
Cayatte, André (m), 456, 2211
Cayla, Eric, 184
Cayrol, Jean, 438
Cecchi D'Amico, Suso (f), 511, 1153, 1180
Cerami, Vincenzo, 1170, 1200
Cercas, Javier, 1629
Cerezo, Enrique, 39, 1594, 1608, 1619, 1626
Cerna, Jana, 552
Cerri, Lionella, 1177
Cespedes, Marcelo, 46
Chabrol, Claude (m), 421, 447, 448, 449, 455, 487, 527, 551, 575, 623, 2314
Chadha, Gurinder (f), 1821, 1874, 2269
Chagoll, Lydia, 120
Chahal-Sabbag, Randa (f), 1313, 1314, 1315
Chahine, Youssef (m), 387, 402
Chaiken, Ilene (f), 2171
Chaiken, Ilya (f), 2306
Chakrapani, 985
Challis, Christopher, 1768
Chamaillard, Benoît, 618
Champetier, Caroline (f), 118, 503, 528, 577, 582, 583, 633, 667
Chan, Alice, 315
Chan, Hanson, 914
Chan, Jackie, 907
Chan, John (m), 922
Chan, Kin Chung, 918
Chan Man-keung, 909, 916
Chan, Susanne, 917
Chan Ying, 909
Chandran, Rajiv, 1057
Chandrasekhar, Priya (f), 1047
Chang, Chih-yuan, 1687
Chang, Eileen (f), 902, 922, 1679
Chang, Guo, 1683
Chang Hui-kung, 1675
Chang, Sylvia (f), 298, 906, 912, 1677, 1684, 1691
Chang, Vivian (f), 1688

Chang Yi (m), 1676
Chang Yuhong, 310
Channing-Williams, Simon, 1838, 1886
Channipa, 1694
Chaplin, Patrice, 2081
Chapman, Jan, 65, 71, 81
Chapman, Leigh (f), 2110
Chapman, Matthew (m), 2092
Chapman, Michael, 2018
Chapot, Jean, 477
Chappell, Peter, 1528
Chapuis, Dominique, 512, 555, 580, 1543
Charbonnet, Patricia, 2234
Charef, Mahdi, 556
Charles, Cliff, 2287
Charny, Ruth (f), 2205, 2265
Chasman, Julia (f), 1803
Chastain, Don, 1983
Chatry, Bertrand, 1533
Chatterjee, Basu (f), 981
Chatterjee, Sudeep, 1050
Chattopadhya, Mohit, 1016
Chaulier, Agnès (f), 484
Cheang, Shu Lea (f), 1269, 2162
Chediak, Enrique, 2283, 2296, 2332
Chekhov, Anton, 1187, 1767
Chen, Huai-en, 1682
Chen Huan Kai, 236
Chen Hung-yu, 319
Chen Jianyu, 259
Chen, Joan (f), 315
Chen Kun-hou, 1678
Chen Kunming, 301
Chen Kuo-fu (m), 1689
Chen Xue, 322
Chen Yuan Bin, 291
Chen Zhengxiang, 239
Cheng, A., 251
Cheng Yin, 234
Cheng Yong, 316
Chénieux, Pierre-Laurent, 525
Chenzira, Ayoka (f), 2149
Chepik, Natalya (f), 1514
Cher (f), 2207
Chéreau, Patrice (m), 489, 572
Chernykh, Aleksandr, 2390
Chernykh, Valentin, 2375
Chetvertkov, Sergei, 1743
Cheung, Mabel (f), 921
Cheung Wai-kung, 1677
Chi Xiaoning, 291, 318
Chiang, Bi-yi, 1682
Chien Hsiang, 1691
Chiesa, Alcides, 836
Chinarbaev, Ermek (m), 2385

Ching Siu-tung, 914, 917
Chionglo, Mel (m), 1427, 1435
Chiron, Dominique, 618
Chitra, Charu, 971
Chitra, Sujata, 999
Chiu Fu-sheng, 284
Chiu Kang Chien, 900
Chiu Shun-ching, 1685, 1688
Chivers, Louise (f), 2082
Cho Min-ho, 1300
Cho Sang-hyun, 1305
Choi, Byung Ryul, 1288
Choi Jong-tae, 1310
Choi Ming Leung, 1677
Choi Seung-woo, 1290
Choi Su-yeong, 1289
Choi, Yeong-hwan, 1307
Chokalingham, S., 1056
Cholodenko, Lisa (f), 2167, 2231, 2324, 2338
Chong, Rae Dawn (f), 2158
Chong Wui Sin, 1266
Chopin, Kate (f), 2007, 2127
Chopra, B. R., 967
Chopra, Joyce (f), 2112
Chor Yuen (m), 900
Chou, Gordon, 2306
Chouikh, Mohamed (m), 14
Chouraqui, Elie (m), 2298
Chouridis, Catherine (f), 596
Chow, Raymond, 916, 918, 921, 923
Chowhani, Jagdish, 1010
Christanell, Linda (f), 2066
Christian, H. R., 1954
Chu Tien-wen, 1277, 1686, 1690
Chubb, Caldecott, 2223
Chukhnov, Vladimir, 2378
Chung, David, 1681
Chung, Henry, 925
Chung Jin-woo, 1294
Chytilová, Vira (f), 347, 349, 350, 352
Cianchetti, Fabio, 1203, 1206, 1880
Ciccone, Anne, 1206
Cicogna, Marina (f), 1156, 1159
Cimino, Michael, 1998
Cipri, Daniele, 1197, 1201
Cissé, Souleymane (m), 1318, 1321
Citti, Sergio, 1146, 1200
Civit, Josep, 566, 1566, 1575, 1577, 1612, 2322
Clara Simo, Isabel (f), 1612
Clark, Chris, 1932
Clark, Curtis, 1312, 2055
Clark, Louise (f), 197
Clark, Penny (f), 1109
Clark, Tony, 79
Class, Joanna McClelland (f), 2271

Claus, Hugo, 109, 124, 1368
Claussen, Jakob, 689
Clayton, Jack (m), 1745, 1752, 1802
Clayton, Susan (f), 1777
Cleary, Stephen, 891
Clegg, Terence A., 2091
Cleitman, René, 2218
Clément, Magali (f), 532
Clemente, Shayne, 1448
Clerval, Denys, 1329
Clifford, Graeme, 2016
Cloquet, Ghislain, 450, 454, 461
Clouzot, Henri-Georges (m), 424
Clouzot, Véra (f), 424
Clowes, Daniel, 2277
Coburn, Randy Sue, 2165
Coe, Fred, 1893
Coen, Ethan, 2200
Coen, Joel, 2200
Coetzee, J. M., 121
Coffey, Joseph F., 1905
Cohen, Albert, 2298
Cohen, Annette (f), 187
Cohen, Catherine (f), 550
Cohen, Charles Zev, 2074
Cohen, Eric, 1141
Cohen, Maxi (f), 91
Coixet, Isabel (f), 220, 2217
Colace, Hugo, 40
Cole, Nigel (m), 1881
Colell, Judith (f), 1612
Colesberry, Robert, 2073
Collet, Paul, 108
Collier, Zena, 2240
Collins, Andy, 1853
Colombani, Laetitia (f), 647
Colombo, Arrigo, 1166
Colomo, Fernando, 1586
Colpaert, Carl, 2164
Columbus, Chris (m), 2236
Combes, Marcel, 428
Comencini, Christina (f), 1193, 1203
Comencini, Francesca (f), 1174, 1208
Comfort, Bob, 2124
Comolli, Jean-Louis, 505
Compton, Juleen (f), 1903, 1968
Conchon, Georges, 489
Coninx, Stijn (m), 1378
Conklin, Betty (f), 1954
Connolly, Robert, 84
Connors, Richard, 2336
Constantiner, Leon, 1336
Contini, Alfio, 1161
Contner, J. Burgi, 1910
Conversi, Fabio, 547, 559

Cook, T. S., 1989
Coolidge, Martha (f), 1966, 2135, 2140, 2156, 2260
Cooper, Lindsay, 1782
Cooper, Natalie (f), 2044
Cooper, Susan, 2033
Copans, Richard, 599
Coppola, Francis (m), 1913, 2061
Corcoran, Sean, 1110
Cordeiro, Margarida (f), 1487
Cordie, Orette, 843
Cordini, Angelo, 1185
Cordoba, Juan, 1607
Coriat, Laurence, 1861, 1877
Cork, John, 2101
Corman, Julie (f), 1985
Corman, Roger, 1916, 1929, 1947, 1996, 2039, 2119
Cornall, Jan (f), 72
Corneau, Alain, 663
Corner, Harry, 1955
Cornwall, Ray, 1779
Corr, Eugene, 2052
Correa, João, 110
Corrington, John William, 1929
Corrington, Joyce Hooper, 1929
Corsi, Tilde, 1198
Corsini, Catherine (f), 613, 640
Cortés, Alberto (m), 1331
Cortés, Busi (m), 1333, 1338
Cortez, Stanley, 1896
Costa e Silva, Manuel, 1489, 1491, 1492, 1494
Costa, João, 2417
Costa, Juan, 1554
Costa, Pedro (m), 1497
Costa-Gavras, 2010, 2102
Costas, Celia, 2253
Costigan, James, 1964
Cotet, Jean, 451
Cottereau, Pierre, 670
Cottringer, Anne (f), 1777, 1781
Coulibaly, Sega (m), 1319
Coulter, Michael, 1830, 2073
Cournihan, Judy, 1377
Courtoy, Carole (f), 116
Cousin, Lionel, 1323
Coutard, Raoul, 422, 426, 434, 437, 439, 444
Cowan, Rob, 2292
Cowan, Tom (m), 48
Cowley, Graeme, 1391
Cox, Paul (m), 54, 56, 66
Crabe, James, 1938, 1989
Craven, Wes (m), 2249
Crawford, Robert, 2035
Cremata Malberti, Juan Carlos (m), 345
Crenshaw, Michelle (f), 2192
Crespo, Mario, 344

Crialese, Emanuele (m), 1207
Crichton, Michael (m), 1977
Cristaldi, Franco, 1165
Cristiani, Gabriella (f), 213
Cristofer, Michael, 2084
Croll, Tony, 2320
Crone, Nina (f), 357
Cronenweth, Jordan, 1934, 1961, 2061
Croner, Karen (f), 2233
Cronyn, Hume, 2033
Crossan, Denis, 1877
Crossley, Rosemary, 53
Crouch, Catherine (f), 2284
Cuarón, Alfonso, 1346
Cuarón, Carlos, 1346
Cuau, Emmanuelle (f), 576
Cubano, Augustin, 847
Cuevas Ortiz, Antonio, 1557
Cukor, George (m), 1964, 2012
Cullen, Paddy, 2319
Cumali, N., 1723
Cundey, Dean, 2141
Cunningham, Michael, 2300
Cunningham Reid, Fiona (f), 1825
Curi, Marcio, 156
Curling, Chris, 1866
Curling, Jonathan, 1777
Curtelin, Jean, 482
Curtis, Richard (m), 2274
Curtis, Sarah (f), 1842, 1851, 1870
Czap, Hans, 171
Czenki, Margit (f), 833

D'Alpuget, Blanche (f), 69
D'Anolfi, Massimo, 1201
D'Erneville, Annette Mbaye (f), 1522
Dabadie, Jean-Loup, 459, 488
Dabal, Wit, 1482
Dadiras, Dimis, 870
Daguet, Nicolas, 600
Dahan, Alain, 115, 464
Dahan, Olivier (m), 666
Dahl, Roald, 2105
Dahlbeck, Eva (f), 1642
Dahlberg, Ingrid (f), 1658
Dahlquist, Lars, 1656
Dailland, Laurent, 624
Daldoul, Hassen, 1353, 1701, 1703
Daldry, Stephen (m), 2300
Dalianidis, Yannis, 860
Dallessandro, James, 834
Dalrymple, Ian, 1749
Dalton, Richard, 1771
Dalvi, Jaywant, 998, 1019
Damic, Irina, 326

Damon, Mark, 2329
Danager-Dorr, Karen, 2140
Danalis, Grigoris, 856
Danalis, Syrokos, 858
Dancigers, Óscar, 443
Danezi-Knutsen, Aliki (f), 887, 892
Dang, Nhat Minh (m), 2403, 2404
Dangarembga, Tsitsi, 2416, 2418
Dangerfield, Yves, 625
Danielewski, Tad, 970
Daniels, Mark, 2079, 2115
Danon, Raymond, 468
Dansereau, Mireille (f), 177, 182, 196
Dardenne, Jean-Pierre, 127
Dardenne, Luc, 127
Dark, Alice Elliott (f), 2265
Darkaoui, Abdel, 1350
Daroudchi, Khalil, 1083
Dart, Iris Rainer, 2087
Darunaratna, Donald, 1635
Dasgupta, Buddhadev (m), 1054
Dash, Julie (f), 2122
Dassin, Jules (m), 851, 871, 1911
Dauman, Anatole, 763
Dauman, Pascale (f), 542
Davey, Bruce, 212
Daviau, Allen, 2042
David, Marjorie (f), 2080
David, Michael, 167
David, Zoltan, 2070
Davidoff, Oded (m), 1137
Davidson, Petter, 1646
Davies, Andrew, 1115, 2274
Davies, Desmond, 1751
Davies, John, 1108, 1796
Davies, Terence (m), 1867
Davis, Alan, 1964
Davis, Bridgett (f), 2213
Davis, DeMane, 2279
Davis, Elliot, 2082, 2132, 2315
Davis, Julie (f), 2246
Davis, Ossie (m), 1939
Davison, Jon, 2013
Davudi, Mohammad, 1090
Dawkins, Willie E., 1692
Day, Ernest, 1789
Day, Janette (f), 1885, 2301
Day, Jenny (f), 68
Dayan, Josée (f), 633, 645
Dayrit, Trina, 1449
De Almeida, Acacio, 224, 578, 1184, 1487, 1488, 1499, 1607
De Andrade, Mario, 22
De Battista, Gérard, 556, 579, 616
De Bernadi, P., 1152

De Besche, Austin, 2017
De Boisrouvray, Albina (f), 458
De Bont, Jan, 2139
De Borman, John, 1857
De Bourbon, Etienne, 538
De Broca, Michelle (f), 459
De Casabianca, Camille (f), 523
De Clermont-Tonnerre, Martine (f), 152
De Felitta, Frank, 2008
De Filippo, Eduardo, 1188
De Gleria, Mile, 2412
De Goeij, Jacqueline (f), 1384
De Gregorio, Eduardo, 465, 473
De Heer, Rolf (m), 79
De Hirsch, Storm (f), 1149
De Kermadec, Liliane (f), 464, 571
De Keyzer, Bruno, 534, 560, 1339, 1807
De Kuyper, Eric, 632, 654
De La Cuadra, José, 405
De La Fuente, Leonardo, 1476
De la Gándara, Beatriz (f), 1421, 1586, 1632
De la Iglesia, Alex (m), 1609
De la Rica, Kiko, 1609
De la Rosa, Arturo, 1332, 1344
De Laurentiis, Guido, 1191
De Leon, Rey, 1445
De Luna, Aureli, 1612
De Macedo, António, 1494
De Maupassant, Guy, 531
De Oliveira, Manoel (m), 1495, 1500
De Palm, Norman, 1364
De Palma, Brian (m), 1936, 2294
De Passe, Suzanne (f), 1932
De Robien, Antoinette (f), 590
De Rooy, Felix (m), 1364
De Santis, Pasqualino, 1182
De Sica, Vittorio (m), 1144, 1159
De Simone, Esa (f), 1161
De Sisti, Vitorio, 1550
De Van, Marina (f), 643, 646, 653
De Volpi, David, 199
De Vos, Pieter, 1359
De Vries, Edwin, 1380
De Weers, Hans, 1377, 1383
Deakins, Roger, 2101, 2147, 2198, 2200, 2237
Deasy, Seamus, 1121
Deboise, Eve (f), 622
Debrauwer, Lieven (m), 129
Debray, Régis, 554
Decaë, Henri, 421, 429, 443
Decharme, Paul-Edmond, 430
Déchet, Bernard, 1213, 1214
Declercq, Jan, 131
Dee, Derek (m), 1434
Dee, Ruby (f), 1911

Deerson, Jack, 1917, 1953
Defoe, Daniel, 1835
Deghidy, Inas. *See* Al-Dighidi, Inas
Degli Esposti, Piera (f), 1173, 1178
Degraeve, Danny, 122
Dehan, Alain, 113
Deitch, Donna (f), 2044
Del Amo, Alvaro (m), 1628
Del Rosario-Corpus, Veronique, 1447
Del Rosario, Vic, 1444
Delahaie, Agnès, 431
Delaney, Shelagh (f), 1746, 1794
Delannoy, Aurique, 571
Delay, Florence (f), 495
Delbonnel, Bruno, 628
Delbosc, Olivier, 643, 646, 664
Delesalle, Bénédicte, 112
Delgado, Evelio, 333
Delgado, Johnny, 1452
Delgado, Livio, 333, 334, 335
Delgado, Teo, 1588, 1604, 1620
Delhomme, Benoit, 576, 592
DeLine, Donald, 2345
Delire, Jean, 106
Delli Colli, Tonino, 677, 1146, 1152, 1166, 1178
Dellora, Daryl (m), 59
Delpeut, Peter (m), 1365
Delsol, Paule (f), 436
Delvaux, André (m), 119
DeMarco, John, 2110
Dembo, Richard, 597
Demers, Gloria (f), 199
Deming, Peter, 2249, 2347
Demme, Jonathan (m), 1947, 1962, 2040, 2093, 2117, 2230
Demy, Jacques (m), 422, 430, 440, 454
Denault, Jim, 2221, 2238, 2310, 2342
Deng Je, 317
Denis, Claire (f), 530, 586, 665
Denis, Jean-Pierre (m), 619
Denny, Jon, 2060
Densham, Pen (m), 1835, 2189
Depardieu, Gérard, 603
Depardon, Raymond (m), 542
Derflinger, Sabine (f), 96
Derobe, Alain, 120, 482
Dery, Rosa, 935
Desai, Babubhai, 994
DeSalvo, Joe, 1684
Deschamps, Jean-Marc, 628
Deshpande, Shashi, 1040
Despentes, Virginie (f), 618
Desplechin, Arnaud (m), 1866
Dester, Mogens, 369
Deubel, Claus, 809, 820

Dev, Vasant, 1004, 1014
Devers, Claire (f), 536
Deville, Michel (m), 531
Deville, Rosalinde (f), 531
DeVito, Danny, 2242
Devlin, Anna (f), 1116
Dexter, Brad, 1932
Dey, Dulal, 1055
Dharankar, Sanjay, 1039
Dharmaraj, Rabindra, 998
Dharmasena, K. A., 1637
Dhawan, Sabrina (f), 2307
Dhouib, Moncef, 1701
Di Clemente, Giovanni, 1180
Di Giulio, Amanda, 2195
Di Leandro, Natalina (f), 213
Di Palma, Carol, 1147
Di Palma, Dario, 1160
Di Venanzo, Gianni, 1150
Diagana, Moussa, 168
Diakite, Moussa Kemoko (m), 895
Díaz Abaya, Marilou (f), 1428, 1431, 1433, 1438, 1440, 1441, 1443
Diaz, Jesús (m), 338
Díaz Torres, Daniel (m), 343
Diaz Yanes, Agustin (m), 1589
Díaz-Salgado, Rafael, 1596
DiCillo, Tom, 2031
Dickerson, Ernest, 1364, 2062
Dickins, Barry, 66
Dickman, Wolfgang, 88
Diderot, Denis, 445
Didion, Joan (f), 1926, 1934
Diego, Constante, 332
Diegues, Carlos (m), 134, 149
Dietrich, Erwin, 1664
Díez, Ana (f), 1599
Dignam, Erin (f), 2226
Dikker, Marianne (f), 1371
Dikongue-Pipa, Jean-Pierre (m), 170
DiLeo, Mario, 834
Dimantas, Melanie (f), 147, 155
Dimopoulos, Dinos, 855, 862, 863
Dinesen, Isak (f), 362, 2049
Ding Xiaoqi, 255
Ding Yah Ming, 1678
Diniz, Carlos Alberto, 137, 142
Dionne, Guylaine (f), 214
Diop Mambéty, Djibril (m), 1529
DiPalma, Dario, 1158
Diver, William, 1116
Dixon, Leslie (f), 2077, 2078, 2321
Djafarian, Hossein, 1076, 1087
Djarot, Eros (m), 1070
Djebar, Assia (f), 5, 13

Dobrowolski, Tomasz, 1484
Docampo Feijóo, Beda, 28
Dod Mantle, Anthony, 375
Doel, Frances, 1962
Dognini, Liana, 1878
Doillon, Jacques (m), 515, 662
Dolinin, Dmitri, 1517, 2359, 2363, 2364, 2369
Dollarhide, Jim, 2311
Dolman, Bob (m), 2288
Donaldson, Gil, 1856
Donaldson, Roger (m), 2046
Donen, Joshua, 2185
Dong Kena (f), 230, 234, 243, 250, 253, 263, 267, 270,
    282, 287, 290
Dong, Pierre-Marie (m), 674
Donkers, Jan, 1369
Donner, Jörn (m), 408, 409, 410, 415, 1648
Donoghue, Mary Agnes (f), 2087, 2315, 2335
Donohue, Walter, 1817
Donovan, Arlene (f), 2038
Donovan, Martin, 2141
Doran, Lindsay (f), 1830, 2128
Doria, Enzo, 1155
Dormael, Jaco van, 566
Dormann, Geneviève (f), 763
Dörrie, Doris (f), 690, 811, 822
Dorst, Tankred, 752
Dostoevsky, Fyodor, 450
Douganov, Marat, 2394
Douglas, Michael, 1989
Doukas, Nikos, 880
Dowd, Nancy (f), 187, 2040
Downs, Clare (f), 1801
Doye, Jacqueline (f), 479
Doyle, Carol (f), 2228, 2335
Doyle, Chris, 920
Doyle, Christopher, 298, 1671
Doyle, Roddy, 1824
Drabble, Margaret (f), 1761
Drabo, Adama (m), 1323
Drach, Michel (m), 4
Dragan Vasile, Vivi, 1505
Dragusin, Adrian, 1507
Drakoularakos, Yannis, 891
Draper, Robert, 2187
Drawe, Hans, 754
Dresen, Andreas (m), 703
Dressel, Roland, 695, 733
Dreujou, Jean-Marie, 594
Dreyer, Carl, 354, 364
Driver, Sara (f), 2063
Drouot, Pierre, 108
Drummond, Randy, 2282
Druout, Pierre, 482, 485
Druyan, Ann (f), 2222

Dryburgh, Stuart, 71, 1392, 1397, 1836, 2274
Du Pré, Hilary, 1852
Duarte de Carvalho, Ruy, 23
Dubey, Satyadev, 991
Dubini, Donatello, 1668
Dubini, Fosco, 1668
Dubroux, Danièle (f), 547
Dufaux, Georges, 173, 189, 200
Dufaux, Guy, 1819
Duff, Alan, 1397
Dufour, Lorraine (f), 216
Dufresne, Michel, 519
Dugowson, Martine (f), 580, 614
Dulat, Isabekov, 1281
Duletic, Vojko (m), 2412
Dumas, Alexandre, 572
Dumayet, Pierre, 456
Dumoulin, Marianne (f), 659
Duncan, Digby, 52
Duncan, Isadora (f), 1761
Dunn, Andrew, 1806
Dunn, Nell (f), 1760, 1790
Dunne, Dominique, 1934
Dunne, John Gregory, 1934
Dunne, Lee, 1106
Dunye, Cheryl (f), 2192, 2284
DuParc, Henri (m), 1210, 1213, 1214
DuParc, Henriette (f), 1214
Dupeyron, François, 603
Dupont, Renelde, 112
Dupouey, Pierre, 588
Dupuis-Mendel, Philippe, 637
Duque, Monino, 1447
Durai (m), 980
Duran, Carlos, 1545
Durán, Jorge, 137
Durant, Alberto (m), 1420, 1421
Duras, Marguerite (f), 461, 463, 467, 480, 500, 531,
    1757
Duru, Süreyya (f), 1715
Dürrenmatt, Friedrich, 740, 1529
Dusart, Philippe, 438, 439
Dutt, Anjan, 1028
Duval, Claire (f), 474
Duvignaud, Jean, 6
Düwel, Dirk, 678
Duy, Tien-hanem (m), 2409
Dwyer, Finola, 1877
Dylewska, Jolanta, 706
Dymek, Janusz, 1460

Eastman, Carole (f), 1920
Eastwood, Clint (m), 2343
Ebersole, P. David, 2280
Ebert, Roger, 1915

Ecaré, Désiré (m), 1212
Echeverría-Torres, Jacobo, 1628
Edson, Margaret (f), 2286
Edwards, Eric Alan, 2190
Edwards, George, 1928
Egelson, Jan (m), 2273
Egoyan, Atom (m), 212
Eguino, Antonio, 132
Ehler, Ursula (f), 752
Ehrenberg, Miguel, 1327
Ehrhardt, Bo, 373
Ehrmann, Käte (f), 705
Eichhammer, Klaus, 804, 845
Eichinger, Bernd, 709
Eisenstadt, Debra (f), 2289
Ekelund, Allan, 1638
El Cheikh, Said, 382
El Degheidy, Inas. *See* Al-Dighidi, Inas
El Fani, Nadia (f), 1704
El Hagar, Khaled, 404
El Khadem, Chirine, 2019
El-Khalek, Ali Abd (m), 398
El-Mahdi, Dia el-Deen, 377
El-Sabban, Rafiq, 403
El-Sebai, Medhat, 394
El-Tayeb, Fatina (f), 691
El Telmessani, Tarek, 390, 394
El-Zurhani, Ali, 378
Elbaum, Diana, 608
Elder, Lonne, 1993
Eldin Wahba, Saad, 377, 380, 382
Elek, Judit (f), 929, 946
Elfand, Martin, 2002
Eliacheff, Caroline (f), 575, 623
Elizalde, Julian, 1624
Elkabetz, Ronit (f), 1141
Elkabetz, Shlomi (m), 1141
Ellefsen, Tove, 1652
Elliot, Grace (f), 629
Elliot, Paul, 68
Elliott, Scott (m), 2248
Ellis, Alice Thomas (f), 1820
Ellis, Bob, 56
Ellsen, Isabel, 2298
Elmer, Jonas (m), 369
Elswit, Robert, 2007, 2044, 2142, 2151
Emigholz, Heinz, 2022
Emil, Anna (f), 1743
Enders, Robert, 1775
Engin, Erdogan, 1719, 1726, 1729
English, Rose, 1782
Enright, Nick, 2144
Entius, Yolanda (f), 1370
Enyedi, Ildikó (f), 949
Enzenberger, Marianne (f), 813, 829

Ephron, Delia (f), 2148, 2259
Ephron, Nora (f), 2028, 2056, 2148, 2259
Erabaci, Metin, 1735
Erdöss, Pal (m), 941, 953
Erenrz, Kaya, 1714
Ergas, Moris, 1142, 1152
Ergun, Cengiz, 1727, 1730
Erichsen, Bente, 1407, 1409, 1412
Ericson, Rune, 1640, 1643, 1654
Eriksen, Gordon (f), 2209
Erkomaishvili, Nugzar, 2376, 2379, 2381, 2386
Erksan, Metin, 1707, 1709
Erlichman, Martin, 1977
Erman, Hürrem, 1710
Erman, John (m), 2118
Ernotte, André, 114
Escamilla, Teodoro, 1547, 1556, 1563, 1569
Escoffier, Jean-Yves, 2205, 2264
Escorel, Lauro, 136, 139
Escriva, Amalia (f), 630
Esparze, Moctesuma, 2227
Espinosa, Pedro, 31
Estébanez, Natacha (f), 2273
Eszterhas, Joe, 2102, 2139
Etchegaray, Françoise (f), 601, 629
Etcherelli, Claire (f), 4
Etienne, Anne-Marie (f), 104, 545
Etxebarría, Lucía (f), 1605
Èuøik, Jan, 349
Euripides, 364, 850, 851, 871, 1156, 1342
Evans, Stephen, 1848
Ewart, William, 2126
Export, Valie (f), 87, 88, 91, 759
Extan, Clive (f), 1761
Eyde, Marianne (f), 1422
Eyre, Richard (m), 1786, 1871
Ezouz, Sari, 1140

Faber, George, 1815, 1878
Faber-Jansen, Maya, 91, 767
Fabre, Jean-Marc, 619, 658
Fabry, Patrick, 1525, 1527
Fadel, Youssef, 1355
Fahmy, Mahmoud, 379
Fakhimi, Mehrdad, 1077
Fakhimzadeh, Mehdi (m), 1079
Falconi, Diego, 405
Faldbakken, Knut, 1409
Fanger, Elisabeth (f), 667
Faragó, Katinka (f), 417
Färberböck, Max (m), 697
Farenc, Laurence, 653
Farès, Nadia (f), 1699
Fargeau, Jean-Pol, 530, 586
Fargnoli, Marco, 2265

Farid, Wahid, 378
Farida, Ida (f), 1060
Färm, Heikki, 418
Farrell, Henry, 1928
Fasano, Frederic, 1204
Fash, Mike, 2083
Fassbinder, Rainer Werner (m), 751, 753, 755, 756, 757, 758, 762, 772, 785, 802
Fatkhulin, Dilshat, 2354
Faucher, Éléonore (f), 670
Faucon, Philippe (m), 626
Faulk, Matthew, 1885
Favrat, François, 651, 657
Faye, Safi (f), 1525, 1527, 1531
Fayolle, Lise, 469
Fei Xiaoping, 316
Feindt, Johann, 821
Feitshans, Buzz, 1951, 1954
Fejerman, Daniela (f), 1614, 1632
Fellini, Federico, 1150
Fellner, Eric, 1811
Fellous, Maurice, 456
Femenia, Paco, 1589, 1619
Feng Yiting, 291
Fengler, Michael, 772
Féret, René, 549
Ferguson, Christina (f), 68
Ferhati, Jilalli (f), 1350
Fernández, Angel Luis, 1558, 1580
Fernández, Catalina (f), 46
Fernandez Cubas, Cristina (f), 1571
Fernández, Evelina (f), 2263
Fernández, Julio, 1591
Fernández Unsáin, José María, 1325
Fernández Violante, Marcela (f), 1332, 1344
Fernández-Berridi, Gonzalo, 1605, 1621
Fernández-Cid, Jaime, 1545
Ferragut, Jean-Noël, 506, 540
Ferrari, Marcio, 150
Ferrari, Paolo, 1205
Ferreira, Patricia (f), 1614
Ferrer, Mel, 1904
Ferreri, Marco, 1173, 1178
Ferris, Beth, 1776
Ferris, Kostas, 869, 874
Ferris, Michael, 2170, 2337
Ferry, Jean, 108
Fetin, Vladimir (m), 2360
Fetoux, Jean-Bernard, 559
Fey Zhao, 284
Fiedler, John, 2132
Field, David, 2250
Field, Sally (f), 2325
Field, Ted, 2077
Fielding, Helen (f), 2274

Fields, Adam, 2239
Fields, Freddie, 1972, 1982, 2054
Fierberg, Andrew, 2312
Fierberg, Steven, 2039, 2312
Fieschi, Jacques, 582, 624, 658
Figueras, Ricard, 1601
Fikru, Nikodimos (m), 407
Filac, Vilko, 607
Filiatrault, Denise (f), 210, 218
Filippova, Nina (f), 1279
Finder, Joseph, 2299
Fine, Billy, 2014
Fine, Russell Lee, 2204
Fink, Margaret (f), 49
Finkiel, Emmanuel (m), 617
Finlayson, Tom, 1388
Finnegan, Bill, 2033
Firth, Michael, 1390
Firth, Tim, 1881
Fischer, Erica (f), 697
Fischer, Jens, 1656
Fishel, Deirdre (f), 2166
Fisher, Carrie (f), 2114
Fisher, Gerry, 511, 1771
Fisk, Jack (m), 1780
Fitch, Janet, 2315
Fitzgerald, Kitty (f), 1814
Fitzpatrick, Peter, 73
Flagg, Fannie (f), 2125
Flannery, Lucy (f), 1840
Flaubert, Gustave, 551, 2393
Flickinger, Lindsay, 2295
Flomenbaum, Sandra, 38
Flores Silva, Beatriz (f), 2350
Fogiel, Yael, 617, 673
Foner, Naomi (f), 2151, 2180
Fong, Eddie, 77, 904
Fong, Mona (f), 901
Fontaine, Anne (f), 558, 658
Fontaine, Stéphane, 671
Fontane, Theodor, 758, 764
Fonteyne, Frédéric, 609
Forbes, Bryan (m), 1748, 1753, 1763
Forbet, Katia (f), 767
Ford, John (m), 1900
Ford, Tracy, 2311
Foreman, John, 1920
Forgash, Adam, 2276
Fornet, Ambrosio, 333
Forsberg, Tony, 1649
Forslund, Bengt, 1646
Forstater, Mark, 1651
Forster, E. M., 1789, 1795
Forster, John, 2031
Forster, Marc (m), 2276

Forsyth, Bill (m), 2073
Forsythe, Kelly (m), 2193
Forte, Kate (f), 2230
Forte, Theirry, 345
Fortunato, Ron, 1844
Forza, Roberto, 1193
Foskolos, Nikos, 873
Fossis, Nikos, 862
Foster, Jodie (f), 2129
Foster, Stan, 2348
Fouad, Sekiena, 384
Fournier, Crystel (f), 672
Fox, Beryl (f), 185
Fox, Robert, 1871, 2300
Fraisse, Robert, 520, 620
Fraker, William, 1909, 1982, 1991, 2067
Frame, Janet (f), 1392
Francia, Luisa (f), 771, 782
Francis, Freddie, 1745, 2100
Franco, Jesus, 1664
Franco, Ricardo, 1596
François, Anne (f), 578
Franju, Georges (m), 433
Frank, Christopher, 520
Frank, Harriet, Jr., 1997
Frank, Hubert, 797
Frank, Laurie (f), 2076, 2130
Frank, Scott, 2129
Frankel, Cyril, 676
Frankenberg, Pia (f), 699
Franklin, Carl, 2233, 2299
Franklin, J. E., 1939
Franklin, Richard (m), 73
Frappier, Roger, 190, 209, 215
Fraser, Angus, 206
Fraser, Julia (f), 2
Frateur, Didier, 130
Frazee, David, 217, 2158
Frears, Stephen (m), 1824
Freedman, Robert, 2285
Freeman, Joan (f), 2039
Freud, Esther (f), 1857
Freyd, Denis, 625
Friedel, Christoph, 706
Friedes, Jennifer, 2340
Friedman, Elyse (f), 217
Friedman, Ken, 2024
Friel, Brian, 1119
Frizzell, John, 197
Frölich, Pea, 772
Frydman, Marc, 2258
Frye, William, 1902
Fryer, Robert, 1764
Fu Jie, 235
Fu Jing Sheng, 265

Fu Xuwen, 275
Fuentes-Berain, Marcela (f), 1627
Fuhrer, Martin, 1798
Fuji, Hiroaki, 1246
Fujimoto, Sanezumi, 1223, 1234
Fujimoto, Tak, 1947, 1992, 2024, 2040, 2093, 2117, 2230
Fukang, Ying, 295
Fukunaga, Takehiko, 1262
Fuller, Diana (f), 48
Fuller, Sam (m), 1896, 2013
Furia, John, 1976
Furie, Sidney J. (m), 1932, 1967, 2008
Furst, Sean, 2276
Fustier-Dahan, Agnès (f), 666

Gábor, Pál (m), 938
Gabrilovich, Yevgeni, 2373
Gade, Nadia (f), 386
Gaffney, Sheila (f), 2214
Gaggero, Jorge, 44
Gagliardi, Laurent, 200
Gagnier, Jacques, 182
Gagnon, André, 201
Gagnon, Claude, 1243
Gaines, Ernest J., 1938
Gainville, René, 2194
Gaitskill, Mary (f), 2312
Galanos, Alekos, 853
Gale, Ricardo Jacques, 1314
Galgócsi, Ersébet (f), 942
Gallagher, Ronan, 1121
Galvin, Brendan, 2335
Ganatra, Nisha (f), 2255
Gandhy, Behroze, 1834
Ganguly, Anil, 987
Gannon, Ben, 63
Ganz, Lowell, 2143
Garay, Aldo, 2351
García de Leániz, Santiago, 1630
Garcia Del Vall, Arnoldo, 1562
Garcia Espinosa, Julio, 331
Garcia, Esther (f), 220, 1587
Garcia Guevara, Mercedes (f), 37
Garcia Joya, Mario, 336, 338, 1420, 1421
Garcia Lorca, Federico, 1570, 1607
Garcia, Luis, 331
García Márquez, Gabriel, 1182, 1329
Garcia, Nicole (f), 545, 624
Garcia, Rodrigo, 1334, 1335, 2164, 2267
Garcia Serrano, Yolanda (f), 1597
Garciadiego, Paz Alicia (f), 1339, 1340, 1342, 1343
Gardel, Louis, 550
Gardelis, Nikos, 853, 857
Gardos, Eva (f), 2272

Garland, Patrick (m), 1771
Garner, Chip, 2209
Garner, Helen (f), 65
Gary, Romain, 1755, 2013
Gasquet, Nicole, 773
Gasser, Yves, 493, 1665
Gassor, Charles, 647
Gasull, Jordi, 1618
Gatti, Marcello, 1148
Gaty, Andrew, 2092
Gauer, Janusz, 1469
Gautier, Eric, 570, 1866
Gautier, Théophile, 1151
Gavala, Maria (f), 877
Gavron, Laurence (f), 91
Gay, Piergiorgio (m), 1195
Gaztambide, Michel, 1577
Ge Gengtana (m), 241
Gearing, Nigel, 1109
Geater, Sara (f), 1800
Gefter, Marina (f), 2294
Gégauff, Paul, 421, 447
Geick, Eberhard, 729
Geiger-Berlet, Uta (f), 784
Geilfus, Frederic, 105
Geissbuhler, Luke, 2316
Geissendörfer, Hans W., 749, 815
Geisslen, Dieter, 783
Gené, Juan Carlos, 25
Genée, Heidi (f), 748, 764
Genée, Peter, 752
Genet, Jean, 1757
Génovès, André, 447, 448, 449
Gentil, Dominique, 896, 897, 1532, 1534
George, K. G. (m), 1003
George, Terry (m), 1118
Georgiades, Vassilas (m), 853
Georgiou, Christos (m), 894
Gerardi, Roberto, 1151
Gerede, Canan (f), 1736
Gerima, Haile (m), 847, 1969
Gerinska, Vesselina (f), 158
Géronimi, Jérôme, 424
Getchell, Robert, 1946, 2051, 2118, 2159
Ghafori, Ebrahim, 2, 1097
Ghalem, Ali, 11
Ghali, Fayez, 390
Ghanem, Ali. *See* Ghalem, Ali
Ghatak, Ritwik (m), 964
Gheerbrant, Denis, 843
Ghibu, Calin, 1509
Gholizadeh, Hassan, 1075
Ghorab-Volta, Zaïda (f), 581, 602, 638
Ghose, Goutam (m), 1020, 1055
Ghosh, Nabendu, 966

Ghosh, Rituparno, 1034
Gialamas, Asimakis, 855
Giannoli, Xavier, 655
Gibb, Andrea (f), 1882
Gibbon, Sharon (f), 207
Gibson, Brian, 2155
Gibson, Sarah (f), 52
Gibson, Sue (f), 1843
Gibson, William, 1893
Gieck, Eberhard, 827
Giedroyc, Corky (f), 1858
Gies, Christoph, 823
Gil, Edgar, 1617
Gil, Edmundo, 1589
Gil, Margarida (f), 1488, 1489, 1493, 1498
Gil, Xavier, 1610, 1611, 1618
Gilaizeau, Claude, 168
Gilbert, Brian (m), 2133
Gilbert, Bruce, 1999, 2058
Gilbert, Lewis (m), 1785, 1810
Giles, Philippa (f), 1808
Gill, François, 177
Gill, Pierre, 218
Gilliat, Penelope, 187
Gilroy, Tony, 2174
Giltay, Goert, 1373
Gimeno, Alphonso, 428
Ginzburg, Valeri, 2358
Giorgi, Francesco, 1171
Giovanni, Marita (f), 2170
Giovannini, Giuseppe, 1190
Giraudoux, Jean, 1763
Girod, Francis (m), 496
Gitai, Amos (m), 1136
Giurato, Blasco, 1200
Glasberg, Jimmy, 641
Glatter, Leslie Linka (f), 2183
Gleason, Michie (f), 2006, 2082
Glenaan, Kenneth, 1887
Glenn, Pierre-William, 652
Glennon, James, 2026, 2197
Glimcher, Arne, 2090
Globus, Menahem, 2080
Globus, Yoram, 1176
Glowna, Vidim, 684
Gluscevic, Maja (f), 325
Gobel, Michael, 811
Godard, Agnès (f), 586, 605, 613, 640, 656, 665
Godard, Jean-Luc, 426, 434, 437, 439, 444, 472
Goded, Ángel, 1330
Godmilow, Jill (f), 2064
Godoy, Coral (f), 2351
Goeffers, André, 106
Gogoberidze, Lana (f), 675, 2370, 2376, 2379, 2381, 2386

Goh Hak Rim (m), 1287
Goikoetxea, Gonzalo, 1560
Gojawiczyñska, Pola (f), 1469
Golan, Menahem, 1125, 1176
Goldbacher, Sandra (f), 1851, 1877
Goldberg, Leonard, 2136, 2241
Golde, Gert, 721
Goldenberg, Billy, 1976
Goldenberg, Jorge, 30, 34
Goldin, Marilyn (f), 529, 1880
Goldman, Bo, 1998, 2040
Goldman, Marianne (f), 366
Goldschmidt, Gilbert de, 427
Goldsman, Akiva, 2159
Goldsmith, John, 1863
Goldsmith, Olivia, 2202
Goldstein, Gary, 2088
Goldstone, John, 1767
Goldwyn, Samuel, Jr., 2118
Golin, Steve, 1836, 2264
Gomes, Flora (f), 896, 897, 1502
Gómez, Andres, 1574, 1578, 1593, 1609, 1620, 1623, 1629
Gómez Urquisa, Manuel, 1326
Gómez Urquisa, Zacarias (m), 1326
Gómez Yera, Sara (f), 331
Gomez-Olea, Antonio, 1562
Gonzalez, Luis, 323
Gonzalez, Marina Feleo (f), 1425
Gonzalez-Sinde, Angeles, 39
Goodman, Brenda (f), 2150
Goodwin, Richard, 1789
Gope, Shankar (m), 1030
Gordon, Bette (f), 91, 2031
Gordon, Rafael, 1613
Gordy, Berry (m), 1965
Gore, Bertrand, 622, 1706
Gören, Serif (m), 1719, 1728
Goretta, Claude (m), 481
Gorey, Lakshman, 977
Gori, Rita Cecchi (f), 1201
Gorky, Maxim, 2380
Gorlov, Boris, 2392
Gornick, Lisa (f), 1876
Gorris, Marleen (f), 1361, 1366, 1377, 1843
Goswami, Goutam, 1028
Gould, Lois (f), 1926
Goupil, Sophie (f), 546
Gouze-Rénal, Christine (f), 429
Gowdy, Barbara (f), 206
Gozon, Francisco, 2350
Gozu, Naoe, 1263
Grace, Anna (f), 2204
Graczyk, Ed, 2015
Graf, Dominik (m), 711, 845

Graf, Roland, 722
Graff, Todd, 2156
Graham, Bob (m), 2007
Granderath, Christian, 703
Grandio, Paula (f), 38
Granier-Deferre, Pierre (m), 468, 520
Granillo, Guillermo, 1340, 1342, 1343
Grant, Jaems, 85
Grant, Susannah (f), 2242, 2253
Grasian, Dolores (f), 482
Grau, Jorge, 1557
Graver, Gary, 324
Gravouil, Denis, 1354
Gray, F. Gary (m), 2216
Gray, James, 209
Gray, Pamela (f), 2249
Gray, Ronald K., 2149
Gray, Valerie (f), 207
Grean, Wendy (f), 2285
Greatrex, Richard, 2270, 2302, 2339
Greatrex, Stephen, 1842
Green, Jack, 2130, 2244
Green, Janet (f), 1900
Green, Sarah (f), 2147
Greenberg, Adam, 1125, 1126
Greenberg, Robbie, 2051, 2340
Greene, Callum, 2297
Greene, Gael, 187
Greenfield, Matthew, 2296
Greenhut, Robert, 2086
Greenberg, Joanne (f), 1979
Greenwald, Maggie (f), 2150, 2283, 2285
Greicius, Ramunas, 348
Greisman, Alan, 2059
Gren, Roman, 208
Grey, Donna, 1782
Griebe, Frank, 698, 1374, 1379
Griffith, Robert, 2153
Grignon, Marcel, 423
Grigor, Barbara, 1816
Grigoriou, Grigoris, 856
Grishman, John, 2159
Grison, Geoffroy, 1138
Grohmann, Martje (f), 782
Grosbard, Ula (m), 2176
Grossman, Vasili, 2358
Groupe de jeunes cinéastes, 1104
Gruault, Jean, 445, 471
Grunstein, Pierre, 579, 593
Grunwald, Anatole de, 1747
Grunwalsky, Ferenc, 934, 955
Gruszynski, Alexander, 359, 2178, 2319
Gschlacht, Martin, 97, 100
Gu Changwei, 259
Guan Hu, 320

Guang Yu, 276
Guangron Zhou, 320
Guard, Candy (f), 1815
Guarnieri, Ennio, 495, 1156, 1159, 1163, 1165, 1173, 1202
Guarnieri, Gianfrancesco, 139
Guay, Richard, 2104, 2124, 2152, 2229
Guédiguian, Robert (m), 584
Guérin, Jean-Pierre, 645
Guerra, José, 42
Guerra, Ruy (m), 1324, 1329
Guerra, Tonino, 1143, 1147, 1182
Guerrica, Jorge, 1609
Guerricaechevarria, Jorge, 1620
Guézel, Yvon, 477
Gugliotta, Sandra (f), 42
Guidone, Marco, 1199
Guidt, Geuorgui, 2385
Guilford, Allen, 1389, 1393
Guillaume, Pierre-Erwan, 608
Guilleaume, Alain, 114
Guillen, Laurice (f), 1430, 1436, 1450, 1452
Guimarães, Ana Luisa (f), 1492
Gulea, Stere, 1511
Gulzar (m), 983, 986, 996, 1001, 1007, 1021, 1038
Gulzar, Meghna (f), 1053
Gulzoy, Umit, 1722
Gundelach, Renée (f), 769, 778, 793, 801, 807, 818, 833, 836, 839
Gunn, Andrew, 2321
Gunnari, Gaute, 1415
Gunther, Egon (m), 723
Guðmundsson, Ágúst (m), 962
Gupta, Dinen, 964
Gupta, Tanika, 1834
Gurfinkel, David, 1124, 1129, 1131
Gurian, Paul, 2061
Gusi, Carles, 1591, 1630, 1631
Gusko, Erich, 723
Gusner, Iris (f), 727, 734
Gutiérrez Alea, Tomas (m), 331, 332, 336
Gutiérrez Aragon, Manuel, 1568, 1602
Gutiérrez, Chus (f), 1581, 1607
Gutowski Gene, 1756
Gyarmarthy, Livia (f), 952
Gye Yong-muk, 1297
Gyllenhaal, Stephen (m), 2151, 2180
Gyöngyössy, Imre, 824
Gyurkó, László, 932

Haak, Dörte (f), 812
Håan, Rolv, 1408
Hach, Heather (f), 2321
Hackford, Taylor (m), 2174
Hadar, Itamar, 1134

Haddad, Patrice, 592
Hagedorn, Jessica (f), 2162
Hagen, Ron, 72
Haggard, Piers (m), 1106
Haggis, Paul, 2343
Hahn, Rob, 2345
Hai Ning, 2405
Hakim, Raymond, 1761
Hakim, Robert, 421, 1761
Hakim, Shafi, 1017
Hale, John, 1768
Halioua, Sarah (f), 345, 1611
Hall, Conrad, 1912, 1956, 2068
Hall, Dolly (f), 635, 1684, 2231
Hall, Jennie (f), 1766
Hall, Peter, 1809
Halldórsdóttir, Guðný (f), 961
Hallström, Lasse (m), 2313
Hamano, Sachi (f), 1267, 1274
Hambly, Glenda (f), 55
Hami, Susumu (m), 1224
Hamid, Abdel, 379
Hamilton, Jane (f), 2248
Hamilton, Strathford (m), 1839
Hammon, Michael, 703
Hamos, Gusztav, 806
Hampton, Christopher, 775, 1771, 1828
Hampton, Orville, 1899
Hamza, Nadia (f), 386
Han Lanfang, 266
Han Sung-won, 1299
Hanák, Dusan (m), 353
Hanalis, Blanche (f), 1902
Handke, Peter (m), 769
Handschin, Jon, 715
Haneke, Michael (m), 95, 101
Hanff, Helen (f), 2053
Hani, Susumu (m), 1233
Hankey, Mark, 2279
Hanks, Tom (m), 2308
Hannan, Peter, 1794, 1802, 2133
Hansberry, Lorraine (f), 1890
Hänsel, Marion (f), 117, 121, 125, 130, 566, 1363
Hanson, Curtis (m), 2013, 2142
Hanson, John (m), 2052
Hardwick, Gary (m), 2319
Hardy, Jonathan, 1385
Hardy, Thomas, 1759
Hare, David, 1806, 2050, 2300
Hare, Ellin (f), 1814
Harlin, Renny (m), 2135, 2210
Harling, Robert, 2103, 2202
Harrington, Curtis (m), 1928
Harrison, George, 1784
Harrison, Harvey, 2105

Harron, Mary (f), 2206
Hart, John, 2238
Harten, Charles, 1888
Hartwig, Horst, 732
Harvey, Anthony (m), 1778
Harvey, Gary, 207
Harwood, Ronald, 221
Has, Wojciech J. (m), 1454
Hasebe, Keiji, 1225, 1226, 1247
Hasegawa, Kyoshi, 1254
Hasfari, Shmuel (m), 1131
Hassapis, Stavros, 869, 876, 884
Hassid, Daniel, 2251
Hatta, Kayo (f), 2184
Hattori, Yoshi, 1250
Hauser, Robert, 1993
Hauser, Thomas, 2010
Hausman, Michael, 2028
Hausner, Jessica (f), 100
Haviv, Yuri, 1980
Hawthorne, Nathaniel, 752
Hayashi, Fumiko (f), 1223
Haydu, Jorge, 342
Hayek, Salma (f), 2295
Hayes, John Michael (m), 1750, 1888, 1892
Hayes, Raphael, 1899
Haynes, Todd (m), 2186, 2293
Hayward, Kevin, 1385
Hazarika, Bhupen, 1021
He Guopu, 300
He Mengtan, 278
He Qin, 255
He Yijie, 258
Head, Murray, 607
Héberlé, Antoine, 600, 610, 636
Hébert, Anne (f), 179
Hébert, Julie (f), 2201
Heche, Anne (f), 2260
Hecht, Marlen, 2257
Hedges, Peter (m), 2248, 2330
Hedmann, Trine, 356
Heer, Johanna (f), 825
Heffernan, Terence, 186
Heffner, Avraham (m), 1129
Hegyes, Stephen, 202
Heidish, Marcy (f), 1993
Heiduschka, Veit, 95, 686
Heiland, Udo, 835
Heinl, Bernd, 830
Heinz, Carl, 863
Hekmat, Manijeh (f), 1100
Held, Wolfgang, 736
Helf, Gerald, 96
Helgar, Anne Marie (f), 361
Hellberg, Martin (m), 719

Heller, Leon, 2007
Heller, Lukas, 1907
Hellinckx, Lieve, 128
Hellman, Lillian (f), 1892, 1981
Hellstenius, Axel, 1414
Helman, Geoffrey (m), 2053
Hencz, Stefan, 1655
Hengge, Paul, 837
Henley, Beth (f), 2054, 2060
Henning-Jensen, Astrid (f), 358
Henriques, Julian (m), 1864
Henry, Buck, 2190
Herd, Kelli (f), 2224
Herholdt, Nick, 1541
Herman, Mark (m), 1853
Herman-Wurmfeld, Charles (m), 2161, 2303, 2325
Hernádi, Gyula (f), 932, 934, 936, 940
Hernández, Humberto, 334, 336, 338, 343
Hernandez, Miguel, 1615
Herrera, Jorge, 328, 329
Herrero, Gerardo, 1611
Herron, Jonathan, 2297
Hershman Leeson, Lynn (f), 1855, 2333
Herzberg, Judith (f), 1357, 1358
Herzer, Sandra Mara (f), 145
Hesse, Jan, 1455
Hewett, Dorothy (f), 48
Hewlett, Jamie, 2189
Heyman, Norma (f), 1820, 1823
Heyns, Katinka (f), 1538, 1542
Hibbin, Sally (f), 1822, 1887
Hickey, Kieran (m), 1110
Hicks, James, 2058
Hidaka, Shinya, 1254, 1256
Hidari, Sachiko (f), 1248
Higashi, Yoichi (m), 1252, 1255
Higgins, Colin (m), 1999
Highsmith, Patricia (f), 815
Higson, Frances (f), 1123
Hilal, Mohaned Hilmi, 400
Hild, Michael, 845
Hildyard, Jack, 1758
Hill, Arthur (m), 2077
Hill, George Roy (m), 2035
Hill, Jack (m), 1941, 1951
Hill, Matt, 2320
Hill, Walter, 1994
Hillenius, Brigit (f), 1418
Himeda, Shinsaku, 1225, 1226, 1240
Hinsch, Jørgen, 361
Hinzman, Bill, 1935
Hirayama, Hideyoshi, 1266
Hiriart, Hugo, 1337
Hirosawa, Ei, 1245
Hirschbiegel, Oliver (m), 714

Hirschfeld, Gerald, 1918, 1943
Hirst, Michael, 1850
Hirszman, Leon (m), 139
Hishigaki, Rokuro, 1234
Hjulström, Lennart, 1653
Ho, Leonard, 913
Ho Nan-hung, 1689
Ho, Nguyen, 2407
Hobby, Amy (f), 2312
Hocevar, Zoran, 1536
Hocking, Jenny (f), 59
Hoermann, Guenter, 744
Höfer, Andreas, 704, 715
Hofer, Arthur, 704
Hoffer, William, 2133
Hoffman, Laura (f), 2170
Hofman, Henner, 1600, 1615
Hogan, David Glenn, 2171
Hogan, P. J. (m), 74
Holch, Christoph, 773
Holdaway, Jim, 1758
Holder, Mary, 197
Holding, Elisabeth Sanxay, 2275
Holender, Adam, 1920, 1930, 2235
Holland, Agnieszka (f), 208, 554, 567, 810, 836, 837, 1463, 2066, 2228
Holmberg, Kaj, 416
Holmberg, Sten, 1653
Holofcener, Nicole (f), 2219, 2305
Hölscher, Heinz, 676
Holst, Per, 363, 368
Holt, Anne (f), 1414
Holt, Robert I., 1106
Holthius, Tinus, 1375
Homes, Amy Michael, 2332
Hondo, Med (m), 165
Honigmann, Heddy (f), 1376
Honkasalo, Pirjo, 410, 411
Hooas, Solrun (f), 62
Hoogesteijn, Solveig (f), 792, 2397, 2399
Hope, Ted, 2219, 2305
Hope, Tony, 902
Hopkins, Ben, 2302
Horak, Edwin, 563
Hormann, Sherry, 845
Hotchkis, Joan (f), 1963
Hou Hsiao-hsien (m), 1277, 1674, 1682, 1686, 1690
Houdyer, Paulette (f), 619
Houis, Shelly, 2104
Houppin, Serge, 563
House, Lynda (f), 74
Houssiau, Michel (m), 116
Hovmand, Annelise (f), 356
Howard, Elizabeth Jane, 1387
Howard, Vivienne (f), 1864

Howard-Carrington, Jane (f), 1904
Howitt, Peter, 1854
Hsiao Li-hung, 1678
Hsin Liang, 235
Hsu Hsiao-ming (m), 1683
Hsu Li-kong, 1689
Hu Huiying, 264
Hu Jian, 280
Hu Ke, 229
Hu Mei, 255
Huang Chunming, 1672
Huang, Jessie, 1683
Huang Jianzhong (m), 247, 311
Huang Shiying, 293
Huang Shuqing (f), 261, 289
Huang Yu Shan (f), 911
Huang Zongying, 245
Huber, Gerd, 690
Huber, Lotti (f), 829
Huete, Angélica, 1581
Huete, Christina (f), 1629
Hughes, Carol, 70
Hughes, David, 1639, 1640, 1643
Hughes, Todd, 2280
Hui, Ann (f), 902, 916, 918, 922, 925, 1681
Huillet, Danièle (f), 683, 745
Humberto Hermosillo, Jaime, 1327
Hume, Alan, 1791, 1810
Hun, Catherine, 918
Hung, Fran Anh (m), 2408
Hung Hung, 1687
Hunt, Judith, 1543
Hunter, Ross, 1750
Huntgeburth, Hermine (f), 679
Huppert, Caroline (f), 522
Hurault, Bertrand (m), 1648, 1655
Hussein, Waris (m), 1820
Huston, Anjelica (f), 1863, 2195
Huth, Hanno, 697
Huth, James (m), 604
Hwang Kyung Sang, 1301
Hyman, Myron, 2100

Ibanez, Adela (f), 1633
Ibarra, Epigmenio, 1627
Ibsen, Henrik, 757, 1078, 1771, 1772
Ibuse, Masuji, 1258
Ice Cube (m), 2234
Ichikawa, Kon (m), 1254, 1256
Ichiyama, Shozo, 1686
Ide, Masato, 1221
Ide, Toshiro, 1220, 1223
Ido, Akio, 1244
Idris, Yusef, 377
Idrizovic, Mirza (f), 2415

Idström, Tove (f), 419
Idziak, Slawomir, 567, 1456, 1476
Idziak, Wojciech, 1468
Iglesias, Roy C., 1451
Iino, Hisao, 1258
Ikbal, Musret, 1707
Ikin, Bridgit (f), 77, 1392
Ilagan, Bonifacio, 1439
Iliesiu, Sorin, 1506
Ilioú, Maria (f), 889, 891
Ilkin, Bridget (f), 1395
Ilyin, Vladimir, 2382
Im Kwon-taek (m), 1292, 1296, 1297, 1298, 1299, 1305
Imamura, Shohei (m), 1225, 1226, 1239, 1253, 1258
Imi, Tony, 697
Imperiale, Laura (f), 1342, 1343
Incalcaterra, Danièle, 581
Indira, M. K., 1002
Infascelli, Fiorella (f), 1184
Ioseliani, Otar (m), 537
Irby, Beverly (f), 2111
Irmas, Matthew (m), 1833
Irola, Judy (f), 2065
Irvin, John (m), 1826
Isa, Androws, 1103
Isaac, Tony, 1386
Isaacs, Susan (f), 2043
Isaka, Satoshi, 1268
Isaksson, Ulla (f), 1649
Ishido, Toshirô, 1218
Ishii, Isao, 1273
Ishii, Sogo (m), 1264
Isohata, Yukio, 1256
Isserman, Aline (f), 519
Itami, Juzo (m), 1257
Itô, Kazunori, 1271
Ito, Naokatsu, 1273
Ito, Takero, 1250
Ivanov, Anatoli, 2367
Ivanov, Stefan, 219, 226
Ivory, James (m), 972, 1783, 1787, 1795, 2278

Jablonski, Dariusz, 1486
Jacinto, Eduardo, 1440, 1443
Jackson, Pamm R. (f), 2062
Jackson, Peter (m), 1396
Jacobsen, Dagmar, 710
Jacobsen, Jürgen-Frantz, 368
Jacques, Catherine (f), 599
Jacquot, Benoît (m), 495, 582, 583, 667
Jaeuthe, Günter, 731
Jafa, Arthur, 2122
Jafarian, Hossein, 1085, 1095
Jaffe, Arthur, 2160

Jaffe, Herb, 1978
Jaffe, Michael, 1993
Jaffe, Robert, 1978
Jaffre, Mathilde, 608
Jago, Barbara, 2417
Jain, Prasann, 1032
Jamal, Anwar, 1056
James, Henry, 495, 1745, 1787, 1836, 1848, 2228, 2278
James, Peter, 2241
James, Terry, 1797
Jancsó, Nyika, 944, 948, 950, 954, 959
Janda, Krystyna (f), 1480
Jang Jun-yeong, 1308
Janger, Lane, 2178
Jankura, Péter, 957
Janne, Dominique, 129
Janni, Joseph, 1754, 1758, 1759, 1760
Jancsó, Miklós, 932
Jancsó, Zoltan, 958
Jaoui, Agnès (f), 596, 671
Japrisot, Sébastien, 510
Jaquillard, Henri, 456
Jarmusch, Jim, 2063
Jarrot, Charles, 1768
Jawarski, Cezany, 2401
Jayalath, Karunasena, 1635
Jean, Raymond, 531
Jebali, Taoufik, 1695
Jee, Sang-hak, 1294
Jeffs, Christine (f), 1883
Jelinek, Elfriede (f), 95
Jénart, Corinne, 113
Jenkins, Patty (f), 2329
Jennings, Christina (f), 1819, 1831
Jensen, Anders Thomas, 374
Jensen, Johnny, 2135, 2140, 2156
Jensen, Peter, 367, 370
Jeon Il-seong, 1292
Jeong Do-hwan, 1298
Jeong Jae-eun (f), 1307
Jeong, Woong-ki, 1293
Jeshel, Jörg, 781
Jett, Sue (f), 2099
Jeturian, Jeffrey (m), 1448
Jeunet, Jean-Pierre (m), 628
Jewison, Norman (m), 2041
Jeyrani, Fereydun, 1076, 1088
Jha, Prakash (m), 1042
Jhabvala, Ruth Prawer (f), 972, 1783, 1787, 1795, 2278
Ji Sang-hak, 1301
Jiang Sheng, 253
Jiang Shensheng, 248
Jie Chen (f), 318
Jiminez, Mary (f), 116, 1419

Jin Seong-man, 1296
Jin Zhonqiang, 320
Jin Zuoxin, 276
Jindal, Suresh, 981
Jo Moon-jin, 1291
Joaquin, Agapito, 1445
Jobin, Daniel, 210
Jodrell, Steve (m), 58
Joffe, Rowan, 1868
Johannesdóttir, Kristín (f), 960
Johansson, Jürgen, 373
Johnson, David, 1852
Johnson, Lamont (m), 1972
Johnson, Liza (f), 701
Johnson, Mark, 2288
Johnston, Heather (f), 2209
Johnston, William, 192
Jolley, Elizabeth, 78
Jones, Amy Holden (f), 2025, 2094, 2215
Jones, Damian, 1873
Jones, David (m), 2053
Jones, Eileen (f), 1855
Jones, Evan, 1758
Jones, Laura (f), 57, 78, 1392, 1836
Jones, Laurie (f), 2111
Jones, Quincy, 2042
Jong, Ate de, 1380
Jönsson, Lars, 1662
Jordá, Joaquín (m), 1591
Jordan, Glenn, 2011
Jordan, Jack, 1644
Jordan, Neil (m), 1788
Joshi, Rajesh, 1023
Josselin, Jean-Francois, 594
Josson, Suma (f), 1043
Jouma, Mustapha, 388
Jovanoska, Vesna, 1879
Judat, Farzad, 1099
Juergensen, Heather (f), 2303
Julaj, Ondrej, 353
Julien, Isaac (m), 1799
Julien, Max, 1940
Jun Jo-myung, 1291
Jung Il-sung, 1297, 1305
Jungmann, Recha (f), 780
Junkersdorf, Eberhard, 687, 800, 1187
Jur, Jeff, 2232, 2308
Jurácek, Pavel, 351
Jürges, Jürgen, 101, 700, 753, 779, 808, 814, 1531, 1736
Juric-Tilic, Ankica (f), 325, 327
Jurriën, Rood, 1356
Juson, Galliano, 1206
Jutra, Claude (m), 179, 185
Jutzeler, Denis, 1667
Kabay, Barna, 824

Kabitzke, Siegfried, 726
Kacíková, Eva (f), 347
Kacou, N-Gouan, 1211
Kaczmarek, Zdzislaw, 1458
Kafka, Franz, 222
Kahan, Marcy (f), 1815
Kahiry, W., 378
Kahn, Cedric, 555
Kahraman, Erdal, 1728, 1731
Kalari, Mahmoud, 1078, 1083, 1084, 1088, 1096
Kalashinikov, Leonid, 2380
Kalem, Toni (f), 2344
Kalicinski, Janusz, 1460
Kälin, Matthias, 167, 1529, 1668, 1670
Källberg, Per, 961
Kálman, Ferenc, 1358
Kam Kwok-leung, 920
Kamarullah, George, 1068
Kambauis, Nikos, 864
Kamenka, Sacha, 436
Kaminski, Janusz, 2177
Kaminski, Zbigniew (m), 1458, 1465
Kamoto, Tetsuya, 1269
Kamwa, Daniel (m), 171
Kan Gotanda, Philip, 2097
Kane, Bob, 2337
Kane, Mary (f), 2260
Kane, Robert G., 1895
Kaneo, Mitsuji, 1245
Kanew, Jeff (m), 2138
Kang Hye-yun, 1305
Kang Liwen, 255
Kaplan, Jonathan (m), 2024, 2085, 2145, 2239
Kaplan, Nelly (f), 451, 457, 477
Kaplan, Susan (f), 2249
Kaplun, Arik (m), 1135
Kapoor, Pradeep, 1004
Kapoor, Ranjit, 1031
Kapoor, Ravi, 1022
Kapoor, Shashi, 997, 1012
Kappen, Barbara (f), 809
Kapur, Shekhar (m), 1007, 1031, 1850
Karabuda, Günes, 1718
Karago, Njeri (f), 1286
Karakulor, Amir (m), 1282
Karall, Luca, 946
Karanth, Prema (f), 1002, 1040
Karayiannis, Kostos (m), 848, 864
Kardos, István, 941, 953, 957
Kardos, Sandor, 947
Karezi, Jenny (f), 866
Karim, Ala (m), 399
Karim, Baker, 1660
Karina, Anna (f), 462
Karjuk, Genadij, 1742

Karlsen, Elizabeth (f), 1853
Karmel, Pip (m), 83
Karmitz, Marin, 460, 527, 551, 567, 574, 575, 623, 1102
Karnad, Girish (m), 1012
Karpinski, Maciej, 1463
Karpov, Aleksandr, 2352
Karya, Teguh (m), 1066, 1068
Karyuk, Gennadi, 1743, 2361, 2365
Kasamatsu, Norimichi, 1264, 1272
Kasander, Kees, 1372
Kasaravalli, Girish (m), 993
Kashara, Ryozo, 1229
Kastelic, Boris, 1536
Kästner, Roland, 734
Katakouzinos, Yiorgas (m), 882
Katanyan, Vasili, 2356
Katritzidatis, Vangelis, 890
Katsouridis, Dinos, 849, 868
Katz, Pamela (f), 717, 718
Katz, Stephen, 2059
Katznelson, David, 1122
Kaufman, Boris, 1901, 1911
Kaufman, Philip (m), 2109, 2347
Kaufman, Rose (f), 2109
Kaufman, Sue, 1918
Kaufmann, Judith (f), 691
Kaukomaa, Tero, 418
Kaul, Mohan, 1022
Kaurismäki, Aki (m), 417
Käutner, Helmut, 739
Kavanaugh, Brian (m), 47
Kavoukidis, Nikos, 855, 862, 868
Kavur, Ömer (m), 1716
Kawalerowicz, Jerzy (m), 1453
Kawamata, Ko, 1218
Kawamata, Takashi, 1258
Kawashima, Yuzo, 1222
Kay, Karyn (f), 2070
Kay, Sandra (f), 2065
Kaygun, Sahin, 1726
Kaysen, Susan, 2244
Kazakos, Kostas, 866
Kazama, Shiori (f), 1273
Kazan, Nicholas, 2292
Kazarenskov, Alexander, 1515
Kaze, Shindô (f), 1270
Kazimierz, Brandys, 1454
Kazmierski, Stephen, 2212
Keaton, Diane (f), 2112, 2259
Keays-Byrne, Hugh (m), 68
Kedzierski, Grzegorz, 1271
Kedzierzawska, Dorota (f), 1475, 1483
Keigel, Léonard, 483
Kelber, Michel, 442

Kelemen, Fred (m), 693
Keller, Bernhard, 98
Kelljian, Bob (m), 1954
Kelly, Nancy (f), 2120
Kemper, Victor J., 1977
Kende, János, 928, 930, 932, 933, 936, 937
Kennedy, A. L., 1858
Kennedy, Anne (f), 84, 1395
Kennedy, Douglas, 1110
Kennedy, Kathleen (f), 2248
Kenny, Jan, 55
Kent, Nicolas, 1852
Kenway, John, 1821
Kerbasch, Roeland, 1360
Kermadec, Liliane de (f), 571
Kernochan, Sarah (f), 1807
Kerrigan, Lodge (m), 2256
Kershner, Irvin (m), 1937
Kerven, Claude, 2132
Keskiner, Abdurrahman, 1718
Keskiner, Arif, 1718
Kesselman, Wendy (f), 1823
Keytsman, Alain, 104
Khamraev, Ali (m), 2354, 2366
Khan, Mohamed (m), 388, 391
Khanna, Amit, 1039
Khin Maung U (m), 169
Khleifi, Michel, 1417
Khmelik, Mariya (f), 2389
Khondji, Darius, 1192
Khosa, Rajan (m), 1847
Khouri, Callie (f), 2137, 2291, 2313
Kiarostami, Abbas (m), 1102
Kibinge, Judy (f), 1286
Kidman, Nicole (f), 2323
Kidron, Beeban (f), 1808, 1815
Kieslowski, Krysztof (m), 567, 574, 1476
Kiesser, Jan, 2138, 2165, 2176
Kikushima, Ryuzo, 1217
Killough, James, 1029
Kilner, Claire (f), 2302
Kim, Anatoli, 2385
Kim Dae-u, 1303
Kim Jin-su (f), 1310
Kim Ki-duk, 1304
Kim Mi-hee, 1309
Kim Myong-joon, 1306
Kim Soo-yang, 1291
Kim Yeong-cheol, 1303
Kim Yeong-ho (m), 1288
Kimenye, Barbara, 1284
Kimmel, Anne (f), 2037
Kimmel, Imogen (f), 1879
Kinagi, Rajan, 999
Kindl, Mina (f), 537

Kindler, Walter, 90
King, Erin, 2255
King, I. Marlene (f), 2183, 2207
King, Jonathan, 2245
King, Stephen, 2174
Kinoshita, Keisuke (m), 1219, 1227
Kinyanjui, Wanjiru (f), 1284
Kiönig, Carl Jörgen (m), 1414
Kiral, Erden, 1720
Kirchhoff, Bodo, 714
Kirkov, Lyudmil (f), 159
Kishimoto, Masahiro, 1265
Kiss, Marian (f), 806
Kittredge, William, 1776
Klap, Hans, 1363
Klausmann, Rainer, 714
Klepikov, Yuri, 2357, 2363
Kleszczewska, Karina, 1535
Klier, Michael (m), 708
Klimenko, Youri, 2377
Klimov, Elem (m), 2378
Klopcic, Matjaz (m), 2413
Klosinski, Edward, 1457
Klotz, Nicolas, 669
Kluge, Alexander (m), 743, 744, 754
Klusák, Jan, 351
Knott, Frederick, 1904
Knouse, Robert, 2088
Knudsen, Mette (f), 355, 356
Ko Chiu-lam, 915
Ko Ko Htay, 169
Ko Shu-ching, 1685
Kobayashi, Setsuo, 1221, 1228, 1232, 1236, 1250
Koch, Douglas, 195, 205
Koch, Howard, 1919
Koch, Karin, 1699
Koch, Vladimir, 2411
Kodar, Oja (f), 324
Koenekamp, Fred, 1915
Koepp, David, 2141
Koerner von Gustorf, Florian, 696
Kofman, Teo (m), 31
Kohlhaase, Wolfgang, 704, 729
Kohon, David (m), 24
Koichumanov, Sapar, 1281
Koji, Kanaya, 1270
Koldauova, Ulzhan (f), 1281
Kollantai, Alexandra (f), 801
Kollek, Amos (m), 2034, 2072
Koltai, Lajos, 221, 931, 934, 935, 938, 941, 943
Kolvig, Lars, 360
Kon, Toko (m), 1216, 1249
Konchalovsky, Andrei (m), 2080, 2357, 2366
Kong Liang, 903
König, Ralf, 1624

König, Klaus, 775
Konner, Lawrence, 2328
Konrad, Cathy (f), 2197
Konstantinovsky, Carolina, 41
Kontelis, Panos, 856
Kontny, Truls, 1415
Konwicki, Tadeusz, 1453
Kopelson, Anne (f), 2347
Korch, Morten, 371
Kore-eda, Hirokazu (m), 1263, 1275
Korkala, Veikko, 412
Kórodi, Ildikó (f), 936, 937, 939
Korotkov, Yuri, 1516
Korshak, Harry, 1967
Korty, John (m), 1938
Kósa, Ferenc, 943
Kosari, Jahangir, 1085, 1092, 1095
Kosh, Yoav, 1130
Kosminsky, Peter (m), 2315
Kosugi, Masao, 1231
Kothari, Rajan, 1042, 1045, 1047
Kotlarski, François, 1284
Kotte, Gabriele, 727, 731
Koules, Stephanie (f), 2214
Koumantareas, Menis, 868
Kouyaté, Dani (m), 168
Kovács, László, 2016, 2047
Kovács, Zsolt Kézdi (m), 933
Kovácsi, János, 2350
Kovensky, Hugo, 148, 150
Koychumanov, Saparbek, 1279
Krabbé, Jeroen (m), 1380
Kramer, Larry, 1765
Kramer, Oscar, 34
Kramo-Lanciné, Fadika (m), 1211
Krasne, Philip, 1106
Krasner, Milton, 1894
Kratz, Käthe (f), 89, 90
Krause, Peter, 962
Krebs, Mario, 796
Kretzner, Tzvika, 1128
Kreuzhage, Andrea (m), 1600
Krim, Rachida (f), 18
Krishnakant (m), 994
Krishtofovich, Vyacheslav (m), 2387, 2395
Kristiansen, Henning, 362
Kristiansen, Terje, 1410
Kristov, Kristo (m), 161
Kromas, Vladimir, 59
Kropf, Yves, 1699
Krost, Barry, 2155
Krueger, Lisa (f), 2181, 2257
Krueger, Tom, 2181, 2257
Krumbachová, Ester (f), 350
Krumov, Alexander, 164

Krumov, Krum, 160
Kruschen, Francesca (f), 178
Ku Jung-mo, 1296, 1298, 1299
Kubo, Shinji, 1271
Kuc, Dariusz, 1478
Kucera, Stepan, 347
Kuchar, Mike, 801
Kuchler, Alwin, 1832, 1878, 1884
Kuer Ya-lei, 307
Kügler, Harald, 692
Kuhn, Toni, 1336, 1337
Kühn, Regine (f), 732, 737
Kühn, Siegfried (m), 735, 737
Kühne, Erich, 722
Kukula, Martin, 712
Kulkarni, Mangesh, 1009
Kumai, Kei (m), 1245, 1249, 1276
Kumar, Ashok (m), 1048
Kumar, Nirmal, 1018
Kumashiro, Tatsumi (m), 1240
Kümel, Harry, 103, 108, 126
Kunin, Vladimir, 2391, 2395
Kurahara, Koreyoshi, 1235
Kurant, Willy, 541, 1840, 1970
Kuras, Ellen (f), 2206, 2207, 2309
Kureishi, Hanif (m), 1884
Kurfirst, Gary, 2081
Kuri, Dulce (f), 1345
Kurihara, Komaki (f), 1245
Kurihara, Taseshi, 1255
Kurita, Toyomichi, 2127, 2191
Kurosawa, Akira, 1276
Kuryla, Mary (f), 2243
Kurys, Diane (f), 497, 509, 559, 607
Kusada, Hiroshi, 1219, 1227
Kusakabe, Goro, 1253
Kusturica, Nina (f), 99
Kuveiller, Luigi, 1189
Kuvera, Jaroslav, 350
Kuzu, Hüseyin,, 1728
Kwan, Stanley, 907, 910, 913
Kwan, Teddy Robin, 908
Kwok, Crystal (f), 924
Kyle, Christopher, 2268

La Russo, Louis, 834
Labadie, Jean, 550
Labate, Wilma (f), 1190, 1194
Laborder, Jean, 457
Labourier, Dominique (f), 465
Labrecque, Jean-Claude, 216
Labruyère-Colas, Catherine (f), 18
LaBute, Neil (m), 2264
Lacambre, Daniel, 1927, 1931, 1944, 1960, 1996
Lachman, Edward, 2045, 2076, 2131, 2227, 2242, 2293

Lackner, Erich, 94
Lacomblez, Antoine, 559, 1798, 2396
Lacor, Jean-Michel, 1339
Lacoste, Christian, 1210
Lafaye, Yves, 490, 492
LaGravenese, Richard, 2211, 2230
Laguna, Mónica (f), 1620
Lähndorf, Silke (f), 814
Lai Miu-suet, Carol (f), 926
Lai, Yiu-fai, 923
Lainé, Pascal, 481
Laing, John (m), 1388
Laing, Robin (f), 1387, 1393, 1394
Laïus, Leida (f), 406
Lake, Diane, 2295
Lakhal, Mahmoud, 11
Lakhdar-Hamina, Mohamed (m), 12
Lam, Ardy, 918
Lam, Charlie, 322
Lamangan, Joel (m), 1439, 1444, 1447, 1451
Lamarque, Alex, 666
Lamasan, Olivia (f), 1441
Lamb, Jan, 920
Lambert, Gavin, 1898, 1979
Lambert, Mary (f), 2081, 2127
Lambert, Susan (f), 52, 72
Lambert, Verity (f), 60
Lambrecht, Marcus, 1739
Lamey, Ihab, 1418
Lampe, Jutta (f), 782
Lampela, Jarmo, 419
Lampert, Micha, 2390
Lamriki, Souad, 662
Lamy, Benoît (m), 485, 1575
Lan, Bo-chow, 1682
Lan, Wu (m), 265
Lancelin, Sabine (f), 632, 654
Lancelot, Dominique, 843
Lanci, Giuseppe, 1170, 1176, 1187, 1191
Lanctôt, Micheline (f), 201
Landau, Ely, 1763
Landau, Saul, 223
Lander, Ned, 80
Landicho, Domingo, 1447
Lane, Charles (m), 2149
Laney, Lanier, 1803
Lang, Charles, 1898, 1904
Lang, Samantha (f), 78, 84
Lang Yun, 301
Lange, Monique (f), 508
Langer, Martin, 718
Langlois, Michel, 189
Langmaack, Beate (f), 841
Langmann, Arlette (f), 536, 576
Lanier, Kate (f), 2155, 2216

Lansing, Sherry (f), 2071, 2085
Lantos, Robert, 221
Lanzmann, Claude, 4
Lao, Armando, 1448
Laou, Julius-Amédée (m), 526
Lapine, James (m), 1807
Lapointe, Yves, 554
Lapoirie, Jeanne (f), 630, 643, 646, 2349
Lappin, Arthur (m), 1863
Lapshov, Anatoli, 2372
Lapsui, Anastasia (f), 420
Lara, Agustin, 1559
Larnaout, Mahmoud, 1699
Larner, Stevan, 452, 1921
Laroche, Pierre, 105
Larreta, Antonio, 32, 1551, 1570, 1619
Larrieu, Jean-Claude, 220, 1706, 2396
Larsen, Kaj, 1659
LaShelle, Joseph, 1900
Laske, Rüdiger, 780
Lasker, Alex, 2172
Laskos, Orestis, 852
Lassally, Walter, 850, 1113, 1746, 1787
Laszlo, Andrew, 1899
Lau Kar-leung (m), 901
Laudadio, Felice (f), 685
Laurant, Guillaume, 628
Laure, Carole (f), 194
Laurence, Margaret (f), 1908
Laurent, Christine (f), 528, 561, 2349
Laurents, Arthur, 1945, 1987
Laverty, Paul, 1869
Law, Alex, 921
Law, Clara (f), 77, 908, 2175
Lawrence, D. H., 1765
Lawton, Charles, Jr., 1890
Lawton, J. F., 2088
Lazar, Andrew, 2196
Lazarkiewicz, Magdalena (f), 1473, 1477, 1484
Lazarkiewicz, Piotr, 1484
Lazmi, Kalpana (f), 1021, 1050
Le Carré, John, 2035
Le Henry, Alain, 497, 509, 569
Le, Hoang (m), 2407, 2410
Le Rigoleur, Dominique (f), 500, 519, 531
Lean, David, 1789
Leary, William C., 1439
Lebègue, Pascal, 539
Leber, Susan (f), 2306
Lebeshev, Pavel, 2395
Lebigre, Thierry, 1355
LeBrocquy, Julie, 2
Lebrun, Francine (f), 210
Lechaptois, Georges, 635
Leclère, Marie-Francois, 511

Leconte, Patrice (m), 627
Lederle, Franz, 797
LeDoux, Patrice, 544, 611
Leduc, Paul (m), 1330
Lee, Ang (m), 1684, 1830
Lee, Angelica (f), 1691
Lee, Cinqué, 2160
Lee, Damian, 2271
Lee Dong-sahm, 1310
Lee Doo-yong (m), 1293, 1295
Lee, Gerard, 61
Lee, Gigo, 924
Lee Jae-yong (m), 1303
Lee, Joie (f), 2160
Lee, Lillian (f), 907, 915
Lee, Mark, 922
Lee Min-yong (m), 1300
Lee Mun-yeol, 1292
Lee, Pin Bing, 304, 1686, 1690, 2408
Lee Ping-ping, 1277
Lee, Raymond, 1449
Lee, Ricardo, 1428, 1430, 1431, 1433, 1434, 1435,
     1436, 1439, 1440, 1441, 1444, 1447, 1449
Lee, Seong-choon, 1293, 1294
Lee, Spike (m), 2062, 2160, 2203, 2262
Lee, Sun-yeol, 1300
Lee Tae-won, 1295, 1299
Lefèbvre, Geneviève (f), 213, 524
Léger, Claude, 213
Legrand, Gilles, 627
Lehmuskallio, Johannes, 420
Lehmuskallio, Markku (m), 420
Leichtling, Jerry, 2061
Leigh, Mike (m), 1838, 1841, 1886
Leigh, Norman, 187
Leightling, Jerry, 2157
Leipzig, Adam, 2194
Leiterman, Richard, 181
Leitner, Isabella (f), 1113
Lembach, Christine, 1178
Lembeck, Michael (m), 2339
Lemmons, Kasi (f), 2223
Lemont, John (m), 1744
Lemos, Lilia, 405
Lenart, Frank, 676
Lencina, Julio, 31
Lenczewski, Ryszard, 1471, 1868
Lennart, Isobel (f), 1906
Lenoir, Denis, 565, 587, 655, 1828
Lent, Dean, 2126
Lenzer, Don, 1966
Leon Garcia, Maryse (f), 1701
Leonard, Elmore, 2225
Leonard, Hugh, 1826
Leonardou, Sotira (f), 874

Leondeff, Doriana (f), 1196
Leone, Lu, 1164
Leonelli, Nadia, 2316
Leopold, Nanouk (f), 1382
Lepetit, Jean-François, 615, 668
Lepicier, Eugene, 433
Lepkowska, Ilona (f), 1473
Lerman, Diego (m), 43
Lermer, Horst, 798
Lerner, Alan Jay, 1919
Lesmes, Eva (f), 1595, 1621
Lesnie, Andrew, 63
Lessing, Doris, 549, 1651
Lessing, Gotthold Ephraim, 719
Lester, Mark (m), 1958
Lester, Richard (m), 1762
Letessier, Dorothée (f), 517
Levangie, Gigi, 2236
Levant, Alain, 445
Lévêque, Josiane (f), 517
Levie, Pierre, 105
Levin, Don, 2025
Levin, Ira, 1909
Levine, Michael, 2338
Levinson, Mark, 2094
Levitin, Jacqueline (f), 193
Lévy, Raoul, 424, 444
Levy, Sandra (f), 57, 78
Leweck Volkmar, 737
Lewenstein, Oscar, 1757
Lewis, Andy, 1924
Lewis, Dave, 1924
Lewis, David, 1839
Lewis, Edward, 2010
Lewis, James, 178
Lewis, Joyce Renee (f), 2318
Lhomme, Pierre, 489, 529, 597, 1856
Li Chengsheng, 246, 283
Li Han-hsiang, 232, 237
Li Kangsheng, 313
Li, Mark, 916
Li Ruquin, 236
Li Shaohong (f), 294, 302
Li Tai-hung, 901
Li Wei, 256
Li Xiaojun (f), 255
Li Xiong, 305, 2290
Li Yu, 316
Li Zhun, 231
Li Ziyu, 261
Liang Xin, 228
Liang Ziyong, 266
Liangio, Shan, 274
Liappa, Frieda (f), 872, 883
Libresco, Caroline (f), 2161

Lidon, Maria Luna (f), 1633
Liebeneiner, Wolfgang, 738
Liénard, Bénédicte (m), 659
Lilamazares, Julio, 1604
Lilar, Suzanne (f), 119
Lim Chung, 1293
Lim, Jae-soo, 1311
Lim Sang Soo (m), 1302
Lima, Walter (m), 135
Limmer, Ulrich, 804
Limpach, Hannelore (f), 829
Lin Cheng-sheng (f), 1685
Lin Deng-fei, 1673, 1678
Lin Hongzhong, 1672
Lin Jong, 268, 1874, 2269
Lin Rongfeng, 1674
Lin Zanting, 1674
Linarès, Maria-Luisa (f), 435
Lind, Graham, 83
Lindblom, Gunnel (f), 1649
Lindenlaub, Karl, 2261
Lindenlaub, Karl Walter, 2288
Lindgren, Göran, 1640, 1643
Lindgren, Hans, 1403
Lindley, John, 2136
Lindon, Lionel, 1902
Lindop, Audrey Erskine (f), 1747
Lindren, Goran, 1639
Lindsell, Patrick, 2418
Lindström, Göran, 1413
Lindstrom, Lisa (f), 2267
Ling Zifeng, 266
Linh Viêt (f), 2406
Link, Caroline (f), 689, 709
Linstead, Hilary, 51
Linta, Branko, 327
Lipman, Jerzy, 1358
Lipp, Adrian, 1592
Lipper, Ken, 1849
Lippold, Eva (f), 730
Liron, Fabien, 83
Lispector, Clarice (f), 141
Littman, Lynne (f), 2022, 2030
Litvinova, Renata (f), 1516, 1742
Liu Bingjian, 317
Liu Heng, 280, 291
Liu Jinxi, 310
Liu Lihua, 258, 300
Liu Meng, 289
Liu, Rene (f), 1691
Liu Xihong, 271
Livnev, Sergei, 1516
Lloyd, Walk, 2097
Loach, Ken (m), 1760, 1811, 1822, 1869
Loader, Kevin, 1884

Lobell, Mark, 2261
Loboguerrero, Camila (f), 323
Lochar, Holger, 713
Locke, Sondra (f), 2110
Loden, Barbara (f), 1922
Lodi, Maurizo, 1145
Lofts, Norah (f), 1900
Loftus, Bryan, 1788, 1792, 1797, 2081
Logan, Bruce, 1962, 1979, 2009
Lohmann, Dietrich, 552, 678, 747, 1117
Lohmann, Paul, 1941, 2033
Loiseleux, Jacques, 491, 626
Løkkeberg, Vibeke (f), 1404, 1410, 1411
Lombardo, Antonio, 128
Lomholdt, Boje, 376
Longo, Francesco, 1181
Loomer, Lisa, 2244
Lope de Vega, Felix, 1594
Lopes-Curval, Julie (f), 651
Lopez, Elizabeth (f), 168
López Garcia, Teo, 1585
Lopez, Josefina (f), 2310
Lopez, Sal, 2263
Lorden, Anne (f), 1356
Loridan-Ivens, Marceline (f), 660
Loriot, Noëlle (f), 469
Lorsac, Olivier, 515
Losey, Joseph (m), 508, 1758, 1771, 1790
Losey, Patricia (f), 1790
Lou Chen Sheng, 260
Louisianna Knop, Patricia (f), 2081
Lourcelles, Jacques, 606
Louvart, Hélène (f), 581, 590, 602, 612, 639, 659, 662, 669
Lowry, Hunt, 2317
Lu Gengxin, 301
Lu Junfu, 251, 292
Lu Le, 289
Lu Ren, 231
Lu Shoujun, 292
Lu Wei (m), 273, 310
Lu Yue, 315
Lubezki, Emmanuel, 1346, 2267
Lubtchansky, William, 472, 473, 503, 505, 545, 561, 683
Lucari, Gianni, 1163
Luciano, Fulvio, 1179
Luedtke, Kurt, 2005, 2049
Lufti, Dib, 135
Lui Baogui, 293
Lukács, Lóránt, 945
Luketic, Robert, 2325
Lumet, Sidney (m), 1901, 2058
Luna, Alicia (f), 1630
Luna, Bigas, 1566
Lupino, Ida (f), 1902

Luret, Jean, 1553
Lurie, Jeffrey, 2138
Lurie, Rod (m), 2258
Lussier, Sylvie (f), 218
Luther, Igor, 763, 810, 2108
Lutic, Bernard, 502, 509, 535
Lutz, Karen (f), 2325
Luzardo, Julio, 1326
Luzuriaga, Camilo (m), 405
Lvovsky, Noëmie, 587
Lyles, Leslie (f), 2146
Lyne, Adrian (m), 2071, 2314
Lyons, John, 2330
Lyttkens, Yngve, 1642

M'Hando, Martin, 1692
Ma Chor-shing, 906
Ma Feng, 267
Ma, Jingle, 908, 912
Maar, Gyula (f), 935
Maas, Audrey (f), 1946
Maas, Peter, 2046
Macák, Jirí, 351
Macau Collective, 68
Maccari, Guiseppe, 1190
Maccari, Ruggero, 1142
Maccarone, Angelina (f), 691
MacDonald, Peter, 1803
Macdonald, Sharman, 1849
Macé, Gaëlle (f), 670
Machuel, Emmanuel, 660, 1497, 1500, 1501
Macias, Alberto, 39
MacIvor, Daniel, 219
MacKenzie, John (m), 1121
Mackie, Suzanne (f), 1881
MacKinnon, Billy, 1857
MacKinnon, Gillies (m), 1857
MacLaverty, Bernard, 1112
MacLean, Alison (f), 1395
MacLean, Stephen (m), 50
MacMillan, Kenneth, 1115, 1119
Madame de la Fayette, 1500
Madden, David, 2142
Madden, John (m), 1842
Maddow, Ben, 1891
Maddox, Brenda, 1120
Mader, Ruth (f), 98
Madsen, Ole Christian (m), 373
Maeda, Yonezo, 1257
Maeztu, Myriam de (f), 1586
Magag, Jose, 1633
Magalhães, Ana Maria (f), 2175
Magdalena, Marianne, 2249
Maggioni, Daniele, 1196
Magill, Mark, 2064

Maglie, Graciela (f), 33
Magni, Luigi, 1151
Mahajan, K. K., 978, 981, 995, 1010, 1011, 1021
Maharaj, Anthony, 2048
Mahfuz, Nagib, 378
Mahmoody, Betty (f), 2133
Maidment, Rex, 1815, 1815, 1820
Maier, Christine, 94
Maigne, Sylvie (f), 168
Maintigneux, Sophie (f), 518, 521, 708, 1493
Majewski, Janusz (m), 1466
Majidi, Majid (m), 1090
Majumdar, Kamal, 1020, 1026
Majumdar, Sunirmal, 1034
Makavejev, Dusan (m), 2414
Makepeace, Ann (f), 2120
Makhmalbaf, Mohsen (m), 1083, 1093, 1097, 1101
Makhmalbaf, Samira (f), 1101
Makk, Károly (m), 783, 942, 959
Makovski, Claude, 451
Malatesta, Andres, 1420
Maldoror, Sarah (f), 22
Malige, Jean, 436
Malik, Ravi, 1020
Malik, Ulrich, 701
Mallawarachchi, Edward, 1636
Malle, Louis (m), 429, 443
Mallet, Marilu (f), 191
Malmros, Nils (m), 368
Malo, René, 213
Maloney, Denis, 2258
Mamani, Abdoulaye, 165
Mañá, Laura (f), 1615
Mandel, Babaloo, 2143, 2270
Mandel, Loring, 2035
Mándy, Iván, 929
Mandzhiyev, Oleg, 1278
Mangiacapre, Lina (f), 1183
Mangold, James (m), 2244
Mangolte, Babette (f), 113, 1782, 1933, 1950, 1971
Maniaci, Teodoro, 2254, 2256
Mann, Daniel (m), 1888, 1905
Mans, Lorenzo, 2063
Mansarova, Aida (f), 2383
Mansuri, Naser, 1086
Mantila, Auli (f), 418
Mantxola, Aitor, 1576
Manuel, Jo, 1826
Manzotti, Achille, 1173, 1178
Mao Xiao (f), 258, 294
Mapashi, R. C., 1009
Maraini, Dacia (f), 1164, 1178, 1187
Marano, Vincenzo, 593, 614
Marboeuf, Jean (m), 589
Marchand, Gilles (m), 661

Marchant, William, 1766
Marco, Armand, 1700
Marcoen, Alain, 127
Marcus, Frank, 1907
Marcus, Laurence, 1762
Margineanu, Nicolae, 1513
Margolis, Seth, 2180
Mari, Pasaquale, 1737
Marian, Susanne (f), 100
Marias, Luis, 1621
Marignac, Martine (f), 528, 553
Marin, Roy, 323
Marincek, Ivan, 2411
Marivaux, Pierre, 528, 1880
Mark, Laurence, 2068, 2237
Marketaki, Tonia (f), 876, 884
Markowitz, Murray, 178
Marmak, Siddiq (m), 2
Marmion, Yves, 569, 631
Marmstedt, Lorens, 1642
Maron, Omri, 1128
Marquard, Brick, 1951, 1954
Marquez, Artemio, 1434
Marquez, Melanie (f), 1434
Marsh-Edwards, Nadine, 1821
Marshall, Alan, 2139
Marshall, Frank, 2248
Marshall, Garry (m), 2078, 2087
Marshall, Penny (f), 2143
Marshall, Tonie (f), 539, 616
Marston, Joshua (m), 2342
Martel, Kenneth, 2070
Martel, Lucretia (f), 40
Märthesheimer, Peter, 755, 772
Marti, Pascal, 898, 1198
Martin, Catherine (f), 216
Martin, Darnell (f), 2178
Martin, Jürgen, 790
Martin, Philippe, 576, 640
Martinetti, Nino Gaetano, 66
Martinez, Arturo, 1559
Martinez, Jesus, 1325
Martoreli, Andres, 1608
Marx, Barbara (f), 1668
Marzouk, Ramses, 396
Marzuq, Said (m), 382
Masahiro, Shinoda (m), 1238
Masini, Mario, 774
Maslin, Sue (f), 86
Mass, Ethan, 1859
Massis, Stephan, 651
Masson, Laëtitia (f), 577, 600, 610, 672
Massuh, Gabriela (f), 33
Mastrosimone, William, 2055
Masumura, Yasuzo (m), 1221, 1228, 1230, 1232, 1236,

1246
Matanic, Dalibor (m), 327
Máthé, Tibor, 949
Matheson, Richard, 2009
Mathew, George, 1056
Matji, Manuel, 1626
Matofsky, Harvey, 1961
Matras, Christian, 433
Matsas, Nestoras, 852
Matsumoto, Tsuneyasu, 1249
Matsuyama, Zenzo, 1220, 1234, 1241
Matthee, Dalene (f), 1538
Matthews, Elizabeth (f), 1839
Matthews, Paul, 1839
Matthews, Ross, 67
Mattsson, Arne (m), 1642
Matyjaszkiewicz, Stefan, 1454
Mauch, Thomas, 625, 699, 754, 766, 788
Maugham, W. Somerset, 221, 2388
Mauriac, François, 433
Mavraki, Isavella (f), 888
Mawuru, Godwin (m), 2416
May, Elaine (f), 1926
Mayfield, Julian, 1911
Maynard, John, 61
Maynard, Joyce (f), 2190
Mayo, Alfredo, 36, 39, 1579, 1602, 1603
Mayron, Melanie (f), 2096
Mazif, Sid Ali (m), 9
Mazursky, Paul (m), 1988
Mazuy, Patricia (f), 625
Mazzoni, Roberta (f), 956, 1179, 1193
Mbengue, Wongue, 1532
McAdam, Trish (f), 1117
McAlpine, Donald, 49, 2236
McCarthy, Mary (f), 1901
McCauley, Sue (f), 1388
McCready, Dale, 1399
McCredie, Elise (f), 85
McCullum, Rich, 1806
McCunn, Ruthanne Lum (f), 2120
McDonald, Anne, 53
McDonnell, Edward, 2337
McFadean, David, 2270
McGarvey, Seamus, 1827, 1849, 2248, 2286, 2300
McGhee, Scott, 2275
McGowan, Catriona (f), 1879
McGowan, Sharon, 211
McGrath, Martin, 74
McGregor, Roy, 1539
McGuckian, Mary (f), 1116
McGuinness, Frank, 1119
McGuire, Sharon (f), 2274
McInnes, Laurie, 52
McKay, Doug, 174

McKay, Jim (m), 1875, 2204, 2284
McLaren, Lucy (f), 85
McLaughlin, Sheila (f), 2022, 2079
McLennan, Gordon, 220
McMillan, Terry (f), 2191, 2232
McMullen, Ken (m), 1797
McMurchy, Megan (f), 72
McMurray, Mary (f), 1792
McNaughton, Bruce, 47
Mecava, Goran, 325, 326
Meckler, Nancy (f), 1823
Meddour, Azzedine, 17
Medeiros, José, 134, 146
Medina, Teresa (f), 1599, 2201, 2217, 2229, 2273
Medrano, Dora (f), 2217
Medioli, Enrico, 1153, 1171
Meerapfel, Jeanine (f), 710, 786, 821, 835, 836
Meeren, Yves, 1417
Meffre, Pomme, 506
Megino, Luis, 1568
Meheux, Phil, 2123
Mehrjui, Dariush (m), 1078, 1081, 1084, 1086, 1098
Mehta, Ashok, 997, 1006, 1012, 1018, 1026, 1031
Mehta, Deepa (f), 1037, 1819
Mehta, Ketan (m), 1017
Mehta, Vijaya (f), 1009, 1019
Mei Changkun, 1672
Meier, Pierre-Alain, 1529
Meily, Lee, 1450
Meiners, Bernd, 679
Meira, Maria (f), 43
Melli, Elide (f), 1200
Melnick, Daniel, 2095
Melnikov, Vitaly (m), 2363, 2368
Meloni, Claudio, 1181
Ménard, Robert, 182
Mendes, Antonio Luiz, 144, 151
Mendoza, Miguel, 328
Ménégoz, Margaret (f), 101, 502, 521, 662
Meng, Xia, 903
Mengel, Vincent (m), 2014
Menges, Chris, 1801, 1804, 2046, 2080
Menkes, David (m), 1605
Menkes, Nina (f), 2057, 2134
Menon, Rajiv (m), 1057
Menoud, Jean-Bernard, 543
Mensah, Charles, 674
Menshov, Vladimir (m), 2375
Merabtine, Rachid, 9
Mercader, Martha (f), 25
Mercer, David, 1771
Merchant, Ismail, 972, 1783, 1787, 1795, 1837, 1856, 2278
Meredith, Anne (f), 2195, 2338
Merezhko, Viktor, 2387

Merimee, Prosper, 1533
Merlet, Agnès (f), 592
Meruisse, Jean-Paul, 500
Meshkini, Marziyeh (f), 1093
Messaad, A., 16
Messick, Dale (f), 2100
Mesuret, Nathalie (f), 622, 1706
Mészáros, Márta (f), 927, 928, 930, 931, 934, 936, 937, 939, 940, 944, 948, 950, 954, 956, 958, 959, 1462
Metter, Izrail, 2372
Meyer, Henrik, 717
Meyer, Michael, 1771
Meyer, Nicholas, 2071
Meyer, Randy, 2101
Meyer, Russ (m), 1915
Meyers, Janet (f), 2121
Meyers, Nancy (f), 2003
Meyjes, Menno, 2042
Mezey, Paul, 2342
Mézières, Myriam (f), 650, 1667
Mezquita, Pedro, 2401
Michaelides, Victor, 853
Michell, Roger (m), 1884
Michlos, Anastas, 2328
Middleton, Gregory, 206, 211
Middleton, Peter, 1864
Middleton, Vanessa (f), 2287
Midler, Bette (f), 2087
Miéville, Anne-Marie (f), 472, 533, 563, 595
Migeat, François, 1212
Mignona, Eduardo (m), 35
Mignot, Pierre, 188, 190, 203, 213, 2015
Miguel, Joëlle (f), 518
Mihailidis, Lakis, 865
Mihalic, Zdravko, 324
Mihaylov, Eugeny (m), 163
Mikesch, Elfi (f), 680, 742, 805, 829, 840
Mikkelsen, Laila (f), 1406, 1408
Milani, Tahmineh (f), 1087, 1096, 1098
Milas, Nikos, 861, 867
Milchan, Arnon, 2159, 2173, 2211
Miller, Claude (m), 631
Miller, George (m), 2084, 2144
Miller, Harvey (f), 2003
Miller, Michael (m), 1970
Miller, Rebecca (f), 2309
Miller, Richard, 2283
Miller, Robert Ellis, 2100
Miller, Sue (f), 2090
Miller, Susan (f), 2074
Millié, Robert, 168
Millman, Sara (f), 2331
Mills, Paul, 1790
Milon, Pierre, 638, 661
Milshtein, Oury, 516

Min Anqi, 289
Minahan, Daniel (m), 2206, 2282
Miner, Michael, 2027
Minh-ha, Trinh T. (f), 2188
Minnelli, Vincente (m), 1919
Minon, Juan, 1567
Minsky, Charles, 2245
Minton, Roy, 1784
Miotto, Jean-Paul, 526
Mireille, Arania (f), 111
Miró, Pilar (f), 1546, 1551, 1583, 1594, 1596
Mirza, Masood, 1049
Mishev, Georgi, 159
Mishima, Yukio, 582, 1235
Mishra, Ashok, 1048
Mishra, Sudhir (m), 1023
Missel, Renée, 2004, 2123
Misselwitz, Helke (f), 688
Mita, Merata (f), 1391
Mitchell, Joni, 187
Mitchell, Sollace (f), 2070
Mitra, Bimal, 965
Mitra, Narendranath, 968
Mitra, Premendra, 1010
Mitra, Subrata, 963, 968, 969, 972
Mitran, Doru, 1508, 1513
Mitro, Kristaq, 3
Mitry, Jean, 428
Miura, Akira, 1240
Miyagawa, Kazuo, 1247
Miyajima, Yoshio, 1216, 1235
Miyamoto, Ken, 1248
Miyazawa, Rie (f), 925
Mizrahi, Moshé (m), 175, 486, 492, 1125
Mizuno, Katsuhiro, 1682
Mo Yan, 259
Modaresi, Majid, 1082
Modica, Antonio, 1183
Moffatt, Tracy (f), 70
Mogel, Siegfried, 726
Mohamed, Khalid, 1032, 1039
Mohammadi, Vahidéa, 1098
Mohan, R., 1049
Mohr, Clifford, 1071
Mohrbutter, Jürgen, 812
Moisnard, Franck, 1502
Moknèche, Nadir, 1611, 1706
Mokri, Amir, 2106
Moktari, Ebrahim (m), 1080
Moland, Hans Petter (m), 1862
Moliavko-Visotsky, Nathalie (f), 214
Molina, Juan, 1571, 1581
Mollberg, Rauni (m), 411, 412
Molloy, Mike, 1805
Molnár, György (m), 951

Momotani, Houko, 1274
Monicelli, Mario (m), 1180
Montanais, Lazeros, 863
Monteiro, João César, 1488, 1489
Montera, Rosa (f), 1627
Monteverde, Lily (f), 1427
Monteverde-Teo, Roselle, 1451
Montgomery, Jennifer (f), 2169
Monti, Adriana (f), 1185
Monti, Felix, 29, 32, 33, 34
Monton, Vincent, 51
Moodley, Shan, 1539
Moodysson, Lukas (m), 1662
Moonjean, Hank, 2009
Moore, Brian (m), 1802
Moore, Demi (f), 2183, 2207
Moore, Simon, 2185
Moore, Susanna, 2323
Moore, Tom (m), 2059
Moorhouse, Jocelyn (f), 74, 2177
Mor, Esther (f), 1126
Morand, Roger, 487
Moravia, Alberto, 437, 1144
Moraz, Patricia (f), 484
Moreau, Jeanne (f), 474, 660
Moreno, Adriano, 2398, 2400
Morgan, Donald, 1967
Morita, Rhett, 2285
Morrill, John Arthur, 1958
Morris, Mary McGarry (f), 2151
Morris, Oswald, 1752
Morris, Reginald, 187
Morrison, Bruce (m), 1385
Morrison, David, 2161
Morrison, Toni (f), 2230
Mortimer, Penelope (f), 1752
Moscati, Italo, 1155
Mosley, Tim, 2287
Mostafavi, Farid, 1095, 1100
Mostert, Dirk, 1537
Mounier, Collin, 1740
Moura, Edgar, 137, 142, 149
Moustapha, Ky, 166
Moyle, Allan, 2130
Mu Deyuan, 249
Mucaj, Ibrahim, 3
Mueller, Kathy (f), 63
Muir, David, 1766
Mukherjee, Abhik, 1046
Mukherjee, Arvind, 974
Mukherjee, Barun, 998
Mukherjee, Prabhat, 963
Mukherjee, Robin, 1847
Mularczyk, Andrzej, 1486
Mullan, Peter (m), 1123

Müller, Christa (f), 735
Muller, Marco, 314
Müller, Robby, 367, 372, 749, 752, 769, 1845
Mulligan, Robert (m), 1894, 1898
Mulvey, Laura (f), 1773
Mulvihill, Queenae Taylor (f), 1692
Mulvihill, Ron, 1692
Münch, Christopher (m), 2265
Mundhra, Jag (m), 1014, 1048
Mungai, Anne (f), 1283
Munjal, Raj, 2304
Munk, Andrzej (m), 1459
Munro, Rona (f), 1822
Murai, Hiroshi, 1222
Murat, Lúcia (f), 151
Muratova, Kira (f), 1742, 1743, 2361, 2365, 2377,
    2388, 2390
Murga, Celina (f), 41
Murphy, Fred, 1776, 1990
Murphy, Geoff, 1387
Murphy, Maeve (f), 1122
Murphy, Pat (f), 1108, 1111, 1120
Murphy, Paul, 67
Murphy, Tab, 2091
Murray, Don, 53
Murray, Forrest, 2187
Murthy, S. R. K., 1024
Murúa, Lautaro, 25
Musina, Shapiga (f), 1280
Mutrux, Gail (f), 2264
Myers, Nancy (f), 2067
Myers, Suzanne (f), 2193
Myhre, James, 2322
Myles, Lynda, 1824
Myulgaut, Valeri, 2388

Na Dohyang, 1295
Nabili, Marva (f), 1073
Nachmias, Limor (f), 1137
Naderi, Amir (m), 2327
Nadja, Zdzislaw, 1475
Nadjari, Raphaël, 1138
Naefe, Vivian (f), 676, 804
Naess, Halvor, 1403, 1412
Nagano, Juichi, 1224, 1233
Nagasaki, Shunichi, 1251
Nagata, Masaichi, 1230
Nai Chung-chou, 1681
Naidu, Damodar, 1033
Nair, Hari, 1043
Nair, Mira (f), 1885, 2131, 2301, 2307
Nakabori, Masao, 1263
Nakagawa, Yoshihisa, 1246
Nannuzi, Armando (m), 740, 1142
Nanus, Susan, 2207

Napolitano, Silvia (f), 1199
Narbey, Leon, 1388, 1394
Narita, Hiro, 2333
Narliev, Khodjakuli (m), 2367
Narusawa, Masashige, 1216
Naruse, Mikio (m), 1217, 1220, 1223, 1229, 1234
Narushima, Toichiro, 1238
Narutskaya, Olga (f), 1517
Nash, Margot (f), 75
Nasr, Abdou, 380
Nasr, Mohsen, 387, 392, 400, 402
Nasrallah, Yousry, 396
Nathan, Robert, 2254
Nathansen, Henri, 360
Natteau, Jacques, 851
Naughton, Edmund, 1925
Nava, Gregory (m), 2007, 2026, 2227, 2295
Navarrete, Beatriz (f), 1628
Navarro, Bertha (f), 1341, 2026
Navarro, Guillermo, 1331, 2210, 2225
Neame, Ronald (m), 1750, 1764
Neau, André, 2064
Neckelbrouch, Jean-Claude, 104, 111, 553
Negrepontis, Yiznnis, 867
Nejjar, Narjiss (f), 1354
Nellis, Alice (f), 348
Nelson, Jessie (f), 2236
Nelson, Peter, 1802
Nepomniaschy, Alex, 2107, 2186, 2194
Néron, Claude, 459
Nettelbeck, Sandra (f), 707
Netzer, Ralph, 1416
Neuenfels, Benedict, 711
Neukirchen, Dorothea (f), 791
Neuman, Tom G., 1770
Neumann, Claus, 732
Neumann, Margarete (f), 93
Neuwirth, Manfred, 93
Neuwirth, Tom, 2074
Névé, Éric, 666
Neven, Bill, 219
Newby, Chris (m), 1818
Newell, Mike (m), 1794, 1815, 2328
Newland, John, 1766
Newman, Paul (m), 1908, 1930
Neyman, Yuri, 2318
Ngor, Peter, 901
Ngu, Nguy, 2410
Nguyen, Huu Tuan, 2409
Nguyen, Kim Cuong, 2409
Nguyen, Lan, 2403
Nguyen, Quang Vinh, 2409
Nhan, Tran Trung, 2405
Ni Zhen, 284, 302
Nicdas, Paul (m), 2014

Nichikawa, Miwa (f), 1275
Nicholas, Gregor (m), 1398
Nichols, Mike (m), 2028, 2056, 2098, 2114, 2286
Nicloux, Guillaume (m), 652
Nicolae, Christiana (f), 1507
Nicolas, Paul, 2014
Nielsen, Jürgen, 354
Nieto, Guillermo, 45
Nig Dai, 314
Nihalani, Govind, 979, 991, 1004, 1041
Nilsson, Göran, 370, 1657
Nimoy, Leonard (m), 2090
Nin, Anaïs (f), 2109
Nini, Soraya (f), 626
Nisal, Shanta (f), 999
Niskanen, Tuija-Maija (f), 413, 414
Nissan, Rosa, 1337
Noda, Kogo, 1215
Noganumo, Mutsuo, 1260
Nogueira, Helena (f), 1539
Nollo, Jacques, 560
Norbert, Paul, 1923
Nordström, Robert, 1661
Norman, Leslie, 1749
Norman, Marc, 1961
Norman, Marsha (f), 2059, 2240
Nothomb, Amélie (f), 663
Novak, David, 1917, 1953
Novak, Emil, 946
Novaro, Beatriz (f), 1334
Novaro, Maria (f), 1334, 1335, 1345
Novarro, Guillermo, 1622
Novion, Pierre, 532
Nowicki, Jan (m), 1462
Nowra, Louis, 80
Noyce, Philip (m), 51
Nozik, Michael, 2089
Nüchtern, Monika (f), 819
Nüchtern, Rüdiger (m), 819
Nugiel, Nellie (f), 2146
Nuñez, Victor (m), 1995, 2154
Nunn, Trevor, 1772
Nunnuzzi, Armando, 1174
Nur, Arifin C., 1059
Nutley, Colin (m), 1656
Nuttgens, Giles, 1037, 2275
Nuytten, Bruno, 463, 467, 476, 480, 493, 504, 515, 529
Nxumalo, Khulile (m), 1544
Nykvist, Sven, 408, 760, 1413, 1638, 1639, 1641, 1645, 1647, 1650, 1658, 2041, 2086, 2313
Nyswaner, Ron, 2036

O'Bannon, Dan, 1994
O'Brien, Edna (f), 187, 1751
O'Brien, Rebecca, 1869

O'Carroll, Brendan, 1863
O'Connor, Gavin (m), 2252
O'Connor, Greg, 2252
O'Connor, Pat (m), 1112, 1115, 1119
O'Dell, David, 1791
O'Hara, John, 1888
O'Hara, Mario (m), 1424, 1426, 1432, 1437, 1445
O'Leary, Ronan (m), 1113
O'Steen, Sam (m), 1974
O'Sullivan, Thaddeus, 1111
Obadia, Agnès (f), 598
Obayashi, Nobuhiko, 1261
Obreshkov, Alexandre (m), 160
Obst, Lynda (f), 2148
Ocak, Esma, 1731
Octavio Gómez, Manuel (m), 330
Oduwa-Imasuen, Lancelot (m), 1402
Off, Michael, 2224
Ogaard, Philip, 1862
Ogawa, Tomoko (f), 1273
Ogborn, Kate (f), 1846
Ogden, Jennifer (f), 2232
Ogier, Bulle (f), 465
Ogita, Yoshihisa, 1263
Oglesby, Marsha (f), 2267
Oguz, Orhan, 1723, 1727, 1733
Oh Hye Young, 1288
Oh Jeong-wan, 1303
Oh, Ki-min, 1307
Ohashi, Rene, 207
Ohrvik, Harald, 1406
Oikawa, Shotaro (m), 1273
Okazaki, Kozo, 1249
Oken, Stuart, 1807
Okomot, Meneko, 1262
Okpako, Branwen (f), 715
Okuhara, Teizo, 1276
Oldman, Gary (m), 1844
Oldoini, Enrico, 1175
Olea, Pedro (m), 1560
Olesen, Annette K. (f), 376
Olgaç, Bilgé (f), 1722, 1724
Olivera, Hector (m), 39
Olivier, Laurence (m), 1767
Olmi, Fabio, 1195
Olsberg, Jonathan, 2302
Olsten, Suzanne (f), 1657
Omedes, David, 1632
Ömer Akad, Lüfti, 1713
Önal, Safa, 1711, 1712
Ondricek, Miroslav, 2028, 2143
Ongören, Vasif, 1711
Onodera, Lisa (f), 2184
Onwurah, Ngozi (f), 1832
Oppé, Felicity, 1815

Oppenheim, Jacques, 166
Ordody, Judit (f), 946
Oristrell, Joaquin, 1565, 1595, 1597
Ormanlar, Kenan, 1720
Ornitz, Arthur, 1988
Orsenna, Erik, 550
Ort-Snep, Joseph, 837
Orthmann, Christel, 694
Osaki, Midori, 1267
Oshii, Mamoru (m), 1271
Oshima, Nagisa, 1218
Osin, Roman, 894
Ost, Gü, 721
Osten, Suzanne (f), 1652
Othmer, Zak, 2199
Otsuka, Kazu, 1235
Ottinger, Ulrike (f), 91, 770, 778, 793, 807, 839
Ouedraogo, Idressa (m), 167
Overton, Julia (f), 76
Owen, Alison, 1883
Oxburgh, Anita, 1661
Oz, Frank (m), 2345
Ozbatur, Zeynep, 1740
Ozbey, Mustafa, 1722
Özgentürk, Ali, 1717
Özgentürk, Isil, 1718
Özkan, Yavuz (m), 1733, 1734
Ozon, François (m), 643, 646, 664
Ozpetek, Ferzan (m), 1198, 1737
Ozsahin, Hüseyin, 1724
Ozu, Yasujiro (m), 1215

Paar, Larry, 1385
Pack, Jill (f), 1781
Packers, Gerald, 1831
Padrón Leonardo, 2401
Page, Anthony (m), 1979
Pagés, Luc, 598
Pakula, Alan J. (m), 1894, 1898, 1924, 2020
Pakulski, Krzysztof, 1473
Pal, Kuljit, 1005
Palatsi, Serge, 1353
Palcy, Euzhan (f), 512
Pamphili, Francesco, 956
Pan, Nalin, 1847
Pan Wenzhan, 235
Panahi, Jafar (m), 1091
Pandit, R.V., 1038
Panfilov, Gleb (m), 2359, 2364, 2371, 2380
Paniagua, Cecilio, 435
Pankov, Vladimir, 2390
Panoussopoulos, Yiogas (m), 878
Pansha, 1316
Panwalker, S. D., 1004
Pao Xiaoran, 242, 296

Paolantonio, José, 25
Papadiamantis, Alexandros, 869
Papakostas, Yiorgas (m), 854, 861
Papamichael, Phedon, 2119, 2218
Papasov, Boyan, 161
Papayiannakis, Kostas, 870
Paré, Lisa Katselas (f), 1843
Parent, Gail (f), 1967
Parenzo, Sandro, 1193
Paretsky, Sara (f), 2138
París, Inéz (f), 1614, 1632
Paris, James, 849
Park Chul-soo (m), 1301
Park Jong-chan, 1292, 1297
Park, Kyung-hee (f), 1311
Parker, Alan (m), 2165
Parker, Laurie, 2323
Parks, Suzan-Lori (f), 2203
Parmet, Phil, 2168
Parolini, Marilu (f), 473
Parson, Belinda (f), 1825
Parsons, Clive, 1840, 1860
Partovi, Kambuzia, 1091
Pascal, Christine (f), 490
Pasolini, Pier Paolo (m), 1146, 1156
Passari, Martina (f), 883
Pataki, Eva (f), 948, 950, 954, 956, 959
Patel, Jabbar (m), 999
Patterson, David, 186
Patterson, John, 53
Patton, Bart, 1913
Pattrea, Purnendu (m), 982
Paul, Evelyn (f), 113
Pauli, Rudolph, 485
Paulino, Justo, 1955
Pauls, Alan, 46
Paulsen, Marit (f), 1406
Pavan, Marcelo, 36
Pavans de Ceccatty, Philippe, 621
Pavel, Samy, 111
Pawlikowski, Pawel (m), 1868
Payan, Inna (f), 1627
Payás, Dolores (f), 1601
Payen, Patrice, 122
Payeur, Bernadette (f), 189
Payne, Alexander (m), 2197
Payvar, Homayun, 1092
Paz, Octavio, 32
Paz, Senal, 2399
Pearce, Larry (m), 1899, 2101
Pearce, Peter, 2166
Pearce, Richard (m), 1776
Pearson, Noel, 1119
Peck, Raoul (m), 898
Pecorini, Nicola, 2298

Pélégri, Pierre, 427
Pelletier, Andrée (f), 213, 1243
Pelletier, Chantal (f), 585
Pellizzari, Monica (f), 76
Peltomaa, Hannu, 411
Penata, George Kanarullah, 1070
Peng Xiaolian (f), 258, 268
Penn, Arthur (m), 1893
Penn, Sean, 2226
Penotti, John, 2235
Penzer, Jean, 115, 225, 464
Peploe, Clare (f), 1169, 1801, 1880
Peploe, Mark (m), 1801
Peralta, Charlie, 1446
Perceval, Elisabeth (f), 669
Pérez, Antonio, 1616
Perez, Cesar, 1422
Pérez Cubero, Raúl, 1550
Pérez Grobet, Xavier, 1627, 2338
Perez Grovas, Jorge, 1332
Peries, Lester, 1634
Peries, Sumitra (f), 1634, 1635, 1636, 1637
Perincioli, Christine (f), 777
Perkins, Rachel (f), 80
Perlmutter, Renée (f), 187
Perr, Harvey, 1975
Perrault, Gilles, 578
Perrein, Michèle (f), 424
Perry, Eleanor, 1918
Perry, Frank (m), 1918, 1934, 2043
Perry, Simon, 1786, 1798
Persey, Jonny, 2418
Persson, Jörgen, 360, 1659
Pervilä, Kristina, 420
Pésary, Bruno, 565, 665
Peschke, Reinhart, 2348
Peschke, Toni, 89
Pesci, Allessandro, 1194
Pesta Sirait, Edward, 1062
Petanyi, Katalin, 824
Peterman, Donald, 2012
Peters, Barbara (f), 1917, 1923, 1953, 1985
Peters, Brock, 1942
Peters, Don, 1916
Petersen, Katia (f), 356
Petersen, Mark, 2208
Petho, Gyorgy, 946
Pétin, Michèle (f), 619
Petit, Jean, 64
Petraglia, Sandro, 1190
Petriccione, Italo, 1199
Petrie, Daniel (m), 1890, 2004
Petrie, Donald (m), 2033, 2094, 2194
Petriga, Anatoly, 1519
Petrycki, Jacek, 208, 1463, 1741

Pezold, Friederika (f), 805
Pfannenschmidt, Christian, 702
Pfarrer, Chuck, 2171
Pfeiffer, Carolyn (f), 2032, 2083, 2127
Pfister, Wally, 2324
Pfundner, Stefan, 99
Pham Thuy Nhon, 2406
Pham, Viet Thanh, 2404
Phelan, Anna Hamilton (f), 2047, 2091, 2244
Phillips, Alex, 2263
Phillips, David, 2279
Phillips, Garry, 84
Pialat, Maurice (m), 499
Picazo, Miguel, 1563
Piccioni, Giuseppe, 1177
Piccone, Ugo, 745
Pichon Riviere, Marcelo, 26
Pichul, Vasil (m), 2389
Pickering, Joseph, 58
Pieiller, Evelyne, 226
Pielmeier, John, 2041
Pierce, Kimberly (f), 2238
Pierce-Roberts, Tony, 1795, 2159, 2278
Pietrangelo, Antonio (m), 1142
Pievar, Homayun, 1080
Pigott, Johanna (f), 1398
Pikser, Jeremy, 2112
Pilinszky, János, 935
Pillai, Alex (m), 1834
Pillsbury, Sarah (f), 2145, 2177
Pine, Lester, 1948
Pine, Tina (f), 1948
Pinelli, Tullio, 1150
Piñeyro, Marcelo (m), 36
Ping Wang (f), 229
Pinhão, Leonor (f), 1503
Pinheiro, José (m), 154, 511
Pinoteau, Claude (m), 597
Pinter, Harold, 1752, 2108
Pinter, Tomislav, 2413, 2414
Pintilie, Lucian (m), 1508, 1509
Pinto, Mercedes (f), 226
Pirhasan, Baris, 1725, 1727
Pirozzi, John, 2326
Pirro, Ugo, 1163
Pirselimoglu, Tayfun (m), 1740
Pisano, Isabel (f), 1633
Piscicelli, Salvatore (m), 1168
Pisier, Marie-France (f), 465
Pita, Dan (m), 1504
Pitof (m), 2337
Pius, Raj, 1032
Piwowski, Marek, 1462
Pizer, Larry, 1837
Pladevall, Tomàs (m), 1590

Planer, Franz, 1892
Platt, Marc, 2325
Platt, Polly (f), 2248
Plattner, Patricia (f), 1670
Pleijel, Agneta (f), 1653
Plenert, Thomas, 688, 728
Plenzdorf, Ulrich, 721, 724
Plessas, Mimis, 860
Plyta, Maria (f), 858
Pogany, Gabor, 1144
Poirier, Anne Claire (f), 180, 183
Poirier, Pierre, 218
Poitier, Sidney (m), 1905
Polanski, Roman (m), 1756, 1909
Poliakoff, Stephen, 1809
Polito, Gene, 1942
Polk, Mimi (f), 2137
Pollack, Christophe, 558, 573, 631, 657, 673
Pollack, Dale, 2216
Pollack, Patsy (f), 1806
Pollack, Sharon (f), 2199
Pollack, Sidney (m), 1945, 2005, 2049
Polon, Vicki (f), 1990
Pons, Maurice, 22
Pons, Ventura (m), 1590
Ponti, Carlo, 422, 425, 426, 437, 1144, 1755
Pool, Lea (f), 189, 190, 200, 203
Poon Hang-sang, 903, 905, 913, 917
Pope, Bill, 2121, 2196
Pope, Dick, 1838, 1841, 1886
Popov, Sergei, 2390
Popovic, Predrag, 835
Porath, Gideon, 1137
Porta, Elvio, 1176
Porter, Dorothy (f), 84
Posmysz, Zofia (f), 1459
Poster, Stephen, 2030
Pot, Bert, 1384
Potter, Sally (f), 1782, 1817, 1845
Pottersman, Vivien (f), 1779
Poucet, Pascal, 622
Poul, Alain, 2402
Poulheim, Achim, 841
Poulsen, Peter, 360
Powell, Lorna (f), 1814
Prakash, J. Om (m), 983, 1013
Prasad, L. V., 973
Prasad, Shree, 1044
Pratt, Roger, 1871
Preiss, Jeff, 813
Prejean, Helen (f), 2198
Preminger, Otto (m), 1926
Premji, 996
Pressman, Edward, 1936, 1991, 2050
Preston, Gaylene (f), 1387, 1393, 1394, 1400

Pretederis, Costas, 855
Preto, Gonsalves, 1491
Prévost, Françoise (f), 501
Price, Frank, 1115
Price, Nancy (f), 2136
Priemikhov, Valery, 2382
Prietor, Jenaro, 2194
Prieto, Rodrigo, 1341, 2295
Prince-Bythewood, Gina (f), 2262
Pringle, Ian (m), 64
Priyono, Ami, 1064
Procacci, Domenico, 1207
Proctor, Elaine (f), 1540, 1543
Proferes, Nicholas T., 1922
Prokopowicz, Bartek, 1485
Prose, Francine (f), 2152
Protat, François, 182
Prouix, Monique (f), 184
Proust, Marcel, 632
Prouty, Olive Higgins (f), 2118
Provelangios, Angelos (m), 885
Puenzo, Luis (m), 29
Punter, Ian, 1808
Pupkewitz, David, 1879
Purcell, Evelyn (f), 1947, 2060
Pürrer, Ursula (f), 93
Purzer, Manfred, 785
Putnam, David, 1112
Putnam, Mark, 2246

Qi Chang, 204
Qi Xu, 245
Qian Jiang, 236
Qiao Xuezhu, 246, 262, 286
Qin Wenju, 256
Qin Yan (f), 281
Qin Yifu, 227
Qin Zhiyu (m), 272, 285, 308
Qiñones, Sarafin, 336
Quarrington, Paul, 1819
Queffélean, Alain, 537, 1329
Queffélec, Yann, 125
Quercy, Alain, 106
Querejeta, Elias, 1602
Querejeta, Gracia (f), 1602
Quill, Michele, 1390
Quindlen, Anna (f), 2233
Quinlan, Richard, 2111
Quinn, Anthony (m), 740
Quinn, Declan, 1885, 2150, 2233, 2253, 2301, 2307
Quintos, Rory B., 1449
Quoc, Doan, 2406

Raab, Kurt, 756
Rabatoni, Tony, 1324

Rabier, Jean, 425, 440, 447, 448, 449, 455, 487, 527, 551
Rabinad, Antonio, 1593
Racine, Jean, 513
Rada, Ricardo, 132
Radclyffe, Sarah (f), 1804
Raddon, Richard, 2344
Rademakers, Fons, 109
Rademakers, Lili (f), 124, 1368
Radnitz, Robert, 2023
Raeburn, Michael (m), 1651
Rafaelyan, Mike, 1708
Rafelson, Bob (m), 2068
Raffe, Alexandra, 195
Rafiyev, Bagir, 102
Rafiyie Jam, Asghar, 1094
Ragályi, Elemér, 929, 939, 2272
Rahardjo, Slamet (m), 1008
Rai, Gulshan, 1033
Rai, Rajiv (m), 1033
Raimi, Sam (m), 2185
Rainer, Yvonne (f), 1933, 1950, 1971, 2115, 2212
Raizman, Yuly (m), 2373
Rajski, Peggy (f), 2129
Rakintzis, Thanassis (m), 886
Raltschev, Rali, 682
Ramaka, Joseph Gai (m), 1533
Ramakrishna, Bhanumathi (f), 977
Ramirez, Ismael, 1699
Ramon, Carlos, 1584
Ramones, Cenen, 1429
Ramos, Francisco, 1605, 1625
Ramsay, Lynne (f), 1878
Ramsay-Levi, Jean-Pierre, 656
Ranasinghe, Tony, 1637
Randall-Cutler, Roger, 1794
Raphael, Frederic (m), 1754, 1759, 1778, 1949
Rapp, Joseph, 2050
Rappaport, Michele (f), 1991
Rapsey, David, 55
Rashidi, Davoud, 1099
Rasker, Frans, 1367
Rasp, Helmut, 822
Rasputin, Valentin, 2378
Rath, Franz, 687, 717, 771, 782, 789, 828
Rathborne, Tina (f), 2099
Rathnam, A. M., 1057
Räty, Harri, 419
Rau, Santha Rammi, 1789
Ravetch, Irving, 1997
Ravi, Rajeev, 1049
Ravier, Jean, 430
Rawlings, Marjorie Kinnan, 1995, 2023
Ray, Satyajit (m), 963, 968, 969
Rayfiel, David, 1972
Rayson, Hannie (f), 73

Razbezhkina, Marina (f), 1520
Read, Melanie (f), 1389
Rebeck, Theresa (f), 2337
Rebes, Andreu, 1601
Red, Eric, 2106
Reeves, Jennifer (f), 2346
Refaie, Nasser, 1099
Refig, Halit (m), 1708, 1710, 1730
Regnier, Sebastien, 639
Reichebner, Harald, 684
Reichman, Rachel (f), 2220
Reiker, Tami (f), 2167, 2193, 2231, 2330
Reilly, William, 2132
Reimann, Brigitte (f), 732
Reis, António (m), 1487
Reisz, Karel (m), 1761, 2051
Reitemeier, Lutz, 321
Reitz, Edgar, 743
Rejtman, Martin (m), 38
Remaudeau, Michel, 1523
Remias, Ricardo, 2048
Renan, Sergio, 1626
Renard, Jacques (m), 465, 546
Rendell, Ruth (f), 575, 631
Renoir, Claude, 469
Renucci, Bernard, 673
Renzi, Maggie, 2017, 2147, 2247
Rerberg, Georgi, 2357
Rescher, Gayne, 1908, 1926, 1948
Reshovsky, Marc, 2216
Resnais, Alain (m), 438, 596
Resnick, Gina (f), 2221
Resnick, Patricia, 1999
Reuss, Karlhans, 757
Revich, Valeri, 1518
Rex, Jytte (f), 357, 359, 365
Rey, Cristina (f), 2208
Rey, Jean-Michel, 672
Rey-Coquais, Cyrille (f), 842
Reynolds, Don, 1389, 1390
Reypens, Magda (f), 109
Reyre, Marie-Laure, 554
Reznikov, Yefim, 2389
Reznikow, Jean, 482
Ribeiro, Jao Ubaldo, 149
Riber, John, 2416
Riber, Louise (f), 2416
Ribes, Federico, 1352, 1565
Rice, Luanne (f), 2140
Rice, Sascha (f), 2326
Rice, Tom (m), 2311
Richards, John C., 2264
Richardson, Robert, 2341
Richardson, Tony, 1746, 1751, 1757, 2157
Richmond, Anthony, 1793, 2195, 2325

Rickman, Alan (m), 1849
Rickman, Thomas, 2000
Rico-Godoy, Carmen (f), 1578
Riga, Elizabetta (f), 1197
Riis, Sharon (f), 192
Rilke, Rainer Maria, 1487
Rintels, David, 2133
Rinzler, Lisa (f), 2072, 2104
Ripert, Jean-Marc, 175
Ripstein, Arturo (m), 1339, 1340, 1342, 1343
Rique, Newton, 133
Risi, Marco (m), 1199
Risi, Nelo (m), 1154
Risquez, Diego, 2401
Ritchie, Michael (m), 1956
Ritschel, Franz, 684
Ritt, Martin (m), 1997, 2023
Ritter von Theumer, Ernst, 834
Rivas, Ray, 2092
Rivera, Frank, 1437
Rives, Federico, 1608
Rivette, Jacques (m), 445, 465, 473, 503, 528, 561
Rivière, Marie (f), 521
Rizzoli, Angelo, 1147, 1150
Robbins, Isen, 1859
Robbins, Tim (m), 2198
Robert, Denise, 200, 218
Roberts, Amanda, 213
Roberts, Peter, 1814
Roberts, Philip, 2417
Robin, Jean-François, 634, 1120
Robinson, Marilynne, 2073
Robinson, Sally (f), 2340
Robsahm, Thomas, 1415
Roch, Antoine, 637
Rocha, Claudio, 2184
Roche, Axel de, 796
Rochefort, Christiane (f), 175
Rodionov, Alexei, 1817
Rödl, Josef, 799
Rodriguez, Ana (f), 344
Rodriguez, Azucema (f), 1586
Rodriguez, Francisco, 1549
Rodríguez, Miguel, 25, 26, 27, 30
Rodriguez, Milagros, 2397
Rodríguez, Nelson, 329, 334, 335
Rodriguez, Raul, 345
Rodriguez, Rosemary (f), 2316
Roeg, Nicolas (m), 1759, 1762, 1793, 2105
Roehler, Oskar (m), 705
Roesch, Christine (f), 684
Roestad, Paul, 1411
Rogue, Elso, 1487
Rohmer, Eric (m), 453, 502, 514, 518, 521, 601, 629, 765

Roiphe, Anne Richardson (f), 1937
Roizman, Owen, 2005
Rojas, Manuel, 1555
Rojas, Orlando (m), 340
Roll, Gernot, 689, 709, 748
Rollin, Dominique, 117
Roman, Tony, 213
Romano, Marcia (f), 643
Römer, Rolf (m), 726
Romero, Eddie (m), 1955
Romero, George (m), 1935
Romero, Nancy (f), 1935
Romero, Rosa (f), 1575, 1577
Romoli, Gianni, 1737
Ronay, Esther (f), 1774
Roño, Chito S. (m), 1446
Rooke, Stephen (m), 1114
Rooks, Pamela (f), 1029
Roos, Don, 2145, 2173
Rosa da Costa, Jean-Paul, 533
Rosaleva, Gabriella (f), 1172
Rose, Alexandra (f), 1997, 2078
Rose, Bernard (m), 591
Rose, Heather (f), 79
Rose, Louisa (f), 1936
Rosella, Gualtiero, 1177
Rosenbaum, Stephanie, 2161
Rosenberg, Aaron, 1968
Rosenberg, Marc, 51
Rosenberg, Pauline (f), 68
Rosenberg, Saturday (f), 63
Rosenman, Howard, 1974
Roshan, Rakesh, 1022
Rosher, Charles, Jr., 1986
Rosi, Francesco, 1182
Rosier, Michèle (f), 476
Ross, Herbert (m), 1987, 2103, 2173
Ross, Lillian Bos (f), 1961
Rossetti, Ann T., 2163
Rossignon, Christophe, 636, 2408
Rossner, Judith (f), 1982
Rossoff, Eduardo, 1600
Rotaeta, Felix, 1577
Rotberg, Dana (f), 1336
Roth, Richard, 1981
Rothman, Stephanie (f), 1921, 1927, 1931, 1944, 1960
Rotunno, Guiseppe, 1167
Roüan, Brigitte (f), 555, 588, 641
Roumel, Katie (f), 2282
Rousselot, Philippe, 497, 523, 572, 604, 2109
Rousset-Rouard, Yves, 508
Roven, Charles, 2024
Rowe, Ashley, 1823, 1826, 1851, 1881
Roxas, Humilde, 1434
Roy, Bimal (m), 966

Roy, Soumendu, 1051
Rozema, Patricia (f), 195, 205
Rozenbaum, Marek, 1129, 1130
Rozewicz, Stanislaw (m), 1470
Rózewicz, Tadeusz, 1477
Ru Shuiren, 285
Ruark, Ann, 2256
Ruban, Al, 1984
Ruben, Andy, 2119
Ruben, Joseph (m), 2136
Ruben, Katt Shea (f), 2119
Rubenstein, Bill, 2172
Rubinstein, Mauricio, 2317
Rücker, Günther (m), 723, 730
Ruddy, Albert, 2110
Rudin, Scott, 2036, 2202
Rudnick, Paul, 2261, 2345
Rudolph, Alan (m), 1992, 2032, 2132
Rudolph, Verena (f), 827
Ruiz, Raoul (m), 222, 223, 225, 226, 513
Ruiz-Gutierrez, Pilar (f), 1631
Rukov, Mogens, 373
Rule, Jane, 2044
Rusic, Lierka (f), 1201
Rusinov, Georgi, 159
Ruslani, Soleh, 1065
Russell, Ken, 1765
Russell, Willy, 1785, 1810
Russo, Aaron, 1998
Rutler, Monique (f), 1491
Ruttenberg, Joseph, 1891
Ruzicka, Viktor, 844
Ruzicková-Steiner, Gudrun (f), 799, 1669
Ryazantseva, Natalya (f), 2355, 2365, 2369
Rydell, Mark (m), 1998
Ryffel, Hugues, 1666
Rygârd, Elisabeth (f), 356
Ryslinge, Helle (f), 361, 363
Rywin, Lew, 1482

Sa'ati, Azia, 1082
Saada, Raoul, 667
Saarinen, Eric, 1985
Sade, Marquis de, 531
Saderman, Alejandro (m), 2400
Sadilova, Larisa (f), 1515, 1519
Sadler, Richard, 1533
Safa, Mohamed Ali, 1103
Sagan, Carl, 2222
Sagan, Françoise (f), 423
Sagel, Hille, 767, 784, 787, 803, 833
Sahar, Gouda, 379
Sahiwal, 1042
Sahraout, Youcef, 12
Sail, Nourredine (m), 1352

Saint Phalle, Niki de (f), 1770
Saint-Blancat, Pierre, 534
Saint-Jean, Michel, 605
Saint-Martin, Virginie (f), 609
Saire, Jean-Pierre, 621
Saito, Yonejiro, 1228
Saiz, Antonio, 1626
Sakamoto, Junji (m), 1272
Sakellarios, Alekos, 857
Saks, Mady (f), 1360, 1367
Sakurai, Myoko, 1260
Salajev, Ajas (m), 102
Salami, Bachir, 19
Salazar, Ramón, 1625
Saldívar, Serguei, 1345
Salerno, Enrico Maria, 1160
Salinas, Martín, 1341
Salles, Murilo, 133
Salles, Walter (m), 152
Salminen, Timo, 417
Salmones, Javier, 1586
Salomon, Amnon, 2034
Salomon, Mikael, 2099
Samanta, Shakti, 974
Samb-Makharam, Ababacar (m), 1522
Sami, Mostafa, 380
Samosiuk, Zygmunt, 1466
Samsom, Cees, 1360
Samsonov, Samson (m), 2374
San Miguel, Santiago, 1552
Sanchez, Carlos, 323
Sanchez, Christian, 223
Sánchez, Jorge, 1334, 1335
Sanchez, Rodolfo, 143, 145, 154
Sander, Helke (f), 91, 767, 794, 812
Sanders-Brahms, Helma (f), 695, 716, 766, 779, 788,
    816
Sandler, Susan, 2089
Sandor, Gregory, 1936
Sandoz, Gilles, 616
Sandrin, Patrick, 225, 226
Sanford, Midge (f), 2045, 2145, 2177
Sanger, Jonathan, 2016
Sani, Asrul (m), 1058, 1061, 1065
Saniewski, Wieslaw, 1472
Sanjines, Jorge, 132
Sankofa Collective, 1799
Santiago, Cirio (m), 2048
Santiago, Digna (f), 1425
Santoni, Tino, 1145
Santos, Malou, 1446
Santos-Concio, Chard, 1440
Santoshi, Rajkumar, 1052
Sanz, Nestor, 1372
Sapir, Esteban, 37

Sarafian, Tedi (f), 2189
Sarde, Alain, 491, 520, 545, 564, 568, 573, 610, 620,
    624, 633, 634, 658, 660, 663
Sargent, Alvin, 1930, 1981, 2237, 2314
Sarin, Vic, 186, 192, 198
Sarmiento, Valeria (f), 224, 225, 226
Sarner, Arlene (f), 208, 2061, 2157
Sarossy, Paul, 212
Sarrazin, Albertine (f), 1331
Sarukawa, Naoto, 1276
Sass, Barbara (f), 1461, 1467, 1469, 1474, 1479, 1481
Sato, Masajuki, 1245
Sato, Midori (f), 1273
Satomi, Ton, 1215
Saubiran, André, 442
Saura, Carlos (m), 1547, 1556, 1574
Sautet, Claude (m), 459, 488
Saux, Yorick, 664
Savin, Lee, 1939
Savoca, Nancy (f), 2104, 2124, 2152, 2207, 2229
Sayag, Pierre, 597
Saydam, Nejat (m), 1711
Sayeed, Malik, 2203, 2234
Sayles, John (m), 1996, 2017, 2147, 2247, 2317
Sayyad, Parviz (m), 1074
Scalella, Luis, 39
Scandurra, Sofia (f), 1164
Scardino, Don (m), 2146
Scavarda, Aldo, 859, 1143
Scborg, Morten, 374
Schaefer, Roberto, 2276
Schäfer, Martin, 794, 812
Schanelec, Angela (f), 696
Schapces, Marcelo, 42
Scharf, Yaron, 1141
Schatzberg, Jerry (m), 1920
Scheibelhofer, Maria (f), 96
Schell, Maximilian (m), 775
Schepsi, Fred (m), 60, 2050
Scherick, Edgar, 1979
Schick, Elliot, 2046
Schierl, Angela Hans (f), 93
Schiff, Paul, 2328
Schiffman, Suzanne (f), 471, 503, 538
Schindler, Deborah (f), 2191, 2328
Schipek, Dietmar, 93
Schlesinger, Günter, 746
Schlesinger, John (m), 1754, 1759
Schliesser, John, 2280
Schlöndorff, Volker (m), 704, 760, 761, 763, 2108
Schlosberg, Leopold, 423
Schlossberg, Julian, 2111
Schmid, Anka (f), 842
Schmidt, Evelyn (f), 733
Schmidt, Hartwig, 1468

Schmidt, Jan (m), 351
Schmidt, Jörg, 792
Schmidt-Reitwein, Jörg, 759
Schmitt, Eric-Emmanuel, 589
Schneider, Bert, 2006
Schneider, Harold, 2008
Schneider, Peter, 687
Scholes, Robin, 1397, 1398
Scholten René, 1373
Schrader, Leonard, 1991
Schrader, Paul (m), 1991, 2075
Schreiber, Nancy (f), 2284
Schröder, Claudia (f), 691, 714
Schroeder, Barbet (m), 453, 465, 475, 503, 765
Schroeter, Werner (m), 649, 750, 795
Schubert, Helga (f), 728
Schubert, Stefan, 1739
Schühly, Thomas, 802
Schulberg, Sandra (f), 2052, 2064
Schuler, Fred, 2001
Schulman, Arnold, 1894
Schultz, Michael, 2348
Schultze-Kraft, Cornelius, 887, 892
Schulze, Berhnard, 757
Schulze-Gerlach, Tine, 731
Schumacher, Joel (m), 1968, 1974, 2009, 2159, 2335
Schwartz, Bernard, 2000, 2051
Schwartz, Jaime, 154
Schwartz, Nadine (f), 213
Schwarzenberger, Xaver, 802
Schyfter, Guita (f), 1337
Scibor-Rylski, Aleksander, 1457
Scola, Ettora (m), 1142
Scorsese, Martin (m), 1929, 1946
Scott, Alex, 1816
Scott, Allan, 2105
Scott, Ann (f), 1815, 1831, 1857
Scott, Cynthia (f), 199
Scott, Ridley (m), 1994, 2137
Scotta, Carole (f), 661
Scotti, Tony, 2074
Seabra, Antonia (f), 1498
Seabra, Toca, 155
Seacat, Sandra (f), 2111
Seale, John, 2091, 2144, 2172
Seaton, Eula, 2007
Seaward, Tracey, 1826
Sechehaye, Margeurite Ardrée (f), 1154
Seeber, Michael, 96
Seefeldt, Renate (f), 690
Segawa, Junichi, 1248
Segre, Daniele, 1205
Segura, Mayra (f), 344
Seguy, Margarita (f), 21
Sehr, Peter (m), 678

Seidelman, Susan (f), 2019, 2045, 2076, 2116, 2240, 2322
Sejfullina, Lidiya (f), 2360
Sekkat, Mohamed, 1349
Selami, Bachir, 17
Sellner, Manuel, 365
Seltzer, David (m), 2095
Sembène, Ousmane (m), 1521, 1523, 1524, 1526, 1532, 1534
Semler, Dean, 2110
Sempé, Wilfrid, 648
Sen, Aparna (f), 997, 1018, 1026, 1035, 1046, 1055
Sen, Asit, 971
Sen, Mala (f), 1031
Sen, Mrinal (m), 995, 1010, 1016, 1028
Sen, Somanth (m), 2304
Sen, Sujit, 1005
Sender, Julie Bergman (f), 2215, 2228
Senje, Riri (f), 1415
Senkay, Ertunc, 1732, 1738
Senna, Orlando, 138
Senter, Hal, 1889
Seo, Jeong-min, 1300
Serdaris, Vangelis (m), 893
Sereny, Julia (f), 219
Serikbayeva, Zhanna (f), 1279
Serlin, Beth (f), 689
Serra, Eduardo, 627, 1848, 2250
Serrano, Antonio (m), 1627
Serrano, Carlos, 1565
Serrano, Marcela, 39
Serrano, Nina (f), 223
Serreau, Coline (f), 540, 634
Sertesen, Melih, 1711
Sethumadhavan, K. S. (m), 975, 985
Seville, Victor, 1749
Sewell, Stephen, 64
Shabazz, Menelik (m), 1779
Shadan, Abdulah, 1
Shafaq, Toryalai, 1
Shagiev, Talgat, 1279
Shah, Piyush, 1847
Shahani, Kumar (m), 978, 1011, 1027
Shahriar, Maryam (f), 1092
Shainberg, Steven, 2312
Shajgardanov, Yuri, 1516
Shakespeare, William, 401
Shamiakin, Ivan, 2374
Shang Xiangin, 238
Shao Qi, 297
Shapiro, Lisa (f), 2167
Shapiro, Susan (f), 1774
Shapiro, Yevgeni, 2360
Sharaqui, Youssef, 1695
Sharashidze, Alexander, 675
Sharma, Eranki (m), 992

Sharma, Tripurari, 1041
Sharma, Vijay (m), 984
Sharon, Rubin, 746
Sharp, Sally (f), 2007
Shashikant, A., 1035
Shatransky, Renée (f), 2031
Shaw, George Bernard, 459
Shaw Run Me, 900
Shaw, Sam, 1959, 2001
Shaw, Sandy, 917
Shayeghi, Syamak, 1075
Shebib, Donald (m), 186
Shechori, Idit (f), 1127
Sheeler, René, 442
Sheldo, Ronald, 1828
Shelton, Angela (f), 2252
Shen Miaorong, 306
Shen Ningyue, 299
Shen Rei-yuan, 1688
Shen Ru-mei, 274
Shepitko, Larisa (f), 2355, 2378
Sheppard, Christopher, 1817, 1845
Sher, Lawrence, 2303
Sherick, Edgar, 2036
Sheridan, Jim (m), 1118, 1863
Sheridan, Michael, 1121
Sherman, Geraldine (f), 1825
Sherman, Martin, 1202, 1820
Shetty, Manmohan, 998
Shi Shujin, 269
Shi Xiaohua (f), 244, 292, 300
Shields, Carol (f), 1831
Shii, Yukiko, 1272
Shimizu, Kunio, 1224
Shimoda, Atsuyuki, 1264
Shin Sang-okk (m), 1289, 1290
Shin Seung-soo (m), 1308
Shindo, Kaneto, 1228, 1230, 1232, 1236
Shinoda, Masahiro, 1231, 1242, 1247
Shirasaka, Yoshio, 1246
Shiva, Gil, 1167
Shivas, Mark, 1778, 2105
Shivers, Louise (f), 2082
Sho Sa, 1673
Shope, Stephani (f), 2208
Shoten, Kadokawa, 1266
Shu Kei (m), 919
Shukla, Vinay (m), 1045
Shukri, Mamduh (m), 381
Shulgina, Albina (f), 2360
Shum, Mina (f), 202
Shumovich, Aleksandr, 1514
Shuqing, Huang (f), 289
Shusett, Ronald, 1994
Shuster, Harry, 1922

Shuvalov, Valeri, 2391
Shyer, Charles (m), 2003, 2067
Si Huang, 276
Sichel, Alex, 2260
Sichel, Sylvia, 2260
Sicot, Marcel, 432
Sidibé, Abdoulaye, 1318
Sidorov, Gennadi, 1515, 1519
Siegel, David, 2275
Sievernich, Lilyan (f), 1117
Sigal, Clancy, 2295
Sigel, Newton Thomas, 681, 2239
Sighvatsson, Sigurjon, 2268
Sigurd, Jacques, 435
Sillart, Jüri, 406
Silveira, Breno, 147, 153
Silver, Amanda, 2142
Silver, Joan Micklin (f), 1952, 2089
Silver, Megan (f), 2182
Silver, Raphael D., 1952
Silvera, Charlotte (f), 535
Silvers, Dean, 2181
Simakov, Vsevolod, 2384
Simenon, Georges, 468
Simmonds, Michael, 2327
Simon Cerezo, Ana, 1585
Simon, Claire (f), 599
Simon, Neil, 2011
Simon, Wolfgang, 87, 832
Simonetti, Marcelo, 24
Simonic, Dodo, 346
Simpson, Geoffrey, 65, 1118, 2125, 2179, 2334
Simpson, Mona (f), 2237
Simpson, Peter, 2158
Simsolo, Noël, 466
Sinai, Khosro (m), 1089
Sinambs, Andreas, 710
Sinclair, Harry (m), 1399
Sinclair, Ingrid (f), 2417
Singer, Raymond, 2340
Singh, Manmohan, 1053
Singh, Sehjo, 1056
Sinha, Tapan, 1051
Sinke, Digna (f), 1363, 1373
Sissoko Oumar, Cheick (m), 1320
Sivan, Sanatosh (m), 1044
Skaggs, Calvin, 2097
Skeet, Mark, 1885
Skelton, Barbara (f), 1840
Skorepová, Jana (f), 346
Skourti, Maria (f), 875
Slabnevich, Igor, 2355, 2375
Slak, Francie, 1535
Slapeta, Ivan, 795
Slater-Ling, Tony, 1887

Slim Riad, Mohamed (m), 8
Slocombe, Douglas, 1748, 1772, 1964, 1981
Slovis, Michael, 2214
Slovo, Robyn (f), 1878
Slovo, Shawn, 1804
Sluizer, George, 1356
Smaragadis, Nikos, 872, 883
Smeds, Barbro (f), 1657
Smihi, Moumen (m), 1349
Smith, Bernard, 1900
Smith, John, 2277
Smith, Kirsten (f), 2325
Smith, Robert, 1108, 1796
Smith, S. Douglas, 2304
Smyth, Karen (f), 1872
So Wai Ching, 1677
Soarez, Elena (f), 153
Sobieski, Carol (f), 2125
Sobocinski, Piotr, 574, 956
Sobocinski, Witold, 1486
Søborg, Morten, 371
Söderberg, Hjalmar, 354
Soderbergh, Steven (m), 2242
Södergran, Edith (f), 413
Softley, Iain (m), 1848
Sohlberg, Kari, 415
Sokol, Yuri, 54, 56
Sokurov, Alexander (m), 2393
Solal, Serge Cohen, 555
Solano, Domingo, 1553, 1572
Solares, Raul, 1325
Solás, Humberto (m), 328, 329, 334, 335
Soldini, Silvio (m), 1196
Solitrenick, Jacob, 156
Solms, Kenny, 1967
Solo, Robert H., 2157
Solomon, Alex, 1512
Solomon, Ed, 2128
Somb-Makharan, Ababacar (m), 1528
Somego, Rodolfo, 1165
Somló, Tamás, 927
Son Hyunchae, 1295
Soner, Ahmet, 1719
Song Gyeong Shik, 1310
Song Il Gon, 1306
Song Kil-han, 1292, 1296, 1298
Songsri, Cherd (m), 1693, 1694
Sonnenfeld, Barry, 2043
Sophiaan, Sophan, 1063
Sophocles, 683, 849, 932, 1155
Soray, Türkan (f), 1712, 1718
Sou, Jacob (m), 166
Southon, Mike, 2129
Spagnoli, Alberto, 1949
Spark, Muriel (f), 1764

Specht, Kenneth, 174
Speeckaert, Glynn, 1879
Spencer, Don, 1921
Sperduti, Marco, 685
Speth, Maria (f), 713
Spicer, Michael, 204
Spiehs, Karl, 676
Spielberg, Steven (m), 1957, 2042
Spiller, Michael, 2219
Spinelli, Anthony, 1899
Spinola, Paolo, 1148
Spinotti, Dante, 1179, 2054, 2087, 2185, 2211
Spragg, Mike, 1834
Sprecher, Jill (f), 2221
Sprecher, Karen (f), 2221
Spring, Sylvia (f), 174
Srour, Heiny (f), 1312
Stacey, Terry, 2266
Stadiem, William (m), 1840
Stafford-Clark, Nigel, 1792
Stagner, Rama Laurie, 2157
Stahl, Frederick, 79
Stambrini, Monica (f), 1206
Stancanelli, Elena, 1206
Stanev, Lyuben, 158
Stanier, John, 2207
Stanley-Smith, Judith (f), 1818
Stantic, Lita (f), 26, 27, 28, 30, 32, 33, 35, 40, 43
Stapleton, Oliver, 1824, 2116
Starger, Martin, 2047
Starhemberg, Heinrich, 1549
Stark, Ray (m), 1906, 1945, 2103
Stark, Wilbur, 1766
Starrett, Jack (m), 1940
Stassen, Willy, 1377
Stavro, Aris, 873
Steel, Judy, 181
Steele, Gunnar, 1889
Stehr, Manuela (f), 708
Steiger, Ueli, 2183
Stein, Gertrude, 1539
Stein, Peter, 2052
Steinbach, Peter, 838
Steinke, Günter, 757
Stephens, John M., 1929
Stephens, Paul, 208
Stern, Stewart, 1908, 1943
Stern, Tom, 2343
Stettner, Patrick (m), 2254
Stevens, Robert, 1747
Stewart, Donald, 2010
Stewart, Olivia, 1867
Steyn, Jacques, 791, 819
Stickelbrucks, Lothar, 783
Stieler, Laila (f), 703

Štiglic, France (f), 2411
Stiles, Mark, 51
Stiller, Tobias, 1379
Stöckl, Ula (f), 682, 747, 773, 774, 818
Stöcklin, Tania (f), 842
Stoffers, Rogier, 2292
Stoloff, Dan, 2252
Stone, Noreen (f), 2100
Stone, Oliver, 2106
Stopkewich, Lynne (f), 206
Storaro, Vittorio, 1169
Storozheva, Vera (f), 1742
Stover, Susan (f), 1859, 2220, 2324
Stradling, Harry, Jr., 1945
Stradling, Harry, Sr., 1906, 1919
Strangio, Benito, 1382
Stratfeld, Susan (f), 2201
Straub, Jean-Marie (m), 683, 745
Streeter, Khari (f), 2279
Streisand, Barbra (f), 2211
Stroh, Valerie (f), 549
Stroppiano, Bruno, 149
Strouvé, Georges, 466
Strugatz, Barry, 2093, 2116
Sturgess, Ray, 1106
Stutterheim, Eliane (f), 1508, 1736
Styron, William, 2020
Su Fannggui, 303
Su Tong, 302
Suárez, Carlos, 1551, 1552, 1628
Suárez, David, 2398
Suárez, Ramon, 524
Sugandhi, Yadi, 1072
Sugarman, Burt, 2055
Sugarman, Sara (f), 1873
Sughand, Jhamu, 1053
Suhrstedt, Tim, 2094
Sukalo, Danijel, 2415
Sukhatankar, Sunil (f), 1036
Suleimenov, Nuraly, 1281
Sullivan, Kevin Rodney (m), 2232
Sumar, Sabiha (f), 1416
Sumathipala, Milina, 1637
Summers, Manuel, 1557
Sun Qian, 267
Sundberg, Bert, 1652, 1653
Sung Kwang-jae, 1301
Surikova, Alla (f), 2384
Surtees, Bruce, 1974, 2013, 2113
Surtees, Robert, 1895, 1987
Suryadi, Tantra, 1008
Susan, Minot (f), 1192
Susanto, Adrian, 1063, 1064
Suschitzky, Peter, 549
Suslov, Mikhail, 2060

Susskind, David, 1890, 1946
Sutherland, Kiefer, 2271
Suzuki, Tatsuo, 1242
Sveen, Karin, 1408
Svensrud, Gunnar, 1405
Svoboda, Victor, 353
Swanson, Glenwood J., 1939
Swartz, Charles, 1927, 1931, 1944, 1960
Swicord, Robin (f), 1803, 2179
Swimar, Barry, 2192
Syaa, Meera, 1821
Sylbert, Anthea (f), 2313
Syrigas, Marc, 613
Szabó, Gabor, 824
Szabó, Ildiko (f), 957
Szabó, István, 221
Szomjas, György, 955
Szwark, Jeannot (m), 1791

Taberna, Helena (f), 1608
Tabío, Juan Carlos (m), 337, 339
Tacer, Cengiz, 1710
Tachenov, Dj., 2352
Tafa, Nexhati, 3
Tafani, Carlo, 1188
Tafori, Renato, 1172
Tagore, Rabindranath, 969
Tahir, Kemal, 1708
Tait, Margaret (f), 1816
Takahashi, Yoko (f), 1245
Takahishi, Kaori, 1262
Takayama, Yukiko (f), 1262
Talalay, Rachel (f), 2189
Tally, Ted, 2117
Tam, William, 909
Tamahori, Lee (m), 1397
Tamai, Masao, 1217
Tamaoki, Yasushi, 1257
Tamaro, Susanna, 1193
Tamdon, Adeep, 1019
Tammes, Diane (f), 1773, 1774
Tan Han-chang, 1679
Tan Xiangiang, 318
Tanaka, Joji, 1267
Tanaka, Kinuyo (f), 1216, 1245
Tanaka, Masako, 1255
Tanaka, Noboru, 1244
Tanaka, Rika (f), 1268
Tanaka, Sumie (f), 1223
Tanaka, Tomoyuki, 1254, 1256
Tang Chi-ming, 1680
Tang, Elsa (f), 304
Tang Shu Shuen, 899
Tanizaki, Junichiro, 1179, 1228, 1254, 1368
Tanner, Alain (m), 650, 1663, 1665, 1666, 1667

Tarantino, Quentin (m), 2225, 2341
Taraporevala, Sooni (f), 2131
Tarazi, A., 2353
Tardini, Ib, 371, 376
Tarr, Béla (m), 947
Tasev, Atanas, 161
Tashiro, Hirotaka, 1259
Taslami, Susan (f), 1661
Tattersall, David, 1835
Tattersall, Gale, 2189
Tattoli, Elda (f), 1158
Tau Tai, 910
Taurand, Gilles, 656
Tavernier, Bertrand (m), 534
Tavernier, Colo (f), 527, 534
Távora, Pilar (f), 1607
Taylor, Edward, 2138
Taylor, Gilbert, 1756
Taylor, Jeffrey, 2269
Taylor, Jim, 2197
Taylor, Sam, 894
Taymor, Julie (f), 2295
Tchalgadjieff, Stéphane, 467, 473
Teague, Lewis (m), 1996
Téchiné, André (m), 464, 493, 564, 656, 2349
Tegopoulos, Apostolos, 859, 861
Teheri, Barbod, 1073
Tei, Yoshinobu, 1266
Teichman, Adam, 2182
Teles, Luis Galvão (m), 1502, 1603
Temenov, Talgat (m), 1278
Templeman, Conny (f), 1798
Tendulkar, Vijay, 999, 1014
Tengberg, Bo, 369
Tennant, Victoria (f), 1833
Tennant, William, 1940, 2082
Terán, Georgina (f), 1338
Teran, Manuel, 64
Terje, Kristiansen, 1411
Tesse, Chris Tsui, 846
Tetley, Graeme, 1393, 1394
Tevet, Akiva (m), 1128
Tewfik, Raoul, 391
Tewkesbury, Joan (f), 1991
Tezuka, Yoshi, 1540
Thackeray, William, 1885
Thatree, Thom, 1693, 1694
Theos, Dimos, 869
Theotokis, Konstantinos, 876
Theron, Charlize (f), 2329
Thibaut, Jean-Claude, 604
Thiel, Nick, 2194
Thiele, Rolf, 741
Thieltges, Gary, 2096
Thijssen, Felix, 1367

Thiombiano, Issaka, 166
Thirard, Armand, 424
Thivel, Caroline, 647
Thom, Robert, 1916, 1962
Thomas, Anna (f), 2026, 2295
Thomas, Betty (f), 2253
Thomas, Jeremy, 1192, 1793
Thomas, Lee, 1875
Thomas, May Miles (f), 1872
Thomas, Michael, 1805
Thomas, Pascal (m), 606
Thomas, Robert, 646
Thomasson, Camille (f), 1600
Thompson, Bob, 911
Thompson, Christopher, 620
Thompson, Danièle (f), 572, 620
Thompson, Emma (f), 1830, 2286
Thompson, J. Lee (m), 1976
Thompson, Peggy (f), 211
Thompson, Tommy, 1107
Thomsen, Christian Braad (m), 355, 361, 365
Thomsen, Preben, 364
Thornton, Warwick, 80
Thorin, Donald, 2173, 2202
Thorn, Jean-Pierre, 843
Thorp, Sarah (f), 2347
Thurman, Uma (f), 2341
Thurmann-Andersen, Erling, 1405, 1407, 1409
Tiappa, Frieda (f), 881
Tibbo, Piret (f), 406
Tickner, Clive, 1109, 1786, 1811
Tie Ning, 283
Tijdink, Stef, 1376
Tilson, Alison (f), 86
Timite, Bassori (m), 1209
Tini, Maurizio, 1194
Tinio, Rolando, 1443
Tirl, George, 2037
Tittel, Volker, 1496
Tlatli, Moufida (f), 1698, 1702
To, Johnny (m), 917
To, Raymond, 905, 919
Tochizawa, Masao, 1239, 1253
Todd, Suzanne, 2207
Todorov, Yatsek, 162
Todorovsky, Pyotr (m), 2391
Todorovsky, Valery, 1516
Tofano, Gilberto (m), 1124
Toledo, Serge, 145
Tolstaya, Tatyana, 1514
Tolstoy, Leo, 591, 2356
Tolstunov, Igor, 1742
Tom, Tim, 99
Tomioka, Taeko, 1238, 1242
Tomlinson, Mike, 1781

Tong, Terry (m), 1680
Tong, Wang (m), 1672
Toole, F. X., 2343
Toon, John, 1398, 1883
Topalov, Kiril, 160
Topor, Tom, 2085
Topping, Angela, 1796
Törhönen, Lauri (m), 416
Tórisson, Snorri, 961
Torre, Roberta (f), 1197, 1201
Torrent, Jordi, 1610
Torrente, Fina (f), 1615
Torres, Fina (f), 585, 2396, 2402
Torres, Miguel, 1324
Torronen, Hannelore (f), 416
Toscan du Plantier, Daniel, 481, 489, 504
Toshiyuki Uno, Michael (m), 2097
Tosi, Mario, 2004
Tovey, Janet, 1815
Tovoli, Luciano, 1171
Towhidi, Juliette (f), 1881
Towne, Robert (m), 2018
Toye, Patrice (f), 128
Toyoda, Shiro (m), 1241
Tozzi, Fausto, 859
Tozzi, Federigo, 1191
Trahey, Jane (f), 1902
Trampe, Tamara (f), 731
Trapero, Pablo, 45
Trebitsch, Katherina (f), 702
Treilhou, Marie-Claude (f), 543
Tremblay, Jean Charles, 193
Tremblay, J.-J., 196
Trenez, Tote, 1616
Treu, Wolfgang, 2035
Treut, Monika (f), 680, 742, 840, 2175
Trevor, William, 212, 1110
Tribuson, Snjezane (f), 325, 326
Trilogchander, A. C. (m), 988
Trinh, Coralie (f), 618
Trintignant, Nadine (f), 578
Troche, Rose (f), 2163, 2332
Trodd, Kenith, 1809
Troell, Jan (m), 1961
Trope, Tzipi (f), 1133
Trow, George, 1837
Trueba, David (m), 1629
Truffaut, Francois (m), 471
Trujillo, Miguel, 1567
Trushkovsky, Vasili, 2387
Tsai Cheng-hui, 1685
Tsiarta, Anna, 892
Tsiolis, Stavros, 879
Tsue, Maisy (f), 912
Tsui Hark (m), 905, 914, 915

Tsukimori, Sennosuke, 1216
Tuber, Joel, 2076
Tucker, Anand (m), 1852
Tuna, Feyzi (m), 1714
Tunca, Çetin, 1717, 1730
Tunhas, Paulo, 1490
Turanli, Gani, 1713
Türkali, Vedat, 1715
Turker, Yildirim, 1735
Turko, Rose-Marie (f), 2027
Turner, Ann (f), 67, 69
Turner, Barbara (f), 1762, 1976, 2176
Turner, Guinevere (f), 2163
Turner, Khahtee (f), 2331
Turner, Tina (f), 2155
Turnheg, Karl, 1747
Turpin, André, 215
Turpin, Gerry, 1753
Twyker, Tom (m), 698, 1374
Tyler, Anne (f), 2344
Tyurin, Rudolf, 2378
Tzavellas, Yorgas (m), 849

Udoff, Yale, 1793
Ufland, Harry, 2133
Ufland, Mary Jane, 2133
Ugar, Ali, 1715
Ujlaki, Tamas, 92
Ullmann, Liv (f), 187, 360, 1413, 1658, 1659
Ulloa, Alejandro, 1564
Uman, Chaerul (m), 1065
Undset, Sigrid (f), 1413
Unger, Kurt, 1769
Uno, Isamu, 1272
Unsworth, Geoffrey, 1767
Updike, John, 2084
Uralskaya, Irina (f), 1520
Urbaniak, Urszula (f), 1485
Urdang, Leslie, 2146
Ureta, Raúl Perez, 343
Urruzola, Maria, 2350
Ursianu, Malvina (f), 1505, 1506, 1510
Ustaoglu, Yesim (f), 1741
Ustinov, Peter, 1755
Utt, Kenneth, 2093
U-wei, Haji Shaari (m), 1316

Vacano, Jost, 761
Vachon, Christine (f), 2186, 2206, 2282, 2293, 2332
Vagenshtain, Plamen, 158
Vaikunth, K., 983, 986, 996
Valchinov, Nikolai, 163
Valdes, Julio, 337, 339, 344
Valenzuela, Jose Luis (m), 2263
Valery-Grossu, Nicole (f), 1513

Valleti, Serge, 505
Valverde, Manuel, 1582
Van Brummelen, Reinier, 1381
Van Damme, Charles, 119, 478
Van de Sande, Theo, 1359, 1362, 2089, 2299
Van den Berghe, Dorothée (f), 131
Van Den Bos, Paul, 124, 1368, 1383
Van den Ende, Walther, 114, 117, 121, 125, 1380
Van der Enden, Eddy, 103, 108, 109, 126
Van der Laan, Heleen (f), 1378
Van der Meulen, Helena (f), 1376
Van der Oest, Paula (f), 1384
Van der Velde, Jean, 1378
Van Druten, John, 2012
Van Eden, Frederik, 1362
Van Grote, Alexandra (f), 817
Van Heijningen, Matthijs, 1357, 1361, 1362, 1366, 1369
Van Hensbergen, Mat, 1356
Van Kraaij, Peter, 131
Van Laer, Michel, 129
Van Oosterhout, Richard, 128
Van Peebles, Melvin (m), 621
Van Reemst, Frank, 1365
Van Rensburg, Manie (m), 1541
Van Sant, Gus, 2190
Van Sickle, Kenneth, 1952
Van Voorst, Suzanne (f), 1376
Vancaillie, Jan, 131
Vance, Leigh, 1744
Vandendries, Paul, 110
Vandeputter, Annemarie (f), 1363
Vanderwildt, Albert, 1363
Vankeerberghen, Laurette, 566
Vanlint, Derek, 1994
Vanni, Carlo, 548
Vanzina, Carlo, 1186
Varda, Agnès (f), 425, 441, 452, 478, 516, 525
Vardalos, Nia (f), 2308, 2339
Varela, Diego, 2351
Varini, Carlo, 1016
Vasile, Turi, 1158
Vasile, Vivi Dragan, 1511
Vassdal, Kjell, 1414
Vassiliadis, Vassilis, 864, 866
Vazquez Figueroa, Alberto, 1559
Vecchiali, Paul (m), 466
Vecsey, George, 2000
Vega, Pastor, 333
Veillot, Claude, 491
Veitia, Hector, 344
Vejnovic, Sanja, 326
Velarde, Alvaro (m), 1423
Velasco, Manuel, 1584, 1598
Velev, Nikola, 157
Velho da Costa, Maria (f), 1493, 1498

Venkatesan, N., 1055
Venu, 1029, 1054
Vera, Gerardo (m), 1623
Verbong, Ben (m), 1359, 1371
Vercruysse, Gérard, 109
Verges, Rosa (f), 1575
Verhoeff, Pieter (m), 1383
Verhoeven, Michal (m), 686, 796
Verhoeven, Paul, 2139
Vernoux, Marion (f), 570
Veroiu, Mircea, 1504
Verzier, René, 176
Vészi, Endre, 938
Veuve, Jacqueline (f), 560
Veysset, Sandrine (f), 590, 639
Vicario, Marco (m), 1165
Vicente, Joana (f), 2282
Vierny, Sacha, 438, 446, 816
Viets, Alexandra (f), 1856
Vieva, Luandino, 22
Vilasis, Mayra (f), 344
Vilenski, V., 2362
Villalobos, Reynaldo, 1999, 2095, 2226, 2262
Villard, Marc, 641
Villaverde, Cirilo, 334
Villaverde, Teresa (f), 1496, 1499, 1501
Villeneuve, Denis (m), 215
Villiers, Francois (m), 435
Vilsmaier, Joseph (m), 702, 838
Vilstrup, Li (f), 356
Vincent, Amy (f), 2223
Vincent, Russel, 1914
Vincze, Ernst, 1784, 1800
Vinokur, Semyon, 1135
Vir, Parminder (f), 1864
Visconti, Luchino, 1153
Vitti, Monica (f), 1189
Vittorio, Gian, 1154
Vitug, Romeo, 1439
Vlachová, Kristina (f), 352
Vlacos, Alex, 2154
Vlail, Frantisek, 352
Vogel, Frank, 722
Vohra, Chander, 973
Vohra, Paromita, 1416
Volodarsky, Eduard, 2383
Von Ackeren, Robert, 808
Von Alemann, Claudia (f), 787
Von Arnim, Elizabeth (f), 1815
Von Brakel, Nouchka (f), 1357, 1362, 1369
Von Garnier, Katja (f), 692, 2340
Von Grote, Alexandra (f), 803
Von Hillern, Wilhelmine, 832
Von Kleist, Heinrich, 765
Von Krusenstjerna, Agnes (f), 1639

Von Präunheim, Rosa (m), 801, 829
Von Scheibner, Raimund, 716
Von Scherler Mayer, Daisy (f), 2214
Von Trier, Lars (m), 364, 367, 372, 375
Von Trotta, Margarethe (f), 677, 685, 687, 717, 718,
    760, 761, 763, 771, 782, 789, 800, 828, 1187
Von Vietinghof, Joachim, 1720
Von Vietinhoff, P., 831
Von Waldenfels, Walburg (f), 694
Von Wolkenstein, Michael, 92
Vonier, Fabienne (f), 582
Voorthuysen, Paul, 1378
Vorschneider, Reinhold, 696, 713
Voss, Christiane (f), 1374
Voss, Kurt (m), 2251, 2266, 2320
Vosser, Silvia (f), 1353
Voufargol, Paul, 475
Voulgaris, Pantelis (m), 868, 880
Vouyouklakis, Takis (m), 865, 873
Vucicevic, Branko, 2414
Vuorinen, Esa, 414, 416

Wachowski, Andy, 2196
Wachowski, Larry, 2196
Waddington, Andrucha (f), 153
Wade, Kevin, 2098
Wagner, Jane (f), 2009
Wagner, Richard, 1762
Wagner, Ulla (f), 706
Wagon, Virginie B. (f), 642
Waite, Ric, 2271
Wajda, Andrzej (m), 810, 1457, 1482
Wakeford, Kent, 1946
Waldekranz, Rune, 408, 1639
Waldleitner, Luggi, 785
Walerstein, Mauricio, 1552
Walker, Alice (f), 2042
Walker, John, 197
Walker, Mandy, 78
Wallace, Earl, 2207
Wallace, Pamela, 2207
Wallace, Stephen (m), 69
Wallis, Hal B., 1768
Wallon, Peter, 561
Walnum, Sven, 1923
Walsh, David, 1940, 2011, 2077
Walsh, Frances, 1396
Walters, Charles, 1891
Walther, Connie (f), 1379
Wan Ren (m), 1674
Wandago, Albert (m), 1285
Wang Haowei (f), 236, 238, 246, 283
Wang Jin (m), 278, 303
Wang Junzheng (f), 262, 286
Wang Lianpin, 276

Wang Lingu, 233
Wang Ping (f), 293
Wang Quan'an, 321
Wang Shifu, 311
Wang Tian-lin, 227
Wang Tianyun, 295
Wang, Wayne (m), 2237
Wang Wei, 288
Wang Wei-wei, 305
Wang, Xiao-yen (f), 2290
Wang Xiaolie (m), 313
Wang Xiaoyan (f), 305
Wang Xinsheng, 273
Wang Zhaoling, 238
Wankowicz, Melchior, 1486
Wargnier, Régis (m), 550, 569
Warneke, Lothar (m), 725, 728, 732, 736
Wassally, Walter, 1783
Watelet, Marilyn, 118
Waters, Mark (m), 2321
Watkin, David, 1757, 1860, 1965, 2049, 2090
Watkins, Christine (f), 1818
Watt, Jeremy, 1784
Watts, Frank, 1785
Wauters, Armand, 107
Wauthion, Claire, 112
Wawrzyn, Lienhard, 820
Waxman, Harry, 1747
Wearing, Michael, 1121
Weber, Alicia (f), 1833
Weibel, Peter, 87, 88
Weiley, John, 48
Weill, Claudia (f), 1990, 2002
Weincke, Jan, 368
Weindler, Helge, 690, 822
Weinstadt, Liliane, 106
Weinstein, Hannah (f), 1948
Weisberg, David, 2241
Weisenfeld, Joe, 185
Weiss, Ida (f), 1536
Weiss, Jiri, 844
Weiss, Maja (f), 1536
Weissman, Aerlyn, 197
Weisz, Frans, 1358
Weldon, Fay (f), 2116
Welin, Hans, 1406, 1648, 1652, 1655
Wells, Audrey (f), 2245, 2334
Wells, Jon, 2315
Wells, Rebecca, 2291
Wen Xiaoyu, 252
Wenders, Wim (m), 752
Wendkos, Paul (m), 1993
Wenig, Ernst, 733
Wertmüller, Lina (f), 1160, 1162, 1166, 1167, 1175,
    1176, 1186, 1188

Wertwijn, Lex, 1371
Wessel, Kai, 841
West, Brian (m), 2053
Westfeld, Jennifer (f), 2303
Weston, Jay, 1905
Wexler, Haskell, 2215, 2247
Wharton, Edith, 1867
Wheeler, Anne (f), 192, 198, 207, 211, 217
Whitaker, Forest, 2191
White, Mike, 2296
Whitehead, Peter (m), 1770
Whitmore, Hugh, 1775
Whitmore, Preston A., II, 2318
Wichard, Michel, 428
Wick, Douglas, 2098, 2244
Wicki, Bernhard, 740
Widitomo, Bambang, 1064
Wiedemann, Katrine (f), 371
Wiedemann, Vinca (f), 371
Wieland, Joyce (f), 181
Wilhelm, Bettina (f), 1669
Wilhelm, Rolf, 741
Wilhelm, Uwe, 692
Wilkening, Thomas, 688
Willems, Paul, 105
Williams, Billy, 1765, 1769, 2118
Williams, David D., 2153
Williams, Matt (m), 2270
Williams, Norman (m), 1744
Williams, Oscar (m), 1942
Willing, Vinay, 1019
Willingham, Calder, 2135
Willis, Gordon, 1924, 1937
Willoughby, Nigel, 1123
Wilson, Barbara (f), 2322
Wilson, Daniel, 2108
Wilson, David, 199
Wilson, Erin Cressida (f), 2312
Wilson, Hugh (m), 2202
Wilson, Kim, 2143
Wilson, Richard (m), 1910
Wilson, Rita (f), 2308
Windeløv, Vibeke (f), 372, 374, 375
Windhäger, Edward, 768
Winding, Andreas, 6, 458, 477
Winding, Romain, 557, 568
Wing, Avra, 2156
Winham, Francine (f), 1774
Winiewicz, Krysztof, 1459
Winkler, Irwin, 1937, 2102
Winschneider, Anna, 838
Winter, John, 75
Winterbottom, Michael (m), 1827, 1861
Winterson, Jeanette (f), 1808
Wirschling, Josef, 976

Wirth, Wolf, 741
Wishman, Doris (f), 1897
Witcombe, Eleanor (f), 49
Witte, Gunther, 771
Wittig, Monique (f), 635
Wittliff, William, 1780
Woff, Clarence, 505
Wojcik, Jerzy, 1453, 1470, 1486
Wojcik-Slak, Hanna A. (f), 1535
Wojtowicz, Piotr, 958
Wolf, Christa (f), 720
Wolf, Konrad (m), 720, 729
Wolitzer, Meg, 2148
Wolkind, Jenny (f), 2100
Wollen, Peter (m), 1773
Wolman, Dan (m), 1126, 1134
Wong, Arthur, 921, 926
Wong, Bill, 907, 910, 919
Wong, Manfred, 923
Wood, Caroline (f), 1882
Wood, Oliver, 2321
Woodcock, Steven, 1865
Woolcock, Penny (f), 1815
Woolf, Jack, 1968
Woolf, James, 1752
Woolf, Virginia, 793, 1817, 1843
Woolley, Stephen, 1805
Worth, Annie Brown (f), 1781
Worth, David (m), 1071
Worth, Jan (m), 1781
Wottitz, Walter, 468
Wouthuysen, Bernd, 1370
Wu Di, 320
Wu Jianxin, 244
Wu Nien-chen, 1675
Wu Nien-jen, 1671, 1681
Wuer Shana (f), 252, 257
Wunstorf, Peter, 202
Wurmfeld, Eden, 2161
Wyler, William (m), 1892, 1906
Wyman, Brad, 2171
Wynn, Tracy Keenan, 1938

Xiao Jian, 288
Xie Fei (f), 265, 293, 296
Xie Jin (m), 228, 233, 239, 240, 245, 251, 277, 306
Xie Tieli, 236
Xie Yang (m), 307
Xu Qingding, 239
Xu Qingdong, 275
Xu Wei, 317
Xu Yali, 260
Xwe Ke, 248
Yaconelli, Steve, 2157

Yafa, Stephen, 1910
Yaguchi, Shinobu (m), 1265
Yahiaoui, Allel, 10, 14, 1697
Yakin, Boaz (m), 2235
Yamada, Nobuo, 1231
Yamamoto, Hideo, 1275
Yamamoto, Michiko, 1452
Yamamoto, Satsuo (m), 1250
Yamamoto, Shugoro, 1276
Yamasaki, Tizuka (f), 137, 140, 142
Yamazaki, Kuninori (f), 1267, 1274
Yameshita, Kasaku, 1237
Yan Cui (f), 204
Yan Geling, 318
Yan Junsheng, 234, 256, 267
Yan Yan Mak (f), 322
Yan Yijun, 321
Yanakiev, Boris, 157
Yang, Edward (m), 1671
Yang, Janet, 2299
Yang, Lun, 280
Yang Wei-han, 1673, 1676, 1679, 1683
Yang Xinji, 299
Yanne, Josée (f), 548
Yannoulis, Stamatis, 889
Yao Yun, 263
Yasumoto, Jun, 1220, 1223, 1229
Yau Ching (f), 319
Yau Tai, 907
Yautai On-ping, 913
Yazaki, Hitoshi, 1251
Ye Dan, 250
Ye Weilin, 278
Yedaya, Karen (f), 1140
Yegin, Mengü, 1707, 1709
Yeshov, Valentin, 2355
Yi Chang (m), 1673
Yi Ling, 309
Yildiz, Bekir, 1715
Yilmaz, Atif (m), 1717, 1721, 1723, 1725, 1727, 1731, 1735
Yim Ho (m), 309, 903
Yip, Raymond (m), 923
Yoda, Yoskitaka, 1249
Yonfan, 925
Yong Bai Xin, 277
Yonova, Eli, 163
York, Susannah (f), 1107
Young, Dalene, 2023
Young, David, 1831
Young, Diana (f), 1983
Young, Freddie, 1775, 1778
Young, John Sacret, 2030
Young, Robert M. (m), 2055
Young, Terence (m), 1904

Yourcenar, Marguerite (f), 763
Youssef, Khaled, 402
Yu Hua, 314
Yu Shan, 269
Yu Shishan, 244
Yuan Wenyao, 272
Yuen Woo-ping (m), 304
Yumeno, Kyusaku, 1264
Yun Zhaogung (m), 241
Yurizditsky, Sergei, 2393

Zagni, Giancarlo, 859
Zaid, Gal, 1137
Zaidi, Shama (f), 1000, 1006, 1047
Zaim, Dervis (m), 1738
Zalaznick, Lauren, 2204
Zamarion, Fabio, 1207
Zambrano, Benito (m), 1616
Zanke, Susanne (f), 92
Zanuck, Richard, 1957
Zanussi, Krzysztof (m), 1455, 1456, 1468
Zappon, Erik, 366
Zarchi, Meir (m), 1980
Zarchy, Bill, 1855
Zarin Dast, Ali Reza, 1081
Zarkhi, Alexander (m), 2356
Zarokosta, Melpo, 870
Zauberman, Yolande (f), 587
Zavattini, Cesare, 1144, 1159
Zdort, Wieslaw, 1461, 1467, 1474, 1479, 1481
Zebrowski, Edward, 1455
Zecevic, George, 2414
Zeffirelli, Franco (m), 1202, 1860
Zei, Lucia Maria (f), 1177
Zeig, Sande (f), 635
Zeitoun, Ariel, 496, 509
Zeitoun, Serge, 1502
Zeltzer, Yuri, 2299
Zemeckis, Robert (m), 2141, 2222
Zeng Nianping, 294, 302
Zeng Zhuangxiang, 1675
Zertsalov, Andrei, 1518
Zervoulakos, Takis, 874
Zervoulakos, Yiorgas, 867
Zetterling, Mai (f), 187, 1639, 1640, 1643, 1654, 1784
Zhang Chang Guang, 274
Zhang Huanqin, 279
Zhang Hui (m), 312
Zhang Jian, 281
Zhang Lun (m), 241
Zhang Manling, 249
Zhang Nuanxing (f), 242, 249
Zhang Songping, 248
Zhang Wenmin, 253
Zhang Xian (m), 272, 285

Zhang Xigui, 314
Zhang Xuan, 308
Zhang Yi. See Chang Yi
Zhang Yimou (m), 259, 280, 284, 291
Zhang Yu (f), 309
Zhang Yuan (m), 281, 314
Zhang Zeming, 271
Zhang Zhenhua, 320
Zhang Zhong Ping, 262
Zhao Fei, 309
Zhao Heqi, 297
Zhao Junhong, 269, 299
Zhao Shi, 248
Zhao Xiaoshi, 278
Zhao Yimin, 297
Zheltukhina, Natalia (f), 1520
Zhelyazkova, Binka (f), 157
Zhen Kang-zhen, 288
Zheng Kangzhen, 271
Zhou Damin, 233
Zhou Jianping, 306
Zhou Jixun, 275
Zhou Xiaowen (f), 273, 301
Zhou Zhiqianq, 264
Zhu Wei, 259
Zhu Yongde, 268
Zhukhovitsky, Leonid, 2361
Zia Lixing, 261
Zidi, Claude, 4
Zieff, Howard, 2003
Ziegler, Regina (f), 683, 786, 828
Zielinski, Jerzy, 1112, 2228
Ziesche, Peter, 736, 737

Zilberstein, Guy, 588
Zimmer, Hedda (f), 737
Zimmer, Markus, 717
Zimre, Peter, 930
Zinai Koudil, Hafsa (f), 16
Zindel, Paul, 1930, 1937
Zinneman, Fred (m), 1981
Zions, Brad, 2303
Ziskin, Laura, 2190
Zito, Luciano, 43
Zitzermann, Bernard, 170, 496, 517, 554, 575, 817
Zlotoff, Lee David (m), 2187
Zobel, Joseph, 512
Zola, Émile, 531, 1484, 1546
Zolkowska, Joanna (f), 1484
Zonca, Erick (m), 605, 642
Zornitsa, Sophia (f), 164
Zschoche, Herrmann (m), 721, 731
Zsigmond, Vilmos, 1107, 1925, 1957, 1998, 2084
Zsures, Éva (f), 945
Zugsmith, Albert, 1889
Zulawski, Andrzej (m), 504
Zúñiga, Ariel (m), 1328
Zurlini, Valerio (m), 1145, 1152
Zuta, Daniel, 2168
Zveryeva, Marina (f), 406
Zweig, Stefanie, 709
Zwerenz, Catharina (f), 808
Zwick, Edward (m), 2128
Zwick, Joel (m), 2308
Zwigoff, Terry (m), 2277
Zylber, Filip, 1478

INDEX OF SUBJECTS

Abandoned, 110, 1086, 1200, 1611, 2412

Abandoned and pregnant, 212, 740, 876, 985, 992, 1135, 1338, 1529, 2270

Abortion, 24, 77, 94, 166, 215, 376, 442, 478, 488, 497, 527, 993, 1408, 1752, 1783, 1894, 2197, 2207

Abortion rights, 1261, 1507

Abortionists, 527, 754, 1072, 1886

Abuse. *See* Addiction; Betrayal; Child abuse; Domestic abuse; Genital mutilation; Incest; Mothers, abusive; Partner abuse; Rape; Spouse abuse

Action films, 43, 58, 68, 86, 304, 310, 544, 611, 655, 698, 900, 901, 905, 914, 917, 918, 923, 1033, 1067, 1071, 1206, 1237, 1308, 1536, 1758, 1791, 1916, 1923, 1929, 1947, 1954, 1957, 1958, 1962, 1970, 1994, 1996, 2100, 2106, 2110, 2117, 2137, 2171, 2172, 2185, 2189, 2210, 2216, 2225, 2241, 2337, 2341. *See also* Blaxploitation films

Actors, 102, 106, 154, 172, 213, 221, 340, 466, 528, 541, 594, 640, 680, 714, 737, 748, 768, 871, 905, 910, 919, 935, 1058, 1129, 1173, 1180, 1184, 1454, 1470, 1474, 1549, 1565, 1580, 1590, 1641, 1643, 1659, 1726, 1866, 1907, 1984, 2011, 2013, 2066, 2147, 2183, 2203, 2209, 2213, 2289, 2305, 2364, 2370, 2386. *See also* Film actors; Stunt actors

Actors, Chinese opera, 261, 919

Adaptations, 445, 635, 1533, 1546, 1981, 2127

Adaptations, comic book, 1758, 1791, 2100, 2189, 2277, 2337

Adaptations, novel, 221, 222, 226, 303, 371, 423, 427, 495, 511, 551, 632, 672, 752, 758, 764, 765, 965, 1040, 1057, 1415, 1484, 1759, 1765, 1789, 1802, 1830, 1835, 1843, 1848, 1867, 1885, 1888, 1949, 2007, 2042, 2108, 2179, 2228, 2278, 2356, 2393

Adaptations, play, 364, 513, 683, 719, 740, 757, 849, 850, 851, 867, 871, 932, 1078, 1155, 1156, 1342, 1529, 1570, 1594, 1607, 1624, 1643, 1767, 1771, 1772, 1880, 2380

Addiction, 1169, 1431, 1535, 1739, 2016. *See also* Alcoholics; Drug addicts

Adoption, 29, 185, 224, 303, 550, 852, 934, 1441, 1742, 1838, 2156, 2180, 2265, 2317

Afghani Canadians, 1097

Afghanistan, 1090, 1097, 1668 (made in), 1–2

Afghanistan, Kabul, 2, 1101

Africa, towns and villages, 537. *See also* names of individual countries

African Americans, 407, 847, 1364, 1890, 1905, 1911, 1938, 1939, 1940, 1942, 1948, 1951, 1965, 1969, 1974, 1993, 2042, 2062, 2101, 2122, 2131, 2149, 2153, 2160, 2191, 2192, 2194, 2203, 2213, 2216, 2223, 2230, 2232, 2234, 2262, 2269, 2279, 2287, 2305, 2318, 2319, 2348. *See also* Blaxploitation films; Race relations

African British, 1779

African French, 526, 669

African Germans, 691

African Italians, 1197

African Portuguese, 1497

African Swedes, 1644, 1657

Age differences. *See* Older man, younger woman; Older woman, younger man; Older woman, younger woman

AIDS, 2173

AIDS activists, 1214, 1436

Akan people, 847

Albania (made in), 3

Albanian French, 562

Alcoholics, 539, 624, 778, 786, 965, 1479, 1589, 1912, 1984, 1998, 2058, 2159, 2253, 2266

Algeria, 555, 1611 (made in), 4–21

Algeria, Algiers, 8, 20, 1706

Algeria, l'Aurès, 19

Algeria, history, 5, 7, 17, 18, 21, 64, 630

Algeria, Kabil, 17

Algeria, towns and villages, 12, 14, 17, 21, 630

Algerian French, 4, 18, 20, 581, 602, 626, 637

Alzheimer's disease. *See* Dementia

Ambition, 50, 204, 243, 699, 772, 1636, 1825, 2343

Americans (U.S.). *See* African Americans; Argentinean Americans; Chinese Americans; Cuban Americans; Czech Americans; Hispanic Americans; Mexican Americans; Indian Americans; Iranian Americans;

Italian Americans; Japanese Americans; Native
    Americans; Norwegian Americans; Vietnamese
    Americans
Amnesiacs, 610, 2078
Amnesty International, 524, 2399
Ancient history. *See* Historical settings, ancient
Androgyny, 793, 1817
Angola (made in), 22–23
Animal testing, 2325
Animism, 1284, 1422, 1526
Anthology films, 24, 91, 187, 320, 329, 344, 386, 549,
    595, 617, 738, 920, 1093, 1105, 1290, 1504, 1688,
    1728, 2175, 2267, 2269, 2309
Anthropologists, 839
Appearances. *See* Androgyny; Beauty; Cross-dressers;
    Fashion
Arab–black relations, 396, 1321, 1701
Arab French, 403
Arab–white relations, 4, 64, 542, 555, 662, 753, 1144
Architects, 732, 1087
Arctic Circle, 1378
Arendt, Hannah, 595
Argentina, 786
    (made in), 24–46
    Argentina, Buenos Aires, 25, 27, 41, 1199, 1845
    Argentina, "disappeared," 29, 33, 46, 836
    Argentina, history, 30
    Argentina, Paraná, 41
    Argentina, Salta, 40
Argentinean Americans, 1617
Argentinean British, 1812
Argentineans. *See* German Argentineans; Italian
    Argentineans
Arsonists, 1757
Art, 943
Art dealers, 1345
Artists, 580, 595, 1240, 2193, 2290, 2306. *See also*
    Actors; Filmmakers; Painters; Photographers;
    Potters; Sculptors
Ashton-Warner, Sylvia, 1390, 1891
Asian–white relations, 62, 86, 137, 202, 207, 550, 2150
Assassinations, 1121, 1421, 1804, 2335
Asylum seekers, 669
Athletes, 209, 242, 349, 1738, 1825, 1874, 1979, 2018,
    2024, 2081, 2143, 2226, 2262, 2343
Aubrac, Lucie, 548, 593
Aung San Suu Kyi, 2172
Aunts, 169, 244, 360, 944, 967, 1089, 1282, 1445,
    1637, 1775, 1783, 2073, 2396
Australia, 1386
    (made in), 47–86
    Australia, Sydney, 75
    Australia, towns and villages, 77
Australians, 1393. *See also* Japanese Australians;
    Native Australians

Austria (made in), 87–101
    Austria, Alps, 100
    Austria, history, Nazi regime, 87
    Austria, towns and villages, 96, 97
    Austria, Vienna, 94, 95, 98, 541, 801, 864, 1793
Austrians. *See* Polish Austrians
Authors, 32, 49, 73, 262, 477, 493, 517, 549, 559,
    631, 644, 664, 749, 787, 800, 815, 881, 956, 972,
    1009, 1013, 1107, 1157, 1223, 1267, 1383, 1386,
    1390, 1517, 1668, 1807, 1831, 1837, 1840, 1879,
    1981, 2049, 2064, 2109, 2121, 2165, 2183, 2261,
    2267, 2300, 2334. *See also* Diarists; Letter writers;
    Novelists; Poets; Romance writers
Autonomy, 9, 25, 49, 63, 81, 109, 153, 170, 198, 246,
    322, 366, 383, 415, 423, 459, 497, 514, 523, 572,
    577, 609, 689, 720, 748, 769, 799, 848, 876, 881,
    1035, 1073, 1192, 1225, 1258, 1325, 1413, 1418,
    1425, 1475, 1477, 1554, 1655, 1672, 1719, 1721,
    1759, 1785, 1840, 1887, 1908, 1913, 2034, 2052,
    2073, 2125, 2154, 2156, 2179, 2182, 2228, 2313,
    2357
Avant-garde films. *See* Experimental films; Non-
    narrative films
Azerbaijan (made in), 102

Bach, Johannes Sebastian, 745
Ballet, 1987
Bankers, 496
Bar owners, 776, 1217, 1239, 1537, 2092
Battered women. *See* Partner abuse; Spouse abuse
Beauty (physical) 74, 210, 218, 226, 274, 422, 425, 481,
    594, 616, 671, 962, 1022, 1192, 1204, 1297, 1408,
    1413, 1678, 1693, 1716, 1754, 1762, 1764, 1793,
    1867, 1924, 1956, 1982, 2124, 2141, 2211, 2305
Beauty parlors, 616, 1756, 1861, 2103, 2149
Beiriz, Anayde, 140
Belgium, 91
    (made in), 103–131
    Belgium, Antwerp, 128, 1380
    Belgium, Brussels, 107, 122, 131
    Belgium, The Hague, 126
Belgium, history, German occupation, 114
    Belgium, Malmédy, 103
    Belgium, Ostend, 108
    Belgium, towns and villages, 124
Berber, Anita, 824
Berber people, 8, 17, 1354
Bernhardt, Sarah, 154
Betrayal, 1, 27, 29, 65, 127, 196, 213, 246, 274, 309,
    329, 363, 369, 384, 392, 398, 435, 441, 482, 495,
    524, 541, 567, 620, 622, 624, 688, 714, 718, 724,
    735, 762, 801, 875, 906, 907, 924, 939, 961, 1005,
    1013, 1069, 1070, 1086, 1137, 1150, 1161, 1198,
    1251, 1296, 1309, 1348, 1454, 1481, 1542, 1547,
    1553, 1608, 1619, 1641, 1683, 1687, 1778, 1802,

1836, 1877, 1912, 1926, 1988, 1995, 2034, 2071, 2157, 2223, 2257, 2263, 2313, 2329, 2334. *See also* Abandoned

Biographies, 523, 597, 611, 702, 913, 991, 1031, 1111, 1120, 1256, 1339, 1390, 1653, 1761, 1768, 1850, 1852, 1855, 1893, 1932, 2000, 2022, 2028, 2051, 2064, 2155, 2206, 2227

Biographies of artists, 464, 529, 592, 1202, 1330, 2295

Biographies of authors, 32, 323, 413, 493, 695, 705, 749, 956, 996, 1009, 1267, 1373, 1383, 1386, 1392, 1654, 1775, 1807, 1837, 1871, 1883, 2023, 2049, 2064, 2109, 2165, 2261

Biographies of political activists, 828, 1393, 1421, 2028, 2401

Birth control, 132, 818, 1106

Birthdays, 342, 366, 604, 946, 1412, 2054, 2209

Births, 533, 779, 847, 936, 1043, 1301, 1639, 1856, 2230

Bisexual women, 515, 1179, 1585, 1687, 2018, 2109

Black–Arab relations. *See* Arab–black relations

Black–white relations, 121, 134, 334, 530, 540, 621, 642, 690, 691, 716, 823, 1134, 1521, 1538, 1541, 1543, 1592, 1604, 1644, 1651, 1657, 1746, 1782, 1838, 1899, 1965, 2006, 2013, 2014, 2021, 2079, 2101, 2115, 2125, 2127, 2145, 2180, 2192, 2220, 2293, 2311

Blaxploitation films, 1940, 1941, 1951, 2213, 2225. *See also* Exploitation films

Blind women, 56, 372, 1311, 1348, 1893, 1904, 2083

Bokma de Boer, Sjoukje, 1383

Bolivia (made in), 132

Book collectors, 2053

Book editors, 2309

Book readers, 426, 531, 682

Booksellers, 2089

Borneo, 1245

Brazil (made in), 133–156
  Brazil, Amazon region, 138
  Brazil, Brazilia, 151
  Brazil, Bélem, 138
  Brazil, history, 134, 140, 144, 147
  Brazil, Minas Gerais, 134
  Brazil, Rio de Janeiro, 156
  Brazil, São Paulo, 137, 141, 150
  Brazil, towns and villages, 149, 156

Brazilians. *See* Japanese Brazilians

Breadwinners, 7, 89, 153, 171, 266, 296, 301, 964, 968, 995, 1023, 1056, 1062, 1119, 1130, 1223, 1248, 1322, 1446, 1448, 1672, 1714, 1869, 2329

Brice, Fanny, 1906

Brides of god, 420, 996. *See also* Nuns

Britain, 30, 664, 972, 997. *See also* United Kingdom

British. *See* Argentinean British; Caribbean British; Indian British

British Indians, 1029, 1887

Brontë sisters, 493

Brothels. *See* Houses of prostitution

Brothers Grimm, 1774

Buddhists, 256, 1299, 2403

Bulgaria (made in), 157–164
  Bulgaria, history, 162
  Bulgaria, towns and villages, 159

Bulimia, 781

Bureaucrats, 229, 238, 240, 248, 287, 345, 732, 1210, 1257, 2046, 2361, 2371, 2390

Burkina Faso (made in), 165–168

Burma (made in), 169

Businesswomen, 105, 250, 258, 272, 296, 299, 427, 438, 485, 508, 624, 636, 653, 708, 857, 910, 968, 1212, 1532, 1572, 1599, 1609, 1611, 1671, 2067, 2194, 2235, 2254. *See also* Bankers; Bar owners; Entrepreneurs; Executives; Farm owners; Managers

Callas, Maria, 1202

Cameroon, 530
  (made in), 170–172

Canada, 627
  (made in), 173–221
  Canada, Alberta, 192
  Canada, British Columbia, 207
  Canada, British Columbia, Vancouver, 211
  Canada, Ontario, 1831
  Canada, Ontario, Toronto, 204, 2158
  Canada, Quebec, 179, 188, 199
  Canada, Quebec, Montreal, 215
  Canada, seaside, 173
  Canada, towns and villages, 207

Canadians. *See* Afghani Canadians; Chilean Canadians; Chinese Canadians; Japanese Canadians

Cancer, 220, 358, 425, 469, 501, 608, 728, 1129, 1379, 1473, 1551, 2029, 2212, 2236, 2265, 2286

Cano, María, 323

Cape Verde, 23

Capital punishment, 157, 372, 527, 1026, 1359, 1439, 1794

Caretakers, 47, 65, 66, 79, 117, 129, 219, 266, 281, 320, 345, 374, 384, 412, 449, 486, 564, 627, 634, 650, 689, 716, 894, 916, 929, 964, 973, 987, 1008, 1010, 1046, 1132, 1170, 1209, 1241, 1282, 1322, 1374, 1470, 1535, 1569, 1641, 1645, 1650, 1738, 1886, 2001, 2134, 2153, 2198, 2233, 2259, 2267, 2400

Caribbean British, 1799

Caribbean French, 526

Caribbean Spanish, 1604

Carpet weavers, 1083, 1092

Carrington, Dora, 1828

Cashiers. *See* Workers, retail

Catholic–Protestant relations, 572, 764, 1110

Catholics, 28, 32, 76, 431, 445, 523, 538, 561, 572, 611, 843, 1106, 1123, 1453, 1481, 1563, 1769, 1982, 2041, 2152
Catt, Carrie Chapman, 2340
Celebrations, 362, 2395. *See also* Birthdays; Holidays; Weddings
Censorship, 1457
Cerebral palsy, 53, 79
Césaire, Aimé, 23
Chiang Kai-shek, 921
Child abuse, 639, 895, 993, 1406, 1434, 1440, 1640, 1642, 1766, 1834, 2195. *See also* Incest
Child abuse victims, 316, 860, 1001, 1114, 1429, 1916, 2042, 2135, 2174, 2348
Childbearing conflicts, 29, 132, 180, 426, 439, 536, 549, 599, 746, 791, 954, 974, 1007, 1069, 1106, 1195, 1220, 1399, 1576, 1724, 1731, 1742, 1752, 1838, 1937, 2180, 2260. *See also* Adoption; Infertility; Mothers, surrogate
Chile (made in), 222–226
    Chile, history, 1973 coup d'etat, 2010
    Chile, Valparaiso, 225
Chilean Canadians, 191
China, 905, 1386, 1673, 1900. *See also* Hong Kong (made in), 227–322
    China, Beijing, 258
    China, Guongdong, 903
    China, Hainan, 228
    China, history, 233, 237, 239, 241, 289, 307
    China, history, Cultural Revolution, 249, 251, 252, 255, 305, 315
    China, history, Japanese occupation, 276, 1675, 1682
    China, history, Second Civil War, 235
    China, Jiangsu, Suzhou, 302, 925
    China, Pearl River, 303
    China, Shandong, Qingdao, 926
    China, Shanghai, 268, 299, 922, 1679, 1686
    China, Tang Dynasty, 311
China, towns and villages, 236, 238, 247, 258, 265, 267, 278, 280, 283, 291, 296, 312, 317, 321, 899, 903, 911, 1680
    China, Zheijiang, Zhuji, 320
Chinese. *See* Japanese Chinese
Chinese Americans, 908, 910, 1684, 2120, 2175, 2290
Chinese Canadians, 202, 204
Chinese–Japanese relations, 288, 300
Chinese–Taiwanese relations, 307
Choosing for oneself. *See* Autonomy
Christ, Lena, 749
Christian revivals, 1908, 2348
Christians, 682, 736, 1216, 1613. *See also* Catholics; Protestants
Christians, orthodox, 2308
Circus performers, 34, 205, 744, 1336

Class differences, 24, 40, 121, 154, 269, 286, 336, 440, 481, 495, 550, 582, 625, 634, 719, 724, 733, 764, 775, 823, 846, 858, 868, 903, 931, 945, 979, 1003, 1005, 1012, 1042, 1048, 1082, 1120, 1162, 1163, 1191, 1307, 1326, 1353, 1396, 1491, 1541, 1565, 1639, 1685, 1698, 1707, 1720, 1725, 1754, 1755, 1785, 1792, 1838, 1848, 1885, 1888, 2078, 2094, 2098, 2118, 2212, 2283, 2288, 2328, 2398. *See also* Classism; Middle class; Poverty; Upper class; Working class; Wealthy women
Classics (humanities), 591, 683, 849, 850, 851, 867, 932, 1624, 1771
Classism, 1, 380, 922, 1031, 1050, 1224, 1305, 1314, 1373, 1594, 1730, 1867, 2115
Claudel, Camille, 529
Cline, Patsy, 2051
Coelho da Cunha, Adelaide, 1491
Colombia, 323
    (made in), 323
Colonialism, 15, 17, 23, 134, 147, 165, 329, 334, 467, 511, 530, 550, 555, 630, 897, 1066, 1070, 1523, 1592, 1783, 1792, 1856, 2417
Comedians, 2095
Comedy, 63, 67, 74, 83, 186, 221, 312, 327, 339, 350, 443, 451, 482, 540, 579, 604, 621, 646, 654, 680, 707, 822, 905, 912, 957, 1006, 1079, 1151, 1188, 1199, 1265, 1275, 1310, 1343, 1369, 1370, 1382, 1423, 1503, 1558, 1573, 1579, 1580, 1587, 1594, 1595, 1597, 1725, 1743, 1758, 1812, 1826, 1875, 1879, 1895, 1902, 1910, 1915, 1918, 1926, 1931, 1942, 1956, 1967, 1985, 1999, 2003, 2009, 2011, 2029, 2037, 2043, 2045, 2056, 2060, 2061, 2067, 2072, 2076, 2077, 2078, 2084, 2088, 2093, 2096, 2098, 2100, 2111, 2112, 2116, 2141, 2148, 2190, 2194, 2202, 2214, 2221, 2232, 2253, 2270, 2274, 2277, 2288, 2291, 2302, 2303, 2305, 2308, 2312, 2321, 2325, 2339, 2387, 2402
"Comfort women." *See* Slavery
Communism, 251, 302, 942, 1481, 2379
Communist "model women," 229, 231, 233, 242, 336, 2371
Communists, 236, 241, 276, 730, 880, 938, 944, 959
Concentration camps, 120, 524, 660, 1161, 1459, 1468, 2020
Concubines, 284, 303, 1290, 1737. *See also* Slaves; Spouses
Conservatism. *See* Class; Marriage; Politicians; Religious fundamentalism; Tradition
Constant, Benjamin, 1373
Contraception. *See* Birth control
Convents, 445, 827, 1413, 1453, 1558, 1563, 1600. *See also* Nuns
Cooks, 362, 707, 2269, 2330, 2357, 2370, 2402
Corbaz, Aloise, 464
Corruption, 238, 402, 445, 1004, 1460

Courtesans, 900, 907, 922, 925, 965, 971, 976, 1000, 1012, 1238, 1260, 1276, 1305, 1686, 1698, 2405. *See also* Prostitutes

Cousins, 156, 1180, 1490

Criminals, 306, 347, 375, 377, 433, 544, 618, 624, 733, 743, 811, 923, 1027, 1031, 1176, 1206, 1272, 1279, 1331, 1564, 1589, 1621, 1753, 1757, 1784, 1801, 1827, 1916, 1929, 1940, 1957, 1962, 1968, 2146, 2164, 2196, 2201, 2294, 2331, 2348, 2382. *See also* Murderers; Thieves

Croatia, 2298, 2411
   (made in), 324–327
   Croatia, rivers, 1536
   Croatia, towns and villages, 324, 327
   Croatia, Zagreb, 325

Croatian New Zealanders, 1398

Cross-cultural relations. *See* Arab–white relations; Arab–black relations; Asian–white relations; Black–white relations; Catholic–Protestant relations; Chinese–Japanese relations; Chinese–Taiwanese relations; Gay–straight relations; Greek Orthodox–Protestant relations; Hindu–Muslim relations; Indian–white relations; Israeli–Palestinian relations; Jewish–Catholic relations; Jewish–Gentile relations; Jewish–Protestant relations; Mixed couples; Mixed parentage; Native–white relations; Serb–Croat relations

Cross-dressers, 2, 25, 103, 232, 261, 681, 706, 905, 1090, 1092, 1151, 1769, 1817, 1880, 2150, 2238, 2339

Cuba (made in), 328–345
   Cuba, Havana, 331, 340
   Cuba, history, 332, 334
   Cuba, towns and villages, 330, 343

Cuban Americans, 338, 2209

Cults, 81, 1818

Curie, Madame, 597

Custody battles, 389, 953, 1357, 1417, 1538, 1899, 2090, 2285, 2338

Cutting, 95, 653, 781. *See also* Genital mutilation

Cyprus, 887, 892

Czech Americans, 2066

Czech Republic (made in), 346–347

Czechoslovakia (made in), 348–353
   Czechoslovakia, Prague, 844

DAI people, 249

Dance, 235, 895, 2370

Dance schools, 1554

Dancers, 422, 526, 829, 970, 1034, 1049, 1505, 1533, 1706, 1761, 1803, 1845, 1933, 1987, 2410

Dancing, belly, 1705

Dandridge, Dorothy, 2203

Dating. *See* Seeking spouses

Daughters, 8, 11, 77, 171, 314, 371, 457, 458, 534, 581, 664, 671, 675, 683, 849, 964, 986, 1138, 1153, 1155, 1171, 1211, 1243, 1249, 1368, 1410, 1496, 1498, 1547, 1552, 1553, 1569, 1661, 1830, 1873, 1888, 1943, 2102, 2396. *See also* Mothers and daughters

Daughters and fathers, 1, 184, 224, 411, 414, 562, 565, 592, 680, 744, 832, 846, 886, 916, 963, 993, 1020, 1082, 1200, 1290, 1338, 1365, 1398, 1407, 1427, 1429, 1444, 1447, 1673, 1701, 1770, 1824, 1834, 1862, 1983, 2025, 2106, 2227, 2228, 2259, 2313, 2354, 2389

Daughters and parents, 689, 762, 1275, 2233

Daughters-in-law, 12, 982, 1047, 1290, 2380

Davies, Sonja, 1393

Death, 206, 926, 1732, 1934

Death of a child, 60, 324, 387, 554, 567, 631, 641, 1041, 1234, 1325, 1504, 1606, 2103, 2168, 2248, 2276

Death of a parent, 75, 80, 150, 225, 277, 533, 539, 565, 865, 886, 1106, 1153, 1351, 1407, 1427, 1451, 1508, 1552, 1571, 1602, 1626, 1639, 1688, 1770, 1846, 1943, 2025, 2185, 2256, 2259

Death of a partner, 1222, 1878, 2260

Death of a spouse, 117, 533, 685, 1030, 1198, 1442, 1471, 1504, 1811, 2264

De Charriere, Madame, 1373

Dementia, 1450, 1871

Denmark (made in), 354–376
   Denmark, Copenhagen, 360
   Denmark, history, 368
   Denmark, towns and villages, 362

Denmark (Danes). *See* French Danes

Dentists, 1344

Depression, 77, 800, 1147, 1605, 1641, 2394

Desert villages, 12, 2367

Detectives, 84, 155, 275, 491, 652, 703, 715, 834, 1137, 1264, 1268, 1414, 1591, 1811, 2068, 2106, 2117, 2130, 2138, 2200, 2322, 2347

Development, 51, 138, 1391, 2378

Devlin, Anne, 1111

Diarists, 815, 944, 948, 950, 1028, 1096, 1193, 1626, 1682

Dietrich, Marlene, 702

Dinesen, Isak, 2049

Diola people, 1523

Disabled, 34, 53, 79, 712, 1164, 1258, 1982, 2059, 2147. *See also* Blind women; Mute women

Disaster, 1435

Disaster survivors, 101, 351, 1016, 2280

Discrimination. *See* Classism; Racism; Sexism

Divorce, 264, 285, 295, 313, 382, 760, 1003, 1357, 1677, 1833, 1922, 1988, 2044, 2232, 2240, 2338

Doctors, 442, 469, 677, 722, 795, 818, 1034, 1040, 1080, 1198, 1210, 1465, 1517, 1648, 1649, 1689, 1692, 1699, 1735, 1747, 1806, 1900, 1977,

2172, 2183, 2267, 2390, 2399. See also Dentists;
    Psychiatrists
Dogon people, 1323
Dollmakers, 2033
Domestic abuse, 12, 16, 99, 384, 455, 556, 573, 779,
    999, 1008, 1095, 1281, 1300, 1329, 1397, 1398,
    1496, 1688, 1882. See also Child abuse; Incest;
    Partner abuse; Spouse abuse
Domestic servants, 30, 40, 44, 78, 103, 146, 154, 192,
    207, 311, 362, 388, 409, 461, 526, 575, 619, 662,
    790, 752, 868, 893, 979, 1003, 1005, 1011, 1042,
    1111, 1134, 1290, 1314, 1380, 1439, 1441, 1443,
    1521, 1623, 1639, 1698, 1703, 1750, 1776, 1823,
    1856, 1886, 1905, 2026, 2135, 2142, 2174, 2240,
    2271. See also Governesses
Drug addicts, 1174, 1362, 1912, 1932, 1998, 2114,
    2119, 2176, 2197, 2231, 2316
Drug culture, 462, 587, 1174, 1366, 1932, 2176, 2231
Drug mules. See Mules (carriers)
Du Pré, Jacqueline, 1852
Duffau, Maria Esther, 25
Duncan, Isadora, 1761
Duras, Marguerite, 633
Dwarfs, 34

Eberhardt, Isabelle, 64
Ecuador (made in), 405
Education, 9, 90, 171, 232, 282, 512, 964, 1099, 1285,
    1353, 1532, 1600, 1696, 1719, 1785, 2046, 2355
Egypt (made in), 377–404
    Egypt, Alexandria, 891
    Egypt, Cairo, 387, 388, 390, 396, 400, 404
    Egypt, towns and villages, 380
El Salvador, 193
Elderly women, 45, 66, 107, 122, 155, 167, 199, 344,
    348, 420, 486, 512, 543, 645, 673, 682, 684, 869,
    929, 935, 947, 997, 1093, 1110, 1205, 1253, 1274,
    1354, 1471, 1487, 1494, 1518, 1730, 1741, 1755,
    1788, 1809, 1814, 1819, 1860, 1884, 2083, 2097,
    2260, 2370, 2378, 2386
Elections, 151, 983, 1310, 2258
Elliot, Grace, 629
Elsner, Gisela, 705
Embroiderers, 670, 961, 1015, 1078, 1678
Emotional dependency, 529, 679, 782, 786, 989, 1119,
    2351
Engineers, 248, 855
Entrepreneurs, 169, 251, 258, 259, 296, 301, 316, 337,
    346, 509, 527, 532, 776, 805, 1027, 1142, 1239,
    1372, 1532, 1714, 1881, 1925, 2194, 2324. See also
    Businesswomen
Environmentalists, 51, 1391, 2091, 2162. See also
    Political activists
Equatorial Guinea, 1592
Escapes, 48, 470, 692, 1050, 1067, 1331, 1784, 1947,

2136, 2173, 2292. See also Flights
Eskimo people, 681
Estonia (made in), 406
Ethiopia (made in), 407
Ethiopian Christians, 1134
Ethnologists, 1668
Euthanasia, 1747, 2343
Evil spirits, 16, 87, 405, 504, 870, 1284, 1364, 1433,
    1453, 1745, 1909, 2008, 2084, 2230, 2281
Ex-convicts, 314, 406, 966, 1091, 1354, 1467, 1992,
    2187
Exchanging bodies, 1530, 1595, 2321
Exchanging lives, 1369, 1580
Executives, 238, 285, 300, 379, 496, 589, 655, 691,
    855, 1079, 1636, 2046. See also Businesswomen
Exorcism, 16, 870, 1073, 1453, 2230
Experimental films, 113, 463, 467, 831, 1149, 1773,
    1933, 1950, 1971, 1973, 2057, 2115, 2212
Exploitation films, 110, 428, 797, 860, 885, 900, 1244,
    1437, 1664, 1889, 1897, 1910, 1914, 1916, 1917,
    1921, 1935, 1944, 1953, 1954, 1955, 1958, 1960,
    1970, 1972, 1980, 1985, 2014, 2039, 2048, 2139,
    2158, 2171, 2282. See also Blaxploitation films

Fairy tales, 187, 218, 454, 915, 1353, 1774, 2182
False convictions, 251
Families, large, 540, 590, 1186, 1752, 1863, 1948
Family. See Aunts; Births; Childbearing; Cousins;
    Custody; Daughters; Mothers; Orphans;
    Pregnancy; Sibling rivalry; Sisters; Spouses;
    Weddings; Widows
Family honor. See Honor
Family planning, 399, 478
Fantasy, 38, 47, 218, 297, 326, 356, 370, 454, 465, 473,
    540, 653, 676, 759, 770, 793, 813, 839, 884, 892,
    907, 915, 917, 949, 951, 984, 1150, 1323, 1353,
    1375, 1503, 1595, 1669, 1763, 1774, 1782, 1788,
    1937, 1963, 1999, 2105, 2141, 2264, 2321
Fantasy worlds, 83, 1385, 1396, 1919, 1979, 2250,
    2264
Farm owners, 188, 601, 636, 838, 1195, 2362
Farmer, Frances, 2016, 2022
Faroe Islands, 368
Fashion models, 574, 847, 1920
Fashion workers, 185, 285, 300, 614, 670, 751, 940.
    See also Embroiderers
Feminist viewpoints, 5, 27, 32, 49, 65, 81, 88, 99, 113,
    143, 165, 177, 195, 197, 273, 347, 349, 350, 352,
    356, 357, 459, 463, 464, 467, 477, 533, 637, 668,
    676, 742, 747, 748, 757, 767, 779, 781, 786, 789,
    794, 828, 831, 948, 950, 1051, 1082, 1085, 1108,
    1198, 1212, 1284, 1300, 1323, 1353, 1361, 1377,
    1392, 1413, 1483, 1518, 1524, 1542, 1578, 1612,
    1643, 1694, 1699, 1728, 1761, 1773, 1799, 1851,
    1858, 1874, 1935, 1947, 1950, 1973, 1988, 1990,

2009, 2021, 2028, 2031, 2057, 2064, 2085, 2115, 2143, 2191, 2192, 2212, 2213, 2231, 2260, 2361

Feminists, 64, 476, 478, 607, 723, 787, 789, 1164, 1595, 1728, 1774, 1786, 1831, 2021, 2031, 2088, 2206, 2260, 2401. *See also* Women's rights advocates

Film actors, 429, 474, 802, 827, 913, 991, 1204, 1256, 1317, 1445, 1474, 1682, 1898, 1934, 1973, 2016, 2022, 2114, 2192

Film within a film, 1317, 1474, 1682, 1973, 2390

Filmmakers, 33, 102, 115, 189, 191, 452, 494, 563, 614, 672, 685, 699, 780, 823, 948, 950, 1005, 1085, 1130, 1457, 1474, 1652, 1660, 1845, 1973, 2079, 2115, 2192

Finland (made in), 408–420

    Finland, history, German occupation, 415

    Finland, towns and villages, 411, 412

First, Ruth, 1804

Fishing villages, 169, 238, 260, 577, 962, 1075, 1104, 1207, 1420, 1422, 1435

Flights, 21, 136, 164, 200, 522, 560, 693, 766, 1128, 1630, 1670, 2128, 2243. *See also* Escapes

Folksingers, 2124

Food, 296, 301, 350, 2269

Food workers. *See* Cooks; Noodle makers; Oil makers; Restaurant managers; Waitresses

Fortune tellers, 1568, 1753, 1872, 2223, 2267

Fossey, Dian, 2091

Frame, Janet, 1392

France, 91, 803, 2064

    (made in), 421–673

    France, Bordeaux, 647

    France, Clermont-Ferrand, 532

    France, Corsica, 711

    France, Fontainbleau, 652

    France, Grenoble, 479

    France, history, 431, 550, 561, 572, 625, 629, 1523

    France, history, German occupation, 546, 548, 593, 656, 817

    France, Lille, 605

    France, Lyon, 509, 540

    France, Marseille, 584, 626, 1521

    France, Normandy, 481, 816

    France, Paris, 4, 172, 403, 421, 428, 432, 439, 444, 446, 465, 473, 496, 503, 508, 553, 566, 580, 581, 585, 587, 596, 606, 607, 614, 628, 629, 635, 665, 669, 817, 940, 1476, 1502, 1553, 1667, 1763, 1837, 2006, 2034

    France, Riviera, 430

    France, Rouen, 460

    France, towns and villages, 449, 451, 491, 516, 527, 637, 651, 670, 1757

French. *See* African French; Algerian French; Spanish French

French Algerians, 555, 630

French Danes, 362

French Japanese, 663

Friends, 9, 10, 29, 57, 175, 177, 186, 204, 210, 230, 252, 253, 271, 302, 321, 361, 362, 465, 478, 482, 484, 502, 575, 605, 634, 638, 670, 735, 736, 806, 809, 812, 813, 836, 871, 925, 934, 937, 1087, 1143, 1164, 1209, 1245, 1251, 1260, 1273, 1278, 1283, 1288, 1313, 1337, 1345, 1352, 1370, 1395, 1460, 1494, 1553, 1554, 1588, 1649, 1669, 1671, 1733, 1778, 1810, 1819, 1820, 1831, 1833, 1841, 1848, 1878, 1953, 1981, 1987, 2025, 2066, 2077, 2101, 2123, 2218, 2232, 2240, 2248, 2288, 2291, 2299, 2301, 2311, 2332, 2361, 2385, 2386, 2414. *See also* Women and gay men

Friends, close, 39, 72, 78, 232, 350, 388, 461, 466, 492, 509, 518, 578, 580, 640, 677, 779, 800, 906, 911, 1053, 1114, 1117, 1175, 1270, 1382, 1396, 1415, 1497, 1517, 1547, 1582, 1592, 1665, 1668, 1813, 1828, 1863, 1877, 1892, 1908, 1990, 2087, 2096, 2125, 2128, 2132, 2137, 2187, 2219, 2239, 2277, 2385, 2417

Friends, groups of, 94, 269, 274, 277, 283, 287, 400, 403, 421, 474, 556, 598, 614, 845, 910, 1115, 1127, 1302, 1306, 1307, 1383, 1403, 1409, 1412, 1438, 1486, 1536, 1543, 1564, 1606, 1621, 1660, 1699, 1700, 1790, 1803, 1815, 1821, 1875, 1901, 1960, 1973, 1988, 2012, 2015, 2094, 2103, 2112, 2164, 2173, 2177, 2183, 2191, 2199, 2204, 2221, 2263, 2287, 2375

Fugitives, 375, 1897

Fundamentalism. *See* Religious fundamentalism

Future, 68, 222, 1978, 2108, 2121

Gabon (made in), 674

Galrâo, Patricia, 144

Gamblers, 430, 651, 1620

Games, 2327

Gangs, 923, 1031, 1308

Gangsters, 1176

Gardens, 1792

Gay men. *See* Women and gay men

Gay–straight relations, 111, 211, 447, 632, 668, 1384, 1414, 2021, 2173, 2216, 2293, 2300

Geishas, 1227, 1276. *See also* Prostitutes

Generals, 561

Genital mutilation, 1210, 1320, 1534

Genres (film). *See* Action; Comedy; Exploitation; Fantasy; Mystery; Non-narrative films; Thrillers

Gentileschi, Artemesia, 592

Georgia, 2376, 2381

    (made in), 675

    Georgia, Tbilisi, 673, 675

    Georgia, towns and villages, 2370

German Argentinians, 786

German Russians, 1278

German Turks, 700
Germans. *See* African Germans; Kenyan Germans;
    Turkish Germans
Germany, 77, 743
    (made in), 676–718
    (made in East Germany), 719–737
    (made in West Germany), 91, 738–845
    Germany, Auschwitz, 120, 660, 1113, 1358, 1459
    Germany, Berlin, 687, 688, 696, 697, 708, 713, 716,
        767, 778, 803, 873, 1179, 1797
    Germany, Dresden, 682
    Germany, Frieburg, 776
    Germany, Hamburg, 678, 679, 707, 759, 1739
    Germany, history, 682, 720, 738, 779, 789, 828
    Germany, history, Nazi regime, 695, 697, 717,
        772, 779, 785, 796, 798, 834, 841, 956, 1161, 1358,
        1459, 2020. *See also* individual countries, history,
        German occupation
    Germany, Munich, 796, 802
    Germany, towns and villages, 740, 780, 799, 842
Ghana (made in), 846–847
    Ghana, slave forts, 847
Ghosts. *See* Evil spirits; Spirits
Goddesses. *See* Spirits
Gonçalves, Antonio Aurelio, 23
Governesses, 30, 1569, 1745, 1750, 1851, 2099
Grandmothers, 45, 214, 268, 346, 348, 472, 512, 533,
    646, 673, 679, 869, 1047, 1193, 1203, 1229, 1329,
    1377, 1442, 1450, 1487, 1518, 1750, 1788, 1962,
    2105, 2140, 2407
Greece, 667, 710, 1801, 1810
    (made in), 848–894
    Greece, Athens, 868, 872, 874, 878, 1152
    Greece, Corfu, 876
    Greece, history, 862, 864, 873, 874
    Greece, history, German occupation, 863, 884
    Greece, islands, 856, 866
    Greece, Piraeus, 853
    Greece, Thessalonica, 890
Greek Orthodox–Protestant relations, 2308
Greek Turks, 1741
Griots. *See* Storytellers
Guatemala, 39
Guerrilla fighters. *See* Rebels
Guerin, Veronica, 1121, 2335
Guilt, 273, 456, 458, 634, 735, 1480, 1500
Guinea (made in), 895
Guinea-Bissau (made in), 896–897, 1502
Gullah, 2122
Gypsies, 1475, 1565, 1728

Hackers, 1704
Haiti, 1664
    (made in), 898
Harems, 1698, 1737

Healers, 526, 538, 963, 2004
Hindu cults, 81, 963
Hindu–Muslim relations, 1055
Hindus, 983, 996, 1002, 1055
Hispanic Americans, 191, 2164, 2178, 2229, 2263,
    2269, 2273. *See also* Mexican Americans
Historical settings, prehistory, 1242
Historical settings, ancient, 513, 683, 849, 850, 867,
    1012, 1624
Historical settings, fourth century to thirteenth
    century, 310, 311, 431, 538, 561, 996, 1012, 1262,
    1413, 1769
Historical settings, fourteenth century, 534, 1293, 1818
Historical settings, fifteenth century, 611, 1613, 1619
Historical settings, sixteenth century, 572, 1249,
    1466, 1563, 1768, 1850
Historical settings, seventeenth century, 32, 592, 752,
    764, 1172, 1405, 1489, 1560, 1594, 1600
Historical settings, eighteenth century, 48, 134, 147,
    368, 445, 594, 625, 629, 679, 945, 1111, 1184,
    1238, 1373, 1835, 1839, 1880, 1885
Historical settings, nineteenth century, 28, 49, 71,
    103, 126, 154, 165, 179, 188, 216, 237, 329, 334,
    360, 362, 371, 413, 458, 471, 523, 529, 551, 591,
    607, 627, 719, 750, 758, 859, 864, 935, 946, 969,
    1000, 1002, 1009, 1020, 1026, 1244, 1260, 1276,
    1415, 1494, 1546, 1642, 1686, 1694, 1759, 1771,
    1776, 1777, 1787, 1807, 1836, 1842, 1848, 1851,
    1866, 1925, 1938, 1949, 1993, 2120, 2127, 2150,
    2179, 2184, 2230, 2268, 2278, 2300, 2356, 2401
Historical settings, 1900s, 17, 64, 137, 245, 303, 630,
    694, 876, 961, 976, 1191, 1250, 1362, 1393, 1410,
    1469, 1726, 1737, 1767, 1795, 2036
Historical settings, 1910s, 89, 181, 265, 413, 443, 763,
    801, 905, 1009, 1064, 1070, 1247, 1411, 1491,
    1639, 1679, 1708, 1727, 1828, 2007, 2042, 2340,
    2360, 2380
Historical settings, 1920s, 19, 144, 235, 280, 284, 307,
    308, 309, 341, 412, 413, 496, 526, 552, 571, 790,
    829, 856, 882, 893, 956, 1009, 1061, 1109, 1116,
    1267, 1295, 1312, 1341, 1509, 1570, 1765, 1783,
    1789, 1815, 1826, 1843, 1906, 1928, 2125, 2358,
    2366, 2379
Historical settings, 1930s, 30, 104, 140, 162, 221, 233,
    235, 289, 329, 341, 375, 378, 675, 695, 702, 737,
    775, 779, 796, 817, 844, 862, 873, 884, 907, 913,
    922, 925, 939, 956, 959, 991, 1009, 1119, 1179,
    1232, 1246, 1254, 1312, 1339, 1386, 1477, 1514,
    1593, 1654, 1668, 1693, 1764, 1797, 1823, 1860,
    1898, 1900, 1901, 1906, 1929, 1932, 1981, 1995,
    2038, 2082, 2109, 2135, 2412
Historical settings, 1940s, 30, 104, 207, 228, 239, 241,
    247, 262, 276, 289, 307, 387, 464, 468, 779, 785,
    902, 939, 944, 1017, 1158, 1166, 1195, 1200, 1291,
    1385, 1386, 1513, 1520, 1623, 1652, 1682, 1780,

1865, 1886, 1906, 2000, 2053, 2143, 2281, 2311, 2385, 2392

Historical settings, 1950s, 4, 18, 25, 62, 90, 156, 256, 289, 302, 307, 411, 509, 549, 550, 555, 781, 802, 827, 846, 880, 938, 942, 950, 962, 964, 968, 1066, 1110, 1126, 1142, 1161, 1281, 1291, 1337, 1349, 1350, 1390, 1393, 1457, 1592, 1596, 1673, 1794, 1820, 1856, 1859, 1890, 1962, 1968, 2000, 2016, 2022, 2044, 2051, 2073, 2101, 2195, 2207, 2228, 2272, 2293, 2300, 2328, 2375

Historical settings, 1960s, 25, 132, 251, 252, 255, 305, 315, 329, 442, 456, 478, 497, 550, 621, 687, 706, 720, 794, 880, 1054, 1105, 1123, 1291, 1472, 1673, 1754, 1803, 1804, 1805, 1863, 1905, 1938, 1967, 1998, 2124, 2145, 2157, 2205, 2206, 2223, 2260, 2261

Historical settings, 1970s, 7, 46, 104, 139, 193, 223, 307, 478, 667, 767, 789, 880, 887, 896, 997, 1041, 1141, 1158, 1195, 1314, 1352, 1380, 1457, 1586, 1598, 1673, 1722, 1734, 1783, 1857, 2010, 2160, 2207, 2260, 2345, 2375, 2417

Historical settings, 1980s, 16, 836, 952, 1028, 1087, 1201, 1314, 2112

History. *See* Colonialism; Historical settings; individual countries, history; Jewish holocaust; Japanese holocaust; World War

Holiday, Billie, 1932

Holidays, 498, 620, 682, 1409, 1567, 2269, 2330. *See also* Vacations

Homeless women, 25, 516, 557, 675, 777, 1499, 2119

Homophobia, 414, 428, 483, 579, 640, 680, 942, 1148, 1160, 1175, 1228, 1357, 1565, 1808, 1892, 2208, 2238, 2260, 2285, 2300

Hong Kong, 77, 319, 432, 1449
(made in), 899–926
Hong Kong, history, Japanese occupation, 902

Honor (family), 275, 396, 961, 1709

Honor beatings, 1095

Honor killings, 12, 294, 759, 1182, 1715, 2366

Horror films, 100, 108, 618, 813, 1107, 1562, 1745, 1788, 1909, 1927, 1928, 1936, 1980, 1983, 1994, 2008, 2048, 2117, 2281, 2282

Horsewomen, 34, 63

Hospitals, 416, 442, 1043, 1157, 1232, 1301, 1473, 1515, 1639, 1977, 1979, 2244, 2286

Hostages, 542

Houses of prostitution, 853, 900, 909, 986, 1006, 1008, 1214, 1225, 1246, 1276, 1296, 1354, 1366, 1593, 1625, 1686, 1932, 2065

Housework, 113, 461, 507, 1676

Housing, crowded, 337, 654, 673, 929, 947, 968, 2363, 2365, 2395

Human sacrifice, 168

Hungary, 2272
(made in), 927–959

Hungary, Budapest, 929, 940, 941, 944, 948, 950, 955

Hungary, history, 939, 940, 945, 950

Hungary, towns and villages, 934

Hunger strikes, 1122

Hyde, Robin, 1386

Hymns, 362

Ibo people, 2122

Iceland, 962
(made in), 960–962

Identity theft, 578

Illness, 219, 469, 560, 738, 821, 1159, 2103, 2212. *See also* Addiction; AIDS; Amnesiacs; Cancer; Cerebral palsy; Dementia; Mental illness

Immigrants, 4, 42, 62, 77, 82, 94, 98, 137, 204, 293, 298, 372, 407, 526, 581, 585, 602, 626, 637, 669, 687, 694, 754, 815, 816, 908, 910, 1032, 1131, 1134, 1197, 1233, 1337, 1355, 1398, 1439, 1521, 1581, 1604, 1610, 1661, 1710, 1727, 1739, 1741, 1799, 1868, 1869, 1887, 1952, 2026, 2066, 2072, 2120, 2131, 2184, 2272, 2273, 2290, 2342

Incest, 454, 500, 549, 842, 1153, 1336, 1368, 1434, 1642, 1766, 1796, 1823, 2042, 2223, 2268

India, 1783, 1856
(made in), 963–1057
India, Assam, 1050
India, Bihar, 1042
India, Chandrapore, 1789
India, Gujarat, 1017
India, history, 1012, 1783
India, Kolkata, 467, 964, 969, 997, 1028, 1041
India, Maharashtra, 991, 1036
India, Maharashtra, Mumbai, 972, 991, 1023, 1040, 1049
India, New Delhi, 81, 968, 1037, 1039, 1847, 2307
India, Orrisa, 1035
India, Rajasthan, 1048
India, towns and villages, 963, 975, 1002, 1017, 1024, 1047, 1054, 1056
India, Uttar Pradesh, Kanpur, 1052
India, Utter Pradesh, Lucknow, 976

Indian Americans, 2131, 2255

Indian British, 1821, 1834

Indian Pakistanis, 1032

Indian Ugandans, 2131

Indian–white relations, 972, 997, 1029, 1610, 1783, 1792, 1856, 1874

Indians. *See* British Indians

Indonesia, 120
(made in), 1058–1072
Indonesia, history, Japanese occupation, 1063
Indonesia, Jakarta, 1068
Indonesia, towns and villages, 1065, 1072
Indonesia, West Sumatra, 1061

Infertility, 398, 643, 939, 1037, 1053, 1084, 1356. *See also* Punishment for no children

Infidelity, 19, 26, 37, 54, 65, 71, 92, 102, 110, 119, 124, 153, 181, 221, 263, 280, 290, 296, 301, 336, 344, 355, 360, 374, 423, 439, 448, 494, 499, 519, 569, 579, 588, 591, 603, 620, 642, 651, 758, 762, 810, 822, 875, 898, 933, 952, 967, 969, 979, 1018, 1021, 1024, 1037, 1138, 1147, 1148, 1162, 1175, 1201, 1216, 1228, 1230, 1238, 1273, 1290, 1303, 1309, 1357, 1371, 1430, 1456, 1462, 1480, 1491, 1495, 1500, 1504, 1573, 1643, 1658, 1659, 1667, 1699, 1717, 1721, 1729, 1760, 1794, 1816, 1865, 1917, 1926, 1953, 2002, 2007, 2017, 2036, 2040, 2056, 2082, 2109, 2220, 2240, 2293, 2296, 2314, 2353, 2354, 2356, 2373, 2388, 2393, 2408

Inheritances, 105, 404, 710, 939, 1254, 1333, 1384, 1602, 1836, 2208, 2228

In-laws, 124, 238, 246, 360, 916, 963, 967, 1023, 1042, 1235, 1241, 1293, 1320, 1518, 1713, 2235, 2416. *See also* Daughters-in-law; Mothers-in-law; Sisters-in-law

Interior decorators, 435

Investigations, 29, 36, 60, 264, 272, 273, 505, 597, 641, 685, 715, 759, 761, 834, 1033, 1194, 1252, 1264, 1268, 1328, 1361, 1407, 1439, 1783, 1793, 1811, 1968, 1977, 1989, 2010, 2031, 2041, 2043, 2117, 2130, 2132, 2159, 2162, 2322, 2388, 2398, 2410

Iran, 1668, 2133
   (made in), 1073–1102
   Iran, Tehran, 1077, 1078, 1079, 1094, 1095, 1099, 1102
   Iran, towns and villages, 1073, 1075, 1082

Iranian Americans, 2133

Iranian Swedes, 1661

Iraq (made in), 1103–1105
   Iraq, towns and villages, 1104

Ireland, 1747
   (made in), 1106–1123
   Ireland, Belfast, 1108, 1109, 1811
   Ireland, County Cork, 1110
   Ireland, Donegal, 1119
   Ireland, Dublin, 1114, 1115, 1116, 1117, 1121, 1751, 1802, 1863, 2335
   Ireland, history, 1109, 1111
   Ireland, Irish Republican Army, 1111, 1112, 1118, 1122
   Ireland, towns and villages, 1826

Israel, 190
   (made in), 1124–1141
   Israel, Haifa, 1141
   Israel, history, 1124
   Israel, Jerusalem, 492, 861, 1136
   Israel, kibbutzim, 497, 1128, 2034
   Israel, Tel Aviv, 617, 1135
   Israel, towns and villages, 1131

Israeli–Palestinian relations, 1126, 1417, 2035

Italian Americans, 2104, 2152

Italian Argentineans, 42

Italians. *See* African Italians

Italy, 827, 1949
   (made in), 1142–1208
   Italy, Alps, 1159
   Italy, Florence, 1860
   Italy, history, 1860
   Italy, islands, 437, 1143, 1162, 1207
   Italy, Milan, 1185
   Italy, Naples, 1168, 1176, 1181, 1183
   Italy, Palermo, 1197, 1201
   Italy, Ravenna, 1147
   Italy, Rome, 437, 1142, 1146, 1149, 1175, 1180, 1550
   Italy, Sicily, 1166, 1182
   Italy, Sienna, 1191
   Italy, towns and villages, 859, 1144, 1207
   Italy, Trieste, 644, 1193
   Italy, Tuscany, 859, 2334
   Italy, Venice, 739, 1848

Ivory Coast, 1321
   (made in), 1209–1214
   Ivory Coast, Abidjan, 1210

Jale, Afife, 1726

Jamaican British, 1864

Japan (made in), 1215–1277
   Japan, Hiroshima, 1258
   Japan, history, 288, 1244, 1262, 1276
   Japan, history, Sino-Japanese War, 1232, 1242. *See also* China; Hong Kong; Indonesia; Korea; Malaysia
   Japan, history, U.S. occupation, 1239
   Japan, Mt. Fuji, 1265
   Japan, Osaka, 1244, 1254
   Japan, Sendai, 1226
   Japan, Tokyo, 663, 1244, 1257, 1273, 1277
   Japan, towns and villages, 1230, 1253, 1263, 1264

Japanese. *See* Chinese–Japanese relations; French Japanese

Japanese Americans, 2097, 2184

Japanese Australians, 62

Japanese Brazilians, 137

Japanese Canadians, 207

Japanese Chinese, 1681

Japanese holocaust, 1258

Japanese Peruvians, 1233

Jealousy, 79, 243, 490, 563, 614, 911, 961, 962, 1114, 1223, 1600, 1642, 1840, 2268. *See also* Sibling rivalry

Jewish–Catholic relations, 1478, 1482, 2411

Jewish–Gentile relations, 35, 492, 697, 717, 785, 837, 844, 884, 1134, 2358

Jewish Holocaust, 120, 617, 660, 686, 717, 786, 837,

844, 939, 956, 1113, 1153, 1358, 1478, 2020, 2411
Jewish–Protestant relations, 695
Jews, 35, 366, 617, 686, 709, 710, 737, 956, 1113,
    1141, 1153, 1482, 1613, 1851, 1866, 2089
    Jews, Ashkenazi, 1337
    Jews, Hasidic, 1380, 2235
    Jews, Orthodox, 1136, 1138, 1337
    Jews, Russian, 620
    Jews, Sephardic, 1125, 1337
Joan of Arc, 431, 561, 611
    Joan of Arc as model, 2099, 2364
Journalists, 64, 69, 142, 151, 222, 287, 381, 383, 402,
    403, 489, 566, 697, 759, 835, 888, 889, 942, 1025,
    1033, 1085, 1121, 1130, 1131, 1132, 1245, 1261,
    1291, 1363, 1369, 1428, 1461, 1479, 1556, 1578,
    1603, 1655, 1781, 1804, 1989, 2005, 2037, 2043,
    2056, 2069, 2080, 2100, 2231, 2233, 2335, 2376,
    2410, 2417

Kafka, Franz, 552
Kahlo, Frida, 1330, 2295
Kazakhstan, 2352, 2353
    (made in), 1278–1282
    Kazakhstan, towns and villages, 1282, 2385, 2394
Keeler, Christine, 1805
Keller, Helen, 1893
Kenya, 709, 2049
    (made in), 1283–1286
    Kenya, Nairobi, 1283, 1284, 1286
    Kenya, towns and villages, 1283, 1284
Kenyan Germans, 715
Kept women, 290, 924, 1007, 1210, 1220, 1222, 1235,
    1778, 1995. *See also* Courtesans
Kidnappings, 43, 135, 310, 457, 470, 542, 631, 811,
    839, 953, 2063, 2181, 2322, 2382
Kikuyu people, 1284
Kirgizstan, 959, 2362
Kohler, Aimée Farberbock, 697
Korea, 1249
    (made in North Korea), 1287–1288
    (made in South Korea), 1289–1311
    Korea, history, 1288, 1293
    Korea, history, Japanese occupation, 1295
    Korea, South, Inchon, 1307
    Korea, South, Pohang, 1304
    Korea, South, Seoul, 1300, 1304
    Korea, towns and villages, 1289, 1292, 1295
Kovalevsky, Sonya, 1653

Labor organizers, 7, 68, 89, 137, 336, 419, 460, 659,
    756, 843, 938, 1015, 1185, 1457, 1800, 1829, 1929,
    1997, 1999, 2028, 2318. *See also* Political activists;
    Workers
Labor strikes, 6, 9, 419, 460, 517, 1528, 1800, 1829
Labor unions, 139, 329, 1015, 1185, 1195, 1869, 1997

Lapp people, 411
Lasker-Schüller, Else, 695
Lawyers, 36, 58, 92, 385, 386, 971, 1285, 1407, 1431,
    1557, 1811, 1862, 2079, 2085, 2087, 2102, 2123,
    2130, 2159, 2201, 2242, 2263, 2299, 2325
Leavings, 27, 175, 268, 714, 1052, 1150, 1583, 1771,
    1913
Lebanese French, 403
Lebanon (made in), 1312–1315
    Lebanon, history, 10, 1314
Lesbian culture, 84, 93, 195, 211, 319, 428, 447, 524,
    541, 579, 598, 691, 751, 770, 839, 840, 919, 923,
    955, 1784, 1825, 1876, 1973, 2018, 2021, 2161,
    2162, 2163, 2170, 2182, 2192, 2199, 2208, 2224,
    2231, 2260, 2303, 2326
Lesbian relationships, 32, 43, 110, 112, 115, 178, 185,
    190, 205, 303, 316, 322, 414, 427, 433, 483, 492,
    515, 579, 635, 681, 697, 751, 773, 778, 803, 817,
    823, 885, 904, 942, 952, 1037, 1092, 1148, 1160,
    1168, 1175, 1228, 1243, 1274, 1279, 1356, 1357,
    1372, 1414, 1539, 1549, 1563, 1565, 1582, 1585,
    1632, 1664, 1685, 1687, 1735, 1782, 1784, 1808,
    1823, 1825, 1827, 1859, 1865, 1889, 1897, 1907,
    1914, 1917, 1953, 1975, 2017, 2042, 2044, 2064,
    2079, 2167, 2170, 2175, 2196, 2212, 2216, 2220,
    2224, 2231, 2238, 2255, 2260, 2267, 2285, 2300,
    2329, 2331
Lesbian women, 1251, 1270, 1892, 1908, 2028,
    2065, 2125. *See also* Friends, close; Gay–straight
    relations; Homophobia; Older woman, younger
    woman
Letter writers, 112, 130, 345, 673, 1373, 1882, 2053,
    2311
Libya, history, 1312
Living Buddha, 256
Love, 179, 187, 354, 1419, 1575. *See also*
    Relationships
Lovelace, Ada, 1855
Luxemburg, Rosa, 828
Lynn, Loretta, 2000

M'Sika, Habiba, 1697
Magic, 1131, 1349. *See also* Witchcraft
Magicians, 465, 2161
Maillart, Ella, 1668
Maintenon, Madame de, 625
Malaysia (made in), 1316–1317
    Malaysia, history, Japanese occupation, 1063
    Malaysia, towns and villages, 1316
Malaysians. See Vietnamese Malays
Male institutions, 1190, 1212, 1291, 1461, 1726
Mali (made in), 1318–1323
    Mali, Bamako, 1318
    Mali, towns and villages, 1319, 1320, 1323
Managers, 230, 240, 250, 423, 485, 550, 616, 937, 999,

1027, 1165, 1176, 1201, 1532, 1550, 1551, 1595, 1800, 2171, 2267, 2313. See also Businesswomen; Executives; Restaurant managers

Manchuria, towns and villages, 260

Mao Zedong, 308

Maori people, 1390, 1397, 1891

Marital boredom, 175, 220, 349, 353, 354, 356, 433, 446, 448, 467, 509, 519, 551, 769, 808, 969, 1021, 1098, 1189, 1196, 1423, 1456, 1458, 1462, 1495, 1548, 1549, 1643, 1772, 1843, 1865, 1918, 1935, 1937, 1963, 2186, 2224, 2235, 2296, 2300, 2309, 2393

Mark, Adrienne, 1837

Marriage, 54, 62, 187, 226, 287, 335, 354, 355, 358, 401, 437, 450, 559, 622, 719, 722, 725, 726, 753, 772, 801, 819, 824, 908, 911, 946, 1014, 1035, 1040, 1078, 1079, 1093, 1141, 1148, 1167, 1182, 1188, 1193, 1195, 1210, 1255, 1297, 1483, 1578, 1677, 1678, 1734, 1759, 1931, 1952, 1963, 2056, 2061, 2097, 2211, 2235, 2412. See also Divorce; Marital boredom; Partners; Polygamy; Spouses; Weddings

Marriage, arranged, 11, 71, 246, 247, 296, 321, 674, 758, 1031, 1233, 1243, 1263, 1350, 1413, 1607, 1634, 1699, 1961, 2184, 2307

Marriage, child, 1048, 2397

Marriage, forced, 11, 259, 265, 279, 284, 766, 832, 1050, 1075, 1089, 1098, 1103, 1125, 1213, 1219, 1283, 1320, 1410, 1444, 1489, 1531, 1673, 1708, 1718, 1820, 2042

Marriage of convenience, 433, 760, 1363, 1684, 2278, 2411

Marriage to make others happy, 188, 360, 371, 440, 517, 1083, 1136, 2104

Martial arts, 304, 900, 901, 905, 914, 917, 918, 923, 1071, 1237, 1940, 1954, 2138, 2341

Martinique, 512

Masaai people, 1283

Masochism, 95, 116, 226, 367, 421, 471, 475, 494, 499, 551, 582, 615, 653, 755, 781, 1158, 1161, 1266, 1793, 1916, 2312

Mathematicians, 1653, 1855

Matriarchies, 159, 303, 537, 1354, 1527, 2088

Matriarchs, 45, 104, 216, 296, 550, 673, 679, 919, 1006, 1077, 1119, 1180, 1193, 1253, 1298, 1327, 1377, 1450, 1534, 1570, 1674, 1702, 1890, 1962, 2029, 2122, 2140, 2230

Memories, 107, 117, 133, 179, 474, 498, 710, 786, 883, 923, 1110, 1131, 1377, 1471, 1487, 1571, 1573, 1598, 1642, 1692, 1698, 1755, 1837, 1843, 2020, 2107, 2383

Menopause, 2115

Mental illness, 30, 61, 114, 173, 373, 391, 410, 416, 430, 464, 481, 484, 511, 529, 576, 622, 700, 781, 788, 795, 829, 879, 1003, 1005, 1023, 1073, 1107,

1110, 1126, 1157, 1173, 1207, 1360, 1388, 1392, 1404, 1411, 1473, 1491, 1522, 1543, 1620, 1647, 1651, 1652, 1654, 1720, 1797, 1809, 1883, 1922, 1934, 1959, 1963, 1979, 2016, 2022, 2092, 2107, 2152, 2157, 2186, 2217, 2244, 2312, 2346. See also Addiction; Cutting; Depression; Neurosis; Psychotherapy, Schizophrenia

Mexican Americans, 1869, 2027, 2310. See also Hispanic Americans

Mexicans. See Polish Mexicans; Turkish Mexicans

Mexico, 197, 1600, 2227, 2295
    (made in), 1324–1346
    Mexico, history, 32, 1556
    Mexico, Mexico City, 1334, 1335, 1337, 1342, 1627
    Mexico, Veracruz, 1335

Middle-aged women, 152, 480, 582, 601, 734, 784, 972, 1150, 1584, 1587, 1984, 2153, 2202, 2218, 2288

Middle class, 16, 26, 29, 126, 175, 383, 396, 423, 446, 483, 813, 816, 903, 931, 1028, 1041, 1077, 1094, 1150, 1160, 1163, 1178, 1224, 1235, 1286, 1327, 1429, 1541, 1543, 1566, 1621, 1639, 1685, 1700, 1728, 1772, 1942, 2223, 2240, 2283, 2288

Midwives. See Nurses

Military, 1190, 1425. See also Soldiers

Military officers, 611, 1070, 2358

Miller, Henry, 2109

Miners, 1829, 2052

Ministers, 376

Missing persons, 600, 1143

Missionaries, 1029, 1900

Mistresses, 441, 590, 934, 1180, 1636, 2042. See also Kept women

Mixed couples, 4, 62, 75, 134, 202, 207, 411, 540, 681, 691, 716, 753, 823, 1197, 1565, 1604, 1782, 1783, 1832, 1899, 2006, 2079, 2127, 2131, 2145, 2150, 2162, 2192, 2215, 2220, 2293

Mixed parentage, 620, 710, 715, 717, 1259, 1600

Mizoguchi, Kenji, 1256

Mongolia, 241, 252, 839, 1347, 1348

Moroccan French, 403, 1351

Moroccan Israelis, 1131

Morocco, 64, 1857
    (made in), 1349–1355
    Morocco, Atlas Mountains, 1354
    Morocco, Fez, 1351
    Morocco, Tangiers, 667, 1349, 1567
    Morocco, towns and villages, 1350, 1352, 1354, 1355

Morticians, 206

Mothers and their children's sexuality, 76, 649, 781, 1160, 1181, 1534, 1569, 1640, 1774, 1808, 2090, 2126, 2149, 2395

Mothers, 27, 29, 55, 60, 101, 104, 148, 150, 176, 180, 208, 220, 281, 282, 301, 310, 327, 344, 359,

364, 373, 377, 387, 462, 527, 530, 545, 590, 591,
634, 656, 686, 725, 801, 819, 836, 852, 861, 917,
937, 960, 968, 1028, 1041, 1095, 1124, 1134,
1141, 1147, 1156, 1176, 1186, 1219, 1220, 1229,
1234, 1253, 1303, 1322, 1371, 1377, 1383, 1404,
1434, 1435, 1446, 1449, 1464, 1471, 1472, 1488,
1496, 1501, 1520, 1538, 1568, 1578, 1606, 1643,
1652, 1673, 1702, 1707, 1713, 1717, 1752, 1808,
1814, 1820, 1863, 1886, 1899, 1948, 1969, 2020,
2046, 2063, 2118, 2122, 2126, 2129, 2133, 2144,
2153, 2168, 2178, 2210, 2229, 2241, 2276, 2338,
2352, 2356, 2372, 2376, 2385, 2398. *See also*
Grandmothers; Single mothers; Widows
Mothers, abusive, 639, 1497, 1679
Mothers, accidental, 194, 297, 384, 412, 707, 967, 987,
1007, 1170, 1177, 1448, 2001, 2064, 2067, 2073,
2138, 2145, 2319, 2369, 2418
Mothers and children, 55, 472, 606, 753, 1068, 1884
Mothers and daughters, 34, 45, 47, 57, 76, 81, 82, 90,
95, 115, 127, 128, 131, 136, 148, 156, 163, 182,
203, 211, 214, 216, 219, 254, 264, 268, 292, 305,
307, 324, 338, 342, 346, 348, 390, 409, 502, 511,
515, 525, 533, 539, 546, 550, 554, 564, 572, 573,
576, 602, 641, 646, 649, 650, 654, 666, 673, 679,
706, 779, 781, 786, 816, 820, 850, 876, 891, 895,
899, 909, 927, 940, 971, 1001, 1010, 1034, 1043,
1046, 1047, 1050, 1054, 1072, 1082, 1139, 1140,
1144, 1160, 1173, 1181, 1193, 1200, 1203, 1208,
1209, 1215, 1225, 1227, 1266, 1288, 1289, 1319,
1327, 1333, 1334, 1337, 1354, 1372, 1389, 1419,
1424, 1440, 1442, 1447, 1452, 1470, 1534, 1544,
1548, 1555, 1568, 1570, 1571, 1576, 1579, 1601,
1602, 1616, 1626, 1628, 1632, 1650, 1662, 1674,
1681, 1688, 1696, 1698, 1701, 1705, 1706, 1731,
1739, 1744, 1773, 1774, 1834, 1844, 1847, 1849,
1853, 1857, 1862, 1866, 1882, 1888, 1908, 1930,
1958, 1962, 2011, 2025, 2029, 2047, 2059, 2075,
2080, 2103, 2140, 2148, 2149, 2152, 2160, 2174,
2177, 2179, 2195, 2218, 2230, 2237, 2252, 2275,
2284, 2291, 2301, 2305, 2310, 2315, 2321, 2330,
2332, 2348, 2351, 2365, 2370, 2380, 2383, 2391,
2395, 2405
Mothers and sons, 16, 113, 125, 130, 194, 296, 360,
396, 438, 507, 554, 560, 693, 712, 768, 928, 947,
1085, 1102, 1118, 1146, 1169, 1203, 1207, 1326,
1416, 1610, 1640, 1740, 1766, 1890, 1946, 2243,
2324, 2363, 2390
Mothers-in-law, 12, 402, 637, 643, 933, 990, 1046,
1062, 1084, 1236, 1280, 1290, 1298, 1589, 1789.
See also In-laws
Mothers, legally incompetent, 399, 731, 1350, 1822,
1957, 2090, 2197
Mothers, neglectful, 55, 57, 128, 376, 406, 606, 706,
882, 919, 1334, 1340, 1397, 1483, 1784, 1922,
1930

Mothers, surrogate, 52, 397, 939, 954, 1053, 1178,
1298, 2108, 2255
Mothers without sons, 12, 1069, 1576, 1731
Mothers working outside the home. *See* Working
outside the home
Motorcycle racing, 576
Motorcycle riders, 58, 90, 1414, 1814, 1923, 2047
Mountain villages, 14, 37, 96, 278, 1253, 1354, 1405,
1622, 1903
Mountains, 96, 100, 809, 1233, 1280, 1628
Moyano, Maria Elena, 1421
Muen, Amdang, 1694
Mules (carriers), 1981, 2239, 2342
Multicultural communities, 68, 1314, 1398, 1784,
2122
Murder victims, 1982, 2238
Murderers, 113, 282, 314, 351, 372, 395, 424, 487,
568, 575, 578, 619, 623, 645, 664, 783, 842, 869,
871, 966, 1253, 1340, 1361, 1365, 1428, 1439,
1718, 1743, 1747, 1756, 1823, 1827, 1897, 1936,
2190, 2268
Murderers, child, 364, 377, 535, 1156, 1342, 1483,
2230
Murderers, parent, 121, 150, 487, 534, 1100, 1206,
1280, 1374, 1396, 1742
Murderers, partner, 147, 200, 424, 604, 650, 1430,
1546, 1794, 2241, 2388
Murderers, serial, 694, 1936, 2068, 2329
Murderers, spouse, 385, 588, 1005, 1089, 1221, 1374,
1428, 1438, 1607, 1675, 2068
Murdoch, Iris, 1871
Muses, 1723
Music composers, 567
Music, popular, 587, 692, 797, 930, 1846, 1864, 1915,
1974, 2000, 2021, 2051, 2176, 2205, 2266, 2320,
2324. *See also* Performers; Singers
Musicals, 228, 235, 372, 440, 596, 895, 974, 984, 985,
986, 996, 1000, 1006, 1015, 1045, 1049, 1057,
1197, 1381, 1502, 1533, 1810, 1864, 1906, 1919,
2021, 2251
Musicians, 10, 71, 95, 116, 287, 341, 461, 567, 585,
671, 689, 792, 854, 874, 960, 1114, 1373, 1632,
1644, 1819, 1847, 1852, 2176, 2205, 2227, 2249,
2283. *See also* Actors; Chinese opera
Musicians, rock, 522, 692, 1915, 2075, 2251, 2320
Muslims, 2, 15, 16, 382, 388, 389, 626, 637, 976, 1047,
1055, 1061, 1101, 1351, 1526, 1567, 1661, 1726,
1887, 2122, 2366
Mute women, 71, 792, 920, 1001, 1318, 1428, 1444,
1516, 1692
Myanmar, 2172
Myanmar, towns and villages, 169
Mystery, 36, 78, 100, 173, 275, 448, 449, 455, 482, 503,
506, 522, 554, 556, 600, 610, 646, 658, 661, 664,
1268, 1333, 1387, 1389, 1420, 1476, 1492, 1564,

1566, 1591, 1596, 1811, 1896, 1924, 1983, 2008, 2035, 2043, 2063, 2068, 2123, 2138, 2159, 2168, 2174, 2200, 2208, 2215, 2250, 2275, 2396

Namibia, 2006
Nannies. See Governesses
Native (peoples). See Akan; Berber; DAI; Diola; Dogon; Eskimo; Ibo; Kikyu; Lapp; Maori; Masaai; Nenet; Roma; Shona; Zulu
Native Americans, 138, 192, 571, 681, 1600, 2122
Native Australians, 68, 70, 80
Native–white relations, 40, 132, 192, 411, 681, 1600
Nenet people, 420
Netherlands (made in), 1356–1384
    Netherlands, Amsterdam, 1361
    Netherlands, history, 1066
    Netherlands, history, German occupation, 1359
    Netherlands, towns and villages, 1367, 1377
Neurosis, 95, 643, 653, 881, 1676, 1852, 2086, 2346
New Zealand, 71
    (made in), 1385–1400
    New Zealand, Auckland, 1385, 1394, 1397, 1398
New Zealanders. See Croatian New Zealanders
Nicaragua (made in), 1401
Nigeria (made in), 1402
Nin, Anaïs, 2109
Ninou, Marika, 874
Nomads, 1083
Non-narrative films, 5, 70, 87, 88, 91, 118, 130, 357, 359, 365, 393, 463, 472, 480, 610, 672, 747, 831, 1183, 1419, 1612, 1723, 1770, 1773, 1799, 1933, 1950, 1971, 2031, 2057, 2115, 2188, 2212, 2327
Noodle makers, 301
Norway, 1862
    (made in), 1403–1415
    Norway, Bergen, 1410
    Norway, history, German occupation, 1406
    Norway, Oslo, 1403, 1409, 1412, 1771
    Norway, towns and villages, 1405, 1415
Norwegian Americans, 2268
Novelists, 119, 607, 633, 705, 1392, 1629, 1654, 1871, 2012, 2023
Nuns, 32, 445, 458, 523, 843, 956, 1123, 1177, 1299, 1453, 1481, 1563, 1593, 1902, 2041, 2198, 2400. See also Brides of god
Nurses, 66, 88, 255, 352, 363, 416, 479, 557, 622, 661, 716, 790, 863, 947, 973, 1232, 1301, 1393, 1425, 1486, 1641, 1900, 1921, 1941, 2147, 2182, 2248, 2391

Objects of desire, 632, 662, 893, 1447, 2135. See also Beauty
Oil makers, 296
Older man, younger woman, 11, 26, 102, 109, 119, 224, 350, 477, 587, 592, 600, 616, 650, 758, 1098, 1230, 1320, 1413, 1495, 1553, 1636, 1657, 1751, 1820, 2169, 2245, 2397
Older woman, younger man, 26, 92, 95, 102, 217, 221, 456, 468, 520, 525, 547, 582, 588, 633, 711, 835, 1018, 1076, 1088, 1112, 1128, 1145, 1239, 1255, 1341, 1373, 1388, 1413, 1553, 1605, 1658, 1666, 1875, 1884, 1964, 2240, 2304, 2324
Older woman, younger woman, 78, 520, 1228, 1356, 1632, 1907, 1914, 2329
Orphans, 675, 927, 1451, 1639, 2418
Osaki, Midori, 1267

Pacifists, 223, 828, 943. See also Political activists
Painters, 190, 289, 403, 464, 592, 647, 1330, 1828, 2295, 2359
Pakistan (made in), 1416
Pakistanis. See Indian Pakistanis
Palestine (made in), 1417–1418
    Palestine, history, 1312
Pan Yuliang, 289
Paraguay, 834
Parker, Dorothy, 2165
Partner abuse, 150, 164, 541, 616, 931, 1300, 1566, 1780, 1897, 1946, 2166, 2173, 2226, 2243. See also Spouse abuse
Paul, Alice, 2340
Pepin sisters, 619, 1823
Performers, 50, 361, 394, 443, 567, 785, 829, 865, 1117, 1211, 1227, 1502, 1574, 1732, 1906, 1919, 1920, 2019, 2087, 2095, 2190, 2265. See also Actors; Circus performers; Comedians; Dancers; Musicians; Singers
Peru, 222, 1233
    (made in), 1419–1423
    Peru, Lima, 1421
    Peru, towns and villages, 1420, 1422
Peruvians. See Japanese Peruvians
Philippine Japanese, 1259
Philippines (made in), 1424–1452
    Philippines, Camarines Norte, 1430
    Philippines, history, Japanese occupation, 1426
    Philippines, Manila, 1429, 1432, 1435, 1447, 1449
    Philippines, towns and villages, 1427, 1435
Philosophical films. See Feminist viewpoints; Non-narrative films
Phoolan Devi, 1031
Photographers, 13, 87, 195, 638, 767, 953, 1132, 1167, 1311, 1389, 1501, 1562, 1816, 1849, 1851, 1990, 2231
Photography, 1189, 2169
Pianists, 116, 279, 866, 1650, 1671
Pilots, 234, 2355
Plath, Sylvia, 1883
Plato, 595
Poets, 32, 84, 140, 323, 413, 695, 996, 1512, 1775,

1883, 2346
Poland, 208
(made in), 1453–1486
Poland, Gdansk, 1457
Poland, history, 1466, 1486
Poland, history, German occupation, 810, 1468, 1478, 1482
Poland, towns and villages, 1471, 1475, 1485
Poland, Warsaw, 958, 1469, 1482
Police, 491, 652, 1591, 1955, 2106, 2110
Polish Austrians, 98
Polish Mexicans, 1337
Political activists, 10, 139, 144, 267, 323, 329, 381, 489, 867, 889, 949, 950, 1029, 1045, 1048, 1287, 1359, 1391, 1393, 1421, 1436, 1457, 1512, 1523, 1556, 1618, 1704, 2374, 2378, 2401
Political activists, Australia, 48, 51, 68, 69
Political activists, Germany, 685, 717, 730, 754, 756, 763, 789, 800, 818, 828
Political activists, Ireland, 1109, 1111, 1112, 1118
Political activists, United Kingdom, 1779, 1790, 1804, 1829
Political activists, United States, 1938, 1945, 1993, 2006, 2028, 2091, 2101, 2172, 2206, 2242, 2325
Political activists, Venezuela, 2398, 2400
Political persecution, 251, 1315
Political prisoners, 22, 29, 46, 157, 675, 718, 730, 880, 1061, 1122, 1328, 1464, 1506, 1513, 1586, 1683, 2374, 2392
Politicians, 165, 237, 572, 898, 983, 1031, 1242, 1310, 1421, 1466, 1526, 1572, 1613, 1657, 1694, 1768, 1842, 1850, 1895, 2258, 2371
Polygamy, 14, 19, 171, 284, 379, 380, 392, 895, 1084, 1213, 1323, 1349, 1444, 1524, 1708, 1724
Pornography, 618, 797, 840, 1240
Portugal (made in) 1487–1503
Portugal, history, 134, 147
Portugal, Lisbon, 578, 1497, 1499, 1503
Portugal, towns and villages, 1488, 1498, 1501
Portuguese. *See* African Portuguese
Potters, 346
Poverty, 89, 141, 224, 240, 309, 317, 331, 377, 557, 590, 625, 639, 669, 693, 754, 958, 998, 1008, 1075, 1091, 1186, 1218, 1224, 1225, 1230, 1253, 1421, 1424, 1435, 1447, 1451, 1467, 1483, 1499, 1525, 1634, 1713, 1714, 1890, 1922, 1969, 2033, 2348, 2372, 2389, 2394, 2398, 2412, 2417, 2418. *See also* Homeless women; Working class
Prayer women, 1452
Pregnancy, 186, 212, 291, 376, 536, 559, 608, 1106, 1301, 1431, 1576, 1639, 1844, 1909, 1937, 2108, 2229, 2299, 2311. *See also* Abandoned and pregnant; Pregnant women, single
Pregnancy, unwanted, 497, 951, 1483, 1978
Pregnant women, 106, 142, 388, 1024, 1043, 1399,

1422, 1432, 1507, 1515, 1746, 2181, 2207, 2282, 2389
Pregnant women, single, 160, 164, 352, 417, 440, 442, 488, 566, 583, 586, 670, 688, 696, 936, 941, 961, 985, 992, 1016, 1104, 1105, 1123, 1135, 1178, 1277, 1285, 1319, 1364, 1408, 1637, 1748, 1798, 1806, 1824, 1861, 1894, 2156, 2197, 2270, 2311, 2358
Princesses. *See* Fairy tales; Upper class
Prisoners, 48, 120, 166, 257, 306, 376, 431, 445, 535, 556, 561, 606, 659, 692, 718, 789, 833, 1100, 1123, 1168, 1279, 1331, 1432, 1437, 1459, 1472, 1481, 1513, 1784, 1868, 1947, 2014, 2121, 2239, 2284, 2318. *See also* Ex-convicts; Political prisoners
Prisons, 157, 222, 257, 376, 431, 535, 561, 730, 880, 1033, 1168, 1432, 1464, 1481, 1509, 1513, 1586, 1784, 1868, 1944, 2014, 2239, 2284, 2392. *See also* Escapes
Profession versus family, 279, 442, 469, 722, 725, 791, 855, 1035, 1080, 1210, 1446, 1551, 1578, 2376
Professors, 88, 95, 252, 1328, 1514, 1653, 1734, 2002, 2086, 2088, 2212, 2286, 2304, 2328
Promiscuity, 175, 197, 271, 367, 436, 551, 615, 649, 788, 1269, 1422, 1431, 1485, 1569, 1597, 1615, 1639, 1846, 1926, 1974, 1982, 2135, 2414
Propaganda, 233, 234, 235, 238, 242, 249, 256, 269, 313, 705, 720, 2379
Prostitutes, 113, 138, 162, 170, 262, 289, 302, 378, 432, 434, 444, 446, 451, 475, 486, 600, 634, 658, 666, 706, 808, 853, 890, 909, 920, 958, 965, 974, 976, 980, 986, 989, 1006, 1008, 1036, 1054, 1059, 1140, 1142, 1146, 1152, 1176, 1197, 1214, 1225, 1244, 1245, 1246, 1276, 1295, 1296, 1304, 1310, 1319, 1329, 1354, 1366, 1428, 1443, 1445, 1452, 1589, 1593, 1625, 1633, 1662, 1670, 1672, 1711, 1716, 1727, 1733, 1735, 1754, 1781, 1805, 1835, 1858, 1888, 1896, 1911, 1924, 1925, 2027, 2039, 2057, 2065, 2119, 2120, 2158, 2256, 2336, 2350, 2391, 2404. *See also* Courtesans
Prostitution, 491, 1042, 1218, 1283, 1331, 1516. *See also* Houses of prostitution, Women as commodity
Protestants, 368, 376, 572, 1109, 1110, 1284. *See also* Catholic–Protestant relations
Proust, Marcel, 790
Psychiatrists, 728, 870, 1154, 1361, 1614, 1617, 1647, 1749, 1979, 2032, 2041
Psychotherapy, 511, 2086
Punishment. *See* Capital punishment; Honor; Sexism; Victims
Punishment for being different, 399, 434, 1032, 1052, 1065, 1073, 1304, 1367, 1522, 2406
Punishment for being raped, 58, 166, 988, 998, 1281, 1293, 1319, 1336, 1709, 1715
Punishment for being unmarried, 538, 1030, 1073,

1123, 1730, 1780
Punishment for no children, 398, 643, 746, 974, 1037,
    1084, 1136, 1294, 1356, 2413
Punishment for sexual expression, 12, 28, 30, 149,
    294, 458, 752, 758, 904, 985, 1123, 1247, 1299,
    1405, 1433, 1485, 1560, 1716, 1834, 1982, 2366

Queen Elizabeth, 1768, 1850
Queen Himiko, 1242
Queen Isabella, 1613
Queen Juana, 1619
Queen Margot, 572
Queen of Scots, Mary, 1768
Queen of the Asnas, 165
Queen Victoria, 1842
Queens, 147, 165, 237, 572, 1183, 1242, 1375, 1466,
    1526, 1619, 1768, 1842
Qui Jin, 245
Qui Yun, 261

Race relations. See Cross-cultural relations;
    Immigrants; Mixed couples; Native (peoples)
Racism, 75, 134, 334, 396, 513, 530, 550, 555, 621,
    697, 709, 753, 847, 1068, 1144, 1321, 1397, 1537,
    1538, 1540, 1541, 1543, 1651, 1657, 1789, 1832,
    1851, 1899, 1932, 2006, 2013, 2115, 2125, 2131,
    2209, 2279, 2311. See also Colonialism; Japanese
    holocaust; Jewish Holocaust
Radio, 1480. See also Journalists
Radio performers, 2021, 2025, 2032, 2265
Rape, 58, 125, 158, 166, 183, 273, 288, 315, 318, 479,
    510, 587, 592, 765, 847, 941, 998, 1031, 1033,
    1040, 1144, 1219, 1252, 1305, 1318, 1397, 1451,
    1485, 1508, 1511, 1665, 1714, 1715, 1720, 1733,
    1966, 1978, 2085, 2137, 2204, 2234, 2254, 2266,
    2348. See also Punishment for being raped
Rape victims, 347, 377, 766, 900, 1194, 1226, 1232,
    1367, 1424, 1583, 1675, 1720, 1932, 1954, 1970,
    1972, 1980
Rawlings, Marjorie Kinnan, 2023
Rebels, 193, 236, 245, 328, 1070, 1401, 1608, 1683,
    2417
Rebirths, 847, 884, 1502
Refugees, 69, 656, 964
Rehabilitation, 736, 2114, 2253
Relationships. See Courtesans; Family; Kept women;
    Lesbian relationships; Marriage; Older man,
    younger woman; Older woman, younger man;
    Older woman, younger woman; Search for;
    Triangles
Religion. See Animism; Catholics; Christians;
    Convents; Cults; Exorcism; Hindus; Ministers;
    Muslims; Nuns; Protestants; Saints; Santería;
    Shamanism; Sikhs; Spirits; Spirituality; Taoism
Religious differences. See Catholic–Protestant

relations Hindu–Muslim relations; Jewish–Catholic
    relations; Jewish–Protestant relations; Sikh–
    Muslim relations
Religious fundamentalism, 2, 15, 16, 1136, 1138, 1364,
    1380, 1416, 1534, 1700, 1706, 1808, 1818, 2108,
    2152, 2197, 2348
Religious intolerance, 32, 256, 330, 538, 561, 572, 626,
    764, 1055, 1109, 1110, 1216, 1284, 1416, 1482,
    1563, 1726, 1887, 2411
Religious workers. See Nuns; Ministers
Researchers, 59, 87, 262, 297, 542, 597, 644, 787,
    1386, 1457, 1539, 1556, 1831, 2283
Resistance, 7, 68, 228, 272, 291, 310, 318, 380, 396,
    414, 434, 450, 637, 684, 763, 792, 873, 936, 996,
    1017, 1020, 1024, 1042, 1064, 1066, 1073, 1089,
    1105, 1155, 1300, 1316, 1320, 1332, 1464, 1509,
    1523, 1528, 1534, 1635, 1707, 1709, 1726, 1993,
    1999, 2108, 2120, 2121
Restaurant managers, 532, 1142, 1568. See also
    Cooks; Waitresses
Revenge, 58, 113, 200, 221, 273, 288, 347, 364, 369,
    417, 418, 432, 451, 510, 618, 645, 718, 740, 834,
    841, 847, 850, 886, 900, 932, 975, 988, 1022, 1031,
    1038, 1071, 1116, 1145, 1156, 1161, 1171, 1176,
    1226, 1231, 1234, 1237, 1308, 1316, 1342, 1365,
    1424, 1428, 1529, 1550, 1557, 1561, 1597, 1733,
    1858, 1910, 1923, 1941, 1951, 1954, 1972, 1980,
    1992, 2048, 2055, 2098, 2116, 2137, 2185, 2202,
    2204, 2234, 2254, 2257, 2292, 2348, 2407
Revolutionaries, 18, 52, 140, 223, 241, 245, 329, 704,
    828, 864, 896, 921, 1111, 1312, 1593, 1608, 1683,
    2021, 2035, 2360, 2379
Reyes, Lucha, 1339
Rice-Davies, Mandy, 1805
Rivas Mercado, Antonieta, 1556
Rivera, Diego, 2295
Road trips, 45, 136, 214, 348, 803, 1308, 1345, 1548,
    1665, 1878, 1962, 2128, 2167, 2252, 2264
Rock music. See Music, popular
Rodin, Auguste, 529
Romance writers, 1587, 2012
Romania (made in), 1504–1513
    Romania, towns and villages, 1509
Romantic love, 83, 326, 354, 591, 688, 804, 831, 846,
    857, 888, 1340, 1483, 1764, 1894, 2025, 2164,
    2344, 2356, 2361, 2393
Royalty. See Rulers; Upper class
Ruan Ling Yu, 913
Rulers, 513, 1353, 2405. See also Queens
Russia, 1767. See also USSR
    (made in), 1514–1520
    Russia, Georgia, 2379
    Russia, history, 801, 1514, 2360, 2379, 2380
    Russia, Jamal Peninsula, 420
    Russia, Leningrad, 1514, 2361

Russia, Moscow, 948, 2365, 2375, 2395
Russia, Nizhny Novogorod, 2380
Russia, Siberia, 2360
Russia, Tbilisi, 2386
Russia, towns and villages, 1515, 1518, 1520, 2357, 2371, 2372, 2378
Russians, 1868. *See also* German Russians

Sacrifice, 306, 987
Safe houses, 777, 999, 1003, 1351, 1834
Saints, 431, 523, 561, 611
Salomon, Charlotte, 1358
Sand, George, 607, 1807
Santería, 334, 2399
Satire. *See* Comedy
Saudi Arabia, 397
Schaft, Hanny, 1359
Schizophrenia, 870, 1154
School, Sophie, 798
Schwarzenbach, Anne Marie, 1668
Science fiction, 52, 93, 222, 351, 465, 566, 807, 1269, 1271, 1855, 1859, 1977, 1978, 1994, 2021, 2061, 2076, 2108, 2171, 2222, 2280, 2333
Scientists, 32, 86, 230, 597, 889, 1462, 1562, 1855, 2091, 2222, 2386. *See also* Engineers; Researchers
Sculptors, 529, 1765
Search (for something), 1177, 1265
Search for a child, 135, 836, 856, 940, 1160, 1328, 1441, 1740
Search for a friend, 152, 1143, 1335, 1610
Search for a lover, 20, 612, 1315, 1710, 1827, 2349
Search for a parent, 562, 565, 887, 927, 959, 1259, 1266
Search for a sister, 1097, 2297
Search for a spouse, 22, 896, 1149, 1199, 1420, 2010, 2298
Search for self, 23, 143, 174, 179, 197, 206, 214, 271, 333, 349, 571, 671, 739, 741, 803, 847, 883, 926, 943, 1041, 1058, 1081, 1159, 1177, 1283, 1306, 1467, 1470, 1488, 1580, 1581, 1601, 1617, 1627, 1658, 1701, 1857, 1876, 1984, 1991, 2086, 2373, 2414
Seducers, 67, 110, 133, 134, 224, 227, 334, 453, 462, 465, 494, 502, 520, 531, 579, 594, 613, 632, 648, 751, 825, 851, 1025, 1064, 1120, 1179, 1184, 1231, 1395, 1415, 1492, 1663, 1762, 1764, 1793, 1805, 1835, 1884, 1927, 2081, 2084, 2139, 2294
Seeking spouses, 35, 55, 188, 254, 274, 311, 321, 337, 390, 502, 604, 678, 734, 811, 846, 857, 868, 902, 981, 1010, 1057, 1083, 1215, 1253, 1262, 1337, 1382, 1415, 1418, 1448, 1469, 1519, 1525, 1594, 1604, 1651, 1689, 1806, 1867, 1875, 1905, 1908, 1967, 2089, 2179, 2191, 2228, 2246, 2274, 2301, 2377
Selena, 2227

Self-mutilation. *See* Cutting
Senegal, 2006
    (made in), 1521–1534
Senegal, Casamance, 1523
Senegal, Dakar, 1532
Senegal, history, 1523
Senegal, towns and villages, 1523, 1527, 1528, 1529, 1531, 1534
Serb–Croat relations, 324
Serial killers. *See* Murderers, serial
Servants. *See* Domestic servants
Sex change, 1530, 1545, 1817
Sex role reversal, 356, 676, 1323, 1895
Sex slavery. *See* Slavery
Sex trafficking, 1014, 1662
Sexism. *See* Punishment for being different; Punishment for being raped; Punishment for being unmarried; Punishment for no children; Punishment for sexual expression; Sexism, cultural; Sexism, institutional
Sexism, cultural, 15, 16, 76, 143, 278, 294, 336, 393, 420, 441, 581, 962, 982, 995, 1019, 1048, 1051, 1052, 1065, 1073, 1081, 1093, 1101, 1190, 1281, 1289, 1299, 1302, 1319, 1324, 1352, 1367, 1431, 1433, 1485, 1551, 1600, 1656, 1696, 2024, 2040, 2262, 2300, 2355
Sexism, institutional, 2, 6, 12, 232, 382, 385, 389, 399, 674, 752, 988, 993, 994, 1024, 1026, 1032, 1057, 1099, 1136, 1247, 1294, 1341, 1350, 1384, 1405, 1507, 1522, 1534, 1560, 1578, 1715, 1727, 1730, 1794, 1830, 2366, 2413
Sexual harassment, 161, 1074, 1087, 1094, 1440, 1690
Sexuality, 28, 32, 85, 108, 109, 116, 133, 145, 178, 184, 187, 197, 206, 249, 273, 289, 319, 322, 344, 354, 367, 411, 443, 446, 475, 477, 494, 520, 531, 549, 554, 582, 588, 592, 609, 615, 616, 643, 647, 665, 668, 680, 742, 770, 840, 878, 893, 904, 914, 1037, 1060, 1083, 1106, 1127, 1192, 1232, 1247, 1267, 1269, 1274, 1302, 1335, 1346, 1371, 1413, 1422, 1477, 1484, 1530, 1536, 1545, 1569, 1573, 1575, 1582, 1594, 1604, 1615, 1619, 1631, 1654, 1658, 1756, 1764, 1765, 1788, 1789, 1817, 1846, 1851, 1859, 1875, 1881, 1884, 1924, 1982, 2018, 2031, 2070, 2079, 2090, 2097, 2109, 2110, 2130, 2135, 2149, 2175, 2203, 2211, 2223, 2230, 2312. *See also* Beauty; Birth control; Bisexual women; Cross-dressers; Lesbian women; Masochism; Mothers and their children's sexuality; Objects of desire; Promiscuity; Punishment for sexual expression; Romantic love; Seducers; Transsexuals
Shakespeare, William, 23
Shamanism, 420, 1692
Sheltered women, 34, 329, 360, 868, 1109, 1569
Shelters. *See* Safe houses
Ship captains, 770, 1994

Shona people, 2416
Sibling rivalry, 61, 65, 82, 149, 1427, 1846, 2176, 2259
Sikh–Muslim relations, 1416
Sikhs, 1874
Silkwood, Karen, 2028
Singers, 10, 57, 189, 198, 341, 425, 478, 671, 702, 729, 785, 797, 854, 873, 991, 1006, 1039, 1059, 1145, 1169, 1339, 1476, 1579, 1644, 1656, 1667, 1697, 1698, 1723, 1736, 1847, 1853, 1864, 1932, 1946, 1974, 1998, 2000, 2051, 2112, 2155, 2176, 2205, 2227, 2247, 2266, 2338. See also Actors, Chinese opera
Singers, opera, 233, 320, 354, 585, 750, 1202, 1282, 1873
Singers, rembetico, 874
Single mothers, 90, 96, 161, 163, 260, 285, 295, 372, 383, 389, 422, 442, 488, 539, 540, 584, 612, 631, 708, 723, 724, 731, 733, 748, 760, 767, 784, 826, 936, 953, 955, 989, 1072, 1082, 1208, 1263, 1268, 1285, 1335, 1345, 1377, 1379, 1381, 1394, 1406, 1463, 1517, 1532, 1537, 1566, 1577, 1584, 1611, 1634, 1643, 1646, 1776, 1780, 1781, 1794, 1829, 1864, 1872, 1882, 1946, 1948, 2027, 2060, 2090, 2113, 2148, 2164, 2230, 2237, 2242, 2247, 2252, 2284, 2301, 2306, 2332, 2350, 2357, 2363, 2365, 2386, 2392, 2395
Single mothers, teenage, 1499
Single women, 25, 38, 41, 83, 95, 100, 112, 126, 131, 141, 152, 155, 202, 255, 315, 317, 326, 343, 344, 363, 366, 369, 392, 400, 403, 410, 421, 422, 435, 436, 449, 471, 490, 498, 506, 514, 516, 521, 538, 553, 558, 574, 577, 610, 613, 616, 628, 651, 653, 665, 667, 675, 678, 687, 690, 711, 713, 726, 734, 735, 739, 804, 814, 815, 848, 854, 855, 857, 860, 865, 872, 897, 944, 966, 978, 981, 990, 1000, 1010, 1015, 1016, 1055, 1074, 1085, 1091, 1123, 1149, 1240, 1243, 1286, 1376, 1377, 1400, 1455, 1469, 1485, 1490, 1519, 1542, 1550, 1555, 1567, 1575, 1581, 1583, 1588, 1622, 1626, 1690, 1691, 1730, 1743, 1754, 1764, 1795, 1802, 1873, 1885, 1949, 1986, 1988, 1991, 2019, 2025, 2052, 2055, 2062, 2069, 2084, 2123, 2124, 2150, 2151, 2154, 2166, 2191, 2246, 2267, 2274, 2287, 2344, 2361, 2384, 2387, 2394. See also Pregnant women, single; Single mothers; Widows
Sisters, 61, 65, 73, 75, 77, 80, 129, 149, 156, 201, 219, 225, 273, 314, 404, 405, 493, 532, 543, 555, 565, 570, 596, 619, 620, 782, 789, 872, 879, 882, 889, 912, 915, 921, 922, 946, 961, 977, 987, 989, 992, 1013, 1036, 1077, 1097, 1119, 1136, 1180, 1187, 1254, 1272, 1303, 1384, 1427, 1451, 1478, 1490, 1552, 1555, 1597, 1602, 1634, 1638, 1645, 1681, 1693, 1741, 1756, 1765, 1767, 1796, 1806, 1846, 1852, 1861, 1869, 1939, 1941, 1983, 2054, 2083, 2143, 2146, 2149, 2176, 2179, 2181, 2201, 2255,
2259, 2297, 2305, 2310, 2313, 2319, 2408
Sisters and brothers, 31, 82, 384, 490, 493, 500, 564, 586, 626, 683, 842, 849, 932, 1153, 1170, 1275, 1599, 1738, 1830, 2418
Sisters-in-law, 1037, 1042, 2268
Sisters, twin, 649, 866, 920, 949, 1936
Slavery, 134, 318, 334, 847, 1014, 1063, 1092, 1123, 1662, 1938, 1993, 2120, 2230. See also Concubines; Women as commodity
Slovakia, 348
Slovenia, 1535, 1536
Smugglers, 894, 1584
Social workers, 107, 240, 478, 625, 937, 955, 1133, 1325, 1649, 2180
Socrates, 595
Södergran, Edith, 413
Solanas, Valerie, 2206
Soldiers, 234, 235, 253, 276, 763, 1044, 1151, 1288, 1593, 1870, 2003, 2355, 2409, 2415. See also Rebels
Soong Ai-ling, 921
Soong Ching-ling, 921
Soong May-ling, 921
South Africa, 1321, 1386
    (made in), 1537–1544
    South Africa, Capetown, 1543
    South Africa, history, 1804
    South Africa, history, apartheid, 1321, 1537, 1539, 1543, 1804
    South Africa, Soweto, 1541
South America, 443, 2401. See also names of individual countries
Space ships, 1994
Spain, 2081
    (made in), 1545–1633
    Spain, Andalusia, 824, 1570
    Spain, Barcelona, 1566, 1585, 1601, 1606, 1610, 2322, 2350
    Spain, Basque region, 1560
    Spain, Brumal, 1571
    Spain, Catalonia, 1554
    Spain, Galacia, 1602, 1614
    Spain, history, 1563, 1574, 1593, 1608, 1613, 1618, 1619, 1622, 1629
    Spain, history, Franco regime, 1569, 1596, 1622, 1623
    Spain, islands, 435
    Spain, Madrid, 1568, 1587, 1590, 1596, 1625
    Spain, Seville, 1616
    Spain, towns and villages, 824, 1554, 1555, 1560, 1571, 1604, 1615, 1622, 1631
Spanish French, 579
Spies, 223, 544, 862, 863, 1071
Spirits, 105, 133, 264, 330, 473, 847, 878, 894, 915, 963, 984, 1116, 1323, 1387, 1502, 1534, 1669. See also Evil spirits

Spirituality, 208, 367, 376, 673, 984, 1284, 1416, 1422, 1452, 1513, 1518, 1692, 2004, 2152, 2198, 2230. *See also* Hymns; Religion

Spouse abuse, 136, 146, 280, 296, 385, 472, 681, 1031, 1042, 1050, 1088, 1133, 1284, 1300, 1397, 1402, 1428, 1438, 1483, 1489, 1540, 1630, 1670, 1675, 1699, 1717, 1762, 1844, 1946, 2046, 2132, 2136, 2155, 2292, 2309, 2338. *See also* Partner abuse

Spouses, 14, 22, 27, 89, 106, 117, 124, 139, 172, 175, 231, 266, 291, 301, 308, 309, 313, 342, 353, 367, 379, 383, 386, 391, 423, 437, 444, 467, 507, 532, 533, 551, 569, 599, 603, 627, 637, 658, 671, 725, 745, 769, 774, 801, 808, 896, 910, 921, 933, 957, 963, 969, 983, 999, 1014, 1041, 1056, 1078, 1096, 1120, 1141, 1147, 1165, 1189, 1199, 1210, 1213, 1221, 1229, 1236, 1248, 1280, 1296, 1349, 1352, 1403, 1409, 1412, 1423, 1462, 1483, 1491, 1501, 1509, 1520, 1521, 1524, 1559, 1582, 1598, 1643, 1676, 1702, 1712, 1714, 1724, 1725, 1733, 1760, 1771, 1772, 1810, 1840, 1909, 1912, 1913, 1918, 1937, 1942, 1943, 1952, 1959, 2009, 2010, 2097, 2125, 2157, 2178, 2220, 2293, 2345, 2368, 2380, 2381, 2397, 2414. *See also* Death of a spouse; Murderers, spouse; Partners; Seeking spouses

Spouses, mail-order brides, 71, 1233, 1961, 2184

Spouses, secondary. *See* Concubines; Polygamy

Spouses, "war brides," 62

Sri Lanka (made in), 1634–1637

St. Therese of Lisieux, 523

Stalkers, 471, 647, 1573, 1992, 2025, 2031

Stein, Edith, 956

Stepmothers, 1007, 2236, 2315

Storytellers, 531, 779, 1211, 1323, 1659, 1774, 1788, 2125, 2182

Strachey, Lytton, 1828

Strippers, 648, 1240, 2234

Students, 9, 269, 344, 518, 890, 1087, 1115, 2177, 2262

Stunt women, 918

Suburbia, 77, 579, 595, 769, 968, 1394, 1912, 1917, 2009, 2030, 2043, 2045, 2095, 2116, 2186, 2218, 2226, 2276, 2293, 2300, 2332, 2345

Suicide, 116, 127, 183, 196, 200, 278, 377, 441, 450, 456, 466, 484, 516, 591, 630, 782, 788, 869, 993, 1028, 1179, 1211, 1253, 1294, 1336, 1521, 1531, 1556, 1570, 1709, 1797, 1816, 2059, 2300, 2356

Sun Yat-sen, 921

Supernatural. *See* Exchanging bodies; Evil spirits; Fortune tellers; Magic; Rebirths; Spirits; Time travel; Witchcraft; Witches, 1595

Survivors, 97, 169, 524, 624, 629, 660, 817, 1022, 1113, 1161, 1174, 1194, 1258, 1510, 1793, 2020, 2030, 2150

Susann, Jacqueline, 2261

Suspense. *See* Mystery

Suttee, 1020, 1026

Sweden, 764, 2391
(made in) 1638–1662
Sweden, Stockholm, 1644
Sweden, towns and villages, 1660

Swedes. *See* African Swedes; Iranian Swedes

Swift, Jonathan, 1116

Switzerland, 464
(made in), 1663–1670
Switzerland, towns and villages, 1172, 1666

Taiwan (made in), 1671–1691
Taiwan, Taipei, 1690

Tanake, Kinuyo, 1256

Tanzania (made in), 1692

Taoism, 904

Taxi drivers, 271, 286, 482, 1102

Teachers, 21, 29, 53, 205, 239, 244, 249, 252, 268, 320, 386, 449, 456, 520, 528, 606, 615, 625, 671, 721, 771, 859, 925, 997, 1004, 1060, 1066, 1110, 1126, 1292, 1385, 1390, 1416, 1493, 1508, 1600, 1631, 1653, 1757, 1764, 1765, 1891, 1892, 1893, 1902, 1908, 1928, 1982, 1987, 2129, 2249, 2304, 2355, 2369, 2390. *See also* Professors

Technology, 805, 1704

Telephone operators, 1781

Television, 151, 301, 326, 805, 806, 920, 1131, 1423, 1551, 1989, 2190, 2229, 2282. *See also* Journalists; Performers

Terrorism, 21, 59

Terrorists, 503, 704, 789, 1038, 1044, 1066, 1543, 1618, 1683, 2035

Thailand, 2239
(made in), 1693–1694
Thailand, towns and villages, 1693

Theater, 221, 262, 340, 1160, 1574, 1726

Thieves, 292, 771, 877, 905, 1076, 1472, 1665, 1688

Thrillers, 84, 150, 212, 418, 470, 504, 505, 640, 657, 685, 694, 703, 715, 759, 806, 1107, 1234, 1387, 1400, 1414, 1557, 1561, 1577, 1599, 1738, 1832, 1904, 1911, 1928, 1936, 1972, 1977, 1989, 2058, 2071, 2074, 2092, 2119, 2130, 2132, 2136, 2139, 2142, 2158, 2196, 2215, 2280, 2292, 2294, 2299, 2323

Tibet, 256, 313

Tilak, Laxmibai, 1009

Time travel, 907, 1312, 1613, 1854, 1855, 1859, 1919, 2061

Tjoet Nya Dien, 1070

Torture, 332

Towns and villages. *See* individual countries; Desert villages; Fishing villages; Mountain villages

Tradition versus modernity, 16, 4, 149, 254, 258, 335, 351, 537, 925, 963, 968, 1002, 1024, 1048, 1083, 1093, 1167, 1210, 1213, 1284, 1292, 1312, 1350,

1402, 1422, 1477, 1502, 1531, 1554, 1661, 1692, 1726, 1874, 2089, 2353, 2354, 2399, 2416. *See also* Marriage; Seeking spouses; Sexism

Translators, 501, 552, 663, 2063

Transsexuals, 145, 184, 1545, 1817

Travel, 37, 39, 81, 115, 199, 203, 208, 283, 517, 571, 598, 667, 739, 809, 830, 1196, 1345, 1370, 1378, 1462, 1536, 1567, 1588, 1599, 1628, 1668, 1789, 1815, 1821, 1949, 1970, 2128, 2133, 2145, 2173, 2239, 2270, 2294. *See also* Road trips

Trials, 53, 424, 431, 561, 630, 1172, 2085, 2299, 2388

Triangles, 65, 102, 142, 227, 263, 287, 316, 423, 439, 515, 553, 558, 569, 579, 587, 588, 677, 906, 955, 981, 1016, 1076, 1114, 1236, 1303, 1343, 1348, 1352, 1490, 1667, 1687, 1717, 1760, 1778, 1806, 2018, 2025, 2069, 2077, 2082, 2109, 2271, 2351

Tristan, Flora, 787

Trotsky, Leon, 1797, 2295

Tuberculosis, 1159

Tubman, Harriet, 1993

Tunisia (made in), 1695–1706
    Tunisia, Djerba, 1702
    Tunisia, towns and villages, 6, 1696
    Tunisia, Tunis, 1695, 1700, 1705, 2006

Turkey, 887, 1668
    (made in), 1707–1741
    Turkey, history, 1737
    Turkey, Istanbul, 1708, 1713, 1726, 1736, 1737
    Turkey, towns and villages, 894, 1707, 1709, 1712, 1715, 1716, 1717, 1718, 1719, 1720, 1721, 1722, 1727, 1741

Turkish Germans, 821, 1739

Turkish Mexicans, 1337

Turkmenistan, 2367

Turks. *See* German Turks; Greek Turks

Turner, Tina, 2155

Uganda, 2091

Ugandans. *See* Indian Ugandans

Ukraine (made in), 1742–1743

United Kingdom (made in), 1744–1887. *See also* British
    United Kingdom, England, history, 1768, 1783, 1818, 1842, 1850, 1870, 1886
    United Kingdom, England, Liverpool, 1800, 1822, 1846
    United Kingdom, England, London, 221, 1160, 1748, 1754, 1781, 1799, 1835, 1838, 1843, 1845, 1848, 1854, 1861, 1864, 1866, 2053, 2300
    United Kingdom, England, towns and villages, 1814, 1865, 1875
    United Kingdom, Scotland, 1858
    United Kingdom, Scotland, Edinburgh, 1764, 1816
    United Kingdom, Scotland, towns and villages, 1849
    United Kingdom, Wales, 1839

United States, 571
    (made in), 1888–2348
    United States, Alabama, Montgomery, 2101
    United States, Alaska, 2247
    United States, Appalachian Mountains, 2283
    United States, Arizona, 1946
    United States, Arizona, Tucson, 2173
    United States, Atlantic islands, 2122
    United States, California, 2242, 2267
    United States, California, Los Angeles, 1845, 1869, 1898, 1934, 1942, 1960, 1969, 1986, 2025, 2026, 2060, 2110, 2114, 2119, 2164, 2201, 2216, 2225, 2226, 2237, 2251, 2262, 2310, 2324
    United States, California, San Francisco, 840, 1762, 2290, 2326, 2331
    United States, Florida, 1995, 2023, 2154, 2266
    United States, history, 223, 2101, 2340
    United States, history, slavery, 847, 1938, 1993, 2230
    United States, Idaho, 2120
    United States, Illinois, Chicago, 2163, 2308
    United States, Louisiana, 2080, 2127, 2223, 2291
    United States, Massachusetts, 752, 2328
    United States, Massachusetts, Boston, 1787, 2273, 2279
    United States, Michigan, Detroit, 2033
    United States, Minnesota, 2052
    United States, Minnesota, Minneapolis, 2200
    United States, Mississippi, 2131
    United States, Nebraska, 2238
    United States, Nevada, Las Vegas, 2134
    United States, Nevada, Reno, 2044
    United States, New Jersey, Atlantic City, 2087, 2112
    United States, New Mexico, 2126
    United States, New York, 2095, 2152, 2300
    United States, New York City, 898, 910, 1581, 1684, 1837, 1859, 1918, 1932, 1948, 1967, 1982, 1988, 2021, 2039, 2053, 2065, 2066, 2072, 2089, 2098, 2106, 2111, 2165, 2178, 2180, 2194, 2203, 2206, 2209, 2212, 2219, 2228, 2253, 2256, 2287, 2289, 2303, 2314, 2316, 2327, 2342
    United States, New York City, Brooklyn, 1364, 2062, 2160, 2229, 2235, 2306, 2346
    United States, North Carolina, 2344
    United States, Ohio, Cincinnati, 2230
    United States, Ohio, Cleveland, 1911
    United States, Oklahoma, 2270
    United States, Oregon, Portland, 2320
    United States, Ozark Mountains, 1903
    United States, Pennsylvania, 1922
    United States, Pennsylvania, Pittsburgh, 2074
    United States, South Carolina, 1803
    United States, Tennessee, 2046
    United States, Texas, 1780, 2224, 2296

United States, Texas, Waxahachie, 2038
United States, towns and villages, 58, 372, 375,
    1892, 1903, 2038, 2042, 2082, 2103, 2187, 2223,
    2238, 2293, 2311, 2344, 2345
United States, Vermont, 2187
United States, Virginia, 2099, 2153
United States, Washington, D.C., 2056
United States, Washington State, 372, 2140
United States, Wisconsin, 2248
United States, Wyoming, 1776
Unrequited love, 471, 897, 1251, 1270, 1419, 1462,
    1655, 1693, 1892. See also Stalkers
Upper class, 1, 28, 44, 103, 277, 380, 457, 541, 625,
    629, 719, 765, 839, 851, 945, 946, 1012, 1018,
    1040, 1082, 1162, 1163, 1179, 1262, 1373, 1526,
    1594, 1639, 1654, 1763, 1795, 1843, 1848, 1860,
    1880, 1892, 1901, 1964, 2228, 2307, 2380
Uruguay, 892
    (made in), 2349–2351
    Uruguay, Montevideo, 2349, 2350
USSR, 1457. See also names of republics
    (made in), 2352–2395
    USSR, history, Stalin regime, 938, 944, 959, 1464,
    1481, 1514, 1520
Uzbekistan, towns and villages, 2354, 2366

Vacations, 409, 521, 545, 620, 643, 711, 809, 839,
    1494, 1536, 1627, 1765, 1798, 1810, 1815, 2232,
    2239
Vampires, 108, 1927
Van Hichtum, Nynke, 1383
Van Zuylen, Belle, 1373
Veiling, 7, 13, 400, 1081, 1093, 2366
Venezuela (made in), 2396–2402
    Venezuela, Caracas, 1552, 2397
Victims, 16, 59, 212, 318, 325, 332, 372, 394, 421, 434,
    450, 455, 513, 542, 762, 837, 922, 964, 999, 1063,
    1067, 1087, 1094, 1113, 1123, 1161, 1172, 1236,
    1258, 1316, 1324, 1338, 1358, 1366, 1453, 1484,
    1491, 1608, 1670, 1679, 1709, 1722, 1724, 1736,
    1818, 1867, 1903, 2020, 2039, 2055, 2070, 2121,
    2169, 2258, 2292, 2294, 2399, 2406. See also Child
    abuse victims; Domestic abuse; Rape victims
Victims' rights, 1344
Vietnam, 550
    (made in), 2403–2410
    Vietnam, Hanoi, 2408
    Vietnam, towns and villages, 2406
    Vietnam, war, 2403, 2404, 2407, 2409
Vietnamese Americans, 2269
Vietnamese Malays, 69
Vintners, 259, 601, 1165
Virginity, 85, 278, 405, 1182, 1329, 2041, 2246. See
    also Punishment for sexual expression
Von Krusenstjerna, Agnes, 1654

Wadkar, Hansa, 991
Waitresses, 88, 96, 583, 621, 628, 952, 1140, 1861,
    2094, 2118, 2124, 2126, 2168, 2187, 2309, 2343
Want ads, 194, 609, 1369, 1689, 2303, 2387
Wardens, 257, 306, 944, 1100, 1459
Wartime, 3, 5, 89, 114, 198, 288, 307, 324, 325, 415,
    546, 548, 593, 656, 763, 772, 779, 796, 798, 810,
    817, 837, 838, 856, 862, 863, 873, 884, 887, 894,
    896, 1124, 1144, 1152, 1219, 1232, 1245, 1258,
    1313, 1314, 1347, 1417, 1426, 1468, 1482, 1486,
    1508, 1514, 1520, 1860, 1981, 2050, 2298, 2362,
    2385, 2403, 2407, 2417
Wealth. See also Inheritances, 2390
Wealthy man–poor woman relations, 662, 979, 1050,
    1082, 1145, 1191, 1326, 2278, 2412
Wealthy woman–poor man relations, 719, 858, 2278
Wealthy woman–poor woman relations, 752
Wealthy women, 30, 44, 105, 196, 215, 277, 335, 623,
    630, 710, 740, 755, 802, 851, 858, 864, 902, 904,
    924, 982, 994, 1041, 1109, 1162, 1220, 1234, 1254,
    1297, 1326, 1368, 1418, 1494, 1529, 1556, 1559,
    1635, 1639, 1640, 1678, 1750, 1763, 1836, 1843,
    1856, 1860, 1926, 1964, 2064, 2228, 2245
Weddings, 11, 766, 1077, 1089, 1117, 1316, 1472,
    1504, 1660, 1722, 1820, 2104, 2161, 2219, 2307
Westerns, 1776, 1839, 1925, 2120, 2150, 2185
Whistleblowers, 2046
White Africans, 709, 1538, 1540, 1543, 2049
White people. See Arab–white relations; Asian–white
    relations; Black–white relations; Indian–white
    relations; Native–white relations
Widows, 17, 26, 33, 113, 133, 149, 339, 368, 390, 399,
    408, 438, 468, 567, 601, 643, 685, 710, 899, 906,
    928, 977, 993, 1002, 1011, 1026, 1030, 1032, 1068,
    1124, 1125, 1128, 1139, 1166, 1215, 1217, 1235,
    1263, 1289, 1320, 1333, 1343, 1350, 1416, 1417,
    1471, 1504, 1505, 1597, 1605, 1623, 1680, 1705,
    1744, 1826, 1839, 1849, 1863, 1878, 1884, 1930,
    1946, 1976, 1995, 2004, 2038, 2113, 2195, 2218,
    2264, 2362, 2367, 2385, 2390, 2403, 2413, 2416
Wilkonson, Iris, 1386
Witch doctors, 405
Witchcraft, 884, 1530, 1818, 2406. See also
    Supernatural
Witches, 167, 538, 1073, 1156, 1172, 1341, 1405,
    1560, 1935, 2105, 2406
Wizemsky, Anne, 476
Women and eunuchs, 1737
Women and former lovers, 438, 1755
Women and gay men, 27, 111, 508, 668, 680, 690,
    701, 763, 1198, 1327, 1335, 1346, 1384, 1431,
    1605, 1624, 1656, 1746, 1765, 1786, 1828, 2275,
    2293
Women and leftist men, 139, 329, 336, 1041, 1383,
    1684, 1799

Women as commodity, 8, 24, 31, 166, 168, 259, 290,
    309, 318, 397, 621, 674, 963, 1017, 1036, 1054,
    1064, 1092, 1103, 1290, 1293, 1447, 1516, 1531,
    1672, 1680, 1731, 2120
Women's rights advocates, 232, 287, 312, 478, 487,
    794, 962, 999, 1031, 1048, 1061, 1108, 1158, 1160,
    1267, 1351, 1393, 1446, 1603, 1643, 1694, 1711,
    1787, 2206, 2260, 2328, 2340, 2401. *See also*
    Feminists; Political activists
Women's shelters. *See* Safe houses
Woolf, Virginia, 2300
Workers, 7, 98, 100, 258, 316, 602, 663, 701, 1248,
    1960, 1986, 2134. *See also* Actors; Artists;
    Athletes; Bureaucrats; Businesswomen; Carpet
    weavers; Doctors; Fortune tellers; Dollmakers;
    Domestic servants; Embroiderers; Engineers;
    Fashion workers; Food workers; Journalists; Labor
    organizers; Lawyers; Miners; Nurses; Prostitutes;
    Religious workers; Taxi drivers; Teachers;
    Telephone operators; Writers
Workers, cleaning, 122, 419, 540, 823, 1616, 1621,
    2216. *See also* Domestic servants
Workers, construction, 2363, 2377
Workers, cultural, 72, 333, 465, 558, 681, 1356, 2214
Workers, dock, 336
Workers, factory, 4, 9, 89, 372, 417, 517, 577, 688,
    727, 889, 930, 931, 934, 936, 938, 941, 1092, 1095,
    1159, 1250, 1519, 1695, 1721, 1879, 1997, 2040,
    2364
Workers, farm, 68, 137, 153, 159, 267, 329, 512, 590,
    1082
Workers, garment, 400, 460, 1460, 1684, 1738, 1777,
    2310
Workers, migrant, 68, 137, 1090, 1134, 1712
Workers, office, 141, 161, 299, 437, 521, 589, 657,
    782, 1208, 1243, 1999, 2098, 2221, 2287, 2302

Workers, postal, 345, 575, 1463
Workers, retail, 97, 123, 243, 327, 400, 421, 509, 1273,
    1800, 2113, 2279
Workers, transportation, 1264, 1287
Working class, 41, 89, 98, 104, 114, 139, 141, 146,
    177, 240, 317, 377, 399, 400, 472, 481, 527, 576,
    584, 612, 669, 724, 729, 754, 848, 903, 931, 955,
    995, 1008, 1082, 1146, 1186, 1218, 1223, 1225,
    1248, 1253, 1307, 1332, 1337, 1404, 1421, 1424,
    1435, 1469, 1483, 1566, 1577, 1581, 1621, 1634,
    1639, 1663, 1685, 1713, 1714, 1717, 1785, 1838,
    1861, 1866, 1872, 1890, 1948, 1965, 1969, 1986,
    2033, 2047, 2094, 2096, 2118, 2132, 2187, 2283,
    2288, 2344, 2348, 2387, 2389, 2394, 2412, 2417.
    See also Poverty; Prostitutes
Working outside the country, 1181, 1439, 1449
Working outside the home, 7, 16, 305, 333, 767, 968,
    1102, 1208, 1446, 1578, 1872, 2046, 2229, 2376
World War I, 335, 464, 763, 1486, 1716, 1843, 1975
World War II, 198, 415, 527, 660, 686, 709, 772, 779,
    796, 817, 837, 838, 884, 939, 1144, 1258, 1393,
    1406, 1454, 1478, 1482, 1514, 1523, 1623, 2040,
    2102, 2367, 2411, 2415
World War II, resistance, 3, 489, 546, 548, 593, 697,
    717, 796, 798, 863, 1359, 1870, 1981, 2050

Yang Kaihui, 308
Yugoslavia, 94, 678
    (made in), 2411–2415

Zetterling, Mai, 476
Zimbabwe, 1651
    (made in), 2416–2418
    Zimbabwe, Harare, 2417
Zoos, 878
Zulu people, 1544

INDEX OF TITLES

1 + 1 = 3, 748
10, 1102
10 Women, 1728
2 secondes, 209
20 : 30 : 40, 1691
21:12 Piano bar, 116
The 24-Hour Woman, 2229
28 Days, 2253
30 Years to Life, 2287
36 Chowringhee Lane, 997
4 Adventures of Reinette and Mirabelle, 518
4 Aventures de Reinette et Mirabelle, 518
7 wanita dalam tugas rahasia, 1067
The 7th Sun of Love, 893
8 femmes, 646
8 Women, 646
84 Charing Cross Road, 2053
9 to 5, 1999
À la folie, pas du tout, 647
À la verticale de l'été, 2408
A Li Ma, 241
Á tout de suite, 667
Á vendre, 600
A, yao lan, 239
Aah, Belinda, 1725
Aakhir kyon, 1013
Aandhi, 983
Aberdeen, 1862
About the Verb Love, 1419
Abraham's Valley, 1495
Abschied von gestern, 743
Absence of Malice, 2005
Absences, 882
Accomplices, 833
The Accused, 2085
Act of Vengeance, 1954
The Actress, 737
Actress, 913, 1256
Actresses, 1590
L'Actrice et son fantôme, 261
Actrius, 1590
Acts of Worship, 2316

Ada of Manila, 1447
Adada, 1297
Adaminte variyellu, 1003
Adam's Rib, 1003, 2395
Ademloos, 1360
Adhexios erastis, 875
Adhikimeni, 854
Adi Vasfiye, 1723
Adj király katonát!, 941
Adoption, 934
Adua and Company, 1142
Adua e le compagne, 1142
The Aesthenic Syndrome, 2390
An Affair, 1303
An Affair of Love, 609
Une Affaire de femmes, 527
Afife Jale, 1726
A.F.R.C.A., 1308
L'Africana, 677
Afrika, 1308
After Love, 559
After Sex, 588
After the Wind Has Gone, 1262
Afternoon Breezes, 1251
Afureru atsui namida, 1259
Afwan ayuha al-qanun, 385
Against the Innocent, 59
Agatha, 500
Agatha et les lectures limitées, 500
Agnes Browne, 1863
Agnes of God, 2041
Agria triandafylla, 885
To Agrimi, 848
Agua e sal, 1501
Ah Fei, 1674
Ah kam, 918
Ah! Nomugi toge, 1250
Ahava mimabat sheni, 1132
Ahavata ha'ahronah shel Laura Adler, 1129
Ahlam Hind wa Kamilya, 388
Ahnungslosen, 715
Ahot zara, 1134

Ai no kawaki, 1235
Ai nü, 900
Ai o kou hito, 1266
Ai zai Beiang de jijie, 908
Aici nu mai locuieste nimeni, 1510
Aika hyva ihmiseksi, 412
Les Ailes de la colombe, 495
Aimée & Jaguar, 697
Ain't Nothing without You, 699
Aje, aje, bara aje, 1299
Akai satsui, 1226
Akai tenshi, 1232
Akelarre, 1560
El Akhar, 402
Akibiyori, 1215
Alas de mariposa, 1576
Alchemy, 2193
Alexandria, 891
Ali, Fear Eats the Soul, 753
Alias Betty, 631
Alice Doesn't Live Here Anymore, 1946
Alice in Wondertown, 343
Alice's Odyssey, 218
Alicia en el pueblo de Maravillas, 343
Alien, 1994
Aliki Dictator, 865
Aliko Dohiktator, I, 865
Alima, 241
All about My Mother, 1606
All Ends Well, 691
All for Love, 746
All for the Best, 977
All Hell Let Loose, 1661
All Mixed Up, 1228
All My Girls, 727
All Night Long, 118
Alle meine Mädchen, 727
Alles wird gut, 691
The All-Round Reduced Personality: Outtakes, 767
Die Allseitig reduzierte Persönlichkeit—Redupers, 767
Alma's Rainbow, 2149
Aloïse, 464
Älskande pär, 1639
Das alte Lied, 682
Amada, 335
L'Amant magnifique, 519
Amar prem, 974
Ambrogio, 1190
Amdaeng Muen kab nai Rid, 1694
Amélia, 154
Amelia Lopes O'Neill, 225
Amélie, 628
An American Rhapsody, 2272
L'Amie, 800

Les Ami(e)s, 1635
La Amiga, 836
Amor a la vuelta de la esquina, 1331
Un Amor en Allemagne, 810
El Amor no es pecado, 1325
Amorosa, 1654
An Amorous Woman of the Tang Dynasty, 904
L'Amour nu, 501
L'Amour plus froid, 1736
L'Amour violé, 479
An Li Xiao, 272
Ana, 1487
Ana and the Others, 41
Ana y los otros, 41
Anacrusa o de como la música viene después del silencio, 1328
Anacrusa or How the Music Comes after the Silence, 1328
Anak, 1449
Anam, 1739
Anatomie de l'enfer, 668
Anatomy of Hell, 668
Anchoress, 1818
And Quiet Rolls the Dawn, 995
And Then There Was Light, 537
And Women Shall Weep, 1744
And Your Mother Too, 1346
Die Andere Frau, 718
Andesu no hanayome, 1233
Angae maul, 1292
L'Ange noir, 568
An Angel at My Table, 1392
Angel de fuego, 1336
Un Ángel de la calle, 1326
Angel of Fire, 1336
Angel of the Street, 1326
Angela, 1201
Angelan sota, 415
Angela's War, 415
Angemaeul, 1292
Angi Vera, 938
Angie, 2156
Änglagård, 1656
L'Anglaise et le duc, 629
Angry Harvest, 837
Angst essen Seele auf, 753
Ani ohev otach Rosa, 1125
El Anillo de niebla, 1562
Anita: Dances of Vice, 829
Anita: Tänze des Lasters, 829
O Anjo da guarda, 1498
Anjuman, 1015
Ankur, 979
Anna, 409, 940, 2066
Anna filmje, 951

Anna Karenina, 591, 2356
Anna Wunder, 706
Anna's Film, 951
Annas sommer, 710
Anna's Summer, 710
Anne Devlin, 1111
Anne Trister, 190
Annie's Coming Out, 53
Another Way, 942
Another Woman, 2086
Ansikte mot ansikte, 1647
Anta mana manchike, 977
Antarjali yatra, 1020
Antigone, 683, 849, 1155
Antigoni, 849
Antigua, My Life, 39
Antigua vida mia, 39
Antonia and Jane, 1813
Antonian maailma, 1377
Antonia's Line, 1377
Antonieta, 1556
Anywhere but Here, 2237
Ao fei si xiao, 299
Ap' ta Ierossolima me agapi, 861
Apa yang kau cari Palupi, 1058
Apenbaringen, 1404
Apeurika, 1308
Apoussies, 882
The Apple Game, 352
The Apple Tree of Paradise, 1469
Apprehension, 728
Après l'amour, 559
April the Nineteenth, 1034
Aquella larga noche, 332
Arais al tein, 1703
Arayiss min kasab, 1350
The Arch, 899
Ardh satya, 1004
Ardor, 1309
I Ariadhni meni sti Lero, 886
Ariadne Lives in Leros, 886
Army Nurse, 255
To Aroma tis violettas, 877
Arous-e atash, 1089
L'Arrache-coeur, 182
Art for Teachers of Children, 2169
Art of Loving, 1454
Artemisia, 592
Arth, 1005
Artificial Insemination, 1559
Die Artisten in der Zirkuskuppel: ratlos, 744
Artists at the Top of the Big Top: Disoriented, 744
Arus atash, 1089
As a Wife, as a Woman, 1220
Ascendancy, 1109

Ashes from Paradise, 36
Así es la vida, 1342
Asiye nasil kurtulur?, 1711
Ask ölümden soguktur, 1736
Assam Garden, 1792
The Associate, 2194
Asteniceskij sindrom, 2390
Asya's Happiness, 2357
At First Sight, 509
At Five in the Afternoon, 1101
Atabit al-sittat, 398
Atalia, 1128
Através da janela, 148
Att älska, 408
L'Attente des femmes, 19
Attracta, 1110
Au pays des Juliets, 556
Auf immer und ewig, 826
August and July, 178
August Moon, 1567
Une Aussi longue absence, 879
Austral, 1389
Auswege, 99
Autobiographia dimionit, 1130
Autobiography of Miss Jane Pittman, 1938
L'Autre, 402
L'Autre femme, 435
L'Autre monde, 20
L'Autre rive, 181
Autumn Almanac, 947
Autumn Milk, 838
Autumn Sonata, 1650
An Autumn Story, 1734
Autumn Sun, 35
Autumn's Tale, 601
Avalon, 1271
Avalum penn thaane, 980
Avanim, 1138
Avargal, 990
Ave Maria, 1600
Avec tout mon amour, 630
L'Avenir d'Émilie, 816
Aventure de Catherine C., 541
Avskedet, 414
L'Avventura, 1143
Awakening, 298
The Awakening, 2007
Ay! Carmela, 1574
Aya, 62
Ayna, 1720
Ayouma, 674
Ayu dan Ayu, 1069
Az én XX szazadom, 949
Azhal auzynda, 1280
Aziza, 1695

Azra, 2415

Bab al-Sama maftouh, 1351
Babae, 1442
Babae sa bubungang lata, 1445
Babette's Feast, 362
Babettes gaestebud, 362
Babs, 1381
Babusya, 1518
Baby Boom, 2067
Babymother, 1864
Bad Girls, 447
Bad Girls Go to Hell, 1897
Bad Timing, 1793
Badis, 1352
Bagdad Cafe, 830
Al Bahethat an al horeya, 403
Baie des anges, 430
Baise-moi, 618
Bal poussière, 1213
Balance Sheet, 1456
The Ballad of Eve, 1181
The Ballad of Little Jo, 2150
The Ballad of Narayama, 1253
La Ballata di Eva, 1181
Balles perdues, 505
Ban sheng yuan, 922
La Bande des quatre, 528
Bandh jharokhe, 1040
Bandini, 966
Bandit Queen, 1031
Bandits, 692
The Banger Sisters, 2288
Banished Orin, 1247
The Banker, 496
Banoo, 1086
Banoo-ye ordibehesht, 1085
La Banquiere, 496
Banu, 1086
Bao gio cho toi thang muoi, 2403
Bar, 892
Bar Girls, 2170, 2410
Bara du och jag, 1657
Baran, 1090
Barb Wire, 2171
Barbara, 368
La Barque, 1104
The Barrister, 1019
Basic Instinct, 2139
Bastard Out of Carolina, 2195
The Bat, 102
Bata, bata ... Paano ka ginawa, 1446
The Battle of the Sacred Tree, 1284
Bavandar, 1048
Bay of Angels, 430

Baya's Mountain, 17
Be Blessed, 160
The Beach of Desire, 1324
Beaches, 2087
Bear Ye Another's Burdens, 736
Le Beau mariage, 502
A Beautiful Sunset, 1628
The Beauty of the Alhambra, 341
The Bed, 117
Beda, 2372
beDevil, 70
Bedrana, 1715
Bedwin Hacker, 1704
Before the Time Comes, 180
Begging for Love, 1266
Der Beginn Aller Schrecken ist Liebe, 812
The Beginning, 2364
Behind the Wall, 1455
Bei gua hong dou, 246
Being Julia, 221
La Bella del Alhambra, 341
Bella Martha, 707
Belladonna, 359
Belle, 1372
Belle de jour, 446
Belle Van Zuylen, 1373
A Belly Full, 621
Beloved, 2230
Belye, belye ajsty, 2354
Belyye, belyye aisty, 2354
Bemani, 1098
Bend It like Beckham, 1874
Bent familia, 1700
Benvenuta, 119
Benzina, 1206
Berdel, 1731
Bérénice, 513
Berget pa manens baksida, 1653
The Berlin Affair, 1179
Die Berührte, 788
The Best Day of My Life, 1203
Der Besuch, 740
Better Than Chocolate, 211
Betty Fisher and Other Stories, 631
Betty Fisher et les autres histoires, 631
Between Heaven and Earth, 566
Between Two Women, 1865
Die Beunruhigung, 728
Beyond Desire, 1623
Beyond Rangoon, 2172
Beyond Silence, 689
Beyond the Door, 1171
Beyond the Valley of the Dolls, 1915
Beyond the Walls, 1563
Bez bebek, 1729

Bez mitosci, 1461
Bez strakha, 2366
Bhadrakali, 988
Bhaji on the Beach, 1821
Bhumika, 991
Biale matzeństwo, 1477
A Bible for Daughters, 254
Les Biches, 447
The Bicycle, 733
The Big City, 968
Bilans kwartalny, 1456
Bildinis einer Trinkerin, 778
Binding Sentiments, 928
Binecuvintata fii inchisoare, 1513
Bir sonbahar hikayesi, 1734
Bir türke gönül verdim, 1710
Bir yudum sevgi, 1721
Birch Tree Meadow, 660
The Bird of Happiness, 1583
Birdcage Inn, 1304
Bird-Walking Weather, 726
Bis daß der Tod Euch scheidet, Leben mit Uwe, 725
Der Biß, 813
Bitches, 957
The Bite, 813
Bitter Day, Sweet Day, 390
Bitter Harvest, 837
The Bitter Spirit, 1219
The Bitter Tears of Petra von Kant, 751
Bittere ernte, 837
Die bitteren Tränen der Petra von Kant, 751
The Black Angel, 568
Black Cat, 544
Black Girl, 1521, 1939
Black Island, 1592
Black Rain, 1258
Black Rose, 1493
Black Shack Alley, 512
Black Tea with Lemon, 1494
Black Widow, 2068
A Blade of Grass in Kunlun Mountain, 230
Blagajnica hoce ici na more, 327
Blanche et Marie, 546
Die bleirne Zeit, 789
Bless You Prison, 1513
Blessed Are Those Who Thirst, 1414
La Blessure, 669
Les Blessures assassinés, 619
Ein Blick—und die Liebe bricht aus, 831
Blind Fairies, 1198
Blind Spot, 787, 1535
The Blonds, 46
Blood Feud, 1166
Blood Flowers, 650
Blood of the Condor, 132

Bloody Mama, 1916
Bloody Morning, 294
Blow for Blow, 460
Blue, 567
Blue Black Permanent, 1816
The Blue Diner, 2273
Blue Eyes of Yonta, 897
Blue Heaven, 346
Blue Sky, 2157
Blue Steel, 2106
The Blue-Veiled, 1082
Blush, 302
The Boat, 1104
Bodi blagoslovena!, 160
A Body in the Forest, 1591
Bolero, 819
Bombay Talkie, 972
Bon bast, 1074
Bona, 1429
Bones, 1497
Le Bonheur, 441
Les Bonnes femmes, 421
Boom boom, 1575
Bord de mer, 651
Border Line, 547
Born in Flames, 2021
Böse Zellen, 97
The Bostonians, 1787
Le Boucher, 449
Boulevard, 2158
Boulevard des Hirondelles, 548
Bound, 2196
A Bowl of Cherries, 136
Boxcar Bertha, 1929
Boys Don't Cry, 2238
Boys on the Side, 2173
Bread and Roses, 1393, 1869
Bread and Tulips, 1196
Breaking the Waves, 367
Breathless, 1360
Brenda Starr, 2100
Una Breve vacanza, 1159
The Bride, 1713
Bride of Fire, 1089
Bride of the Andes, 1233
A Bride of the Seventh Heaven, 420
Bride to Be, 1337
The Bridge, 603
Bridget Jones's Diary, 2274
Brief Encounters, 2361
A Brief Vacation, 1159
Bright Ocean Pearl, 238
Broadcast News, 2069
Der Brocken, 684
Brodeuses, 670

Brokedown Palace, 2239
Broken English, 1398, 2006
Broken Mirrors, 1366
The Broken Mountain, 684
Broken Silence, 1622
Broken Wings, 1139
The Brontë Sisters, 493
La Bru, 1713
Brumal, 1571
Brutal, 1428
Bubbling Spring, 244
La Bûche, 620
Bukan isteri pilihannya, 1062
Bulaklak ng City Jail, 1432
Bulaklak ng Maynila, 1447
Bulutlari beklerken, 1741
Bürgschaft für ein Jahr, 731
Burning an Illusion, 1779
Burning Angel, 416
Bury Me an Angel, 1923
Bush Mama, 1969
A Business Affair, 1840
Business as Usual, 1800
The Business of Strangers, 2254
The Butcher, 449
Butterfield 8, 1888
Butterfly, 322
Butterfly Kiss, 1827
Butterfly Wings, 1576
By Design, 185
By the Seaside, 1488
Bye Bye Blues, 198
Byeda, 2372
Byegushaya Mishen, 1278

C'est la vie, 1342
C't'a ton tour Laura Cadieux, 210
Cactus, 56
Café Lumière, 1277
Caged Heat, 1947
Cal, 1112
Calé, 1565
Calendar Girls, 1881
Call Me, 2070
Callas Forever, 1202
Cama adentro, 44
Cambio de sexo, 1545
Camila, 28
Camilla, 1819
Camille Claudel, 529
Le Camion, 480
Camorra: The Naples Connection, 1176
The Camp Followers, 1152
Canale Grande, 805
Canary Season, 163

Cannibal Women in the Avocado Jungle of Death,
    2088
I Cannibali, 1155
The Cannibals, 1155
The Cannibal's Daughter, 1627
La Captive, 632
La Captive du désert, 542
Captive of the Desert, 542
Career Girls, 1841
Cari genitori, 1160
Carla, 721
La Carnada, 1422
Carolota Joaquina, Princesa do Brazil, 147
Carra 30, 378
Carrington, 1828
La Carta, 1500
La Casa de Bernarda Alba, 1570
Casa de los Babys, 2317
A Case of High Treason, 862
The Case of Lena Christ, 749
The Cashier Wants to Go to the Seaside, 327
The Cat Has Nine Lives, 747
Catherine Chérie, 797
Catwoman, 2337
Cavedweller, 2338
Cecilia, 334
Ceddo, 1526
Celeste, 790
Celestial Clockwork, 585
Céline, 557
Celine and Julie Go Boating, 465
Céline et Julie vont en bateau, 465
Cenizas del paraiso, 36
Center Stage, 913
Central do Brasil, 152
Central Station, 152
Il Cerchio, 1091
La Cérémonie, 575
The Ceremony, 575
Le Cerf volant, 1315, 1407
César et Rosalie, 459
Cet amour-là, 633
Cette femme-là, 652
Chá forte com limã o, 1494
Chained Heat, 2014
Chair á bon marché, 397
Chakra, 998
Chalk Garden, 1750
The Challenge, 389
La Chambre de mariage, 1722
Chandni Bar, 1049
Chang bei, 901
Chant d'exile, 921
Chaos, 634
Characters, 990

Le charbonnier, 7
Charlotte, 1358
Charlotte Gray, 1870
Charulata, 969
Chatarra, 1577
Chaverim shel Yana, ha, 1135
Cheap Flesh, 397
Check to the Queen, 1549
Le Chêne, 1508
El Chergui, 1349
Cherie, I'm Not Well, 806
Cherie, mir ist schlecht, 806
Una Chica llamada Marilyne, 1553
Chilakamma cheppindi, 992
Children of the Century, 607
The Children's Hour, 1892
Chili Bouquet, 1017
Chimère, 536
Chin Up!, 608
The China Syndrome, 1989
Chinese Chocolate, 204
Chinese Roulette, 762
Chinesisches Roulette, 762
Chocolat, 530
Choose Me, 2032
Chornique d'une mort annoncée, 1182
Choses secretes, 648
Christines Schwester, 814
Christine's Sister, 814
Ta Chronia tis megalis zestis, 883
Chronicle of a Death Foretold, 1182
Chronicle of Love, 1133
Chronicles of Anna Magdalena Bach, 745
Chronik de Anna Magdalena Bach, 745
Chronika shel ahava, 1133
Chu jia nü, 278
Chun tao, 266
Chunhyang, 1305
Chunyeo dului gernyuk siksa, 1302
La Chute d'une femme, 394
Chutney Popcorn, 2255
Chuvanna vithukal, 989
Chuzhiye pisma, 2369
La Ciénaga, 40
De cierta manera, 331
La Ciociara, 1144
The Circle, 1091
Circle of Friends, 1115
Circuit carole, 576
The Citadel, 14
Citizen Ruth, 2197
A City's Child, 47
Civil Brand, 2318
Civilized People, 1314
Civilizées, 1314

Claire Dolan, 2256
Claudia, 107
Claudine, 1948
Clay Dolls, 1703
Clean Sweep, 1137
Cléo de 5 à 7, 425
Cleo from 5 to 7, 425
Cleopatra Jones, 1940
The Client, 2159
Clockwatchers, 2221
Closet Land, 2121
Cloth Doll, 1729
The Clothes in the Wardrobe, 1820
The Cloud Capped Star, 964
Clouds: Letters to My Son, 130
Clubbed to Death, 587
Clumsy Lover, 875
Co gai tren song, 2404
Coal Miner's Daughter, 2000
The Coalburner, 7
Cocktail Molotov, 497
Codou, 1522
Coeurs à l'envers, 186
Coeurs flambés, 363
Coffy, 1941
La Colonia penal, 222
The Color of the Soul, 716
The Color Purple, 2042
Coma, 1977, 2392
Come Back to My Side, 1602
Come Back to the 5 and Dime Jimmy Dean, Jimmy
    Dean, 2015
Come, Come, Come Upward, 1299
The Comeback, 1712
Comme une image, 671
Comment sauver Asiye?, 1711
The Commissar, 2358
Committed, 2022, 2257
A Common Thread, 670
Common Wealth, 1609
Commotion, 2370
Cómo ser mujer y no morir en el intento, 1578
The Company of Strangers, 199
The Company of Wolves, 1788
Compassionate Sex, 1615
A Completely Neglected Girl, 768
Un Complicato intrigo di donne, vicoli e delitte,
    1176
Compromising Positions, 2043
La Comunidad, 1609
Con gli occhi chiusi, 1191
Conceiving Ada, 1855
Congregation, 1015
Connie and Carla, 2339
Constance, 1385

Contact, 2222
Conte d'automne, 601
Le Conte du ventre plein, 621
Contempt, 437
The Contender, 2258
A Cooler Climate, 2240
Coraje, 1421
Corazon de la Cruz, 1425
Corps plongés, 898
Cory scescie, 958
Un Cos al bosc, 1591
Costa Brava, 1585
Coto de caza, 1557
Cotton Mary, 1856
La Couleur de l'ame, 716
Coup de foudre, 509
Coup de grâce, 763
Coup pour coup, 460
Courage, 1421
Cours privé, 520
Le Couteau, 2407
The Cradle, 239
Crazy in Love, 2140
Crazy Mama, 1962
Credo, 370
De Criada a señora, 1550
Cries and Whispers, 1645
Crimes of the Heart, 2054
Crocodiles in Amsterdam, 1370
Cronaca di u na morte annunciata, 1182
Crooklyn, 2160
Cross Creek, 2023
Crossing Delancey, 2089
The Cruel Embrace, 125
Crush, 1395, 1875
Cry in the Dark, 60
Cry No More, 1354
Crying Women, 317
Crystal Nights, 884
Csajok, 957
A Csalás gyönyöre, 952
Csókkal es körömmel, 955
Cuando vuelvas a mi lado, 1602
Cuerpo en el bosque, 1591
The Curse, 1524
Custody, 1472
Czlowiek z marmuru, 1457
Czlowiek z zelaza, 1457

D'une Femme a l'autre, 1840
Da hong deng long gao gao gua, 284
Dabbel Trabbel, 791
Daddy, 1770
Daehan minguk, 1310
Dagboek van een oude dwaas, 1368

Dahil mahal kita, 1436
Daichi no komoruta, 1246
Daisies, 350
Daisy Miller, 1949
Dallas Doll, 67
Daman, 1050
La Dame, 1730
Dançar Até Morrer, 587
Dance Me to My Song, 79
Dance of the Wind, 1847
Dance with a Stranger, 1794
Dancer in the Dark, 372
Dancing at Lughnasa, 1119
Dancing in the Dust, 1213
Dangerous Affair, 1286
Dangerous Climb, 809
A Dangerous Woman, 2151
Dans ma peau, 653
Danzón, 1335
Dao ma dan, 905
Dark Habits, 1558
The Dark Side of Tomorrow, 1917
Darling, 1754
Dau an cua quy, 2406
The Daughter of a Good Family, 1700
Daughter of Luck, 958
The Daughter-in-Law, 2367
Daughters of the Dust, 2122
Daughters of the Sun, 1092
Daughters of the Wind, 156
Daughters of This Century, 1051
Dawn, 999
The Day I Became a Woman, 1093
Day Longer Than Night, 2381
Day of Birth, 1043
Day of the Idiots, 795
Day of the Woman, 1980
Daydream Believer, 63, 2289
Dayereh, 1091
The Days Between, 713
Days of Water, 330
Days to Remember, 835
De qué se ríen las muferes?, 1597
Dead End, 1074
Dead Man Walking, 2198
Deadly Game, 783
Deadly Maria, 1374
Deaf to the City, 196
Dear, Dearest, Beloved, Unique . . ., 2382
Dear Frankie, 1882
Dear Irene, 355
Dear Ladies!, 393
Dear Parents, 1160
Death Becomes Her, 2141
Death of Maria Malibran, 750

Death Sentence, 1042
The Debut, 2364
Deception, 967
Deep Crimson, 1340
The Deep End, 2275
Defenseless, 2123
Le Défi, 389
Degirmen, 1727
Deliver Us from Eva, 2319
Demain on déménage, 654
Demasiado miedo a la vida o Plaff, 339
Il Demino clandestino, 1186
La Demoiselle sauvage, 200
Démon au féminin, 16
Demon Seed, 1978
Demonlover, 655
Den dlinnee notchi, 2381
Den Muso, 1318
Den Vita Väggen, 1646
La Dentellière, 481
Departed Love in the Evening, 1332
The Deputy, 1572
La Derive, 436
Derman, 1719
Le Dernier baiser, 482
Le Dernier harem, 1737
Déryné, hol Van?, 935
Deseo, 1623
Desert Blanc, 260
Desert Hearts, 2044
Deserto rosso, 1147
Desire in Motion, 203
Desirée, 1364
Désolé, c'est la loi, 385
Desperately Seeking Susan, 2045
Despoinis dieuthyntes, 855
Le Destin, 1319
Destin éphémère, 2405
El Destino no tiene favoritos, 1423
Destiny, 1319
Destiny Has No Favorites, 1423
Det Storste i verden, 1415
Deutschland bleiche Mutter, 779
Deutschland kann manchmal sehr schön sein, 792
Deux, 649
Deux actrices, 201
Deux femmes, 1087
Deux ou trois choses que je sais d'elle, 444
Deveti Krug, 2411
Devi, 963
The Devil and the Nun, 1453
The Devil's Mark, 2406
The Devils, the Devils, 1475
I Dhaskalitsa me tin kali kardhia, 859
I Dhemonisement, 870

Dhio manes sto stavro tou ponou, 852
Dhiogmos, 856
Dhromi ke portokalia, 887
I Dhromi tis agapis ine nihterini, 872
Di yi you huo, 295
Un Día de suerte, 42
Diably, diably, 1475
Diario di una schizofrenica, 1154
Diario inconcluso, 191
Diary for My Children, 944
Diary for My Father and Mother, 950
Diary for My Loves, 948
Diary of a Mad Housewife, 1918
Diary of a Mad Old Man, 1368
Diary of a Schizophrenic Girl, 1154
Diary of a Woman in White, 442
Diary of Lady M, 1667
Didone non è morta, 1183
Dieu de tonnerre, 1523
Dignity, 1528
La Dilettante, 606
Dime una mentira, 1580
Dimeri i fundit, 3
Ek din prati din, 995
La Diputada, 1572
Dirty Dishes, 507
Dirty Mary, 451
Disaster, 2372
Discombobbled, 2290
Disparen a matar, 2398
Disturbance, 2370
Divided Heaven, 720
Divine Secrets of the Ya-Ya Sisterhood, 2291
Dix femmes, 1728
Djeli, 1211
Djeli, conte d'aujourd'hui, 1211
Do I Love You?, 1876
Do Zan, 1087
Doces poderes, 151
Docteur Françoise Gailland, 469
Doea tanda mata, 1066
Dog in the Manger, 1594
Dogfight, 2124
Doghi, 1036
A Dog's Life, 1555
Dogs of the Night, 31
Dogville, 375
Dokhtaran khorshid, 1092
Dolgiye provody, 2365
The Dollmaker, 2033
Doll's Eye, 1781
A Doll's House, 757, 1078, 1771
Dolores Claiborne, 2174
The Dolzura Cortez Story, 1436
Dom na peske, 1514

Domenica, 1194
Dona Flor and Her Two Husbands, 133
Dona Flor e seus dois maridos, 133
Doña Herlinda and Her Son, 1327
Doña Herlinda y su hijo, 1327
Dong fu ren, 899
Donkey's Skin, 454
Don't Cry, 1282
Don't Cry, Pretty Girls, 930
Dönüs, 1712
A Door in Heaven, 1351
Dorian Gray im Spiegel der boulevard Presse, 807
Une Dot pour Robab, 1075
Double Happiness, 202
Double Jeopardy, 2241
The Double Life of Veronique, 1476
Double Suicide, 1238
Double Trouble, 791
Le Double vie de Véronique, 1476
Down & Out with the Dolls, 2320
Dowry for Robaab, 1075
Dream Life, 177
Dream of a Waltz, 143
A Dream of Passion, 871
The Dream of the Elk, 735
Dream On, 1814
The Dreamlife of Angels, 605
Dreams of Hind and Camelia, 388
Drei Sterne, 707
Der Dritte, 723
Drive to Win, 242
Du shen nü ren, 285
Du shi sha ke si feng, 300
Du verbe aimer, 1419
Duelle, 473
Dus gezginleri, 1735
Dust, 121
Duvata Mawaka Misa, 1637
Dziewczeta z Nowolipek, 1469

Each Other, 492
Earth Is a Sinful Song, 411
East on the Compass, 1610
L'École de la chair, 582
Les Écrans de sable, 1313
Edie and Pen, 1833
Edith's Diary, 815
Ediths Tagebuch, 815
Edna Zhena na trideset i tri, 161
Educating Rita, 1785
The Effect of Gamma Rays on Man-in-the-Moon
　　Marigolds, 1930
Effi Briest, 758
Les Égarés, 656
Egymásra nézve, 942

Die Ehr der Maria Braun, 772
Eien no hito, 1219
Eiga joyu, 1256
Eighteen Springs, 922
Eila, 419
Einer trage des anderen Last, 736
Eine einfache Geschichte, 488
The Eldest Daughter, 1636
Electra, 850, 932
Elektra, 932
Elephants and Grass, 1738
Les Eléphants et la pelouse, 1738
Eles não usam black-tie, 139
Eline Vere, 126
Elisa, My Life, 1547
Elisa vida mia, 1547
Elise or Real Life, 4
Elise, ou la vraie vie, 4
Elizabeth, 1850
Ellas, 1603
Elle, 226
Elle est des nôtres, 657
Elsker dig fo evigt, 374
Eltávozott nap, 927
Elyes, baccar, 581
Em dic Sara, 1601
Un Embrujo, 1341
Emine, the Leaning One, 1716
Emitai, 1523
Emma Zunz, 1365
Emotional Crack, 1402
The Empress Dowager, 237
Emraa ayla lel sekout, 394
Emraa waheda la takri, 392
Emtehan, 1099
En Avoir (ou pas), 577
En decouvrant le caste monde, 2377
En Kaerligheds historie, 373
En la puta vida, 2350
Enchanted April, 1815
The End of August, 2007
The End of August at the Hotel Ozone, 351
End of Innocence, 2107
The End of the World (In Our Usual Bed in a Night
　　Full of Rain), 1167
Les Enfants du siècle, 607
The Engagement of Anna, 868
The Engagement Party, 1546
Engelchen, 688
Enough, 2292
Enskilda samtal, 1658
The Entity, 2008
Entre el cielo y la tierra, 566
Entre nous, 509
Entre rojas, 1586

Entre tinieblas, 1558
Ephemeral Fate, 2405
Epiphany Sunday, 543
Epitafium la Barbary Radizwillowny, 1466
The Epitaph for Barbara Radizwill, 1466
L'Erdità Ferramonti, 1163
Erendira, 1329
Erikas Leidenschaften, 773
Erika's Passions, 773
Erin Brockovich, 2242
Ermo, 301
Erotic Symphony, 866
Erotiki symfonia, 866
Érotique, 2175
The Escape, 1148
De eso no se habla, 34
La Espera, 2351
El Este de la brujula, 1610
Esther Kahn, 1866
Et la lumière fut, 537
L'Été meurtrier, 510
Eternamente Pagu, 144
L'Eternel retour, 682
Etwas tut weh, 780
Eu, tu, eles, 153
Eva Guerillera, 193
L'Evanouie, 560
O Evdemos ilios tou erota, 893
Every Other Weekend, 545
Everyone's Child, 2418
Everything Is Dark, 1599
Everything Put Together, 2276
Everything Relative, 2199
Eve's Bayou, 2223
Exam, 1099
The Executioners, 917
The Experiment, 1105
Extramuros, 1563
Extremities, 2055
Eyes of Beauty, 320

Faat-Kine, 1532
Le Fabuleux destin d'Amélie Poulain, 628
Face, 1272
Face to Face, 1512, 1647
Faces of women, 1212
Fad'jal, 1527
El Fahham, 7
Das Fahrrad, 733
A Faithful and True Rehabilitation, 1489
Faithless, 1659
Der Fall Lena Christ, 749
Fall of a Woman, 394
Falling Bodies, 898
Famila rodante, 45

Family Album, 1585
Fan mu an kao, 1680
Fanci's Persuasion, 2161
Der Fangschuss, 763
Fanny "Pelopaja," 1561
Fanta, 172
Les Fantômes des trois Madeleine, 214
Far Away and Close, 1648
Far from Heaven, 2293
Far from the Barbarians, 562
Far from the Madding Crowd, 1759
The Far Road, 1248
Far Shore, 181
Faraw! Mother of the Dunes, 1322
Faraw, une mère de sable, 1322
Die Farbe der Seele, 716
The Farewell, 414, 2378
Farewell China, 908
Farewell to Maria, 1478
Fargo, 2200
Fata în fata, 1512
Fatal Attraction, 2071
Le Fate ignoranti, 1198
The Fatima Buen Story, 1437
Un Fatto di sangue fra due uomini per cause di una vedova—si sospettano moventi politici, 1166
Fear and Trembling, 663
Felicia's Journey, 212
Félicité, 490
Der Felsen, 711
Female Perversions, 2201
Féminin-Féminin, 110
La Femme au couteau, 1209
Une Femme d'exterieur, 622
La Femme de l'hotel, 189
Une Femme de la province, 1471
La Femme de Rose Hill, 1666
Une Femme douce, 450
La Femme du Gange, 463
Une Femme est une femme, 426
Femme Fatale, 2294
La Femme flic, 491
Une Femme francaise, 569
La Femme infidèle, 448
Une Femme mariée, 439
La Femme Nikita, 544
Une Femme pour mon fils, 11
Une Femme, un jour, 483
Les Femmes, 386
Femmes femmes, 466
Feng kang de dai jia, 273
Fényérzékeny történet, 953
Fernweh, 701
Fertility, 1047
The Festival, 1012

Fetch a Pail of Water, 1448
The Fiancee, 730
La Fiancée du pirate, 451
Fiela se Kind, 1538
Fiela's Child, 1538
Filhaal, 1053
Filhas do Vento, 156
La Fille, 1318
La Fille aux yeux d'or, 427
La Fille seule, 583
Filler ve çimen, 1738
Film about a Woman Who . . ., 1950
Les Fils de Marie, 194
La Fine del mondo nel nostro solito letto in una
    notte piena di pioggia, 1167
Finzan, 1320
Fire, 1037
Fire in Their Hearts, 1539
The First Amendment, 1310
First Attraction, 295
The First Steps, 784
The First Wives Club, 2202
First Woman in the Forests, 262
Fish and Elephant, 316
Fistful of Flies, 76
Five Faces of Kadarwati, 1063
Five on the Black Hand Side, 1942
Flamberede hjerter, 363
Die flambierte Frau, 808
Flame, 2417
Flaming Ears, 93
Flaming Hearts, 363
Fleurs de sang, 650
Flight, 1834
Flikorna, 1643
The Floating Landscape, 926
Floating Life, 77
The Flor Contemplacion Story, 1439
La Flor de mi secreto, 1587
À Flor do mar, 1488
Flores de otro mundo, 1604
A Flower in the Rainy Night, 1672
Flower Island, 1306
The Flower of My Secret, 1587
Flowers from Another World, 1604
Flowers of Shanghai, 1686
Flowers of the City Jail, 1432
Flugel und Fesseln, 816
Foetus, 954
Folle à tuer, 470
Follow Your Heart, 1193
Following Desire, 1240
I Fonissa, 869
Footsteps Disappear on the Horizon, 2353
For Better or for Worse, 1961

For Ever and Ever, 826
For Love of Ivy, 1905
For Sale, 600
For the Moment, 198
Forbrydelser, 376
A Foreign Body, 599
Foreign Sister, 1134
Forever, Lulu, 2072
Forfolgelsen, 1405
Four Faces of Eve, 920
Four Women, 1660
Four Women in a Harem, 1708
The Fourth Sex, 428
Foxy Brown, 1951
Fragments of Isabella, 1113
Fran, 55
Frances, 2016
Francesca, 827
Eine Frau fürs ganze Leben, 738
Eine Frau mit Verantwortung, 774
Eine Frau namens Harry, 676
Freak Orlando, 793
Freak Weather, 2243
Freaky Friday, 2321
Free Radicals, 97
A Free Woman, 760
Freedom Fighters, 1593
French Twist, 579
A French Woman, 569
Fresh Kill, 2162
Freud flyttar hemifrån, 366
Freud Leaves Home, 366
Freud quitte la maison, 366
Frida, 1330, 2295
Friday Night, 665
Fried Green Tomatoes, 2125
Friends, 1543, 1635
From Jerusalem with Love, 861
From Maid to Lady, 1550
Frontier Women, 1401
Frost, 693
Fruen på Hamre, 371
Fu chu de nü ren, 288
Fu rong zhen, 251
Fu sheng, 77
La Fuga, 1148
Fugueuses, 578
Full Circle, 2386
Full Moon in New York, 910
Full Moon in Paris, 514
Fünf letzte Tage, 798
Funny Girl, 1906
Fuori dal mondo, 1177
Für immer: Lulu, 2072
Fürchten und Lieben, 1187

The Future Is Woman, 1178
The Future of Emily, 816
Il Futuro è donna, 1178
Fyra kvinnor, 1660

Gabbeh, 1083
Gai nhay, 2410
Gaijin, 137
Gaijin, caminhos de liberdade, 137
Gal Young 'Un, 1995
Game Reserve, 1557
Gan no tera, 1222
The Gang of Four, 528
Ein ganz und gar verwahrlostes Mädchen, 768
The Garage, 399
Gary Cooper que estás en los cielos, 1551
Gary Cooper Who Art in Heaven, 1551
Gas Food Lodging, 2126
Gasoline, 1206
Gates of Europe, 1486
Gaudi Afternoon, 2322
Gazala, 1103
Gazon maudit, 579
Gebroken spiegels, 1366
Geh wohin dein herz dich Trägt, 1193
Gehenu Lamai, 1634
Die Geirwally, 832
Gelegenheitsarbelt einer Sklavin, 754
Gelin, 1713
Genesis, 1016
Gentili Signore, 1185
A Gentle Woman, 450
The Geography of Fear, 418
Georgette Meunier, 842
Georgia, 2176
Georgia Georgia, 1644
German Dreams, 820
The German Sisters, 789
Germany Can Sometimes Be Very Nice, 792
Germany Pale Mother, 779
Gertrud, 354
Gesches, 694
Geschichten aus dem Wienerwald, 775
Der geteilte Himmel, 720
Getting to Know the Big Wide World, 2377
Ggot seom, 1306
Ghattashraddha, 993
Ghermez, 1088
Ghost World, 2277
Gib mir Liebe, 746
Gift, 694
Gina Wildcat, 776
Gina Wildkatze, 776
The Girl, 635, 927, 1318
Girl 6, 2203

A Girl Called Marilyne, 1553
Girl from Heaven, 247
Girl from Hunan, 265
Girl from Paris, 636
Girl, Interrupted, 2244
Girl on the River, 2404
Girl Student Dormitory, 269
The Girl Who Came Late, 63
Girl with Green Eyes, 1751
The Girl with the Golden Eyes, 427
The Girl with the Red Hair, 1359
The Girl with the Red Scarf, 1717
The Girl with the Suitcase, 1145
The Girlfriend, 836
Girlfriends, 1990
The Girls, 421, 1634, 1643
Girls from Nowolipki Street, 1469
Girls' Night Out, 1302
The Girls to Be Married, 278
Girls Town, 2204
Giulietta degli spiriti, 1150
Gloria, 2001
Go Fish, 2163
Go Where the Heart Leads You, 1193
The Goddess, 963
Godmother, 1045
Gold Diggers, 1782
The Golden Bowl, 2278
Golden Eighties, 123
Golden Fingernails, 274
Golden Youth, 638
Golpes a mi puerta, 2400
Good Day, Bad Day, 390
The Good Girl, 2296
A Good Marriage, 502
Good Men, Good Women, 1682
The Good Mother, 2090
Goodbye, 1376
Goodbye in the Mirror, 1149
Goodbye Lenin, 712
Goodbye New York, 2034
Gorillas in the Mist, 2091
Die Gottesanbeterin, 842
Une Gouette d'amour, 1721
The Governess, 1851
Go-yang-i-rul boo-tak-hae, 1307
Grace of My Heart, 2205
Le Grain de sable, 506
Grain of Sand, 506
Grand Isle, 2127
Granny, 1518
Gräset Sjunger, 1651
Grass Grows on the Kunlun Mountains, 230
The Grass Is Singing, 1651
Grat Wanderung, 809

The Grave, 1714
The Greatest Thing, 1415
The Green Ray, 521
Green Snake, 915
Grenzenlos, 799
Grete Minde, 764
The Griot, 1211
The Group, 1901
Group Marriage, 1931
Growing Up, 1406
Gu huo zai qing yi pian zhi hong xing shi san mei, 923
Guarda il cielo, 1195
Guardian of the Frontier, 1536
Guernica, 943
The Guest, 1157
Gui ge qing yuan, 279
The Guide, 970
Guihuaxiang, 1678
Guilt, 158
Guinevere, 2245
Gülüsan, 1724
Gumrah, 967
Guo nian hui jia, 314
Guruku contik sekali, 1060
Gyae-got-un nalui ohu, 1300
Gypsy, 1565

Ha megjön József, 933
Habiba M'sika, 1697
Hai shang hua, 1686
Hai shang ming zhu, 238
Hai tan de yi tian, 1671
Hai xia, 236
Half of Heaven, 1568
Half Truths, 1004
Ham and Chips, 485
Hamsar, 1079
Hanaoka Seishu no tsuma, 1236
Hanare goze Orin, 1247
The Hand That Rocks the Cradle, 2142
The Handmaid's Tale, 2108
Hanging Offense, 652
Hanging Up, 2259
Hanim, 1730
Hao nan hao nü, 1682
Happiness, 441
Happy Birthday, 1515
The Happy Ending, 1912
Happy Here and Now, 2297
El Haram, 377
Harem of Madame Osmane, 1611
Harem suare, 1737
Häremde dört kadýn, 1708
El Harén de Madame Osmane, 1611

Hari bhari, 1047
Harrison's Flowers, 2298
Harry and Harriette, 676
Harvest Time, 1520
Hasta cierto punto, 336
Hauptsache Leben, 1379
Haut les coeurs!, 608
Hazaar chaurasi ki maa, 1041
H'Biba M'Sika, 1697
He Loves Me, He Loves Me Not, 647
The Healer, 208
Heart like a Wheel, 2024
Heart of Midnight, 2092
Heart of the Country, 121
Heartaches, 186
Heartbreak, 182
Heartbreak Island, 1683
Heartburn, 2056
Heartland, 1776
Heat and Dust, 1783
Heatwave, 51
Heavenly Creatures, 1396
Heavy Weather, 589
Hebi ichigo, 1275
Hedda, 1772
Hedwig, or the Cool Lakes of Death, 1362
Heidi M., 708
The Heiresses, 939
Hell Hunters, 834
Heller Wahn, 800
Henry and June, 2109
Her Lonely Lane, 1223
L'Herbe sauvage, 1210
Herbstmilch, 838
Les Heritieres, 939
The Heroic Trio, 917
Hester Street, 1952
Hi, Are You Alone?, 1588
Hibiscus Town, 251
Hibotan bakuto, 1237
Hiçbiryerde, 1740
Hidden Agenda, 1811
The Hidden Half, 1096
Hidden River, 37
Hidden Star, 964
Hidden Whisper, 1688
Hideous Kinky, 1857
High Art, 2231
High Crimes, 2299
High Heels, 1579
High Season, 1801
High Tide, 57
La Hija del canibál, 1627
Hikinige, 1234
Hilary and Jackie, 1852

Hill on the Dark Side of the Moon, 1653
Himiko, 1242
Himutsu no hanazono, 1265
Une Hirondelle a fait le printemps, 636
L'Histoire d'Adèle H, 471
Histoire d'Orokia, 166
Une Histoire simple, 488
Les Histoires d'amour finissent mal . . . en général, 558
Historia niemoralna, 1474
La Historia oficial, 29
Historias de mujeres, 1552
History of Postwar Japan, 1239
Hit and Run, 1234
A Hjara veraldar, 960
Ho yuk, 319
Hob el banat, 404
Hola, estàs sola?, 1588
Hold Up, 1621
Holdudvar, 928
Holy Smoke!, 81
Holy Week, 1482
Homecoming, 903
Un Homme et deux femmes, 549
Honey and Ashes, 1699
Hong fen, 302
Hong gao liang, 259
Hong niang, 311
Hong se niang zijun, 228, 235
The Honor, 1281
Honor of the House, 961
A Hora da estrela, 141
Horoki, 1223
Hostess, 726
Höstsonaten, 1650
Hot Land, 1715
The Hot Roof, 1300
Hot Spices, 1017
Hotel, 100
Hotel Central, 162
Hotel Sorrento, 73
Hotel Tsentral, 162
Hour of the Star, 141
The Hours, 2300
House Built on Sand, 1514
House for Swap, 337
House of Angels, 1656
The House of Bernarda Alba, 1570
House of Memories, 1046
The House of Mirth, 1867
The Houseguest and My Mother, 1289
Household Saints, 2152
Housekeeping, 2073
How Stella Got Her Groove Back, 2232
How to Be a Woman and Not Die Trying, 1578

How to Be Loved, 1454
How to Make an American Quilt, 2177
Hra o jablko, 352
Hsiang hun nü, 296
Hu du men, 919
Hua hun, 289
Huai shi zhuang, 229
Huan nü, 297
Huang se gu shi, 1677
Huang tu po de po yi, 267
Huang yuan, 260
Hubog, 1451
Hud, 1410
Human Woman, 88
Hunger Years, 781
Hungerjahre—in einem reichen Land, 781
Hungry for Love, 1142
Hungry Wives, 1935
A Hunter's Family, 1280
Hus i helvete, 1661
Hustruer, 1403
Hustruer ti ar etter, 1409
Hustruer III, 1412
Hyenas, 1529
Hyènes, 1529
Hysterical Blindness, 2301

I Am Living, 1023
I Belong to Me, 1164
I Can't . . . I Can't, 1106
I Don't Want to Talk About It, 34
I Have Found It, 1057
I Know Who You Are, 1614
I Like It like That, 2178
I Love to Work, 1208
I Love You All, 498
I Love You . . . Don't Touch Me!, 2246
I Love You Rosa, 1125
I Loved a Turk, 1710
I Never Promised You a Rose Garden, 1979
I Shot Andy Warhol, 2206
I Spit on Your Grave, 1980
I Thank a Fool, 1747
I, the Worst of All, 32
I Want a Solution, 382
I Want to Be a Woman, 1545
I Will Survive, 1605
Ibunda, 1068
Ich bin dir Verfallen, 843
Ichijo sayuri: nureta yokujo, 1240
If These Walls Could Talk, 2207
If These Walls Could Talk 2, 2260
Ijo yeoinjanhoksa, 1290
Ika-11 utos: Mahalin mo asawa mo, 1438
Iki kadýn, 1733

I.K.U., 1269
Îles flottantes, 1382
Illusive Girl, 297
Im Kreise der Lieben, 679
I'm Your Slave, 843
The Image of Dorian Gray in the Yellow Press, 807
Images, 1107
Imagined Autobiography, 1130
Immacolata e concetta, 1168
An Immoral Story, 1474
Immortal Love, 974, 1219
Impasse de la vignette, 104
Impromptu, 1807
Impulse, 2110
Imraa la ibni, 11
Imra'ah wahidah la takfi, 392
In den Tag hinein, 713
In Heaven as on Earth, 566
In My Skin, 653
In Nowhereland, 1740
In Praise of Mother Santoshi, 984
In Self Defense, 1465
In the Country of Juliets, 556
In the Cut, 2323
In the Gorge, 2412
In the Heart of the Country, 121
In the Spirit, 2111
In the Wings, 935
In Your Hands, 376
Ina, kapatid, anak, 1427
Inay, 1434
Inch'Allah dimanche, 637
Inch'Allah Sunday, 637
The Incredible Shrinking Woman, 2009
The Indecent Woman, 1371
India Song, 467
The Indians Are Still Far Away, 484
Les Indiens sont encore loin, 484
Indochine, 550
L'Infidele, 1659
The Inheritance, 939, 1163
Inn Trouble, 2208
Innocent, 1007
The Innocents, 1745
Insect Woman, 1225
Inseminacion artificial, 1559
Insiang, 1424
Inside Daisy Clover, 1898
Intentions of Murder, 1226
Interdevochka, 2391
Intergirl, 2391
Interno Berlinese, 1179
The Interrogation, 1464
Intimate Confessions of a Chinese Courtesan, 900
Invisible Adversaries, 87

Io sono mia, 1164
Ipaglaban mo, 1440
Iracema, 138
Iris, 1367, 1386, 1871
Iron Jawed Angels, 2340
Isabel, 173
Isabelle Eberhardt, 64
Isadora, 1761
Iskrenne vash . . ., 2384
Island Militia Women, 236
Island on the Continent, 929
Isn't She Great, 2261
Isolde, 365
Istakusa, 401
Istoriya Asi Klyachinoi kotoraya lyubila, da ni vyshla
    zamuzh, 2357
It Was Cold and Raining, 1732
Itan enas issihos thanatos, 881
It's in the Water, 2224
It's My Turn, 2002
It's Raining in My House, 105
It's Your Turn, Laura, 210
I've Heard the Mermaids Singing, 195

Jackie Brown, 2225
Jack's Wife, 1935
Jackson County Jail, 1970
Jade Women, 1673
Die Jager, 783
Jahizieh bara-ye Robab, 1075
Jai Santoshi maa, 984
Jak byæ kochana, 1454
Jambon d'Ardenne, 485
James Joyce's Nora, 1120
Janice Beard, 2302
Janmadinam, 1043
Japanese Story, 86
Jaque la dama, 1549
Al Jaraj, 399
Je demande la parole, 2371
Je demande une solution, 382
Je tu il elle, 112
Je vous aime, 498
A Jealous Man, 1175
Jeanne Dielman, 23 Quai du Commerce, 1080
    Bruxelles, 113
Jeanne la pucelle, 561
Jeanne's House, 532
Jenseits der Stille, 689
Jeongsa, 1303
Jeunesse dorée, 638
Jia zhuang mei gan jue, 268
Jin lu er, 243
Jin nian xia tian, 316
Jin se de zhi, 274

Jingzhe, 321
Joan of Arc of Mongolia, 839
Joan the Maid, 561
Johanna d'Arc de Mongolia, 839
Johanna d'Arc of Mongolia, 839
Jom, 1528
Le Jour des rois, 543
Journal d'un vieux fou, 1368
Le Journal d'une femme en blanc, 442
Le Journal de Lady M, 1667
Journey among Women, 48
Journey of Arian, 1618
The Journey to Kafiristan, 1668
The Journey to the Western Zia Empire, 310
Ju Dou, 280
Juana la loca, 1619
Juana the Mad, 1619
Judgment in Stone, 575
Judith Therpauve, 489
El Juego de Luna, 1620
Julia, 1981
Julie, 985
Julie's Geist, 1669
Julie's Ghost, 1669
Juliet of the Spirits, 1150
Jumalan morsian, 420
Jument vapeur, 507
The Junction, 1485
Die Jung Frauenmaschine, 840
Jupon rouge, 524
Just the Two of Us, 1953
Just You and Me, 1657
Jylama, 1282

Kadarwati, wanita dengan lima nama, 1063
Kaddu beykat, 1525
Kadosh, 1136
Kaere Irene, 355
El Kahira thalatin, 378
El Kalaa, 14
Kamla, 1014
Kamouraska, 179
Kan hai de rizi, 1672
Kandahar, 1097
Kandukondain, kandukondain, 1057
Al Kanour ayuha al-qanun, 385
Kao, 1272
Karamat zawgati, 379
Karla, 721
Karmen, 1533
Karmen Geï, 1533
Karnal, 1433
Die Karwoche, 1482
Kasba, 1027
Kasei-no kanon, 1273

Kasik Düsmani, 1722
Kaskade rückwärts, 734
Kataskopos Nelly, 873
Kato apo t'astra, 894
Kaze no katami, 1262
Kazetachi no gogo, 1251
Ke tu chiu hen, 1681
Keïd ensa, 1353
Keiko, 1243
Keiner liebt mich, 690
Khak-e mohr shode, 1073
Khamosh pani, 1416
Khandar, 1010
Khilona, 973
Khoon bhari maang, 1022
Khuin kholboo, 1348
Kiep phu du, 2405
Kilenc hónap, 936
Kill Bill Vols. 1 and 2, 2341
Killing Heat, 1651
Killing Mad Dogs, 1094
The Killing of Sister George, 1907
Killing Rabids, 1094
Kira's Reason: A Love Story, 373
Kissed, 206
Kisses and Scratches, 955
Kisses for My President, 1895
Kissing Jessica Stein, 2303
Kisvilma: az utolsó napló, 959
The Kite, 1315
Kizgin toprak, 1715
Klute, 1924
Knafayim shvurot, 1139
The Knife, 2407
Knife Horse Dawn, 905
Knocks at My Door, 2400
Kobieta i kobieta, 1460
Kobieta samotna, 1463
Kobieta w kapeluszu, 1470
Kobieta z prowincji, 1471
Kodou, 1522
Koge, 1227
Kôhî jikô, 1277
Ta Kokkina fanaria, 853
Koks i kulissen, 361
Koma, 2392
Komissar, 2358
Komplizinnen, 833
Konec srpna v Hotelu Ozon, 351
Konojo to kare, 1224
Konserto yia polivola, 862
Korotkie vstrechi, 2361
Kototsu no hito, 1241
Κραυγή yuvalkóv, 871
Kravyi yinekon, 871

Kristallines nichtes, 884
Kristin Lavransdatter, 1413
Kristina Talking Pictures, 1971
Krokodillen in Amsterdam, 1370
Krugovorot, 2386
Krylia, 2355
Krzyk, 1467
Kseniya, Beloved Wife of Feodor, 2368
Kseniya, lyubimaya zhene Fyordora, 2368
Ku qi de nü ren, 317
Kuei-hua hsiang, 1678
Kuei mei, 1673
Kulavadhu, 994
Die Kümmeltürkin geht, 821
Kung Fu Master, 525
Kunlun shan shang yike cao, 230
Kuroi ame, 1258
Kuyu, 1709

Labyrinth of Dreams, 1264
The Lacemaker, 481
Ladies on the Rocks, 361
Ladies Room, 213
Ladies' Threshold, 398
The Lady, 1086
The Lady and the Duke, 629
Lady Beware, 2074
Lady Dragon, 1071
Lady from Constantinople, 929
The Lady in Red, 1996
Lady L., 1755
The Lady of Hamre, 371
Lady Ogin, 1216
Lady Sings the Blues, 1932
Ladybird, Ladybird, 1822
Laham rakhis, 397
Laisse un peu d'amour, 602
Lajja, 1052
The Land of the Deaf, 1516
Land That Does Not Exist, 413
Landet som icke är, 413
Langouste, 401
Långt Borta och Nära, 1648
The Last Aristocrats, 277
The Last Days of Chez Nous, 65
The Last Five Days, 798
The Last Harem, 1737
The Last Kiss, 482
Last Resort, 1868
The Last Winter, 3
The Last Word, 157
Late Autumn, 1215
Laufen lernen, 784
Laura Adler's Last Love Affair, 1129
Laurel Canyon, 2324

Layar lara, 1317
Laylat el-kaped alla Fatma, 384
Leaden Times, 789
A League of Their Own, 2143
Leap Backward, 734
Leap into the Void, 1170
Lea's Story, 1446
Learning to Run, 784
Leaving in Order to Arrive, 803
Leaving Normal, 2128
La Lectrice, 531
Leela, 2304
Left Luggage, 1380
The Left-Handed Woman, 769
Legacy, 1963
Legally Blonde I, 2325
Legally Blonde II, 2325
The Legend of Paul and Paula, 724
The Legend of Rita, 704
Legend of Tianyun Mountain, 240
Die Legende von Paul und Paula, 724
Leila, 1084
Leila and Others, 9
Leila and the Wolves, 1312
Leila est les autres, 9
Leila wa alchwatouha, 9
Leila wal ziab, 1312
Lejania, 338
Lejos de África, 1592
Lemon Sisters, 2112
Lena's Dreams, 2209
Let's Get Lost, 369
Let's Go Barbara, 1548
Let's Hope It's a Girl, 1180
Let's Love Hong Kong, 319
The Letter, 1500
Letter from the Wife, 982
Lettre Paysanne, 1525
Les Lèvres rouges, 108
Li Shuang-shuang, 231
Une Liaison pornographique, 609
Lian ai li jie, 252
Lian zhi feng jing, 926
Liang jia fu nü, 247
Liang Shan-bo yu Zhu Ying-tai, 232
Lianna, 2017
Liberation, 1024
Libertarias, 1593
Licht, 1378
Lie t Me, 1580
Eine Liebe in Deutschland, 810
Le Lien maternel, 1348
Life Is a Woman, 1279
Life Is the Main Thing, 1379
Life . . . My Passion, 400

Lift, 2279
Light of Day, 2075
A Light on the 10th Floor, 1506
A Light Sensitive Story, 953
Like a Bride, 1337
Lili Marleen, 785
Lillian, 2153
Lily Festival, 1274
Lilya 4-Ever, 1662
Limbo, 2247
Die linkshändige Frau, 769
Lions Love, 452
Lipstick, 1972
A Lira do delirio, 135
Lisístrata, 1624
Le Lit, 117
Liten Ida, 1406
Little Angel, 688
A Little Color, 1670
The Little Drummer Girl, 2035
Little Ida, 1406
Little Man Tate, 2129
Little Raoul, 25
The Little Republic, 1056
Little Vera, 2389
Little Vilma: The Last Diary, 959
Little Voice, 1853
Little Women, 2179
På Liv och död, 1655
Live-In Maid, 44
Lives of Performers, 1933
Living Together, 462
Living with Uwe, 725
Lobster, 401
Locust Tree Village, 229
Loin des barbares, 562
Lokuduwa, 1636
Lola, 422, 1334, 1566
Lola rennt, 698
Lonely Lane, 1223
The Lonely Passion of Judith Hearne, 1802
The Lonely Wife, 969
The Lonely Woman, 1463
A Lonely Woman Seeks a Lifetime Companion, 2387
The Long Farewell, 2365
The Long Kiss Goodnight, 2210
The Long Silence, 685
Long Walk Home, 2101
Longing for Chalila, 313
Longue vie, 1515
Look at Me, 671
Look Back, 2383
Looking for Mr. Goodbar, 1982
Loose Connections, 1786
The Lord, His Wife and Slave, 965

Lorenzo's Oil, 2144
Los Días del agua, 330
Los Nombres de Alicia, 1631
Los Rubios, 46
Losing Isaiah, 2180
The Lost Dream, 282
Lost Honor of Katharina Blum, 761
Lou Didn't Say No, 563
Lou n'a pas dit non, 563
Loulou, 499
Love, 187
Love Affairs Usually End Badly, 558
Love among the Ruins, 1964
Love and Basketball, 2262
Love and Faith, 1249
Love and Fear, 1187
Love around the Corner, 1331
Love at Second Sight, 1132
Love Brewed in the African Pot, 846
Love Colder Than Death, 1736
Love Crimes, 2130
The Love Eterne, 232
Love Field, 2145
Love in a Fallen City, 902
A Love in Germany, 810
Love Is Not a Sin, 1325
Love Is the Beginning of All Terror, 812
Love Juice, 1270
Love Letters, 2025
Love Me, 610
The Love of Three Oranges, 1687
Love under the Crucifix, 1216
Love Wanders in the Night, 872
Love with the Proper Stranger, 1894
Loved, 2226
Lovely and Amazing, 2305
Loves of Isadora, 1761
Loving Couples, 1639
Loyalties, 192
The L-Shaped Room, 1748
Lucía, 329
Lucia, 1435
Lucía, Lucía, 1627
Lucie Aubrac, 593
A Lucky Day, 42
Lullaby of the Earth, 1246
Lumière, 474
O Lumina la etajul 10, 1506
Luminarias, 2263
La Luna, 1169
Luna de Agosto, 1567
Luna's Game, 1620
Il Lungo silenzio, 685
Luoi dao, 2407
The Lyre of Delight, 135

Lysistrata, 867, 1624, 1643
Lyssistrati, 867

Ma femme est PDG, 379
Ma nim, 1294
Ma saison preferée, 564
Maa jota ei ole, 413
Maa on syntinen laulu, 411
Maachis, 1038
Ma'agalim shel shishabat, 1127
Een Maand later, 1369
Maangamizi: The Ancient One, 1692
Maborosi, 1263
Die Macht der Männer ist die Geduld der Frauen, 777
Macu, la mujer del policia, 2397
Macu, the Policeman's Wife, 2397
Mad Enough to Kill, 470
Mad Love, 1619
Madam, 1730
Madame Bovary, 551
Madame Bovary, It's Me, 1458
Madame de Charriere, 1373
Madame Dery, 935
Madame P, 122
Madame Rosa, 486
Madame X: An Absolute Ruler, 770
Madame X—Eine absolute Herrscherin, 770
Madamigella di Maupin, 1151
Madeleine Is . . ., 174
Mademoiselle, 1757
Mademoiselle de Maupin, 1151
Mademoiselle Ogin, 1249
Madwoman of Chaillot, 1763
Maelström, 215
Maeve, 1108
The Mafu Cage, 1983
Magdalena, the Unholy Spirit, 1452
Magdalena Viraga, 2057
Magdalene Sisters, 1123
A Magzat, 954
Mahajan, K. K., 1027
Mahanagar, 968
Mahaprithivi, 1028
Mahogany, 1965
Maiden Rose, 307
Main azaad hoon, 1025
Main zinda noon, 1023
Main-ma le thein kywe, 169
Maisat sam lam, 924
La Maison de Jeanne, 532
Maitresse, 475
Måker, 1411
Making Mr. Right, 2076
The Makioka Sisters, 1254

Malabrigo, 1420
Male Director in the Women's Department, 312
Malenkaya Vera, 2389
Malou, 786
Mama, 281
Mama Got Married, 2363
Mama, There's a Man in Your Bed, 540
Mama vyshla zamuzh, 2363
Mamma, 1652
Mamma Roma, 1146
Mammo, 1032
Mamta, 971
Mamza, 1537
A Man and Two Women, 549
Man of Iron, 1457
Man of Marble, 1457
Manda meyer upakhyan, 1054
Mandi, 1006
Mando mavroyenous, 864
Mango Kiss, 2326
Manía, 878
Manji, 1228
Männer, 822
Manny and Lo, 2181
Manuela, 328
Manuela Sáenz, 2401
Manuela's Loves, 524
A Map of the Heart, 711
Map of the World, 2248
Mar de rosas, 136
Marathon, 2327
Marcides, 396
Margarita Happy Hour, 2306
María Cano, 323
Maria Chapdelaine, 188
Maria Electra, 890
Maria Full of Grace, 2342
Maria nap, 946
Mariages, 216
Marianne and Juliane, 789
Marianne eidn Recht für alle, 89
Marianne One Law for All, 89
Marianne un droit pour tous, 89
Maria's Day, 946
Marie, 2046
Marie Antoinette Is Not Dead, 1375
Marie-Antoinette is niet dood, 1375
Marie's Sons, 194
Marion Bridge, 219
Marius and Jeanette, 584
Marius et Jeanette, 584
Marja Pieni, 410
A Market Woman and a Poet, 2374
Marketplace, 1006
Marlene, 702

Marlene: der Amerikanishe Traum, 90
Marlene, the American Dream, 90
La Marque du démon, 2406
Marquise, 594
The Marquise of O, 765
Die Marquise von O, 765
The Marriage of Maria Braun, 772
Marriages, 216
Married to a Child, 265
Married to the Mob, 2093
A Married Woman, 439
The Mars Canon, 1273
Mars Turkey, 1137
Martha, 755
Martha and Me, 844
Martha Jellneck, 841
Martha . . . Martha, 639
Martha und ich, 844
Maruhi: shikijo mesu ichiba, 1244
Marusa no onna, 1257
Mary from Beijing, 298
Mary, Queen of Scots, 1768
La Maschera, 1184
La Maschera di scimmia, 84
The Mask, 1184, 2047
Masoom, 1007
The Match Factory Girl, 417
The Matchmaker, 311
The Maternal Link, 1348
Matka Joanna od aniolóu, 1453
Matriarchy, 159
Matriarhat, 159
A Matter of Life and Death, 1655
Matzor, 1124
Mauri, 1391
Mausam, 986
Mávahlátur, 962
May I Have the Floor, 2371
The May Lady, 1085
May Motherhood Be Yours, 1441
May nag mamahal sa iyo, 1441
Maya darpan, 978
McCabe and Mrs. Miller, 1925
Me and Veronica, 2146
Me llamo Sara, 1601
Me Myself I, 83
Me without You, 1877
Me You Them, 153
The Meaning, 1005
Mécaniques célestes, 585
Medea, 364, 871, 1156, 1342
Meera, 996
Meghe dhaka tara, 964
Mei-li zai chang ge, 1685
Mein Herz—Niemandem!, 695

Mein letzter, 714
Meisje, 131
Het meisje met het rode haar, 1359
Melek leaves, 821
Mementos, 1066
Memory Episodes, 1009
Men, 822
Men Don't Leave, 2113
Menschen Frauen, 88
Menuet, 124
Le Mépris, 437
Merci pour le chocolat, 623
La Mère porteuse, 1298
Mesdames et mesdemoiselles, 393
The Message from the Islands, 23
The Messenger: The Story of Joan of Arc, 611
Messidor, 1665
Metamo, 1285
Metropolitan Saxophone, 300
Mi boda contigo, 224
A mi madre le gustan las mujeres, 1632
Mi piace lavorare (mobbing), 1208
Mi Vida Loca, 2164
Mia gynaika stin antistassi, 863
Mia tosso makrini apoussia, 879
Miao jie huang hou, 909
Michael sheli, 1126
Midori, 1267
The Midwife's Tale, 2182
Miel et cendres, 1699
Mila from Mars, 164
Mila ot Mars, 164
Milae, 1309
Milagros, 1443
Milena, 552
Millennium Mambo, 1690
Million Dollar Baby, 2343
Milyi, dorogoi, lyubimyi, yedinstvennyi . . ., 2382
Mina Tannenbaum, 580
Minna von Barnhelm, 719
Minna von Barnhelm oder das Soldatenglück, 719
Mins'y isang gamu-gamo, 1425
Minuet, 124
Mira, 109
Mira de Teleurgang van de waterhoek, 109
The Miracle Worker, 1893
The Miraculous Policemen and the Magical Thief, 292
Mirch marsala, 1017
Le Miroir, 1720
The Mirror, 1720
The Mirror Has Two Faces, 2211
The Mirror Image of Dorian Gray, 807
Mirror of Illusion, 978
Miso, 1311
Miss An Li, 272

Miss Beatty's Children, 1029
Miss Director, 855
Miss Mary, 30
Miss O'Gynie and the Flower Men, 111
Miss O'Gynie et les hommes fleurs, 111
Missing, 2010
Mississippi Masala, 2131
The Mistress, 924
The Misty Village, 1292
La Mitad del cielo, 1568
Mitten ins Herz, 811
Mix Me a Person, 1749
Modern Cinderella, 857
Moderna stahtopouta, 857
Modesty Blaise, 1758
Modré z neba, 346
Mogliamante, 1165
Mogzitwa, 407
Mohra, 1033
Le Moine et la sorcière, 538
Moko-dakhan, 1319
Moll Flanders, 1835
Le Môme Singe, 305
A Moment, 358, 1021
Momentos, 26
Moments, 492
Mon cher sujet, 533
Mon coeur est rouge, 476
Mon nuit chez Maud, 453
Mona Lisa Smile, 2328
Monkey Kid, 305
The Monkey's Mask, 84
Monsieur Hawarden, 103
Monsoon Wedding, 2307
Monster, 2329
La Montagne de Baya, 17
Montenegro, 2414
A Month Later, 1369
Moolaadé, 1534
Moral, 1431
The Morning After, 2058
Mortal Thoughts, 2132
Mortu Nega, 896
Morvern Callar, 1878
Mosaferan, 1077
Moscow Does Not Believe in Tears, 2375
Moskva slezam ne verit, 2375
Mossane, 1531
Mostly Martha, 707
Mothballs, 1554
Mother, 1068, 1884
A Mother Alone, 1637
Mother and Daughter, 940
Mother Joan of the Angels, 1453
Mother Kuster Goes to Heaven, 756

Mother of 1084, 1041
Mother, Sister, Daughter, 1427
Mother Viper, 1200
A Mother's Epic, 2352
The Mother's Field, 2362
Les Mots pour le dire, 511
Moul le ya, moul le ya, 1293
Le moulin, 1727
Mount Venus, 741
Mourir à tue-tête, 183
Mourir d'aimer, 456
Mouvements du desír, 203
Mr. and Mrs. Iyer, 1055
Mr. Wrong, 1387
Mrityudand, 1042
Mrs. Brown, 1842
Mrs. Dalloway, 1843
Mrs. Parker and the Vicious Circle, 2165
Mrs. Soffel, 2036
Mua he chieu thang dung, 2408
Muen and Rid, 1694
Mujer transparente, 344
Mujeres al bordo de un ataque de nervios, 1573
Mujeres de la frontera, 1401
The Mulberry Tree, 1295
A Mulher que acreditava ser presidente dos EUA, 1503
Mung sing si fan, 298
MURDER and murder, 2212
The Murderess, 395, 869
Murderous Maids, 619
Muriel, 438
Muriel, ou le temps d'un retour, 438
Muriel's Wedding, 74
Murmur of Youth, 1685
Un Muro de silencio, 33
Music Box, 2102
Music of the Heart, 2249
The Mutants, 1499
Mutter Küsters Fahrt zum Himmel, 756
Mutters Courage, 686
My 20th Century, 949
My Big Fat Greek Wedding, 2308
My Brilliant Career, 49
My Crazy Life, 2164
My Father Is Coming, 680
My Favorite Season, 564
My Favorite Story, 533
My First Wife, 54
My Happiness, 1288
My Heart Is Mine Alone, 695
My Last Film, 714
My Life, My Passion, 400
My Life to Live, 434
My Life without Me, 220

My Lover, My Son, 1766
My Michael, 1126
My Mother, 1739
My Mother and Her guest, 1289
My Mother Likes Women, 1632
My Mother's Courage, 686
My Name Is Sara, 1601
My Night with Maud, 453
My Secret Garden, 1265
My Sister Lucy, 2385
My Teacher Is Very Pretty, 1060
My Voice, 1502
My Wife Is Director-General, 379
My Young Aunt, 901
Mystic Pizza, 2094

Na Klancu, 2412
Na koniec swiata, 1484
Nabantwa bam, 1544
Nachalo, 2364
Nada mas, 345
Nadia and the Hippos, 612
Nadia et les hippopotames, 612
Nadie hablara de nosotras cuando hayamos muerto, 1589
Nadzór, 1472
Naeui haengbok, 1288
Naftalina, 1554
Nahla, 10
Naitou, 895
Naked Acts, 2213
The Naked Kiss, 1896
Naked Vengeance, 2048
The Nameless Castle, 945
Namis, 1281
Namkeen, 1001
Nan fu nü zhu ren, 312
The Nanny, 407
Nanny Dear, 1569
Nanou, 1798
The Naples Connection, 1176
Napló apámnak anyámnak, 950
Napló gyermekeimnek, 944
Napló szerelmeinmnek, 948
Narayama bushiko, 1253
Nargess, 1076
Narrow Bridge, 1065
Nathalie, 658
Nathalie Granger, 461
Nattlek, 1640
Néa, 477
Near and Far Away, 1648
O něčem jiném, 349
Nelly, the Spy, 873
Nénette and Boni, 586

Neria, 2416
Neskolko interviu palichnim voprosam, 2376
Neun Leben hat die Katze, 747
Never Again, 120
Never Again Alone, 106
Nevestka, 2367
Névtelen vär, 945
The New Eve, 613
A New Life, 565
The New Women, 2280
Nga ba Dong Loc, 2409
Nha fala, 1502
Nic, 1483
Nicht nichts ohne Dich, 699
Night and Day, 553
Night Full of Rain, 1167
Night Games, 1640
'Night, Mother, 2059
Night Porter, 1161
The Night They Arrested Fatma, 384
Nightcap, 623
Nikita, 544
O Nikitis, 858
Nil by Mouth, 1844
Nimeh-ye penhan, 1096
Nine Months, 936
Nine to Five, 1999
The Ninth Circle, 2411
Nippon konchuki, 1225
Nippon sengoshi, 1239
Nirgendwo in Afrika, 709
Al Nissa, 386
No Cordiality for the Woman, 383
No Ford in the Fire, 2359
No Mercy, No Future, 788
No Place to Go, 705
Nobody Lives Here, 1510
Nobody Loves Me, 570, 690
Nobody Will Speak of Us When We're Dead, 1589
Nobody's Fool, 2060
Nobody's Wife, 27
Les Noces barbares, 125
Nocturnal Uproar, 494
Nocturno amor que te vas, 1332
La Noire de . . ., 1521
Nomugi Pass, 1250
Nora, 1120
Nora Helmer, 757
Nordrand, 94
Norma Rae, 1997
El Norte, 2026
North China Red Beans, 246
Northern Skirts, 94
Nosotras, 1612
Not a Pretty Picture, 1966

Not for Publication, 2037
Not of This World, 1177
Not the Wife of His Choice, 1062
Not without My Daughter, 2133
Nothing, 345, 1483
Notre fille, 171
Notre mariage, 224
La Nouba des femmes du Mont Chenoua, 5
The Nouba Women of Mount Chenou, 5
Noubat al Nissa Djebel Chenoua, 5
Nous sommes tous encore ici, 595
Nouveau départ, 803
Le Nouveau journal d'une femme en blanc, 442
La Nouvelle Eve, 613
Une Nouvelle vie, 565
A Nova Eva, 613
November Moon, 817
Novembermond, 817
Novia que te vea, 1337
Now and Then, 2183
Now or Never, 826
Nowhere in Africa, 709
Nü bing yuan wu qu, 253
Nü da xue shena su she, 269
Nü er gu, 306
Nü er hong, 307
Nü er jing, 254
Nü er lou, 255
Nü feisingyuan, 234
Nü huang ling xia de feng liu niang men, 290
Nü huo fuo, 256
Nü qiu da dui, 257
Nü ren de gushi, 258
Nü ren de li liang, 248
Nü ren hua, 303
Nü ren taxi, nü ren, 286
Nü ren si shi, 916
Nü shen tan bao gaiding, 275
Nü xing shi jie, 287
Nü zi bie dong dui, 276
Nuages, 1492
Nuages, lettres à mon fils, 130
Nuit et jour, 553
Les Nuits de la pleine lune, 514
Numéro deux, 472
The Nun, 445
Nunta de piatra, 1504
Nurse Betty, 2264
Nuvem, 1492
Nynke, 1383

The Oak, 1508
Øbjeblikket, 358
Obsession, 273
Occasional Work of a Female Slave, 754

October Won't Return, 2403
Odin den i vsya zhian, 2379
Odinokaya zhenshchina zhelayet poznakomitsya, 2387
L'Odyssée d'Alice Tremblay, 218
Of the Flesh, 1433
Office Girls, 299
The Official Story, 29
Oginsama, 1216, 1249
Oglianis, 2383
Ök Ketten, 937
Old Boyfriends, 1991
Old Havana Waltz, 342
Old Women, 1205
Olivier, Olivier, 554
Oltre la porta, 1171
L'Ombre, 1347
On a Clear Day You Can See Forever, 1919
On connait la chanson, 596
On Guard, 52
On kadin, 1728
On Probation, 731
On the Hill of Desire, 2412
On the Left Bank of the Blue Danube, 1505
On the Move, 1462
On the Way, 1462
On the Wire, 1540
Once Were Warriors, 1397
One Day and a Whole Life, 2379
One Deadly Summer, 510
One Life Stand, 1872
One Look and Love Breaks Out, 831
One Potato, Two Potato, 1899
One Sings, the Other Doesn't, 478
One Summer after Another, 104
One True Thing, 2233
One Way or Another, 331
One Woman Is Not Enough, 392
One's Own Shadow, 1517
De onfatsoenlijke vrouw, 1371
Only Fear, 1479
Only When I Laugh, 2011
Onna ga kaidan o agaru toki, 1217
Onna keiji riko: seibo no fukako fuchi, 1268
Onna no rekishi, 1229
Onna zakari, 1261
Open Hearts, 374
Opening Night, 1984
The Opposite of Homesick, 701
Or (mon trésor), 1140
Or (My Treasure), 1140
Oranges Are Not the Only Fruit, 1808
Oriana, 2396
Orlando, 1817
Örökbefogadás, 934

Örökség, 939
Oromtriali, 2386
Oru penninte katha, 975
Os Cafajestes, 1324
Os Mutantes, 1499
Osama, 2
Osmanthus Alley, 1678
L'Ospite, 1157
Ossos, 1497
Öszi almanach, 947
The Other, 402
Other Halves, 1388
The Other Side of the Street, 155
The Other Woman, 435, 718
The Other World, 20
The Others, 2281
Oultougan, 2394
Our Daughter, 171
Our Marriage, 224
Our Rail Ticket Clerk, 1287
Our Short Life, 732
Ouridou hallan, 382
Out of Africa, 2049
Out of Rosenheim, 830
Out of Time, 1386
The Outcome, 1598
An Outgoing Woman, 622
Outrageous Fortune, 2077
Outremer, 555
O Outro lado da rua, 155
Al Ouyoune al jaffa, 1354
Overboard, 2078
Overseas, 555

Paint My Heart Red, 476
The Painter, 289
El Pájaro de la felicidad, 1583
Pakeezah, 976
Ek Pal, 1021
Palava enkeli, 416
Les Palmes de M. Shutz, 597
El Palo, 1621
Pane e tulipani, 1196
Panj é asr, 1101
Papa, les petits bateaux, 457
Papa, the Little Boats, 457
Papeles secundarios, 340
Paper Bird, 1407
Papirfügien, 1407
Para perintis kemerdekaan, 1061
Paradistorg, 1649
Parahyba, a Macho Woman, 140
Parahyba, mulher macho, 140
Paran daemun, 1304
Les Parapluies de Cherbourg, 440

Le Parfum de l'encens, 1227
Pari, 1081
Paroma, 1018
Paromitar ek din, 1046
Une Part du ciel, 659
Part Time Work of a Domestic Slave, 754
Parting of the Ways, 338
Party Girl, 2214
Pasázerka, 1459
Pasir berbisik, 1072
A Passage to India, 1789
The Passenger, 1459
Passion, 906
La Passion Béatrice, 534
Passion Fish, 2147
Passion of Beatrice, 534
Passion of Mind, 2250
The Passion of Remembrance, 1799
Pasti, pasti, pastiky, 347
Patriamada, 142
Paulina 1880, 458
Pauline and Paulette, 129
Pauline en Paulette, 129
Paura e amore, 1187
Pe malul stîng al Dunarii albastre, 1505
Pean d'ane, 454
Peasant Letter, 1525
Le Péché, 377
Peggy Sue Got Married, 2061
La peintre, 289
Peking Opera Blues, 905
Pelon maantiede, 418
The Penal Colony, 222
Pentimento, 539
Peony Pavilion, 925
La Perdición de los Hombres, 1343
Peremena uchasti, 2388
Perempuan, isteri dan . . .?, 1316
Perepolokh, 2370
Perfect Strangers, 1400
Peros de la noche, 31
Perras callejeras, 1564
El Perro del hortelano, 1594
Persecution, 856
Persona, 1641
Personal Best, 2018
Personal Velocity, 2309
The Personals, 1689
Personne ne m'aime, 570
Pestka, 1480
La Peticion, 1546
Le Petit amour, 525
La Petite Lola, 587
La Petite prairie aux bouleaux, 660
Les Petites couleurs, 1670

Petrina chronia, 880
Petulia, 1762
Phaedra, 851
Phaniyamma, 1002
Pianeta Venere, 1158
La Pianiste, 95
The Piano, 71
The Piano Teacher, 95
Pianoforte, 1174
Picture Bride, 2184
A Piece of the Sky, 659
Pieces of April, 2330
Piedras, 1625
De piel de víbora, 1344
Piera's Story, 1173
Pila balde, 1448
Pioneers of Freedom, 1061
Pip, 1480
La Pirate, 515
La Piste du télégraphe, 571
Il più bel giorno della mia vita, 1203
La Pivoine rouge, 1237
Place Vendôme, 624
Places in the City, 696
Places in the Heart, 2038
Plaff! Or Too Afraid of Life, 339
Le Plaisir de tromper, 952
Planet Venus, 1158
The Plastic Dome of Norma Jean, 1903
Plätze in Städten, 696
Play It as It Lays, 1934
The Players Club, 2234
Plenty, 2050
Il pleut dans ma maison, 105
Plus jamais seul, 106
Po Drodze, 1462
Point of No Return, 544
Pokuszenie, 1481
The Policewoman, 703
Die Polizisten, 703
Pomegranate Siestas, 1701
Pong, 1295
Ponirah, 1008
Le Pont du Nord, 503
Un Pont entre deux rives, 603
Poor Cow, 1760
Pope Joan, 1769
Por un hombre en tu vida, 1595
Il Portiere di notte, 1161
Portland Street Blues, 923
Portrait of a Female Alcoholic, 778
Portrait of a Lady, 1836
Portrait of Teresa, 333
Portraits chinois, 614
Poslednata Duma, 157

Possessed Woman, 870
Possession, 504
Postcards from the Edge, 2114
Post-coitum, animal triste, 588
Poupeés d'argile, 1703
Poupées de roseaux, 1350
Pourquoi (pas) le Brésil, 672
The Power of Men Is the Patience of Women, 777
Pozegnanie z Maria, 1478
Poznavaia bely svet, 2377
Practice of Love, 759
Die Praxis der Liebe, 759
Una Preciosa puesta de sol, 1628
La Premiere femme de la foret, 262
Prénom Vasfiyé, 1723
Prepoznavanje, 325
Pretty Good for a Human Being, 412
A Price Above Rubies, 2235
The Price of Freedom, 170
The Price of Love, 876
Primal Fear, 183
O Primavara de neuitat, 1509
The Prime of Miss Jean Brodie, 1764
The Princess, 941
Prisonnières, 535
Private Benjamin, 2003
Private Class, 520
Private Confessions, 1658
Privilege, 2115
Le Prix de la folie, 273
Le Prix de la liberté, 170
Procès de Jeanne d'Arc, 431
Il Processo di Caterina Ross, 1172
Profundo carmesi, 1340
La Proie pour l'ombre, 423
The Promise, 687
The Promised Life, 666
The Proposition, 1839
The Proprietor, 1837
Proshchanie, 2378
Proshu slova, 2371
La Prostitution, 432
A Provincial Woman, 1471
To Proxenio tis Annas, 868
Przesluchanie, 1464
Przez dotyk, 1473
Puen and Paeng, 1693
Puen-Paeng, 1693
Le Puits, 1709
The Pumpkin Eater, 1752
Punchline, 2095
Pure Heart, 976
Push! Push!, 1301
Put a Man In Your Life, 1595
Yo Puta, 1633

Puzzle of a Downfall Child, 1920

Al Qatilla, 395
Qian xi man bo, 1690
Qing cheng zhi lian, 902
Qing she, 915
Qing shun ji, 249
Qinq guo qing cheng, 237
Qiu Jin, 245
Qiu Jin: A Revolutionary China, 245
Qiu Ju da guansi, 291
Quarterly Balance-Taking, 1456
Quartier Mozart, 1530
Les Quatres soeurs, 1254
Le Quatrième sexe, 428
Que hacer?, 223
Queen Isabella in Person, 1613
Queen Margot, 572
Queen of Diamonds, 2134
Queen of Temple Street, 909
Queen of the Night, 1339
Quest for Truth, Quest for Love, 1539
A Question of Silence, 1361
Qui a tué Bambi?, 661
The Quick and the Dead, 2185
A Quiet Death, 881
Quiet Joy, 353
Qunian dong tian, 1683

Rabeia e Balkhi, 1
Rabia of Balkh, 1
Rachel, Rachel, 1908
Rachida, 21
Radiance, 80
The Rag Doll, 1729
La Ragazza con la valiglia, 1145
Rage to Kill, 834
Raggedy Man, 1780
Rain, 1090
The Rain People, 1913
Rainbow's End, 960
Raise the Red Lantern, 284
Raisin in the Sun, 1890
Raja, 662
Rajanigandha, 981
Rajska Jablòn, 1469
Rambling Rose, 2135
Ramparts of Clay, 6
Rana's Wedding, 1418
Rao Saheb, 1019
The Rape, 1252
Rape Me, 618
Rape of Love, 479
Rape Squad, 1954
Rapeseed Girl, 1674

Rapture of Deceit, 952
Rapunzel Let Down Your Hair, 1774
La Raulito, 25
Le Rayon vert, 521
The Reader, 531
Real Women Have Curves, 2310
Reason Asleep, 818
Rebro Adama, 2395
O Recado das ilhas, 23
Recognition, 325
Une Recontre volée, 406
Red, 574, 1088
The Red Angel, 1232
The Red Desert, 1147
Red Detachment of Women, 228, 235
The Red Lanterns, 853
Red Lips, 108
Red Love, 801
Red Peony Gambler, 1237
Red Satin, 1705
Red Seedling, 989
The Red Skirt, 524
Red Sorghum, 259
Redeem Her Honor, 1440
The Redhead, 739
Redupers—Die Allseitig reduzierte Persönlichkeit, 767
The Reed Dolls, 1350
Regaeim, 492
Regrouping, 1973
La Reina de la noche, 1339
La Reina Isabel en persona, 1613
La Reine Margot, 572
La Reipu, 1252
Die Reise nach Kafiristan, 1668
Die Reise nach Lyon, 787
Relacão fiel e verdadeira, 1489
La Religieuse, 445
Rembetiko, 874
Remember My Name, 1992
Remparts d'Argile, 6
Ren, gui, qing, 261
Ren zai niu yue, 910
Rendez-vous d'Anna, 115
La Répétition, 640
Repulsion, 1756
The Request, 1546
Resistance, 68
Respiro, 1207
Resultado final, 1598
Resurrection, 2004
Retrato de Teresa, 333
Revelation, 1404
Revenge of the Serpents, 1707
Rich and Famous, 2012

Rich Man's Wife, 2215
Richard's Things, 1778
Riddance, 931
Riddles of the Sphinx, 1773
Right in the Heart, 811
Right Now, 667
Rihaee, 1024
Rihatee, 1024
Riko, 1268
The Ring of Mist, 1562
Río Escondido, 37
The Rising Place, 2311
Risk, 2166
The Ritual, 993
Roads and Oranges, 887
Robin's Hood, 2331
Rok spokojnego słońca, 1468
The Role, 991
Rolling Family, 45
Romaine, 598
Romance, 615
Romance da Empregada, 146
Romelia's Secret, 1333
Romuald & Juliette, 540
A Room with a View, 1795
Roozi khe zan shodam, 1093
Roro Mendut, 1064
Rosa Luxemburg, 828
Rosa negra, 1493
The Rose, 1998
Rosemary's Baby, 1909
Rosenstrasse, 717
Rosetta, 127
Rosie, 128
Rosine, 573
Die Rote, 739
Rote Liebe, 801
Rote Ohren fetzen durch Asche, 93
Rouge, 907
Rouge of the North, 1679
Rousari-abi, 1082
Ruan Ling Yu, 913
Ruby and Rata, 1394
Ruby in Paradise, 2154
Die Rückkehr, 677
Rue Cases Nègres, 512
Rue Haute, 114
Rue Princesse, 1214
Der Ruf der blonden Göttin, 1664
The Ruination of Men, 1343
The Ruins, 1010
Run Lola Run, 698
The Running Target, 1278
La Rupture, 455
Ryah El Janoub, 8

S dnjom rozhdenya, 1515
S ljubov'ju, Lilya, 1519
Sa mère, la pute, 641
Sa propre ombre, 1517
Sabato, Domenica, Lunedi, 1188
Sacrificed Youth, 249
Safar e ghandehar, 1097
Safe, 2186
Safety of Objects, 2332
Sagkoshi, 1094
Sahib bibi aur ghulam, 965
Saikati, 1283
Saint-Cyr, 625
La Saison des amours, 252
La Saison des hommes, 1702
The Salamander, 1663
La Salamandre, 1663
Salige er de som törster, 1414
Salmonberries, 681
Salome, 1430
Salto nel vuoto, 1170
Sama, 1696
Samancynyn zolu, 2362
Sambizanga, 22
Same Old Song, 596
Samia, 626
San bu in koa, 1301
San ge nü: ren, 258
San ju chi lian, 1687
San toit ni loi, 516
Sand Screens, 1313
Sand Storm, 12
Sanda, 1507
Sandakan 8, 1245
Sandakan hachiban shokan: bokyo, 1245
Sandra, 1153
The Sandstorm, 1048
Sankofa, 847
Santa Santita, 1452
Santera, 2399
Santeria, 2399
Sappho, Darling, 1889
Sara, 1078
Sarah dit . . . Leila dit, 120
Sarang bang sonnim omoni, 1289
Sardari Begum, 1039
Sarraounia, 165
Sasame yuki, 1254
Sati, 1026
Satin Rouge, 1705
Saturday, Sunday, Monday, 1188
Le Saut dans le vide, 1170
Sauvage, sauvage est la rose, 227
Savage Sisters, 1955

Savage Woman, 200
Save and Protect, 2393
Sayyidati anisati, 393
Scandal, 1805
Scandalo Segreto, 1189
The Scar, 1829
Scarlet Diva, 1204
The Scarlet Letter, 752
Scarred, 2027
The Scent of Incense, 1227
The Scent of Violets, 877
Der scharlachrote Buchstabe, 752
Die Schauspielerin, 737
Der Schlaf der Vernunft, 818
The School of Flesh, 582
Schwestern oder die Balance des Glücks, 782
Scorpian Woman, 92
Scrap Metal, 1577
The Scream, 1467
A Scream from Silence, 183
Scrubbers, 1784
Se permuta, 337
Sé quién eres, 1614
The Sea Is Watching, 1276
Sea of Roses, 136
Seagulls, 1411
Seagull's Laughter, 962
The Sealed Soil, 1073
Seance on a Wet Afternoon, 1753
Seaside, 651
Season of Love, 252
Season of Men, 1702
Season of the Witch, 1935
The Second Awakening of Christa Klages, 771
Second Class Citizens, 1743
Second Love, 1255
The Second Wife, 380
La Seconde épouse, 380
Le Secret, 642
Secret Chronicle: Shebeast Market, 1244
Secret Scandal, 1189
Secret Society, 1879
Secret Things, 648
Secretary, 2312
El Secreto de Romelia, 1333
Secrets & Lies, 1838
Secrets of Women, 527
Sedmikrásky, 350
Seduction: The Cruel Woman, 742
The Seedling, 979
Die Sehnsucht der Veronika Voss, 802
Seisaku no tsuma, 1230
Seisaku's Wife, 1230
Sekando rabu, 1255
Sekten, 370

Selena, 2227
Selvi boylum al yazmalim, 1717
Señora de nadie, 27
Sense and Sensibility, 1830
Sequins, 670
The Serbian Girl, 678
Das serbische Mädchen, 678
Serial Lover, 604
Series 7, 2282
Serpientes y escaleras, 1338
Serving Time, 833
Sestra moja Ljusia, 2385
Set It Off, 2216
La Settima stanza, 956
Une Seule femme ne suffit pas, 392
Seven Women, 1900
Seven Women on a Secret Mission, 1067
Seven Women Seven Sins, 91
Seventeen Years, 314
The Seventh Chamber, 956
The Seventh Year, 722
Sex Change, 1545
The Sex of the Stars, 184
Le Sexe des étoiles, 184
Sexo por compasión, 1615
Sezonat na kanarchetat, 163
Sha fu, 1675
Sha Ou, 242
Sha sha jia jia zhan qi lai, 912
Shadow of Adultery, 423
Shadows in a Conflict, 1584
Shag, 1803
Shame, 58
Shamt al kushur, 1698
Shan lin zhong tou yi ge nü ren, 262
Shanghai Women, 268
Shao nü Siao Yu, 1684
She and He, 1224
She Must Be Seeing Things, 2079
She Too Is a Woman, 980
She Was Wronged, 854
She-Devil, 2116
Sheer Madness, 800
Shei shi di san zhe, 263
Sheila Levine Is Dead and Living in New York, 1967
Shen jing qi tou, 292
She-pen, 1291
She's Been Away, 1809
She's Gotta Have It, 2062
She's One Of Us, 657
Sh'hur, 1131
Shi qu de meng, 282
Shinjû ten no amijima, 1238
Shirin's Wedding, 766
Shirins Hochzeit, 766

Shirley Valentine, 1810
Shoot to Kill, 2398
Short Encounters, 2361
Shui shi disanzhe, 270
Shwet paatharer thaalaa, 1030
Shy People, 2080
Si mian xia wa, 920
Si shui liu nian, 903
Sia, le rêve du python, 168
Sia, the Dream of the Python, 168
Siao bai wa jin ju, 1688
Siao Yu, 1684
Sibaji, 1298
Sidhi, 1444
Das siebente Jahr, 722
Siege, 1124
Siesta, 2081
Les Siestes grenadine, 1701
Sign of Escape, 99
Signé Charlotte, 522
The Silence, 1638
The Silence of the Lambs, 2117
The Silences of the Palace, 1698
Silencio roto, 1622
Silent Grace, 1122
Silent Ocean, 1363
The Silent Pacific, 1363
Silent Waters, 1416
Silkwood, 2028
Silvia Prieto, 38
A Simple Story, 488
The Sin, 377
Sin dejar huella, 1345
Since Otar Left, 673
Sincerely Yours . . ., 2384
Single Girl, 583
A Single Woman, 285
Sinon, oui, 599
Siódmy pokój, 956
A Sip of Love, 1721
Sister My Sister, 1823
Sisters, 1936
Sisters of the World Unite, 912
Sisters or the Balance of Happiness, 782
Le Sixième jour, 387
The Sixth Day, 387
Skaz o materi, 2352
Skin, 1410
Skirt Power, 1323
Die Skorpionfrau, 92
Sledy ukhodiat za gorizont, 2353
Sleep of Reason, 818
Sleeping with the Enemy, 2136
Sleepwalk, 2063
Sleepy Time Gal, 2265

Slepa pega, 1535
Sliding Doors, 1854
A Slipping-Down Life, 2344
Small Happiness, 202
A Smart Lady, 169
Smile, 1311, 1956
Smithereens, 2019
Smriti chitre, 1009
Snakes and Ladders, 1117, 1338
The Snapper, 1824
Snart Sjutton, 1408
Snowy Wilderness, 260
Sobreviviré, 1605
Sobstvennaya tien, 1517
Les Soeurs Brontë, 493
Sofie, 360
Soft Fruit, 82
Softly, softly, 1175
Soguktu ve yagmur ciseliyordu, 1732
Soif d'amour, 1235
Sol de otoño, 35
Solas, 1616
Soldados de Salamina, 1629
Le Soldatesse, 1152
Soldiers of Salamina, 1629
La Soledad era esto, 1626
Solo de violino, 1491
Solo Sunny, 729
Sombras en una batalla, 1584
Some Interviews on Personal Matters, 2376
Some Mother's Son, 1118
Something Different, 349
Something Hurts, 780
Something to Talk About, 2313
Song jia huang chao, 921
Song of Algerian Women, 15
Song of the Exile, 1681
The Song of the Shirt, 1777
Songcatcher, 2283
Songs of Forgetting, 13
Sonho de valsa, 143
Soong Sisters, 921
Sophie's Choice, 2020
The Sorceress, 538
Sorrento Beach, 73
Sorry, It's the Law, 385
Sotto, sotto . . . strapazzato da anomala passione,
    1175
The Soul of a Painter, 289
Le Sourd dans la ville, 196
Sous la sable, 643
Sous les pieds des femmes, 18
South Side Story, 1197
The South Wind, 8
Souvenir, 2167

Souviens-toi de moi, 581
Sparkle, 1974
Spasi i sokhrani, 2393
Speriamo che sia femmina, 1180
Spices, 1017
The Spinster, 1891
The Spitfire Grill, 2187
Spoon Enemy, 1722
The Spouse, 1079
Le Stade de Wimbledon, 644
Stage Door, 919
Stakoza, 401
Les Stances à Sophie, 175
Stare de fapt, 1511
Starry Sky, 150
Starstruck, 50
State of Things, 1511
Stay Alive, 1098
Stealing Beauty, 1192
Steaming, 1790
Steel Magnolias, 2103
Stefania, 860
Stella, 2118
Stella Does Tricks, 1858
Step on It, 96
The Stepford Wives, 2345
Stepmom, 2236
Stevie, 1775
Sticky Fingers, 2096
The Sticky Fingers of Time, 1859
Die Stille nach dem Schuß, 704
De Stille oceaan, 1363
De Stilte rond Christine M., 1361
Stir patra, 982
Stolen Meeting, 406
Stone Wedding, 1504
Stone Years, 880
Stones, 1138, 1625
Storia di Piera, 1173
Die Storie van Klara Viljee, 1542
Stories of the Vienna Woods, 775
The Storm, 983
Story of a Woman, 975, 1677, 2360
The Story of Adele H, 471
The Story of Ah, 1444
The Story of Ermei, 321
Story of Fausta, 146
The Story of Klara Viljee, 1542
Story of Qiu Ju, 291
Story of Women, 258, 527
Straight to the Heart, 811
Strana gluchich, 1516
Strange Fits of Passion, 85
Strange Letters, 2369
A Strange Woman, 2373

Stranger Inside, 2284
Strannaya zhenshchina, 2373
Strapless, 1806
Stray Bullets, 505
Strayed, 656
Street Bitches, 1564
Streets, 2119
Streetwalkin', 2039
Strohfeuer, 760
Struggle, 98
Student Nurses, 1921
The Stuntwoman, 918
Stupeur et tremblements, 663
Subah, 999
The Subjective Factor, 794
Der subjektive Faktor, 794
Sublet, 1581
Sublet (Realquiler), 1581
Succession of Events, 2386
Such Good Friends, 1926
Such Is Life, 1342
Suci sang primadona, 1059
Suci the Divine Primadonna, 1059
Sud side stori, 1197
Suddenly, 43
Suddenly Naked, 217
Sugar Cane Alley, 512
Sugar Hat, 804
Sugar Town, 2251
Sugarbaby, 825
Sugarland Express, 1957
Summer Heat, 2082
The Summer House, 1820
Summer Lightning, 760
Summer Paradise, 1649
Summer School Teachers, 1985
Summer Snow, 916
Summer Wishes, Winter Dreams, 1943
Sun and Rain, 271
The Sun Has Ears, 309
Sun on the Roof of the World, 293
The Sung Sisters, 921
The Sun's Burial, 1218
Sunshine and Showers, 271
Supergirl, 1791
Supporting Roles, 340
Sur la terre comme au ciel, 566
The Surrogate Woman, 1298
Suuder, 1347
The Swamp, 40
Swann, 1831
Swaraaj, 1056
Sweet 17, 1408
Sweet Dreams, 2051
Sweet Power, 151

Sweet Snow, 283
Sweetheart, Dear, Beloved, the Only One . . ., 2382
Sweetie, 61
Swept Away . . . By an Unusual Destiny in the Blue
    Sea of August, 1162
Swimming Pool, 664
Swimming with Tears, 1259
Swing Shift, 2040
Swordman II, 914
Sylvia, 1390, 1883
Szabad lélegzet, 931
Szép lányok, ne sirjatok, 930
Szerelmem, Electra, 932
A Szerencse lányai, 958
Sziget a szárazföldön, 929

Ta' det som en mand, frue!, 356
Taafe fanga, 1323
Tacones lejanos, 1579
Der Tag der Idioten, 795
Al Tahaddi, 389
Tai yang you er, 309
Tai yang yu, 271
Taiyo no hakaba, 1218
Take Care of My Cat, 1307
Take It like a Man, Ma'am, 356
Take My Eyes, 1630
Tale of a Naughty Girl, 1054
A Tale of Autumn, 601
Tale of Love, 2188
Talk, 72
Tan de repente, 43
The Tango Lesson, 1845
Taning yaman, 1450
Tank Girl, 2189
Tante Tao quan shui ding dong, 244
Tapage nocturne, 494
Tapasya, 987
Tarang, 1011
Tarfaya, 1355
Taste of Honey, 1746
Tata mia, 1569
Tatlong taong walong Diyos, 1426
Taxi pour Soweto, 1541
Taxi to Soweto, 1541
A Taxing Woman, 1257
Taxo to Soweto, 1541
Te doy mis ojos, 1630
Tea with Mussolini, 1860
The Teachers with the Golden Heart, 859
Al Tejruba, 1105
Teknolust, 2333
The Telegraph Route, 571
Le Temple des oies sauvages, 1222
Temple of the Wild Geese, 1222

Le temps, 1321
Temps de chien, 589
Le Temps de l'avant, 180
Le Temps du loup, 101
Le Temps pour . . ., 324
Temptation, 1481
Ten, 1102
Ten Girls of Dong Loc, 2409
Terminal Island, 1944
Terms of Endearment, 2029
La Terre brullante, 1715
The Terrorist, 1044
Testament, 2030
That Day on the Beach, 1671
That Long Night, 332
That Tender Touch, 1914
That Was Loneliness, 1626
Thelma and Louise, 2137
Thérèse, 523
Thérèse Desqueroux, 433
They Don't Wear Black Tie, 139
Thin Ice, 1825
Things behind the Sun, 2266
Things I Never Told You, 2217
Things You Can Tell Just By Looking at Her, 2267
The Third, 723
The Thirst for Love, 1235
This Is My Life, 2148
This Love of Mine, 1676
This Side of Heaven, 318
A Thoroughly Neglected Girl, 768
A Thousand Pieces of Gold, 2120
Three Godless Years, 1426
Three in the Attic, 1910
The Three Madeleines, 214
The Three Men of Melita Zganjer, 326
Three Minus Me, 1490
Three Seasons, 889
Three Siblings, 1496
Three Sisters, 1187, 1767
Three Stories, 1742
Three Times Ana, 24
Three Wives, 1199
Three Women, 1986
The Threshold, 999
The Thundergod, 1523
Tian yu, 315
Tian yun shan chan qi, 240
Tichá radost, 353
Ticket, 1296
Ticket of No Return, 778
Tieta do Agreste, 149
Tieta of Agreste, 149
Tiger, Lion, Panther, 845
Tiger, Löwe, Panther, 845

La Tigra, 405
The Tigress, 405
Time, 1321
The Time For . . ., 324
The Time of the Wolf, 101
The Time We Killed, 2346
Time's Up!, 1617
I Timi tis agapis, 876
Titan serambut dibelah tujuh, 1065
Tjoet Nya Dien, 1070
To Crush the Serpent, 1718
To Die For, 2190
To Die of Love, 456
To Have (or Not), 577
To ja Pani Bavary, 1458
To Love, 408
To Save Nine, 1186
To Take a Wife, 1141
To the End of the World, 1484
Der Tod der Maria Malibran, 750
Die tödliche Maria, 1374
Todo está oscuro, 1599
Todo sobre mi madre, 1606
Toi ippon no michi, 1248
Tomboy Paula, 25
Tomorrow We Move, 654
Tong chiu ho fong nü i, 904
Topless Women Talk about Their Lives, 1399
Torgovka i poet, 2374
Torowisko, 1485
Tot ziens, 1376
A Touch of Spice, 1017
Touchia, 15
Touching, at a Touch, 1473
Toute une nuit, 118
Towhaired Fanny, 1561
Τράίto, 888
The Trace, 1696
Trampa para una esposa, 1582
Transatlantic, 2349
Transatlántico, 2349
Transatlantique, 2349
Transit, 888
Transparent Woman, 344
Tranzito, 888
Trap for a Wife, 1582
Traps, 347
Der Traum vom Elch, 735
Travolti da un insolito destino nell'azzurro mare
    d'Agosto, 1162
Tre moglie, 1199
The Tree of Adultery, 1294
Três irmãos, 1496
Três menos eu, 1490
Tres veces Ana, 24

Tri istorii, 1742
Tri muskarca Melite Zganger, 326
The Trial of Caterina Ross, 1172
Trial of Joan of Arc, 431
Trial Run, 1389
The Tricky Life, 2350
The Trio, 679
Le Trio terrible, 679
Tris epoches, 889
Triumph of Love, 1880
Troc de mariées, 1731
Trois couleurs: Bleu, 567
Trois couleurs: Rouge, 574
Trois saisons, 889
Trolösa, 1659
The Trouble with Angels, 1902
The Trouble with Love, 812
The Trout, 508
Truck Stop Women, 1958
True Love, 2104
The True Nature of Bernadette, 176
La Truite, 508
Truth, 424
Trå Kvinnor: den Vita Väggen, 1646
Tsuma toshite onna toshite, 1220
Tsuma wa kokuhaku sura, 1221
Tu ecraseras le serpent, 1718
Tu nombre en venena mis sueños, 1596
Tube Rose, 981
Tulitikkutehtaan tyttö, 417
Tumbleweeds, 2252
The Turkish Spice Lady Is Leaving, 821
The Turning Point, 1261, 1987
Turtle Beach, 69
Twee koffers, 1380
Twee vrouen, 1356
Twice a Woman, 1356
Twilight Years, 1241
The Twin Bracelets, 911
Twist of Fate, 2388
Twisted, 2347
Two, 649
Two A.M., 264
Two Actresses, 201
Two Brothers, My Sister, 1496
Two Loves, 1891
Two Mothers on the Cross, 852
Two of Them, 937
Two or Three Things I Know about Her, 444
Two Small Bodies, 2168
Two Stage Sisters, 233
Two Women, 1036, 1087, 1144, 1733
Two Women in Love, 1168
Tylko strach, 1479
Tystnaden, 1638

Ualla azae lel sayedat, 383
Udju azul di Yonta, 897
Ukradennoye svidaniye, 406
Um Céu de estrelas, 150
Umbartha, 999
The Umbrellas of Cherbourg, 440
Umi wa miteita, 1276
Umrao jaan, 1000
L'Un chante, l'autre pas, 478
Die Unberührbare, 705
Under a Spell, 1341
Under the City's Skin, 1095
Under the Skin, 1846
Under the Skin of the City, 1095
Under the Stars, 894
Under the Sun, 643
Under the Tuscan Sun, 2334
Undercurrents, 1114
Unfaithful, 2314
The Unfaithful Wife, 448
Unfinished Diary, 191
An Unforgettable Summer, 1509
Ungfrúin góða og húsið, 961
Unholy Desire, 1226
Unhook the Stars, 2218
Unishe April, 1034
An Unmarried Woman, 1988
Unser kurzes Leben, 732
Unsichtbare Gegner, 87
Up the Sandbox, 1937
Up Tight!, 1911
Up to a Certain Point, 336
Uridu hallan, 382
Ursula and Glenys, 1796
Útközben, 1462
Utsav, 1012
Utsukushisa to kanashimi to, 1231

V. I. Warshawski, 2138
V ogne broda net, 2359
Va' dove ti porta il cuare, 1193
Vacant Possession, 75
Vagabond, 516
Vaghe stelle dell'Orsa, 1153
Vale Abraão, 1495
Valley of the Innocent, 715
Vals de la Habana Vieja, 342
Une Valse au bord de la Petchora, 675
Vámonos, Barbara, 1548
Vanity Fair, 1885
El varano de Anna, 710
Varastatud kohtumine, 406
Variety, 2031
Varuh meje, 1536
Vassa, 2380

Vdovstvo Karoline Zasler, 2413
Vecchie, 1205
Ve'lakhta lehe isha, 1141
The Velvet Vampire, 1927
Ven de koele meren des doods, 1362
Vendredi soir, 665
La Vengeance des serpents, 1707
Vent de sable, 12
Le Vent du sud, 8
Vénus Beauté Institut, 616
Venus Beauty Institute, 616
Venus Beauty Salon, 616
Venusberg, 741
Vera, 145
Vera Drake, 1886
Verführung: Die grausame Frau, 742
La Vérité, 424
Die Verliebten, 835
Die Verlobte, 730
Die verlorene Ehre der Katharina Blum, 761
Veronica Guerin, 2335
Veronicas svededug, 357
Veronica's Veil, 357
Veronika Voss, 802
Das Versprechen, 687
The Vertical Ray of the Sun, 2408
Very Annie Mary, 1873
A Very Curious Girl, 451
A Very Long Absence, 879
A Very Private Affair, 429
Le Veut à laisse une trace, 1262
La Veuve Couderc, 468
La Veuve de Saint-Pierre, 627
Viaje de Arián, 1618
Vibrations, 1011
Vicious Circle, 998
Vida perra, 1555
La Vie devant soi, 486
Vie privée, 429
La Vie promise, 666
La Vie rêvée, 177
Vie rêvée des anges, 605
La Vieille quimboiseuse et le majordome, 526
Vilde, the Wild One, 1410
Le Village de l'Acacia, 229
Village in the Mist, 1292
Vinata, 158
The Violent Silence, 1349
Violette Nozière, 487
Violin Solo, 1491
Vipera, 1200
The Virgin Machine, 840
The Virginia Hill Story, 1968
Virineya, 2360
Visages de femmes, 1212

The Visit, 740
Visitor at Dawn, 381
Viskningar och Rop, 1645
Viva Algeria, 1706
Viva Laldjérie, 1706
Viva Maria!, 443
Vivre ensemble, 462
Vivre sa vie, 434
Vollgas, 96
Voodoo Passion, 1664
Voyage à Paimpol, 517
Voyage Beyond, 1020
Voyages, 617
Les Voyageurs, 1077
La Vraie nature de Bernadette, 176
Vremya zhatvy, 1520
Vrijeme za . . ., 324
Een Vrouw als Eva, 1357
Vtorostepenniye lyudi, 1743
Výlet, 348

W obronie wlasnej, 1465
Waati, 1321
The Wait, 2351
Wait until Dark, 1904
Waiting for the Clouds, 1741
Waiting for the Moon, 2064
Waiting to Exhale, 2191
Walking after Midnight, 1735
Walking and Talking, 2219
A Wall of Silence, 33
Walsi Petschorase, 675
Waltzing on the River Pecora, 675
Wanda, 1922
A Wandering Life, 1223
War between Us, 207
The War Widow, 1975
Wara mandel, 1847
The Wash, 2097
Washington Square, 2228
Watch the Sky, 1195
Water and Salt, 1501
Watermelon Woman, 2192
Wave, 1011
The Way We Were, 1945
The Wedding Chamber, 1722
Wedding Night, 1106
Weekend Circles, 1127
Un Weekend sur deux, 545
Weggehen um Anzukommen, 803
Weight of Water, 2268
Die weiße Rose, 796
Welcome to the Terrordrome, 1832
The Well, 78, 1709
We're All Still Here, 595

The Whales of August, 2083
What Alice Found, 2336
What Are Women Laughing About?, 1597
What Are You Searching for, Palupi?, 1058
What Do You Search for, Palupi?, 1058
What Is to Be Done?, 223
What Makes a Family, 2285
What the Sea Said, 1035
What's Cooking?, 2269
What's Love Got to Do with It?, 2155
What's the Matter with Helen?, 1928
The Wheel, 1293
When a Woman Ascends the Stairs, 1217
When Joseph Returns, 933
When Night Is Falling, 205
When the 10th Month Comes, 2403
When the Light Comes, 1378
When the Sky Falls, 1121
Where Are you, Mrs. Dery, 935
Where the Heart Is, 2270
Where Women Tread, 18
Whispering Sands, 1072
The White Cranes, 2354
White Dog, 2013
White Marriage, 1477
White Oleander, 2315
The White Rose, 796
The White Wall, 1646
The White, White Storks, 2354
Who Is the Third Party?, 263, 270
Who Killed Bambi?, 661
Who Slew Auntie Roo?, 1928
Whore, 1633
Why (Not) Brazil?, 672
The Widow, 1976
The Widow Couderc, 468
The Widow of St. Pierre, 627
Widowhood of Karolina Zasler, 2413
Widow's Peak, 1826
Wielki tydzien, 1482
A Wife for My Son, 11
Wife of an Important Man, 391
The Wife of Seishu No Tsuma, 1236
Wifemistress, 1165
A Wife's Confession, 1221
Wild Berries, 1275
Wild Grass, 1210
Wild Roses, 885
The Wild Wild Rose, 227
The Wildcat, 848
Wildrose, 2052
Will It Snow for Christmas?, 590
Wimbledon Stadium, 644
The Window Across, 148
Wing Chun, 304

Wings, 2355
Wings of the Dove, 495, 1848
The Winner, 858
Winter Guest, 1849
A Winter Tan, 197
Wit, 2286
Witch Hunt, 1405
The Witches, 2105
The Witches of Eastwick, 2084
Witches' Sabbath, 1560
With All My Children, 1544
With All My Love, 630
With Beauty and Sorrow, 1231
With Closed Eyes, 1191
Without a Trace, 1345
Without Fear, 2366
Without Love, 1461
With Love, Lilya, 1519
Wives, 1403
Wives: Ten Years After, 1409
Wives III, 1412
Wo te ai, 1676
The Wolf's Bride, 823
Die Wolfsbraut, 823
Woman, 1442
A Woman Alone, 1463
A Woman and a Woman, 1460
A Woman and Seven Husbands, 1680
Woman as the Devil, 16
A Woman at 33, 161
The Woman Banker, 496
Woman Called Moses, 1993
Woman Commando, 276
The Woman Cop, 491
Woman, Demon, Human, 261
Woman Detective, 275
A Woman for Life, 738
A Woman for Two, 266
The Woman from Africa, 677
Woman from Rose Hill, 1666
A Woman in Flames, 808
A Woman in the Resistance, 863
A Woman in Transit, 189
A Woman Is a Woman, 426
A Woman like Eve, 1357
Woman Living Buddha, 256
Woman of Darkness, 1642
Woman of Good Family, 247
Woman of the Ganges, 463
Woman of Wrath, 1675
Woman on a Tin Roof, 1445
A Woman on Her Own, 1463
Woman on Top, 2402
A Woman, One Day, 483
A Woman Pianist's Story, 279

A Woman Reporter, 1291
Woman Sesame Oil Maker, 296
Woman Soldiers Song, 253
Woman, Taxi, Woman, 286
Woman Thou Art Loosed, 2348
A Woman Under the Influence, 1959
Woman Wanted, 2271
The Woman Who Imagined She Was President of
    the United States, 1503
Woman, Wife, and Whore, 1316
The Woman with a Hat, 1470
The Woman with a Knife, 1209
A Woman with Responsibility, 774
Woman's Power, 248
A Woman's Story, 1229
A Woman's Tale, 66
Women, 386, 1603, 1612
Women Avengers, 288
Women Flowers, 303
Women from the Lake of Scented Souls, 296
Women in Love, 1765
Women in Search of Freedom, 403
Women in Tropical Places, 1812
Women of the Chosun Dynasty, 1290
The Women of Yellow Earth, 267
Women on the Verge of a Nervous Breakdown,
    1573
Women Pilots, 234
Women Women, 466
Women's Expectations, 19
Women's Group, 257
Women's Love, 404
Women's Prison, 1100
Women's Story, 258, 1552
Women's Valley, 306
Women's Wiles, 1353
Women's World, 287
Wonderland, 1861
The Words to Say It, 511
Words upon the Window Pane, 1116
Work, 2220
Working Girl, 2098
Working Girls, 1960, 2065
A World Apart, 1804
World Within, World Without, 1028
The Wound, 669
Wretched Lives, 1451
Wrota Europy, 1486
Wu die, 322
Wu tai jie mei, 233
Wu ye liang dian, 264

Xala, 1524
O! Xi ang xue, 283
Xi shi yan, 320

Xi xia lu tiao tiao, 310
Xian dai bao xia zhuan, 917
Xiang nü xiao xiao, 265
Xiang si nü zhi ke dian, 250
Xiangsi Woman's Hotel, 250
Xiao ao jiang hu zhi dong fang bu bai, 914
Xiao Yu, 1684
Xica da Silva, 134
Xiu Xiu: The Sent Down Girl, 315
Xuese qing chen, 294

Y aura-t-il de la neige à Noël?, 590
Y fargen, 1839
Y tu mamá también, 1346
Ya donya ya gharmi, 400
Yaaba, 167
Yahalou yeheli, 1635
Yan kou, 907
Yana's Friends, 1135
Yang Kaihui, 308
Yao wang Chalila, 313
Yara, 700
Yarasa, 102
Yasmin, 1887
Yatik Emine, 1716
Yawar Mallku, 132
Yawm murr yawm hulu, 390
Ye meigui zhi lian, 227
Year of the Quiet Sun, 1468
Yearning, 1260
Years of Hunger, 781
The Years of the Big Heat, 883
Yeogija 20nyeon, 1291
Yerma, 824, 1607
Yesterday Girl, 743
Les Yeux secs, 1354
Yilani oldürseler, 1718
Yilanlarin öcü, 1707
Yin ji kau, 907
Yngsjömordet, 1642
Yo, la peor de todas, 32

Yoinchanhoksa: moul le ya moul le ya, 1293
Yong Chun, 304
You ma caizi, 1674
You yuan jing meng, 925
Al-Youm as-Sadiss, 387
A Young Emmanuelle, 477
Your Name Poisons My Dreams, 1596
Yoyes, 1608
Yuan nü, 1679
Yuen ling-juk, 913
Yugant, 1035
Yume no ginga, 1264
Yume no onna, 1260
Yurisai, 1274

Za sciana, 1455
Zaide, 645
Zaïde, un petit air de vengeance, 645
Za'ir al-Fajr, 381
Al Zakira al khasba, 1417
Zandy's Bride, 1961
Al Zawga el tania, 380
Zawgati, mudir am, 379
Zawjat rajul muhim, 391
Al Zawraq, 1104
Zeit des zorns, 685
Zelly and Me, 2099
Zendan-e zanan, 1100
La Zerda ou les chants de l'oublie, 13
Zhena na trideset i tri, 161
Zheng hun qi shi, 1689
Zhizn-zhenshchina, 1279
Zina, 1797
Zinat, 1080
Zir-e poost-e shahr, 1095
Zuckerbaby, 825
Zuckerhut, 804
Zui hou de gui zu, 277
Die Zukunft, 1178
Zus & Zo, 1384
Das zweite Erwachen der Christa Klages, 771

ABOUT THE AUTHOR

Jane Sloan has an MA in library science and an MA in film studies. She is the media librarian, cinema studies selector, and head of multimedia studies at Rutgers University Libraries. She is the author of *Robert Bresson: A Guide to References and Resources* (1983) and *Alfred Hitchcock: A Filmography and Bibliography* (1995).